COMPLETE
PRICE GUIDE TO
WATCHES

BY

COOKSEY SHUGART & RICHARD E. GILBERT

EDITED BY MARTHA SHUGART

Important Notice. All of the information, including valuations, in this book has been compiled from the most reliable sources, and every effort has been made to eliminate errors and questionable data. Nevertheless, the possibility of error, in a work of such immense scope, always exists. The publisher or authors will not be held responsible for losses which may occur in the purchase, sale, statements of its advertisers or other transaction of items, because of information contained herein. Readers who feel they have discovered errors are invited to write and inform us, so they may be corrected in subsequent editions.

The Complete Price Guide To Watches is published independently and is not associated with any watch manufacturer.

This book endeavors to be a **Guide** or helpful manual and offers a wealth of material and information to be used as a tool not as a absolute document. The Complete Price Guide To Watches is like some *watches*, the worst may be better than none at all, but at best cannot be expected to be 100% accurate.

Published by: **COOKSEY SHUGART PUBLICATIONS**
P. O. BOX 3147
CLEVELAND, TN. 37320-3147
TEL. OR FAX (423) 479 – 4813

Distributed by: **COLLECTOR BOOKS**
P. O. BOX 3009
5801 KENTUCKY DAM ROAD
PADUCAH, KY. 42001

ISBN 0 – 89145 – 777 – 1
SEVENTEENTH EDITION: JAN., 1997

European Distributor: **BUSHWOOD BOOKS**
84 Bushwood Road, Kew Gardens, Surrey TW9 3BQ (U. K.)

Manufactured in the United States of America

ABOUT COVER see page 567

COOKSEY SHUGART

RICHARD E. GILBERT

ABOUT THE AUTHORS

The Complete Price Guide To WATCHES, published by Shugart Publications, and co-authored by Cooksey Shugart and Richard E. Gilbert. Mr. Gilbert holds both Bachelor's and Master's degrees in Science. Richard Gilbert is the owner of Ashland a multi-million dollar international mail order business, he has an impeccable reputation for honesty and integrity, and has been sought after for years by other dealers as a guide to establishing prices.

Both authors have been active watch buyers since the early 1960's. The authors have been Horologists and members of the National Association of Watch and Clock Collectors since the early 1970's. Both have searched for fine timepieces all over the world and are the foremost experts in the field of antique pocket and wrist watches. Both have enjoyed broadening their knowledge in horology while traveling in Europe.

The co-authors travel extensively to auctions throughout the United States and Europe, to regional and national conventions, meets and shows, and keep an up-to-date pulse of the watch market. They continually expand their horological reference library and their extensive selection of watch photographs. Because of the unique knowledge of the market these two co-authors possess, this volume should be considered one of the most authoritative watch references on the market today. Each edition contains updated and revised information and prices, and has become the accepted standard reference work of the watch market. "We see this book as an extension of the information we have been gathering for years and take great pride in sharing it with other collectors who have a deep and abiding interest in watches," the authors stated.

Mr. Shugart resides in Cleveland, Tennessee, and Mr. Gilbert lives in Sarasota, Florida.

TABLE OF CONTENTS

4

ACKNOWLEDGMENTS

I am especially appreciative of **Bob Overstreet**, author of The Overstreet Comic Book Price Guide, for his encouragement.

To my wife **Martha**, for her complete understanding and assistance in compiling this book.

To best friend **TOM ENGLE** whose help is invaluable a very special thanks.

A very special thanks to Henry B. Fried, Adolphe Chapiro and Dan Crawley.

To the NAWCC Museum, Hamilton Watch Co., and Bowman Technical School, for allowing us to photograph their watches.

To Christie's, Osvaldo Patrizzi, Dr. H. Crott and Joseph Auctions for photographs of watches.

And to the following people whose help was invaluable and will be long remembered: Frank Irick, John Cubbins, Harold Harris, Paul Gibson, Robert L. Ravel, M.D., William C. Heilman Jr., M.D., Thomas McEntyre, Paul Morgan, Bill Selover, Oscar Laube, Ed Kieft, Charles Wallace, Bob Walters, Jack Warren, Howard Schroeder, Edward M. McGinnis, James Gardner, Paul Zuercher, Irving E. Roth, Don Bass, Stephen Polednak, Dick Stacy, Ernest J. Lewis, Herbert McDonald, David Steger, Fred Favour, Ralph Warner, Estus Harris, Charles Cleves, Tom McIntyre, Ralph Ferone, Arnold C. Varey, Jeffrey Ollswang, Tom Rohr, Leon Beard, Glenn Smith, Kenneth Vergin, Thomas Rumpf, Frank Diggs, Tom Thacker, Bob Lavoie, Constantin Tanasecu, Rod Minter, Ernest Luffman, John Amneus, Lawrence D. Harnden, Mike Kirkpatrick, Clint B. Geller, Art W. Rontree, and a special thanks to Peter Kushnir, Dr. J. Mauss, Robert D. Gruen, Jeff Hess, Col. R. A. Mulholland, Dick Ziebell, Jack Warren, Dick Flaute, Ralph Vinge, Edward Fletcher, Richard Walker, Alex Wolanguk, Carl Goetz, Miles Sandler, Dave Mycko, Martin & Patrick Cullen, Benjy Rook, Phillip Welsh, Paul Craft, Fred Fox, Fred Andrus, Ellis Gifford, Steve Berger, Bruce Ellison, Lawrence D. Harnden, Geoff White, Bob & Pat Wingate, David Searles, Ray R. Tyulty Jr., Don Levison, Robert M. Toborowsky M.D., Dr. John R. Dimar, Jonathan Snellenburg, Tom Reindl, Paul A. Duggan, Gregory A. Hill, Don & Sandy Robbins, Bernie Kraus, Veron Willams, Fred Hansen, Drew Schmidt, Norman Howard, Harry Blair.

*   *   *

Send only corrections, additions, deletions and comments to
COOKSEY SHUGART, P. O. BOX 3147, CLEVELAND, TN. 37320-3147.
*When **corresponding**, please send a* ✉ *self-addressed, stamped envelope.*

JIM WOLF
Special Consultant

INTRODUCTION

This book is dedicated to all watch collectors who we hope will find it an enjoyable and valuable reference to carry on buying trips or to trace the lost history of that priceless family heirloom.

The origin of this book began when I was given a pocket watch that had been in our family for many years. After receiving the prized heirloom I wanted to know its complete history, and thus the search began. Because of the lack of a comprehensive reference on American pocket watches the venture took me through volume after volume. Over the course of ten years many hours were accumulated in running down the history of this one watch. The research sparked my interest in the pocket watch field and pointed to the need for a book such as this one. We hope it will provide the information that you are looking for.

— The Authors

Watches are unique collectibles and since the beginning of civilization man has held a fascination for time. When man scooped up a handful of sand and created the hourglass, portable timepieces have been in demand for the wealthy and poor alike. Man has sought con-stantly to improve his time-measuring instruments and has made them with the finest metals and jewels. The pocket watch, in particular, became an orna-mentation and a source of pride, and this accounts for its value among families for generation after generation.

The watch has become precious and sentimental to so many because it is one of the true personal compan-ions of the individual night and day. Mahatma Gandhi, the father of India and one of the rare people in history who was able to renounce worldly possessions, was obsessed with the proper use of his time. Each minute, he held, was to be used in the service of his fellow man. His own days were ordered by one of his few personal possessions, a sixteen-year-old, eight-shilling Ingersoll pocket watch that was always tied to his waist with a piece of string.

Another factor that has made watches unique collectibles is the intricate artisanship with which they are put together. Many of the watches of yester-year, which were assembled with extreme accuracy and fine workmanship, continue to be reliable timepieces today. They stand out as unique because that type of watch is no longer hand made. In today's world of mass produc-tion, the watch with individual craftsmanship containing precious jewels and metals can rarely be found—and, if found, it is rarely affordable.

The well-made watch is a tribute to man's skills, artisanship and crafts-manship at their finest level. That is why the watch holds a special place in the collectible field.

In America, there are about 80,000 avid watch collectors. About 5 million people own two or more watches, and an untold number possess at least one of these precious heirlooms.

The Complete Price Guide to Watches does not attempt to establish or fix values or selling prices in the watch trade market.

It does, however, reflect the trends of buying and selling in the collector market. Prices listed in this volume are based on data collected and analyzed from dealers and shops all over the country.

These prices should serve the collector as a **guide** only. The price you pay for any watch will be determined by the value it has to you. The intrinsic value of any particular watch can be measured only by you, the collector, and a fair price can be derived only after mutual agreement between both the buyer and the seller.

Keep in mind the fair market **values** as outlined in this price guide and buying wisely, but don't hesitate, as the better and scarce pieces are quickly sold.

It is our hope that this volume can help make your watch collecting venture both pleasurable and profitable.

Information contained herein may not necessarily apply to every situation. Data is still being found, which may alter statements made in this book. These changes, however, will be reflected in future editions.

Hopefully, everyone interested in horology will research the watch and add to his library on the subject.

COLLECTAMANIA
Hobby — Business — Pastime — Entertainment

Just name it. More than likely someone will want to buy or sell it: books, coins, stamps, bottles, beer cans, gold, glassware, baseball cards, guns, clocks, watches, comics, art, cars, and the list goes on and on.

Most Americans seem to be caught up in collectamania . More and more Americans are spending hour after hour searching through antique shops, auctions, flea markets and yard sales for those rare treasures of delight that have been lying tucked away for generations just waiting to be found.

This sudden boom in the field of collecting may have been influenced by fears of inflation or disenchantment with other types of investments. But more people are coming into the field because they gain some degree of nostalgic satisfaction from these new tangible ties with yesteryear. Collecting provides great fun and excitement. The tales of collecting and the resultant "fabulous finds" could fill volumes and inspire even the non-collector to embark upon a treasure hunt.

Collecting for the primary purpose of investment may prove to have many pitfalls for the amateur. The lack of sufficient knowledge is the main cause of disappointment. The inability to spot fakes or flawed merchandise can turn excitement into disappointment. And, in many fields, high-class forgers are at work, doing good and faithful reproductions in large quantities that can sometimes fool even the experts the first time they see them.

Collecting for fun and profit can be just that if you observe a fair amount of caution. Always remember, amidst your enthusiasm, that an object may not be what it would first appear. Next are a few guidelines that may be helpful to you.

FOCUS - LEARN - CONDITION - TRUST

" LOOK UNDER THE HOOD"

1. **Make up your mind** and **FOCUS** on what you want to collect and concentrate in this area. Your field of collecting should be one that you have a genuine liking for, and it helps if you can use the objects. It may also help to narrow your field even further, for instance, in collecting watches, to choose only one company or one type or style and have a method of collecting.

2. **Gain all the knowledge you can** and **LEARN** all about the objects you collect. The more knowledge you have the more successful you will be in finding valuable, quality pieces. Amassing the knowledge required to be a good collector is easier if you have narrowed your scope of interest. Otherwise, it may take years to become an "expert." Don't try to learn everything there is to know about a variety of fields. This will end in frustration and disappointment. Specialize and **learn** fair market **values**.

3. **Buy the best CONDITION you can afford**, assuming the prices are fair. The advanced collector may want only mint articles; but the novice collector may be willing to accept something far less than mint condition due to caution and economics. Collectible items in better condition continue to rise in value at a steady rate.

4. **Deal with reputable dealers** whom you can **TRUST**. Talk with the dealer; get to know the seller; get a business card; know where you can contact the dealer if you have problems, or if you want the dealer to help you find something else you may be looking for.

FAIR MARKET PRICE: Fair price may be defined as a fair **reasonable** range of prices usually paid for a watch or a watch of **good value** as used in this book (*at the RETAIL LEVEL*). This market level includes a particular time frame, desirability, condition and quality. A guide to fair purchase prices is subject to sales and transaction between a large number of buyers and sellers who are informed, up to date on all normal market influences (while keeping in mind the difference between compulsiveness and acceptable buying), and buy and sell on a large scale from coast to coast. A willing buyer and a willing seller acting carefully and judiciously in their own best interest while, doing business in a normal and fair manner and preferable with payment immediately.

Keep in mind the fair market **values** as outlined in this price guide and buying wisely, but don't *hesitate*, as the better and scarce watches are *quickly* sold.

HOW TO USE THIS BOOK

The Complete Price Guide to Watches is a simple reference, with clear and carefully selected information. The first part of the book is devoted to history, general information, and a how-to section. The second part of the guide consists mainly of a listing of watch manufacturers, identification guides, and prices. This is a unique book because it is designed to be taken along as a handy pocket reference for identifying and pricing watches. With the aid of this book, the collector should be able to make on-the-spot judgments as to identification, age, quality, and value. This complete guide and a pocket magnifying glass will be all you need to take on your buying trips.

Watch collecting is fast growing as a hobby and business. Many people collect for the enjoyment and profit. The popularity of watches continues to rise because watches are a part of history. The American railroad brought about the greatest watch of that time, the railroad pocket watch. Since that time America has produced some of the best quality pocket watches that money could buy. The gold-filled cases made in America have never been surpassed in quality or price in the foreign market. With the quality of movement and cases being made with guaranteed high standards as well as beauty, the American pocket watch became very desirable. Because they are no longer being made in the U. S. A., pocket watches continue to rise in value.

The watch is collected for its beauty, quality in movement and case, and the value of metal content. Solid gold and platinum are the top of the line; silver is also very desirable. (Consider that some watches in the early 1900's sold between $700 and $1,000. This is equal to or greater than the price of a good car of the same period.)

As with limited edition prints, a watch of supreme excellence is also limited and will increase in value. There is universal appeal and excitement in owning a piece of history, and your heirloom is just that. At one time pocket watches were a status symbol. Everyone competed for beauty and quality in the movement and case. Solid gold cases were adorned with elaborate engraving's, diamonds, and other precious jewels. The movements were beautiful and of high quality. Manufacturers went to great lengths to provide movements that were both accurate and lovely. Fancy damaskeening on the back plates of nickel with gold lettering, 26 jewels in gold settings, and a solid gold train (gears) were features of some of the more elaborate timepieces. The jewels were red rubies, or diamond-end stones, or sapphires for the pallet stones. There were gold timing screws, and more. The faces were made by the best artisans of the day. Hand-painted, jewel-studded, with fancy hands and double-sunk dials made of enamel and precious metals.

HOW TO DETERMINE MANUFACTURER

When identifying a watch, look on the face or dial for the name of the company and then refer to the alphabetical list of watch companies in this book. If the face or dial does not reveal the company name you will have to seek information from the movement's back plate. First determine from what country the watch originated. The company name or the town where it was manufactured will likely be inscribed there. The name engraved on the back plate is referred to as the "signature." After locating the place of manufacture, see what companies manufactured in that town. This may require reading the histories of several companies to find the exact one. Use the process of elimination to narrow the list. Note: Some of the hard-to-identify watches are extremely collectible and valuable. Therefore, it is important to learn to identify them.

In order to establish the true manufacturer of the movement, one must study the construction, taking note of the shape, location, plate layout (is it full or 3/4), shape of the balance cock and the regulator, location of jewels, location of screws, etc. Compare and match your watch movement with every photograph or drawing from each watch company in this volume until the manufacturer is located.

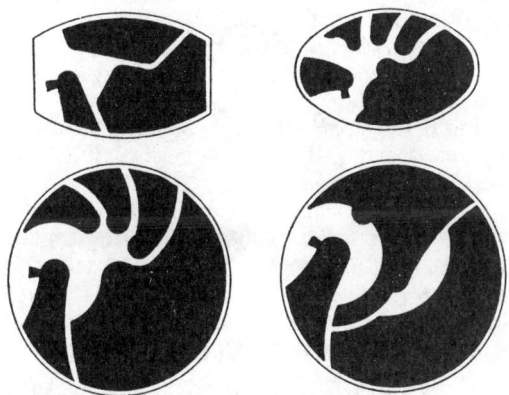

HOW TO DETERMINE AGE

After establishing the name of the manufacturer, you may be interested in the age of the watch (where production tables are listed). This information can be obtained by using the serial number inscribed on the back movement plate and referring to the production table. It is often difficult to establish the exact age, but this method will put you within a two or three-year period of the date of the manufacture.

To establish the age of a pre-1850 watch there are many points to be considered. The dial, hands, pillars, balance cock and pendant, for example, contain important clues in determining the age of your watch. However, no one part alone should be considered sufficient evidence to draw a definite conclusion as to age. The watch as a whole must be considered. First determine from what country the case originated and from what country did the movement originate for example, an English-made silver-cased watch will have a hallmark inside the case. It is quite simple to refer to the London Hallmark Table for hallmarks after 1697. The hallmark will reveal the age of the case only. This does not fix the age of the movement. Many movements are housed in cases made years before or after the movement was produced.

The case that houses the movement is not necessarily a good clue to the origin of the movement. It was a common practice for manufacturers to ship the movements to the jewelers and watchmakers uncased. The customer then married the movement and case. That explains why an expensive movement can be found in a cheaper case or vice versa.

If the "manufacturer's" name and location are no help, the inscription could possibly be that of a jeweler and his location. Then it becomes obvious there is no quick and easy way to identify some American made watches. However, the following steps may be helpful. Some watches can be identified by comparing the models of each company until the correct model is found. Start by sizing the watch and then comparing the varied plate shapes and styles. The cock or bridge for the balance may also be a clue. The general arrangement of the movement as to jeweling, whether it is an open face or hunting case, and style of regulators may help to find the correct identification of the manufacturer of the movement.

Numbers on a watch case should not be considered as clues to the age of the movement because cases were both American and foreign made, and many of the good watches were re-cased through the years.

WHAT'S MY WATCH WORTH

Watch collecting is still young when compared to fields of the standard collectibles: coins and stamps. The watch collecting field is growing but information is still scarce, fragmented, and sometimes unreliable. To be knowledgeable in any field, one must spend the time required to study it.

The value of any collectible is determined first by demand. Without demand there is no market. In the watch trade, the law of supply and demand is also true. The supply of the American watches has stopped and the demand among collectors continues to rise. There are many factors that make a watch desired or in demand. Only time and study will tell a collector just which pieces are most collectible. After the collector or investor finds out what is desirable, then a value must be placed on it before it is sold. If it is priced too high, the watch will not sell; but, on the other hand, if it is priced too low, it will be hard to replace at the selling price. The dealer must arrive at a fair market price that will move the watch. As with limited edition prints, a watch of supreme excellence is also limited and will increase in value. There is universal appeal and excitement in owning a piece of history, and your heirloom is just that. At one time pocket watches were a status symbol. Everyone competed for beauty and quality in the movement and case. Solid gold cases were adorned with elaborate engraving's, diamonds, and other precious jewels.

The movements were beautiful and of high quality. Manufacturers went to great lengths to provide movements that were both accurate and lovely. Fancy damaskeening on the back plates of nickel with gold lettering, 26 jewels in gold settings, and a solid gold train (gears) were features of some of the more elaborate timepieces. The jewels were red rubies, or diamond-end stones, or sapphires for the pallet stones. There were gold timing screws, and more. The faces were made by the best artisans of the day. Hand-painted, jewel-studded, with fancy hands and double-sunk dials made of enamel and precious metals.

There are no two watches alike. This makes fair market value more difficult and often-times arbitrary. But there are certain guidelines one can follow to arrive at a fair market price. When watches were manufactured, most companies sold the movements to a jeweler, and the buyer had a choice of dials and cases. Some high-grade movements were placed in a low-grade case and vice versa. Some had hand-painted multi-colored dials; some were plain. The list of contrasts goes on. Conditions of watches will vary greatly, and this is a big factor in the value. The best movement in the best original case will bring the top price for any type of watch.

Prices are constantly changing in the watch field. Gold and silver markets affect the price of the cases. Scarcity and age also affect the value. These prices will fluctuate regularly.

VALUATION GUIDELINES

Demand, supply, condition, and value to collectors must be the prime factors in **determining** what's my watch worth.

Demand is the most important element. Demand can be determined by the number of buyers for the particular item. A simple but true axiom is that value is determined by the price someone is willing to pay.

In order to obtain a better knowledge in collectable value and judging watches, the following guidelines are most useful. Consider all these factors before placing a value on the watch. (There is no rank or priority to the considerations listed.)

1. **Demand:** Is it high or low?
2. **Supply** or **Availability:** How **rare** or scarce is the watch?
   How many of the total production remain?
3. **Condition** of the case, dial and movement (very important).
4. Low serial numbers: The first one made would be more
   valuable than later models.
5. Historical value, first run, famous owners and etc.
6. Age: When was movement and case made? (Are they the same age?)
7. Value of **metal** content, style or type of case, beauty and eye appeal.

8. Is it in its **original** case? (very important).
9. Is it an early handmade watch, railroad watch or private label watch?
10. Complications: Repeaters, for example.
11. Type of **escapement**.
12. Size, number of jewels, type of plates (3/4, full and bridge), type of balance, type of winding (key-wind, lever-set, etc.), number of adjustments, gold jeweled settings, damaskeening, gold train.
13. What grade of condition is it? Pristine, Mint, Extra Fine, Average, Fair, or Scrap?
14. Identification ability. (For parts) (What country American Swiss etc.)
15. Future potential as an investment.
16. Quality (high or low grade), or low cost production watches (dollar watch).
17. How much will this watch & case scrap for?
18. Original box with Original papers.

GRADING WATCHES

Pricing in this book is based on the following grading system:

PRISTINE MINT (G-10): *NEW OLD STOCK.* Absolutely factory new; sealed in factory box with wax paper still intact & all tags & papers etc.

MINT PLUS (G-9): Still in factory box *"BUT LOOKS UNUSED"*.

MINT (G-8): Same as factory new but with very little use; no faint scratches; is original in every way crystal, hands, dial, case, movement; used briefly and stored away; may be in box.

NEAR MINT (G-7): Completely original in every way; faint marks may be seen with a loop only; expertly repaired; movement may have been cleaned and oiled.

EXTRA FINE (G-6): May or may not be in factory box; looks as though watch was used very little; crystal may have been replaced; original case, hands, dial, and movement. If watch has been repaired, all original replacement parts have been used. Faint case scratches are evident but hard to detect with the eye. No dents and no hairline on dial are detectable.

FINE (G-5): May have new hands and new crystal, but original case, dial and movement; faint hairline in dial; no large scratches on case; slight stain on movement; movement must be sharp with only minor scratches.

AVERAGE (G-4): Original case, dial and movement; movement may have had a part replaced, but part was near to original; no brass showing through on gold-filled case; no rust or chips in dial; may have hairlines in dial that are hard to see. All marks are hard to detect, but may be seen without a loop.

FAIR (G-3): Hairlines in dial and small chips; slight amount of brass can be seen through worn spots on gold-filled case; rust marks in movement; a small dent in case; wear in case, dial, and movement; well used; may not have original dial or case.

POOR (G-2): Watch not working; needs new dial; case well worn, with many dents; hands may be gone; replacement crystal may be needed.

SCRAP (G-1): Movement not working; bad dial; rusty movement; brass showing badly; may not have case; some parts not original; no crystal or hands. Good for parts only.

🕐 Pricing in this Guide are for **COMPLETE** watches in **MINT**= (G-8), **EX. FINE**= (G-6), & **AVERAGE**= (G-4) condition.
Below is an example of how the price is affected by the different grades of the same watch:

Hamilton 992B

G-10	$465
G-9	$435
G-8	**$425**
G-7	$375
G-6	**$365**
G-5	$335
G-4	**$325**
G-3	$200
G-2	$95
G-1	$65

The value of a watch can only be assessed after the watch has been carefully inspected and graded. It may be difficult to evaluate a watch honestly and objectively, especially in the rare or scarce models.

If the watch has any defects, such as a small scratch on it, it can not be Pristine. It is important to realize that older watches in grades of Extra Fine or above are extremely rare and may never be found.

Watches listed in this book are priced at the collectable retail level, as **COMPLETE** watches having an original 14k gold-filled case and Key Wind with silver, an original white enamel single sunk dial, and with the entire original movement in good working order with no repairs needed.

Keep in mind the fair market **values** as outlined in this price guide and buying wisely, but don't *hesitate*, as the better and scarce watches are *quickly* sold.

COLLECTING ON A LIMITED BUDGET

Most collectors are always looking for that sleeper, which is out there waiting to be found. One story goes that the collector went into a pawn shop and asked the owner if he had any gold pocket watches for sale. The pawn broker replied, ''No, but I have a 23J silver cased pocket watch at a good price.'' Even though the pocket watch was in a cheaper case, the collector decided to further explore the movement. When he opened the back to look at the movement, there he saw engraved on the plates 24J Bunn Special and knew immediately he wanted to buy the pocket watch. The movement was running, and looked to be in first grade shape. The collector asked the price. The broker said he has been trying to get rid of the pocket watch, but had no luck and if he wanted it, he would sell it for $35. The collector took the pocket watch and replaced the bent-up silver case for a gold-filled J. Boss case, and sold it a month later for $400. He had a total of $100 invested when he sold it, netting a cool $300 profit.

Most collectors want a pocket watch that is in mint or near-mint condition and original in every way. But consider the railroad pocket watches such as the Bunn Special in a cheaper case. The railroad man was compelled to buy a watch with a quality movement, even though he may have only been able to afford a cheap case. The railroad man had to have a pocket watch that met certain standards set by the railroad company. A watch should always be judged on quality and performance and not just on its appearance. The American railroad pocket watch was unsurpassed in reliability. It was durable and accurate for its time, and that accounts for its continuing value today.

If you are a limited-budget collector, you would be well advised not to go beyond your means. But watch collecting can still be an interesting, adventurous, and profitable hobby. If you are to be successful in quadrupling your purchases that you believe to be sleepers, you must first be a hard worker, have perseverance and let shrewdness and skill of knowledge take the place of money. A good starting place is to get a working knowledge of how a pocket watch works. Learn the basic skills such as cleaning, mainspring and staff replacement. One does not have to be a watchmaker, but should learn the names of parts and what they do. If a watch that you are considering buying does not work, you should know how and what it takes to get it in good running order or pass it by. Stay away from pocket watches that do not wind and set. Also avoid ''odd'' movements that you hope to be able to find a case for.

Old watches with broken or missing parts are expensive and all but impossible to have repaired. Some parts must be made by hand. The odd and low-cost production watches are fun to get but hard to repair. Start out on the more common basic-jeweled lever pocket watches. The older the watch, the harder it is to get parts. Buy an inexpensive pocket watch movement that runs and play with it. Get the one that is newer and for which parts can be bought; and get a book on watch repairing.

You will need to know the history and **demand** of a watch. Know what collectors are looking for in your area. If you cannot find a buyer, then, of course, someone else's stock has become yours.

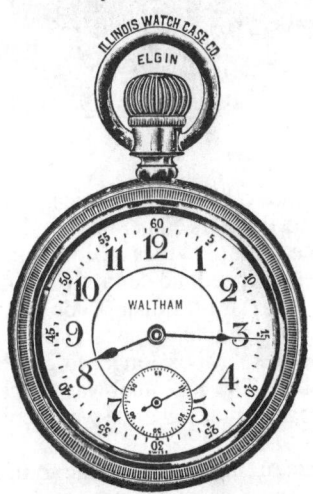

JOIN THE NAWCC®

The authors of this book Mr. Cooksey Shugart and Mr. Richard E. Gilbert recommend you join the NAWCC ® today and share a fascination for watches with other members.

The National Association of Watch and Clock Collectors (NAWCC ®) is a non-profit, scientific and educational corporation founded in 1943 and now serving the horological needs and interests of about 35,000 members (professional horologists and **amateurs**) in the United States and 40 others countries. Help to its members is only a telephone call away.

Participation in National & Regional *Conventions* also Local *Activities* and *Seminars*.

A **PUBLICATION** sent to you each month.

The **NAWCC ® Mart Sent to you every odd - month**

The **NAWCC ® Bulletin Sent to you every even - month**

The **Bulletin** sent to you every even - month is an absorbing, abundantly illustrated articles on historic, artistic and technical aspects of time keeping, answers by experts to your questions in the "Answer Box" , concise reviews of horological books, members' opinions and comments in "VOX TEMPORIS", research findings and request, slide programs available to Chapters, news and announcements of local Chapters, Regional and National activities.

The **Mart** sent to you every odd - month. An informal medium of exchange in which, for a nominal fee, you can list any horological item you may wish to **buy, sell or trade**... an absorbing and entertaining way to find items to fill out your collection or dispose of pieces you no-longer want. Announcements of Regional and National **Conventions & Seminars.**

TO JOIN THE NAWCC ® Call or Send for a FREE copy of their brochure with additional information on the NAWCC ®, membership and benefits.

NAWCC, INC.
514 Poplar Street
Columbia, PA   17512
(717) 684-8261

Recommended by member COOKSEY SHUGART membership number - **23,843.**
Also see AD in the ADVERTISING SECTION of this book.

THAT GREAT AMERICAN
RAILROAD POCKET WATCH

It was the late nineteenth century in America. The automobile had not yet been discovered. The personal Kodak camera was still not on the market. Women wore long dresses, and the rub board was still the most common way to wash clothes. Few homes had electricity, and certainly the radio had not yet invaded their lives. Benjamin Harrison was president. To be sure, those days of yesteryear were not quite as nostalgically simple as most reminiscing would have them be. They were slower, yes, because it took longer to get things done and longer to get from one place to another. The U.S. mail was the chief form of communication linking this country together, as America was inching toward the Twentieth Century.

The tremendous impact of the railroad on the country during this era should  not be under estimated. Most of the progress since the 1830s had chugged along on the back of the black giant locomotives that belched steam and fire, up and down the countryside. In fact, the trains brought much life and hope to the people all across the country, delivering their goods and food, bringing people from one city to another, carrying the U.S. mail, and bringing the democratic process to the people by enabling candidates for the U.S. Presidency to meet and talk with people in every state.

Truly the train station held memories for most everyone and had a link with every family.

In 1891, the country had just eased into the period that historians would later term the ''Gay Nineties.'' It was on April 19 of that year that events occurred near Cleveland, Ohio, that clearly pointed out that the nation's chief form of transportation was running on timepieces that were not reliable. The time had come for strict standards and guide lines for accurate pocket watches to be used by the railroad men and the railroad industry with precision in time keeping.

From the ashes of this smoldering Ohio disaster rose the phoenix in the form of the great American railroad pocket watch, a watch unrivaled in quality and reliability.

That April morning the fast mail train, known as No. 4, was going East. On the same track an accommodation train was going West. It was near Elyria, about 25 miles from Cleveland, Ohio, that the engineer and conductor of the accommodation train were given written orders to let the fast mail train pass them at Kipton, a small station west of Oberlin.

As the accommodation train was leaving the station at Elyria, the telegraph operator ran to the platform and verbally cautioned the engineer and conductor, "Be careful, No. 4 is on time." The conductor replied, "Go to thunder. I know my business."

The train left Elyria on time according to the engineer's watch. What was not known was that the engineer's watch had stopped for four minutes and then started up again. Had the conductor looked at his own watch, the impending disaster could have been avoided.

The two trains met their destiny at Kipton; the accommodation train was under full brakes, but the fast mail was full speed ahead. Both engineers were killed as well as nine other people. The railroad companies (Lake Shore Railroad and Michigan Southern Railway) sustained great losses in property as did the U.S. Post Office.

Following this disaster, a commission was appointed to come up with standards for timepieces that would be accepted and adopted by all railroads. The commission learned that, up to the time of the Kipton crash, conductors on freight trains were depending on cheap alarm clocks. The railroading industry had grown, fast new trains were now in service, and the same lines were used by several different railways. Very often, in only a short space of time, two trains would cover the same track. The industry now had to demand precision in its time keeping.

By 1893 the General Railroad Timepiece Standards were adopted, and any watch being used in rail service by railroaders responsible for schedules was required to meet the following specifications:

Be open faced, size 18 or 16, have a minimum of 17 jewels, adjusted to at least five positions, keep time accurately to within a gain or loss of only 30 seconds a week, adjusted to temperatures of 34 to 100 degrees Fahrenheit, have a double roller, steel escape wheel, lever set, micrometric regulator, winding stem at 12 o'clock, grade on back plate, use plain Arabic numbers printed bold and black on a white dial, and have bold black hands.

Some also wanted a Breguet hairspring, adjusted to isochronism and 30 degrees Fahrenheit with a minimum of 19 jewels.

The railroad man was compelled to buy a timepiece more accurate than many scientific instruments of precision used in laboratories. The American pocket watch industry was compelled to produce just such an instrument which it did. The railroad watch was a phenomenal timekeeper and durable in long life and service. It had the most minute adjustments, no small feat because watchmaking was rendered far more difficult than clock making, due to the fact that a clock is always in one position and powered by a constant force-it's weights,while watches must be accurate in several positions with a variable power source.

The 1893 railroad pocket watch standards were adopted by almost every railroad line. While each company had its individual standards, most all of them included the basic recommendations of the commission.

The key figure in developing the railroad watch standards was Webb C. Ball of Cleveland, Ohio, the general time inspector for over 125,000 miles of railroad in the U.S., Mexico, and Canada. Ball was authorized by railroad officials to establish the timepiece inspection system. After Ball presented his guidelines, most American manufacturers set out to meet those standards and a list of the different manufacturers producing watches of the grade that would pass inspection, was soon available.

According to the regulations, if a watch fell behind or gained 30 seconds in 7 to 14 days, it must be sent in for adjustment or repair. Small cards were given to the engineers and conductors the railroad timekeepers and a complete record of the watch's performance was written in ink. All repairs and adjustments were conducted by experienced and approved watchmakers; inspections were conducted by authorized inspectors.

Because this system was adopted universally and adhered to, and because American watch manufacturers produced a superior railroad watch, the traveling public was assured of increased safety and indeed the number of railroad accidents occurring as a result of faulty timepieces was minimized.

Prior to the 1891 collision, some railroad companies had already initiated standards and were issuing lists of those watches approved for railroad use. Included were the Waltham 18s, 1883 model, Crescent Street Grade, and the B.W. Raymond, 18s, both in open & hunter cases with lever or pendant set.

By the mid 1890s hunter cases were being turned down as well as pendant set. Watches meeting approval then included Waltham, 18s, 1892 model; Elgin, 7th model; and Hamilton, 17j, open face, lever set.

Hamilton Grade 992, 16 size, 21 jewels, nickel 3/4 plate movement, lever set only, gold jewel settings, gold center wheel, steel escape wheel, micrometric regulator, double roller, compensating balance. Adjusted to temperature, isochronism and 5 positions. Marked *Elinvar* under balance wheel. Serial number 2584307 & listed as 992E under the "Hamilton serial numbers and grades" section.

By 1900 the double roller sapphire pallets and steel escape wheels with a minimum of five positions were required.

The early Ball Watch Co. movements, made by Howard, used initials of railroad labor organizations such as "B. of L.E. Standard" and "B. of L.F. Standard." Ball also used the trademark "999" and "Official Railroad Standard." Some watches may turn up that are marked as "loaners." These were issued by the railroad inspectors when a watch had to be kept for repairs.

By 1920 the 18 size watch had lost popularity with the railroad men and by 1950 most railroad companies were turning them down all together.

In 1936 duty on Swiss watches were lowered by 50 percent, and by 1950 the Swiss imports had reached a level of five million a year.

In 1969 the last American railroad pocket watch was sold by Hamilton Watch Co.

NOTE: Railroad Standards, Railroad Approved & Railroad Grade **terminology,** as defined and used in this _BOOK_. **RAILROAD STANDARDS** = A commission or board appointed by the railroad companies outlined a set of **guidelines** to be accepted or approved by each railroad line. **RAILROAD APPROVED** = A _LIST_ of watches each railroad line would approve if purchased by their employee's. (this list changed through the years). **RAILROAD GRADE** = A watch made by manufactures to met or exceed the railroad **standards.** Grade such as 992, Vanguard and B.W. Raymond etc.
Some GRADES **exceeded** the R.R. standards such as 23 jewels, diamond end stone, gold train, raised gold jewel settings, double sunk dial and the list goes on. Examples: such as Veritas, Sangamo, 950 & Riverside Maximus and many others.

RAILROAD GRADE WATCH ADJUSTMENTS

The railroad watch, as well as other fine timepieces, had to compensate for several factors in order to be reliable and accurate at all times. These compensations, called adjustments, were for heat and cold, isochronism, and five to six different positions. These adjustments were perfected only after experimentation and a great deal of careful hand labor on each individual movement.

All railroad grade watches were adjusted to a closer rate to compensate for heat and cold. The compensation balance has screws in the rim of the balance wheel which can be regulated by the watchmaker. The movement was tested in an ice box and in an oven, and if it did not keep the same time in both temperature extremes, as well as under average conditions, the screws in the balance wheel was shifted or adjusted until accuracy was achieved.

The isochronism adjustment maintained accuracy of the watch both when the mainspring was fully wound up and when it was nearly run down. This was achieved by selecting a hairspring of exact proportions to cause the balance wheel to give the same length of arc of rotation regardless of the amount of the mainspring that had been spent.

Railroad watches were adjusted to be accurate whether they were laying on their face or back, or being carried on their edges with pendants up or down, or with the three up or the nine up. These adjustments were accomplished by having the jewels, in which the balance pivots rest, of proper thickness in proportion to the diameter of the pivot and, at the same time, equal to the surface on the end of the pivot which rests on the cap jewel. To be fully adjusted for positions, the balance wheel and the pallet and escape wheel must be perfectly poised. Perfect poise is achieved when the pivots can be supported on two knife-edged surfaces, perfectly smooth and polished and when the wheel is placed in any edge, it will remain exactly as it is placed. If it is not perfectly poised, the heaviest part of the wheel will always turn to the point immediately under the lines of support.

Example: Of a Bunn 16 size, 17-19 jewels, nickel 3/4 plate movement, lever set, gold jewel settings, gold center wheel, double roller, steel escape wheel, micrometric regulator, compensating balance. Adjusted to temperature, isochronism and 5 positions, artistically damaskeened.

🕐 NOTE: Railroad grade watches had a compensation balance made of brass and steel. Brass was used on the outside rim and steel on the inside. Brass is twice as sensitive to temperature changes and twice as thick as the steel balance (one-piece is welded to the steel balance wheel) and after finishing, the rim is cut at one end near the arm of the balance and at the same spot 180 across. In higher temperature, the dominant brass would "grow" longer but welded to the steel rim, it would curve inward, thus, in effect, placing the mass of the balance closer to the center of the balance wheel. This would cause the balance to go faster. However, the steel hairspring in rising temperature would also grow longer but more important would also lose some of its resilience. This would cause the watch to lose time. The balance, remember under the same condition, in effect became smaller and this action by the balance compensated for the loss of the hairspring's elasticity and lengthening. In cold temperatures, the opposite effect took place. This is why the balance is called a "compensation" balance. (It compensates for the temperature errors in the hairspring.)

The micrometric regulator or the patent regulator is a device used on all railroad grade and higher grade watches for the purpose of assisting in the finer manipulation of the regulator. It is arranged so that the regulator can be moved the shortest possible distance without fear of moving it too far. There is always a fine graduated index attached which makes it possible to determine just how much the regulator has been moved.

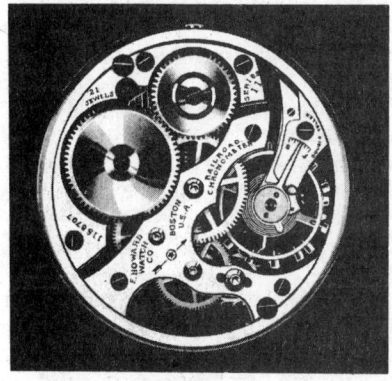

E. Howard Watch Co. Railroad Chronometer, Series 11, 16 size, 21 jewels, expressly designed for the railroad trade.

The hairspring used on the so-called ordinary and medium-grade watches is known as the flat hairspring. The Breguet hairspring was an improvement over the flat hairspring and was used on railroad and high-grade watches. The inside coil of any hairspring is attached to a collet on the balance staff and the end of the outside coil of the hairspring is attached to a stud which is held firmly by a screw in the balance wheel bridge. Two small regulator pins are fastened to the regulator. These pins clasp the outer side of the hairspring a short distance from the hairspring stud. If the regulator index is moved toward the ''S,'' the regulator pins will move, allowing the hairspring to lengthen and the balance wheel to make a longer arc of rotation. This causes the watch to run slower because it requires a longer time for the wheel to perform the longer arc.

Bunn Special

18 Size, 21 Jewels, Adjusted 6 Positions

21 ruby and sapphire jewels; gold settings; adjusted to temperature, SIX positions and isochronism; compensating balance; gold screws including timing screws; double roller; steel escape wheel; Breguet hairspring, patent micrometric screw regulator, safety screw center pinion, beautifully damaskeened with black enamel lettering, double sunk dial.

When the regulator is moved toward the "F" these regulator pins are moved from the stud which shortens the hairspring and makes shorter arcs of the balance wheel, thus causing the movement to run faster. Sometimes, after a heavy jolt, the coil next to the outside one will catch between these regulator pins and this will shorten the length of the hairspring just one round, causing a gaining rate of one hour per day. When this occurs, the hairspring can be easily released and will resume its former rate.

The Breguet <u>overcoil</u> hairspring, which is used on railroad grade movements, prevented the hairspring from catching on the regulator pins and protected against any lateral or side motion of the balance wheel ensuring equal expansion of the outside coil.

Railroad grade watches also used the patent or safety pinion which was developed to protect the train of gears from damage in the event of breakage of the mainspring. These pinions unscrewed in event of mainspring breakage, allowing the force to be harmlessly spent by the spinning barrel.

Some earlier railroad grade watches had non-magnetic movements. This was achieved by the use of non-magnetic metals for the balance wheel, hairspring, roller table and pallet. Two of the metals used were iridium and palladium, both very expensive.

Rockford Grades 805-Hunting case & 905-Open Face case, 18 size, 21 ruby jewels in gold settings, beautifully damaskeened, nickel plates, gold lettering, adjusted to temperature, isochronism and 5 positions, Breguet hair spring, double roller, steel escape wheel, sapphire pallets, micrometric regulator, compensating balance in recess.

Ball Watch Co. Motto: "Carry a Ball and Time Them All." This case is an example of Ball's patented Stirrup Bow. With the simple easy to read dial, this watch was a favorite among railroad men.

RAILROAD WATCH DIALS

Railroad watch dials are distinguished by their simplicity. A true railroad watch dial contained no fancy lettering or beautiful backgrounds. The watches were designed to be functional and in order to achieve that, the dials contained bold black Arabic numbers against a white background. This facilitated ease of reading the time under even the most adverse conditions.

True railroad watches had the winding stem at the 12 o'clock position. The so-called "side winder," that winds at the 3 o'clock position, was not approved for railroad use. (The side winder is a watch movement designed for a hunter case but one that has been placed in an open-faced case.)

One railroad watch dial design was patented by a Mr. Ferguson. On this dial, the five minute numbers were much larger than the hour numbers which were on the inside. This dial never became very popular.

About 1910 the Montgomery dials began to appear. The distinguishing feature of the Montgomery dial is that each minute is numbered around the hour chapter. The five-minute divisions were in red, and the true Montgomery dial has the number "6" inside the minute register. These dials were favored by the railroad men.

The so-called Canadian dial had a 24-hour division inside the hour chapter.

The double-time hands are also found on some railroad grade watches. One hour hand was in blue or black and the other was in red or gold, one hour apart, to compensate for passing from one time zone to another.

Rockford Watch Co., Enamel **Railroad** double sunk dial, with two hour hands for a second time zone the hour hand at 2 O'clock is BLUE, the hour hand at 3 O'clock is RED or GOLD.

This style Illinois railroad watch cases were fitted with movements, rerated and timed in their specially designed case at the factory as complete watches in a gold filled case with screw back & hinged bezel. Note: Montgomery dial.

RAILROAD WATCH CASES

Open face cases were the only ones approved for railroad use. Railroad men sought a case that was tough and durable; one that would provide a dust-free environment for the movement.

The swing-out case offered the best protection against dust, but the screw-on back and bezel were the most popular open-face cases.

The lever-set was a must for railroad-approved watches and some of the case manufacturers patented their own styles of cases, most with a heavy bow. One example is the Stirrup Bow by the Ball Watch Co. Hamilton used a bar above the crown to prevent the stem from being pulled out. Glass was most commonly used for the crystal because it was not as likely to scratch.

RAILROAD GRADE OR
RAILROAD SERVICE

Note: Not all railroad GRADE watches were railroad APPROVED, to be approved each railroad line or company made a list of watch grades that they would approve for example, Southern Railway, Lake Shore Railroad & Santa Fe Railway System etc. Not all watches listed here are railroad approved, even though all are railroad grade.

BALL
All official R.R. standard with 19, 21, & 23J, hci5p, 18 &16S, open face.

COLUMBUS WATCH CO.
Columbus King, 21, 23, 25J; Railway King, 17-25J; Time King, 21-25J, 18S; Ruby Model, 16S.

ELGIN
1. "Pennsylvania Railroad Co." on dial, 18S, 15J & 17J, KW-KS, first model "B. W. Raymond."
2. "No. 349," 18S, seventh model, 17-21J.
3. Veritas, B. W. Raymond, or Father Time, 18S, 21-23J.
4. Grades 162, 270, 280, or 342 marked on back plate, 16S, 17-21J.
5. Veritas, Father Time, or Paillard Non-Magnetic, 16S, 19-23J.
6. 571, 21J or 572, 16S, 19J., also All wind indicator models.

HAMILTON
1. 18S= Grade 946= 23J, & 940, 942= 21J, & 944= 19J, & 924, 926, 934, 936, 938, 948 = 17J.
2. 16S = Grades 950, 950B, 950E= 23J, & 992, 992B, 992E, 954, 960, 970, 994, 990= 21J.
3. 16S = Grade 996= 19J & 972, 968, 964= 17J.

HAMPDEN
1. Sp. Railway, 17J, 21J, 23J; New Railway, 23J & 17J; No. Am. RR22J.,
   Wm. McKinley, 21J; John Hancock, 21J & 23J; John C. Duber, 21J, 18S
2. 105, 21J; 104, 23J; John C. Duber, 21J; Wm. McKinley, 17, 21, & 23J;
   New Railway, 21J; Railway, 19J; Special Railway, 23J, 16S.

E. HOWARD & CO.
1. All Howard models marked "Adjusted" or deer symbol.
2. Split plate models, 18S or N size; 16S or L size.

HOWARD WATCH CO.
All 16S with 19, 21, & 23J.

ILLINOIS
1. Bunn 15J marked "Adjusted," & Stuart, 15J marked "Adjusted," 18S.
2. Benjamin Franklin,17-26J; Bunn 17-21, 24J; Bunn Special,21-26J; Chesapeake & Ohio Sp.,24J;
   Interstate Chronometer, 23J;Lafayette, 24J; A. Lincoln, 21J; Paillard W. Co., 17-24J;
   Trainsmen, 23J; Pennsylvania Special 17-26J; The Railroader & Railroad King, 18S.
3. Benjamin Franklin,17-25J; Bunn,17-19J; Bunn Special,21-23J; Diamond Ruby Sapphire,21-23J;
   Interstate Chronometer,23J; Lafayette,23J; A.Lincoln,21J; Paillard Non-MagneticW.Co.,17-21J;
   Pennsylvania Special, 17, 21, & 23J; Santa Fe Special, 21J; Sangamo, 21-26J;
   Sangamo Special, 19-23J; grades 161, 161A=21J;163, 163A=23J & 187, and 189, 17J, 16S.

PEORIA WATCH CO.
15 & 17J with a patented regulator, 18S.

ROCKFORD
1. All 21 or more jewels, 16-18S, All and wind indicators.
2. Grades 900, 905, 910, 912, 918, 945, 200, 205, 18S.
3. Winnebago, 17-21J, 505, 515, 525, 535, 545, 555, 16S.

SETH THOMAS
Maiden Lane, 21-28J; Henry Molineux, 20J; 260 Model, 18S.

SOUTH BEND
1. Studebaker 329, Grade Nos. 323, and 327, 17-21J, 18S.
2. Studebaker 229, Grade Nos. 223, 227, 293, 295, 299, 17-21J, Polaris,21J; 16S.

UNITED STATES WATCH CO., MARION
United States, 19J, gold train.

U. S. WATCH CO., WALTHAM
The President, 17J, 18S.

WALTHAM
1. 1857 KW with Pennsylvania R.R. on dial, Appleton Tracy & Co. on movement.
2. Crescent Street, 17-23J; 1883 & 1892 Models; Appleton Tracy & Co., 1892 Model; Railroader,
   1892 Model; Pennsylvania Railroad; Special RR, Special RR King, Vanguard, 17 -23J, 1892
   Model; Grade 845, All wind indicators 18S.
3. American Watch Co., 17-21J, 1872 Models; American Watch Co., All wind indicators,
   17-23J, Bridge Models; Crescent Street, 17-21J, 1899 & 1908 Models;
   Premier Maximus; Railroader; Riverside Maximus, 21-23J; Vanguard, 19-23J; 645 16S.

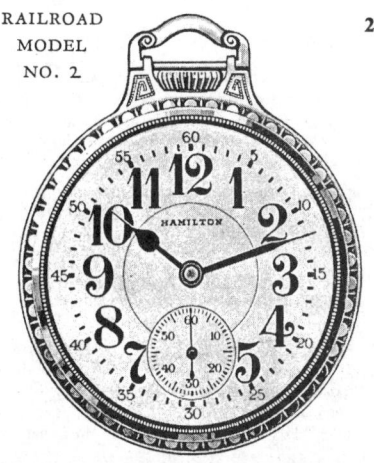

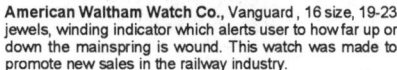

American Waltham Watch Co., Vanguard, 16 size, 19-23 jewels, winding indicator which alerts user to how far up or down the mainspring is wound. This watch was made to promote new sales in the railway industry.

Hamilton Watch Co., This was a favorite railroad style case by Hamilton model NO. 2 supplied in 10K or 14K gold filled. Note the Railroad style dial with red marginal figures as well as the bar-over-crown with "Hamilton Railroad" on crown.

CANADIAN PACIFIC SERVICE
RAILROAD APPROVED WATCHES 1899

WALTHAM
Vanguard, 18-16S, 19-21-23 jewels
Crescent St., 18S, 19J; 18-16S, 21J
Appleton-Tracy 17J; also No. 845, 21J
Riverside 16S, 19J; Riverside Maximus, 16S, 23J;
No. 645, 16S, 21J, C. P. R. 18-16S, 17J; C.T. S. 18-16S, 17J
ELGIN
Veritas, 18-16S, 21-23J
B. W. R. 18-16S, 17-19-21J
Father Time 18-16S, 21J
Grade 349, 18S, 21J
HAMILTON
18S, 946, 23J; 940-942, 21J; 944, 19J; 936-938, 17J
16S, 950, 23J; 960-990-992, 21J; 952, 19J; 972, 17J
SOUTH BEND
18S, 327-329, 21J; 323, 17J
16S, 227-229, 21J; 223, 17J
BALL
All Balls 18S, 16S, 17-19-21-23J
ILLINOIS
Bunn Special, 18-16S, 21-23J; also Bunn 18-16S, 17-19J
A. Lincoln, 18-16S, 21J; Sangamo Special, 16S, 19-21-23J
SETH THOMAS
Maiden Lane, 18S, 25J; No. 260, 21J; No. 382, 17J
E. HOWARD WATCH CO.
16S Series, 0-23J, 5-19J, 2-17J, 10-21J; also No. 1, 21J
ROCKFORD
18S, Grade 918-905, 21J; Winnebago, 17J; also Grade 900, 24J
16S, Grades 545, 525, 515, 505, 21J; 655 W.I., 21J; and Grade 405, 17J
LONGINES
18S, Express Monarch, 17-19-21-23J
16S, Express Monarch, 17-19-21-23J
BRANDT-OMEGA
18S, D.D.R., 23J; C.C.C.R., 23J; C.D.R., 19J; C.C.R., 19J

Double Hour Time Zone Hands, used on railroad watches and were reversible in RED & BLUE or GOLD & BLACK.

AMERICAN RAILROAD APPROVED WATCHES 1930

The following requirements for railroad approved watches are outlined by Mr. R. D. Montgomery, General Watch Inspector of the Santa Fe Railway System:

"The regulation watch designated as of 1930 to be standard is described as follows:"

"16 size, American, lever-setting, 19 jewels or more, open face, winding at "12", double-roller escapement, steel escape wheel, adjusted to 5 positions, temperature and isochronism, which will rate within a variation not exceeding 6 seconds in 72 hour tests, pendant up, dial up and dial down, and be regulated to run within a variation not exceeding 30 seconds per week."

"The following listed makes and grades meet the requirements and comprise a complete list of watches acceptable. Watches bearing the name of jewelers or other names not standard trade marks or trade numbers will not be accepted:"

AMERICAN WALTHAM W. CO.
(16 Size)
23J Premier Maximus
23J Riverside Maximus
23J Vanguard
　　6 position
　　winding indicator
23J Vanguard
　　6 position
21J Crescent Street
21J No. 645
19J Vanguard
19J Riverside

BALL WATCH CO.
(16 Size)
23J Official R.R. Standard
21J Official R.R. Standard
19J Official R.R. Standard

ELGIN WATCH CO.
(16 Size)
23J Veritas
21J Veritas
21J B. W. Raymond
21J Father Time
21J No. 270

HAMILTON WATCH CO.
(16 Size)
23J No. 950
21J No. 990
21J No. 992
19J No. 952
19J No. 996

HAMPDEN WATCH CO.
(16 Size)
23J Special Railway
21J New Railway
19J Railway

HOWARD WATCH CO.
(16 Size)
All 23J
All 21J
All 19J

ILLINOIS WATCH CO.
(16 Size)
23J Sangamo Special
23J Sangamo
23J Bunn Special
21J Bunn Special
21J Sangamo
21J A. Lincoln
19J Bunn

SOUTH BEND WATCH CO.
(16 Size)
21J No. 227
21J No. 229
21J No. 295
19J No. 293

APPROVED POCKET WATCHES IN
CP RAIL SERVICE AS OF FEBRUARY 1, 1957

WALTHAM (16 SIZE)
23J Vanguard S. # 29, 634, 001 and up

ELGIN (16 Size)
21J B.W.R.
21J No. 571

HAMILTON (16 SIZE)
23J No. 950B
21J No. 992B

BALL W. Co.(16 Size)
21J (Hamilton) No. 992C
21J No. 435C

ZENITH (16 Size)
21J Extra RR 56

APPROVED WRIST WATCHES IN
CP RAIL SERVICE

CYMA
17J RR 2852 M
25J RR 2872 A

GIRARD PERREGAUX
17J CP 307H.F.

LONGINES
17J RR 280

UNIVERSAL
19J RR 1205

ZENITH
18J RR 120 T

FERGUSON Patented Railroad Dial : Patent number on back. Valued at ; BALL = $350 to $550 and A.W.W.Co., Elgin, Hamilton, Illinois, etc., = $200 to 350 for MINT dials.

ELGIN WATCH CO., Montgomery Railroad Dial with red marginal numbers at 5, 10, 15, 20, 25, 30, 35, 40, 45, 50, 55, & 60. Valued at $75 to $135.

APPROVED WRIST WATCHES IN
CP RAIL SERVICE 1965
BATTERY POWERED

BULOVA ACCUTRON
17J 214
17J 218 Calendar

RODANIA
13J RR 2780 Calendar

WITTNAUER
13J RR 12 WT Calendar

APPROVED WRIST WATCHES SEMI-MECHANICAL
QUARTZ ANALOG BATTERY POWERED
IN CP RAIL SERVICE AS OF 1978

CYMA
7J Calendar RR 9361 Q
6J Calendar RR 960 Q

BULOVA
7J Calendar RR 9362 Q
6J Calendar RR 960.111Q

RODANIA
6J Calendar 9952.111RR
7J Calendar RR 9361 Q

ROTARY
7J Calendar RR 9366 Q

WYLER
7J Calendar RR 9361 Q

WITTNAUER
7J Calendar RR 2 Q 115 C

A D J U S T M E N T S

There are **nine** basic adjustments for watch movements. They are:

heat 1
cold 1
isochronism 1
positions 6
TOTAL 9

THE SIX POSITION ADJUSTMENTS ARE:

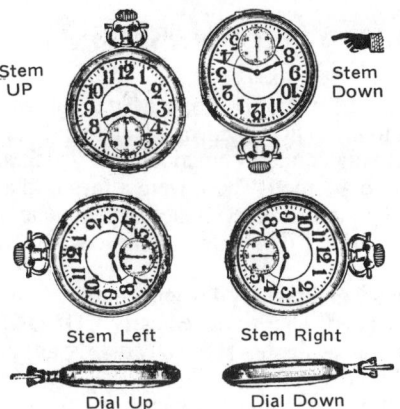

Stem UP

Stem Down

This position adjustment not required on railroad watches.

Stem Left   Stem Right

Dial Up   Dial Down

🕐 A watch marked as **5 positions** is equivalent to one marked *eight adjustments* (the most common found on RR watches) and will be listed in this book as: **"Adj.5P"** (adjusted to heat,cold, isochronism and 5 positions). A watch marked as **nine adjustments** is equivalent to one marked *6 positions* & listed as **"Adj.6P"** (adjusted to heat,cold, isochronism and 6 positions). A watch that is marked as *ADJUSTED* only is adjusted to isochronism & in poise in all temperatures & is listed as **"Adj."**. Later some manufactures used a variations of **8 adjustments**, six to position = 1-isochronism, 1-temperature, & 6 positions (*temperature* of heat & cold combined to = one adjustment not two).

🕐 Not all railroad GRADE watches were railroad **APPROVED**, to be approved each railroad line or company made a list of watch grades that they would **approve** for example, Southern Railway, Lake Shore Railroad & Santa Fe Railway System etc.

WRIST WATCHES POSITION ADJUSTMENTS

CROWN UP - CROWN DOWN- CROWN LEFT - CROWN RIGHT - DIAL DOWN - DIAL UP

Main vertical position: Wrist Watches = CROWN DOWN & Pocket Watches = PANDANT UP.

The total number of pocket watches made for the railroad industry was small in comparison to the total pocket watches produced. Generally, watches defined as "Railroad Watches" fall into five categories:

1. **Railroad Approved-** Grades and Models approved by the railway companies.
2. **Railroad Grade-**Those advertised as being able to pass railroad inspection.
3. **Pre-Commission Watches-**Those used by the railroads before 1893.
4. **Company Watches-**Those with a railroad logo or company name on the dial.
5. **Train Watches-**Those with a locomotive painted on the dial or inscribed on the case.

*   *   *   *   *

1. Not all railroad employees were required to purchase or use approved watches, just the employees that were responsible for schedules. But many employees did buy the approved watches because they were the standard in reliability.

2. These were used primarily by those railroaders who were not required to submit their watches for inspection.

3. There were many watches made for railroad use prior to 1893. Some of the key wind ones, especially, are good quality and highly collectible.

4. Some manufacturers inscribed terms such as railroader, special railroad, dispatcher, etc. on the back plates of the movements.

COLONIAL WATCHMAKERS

(PRE—1850)

Early American watchmakers came from Europe; little is known about them, and few of their watches exist today. Their hand-fabricated watches were made largely from imported parts. It was common practice for a watchmaker to use rough castings made by several craftsmen. These were referred to as Ebauches or "movements in the gray." The watchmaker finished the Ebauches movements and parts and assembled them to make a complete watch. He would then engrave his name on the finished timepiece.

Some of the early American watchmakers designed the cases or other parts, but most imported what they needed. The so called early **COLONIAL** watchmakers showed little originality as designers and we can only guess how many watches were really made in America.

These early hand-made watches are almost non-existent; therefore, only the name of the watchmaker will be listed. This compilation comes from old ads in newspapers and journals and other sources. It is not considered to be complete. Because of the rarity and condition of these early watches, prices may vary widely from $400 to $2,000.

As early as 1775 the first Swiss made watches came into the U.S.A. in the London style. In 1830, Vacheron & Constantin established a connection in New York through Jean Magnin. Later in mid 1830's extending their trade to Philadelphia and New Orleans and by 1838 Agassiz and later Jurgensen.

Early in the 1860's Swiss watches were sent to America. The Swiss Firms of Cortebert, E. Borel and Courvoisier made and **designed** watches to closely resemble the style of American watch case and movement. Examples the Ohio Watch Co. was distributed by Leon Lesquereaux and son (Junior) of Columbus, Ohio. E. Borel & Co. produced American style watches and shipped them to Lucien Morel & Ed. Droz at New York. These were followed later by the entirely original designs of Omega, Tissot, Movado and Zenith.

George Bowen, Boston Mass., engraved on movement "Chronometer Maker", KW KS, Spring Detent., Ca. 1850.

Davis Watson & Co. Boston, Fusee with right angle escapement lever, serial No. 8028 Ca. 1850.

Example of watch paper placed inside a pair-cased watch by a watch maker. This was a form of advertisement placed in the watch after repair was made.

Ephraim Clark, 18 size, non-jeweled, made between 1780-1790; a good example of a colonial watch. These early watches usually included chain driven fusees, verge type escapements, hand pierced balance cock, key wind & set; note the circular shaped regulator above the balance Cock.

Effingham Clark, New York, on dial & movement, the inner with Roman hour chapter and a sweep second outer dial, diamond stone, serial No. 720, Ca. 1815.

E. EMBREE, NEW YORK engraved on movement, serial # 790, chain driven fusee, silver pair cased watch, ca. early 1800's.

B. F. S. Patten, Bangor, Maine, LEFT & RIGHT; left a 48mm, 6 jewels, <u>Cylinder</u> escapement bar style Ebauche movement which may have been manufactured by Japy Freres with branches in France, Switzerland & England. Right; showing the movement cover that reads four holes jeweled but 6 jewels exits, Ca.1855 to 1865.("Continental Watch")

GREENLEUF & OAKES, Hartford, Ca. 1805, Greenleuf & Oakes formed a partnership in 1804, verge, pierced cock.

MARQUAND & CO. , New York, Ca. 1850s, gold case, right angle lever escapement, fusee, gold dial.

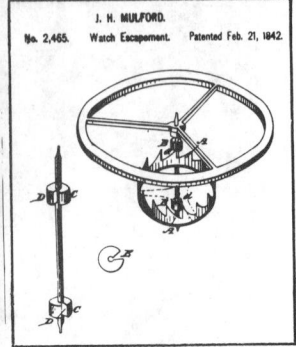

J. H. MULFORD, Albany, N. Y., produced watches from about 1835 to 1875, the two watch movements (A & B) are illustrated, A is about size 18, KWKS, gold jewel settings, compensated balance with gold screws. Movement B is 3 arm balance, diamond end stone. Note the J. H. Mulford patented verge style escapement patented # 2465,dated Feb. 21, 1842. illustrated to the far right.

EARLY AMERICAN WATCHMAKERS
(With Location and Approximate Date)

Adams, Nathan (Boston, MA, 1800)
Adams, William (Boston, MA, 1810)
Alden, & Eldridge (Bristol, Conn., 1820)
Aldrich, Jacob (Wilmington, DE, 1802)
Alrichs, Jonas (Wilmington, DE, 1880)
Allebach, Jacob (Phila., PA, 1825-1840)
Amant, Fester (Phila., PA, 1793)
Atherton, Nathan (Phila., PA, 1825)
Atkins & Allen (Bristol, Ct., 1820)
Atkinson, James (Boston, MA, 1745)
Austin, Isaac (Phila., PA, 1785)
Backhouse, John (Lancaster, PA, 1725)
Bagnall, Benjamin (Phila., PA, 1750)
Bailey, John (Boston, MA, 1810)
Bailey & Kitchen:(Phila,PA, 1832-46) name
changed toBailey, Banks & Biddle
Bailey, William (Phila., PA, 1820)
Baker, Benjamin (Phila., PA, 1825)
Banks, Joseph (Phila., PA, 1790)
Banstein, John (Phila.,PA, 1790)
Barnes, Timothy (Litchfield, Conn. 1790)
Barnhill, Robert (Phila., PA, 1775)
Barrow, Samuel (Phila., PA, 1771)
Barry, Standish (Baltimore, MD, 1785)
Basset, John F. (Phila., PA, 1798)
Batterson, James (New York 1705-30)
Bayley, Simeon C., (Phila., PA 1795)
Beard, Duncan (Appoquinemonk, Del.1765)
Belk, William (Phila., PA 1796)
Belknap, William (Boston, MA, 1815)
Bell, William (Phila., PA, 1805)
Benedict, S. W. (New York, NY, 1835)
Bigger & Clarke (Baltimore, MD, 1783)
Billion, C. (Phila., PA, 1775-1800)
Billow, Charles & Co. (Phila., PA 1796
Bingham & Bricerly (Phila., PA, 1778-1799)
Birge, Mallory & Co. (Bristol, Conn. 1830)
Birge, Peck & Co. (Bristol, Conn. 1830)
Birnie, Laurence (Phila., PA, 1774)
Blundy, Charles (Charleston, SC, 1750)
Blunt & Nichols (New York, NY, 1850)
Boardman, Chauncey (Bristol, Conn.1815)
Boardman, & Dunbar (Bristol, Conn. 1811)
Boardman, & Wells (Bristol, Conn. 1815)
Bode, William (Phila., Pa 1796)
Bogardus, Evarardus (New York, 1698)
Bond, William (Boston,MA, 1800-1810)
Bonnaud (Phila., PA, 1799)
Bower, Michael (Phila., PA, 1790-1800)
Bowman, Joseph (Lancaster, PA, 1821-44)
Boyd & Richards (Phila., PA, 1808)
Boyter, Daniel (Lancaster, PA, 1805)
Brands & Matthey (Phila., PA, 1799)
Brandt, Aime (Phila., PA, 1820)
Brant, Brown & Lewis (Phila., PA, 1795)
Brazier, Amable (Phila., PA, 1795)
Brearley, James (Phila., PA, 1790-1800)
Brewer, William (Phila., PA, 1785-1791)
Brewster, Abel (Norwich, CT) 1802
Brewster &Ingraham(Bristol,CT,1827-39)
Brown, Garven (Boston, MA, 1767)
Brown, John (Lancaster, PA, 1840)
Brown, Samuel (New York, 1820-1850)
Brownell, A. P. (New Bedford, MA.1840-60)
Burkelow, Samuel (Phila., PA, 1791-1799)
Burnop, Daniei (E. Windsor, Conn., 1793)

Bush, George (Easton, PA, 1790-1800)
Campbell, Charles (Phila., PA, 1796)
Campbell, William (Carlisle, PA, 1765)
Canby, Charles (Wilmington, Del., 1825)
Capper, Michael (Phila., PA, 1799)
Carey, James (Brunswick, ME, 1830)
Carrell, John (Phila., PA, 1791-1793)
Carter, Jacob (Phila., PA, 1805)
Carter, Thomas (Phila., PA, 1823)
Carver, Jacob (Phila., PA, 1790)
Carvill, James (New York, NY, 1803)
Chandlee, John(Wilmington,DE,1795-1810)
Chaudron, Co., (Phila., PA, 1799- 1815)
Chauncey & Joseph Ives (Bristol, CT, 1825)
Cheney, Martin (Windsor, VT, 1800)
Chick, M. M. (Concord, NH, 1845)
Clark,Benjamin(Wilmington,DE,1737-1750)
Clark, Charles (Phila., PA 1810)
Clark, Ephraim (Phila., PA, 1780-1800)
Clark, John (New York, NY, 1770-1790)
Clark, John (Phila., PA, 1799)
Clark, Thomas (Boston, MA, 1764)
Claudon,John-George (Charleston SC,1773)
Cook, William (Boston, MA, 1810)
Crow, George (Wilmington, DE, 1740-1770)
Crow, John (Wilmington, DE, 1770-1798)
Crow, Thomas (Wilmington, DE, 1770-98)
Currier & Trott (Boston, MA, 1800)
Curtis, Solomon (Phila., PA, 1793-1795)
Dakin, James (Boston, MA, 1795)
Davis, Samuel (Boston, MA, 1820)
Davis,Watson & Co.(Boston, 1840-1850)
Delaplaine, James K.(New York, 1786-1800)
DeVacht, Joseph & Frances
        (Gallipolis, OH,   1792)
Dix, Joseph (Phila., PA, 1770)
Downes, Anson (Bristol, CT, 1830)
Downes, Arthur (Charleston, SC, 1765)
Downes, Ephraim (Bristol, CT, 1830)
Droz, Hannah (Phila., PA, 1840)
Droz, Humbert (Phila., PA, 1793-1799)
Duffield, Edward W. (Whiteland, PA, 1775)
Dunheim, Andrew (New York, NY, 1775)
Dupuy, John (Phila., PA, 1770)
Dupuy, Odran (Phila., PA, 1735)
Dutch, Stephen, Jr. (Boston, MA.1800-10)
Eberman, George (Lancaster, PA, 1800)
Eberman, John (Lancaster, PA, 1780-1820)
Ellicott, Joseph (Buckingham, PA, 1763)
Elsworth, David (Baltimore, MD.1780-1800)
Embree, Effingham (New York, NY, 1785)
Evans, David (Baltimore, MD, 1770-1773)
Fales, James (New Bedford, MA.1810-20)
Ferris, Tiba (Wilmington, DE, 1812-1850)
Fessler, John (Phila., PA, 1785-1820)
Feton, J. (Phila., PA, 1825-1840)
Filber, John (Lancaster, PA, 1810-1825)
Fister, Amon (Phila., PA, 1794)
Fix, Joseph (Reading, PA, 1820-1840)
Fowell, J & N (Boston, MA, 1800-1810)
Frances, Basil & Alexander Vuille
        Baltimore, MD, 1766)
Galbraith, Patrick (Phila., PA, 1795)
Gibbons, Thomas (Phila., PA, 1750)
Goodfellow, William (Phila., PA,1793-1795)
Goodfellow & Son, William (Phila., PA,1796)

Gooding, Henry (Boston, MA, 1810-1820)
Green, John (Phila., PA, 1794)
Griffen, Henry (New York, 1790)
Groppengeiser, J. L. (Phila., PA, 1840)
Grotz, Issac (Easton, PA, 1810-1835)
Hall, Jonas (Boston, MA, 1848-1858)
Harland, Theodore (Norwich, CT,1750-90)
Harland, Thomas (New York, 1805)
Harland, Thomas (Norwich, CT, 1802)
Harrison, James (Shrewbury, MA, 1805)
Hawxhurst, Nath. (New York, NY, 1784)
Heilig, Jacob (Phila., PA, 1770-1824)
Heilig, John (Germantown, PA, 1824-1830)
Hepton, Frederick (Phila., PA, 1785)
Heron, Isaac (New York, NY, 1770-1780)
Hill, D. (Reading, PA 1830)
Hodgson, William (Phila., PA, 1785)
Hoff, John (Lancaster, PA, 1800)
Hoffner, Henry (Phila., PA, 1791)
Howard, Thomas (Phila., PA, 1789-1791)
Howe, Jubal (Shrewbury, MA, 1800)
Huguenail, Charles (Phila., PA, 1799)
Hunt, Hiram (Robbinston, ME, 1800)
Hutchins, Abel (Concord, MA, 1785-1818)
Hutchins, Levi (Concord, MA, 1785-1815)
Hyde, John E. (New York, NY, 1805)
Hyde & Goodrich (New Orleans, LA, 1850)
Ingersoll, Daniel B. (Boston, MA, 1800-10)
Ingold, Pierre Frederick (NY, NY,1845-50)
Ives, Chauncy & Joseph (Bristol, CT, 1825)
Jacob, Charles & Claude (Annapolis,MD, Ca.1775)
Jackson, Joseph H. (Phila., PA, 1802-1810)
Jessop, Jonathan (Park Town, PA, 1790)
Jeunit, Joseph (Meadville, PA, 1763)
Johnson, Chauncy (AlbanyN.Y., 1825-1840
Johnson, David (Boston, MA, 1690)
Johnson, John (Charleston, SC, 1763)
Jones, George (Wilmington, DE, 1815-35)
Jones, Low & Ball (Boston, MA, 1830)
Keith, William (Shrewbury, MA, 1810)
Kennedy, Patrick (Phila., PA, 1795-1799)
Kincaid, Thomas (Christiana Bridge, DE, Ca. 1175)
Kirkwood, John (Charleston, SC, 1761)
Kumble, Wm. (New York- 1776)
Launy, David F. (Boston & N. Y., 1800)
Leavenworth, Mark (Waterbury, CT, 1820)
Leavenworth, Wm. (Waterbury, CT, 1810)
Leslie & Co., Baltimore, MD, 1795)
Leslie & Price (Phila., PA, 1793-1799)
Leslie, Robert (Baltimore, MD, 1788-1791)
Levely, George (Phila., PA, 1774)
Levi, Michael & Issac (Baltimore,MD,1785)
Limeburner, John (Phila., PA, 1790)
Lind, John (Phila., PA, 1791-1799)
Lowens, David (Phila., PA, 1785)
Ludwig, John (Phila., PA, 1791)
Lufkins & Johnson (Boston, MA, 1800-10)
Lukins, Isaac (Phila., PA, 1825)
Macdowell, Robert (Phila., PA, 1798)
MacFarlane, John (Boston, MA, 1800-1810)
Mahve, Matthew (Phila., PA, 1761)
Manross, Elisha (Bristol, CT, 1827)
Martin, Patrick (Phila., PA, 1830)
Mathey, Louis (Phia., PA, 1800)
Maunroe & Whitney (Concord,MA,1800's)
Maus, Frederick (Phila., PA, 1785- 1793)

Maynard, George(New York,NY,1702-1730)
McCabe, John (Baltimore, MD, 1774)
McDowell, James (Phila., PA, 1795)
McGraw, Donald (Annapolis, MD, 1767)
Mends, James (Phila., PA, 1795)
Merriman, Titus (Bristol, CT, 1830)
Merry, Charles F. (Phila., PA, 1799)
Meters, John(Fredricktown, MD,1795-1825)
Miller, Abraham (Easton, PA, 1810-1830)
Mitchell & Atkins (Bristol, CT, 1830)
Mitchell, Henry (N. Y., NY, 1787-1800)
Mohler, Jacob (Baltimore, MD, 1773)
Moir, J & W (Waterbury, CT, 1790)
Montandon, Julien (Shrewbury, CT, 1812)
Moollinger, Henry (Phila., PA, 1794)
Morgan, Thomas (Phila. & Balti., 1774-93)
Moris, William (Grafton, MA, 1765-1775)
Mulford, J. H. (Albany, NY, 1845)
Mulliken, Nathaniel (Boston, MA, 1765)
Munroe & Whitney (Concord, MA, 1820)
Narney, Joseph (Charleston, SC, 1753)
Neiser, Augustine (Phila., PA, 1739-1780)
Nicholls, George (New York, NY, 1728-50)
Nicollette, Mary (Phila., PA, 1793-1799)
O'Hara, Charles (Phila., PA, 1799)
Oliver, Griffith (Phila., PA, 1785-1793)
Ormsby, James (Baltimore, MD, 1771)
Palmer, John (Phila., PA, 1795)
Palmer, John Peter (Phila., PA, 1795)
Park, Seth (Parktown, PA, 1790)
Parke, Solomon (Phila., PA, 1791-1795)
Parke, Solomon & Co. (Phila., PA, 1799)
Parker, James (Cambridge, OH, 1790)
Parker, Thomas (Phila., PA, 1783)
Parry, John J. (Phila., PA, 1795-1800)
Patton, Abraham (Phila., PA, 1799)
Patton, David (Phila., PA, 1800)
Payne, Lawrence (New York, NY,1732-55)
Pearman, W. (Richmond, VA, 1834)
Perkins, Thomas (Phila., PA. 1785-1800)
Perry, Marvin (New York, NY, 1770-1780)
Perry, Thomas (New York, NY, 1750-1775)
Phillips, Joseph (New York, NY, 1713-35)
Pierret, Mathew (Phila., PA, 1795)
Pope, Joseph (Boston, MA, 1790)
Price, Philip (Phila., PA, 1825)
Proctor, Cardan (New York, NY.1747-75)
Proctor, William (New York,NY.1737-1760)
Proud, R. (Newport, RI, 1775)
Potter, J.O.&J.R. (Providence,R.I.1849-59)
Purse, Thomas (Baltimore, MD, 1805)
Quimby, Phineas & William (Belfast, ME, Ca. 1825)
Reily, John (Phila., PA, 1785-1795)
Rich, John (Bristol, CT, 1800)
Richardson, Francis (Phila., PA, 1736)
Ritchie, George (Phila., PA, 1785-1790)
Roberts, John (Phila., PA, 1799)
Roberts, S & E (Trenton, NJ, 1830)
Rode, William (Phila., PA, 1785)
Rodger, James (New York, NY, 1822-1878)
Rodgers,Samuel (Plymouth,MA, 1800's)
Russell, George (Phila., PA, 1840)
Saxton & Lukens (Phila., PA, 1828)
Schriner, Martin (Lancaster, PA.1790-1830)
Schriner, M & P (Lancaster, PA, 1830-40)
Seddinger, Margaret (Phila., PA, 1846)
Severberg, Christian (NY, NY, 1755-1775)

Sherman, Robert(Wilmington, DE.1760-70)
Sibley, O. E. (New York, NY, 1820)
Simpson, Saml. (Clarksville,Tenn - 1855)
Smith, J. L. (Middletown, CT, 1830)
Smith & Goodrich (Bristol, CT, 1827-1840)
Soloman, Henry (Boston, MA, 1820)
Souza, Sammuel (Phila., PA, 1820)
Sprogell, John (Phila., PA, 1791)
Spurck, Peter (Phila., PA, 1795-1799)
Stanton, Job (New York, NY, 1810)
Stein, Abraham (Phila., PA, 1799)
Stever & Bryant (Wigville, CT, 1830)
Stillas, John (Phila., PA, 1785-1793)
Stinnett, John (Phila., PA, 1769)
Stokel, John (New York, NY, 1820-1840)
Store, Marmaduke (Phila., PA, 1742)
Strech, Thomas (Phila., PA, 1782)
Syderman, Philip (Phila., PA, 1785)
Taf, John James (Phila., PA, 1794)
Taylor, Samuel (Phila, PA, 1799)
Tonchure, Francis (Baltimore, MD, 1805)

Townsend, Charles (Phila., PA, 1799)
Townsend, David (Boston, MA, 1800)
Trott, Andrew (Boston, MA, 1800-1810)
Turrell, Samuel (Boston, MA, 1790)
Voight, Henry (Phila., PA, 1775-1793)
Voight, Sebastian (Phila., PA, 1775-1799)
Voight, Thomas (Henry's son) (Phila., PA, 1811-1835)
Vuille, Alexander (Baltimore, MD, 1766)
Warner, George T. (New York, NY, 1795)
Watson, Davis (Boston, 1840-50)
Weller, Francis (Phila., PA, 1780)
Wells, George & Co. (Boston, MA, 1825)
Wells, J.S. (Boston, MA, 1800)
Wetherell, Nathan (Phila., PA, 1830-1840)
Wheaton, Caleb (Providence, RI, 1800)
White, Sebastian (Phila., PA, 1795)
Whittaker, William (NY, NY, 1731-1755)
Wood, John (Phila., PA, 1770-1793)
Wright, John (New York, NY, 1712-1735)
Zahm, G.M. (Lancaster, PA, 1865)

Watch made by Andrew, Dunheim of New York in about 1775. Note the hand pierced case.

Louis Mathey, Philadelphia engraved on movement, about 18 size, very thin movement, **Virgule** escapement, key wind & set from back, Ca.1795-1805.

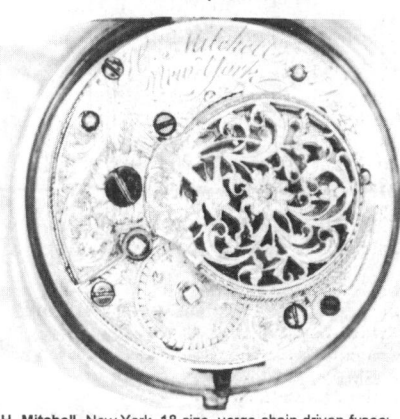

H. Mitchell, New York, 18 size, verge chain driven fusee; note the regulator below hand-pierced cock, Ca. 1790.

MILLIMETERS

AMERICAN MOVEMENT SIZES
LANCASHIRE GAUGE

Size	Inches	Inches	mm	Lignes	Size	Inches	Inches	mm	Lignes
18/0	18/30	.600	15.24	6 3/4	2	1 7/30	1.233	31.32	13 7/8
17/0	19/30	.633	16.08	7 1/8	3	1 8/30	1.266	32.16	14 1/4
16/0	20/30	.666	16.92	7 1/2	4	1 9/30	1.300	33.02	14 7/8
15/0	21/30	.700	17.78	7 7/8	5	1 10/30	1.333	33.86	15 1/8
14/0	22/30	.733	18.62	8 1/4	6	1 11/30	1.366	34.70	15 3/8
13/0	23/30	.766	19.46	8 5/8	7	1 12/30	1.400	35.56	15 3/4
12/0	24/30	.800	20.32	9 1/8	8	1 13/30	1.433	36.40	16 1/8
11/0	25/30	.833	21.16	9 3/8	9	1 14/30	1.466	37.24	16 1/2
10/0	26/30	.866	22.00	9 3/4	10	1 15/30	1.500	38.10	16 7/8
9/0	27/30	.900	22.86	10 1/8	11	1 16/30	1.533	38.94	17 1/4
8/0	28/30	.933	23.70	10 1/2	12	1 17/30	1.566	39.78	17 5/8
7/0	29/30	.966	24.54	10 7/8	13	1 18/30	1.600	40.64	18 1/8
6/0	1	1.000	25.40	11 1/4	14	1 19/30	1.633	41.48	18 3/8
5/0	1 1/30	1.033	26.24	11 5/8	15	1 20/30	1.666	42.32	18 3/4
4/0	1 2/30	1.066	27.08	12 1/8	16	1 21/30	1.700	43.18	19 1/8
3/0	1 3/30	1.100	27.94	12 3/8	17	1 22/30	1.733	44.02	19 1/2
2/0	1 4/30	1.133	28.78	12 3/4	18	1 23/30	1.766	44.86	19 7/8
0	1 5/30	1.166	29.62	13 1/8	19	1 24/30	1.800	45.72	20 1/4
1	1 6/30	1.200	30.48	13 1/2	20	1 25/30	1.833	46.56	20 3/4

SWISS MOVEMENT SIZES
Lignes With Their Equivalents in Millimeters and Decimal Parts of an Inch

Lignes	Inches Decimals	Millimeters
7	.622	15.79
8	.710	18.05
9	.799	20.30
10	.888	22.56
11	.977	24.81
12	1.066	27.07
13	1.154	29.32
14	1.243	31.58
15	1.332	33.84
16	1.421	36.09
17	1.510	38.35
18	1.599	40.60
19	1.687	42.86
20	1.776	45.11
21	1.865	47.37
22	1.954	49.63

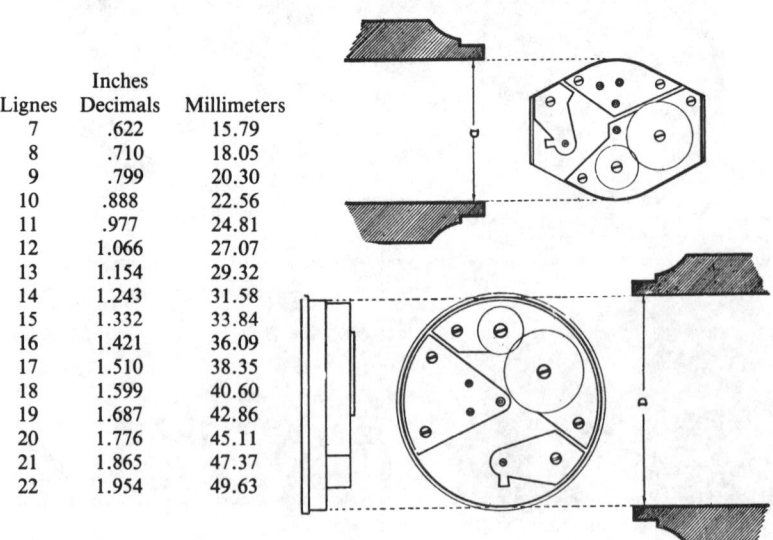

GAUGES FOR MEASURING YOUR WATCH SIZE

The size of a watch is determined by measuring the outside diameter of the dial side of the lower pillar plate. The gauges below may be placed across the face of your watch to calculate its approximate size.

AMER. MOVEMENT SIZES

SWISS MOVEMENT SIZES
LIGNES

SOLID GOLD MARKS

IMPORTANT NOTE: Have your watch case TESTED to made sure of gold quality or Karat.

The term **KARAT** is a word of definition in regards to the quality of gold, one 24th part (of pure gold). For example: Pure or fine gold is 24 karats; 18 Karat (abbreviated 18 K)consist of 18 parts of pure gold and mixed with 6 parts of other metal. The term **CARAT** is a unit of weight for gemstones, 200 milligrams equal 1 Carat. Karat = gold content & Carat = weight of GEMS.

GOLD-FILLED CASES

The first patent for gold-filled cases was given to J. Boss on **May 3, 1859.** Gold-filled cases are far more common than solid gold cases. Only about 5 percent of the cases were solid gold. In making the gold-filled case, the following process was used: two bars of gold, 12'' long, 2'' wide, and 1/2 '' thick were placed on either side of a bar of base metal. The bar of base metal was 3/4'' thick and the same length and width as the gold bars. These three bars were soldered together under pressure at high temperature. The bars were sent through rolling mills under tremendous pressure; this rolling was repeated until the desired thickness was reached. The new sandwich-type gold was now in a sheet. Discs were punched out of the sheet and pressed in a die to form a dish-shaped cover. Finally the lip, or ridge, was added. The bezel, snap, and dust caps were added in the finishing room. Gold-filled cases are usually 10k or 14k gold. The cases were marked ten-year, fifteen-year, twenty-year, twenty-five-year, or thirty-year. The number of years indicated the duration of guarantee that the gold on the case would not wear through to the base metal. The higher the number of years indicates that more gold used and that a higher original price was paid.

In 1924 the government prohibited any further use of the guarantee terms of 5, 10, 15, 20, 25, or 30 years. After that, manufacturers marked their cases 10k or 14k Gold-Filled and 10k Rolled Gold Plate. Anytime you see the terms ''5, 10, 15, 20, 25 and 30-year,'' this immediately identifies the case as being gold-filled. The word ''guaranteed'' on the case also denotes gold-filled.

Rolled Gold

Rolled gold involved rolling gold into a micro thinness and, under extreme pressure, bonding it to each sheet of base metal. Rolled gold carried a five-year guarantee. The thickness of the gold sheet varied and had a direct bearing on value, as did the richness of the engraving.

Gold Gilding

Brass plates, wheels and cases are often gilded with gold. To do this, the parts are hung by a copper wire in a vessel or porous cell of a galvanic battery filled with a solution of ferro-cyanide of potassium, carbonate of soda, chloride of gold, and distilled water. An electric current deposits the gold evenly over the surface in about a six-minute period. One ounce of gold is enough for heavy gilding of six hundred watches. After gilding, the plates are polished with a soft buff using powdered rouge mixed with water and alcohol. The older method is fire-gilt which uses a gold and mercury solution. The metal is subjected to a high temperature so the mercury will evaporate and leave the gold plating. This is a very dangerous method, however, due to the harmful mercury vapor.

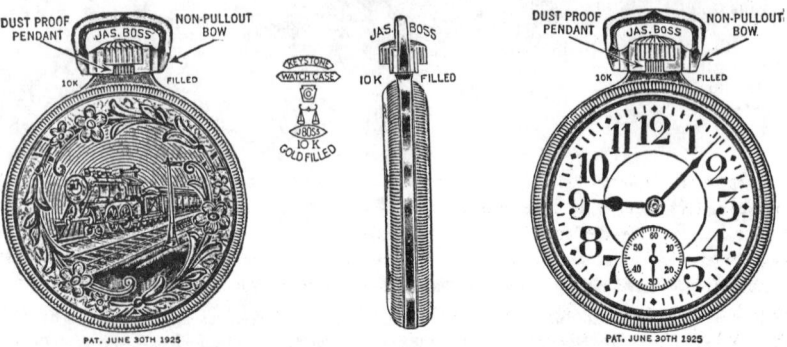

JAS. BOSS Railroad Model 10K Gold Filled cases sold for $14.00 in 1927

GOLD-FILLED MARKS

The following gold-filled and rolled gold plate marks are not complete, but if you have any doubt that the case is solid gold, **pay** only the *gold-filled* price.

Important Notice. All of the information, including valuations, in this book has been compiled from the most reliable sources, and every effort has been made to eliminate errors and questionable data. Nevertheless, the possibility of error, in a work of such immense scope, always exists. The publisher or authors will not be held responsible for losses which may occur in the purchase, sale, or other transaction of items, because of information contained herein. Readers who feel they have discovered errors are invited to write and inform us, so they may be corrected in subsequent editions.

GOLD FILLED MARKS

☆ 10K ROLLED GOLD PLATE

BEE HIVE

(14K. Filled.)

(Jas. Boss 10K. Filled. 20 Years.)

(Keystone Extra, Substitute for All-Gold Case.)

CROWN 14K. FILLED
(25 Years.)

CROWN 10K. FILLED
(20 Years.)

(Rolled Gold.)

(Jas. Boss 14K. Filled. 25 Years.)

(10 Years.)

EMPRESS
(Gold Filled, 10 Years.)

FORTUNE
(Gold Filled, 20 Years.)

PREMIER
(Gold Filled, 25 Years.)

(14K. Filled.)

V.

XV.

(15 Years.)

THE BELL 14K.
(25 Years.)

XX.

(20 Years.)

(25 Years.)

CASHIER
(Gold Filled, 25 Years.)

THE COMET
(10 Years.)

WARRANTED
N.A.W.Co.
20 YEARS

(10K. Gold Filled.)

(5 Years.)

SILVER CASE MARKS

AMERICAN WATCH CO.
WALTHAM, MASS.

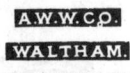

A.W.W.CO.
WALTHAM.
STERLING.

A.W. CO.
STERLING.

A.W.W. CO.
COIN.

WALTHAM, MASS.
STERLING

AMERICAN WATCH CO. WALTHAM, MASS.
WARRANTED
STERLING SILVER.

AMERICAN WALTHAM CO.

STERLING

AMERICAN WALTHAM CO.

STERLING

A.M.WATCH CO. WALTHAM, MASS.
WARRANTED
COIN-SILVER.

DUEBER STERLING
(Discontinued.)

925
(Discontinued.)

NEWPORT
COIN

(Coin Silver with Albata Cap)
(Discontinued.)

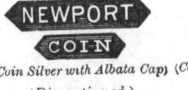

DUEBER COIN
(Coin Silver with Silver Cap)
(Discontinued.)

CHAMPION
COIN.

STAR W.C.CO.

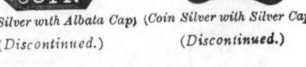

STERLING
925/1000
FINE

(Coin Silver, with Silver Caps,
Gold Joints and Crowns.)

N.A.W.Co.
STERLING
(Sterling Silver.)

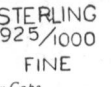

DUEBER
STERLING

925

Sterling Silver

IMPORTANT NOTE: Have your watch case TESTED to made sure of gold quality or Karat.

NICKEL SILVER is 66% Copper, 24% Zinc, and 10% Nickel (also known as <u>**Silveroid**</u> etc.)

SILVER CASE MARKS

(*Sterling Silver*.)

STERLING
SILVER
UNITED STATES
ASSAY
925./1000
FINE.

ILLINOIS
W.C.CO,
ELGIN
STERLING

HUNTING CASES

A hunting case is identified by a cover over the face (concealed dial) of the watch. The case is opened by pressing the stem or the crown of the watch. The hunter style watch was used for protection of the watch and carried by men of status and used as a dress watch.

HOW TO HANDLE A HUNTING CASE WATCH

Hold the watch in your right hand with the bow or swing ring between the index finger and thumb. Press on the pendant-crown with the right thumb to release the cover exposing the face.

When closing, do not **SNAP** the cover. Press the crown to move the catch in, close the cover, then release the crown. This will prevent wear to the soft gold on the rim and catch.

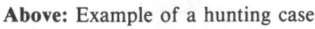

Above: Example of a hunting case

Right: Example of a swing-out case

SWING-OUT MOVEMENT

On some pocket watches the movement swings out from the front. On these type watches the movement can be swung out by unscrewing the crystal and pulling the stem out to <u>release</u> the movement. **SEE EXAMPLE ABOVE.**

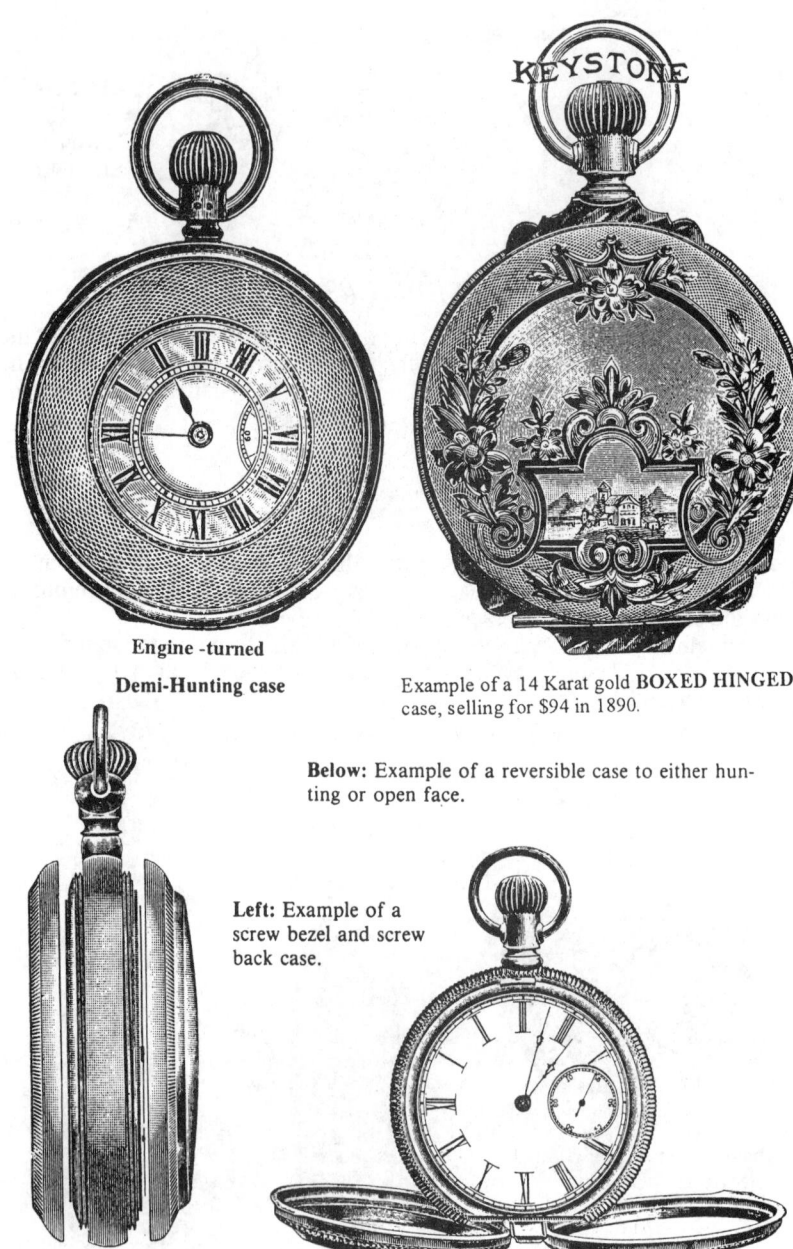

Engine -turned

Demi-Hunting case

Example of a 14 Karat gold **BOXED HINGED** case, selling for $94 in 1890.

Below: Example of a reversible case to either hunting or open face.

Left: Example of a screw bezel and screw back case.

Note: The screw on bezel was invented by E. C. Fitch in 1886.

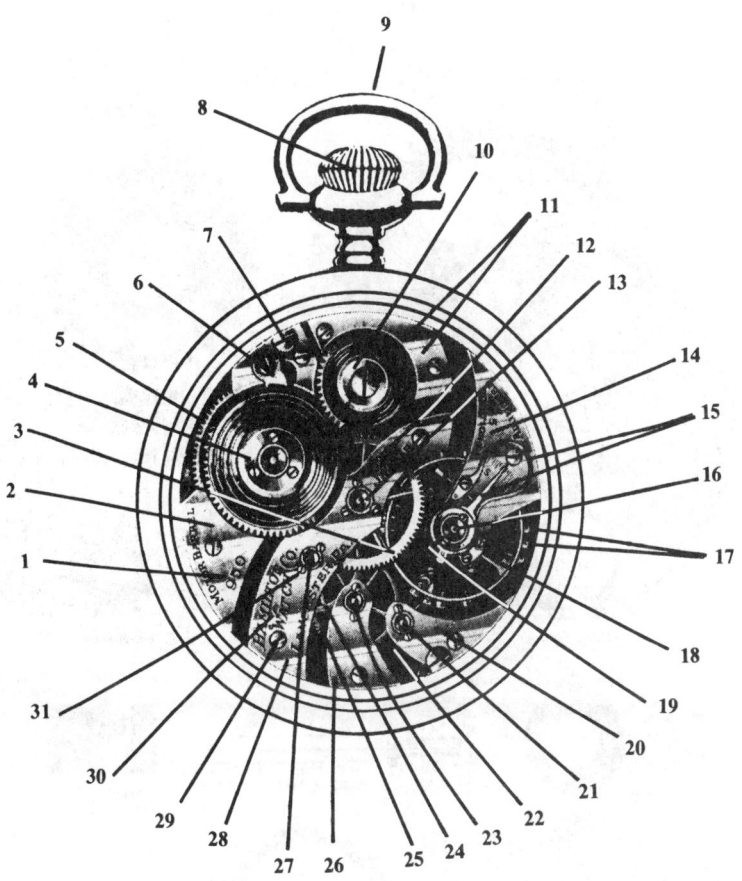

MOVEMENT IDENTIFICATION

1. Grade Number. **2.** Nickel Motor Barrel Bridge. **3.** Center Wheel (2nd Wheel). **4.** Winding Wheel with Jewel Setting. **5.** First Barrel Wheel. **6.** Winding Click. **7.** Case Screw. **8.** Pendant Crown. **9.** Pendant Bow or Swing Ring. **10.** Crown Wheel with Screw. **11** Damaskeening-horizontal pattern. **12.** Number of Jewels. **13.** Center Wheel Jewel with Setting. **14.** Adjusted to Heat, Cold, Isochronism & 5 Positions. **15.** Patented Regulator with Index & Spring. **16.** Balance End Stones (Diamonds, Rubys, & Sapphires were used). **17.** Balance Screws. **18.** Compensating Balance Wheel. **19.** Hairspring. **20.** Escapement Bridge. **21.** Escapement Wheel Jewel with Setting (Diamonds, Rubys, & Sapphires were used). **22.** Escapement Wheel. **23.** Fourth Wheel Jewel with Setting. **24.** Third Wheel. **25.** Fourth Wheel. **26.** Fourth Wheel Bridge. **27.** Third Wheel Jewel with Setting. **28.** Center & Third Wheel Bridge. **29.** Bridge Screw. **30.** Manufacturers Name & Location. **31.** Jewel Setting Screw.

NOMENCLATURE
OF
WATCH PARTS

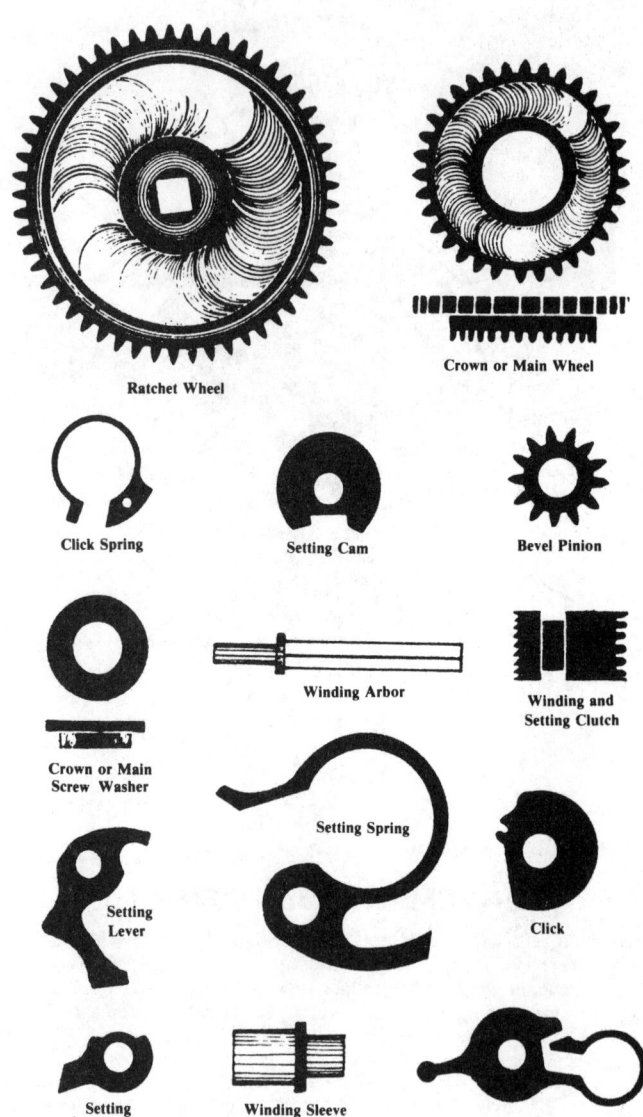

Ratchet Wheel

Crown or Main Wheel

Click Spring

Setting Cam

Bevel Pinion

Crown or Main
Screw Washer

Winding Arbor

Winding and
Setting Clutch

Setting
Lever

Setting Spring

Click

Setting
Spring Cam

Winding Sleeve

Clutch Lever

NOMENCLATURE
OF
WATCH PARTS

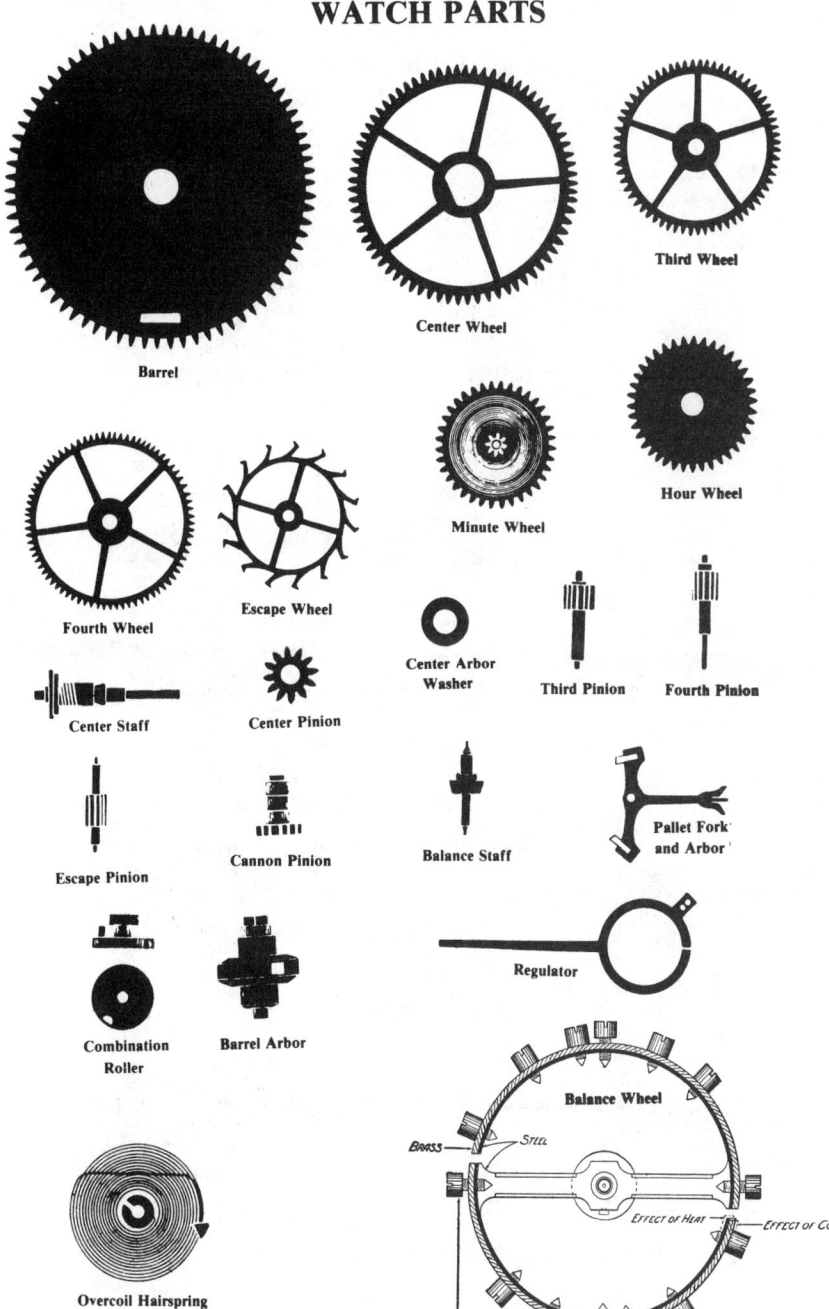

Barrel

Center Wheel

Third Wheel

Fourth Wheel

Escape Wheel

Minute Wheel

Hour Wheel

Center Staff

Center Pinion

Center Arbor Washer

Third Pinion

Fourth Pinion

Escape Pinion

Cannon Pinion

Balance Staff

Pallet Fork and Arbor

Combination Roller

Barrel Arbor

Regulator

Balance Wheel

BRASS   STEEL

EFFECT OF HEAT   EFFECT OF COLD

Overcoil Hairspring

MEAN TIME SCREWS

CASE PRICES

Case prices are for complete cases with bezel, crystal, stem, crown and bow. Hunting case style watches must have workable lift spring.

SILVEROID CASES

Size and Style	Avg	Ex-Fn	Mint
18S, OF, SW	$15	$20	$30
18S, OF, KW	35	40	50
18S, HC, SW	40	50	65
18S, HC, KW	50	60	80
16S, OF	20	25	30
16S, HC	40	45	50
12S, OF	10	15	20
12S, HC	40	45	50
6S-0S, OF	10	15	20
6S-0S, HC	35	40	50

COIN-SILVER CASES

Size and Style	Avg	Ex-Fn	Mint
18S, OF, SW	$50	$60	$75
18S, OF, KW	60	70	85
18S, HC, SW	70	80	95
18S, HC, KW	80	95	120
16S, OF	40	50	65
16S, HC	50	60	75
12S, OF	20	25	35
12S, HC	35	45	60
6S & 0S, OF	15	20	25
6S & 0S, HC	30	40	50

GOLD-FILLED CASES

Size and Style	Avg	Ex-Fn	Mint
18S, OF, Plain	$65	$75	$95
18S, OF, Fancy or RR or Ex-Heavy	90	110	135
18S, HC, Plain	85	95	160
18S, HC, BOX & Fancy or Ex-Heavy	150	175	235
18S, HC, MULTI-COLOR BOX & Fancy	350	400	500
16S, OF, Plain	60	70	85
16S, OF, Fancy or RR or Ex-Heavy	85	100	125
16S, HC, Plain	85	100	135
16S, HC, BOX & Fancy or Ex-Heavy	200	250	325
16S, HC, MULTI-COLOR BOX & Fancy	250	300	400
12S, OF, Plain	30	40	50
12S, OF, Fancy or Ex-Heavy	35	45	55
12S, HC, Plain	45	55	75
12S, HC, Fancy or Ex-Heavy	60	70	95
6S & 0S, OF, Plain	25	35	50
6S & 0S, OF, Fancy or Ex-Heavy	30	40	60
6S & 0S, HC, Plain	35	40	65
6S & 0S, HC, BOX or Ex-Heavy	75	90	150
6S & 0S, HC, MULTI-color BOX	135	165	225

🕐 **Note:** Plain enamel single sunk dial bring $15 to $30.

14K SOLID GOLD CASES

Size and Style	Avg	Ex-Fn	Mint
18S, OF, Plain	$300	$350	$425
18S, OF, Fancy or RR or Ex-Heavy	350	375	450
18S, HC, Plain	375	425	475
18S, HC, Fancy or Ex-Heavy	400	450	575
18S, HC, BOX & Fancy	575	800	1,000
16S, OF, Plain	250	275	350
16S, OF, Fancy or RR or Ex-Heavy	300	325	375
16S, HC, Plain	350	375	400
16S, HC, Fancy or Ex-Heavy	375	400	450
16S, HC, BOX & Fancy	425	550	750
12S, OF, Plain	150	160	175
12S, OF, Fancy or Ex-Heavy	200	235	285
12S, HC, Plain	225	255	300
12S, HC, Fancy or Ex-Heavy	265	285	325
6S & 0S, OF,	125	155	185
6S & 0S, HC, Plain	155	185	225
6S & 0S, HC, BOX or Heavy	200	225	300

18K SOLID GOLD CASES

Size and Style	Avg	Ex-Fn	Mint
18S, OF, Plain	$500	$550	$625
18S, OF, Fancy or RR or Ex-Heavy	550	600	725
18S, HC, Plain	650	700	800
18S, HC, Fancy or Ex-Heavy	750	800	1,000
18S, HC, BOX & Fancy	1,000	1,200	1,500
16S, OF, Plain	400	450	500
16S, OF, Fancy or RR or Ex-Heavy	450	500	625
16S, HC, Plain	500	600	725
16S, HC, Fancy or Ex-Heavy	550	650	825
16S, HC, BOX & Fancy	650	725	900
12S, OF, Plain	250	275	335
12S, OF, Fancy or Ex-Heavy	275	300	335
12S, HC, Plain	350	375	425
12S, HC, Fancy or Ex-Heavy	400	450	500
6S & 0S, OF,	155	185	225
6S & 0S, HC, Plain	200	250	300
6S & 0S, HC, BOX or Heavy	300	365	450

14K MULTI-COLOR SOLID GOLD CASES

Size and Style	Avg	Ex-Fn	Mint
18S, OF, Plain	$650	$700	$800
18S, OF, BOX or Ex-Heavy	1,000	1,200	1,500
18S, HC, Plain	850	900	950
18S, HC, BOX	1,500	2,000	2,500
18S, HC, BOX & Fancy or Ex-Heavy	2,000	3,000	4,000
16S, OF, Plain	500	650	700
16S, OF, BOX or Ex-Heavy	650	700	750
16S, HC, Plain	700	800	900
16S, HC, BOX	800	900	1,100
16S, HC, BOX & Fancy or Ex-Heavy	900	1,200	1,500
6S & 0S, OF,	300	350	400
6S & 0S, HC, Plain	400	450	500
6S & 0S, HC, BOX & Fancy or Ex-Heavy	450	500	575

INSPECTING OPEN-FACED WATCHES

For watches with a screw-on front and back, as in railroad models, hold the watch in the left hand and, with the right hand, turn the bezel counter clockwise. While removing the bezel, hold onto the stem and swing ring in order not to drop the watch. Lay the bezel down, check the dial for cracks and crazing, nicks, chips, etc. Look for lever and check to see that it will allow hands to be set. After close examination, **replace** the bezel and turn the watch over. Again, while holding the stem between the left thumb and index finger, remove the back cover. If it is a screw-on back cover, turn it counter clockwise. If it is a snap on cover, look for the lip on the back and use a pocket knife to pry the back off.

Left: Example of **OPEN FACE** case.　　　**Right**: Example of **DAMASKEENING**.

DAMASKEENING

A special American factory terminology used in all their advertisements or a American *IDIOM* or expression. Damaskeening (pronounced dam-a-skeening) is the process of applying ornate designs on metal by inlaying gold or by etching. Damaskeening on watch plates became popular in the late 1870s. This kind of beauty and quality in the movement was a direct result of the competition in the watch industry. Illinois, Waltham, Rockford, and Seth Thomas competed fiercely for beauty. Some damaskeening was in two colors of metal such as copper and nickel. The process may derive its name from Damascus, a city in Syria, most famous for its metal work. Damascening is a type of steel that was made with designs of wavy or variegated lines etched or inlaid on their swords.

🕐 **Damaskeening** is a special American terminology or a American idiom. In European terminology the word *Fausse Cotes* or *Geneva Stripes* is used.

DISPLAY CASE WATCHES

Display case watches were used by salesmen and in jewelry stores to show the customer the movement. Both front and back had a glass crystal. These are not rare, but they are nice to have in a collection to show off a watch movement.

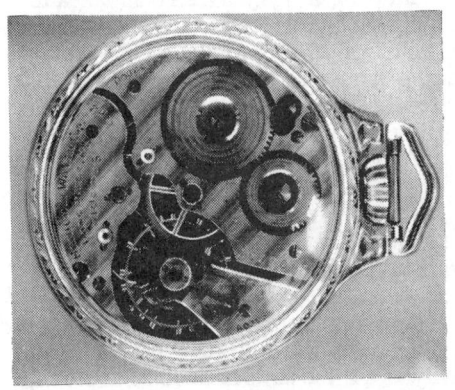

DISPLAY CASE with a bezel & glass crystal to view movement.

WATCH CASE PRODUCTION

Before the Civil War, watchmaking was being done on a very small scale, and most of the companies in business were making their own movements as well as their own cases. After the War, tradesmen set up shops specializing exclusively in cases, while other artisans were making the movements. The case factories, because of mass production, could supply watch manufacturers with cases more economically than the manufacturers could produce their own.

A patent granted to James Boss on May 3, 1859, were not the first gold-filled cases made from sandwich-type sheets of metal, but Boss did invent a new process that proved to be very successful, resulting in a more durable case that he sold with a 20-year money-back guarantee.

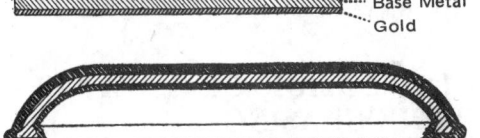

Gold
Base Metal
Gold

The illustrations at left is a sandwiched type gold-filled case.

GOLD CASE WEIGHTS BY SIZE

Size & Style of Case	Pennyweights (DWT)				
	Ex. Heavy	Heavy	Medium	Light	Ex. Light
18 size Hunting Case	60 to 65	50 to 55	45 to 50	40 to 45	35
16 size Hunting Case	55 to 60	45 to 50	40 to 45	35 to 40	32
18 size Open Face Case		40 to 45	38	35	
16 size Open Face Case		40	36	30	
12 size Open Face Case (Thin)					14
6 size Hunting Case	24	22	20	18	
0 size Hunting Case					14 to 16

An 18 size movement with a full plate weighs 50 DWT; a 16 size movement with a ¾ plate weighs 35 DWT. These weights do not include the case.

TROY WEIGHT = 24 grains=1dwt., 1 Grain= 0.0648 grams, 20dwt = 1 OZ., 12oz = 1 LB.
NOTE: Gold & Silver Standards Vary from Country to Country. U.S.A. Coin Gold =.900 or 21 3/5K, Silver Coin=.900.
Gold Standards: 24K=1,000%or 1.0, 23K=.958 1/3, 22K=.916 2/3, 21K=.875, 20K=.833 1/3, 19K=.791 2/3, 18K=.750,
17K=.708 1/3, 16K=.666 2/3, 15K=.625, 14K=.583 1/3, 13K=.541 2/3, 12K=.500, 11=.458 1/3, 10K=.416 2/3, 9K=.375.
8K=.333 1/3, 7K=.291 2/3, 6K=.250, 5K=.208 1/3, 4K=.166 2/3, 3K=.125, 2K=.83 1/3, 1K=.41 2/3.

CARE OF WATCHES

To some people a watch is just a device that keeps time. They do not know the history of its development nor how it operates. They have no appreciation for improvements made over the years. That the watch is a true miracle of mechanical genius and skill, is seldom more than a fleeting thought. The average person will know it must be wound to run, that it has a mainspring and possibly a hairspring. Some even realize there are wheels and gears and, by some strange method, these work in harmony to keep time. If for some reason the watch should stop, the owner will merely take it to a watch repair shop and await the verdict on damage and cost.

To be a good collector one must have some knowledge of the components of a watch and how they work and the history of the development of the watch. To buy a watch on blind faith is indeed risky, but many collectors do it every day because they have limited knowledge.

How does a watch measure time and perform so well? Within the case one can find the fulcrum, lever, gear, bearing, axle, wheel, screw, and the spring which overcomes nature's law of gravity. All these parts harmonize to provide an accurate reading minute by minute. A good collector will be able to identify all of them.

After acquiring a watch, you will want to take good care of it. A watch should be cleaned inside and out. Dirt will wear it out much faster, and gummy oil will restrict it and keep it from running all together. After the watch has been cleaned it should be stored in a dry place. Rust is the No. 1 enemy. A watch is a delicate instrument but, if it is given proper care, it will provide many years of quality service. A pocket watch should be wound at regular intervals about once every 24 hours, early each morning so the mainspring has its full power to withstand the abuse of daily use. Do not carry a watch in the same pocket with articles that will scratch or tarnish the case. A fully wound watch can withstand a jar easier than a watch that has been allowed to run down. Always wind a watch and leave it running when you ship it. If you are one who enjoys carrying a watch be sure to have it cleaned at least once every two years.

EXAMINATION AND INSPECTION OF A WATCH BEFORE PURCHASING

The examination and inspection of a watch before purchasing is of paramount importance. This is by no means a simple task for there are many steps involved in a complete inspection.

The first thing you should do is to listen to a watch and see how it sounds. Many times the trained ear can pick up problems in the escapement and balance. The discriminating buyer will know that sounds cannot be relied on entirely because each watch sounds different, but the sound test is worthwhile and is comparable to the doctor putting the stethoscope to a patient's heart as his first source of data.

Check the bow to see if it is securely fastened to the case and look at the case to see if correction is necessary at the joints. The case should close firmly at both the back and front. (Should the case close too firmly, rub the rim with beeswax which will ease the condition and prolong the life of the rim.)

Take note of the dents, scratches, wear and other evidences of mis-use. Does the watch have a generally good appearance? Check the bezel for proper fit and the crystal to see if it is free of chips.

Remove the bezel and check the dial for chips and hairline cracks. Look for stains and discoloration; and check to see if the dial is loose. It is important to note that a simple dial with only a single sunk dial is by nature a stronger unit due to the fact that a double sunk dial is constructed of three separate pieces.

If it is a stem-winder, try winding and setting. Problems in this area can be hard to correct. Parts are hard to locate and may possibly have to be handmade. If it is a lever set, pull the lever out to see if it sets properly into gear. Also check to see that the hands have proper clearance.

Now that the external parts have been inspected, open the case to view the movement. Check to see that the screws hold the movement in place securely. Note any repair marks and any missing screws. Make a visual check for rust and discoloration, dust, dirt and general appearance. If the movement needs cleaning and oiling, this should be deducted from the price of the watch, as well as any repair that will have to be made.

Note the quality of the movement. Does it have raised gold jewel settings or a gold train (center wheel or all gears)? Are the jewels set in or pressed in? Does it have gold screws in the balance wheel? Sapphire pallets? Diamond end stones? Jeweled motor barrel? How many adjustments does it have? Does it have overall beauty and eye appeal?

Examine the balance for truth. First look directly down upon the balance to detect error truth in the roundness. Then look at it from the side to detect error in the flat swing or rotation. It should be smooth in appearance.

Examine the hairspring in the same manner to detect errors in truth. When a spring is true in the round, there will be no appearance of jumping when it is viewed from the upper side. The coils will appear to uniformly dilate and contract in perfect rhythm when the balance is in motion. Check the exposed portion of the train wheels for burred, bent, or broken teeth. Inspect pinions and pivots for wear. If a watch has complicated features such as a repeater, push the slides, plungers, and buttons to see that they are in good working order.

After the movement and case have been examined to your satisfaction and all the errors and faults are found, talk to the owner as to the history and his personal thoughts about the watch. Is the movement in the original case? Is the dial the original one? Just what has been replaced?

Has the watch been cleaned? Does it need any repairs? If so, can the seller recommend anyone to repair the watch?

Finally, see if the seller makes any type of guarantee, and get an address and phone number. It may be valuable if problems arise, or if you want to buy another watch in the future.

HOW A WATCH WORKS

There are five basic components of a watch:
1. The mainspring, and its winding mechanism, which provides power.
2. The train which consists of gears, wheels & pinions that turn the hands.
3. The escapement consisting of the escape wheel and balance that regulates or controls.
4. The dial and hands that tell the time & setting mechanism.
5. The housing consisting of the case and plates that protect.

A watch is a machine with a power source that drives the escapement through a train of gears, and it has a subsidiary train to drive a hand. The motion of the balance serves the watch the same as a pendulum serves a clock. The balance wheel and roller oscillate in each direction moving the fork and lever by means of a roller jewel or pin. As the lever moves back and forth it allows the escape wheel to unlock at even intervals (about 1/5 sec.) and causes the train of gears to move in one direction under the power of the mainspring. Thus, the mainspring is allowed to be let down or unwind one pulse at a time.

WATCH MOVEMENT PARTS

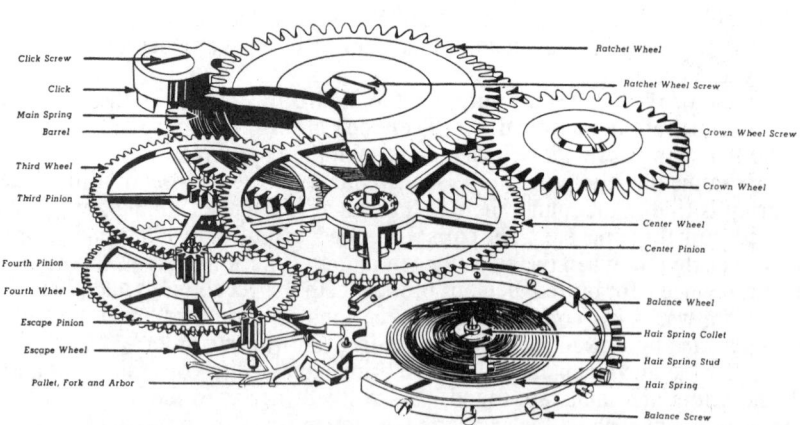

Mechanical watches are small engines powered by a main spring, which keeps the balance in motion. The **uniformity** of this motion relies on the <u>balance</u> and <u>escapement</u>; the **durability** rests on the quality of <u>material</u> and <u>construction</u> of the complete movement.

TRAIN OF A ELGIN MOVEMENT
& EACH PART NAMED

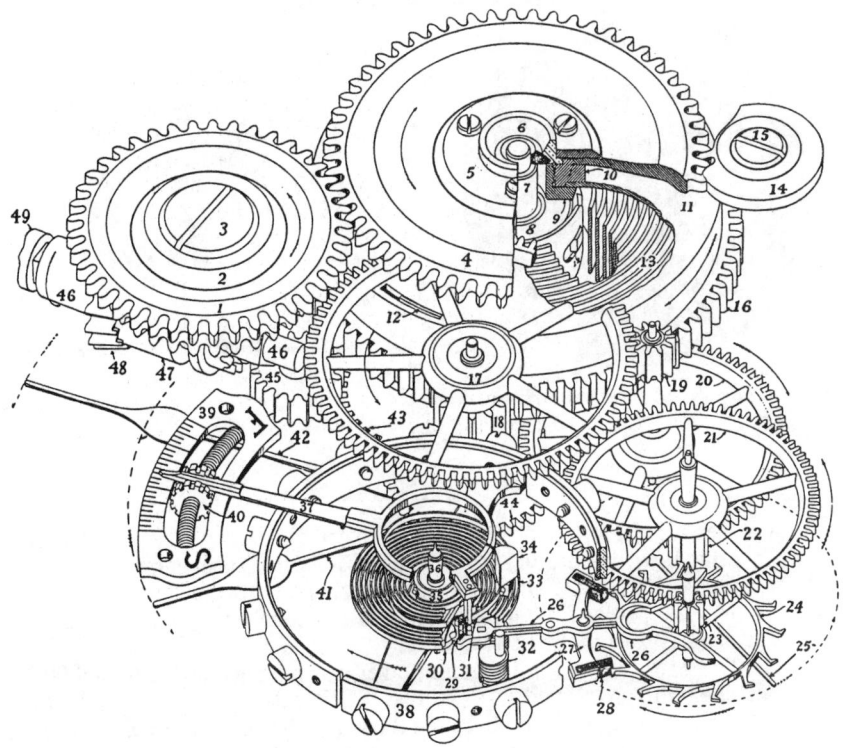

1 Main Wheel.	26 Fork.
2 Main Wheel Washer.	27 Pallet.
3 Main Screw.	28 Pallet Stones.
4 Ratchet Wheel.	29 Roller Jewel Pin.
5 Ratchet Wheel Washer.	30 Safety Roller.
6 Jewel Setting.	31 Table Roller.
7 Barrel Arbor.	32 Banking Screws.
8 Barrel Arbor Hub.	33 Breg. Hair Spring.
9 Barrel Hub Screw.	34 Hair Spring Stud.
10 Barrel Hub.	35 Hair Spring Collet.
11 Barrel.	36 Balance Staff.
12 Main Spring Hooked.	37 Regulator.
13 Main Spring.	38 Balance.
14 Recoiling Click.	39 Index.
15 Click Screw.	40 Reg. Adj. Nut.
16 First Wheel.	41 Hour Hand.
17 Center Wheel.	42 Minute Hand.
18 Center Pinion.	43 Minute Wheel.
19 Third Pinion.	44 Hour Wheel.
20 Third Wheel.	45 Setting Wheel.
21 Fourth Wheel.	46 Winding Arbor.
22 Fourth Pinion.	47 Wind. & Set. Clutch.
23 Escape Pinion	48 Bevel Pinion.
24 Escape Wheel.	49 Pendant Bar.
25 Second Hand.	

First Wheel 78 Teeth, 1 Rev. in 6 Hours, 30 Minutes.
Center Pinion 12 Teeth, 1 Rev. in 1 Hour.
Center Wheel 80 Teeth, 1 Rev. in 1 Hour.
3rd Pinion 10 Teeth, 1 Rev. in 7½ Minutes.
3rd Wheel 75 Teeth, 1 Rev. in 7½ Minutes.
4th Pinion 10 Teeth, 1 Rev. in 1 Minute.
4th Wheel 80 Teeth, 1 Rev. in 1 Minute.
Escape Pinion 8 Teeth, 1 Rev. in 6 Seconds.
Escape Wheel 15 Teeth, 1 Rev. in 6 Seconds.
Balance Vibrates 30 times in 6 Seconds.
300 times in 1 Minute.
18,000 times in 1 Hour.
432,000 times in 1 Day.
157,680,000 times in 1 Year.

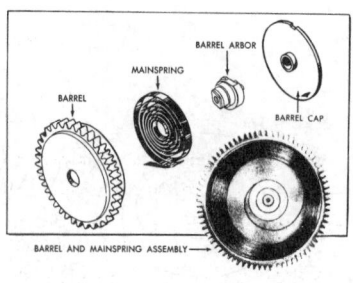

Power unit for modern watch showing the various parts.

Early style watch with a stackfreed (tear shaped cam). Note the balance is dumbbell shaped.

THE MAINSPRING

Watches were developed from the early portable clocks. The coiled spring or mainspring provided the drive power. The first coiled springs were applied to clocks about 1450. For the small portable watch, coiled springs were first used about 1470. The power from a mainspring is not consistent and this irregular power was disastrous to the first watches.

The Germans' answer to irregular power was a device called a stackfreed. Another apparatus employed was the fusee. The fusee proved to be the best choice. At first catgut was used between the spring barrel and fusee. By around 1660 the catgut was replaced by a chain. Today, the fusee is still used in naval chronometers. One drawback to the fusee is the amount of space it takes up in the watch. Generally, the simplest devices are best.

The mainspring is made of a piece of hardened and tempered steel about 20 inches long and coiled in a closed barrel between the upper and lower plates of the movement. It is matched in degree of strength, width, and thickness most suitable for the watch's need or design. It is subject to differing conditions of temperature and tensions (the wound-up position having the greatest tension). The lack of uniformity in the mainspring affects the time keeping qualities of a watch.

The power assembly in a watch consists of the mainspring, mainspring barrel, arbor, and cap. The mainspring furnishes the power to run the watch. It is coiled around the arbor and is contained in the mainspring barrel, which is cylindrical and has a gear on it which serves as the first wheel of the train. The arbor is a cylindrical shaft with a hook for the mainspring in the center of the body. The cap is a flat disk which snaps into a recess in the barrel. A hook on the inside of the mainspring barrel is for attaching the mainspring to the barrel.

The mainspring is made of a long thin strip of steel, hardened to give the desired resiliency. Mainsprings vary in size but are similar in design; they have a hook on the outer end to attach to the mainspring barrel, and a hole in the inner end to fasten to the mainspring barrel arbor.

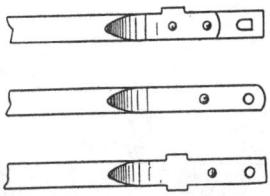

Mainspring Bridles showing a few different designs.

By turning the crown clockwise, the barrel arbor is rotated and the mainspring is wound around it. The mainspring barrel arbor is held stationary after winding by means of the ratchet wheel and click. As the mainspring uncoils, it causes the mainspring barrel to revolve. The barrel is meshed with the pinion on the center wheel, and as it revolves it sets the train wheels in motion. Pocket and wrist watches, in most cases, will run up to 40 hours on one winding.

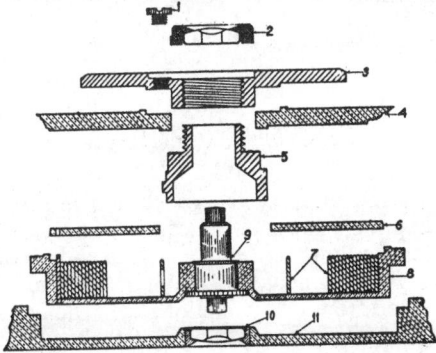

Jeweled Motor Barrel Unit: 1. Barrel top jewel screw. 2. Barrel top jewel and setting. 3. Ratchet wheel. 4. Barrel bridge. 5. Barrel hub. 6. Barrel head. 7. Mainspring (in barrel). 8. Barrel. 9. Barrel arbor (riveted to barrel). 10. Barrel lower jewel and setting. 11. Pillar plate.

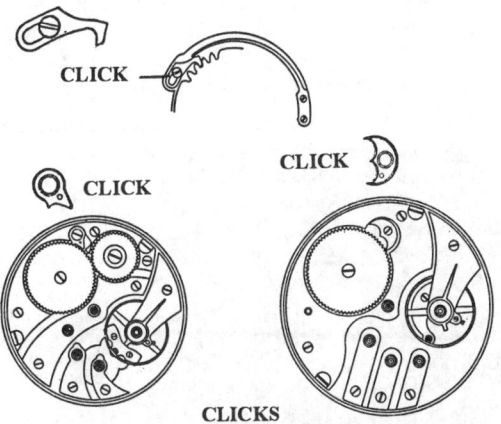

CLICKS

A **click** acts on the teeth of the ratchet wheel, so that the barrel-arbor can turn in one direction only, that of the winding. The click is made to mesh constantly with the ratchet teeth by the click spring. In older watches a device known as **stop-work** which restricted the two extremes of the mainspring was used. A modern watch uses the **click-work** which prevents the mainspring from being *over wound* by a certain amount of recoil.

Curb pins adjusted
to vary the length
of hairspring

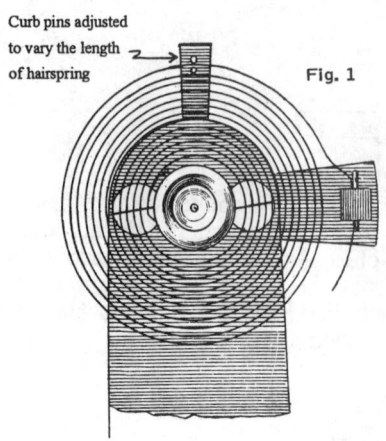

Fig. 1

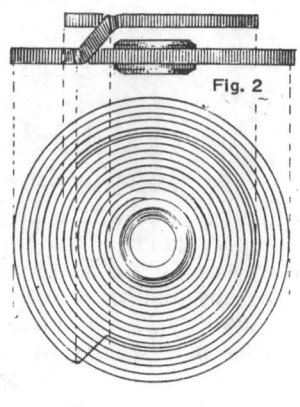

Fig. 2

Fig. 1. Bottom view of Hairspring & cock
Fig. 2. Aside and top view of hairspring

THE HAIRSPRING

The hairspring is the brain of the watch and is kept in motion by the mainspring. The hairspring is the most delicate tension spring made. It is a piece of flat wire about 12 inches long, 1/100th of an inch wide, 0.05mm or 0.0019685 inches thick, and weighs only about 1/9,000th of a pound. Thousands of these hairsprings can be made from one pound of steel. The hairspring controls the action of the balance wheel. The hairspring steel is drawn through the diamond surfaces to a third the size of a human hair. There are two kinds of hairsprings in the watches of later times, the flat one and the Breguet. The Breguet (named for its French inventor) is an overcoil given to the spring.

There are two methods for overcoil, the oldest is the way the spring is bent by hand; and with the other method the overcoil is bent or completed in a form at one end and at the same time is hardened and tempered in the form. The hairspring contracts and expands 432,000 times a day.

A modern style (Am. Waltham) regulator. Note the triangular shaped hairspring stud which is located on the balance bridge between the screw and curb pin.

REGULATORS
Identification

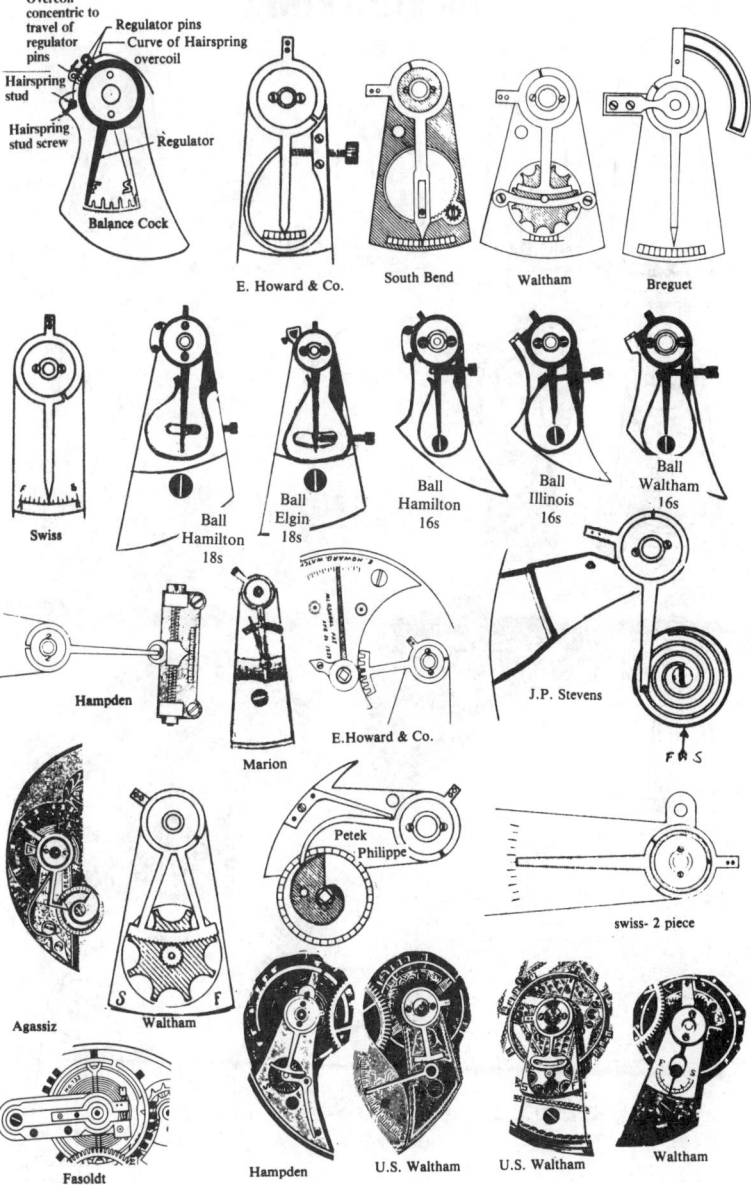

Overcoil concentric to travel of regulator pins
Regulator pins
Curve of Hairspring overcoil
Hairspring stud
Hairspring stud screw
Regulator
Balance Cock

E. Howard & Co.

South Bend

Waltham

Breguet

Swiss

Ball Hamilton 18s

Ball Elgin 18s

Ball Hamilton 16s

Ball Illinois 16s

Ball Waltham 16s

Hampden

Marion

E.Howard & Co.

J.P. Stevens

F & S

Agassiz

Waltham

S   F

Petek Philippe

swiss- 2 piece

Fasoldt

Hampden

U.S. Waltham

U.S. Waltham

Waltham

REGULATORS
Identification

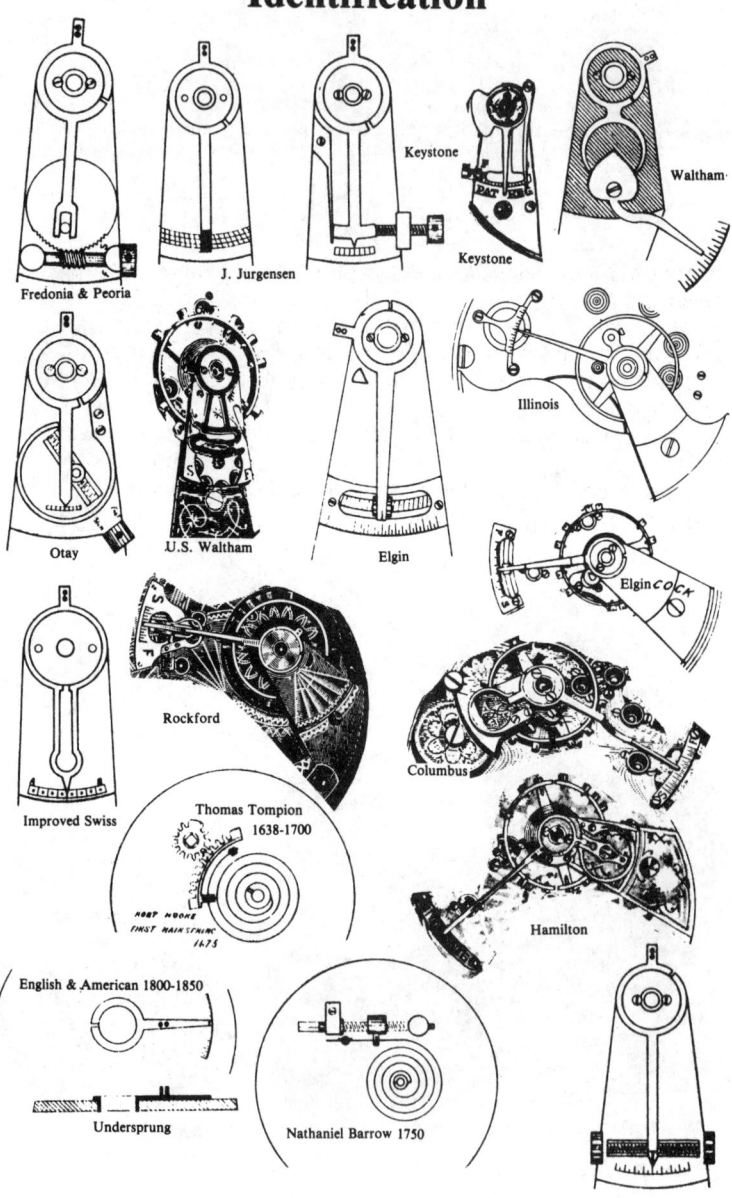

Fredonia & Peoria

J. Jurgensen

Keystone

Keystone

Waltham

Otay

U.S. Waltham

Elgin

Illinois

Elgin COCK

Rockford

Columbus

Improved Swiss

Thomas Tompion
1638-1700

Hamilton

English & American 1800-1850

Undersprung

Nathaniel Barrow 1750

Grossman Glasshutte

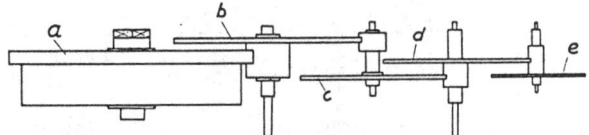

Elevation of a **GEAR-TRAIN**

(a.) barrel, (b.) center wheel (carries Minute hand), (c.) third wheel, (d.) fourth wheel (carries seconds hand), (e.) escape wheel
8 day watches use a *intermediate* (8 day wheel) placed between the barrel and the center wheel.

THE TRAIN

The time train consists of the mainspring barrel, center wheel and pinion, third wheel and pinion, fourth wheel and pinion, and escape wheel which is part of the escapement. The function of the time train is to reduce the power of the mainspring and extend its time to 36 hours or more. The mainspring supplies energy in small units to the escapement, and the escapement delays the power from being spent too quickly.

The long center wheel arbor projects through the pillar plate and above the dial to receive the cannon pinion and hour wheel. The cannon pinion receives the minute hand and the hour wheel the hour hand. As the mainspring drives the barrel, the center wheel is rotated once each hour.

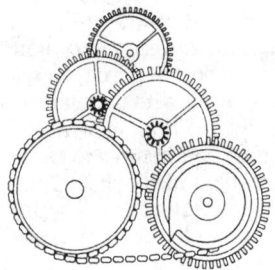

Alignment of chain driven fusee with train. **Fusee** at right and main-spring barrel at left. Note chain between fusee and main-spring barrel.

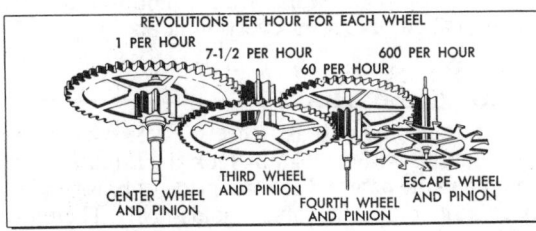

Actual alignment of **Train Unit**

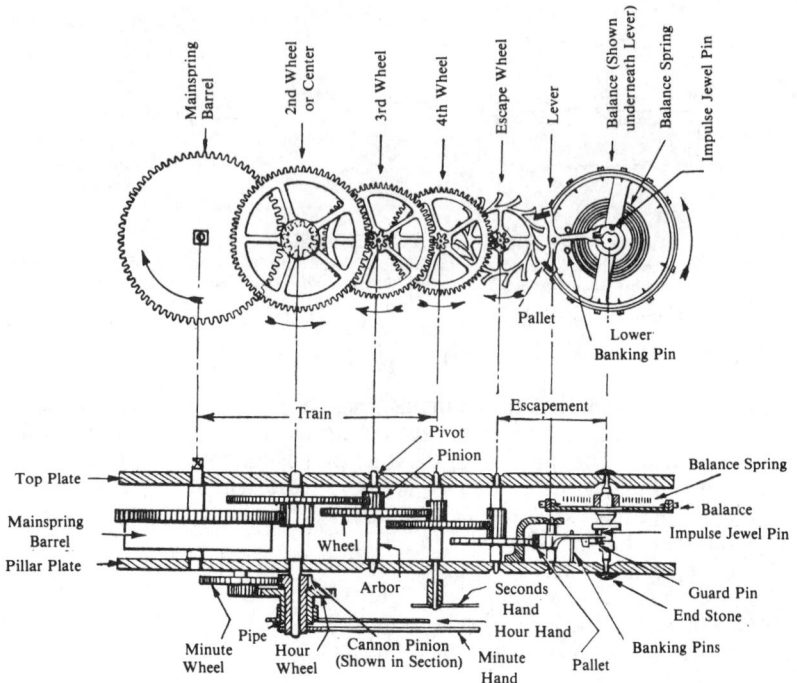

The second or center wheel of the watch turns once every hour. It is the second largest wheel in the watch, and the arbor or post of the center wheel carries the minute hand. The center wheel pinion is in mesh with the mainspring barrel (pinions follow and the wheel supplies the power). The center wheel is in mesh with the third wheel pinion (the third wheel makes eight turns to each turn of the center wheel). The third wheel is in mesh with the fourth wheel pinion, and the fourth wheel pinion is in mesh with the escape wheel pinion. The fourth wheel post carries the second hand and is in a 1:60 ratio to the center wheel (the center wheel turns once every hour and the fourth wheel turns 60 turns every hour). The escape wheel has 15 teeth (shaped like a flat foot) and works with two pallets on the lever. The two pallet jewels lock and unlock the escape wheel at intervals (1/5 sec.) allowing the train of gears to move in one direction under the influence of the mainspring. The lever (quick train) vibrates 18,000 times to one turn of the center wheel (every hour). The hour hand works from a motion train. The mainspring barrel generally makes about five turns every 36 hours.

SOLID GOLD TRAIN

Some watches have a gold train instead of brass wheels. These watches are more desirable. To identify gold wheels within the train, look at a Hamilton 992; the center wheel is made of gold and the other wheels are made of brass. Why a gold train? Gold is soft, but it has a smooth surface and it molds easily. Therefore, the wheels have less friction. These wheels do not move fast, and a smooth action is more important than a hard metal. Gold does not tarnish or rust and is non-magnetic. The arbors and pinions in these watches will be steel. Many watches have some gold in them, and the collector should learn to distinguish it.

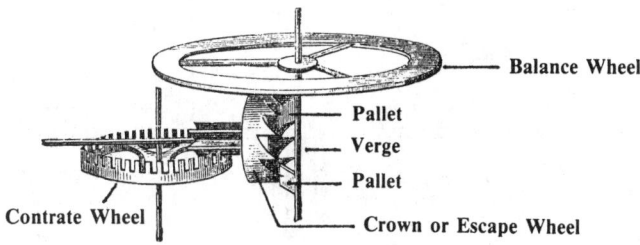

ABOVE: **Verge Escapement**

TYPES OF ESCAPEMENTS

The verge escapement is the earliest form of escapement. It was first used in clocks as far back as the early 1300s. The verge escapement consists of a crown escape wheel, a verge which has two flags called pallets, and a balance. Early German watches had a balance shaped like a dumbbell, called a "foliot." Later most other watches used a balance shaped like a wheel. The crude weights of the foliot could be adjusted closer to or farther from the center of the balance for better time keeping. Another design from that period was the circular balance. The circular balance was used by Christian Huygens in 1675 when he introduced the hairspring. This remarkable invention was used from that time onward.

The verge escapement was used by Luther Goddard in America as well as most of the Colonial watchmakers.

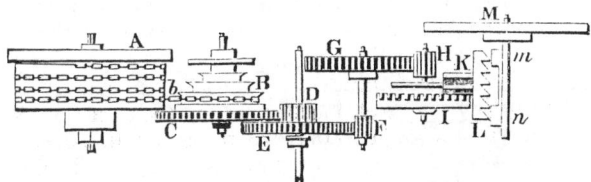

Movement of the common chain driven fusee & verge escapement.

A- is the **barrel** containing the mainspring. **B** - is the **fusee**, to which the key is applied in winding, and which is connected with the barrel by the chain **b**. **C**- is the **fusee-wheel**, called also the **first** or **great wheel**, which turns with the fusee, and works into the pinion **D**, called the **center-wheel pinion**. This pinion, with the **center-wheel**, or **second wheel**, **E**, turns once in an hour. The center-wheel E works into the **third-wheel** pinion **F**; and on the same arbor is **G**, the **third wheel**, which drives the **fourth** or **contrate-wheel pinion H**, and along with it the **contrate wheel I**. The teeth of this wheel are placed at right angles to its plane, and act in the pinion **K**, called the **balance-wheel pinion, L** being the **balance-wheel, escape-wheel**, or **crown-wheel**. The escape-wheel acts on the two **pallets, m** and **n**, attached to the **verge**, or arbor, of the balance **M**, which regulates the movement.

Cylinder

ABOVE: **Cylinder Escapement**

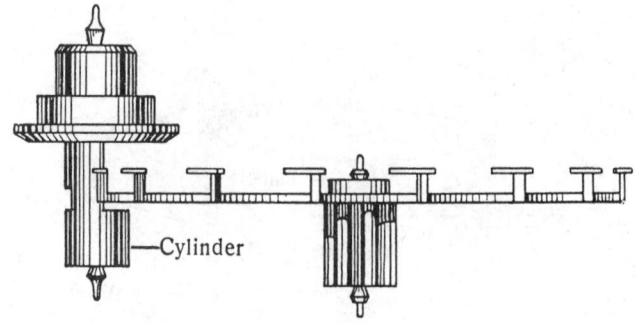

About 1725 the cylinder escapement was invented by George Graham, an Englishman. His cylinder escapement was a great improvement over the verge. Even so, the cylinder escapement was not popular until Abraham Louis Breguet adopted the idea in the late 1790s.

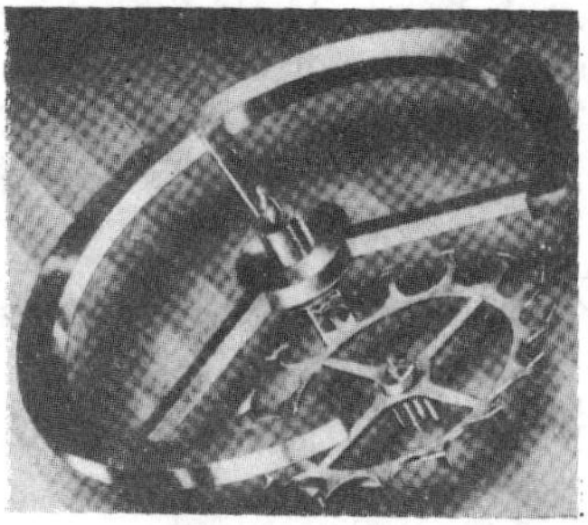

Cylinder Escapement

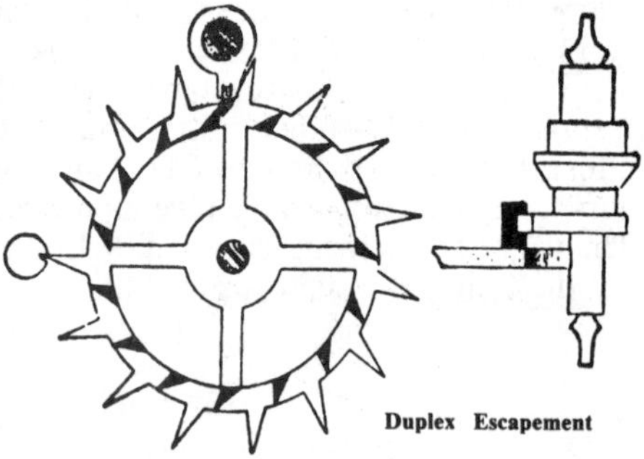

Duplex Escapement

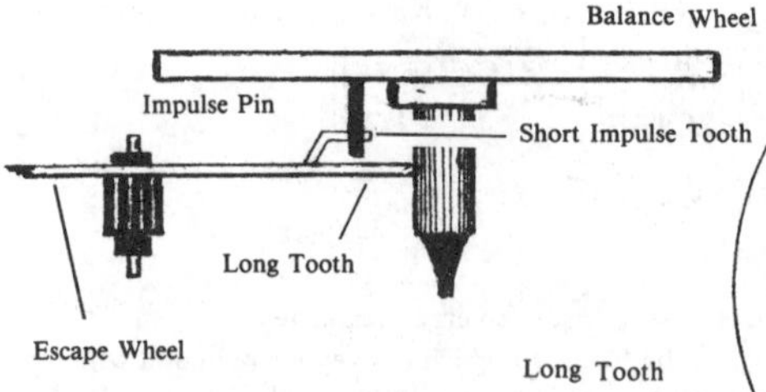

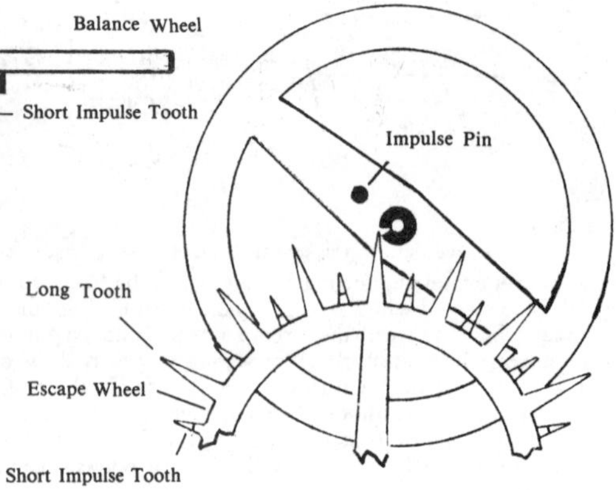

Balance Wheel
Impulse Pin
Short Impulse Tooth
Long Tooth
Escape Wheel

Impulse Pin
Long Tooth
Escape Wheel
Short Impulse Tooth

Illustrating and American form of the **Duplex Escapement** as first employed by the Waterbury Watch Co.

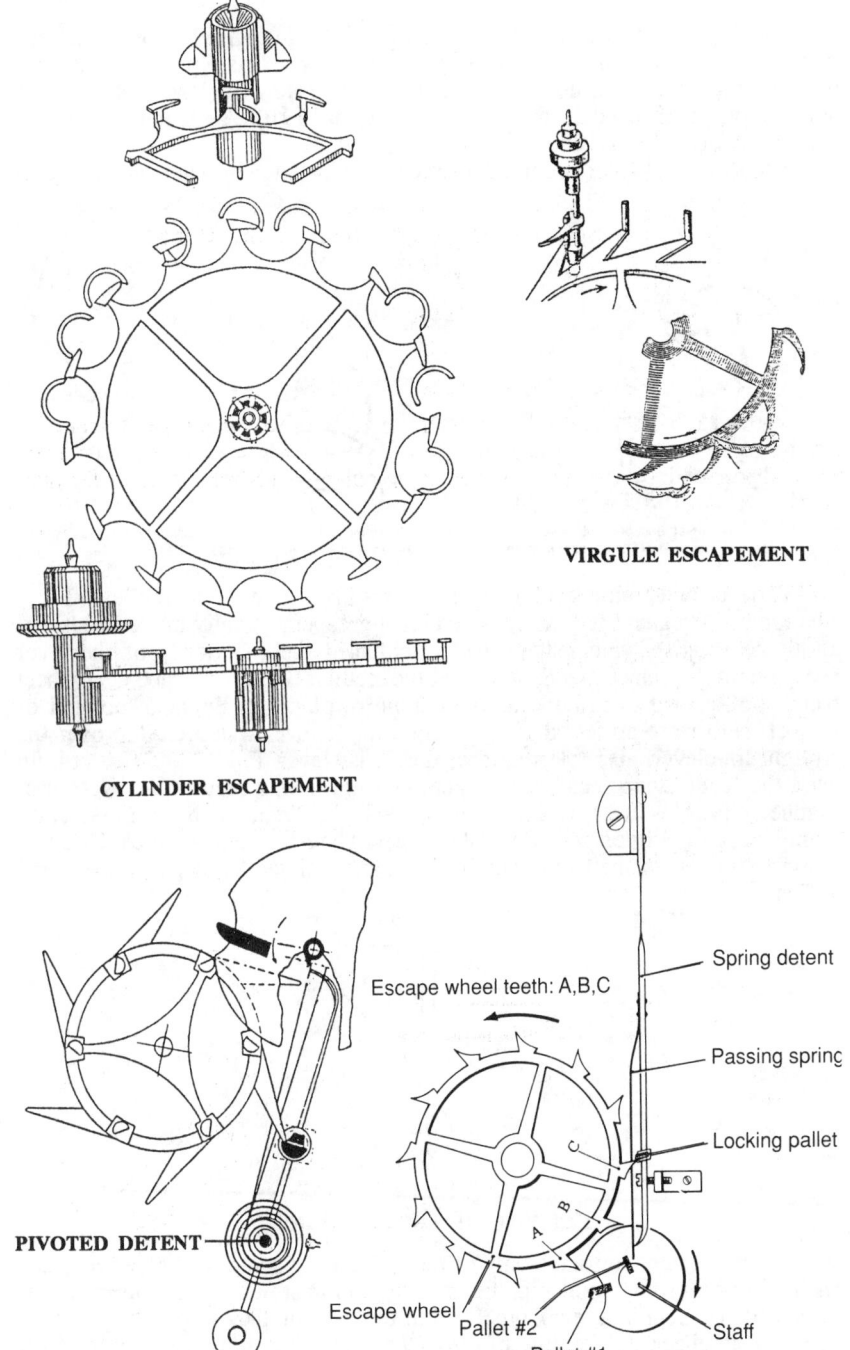

VIRGULE ESCAPEMENT

CYLINDER ESCAPEMENT

PIVOTED DETENT

Escape wheel teeth: A,B,C

Spring detent

Passing spring

Locking pallet

Escape wheel

Pallet #2

Pallet #1

Staff

SPRING DETENT (chronometer escapement)

The duplex escapement is accredited generally to Pierre LeRoy, a Frenchman, around 1750, but was never popular in France. This type of escapement was favored in England up to the mid 1850s. The New England Watch Co. of Waterbury, Conn., used the duplex from 1898 until 1910. The Waterbury Watch Company used it from 1880 to 1898.

The roller and lever action escapement was invented by Thomas Mudge in 1750.

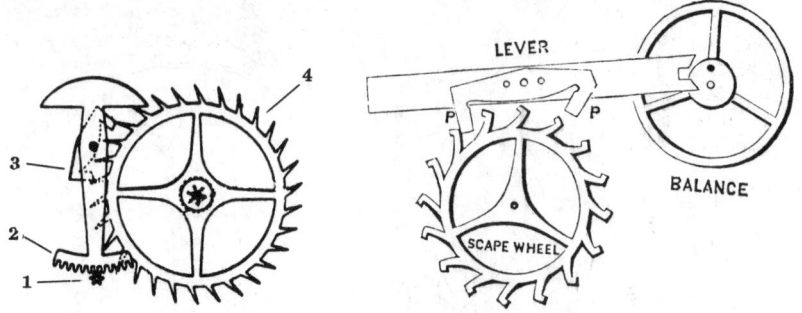

Rack and pinion lever escapement. 1. Balance wheel pinion. 2. Rack. 3. Lever. 4. Ratchet escape wheel.

Right Angle Lever or Detached Escapement which was used in earlier American made watches. P = *pallet.*

The rack and pinion lever escapement was invented by Hautefeuille in 1722. The famous Breguet used the detached lever escapement early in the 1800s. By 1830 the English watchmakers had established the superiority of the lever escapement. In France and Switzerland the teeth of the lever escapement wheel were boot-shaped to provide a wider impulse plane. In England, pointed or ratchet teeth were preferred, and the right-angle lever was preferred over the straight line lever, also referred to as the Swiss lever. Pitkins and Custer both used the lever escapements. The right-angle lever was used in the Warren & Samuel Curtis as well as early Elgin, Newark, Tremont, New York, early Hampden, early Illinois, and Cornell watches. The American factories settled on a Swiss style escapement (straight line lever and club tooth escape wheel) by the 1870s.

Purpose of Escape Wheel

If a movement consisted only of the mainspring and a train of wheels, and the mainspring were wound up, the train would run at full speed resulting in the power being spent in a few moments. For this reason, the escapement has been arranged to check it. The duty of the escapement is to allow each tooth of the escape wheel to pass at a regulated interval. The escapement is of no service alone and, therefore, must have some other arrangement to measure and regulate these intervals. This is accomplished by the balance assembly.

The escape wheel is in most cases made of steel and is staked on a pinion and arbor. It is the last wheel of the train and connects the train with the escapement. It is constructed so that the pallet jewels move in and out between its teeth, allowing but one tooth to escape at a time, turnstile fashion. The teeth are club-foot-shaped because of the addition of impulse face to the end of the teeth.

The pallet jewels are set at an angle to make their inside corners reach over three teeth and two spaces of the escape wheel. The outside corners of the jewels will reach over two teeth and three spaces of the escape wheel with a small amount of clearance. At the opposite end of the pallet, directly under the center of the fork slot, is a steel or brass pin called the guard pin. The fork is the connecting link to the balance assembly.

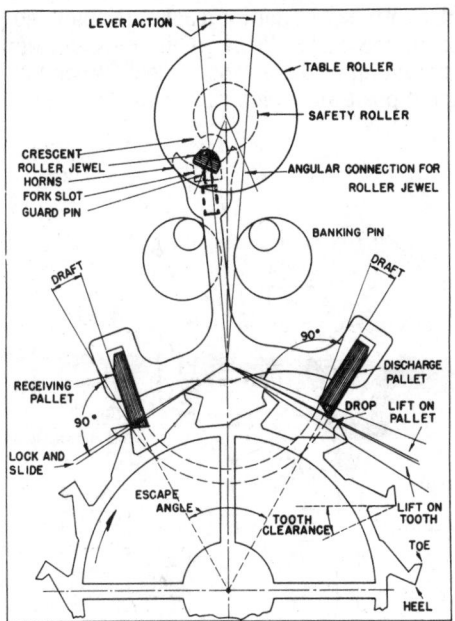

BALANCE AND HAIRSPRING

The rotation of the balance wheel is controlled by the hairspring. The inner end of the hairspring is pinned to the collet, and the collet is held friction-tight

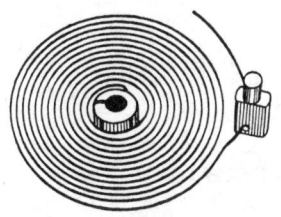

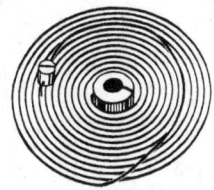

EXAMPLE OF FLAT HAIRSPRING   EXAMPLE OF BREGUET OR OVERCOIL HAIRSPRING

on the staff above the balance wheel. The outer end of the hairspring is pinned to a stud which is held stationary on the balance cock by the stud screw. The roller jewel is cemented in the large roller assembly, which is mounted on the staff directly under the balance wheel. Under the first roller is a smaller one which acts as a safety roller. This is necessary because of the crescent cut out in the roller table which allows the guard pin of the escapement assembly to pass through.

The balance wheel rotates clockwise and counterclockwise on its axis by means of the impulse it receives from the escapement. The motion of the balance wheel is constant due to the coiling and uncoiling of the hairspring. The impulse, transmitted to the roller jewel by the swinging of the pallet fork to the left, causes the balance to rotate in a counterclockwise direction. The position of the fork allows the roller jewel to move out of the slot of the fork freely and in the same direction. The fork continues on until it reaches the banking pin. Meanwhile the balance continues in the same direction until the tension of the hairspring overcomes the momentum of the balance wheel. When this occurs the balance returns to its original position, which causes the roller jewel to again enter the slot of the fork.

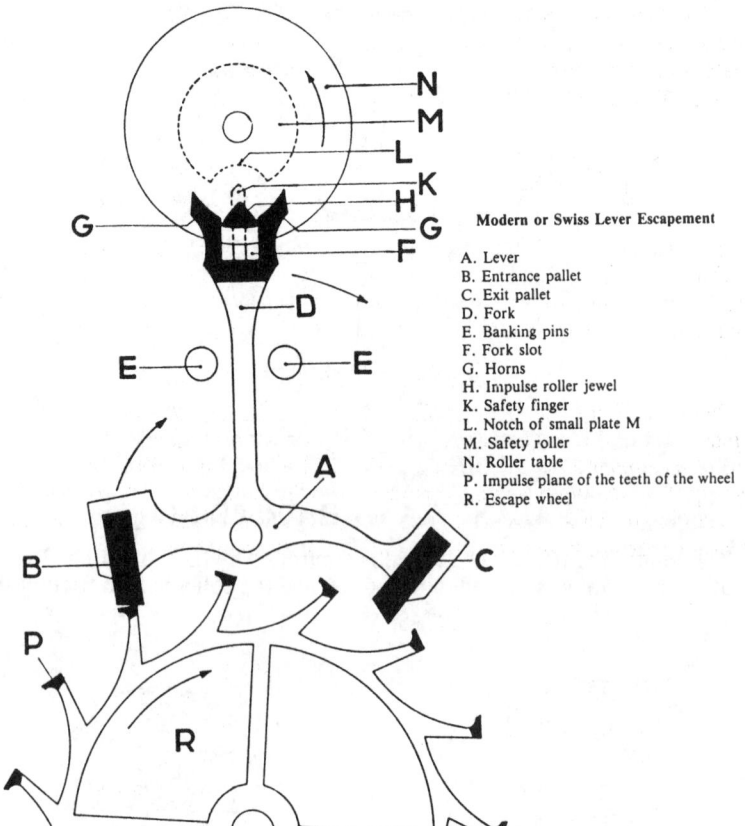

Modern or Swiss Lever Escapement

A. Lever
B. Entrance pallet
C. Exit pallet
D. Fork
E. Banking pins
F. Fork slot
G. Horns
H. Impulse roller jewel
K. Safety finger
L. Notch of small plate M
M. Safety roller
N. Roller table
P. Impulse plane of the teeth of the wheel
R. Escape wheel

Pallet and Escape Tooth Action. The momentum that has been built up during the return of the balance, causes the roller pin to impart an impulse on the inside of the fork slot. This impulse is great enough to push the fork away from its position against the banking pin. As the fork is pushed away, it causes the pallet stone to slide on the toe of the escape wheel tooth. When the pallet stone has slid down to its edge, it frees the escape wheel tooth, thereby unlocking the escape wheel. The escape wheel, being impelled by the force of the mainspring, starts to rotate. As the escape wheel turns, the tooth glides along the impulse face of the pallet jewel, forcing it to move out of the way. The moving pallet carries the fork with it and imparts the impulse to the roller jewel. The right pallet stone intercepts a tooth of the escape wheel to lock it, as the fork moves toward the banking pin. Having a short "run" left to the banking pin, the pressure of the escape wheel tooth against the locking face of the pallet jewel draws the stone deeper into the escape wheel and, therefore, causes the fork to complete its run and holds it against the banking pin. Meanwhile the balance continues in a clockwise direction until the tension of the hairspring overcomes the momentum of the balance and returns it to its original position.

Rate of Escape Tooth Release. Through the motion of the escapement, the mainspring keeps the balance vibrating, and the balance regulates the train. The escape wheel has 15 teeth and is allowed to revolve 10 turns per minute. Thus, 150 teeth glide over each pallet stone in 1 minute. The gliding of the escape wheel teeth over the impulse faces of the pallet stones will cause the balance to vibrate 300 vibrations or beats per minute. These vibrations will continue until the force of the mainspring is spent.

SCREWS

Screws used in watches are very small and precise. These screws measure 254 threads to the inch and 47,000 of them can be put into a thimble. The screws were hardened and tempered and polished to a cold hard brilliance. By looking at these screws through a magnifying glass one can see the uniformity.

EQUIDISTANT ESCAPEMENT

The term Equidistant Escapement is a form of lever escapement. The locking of each pallet takes place at the same distance from the pallet arbor. A similar form of escapement is the circular pallet with the circular form of escapement. The impulses are given at equal distance from the center line. The Swiss preferred the equidistant while the Americans preferred the circular. There is little difference in performance between these two types of escapement.

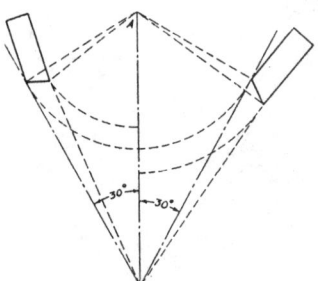

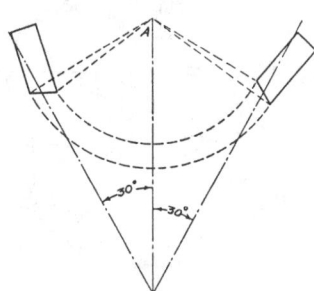

Equidistant form of Escapement   Circular form of Escapement

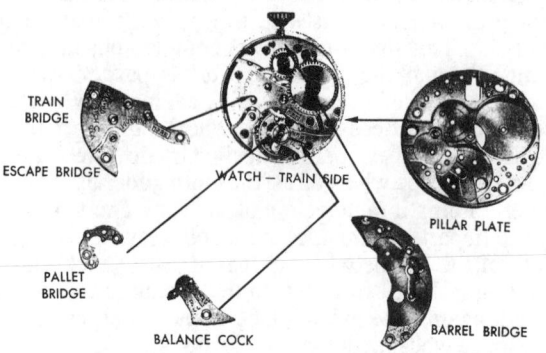

TRAIN
BRIDGE

ESCAPE BRIDGE

WATCH — TRAIN SIDE

PILLAR PLATE

PALLET
BRIDGE

BALANCE COCK

BARREL BRIDGE

The plates and bridges which hold all the parts in proper relation to each other.

THE PLATES

The movement of a watch has two plates and the works are sandwiched in between. The plates are called the top plate and the pillar plate. The top plate fully covers the movement. The 3/4 plate watch and the balance cock are flush and about 1/4 of a full plate is cut out to allow for the balance, thus the 3/4 plate. The bridge style watch has two or three fingers to hold the wheels in place and together are called a bridge. The term bridge (horologically) is one that is anchored at both ends. A cock is a wheel support that is attached at one end only. English balance cock for verge watches and lever watches have but one screw. French and Dutch verge watches have their balance bridges secured at both ends. The metal is generally brass, but on better grade watches, nickel is used. The full plate is held apart by four pillars. In older watches the pillars were very fancy, and the plates were pinned, not screwed, together. The plates can be gilded or engraved when using brass. Some of the nickel plates have damaskeening. There are a few watches with plates made of gold. The plates are also used to hold the jewels, settings, etc. Over 30 holes are drilled in each plate for pillars, pivots, and screws.

The pinion is the smaller of the two wheels that exist on the shaft or arbor. They are small steel gears and usually have six teeth called leaves. Steel is used wherever there is great strain, but where there is much friction, steel and brass are used together; one gear of brass, and a pinion of steel. After the leaves have been cut, the pinions are hardened, tempered, and polished.

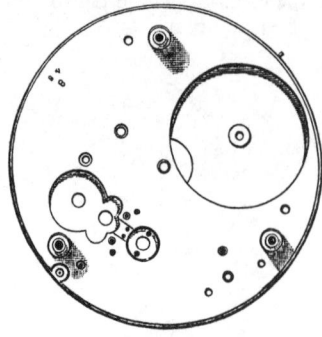

LEFT = PILLAR PLATE   RIGHT = TOP PLATE -(3/4 plate)

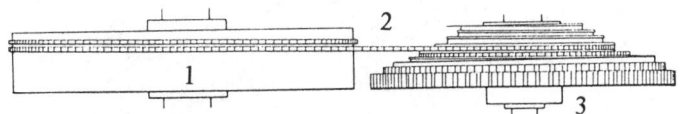

THE FUSEE WAS INVENTED IN 1525
1. MAINSPRING BARREL   2. FUSEE CHAIN   3. FUSEE WHEEL

THE FUSEE

A mainspring gives less and less power as it lets down. To equalize the power a fusee was first used. Fusee leverage increases as the main spring lets down. A fusee is smaller at the top for a full mainspring. When the chain is at the bottom, the mainspring is almost spent, and the fusee has more leverage. Leonardo da Vinci is said to have invented the fusee.

When the mainspring is fully wound, it also pulls the hardest. At that time the chain is at the small end of the fusee. As the spring grows weaker, the chain descends to the larger part of the fusee. In shifting the tension, it equalizes the power.

On the American watch, the fusee was abandoned for the most part in 1850 and an adjustment is used on the hairspring and balance wheel to equalize the power through the 24 hours. When a watch is first wound the mainspring has no more power than it does when it is nearly run down. With or without the fusee, the number of parts in a watch are about the same: close to 300.

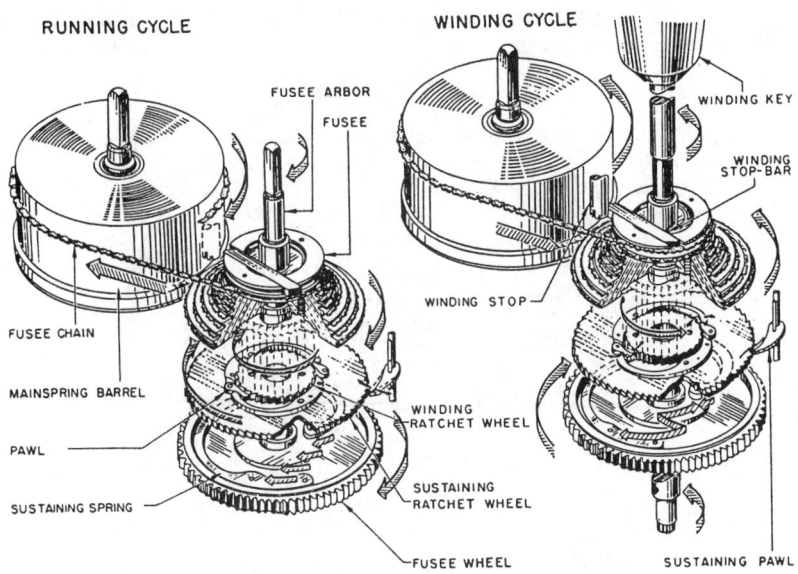

The above is a HAMILTON MODEL 21 **FUSEE** used in a Ships **Chronometer**.

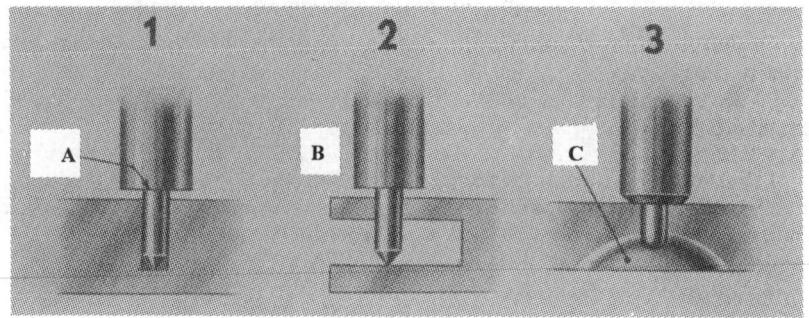

1. Illustration of pivot before 1700. 2. Pivot used in early 1700s. 3. Pivot used in late 1700s to present

JEWELS AND PIVOTS

Before 1700, holes were drilled only part way into the plates and the pivot rested directly on the bottom of the hole, as in Illustration No. 1. The shoulder of the pivot was above the plate, however, reducing part of the function, as in Illustration No. 1A.

In the early 1700s, a French watchmaker, Sully, improved the pivot friction as seen in Illustration No. 2B. Illustration No. 3 shows a later improvement. Perfected by Julien Le Roy.

N.F. de Duiller of Geneva, in conjunction with Peter and Jacob Debaufre, French immigrants living in London, developed a method of piercing jewels. This method was patented in 1704; however, it was not until around 1800 that holed jewels started to appear in watch movements and then only in high grade watches.

In the mid-1800s experiments were already being made for artificial rubies. In 1891 Fremy solved the problem and by the early 1900s the reconstructed ruby was popular.

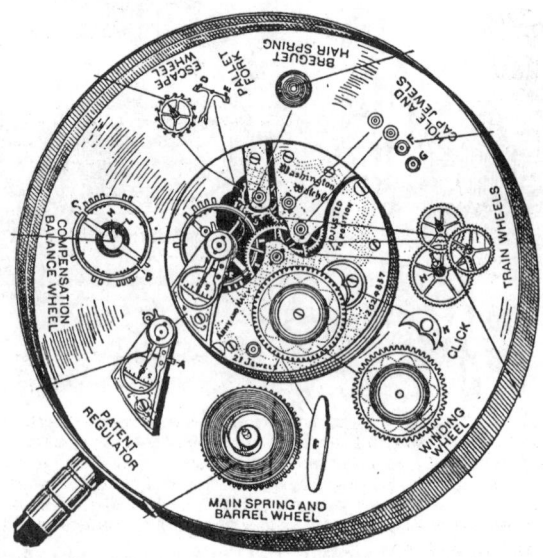

A WASHINGTON WATCH CO. WATCH UNDER A MAGNIFYING GLASS

SHOCK ABSORBERS

When a watch is dropped or subjected to a hard shock, the balance and pivots usually suffer the most.

A shock-resisting device was invented by Breguet in 1789; he called it a parachute. This device was a spring steel arm supporting the endstone. The parachute gives a cushioning effect to the balance staff.

The American pocket watch industry tried to find a device to protect pocket watch pivots, but it was the Swiss who perfected the devices for wristwatches around 1930.

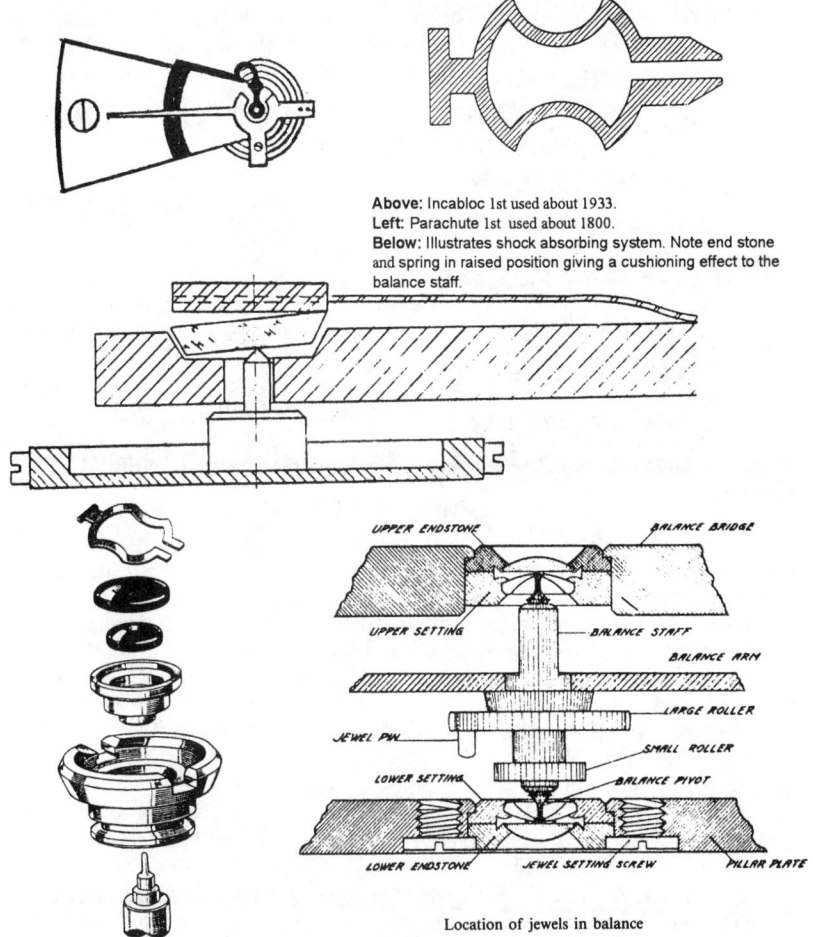

Above: Incabloc 1st used about 1933.
Left: Parachute 1st used about 1800.
Below: Illustrates shock absorbing system. Note end stone and spring in raised position giving a cushioning effect to the balance staff.

Location of jewels in balance

Above LEFT : Incabloc spring, cap-jewel, hole jewel, bearing block & balance-staff.

NOTE: Collectable watches with a higher jewel count usually demand a greater price, *when watches were produced the higher the jewel count the higher the cost*, however, lower production of some models this <u>collectable</u> **rule** does not apply. Example 7, 11 and 15 jewel Hamiltons will bring higher prices than a 17 jewel Hamilton, also a 19 jeweled "Sangamo Special" will bring a higher price than 21 jeweled "Sangamo Special". Most American made watches with 15 jewels and up are marked. **(Generally speaking it is accepted that good to medium quality watches have 15 to 17 jewels and are said to be "fully jeweled".**)
When counting **VISIBLE** jewels beware that some manufactures added <u>non-functional</u> jewels for eye appeal, disassembling the watch is the only way to get a true accurate count.

TYPES OF JEWELS.

Watch jewels are of four distinct types, each type having a particular function.

(1) **HOLE JEWELS.** Hole jewels are used to form the bearing surface for wheel arbors and balance staff pivots.

(2) **CAP JEWELS.** Cap jewels (also called end stones) are flat jewels. They are positioned at the ends of wheel staffs, outside the hole jewels, and limit the end thrust of the staff.

(3) **ROLLER JEWELS.** The roller jewel (pin) is positioned on the roller table to receive the impulse for the balance from the fork.

(4) **PALLET JEWELS.** The pallet jewels (stones) are the angular shaped jewels positioned in the pallet to engage the teeth of the escape wheel.

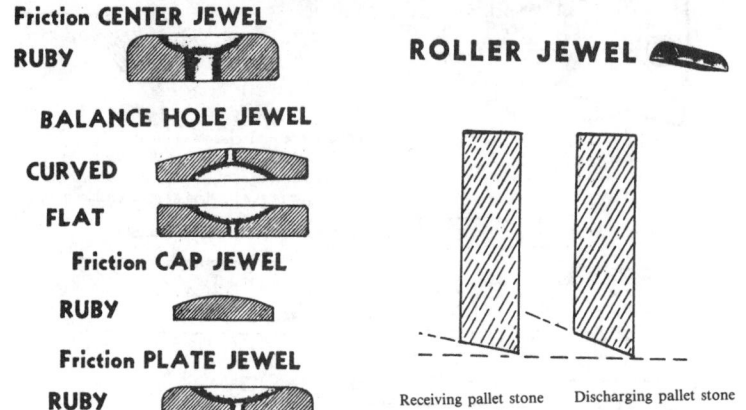

Friction CENTER JEWEL

RUBY

ROLLER JEWEL

BALANCE HOLE JEWEL

CURVED

FLAT

Friction CAP JEWEL

RUBY

Friction PLATE JEWEL

RUBY

Receiving pallet stone   Discharging pallet stone

JEWEL COUNT

Jewels are used as bearings to reduce metal-to-metal contacts which produce friction and wear. They improve the performance and accuracy of the watch, and materially prolong its usefulness. The materials used for making watch jewels are diamonds, sapphires, rubies, and garnets. The diamond is the hardest but is seldom used except for cap jewels. The sapphire is the next in hardness and is the most commonly used because of its fine texture. Garnets are softer than sapphires and rubies.

Number and Location of Jewels. Most watches have either 7, 9, 11, 15, 17, 19, 21, or 23 jewels. The location of the jewels varies somewhat in different makes and grades, but the general practice is as follows:

7-JEWEL WATCHES. Seven-jewel watches have: one hole jewel at each end of the balance staff; one cap jewel at each end of the balance staff; one roller jewel; and two pallet jewels.

9-JEWEL WATCHES. These have the seven jewels mentioned in 7-jewel watches, with the addition of a hole jewel at each end of the escape wheel.

11-JEWEL WATCHES. In these, seven are used in the escapement as in 7-jewel watches. In addition, the four top pivots (the third wheel, the fourth wheel, the escape wheel, and the pallet) are jeweled.

15-JEWEL WATCHES. These watches have the nine jewels found in 9-jewel watches, with the addition of the following: one hole jewel at each end of the pallet staff; one hole jewel at each end of the fourth wheel staff; and one hole jewel at each end of the third-wheel staff.

17-JEWEL WATCHES. The 15 jewels in 15-jewel watches are used with the addition of one hole jewel located at each end of the center wheel staff.

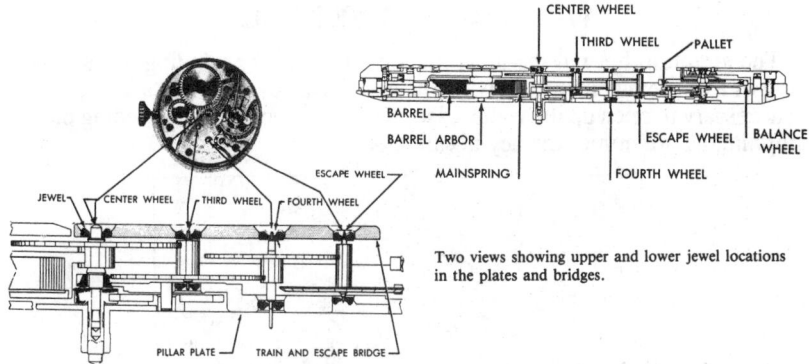

Two views showing upper and lower jewel locations in the plates and bridges.

19-JEWEL WATCHES. In these watches, the jewels are distributed as in the 17-jewel watch, with the addition of one for each pivot of the **barrel & mainspring.**

21-JEWEL WATCHES. The jewels in these are distributed as in the 17-jeweled grade, with the addition of two cap jewels (**USUALLY** placed on the pallet arbor and escape wheel) or 2 jewels for the barrel & mainspring.

Center Wheel — 2	Center Wheel— 2	Center Wheel— 2	Center Wheel— 2
Third Wheel — 2	Third Wheel — 2	Third Wheel — 2	Third Wheel — 2
Fourth Wheel — 2	Fourth Wheel— 2	Fourth Wheel— 2	Fourth Wheel— 2
Escape Wheel— 2	Escape Wheel—2	Escape Wheel—2+2	Escape Wheel— 2+2
Pallet & Arbor— 4	**Barrel Arbor — 2**	Pallet & Arbor— 4+2	**Barrel Arbor — 2**
Balance Staff — 4	Pallet & Arbor— 4	Balance Staff — 4	Pallet & Arbor— 4+2
Roller jewel — 1	Balance Staff — 4	Roller jewel — 1	Balance Staff — 4
TOTAL — 17J	Roller jewel — 1	TOTAL—21J	Roller jewel — 1
	TOTAL — 19J		TOTAL— 23J

23-JEWEL WATCHES. The jewels are distributed as in the 21-jewel watch, with the addition of one for each pivot of the **barrel & mainspring**.

24J., 25J., and 26 JEWEL WATCHES. In all of these watches, the additional jewels were distributed as cap jewels. These were not very functional but were offered as **prestige** movements for the person who wanted more.

In many cases, these jewel arrangements varied according to manufacturer. All jeweled watches may NOT fit these descriptions.

Collectable watches with a higher jewel count usually demand a greater price, *when watches were produced the higher the jewel count the higher the cost,* however, lower production of some models this collectable **rule** does not apply. Example 7, 11 and 15 jewel Hamiltons will bring higher prices than a 17 jewel Hamilton, also a 19 jeweled "Sangamo Special" will bring a higher price than 21 jeweled "Sangamo Special". Most American made watches with 15 jewels and up are marked. (**Generally speaking it is accepted that good to medium quality watches have 15 to 17 jewels and are said to be "fully jeweled".**)

When counting **VISIBLE** jewels beware that some manufactures added non-functional jewels for eye appeal, disassembling the watch is the only way to get a true accurate count.

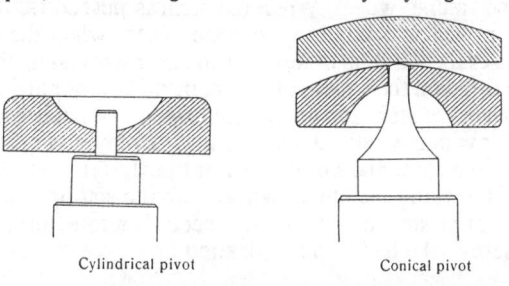

Cylindrical pivot   Conical pivot

WINDING AND SETTING

The simplest, but not the most practical method for winding up the mainspring of a pocket watch was to wind the barrel staff by means of a key, but then it is necessary to open up the watch case. And the key method of winding proved unpopular, as oftentimes the key became lost.

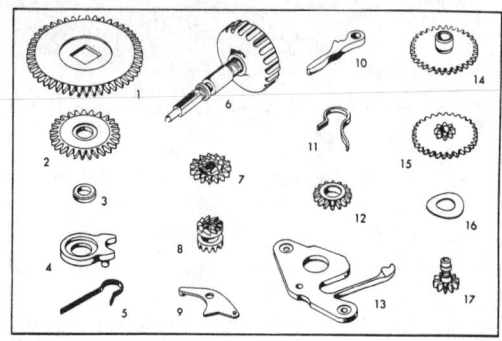

WINDING & SETTING PARTS

1. Ratchet Wheel	6. Stem and Crown	10. Clutch Lever	14. Hour Wheel
2. Crown Wheel	7. Winding Pinion	11. Clutch Lever Spring	15. Minute Wheel
3. Crown Wheel Center	8. Clutch Wheel	12. Setting Wheel	16. Dial Washer
4. Click	9. Setting Lever	13. Yoke	17. Cannon Pinion
5. Click Spring			

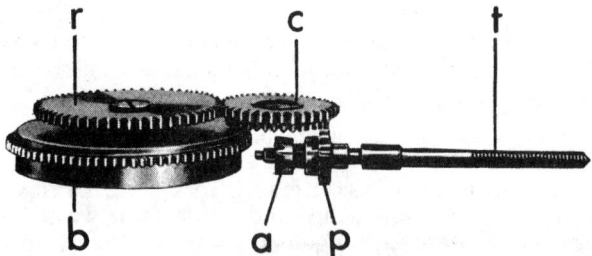

WINDING MECHANISM. a-Winding and setting clutch. p-Winding pinion. b-Barrel. r-Ratchet wheel. c-Crown or main wheel. t- Winding arbor.

The modern principle of the winding of the mainspring and hand setting by pulling on the crown, dates back to 1842. We owe this combination to Adrian Philippe, associate of Patek, of Geneva.

The winding and setting mechanism consists of the stem, crown, winding pinion, clutch wheel, setting wheel, setting lever, clutch lever, clutch spring, crown wheel, and ratchet wheel. When the stem is pushed in, the clutch lever throws the clutch wheel to winding position. Then, when the stem is turned clockwise, it causes the winding pinion to turn the crown and ratchet wheels. The ratchet wheel is fitted on the square of the mainspring arbor and is held in place with a screw. When the stem and crown are turned, the ratchet wheel turns and revolves the arbor which winds the mainspring, thereby giving motive power to the train. Pulling the stem and crown outward pushes the setting lever against the clutch lever, engaging the clutch wheel with the setting wheel. The setting wheel is in constant mesh with the minute wheel; therefore, turning the stem and crown permits setting the hands to any desired time.

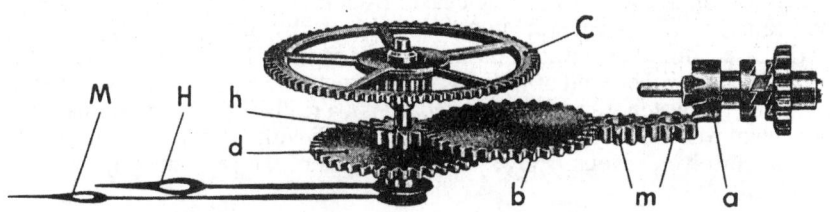

SETTING MECHANISM. Clutch a. meshes with m. and the minute works wheel b. The minute works wheel meshes with the cannon pinion h. The hour cannon d. bears the hour hand H. C. center wheel M. Minute hand.

The dial train consists of the cannon pinion, minute, and hour wheels. The cannon pinion is a hollow steel pinion which is mounted on the center wheel arbor. A stud which is secured in the pillar plate holds the minute wheel in mesh with the cannon pinion. A small pinion is attached to the minute wheel which is meshed with the hour wheel.

The center arbor revolves once per hour. A hand affixed to the cannon pinion on the center arbor would travel around the dial once per hour. This hand is used to denote minutes. The hour wheel has a pipe that allows the hour wheel to telescope over the cannon pinion. The hour wheel meshes with the minute wheel pinion. This completes the train of the cannon pinion, minute wheel, and hour wheel. The ratio between the cannon pinion and the hour wheel is 12 to 1; therefore, the hand affixed to the hour wheel is to denote the hours. With this arrangement, time is recorded and read.

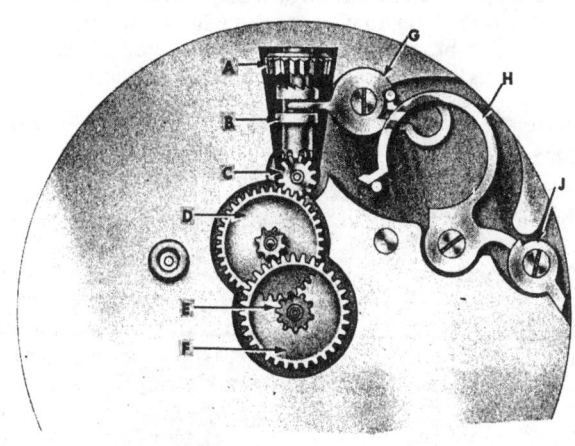

A—PINION
B—CLUTCH WHEEL
C—SETTING WHEEL
D—MINUTE WHEEL
E—CANNON PINION
F—HOUR WHEEL
G—CLUTCH LEVER
H—SETTING SPRING
J—SETTING SPRING CAM

AUTOMATIC WINDING.

The self-winding watch uses the movements of the body in order to wind up the mainspring slowly and nearly continuously. The first pocket self-winding watches were executed by a watchmaker from Le Locle, Abraham-Louis Perrelet, around 1770. They were improved soon after by Abraham-Louis Breguet. In the case of the pocket watch, the movements causing the winding of the watch were essentially the result of walking. This system of winding was never widely adopted. The watch was a fancy model and not a really useful one. Herman von der Heydt was the only maker in America to work with the self-winding pocket watch. However, inventors always kept the idea of the self-winding watch in mind.

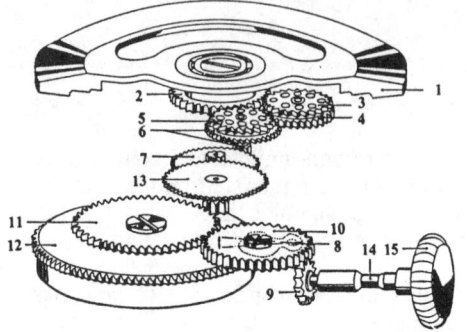 

Early self wind pocket watch by Breguet.

ETERNA-MATIC AUTOMATIC WINDING MECHANISM. 1–Oscillating weight. 2–Oscillating gear. 3–Upper wheel of auxiliary pawl-wheel. 4–Lower wheel of auxiliary pawl-wheel. 5–Pawl-wheel with pinion. 6–Lower wheel of pawl-wheel with pinion. 7–Transmission-wheel with pinion. 8–Crown-wheel yoke. 9–Winding pinion. 10–Crown-wheel. 11–Ratchet-wheel. 12–Barrel. 13–Driving runner for ratchet-wheel. 14–Winding stem. 15–Winding button.

In 1923, the British firm Harwood took up once again the solution of the problem of automatic winding, for wrist watches. This was the spark which rapidly resulted in research to improve and simplify this type of mechanism. A company was formed in London to manufacture Harwood's watch, and before long over 500 jewelers in the United Kingdom were selling his automatic watch. A second company was formed in France, and a third in the United States. The business flourished about two and one-half years. Then, in 1931, these companies were liquidated.

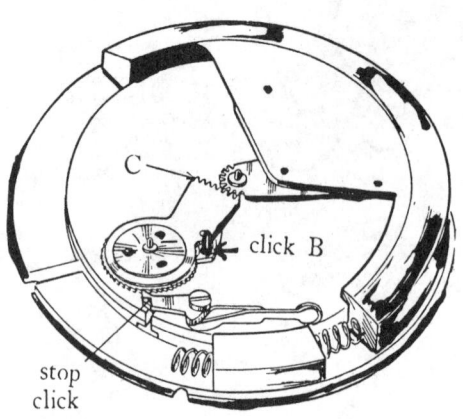 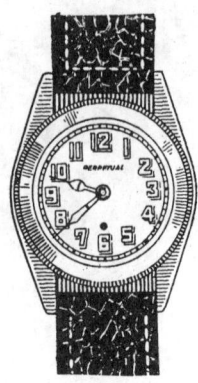

Illustration of Self Winding mechanism used by Harwood.
NOTE: The 2 BUFFER springs used on earlier movements.

This 1931 wrist watch made by Perpetual Self-Winding Watch Co. of America originally sold for $29.75.

THE BALANCE ARC OF VIBRATION

If the watch is to function with any degree of satisfaction, the proper arc of motion of a balance must be no less than 225 degrees in a single vibration direction. Wind up the watch, stop the balance; upon releasing the balance, carefully observe the extent of the swing or vibration. After 30 seconds it should have reached its maximum. If it takes longer, the full power of the mainspring is not being communicated strongly enough. With the watch fully wound, the balance should vibrate between 225 degrees and 315 degrees in a single vibration direction.

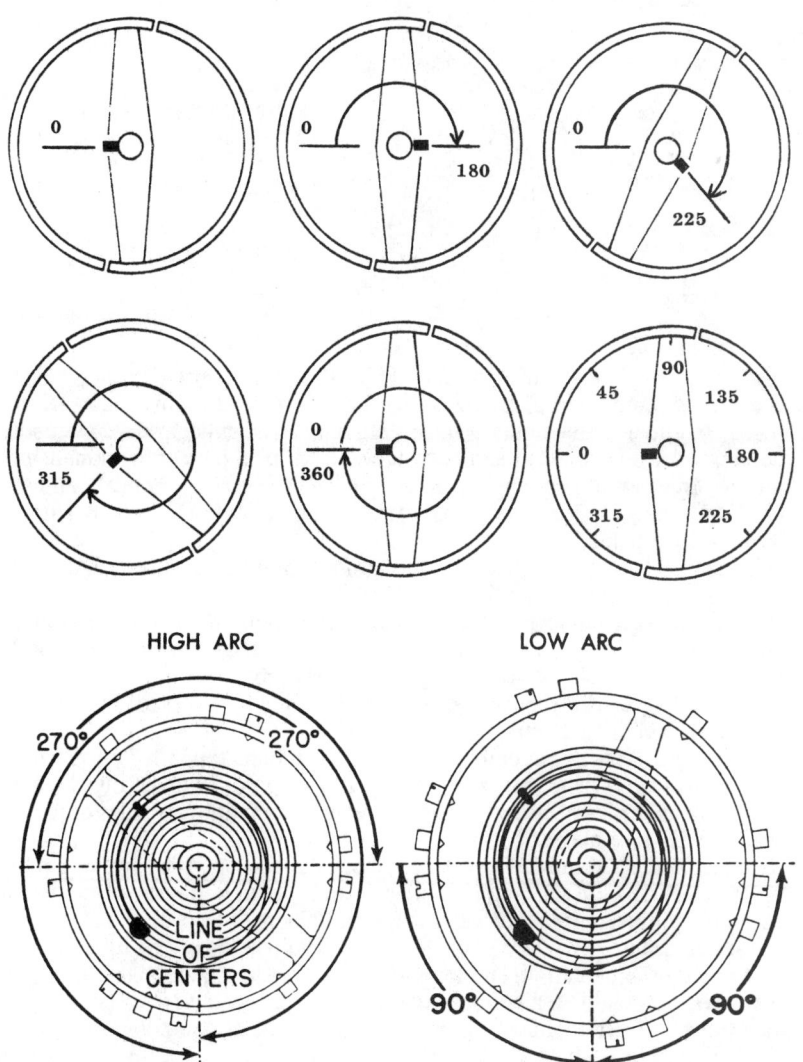

JUDGING QUALITY

Judging the quality of a watch need not be difficult. While observing a watch movement there are two major determining factors to keep in mind. (1.) The quality or precious material. (2.) The amount of workmanship and time it takes to produce the parts for the movement . The precious materials such as 18k or 14k gold, diamond or rubies, gold jewel settings or brass jewel settings. The amount of labor may be measured by the finished parts of the movement such as polishing, chamfered parts (removing sharp edges), and bluing of screws. The collector must learn to compare watches from the same time period because changes were made to improve the time keeping. To assist you the partial list below may be helpful in judging the quality of a watch.

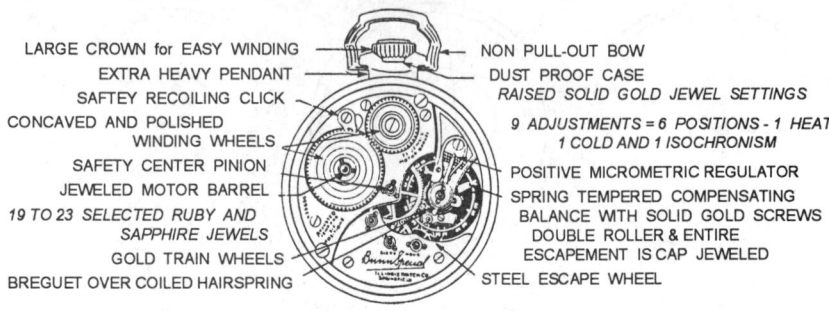

LARGE CROWN for EASY WINDING — NON PULL-OUT BOW
EXTRA HEAVY PENDANT — DUST PROOF CASE
SAFTEY RECOILING CLICK — RAISED SOLID GOLD JEWEL SETTINGS
CONCAVED AND POLISHED — 9 ADJUSTMENTS = 6 POSITIONS - 1 HEAT
WINDING WHEELS — 1 COLD AND 1 ISOCHRONISM
SAFETY CENTER PINION
JEWELED MOTOR BARREL — POSITIVE MICROMETRIC REGULATOR
19 TO 23 SELECTED RUBY AND — SPRING TEMPERED COMPENSATING
SAPPHIRE JEWELS — BALANCE WITH SOLID GOLD SCREWS
GOLD TRAIN WHEELS — DOUBLE ROLLER & ENTIRE
ESCAPEMENT IS CAP JEWELED
BREGUET OVER COILED HAIRSPRING — STEEL ESCAPE WHEEL

Escapement: detent, lever or cylinder; gold, steel or brass escape wheel. *Balance wheel;* number of platinum, gold or brass screws, expansion cut, 1/2 cut or uncut. In older movements gold or brass balance wheel. *Balance cock;* diamond or ruby end stone, amount of engraving or hand pierced workmanship. *Regulator;* free sprung, precision or simple. *Hair spring;* helical, elinvar, overcoil or flat. *Adjustments;* Isochronism, temperature, 6 to 3 positions, adjusted or unadjusted.

The train of gears: Highly polished, gold or brass gear; chamfered above & below, rounded, beveled or flat spokes. Wolf tooth gearing.

Finish to the plates: Engraved, carved, skeletonized, damaskeened is it lavished or conservative finished, highly finished or polished, nickel, brass, gold inlaid, gilt or frosted plates. Hardening of various parts.

Screws: Highly finished or polished, chamfered or beveled, oval or flat heads, blued or plain, also chamfered screw holes.

Jewels and settings: Number of jewels; diamond, sapphire, ruby, other semi-precious jewels as garnet, aquamarine. Raised gold jewel settings held by screws, flush gold jewel settings held by screws, composition settings or jewels pressed directly into plates.

Dials: *Enamel;* enamel on gold or copper, harden or glass; triple, double single or unsunk. *Metal dial;* gold or silver, hand carved or engraved, etched or plated; applied, raised, inlaid or hand painted numbers.

Cases: Platinum or white gold, 18k or 14k gold & heavy or light weight, raised applied ornamentation, engraved or engine turned, diamonds or semi-precious jewels, porcelain, enamel or painted, gold or brass inter-dust cover, gold or brass bow, and silver or silveroid cases. Cases made of composition material that look like gold such as "Pinchbeck gold". (Alloy of copper & zinc that is made to look like gold, but is not.)

Metals used in watches: Bell metal or bronze, Beryllium white colored alloyed with iron, cobalt, copper, etc.; Bi-metallic (brass fused to steel), Brass, Carbon steel, Chromium, Chrome steel, Copper; Elinvar, German metal, gilding metal, Glucinum, Gold, Gold-filled, Gunmetal, Invar, Iron, Nickel, Palladium, Platinum, Pinchbeck, Silver, Silveroid, Silver plated, Stainless steel, Steel, Tin, White gold, and Zinc.

OFFER VERSUS APPRAISALS

When you want to sell your watches you need a offer, not an appraisal. An offer is the actual price someone will pay for your item at a given point in time. The price will be determined by several factors: quality, size, age, metal content, style, grade, rarity and the collect ability at that time. Timing may be very critical in determining the price.

Jewelers and most appraisers use the insurance replacement cost, (an estimate of the retail replacement price). This type of appraisal is fine for contemporary watches and jewelry, but not for collectable watches and antique jewelry items. The "FAIR MARKET" value is a more realistic estimate of price. If done by an appraiser with "current market" knowledge, then a FAIR MARKET appraisal will be the correct evaluation of the dollar level at that *time* for your items.

Selling your watches may be a new experience. The task requires experience in the sale of watches. There is a market for watches, but as in any area of sales, knowledge of your BUYER is important. Collectors may not advertise that they are willing buyers; Collectors may not have enough ready cash at the time. Sending watches to a prospective buyer is a judgment call-- is the buyer trustworthy? Will it be worth the time involved? As a seller, you must guarantee the watch to work, offer return privileges, and refunds. The task of selling requires a knowledge of repair, shipping, the cost of advertising, time to market the watch, and someone standing by to talk to the collector. This is a short list and almost imperative that the seller be in the business of selling watches to be successful at selling. The collector may pay a higher price than a dealer, but the collectors are hard to find and may not have the ready cash at that time.

Selling to dealers may be more pleasant. Dealers will have a qualified staff, including buyers and seller, ready to respond to ads, as well as, a cash reserve for purchases. When dealing with an established business, that can provide you with good references and has a trustworthy record. Each customer is handled in a professional manner by a competent staff member. A dealer understands that selling maybe a new experience and will take you through the process one step at a time. Summation: Considering the cost, time and attempting to find a willing collector, you may be ahead to sell your watches to a qualified dealer.

When selling your watches to collectors or dealers it may involve sending the watch from one place to another. To receive the best price it will be vital to see the watches before a offer is made, this is a common practice in the watch market. Suggestions for mailing your package to the buyer. Make a detailed list of the items you are sending. Keep a copy and send a copy also list your name, address and daytime phone number. The jewelry industry sends millions of dollars worth of jewelry by REGISTERED MAIL. The Post Office Service has close control of the registered mail. Each person who handles the package must sign for it and be responsible for it's safety. Your package will be kept in a secure area much like a bank vault. Your package may be insured up to $25,000.00. Your package must also be able to withstand the shipping stress. Before sealing the box make sure to leave a inch of padded space between your watch and the sides, bottom and top of the box. Cushion these spaces with newspaper, tissue, cotton, bubble or foam padding. Seal the box securely then wrap the outside with gummed PAPER tape that can be written on.

When your package arrives at the dealer the mail staff will open and inspect your package, and log each item. One of the experts in charge will examine each item and call as soon as possible with the offer. If you accept the offer a check will be delivered to you. If the offer is turned down the items will be returned.

When buying watches for RESALE **know what the buyer will pay**. How many buyers are there for, prices above $1,000.00, $2,000.00, $5,000.00 $10,000.00 or as high as $50,000.00 to $100,000.00 and do they have ready cash. Can you find the collector that will pay more or pay your asking price. **The collector may be just as rare as your rare watch! (SUPPLY & DEMAND)**

BRISTOL WATCH CO., KW & KS, serial # 3056. **(SWISS FAKE)**

"The Nassau" on dial and on movement "Hartford, adjusted, jewels, heat & cold. **"(SWISS FAKE)**

COTTAGE INDUSTRY WATCHMAKING
IN COLONIAL AMERICA

The cottage industry (pre-1700s to 1800s) consisted of organized, skilled craftsmen having separate divisions for the purpose of producing watches. The movements were handmade using manpowered tools. The parts generally were not given a final finish. The cottage industries were in most countries including France, England, Switzerland, Germany, and others, but not in America. Each skilled parts maker specialized in a specific part of the watch. There were fusee makers, wheel makers, plate and cock makers, spring makers, case makers and enamelers, to name a few. In the cottage industry each maker became an expert in his field. Expenses and overhead were less because fewer tools and less labor were required. Because all components were produced separately, a larger volume of watches resulted.

The enterprising colonial watchmaker in America would order all the parts and assemble them to complete a finished movement. This finisher, or watchmaker, would detail the parts, such as filing them to fit, polishing and gilding the parts, fitting the movement to a case, installing a dial, and adjusting the movement to perform. The finisher would then engrave his name and town of manufacture to the movement or dial. The finisher determined the time keeping quality of the completed watch, thus gaining a good reputation for some watchmakers.

Most watchmakers used this system during this period; even, to some extent, Abraham L. Breguet. A colonial watchmaker or finisher could produce about 50 watches a year. There were few colonial watchmakers because only the wealthy could afford such a prized possession as a watch. Most colonial watchmakers struggled financially, and supplemented their businesses with repair work on European-made watches. Since most of them understood the verge escapement, and imported this type of part from England to produce watches, many colonial watches have the verge escapement. Few colonial watches survive today.

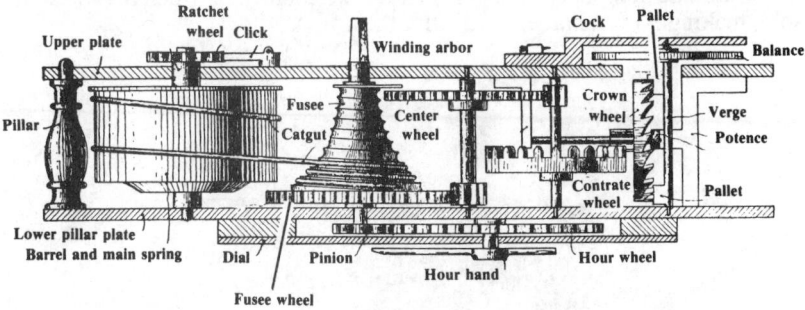

Side-view of 17th Century single-hand movement with fusee and catgut line to barrel. This three-wheel movement normally ran from 15 to 16 hours between windings. Also note the balance has no hairspring.

EBAUCHES

The stamping out of plates and bridges began with Frederic Japy of Beaucort, France, around 1770. At first, ebauches consisted of two plates with barrel and train bridges, the cock and fusee, pillars, and the clicks and assembly screws. The ebauches were stamped-out or rough movements. Japy invented machinery a common laborer could operate, including a circular saw to cut brass sheets into strips, a machine for cutting teeth in a wheel, a machine for making pillars, a press for the balance, and more. These machines were semi-automatic and hard to keep in alignment or register. But, with the aid of these new machines the principal parts of the movement could be produced in a short period of time with some precision. However, the parts of watches at this time were not interchangeable. These movements in the rough or ''gray'' were purchased by finishers. The finisher was responsible for fitting and polishing all parts and seeing to the freedom and depth of these wheels and working parts. He had to drill the holes to fit the dial and hands. The plates, cock and wheel, after being fitted and polished, were gilded. After the parts were gilded, the movement would be reassembled, regulated for good time keeping, and placed in a case. The finisher had to be a master watchmaker.

In England, during the 1800s, Lancashire became the center of the movement trade. One of the better known English ebauche makers was Joseph Preston & Sons of Prescot. The movements were stamped J. P. Some Swiss ebauches would imitate or stylize the movement for the country in which they were to be sold, making it even harder to identify the origin.

As the watch industry progressed, the transformation of the ebauche to a more completed movement occurred. Automation eventually made possible the watch with interchangeable parts, standard sizing, and precision movements that did not need retouching. This automation began about 1850 (in America) with such talented mechanics as Pierre Fredric Ingold, the Pitkins Brothers, A. L. Dennison, G. A. Leschot with Vacheron and Constantin, Patek, Philippe, and Frederic Japy of Beaucount. The pioneers in the 1850s who set the standards for modern watchmaking included the American Pitkin Brothers, Dennison, Howard, and Jacob Custer. By 1880 most other countries had begun to follow the lead of America in the manufacture of the complete pocket watch with interchangeable parts.

In Switzerland there are four major categories of watch producers : **1. Complete, 2. Ebauche, 3. Parts** or **Specialized 4. Finishers.** *Complete* watch producers manufacture entirely on their own premises as Le Coultre. *Ebauche* produce rough movements or movements in the gray called ebauche or blank movements such as ETA in Grenchen. These are made in the valley of Joux and Val-de-Ruz regions, in and around the towns of Granges, Grenchen, La Chaux-de-Fonds, Le Locle and Solothurn, in the Bernese Jura, the valley of St. Imier, Val-de-Travers, at Preseux, in the Ticino, and elsewhere. *Specialized or Parts* are made more or less all over the Swiss regions. Balances more so in Valley of Sagne and at Les Ponts. Lever assortments as the escape wheel, fork, & roller in Jour Valley,at Bienne, in Bernese Jura and especially, at Le Locle. Hairsprings are made at La Chaux-de-Fonds, Geneva, Bienne and St. Imier. Mainspring, dial, hands, cases, jewels, pendant, bow, crowns, crystals, screws, pins, generally speaking are made throughout Switzerland. *Finishers* buy blank movements parts cases etc. and finish the watch as a complete watch with their own name engraved on the watch as *Tiffany & Co., Ball W. Co.* and Etc..

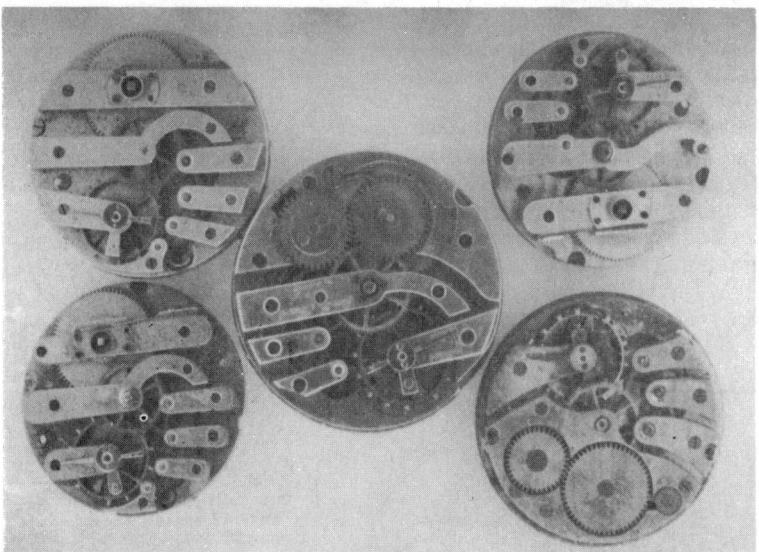

Five typical Ebauches. Three with bar movements, one with a three -quarter plate, one with a half plate. Four with lever escapements, one with a cylinder escapement. The age ranges from 1860 to 1890.

Ebauches S.A.

Ebauches S.A. with its main office in Neuchatel, Switzerland, at one time the following 17 affiliated firms were part of Ebauche S.A. and in the year of 1968 they had produced ABOUT- 40,000, 000 WATCHES.

 A. Schild S.A., Grenchen

 Fabrique d'Horlogerie de Fontainemelon, fontainemelon

 Eta S.A., Fabrique d'Ebauches, Grenchen

 Fabrique d'Horlogerie de Fontainemelon, Succursale du Landeron, Le Landeron

 A. Michel S.A., Grenchen

 Felsa S.A., Grenchen

 Fabriques d'Ebauches Bernoises S.A., Etablissement Aurore, Villeret

 Fabrique d'Ebauches Venus S.A., Moutier

 Fabrique d'Ebauches Unitas S.A., Tramelan

 Fabrique d'Ebauches de Fleurier S.A., Fleurier

 Fabrique d' Ebauches de Peseux S.A., Peseux

 Fabriques d'Ebauches Reunies Arogno S.A., Arogno

 Fabriques d'Ebauches de bettlach, Bettlach

 Fabrique d'Ebauches de Chezard S.A., Chezard

 Derby S.A., La Chaux-de-Fonds

 Nouvelle Fabrique S.A., Tavannes

 Valjoux S.A., Les Bioux

 FRENCH EBAUCHE

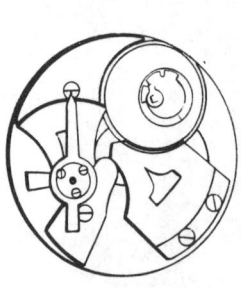

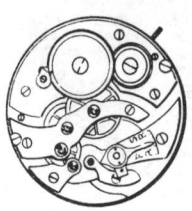

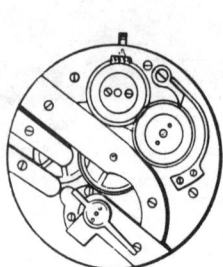

Examples of four ebauches: **Upper left:** Example of a Chinese duplex. **Lower left:** An ebauche circa 1900-1930. **Upper right:** A three-finger bridge movement, circa 1890-1910. **Lower right:** Bridge movement, circa 1885-1900.

WORM GEAR ESCAPEMENT

This oddity was advertised as, "The Watch With a Worm in It," Robert J. Clay of Jersey City was given a patent on October 16, 1886. Mr. Clay said, "The principal object of my invention is to provide a watch movement that is very simple and has but few parts." The worm gear or continuous screw was by no means simple. Mr. Clay and William Hanson of Brooklyn revamped the original worm gear and obtained another patent on January 18, 1887.

The first watch containing a worm gear escapement reached the market in 1887. However, the New York Standard Watch Co. soon converted to a more conventional lever escapement. About 12,000 watches with the worm gear were made, but few survived.

Enlarged **worm gear escapement.** Note endless screw was referred to by the New York Watch Co. as "a watch with a worm in it."

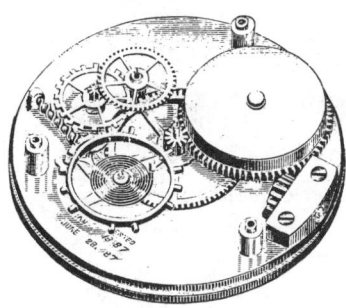

Movement with top plate removed.

DIAL MAKING

Watch dials were basically hand produced. The base is copper and the coating is generally enamel. In the process the copper plate is covered with a fine white enamel, spread with a knife to a thickness of 3/100ths of an inch. It is then allowed to dry at which time it is placed on a plate and inserted into a red hot furnace. The dial is turned frequently with a pair of long tongs. The copper would melt if it were not coated with the enamel. After the dial has been in the furnace for one minute it is removed and the resulting enamel is soft. The dial is now baked onto the copper plate or "set." The surface is rough after cooling, and it is sanded smooth with sandstone and emery, then baked again. The dial is now ready for the painter, who draws six lines across the dial using a lead pencil. Then, with a pencil of black enamel, he traces the numbers, finishing the ends to make them symmetrical. Then the minute marks are made. Lastly, the name of the watch company is painted onto the dial. The dial is glazed and fired again, then polished. The dial artist used a magnifying glass and a fine camel hair brush to paint the dials and produced about one dozen per hour.

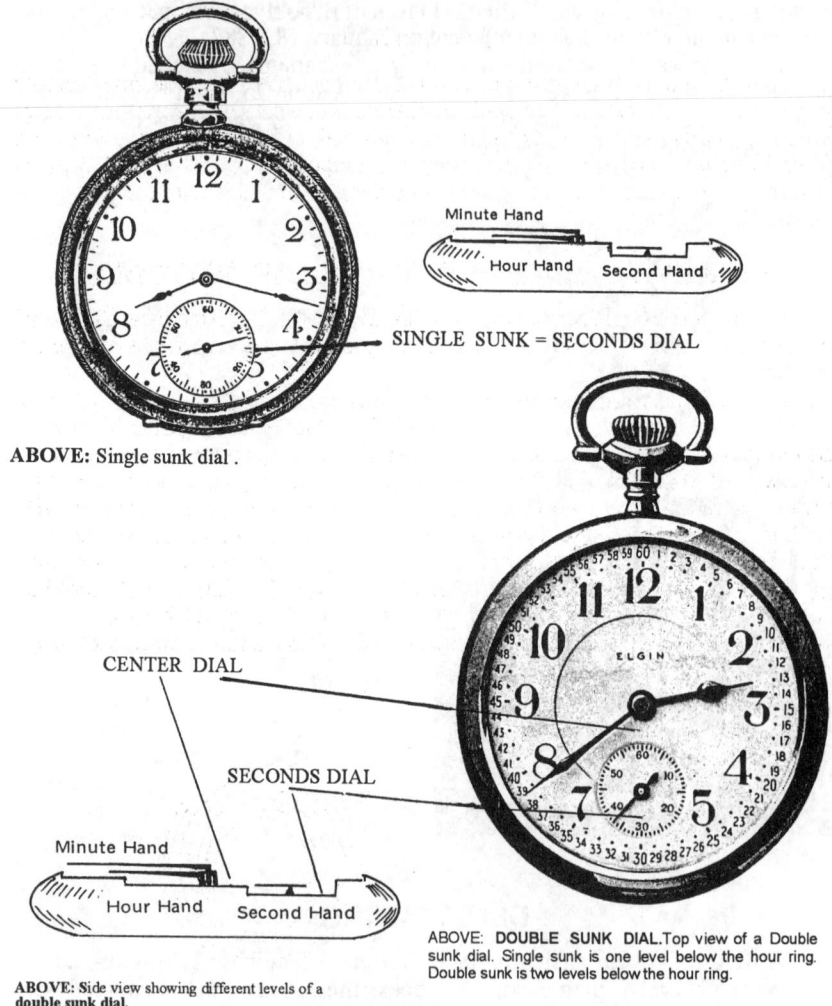

SINGLE SUNK = SECONDS DIAL

ABOVE: Single sunk dial .

CENTER DIAL

SECONDS DIAL

ABOVE: **DOUBLE SUNK DIAL.** Top view of a Double sunk dial. Single sunk is one level below the hour ring. Double sunk is two levels below the hour ring.

ABOVE: Side view showing different levels of a **double sunk dial.**

Note: Some single sunk dial have inner marked circle made to look like double sunk dial.

FIRST DIALS

Thomas Gold was the first to make enamel dials in America in about 1838 in New York City. Thomas had a partner from 1846-51 named Thomas Reeves of Brooklyn. American Watch Co. (Waltham) made their own dial from the beginning by dial-makers John Todd & John T. Gold. Henry Foucy found employment in 1856 with the American Watch Co. he was from Geneva.

CRAZING

The word "craze" means a minute crack in the glaze of the enamel. This is not a crack in the dial because the dial has a backing of copper. Crazing does little damage to the structure of the enamel, even though it may go all the way through to the copper.

ENAMEL

Enamel may be transparent or colored. Enamel acts as a protective surface on the metals. It is resistant to acid, corrosion, and weather. Enamel is made of feldspar, quartz, silica, borax, lead, and mineral oxides. These materials are ground into a fine powder and then fired at a temperature of about 1500 degrees Fahrenheit. The heat melts the enamel powder and unites it with the surface of the metal.

PIN LEVER ESCAPEMENT (DOLLAR WATCHES)

The pin lever escapement is sometimes erroneously referred to as "Roskopf escapement" and watches with pin lever escapements are sometimes referred to as "Roskopf watches."
The original Roskopf watch, which was publicly exhibited at the Paris Exposition in 1867, was a rugged "poor man's watch." The chief Roskopf patent, decreases the number of wheels by creating a large barrel whose diameter encroached upon the center of the watch. The loose cannon pinion and hour wheel were driven by a friction-clutch minute wheel mounted to the barrel cover and enmeshing with the loose cannon pinion and hour wheel. The cannon pinion rode loosely on a steel pin threaded to the center of the main plate. The true term, "Roskopf" applies to the barrel with its clutch fitted minute wheel driving the dial train. The Roskopf ebauches watch was made by **Cortebert** factory in La Chaux-de-Fonds, Switzerland. The first Roskopf watch was sold for 25 franks in January of 1870.
⏱NOTE: Some fakes use the name **"Rosskopf."**

86

LOW COST PRODUCTION WATCHES
(DOLLAR WATCHES)

Jason R. Hopkins hoped to produce a watch that would sell for no more than 50 cents as early as the 1870s. He had a plan for which he received a patent (No. 161513) on July 20, 1875. It was a noble idea even though it was never fully realized. In 1876, Mr. Hopkins met a Mr. Fowle who bought an interest in the Hopkins watch. The movement was developed by the Auburndale Watch Co., and the Auburndale Rotary Watch was marketed in 1877. It cost $10, and 1,000 were made. The 20 size had two jewels and was open-face, pendant wind, lever set, and detent escapement. The 18 size had no jewels and was open-face.

In December, 1878, D. A. A. Buck introduced a new watch, at a record low price of $3.50, under the name of Benedict and Burnham Manufacturing Co. It was a rotary watch, open-face, with a skeleton dial which was covered with paper and celluloid. The movement turned around in the case, once every hour, and carried the minute hand with it. There were 58 parts and all of them were interchangeable. They had no jewels but did have a duplex style escapement. The teeth on the brass escape wheel were alternately long and short, and the short teeth were bent down to give the impulse. The main spring was about nine feet long and laid on a plate on the bed of the case. The click was also fastened to the case. The extremely long mainspring took 140 half turns of the stem to be fully wound. It came to be known as the "long wind" Waterbury and was the source of many jokes, "Here, wind my Waterbury for awhile; when you get tired, I'll finish winding it."

"Trail Blazer" by E. Ingraham Co. TOP view is the original Box, bottom. LEFT is Fob "Wings Over The Pole". RIGHT: Watch has original green crystal. Note: engraving on the back of watch is same scene as depicted on box.

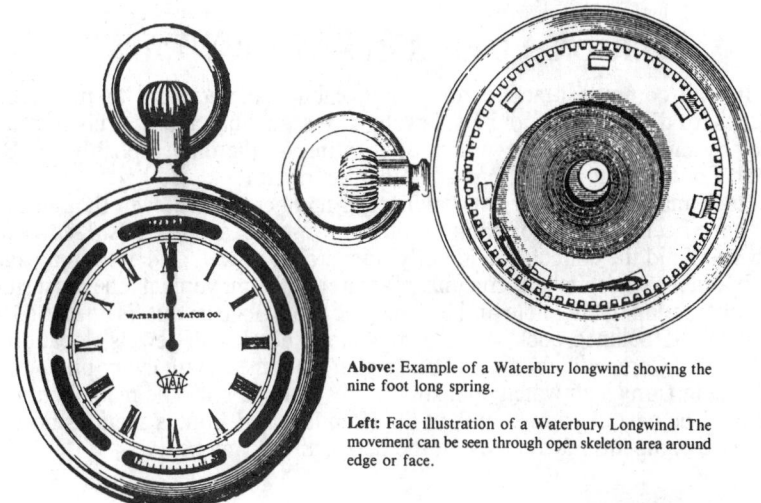

Above: Example of a Waterbury longwind showing the nine foot long spring.

Left: Face illustration of a Waterbury Longwind. The movement can be seen through open skeleton area around edge or face.

Right: Example of a two wheel train rather than the standard four wheel train.

Left: Example of the escape wheel for the duplex escapement.

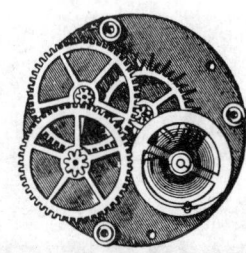

In 1892 R. H. Ingersoll ordered 1,000 watches produced at a cost of 85 cents each. He offered the watch for sale in his mail-order catalog for $1 each and advertised it as, "The Watch that Made the Dollar Famous." These watches were thick, sturdy and noisy and were wound from the back like a clock. The wages in 1892 were about 8 cents per hour, so it took some 13 hours of work to buy a Dollar Watch.

The E. N. Welch Manufacturing Co. was the next low cost production watch manufacturer. Then came the New York City Watch Co., who in 1895, produced a watch with a unique pendant crank to wind the movement. In 1899 came the Western Clock Mfg. Co., which later became the Westclox Corporation.

Also, among the low cost production watches were the "comic character" watches. They have become prime collectibles in recent years.

About 70 percent of the watches sold in the U. S. were Dollar type. These watches were characterized by the pin lever, non-jeweled (for the most part), and with a face of paper or other inexpensive material. These watches were difficult to repair and the repairs cost more than the price of a new one. Thus they were thrown away, and today it is hard to find one in good condition.

DOLLAR WATCH CHARACTERISTICS:

1. Sold at a price that almost everyone could afford.
2. Used pin lever or duplex escapement.
3. Stamped or pressed out parts; also used fewer parts overall.
4. Were non-jeweled (except for a few) but rugged and practical.
5. Dial made of paper or other inexpensive material.
6. Case and movement were sold as one unit.

PERSONALIZED & CUSTOM WATCHES

It was common practice for some watch manufacturers to personalize watches for **distributors**, jobbers, jewelry firms, and individuals. This was done either by engraving the movement or painting on the dial. Probably the Ball Watch Co. did more of this than any other distributor.

Each manufacturer used its own serial number system even though there may have been a variety of names on the movements and/or dials. Knowledge of this will aid the collector in identifying watches as well as determining age.

In order to establish the true manufacturer of the movement, one must study the construction, taking note of the shape, location, plate layout (is it full or 3/4), shape of the balance cock and the regulator, location of jewels, location of screws, etc. Compare and match your watch movement with every photograph or drawing from each watch company in this volume until the manufacturer is located. The best place to start is at the Hamilton and Illinois sections because these two companies made most of the personalized watches.

"Remington Watch Co."-marked on movement and case, made by N.Y. Standard Watch Co., NOTE: The CROWN wheel and RATCHET without a CLICK, these visible wheels are for show only, 16 size, 11 jewels.

"E.F. Randolph"-marked on movement, made by Illinois Watch Co., 23j, hunting, model No. 4.

16 size, No. 390, made by New York Standard Watch Co. Same model as above.

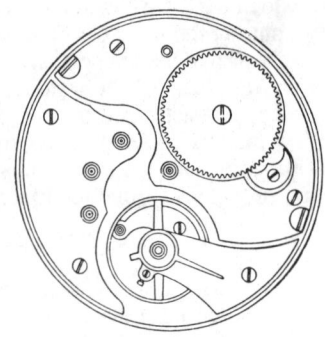

Model 4, 16 size, made by Illinois Watch Co. Same model as above.

Personalized watch movement by ILLINOIS, engraved on movement & on dial B.A. BELL Chattanooga, Tenn., 18 size, adjusted, 15 jewels, OF.

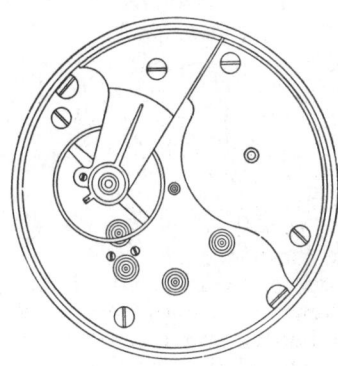

MODEL 4, 18 size, open face, fine train, this matches the watch on the LEFT

Personalized watch movement by ROCKFORD. Engraved on movement. "W.G. Gane, Special Railway, 17j, Adj, serial No. 344551." To identify, see the Identification of Movement section of all watch companies, noting plate design & screw locations to determine that it is a ROCKFORD Model No. 8.

Personalized watch movement by HAMILTON. Engraved on movement, "Mayer, Chattanooga, Tenn., Adjusted, 21 jewels, serial No. 254507." To identify, see the Identification of Movement section of all watch companies, noting plate design & screw locations to determine that it is an 18 size, open face HAMILTON model. Then by using the serial number, the grade can be determined.

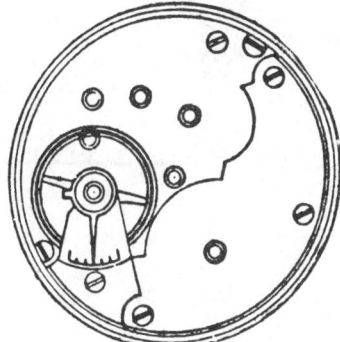

Model 8, 18 size, Rockford, full plate, hunting, lever set. This illustration from the identification section matches the model above.

Grade 936, 18 size, Hamilton, open face. This matches the model above.

The basic **model** will have the key mechanical features and construction. The *decoration,* damaskeening and jewel count determine the **_grade._** Basic models will have such things as, size, hunting or open face, key or stem wind, lever or stem set, and basic layout design. The 18 size may be Transition models and note the location of the cock to the barrel bridge. The 16 size consider the winding parts may not be seen or they could be exposed (crown & ratchet wheel).

Example: Washington Watch Co. 16 size, 17 jewel, Senate grade. Illinois Watch Co. made a custom watch for (Montgomery Ward) using the name Washington Watch Co. and altered the appearance of the movement, however, the basic model was not significantly changed. The mechanical function remain the same to allow the parts to fit the altered model.

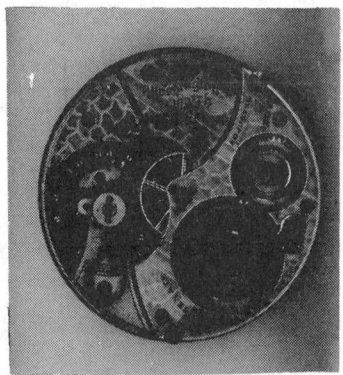 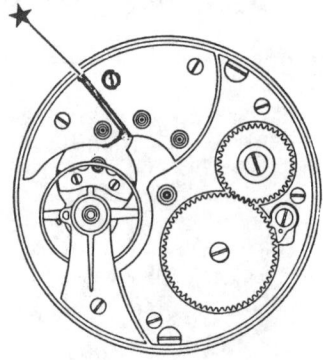

Washington Watch Co. , SENATE, 16 size, 17J, Adj. 3P, HC, polished jewel settings, damaskeen finish, double sunk enamel dial, pendent set, serial # 2457094.

ALTERED drawing of Illinois W. Co., this matches the watch to the left. NOTE: The extra screw & cut out . This also is the same model as below (MODEL # 6)

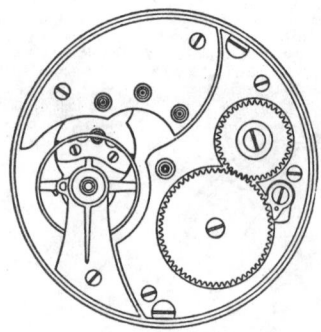

BASIC Illinois Watch Co. **MODEL** 6 as shown in the Illinois W. Co. section this drawing is NOT altered.

After the correct manufacturer has been determined, the serial number can be used to determine the age. Taking the age, grade, size, and manufacturer into consideration, the approximate value can be determined by comparing similar watches from the parent company. If a jeweler's name and location are on the watch, this particular watch will command a higher price in that area.

The custom or personalize watches are really just variations of a type or style of a grade and may show the serial number production dates. The production run may have called for 1,000 movements of a basic model and grade that may contain 700 with the Watch Co. name on movement and 300 of the custom or personalize watches with customers name on the watch. Therefore it difficult to determine how many of this type of custom made watches were produced. Usually the differences between the custom and basic grades can be seen with out a tear down of the movement. Unfortunately it may require a disassembling of the watch and you may want to have a watchmaker to help to make positive identification.

Compare and match the following list which may aid you in the identification of your watches: first determine SIZE, then hunting or open face model, key or lever or pendant set, location of balance cock to winding barrel, location of jewels, location of screws, full, 3/4, 1/2, plate or bridge model. **Grade** differences may include: number of jewels (7-23J.), unadjusted - Adjusted to 3-5 positions, style of regulator & click, (some regulators and click were patented), style of decoration as damaskeening, *no name* or grade name. The grade without a name were the generic type or style of grade. Generic, nameless, Personalized Jobber Watches or unmarked grades for watch movements are listed under the Company name or initials of the Company, etc. by size, jewel count and description.

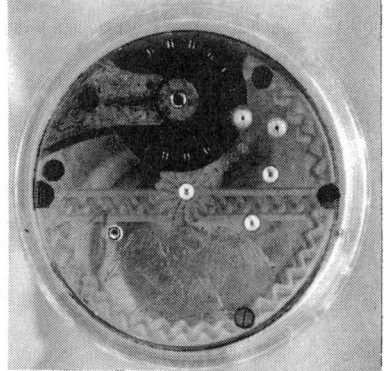

(A): ON MOVEMENT: J. P. STEVENS & BRO. 15 jewels, ON DIAL J.P. STEVENS & BRO. ATLANTA, GA. the size is 18 Size, hunting case model = a **Aurora new model**.

(B): ON DIAL *EAGLE* , On movement illustration of a *EAGLE* and serial number 512929, hunting case model and the is 18 size this is a **Seth Thomas model # 7**.

⊕ Generic, nameless, Personalized Jobber Watches or unmarked grades for watch movements are listed under the Company name or initials of the Company, etc. by size, jewel count and description.

FAKE 21 & 23 JEWEL WATCHES

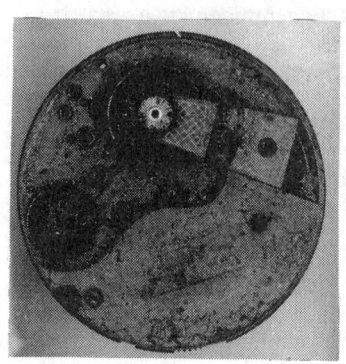

MARKED: 21 jewels, adjusted, R. R. SPECIAL on movement, the watch has 21 fake jewels and is not adjusted also the R. R. SPECIAL implies it is a railroad watch. Also a Locomotive is depicted on movement. (Swiss movement)

MARKED: 23 jewels adjusted, Locomotive Special Chicago U.S.A. on movement, the watch has 23 fake jewels and is not adjusted also Locomotive which implies it is a railroad watch. This is a Trenton M # 6, 18 size, OF.

SWISS IMPORTED FAKES

Before 1871 a flood of pocket watches were made with names strikingly similar to many well-known American watches. These were made in foreign countries as well as in America and looked and sounded like high quality watches. But they were fakes, inferior in quality.

These key-wind imitations of American pocket watches are a fascinating and inexpensive watch type that would make a good collection. The watches closely resembled the ones they were intended to emulate. Names such as "Hampton Watch Company" might fool the casual buyer into thinking he had purchased a watch from Hampden. "Rockville Watch Co." could easily be mistaken for the American Rockford Watch Co. Initials were also used such as H. W. Co., R. W. Co., and W. W. Co., making it even harder to determine the true identity.

In 1871 Congress passed a law requiring all watches to be marked with the country of origin. The Swiss tried to get around this by printing "Swiss" so small on the movement that it was almost impossible to see. Also the word "Swiss" was printed on the top of the scroll or on a highly engraved area of the movement, making it difficult to spot.

By 1885 these Swiss imitations were of better quality and resembled even more closely what was popular in America. But the Swiss fakes did not succeed, and by 1900 they were no longer being sold here.

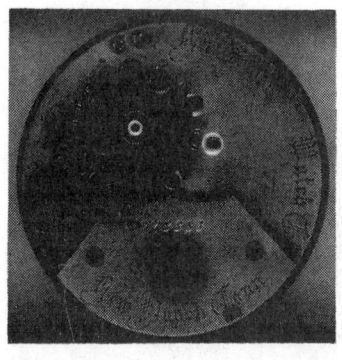

Example of a Swiss imported fake. Note misspelled signature "P.S. Barrett." The authentic American Waltham watch is spelled "P.S. Bartlett."

Example of a NEW HAVEN WATCH CO. imported Swiss fake. Marked on movement New Haven Watch Co. New Haven Conn. Serial # 778883.

HOW TO IDENTIFY A SWISS FAKE

1. At first they were keywind and keyset; then they became stem wind, full plate, about 18 size, large jewels on the plate side, and used Roman numerals.

2. Most had American-sounding names so close to the original that it looks merely like a misspelling.

3. The material was often crudely finished with very light gilding.

4. The dial used two feet; American watches used three.

5. The balance wheel was made to look like a compensated balance, but it did not have the cut in the balance wheel.

6. The large flat capped jewels were blue in color.

These characteristics are not present with all imported fakes. Some or none of these factors may be present. The later the date, the more closely the fake resembled the American watch.

Ohio Watch Co. imported Swiss fake distributed by Leon Lesquereaux of Columbus Ohio. This style watch may have been made by E. Borel & Co. (Swiss) about 1860.

Brooklyn Watch Co. New York serial # 6423, note the similarity to E. Howard & Co. Boston watch movement.

High Grade Movements.

MANUFACTURED BY THE

HAMPDEN WATCH COMPANY.

1898 AD

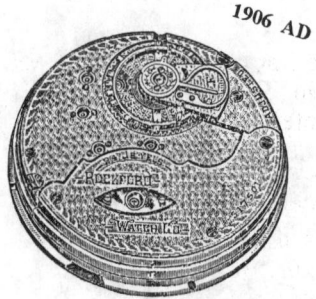

1906 AD

18 Size Movements. O. F. and Htg.

Special Railway	23 Jewels, Nickel Adj.			$35.00
New Railway	23	"	"	28.00
John Hancock	21	"	"	23.00
Special Railway	17	"	"	30.00
New Railway	17	"	"	20.00
Anchor	17	"	"	16.00
No. 48 or 68	17	"	"	16 00
John C. Dueber Special	17	"	"	15.00
No. 47 or 67	17	"	"	15.00
John C. Dueber	17	"	"	12.00
No. 43 or 63	17	"	"	12.00
No. 80 or 81	17	"	"	10.00
No. 49 or 69	17	" Gilt	"	9.50
Dueber	17	" Nickel		8.00
The Dueber Watch Co.	15	" "		6.50
No. 45 or 65	11	" "		5.00
No. 46 or 66	11	" Gilt,		4.75
Champion	7	" "		3.00

John C. Dueber, No. 43 and 63, damaskeened in two colors when specially ordered.

18 Size

No. 800 Hunting }
No. 900 Open Face }   **$60.00**

24 extra fine ruby and sapphire jewels in gold settings, sapphire jewel pin, double roller escapement, steel escape wheel, sapphire exposed pallets, compensating balance in recess, adjusted to temperature, isochronism and five positions, mean time screws, Breguet hair spring, patent micrometric regulator, safety pinion, poised pallet and fork, handsomely damaskeened nickel plates, gold lettering, champfered steel parts, double sunk glass, enamel dial with red marginal figures, Roman or Arabic, elegantly finished throughout. Certificate of rating furnished upon application.

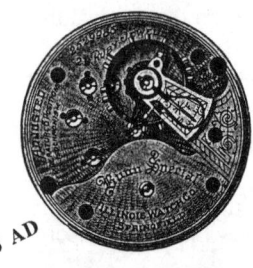

1926 AD

BUNN SPECIAL

9 Adjustments   21 Jewels

$45.00

SUGGESTED PRICES: Complete in any plain screw—
10K Filled Case, $55.00   14K Filled Case, $65.00
Fancy Cases and Fancy Dials Proportionately More.

21 ruby and sapphire jewels; gold settings; adjusted to SIX positions, heat, cold and isochronism; compensating balance; gold screws including timing screws; double roller; steel escape wheel; Breguet hairspring; patent micrometric screw regulator; safety screw center pinion; beautifully damaskeened with black enamel lettering; double sunk dial.

———

No. 89

17 Jewels, Adjusted to Temperature

$22.50

SUGGESTED PRICES: Complete in any plain screw—
10K Filled Case, $32.50   14K Filled Case, $40.00
Fancy Cases and Fancy Dials Proportionately More.

17 jewels; polished settings; adjusted to temperature; compensating balance with timing screws; Breguet hairspring; patent regulator; safety screw center pinion; polished steel work; damaskeened in attractive pattern; double sunk dial.

1926 AD

THE 60 HOUR 6 POSITION
BUNN SPECIAL

23 Jewels, $58.00 ⁛ 21 Jewels, $50.00
9 ADJUSTMENTS

SUGGESTED PRICES: Complete in any plain screw cases:
23J., 10K Filled Case, $65.00   14K Filled Case, $72.50
21J., 10K Filled Case, $57.50   14K Filled Case, $65.00
Special or Fancy Cases and Fancy Dials Proportionately More.

Ruby and sapphire jewels; raised gold settings; adjusted to SIX positions, heat, cold and isochronism; spring tempered compensating balance with gold screws including timing screws; double roller; steel escape wheel; gold train wheels; safety screw center pinion; Illinois superior motor barrel; patent micrometric screw regulator; recoiling safety click; concaved and polished winding wheels; double sunk dial.

The 23 jewel grade contains the Illinois Superior Jeweled Motor Barrel and two jewels in which barrel staff pivots operate.

THE 60 HOUR
BUNN

8 Adjustments   19 Jewels

$43.50

SUGGESTED PRICES: Complete in any plain screw—
10K Filled Case, $50.00   14K Filled Case, $57.50
Fancy Cases and Fancy Dials Proportionately More.

19 ruby and sapphire jewels; raised gold settings; adjusted to five positions, heat, cold and isochronism; special quality hardened and tempered compensating balance with gold screws, including mean time screws; gold train wheels; double roller escapement; steel escape wheel; Breguet hairspring; safety screw center pinion; Illinois superior mainspring; patent micrometric screw regulator; recoiling click; Illinois superior jeweled motor barrel; concaved and polished winding wheels; double sunk dial.

MARKET REPORT
1996

The Pocket Watch Market underwent a leveling off period throughout 1996. The American material (railroad watches, key winds, gold filled Hunter's, etc.) stabilized after a two-year period of steady increases. This trend is likely to carry over in 1997, yet prices for rare and exotic American watches could rise rapidly. Gold cased American and Swiss pocket watches continue to be the **sleepers**. They are currently being passed over in favor of railroad and other non-gold watches, yet they are extremely reasonable in price and offer exceptional value to collectors for the future.

Repeaters and better European pieces continue to bring strong prices. Early pre-1750 watches went up significantly in price. Choice material is becoming very scarce and desirable.

The Wrist Watch Market became more active and new trends developed in 1996. Early Rolex models, better name chronographs, moon phase calendars, alarms, and quality automatics are all commanding better prices and they are quick to sell. Breitling, Le Coultre, Omega, U. Nardin, and International W. Co. are among the **hot** names. Hamilton, Illinois, and other U.S. classical watches made before 1930-1950 are also generating more activity than in previous years.

Ultra rare and Fine classical period wrist watches are not surfacing as in years past--this corner of the market continues to bring very strong prices.

High-end contemporary wrist watches are beginning to surface more regularly in the market place. These will be the future collectibles and the popular models are bringing solid prices at auctions.

Character watches continued on a level basis. Interesting early material and **original boxed** items are almost non-existent on the second-hand market. The early classical pieces in this area of collecting still continue to be solid.

NOV. 15th 1996

🕐 The 1996 Basel World Watch, Clock and Jewelry Show was one of the highlights of the annual Henry Fried Memorial 23rd Horological Tour and professionally guided by Nick Lerescu of Advantage Tours. The Basel Show had 80,000 visitors, 2,433 exhibitors with 249 watch exhibitors. The tour included Horological museums in France, Switzerland, Italy & Austria with expert guides as Adolphe Chapiro. In the Vallee de Joux we visited in Philippe Dufour's workshop & with Ron DeCorte who studied under Mr. Dufour for about six months before returning to the U.S.A. & in Solothurn a visit with Derek Pratt. Mr. Dufour, Mr. DeCorte & Mr. Pratt are master watchmakers. The Jaeger-Lecoultre and Girard-Perregaux factories conducted extensive tours of their state of the art and up to date manufacturing of watches. Our group of 45 who all have a interest in Horology enjoyed sharing their knowledge. Our host Harry Blair arranged discussions for the group to hear from the fellow members filling each day of the tour with their knowledge and common interest of horology. This personal guided tour included meeting with other Horological Associations, picturesque city tours, shopping, good food & hotels, all in all, a great time & a richer appreciation of **Time**, history, European culture & important places.
Cooksey and Martha Shugart

AMERICAN LISTINGS
Pricing At Collectable Fair Market Value At Retail Level
(As Complete Watches With Case & Movement)

Watches listed in this book are priced at the collectable fair market value at the retail level (What a collector may expect to pay for a watch from a watch dealer) and as complete watches, having an original 14k gold-filled case with an original white enamel single sunk dial. The entire original movement is in good working order with no repairs needed, unless otherwise noted. Watches listed as 14k and 18k are solid gold cases. Coin or silveroid-type and stainless steel cases will be listed as such. Keywind and keyset watches are listed as having original coin silver cases. Dollar-type watches or low cost production watches are listed as having a base metal type case and a composition dial. Wrist watches are priced as having original gold-filled case with the movement being all original and in good working order, and the wrist watch band being made of leather except where bracelet is described.

Many of the watch manufacturers were commissioned to put jewelers' or jobbers' names on their movements in place of their own. Due to this practice, the true manufacturers of these movements are difficult to identify. These watch models are listed under the original manufacturer and can be identified by comparison with the model sections under each manufacturer. See "Personalized Watches" for more detailed information.

These watch manufacturers which personalize watches for jobbers or jewelry firms, with exclusive private signed or marked movements must first be found by using a illustration and matched to the manufacture shown in this book. After you identify the movement now the value can be determined. The valuable collectable watches are listed under the signed or marked movement. Other exclusive private signed or marked movements will have equivalent value are only slightly higher value and should be compared to Generic or Nameless movements. Railroad signed or marked (dials & movements) are usually more collectable & higher in value .

The prices shown were averaged from dealers' lists just prior to publication and are an indication of the collectable retail level or what collectors will pay. Prices are provided in three categories: average condition, extra fine, and mint condition, and are shown in whole dollar amounts only. The values listed are a guide for the *collectable* retail level and are provided for your information only. **Dealers** will not necessarily pay **full retail price**. Prices listed are for watches with original cases and dials.

Important Notice. All of the information, including valuations, in this book has been compiled from the most reliable sources, and every effort has been made to eliminate errors and questionable data. Nevertheless, the possibility of error, in a work of such immense scope, always exists. The publisher or authors will not be held responsible for losses which may occur in the purchase, sale, statements of its advertisers, or other transaction of items, because of information contained herein. Readers who feel they have discovered errors are invited to write and inform us, so they may be corrected in subsequent editions.

🕐 Descriptions and serial number ranges listed for early watches cannot be considered 100 percent accurate due to the manner in which records were kept by these companies.

INFORMATION NEEDED: We are interested in any facts and information you might have that should possibly be considered for future editions. Documented facts are needed, so please send photo or sources of information. Send to: Cooksey Shugart, P. O. BOX 3147, Cleveland, Tennessee 37320-3147. *(WHEN CORRESPONDING, PLEASE INCLUDE A* 🖃 *SELF-ADDRESSED, STAMPED ENVELOPE.)*

ABBREVIATIONS USED IN
THE COMPLETE PRICE GUIDE TO WATCHES

🕐 – IMPORTANT NOTE.

★★★★★—only **ONE to FIVE** known to exist (proto type models etc.)

★★★★—**Extremely Rare**; less than 25 to 50 known to exist.

★★★—**Rare**; less than 100 to 200 known to exist.

★★—**Scarce**; less than 500 known to exist.

★—**Uncommon**; less than 2,500 known to exist.

ADJ —Adjusted (to temperature, heat and cold, also isochronism). Adj.5P = Adjusted to 5 positions, 3 positions or 4 positions etc.

BASE—Base metal used in cases; e.g., silveroid

BB —Bubble Back (Rolex style case)

BRG—Bridge plate design movement

Ca. — Circa (about or approximate date)

Cal. —Calendar also Calibre (model)

C&B — Case and Band

Chrono.—Chronograph

Co.—Company

COIN—Coin silver

DES—Diamond end stones

DMK—Damaskeened

DSD—Double sunk dial

DR—Double roller

DWT—Penny weight: 1/20 Troy ounce

ETP—Estimated total production

ESC.—Escapement

EX—Extra nice; far above average

FULL—Full plate design movement

3/4—3/4 plate design movement

F brg—One finger bridge design and a 3/4 plate (see Illinois 16s M#5)

2F brg—Two finger bridge design

3F brg—Three finger bridge design

GF—Gold filled

GJS—Gold jewel settings

G#—Grade number

GT—Gold train (gold gears)

GCW—Gold center wheel

GRO—Good running order

HC—Hunter case

id. — identification

(illo.) —Illustration of watches

J—jewel (as 21J)

K—Karat (as 14k solid gold—not gold filled)

K(w) —WHITE GOLD as in 14K(w)

KS—Key set

KW—Key wind

KW/SW— (Key wind/stem wind) transition

LS—Lever set

MCC—Multi-color case

MCD—Multi-color dial

M#—Model number

mm —Millemeter (over all case size)

Mvt.— Only Dial and movement; no case

NI—Nickel plates or frames

OF—Open face

P—as Adj.5P = Adjusted to 5 positions, 3 positions or 4 positions etc.

PORC—Porcelain (porc. dial)

PS—Pendant set

PW — Pocket Watch

RF# —Reference Factory number

Reg.—Register on a chronograph

REP.—Repeater

RGJS—Raised gold jewel setting

RGP—Rolled gold plate

RR—Railroad

S—Size as 16S = 16 size

SBB—Screw back and bezel

SRC—Swing ring case

SS—Stainless steel

SSD—Single Sunk Dial

SW—Stem wind

S#—Serial number

TEMP—Temperature

TP—Total production

2T—Two-tone

W/ = WITH

WGF—White gold filled

W.I. also W. Ind. —Wind indicator or (up and down indicator)

WW—Wrist watch

YCF—Yellow gold filled

Railroad Standards, Railroad Approved & Railroad Grade "TERMINOLOGY"
NOTE: Railroad Standards, Railroad Approved & Railroad Grade **terminology,** as defined and used in this *BOOK.*

1. **RAILROAD STANDARDS** = A commission or board appointed by the railroad companies outlined a set of **guidelines** to be accepted or approved by each railroad line.

2. **RAILROAD APPROVED** = A *LIST* of watches each railroad line would approve if purchased by their employee's. (this list changed through the years).

3. **RAILROAD GRADE** = A watch made by manufactures to met or exceed the guidelines set by the railroad **standards.** Grade such as 992, Vanguard and B.W. Raymond etc.

🕐 Some GRADES **exceeded** the R.R. standards such as 23 jewels, diamond end stone, gold train, raised gold jewel settings, double sunk dial and the list goes on. Examples: such as Veritas, Sangamo, 950 & Riverside Maximus and many others.

Generic, Nameless or Unmarked grades for watch movements are listed under the Company name or initials of the Company, etc. by size, jewel count and description. Such as American Watch Co. or Amn Watch Co. or A.W.W.Co., Elgin W. Co. or Elgin National W. Co., Hampden W.Co. or Duber W.Co., Illinois W. Co.or I.W.Co., Rockford or R.W.Co., South Bend.
Example name on movement Illinois Watch Co. and the watch is 18 size, 15 jewels, stem wind, adjusted, nickel damaskeened this watch can be found and will be listed under Illinois Watch Co. next look under the18 Size unmarked grade section as Illinois Watch Co., 15J, SW, ADJ, NI, DMK These are Generic or unmarked grades. Movements with a grade **name** such as Bunn it would be found and listed under Bunn grade.

ABBOTT'S STEM WIND

Henry Abbott first patented his stem wind attachment on June 30, 1876. The complete Abbott's stem wind mechanism is arranged in such a way as to convert key wind to stem wind. He also made a repeater-type slide mechanism for winding. On January 18, 1881, he received a patent for an improved stem wind attachment. On the new model the watch could be wound with the crown. Abbott sold over 50,000 of these stem-wind attachments, and many of them were placed on Waltham, Elgin, and Illinois watches.

 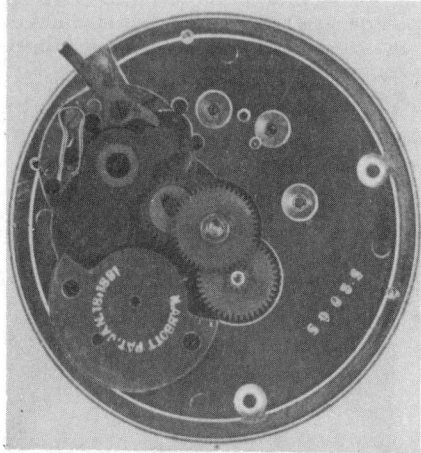

Abbott Stem Wind Attachment. LEFT: normal view of an Illinois watch movement with 'hidden' Abbott Stem Wind Attachment (pat. Jan., 18th, 1881). **RIGHT:** Same watch with dial removed exposing the Abbott Stem Wind Attachment. Serial number 52045. Add $100 to $250 to value of watch with this attachment.

ABBOTT WATCH CO.
(MADE BY HOWARD WATCH CO.) 1908 - 1912

Abbott Sure Time Watches were made by the E. Howard Watch Co.(Keystone), and are similar to Howard Watch Co. 1905 model. These watches sold for $8.75 and had 17 jewels. Some of the open face watches are actually hunting case models without the second bits register.

Description	Avg	Ex-Fn	Mint
Abbott Sure Time, 16S, 17J, OF, GF Case	$195	$265	$350
Abbott Sure Time, 16S, 17J, HC, GF Case	245	325	400
Abbott Sure Time, 16S, 17J, 14K **Abbott** HC .... ★ ★	495	600	750

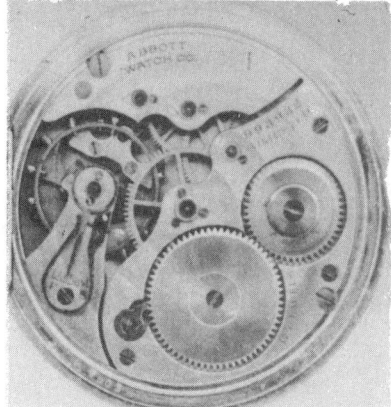 

Abbott Watch Co., 16 size, 17 jewels, gold jeweled settings, hunting case. Note similarity to the Howard Watch Co. model 1905. Serial number 993932.

Abbott Watch Co., 16 size, 17 jewels, gold jeweled settings, open face. Note similarity to the Howard Watch Co. series 9.

ADAMS AND PERRY WATCH MANUFACTURING CO.

Lancaster, Pennsylvania

1874 - 1877

This company, like so many others, did not have sufficient capital to stay in business for long. The first year was spent in setting up and becoming incorporated. The building was completed in mid-1875, and watches were being produced by September. The first watches were limited to three grades, and the escapement and balance were bought from other sources. By December 1875, the company was short of money and,by the spring of 1876, they had standardized their movements to 18 size. The first movement went on sale (**very few watches were sold from this factory name**) April 7, 1876. The next year the company remained idle. In August 1877, the company was sold to the Lancaster Watch Company, after making only about 800 to 1,000 watches. In 1892 Hamilton acquired the assets.

Description		Avg	Ex-Fn	Mint
20S, 20J, GJS, PS, KW, 18K original	★ ★ ★	$2,200	$2,700	$3,300
18S, 20J, GJS, PS	★ ★ ★	1,200	1,600	2,200
18S, 17J, GJS, PS	★ ★	800	1,200	1,600
18S, 17J, GJS, PS, Coin, Original	★ ★	900	1,400	2,000

Adams & Perry Watch Co. movement. This basic model consists of 20 jewels, gold jeweled settings, key wind and pendant set, serial number 1681.

J. H. ALLISON movement 16 jewels,gold train and escape wheel with a pivoted detent, key wind and key set, serial number 19.

J. H. ALLISON

Detroit, Michigan

1853 - 1890

The first watch J. H. Allison made was in 1853; it was a chronometer with full plate and a fusee with chain drive. The balance had time screws and sliding weights. In 1864, he made a 3/4 plate chronometer with gold wheels. He also damaskeened the nickel movement. He produced only about 25 watches, of which 20 were chronometers. By 1883 he was making 3/4 plate movements with a stem wind of his own design.Allison made most of his own parts and designed his own tools. He also altered some key wind watches to stem wind. Allison died in 1890.

Description		Avg	Ex-Fn	Mint
Full Plate & 3\4 Plate, GT, NI, DMK	★ ★ ★ ★ ★	$6,500	$8,000	$10,000
Detent Chronometer Escapement, 16J, KW/KS, GT	★ ★ ★ ★ ★	10,000	12,000	14,000

AMERICAN REPEATING WATCH CO.

Elizabeth, New Jersey
1885 - 1892

Around 1675, a repeating mechanism was attached to a clock for the first time. The first repeating watch was made about 1687 by Thomas Tompion or Daniel Quare. Five-minute, quarter-hour and half-hour repeaters were popular by 1730. The minute repeater became common about 1830.

Fred Terstegen applied for a patent on August 21, 1882, for a repeating attachment that would work with any American key-wind or stem-wind watch. He was granted three patents: No. 311,270 on January 27, 1885; No. 421,844 on February 18, 1890; and No. 436,162 in September 1890. Waltham was the only watch company to fabricate repeating watches in America. It is not known how many repeaters were made, but it is estimated to be about 500 to 1,000.

18 SIZE, with REPEATER ATTACHMENT

Name — Description	Avg	Ex-Fn	Mint
HOWARD, w/ 5 min. repeater attachment, COIN ★★	$3,500	$3,800	$4,250
GOLD CASE ★★	5,000	5,500	6,250
Keystone,or Lancaster, w/ 5 min. rep. attachment, COIN ★★	2,500	2,700	3,000
GOLD CASE ★★	3,500	3,700	4,000
SETH THOMAS,w/ 5 min. repeater attachment, COIN ★★	3,000	3,500	4,250
GOLD CASE ★★	4,000	4,300	4,800

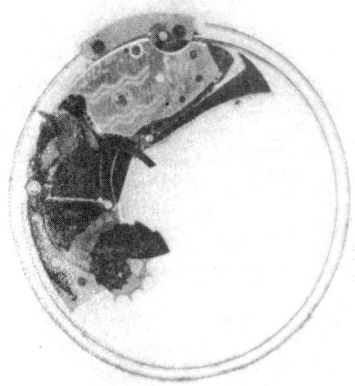 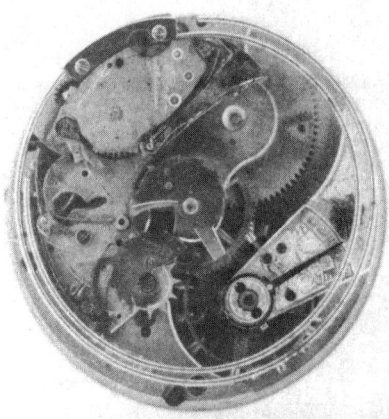

American Repeating Attachment. illustration at LEFT shows Terstegen's patented repeating attachment only. Illustration at RIGHT shows attachment as normally found on movement. The two outside circles on left illustration are wire gongs. The hammer can be seen at upper LEFT Illustration in the shape of a boot.

🕐 Watches listed in this book are priced at the **collectable fair market value** at the RETAIL level, as complete watches having an original 14k gold filled case, KEY WIND with silver, an original white enamel single sunk dial, and with the entire original movement in good working order with no repairs needed, unless otherwise noted.

🕐 Some grades are not included. Their values can be determined by comparing with **similar** age, size, metal content, style, models and grades listed.

16 SIZE, with REPEATER ATTACHMENT

Name — Description		Avg	Ex-Fn	Mint
COLUMBUS, w/ 5 min. rep. attachment, GF or COIN	★★	$2,500	$2,700	$3,000
GOLD CASE	★★	4,000	4,200	4,500
ELGIN, w/ 5 min. rep. attachment, GF or COIN	★★	1,800	2,000	2,500
GOLD CASE	★★	3,500	3,700	4,200
HAMPDEN, w/ 5 min. rep. attachment, GF or COIN	★★	1,800	2,000	2,500
GOLD CASE	★★	3,000	3,300	3,800
HOWARD, w/ 5 min. rep. attachment, GF or COIN	★★	2,500	3,000	3,500
GOLD CASE	★★	4,500	4,700	5,000
ILLINOIS, w/ 5 min. rep. attachment, GF or COIN	★★	2,200	2,500	2,900
GOLD CASE	★★	3,500	3,800	4,250
Non-magnetic (Paillard),w/ 5 min. rep. attachment, gold-filled	★★	2,000	2,200	2,600
GOLD CASE	★★	3,000	3,500	4,000
WALTHAM, w/ 5 min. rep. attachment, GF or COIN	★★	1,800	2,000	2,500
GOLD CASE	★★	3,500	3,700	4,200

🕐 Watches listed in this book are priced at the **collectable fair market value** at the RETAIL level, as complete watches having an original 14k gold filled case, KEY WIND with silver, an original white enamel single sunk dial, and with the entire original movement in good working order with no repairs needed, unless otherwise noted.

🕐 Some grades are not included. Their values can be determined by comparing with **similar** age, size, metal content, style, models and grades listed.

THE AMERICAN WALTHAM WATCH CO.
1851 - 1957

To trace the roots of the Waltham family one must start with the year 1850 in Roxbury, Massachusetts, No. 34 Water Street. That fall David Davis, a Mr. Dennison, and Mr. Howard together formed a watch company. Howard and Dennison had a dream of producing watches with interchangeable parts that were less expensive and did not result in less quality.

Aaron L. Dennison.

Edward Howard.

Howard served an apprenticeship to Aaron Willard Jr. in about 1829. Several years later, in 1842, Howard formed a clock and balance scale manufacturing company with Davis. Howard and Dennison combined their ideas and, with financing provided by Samuel Curtis, the first of their watches was made in 1850. But they had problems. They were trying out ideas such as using jewels, making dials, and producing steel with mirror finishes. This required all new machinery and resulted in a great financial burden. They discovered, too, that although all watches were produced on the same machines and of the same style, each watch was individual with its own set of errors to be corrected. This they had not anticipated. It took months to adjust the watches to the point they were any better than any other timepieces on the market.

Example of a Warren model, about 18 size, 15 jewels, engraved on the movement *Warren N0 44 BOSTON,* plain dial, under sprung, steel balance, right angle lever, escape wheel has pointed teeth, key wind & key set from front, Ca.1853. Note: This movement was made to fit an English size case and will not fit a standard 18 size American case.

But Howard had perfected and patented many automatic watchmaking machines that produced precision watch parts. In 1851 the factory building was completed and the name American Horology Company was chosen. It was not until late 1852 that the first watches were completed bearing the signature "The Warren Mfg. Co.," after a famed Revolutionary War hero. The first 17 watches were not placed on the market but went to officials of the company. Watches numbered 18 through 110 were marked "Warren Boston;" the next 800 were marked "Samuel Curtis;" a few were marked "Fellows & Schell" and sold for $40.

The name was changed to the Boston Watch Company in September 1853, and a factory was built in Waltham, Massachusetts, in October 1854. The movements that were produced here carried serial numbers 1,001 to 5,000 and were marked "Dennison, Howard & Davis," "C. T. Parker," and "P. S. Bartlett." Boston Watch Company failed in 1857 and was sold at a sheriff's auction to Royal E. Robbins. In May 1857, it was reorganized as the Appleton, Tracy & Co., and the watches produced carried serial numbers 5,001 to 14,000, model 1857. The first movements were marked Appleton, Tracy & Co. The C. T. Parker was introduced as model 1857 and sold for $12.00, 399 of these models were made. Also 598 chronodrometers were produced and in January 1858 the P. S. Bartlett watch was made.

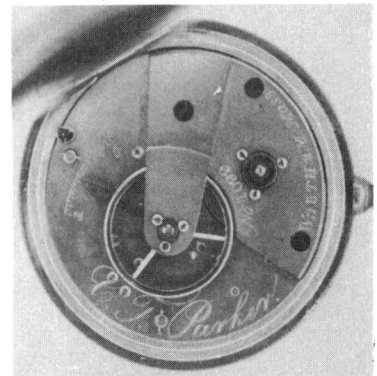

Engraved on movement **SAMUEL CURTIS ROXBURY.**
NO 112, 18 size, 15 jewels, under sprung, steel balance, Ca. 1853. This movement was made to fit in the typical English size case.

Engraved on movement **"C.T. PARKER WALTHAM MASS. NO 1099"**, 7 jewels, under sprung, steel balance, Ca. November 1857. Note: Balance cock not engraved.

In January 1859, the Waltham Improvement Co. and the Appleton, Tracy & Co. merged to form the American Watch Company. In 1860, as Lincoln was elected president and the country was in Civil War, the American Watch Co. was faced with serious problems. The next year, business came to a standstill. There seemed to be little hope of finding a market for watches, and bankruptcy again seemed close at hand. At this point it was decided to cut expenditures to the lowest possible figure and keep the factory in operation.

American horology owes much to members of the Waltham Watch group such as Bacon, Church, Dennison, Fogg, Howard Marsh, Webster, and Woerd, who contributed much to its development and success. In early 1861, the name "J. Watson" appeared on model 1857 (first run: Nos. 23,601 to 24,300 total production 1,200).

The next model 1857 was the "R. E. Robbins" of which 2,800 were made. The William Ellery, marked "Wm. Ellery," (model 1857) was then introduced with the first serial number of 46,201. It was key wind and key set and had 7 to 15 jewels.

A size 10 woman's watch was made in July of 1861 with first serial numbers of 44,201. It was marked "Appleton, Tracy & Co." gold balance, key wind and key set, 3/4 plate, 13 to 15 jewels. Some were marked "P. S. Bartlett" and a 15 jewel was marked "Appleton, Tracy & Co." A special model, 10 size, serial numbers of 45,801 to 46,200, is extremely rare. The first stem wind, beginning with serial number 410,698, was produced in 1868. By 1880 all watches were quick train. The last key wind was serial No. 22,577,000, about 1919, 18 size, 1883 model, 7J, sterling, produced for export.

WALTHAM ESTIMATED SERIAL NUMBERS AND PRODUCTION DATES

DATE — SERIAL NO.	DATE — SERIAL NO.	DATE — SERIAL NO.
1852 – 50	1888 – 3,800,000	1924 – 24,550,000
1853 – 400	1889 – 4,200,000	1925 – 24,800,000
1854 – 1,000	1890 – 4,700,000	1926 – 25,200,000
1855 – 2,500	1891 – 5,200,000	1927 – 26,100,000
1856 – 4,000	1892 – 5,800,000	1928 – 26,400,000
1857 – 6,000	1893 – 6,300,000	1929 – 26,900,000
1858 – 10,000	1894 – 6,700,000	1930 – 27,100,000
1859 – 15,000	1895 – 7,100,000	1931 – 27,300,000
1860 – 20,000	1896 – 7,450,000	1932 – 27,550,000
1861 – 30,000	1897 – 8,100,000	1933 – 27,750,000
1862 – 45,000	1898 – 8,400,000	1934 – 28,100,000
1863 – 65,000	1899 – 9,000,000	1935 – 28,600,000
1864 – 110,000	1900 – 9,500,000	1936 – 29,100,000
1865 – 180,000	1901 –10,200,000	1937 – 29,400,000
1866 – 260,000	1902 –11,100,000	1938 – 29,750,000
1867 – 330,000	1903 –12,100,000	1939 – 30,050,000
1868 – 410,000	1904 –13,500,000	1940 – 30,250,000
1869 – 460,000	1905 –14,300,000	1941 – 30,750,000
1870 – 500,000	1906 –14,700,000	1942 – 31,050,000
1871 – 540,000	1907 –15,500,000	1943 – 31,400,000
1872 – 590,000	1908 –16,400,000	1944 – 31,700,000
1873 – 680,000	1909 –17,600,000	1945 – 32,100,000
1874 – 730,000	1910 –17,900,000	1946 – 32,350,000
1875 – 810,000	1911 –18,100,000	1947 – 32,750,000
1876 – 910,000	1912 –18,200,000	1948 – 33,100,000
1877 – 1,000,000	1913 –18,900,000	1949 – 33,500,000
1878 – 1,150,000	1914 –19,500,000	1950 – 33,560,000
1879 – 1,350,000	1915 –20,000,000	1951 – 33,600,000
1880 – 1,500,000	1916 –20,500,000	1952 – 33,700,000
1881 – 1,670,000	1917 –20,900,000	1953 – 33,800,000
1882 – 1,835,000	1918 –21,800,000	1954 – 34,100,000
1883 – 2,000,000	1919 –22,500,000	1955 – 34,450,000
1884 – 2,350,000	1920 –23,400,000	1956 – 34,700,000
1885 – 2,650,000	1921 –23,900,000	1957 – 35,000,000
1886 – 3,000,000	1922 –24,100,000	
1887 – 3,400,000	1923 –24,300,000	

🕐 The above list is provided for determining the **APPROXIMATE** age of your watch. Match serial number with date. Watches were not necessarily *SOLD* and *DELIVERED* in the exact order of manufactured or production dates.

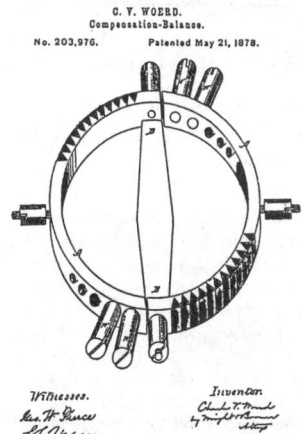

C. V. WOERD.
Compensation-Balance.
No. 203,976.   Patented May 21, 1878.

Witnesses.

Inventor

HOWARD, DAVIS & DENNISON: 20 Size, 15 Jewels, 8 day, two mainsprings and gilt movement. The first 17 were made for the officials of the company, Ca. 1852.

Woerd's patented compensating balance the above illustration is a copy of the blue print of Mr. Woerd's patented SAW TOOTH BALANCE. The Saw Tooth Balance may be found on some 16 size 1872 models. (**VERY RARE**)

🕐 Generic, nameless or unmarked grades for watch movements are listed under the Company name or initials of the Company, etc. by size, jewel count and description.

20 SIZE
MODEL 1862,-20-KW
T. P. 3,500

Grade or Name–Description	Avg	Ex -Fn	Mint
American Watch Co., 19J, KW, 18K, HC, all original .... ★★★	$3,800	$4,500	$6,000
American Watch Co., 15 to19J, KW, KS,3/4, vibrating hair-spring stud, silver case..................... ★★	1,400	2,000	2,500
American Watch Co., 15 to 19J, KW, KS, 3/4, vibrating hair-spring stud, 18K HC, all original .... ★★	3,500	4,000	5,500
American Watch Co., 15 & 17J,3/4, KW, ADJ...........................★	500	650	900
American Watch Co., 19J,3/4, KW, ADJ .... ★★	2,200	2,600	3,200
American Watch Co., 19J,3/4, KW, ADJ, with Maltese cross stopwork, all original silver case...................................... ★★	2,800	3,200	4,000
American W. Co., 15J,3/4, KW ....★	450	550	800
American W. Co., 7-11J,3/4, KW..★	300	400	550
American W. Co., 19J,3/4W, Stratons Pat. Barrel.................... ★★	2,000	2,500	3,500
American W. Co., Nashua S# under dial, (below 51,000).... ★★★	4,000	5,000	6,000
American W. Co., Woerd's Pat., Cam Reg........................ ★★★	2,200	2,500	3,300
Am'n W. Co., 15J, KW,3/4, coin case ....★	425	500	600
Am'n W. Co., 15J, KW,3/4, Mvt. only..	200	250	350
Appleton, Tracy & Co., 15J,3/4, KW, with Maltese cross stopwork, all original...★	500	650	900
Appleton, Tracy & Co., 15 & 17J,3/4,KW gold balance...............★	650	775	950
Appleton, Tracy & Co., 15 & 17J,3/4, KW	400	500	650
Appleton, Tracy & Co., 15 & 17J,3/4, KW, vibrating hair spring stud, silver case....................................... ★★	1,000	1,200	1,600
Appleton, Tracy & Co., 15 & 17J,3/4, KW, vibrating hair spring stud, 18K HC .... ★★★	2,800	3,200	3,600
Appleton Tracy & Co., 15J, KW, Vibrating hairspring stud Straton barrel, Foggs Pat. .... ★★	800	1,000	1,200
Appleton Tracy & Co., 15J, KW,3/4, **Mvt. only no case**	200	265	350
Appleton Tracy & Co., 19J, KW,3/4... ★★	500	600	800
Howard, Davis & Dennison, S#1-17, 8 day, Ca.1852.... ★★★★★	30,000	40,000	58,000

🕐 Generic, nameless or unmarked grades for watch movements are listed under the Company name or initials of the Company, etc. by size, jewel count and description.

NOTE: **RARE** in original gold cases add ($1,200.00 in 14K) & ($1,600.00 in 18K).

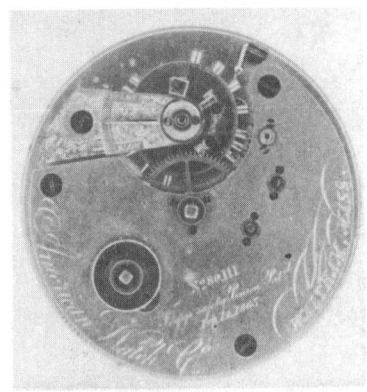

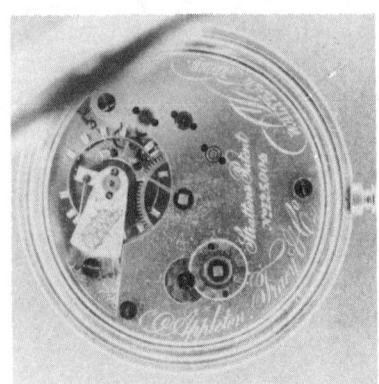

American Watch Co., Model 1862, 20 size, 17 jewels, gold balance and escape wheel, gold jeweled settings, key wind, key set from back, serial number 80111.

Appleton Tracy & Co., Model 20KW, 20 size, 15 jewels, serial number 125004. Note vibrating hairspring stud.

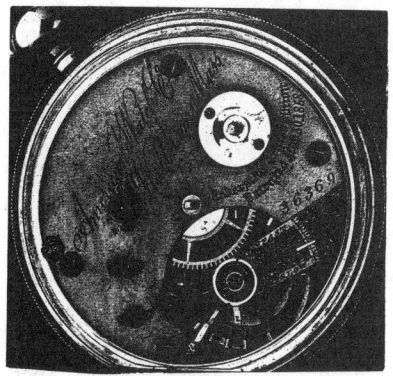

AMERICAN WATCH CO., Model 18KW, 18 size, 15 jewels, serial number 36369. Reversible center pinion, patented Nov. 30th, 1858.

Model 1857, 18 size, 15-16 jewels, "Chronodrometer" on dial, "Appleton Tracy & Co." or "P.S. Bartlett, key wind & set, 1/4 jump seconds, S.# 14,752 . Listed under "Appleton Tracy & Co. Chronodrometer", lst serial # 13,701.

18 SIZE
MODELS 1857, 18KW =1859, 1870, 1877, 1879, 1883, 1892

Grade or Name – Description	Avg	Ex-Fn	Mint
American Watch Co., 17J,3/4, KW, M#18, KW .... ★ ★ ★	$1,400	$1,700	$2,200
American Watch Co., 19J, M#1859, 3/4............................★ ★ ★ ★	2,800	3,400	4,200
American Watch Co., 19J, M#1888, HC, silver.......................★ ★	800	1,000	1,400
American Watch Co.,15-16-17J, M#1883	75	100	150
American Watch Co., 21J, M#1883, Special, ADJ, GJS ...... ★ ★ ★	400	525	700
American Watch Co., 15J, M#1859,3/4, Pat. Nov. 30, 1858,			
Reversible center pinion, original silver case .... ★ ★ ★	3,000	3,300	4,000
American Watch Co., 17J, M#1859,3/4, KW, Fitts Pat.			
Reversible center pinion, Originial 18K case .... ★ ★ ★ ★	4,000	4,800	6,000
American Watch Co., 15J, M#1870, KW	225	275	395

🕐 Generic, nameless or unmarked grades for watch movements are listed under the Company name or initials of the Company, etc. by size, jewel count and description.

AMn. Watch Co., 15J, M#1857, KW, KS	$95	$125	$200
AMn. Watch Co., 17J, M#1857, KW, KS ....★	250	300	400
AMn. Watch Co., 14K, HC, heavy box hinged, multi-color			
(4 colors)	2,200	2,400	3,200
AMn. Watch Co., 11J, thin model, KW, 3/4 plate ....★	200	300	500
AMn. Watch Co., 15 & 17J, M#1870, KW, ADJ	175	225	300
AMn. Watch Co., 17J, M#1892	95	125	175
AMn. Watch Co., 21J, M#1892	225	265	325
AMn. Watch Co., 7J, M#1877	95	125	155
AMn. Watch Co., 11J, M#1877	95	125	155
AMn. Watch Co., 7J, M#1883, SW/ KW	95	125	155
AMn. Watch Co., 11-13J, M#1883, SW/ KW.............................	95	125	155
AMn. Watch Co., 15J, M#1883, SW/ KW	100	125	195
AMn. Watch Co., 15J, M#1857, (*Waltham W. Co.*), SW / KW..★	250	325	450
AMn. Watch Co., 15J, M#1857, (*Waltham W. Co.*), SW / LS.......	195	225	295
Appleton, Tracy & Co., 15J, M#1857, SW / LS.............................	150	195	250
Appleton, Tracy & Co., 7-11J, KW, M#1857	150	175	225
Appleton, Tracy & Co., 11J, thin model, KW,3/4 ....★	250	350	450
Appleton, Tracy & Co., 15J, M#1857, KW	150	175	225
Appleton, Tracy & Co., 15J, M#1857, KW, serial # below 10,000.	250	300	395

🕐 Some watch manufacturers personalize watches for jobbers or jewelry firms, with exclusive private signed or marked movements. The valuable collectable watches are listed under the signed or marked movement. Other exclusive private signed or marked movements will have equivalent value are only slightly higher value and should be compared to Generic or Nameless movements. Railroad signed or marked (dials & movements) are usually more collectable & higher in value.

Grade or Name–Description	Avg	Ex-Fn	Mint
Appleton, Tracy & Co., 15J, M#1859, 3/4, reverse pinion,			
Pat. Nov. 30, 1858, orig. silver case .... ★★★	$1,200	$1,450	$1,800
Appleton, Tracy & Co., 11-15-16-17J, KW, 3/4 ....★	295	365	495
Appleton, Tracy & Co., 16J, M#1857, Ist run (5,001-5,100)			
Am. W. Co. (Eagle) silver HC .... ★★	600	675	800
Appleton, Tracy & Co., 15J, M#1857, KW, 18K HC	600	700	1,000
Appleton, Tracy & Co., 16J, M#1857, KW	225	250	375
Appleton, Tracy & Co., 15J, 3/4, KW, with vibrating hairspring stud,			
Stratton's Pat., coin case .... ★★★	1,400	1,600	2,000
Appleton, Tracy & Co., 15J, 3/4, KW, with vibrating hairspring stud,			
orig. 18K case .... ★★★	2,000	2,400	2,800
Appleton, Tracy & Co., Sporting, (Chronodrometer), M#1857,			
16J, KW, KS, orig. case, with stop feature .... ★★	1,500	1,900	2,500
Appleton, Tracy & Co., 15J, KW, Fitts Pat., pinion............ ★★	400	475	600
Appleton, Tracy & Co., 15J, 3/4, KW............★	175	225	295
Appleton, Tracy & Co., 11-15J, M#s 1877, 1879, SW	85	100	125
Appleton, Tracy & Co., 15J, M#1877, KW	90	125	135
Appleton, Tracy & Co., 15J, M#s 1877-1879, SW, OF	85	95	125
Appleton, Tracy & Co., 15J, M#s 1877-1879, SW, HC	100	125	165
Appleton, Tracy & Co., 15J, M#1883, SW, OF	85	110	135
Appleton, Tracy & Co., 15J, M#1883, SW, non- magnet, OF	100	125	165
Appleton, Tracy & Co., 15J, M#1883, SW, HC	100	125	175
Appleton, Tracy & Co., 15J, M#1892, SW, OF	90	115	135
Appleton, Tracy & Co., 17J, m#1863,LS ....★	175	225	325
Appleton, Tracy & Co., 17J, M#1892, SW, Premiere	95	120	175
Appleton, Tracy & Co., 17J, M#1892, SW, OF	90	115	150
Appleton, Tracy & Co., 17J, M#1883, SW, 2 tone mvt.			
Lehigh Valley Railroad ....★	500	650	800
Appleton, Tracy & Co., 17J, M#1883, SW, HC............	100	125	185
Appleton, Tracy & Co., 17J, M#1883, OF	90	115	125
Appleton, Tracy & Co., 17J, M#1892, SW, HC	100	125	165
Appleton, Tracy & Co., 19J, M#1892, SW, OF	175	200	235
Appleton, Tracy & Co., 19J, M#1892, SW, HC	200	225	295
Appleton, Tracy & Co., 21J, M#1892, SW, OF	225	275	335
Appleton, Tracy & Co., 21J, M#1892, SW, HC	335	355	435

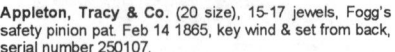

Appleton, Tracy & Co. (20 size), 15-17 jewels, Fogg's safety pinion pat. Feb 14 1865, key wind & set from back, serial number 250107.

P. S. Bartlett, Model 18KW or 1859, 18 size, 11 jewels, key wind & set from back, serial number 41597.

🕐 Generic, nameless or unmarked grades for watch movements are listed under the Company name or initials of the Company, etc. by size, jewel count and description.

Grade or Name – Description	Avg	Ex-Fn	Mint
A. W. W. Co., 7-9J, M#1883, KW, OF	$95	$115	$125
A. W. W. Co., 7-9J, M#1883, SW, OF	85	95	100
A. W. W. Co., 11-13J, LS, HC	100	125	165
A. W. W. Co., 11-13J, M#1879, OF	80	85	100
A. W. W. Co., 11-13J, M#1883, SW, OF	80	85	100
A. W. W. Co., 15J, OF	85	90	110
A. W. W. Co., 15J, HC	100	125	175
A. W. W. Co., 15J, 14K multi-color boxcase HC	2,000	2,300	2,750
A. W. W. Co., 15J, M#1879, OF	85	95	125
A. W. W. Co., 15J, M#1883, OF	85	95	125
A. W. W. Co., 16J, OF or HC	95	125	175
A. W. W. Co., 17J, M#1857, gold bal. wheel, GJS, ★	275	350	475
A. W. W. Co., 17J, "for R.R. Service" on dial ★	235	300	375
A. W. W. Co., 17J, M#1883, OF	90	110	135
A. W. W. Co., 17J, M#1892, LS, OF	100	120	165
A. W. W. Co., 17J, M#1892, PS, OF	100	120	165
A. W. W. Co., 17J, M#1892, HC	120	150	195
A. W. W. Co., 19J, M#1892	125	150	225
A. W. W. Co., 21J, M#1892	235	250	295
A. W. W. Co., 23J, M#1892	295	325	395

P.S. Bartlett, 18 size, 15 jewels, Model 1857, Engraved on back "4 PR. Jewels." Serial number 13446.

Canadian Railway Time Service, Model 1892, 18 size, 17 jewels, serial number 22,017,534.

Grade or Name – Description	Avg	Ex-Fn	Mint
P. S. Bartlett, 7J, M#1857, KW, 1st Run (1,401-1,500 ★★			
Am.W. Co. (Eagle) silver HC	$750	$850	$1,000
P. S. Bartlett, 15J, M#1857, KW, 2nd Run (1,551-1,650)			
Am.W. Co. (Eagle) silver HC ★★	600	700	850
P. S. Bartlett, 11J, M#1857, KW, 2nd-3rd Run ★	400	475	550
P. S. Bartlett, 15J, M#1857, KW, 2nd-3rd Run ★	425	550	685
P. S. Bartlett, 11J, LS, HC, 14K	550	650	850
P. S. Bartlett, 15J, M#1857, KW, below S#8,000	395	435	500
P. S. Bartlett, 11J, M#1879, KW	85	95	135
P. S. Bartlett, 11J, M#1857, KW, Eagle inside case lid	155	175	225
P. S. Bartlett, 15J, M#1857, SW / LS, (note let down screw)	165	200	275
P. S. Bartlett, 15J, M#1879, KW	95	110	150

Grade or Name – Description	Avg	Ex-Fn	Mint
P. S. Bartlett, 15J, M#1879, SW	$85	$95	$110
P. S. Bartlett, 11-15J, M#1870, SW	95	110	135
P. S. Bartlett, 11-15J, M#1877, KW	125	150	200
P. S. Bartlett, 11J, M#1883, SW	80	90	120
P. S. Bartlett, 15J, M#1883, KW	90	120	150
P. S. Bartlett, 15J, M#1883, SW	85	95	135
P. S. Bartlett, 17J, M#1883, SW	100	125	165
P. S. Bartlett, 11J, M#1859, 3/4, thin model, KS from back	285	365	475
P. S. Bartlett, 11J, M#1859, 3/4, Pat. Nov. 30, 1858	400	500	625
P. S. Bartlett, 15J, **pinned plates**, M#1857, KW ....★	700	800	1,000
P. S. Bartlett, 15J, M#1892, SW	90	100	125
P. S. Bartlett, 17J, M#1892, SW, OF, LS	95	110	135
P. S. Bartlett, 17J, M#1892, SW, HC	150	175	215
P. S. Bartlett, 17J, M#1892, SW, OF, PS	95	110	135
P. S. Bartlett, 17J, M#1892, SW, 2-Tone	100	125	150
P. S. Bartlett, 19J, M#1892, SW	175	200	235
P. S. Bartlett, 21J, M#1892, SW	225	260	295
P. S. Bartlett, 21J, M#1892, SW, 2-Tone	275	300	365
Broadway, 7J, M#1857, KW, HC	95	125	160
Broadway, 11J, M#1857, KW, HC	125	150	175
Broadway, 7-11J, M#1877, KW, SW, NI, HC	125	150	175
Broadway, 7J, M#1883, KW, HC	125	150	175
Broadway, 11J, M#1883, KW, HC	125	150	175
Broadway, 11J, M#1883, SW, HC	125	150	175
Canadian Railway Time Service, 17J, M#1883-1892, Adj.5P	355	395	465
Central Park, 15J, M#1857, KW	160	185	245
Champion, 15J, M#1877, OF	65	85	100
Chronometro, 21J, M#1892, OF	300	350	425
Crescent Park, 15J, M#1857	185	225	285
Crescent Street, 15J, M#1870, KW	175	200	255
Crescent Street, 15J, M#1870, **pin or nail set**	180	215	275
Crescent Street, 17J, M#1870, KW ....★	225	255	335

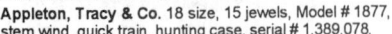

Appleton, Tracy & Co. 18 size, 15 jewels, Model # 1877, stem wind, quick train, hunting case, serial # 1,389,078.

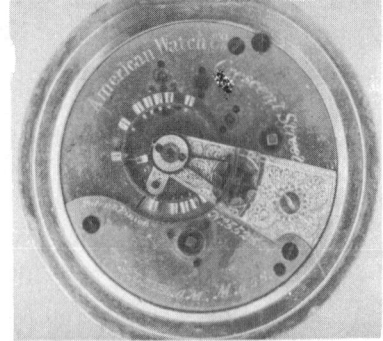

Crescent Street, Model 1870, 18 size, 15 J., Key wind & set from back, serial number 552,526. This grade was the first American watch to be advertised as a railroad watch.

IMPORTANT NOTE: Railroad Standards, Railroad Approved & Railroad Grade **terminology,** as defined and used in this ***BOOK***.
1. **RAILROAD STANDARDS** = A commission or board appointed by the railroad companies outlined a set of **guidelines** to be accepted or approved by each railroad line.
2. **RAILROAD APPROVED** = A ***LIST*** of watches each railroad line would approve if purchased by their employee's. (this list changed through the years).
3. **RAILROAD GRADE** = A watch made by manufactures to met or exceed the guidelines set by the railroad **standards**. Grade such as 992, Vanguard and B.W. Raymond etc.
☉ Some GRADES **exceeded** the R.R. standards such as 23 jewels, diamond end stone, gold train, raised gold jewel settings, double sunk dial and the list goes on. Examples: such as Veritas, Sangamo, 950 & Riverside Maximus and many others.

Grade or Name–Description	Avg	Ex-Fn	Mint
Crescent Street, 15J, M#1870, SW	$150	$175	$225
Crescent Street, 15J, M#1883, SW, non-magnetic, OF	125	165	235
Crescent Street, 15J, M#1883, SW, non-magnetic, HC	150	175	255
Crescent Street, 15J, M#1883, SW, 2-Tone	125	155	225
Crescent Street, 17J, M#1883, SW, OF	95	125	175
Crescent Street, 17J, M#1883, SW, HC	125	155	200
Crescent Street, 19J, M#1883 ★	300	350	425
Crescent Street, 17J, M#1892, SW, GJS	125	150	200
Crescent Street, 17J, M#1892, SW, OF	100	125	155
Crescent Street, 17J, M#1892, SW, HC	135	155	200
Crescent Street, 19J, M#1892, SW, Adj.5P, GJS ,OF	175	200	230
Crescent Street, 19J, M#1892, SW, Adj.5P, GJS ,HC	225	265	275
Crescent Street, 21J, M#1892, SW, Adj.5P, GJS, OF	225	255	335
Crescent Street, 21J, M#1892, SW, Adj.5P, GJS, HC	300	335	395
Crescent Street, 21J, M#1892, Wind Indicator	900	1,100	1,500
Samuel Curtis, 11-15J, M#1857, KW, S# less than200, original 17S silver case ★★	3,000	3,500	4,000
Samuel Curtis, 11-15J, M#1857, KW, S# less than 400, original 17S silver case ★★	2,500	3,000	3,800
Samuel Curtis, 11-15J, M#1857, KW, S# less than 600, original 17S silver case ★★	2,300	2,700	3,500
Samuel Curtis, 11-15J, M#1857, KW, S# less than 1,000, original 17S silver case ★	2,000	2,500	3,200
(Samuel Curtis "not" in original silver case, deduct $800 to $1,000 from value)			
Dennison, Howard, Davis, 7J, M#1857, KW, W/original case	900	1,000	1,200
Dennison, Howard, Davis, 11-13J, M#1857, KW, W/original case	950	1,100	1,300
Dennison, Howard, Davis, 15J, M#1857, KW, W/original case	1,000	1,200	1,450
Dennison, Howard, Davis, 15J, M#1857, KW, 1st. run (1,002-1,100) W/original case Am.W. Co. (Eagle)silver HC ★★	1,200	1,400	1,800
Dennison, Howard, Davis, 15J, M#1857, KW, S# less than 2,000, W/original case Am.W. Co. (Eagle)silver HC ★	1,000	1,200	1,450

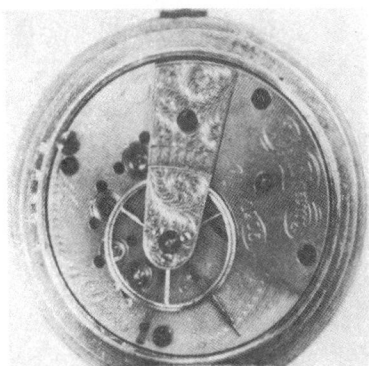

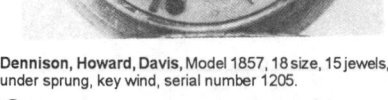

Dennison, Howard, Davis, Model 1857, 18 size, 15 jewels, under sprung, key wind, serial number 1205.

Howard & Rice, Model 1857, 18 size, 15 jewels, under sprung, serial number 6003.

🕓 Watches listed in this book are priced at the collectable retail level, as **complete** watches having an original 14k gold-filled case and Key Wind with silver, an original white enamel single sunk dial, and with the entire original movement in good working order with no repairs needed.

🕓 Some watch manufacturers personalize watches for jobbers or jewelry firms, with exclusive private signed or marked movements. The valuable collectable watches are listed under the signed or marked movement. Other exclusive private signed or marked movements will have equivalent value are only slightly higher value and should be compared to Generic or Nameless movements. Railroad signed or marked (dials & movements) are usually more collectable & higher in value.

Grade or Name –Description	Avg	Ex-Fn	Mint
Denver & Rio Grande, 21J, M#1892, GJS, Adj.3P	$950	$1,200	$1,500
Dominion Railways, 15-17J, M#1883, OF, SW, train on dial	700	900	1,200
Wm. Ellery, 7-11J, M#1857, Boston, Mass. all original silver HC case			
with Am. Watch Co.& eagle, serial # below 46,600 .... ★ ★	350	450	600
Wm. Ellery, 7-11J, M#1857, Boston, Mass.	100	125	175
Wm. Ellery, 7-11J, M#KW, 3/4	175	200	265
Wm. Ellery, 15J, KW, 3/4 ....★	350	400	465
Wm. Ellery, 7-11J, M#18KW, KW-KS from back, 18K, HC	1,000	1,200	1,500
Wm. Ellery, 7J, M#1857, KW, KS from back	200	225	295
Wm. Ellery, 15J, M#1857, SW / LS, (note let down screw)........ ★	225	300	425
Wm. Ellery, 7-15J, M#1877, M#1879, KW	95	125	165
Wm. Ellery, 11-15J, M#1877 & 1879, SW	95	125	165
Wm. Ellery, 7-13J, M#1883	85	95	125
Excelsior, M#1877, KW	100	125	150
Export, 7-11J, M#1877	85	100	125
Export, 7-11J, M#1883, KW	100	125	155
Express Train, 15-17J, M# 1883, LS, OF	200	235	300
Favorite, 15J, M#1877	100	125	155
Fellows & Schell, 15J, KW, KS .... ★ ★ ★	1,500	1,700	2,000
Franklin, 7J, M#1877, SW..............................	150	175	225
Home Watch Co., 7-15J, M#1857-1883, KW	100	125	155
Home Watch Co., 7J, M#1877, KW	100	125	155
Home Watch Co., 7-11J, M#1879, SW.............................	100	125	155
Howard & Rice, 15J, M#1857, KW, KS (serial numbers range			
from 6000 to 6500)........................... ★ ★	1,500	1,700	2,000
E. Howard & Co., Boston (on dial & mvt.), English style escape			
wheel, upright pallets, 15J, M#1857, KW, KS,			
S#s about 6,400 to 6,500 .... ★ ★ ★ ★	2,500	2,800	3,500
Martyn Square, 7-15J, M#1857-1877-1879, KW, SW (exported) ..	125	150	200
Mermod, Jaccard & KingParagon Timekeeper, 23J, M#1892,			
Vanguard, LS, GJS, HC	425	475	535

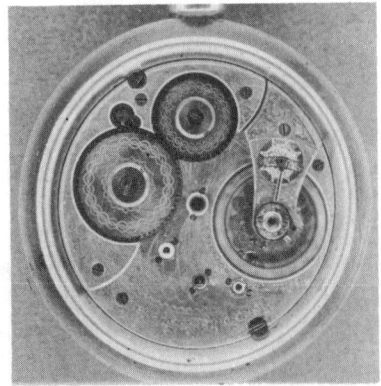

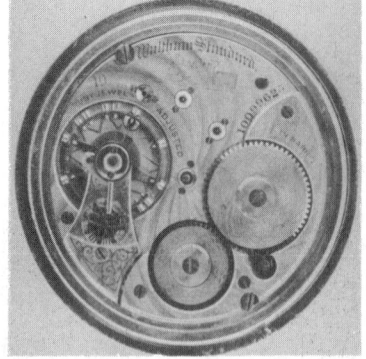

Pennsylvania Special, Model 1892, 18 size, 21 jewels, serial number 14,000,015.

Waltham Standard, Grade 1892, 18 size, 19 jewels, Adj5P, open face, note engine & coal car engraved on movement, serial number 10,099,625.

🕐 Some watch manufacturers personalize watches for jobbers or jewelry firms, with exclusive private signed or marked movements. The valuable collectable watches are listed under the signed or marked movement. Other exclusive private signed or marked movements will have equivalent value are only slightly higher value and should be compared to Generic or Nameless movements. Railroad signed or marked (dials & movements) are usually more collectable & higher in value.

Grade or Name –Description	Avg	Ex-Fn	Mint
Non-Magnetic, 15J, SW, LS, NI	$125	$150	$185
Non-Magnetic, 17J, M#1892, SW, LS	150	175	250
Paragon, 15J, M#1883, HC	125	150	185
C. T. Parker, 7-11J, M#1857, KW, silver HC	400	550	800
Chas. T. Parker, 11-15J, M#1857, KW, HC	350	450	600
C. T. Parker, 7-11J, M#1857, KW, Am.W. Co. (Eagle)silver HC serial # below 1,200 ★★	1,200	1,400	1,800
C. T. Parker, 7-11J, M#1857, KW, 18K, HC serial # below 1,400 ★★	1,800	2,00	2,500
Pennsylvania R.R. on dial, Appleton, Tracy & Co. on Mvt., KW, KS, M# 1859 ★★	2,500	2,900	3,600
Pennsylvania Special, 21J, M#1892, HC ★★★	1,400	1,600	2,000
Pennsylvania Special, 21J, M#1892, OF ★★★	1,400	1,600	2,000
Pennsylvania Special, 21J, M#1892, HC GOLD DAMASKEENED, gold train ★★★★	10,000	12,000	15,000
Pennsylvania Special, 23J, M#1892, OF ★★★	2,000	2,200	2,600
Pioneer, 7J, M#1883	80	95	125
Premier, 17J, M#1892, LS, OF	135	155	195
Railroad, 17J, M#1892, LS	300	350	425
Railroad, 21J, M#1892, LS,	350	425	550
Railroad inspector, 21J, M#1892, LS, (loaner with # on case)	400	450	600
Railroader, 17J, M#1892, LS,Adj,GJS, OF ★★	650	800	1,000
Railroad King, 15J, M#1883, LS	200	250	350
Railroad King, 15J, M#1883, 2-Tone	250	300	400
Railroad King, 17J, Special, M#1883, LS	300	350	450
Railroad Standard, 19J, G#1892, OF ★	600	700	900
(Railroad Watches with R.R. names on dial and movement as follows:)			
Canadian Pacific R.R., 17J, M#1883	335	375	450
Canadian Pacific R.R., 17J, M#1892-1908	375	450	575
Canadian Pacific R.R., 21J, M#1892	500	550	650
Santa Fe Route, 17J, M#1883	425	500	625
Santa Fe Route, 17J, M#1892 ★	525	650	800
Santa Fe Route, 21J, M#1892 ★	625	750	900
Conklins Railroad Special, 21J, G#1892	500	550	625
Rio Grande Western, 17J, G#1892, OF ★	850	900	1,000
Riverside, 7J, M#1857	125	150	200
Riverside, 17J, M#1892 ★	300	350	450
Roadmaster, 17J, M#1892, LS ★	350	400	475
R. E. Robbins, 11-15J, M#1857, KW S# (25,101-25,200) ★	600	700	800
R. E. Robbins, 13-15J, M#1877, KW	200	250	350
R. E. Robbins, 13J, M#1883	100	125	175

Sidereal, model #1892, 17j, 24 hour dial used by astronomers. (marked Sidereal on dial)

Vanguard, Model 1892, 18S, 23J, diamond end stone, gold jewel settings, exposed winding gears, S# 10,533,465.

Grade or Name – Description	Avg	Ex-Fn	Mint
Royal, 17J, M#1892, OF	$95	$110	$150
Royal, 17J, M#1892, HC	150	175	225
Sidereal, M#1892, 19J, (marked **Sidereal** on dial) OF ★★★	1,200	1,500	2,000
M#1892, 17J, Astronomical (marked **Sidereal** on dial) OF.. ★★★	1,000	1,300	1,800
Sol, 7-11J, M#1883, OF	85	95	110
Sol, 17J, OF, PS	95	110	135
Special Railroad, 17J, M#1883, LS, OF	325	365	475
Special R. R. King, 15-17J, M#1883	365	400	550
Special R. R. King, 15-17J, M#1883, HC	450	500	650
Sterling, 7J, M#1857, KW, Silver	100	110	150
Sterling, 7-11J, M#1877, M#1879	75	85	100
Sterling, 7-11J, M#1883, KW	75	85	110
Sterling, 11-15J, M#1883, SW	75	85	100
Tourist, 11J, M#1877	75	85	100
Tourist, 7J, M#1877	75	85	100
Tracy, Baker & Co., 15J, 18K original A.W.W. Co. case ★★★★	4,900	5,500	6,300
Vanguard, 17J, M#1892, GJS, HC ★★★	400	500	650
Vanguard, 17J, M#1892, LS, Adj.5P, DR, GJS, OF ★★	300	400	550
Vanguard, 17J, M#1892, Wind Indicator, Adj.5P, DR, GJS	800	1,000	1,200
Vanguard, 19J, M#1892, LS, Adj.5P, Diamond end stones	200	225	275
Vanguard, 19J, M#1892, LS, Adj.5P, DR, GJS, OF	200	225	275
Vanguard, 19J, M#1892, **Wind Indicator,** LS, Adj.5P, DR, GJS ..	1,500	1,700	2,000
Vanguard, 19J, M#1892, Adj.5P, GJS, HC ★	325	375	485
Vanguard, 21J, M#1892, Adj.5P, PS	235	275	325
Vanguard, 21J, M#1892, GJS, Adj.5P, HC	325	350	400
Vanguard, 21J, M#1892, LS, Adj.5P, DR, GJS, OF	235	275	325
Vanguard, 21J, M#1892, LS, Adj.5P, Diamond end stone	245	295	350
Vanguard, 21J, M#1892, **Wind Indicator**, Adj.5P, GJS, OF ★	1,800	1,950	2,200
Vanguard, 23J, M#1892, LS, Adj.5P, DR, GJS, OF	300	350	400
Vanguard, 23J, M#1892, LS, Adj.5P, DR, GJS, HC ★	375	450	500
Vanguard, 23J, M#1892, LS, Adj.5P, DR, GJS, Diamond end stone	335	375	450
Vanguard, 23J, M#1892, PS, Adj.5P, DR, GJS, OF	300	350	400
Vanguard, 23J, M#1892, **Wind Indicator**, LS, Adj.5P, DR,GJS. ★	2,000	2,400	2,800
Waltham,17J, Adj., G#1892, (**non magnetic**), OF	150	175	210
Waltham Standard,17J, Adj., G#1892, OF	150	175	210
Waltham Standard,19J, Adj., G#1892, (locomotive), OF ★	250	300	375
Waltham Watch Co., 15J, **M#1857**, SW / LS, (let down screw)	200	250	300

American Waltham Watch Co., Model 1883, 18 size, 15 jewels, serial number 3,093,425

Grade 845, Model 1892, 18 size, 21 jewels, railroad grade, Adj.5P, serial number 15,097,475

🕐 Watches listed in this book are priced at the collectable retail level, as **complete** watches having an original 14k gold-filled case and Key Wind with silver, an original white enamel single sunk dial, and with the entire original movement in good working order with no repairs needed.

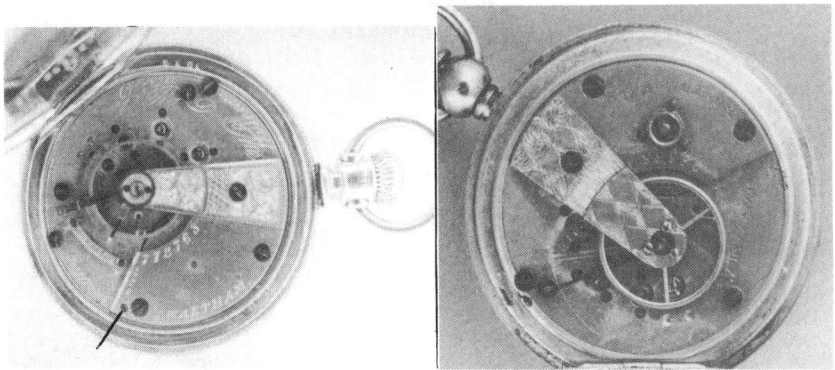

Waltham Watch Co., model 1857 with factory stem wind, 18S, 15J, S# 778763, Fogg's Patent, This is not a Abbott's stem wind conversion. NOTE **let down screw.**

J. WATSON, Boston Mass engraved on movement, 18 size, 11 jewels, hunting case, key wind key set, serial number 28,635, Ca. April 1863.

Grade or Name – Description	Avg	Ex-Fn	Mint
Warren, 15J, M#1857, KW, KS, S#18-29, original 17S			
silver case... ★★★★★ $20,000	$20,000	$24,000	$30,000
Warren, 15J, M#1857, KW, KS, S#30-60, original 17S			
silver case... ★★★★ 15,000	15,000	18,000	22,000
Warren, 15J, M#1857, KW, KS, S#61-90, original 17S			
silver case... ★★★★ 12,000	12,000	14,000	18,000
Warren, 15J, M#1857, KW, KS, S#91-110, original 17S			
silver case... ★★★ 9,000	9,000	12,000	16,000
(Warren not in original silver case, deduct $1,000 to $2,500)			
George Washington, M#1857, KW...	275	350	450
J. Watson, 7J, M#1857, KW, "Boston" S# (28,201-28,270)........ ★	500	700	1,000
J. Watson, 7-11J, M#1857, KW, "London" S# (23,700-23,800) . ★	500	700	1,000
454, 21J, GT, 3/4, ...	200	250	325
845, 21J, M#1892, OF..	225	250	300
845, 21J, M#1892, HC..	250	300	350
836, 17J, DR, Adj.4P, LS, OF..	85	100	135

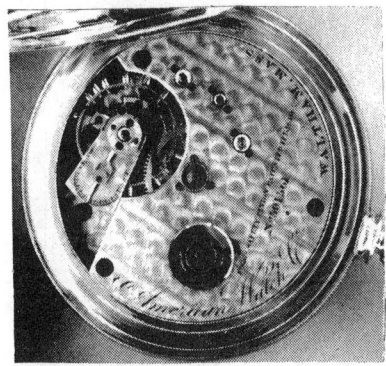

American Watch Co., Model 16KW or Model 1868, 16 size, key wind and set from back, Gold Train, serial number 501,561.

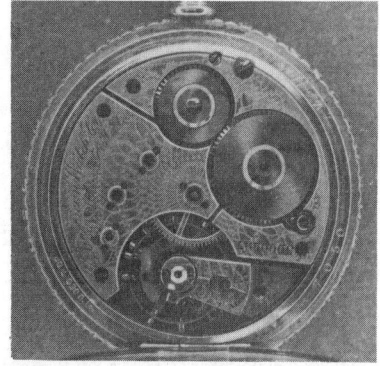

American Watch Co., Model 1888, 16 size, 19 jewels, gold jewel settings, gold train, high grade movement, serial number 5,000,297.

🕐 Some watch manufacturers personalize watches for jobbers or jewelry firms, with exclusive private signed or marked movements. The valuable collectable watches are listed under the signed or marked movement. Other exclusive private signed or marked movements will have equivalent value are only slightly higher value and should be compared to Generic or Nameless movements. Railroad signed or marked (dials & movements) are usually more collectable & higher in value.

16 SIZE

MODELS 16KW = 1860, 1868, 1872, 1888,
1899, 1908, BRIDGE MODEL

Grade or Name – Description	Avg	Ex-Fn	Mint
AMn. Watch Co., 7-15J, M#1872, KW KS, sweep sec. with a slide stop button ★ ★	$500	$600	$750
AMn. Watch Co., 7-11J, M#1888, 3/4, SW	70	80	100
AMn. Watch Co., 7-11J, M#1888-1899	70	80	100
AMn. Watch Co., 11J, M#16KW or 1868, KW & KS from back, original silver case ★ ★	400	450	575
AMn. Watch Co., 11J, M#1868, 3/4, KW	175	200	250
AMn. Watch Co., 13J, M#1888-1899	70	80	100
AMn. Watch Co., 15-17J, M#1868, 3/4, KW	200	225	275
AMn. Watch Co., 15J, M#1868-1872, 3/4, SW	100	125	175
AMn. Watch Co., 15J, M#16KW, KW & KS from back ★ ★	400	450	575
AMn. Watch Co., 15-16J, M#1888-1899, HC	100	125	175
AMn. Watch Co., 15J, M#1888-1899, SW, HC	100	125	175
AMn. Watch Co., 15J, M#1888-1899, SW,	70	80	100
AMn. Watch Co., 16-17J, M#1872, 3/4, SW	150	175	225
AMn. Watch Co., 17J, M#1888-1899	85	100	125
AMn. Watch Co., 19J, M#1872, 3/4, SW ★ ★ ★	600	775	1,000
AMn. Watch Co., 19J, M#1899	125	150	185

🕐 Generic, nameless or unmarked grades for watch movements are listed under the Company name or initials of the Company, etc. by size, jewel count and description.

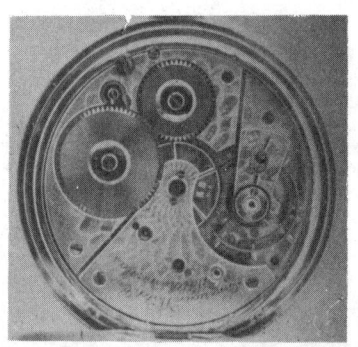

American Watch Co., Model 1888, 16 size, 21 jewels, gold train, note tadpole regulator.

American Watch Co., Bridge Model, 16size, 23 jewels gold train, Adj.5P.

Grade or Name –Description	Avg	Ex-Fn	Mint
American Watch Co., 19J Maltese cross stopwork, gilt mvt. all original 1860 Model, 18K ★ ★	$1,500	$1,800	$2,200
American Watch Co., 17-19J, 3/4, KW & KS from back, vibrating hairspring stud, 1860 Model, 18K ★ ★ ★	1,200	1,500	1,900
American Watch Co., 19J, 3/4 , KW & KS from back, nickel mvt. 1860 Model, original case, 18K ★ ★ ★	2,500	2,800	3,500
American Watch Co., 15J, M#1868, 3/4, KW, Silver ★ ★ ★	300	350	475
American Watch Co., 17J, M#1872,3/4,SW,HC,14K ★	900	1,100	1,250
American Watch Co., 17J, M#1868, 3/4, KW, ADJ, Silver ★ ★	400	425	550
American Watch Co., 17J, M#1899, Adj.5P, ★	250	275	325
American Watch Co., 18J, M#1868, SW, nickel mvt.	450	500	600
American Watch Co., 19J, M#1868, SW, nickel mvt. Silver case ★ ★ ★	1,500	1,800	2,400
American Watch Co., 19J, M#1888, SW, nickel mvt. ★	400	450	550
American Watch Co., 19J, M#1899, SW, nickel mvt. ★	550	600	700

Grade or Name — Description	Avg	Ex-Fn	Mint
American Watch Co., 19J, M#1872, 3/4, SW .... ★★★	$600	$700	$900
American Watch Co., 19-21J, M#1868-1872, 3/4, GJS, "Woerd's pat.			
compensating bal.", **With sawtooth bal.**, all original . ★★★	2,000	2,500	3,200
American Watch Co., 19-21J, M#1868-1872, 3/4, GJS, "Woerd's pat.			
compensating balance" on movt. **without sawtooth bal.**	1,200	1,350	1,550
American Watch Co., 19-21J, M#1872, 3/4, SW .... ★★	1,200	1,350	1,550
American Watch Co., 19-21J, M#1872, 3/4, SW, 18k .... ★★	1,500	1,800	2,200
American Watch Co., 19J, M#1888, 14K .... ★★	700	850	1,050
American Watch Co., 19J, M#1888 ....★	300	400	550
American Watch Co., 21J, M#1888, NI, 3/4 .... ★★	400	500	700
American Watch Co., 23J, M# 1899, Adj.5P, GT, GJS	600	675	800
American Watch Co., 23J, BRG, Adj.5P, GT, GJS, 14K			
original case .... ★★★	1,300	1,800	2,200
American Watch Co., 23J, BRG, Adj.5P, GT, GJS, 18K			
original case .... ★★★	1,500	1,900	2,400
American Watch Co., 23J, BRG, Adj.5P, GT, GJS .... ★	900	1,200	1,600
American Watch Co., 21J, BRG, Adj.5P, GT, GJS .... ★	600	650	750
American Watch Co., 19J, BRG, Adj.5P, GT, GJS .... ★	450	495	550
American Watch Co., 17J, BRG, Adj.5P, GT, GJS .... ★	300	335	450
Appleton, Tracy & Co., 15J, M#1860, 3/4, KW & KS from			
back, all original silver case	500	575	700
Appleton, Tracy & Co., 15J, M#1868, 3/4, KW	300	350	450
Appleton, Tracy & Co., 15J, 3/4, KW, with vibrating			
hairspring stud, all original, silver case .... ★★	700	850	1,200
Appleton, Tracy & Co., 15J, 3/4, KW, with vibrating			
hairspring stud, 18K, original case .... ★★	1,200	1,500	2,200

🕐 Generic, nameless or unmarked grades for watch movements are listed under the Company name or initials of the Company, etc. by size, jewel count and description.

A. W. Co., 7J, M#1872, SW, HC	100	125	175
A. W. W. Co., 7J, SW, M#1888	65	75	95
A. W. Co., 7J, SW, DMK	65	75	95
A. W. W. Co., 9J, SW, ...	65	75	95
A. W. W. Co., 11-13J, SW	65	75	95
A. W. Co., 11J, M#1899, SW	65	75	95
A. W. W. Co., 11-15J, M#1872, SW, HC	100	125	175
A. W. W. Co., 13J, M#1888-99, OF	65	75	95

RIGHT: **Woerd's pat. compensating balance,** this isa illustration copied from a blue print of Mr. Woerd's patented **Saw Tooth Balance.** This balance **must** be in watch for top prices.

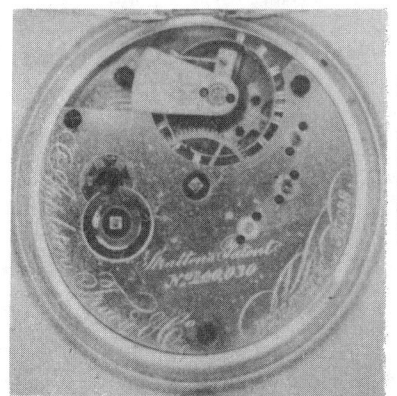

Appleton, Tracy & Co. (16 size), 15J, with viberating hairspring stud, key wind & set from back, S# 140030.

Crescent Street, Model 16–S (CENTER SECONDS), 16 size, movement, 22J, Adj6p, lever set, Wind indicator.

🕐 Generic, nameless or unmarked grades for watch movements are listed under the Company name or initials of the Company, etc. by size, jewel count and description.

Grade or Name—Descripion	Avg	Ex-Fn	Mint
A. W. W. Co., 15J, M#1899, OF	$75	$85	$100
A. W. W. Co., 15J, M#1888, SW, HC	85	100	125
A. W. W. Co., 16J, M#1888, SW, OF	75	80	110
A. W. W. Co., 16J, M#1899, SW, DMK, HC	85	100	125
A. W.W. Co., 17J, M#1872, SW, DMK, GJS, DES, HC ★	200	300	450
A. W. W. Co., 17J, SW, OF	85	95	125
A.W.W.Co., 19J, Adj.5P, LS, OF	150	175	200
A.W.W.Co., 19J, Adj.5P, LS, HC	175	200	250
A.W.W.Co., 21J, Adj.5P, PS, OF	200	225	250
A.W.W.Co., 21J, Adj.5P, PS, HC	225	250	300
A.W.W.Co., 23J, Adj.5P, PS, OF	225	250	300
A.W.W.Co., 23J, Adj.5P, PS, HC	250	275	325
P. S. Bartlett, 17J, M#1899, OF	85	95	110
P. S. Bartlett, 17J, M#1899, HC	100	125	175
P. S. Bartlett, 17J, M#1908, OF	85	95	110
Bond St., 7J, M#1888	60	65	75
Bond St., 11J, M#1888	65	75	100
Bond St., 15J, M#1888	75	85	100
Bond St., 7J, M#1899	50	55	65
Canadian Railway Time Service, M#1908 ★	275	350	450
CHRONOGRAPH are listed as 14 SIZE SEE Chronograph under 14 size			
Chronometro Superior, 21J, M#1899, LS, OF	300	375	500
Chronometro Victoria, 21J, M#1899, HC	350	425	550
Chronometro Victoria, 15J, M#1899, PS, OF	125	150	185
Crescent St., 19J, M#1899, Adj.5P, LS, OF	175	200	250
Crescent St., 19J, M#1899, Adj.5P, PS, OF	175	200	250
Crescent St., 19J, M#1899, Adj.5P, LS, HC	200	250	300
Crescent St., 19J, M#1899, Adj.5P, PS, HC	200	250	300
Crescent St., 21J, M#1899, Adj.5P, PS, OF	225	250	295
Crescent St., 21J, M#1899, Adj.5P, LS, OF	225	250	295
Crescent St., 21J, M#1899, Adj.5P, PS, HC	275	300	335
Crescent St., 19J, M#1908, Adj.5P, LS, OF	175	200	250
Crescent St., 19J, M#1908, Adj.5P, PS, OF	175	200	250
Crescent St., 21J, M#1908, Adj.5P, LS, OF	225	250	295
Crescent St., 21J, M#1908, Adj.5P, PS, OF	225	250	295
Crescent St., 21J, M#1908, Adj.6P, LS, OF	225	250	295
Crescent St., 21J, M#1908, Adj.5P, PS, HC	275	325	400
Crescent St., 21J, M#1908, Adj.5P, LS, **Wind Indicator**	650	725	800
Crescent St., 21J, M#1912, Adj.5P, LS, **Wind Indicator**	650	725	800
Crescent St., 22J, M#16–S, Adj.6P, **DECK WATCH**			
LS, center sec., **Wind Indicator** ★★★★	800	950	1,200
Diamond Express, 17J, M#1888, PS, OF, **Diamond End Stones** ★	400	465	550
Electric Railway, 17J, OF, LS, Adj.3P	160	185	235
Equity, 7-11J, PS, OF, 16 1/2 Size	60	65	75
Equity, 7-11J, PS, HC, 16 1/2 Size	60	65	85
Equity, 15-17J, PS, OF, 16 1/2 Size	75	85	95
Equity, 15-17J, PS, HC, 16 1/2 Size	90	100	125
Gaint, 7-11J, PS, OF, 16 1/2 Size	60	75	85
Gaint, 7-11J, PS, HC, 16 1/2 Size	70	85	125
Hillside, 7J, M#1868, ADJ	100	125	175
Hillside, 7J, M#1868-1872, sweep sec. & STOP ★★	450	600	850
Marquis, 15J, M#1899, LS	65	75	100
Marquis, 15J, M#1908, LS	65	75	100
Non-Magnetic, 15J, NI, HC	135	155	185
Park Road, 11-13-15J, M#1872, PS	90	110	135
Park Road, 16J, M#1872, PS	100	145	200

Premier Maximus, "Premier" on movement. "Maximus" on dial, 16 size, 23 jewels (two diamond end stones), open face, pendant set, serial number 17,000,014.

American Waltham Watch Co., 5 minute repeater, 16 size, 16 jewels, 3/4 plate, grade 1888, adj, 2 gongs, ca. 1900.

Grade or Name — Description	Avg	Ex-Fn	Mint
Premier, 9J, M#1908, PS, OF	$65	$70	$90
Premier, 11J, M#1908	65	70	95
Premier, 15J, M#1908, LS, OF	80	95	110
Premier, 17J, M#1908, PS, OF	85	100	125
Premier, 17J, M#1908, PS, OF, Silveroid	75	80	95
Premier, 21J, M#1908,	200	235	255
Premier, 22J, M#1908, LS, Adj.6P, **Stainless steel case,** OF	175	200	235
Premier, 23J, M#1908, LS, OF	250	275	300
Premier Maximus, 23J, M#1908, GT, gold case, LS,GJS, Adj.6P, WI, DR, 18K Maximus case,box & papers ★★	8,000	9,000	10,000
Premier Maximus, 23J, M#1908, GT, gold case, LS, GJS,Adj.6P, WI, DR, 18K Maximus case, no box ★★	6,000	7,000	8,000
Premier Maximus, 23J, M#1908, GT, gold case, LS,GJS, Adj.6P, WI, DR, 18K Maximus case, sterling box and papers, extra crystal & mainspring ★★	9,000	10,000	11,000
Premier Maximus, 23J, M#1908, GT, YGF recased	2,000	2,400	3,000
Railroader, 7J, M# 1883	125	150	200
Railroader, 17J, M#1888 or 1892, LS, NI ★★	500	600	750
Railroad King, 17J, 2-Tone ★	325	375	425
Railroad Time, 15-17J, ADJ, OF	200	235	285
Railroad Watches with R. R. names on dial and movement, such as Canadian Pacific RR, Santa Fe Route, etc., M#s 1888, 1899, 1908 ★	425	475	650
Repeater, 16J, M#1872, original gold filled case, 5 min. ★★	2,000	2,500	3,000
Repeater, 16J, M#1872, original coin case, 5 min. ★★	2,200	2,700	3,200
Repeater, 16J, M#1888, 5 Min., 14K ★★	4,000	4,750	5,500
Repeater, 16J, M#1872, 5 min., 18K ★★★	4,500	5,200	6,000
Repeater, 16J, M#1872, 5 min., chronograph with register, 18K ★★★★	6,000	7,000	8,000
Repeater, 1 min. moon phase, M#1872, Perpetual Cal., 18K case, all original ★★★★	30,000	35,000	45,000

🕐 Watches listed in this book are priced at the collectable retail level, as **complete** watches having an original 14k gold-filled case and *Key Wind* with silver, an original white enamel single sunk dial, and with the entire original movement in good working order with no repairs needed.

🕐 Some watch manufacturers personalize watches for jobbers or jewelry firms, with exclusive private signed or marked movements. The valuable collectable watches are listed under the signed or marked movement. Other exclusive private signed or marked movements will have equivalent value are only slightly higher value and should be compared to Generic or Nameless movements. Railroad signed or marked (dials & movements) are usually more collectable & higher in value.

Grade or Name — Description	Avg	Ex-Fn	Mint
Riverside, 15J, M#1872, PS, NI, OF	$85	$100	$155
Riverside, 15J, M#1872, PS, **gilted**, OF	75	95	125
Riverside, 16-17J, M#1888, NI, OF, 14K	400	475	600
Riverside, 16-17J, M#1888, NI, OF	95	125	150
Riverside, 17J, M#1888, gilded, OF	95	125	150
Riverside, 15J, M#1888, gilded, OF	95	125	150
Riverside, 17J, M#1888, checker goldtone DMK, raised gold jewel settings, OF	150	175	225
Riverside, 17J, M#1899, LS, DR, OF	95	125	150
Riverside, 17J, M#1899, LS, DR, HC	125	150	200
Riverside, 19J, M#1899, LS, DR, OF	150	175	210
Riverside, 19J, M#1908, Adj.5P, LS, DR	175	200	235
Riverside, 19J, M#1908, Adj.5P, PS, DR, HC ★	200	250	325
Riverside, 21J, M#1888-1899-1908, LS, DR, OF	200	225	285
Riverside, 21J, M#1888-1899-1908, LS, DR, HC	250	275	325
Riverside Maximus, 21J, M#1888, LS, GT, Diamond end stones, OF ★★	550	675	750
Riverside Maximus, 21J, M#1888, LS, ADJ, GJS, GT, DR, HC, GF ★★	600	700	850
Riverside Maximus, 21J, M#1888, LS, ADJ, GJS, GT, DR, HC, 14K ★★	1,000	1,100	1,250
Riverside Maximus, 21J, M#1899, PS, Adj.5P, GJS, GT, DR	375	450	600
Riverside Maximus, 21J, M#1899, LS, Adj.5P, GJS, GT, DR	375	450	600
Riverside Maximus, 21J, M#1899,LS,GT,Diamond end stone, OF ★	400	475	625
Riverside Maximus, 21J, M#1899, LS, GT, Diamond end stone, HC ★	600	650	750
Riverside Maximus, 23J, M#1899, LS, Adj.6P, GJS, GT, DR	400	500	650
Riverside Maximus, 23J, M#1908, PS, Adj.6P, GJS, GT, DR	400	500	650
Riverside Maximus, 23J, M#1908, LS, Adj.6P, GJS, GT, DR	400	500	650
Riverside Maximus, 23J, M#1908, Adj.6P, GJS, GT, **14K OF**	850	1,000	1,200
Riverside Maximus, 23J, M#1908, PS, Adj.6P, GJS, GT, DR, HC, GF ★	600	700	850
Riverside Maximus, 23J, M#1908, PS, Adj.6P, GJS, GT, DR, **14K, HC** ★	1,100	1,200	1,400
Riverside Maximus, 23J, M#1899 or 1908, Adj.6P, **Wind Indicator**, OF ★★	4,000	5,000	6,000

American Watch Co., model 1872, 16 size, marked 17 jewels, gold train, Ca. Dec. 1876, serial number 871,199. NOTE: 1872 model is about 17 size. However, factory referred to it as 16 size. Most 1872 models the jewel count is not marked on movement.

Vanguard, Model 1908, 16 size, 23 jewels, diamond end stone, gold jewel settings, exposed winding gears, serial number 11,012,533.

🕐 Some grades are not included. Their values can be determined by comparing with similar age, size, metal content, style, models and grades listed.

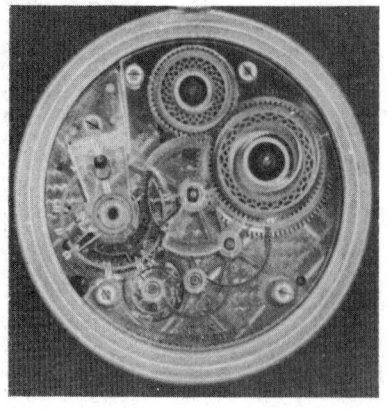

Stone Mountain, 16 size, 17 jewels, crystal plates, Model 1872, gold train, gold jeweled settings, Adj5p, serial # 20.

Vanguard, 16 size, 23 jewels, Adj6p, note pressed-in jewels rather than gold jewel settings. c. 1945.

Grade or Name — Description	Avg	Ex-Fn	Mint
Roadmaster, 17J, M#1899, LS, OF GJS ....★	$200	$245	$350
Royal, 15J, M#1872, PS, OF	70	90	120
Royal, 17J, M#1888, PS, OF	75	95	125
Royal, 17J, M#1888, PS, HC	100	120	150
Royal, 17J, M#1899, Adj.3P, OF	75	95	125
Royal, 17J, M#1899-1908, Adj.5P, OF	80	90	135
Royal, 17J, M#1899-1908, Adj.5P,HC	95	125	165
Royal Special, 17J, M#1888	100	125	175
Sol, 7J, M#1888	50	65	85
Sol, 7J, M#1908	50	65	85
Special Railroad King, 15-17J, M# 1883, OF........................	225	255	350
Special Railroad King, 15-17J, M# 1883, HC	275	325	400
Stone Mountain, 17J, M#1872, GT, Crystal plates ....★★★★	7,000	9,000	15,000
SWISS made, 17-25J, ...	40	50	65
Traveler, 7J, M#1888, 1899, 1908 & 16 1/2 size(Equity).............	40	50	65
Tennyson,15J, M#1888, OF........................	125	150	195
Vanguard, 19J, M#1899, PS, LS, Adj.5P, GJS, DR, OF	175	200	235
Vanguard, 19J, M#1899, PS, LS, Adj.5P, GJS, DR, HC	225	250	295
Vanguard, 21J, M#1899, Adj.5P, OF	225	250	295
Vanguard, 21J, M#1899, Adj.5P, HC	265	300	350
Vanguard, 23J, M#1899, Adj.5P, OF........................	325	350	400
Vanguard, 23J, M#1899, Adj.6P, OF........................	250	295	350
Vanguard, 23J, M#1899, LS, Adj.5P, GJS, DR, OF	250	295	350
Vanguard, 23J, M#1899, PS, Adj.5P, GJS, DR, OF	250	295	350
Vanguard, 23J, M#1899, PS, **Wind Indicator,** Adj.5P, GJS, DR★	650	700	800

🕐 Watches listed in this book are priced at the collectable retail level, as **complete** watches having an original 14k gold-filled case and *Key Wind* with silver, an original white enamel single sunk dial, and with the entire original movement in good working order with no repairs needed.

🕐 Some grades are not included. Their values can be determined by comparing with similar age, size, metal content, style, models and grades listed.

Grade or Name — Description	Avg	Ex-Fn	Mint
Vanguard, 19J, M#1908, LS & PS, Adj.5P, GJS, DR	$200	$225	$265
Vanguard, 21J, M#1908, Adj.5P, GJS, DR, Diamond end stone	225	275	350
Vanguard, 21J, M#1908, Adj.5P, GJS, DR, PS, LS, OF	225	250	300
Vanguard, 21J, M#1908, Adj.5P, GJS, DR, PS, LS, HC	300	350	425
Vanguard, 23J, M#1908, LS, Adj.5P, GJS, DR, OF	275	325	375
Vanguard, 23J, M#1908, LS, Adj.5P, GJS, DR, HC	350	400	450
Vanguard, 23J, M#1908, PS, Adj.5P, GJS, DR	275	325	375
Vanguard, 23J, M#1908, Adj.5P, **Wind Indicator**, GJS, DR	650	700	800
Vanguard, 23J, M#1908, Adj.5P, GJS , Diamond end stone	275	325	385
Vanguard, 23J, M#1908, Adj.5P, GJS, HC	325	350	425
Vanguard, 23J, OF, LS or PS, 14K	600	650	700
Vanguard, 23J, M#1908, Adj.6P, **Wind Indicator**, GJS, DR	650	700	800
Vanguard, 23J, M#1908, Adj.6P, **Wind Ind.**, **Lossier**, GJS,DR	675	725	825
Vanguard, 23J, M#1912, Press Jewels	250	300	350
Vanguard, 23J, M#1912, PS, military (case), **Wind Indicator**	650	700	800
Vanguard, 24J, also marked 9J., center sec., 10 made .... ★★	700	800	950
George Washington, 11J, M#1857 ....★	225	295	375
Weems, 21J, Navigation watch, **Wind Indicator** .... ★★★	650	750	875
Weems, 23J, Navigation watch, **Wind Indicator** .... ★★★	750	885	1,000
M#1888, G #s 650, 640	60	70	85
M#1899, G #s 615, 618, 620, 625, 628, ...	60	70	85
M#1908, G #s 611, 613, 614, 618, 621, 623,			
628, 630, 641, 642	60	70	85
G#637-640=3 pos., G#636=4pos., G#1617=2 pos., ALL=17J.	60	70	85
G#610=7-11J., un Adjusted & 620=15J.	55	60	75
G#625-630-635=17J., Adj., OF...	60	70	85
G#645, 21J, GCW, OF, LS	225	250	295
G#645, 21J, GCW, OF, LS, **wind indicator**...................................	650	700	800
G#645, 19J, OF, LS	100	125	165
G#665, 19J, GJS, BRG, HC .... ★★	600	695	800
G#16-A, 22J, Adj.3P, LS	200	250	285
G#16-A, & G#1024, 17J, Adj.5P	100	110	135
G#1621, 21J, Adj.5P	200	225	265
G#1622, 22J, Adj.5P	200	225	265
G#1623, 23J, Adj.5P	275	300	350

Weems Navigation watch, 21j, Weems pat. seconds dial, pusher for seconds scale setting, ca. 1942.

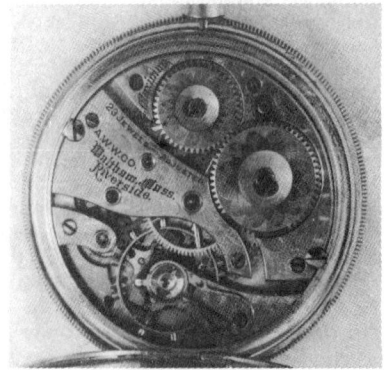

Riverside Maximus, Model 1899, 16 size, 23 jewels, gold train, raised gold jewel settings, a diamond end stone, adjusted to 5 positions, hunting case, serial # 12,509,200.

14 SIZE
MODELS 14KW FULL PLATE, 1874,
1884, 1895, 1897, COLONIAL-A

Grade or Name — Description	Avg	Ex-Fn	Mint
Adams Street, 7J, M#14KW, full plate, KW, Coin	$100	$125	$175
Adams Street, 11J, M#14KW, full plate, KW, Coin	100	125	175
Adams Street, 15J, M#14KW, full plate, KW	100	125	175

🕐 Generic, nameless or unmarked grades for watch movements are listed under the Company name or initials of the Company, etc. by size, jewel count and description.

	Avg	Ex-Fn	Mint
A. W. Co., 7-11J, M#14KW, full plate, KW	60	80	100
A. W. W. Co., 7-11J, M#1874, SW, LS, HC	75	95	125
A. W. Co., 7-11J, M#s FP, 1884, & 1895	50	60	75
A. W. Co., 13J, M#1884	50	60	75
A. W. Co., 15-16J, M#1874, SW	60	70	95
A. W. Co., 17J, SW , OF	65	75	95
A.W.Co., 19J, GJS, GCW	100	120	150
Am. Watch Co., 7-11J, KW,	60	75	90
Am. Watch Co., 13J, M#1874-84, SW	65	75	95
Am. Watch Co., 15J, M#1874-84,	80	90	125
Am. Watch Co., 16J, M#1874, SW	80	90	125
Am. Watch Co., 7-11J, M#14KW, **Full Plate**, KW	75	95	125
Am. Watch Co., 16J, M#1884, SW	75	85	125
Am. Watch Co., 15J, M#1897, SW	55	65	90
Bond St., 7-11J, M#1895, SW	50	55	75
Bond St., 9-11J, M#1884, KW	75	95	125
Bond St., 7J, M#1884, SW, PS	50	60	90
Beacon, 15J, M#1897, SW	55	65	90
Chronograph, 13J, 1874, 14K, OF, **Am. W. Co. case**	600	750	1,000
Chronograph, 13J, 1884, 14K, HC, **Am. W. Co. case**	700	900	1,100
Chronograph, 13J, 1884, 18K, HC, **Am. W. Co. case** ★	1,000	1,200	1,400
Chronograph, 13J, 1874, 14K, OF, W/ register, **Am. W. Co. case**	750	950	1,150
Chronograph, 13J, 1874, 14K, HC, W/ register, **Am. W. Co. case**	850	950	1,350
Chronograph, 13J, 1874, 18K, HC, W/ register, **Am. W. Co. case** ★	1,200	1,350	1,600

Chronograph, Model 1874, split-second, 14 size. Note two split second hands on dial.

Hillside, 14 size, 13 jewels, M#1874, stem wind, hunting case, Woerds Pat., serial number 1,696,188, 18K.

🕐 This book endeavours to be a GUIDE or helpful manual and offers a wealth of material to be used as a tool not as a absolute document. Price Guides are like watches the worst may be better than none at all, but at best cannot be expected to be 100% accurate.

Grade or Name — Description	Avg	Ex-Fn	Mint
Chronograph, 13J, M#1874, **SILVER HC,** *Am. W. Co. case*	$250	$325	$375
Chronograph, 13J, M#1874-1884 , OF	175	225	300
Chronograph, 13J, M#1874-1884, HC	200	250	350
Chronograph, 15J, M#1874-1884 , OF	185	250	335
Chronograph, 15J, M#1874-1884, HC	200	275	375
Chronograph, 17J, M#1874-1884 , OF	195	270	365
Chronograph, 17J, M#1874-1884, HC	250	300	400
Chronograph, 17J, split second, Am. W. Co. case ★★★	350	425	600
Chronograph, 15J, split sec., **14K,** HC ★★★	1,200	1,400	1,600
Chronograph, 15J, split second, **min. register, 14K** Am. W. Co. HC ★★★	1,400	1,600	2,000
Chronograph, 16J, double dial, M#1874, **"coin",** Am. W. Co. case	2,000	2,200	2,500
Chronograph, 16J, double dial, M#1874, **18K,** Am. W. Co. case ..	2,500	3,000	4,000
Chronometro Victoria, 15J, M#1897, ★★	100	135	175
Church St., 7J, M#1884,	80	100	125
Crescent Garden, 7-11J, M#14KW, KW	70	85	100
Crescent Garden, 7J, Full Plate, KW	80	100	130
Wm. Ellery, 7J, M#1874, SW	60	70	85
Gentleman, 7J, M#1884, SW	75	85	100
Hillside, 7-15J, M#1874, SW	60	70	95
Hillside, 7-11J, M#FP, SW	60	70	95
Hillside, 7-13J, M#1884, KW	60	70	95
Hillside, 9-11J, M#1884, KW	60	70	95
Hillside, 15J, M#1884, SW	75	85	110
Hillside, 16J, M#1874, (calendar date only on outside chapter) SW, GJS, OF,(calendar sets from back with lever)... ★★★★	500	600	750
Maximus, 21J, Colonial A	145	185	275
Maximus, 21J, Colonial A, 14K	300	400	575
Night Clock, 7J, M#1884, KW	80	100	150

Chronograph, M# 1884-double dial, 14 size, 15 jewels, hunting case.

Chronograph, Model 1884-Split Second, 14 size, 15 jewels, open face, gold escape wheel, gold train, serial number 303,094.

🕐 Watches listed in this book are priced at the collectable retail level, as **complete** watches having an original 14k gold-filled case and Key Wind with silver, an original white enamel single sunk dial, and with the entire original movement in good working order with no repairs needed.

🕐 Some watch manufacturers personalize watches for jobbers or jewelry firms, with exclusive private signed or marked movements. The valuable collectable watches are listed under the signed or marked movement. Other exclusive private signed or marked movements will have equivalent value are only slightly higher value and should be compared to Generic or Nameless movements. Railroad signed or marked (dials & movements) are usually more collectable & higher in value.

Five Minute Repeater, Model 1884, 14 size, 13-15 jewels, hunting case, slide activated, serial number 2,809,551.

Chronograph, 14 size, Model # 1874, Lugrin Pat., Sept. 28, 1880, serial number 3162800.

Grade or Name — Description	Avg	Ex-Fn	Mint
Repeater (5 min.), 16J, M#1884, SW, LS, 14K ....★	$4,000	$4,700	$5,500
Repeater (5 min.), 16J, M#1884, SW, LS, 18K ....★	4,500	5,700	6,500
Repeater (5 min.), 16J, M#1884, split second chronograph, 18K case ....★ ★	7,000	8,000	10,000
Repeater (5 min.), 16J, M#1884, SW, LS, chronograph, with register, 14K Am. W. Co. case	5,000	5,500	6,000
Repeater (5 min.), 16J, M#1884, SW, LS, chronograph, with register, 18K Am. W. Co. case	5,500	6,000	6,500
Repeater (5 min.), 16J, M#1884, SW, LS, original Coin case	3,000	3,500	4,000
Repeater (5 min.), 16J, M#1884, SW, LS, original gold filled case	2,400	2,800	3,200
Repeater (5 Min.), 18K, HC ....★ ★	4,500	5,500	6,500
Repeater (1 Min.), perpetual calendar, moon ph., 18K .... ★ ★ ★	30,000	37,000	50,000
Riverside, 11-15J, M#s 1874, HC ....★	150	175	250
Riverside, 15J, M#1884, OF	65	80	100
Riverside, 19-21J, Colonial A, OF ....★ ★	150	175	250
Royal, 11-13-15J, M#s 1874, 1884	55	65	90
Seaside, 7-11J, M#1884, SW	55	65	80
Special, 7J, M#1895, HC	75	95	125
Sterling, 7J, M#1884	55	65	80
Waltham, Mass., 7J, Full Plate, KW	95	125	150

12 SIZE
MODELS KW, 1894, BRIDGE, COLONIAL SERIES

Grade or Name — Description	Avg	Ex-Fn	Mint
A. W. W. Co., 7J, M#1894, **14K,** OF	$200	$225	$275
A. W. W. Co., 11J, M#1894, also Colonial model	50	55	75
A. W. W. Co., 15J, M#1894, also Colonial model	50	55	75
A. W. W. Co., 15J, M#1894, Colonial, **14K,** HC	250	275	350
A. W. W. Co., 17J, M#1894, also Colonial model	50	55	75
A. W. W. Co., 17J, M#1894, also Colonial, **14K** OF	200	225	275
A. W. W. Co., 19J, OF	70	85	100
A. W. W. Co., 21J, OF	80	100	125
A. W. W. Co., 23J, OF	125	150	175
P. S. Bartlett, 19J, M#1894, **14K,** HC	300	335	400
P. S. Bartlett, 19J, M#1894	75	90	125
Bond St., 7-13J, M#1894	50	55	75
Bridge Model, 19J, GJS, Adj.5P, GT	100	135	200
Bridge Model, 19J, GJS, Adj.5P, GT, **18K,** HC .... ★ ★ ★	500	550	575
Bridge Model, 21J, GJS, Adj.5P, GT, OF	150	175	250
Bridge Model, 21J, GJS, Adj.5P, GT, **14K,** HC .... ★ ★	600	700	850
Bridge Model, 23J, GJS, Adj.5P, GT	200	250	310

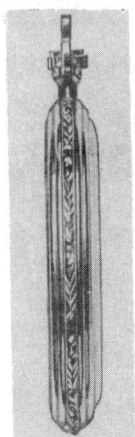

Actual size illustration of a cushion style shaped watch depicting thinness with emphasis on style and beauty. This watch was popular in the 1930s.

Grade or Name — Description	Avg	Ex-Fn	Mint
Duke, 7-15J, M#1894	$70	$90	$100
Digital Hour & Second Window, 17J	75	100	125
Elite, 17J, OF	60	75	95
Ensign, 7J, OF	60	75	95
Equity, 7J,adj.	60	70	80
Martyn Square, 7-11J, M#KW	100	125	175
Maximus, 21J, GJS, GT	225	275	350
Premier, 17-19J, M#1894	75	80	100
Premier, 21J, M#1894	100	150	250
Riverside, 17-19J, M#1894, Colonial	70	80	95
Riverside, 21J, M#1894, Colonial	100	135	165

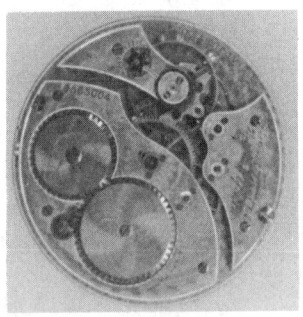

A.W.W.Co., Model 1894, 12 size, 7-11 jewels, open face, serial number 7,565,004.

Riverside, Colonial series, 12 size, 19 jewels, open face or hunting, Adj5p, double roller.

Grade or Name – Description	Avg	Ex-Fn	Mint
Riverside, 19-21J, M#1894, Colonial, 14K, HC	$395	$450	$500
Riverside Maximus, 21J, M#1894, Colonial, GT, GJS, 14K	450	500	600
Riverside Maximus, 21J, M#1894, Colonial, GT, GJS	275	300	325
Riverside Maximus, 23J, M#1894, Colonial, GT, GJS ★	295	325	375
Riverside Maximus, 23J, M#1894, Colonial, GT, GJS, 14K ★	475	525	625
Royal, 17J, OF, PS, Adj, or Adj.3P	55	65	75
Royal, 19J, OF, PS, Adj.3P	65	70	85
Secometer, 17J, (revolving seconds dial only) OF	75	85	100

THE OPERA WATCH
10-12 size case & a 6/0 size Jewel Series movement

Grade or Name – Description	Avg	Ex-Fn	Mint
12-6/0 size, 17-19J, Adj, **18K gold case**	$500	$600	$750
12-6/0 size, 17-19J, Adj, **14K gold case**	300	350	400
12-6/0 size, 17-19J, Adj, **Platinum case**	550	650	800
12-6/0 size, 17-19J, Adj, **gold filled case**	135	150	200

A unique designed Gents dress watch about 10-12 size case with a **fancy framed** 6/0 movement (Jewel Series).

10 SIZE
MODEL KW, 1861, 1874

Grade or Name – Description	Avg	Ex-Fn	Mint
Am. W. Co., 7-15J, M#1874-1878, KW, **14K**	$200	$250	$350
A. W. Co., 7-11J, SW , OF	65	75	95
A. W. Co., 15-17J, SW , OF	75	85	110
A. W. Co., 19-21J, SW , OF	95	110	135
American Watch Co., 11-15J, M#1874, 14K, **HC**	275	325	425
Appleton, Tracy & Co., 15J, M#1861 or 1874, **14K**	200	250	350
Appleton, Tracy & Co., 15J, M#1861, 18K multi-color box case ★ ★	650	750	900
P. S. Bartlett, 7-11J, M#1861, KW, **14K**	275	300	375
P. S. Bartlett, 13J, M#KW, gold balance, 1st S# 45,801, last 46,200, **14K**, Pat. Nov. 3, 1858 ★ ★	300	375	525
P. S. Bartlett, 13J, M#KW, gold balance, 1st S#45,801, last 46,200, **18K**	600	750	850
P. S. Bartlett, 13J, M#1861, KW, **14K**	200	250	300

Appleton Tracy & Co., Model 10KW, 10 size, 7-15 jewels, key wind and set from back, serial number 370,411.   P. S. Bartlett, 10 size, 7-15 jewels, serial number 181602.

NOTE: These watches (excluding Colonial) are usually found with solid gold cases, and are therefore priced accordingly. Without cases, these watches have very little value due to the fact that the cases are difficult to find. Many of the cases came in octagon, decagon, hexagon, cushion and triad shapes.

Grade or Name – Description	Avg	Ex-Fn	Mint
Colonial A , 21J,OF	$70	$85	$100
Crescent Garden, 7J, M#1861, KW, 14K	200	250	300
Wm. Ellery, 7,11,15J, M#1861, KW, 14K	200	250	300
Home W. Co., 7J, M#1874, KW, 14K	200	250	300
Martyn Square, 7-11J, M#1861, 14K	200	250	350
Maximus "A", 21J, 14K ★★	400	475	600
Maximus "A", 23J, 14K ★★	425	500	600
Riverside, 19–21J, Adj.5P, GF	125	135	165
Riverside Maximus, 19-21J, Adj.5P, GJS, GF	150	200	275
Riverside Maximus, 19-21J, Adj.5P, GJS, **18K**	450	525	625
Riverside Maximus, 23J, Adj.5P, GJS, GF	225	275	375
Royal, 15J, Adj.5P, GF	65	75	90

8 SIZE
MODEL 1873

NOTE: Collectors usually want solid gold cases in small watches.

Grade or Name – Description	Avg	Ex-Fn	Mint
Am. W. Co., 15-17J, M#1873, **14K, Multi-Color Box Hinged case**	$500	$700	$900
Am. W. Co., 15-16J, M#1873	75	85	95
P. S. Bartlett, 15-16J, M#1873	50	60	70
Wm. Ellery, 7-11J, M#1873	50	60	70
Wm. Ellery, 7J, **14K, HC**	200	275	350
Riverside, 7-11J, M#1873, **18K, HC**	325	400	600
Riverside, 7-11J, M#1873	75	85	100
Royal, 7-16J, M#1873	50	60	70
Victoria, 11-15J, tu-tone movement, **18k HC** ★	325	400	600

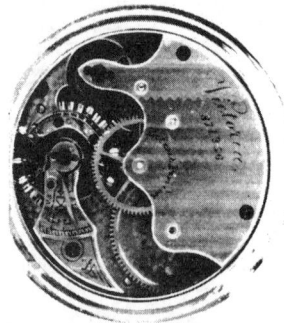

VICTORIA, 8 size 1873 model, 11-15 jewels, tu-tone high grade movement, HC, S# 871256

6 size Ladies movement this basic model came in the following grades: J=7 jewels, gilt; Y=7 jewels, nickel; N=15 jewels,gilded or nickel; X=15 jewels, nickel, gold jewel settings; K=16 jewels nickel, raised gold settings; RIVERSIDE=17 jewels, nickel, raised gold settings.

6 SIZE
MODEL 1873, 1889, 1890

Grade or Name – Description	Avg	Ex-Fn	Mint
A,B,C,D,E,F,G,H,J,K	$75	$80	$100
A,B,C,D,E,F,G,H,J,K, **14K, HC**	200	275	325
A. W. W. Co., 19J, **18K, HC**	325	400	475
A. W. W. Co., 19J, **14K, Multi-Color gold case**	450	600	800
A. W. W. Co., 7J, M#1873	60	70	95

Grade or Name – Description	Avg	Ex-Fn	Mint
A. W. W. Co., 15J, multi-color GF, HC	$185	$225	$275
A. W. W. Co., 15J, 2 tone mvt., HC	85	110	165
A. W. W. Co., 11J, HC, LS	85	110	160
Am. W. Co., 7-11J, M#1889 -1890	50	65	75
American W. Co., 7J, KW & KS from back, 10K, HC	225	250	300
Wm. Ellery, 7J, M#1873	50	60	85
Lady Waltham, 16J, M#1873, Demi, HC, 14K	300	350	400
Lady Waltham, 16J, M#1873, 18K	350	375	450
Riverside Maximus, 19J, GT, Adj., DR, HC	225	250	300
Riverside, 15-17J, PS	70	85	125
Seaside, 7-15J, M#1873	60	75	95
Royal, 16J, HC	85	100	135

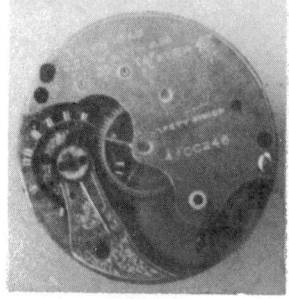

American Watch Co., Model 1889, 6 size 7 jewels, serial number 4,700,246.

Stone Movement or Crystal Plate movement, size 4, 16 jewels, gold train, open face, serial number 28.

4 SIZE

Grade or Name – Description	Avg	Ex-Fn	Mint
Stone Movement or crystal movement, 4 size, crystal, 16 ruby jewels in gold settings, gold train, exposed pallets, compensation balance adjusted to temperature, isochronism, positions, Breguet hairspring, and crystal top plate, 14K case ★ ★ ★	$4,000	$5,000	$6,000

🕐 Watches listed in this book are priced at the collectable retail level, as **complete** watches having an original 14k gold-filled case and *Key Wind* with silver, an original white enamel single sunk dial, and with the entire original movement in good working order with no repairs needed.

1 SIZE & 0 SIZE
MODELS 1882, 1891, 1900, 1907

Grade or Name – Description	Avg	Ex-Fn	Mint
A.W.Co., 7-16J, OF	$70	$80	$95
A.W.Co., 7-16J, HC	100	125	165
A.W.Co., 7-15J, multi-color 14K HC	350	475	600
A. W. Co., 7J, 14K, HC	175	250	350
American Watch Co., 15J, SW, OF &HC	95	125	175

🕐 Generic, nameless or unmarked grades for watch movements are listed under the Company name or initials of the Company, etc. by size, jewel count and description.

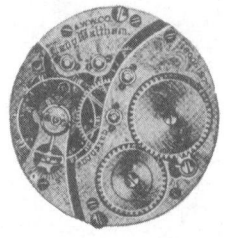

Lady Waltham, Model 1900, 0 size, 16 jewels, open face or hunting, adjusted, stem wind, pendant set.

A.W. Co., Model 1891, 0 size, 7 jewels, stem wind, originally sold for $13.00.

Grade or Name – Description	Avg	Ex-Fn	Mint
American Watch Co., 15J, S.W., **14K, HC**	$200	$275	$350
P. S. Bartlett, 11J, M#1891, OF, **14K**	150	175	200
P. S. Bartlett, 16J, **14K, HC**	200	275	350
Lady Waltham, 15J, SW, **14K, HC**	200	275	350
Lady Waltham, 15-16J, SW, HC	125	150	200
Maximus, 19J, SW, HC	150	175	225
Riverside, 15J,16J,17J, SW, HC	125	150	200
Riverside, 15J,16J,17J, SW, **14K, HC**	200	275	350
Riverside Maximus, 21J, GT, **multi-color gold HC, 14K** ★★	600	750	850
Riverside Maximus, 21J, GT	200	225	275
Riverside Maximus, 19J, SW, HC	175	200	250
Riverside Maximus, 19J, SW, **14K, HC** ★	275	350	475
Royal, 16J, SW, HC	85	125	150
Seaside, 15J, SW, **14K, HC**	175	275	350
Seaside, 11J, SW, OF, **multi-color dial, no chips**	150	200	250
Seaside, 11J, SW, HC	85	125	150
Seaside, 7J, HC	75	95	125
Seaside, 7J, **14K, HC**	200	275	350
Special, 11J, M#1891, **14K, OF**	150	200	225

Riverside, Jewel Series, 6/0 size, 17 ruby jewels, raised gold settings, gold center wheel.

Ruby, Jewel Series, 6/0 size, 15 jewels, adjusted to temperature, open face or hunting.

JEWEL SERIES or 6/0 SIZE

Grade or Name – Description	Avg	Ex -Fn	Mint
Diamond, 15J, Jewel Series, **14K, HC**	$200	$250	$300
Patrician, 15J, pin set, GJS, **18K, OF** ★	300	350	425
Riverside, 17J, Jewel Series, **14K, HC**	200	250	300
Ruby, 15J, Jewel Series, **14K, OF**	150	200	250
Sapphire, 15J, Jewel Series, **14K, OF**	150	200	250

RF # 1A
gold filled : $90 - $100 - $120

RF # 2B
gold filled : $95- $110 - $130

RF # 3C
gold plate: $70 - $80 - $95

RF # 4D
gold filled : $100 - $115 - $120

RF # 5E
gold filled : $110 - $120 - $135

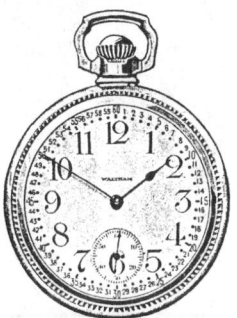

RF # 6F
gold filled : $90 - $100 - $120

MONTGOMERY DIAL

RF # 7G
LOCOMOTIVE model
gold filled : $110 - $120 - $135

1A, 2B, = Gold Filled White or Yellow
3C = Yellow Gold Rolled Plate
4D, 5E, 6F, 7G = Yellow Gold Filled.

🕐 NOTE: Factory Advertised as a complete watch and were fitted with cases of exclusive and unusual design with special heavy bow & movement timed and rated at the factory. The factory also sold _uncased_ movements to **JOBBERS** such as Jewelry stores & they cased the movement in a case styles the **CUSTOMER requested.** All the factory advertised complete watches came with the dial **SHOWN or CHOICE** of other **Railroad** dials.

AMERICAN WALTHAM WATCH CO.
IDENTIFICATION OF MOVEMENTS
BY MODEL NUMBER

How to Identify Your Watch: Compare the movement of your watch with the illustrations in this section. Upon matching the movement exactly, the model number and size can be determined. When comparing, note the location of the balance, jewels, screws, gears and type of back plate (Full, ¾, Bridge) which will be clues to identifying the movement you have. Having determined the size and model number, you can now find your watch in the main price listing by name or number (which is engraved on the movement).

20 size, 1862 or KW 20 model. Note vibrating hairspring stud. 1st serial number 50,001

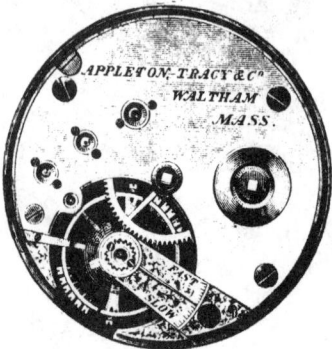

18 size, key wind model
1st serial number 28,821

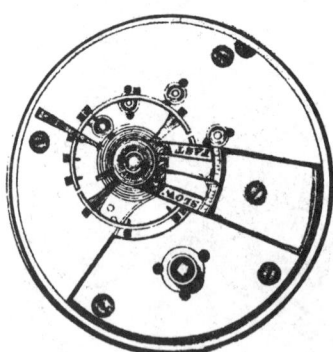

Model 1857, KW, KS. 1st serial number 1,001

Model 1870, KW, KS from back
1st serial number 500,001

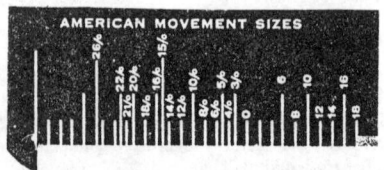

Model 1877, 18 size

Model 1879, 18 size

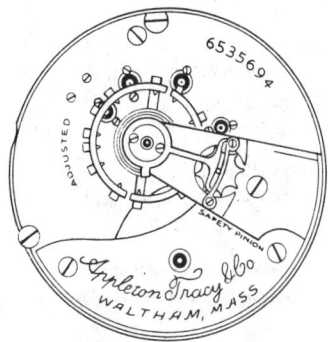

Model 1883, hunting
1st serial number 2,354,001

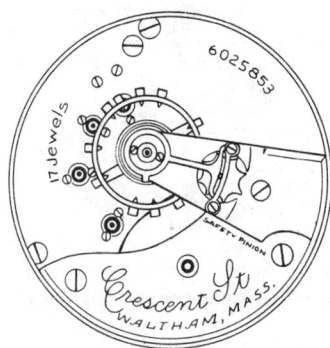

Model 1883, open face

Model 1892, open face

Model 1892, hunting.
1st serial number 6,026,001

16½ size, Equity open face

**Model 1868 or Model 16KW,
16 size**

Model 1872, 16 size open face

Model 1872, 16 size hunting case

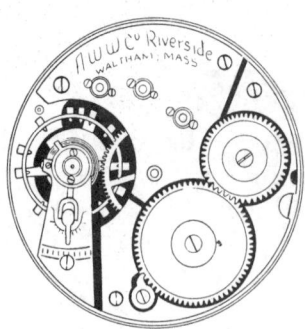

Model 1888, 16 size, hunting

Bridge Model, 16 size

**Model 1899 or Model 1908,
16 size, open face**

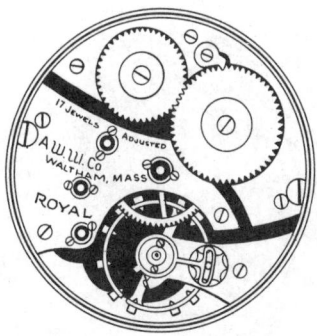

**Model 1899 or Model 1908,
16 size, hunting**

**Model 1899 or Model 1908,
16 size, open face**

Model 16-A, 16 size

**Model 1622, Deck Watch
16 size, sweep second**

Model 1874 & 1884, 14 size

Model 1874, 14 size, hunting

Model 1884, 14 size, open face

5 Minute Repeater, 14 size

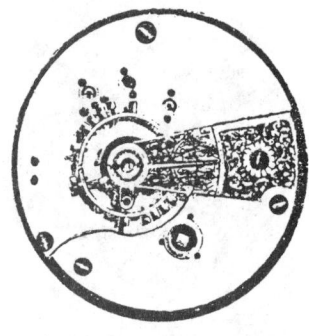

14 SIZE FULL PLATE KW KS
1 st. SERIAL # 909,001

Model 1874, 14 size

Model 1884, 14 size

**Model 1895, 14 size,
open face**

Model 1897, 14 size

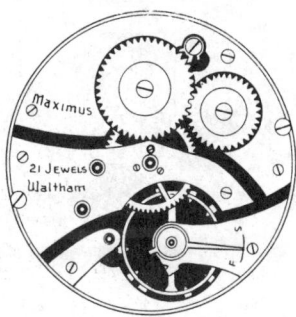

Colonial A Model, 14 size

Colonial Series, 14 size

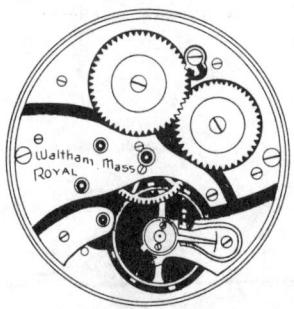

Model 1924, The Colonial

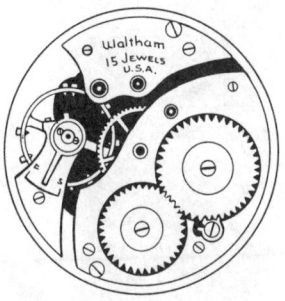

Model 1894, 12 size

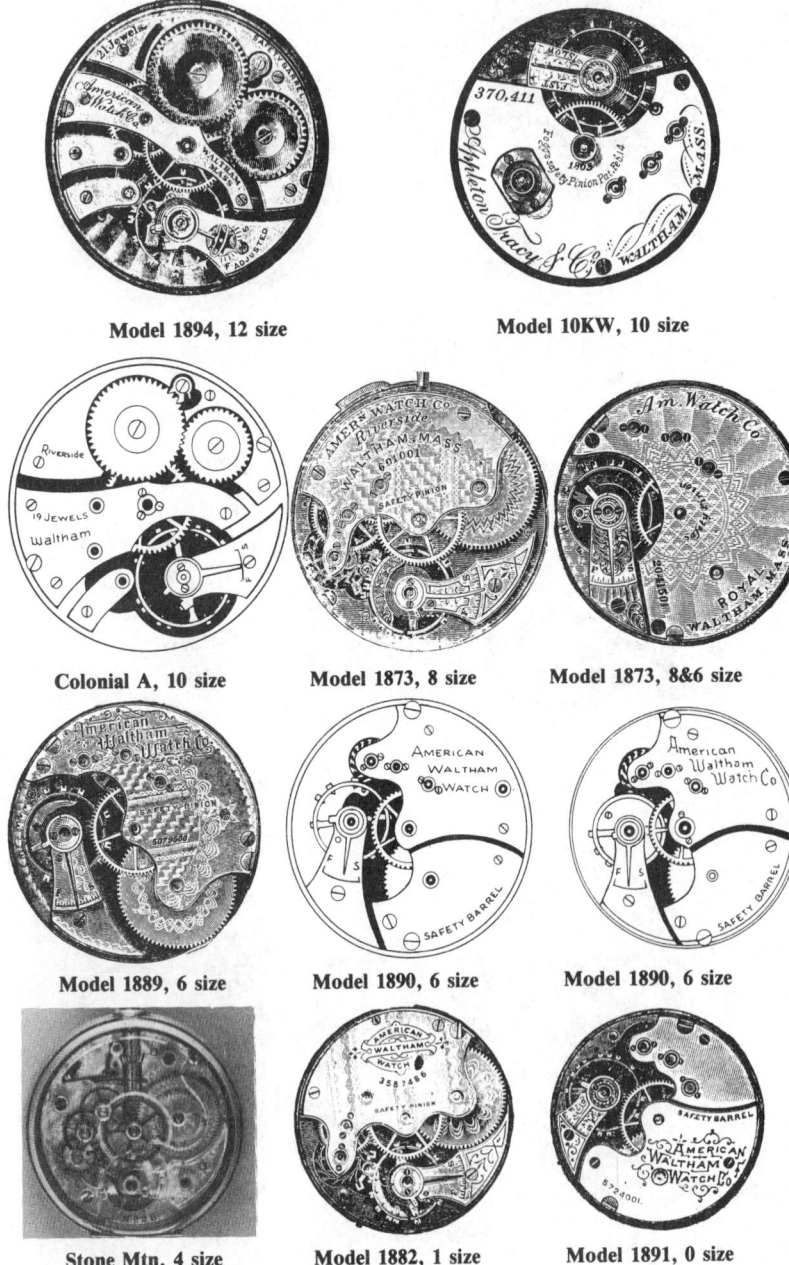

Model 1894, 12 size

Model 10KW, 10 size

Colonial A, 10 size

Model 1873, 8 size

Model 1873, 8&6 size

Model 1889, 6 size

Model 1890, 6 size

Model 1890, 6 size

Stone Mtn, 4 size

Model 1882, 1 size

Model 1891, 0 size

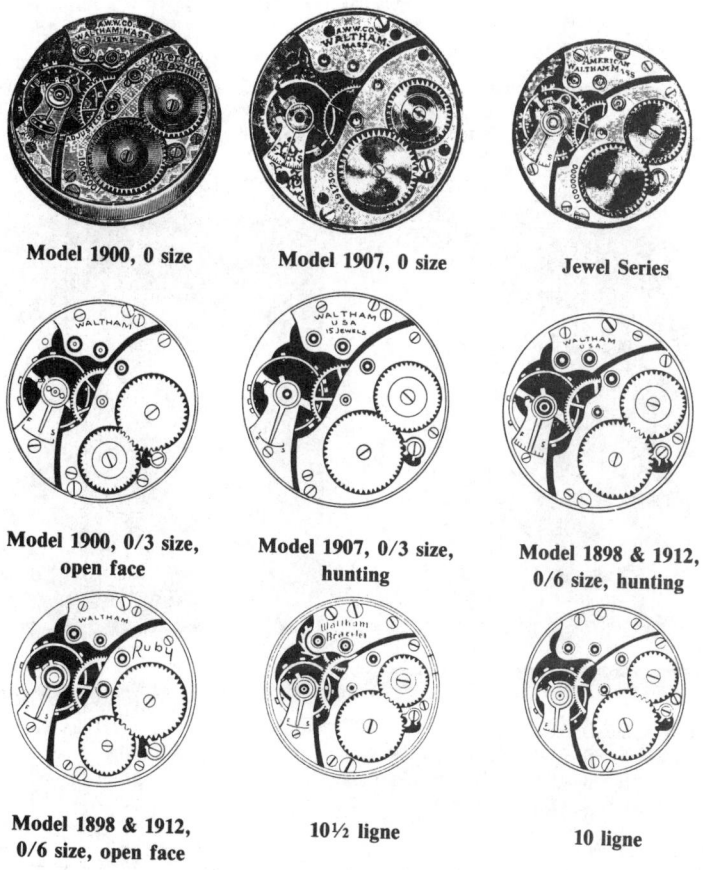

Model 1900, 0 size   **Model 1907, 0 size**   **Jewel Series**

Model 1900, 0/3 size,   **Model 1907, 0/3 size,**   **Model 1898 & 1912,**
open face   **hunting**   **0/6 size, hunting**

Model 1898 & 1912,   **10½ ligne**   **10 ligne**
0/6 size, open face

⊕ Generic, nameless or unmarked grades for watch movements are listed under the Company name or initials of the Company, etc. by size, jewel count and description.

⊕ Some grades are not included. Their values can be determined by comparing with similar age, size, metal content, style, models and grades listed.

⊕ Watches listed in this book are priced at the collectable retail level, as complete watches having an original 14k gold-filled case and Key Wind with silver, an original white enamel single sunk dial, and with the entire original movement in good working order with no repairs needed.

⊕ This book endeavours to be a GUIDE or helpful manual and offers a wealth of material to be used as a tool not as a absolute document. Price Guides are like watches the worst may be better than none at all, but at best cannot be expected to be 100% accurate.

⊕ Characteristics of watches differ for the same age of both case and movement, because these features vary it may not be accurate to date a watch by one single influence. Example: the second hand was not commonly found on watches before 1750, but common about 1800. The first second hand appeared in 1665 and another in 1690. Therefore statements are broad rather than accurate.

ANSONIA CLOCK CO.

Brooklyn, New York
1896 - 1929

The Ansonia Watch Co. was owned by the Ansonia Clock Company in Ansonia, Connecticut. Ansonia started making clocks in about 1850 and began manufacturing watches in 1896. They produced about 10,000,000 dollar- type watches. The company was sold to a Russian investor in 1930. "Patented April 17, 1888," is on the back plate of some Ansonia watches.

Ansonia Watch Company. Example of a basic movement, 16 size, stem wind.

Ansonia Watch Co., Sesqui-Centennial model.

Grade or Name–Description	Avg	Ex-Fn	Mint
Ansonia watch with a White Dial in Nickel case	$40	$50	$75
Ansonia watch with a Radium Dial in Nickel case	50	60	90
Ansonia watch with a Black Dial in Nickel case	40	50	75
Ascot	40	50	75
Bonnie Laddie Shoes	60	95	120
Dispatch	30	40	65
Faultless	40	50	75
Guide	40	50	75
Lenox	35	40	55
Mentor	35	45	60
Piccadilly	45	60	80
Rural	40	50	75
Sesqui-Centennial	250	275	350
Superior	45	60	80
Tutor	45	60	80

🕐 Some grades are not included. Their values can be determined by comparing with similar age, size, metal content, style, models and grades listed.

APPLETON WATCH CO.

(REMINGTON WATCH CO.)

Appleton, Wisconsin

1901 - 1903

In 1901, O. E. Bell bought the machinery of the defunct Cheshire Watch Company and moved it to Appleton, Wisconsin, where he had organized the Remington Watch Company. The first watches were shipped from the factory in February 1902; production ceased in mid-1903 and the contents were sold off before the end of that year. Most movements made by this firm were modified Cheshire movements and were marked "Appleton Watch Company." Advertisements for the firm in 1903 stated that they made 16 and 18 size movements with 11, 15, or 17 jewels. Serial numbers range from 90,000 to 104,950. During the two years they were in business, the company produced about 2,000 to 3,000 watches.

 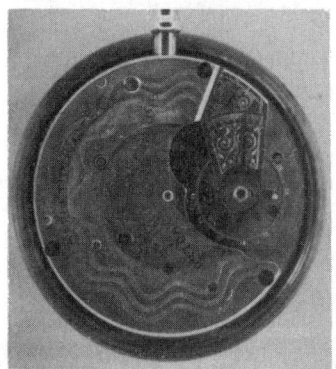

Appleton Watch Co., 18 size, 7 jewels, "The Appleton Watch Co." on dial. Engraved on movement "Appleton Watch Co., Appleton, Wis." Note that the stem is attached to movement. Serial number 93,106.

Description		Avg	Ex-Fn	Mint
18S, 7J, OF, NI, 3/4, DMK, SW, PS, stem attached	★★★	$450	$500	$600
18S, 7J, OF, NI, 3/4, DMK, SW, PS, Coin, OF	★★★	400	500	600
18S, 15J, NI, LS, SW, 3/4, M#2	★★★★	500	600	700
16S, 7-11J, 3/4, stem attached	★★★	450	550	750

Note: With **ORIGINAL APPLETON** cases add **$150 to $250** more. This case is **difficult** to find.

AUBURNDALE WATCH CO.

Auburndale, Massachusetts

1876 - 1883

This company was the first to attempt an inexpensive watch. Jason R. Hopkins was issued two patents in 1875 covering the "rotary design." The rotary design eliminated the need of adjusting to various positions, resulting in a less expensive watch. The company was formed about 1876, and the first watches were known as the "Auburndale Rotary." In 1876, equipment was purchased from the Marion Watch Co., and the first rotary designed watches were placed on the market for $10 in 1877. Auburndale produced about 6,000 watches before closing in 1883.

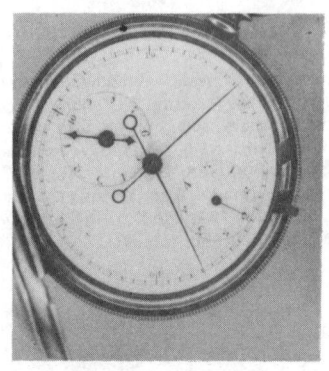

Auburndale Timer, 18 size, 7 jewels, stem wind, 10 minute, second jump timer.

Auburndale 10 min. Timer, 1/4 beat jump seconds, sweep second hand, stop & fly back, back wind.

Grade or Name – Description	Avg	Ex-Fn	Mint
Auburndale Rotary, 20S, 2J, LS, SW, NI case, detent ...... ★★★★	$1,900	$2,500	$3,200
Auburndale Rotary, 18S, 2J, SW, LS, NI case, lever .... ★★★	1,200	1,800	2,500
Bentley, 18S, 7J, LS, NI case, SW, 3/4............................ ★★	600	800	1,100
Lincoln, 18S, 7J, LS, NI case, KW, 3/4............................ ★★	600	800	1,100
Auburndale Timer, 18S, 5-7J, SW, NI case, 10 min. timer, 1/4 sec. jump second..	325	375	425
Auburndale Timer, 18S, 5-7J, SW, NI case, 10 min. timer, 1/4 sec. jump seconds, with a 24 hour dial ....★	400	500	600
Auburndale Timer, 18S, 5-7J, KW, NI case, 10 min. timer, 1/4 sec. jump seconds, **with split seconds** .... ★★	600	750	950
Auburndale Timer,18S, marked "207", gold balance, OF	325	375	425

Bentley, 18 size, 7 jewels, 3/4 plate, stem wind, serial number 2.

Auburndale Rotary, 18 size, 2 jewels, stem wind, lever set, serial number 448.

AURORA WATCH CO.

Aurora, Illinois
1883 - 1892

Aurora Watch Co. was organized in mid-1883 with the goal of getting one jeweler in every town to handle Aurora watches. The first movements were 18S, full plate, and were first sold in the fall of 1884. There were several watches marked No. 1. The total production was about 215,000; over 200,000 were 18 Size, and some were 6 size ladies' watches. For the most part Aurora produced medium to low grade; and at one time made about 150 movements per day. The Hamilton Watch Co. purchased the company on June 19, 1890.

AURORA WATCH CO.
Estimated Serial Nos. and Production Dates

1884 – 10,001	1888 – 200,000
1885 – 60,000	1889 – 215,000
1886 – 101,000	1891 – 230,901
1887 – 160,000	

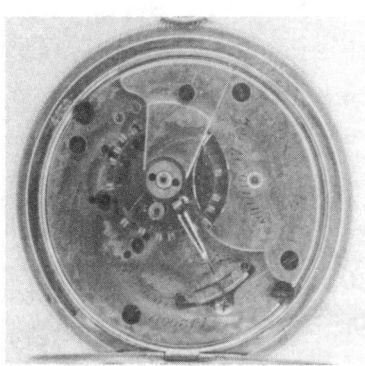
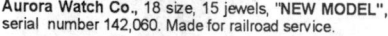

Aurora Watch Co., 18 size, 15 jewels, "NEW MODEL", serial number 142,060. Made for railroad service.

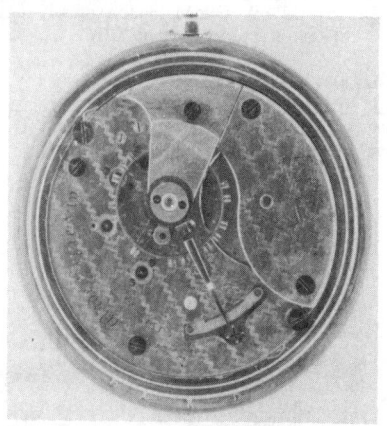

Aurora Watch Co., 18 size, 15 jewels, Adj, engraved on movement "Made expressly R.J.A.," 5th pinion serial number 73,529.

Description	Avg	Ex-Fn	Mint
18S, 7J, KW, KS, Gilded, OF	$150	$180	$230
18S, 7J, KW, KS, Gilded, HC	175	200	250
18S, 7J, 5th pinion, Gilded, LS, SW, OF	135	160	195
18S, 7J, LS, SW, Gilded, new model, HC	200	250	325
18S, 11J, KW, KS, Gilded, HC	175	200	250
18S, 11J, KW, KS, Gilded, OF	150	180	230
18S, 11J, 5th pinion, LS, SW, Gilded, new model, OF	145	175	225
18S, 11J, 5th pinion, LS, SW, NI, GJS, OF	160	200	250
18S, 11J, 5th pinion, LS, SW, NI, GJS, new model, OF	150	180	230
18S, 11J, LS, SW, Gilded, made expressly for the guild, HC	225	275	325
18S, 11J, 5th pinion, LS, SW, NI, made expressly for the guild, OF	225	275	325
18S, 15J, KW, KS, NI, GJS, DMK, OF or HC ★	225	275	350
18S, 15J, 5th pinion, LS, SW, Gilded, OF	200	250	325
18S, 15J, 5th pinion, LS, SW, NI, GJS, DMK, ADT, OF	225	275	350
18S, 15J, 5th pinion, LS, SW, NI, GJS, DMK, ADJ, new model, OF	300	350	400
18S, 15J, LS, SW, NI, GJS, DMK, ADJ, new model, HC	300	350	400
18S, 15J, LS, SW, NI, GJS, ADJ, 2 Tone DMK, checkerboard or snowflake, Ruby Jewels, HC	325	375	425
18S, 15J, LS, SW, NI, GJS, ADJ, 2 Tone DMK, checkerboard or snowflake, 5th pinion, Ruby Jewels, OF ★	400	550	750

"RUBY JEWELS", MARKED = Auroras highest grade.

Size and Description	Avg	Ex-Fn	Mint
18S, 15J, LS, SW, NI, GJS, DMK, ADJ, Railroad Time Service or Caufield Watch, new model, HC ....★	$400	$550	$675
18S, marked **15 Ruby Jewels** but has 17J, 5th pinion, LS, SW, NI, GJS, 2 Tone, ADJ, OF ....★★	600	700	900
18S, marked **15 Ruby Jewels,** only 15J, LS, SW, NI, GJS, 2 Tone DMK, ADJ, HC..........	400	500	600
18S, marked **15 Ruby Jewels,** only 15J, LS, SW, NI, GJS, ADJ, 2 Tone DMK, OF ....★	450	525	600
18S, 15J, Chronometer, LS, SW, NI, DMK, ADJ, new model HC.......★★	400	500	625
18S, 15J, Chronometer, LS, SW, NI, GJS, DMK, ADJ, HC ....★	375	450	525
18S, 15J, LS, Gilded, "Eclipse, Chicago", new model, HC..........	275	300	385
18S, 15J, LS, SW, NI, DMK, made expressly for the guild, HC.....	250	300	375
18S, 15J, 5th pinion, LS, SW, Gilded, made expressly for the guild, OF	300	350	400
18S, 15J, LS, SW, Gilded, made expressly for the "RJA" (Retails Jeweler's Assoc.), HC.......	400	500	600

Size and Description	Avg	Ex-Fn	Mint
6S, 11-15J, LS, SW, Gilded, 3/4, HC	$125	$150	$200
6S, 11-15J, LS, SW, NI, GJS, DMK, 3/4, HC.......	150	175	225
6S, 11-15J, LS, SW, 3/4 plate, **14K, HC**.......	250	300	400

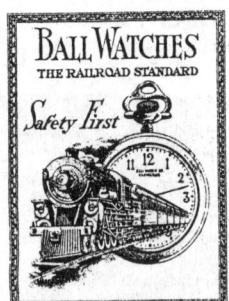

BALL WATCH CO.

Cleveland, Ohio

1879 - 1969

The Ball Watch Company did not manufacture watches but did help formulate the specifications of watches used for railroad service. Webb C. Ball of Cleveland, Ohio, was the general time inspector for over 125,000 miles of railroad in the U. S., Mexico, and Canada. In 1891 there was a collision between the Lake Shore and Michigan Southern Railways at Kipton, Ohio. The collision was reported to have occurred because an engineer's watch had stopped, for about four minutes, then started running again. The railroad officials commissioned Ball to establish the timepiece inspection system. Ball knew that the key to safe operations of the railroad was the manufacturing of sturdy, precision timepieces. He also knew they must be able to withstand hard use and still be accurate. Before this time, each railroad company had its own rules and standards. After Ball presented his guidelines, most American manufacturers set out to meet these standards and soon a list was made of the manufacturers that produced watches of the grade that would pass inspection. Each railroad employee had a card that he carried showing the record of how his watch performed on inspection. Ball was also instrumental in the formation of the Horological Institute of America.

🕐 NOTE: BALL WATCHES ARE PRICED AS HAVING A ORIGINAL BALL DIAL.

ESTIMATED SERIAL NUMBERS AND PRODUCTION DATES
FOR RAILROAD GRADE WATCHES

(Hamilton) Date – Serial #	(Waltham) Date – Serial #	(Elgin) 1904-1906 S # range:
1895 - 13,000	1900 - 060,700	11,853,000 - 12,282,000
1897 - 20,500	1905 - 202,000	
1900 - 42,000	1910 - 216,000	
1902 - 170,000	1915 - 250,000	
1905 - 462,000	1920 - 260,000	(E. Howard & C0.)
1910 - 600,000	1925 - 270,000	1893-1895
1915 - 603,000		S # range:
1920 - 610,000		226,000 - 308,000
1925 - 620,000		
1930 - 637,000	(Illinois)	
1935 - 641,000	Date – Serial #	(Hampden)
1938 - 647,000	1929 - 800,000	1890-1892
1939 - 650,000	1930 - 801,000	S # range:
1940 - 651,000	1931 - 803,000	626,750 - 657,960 -
1941 - 652,000	1932 - 804,000	759,720
1942 - 654,000		

The above list is provided for determining the **APPROXIMATE** age of your watch. Match serial number with date. Watches were not necessarily sold in the exact order of manufactured date.

BALL — AURORA
18 SIZE

Description		Avg	Ex-Fn	Mint
15-17J, OF, marked Webb C. Ball .... ★ ★		$1,500	$1,750	$2,000
15-17J, HC, marked Ball .... ★ ★ ★		2,200	2,500	3,000

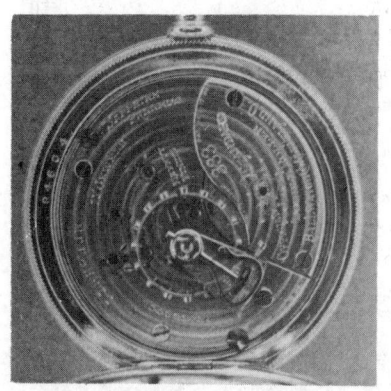

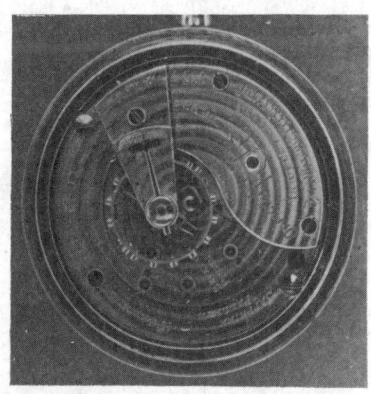

Ball-Elgin, Grade 333, 18 size, 17 jewels, rare hunting case model, serial number 11,958,002.

Ball-Elgin, Grade 333, 18 size, 17 jewels, open face model, serial number 11,856,801.

BALL — ELGIN
18 SIZE G. F. CASES

Description		Avg	Ex-Fn	Mint
16J, G#327, Commercial Standard, LS, OF .... ★		$275	$350	$475
17J, G#328, Commercial Standard, LS, HC .... ★		300	375	500

Description	Avg	Ex-Fn	Mint
17J, G#328, Coin, LS, HC ....★	$250	$325	$450
17J, G#329, NI, Adj.5P, LS, HC .... ★★	1,200	1,500	1,800
21J, G#330, LS, Official RR std., HC ....★★★★	2,000	2,500	3,000
16J, G#331, NI, OF, Adj.5P, PS, Commercial Std. ....★★	375	425	550
16J, G#331, NI, HC, Adj.5P, PS, Commercial Std ....★★	400	500	600
17J, G#331, NI, OF, Adj.5P, PS	200	275	350
17J, G#332, Commercial Std, OF, PS...........................★	300	350	400
17J, G#333, NI, OF, Adj.5P, LS	200	265	325
17J, G#333, NI, HC, Adj.5P, LS .... ★★★	1,300	1,600	1,900
21J, G#333, NI, OF, Adj.5P, LS	325	350	400
21J, G#334, NI, OF, Adj.5P, LS	375	450	500

🕐 Note: 18 Size Ball watches in hunting cases are scarce.

BALL — HAMILTON
18 SIZE G. F. CASES

Description	Avg	Ex-Fn	Mint
17J, M#936, Superior Grade,**first trial run S# 601 to 625**.. ★★★	$2,000	$3,000	4,500
17J, M#938, NI, OF, DR, ...★★	575	625	750
17J, M#-937-939, Official RR std, LS, Adj., HC ....★★	2,000	2,500	3,200
17J, M#999, Commercial Standard	300	400	500
17J, Off. Ball marked jewelers name on dial & mvt., OF ....★	350	450	575
17J, M#999, NI, Official RR std, OF, Adj.5P, LS, Coin.................	250	300	365
17J, M#999, Official RR std, NI, OF, Adj.5P, LS............................	250	300	365
17J, M#999, "A" model adj. ....★	350	400	500
17J, M#999, NI, OF, Adj.5P, marked "Loaner" on case	250	300	365
19J, M#999, Official RR std, NI, OF, Adj.5P, LS..........................	375	425	500
21J, M#999, Official RR std, NI, OF, Adj.5P, LS..........................	400	450	550
23J, M#999, NI, OF, Adj.5P, LS, Gold Filled Case	4,000	5,000	6,000
23J, M#999, NI, OF, Adj.5P, LS ,14K case .... ★★★	6,000	7,500	10,000
23J, M#999, NI, HC, Adj.5P, LS,14K case .... ★★★★	7,000	9,000	12,000
Early Ball & Co., 16-17J, (low serial # 13,001 to 13,400), OF **marked** dial & mvt. *Railroad Watch Co.* (second run).. ★★	1,000	1,300	1,850
Early Ball & Co., 16-17J, (low serial # 14,001 to 15,000), OF **marked** dial & mvt. *Railroad Watch Co.* (third run) ....★	900	1,200	1,550
Ball & Co., 16-17J, SR, **marked** dial & mvt. *Railroad Watch Co*	450	600	800
Brotherhood of Locomotive Engineers, 17J, OF..............................	500	600	775
Brotherhood of Locomotive Engineers, 19J, OF..............................	600	700	875

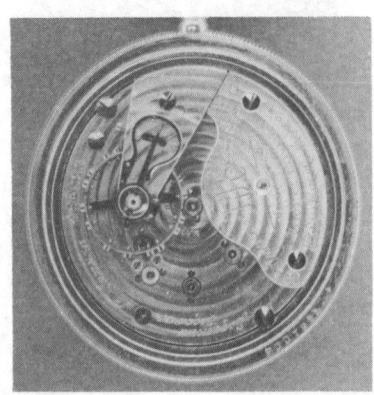
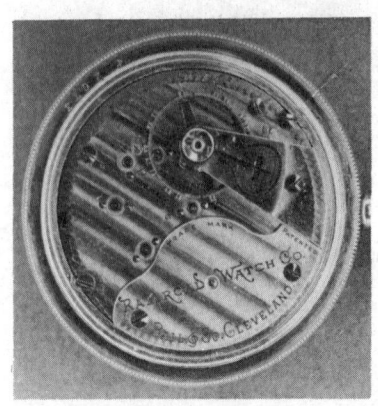

BALL-HAMILTON, Grade 999, 18 size, 17 jewels, serial number 458,623

BALL-HAMILTON, Grade 999, 18 size, 17 jewels, marked *"Railroad Watch Co."* Ca. 1896, serial number 20,793.

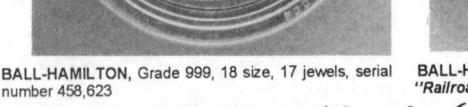

Ball-Hamilton serial number 601 is known to exist.

Ball Watch Co., Brotherhood of RR trainmen, 18 size, 17J, movement made by Hamilton, serial number 13,020.

Ball Watch Co. (Hamilton). Grade 999, 18 size, 21-23 J., sun ray damaskeening, serial number 548,157, c.1906.

Description	Avg	Ex-Fn	Mint
Brotherhood of Locomotive Engineers, 21J, OF	$700	$800	$975
Brotherhood of Locomotive Firemen, 17J, OF	500	600	775
Brotherhood of Locomotive Firemen, 19J, OF	600	700	875
Brotherhood of Locomotive Firemen, 21J, OF	700	800	975
Brotherhood of Railroad Trainsmen, 17J, OF	500	600	775
Brotherhood of Railroad Trainsmen, 19J, OF	600	700	875
Brotherhood of Railroad Trainsmen, 21J, OF	700	800	975
Order of Railroad Conductors, 17J, OF	500	600	750
Order of Railroad Conductors, 19J, OF	600	700	850
Order of Railroad Conductors, 21J, OF	700	800	950
Order of Railroad Telegraphers, 17J, OF	500	600	750
Order of Railroad Telegraphers, 19J, OF	700	800	950
Order of Railroad Telegraphers, 21J, OF	600	700	850
Private Label or Jewelers name, 17J, Adj., OF	375	425	500

BALL WATCH Co. (OFFICIAL R.R. STANDARD) Dial, NOTE: 20th Century bow, W/ snap back.

BALL WATCH Co. DIAL (Order of Railroad Conductors), 18 size.

BALL– DeLONG ESCAPEMENT
16 SIZE

Description	Avg	Ex-Fn	Mint
21J, **14K OF Case** ....★★★★★	$2,000	$2,500	$3,000

Ball-Hamilton, Model 998 Elinvar, 16 size, 23 jewels, with center bridge.

BALL W. CO.(HAMILTON),16 size, 21jewels, official RR standard, ADJ.5p, serial no. B611429.

BALL — HAMILTON
16 SIZE G. F. CASES

Description	Avg	Ex-Fn	Mint
16J, M#976, 977, NI, OF, LS	$200	$250	$300
17J, M#974, NI, OF, LS	150	200	265
17J, Official RR Standard, OF	175	225	285
19J, Official RR Standard, OF	250	300	355
19J, M#999, NI, Off. RR Stan., OF, LS..	250	300	355
21J, M#999, NI, Off. RR Stan., OF, LS..	350	375	425
21J, M#**999B-marked**, Off. RR Stan., OF, **marked-Adj.6P**	375	400	450
21J, M#999, Off. RR Stan., Coin case	350	375	425
21J, M#999 , Off. RR Stan., marked Loaner, coin case ....★★	375	425	475
21J, M#992B, NI, marked **992B** & Off RR Stan. **Adj.6P**.....★★★	750	850	1,100
23J, M#999B, Off. RR Stan., NI, OF, LS, Adj.6P	675	775	825
23J, M#998 **marked-Elinvar**, Off. RR Stan., Adj.5P	775	825	925
23J, M#999, NI, Off. RR Stan., OF, LS..	675	750	825
Brotherhood of Locomotive Engineers, OF...................................	700	765	850
Brotherhood of Locomotive Firemen, OF	700	765	850
Brotherhood of Railroad Trainmen, OF...	700	765	850
Order of Railroad Conductors, OF...	700	765	850
17-19J, Brotherhood or Order, HUNTING CASE ....★★	900	1,000	1,100
Private Label or Jewelers name, 21J, Adj., OF...............................	275	300	335

BALL — HAMPDEN
18 SIZE

Description	Avg	Ex-Fn	Mint
15-17J, LS, SW, HC, marked **Superior Grade** ....★★★	$1,250	$1,400	$1,850
15-17J, LS, SW, OF, marked **Superior Grade** ....★★	1,000	1,200	1,600
15-17J, LS, SW, OF..★	400	450	550
15-17J, LS, SW, HC ....★★★	650	700	850

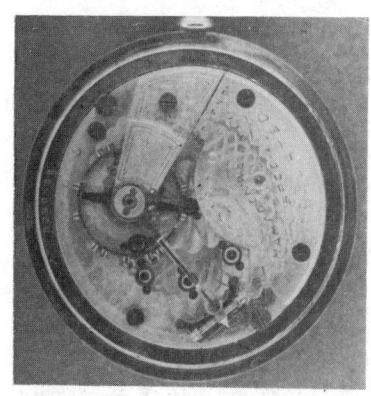

Ball-Hampden, 18 size, 17 jewels, serial number 759,728.

BALL & CO. (E. HOWARD & CO.), Series VIII, 18 size, 17 jewels. Order of Railway Conductors, serial number 307,488. c.1900.

BALL — E. HOWARD & CO.
18 SIZE

Description		Avg	Ex-Fn	Mint
17J, 3/4, HC, PS, GJS, **18K,** VII, orig. gold HC .... ★ ★ ★		$4,500	$5,500	$7,500
17J, 3/4, OF, PS, GJS, **14K,** VIII, Brotherhood of Locomotive Engineers, or Order of Railroad Conductors .... ★ ★ ★		3,000	4,000	6,000
17J, 3/4, OF, PS, GJS, series VIII...		650	700	850

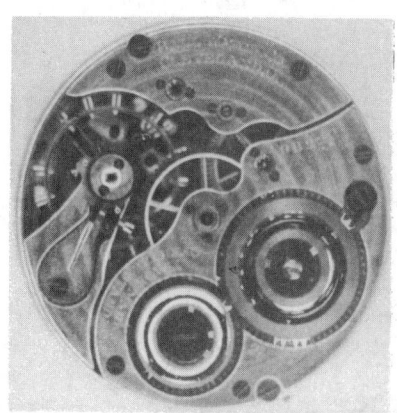

BALL W. Co. (E. HOWARD WATCH CO.), 16 size, 21J. (KEYSTONE). This watch believed to be one-of-a-kind prototype, serial number 982,201.

Ball Watch Co., Illinois Model, 16 size, 23 jewels. Note: The CORRECT HANDS FOR BALL ILLINOIS WATCH.

⊕ Some grades are not included. Their values can be determined by comparing with similar age, size, metal content, style, models and grades listed.

⊕ BALL Watches are priced as having a **ORIGINAL BALL DIAL & CASE.**

BALL — E. HOWARD WATCH CO. (Keystone)
16 SIZE

Description	Avg	Ex-Fn	Mint
17J, OF, GJS	$2,000	$2,500	$3,500
21J, KEYSTONE, Adj, GJS, OF .... ★★★★★	2,500	3,000	4,500

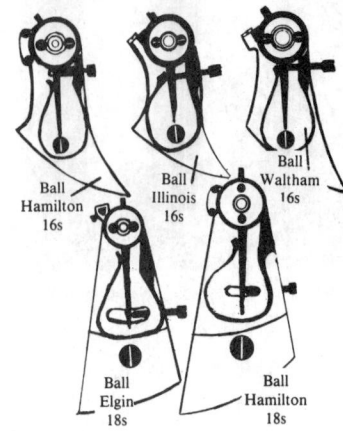

Ball Watch Co., Illinois Model, 16 size, 23 jewels. To identify, note back plates that circle around balance wheel, serial number B801,758.

BALL regulator identification, note: styles and location of hairspring stud.

BALL — ILLINOIS
18 & 16 SIZE

Description	Avg	Ex-Fn	Mint
18 size, 11-15J. or (Garland model), OF...	$175	$195	$225
16 size, 23J, 3/4, LS, Off. RR Stan., Adj. 5P, GJS, OF............ ★★	1,200	1,300	1,500

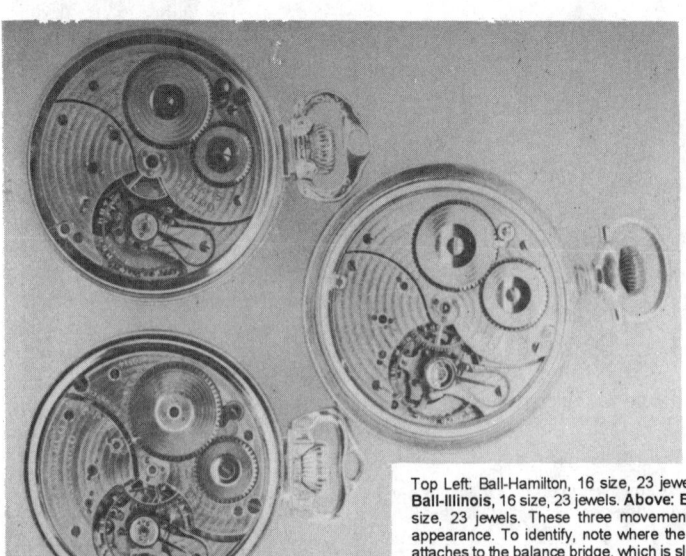

Top Left: Ball-Hamilton, 16 size, 23 jewels. Bottom left: Ball-Illinois, 16 size, 23 jewels. Above: Ball Waltham, 16 size, 23 jewels. These three movements are similar in appearance. To identify, note where the hair spring stud attaches to the balance bridge, which is slightly different on each movement.

BALL — SETH THOMAS
18 SIZE

Description		Avg	Ex-Fn	Mint
17J, M#3, LS, OF,3/4, GJS	★★★★	$3,200	$3,800	$4,500

BALL — WALTHAM
18 SIZE

Description		Avg	Ex-Fn	Mint
1892, 15-17J, OF, LS, SW, marked Webb C. Ball, Cleveland	★★	$1,500	$1,700	$2,200

BALL — WALTHAM
16 SIZE

Description		Avg	Ex-Fn	Mint
15J, Commercial Std.,3/4,HC, GCW	★★	$325	$400	$550
15-16J, Commercial std., OF		125	150	175
16J, Commercial std., HC		175	200	250
17-19J, Commercial std., OF		100	150	175
17-19J, Commercial std., HC		175	200	250
17J, LS, 3/4, Adj.5P, Multi-color case, GF, OF		250	300	400
17J, LS, 3/4, Adj.5P, Off. RR Stan., OF		150	200	275
17J,Official RR std., HC	★★	800	1,000	1,300
19J,Official RR std., LS, GCW,GJS, OF		250	270	325
19J,Official RR std., LS, GCW,GJS, HC		375	475	600

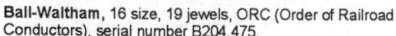

Ball-Waltham, 16 size, 19 jewels, ORC (Order of Railroad Conductors), serial number B204,475.

BALL–WALTHAM, 23 jewels, Official Railroad Standard, lever set, Adjusted to 5 positions, serial# B060,915.

Description		Avg	Ex-Fn	Mint
19J, Off. RR Stan., GJS, HC	★★	$900	$1,100	$1,400
19J, OF, LS, Off. RR Stan., **14K**		600	675	775
19J, OF, LS, Off. RR Stan., stirrup style case		275	325	375
19J, OF, LS, Off. RR Stan., Coin		250	300	355
19J, HC, LS, 3/4, Adj.5P, Off. RR Stan., **HC**	★	365	450	600
19J, OF, LS, 3/4, Adj.5P, Off. RR Stan., Wind Indicator	★★	3,000	3,500	4,250

🕐 Some grades are not included. Their values can be determined by comparing with similar age, size, metal content, style, models and grades listed.

Watches MARKED "BALL & Co." are more difficult to find than BALL WATCH Co.

Description	Avg	Ex-Fn	Mint
21J,Official RR std., LS, GCW,GJS, OF	$375	$400	$450
21J, OF, LS, 3/4, Adj.5P, Off. RR Stan.,	375	400	450
21J, LS, OF, Adj.5P, Off. RR Stan., marked Loaner	375	400	450
17J, Brotherhood, marked ORC, BOFLE & *other etc. dials*, OF....	450	500	575
19J, Brotherhood, marked ORC, BOFLE & *other etc. dials*, OF....	500	600	725
17-19J, Brotherhood, marked ORC, BOFLE & *other etc. dials*,HC	700	800	1,000
21J, Brotherhood, marked ORC, BOFLE & *other etc. dials*, OF....	600	700	850
23J, LS, OF, Adj.5P, NI, GJS, Off. RR Stand.,			
only one known to exist, **Ex. rare** ......★★★★★	4,000	6,000	8,500

Ball Watch Co. by Waltham, 12 size, 19 jewels, open face, digital seconds

Record Watch Co. (BXC), 16 size, 21jewels, M#477-B, Adj.6P, Swiss made Ca.1961.

12 SIZE
(Not Railroad Grade)

Description	Avg	Ex-Fn	Mint
19J, Illinois, OF, PS	$135	$175	$250
19J, Illinois, HC, PS	200	300	450
15J, Waltham,Commercial Standard, OF, PS,	150	200	250
16J, Waltham,Commercial Standard, OF, PS,	160	210	260
17J, Waltham, Commercial Standard, OF, PS,	150	160	180
19J, Waltham, OF, PS, rotating digital sec	200	250	300

NO. 333
NO. 999

   B OF LE

STANDARD B OF RT

O OF RC

OFFICIAL RR STANDARD

The B. of L. E. Standard Watch.
The B. of L. F. Standard Watch.
The B. of R. T. Standard Watch.
The O. of R. C. Standard Watch.
The Official R. R. Standard Watch.
The O. of R. T. Standard Watch.

B OF LF

 SAFETY

OFFICIAL TIME SERVICE STANDARD

 FIRST

TRADE MARKS REGISTERED IN U. S. PATENT OFFICE

Ball-Audemars Piguet & Co., 14 size, 31 jewels, minute repeater, open face, serial number 4,220.

Ball-Vacheron & Constantin, 43mm, 18 jewels, hunting; note wolf-teeth winding.

BALL — SWISS
16 SIZE

Description	Avg	Ex-Fn	Mint
17J, "Garland"...	$100	$125	$175
21J, Time Ball Special,OF...	60	75	100
21J, M#435-B, OF, LS, Adj.6P, Ball case, stirrup bow	200	225	275
21J, M#435-C, OF, LS, Adj.6P, Ball case, stirrup bow	200	225	275
21J, M#477-B, Adj.6P (BXC-Record Watch Co.)	200	225	250
40mm Audemar Piguet, min. repeater, jeweled thru hammers, 18K, OF, triple signed Webb C. Ball	6,000	7,500	9,500
43mm Vacheron & Constantin, 18J, HC, 18K	1,000	1,200	1,400

0 SIZE
(Not Railroad Grade)

Description	Avg	Ex-Fn	Mint
17-19J, Waltham, OF, PS	$225	$275	$375
19J, HC, PS, "Queen" in Ball case..	350	400	550

20 th CENTURY CASE

18 size: 14K=$450 - $500 - $600
18 size: gold filled= $120 - $130 - $150
16 size: 14K=$350 -$375 - $450
16 size: gold filled= $95 - $110 - $140

PATENT SAFETY BOW

ANTIQUE STIRRUP BOW

18 size: 14K=$450 - $500 - $600
18 size: gold filled= $120 - $130 - $150
16 size: 14K= $350 -$375 - $450
16 size: gold filled= $95 - $110 - $140

CATALOG CASE # 106
gold filled case $125 - $150 - $185

CATALOG CASE # 110
gold filled case $150 - $175 - $225

"BOX CAR" Dial
dial found on Hamilton & Illinois made Ball

CATALOG CASE # 114
gold filled case $150 - $175- $200

CATALOG CASE # 118
gold filled case $175 - $200 - $250

🕐 NOTE: A 1902 advertisement for Ball Watch Company read, ''We do not sell movements or cases separately. BALL Advertised as a **COMPLETE** watch with a choice of BALL dials and was fitted with a certain matched, timed and rated movement and sold in the BALL designed case style as a **COMPLETE** watch. **ALL THE ABOVE CASES ARE GOLD FILLED.**

CATALOG CASE # 122
gold filled case $175 - $200 - $225

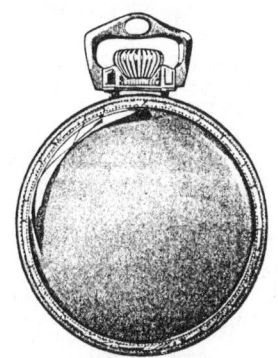

CATALOG CASE # 126
gold filled case $125 - $150 - $175

CONVENTIONAL Dial
dial found on Waltham made Ball

CATALOG CASE # 130
gold filled case $150 - $175 - $200

CATALOG CASE # 134
gold filled case $175 - $200 - $225

🕐 NOTE: A 1902 advertisement for Ball Watch Company read, "We do not sell movements or cases separately. BALL Advertised as a **COMPLETE** watch with a choice of BALL dials and was fitted with a certain matched, timed and rated movement and sold in the BALL designed case style as a **COMPLETE** watch.   **ALL THE ABOVE CASES ARE GOLD FILLED.**

BANNATYNE WATCH CO.
1905 - 1911

Mr. Bannatyne had previously worked for Ansonia, in charge of watch production. Bannatyne made non-jeweled watches that sold for about $1.50. Ingraham bought this company in 1912.

ESTIMATED SERIAL NUMBERS AND PRODUCTION DATES

Date	Serial No.	Date	Serial No.	Date	Serial No.
1906	40,000	1908	140,000	1910	250,000

Description		Avg	Ex-Fn	Mint
18-18S, OF, SW, NI- case	★ ★	$300	$375	$500
12-14S, OF, SW, NI- case	★ ★	200	275	325

Bannatyne Watch Co. (left), Ingraham Watch Co. (right). Note similarity of movements. Both patented Aug. 27th, 1907 & Sept. 3rd, 1907.

BENEDICT & BURNHAM MFG. CO.
Waterbury, Connecticut
1878 - 1880

This name will be found on the dial of the first 1,000 "long wind" Waterbury watches made in 1878. These watches had skeleton type movements with open dials that made the works visible. They contained 58 parts and were attractive. The company was reorganized in March 1880 as the Waterbury Watch Co. and in 1886 became the New England Watch Co.

🕐 Watches listed in this book are priced at the collectable retail level, as **complete** watches having an original 14k gold-filled case & *KEY WIND* with silver case, an original white enamel single sunk dial, and with the entire original movement in good working order with no repairs needed.

Benedict & Burnham Mfg. Co. dial & movement, 18 size, long wind, skeletonized dial.

Description	Avg	Ex-Fn	Mint
18S, duplex escapement, movement rotates as time advances			
long wind,Nickel OF case .... ★ ★ ★ ★	$850	$1,000	$1,300

BOWMAN WATCH CO.

Lancaster, Pennsylvania

1879 - 1882

In March 1877, Ezra F. Bowman, a native of Lancaster, Pa., opened a retail jewelry and watch business. He employed William H. Todd to supervise his watch manufacturing. Todd had previously been employed by the Elgin and Lancaster Watch companies. Bowman made a 17S, 3/4 plate, fully-jeweled movement. The escape wheel was a star tooth design, fully capped, similar to those made by Charles Frodsham, an English watch maker. They were stem wind with dials made by another company. Enough parts were made and bought for 300 watches, but only about 50 watches were completed and sold by Bowman. These watches performed very well. The company was sold to J. P. Stevens of Atlanta, Ga.

Description	Avg	Ex-Fn	Mint
18S, 17J, Hamilton 928, OF, marked E. F. Bowman .... ★ ★	$400	$500	$650
17S, 19-21J, 3/4, GJS, NI, LS, SW .... ★ ★ ★ ★	9,000	11,000	16,000
16S, 21J, Hamilton 960, OF, marked E. F. Bowman .... ★ ★	450	500	650
16S, 21J, Hamilton 961, HC, marked E. F. Bowman .... ★ ★ ★	500	600	750

Bowman Watch Co., 16-18 size, 19-21 jewels, 3/4 plate, gold jewel settings, lever set, stem wind. Note free sprung balance. Serial number 17, c.1880.

CALIFORNIA WATCH CO.

San Francisco - Berkeley, California
1876 - 1877

The Cornell Watch Co. was reorganized in early 1876 as the California Watch Co. The new company bought machinery to make watch cases of gold and silver. In a short time the company was in bad financial trouble and even paid its employees with watches. The business closed in the summer of 1876. Albert Troller bought the unfinished watches that were left. In about four months, he found a buyer in San Francisco. The factory was then closed and sold to the Independent Watch Co. Only about 5,000 watches were made by the California Watch Company. Serial numbers range from 25,115 to 30,174. Inscribed on the movements is "Berkeley."

Description		Avg	Ex-Fn	Mint
18S, 15J, FULL, KW, KS, "Berkeley" .... ★★		$1,300	$1,600	$2,000
18S, 11-15J, FULL, KW, KS or SW............................ ★		1,000	1,200	1,600
18S, 19J, FULL, KW, KS or SW .... ★★★		1,200	1,400	1,900

California Watch Co., 18 size, 15 jewels, full plate.

California Watch Co., 18 size, 7 jewels, full plate, serial number 29,029.

CHESHIRE WATCH CO.

Cheshire, Connecticut
1883 - 1890

In October 1883, the Cheshire Watch Company was formed by George J. Capewell with D. A. A. Buck (designer of the long-wind Waterbury) as superintendent. Their first movement was 18S, 3/4 gilt plate, stem wind, stem set, with the pendant attached to the movement. It fit into a nickel case which was also made at the Cheshire factory. The first watches were completed in April 1885. A new 18S nickel movement with a second hand was made to fit standard size American cases, and was introduced in 1887. By that date production was at about 200 watches per day.

NOTE: George J. Capewell inventor of the Capewell horse shoe nail.

Serial numbers range from 201 to 89,650. All Cheshire watches were sold through L. W. Sweet, general selling agent, in New York City. The factory closed in 1890, going into receivership. The receiver had 3,000 movements finished in 1892. In 1901 O. E. Bell bought the machinery and had it shipped to Appleton, Wisconsin, where he had formed the Remington Watch Company. The watches produced by Remington are marked ''Appleton Watch Co.'' on the movements.

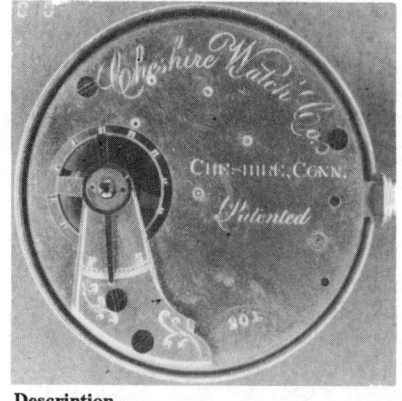

Cheshire Watch Co., 20 size, 4 jewels, model number 1. Note stem attached and will not fit standard size case, serial number **201**. NOTE: Closed top plate near balance.

Description	Avg	Ex-Fn	Mint
20S, 4-7J, FULL, OF, SW, NI case, stem attached, low serial #			
1st model, closed top plate (S # 201 to 300)............... ★★★	$550	$700	$900
20S, 4-7J, FULL, OF, SW, NI case, stem attached,			
1st model, closed top plate .... ★★	450	550	700
18S, 4-7J, 3/4, SW, OF, NI case, stem attached, 2nd model .... ★	300	350	450
18S, 4-7J, HC/ OF fits standard case, 3rd model.......................... ★	250	300	375
18S, 11J, HC/ OF, standard case, 3rd model .... ★	275	325	400
18S, 15J, HC/ OF, NI, ADJ, standard case, 3rd model .... ★	300	350	450
18S, 21J, HC / OF, SW, Coin, standard case, 3rd model .... ★★	400	450	550
6S, 3/4, HC/ OF, SW, NI case.. ★	200	275	350

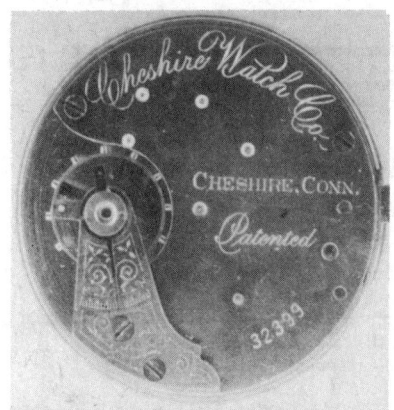

Cheshire Watch Co., 18 size, 4-7 jewels. This model number 2 was manufactured with the stem attached and requires a special case. NOTE: open top plate at Balance.

Cheshire Watch Co., 18 size, 4-7 jewels. This model fits standard 18 size cases. Model number 3.

🕐 1st & 2nd model Cheshire movements will not fit standard 18 size cases.

Model # 1, S# 201 to 4,000 - Model # 2, S # 30,001 to 40,000 - Model # 3, S # 50,001 to 89,650.

CHICAGO WATCH CO.

Chicago, Illinois
1895 - 1903

The Chicago Watch Company's watches were 18 size, 7-15J & 12 size were made by other manufacturer Companies and sold by Chicago Watch Co.

Description	Avg	Ex-Fn	Mint
18S, 7J, OF	$100	$145	$200
18S, 7-11J, HC or OF, Swiss	50	60	75
18S, 11J, KW	325	375	450
18S, 15J, OF, SW	175	200	300
Columbus, 18S, 15J, SW, NI, OF ★	200	250	325
Columbus, 18S, 15J, SW, NI, HC ★★	275	300	350
Illinois, 18S, 11J, SW, NI ★★	200	250	325
Waltham, 18S, 15J ★★	200	250	325
12S, 15J, OF	100	145	200
12S, 15J, YGF, HC	200	250	325

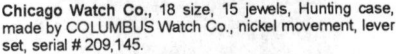

Chicago Watch Co., 18 size, 15 jewels, Hunting case, made by COLUMBUS Watch Co., nickel movement, lever set, serial # 209,145.

Columbia Watch Co., 0 size, 4 jewels, stem wind, open face and hunting, duplex escapement, the escape wheel teeth were milled to give better quality than the Waterbury movements.

COLUMBIA WATCH CO.

Waltham, Massachusetts
1896 - 1899

The Columbia Watch Company was organized in 1896 by Edward A. Locke, formerly General Manager of the Waterbury Watch Company. The firm began manufacturing an 0-size, 4-jewel gilt movement with duplex escapement in 1897. These movements were marked "Columbia Watch Co., Waltham, Mass." The firm also made movements marked "Hollers Watch Co., Brooklyn, NY," as well as nickeled movements marked "Cambridge Watch Co., New York."

Locke turned the business over to his son-in-law, Renton Whidden, in 1898, and the firm changed to an 0-size, 7- jewel nickel movement with lever escapement called the Suffolk. The firm name was not changed until early 1901.

Description	Avg	Ex-Fn	Mint
0S, 4J, SW, OF, HC, Duplex, gilded	$50	$60	$75
0S, 7J, SW, OF, lever escapement	60	75	85

COLUMBUS WATCH CO.

Columbus, Ohio
1874 - 1903

Dietrich Gruen, born in Osthofen, Germany in 1847, started a business as the Columbus Watch Co. on Dec. 22 of 1874 in Columbus, Ohio. At the age of 27, he received a U.S. patent for an improved safety pinion. The new company finished movements made from Madretsch, Switzerland, a suburb of Beil. The imported movements were made in a variety of sizes and were in nickel or gilt. The early watches usually had the initials C.W.CO. intertwined in script on the dial. The serial numbers generally ran up to around 20,000's a few examples are in the 70,000's.

D. Gruen and W.J. Savage decided in late 1882 to manufacture watches locally. By August of 1883 the first movements were being produced with a train consisting of 72 teeth on the barrel, 72 on the center wheel, 11 on the center pinion, 60 on the third wheel with a pinion of 9, 70 on the fourth wheel with a pinion of 9 with a 7 leaf escape pinion. The new manufacture primarily made 18 size movements but also pioneered the 16 size watch while reducing the size and thickness. Several new innovations were used into the design including a completely covered main spring barrel, a new micrometric regulator and the ability to change the main spring without removing the balance cock. By 1884 they were making their own dials, but no cases were ever manufactured.

The company went into receivership in 1894 with new management. That same year Frederick Gruen started again as D. Gruen & Son. They had PAUL ASSMANN to produce 18 size & 16 size movements with 18 & 21 jewels with the escapement designed by Moritz Grossman of Glasshute. Soon after this time movements were obtained from Switzerland and the new Gruen veri-thin movement was developed. In 1898 this company moved to Cincinnati.

From 1894 through February 14, 1903 the Columbus Watch Co. produced watches both under the Columbus Watch Co. and the New Columbus Watch Co. name. The re-organized company produced the same models, but switched primarily to named grades such as Time King, Columbus King, etc. The higher grade watches were assigned a special block of serial numbers from 500,000 to 506,000 . In keeping with the industry several models with 25 jewels were produced in this block of serial numbers.

In 1903 the Columbus Watch Co. was sold to the Studebakers and the South Bend Watch Co. started. The machinery, unfinished movements, parts and approximately 3/4 of the 150 employees moved to South Bend, Indiana. Some marked Columbus Watch Co. movements were finished by the South Bend W. Co. Examples exist of dials made in the South Bend style and movements marked Columbus Watch Co.

COLUMBUS WATCH CO., 19 Lignes or about 14-16 size, 16 jewels, gold jewel settings, marked Gruen's Pat. pinion, OPEN FACE model, serial # 5,387. (Swiss contract)

1874

COLUMBUS WATCH CO., 19 Lignes or about 14-16 size, 15 jewels, hunting case, engraved on movement *"1874"* .

COLUMBUS
ESTIMATED SERIAL NUMBERS AND PRODUCTION DATES

DATE— SERIAL NO.	DATE— SERIAL NO.	
1874----- 1	1888 – 97,000	
1875– 1,000	1889 – 119,000	
1876– 3,000	1890 – 141,000	
1877– 6,000	1891 – 163,000	SPECIAL BLOCK
1878– 9,000	1892 – 185,000	OF SERIAL NOS.
1879– 12,000	1893 – 207,000	DATE— SERIAL NO.
1880– 15,000	1894 – 229,000	1894 – 500,001
1881– 18,000	1895 – 251,000	1896 – 501,500
1882– 21,000	1896 – 273,000	1898 – 503,000
1883 – 25,000	1897 – 295,000	1900 – 504,500
1884 – 30,000	1898 – 317,000	1902 – 506,000
1885 – 40,000	1899 – 339,000	
1886 – 53,000	1900 – 361,000	
1887 – 75,000	1901 – 383,000	

The above list is provided for determining the **APPROXIMATE** age of your watch. Match serial number with date. Watches were not necessarily *SOLD* and *DELIVERED* in the exact order of manufactured or production dates.

SWISS, 3/4 PLATE, & MADE FROM 1874–1883

Most marked COL. WATCH CO. with single sunk dials and may be SW/KW Transitional, serial # up to 20,000.

Grade or Name — Description	Avg	Ex-Fn	Mint
18S, 7J, pressed J., nickel or gilded, OF	$125	$150	$175
18S, 7J, pressed J., nickel or gilded, HC	150	175	200
18S, 11J, pressed J., nickel or gilded, OF	125	150	175
18S, 11J, pressed J., nickel or gilded, HC	150	175	200
18S, 15J, GJS or pressed J., nickel, Adj., OF/HC	225	250	300
18S, 16J, raised GJS, 2 tone or nickel, Adj., OF/HC	250	300	350
16S, 11J, pressed J., nickel, OF/HC	200	225	250
16S, 15J, pressed J. or GJS, Adj., nickel, OF/HC	250	275	300
16S, 16J, raised GJS, Adj., nickel, OF/HC	275	325	350
14S, 16J, GJS, nickel, Adj., OF/HC	200	225	275
9S, 15J, GJS or pressed J., nickel, Adj., OF/HC	175	200	225
8S, 11J, pressed J., nickel, OF/HC	150	175	200
8S, 15J, pressed J., nickel, OF/HC	175	200	225

FOR ABOVE HUNTING CASED MODEL ADD **$25.00 to $50.00**

NOTE: These Odd size movements are difficult to case.

COLUMBUS WATCH CO., 19 Lignes or about 16 size, 15 jewels, exposed winding wheels, marked Gruen Patent, OPEN FACE model, serial # 1,661. (Swiss contract)

COLUMBUS WATCH CO., about 14 size, 16 jewels, gold jewel settings, nickel plates, marked Gruen's pat. pinion, HUNTING CASE model. (Swiss contract)

18 SIZE-KW, FULL PLATE, MODEL # 1 & TRANSITIONAL

Serial # up to 100,000, balance cock set flush to barrel bridge and may have pinned dial.

Marked Col. Watch Co., Ohio Columbus Watch Co.

Grade or Name — Description	Avg	Ex-Fn	Mint
11-13J, KW / KS, gilded, OF/HC	$325	$375	$400
13J, KW / KS, nickel,(marked 13 jewels), OF/HC ★★	600	675	775
15J, KW / KS, gilded, Adj., OF/HC	375	400	450
16J, KW / KS, gilded, OF/HC ★	425	475	525
11-13J, SW/ KW, gilded or nickel, OF/HC	200	225	250
15J, SW/ KW, gilded or nickel, GJS, OF/HC	225	250	275
16J, SW/ KW, gilded or nickel, GJS, OF/HC	250	275	300

FOR ABOVE HUNTING CASED MODEL ADD **$25.00 to $50.00**

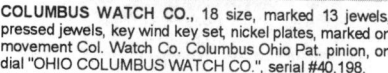

COLUMBUS WATCH CO., 18 size, marked 13 jewels, pressed jewels, key wind key set, nickel plates, marked on movement Col. Watch Co. Columbus Ohio Pat. pinion, on dial "OHIO COLUMBUS WATCH CO.", serial #40,198.

COLUMBUS WATCH CO., 18 size, 15 jewels, key wind key set, hunting case, on movement "Columbus Watch Co. Columbus, Ohio Pat. Pinion", serial # 66,577.

18 SIZE, FULL PLATE, PRE-1894

Marked "Columbus Watch Co. Columbus, Ohio", all marked Safety Pinion

Grade or Name — Description	Avg	Ex-Fn	Mint
7J, G#90, pressed J., OF	$100	$125	$150
7J, G#20, pressed J., HC	100	125	150
11J, G#92, pressed J., nickel, OF	100	125	150
11J, G#22, pressed J., nickel, HC	125	150	195
15J, G#64 / G#93, gilded, OF	100	125	150
15J, G#24 / G#32, gilded, HC	125	150	195
15J, G#63 / G#94, nickel, Adj., OF	100	125	150
15J, G#23 / G#33, nickel, Adj., HC	125	150	195
15J, G#95, nickel, Adj., D.S. dial, OF	125	150	175
15J, G#34, nickel, Adj., D.S. dial, HC	150	175	225
16J, G#97, GJS, nickel, Adj., D.S. dial, OF	175	200	225
16J, G#27, GJS, nickel, Adj., D.S. dial, HC	200	225	250
16J, G#98, raised GJS, 2 tone nickel, Adj., D.S. dial, OF	200	225	250
16J, G#28, raised GJS, 2 tone nickel, Adj., D.S. dial, HC	225	250	285
16J, G#99, raised GJS, 2 tone nickel, Adj., D.S. dial, OF	225	250	325
16J, G#18, raised GJS, 2 tone nickel, Adj., D.S. dial, HC	250	300	365

18 SIZE-FULL PLATE, POST-1894
Some Marked "New Columbus Watch Co. Columbus Ohio"

Grade or Name — Description	Avg	Ex-Fn	Mint
7J, G#10, pressed J., gilded, OF	$100	$125	$150
7J, G#9, pressed J., gilded, HC	125	150	185
11J, G#8, nickel, OF	100	125	150
11J, G#7, nickel, HC	125	150	185
16J, G#6, nickel, OF	125	150	175
16J, G#5, nickel, HC	150	175	200
16J, G#4, GJS, 2 tone nickel, Adj., D.S. dial, OF	175	200	225
16J, G#3, GJS, 2 tone nickel, Adj., D.S. dial, HC	200	225	250
17J, G#204, GJS, 2 tone nickel, Adj., D.S. dial, OF	175	200	225
17J, G#203, GJS, 2 tone nickel, Adj., D.S. dial, HC	200	225	250
17J, G#2, raised GJS, 2 tone nickel, Adj., D.S. dial, OF	225	275	325
17J, G#1, raised GJS, 2 tone nickel, Adj., D.S. dial, HC	250	300	365

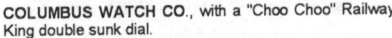

COLUMBUS WATCH CO., with a "Choo Choo" Railway King double sunk dial.

COLUMBUS WATCH CO., Railway King, 18 size, 17 jewels, 2 tone, serial # 313,005.

18 SIZE FULL PLATE, NAMED GRADES
Marked Names, Double Sunk Dials

Grade or Name — Description	Avg	Ex-Fn	Mint
Am. Watch Club, 15J, 2 tone, Adj., D.S. dial, OF/HC	$275	$325	$375
Burlington Route C.B. & QR.R., 15J, nickel, Adj., D.S. dial, OF	650	725	835
Champion, 15J, Nickel, Adj., D.S.dial, OF	150	175	200
Champion, 15J, Nickel, Adj., D.S.dial, HC	175	200	225
Champion, 15J, gilded, Adj., D.S.dial, OF	125	150	175
Champion, 15J, gilded, Adj., D.S.dial, HC	150	175	200
Champion, 16J, Nickel, Adj., D.S.dial, OF	175	200	225
Champion, 16J, Nickel, Adj., D.S.dial, HC	200	225	265

* Chicago W. Co. (see listing under Chicago W. Co. HEADING)

🕐 Watches listed in this book are priced at the collectable retail level, as **complete** watches having an original 14k gold-filled case & *KEY WIND* with silver case, an original white enamel single sunk dial, and with the entire original movement in good working order with no repairs needed.

Grade or Name — Description	Avg	Ex-Fn	Mint
Columbus King, 17J, raised GJS, nickel, Adj., D.S. dial, OF	$300	$350	$400
Columbus King, 17J, raised GJS, nickel, Adj., D.S. dial, HC	350	400	450
Columbus King, 17J, raised GJS, nickel, Adj., choo choo D.S. dial, OF	425	475	525
Columbus King, 17J, raised GJS, nickel, Adj., Angled choo choo D.S. dial, OF	475	525	600
Columbus King, 21J, raised GJS, nickel, Adj., D.S. dial, OF	475	525	575
Columbus King, 21J, raised GJS, nickel, Adj., D.S. dial, HC	400	450	500
Columbus King, 23J, raised GJS, nickel, Adj., D.S. dial, OF ★	950	1,100	1,300
Columbus King, 23J, raised GJS, nickel, Adj., D.S. dial, HC ★	950	1,100	1,300
Columbus King, 25J, raised GJS, nickel, Adj., D.S. dial, OF ★★★★	4,000	4,500	5,000
Columbus King, 25J, raised GJS, nickel, Adj., D.S. dial, HC ★★★★	3,500	4,000	4,500
F.C. & P.R.R., 17J, GJS, nickel, Adj., D.S. dial, OF ★	500	600	700
Jackson Park, 15J, 2 tone, Adj., D.S. dial, OF ★	325	425	500
Jay Gould the Railroad King, 15J, nickel, Adj., D.S. dial, OF ★	500	625	750
New York Susquehanna &Western R.R.,16J, GJS, SW/KW, gold flash, D.S. dial, OF ★★	900	1,000	1,200
Non-magnetic, 16J, raised GJS, 2 tone, Adj., OF/HC	300	400	500
North Star, 11J, gilded, OF	100	125	150
North Star, 11J, gilded, HC	125	150	175
North Star, 11J, nickel, OF	95	125	150
North Star, 11J, nickel, HC	125	150	175
North Star, 15J, nickel, OF	100	125	150
North Star, 15J, nickel, HC	150	175	200
The President, 17J, GJS, Adj, 2 tone, D.S. dial, OF	475	550	575
Railroad Regulator, 15J, GJS, nickel, Adj., D.S. dial, OF ★	450	550	600
Railroad Regulator, 16J, GJS, nickel, Adj., D.S. dial, OF ★	450	500	600
Railway, 17J, GJS, 2 tone, Adj., D.S. dial, OF ★	400	475	525

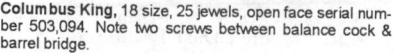
Columbus King, 18 size, 25 jewels, open face serial number 503,094. Note two screws between balance cock & barrel bridge.

Railway King, 18 size, 23 jewels, adjusted, stem wind, hunting case, serial number 503,315. Note one screw between balance cock & barrel bridge.

🕒 Watches listed in this book are priced at the collectable retail level, as **complete** watches having an original 14k gold-filled case & *KEY WIND* with silver case, an original white enamel single sunk dial, and with the entire original movement in good working order with no repairs needed.

Grade or Name — Description	Avg	Ex-Fn	Mint
Railway King, 16J, GJS, 2 tone nickel, Adj., D.S. dial, HC	$300	$325	$375
Railway King, 16J, GJS, 2 tone nickel, Adj., D.S. dial, OF	275	300	350
Railway King, 16J, GJS, 2 tone nickel, Adj., (black red blue) choo chooD.S. dial, HC	375	400	450
Railway King, 16J, GJS, 2 tone nickel, Adj., (black red blue) choo chooD.S. dial, OF	350	375	400
Railway King, 16J, GJS, 2 tone nickel, Adj., Angled choo choo dial, HC	475	550	600
Railway King, 16J, GJS, 2 tone nickel, Adj., Angled choo choo dial, OF	425	500	575
Railway King, 17J, raised GJS, nickel, Adj., D.S. dial, OF	300	350	400
Railway King, 17J, raised GJS, nickel, Adj., D.S. dial, HC	350	375	450
Railway King, 21J, raised GJS, nickel, Adj., D.S. dial, OF	450	500	550
Railway King, 21J, raised GJS, nickel, Adj., D.S. dial, HC	500	550	600
Railway King, 23J, raised GJS, nickel, Adj., Railway King D.S. dial, OF ★★★	1,200	1,300	1,500
Railway King, 23J, raised GJS, nickel, Adj., Railway King D.S. dial, OF ★	1,100	1,250	1,500
Railway King, 25J, raised GJS, nickel, Adj., Railway King D.S. dial, OF ★★★★	3,000	3,500	4,000
Railway King, 25J, raised GJS, nickel, Adj., Railway King D.S. dial, HC ★★★★	3,500	4,500	5,000
Railway King Special, 17J, GJS, nickel, Adj., D.S. dial, OF	325	375	450
Railway Monarch, 17J, GJS, nickel, Adj., D.S. dial, OF ★	300	375	475
Railway Time Service, 17J, GJS, nickel, Adj., D.S. dial, OF ★	375	450	500
The Regent, 15J, D.S. dial, OF	225	250	300
R.W.K. Special, 15J, GJS, Adj., 2 tone, D.S. dial, OF	250	300	350
R.W.K. Special, 15J, GJS, Adj., 2 tone, D.S. dial, HC	275	325	375
R.W.K. Special, 16J, GJS, Adj., 2 tone, D.S. dial, OF	250	285	325
R.W.K. Special, 16J, GJS, Adj., 2 tone, D.S. dial, HC	275	300	350
Springfield Mo.W. Club, 16J, GJS, nickel, Adj., D.S. dial, HC	275	350	400
Special, 17J, GJS, nickel, D.S. dial, OF	200	250	300
J.P. Stevens & Co. (see listing under J.P. Stevens & Co. **HEADING**)			
The New Menlo Park, 15J, HC	100	120	150
The Star, 11J, nickel, OF/HC	175	200	250
Time King, 21J, raised GJS, 2 tone nickel, Adj., D.S. dial, OF	425	475	550
Time King, 21J, raised GJS, 2 tone nickel, Adj., D.S. dial, HC	450	500	600
U.S. Army, 15J, nickel, HC	250	285	325

18 Size, 21 Jewels.

NEW COLUMBUS TIME KING.

Nickel, 21 Genuine Ruby Jewels, set in red, Solid Gold Raised Settings, Escapement Cap Jeweled, Adjusted to temperature, Positions and Isochronism, Breguet Hair Spring, Patent Center Pinion, Patent Regulator, Polished Dust Band and Stem Wind, Beveled Steel Work, Pearled Plates; fine, white, cut and beveled edge, hard enameled, double sunk, Red marginal figured Roman or Arabic Dial; handsomely damaskeened in Gold on Nickel $25 00

Hunting and Open Face.

1895 AD

16 SIZE, 3/4 Plate

Marked "New Columbus Watch Co. Columbus Ohio"

Grade or Name — Description	Avg	Ex-Fn	Mint
7J, G#80 / G#20, gilded, OF	$100	$125	$150
7J, G#40 / G#19, gilded, HC	125	150	175
11J, G#81, gilded, OF	100	125	150
11J, G#41, gilded, HC	125	150	175
11J, G#83 / G#18, nickel, OF	100	125	150
11J, G#43 / G#17, nickel, HC	125	150	175
15J, G#84, Adj., gilded, OF	125	150	175
15J, G#44, Adj., gilded, HC	150	175	200
15J, G#86, GJS, Adj., nickel, D.S. dial, OF	125	150	175
15J, G#46, GJS, Adj., nickel, D.S. dial, HC	150	175	200
16J, G#87 / G#316, GJS, Adj., nickel, D.S. dial, OF	150	175	200
16J, G#47 / G#315, GJS, Adj., nickel, D.S. dial, HC	175	200	225
16J, G#14, GJS, Adj., 2 tone nickel, D.S. dial, OF	200	225	250
16J, G#13, GJS, Adj., 2 tone nickel, D.S. dial, HC	225	275	300
16J, G#88, raised GJS, Adj., 2 tone nickel, D.S. dial, OF	175	225	250
16J, G#48, raised GJS, Adj., 2 tone nickel, D.S. dial, HC	225	250	300
17J, G#12, raised GJS, Adj., 2 tone nickel, D.S. dial, OF	175	225	250
17J, G#11, raised GJS, Adj., 2 tone nickel, D.S. dial, HC	225	250	300
Ruby, 21J, raised GJS, Adj., 2 tone nickel, D.S. dial, OF ★★	600	650	750
Ruby, 21J, raised GJS, Adj., 2 tone nickel, D.S. dial, HC ★	650	700	800

NEW Columbus Watch Co., 16 size, 16 jewels, gold train, 2-tone, serial number 341,339.

Columbus Watch Co., Ruby Model, 16 size, 21 jewels, three quarter plate, gold jewel settings, gold train, Adj.6p.

⊕ Some grades are not included. Their values can be determined by comparing with similar age, size, metal content, style, models and grades listed.

⊕ This book endeavours to be a GUIDE or helpful manual and offers a wealth of material to be used as a tool not as a absolute document. Price Guides are like watches the worst may be better than none at all, but at best cannot be expected to be 100% accurate.

⊕ Characteristics of watches differ for the same age of both case and movement, because these features vary it may not be accurate to date a watch by one single influence. Example: the second hand was not commonly found on watches before 1750, but common about 1800. The first second hand appeared in 1665 and another in 1690. Therefore statements are broad rather than accurate.

6 SIZE

Grade or Name — Description	Avg	Ex-Fn	Mint
7J, G#102, gilded, OF	$100	$125	$150
7J, G#102, gilded, HC	125	150	185
11J, G#101 / G#51 / G#53, nickel or gilded, HC	125	150	185
13J, G#103, nickel, HC	125	150	185
15J, G#104 / G#55, GJS, nickel, D.S. dial, HC	150	175	200
16J, G#57, raised GJS, nickel, D.S. dial, OF/HC	150	200	225
16J, G#100, raised GJS, 2 tone, D.S. dial, (marked 16J.), OF	250	300	350
16J, G#100, raised GJS, 2 tone, D.S. dial, (marked 16J.), HC	200	250	275

Columbus Watch Co., 8-10 size, 13 jewels, 3/4 plate, stem wind, serial number 13,372. For price see 2nd page of Columbus W. Co. under Swiss, 3/4 plate (1874-1883).

New Columbus Watch Co. Example of a basic model for 6 size, 3/4 plate, 7-16 jewels, gilded and nickel.

4 SIZE

Grade or Name — Description	Avg	Ex-Fn	Mint
11J, nickel or gilded, OF/HC ★	$175	$225	$275
15J, nickel or gilded, OF/HC ★	200	250	300

🕐 Watches listed in this book are priced at the collectable retail level, as **complete** watches having an original 14k gold-filled case & *KEY WIND* with silver case, an original white enamel single sunk dial, and with the entire original movement in good working order with no repairs needed.

CORNELL WATCH CO.

Chicago, Illinois
1870 - 1874
San Francisco, California
1875 - 1876

The Cornell Watch Co. bought the Newark Watch Co. and greatly improved the movements being produced. In the fall of 1874, the company moved to San Francisco, Calif., with about 60 of its employees. The movements made in California were virtually the same as those made in Chicago. The company wanted to employ Chinese who would work cheaper, but the skilled employees refused to go along and went on strike. The company stayed alive until 1875 and was sold to the California Watch Co. in January 1876. But death came a few months later.

The Chronology of the Development of Cornell Watch Co.
Newark Watch Co. 1864-1870; S#s 6901-12,000.
Cornell Watch Co., Chicago, Ill. 1870-1874; S#s 12,001 to 25,000.
Cornell Watch Co., San Francisco, Calif. 1874-Jan. 1876; S# s 25,001 to 35,000.
California Watch Co., Jan. 1876-mid 1876.

Cornell Watch Co., J.C. Adams, 18 size, 11 jewels, key wind & set, made in Chicago, Ill, serial number 13,647.

Cornell Watch Co., 18 size, 15 jewels, key wind & set, marked "John Evans," serial number 16,868.

18 SIZE

Grade or Name — Description		Avg	Ex-Fn	Mint
J. C. Adams, 11J, KW	★	$400	$500	$650
C. T. Bowen, FULL, KW	★	350	450	600
C. M. Cady, 15J, SW	★	400	500	650
Cornell W. Co., 7J, San Francisco on mvt., KW	★	900	1,100	1,400
Cornell W. Co., 11J, KW	★	350	400	550
Cornell W. Co., 11J, San Francisco on mvt., KW	★	900	1,100	1,400
Cornell W. Co., 15J, KW	★	350	450	600
Cornell W. Co., 15J, San Francisco on mvt., KW	★	1,100	1,300	1,600

Grade or Name — Description	Avg	Ex-Fn	Mint
Cornell W. Co., 15J, San Francisco on mvt., SW .... ★★	$1,200	$1,400	$1,800
Paul Cornell, 19J, GJS, HCI5P, SW .... ★★★	1,500	1,900	2,500
John Evans, 15J, KW.. ★	350	450	600
Excelsior, 15J, FULL, KW, KS.............................. ★	350	400	550
H. N. Hibbard, 11J, KW, ADJ.............................★	400	500	650
C.L. Kidder, 7J, KWKS, OF ....★	350	400	500
George F. Root, 15J, KW ....★	550	700	900
George Waite, 7J, (Hyde Park), KW.................. ★★	400	550	650
E. J. Williams, 7J, KW ....★	350	450	600
Ladies Stemwind.............................★	150	200	300
Eugene Smith, 17J ....★	350	450	600

JACOB D. CUSTER

Norristown, Pennsylvania

1840 - 1845

At the age of 19, Jacob Custer repaired his father's watch. He was then asked to repair all the watches within his community. Custer was basically self-taught and had very little formal education and little training in clocks and watches. He made all the parts except the hairspring and fusee chains. The watches were about 14 size, and only 12 to 15 watches were made. The 14S fusee watches had lever escapement, 3/4 plate and were sold in his own gold cases. He made a few chronometers, one with a helical spring.

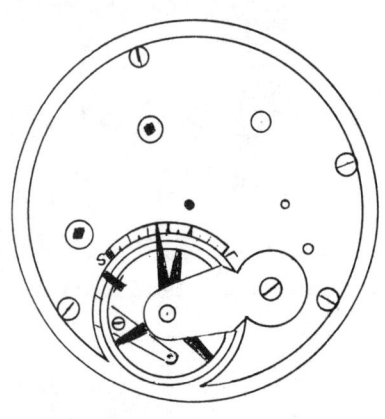

J.D. Custer, 14-16 size, engraved on movement "J.D. Custer, Norristown, Pa. Patented Feb. 4, 1843.

Description	Avg	Ex-Fn	Mint
14S, OF, engraved on mvt. *J. D. Custer, Patented Feb. 4, 1843*			
very RARE watch....................................... ★★★★★	$8,500	$12,000	$18,000

DUDLEY WATCH CO.
Lancaster, Pennsylvania
1920 - 1925

William Wallace Dudley became interested in watches and horology at the age of 13 and became an apprentice making ship chronometers in Canada. When he moved to America, he worked for the South Bend and Illinois Watch companies and the Trenton Watch Co. before going to Hamilton Watch Co. in Lancaster. He left Hamilton at age 69 to start his own watch company. In 1922 his first watches were produced; they were 14S, 19J, and used many Waltham Model 1894 – 1897, 14 size parts, including the train and escapement. The plates and winding mechanism were made at the Dudley plant. Dials and hands were made to Dudley's specifications in Switzerland. At first jewels were obtained from a manufacturer in Lancaster, but by 1925 they were Swiss supplied. The cases came from Wadsworth Keystone and the Star Watch Case Co. Dudley also made a 12S, 19J watch. By 1924, the company was heavily in debt, and on February 20, 1925, a petition for bankruptcy was filed. The Masonic Watch was his most unusual watch.

DUDLEY WATCHES			TOTAL PRODUCTION
Dudley Watch Co.	1920-1925	Model No.1 = S# 500—1,900	= 1,400
P. W. Baker Co.	1925-1935	Model No.2 = S# 2,001—4,800	= 1,800
XL Watch Co., N.Y.	1935-1976	Model No.3 = S# 4,801—6,500	= 1,500
		Total	4,800

Model No. 1, 14S, 19J, OF, can be distinguished by the "Holy Bible" engraved on the winding arbor plate, and a gilded pallet bridge matching the plates.

Model No. 2, 12S, 19J, used the 910 and 912 Hamilton wheels and escapement, has a flat silver-colored Bible.

Model No. 3, 12S, can be distinguished by the silver Bible which was riveted in place and was more three-dimensional. The 3rd wheel bridge was rounded off at one end.

 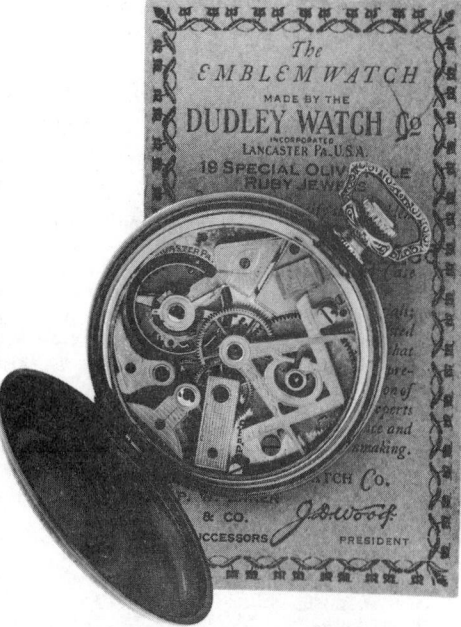

Dudley Watch Co., Model 1, 14 size, 19J., open face, Masonic form plates, flip back, serial # 1232, Ca. 1924.

Dudley Watch Co., Model 2, 14 size, 19J., open face, with original paper. The watch also came with a keystone shaped box, Ca 1927.

12 SIZE - 14 SIZE
"MASONS" MODEL

Grade or Name — Description	Avg	Ex-Fn	Mint
14S, Dudley, 19J, 14K, flip open back, Serial #1 (made 5 experimental models with Serial #1) .... ★	$5,000	$7,000	$10,000
14S, M#1, 19J, OF, 14K, flip open back .... ★	3,000	3,400	3,800
14S, M#1, 19J, OF, 14K, flip open back, w/box & papers .... ★	3,500	4,000	4,500
12S, M#2, 19J, OF, flip open back, GF .... ★	2,000	2,200	2,400
12S, M#2, 19J, OF, 14K, flip open back case .... ★	2,200	2,400	2,600
12S, M#2, 19J, OF, 14K display case .... ★	2,000	2,200	2,400
12S, M#3, 19J, OF, display case, GF .... ★	2,000	2,200	2,400
12S, M#3, 19J, OF, 14K flip open case .... ★	2,200	2,400	2,600

Dudley Watch Co., Model 2, 12 size, 19 jewels, open face, serial number 2,420.

Dudley Watch Co., Model 3, 12 size, 19 jewels, open face. NOTE: 3rd wheel bridge is rounded off at one end.

ELGIN WATCH CO.

(NATIONAL WATCH CO.)

Elgin, Illinois

1864 - 1964

This was the largest watch company in terms of production; in fact, Elgin produced half of the total number of pocket watches (dollar-type not included). Some of the organizers came from Waltham Watch Co., including P. S. Bartlett, D. G. Currier, Otis Hoyt, Charles H. Mason and others. The idea of beginning a large watch company for the mid-West was discussed by J. C. Adams, Bartlett and Blake. After a trip to Waltham, Adams went back to Chicago and approached Benjamin W. Raymond, a former mayor of Chicago, to put up the necessary capital to get the company started. Adams and Raymond succeeded in getting others to pledge their financial support also. The National Watch Co. (Elgin) was formed in August 1864. The factory site was in Elgin, Illinois, where the city had donated 35 acres of land. The factory was completed in 1866, & the 1st. movement was a B. W. Raymond, 18 size, full plate design.

Elgin Movements

	1st. App.	1st S#		1st. App.	1st. S#
18S B. W. Raymond	April 1867	101	10S Lady Elgin	Jan. 1869	40,001
18S H. Z. Culver	July 1867	1,001	10S Frances Rubie	Aug. 1870	50,001
18S J. T. Ryerson	Oct. 1867	5,001	10S Gail Borden	Sept. 1871	185,001
18S H. H. Taylor	Nov. 1867	25,001	10S Dexter Street	Dec. 1871	201,001
18S G. M. Wheeler	Nov. 1867	6,001	First Stem Wind	June 1873	
18S Matt Laflin	Jan. 1868	9,001	1st Nickel Movement	Aug.15, 1879	
18S Father Time	No date	2,300,001	Convertible	Fall 1878	
18S Veritas	No date	8,400,001			

The first watch a **B.W. Raymond** was sold April 1, 1867, selling for about $115.00, and was a 18 size, KW and quick train serial # 101. This **First** Pocket Watch, Serial No. 101, **was once again sold** for **$12,000.00** in 1988 at a SELL in NEW YORK. The first stem wind model was an H. Z. Culver with serial No. 155,001, lever set and quick train. In 1874, the name was changed to the Elgin National Watch Co., and they produced watches into the 1950s. The first **WRIST WATCH** made by Elgin was sold in 1910.

Some Serial Nos. have the first two numbers replace by a letter; i.e., 49,582,000 would be F 482,000.

X= 38 & 39	F= 49
C,E,T & Y= 42	S= 50
L= 43	R= 51
U= 44	P= 52
J= 45	K= 53
V= 46	I = 54
H= 47	
N= 48	

If the letters do not match the list above; the movement was produced after 1954.

ELGIN ESTIMATED SERIAL NUMBERS
AND PRODUCTION DATES

DATE – SERIAL #	DATE–SERIAL #	DATE–SERIAL #
1867 ––– 10,000	1897 – 7,000,000 Oct.28th	1927 – 30,050,000
1868 –– 25,001-Nov.20th	1898 – 7,494,001 May 14th	1928 – 31,599,001-Jan.11
1869 –– 40,001-May 20th	1899 – 8,000,000 Jan.18th	1929 – 32,000,000
1870 ––– 50,001-Aug.24th	1900 – 9,000,000 Nov.14th	1930 – 32,599,001-July
1871 – 185,001-Sep. 8th	1901 – 9,300,000	1931 – 33,000,000
1872 – 201,001-Dec.20th	1902 – 9,600,000	1932 – 33,700,000
1873 – 325,001	1903 – 10,000,000 May 15th	1933 – 34,558,001-July 24th
1874 – 400,001-Aug.28th	1904 – 11,000,000 April 4th	1934 – 35,000,000
1875 – 430,000	1905 – 12,000,000 Oct.6th	1935 – 35,650,000
1876 – 480,000	1906 – 12,500,000	1936 – 36,200,000
1877 – 520,000	1907 – 13,000,000 April 4th	1937 – 36,978,001-July 24th
1878 – 570,000	1908 – 13,500,000	1938 – 37,900,000
1879 – 625,001-Feb.8th	1909 – 14,000,000 Feb.9th	1939 – 38,200,000
1880 – 750,000	1910 – 15,000,000 April 2nd	1940 – 39,100,000
1881 – 900,000	1911 – 16,000,000 July 11th	1941 – 40,200,000
1882 – 1,000,000- March,9th	1912 – 17,000,000 Nov.6th	1942 – 41,100,000
1883 – 1,250,000	1913 – 17,339,001- Apr.14th	1943 – 42,200,000
1884 – 1,500,000	1914 – 18,000,000	1944 – 42,600,000
1885 – 1,855,001-May 28th	1915 – 18,587,001-Feb.11th	1945 – 43,200,000
1886 – 2,000,000- Aug. 4th	1916 – 19,000,000	1946 – 44,000,000
1887 – 2,500,000	1917 – 20,031,001-June 27th	1947 – 45,000,000
1888 – 3,000,000 June 20th	1918 – 21,000,000	1948 – 46,000,000
1889 – 3,500,000	1919 – 22,000,000	1949 – 47,000,000
1890 – 4,000,000 Aug.16th	1920 – 23,000,000	1950 – 48,000,000
1891 – 4,449,001-Mar.26th	1921 – 24,321,001-July 6th	1951 – 50,000,000
1892 – 4,600,000	1922 – 25,100,000	1952 – 52,000,000
1893 – 5,000,000 July 1st	1923 – 26,050,000	1953 – 53,500,000
1894 – 5,500,000	1924 – 27,000,000	1954 – 54,000,000
1895 – 6,000,000 Nov.26th	1925 – 28,421,001-July 14th	1955 – 54,500,000
1896 – 6,500,000	1926 – 29,100,000	1956 – 55,000,000

The above list is provided for determining the **APPROXIMATE** age of your watch. Match serial number with date. Watches were not necessarily **SOLD** and **DELIVERED** in the exact order of manufactured or production dates.

It required several months for raw material to emerge as a finished movement. All the while the factory is producing all sizes, models and grades. The numbering system was basically "consecutive", due to demand a batch of movements could be side tracked, thus allowing a different size and model to move ahead to meet this demand. Therefore, the dates some movements were __sold__ *and delivered to the trade, may not be "consecutive".*

Generic, nameless or unmarked grades for watch movements are listed under the Company name or initials of the Company, etc. by size, jewel count and description.

Some collectors seek out low serial numbers and will usually pay a premium for them. The lower the number, the more desirable the watch. The table shown below lists the first serial number of each size watch made by Elgin.

Size	1st Serial Nos.	Size	1st Serial Nos.
18	101	10	40,001
17	356,001	6	570,001
16	600,001	0	2,889,001
14	351,001		

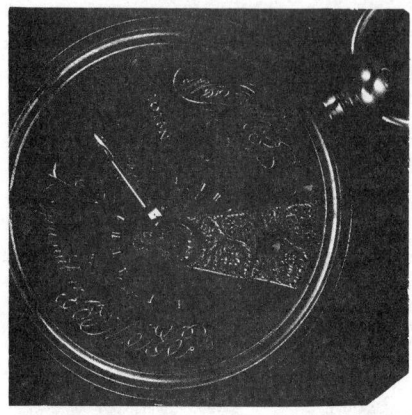

B.W. Raymond, 18 size, 15 jewels, model # 1, key wind & set, 1st. run in April of 1867, **serial number 101.**

Father Time, 18 size, 21 jewels, model #8 with wind indicator, free sprung model, serial number 22,888,020

18 SIZE

Grade or Name — Description	Avg	Ex-Fn	Mint
Advance, 11J, gilded, KW, HC, FULL	$95	$125	$150
Atlas Watch Co., 7J, HC, LS, FULL	95	125	150
California Watch, 15J, gilded, HC, KW, KS, FULL	175	200	250
Chief, 7J, gilded, KW, FULL, HC	95	125	150
Convertible, 7J, G#98	150	175	235
H. Z. Culver, 15J, gilded, KW, KS, FULL, HC, ADJ, low S#	225	275	350
H. Z. Culver, 15J, gilded, KW, KS, FULL, HC, ADJ	150	195	225
H. Z. Culver, 15J, KW, KS, **14K, HC**	725	800	900
H. Z. Culver, 15J, gilded, KW, KS, FULL, HC	150	175	225
H. Z. Culver, 15J, gilded, SW, FULL, HC	95	125	150
H. Z. Culver, 15J, gilded, KW, FULL, LS, HC	95	125	150

🕐 Generic, nameless or unmarked grades for watch movements are listed under the Company name or initials of the Company, etc. by size, jewel count and description.

Grade or Name — Description	Avg	Ex-Fn	Mint
Elgin W. Co., 7J, OF, SW	$75	$100	$125
Elgin W. Co., 7J, KW, gilded, HC	95	125	150
Elgin W. Co., 11J, KW, LS	75	100	125
Elgin W. Co., 11J, LS, SW, **HC, 9K-10K**	350	400	500
Elgin W. Co., 11J, LS, SW, HC, Silveroid	75	100	125
Elgin W. Co., 11J, LS, , SW, OF	75	100	125
Elgin W. Co., 13J, SW, PS/LS, Silveroid	75	100	125
Elgin W. Co., 13J, SW, PS/LS	75	100	125
Elgin W. Co., 15J, SW, LS, OF	85	110	135
Elgin W. Co., 15J, KW, LS, HC	125	150	165
Elgin W. Co., 15J, SW, LS, HC	125	150	165
Elgin W. Co., 15J, KW, **hidden key, COIN silver case**	150	185	225

🕐 Watches listed in this book are priced at the collectable retail level, as **complete** watches having an original 14k gold-filled case and *Key Wind* with silver, an original white enamel single sunk dial, and with the entire original movement in good working order with no repairs needed.

Elgin W. Co., engraved on movement California Watch, 18 size, 15 jewels, gilded, key wind & set, serial # 200,700.

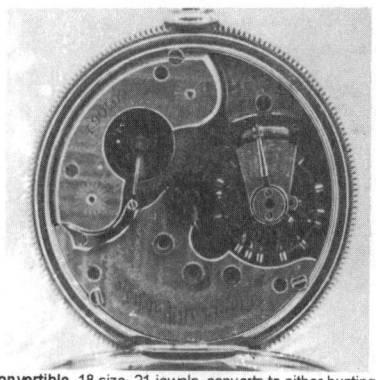

Convertible, 18 size, 21 jewels, converts to either hunting or open face.

Grade or Name — Description	Avg	Ex-Fn	Mint
Elgin W. Co., 15-17J, SW, LS, **box–hinge YGF, HC**	$275	$300	$385
Elgin W. Co., 15-17J, SW, LS, **box–hinge 14K, HC**	1,000	1,200	1,600
Elgin W. Co., 15-17, SW, LS, **Multi-color box YGF, HC**	450	550	650
Elgin W. Co., 15-17J, SW, **14K case, OF**	425	525	625
Elgin W. Co., 15-17J, SW, **14K case, HC**	600	700	900
Elgin W. Co., 15-17J, SW, **18K case, HC**	700	800	1,000
Elgin W. Co., 15-17J, SW, **Multi-color, 14K, HC**	1,800	2,200	2,800
Elgin W. Co., 15-17J, SW, LS, **COIN Silver** 6 oz, OF	200	250	295
Elgin W. Co., 15-17J, SW, LS, **COIN Silver"** , OF	100	150	200
Elgin W. Co., 17J, SW, LS, OF	95	125	150
Elgin W. Co., 17J, SW, LS or PS, HC	135	165	225
Elgin W. Co., 21J, SW, LS or PS, OF	225	250	275
Elgin W. Co., 21J, SW, LS, **box case, GF,OF**	325	350	400
Elgin W. Co., 21J, LS, **HC, 14K**	700	800	900
Elgin W. Co., 21J, SW, LS, Silveroid	225	250	275
Elgin W. Co., 21J, SW, LS, HC	325	350	400
Elgin W. Co., 21J, **Wind Indicator**	1,000	1,200	1,500
Elgin W. Co., 21J, **Wind Indicator, free sprung**	1,200	1,500	1,700
Elgin W. Co., 23J, SW, LS, OF	350	385	435
Elgin W. Co., 23J, SW, LS, HC ★	385	435	495

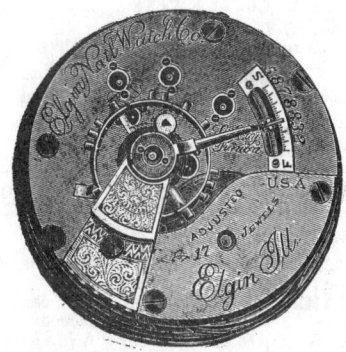

Example of the *nameless* or unmarked *grades* for watch movements which are listed under the Company **name or initials** of the Company, (Elgin W. Co.) etc. by size, jewel count & description.

⊕ Generic, nameless or unmarked grades for watch movements are listed under the Company name or initials of the Company, etc. by size, jewel count and description.

Pennsylvania Railroad Co. on dial. B.W. Raymond on movement. One of the first railroad watches commissioned by Penn. RR Co., 18 size, 15 jewels, key wind and set, serial number 123,245, CA. 1874.

Grade or Name — Description	Avg	Ex-Fn	Mint
Charles Fargo, 7J, gilded, KW, HC..	$175	$200	$225
J. V. Farwell, 11J, gilded, KW, HC .... ★	275	300	375
Father Time, 17J, NI, KW, FULL, HC .... ★	300	350	450
Father Time, 17J, NI, FULL, OF	125	150	200
Father Time, 17J, SW, OF, Silveroid.......................................	125	150	200
Father Time, 17J, SW, HC	150	200	225
Father Time, **20J**, NI, SW, FULL, HC .... ★	300	375	475
Father Time, 21J, NI, SW, FULL, GJS, OF	250	275	300
Father Time, 21J, NI, SW, 3/4, GJS, DMK, HC	325	375	425
Father Time, 21J, NI, SW, 3/4, GJS, OF	250	275	300
Father Time, 21J, GJT, ADJ.5P, Diamond end stone, OF	250	285	325
Father Time, 21J, NI, SW, 3/4, OF, GJS, **wind indicator**	1,250	1,450	1,750
Father Time, 21J, SW, 3/4, GJS, **wind indicator, HC**	1,650	1,850	2,100
Father Time, G#367, 21J, NI, SW, 3/4, OF, GJS, military style, **wind indicator**, free sprung, **602 sterling case**	1,450	1,650	1,950
Father Time, G#367, 21J, NI, SW, 3/4, OF, GJS, military style, **wind indicator**, free sprung, **35 size with gimbals & Box** ...	1,250	1,450	1,650
85 size, Model# 600, 14J, **free sprung,** helical hair spring, dent escapement , **wind indicator**, Gimbals & Box...	1,350	1,500	1,750
W. H. Ferry, 15J, gilded, KW, HC......................................	145	175	200
W. H. Ferry, 11J, gilded, KW, HC......................................	145	175	200
Mat Laflin, 7J, gilded, KW, HC	145	175	200
National W. Co., 7J, KW, KS..	95	125	150
National W. Co., 11J, KW, KS	95	125	150
National W. Co., 15J, KW, KS	100	135	165
M. D. Ogden, 15J, KW, HC	125	145	175
M. D. Ogden, 11J, gilded, KW, HC.....................................	125	145	175
Order of Railway Conductors, 17J, LS, OF ....★	195	225	275
Overland, 17J, NI, KW, HC..	175	200	225
Overland, 17J, NI, SW, HC...	125	150	200
Pennsylvania Railroad Co. on dial, B. W. Raymond on mvt., 15J, KW, KS (1st RR watches) ....★★★	950	1,200	1,500
Railway Timer, 15J, FULL, HC..★	350	400	525

IMPORTANT NOTE: Railroad Standards, Railroad Approved & Railroad Grade **terminology,** as defined and used in this *BOOK*.
1. **RAILROAD STANDARDS** = A commission or board appointed by the railroad companies outlined a set of **guidelines** to be accepted or approved by each railroad line.
2. **RAILROAD APPROVED** = A *LIST* of watches each railroad line would approve if purchased by their employee's. (this list changed through the years).
3. **RAILROAD GRADE** = A watch made by manufactures to met or exceed the guidelines set by the railroad **standards**. Grade such as 992, Vanguard and B.W. Raymond etc.
☉ Some GRADES **exceeded** the R.R. standards such as 23 jewels, diamond end stone, raised gold jewel settings, double sunk dial and the list goes on. Examples: such as Veritas, Sangamo, 950 & Riverside Maximus and many others.

B.W. Raymond, 18 size, 23 jewels, wind indicator. Note small winding indicator gear next to crown wheel.

H.H. Taylor, 18 size, 15 jewels, key wind & set, serial number 288,797.

Grade or Name — Description	Avg	Ex-Fn	Mint
B. W. Raymond, 15-17J, KW, low S# under 200	$650	$800	$1,000
B. W. Raymond, 15-17J, KW, low S# under 1000	350	425	550
B. W. Raymond, 15J, gilded, KW, FULL, HC	145	175	200
B. W. Raymond, 17J, gilded, KW, FULL, HC	145	175	200
B. W. Raymond, 15J, SW, HC	95	125	150
B. W. Raymond, 17J, all G#s, NI, FULL, OF	75	100	125
B. W. Raymond, 17J, Silveroid	75	95	125
B. W. Raymond, 17J, NI, FULL, HC	125	175	200
B. W. Raymond, 15J, **box case 14K**	900	1,200	1,400
B. W. Raymond, 17J, gilded, NI, SW, FULL, ADJ	95	125	150
B. W. Raymond, 19J, NI, 3/4, SW, OF, GJS, G#240, GT	200	225	250
B. W. Raymond, 19J, 3/4, GJS, **jeweled barrel, Wind Indicator**	800	900	1,000
B. W. Raymond, 19J, 3/4, GJS, GT, Diamond end stone	150	175	225
B. W. Raymond, 21J, 3/4, GJS, GT, Diamond end stone, OF	250	275	325
B. W. Raymond, 21J, SW, Silveroid	200	250	275
B. W. Raymond, 21J, SW, GJS, GT, Diamond end stone, HC	325	375	425
B. W. Raymond, 21J, NI, 3/4, SW, GJS, G#389 & 390, GT, OF	225	275	335
B. W. Raymond, 21J, NI, 3/4, SW, GJS, **Wind Indicator**, DMK	1,100	1,300	1,600
J. T. Ryerson, 7J, gilded, FULL, KW, HC	125	145	175
Solar W. Co., 15J, Multi-color dial	135	165	185
Standard, 17J, OF, LS	125	150	175
Sundial, 7J, SW, PS	75	95	125
H. H. Taylor, 15J, gilded, FULL, KW, HC	125	150	200
H. H. Taylor, 15J, NI, FULL, KW, HC, DMK	125	150	200
H. H. Taylor, 15J, NI, FULL, SW, HC, DMK, quick train	125	150	200
H. H. Taylor, 15J, SW, Silveroid	95	125	150
H. H. Taylor, 15J, SW, slow train	95	125	150

🕐 Some watch manufacturers personalize watches for jobbers or jewelry firms, with exclusive private signed or marked movements. The valuable collectable watches are listed under the signed or marked movement. Other exclusive private signed or marked movements will have equivalent value are only slightly higher value and should be compared to Generic or Nameless movements. Railroad signed or marked (dials & movements) are usually more collectable & higher in value.

🕐: Generic, nameless or unmarked grades for watch movements are listed under the Company name or initials of the Company, etc. by size, jewel count and description.

🕐 Some grades are not included. Their values can be determined by comparing with **similar** age, size, metal content, style, models and grades listed.

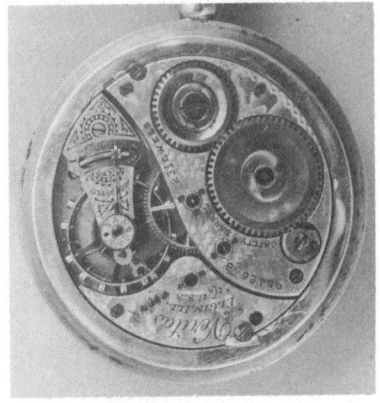

Veritas, 18 size, 23 jewels, solid gold train, gold jewel settings, diamond end stone, serial number 9,542,678.

G.M. Wheeler, Grade 369, 18 size, 17 jewels, open face, gold jewel settings, serial number 14,788,315

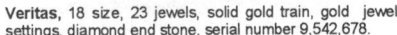

Grade or Name — Description	Avg	Ex-Fn	Mint
Veritas, 21J, 3/4, NI, GJS, DMK, GT, G#239, OF	$275	$300	$335
Veritas, 21J, 3/4, GJS, GT, Diamond end stones.	285	325	365
Veritas, 21J, SW, PS, GJS, GT, HC	350	400	450
Veritas, 21J, SW, LS, GJS, GT, HC	350	400	450
Veritas, 21J, 3/4, GJS, GT, Diamond end stones, G#274, HC	350	425	475
Veritas, 21J, 3/4, NI, GJS, **Wind Indicator**, DMK, G#239, OF	1,500	1,700	2,000
Veritas, 21J, 3/4, NI, GJS, **Wind Indicator**, DMK, G#274, HC . ★	2,200	2,500	3,000
Veritas, 23J, 3/4, NI, GJS, OF, DMK, GT	400	450	500
Veritas, 23J, 3/4, NI, GJS, OF, DMK, GT, Diamond end stone	400	465	525
Veritas, 23J, 3/4, **Wind Indicator**, GJS, DMK, GT, **OF, 14K**	1,900	2,100	2,500
Veritas, 23J, G#214, 3/4, NI, GJS, **Wind Indicator**, DMK, OF	1,500	1,600	1,700
Veritas, 23J, **G#214**, SW, OF	400	450	525
Veritas, 23J, 3/4, SW, NI, GJS, GT, LS, HC ★★	550	550	700
Veritas, 23J, SW, **OF, 14K**	725	800	950
The word **VERITAS** translated is "TRUTH".			
G. M. Wheeler, 11J, gilded, KW, HC	75	100	150
G. M. Wheeler, 13-15J, gilded, FULL, KW, SW	75	100	150
G. M. Wheeler, 15J, NI, FULL, KW, DMK, HC	100	125	175
G. M. Wheeler, 15J, SW, NI, FULL, DMK, OF	55	75	100
G. M. Wheeler, 17J, KW, NI, FULL, DMK, OF	100	125	175
G. M. Wheeler, 17J, SW, NI, DMK, OF	75	100	135
G. M. Wheeler, 17J, SW, NI, DMK, **Wind inicator** ★	700	800	950

MOVEMENTS WITH NO NAME

Grade or Name — Description	Avg	Ex-Fn	Mint
No. 5 & No. 17, 7J, gilded, FULL, HC	$75	$95	$125
No. 23 & No. 18, 11J, gilded, FULL, HC.	85	110	125
No. 69, 15J, M#1, KW, quick train, HC	95	125	150
No. 150, 21J, full plate, GJS, LS	200	225	260
No. 274, 21J., marked **274**, GT, Adj.5p, diamond end stone	225	250	325
No. 316, 15J, NI, FULL, HC, DMK	100	125	150
No. 317, 15J, NI, FULL, ADJ, OF, DMK	100	125	150

⊕: Generic, nameless or unmarked grades for watch movements are listed under the Company name or initials of the Company, etc. by size, jewel count and description.

⊕ Watches listed in this book are priced at the collectable retail level, as **complete** watches having an original 14k gold-filled case and *Key Wind* with silver, an original white enamel single sunk dial, and with the entire original movement in good working order with no repairs needed.

🕐 Generic, nameless or unmarked grades for watch movements are listed under the Company name or initials of the Company, etc. by size, jewel count and description.

Grade or Name — Description	Avg	Ex-Fn	Mint
No. 316 & No. 317, 15J, Silveroid	$75	$100	$125
No. 326, 15J, OF	85	100	125
No. 327, 15J, HC	100	125	150
No. 335, 17J, HC	95	125	150
No. 336, 17J, NI, FULL, OF, DMK	95	125	150
No. 345, 19J, GJS, 2-Tone, HC ★	600	700	900
No. 348, 21J, NI, FULL, GJS, DMK, HC	225	250	275
No. 349, 21J, , LS, MARKED LOANER, OF	225	250	300
No. 378, 19J, NI, FULL, HC, DMK	125	150	185
No. 379, 19J, OF	125	150	185

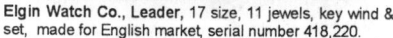

Elgin Watch Co., Leader, 17 size, 11 jewels, key wind & set, made for English market, serial number 418,220.

Elgin Watch Co., 17 size, 7 jewels, key wind & set, serial number 199,076. Made for Kennedy & Co.

17 SIZE

Grade or Name — Description	Avg	Ex-Fn	Mint
Avery, 7J, gilded, KW, FULL, HC	$85	$100	$150
Inter-Ocean, 7J, KWKS, HC	95	110	160
Leader, 7J, gilded, KW, FULL, HC	85	100	150
Leader, 11J, gilded, KW, FULL, HC,	85	100	150
Sunshine, 15J, KW, KS from back	100	125	175
The Age, 7J, gilded, KW, FULL, HC	125	175	225
M#11, 14, 15, 51, 59, 7J, gilded, KW, FULL, HC	100	125	175
17 Size, KW, Silveroid	85	95	135

16 SIZE

Grade or Name — Description	Avg	Ex-Fn	Mint
Blind Man's Watch, 9-17J, HC	$125	$150	$200
Convertible Model, 11J, BRG, OF	100	125	150
Convertible Model, 13J, BRG, OF	100	125	150
Convertible Model, 15J, BRG, ADJ, 14K, HC	600	650	725
Convertible Model, 15J, ADJ, DMK, GJS, 3F BRG, HC	175	200	250
Convertible Model, 15J, 3/4, ADJ, DMK, GJS	125	150	200

🕐 Some watch manufacturers personalize watches for jobbers or jewelry firms, with exclusive private signed or marked movements. The valuable collectable watches are listed under the signed or marked movement. Other exclusive private signed or marked movements will have equivalent value are only slightly higher value and should be compared to Generic or Nameless movements. Railroad signed or marked (dials & movements) are usually more collectable & higher in value.

Elgin Watch Co., 16 size, 21 jewels, converts to open face or hunting case, serial number 607,061.

Elgin W. Co., 16 size, 21 jewels, three-fingered bridge model, adjusted, gold jewel settings, gold train, serial number 6,469,814.

Grade or Name — Description	Avg	Ex-Fn	Mint
Convertible Model, 15J, Silveroid	$100	$125	$150
Convertible Model, 15J, 3F BRG, OF	125	150	175
Convertible Model, 21J, 3F BRG ★	900	1,100	1,450
Convertible Model, 21J, G#72, 3/4, ADJ, GJS, **14K** ★ ★	1,200	1,450	1,800
Convertible Model, 21J, G#91, 3F BRG, **14K** ★ ★	1,500	1,900	2,400
Doctors Watch, 15J, 4th Model, NI, GT, sweep second hand, **GF case**	300	350	425
Doctors Watch, 15J, 4th Model, gilded, sweep second hand, **coin silver case**	300	350	425
Doctors Watch, 15J, 4th Model, sweep second hand, **14K, OF**	650	725	900

Elgin Watch Co., 16 size, Multi- Color Gold hunting case, the locomotive has a diamond in the lantern, the case has white, yellow, rose flowers & green leaf designs, Ca.1880.

Doctors Watch, 16 size, 15 jewels, fourth model, gold jewel settings, gold train, sweep second hand, serial number 926,458.

🕐 Generic, nameless or unmarked grades for watch movements are listed under the Company name or initials of the Company, etc. by size, jewel count and description.

Grade or Name — Description	Avg	Ex-Fn	Mint
Elgin W. Co., 7-9J, OF	$75	$95	$125
Elgin W. Co., 7-9J, HC	100	125	150
Elgin W. Co., 11J, OF	85	100	125
Elgin W. Co., 11J, HC	100	135	165
Elgin W. Co., 13J, OF	85	100	125
Elgin W. Co., 13J, OF, Silveroid	85	100	125
Elgin W. Co., 13J, HC	100	125	150
Elgin W. Co., 15J, HC	100	150	175
Elgin W. Co., 15-16J, OF	95	125	150
Elgin W. Co., 15J, OF 14K case	285	325	400
Elgin W. Co., 15J, HC, 14K	450	550	600
Elgin W. Co., 15J, multi-color gold +diamond, HC, 14K	2,500	3,000	3,500
Elgin W. Co., 17J, OF	95	125	150
Elgin W. Co., 17J, LS, multi-color HC, YGF	250	300	400
Elgin W. Co., 17J, multi-color HC, 14K	1,000	1,200	1,600
Elgin W. Co., 17J, 14K, HC	450	550	600
Elgin W. Co., 17J, G#280, 9th model, ADJ5P	125	150	185
Elgin W. Co., 17J, HC	125	165	195
Elgin W. Co., 19J, OF, LS	125	150	175
Elgin W. Co., 21J, HC	300	350	375
Elgin W. Co., 21J, OF, Silveroid	195	225	250
Elgin W. Co., 21J, OF	225	250	295
Elgin W. Co., 23J, OF	325	375	450
3F Bridge Model, 15J, NI, DMK	75	125	150
3F Bridge Model, 17J, Adj.3P, NI, DMK, GJS	100	125	150
3F Bridge Model, 17J, Adj.5P, NI, DMK, GJS, GT	125	150	195
3F Bridge Model, 21J, Adj.5P, NI, DMK, GJS, GT	300	325	375
Father Time, 17J, 3/4, NI, OF, GJS, DR, DMK	125	150	200
Father Time, 21J, 3/4, NI, HC, GJS, DR, DMK, ADJ.5P	225	250	300
Father Time, 21J, 3/4, NI, OF, GJS, DR, Wind Indicator	750	850	950
Father Time, 21J, 3/4, NI, GJS, DR, pendent set, ADJ.5P, OF ... ★	250	300	375
Father Time, 21J, NI, GJS, DR, ADJ.5P, GT, OF	225	250	300
Lord Elgin, 21J, GJS, DR, Adj.5P, 3F BRG, 14K, OF .... ★★	1,450	1,750	2,250
Lord Elgin, 23J, GJS, DR, Adj.5P, 3/4, 14K, OF .... ★★	1,500	1,800	2,300
Lord Elgin, 23J, GJS, DR, Adj.5P, 3/4, Gold filled OF	850	950	1,200

ELGIN W. Co., CHRONOGRAPH, 16 size, 16 jewels, model # 4, lever set.

Father Time, 16 size, 21 jewels, gold train; Note model 19 up and down wind indicator movement does not show the differential wheel as does the 18 size, S# 18,106,465.

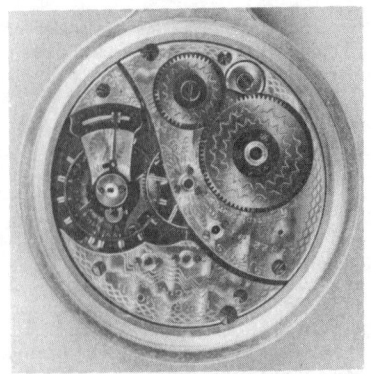

Lord Elgin, 16 size, 21 jewels, gold train, raised gold jewel settings, 3 finger bridge, serial number 10,249,819.

B.W. Raymond, 16 size, 19 jewels, gold jewel settings, Grade 350, serial number 17,822,991.

Grade or Name — Description	Avg	Ex-Fn	Mint
B. W. Raymond, 17J, 3/4, GJS, **14K, OF**	$500	$550	$650
B. W. Raymond, 17J, 3/4, GJS, SW, HC	225	275	350
B. W. Raymond, 17J, 3F BRG ★ ★	400	500	650
B. W. Raymond, 17J, LS, NI, **Wind Indicator** ★	600	650	700
B. W. Raymond, 17J, GJS, SW, ALL G#s, OF	175	200	250
B. W. Raymond, 17J, 3/4, GJS, DR, Adj.5P, DMK	195	225	275
B. W. Raymond, 19J, 3/4, GJS, DR, Adj.5P, DMK, OF	175	225	250
B. W. Raymond, 19J, (Elgin The Railroader on dial) Adj.5P, OF...	200	235	275
B. W. Raymond, 19J, OF, **14K, 30 DWT**	500	550	600
B. W. Raymond, 19J, 3/4, GJS, DR, HCI5P, DMK, **Wind Indicator**	675	725	800
B. W. Raymond, 19J, M#8, G# 372, 455, Adj.5P, OF	175	200	255
B. W. Raymond, 19J, GJS, G#371, 401,Adj.5P, HC	200	250	295
B. W. Raymond, 21J, **14K, OF**	525	575	650
B. W. Raymond, 21J, G#389, 390, 391, 472, 478, 506, G#571, 581, 590, 3/4, Adj.5P, OF	250	275	300
B. W. Raymond, 21J, 3/4, GJS, DR, Adj.5P, HC	300	325	385
B. W. Raymond, 21J, 3/4, GJS, DR, Adj.5P, DMK, OF	225	250	295
B. W. Raymond, 21J, 3/4, GJS, DR, Adj.5P, DMK,**Wind Indicator**	725	825	950
B. W. Raymond, 21J, 3/4, GJS, DR, **Adj.6P**, DMK,**Wind Indicator**	735	835	975
B. W. Raymond, 22J, WWII Model, sweep second hand	275	295	325
B. W. Raymond, 23J, 3/4, GJS, DR, Adj.5P, G#376, 494, 540	375	425	485
B. W. Raymond, 23J, 3/4, GJS, DR, Adj.5P, DMK, **Wind Indicator**	775	825	975
B. W. Raymond, 23J, 3/4, GJS, DR, **Adj.6P**, DMK, **Wind Indicator**	800	875	1,100
B. W. Raymond, 23J, 3/4, GJS, DR, Adj.5P, DMK,**Wind Indicator** military style	725	775	850

14K White or Green
Gold Filled
Specially Designed
Screw Case

Price $35.30

12K-Gold Filled
Specially Designed
Screw Case

Price $31.65

10K-Gold Filled
Specially Designed
Screw Case

Price $31.65

Winding Indicator $3.50 extra

AD
Oct. 15th 1926

B. W. Raymond Movement
16 Size
21 Jewels
8 Adjustments, 5 of them position
Supplied with Montgomery Dial if desired

Veritas, 16 size, 23 jewels, solid gold train, gold jeweled settings, S# 16,678,681. (Veritas translated "Truth")

Elgin Watch Co., LORD ELGIN, Grade 351, 16 size, 23 jewels, gold train, gold jewel settings, serial number 12,718,340 (1st run).

Grade or Name — Description	Avg	Ex-Fn	Mint
Veritas, 19J, G# 401, GJS, Adj.5P., HC ....★	$325	$400	$475
Veritas, 21J, GJS, DR, Adj.5P, DMK, 3/4, **Wind Indicator**	800	900	1,000
Veritas, 21J, 3F brg, GJS, G#360.................................★	375	400	475
Veritas, 21J, GJS, DR, Adj.5P, DMK, 3/4, G#401, HC.................	325	400	475
Veritas, 21J, GJS, SW, Grade 360 ....★	375	400	475
Veritas, 21J, GJS, SW, Adj.5P, OF, Grade 270 & 375	250	300	365
Veritas, 23J, GJS, Adj.5P, **14K, OF**	600	675	800
Veritas, 23J, GJS, Adj.5P, **HC**	500	550	650
Veritas, 23J, GJS, DR, Adj.5P, 3/4, G# 375- 376- 453, OF...........	425	475	575
Veritas, 23J, GJS, DR, Adj.5P, DMK, 3/4, Diamond end stone, Grade 350 ....★	425	475	575
Veritas, 23J, GJS, DR, Adj.5P, Grade 453 & 376 DMK, 3/4, **Wind Indicator**	1,000	1,200	1,500
G. M. Wheeler, 17J, DR, Adj.3P, DMK, 3/4...........................	95	125	150
G. M. Wheeler, 17J, 3F BRG	95	125	150
G. M. Wheeler, 17J, **HC, 14K**	450	475	525
WWII Model, 17J, OF..	125	150	175
WWII Model, 21J, OF..	200	225	275
M#13, 9J, HC...	85	100	150
M#48, 13J, HC...	85	100	150

(Add $50 to $75 to hunting case models listed as open face)

MODELS WITH NO NAMES

Grade or Name — Description	Avg	Ex-Fn	Mint
Grade #72, 21J, ADJ, 3/4, HC.................................★	$450	$600	$800
Grade #91, 21J, 3F BRG ....★★	450	550	700
Grade #145, 19J, GJS, BRG, HC ....★★	650	750	900
Grade #155, 17J, GT, GJS, HC...................................	100	120	150
Grade #156, 21J, 3/4, NI, DR, DMK, GT, GJS, HC ....★	375	425	500
Grade #156, 21J, 3/4, NI, DR, DMK, GT, GJS, HC, **14K** ....★	550	600	700
Grade #162, 21J, SW, PS, NI, GJS, GT, OF ....★	300	365	425
Grade #270, 21J, 3F BRG, GJS, marked mvt.	275	325	375
Grade #280, 17J, marked on mvt.	125	150	200
Grade #290 & #291, 7J, 3/4, NI, DMK, OF	75	95	125

🕀 Generic, nameless or unmarked grades for watch movements are listed under the Company name or initials of the Company, etc. by size, jewel count and description.

🕀 Watches listed in this book are priced at the collectable retail level, as complete watches having an original 14k gold-filled case and Key Wind with silver, an original white enamel single sunk dial, and with the entire original movement in good working order with no repairs needed.

Grade or Name — Description	Avg	Ex-Fn	Mint
Grade #291, 7J, 3/4, HC, **14K**	$400	$450	$550
Grade #312 & #313, 15J, 3/4, NI, DR, DMK, OF	75	95	125
Grade # 340, 17J, 3 finger bridge, OF	95	100	150
Grade #372, 19J, M#15, LS, OF, Adj.5P	250	300	375
Grade #374, 21J, M#15, LS, OF, Adj.5P	275	325	400
Grade #381 & #382, 17J, 3/4, NI, DR, DMK, OF	85	125	135
Grade #571, 21J, Adj.5P, OF	200	225	265
Grade #540, 23J, Adj.5P, OF	200	250	310
Grade #572, 19J, Adj.5P, OF	135	150	195
Grade #573, 17J, Adj.5P, OF	90	110	125
Grade #575, 15J, Adj.3P, OF	75	90	110
Grade #581, 21J, Adj.5P, center sec, hacking, Army, OF	135	175	225

14 SIZE

Grade or Name — Description	Avg	Ex-Fn	Mint
Lord Elgin, 17J, SS, OF	$225	$250	$300
7J, M#1, gilded, KW, **14K, HC**	300	350	400
7J, M#1, gilded, KW, YGF, HC	95	125	150
11J, M#1, gilded, KW, YGF, HC	95	125	150
11J, M#1, gilded, KW, YGF, OF	60	85	100
13J, M#1, gilded, KW, OF	60	85	100
15J, M#1, gilded, KW, OF	60	85	100
7J, M#2, SW, OF	60	85	100
15J, M#2, SW, OF	60	85	100
15J, M#2, SW, **14K, HC**	275	325	375
15J, M#1, grade # 46, KW, 3/4, HC	95	125	150

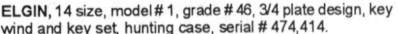

ELGIN, 14 size, model # 1, grade # 46, 3/4 plate design, key wind and key set, hunting case, serial # 474,414.

ELGIN EIGHT DAY, 12 size, 21 jewels, wind indicator, bridge movement, open face, serial number 12,345,678.

12 SIZE

Grade or Name — Description	Avg	Ex -Fn	Mint
Eight Day, 21J, 8-Day Wind Indicator, BRG .... ★★★★★	$2,500	$3,000	$3,500

ELGIN W. Co., dial signed "U.S. Calendar Watch Co.", 12 size, hand for date of month & day of week.   ELGIN W. Co., 12 size with Masonic dial, Ca. 1930.

🕑 Generic, nameless or unmarked grades for watch movements are listed under the Company name or initials of the Company, etc. by size, jewel count and description.

Grade or Name — Description	Avg	Ex-Fn	Mint
Elgin W. Co. #30, 7J, gilded, KW, OF	$65	$75	$120
Elgin W. Co. #189, 19J, HC	85	100	150
Elgin W. Co. #190-194, 23J, GJS, Adj.5P, NI, DMK, GT, OF	150	175	200
Elgin W. Co. #190-194, 23J, GJS, Adj.5P, NI, DMK, GT, HC	175	200	250
Elgin W. Co. #236 & #237, 21J, GJS, Adj.5P, NI, DMK, GT, OF	100	125	175
Elgin W. Co. #236 & #237, 21J, GJS, Adj.5P, NI, DMK, GT, HC.	125	150	200
Elgin W. Co. #301 & #302, 7J, HC	75	85	125
Elgin W. Co. #314 & #315, 15J, HC	100	125	175
Elgin W. Co. #383 & #384, 17J, HC	75	85	125
Elgin W. Co., 7-15J, **14K, Multi-color**	500	600	750
Elgin W. Co., 7-15J, OF, GF	65	75	120
Elgin W. Co., 7-15J, **HC, 14K**	300	350	425
Elgin W. Co., 17J, OF, GF	85	100	125
Elgin W. Co., 17J, **OF, 14K**	275	300	350
Elgin W. Co., 19J, OF, gold filled	100	130	165
Elgin W. Co., 19J, HC, gold filled	110	150	175
Elgin W. Co., 19J, **HC, 14K**	325	375	450
Elgin W. Co., 19J, **14K, OF**	275	300	350
Elgin W. Co., 21J, OF, gold filled	110	135	175
12 size Model 2 & 3 spread to 16 size			
Elgin W. Co., 15-17J, Model 2 **spread to 16 size**, OF	$65	$75	$120
Elgin W. Co., 15-17J, Model 2 **spread to 16 size**, HC	100	125	165
Elgin W. Co., 19-21J, Model 2 **spread to 16 size**, OF	100	135	175
Elgin W. Co., 19-21J, Model 3 **spread to 16 size**, HC	125	150	225
12 SIZE (continued)			
Elete, 17J, GJS, Adj,4P, OF	$55	$65	$85
C. H. Hulburd, 19J, thin BRG model (12 /14 size) **18K case** ...... ★	800	1,000	1,200
C. H. Hulburd, 19J, thin BRG model (12 /14 size) **Platinum** .... ★	1,000	1,200	1,400
Lord Elgin, 23J, GJS, DR, Adj.5P, DMK, NI, HC	225	250	325
Lord Elgin, 17J,	95	125	150
Lord Elgin, 19J, HC	125	150	185
Lord Elgin, 21J, **14K, OF**	275	300	375
Lord Elgin, 21J, HC	200	225	275
Masonic dial, 15-17J, OF	175	195	225

🕑 Watches listed in this book are priced at the collectable retail level, as **complete** watches having an original 14k gold-filled case and *Key Wind* with silver, an original white enamel single sunk dial, and with the entire original movement in good working order with no repairs needed.

Lord Elgin, 12 size, 23 jewels, gold jewel settings, Adj.5p, originally sold for $110.00.

G.M. Wheeler, 12 size, 17 jewels, Adj3p, originally sold for $27.00.

Grade or Name — Description	Avg	Ex-Fn	Mint
Pierce Arrow, 17J, OF	$150	$175	$200
B. W. Raymond, 19J, GJS, Adj.5P, DR, DMK, NI, OF	125	135	175
B. W. Raymond, 19J, GJS, Adj.5P, DR, DMK, NI, HC	135	155	195
G. M. Wheeler, 17J, DR, Adj.5P, DMK, NI, OF	60	75	95
G. M. Wheeler, 17J, DR, Adj.5P, DMK, NI, HC	90	110	125
193, 19J, DR, GJS, Adj.5P, DMK, NI, OF	185	200	250

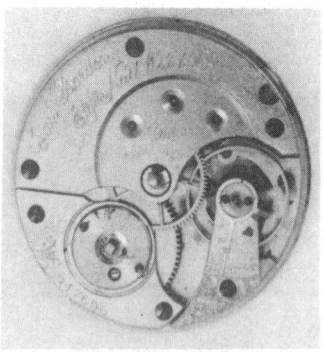

Frances Rubie, Grade 23, 10 size, 15 jewels, key wind & set.

Gail Borden, Grade 22, 10 size, 11 jewels, key wind & set, serial number 947,696.

10 SIZE
(HC)

Grade or Name — Description	Avg	Ex-Fn	Mint
Dexter St., 7J, KW, HC, **14K**	$200	$275	$325
Dexter St., 7J, KW, HC, **18K**	250	325	375
Dexter St., 7J, gilded, KW, HC, gold filled	75	100	125
Frances Rubie, 15J, gilded, KW, HC, **14K** ★	550	600	700
Frances Rubie, 15J, KW, HC, **18K** ★ ★	600	650	750

🕐 Watches listed in this book are priced at the collectable retail level, as **complete** watches having an original 14k gold-filled case and *Key Wind* with silver, an original white enamel single sunk dial, and with the entire original movement in good working order with no repairs needed.

Grade or Name — Description	Avg	Ex-Fn	Mint
Gail Borden, 11J, gilded, KW, HC, **14K**	$225	$300	$350
Gail Borden, 11J, KW, HC, gold filled	75	100	125
Gail Borden, 11J, KW, HC, **18K**	270	325	400
Lady Elgin, 15J, gilded, KW, HC, **14K**	225	275	350
Lady Elgin, 15J, KW, HC, **18K**	275	325	400
Grade # 21 or 28, 7J, gilded, KW, HC, gold filled	75	100	125
Elgin, **multi-color case, gold filled**, HC	200	225	275
Elgin, 15J, Silveroid, HC	50	75	95
Elgin, 15J, YGF, HC	75	100	125

Elgin W. Co., Grade 121, 6 size, 15 jewels, hunting, serial number 4,500,445.

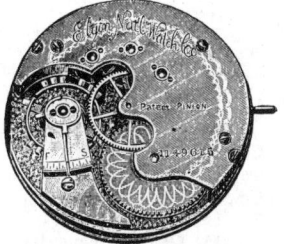

Elgin W. Co., Grade 67, 6 size, 11 jewels, serial number 1,149,615.

6 SIZE
(HC Only)

Grade or Name — Description	Avg	Ex-Fn	Mint
Atlas, 7J, HC	$75	$95	$135
Elgin W. Co. #286, 7J, HC, DMK, NI	75	100	135
Elgin W. Co. #295, 15J, HC, DMK, NI	75	100	135
Elgin W. Co. #168, 16J, HC	100	125	150
Elgin W. Co., 7J, HC, **14K**	200	225	300
Elgin W. Co., 11J, HC, **14K**	200	225	300
Elgin W. Co., 15J, YGF, HC	75	100	135
Elgin W. Co., 15J, YGF demi-HC	95	100	150
Elgin W. Co., 15J, HC, **YGF** multi-color case	200	225	275
Elgin W. Co., 15J, HC, **10K**	175	200	235
Elgin W. Co., 15J, HC, **14K**	225	250	335
Elgin W. Co., 15J, **14K, Multi-color HC**	450	500	650
Elgin W. Co., 15J, HC, **18K**	300	350	435
Elgin W. Co., 15J, SW, HC, **Enamel case, 18K**	800	1,000	1,300

🕐: Generic, nameless or unmarked grades for watch movements are listed under the Company name or initials of the Company, etc. by size, jewel count and description.

Elgin W. Co., 6 size, 15 jewels

Elgin W. Co., Grade 201-HC, 205-OF, 0 size, 19 jewels, gold train.

Elgin W. Co., Grade 200-HC, 204-OF, 0 size, 17 jewels, gold jewel settings.

0 SIZE

Grade or Name — Description	Avg	Ex-Fn	Mint
Atlas W. Co., 7J, HC	$100	$135	$175
Elgin W. Co., 7J, NI, DR, DMK, OF	55	70	90
Elgin W. Co., 15J, NI, DR, DMK, OF	70	80	125
Elgin W. Co., 15J, NI, DR, DMK, HC	100	135	175
Elgin W. Co., 17J, NI, DR, DMK, ADJ, OF	75	90	140
Elgin W. Co., 19J, NI, DR, DMK, GJS, ADJ, OF	55	75	95
Elgin W. Co., 15J, OF, **14K**	155	175	225
Elgin W. Co., 15J, HC, **14K**	200	225	300
Elgin W. Co., 15J, HC, multi-color **GF**	175	200	250
Elgin W. Co., 15J, OF, multi-color **dial**	100	135	175
Elgin W. Co., 15J, HC, **10K**	150	175	225
Elgin W. Co., 15J, **14K**, Multi-color case	400	450	525
Elgin W. Co., 15J, **14K**, Multi-color case +diamond	500	550	625
Frances Rubie, 19J, HC ★	200	225	300

Lady Elgin, 5/0 size, 17 jewels, gold jewel settings, originally sold for $42.50.

Lady Raymond, 5/0 size, 15 jewels, originally sold for $24.20.

3/0 and 5/0 SIZE
(HC ONLY)

Grade or Name — Description	Avg	Ex-Fn	Mint
Lady Elgin, 15J, PS, HC	$75	$100	$150
Lady Elgin, 15J, 14K, HC	200	225	275
Lady Raymond, 15J, PS, HC	75	100	150
Elgin W. Co., 7J, HC	75	100	150

🕐: Generic, nameless or unmarked grades for watch movements are listed under the Company name or initials of the Company, etc. by size, jewel count and description.

STYLE NO. 40
gold filled : $90 - $100 - $120

STYLE NO. 39
gold filled : $95- $110 - $120

STYLE NO. 38
gold filled : $95- $110 - $120

STYLE NO. 19
gold filled : $90 - $100 - $125

STYLE NO. 18
CHROME: $25 - $35 - $45

STYLE NO. 25
gold filled : $95- $110 - $130

STYLE NO. 26
gold filled : $90 - $100 - $120

ANTIQUE BOW
gold filled : $95- $110 - $130

RIGID BOW
gold filled : $100- $125 - $140

GOLD FILLED CASES = 40, 39, 38, 19, 25, 26, and some came with a **solid gold** bow.
CHROME CASES = 18   and   ANTIQUE BOW & RIGID BOW= 20 year gold filled case

🕐 NOTE: Factory Advertised as a **complete** watch and was fitted with a certain matched, timed and rated movement and sold in the factory designed case style as a **complete** watch. The factory also sold <u>uncased</u> movements to **JOBBERS** such as Jewelry stores & they cased the movement in a case styles the **CUSTOMER requested.** All the factory advertised **complete** watches came with a enamel dial **SHOWN or CHOICE** of other **Railroad** dials.

ELGIN NATIONAL WATCH CO.
IDENTIFICATION OF MOVEMENTS
BY MODEL NUMBER

How to Identify Your Watch: Compare the movement of your watch with the illustrations in this section. Upon matching the movement exactly, the model number and size can be determined. While comparing, note the location of the balance, jewels, screws, gears and type of back plate (Full, ¾, Bridge) which will be clues in identifying the movement you have. Having determined the size and model number, you can now find your watch in the main price listing by name or number (which is engraved on the movement).

Model 1, 18 size, full plate, hunting, key wind & set, first serial number 101, Apr., 1867.

Model 2-4, 18 size, full plate, hunting, lever set, first serial number 155,001, June, 1873.

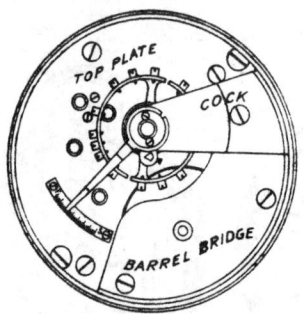

Model 5, 18 size, full plate, open face, pendant set, first serial number, 2,110,001, Grade 43, Dec., 1885.

Model 6, 18 size, three-quarter plate, hunting, open face, pendant set.

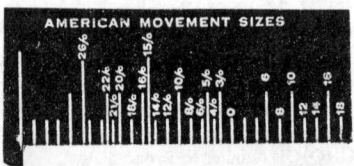

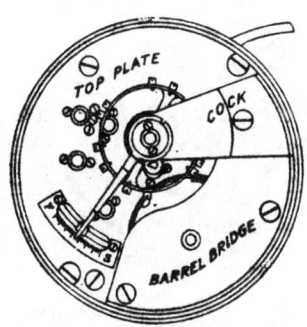

Model 7, 18 size, full plate, open face, lever set, first serial number 6,563,821, Grade 265, Apr., 1897.

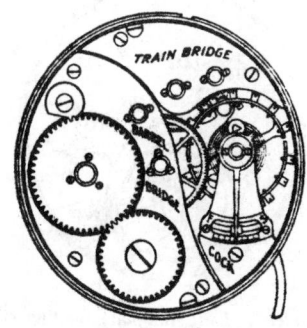

Model 8, 18 size, three-quarter plate, open face, lever set, first serial number 8,400,001, Grade 214, Dec., 1900.

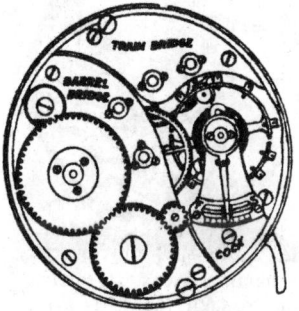

Model 8, 18 size, three-quarter plate, open face, lever set with winding indicator.

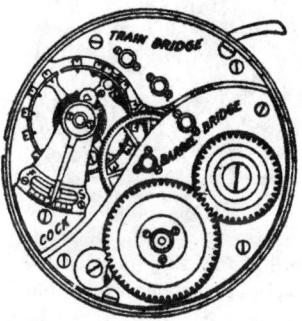

Model 9, 18 size, three-quarter plate, hunting, lever set, first serial number 9,625,001, Grade 274, May, 1904.

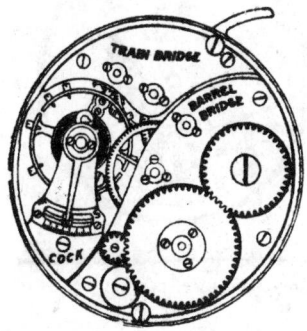

Model 9, 18 size, three-quarter plate, hunting, lever set with winding indicator.

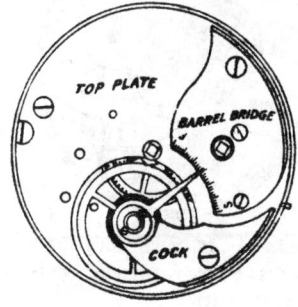

Model 1, 17 size, full plate, hunting, key wind and set.

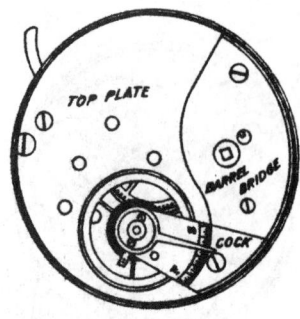

Model 2, 17 size, full plate, hunting, lever set.

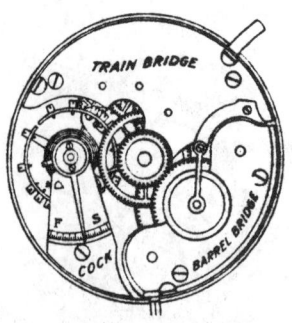

Model 1, 16 size, three-quarter plate, hunting & open face, lever set.

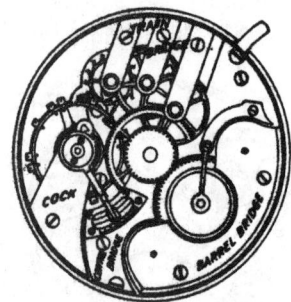

Model 2, 16 size, three-quarter plate, bridge, hunting & open face, lever set.

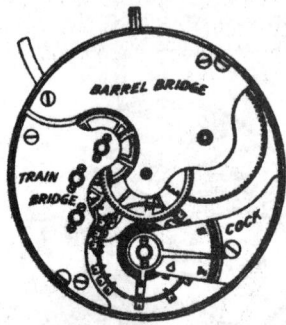

Model 3, 16 size, three-quarter plate, hunting, lever set, first serial number 625,001, Grade 1, Feb., 1879.

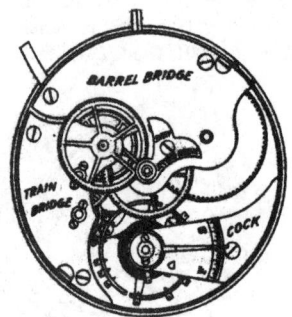

Model 4, 16 size, three-quarter plate, sweep second, hunting & open face, lever set.

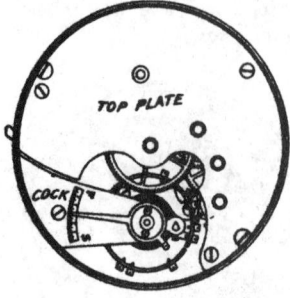

Model 5, 16 size, three-quarter plate, open face, pendant set.

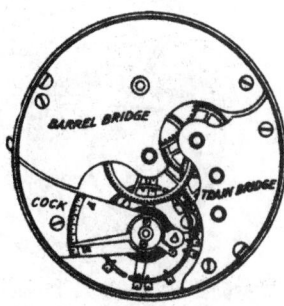

Model 5, 16 size, three-quarter plate, open face, pendant set, first serial number 2,811,001, Grade 105, Oct., 1887.

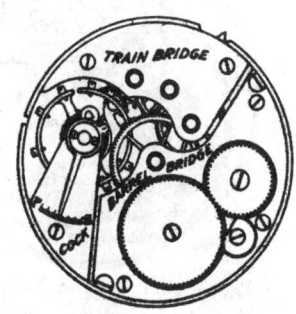

Model 6, 16 size, three-quarter plate, hunting, pendant set, first serial number 6,458,001, Grade 151, Aug., 1895.

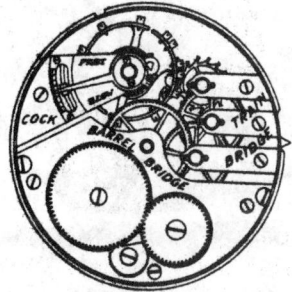

Model 6, 16 size, three-quarter plate, bridge, hunting, pendant set, first serial number 6,463,001, Grade 156, May, 1896.

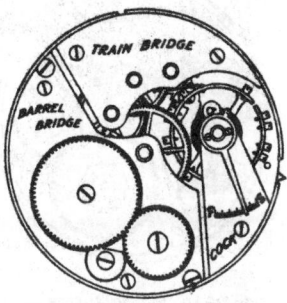

Model 7, 16 size, three-quarter plate, open face, pendant set, first serial number 6,464,001. Grade 157, Sept., 1895.

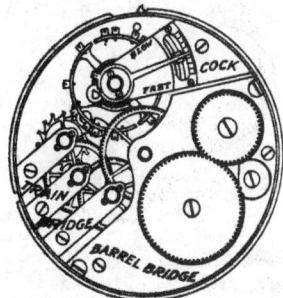

Model 7, 16 size, three-quarter plate, bridge, open face, pendant set, first serial number 6,469,001, Grade 162, Apr., 1896.

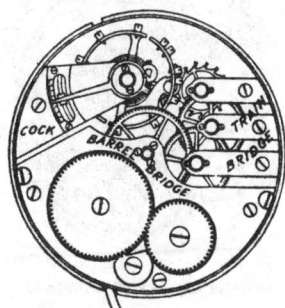

Model 8, 16 size, three-quarter plate, bridge, hunting, lever set, serial number 12,283,001, Grade 341, Jan., 1907.

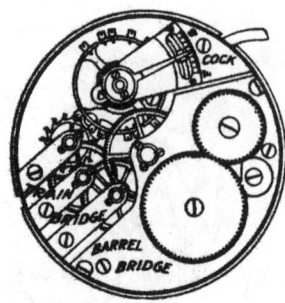

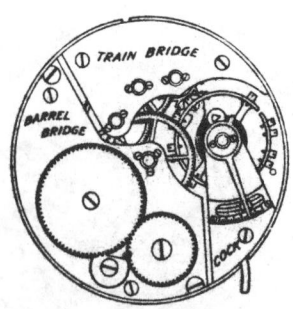

Model 9, 16 size, three-quarter plate, bridge, open face, lever set, first serial number 9,250,001, Grade 270, July, 1902.

Model 13, 16 size, three-quarter plate, open face, lever set, first serial number 12,717,001, Grade 350, June, 1908.

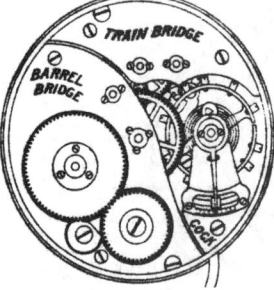

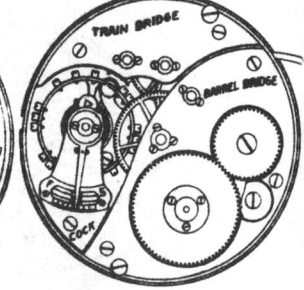

Model 14, 16 size, three-quarter plate, hunting, lever set.

Model 15, 16 size, three-quarter plate, open face, lever set.

Model 17, 16 size, three-quarter plate, hunting, lever set.

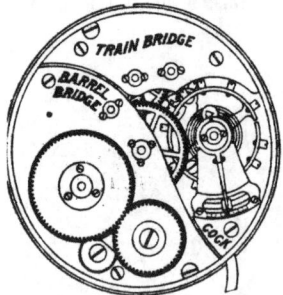

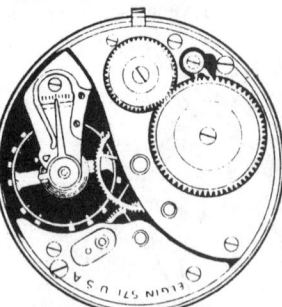

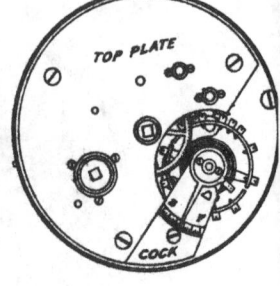

Model 19, 16 size, three-quarter plate, open face, lever set with winding indicator.

Model 20, 16 size, three-quarter plate, open face, Grades 571, 572, 573, 574, 575, 616.

Model 1, 14 size, three-quarter plate, hunting, key wind and set.

Model 2, 14 size, three-quarter plate, open face, pendant set.

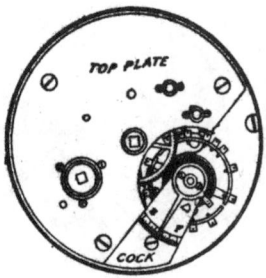

Model 1, 12 size, three-quarter plate, hunting, key wind and set.

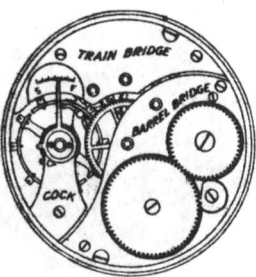

Model 2, 12 size, three-quarter plate, hunting, pendant set, first serial #7,410,001, Grade 188, Dec., 1897.

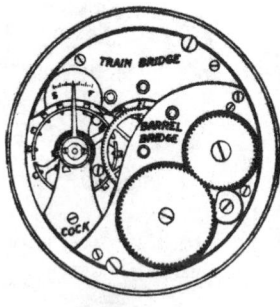

Model 2, 12 size, three-quarter plate, spread to 16 size, hunting, pendant set.

Model 3, 12 size, three-quarter plate, open face, pendant set, serial number 7,423,001, Grade 192, May 1898.

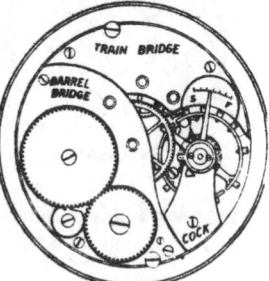

Model 3, 12 size, three-quarter plate, spread to 16 size, open face, pendant set.

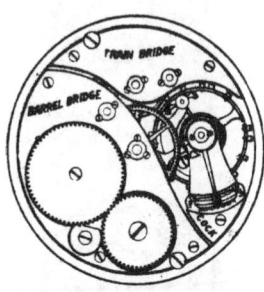

Model 4, 12 size, three-quarter plate, open face, pendant set, serial number 16,311,001, Grade 392, July, 1912.

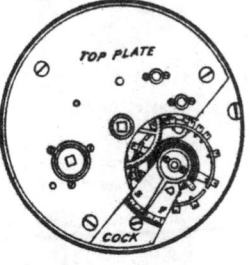

Model 1, 10 size, three-quarter plate, style 1, hunting, key wind and set.

Model 2, 10 size, three-quarter plate, hunting, key wind and set.

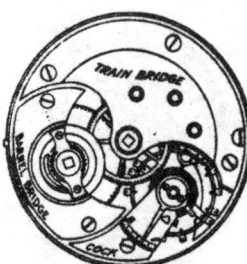

Model 3, 10 size, three-quarter plate, hunting.

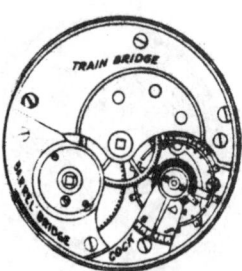

Model 4, 10 size, three-quarter plate, hunting.

Model 5 & 6, 10 size, three-quarter plate.

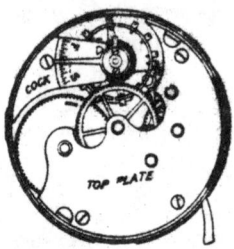

Model 1, 6 size, three-quarter plate, hunting.

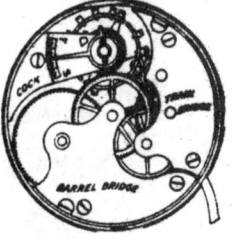

Model 1, 6 size, three-quarter plate, hunting.

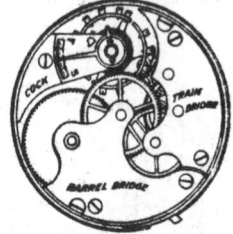

Model 2, 6 size, three-quarter plate, hunting.

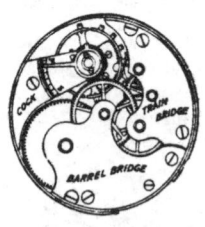

Model 1, 0 size, three-quarter plate, hunting.

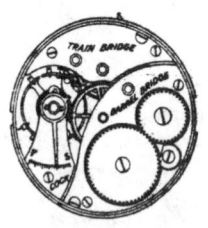

Model 2, 0 size, three-quarter plate, hunting.

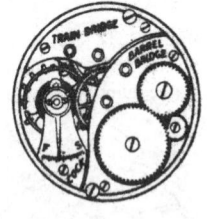

Model 2, 0 size, three-quarter plate, hunting.

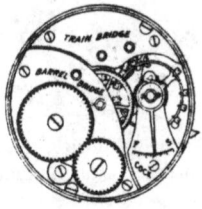

Model 3, 0 size, three-quarter plate, open face.

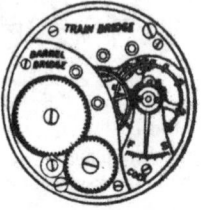

Model 3, 0 size, three-quarter plate, open face.

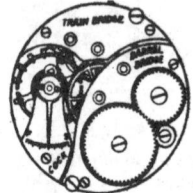

Model 2, 3-0 size, three-quarter plate, hunting.

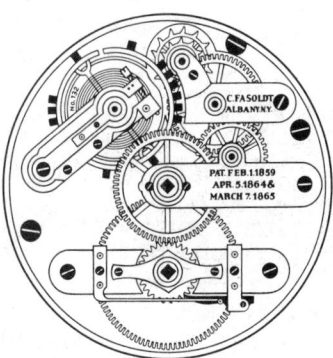

Charles Fasoldt's double escape wheel with odd shaped lever.

Charles Fasoldt, 18-20 size, 16 jewels, key wind & set, bar movement; note patented regulator, series II.

CHARLES FASOLDT WATCH CO.
Rome, New York   1849 - 1861
Albany, New York   1861 - 1878

Charles Fasoldt came to the United States in 1848. One of his first watches, Serial No. 27, was for General Armstrong and was an eight-day movement. At about that same time, he made several large regulators and a few pocket chronometers. He displayed some of his work at fairs in Utica and Syracuse and received four First-Class Premiums and two diplomas. In 1850, he patented a micrometric regulator (generally called the Howard Regulator because Howard bought the patent). He also patented a chronometer escapement in 1859-1865, a watch regulator in 1864, and a hairspring stud in 1877. He was also known for his tower clocks, for which he received many awards and medals. He made about 500 watches in Albany and about 50 watches in Rome.

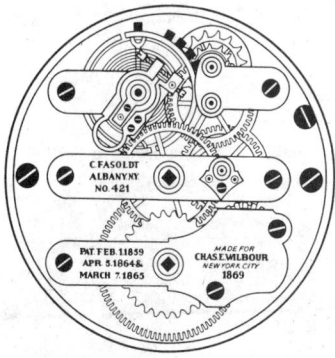
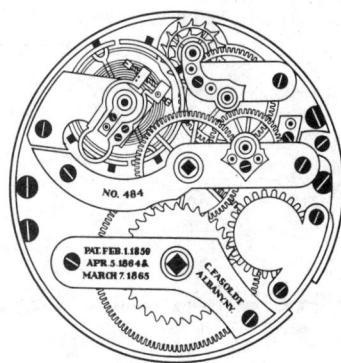

Charles Fasoldt, 18-20 size, 16 jewels, stem wind, key set, bar movement, series III.

Charles Fasoldt, 18-20 size, 16 jewels, stem wind, key set, bar movement, series III.

Year	Model	Style	Serial # Range
1855 - 1864	Series I	KW, ½ plate	5- 40
1865 - 1868	Series II	KW, Bar	41-330
1868 - 1878	Series III	SW, Bar	331-540

Grade or Name — Description	Avg	Ex-Fn	Mint
18 - 20 SIZE, 22J, chronograph,dual mainsprings & dual train, GJS, KW or SW, **18K case**......................★★★★	$15,000	$20,000	$25,000
18 - 20 SIZE, 16J, GJS, KW, KS, double escape wheel, **18K case**..★★★	12,000	15,000	18,000
10 - 12 SIZE, 16J, GJS, KW & SW, KS, **14K**.................................	3,500	4,000	5,000
Otto H. Fasoldt, 18S, 15J, SW, Swiss made or American	175	200	250

FITCHBURG WATCH CO.

Fitchburg, Massachusetts

1875 - 1878

In 1875, S. Sawyer decided to manufacture watches. He hired personnel from the U. S. Watch Company to build the machinery, but by 1878 the company had failed. It is not known how many, if any, watches were made. The equipment was sold to Cornell and other watch companies.

E. H. FLINT

Cincinnati, Ohio

1877 - 1879

The Flint watch was patented September 18, 1877, and about 100 watches were made. The serial number is found under the dial.

Grade or Name — Description	Avg	Ex-Fn	Mint
18 Size, 4–7J, KW, Full Plate, OF, Coin ....★★★	$2,000	$2,500	$3,500
18 Size, 4–7J, KW, Full Plate, 14K, HC ....★★★	4,000	4,500	5,500

 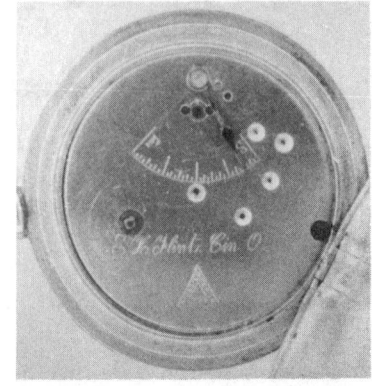

E.H. Flint dial and movement, 18 size, 4-7 jewels, open face, key wind & set, "Lancaster Pa." on dial, "Patented Sept. 18th,1877" on movement.

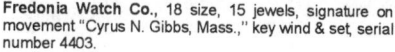

Fredonia Watch Co., 18 size, 15 jewels, signature on movement "Cyrus N. Gibbs, Mass.," key wind & set, serial number 4403.

Fredonia Watch Co., 18 size, 15 jewels, adjusted, serial number 8,368. NOTE: FREDONIA Regulator disc will have teeth all around the disc.

FREDONIA WATCH CO.

Fredonia, New York
1881 - 1885

This company sold the finished movements acquired from the Independent Watch Co. These movements had been made by other companies. The Fredonia Watch Company was sold to the Peoria Watch Co. in 1885, after having produced approximately 20,000 watches.

Chronology of the Development of Fredonia:

Independent Watch Co.	1875 –1881	
Fredonia Watch Co.	1881 –1885	
Peoria Watch Co.	1885 –1889	

Fredonia Watch Co., with a reversible case; changes to either hunting or open face.

Grade or Name — Description	Avg	Ex-Fn	Mint
18S, 7J, SW, OF	$200	$250	$350
18S, 7J, SW, HC	225	275	375
18S, 9J, SW, OF	250	300	375
18S, 9J, SW, HC	225	275	375
18S, 11J, SW, OF	250	300	375
18S, 11J, KW, KS, HC, Coin	225	275	375
18S, 15J, SW, Multi-color, **14K, HC**	1,600	1,800	2,200
18S, KW, Reversible case	500	550	600
18S, 15J, SW, LS, **Gilt,** OF	225	250	350
18S, 15J, straight line escapement, NI, marked **Adjusted**	350	400	500
18S, 15J, SW, LS, **Gold Plated,** OF	350	400	500
18S, 15J, HC, low serial number	350	400	500
18S, 15J, personalized mvt.	300	325	425
18S, 15J, KW, HC, marked Lakeshore W. Co.	300	350	450
18S, 15J, Anti-Magnetic, OF	350	400	500
18S, 15J, Anti-Magnetic, HC	375	425	525
18S, 15J, Special Superior Quality - Anti-Magnetic, OF	375	425	525
18S, 15J, Special Superior Quality - Anti-Magnetic, HC	400	450	550
18S, Mark Twain, 11J, KW, KS ★★	500	650	800

FREEPORT WATCH CO.

Freeport, Illinois

1874 - 1875

Probably less than 20 nickel watches made by Freeport have survived. Their machinery was purchased from Mozart Co., and a Mr. Hoyt was engaged as superintendent. The building erected was destroyed by fire on Oct. 27, 1875. A safe taken from the ruins contained 300 completed brass movements which were said to be ruined.

Grade or Name — Description	Avg	Ex-Fn	Mint
18S, 19J, KW, SW, gold train, raised gold jewel settings 18K case ★★★★	$6,000	$7,000	$8,000
18S, 15J, KW, KS, gold train, friction jewels 18K case ★★★★	$5,500	$6,000	$7,000
Geo. P. Rose, Dubuque, Iowa, 18S, 15J, KW, KS, gold train, friction jewels, 18K case ★★★★	$5,500	$6,000	$7,000

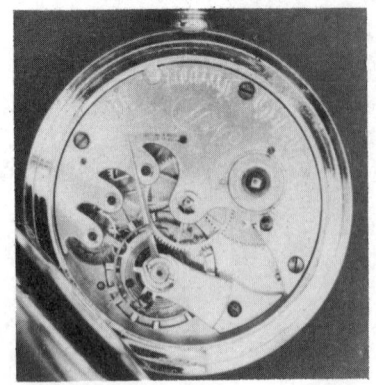

Freeport Watch Co., Example of a basic movement, 18 size, 15 jewels, key wind & set, pressed jewels, gold train, high grade movement, serial number 11.

Freeport Watch Co., 15 jewels, gold train, damaskeened, large over coiled hairspring with a floating stud, steel lever & escape wheel with single roller.

SMITH D. FRENCH

Wabash, Indiana

1866 - 1878

On August 21, 1866, Mr. French was issued a patent for an improved escapement for watches. The escape wheel has triangular shaped pins and the lever has two hook-shaped pallets. The pin wheel escapement was probably first used by Robert Robin, about 1795, for pocket watches. Antoine Tavan also used this style escape wheel around 1800. Mr. French's improved pin wheel and hook shaped lever (about 70 total production) can be seen through a cutout in the plates of his watches.

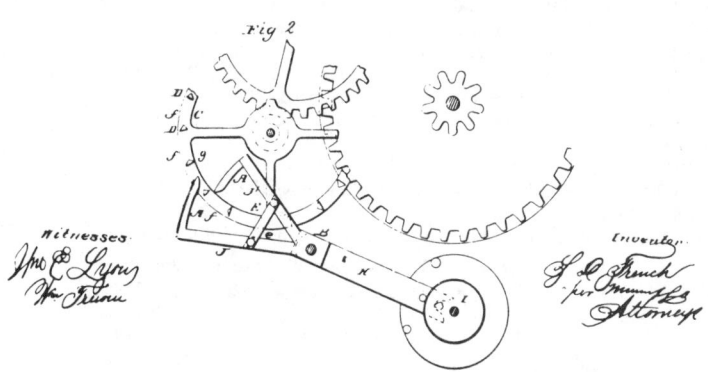

Illustration from the patent office, patent number 57,310, patented Aug. 21, 1866. Note pin wheel escapement with adjustable hook shaped lever.

Grade or Name — Description		Avg	Ex-Fn	Mint
18S, 15J, 3/4, KW, KS, gilt, pin wheel escapement, Silver case	★★★★	$4,000	$5,500	$6,000
18S, 15J, 3/4, KW, KS, gilt, pin wheel escapement, 18K case	★★★★★	5,000	6,500	8,000

S.D. French, about 18 size, 15 jewels, gilt 3/4 movement, key wind & set, with pin wheel escapement, engraved on movement "S.D. French, Wabash Ind., Aug. 21. 1866, No. 24."

L. Goddard, 55mm, 7 jewels, full plate movement with solid cock, chain driven fusee, flat steel balance, serial number 235, ca. 1809-1817.

LUTHER GODDARD

Shrewsbury, Massachusetts

1809 - 1825

The first significant attempt to produce watches in America was made by Luther Goddard. William H. Keith, who became president of Waltham Watch Co. (1861 -1866) and was once apprenticed to Goddard, said that the hands, dials, round and dovetail brass, steel wire, mainsprings and hairsprings, balance, verge, chains, and pinions were all imported. The plates, wheels, and brass parts were cast at the Goddard shop, however. He also made the cases for his movements which were of the usual style open faced, double case-and somewhat in advance of the prevalent style of thick bull's eye watches of the day. About 600 watches were made which were of good quality and more expensive than the imported type. The first watch was produced about 1812 and was sold to the father of ex-governor Lincoln of Worcester, Massachusetts. In 1820 his watches sold for about $60.00.

Goddard built a shop one story high with a hip roof about 18' square; it had a lean-to at the back for casting. The building was for making clocks, but a need for watches developed and Goddard made watches there. He earned the distinction of establishing the first watch factory in America.

His movements were marked as follows: L. GODDARD, L.GODDARD & CO., LUTHER GODDARD & SON, P. GODDARD, L. & P. GODDARD, D.P. GODDARD & CO., D. & P. GODDARD.

Frank A. Knowlton purchased the company and operated it until 1933.

Chronology of the Development of Luther Goddard:

Luther Goddard, L. Goddard, L. Goddard & Son 1809-1825
L. Goddard & Son 1817-1825
P.& D. Goddard 1825-1842
D. Goddard & Son 1842-1850
Luther D. Goddard 1850-1857
Goddard & Co. 1857-1860
D. Goddard & Co., & Benj'n Goddard 1860-1872

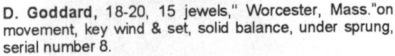

D. **Goddard**, 18-20, 15 jewels," Worcester, Mass."on movement, key wind & set, solid balance, under sprung, serial number 8.

L. **Goddard & Co.**,16-18 size, pair case, open face-thick bulls-eye type, and of high quality for the time.

NOTE: Watches listed below are with original silver cases.

Grade or Name — Description	Avg	Ex-Fn	Mint
Benj'n Goddard..	$1,000	$1,200	$1,500
Luther Goddard, S#1-35 with eagle on balance bridge ...... ★★★★	5,000	6,000	7,500
Luther Goddard without eagle on cock.................................... ★★	2,500	3,000	3,500
Luther Goddard,L.Goddard, Luther Goddard & Son .... ★	2,000	3,200	4,200
L. Goddard & Co., D. Goddard & Son .... ★	1,200	1,400	1,700
Luther D. Goddard, Goddard & Co., D. Goddard & Co. .... ★	1,000	1,200	1,500
P. Goddard, with eagle on cock.. ★	1,000	1,200	1,500
P & D Goddard, 7J., (Worcester), fusee, KWKS, OF	800	900	1,200

L. Goddard & Son. Example of basic movement, about 18 size, open face, pair case; most of the parts are made in America but resemble the English style CA.1815.

L. Goddard & Son, about 18 size, pair case, verge escapement, engraved on movement "L. Goddard & Son, Shrewsbury," serial number 460.

JONAS G. HALL
Montpelier, Vermont 1850 - 1870
Millwood Park, Roxbury, Vermont 1870 - 1890

Jonas G. Hall was born in 1822 in Calais, Vermont. He opened a shop in Montpelier where he sold watches, jewelry, silverware, and fancy goods. While at this location, he produced more than 60 full plate, lever style watches. Hall, later established a business in Roxbury, where he manufactured watch staking tools and other watchmaking tools. At Roxbury, he made at least one watch which was a three-quarter plate model. He also produced a few chronometers, about 20-size with a fusee and detent escapement and a wind indicator on the dial.

Hall was employed by the American Waltham Watch Co. for a short time and helped design the first lady's model. He also worked for Tremont Watch Co., E. Howard & Co., and the United States Watch Co. of Marion, New Jersey.

Style or Name–Description		Avg	Ex-Fn	Mint
18S, 15J, Full plate, KW KS	★ ★ ★	$1,500	$2,000	$2,800
18S, 15J, 3/4 plate, gilded, KW KS	★ ★ ★	2,500	3,000	3,600
20S, 15J, Detent Chronometer, KW KS	★ ★ ★ ★	4,000	5,000	7,500

 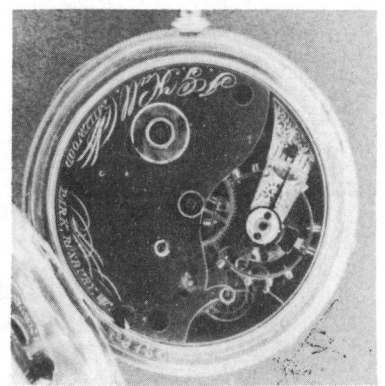

J.G. Hall, 18 size, 15 jewels, full plate, key wind & set, engraved on movement "J.G. Hall, Montpelier, VT.," serial number 25, ca. 1857.

J.G. Hall, 18 size, 15 jewels, 3/4 plate, key wind and set, engraved on movement "J.G. Hall, Millwood Park, Roxbury, VT," no serial number, ca. 1880.

HAMILTON WATCH CO.

Lancaster, Pennsylvania
December 14, 1892 - Present

Hamilton's roots go back to the Adams & Perry Watch Manufacturing Co. On Sept. 26, 1874, E. F. Bowman made a model watch, and the first movement was produced on April 7, 1876. It was larger than an 18S, or about a 19S. The movement had a snap on dial and the patented stem-setting arrangement. They decided to start making the watches a standard size of 18, and no more than 1,000 of the large-size watches were made. Work had commenced on Sept. 1, 1877, at the Lancaster Watch Co. The watches were designed to sell at a cheaper price than normal. It had a one-piece top 3/4 plate and a pillar plate that was fully ruby-jeweled (4 1/2 pairs). It had a gilt or nickel movement and a new stem-wind device designed by Mosely & Todd. By mid-1878, the Lancaster Watch Co. had made 150 movements. Four grades of watches were produced: Keystone, Fulton, Franklin, and Melrose. In September 1879 the company had manufactured 334 movements. In 1880 some 1,250 movements had been made. In mid-1882, about 17,000 movements had been assembled. All totaled, about 20,000 movements were made.

Grade 936, 18 size, 17 jewels, serial number 1. c. 1893.   Grade 936, 18 size, 17 jewels, serial number 2, c. 1893.

The first Hamilton movement to be sold was No. 15 to W. C. Davis on January 31, 1893. The No. 1 movement was finished on April 25, 1896, and was never sold. The No. 2 was finished on April 25, 1893, and was shipped to Smythe & Ashe of Rochester, N. Y. Nos. 1 & 2 are at the N.A.W.C.C. museum.

Chronology of the Development of Hamilton:

Adams & Perry Watch Co....................Sept. 1874-May 1876
Lancaster, Pa., Watch Co. ....Aug. 1877-Oct. 1887
Lancaster, Pa., Watch Co. ....Nov. 1877-May 1879
Lancaster Watch Co. ....May 1883-1886
Keystone Standard Watch Co..................................1886-1890
Hamilton Watch Co. ....Dec. 14, 1892-Present

In 1893 the first watch was produced by Hamilton. The watches became very popular with railroad men and by 1923 some 53 percent of Hamilton's production were railroad watches. The 940 model watch was discontinued in 1910. Most Hamilton watches are fitted with a 42-hour mainspring.

Grade 937, 18 size, 17 jewels, hunting case. Note serial   Hamilton Watch Co., 18 size, 7 jewels, serial number 2934.
number 1047.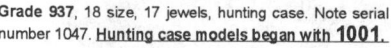

The 950B was introduced in 1940 and by this time a total of about 25,000 grade (950) had been sold. The 992 watch sold for about $60.00 in 1929, the price remained the same $60.00 until 1940.

The Elinvar hairspring was patented in 1931 and used in all movements thereafter. On October 15, 1940, Hamilton introduced the 992B which were fitted with the Elinvar hairspring. Elinvar and Invar are trade names and are the same 36 percent nickel steel. Although the Hamilton Watch Co. is still in business today making modern type watches, they last produced American made watches in about 1969.

HAMILTON ESTIMATED SERIAL NUMBERS
AND PRODUCTION DATES

Date–Serial No.	Date–Serial No.	Date–Serial No.	Date–Serial No.
1893 ---1-2,000	1906 --- 590,000	1919---1,700,000	1932---2,500,000
1894 --- 5,000	1907 --- 756,000	1920---1,790,000	1933---2,600,000
1895 --- 11,500	1908 --- 921,000	1921---1,860,000	1934---2,700,000
1896 --- 16,000	1909---1,087,000	1922---1,900,000	1935---2,800,000
1897 --- 27,000	1910---1,150,500	1923---1,950,000	1936---2,900,000
1898 --- 50,000	1911---1,290,500	1924---2,000,000	1937---3,000,000
1899 --- 74,000	1912---1,331,000	1925---2,100,000	1938---3,200,000
1900---104,000	1913---1,370,000	1926---2,200,000	1939---3,400,000
1901---143,000	1914---1,410,500	1927---2,250,000	1940---3,600,000
1902---196,000	1915---1,450,500	1928---2,300,000	1941---3,800,000
1903---260,000	1916---1,517,000	1929---2,350,000	1942---4,025,000
1904---340,000	1917---1,580,000	1930---2,400,000	
1905---425,000	1918---1,650,000	1931---2,450,000	

The above list is provided for determining the APPROXIMATE age of your watch. Match serial number with date. Watches were not necessarily **SOLD** in the exact order of manufactured date.

Some serial numbers have the first numbers replaced by a (date) letter such as A, B, C, E, F, G, H, J, L, M, N, R, S, T, V, W, X, Y, CY, HW. These letters were used from late 30's to about late 50's. The date letter "2B + Ser.#" found on 950B = **1940 to 1942,** the date letter "C + Ser.#" found on 992B = **1940 to 1952,** the date letter "S + Ser.#" found on 950B = **1943 to 1952** and HA = SWISS.

992B with first letter of C + serial no.	950B with first letter of 2B + serial no.
1940=C001	1940=2B001
1941=C75000	1941=2B400
1942=C160000	1942=2B800
1943=C185000	950B with first letter of S + serial no.
1944=C200000	1943=S001
1945=C220000	1944=S1500
1946=C235000	1945=S2900
1947=C255000	1946=S4000
1948=C275000	1947=S4500
1949=C290000	1948=S6500
1950=C300000	1949=S7500
1951=C310000	1950=S8900
1955=C396300	1951=S10000
	1955=S18700

NOTE: *It required several months for raw material to emerge as a finished movement. All the while the factory is producing all sizes, models and grades. The numbering system was basically "consecutive", due to demand a batch of movements could be side tracked, thus allowing a different size and model to move ahead to meet this demand. Therefore, the dates some movements were __sold__ and delivered to the trade, the serial numbers may not be "consecutive".*

The Hamilton Masterpiece

The adjoining illustration shows the Hamilton Masterpiece. The dial is sterling silver with raised gold numbers and solid gold hands. This watch sold for $685.00 in 1930. All 922 **MP** Models included the following: 12 size, 23 jewels, were adjusted to heat, cold, isochronism, and five positions, with a motor barrel, solid gold train, steel escape wheel, double roller, sapphire pallets and a micrometric regulator.

HAMILTON SERIAL NUMBERS AND GRADES

To help determine the size and grade of your watch, the following serial number list is provided. Serial numbers 30,001 through 32,000, which are omitted from the list, were not listed by Hamilton. To identify your watch, simply look up its serial number which will identify the grade. After determining the grade, your watch can be easily located in the pricing section.

Serial	Grade	Serial	Grade	Serial	Grade	Serial	Grade
1-20	936	27001-28000	929	56801-900	974	73001-200	975
21-30	932	28001-29000	999	56901-57000	976	73201-300	973
31-60	936	29001-800	927	57001-300	977	73301-74000	977
61-400	932	29801-30000	935	57301-500	975	74001-400	974
401-1000	936	32001-300	926	57501-600	973	74401-600	972
1001-20	937	32301-700	930	57601-800	975	74601-75000	976
1021-30	933	32701-33000	934	57801-58000	977	75001-76799	HWW*
1031-60	937	33001-500	931	58001-100	972	76002-76800	HWW*
1061-1100	933	33501-800	927	58101-200	974	77001-100	969
1101-300	937	33801-34000	935	58201-300	972	77101-300	973
1301-600	933	34001-500	928	58301-400	966	77301-500	975
1601-2000	937	34501-700	930	58401-500	976	77501-600	971
2001-3000	7J	34701-800	926	58501-600	972	77601-700	973
3001-100	931	34801-35000	934	58601-800	974	77701-900	975
3101-500	935	35001-800	931	58801-59000	976	77901-78000	977
3501-600	931	35581-36000	935	59001-300	973	78001-500	970
3601-900	935	36001-37000	928	59301-500	967	78501-700	972
3901-4000	931	37001-38000	929	59501-700	975	78701-900	974
4001-300	930	38001-500	926	59701-60000	977	78901-79000	976
4301-5100	934	38501-600	930	60001-500	976	79001-100	973
5101-400	926	38601-900	934	60501-700	974	79101-300	975
5401-600	934	38901-39000	926	60701-61000	976	79301-700	977
5601-6000	930	39001-200	931	61001-200	975	79701-900	975
6001-600	936	39201-500	935	61201-500	977	79901-80000	973
6601-700	938	39501-700	927	61501-600	973	80001-200	972
6701-800	936	39701-900	935	61601-800	975	80201-400	974
6801-7000	932	39901-40000	931	61801-62000	977	80401-600	970
7001-10	17J	40001-200	930	62001-100	972	80601-700	972
7011-600	937	40201-500	934	62101-300	974	80701-900	974
7601-700	939	40501-41000	926	62301-500	976	80901-81000	976
7701-800	937	41001-500	929	62501-700	974	81001-300	961
7801-8000	933	41501-42000	927	62701-900	972	81301-500	965
8001-700	936	42001-43000	999	62901-63000	974	81501-82000	961
8701-800	938	43001-300	941	63001-500	977	82001-300	972
8801-9000	936	43301-500	943	63501-600	975	82301-500	974
9001-300	937	43501-700	937	63601-800	977	82501-600	970
9301-600	939	43701-900	941	63801-900	975	82601-700	972
9601-800	937	43901-44000	943	63901-64000	973	82701-800	974
9801-900	933	44001-02	21J	64001-100	976	82801-900	968
9901-10000	939	44003-400	938	64101-200	972	82901-83000	976
10001-200	938	44401-500	942	64201-300	974	83001-400	977
10201-400	936	44501-45000	936	64301-600	972	83401-500	971
10401-50	932	45001-46000	929	64601-700	976	83501-700	975
10451-500	936	46001-500	926	64701-900	974	83701-800	973
10501-700	938	46501-800	934	64901-65000	976	83801-900	975
10701-900	936	46801-47000	930	65001-200	973	83901-84000	969
10901-11000	938	47001-500	927	65201-300	977	84001-400	974
11001-12000	936	47501-700	935	65301-400	975	84401-500	970
12001-200	939	47701-48000	931	65401-500	973	84501-700	972
12201-13000	937	48001-05	942	65501-700	977	84701-800	968
13001-400	999	48006-300	940	65701-900	975	84801-85000	976
13401-14000	938	48301-500	942	65901-66000	977	85001-200	937
14001-15000	999	48501-900	940	66001-200	976	85201-900	941
15001-300	939	48901-49000	942	66201-300	974	85901-86000	943
15301-15401	21J	49001-400	927	66301-500	972	86001-87000	928
15302-700	937	49401-900	925	66501-600	976	87001-88000	929
15701-16000	933	49901-50	11J	66601-700	974	88001-500	926
16001-100	931	50071-500	962	66701-800	972	88501-89000	930
16101-200	930	50501-750	960	66801-67000	074	89001-500	941
16201-300	927	50751-50850	964	67001-100	977	89501-90000	937
16301-400	931	50851-51000	960	67101-300	975	90001-100	926
16401-600	927	51001-51300	16s	67301-600	973	90101-950	999
16601-17000	931	51301-400	963	67601-800	975	91001-92000	925
17001-500	929	51401-650	961	67801-68000	977	92001-200	940
17501-18000	931	51651-750	965	68001-800	960	92201-93000	936
18001-200	928	51751-52000	961	68801-69000	964	93001-94000	927
18201-300	926	52001-300	16s	69001-100	977	94001-003	934
18301-500	928	52301-500	976	69101-200	975	94004-95000	928
18501-19500	930	52501-700	974	69201-400	973	95001-96000	923
19501-700	926	52701-800	966	69401-600	975	96001-100	942
19701-20000	930	52801-53000	976	69601-70000	977	96101-700	940
20001-300	934	53001-53070	16s	70001-200	976	96701-97000	936
20301-500	926	53071-53500	977	70201-400	970	97001-900	929
20501-21000	999	53501-900	975	70401-600	968	97901-98000	927
21001-300	935	53901-54000	967	70601-900	972	98001-99000	924
21301-500	927	54001-200	972	70901-71000	974	99001-100000	925
21501-800	935	54201-300	974	71001-200	975	100001-101000	924
21801-22500	927	54301-500	976	71201-500	971	101001-102000	925
22501-800	931	54501-700	974	71501-700	975	102001-103000	922
22801-23000	935	54701-800	968	71701-90	973	103001-104000	927
23001-200	928	54801-55000	976	71791-800	969	104001-105000	940
23201-500	7J	55001-300	973	71801-900	977	105001-500	925
24001-500	926	55301-600	977	71901-72000	975	105501-106000	927
24501-25000	934	55601-700	969	72001-100	974	106001-107000	940
25001-100	11J	55701-800	977	72101-300	976	107001-400	941
25101-400	927	55801-56000	975	72301-600	974	107401-500	943
25401-800	931	56001-300	974	72601-700	968	107501-800	941
25801-26000	935	56301-500	976	72701-900	976	107801-108000	943
26001-500	930	56501-600	966	72901-73000	972	108001-200	928
26501-27000	928	56601-800	972				

Serial	Grade	Serial	Grade	Serial	Grade	Serial	Grade
108201-109000	926	186001-187000	942	275202-460	HWW*	322001-323000	974
109001-500	927	187001-188000	927	275462-500	HWW*	323001-700	975
109501-110000	925	188001-189000	924	276001-277000	940	323701-324000	973
110001-900	940	189001-190000	925	277001-278000	941	324001-325000	960
110901-111000	942	190001-191000	926	278001-279000	940	325001-100	965
111001-500	937	191001-192000	927	279001-280000	925	325101-326000	961
111501-112000	941	192001-193000	924	280001-281000	936	326001-327000	974
112001-200	928	193001-194000	925	281001-282000	927	327001-300	971
112201-113000	926	194001-195000	926	282001-283000	926	327301-500	973
113001-114000	925	195001-500	935	283001-284000	925	327501-328000	975
114001-003	940	195501-196000	927	284001-500	934	328001-300	992
114004-115000	936	196001-197000	926	284501-900	924	328301-500	990
115001-116000	927	197001-198000	937	284901-285000	999	328501-329000	992
116001-117000	940	198001-199000	936	285001-286000	925	329001-330000	975
117001-118000	925	199001-200000	925	286001-287000	940	330001-100	992
118001-119000	999	200001-201000	926	287001-288000	927	330101-500	990
119001-120000	925	201001-202000	925	288001-289000	940	330501-331000	992
120001-121000	924	202001-500	926	289001-290000	927	331001-200	973
121001-500	941	202501-203000	934	290001-800	936	331201-400	975
121501-122000	943	203001-204000	927	290801-291000	938	331401-500	969
122001-300	940	204001-100	934	291001-292000	925	331501-700	971
122301-400	942	204101-500	926	292001-500	940	331701-800	973
122401-123000	940	204501-205000	934	292501-293000	942	331801-332000	975
122301-124000	941	205001-206000	941	293001-294000	925	332001-200	992
124001-100	942	206001-207000	940	294001-295000	926	332201-800	972
124101-800	940	207001-208000	927	295001-296000	927	332801-333000	974
124801-125000	942	208001-900	999	296001-297000	940	333001-500	975
125001-126000	927	208901-209000	940	297001-298000	927	333501-700	971
126001-127000	924	209001-210000	925	298001-299000	940	333701-900	973
127001-128000	941	210001-211000	940	299001-300000	925	333901-334000	975
128001-129000	936	211001-212000	927	300001-300	972	334001-200	972
129001-130000	925	212001-213000	940	300301-500	970	334201-800	992
130001-500	924	213001-500	941	300501-900	974	334801-335000	990
130501-131000	926	213501-600	937	300901-301000	968	335001-600	975
131001-132000	925	213601-214000	925	301001-400	975	335601-800	971
132001-100	926	214001-215000	924	301401-500	971	335801-900	973
132101-200	934	215001-216000	927	301501-302000	973	335901-336000	975
132201-600	926	216001-217000	940	302001-100	990	336001-200	972
132501-133000	924	217001-218000	927	302101-200	992	336201-337000	974
133001-134000	937	218001-219000	940	302201-300	990	337001-338000	975
134001-135000	924	219001-220000	925	302301-900	992	338001-200	974
135001-136000	925	220001-221000	924	302901-303000	990	338201-900	992
136001-137000	926	221001-222000	927	303001-100	973	338901-339000	990
137001-100	11J	222001-223000	926	303101-300	971	339001-300	971
137101-138000	927	223001-02	927	303301-800	975	339301-500	973
138001-139000	940	223003-04	941	303801-304000	973	339501-340000	975
139001-140000	937	223005	937	304001-100	970	340001-200	974
140001-300	938	223006-224000	927	304101-400	972	340201-300	972
140301-141000	942	224001-225000	924	304401-305000	974	340301-600	970
141001-142000	941	225001-226000	927	305001-100	973	340601-341000	974
142001-143000	940	226001-227000	940	305101-200	971	341001-200	973
143001-100	927	227001-228000	925	305201-300	969	341201-342000	975
143101-144000	925	228001-229000	924	305301-900	975	342001-300	990
144001-145000	924	229001-230000	925	305901-306000	973	342301-343000	992
145001-146000	925	230001-500	926	306001-400	972	343001-344000	975
146001-400	934	230501-231000	924	306401-307000	974	344001-200	970
146401-147000	924	231001-565	937	307001-100	975	344201-400	972
147001-148000	927	231566-232000	927	307101-300	971	344401-345000	974
148001-149000	940	232001-233000	940	307301-400	975	345001-346000	975
149001-150000	925	233001-234000	941	307401-500	973	346001-300	992
150001-151000	924	234001-235000	940	307501-600	975	346301-347000	974
151001-400	927	235001-236000	941	307601-700	971	347001-180	993
151401-500	935	236001-237000	936	307701-900	975	347181-200	991
151501-152000	927	237001-238000	941	307901-308000	969	347201-300	975
152001-153000	936	238001-239000	926	308001-700	990	347301-400	973
153001-154000	941	239001-500	943	308701-309000	992	347401-700	993
154001-155000	936	239501-240000	941	309001-100	971	347701-900	991
155001-156000	927	240001-241000	940	309101-400	973	347901-348000	973
156001-157000	940	241001-242000	941	309401-310000	975	348001-200	970
157001-158000	925	242001-243000	940	310001-400	970	348201-800	974
158001-159000	940	243001-244000	927	310401-311000	974	348801-349000	972
159001-160000	941	244001-245000	936	311001-700	975	349001-350000	975
160001-161000	940	245001-246000	925	311701-312000	973	350001-300	990
161001-162000	941	246001-247000	940	312001-200	970	350301-400	974
162001-163000	926	247001-248000	927	312201-500	972	350401-600	990
163001-164000	943	248001-249000	940	312501-600	968	350601-351000	992
164001-165000	940	249001-250000	927	312601-313000	974	351001-352000	975
165001-166000	925	250001-251000	926	313001-100	973	352001-100	968
166001-167000	924	251001-252000	927	313101-400	971	352101-353000	974
167001-168000	927	252001-253000	924	313401-600	969	353001-354000	975
168001-169000	940	253001-254000	925	313601-314000	975	354001-400	992
169001-400	935	254001-255000	940	314001-600	974	354401-355000	974
169401-170000	927	255001-256000	925	314601-900	972	355001-800	975
170001-171000	999	256001-257000	926	314901-315000	970	355801-900	973
171001-172000	925	257001-258000	941	315001-100	971	355901-356000	993
172001-100	934	258001-259000	924	315101-400	973	356001-500	990
172101-173000	926	259001-260000	941	315401-316000	975	356501-357000	974
173001-174000	940	260001-261000	940	316001-200	992	357001-358000	975
174001-175000	924	261001-262000	927	316201-300	972	358001-359000	974
175002-176000	HWW*	262001-263000	926	316301-500	992	359001-360000	975
175001-699	HWW*	263001-264000	925	316501-317000	972	360001-550	960
176001-177000	940	264001-265000	940	317001-600	975	360801-361000	960
177001-178000	927	265001-266000	927	317601-700	969	361001-100	993
178001-179000	942	266001-267000	940	317701-318000	973	361101-300	991
179001-500	935	267001-268000	925	318001-100	973	361301-400	993
179501-180000	927	268001-269000	940	318101-900	972	361401-700	975
180001-181000	940	269001-270000	927	318901-319000	970	361701-20	973
181001-182000	941	270001-271000	940	319001-100	971	361721-362000	975
182001-300	926	271001-272000	925	319101-320000	975	362001-900	974
182301-400	934	272001-273000	926	320001-300	972	362901-363000	990
182401-183000	926	273001-274000	941	320301-400	968	363001-364000	975
183001-184000	941	274001-275000	924	320401-321000	974	364001-365000	974
184001-185000	940	275002-100	HWW*	321001-200	973	365001-100	975
185001-186000	925	275102-200	HWW*	321201-322000	975	365101-300	973

Serial Range	No.
365301-366000	975
366001-367000	974
367001-500	975
367501-368000	993
368001-369000	974
369001-370000	992
370001-100	990
370101-400	992
370401-500	974
370501-800	990
370801-371400	992
371401-500	972
371501-373500	974
373501-700	990
373701-374000	992
374001-200	974
374201-700	990
374701-375000	974
375001-100	993
375101-500	991
375501-376000	975
376001-200	972
376201-500	974
376501-377000	992
377001-200	973
377201-378000	975
378001-379000	974
379001-380800	992
380801-381000	990
381001-382000	992
382001-100	990
382101-383000	974
383001-300	992
383301-700	990
383701-384000	972
384001-700	974
384701-900	972
384901-385000	974
385001-600	972
385601-900	974
385801-386000	990
386001-800	974
386801-900	992
386901-387000	972
387001-100	990
387101-900	992
387901-388000	972
388001-400	990
388401-389000	992
389001-391000	974
391001-300	972
391301-392000	974
392001-800	992
392801-393000	990
393001-400	975
393401-600	973
393601-394000	993
394001-200	972
394201-395000	974
395001-100	993
395101-900	991
395901-396000	993
396001-397000	992
397001-200	990
397201-398000	992
398001-200	972
398201-399000	992
399001-600	993
399601-400000	975
400001-401000	924
401001-402000	940
402001-404000	924
404001-405000	926
405001-406000	924
406001-407000	940
407001-408000	926
408001-416000	940
416001-417000	926
417001-418000	940
418001-419000	926
419001-420000	941
420001-421000	940
421001-422000	926
422001-423000	924
423001-425000	926
425001-426000	940
426001-500	936
426501-427000	944
427001-428000	924
428001-429000	926
429001-430000	925
430001-431000	924
431001-432000	925
432001-433000	924
433001-434000	924
434001-500	940
434501-600	942
434601-435000	946
435001-436000	924
436001-438500	940
438501-800	946
438801-900	942
438901-440000	926
440001-441000	924
441001-442000	940
442001-400	946
442401-500	942
442501-443000	946
443001-444000	926
444001-445000	924
445001-446000	927
446001-447000	924
447001-448000	925
448001-449000	926
449001-450000	924
450001-451000	926
451001-452000	925
452001-453000	940
453001-454000	924
454001-456000	940
456001-457000	999
457001-458000	940
458001-459000	999
459001-110	946
459111-118	942
459119-200	946
459201-700	942
459701-460000	946
460001-461900	940
461901-462000	940
462001-463000	999
463001-500	940
463501-464000	940
464001-466000	926
466001-467000	924
467001-468000	926
468001-469000	940
469001-470000	924
470001-471000	926
471001-472000	946
472001-473000	924
473001-474000	940
474001-475000	924
475001-476000	940
476001-477000	924
477001-478000	940
478001-479000	926
479001-480000	944
480001-481000	926
481001-482000	927
482001-483000	924
483001-484000	926
484001-485000	940
485001-486000	925
486001-487000	999
487001-488000	924
488001-489000	999
489001-492000	924
492001-493000	940
493001-494000	946
494001-495000	944
495001-496000	940
496001-497000	925
497001-498000	999
498001-499000	936
499001-501000	940
501001-900	926
501901-502000	934
502001-503000	926
503001-504000	999
504001-507000	940
507001-508000	999
508001-509000	940
509001-510000	942
510001-511500	940
511501-700	942
511701-517000	940
517001-519000	924
519001-521000	925
521001-523000	944
523001-524000	946
524001-531000	940
531001-532000	926
532001-10	934
532011-533000	926
533001-535500	999
535501-536000	940
536001-537000	936
537001-538000	924
538001-543000	940
543001-544000	927
544001-200	934
544201-545000	926
545001-546000	925
546001-547000	924
547001-548000	940
548001-549000	999
549001-551000	940
551001-553000	944
553001-555000	940
555001-556000	936
556001-558000	924
558001-560000	925
560001-561000	999
561001-562000	926
562001-564000	924
564001-565000	926
565001-568000	940
568001-569000	936
569001-571000	924
571001-576000	940
576001-200	942
576201-578000	940
578001-580000	924
580001-582000	926
582001-584000	925
584001-585000	927
585001-587000	999
587001-592000	940
592001-593000	926
593001-594000	924
594001-601000	940
B600001-601000	999 Ball
601001-601800	926
B601001-601800	999 Ball
601801-602000	934
B601801-602000	999 Ball
602001-603000	926
B602001-603000	999 Ball
603001-604000	926
B603001-604000	999 Ball
604001-605000	926
B604001-605000	999 Ball
605001-606000	925
B605001-606000	999 Ball
606001-607000	925
B606001-607000	999 Ball
607001-608000	925
B607001-608000	999 Ball
608001-613000	924
B608001-613000	999 Ball
613001-614000	925
B613001-614000	999 Ball
614001-616500	924
B614001-616500	999 Ball
616501-617000	934
B616501-617000	999 Ball
617001-619000	926
B617001-619000	999 Ball
619001-620000	927
B619001-620000	999 Ball
620001-622700	940
B620001-622700	999 Ball
622701-623000	942
B622701-623000	999 Ball
623001-624000	941
B623001-624000	999 Ball
624001-625000	936
B624001-625000	999 Ball
625001-626000	925
B625001-626000	999 Ball
626001-627000	926
B626001-627000	999 Ball
627001-629000	924
B627001-629000	999 Ball
629001-630800	925
B628001-630800	999 Ball
631001-636000	940
B631001-636000	999 Ball
636001-637000	941
B636001-637000	999 Ball
637001-638000	936
B637001-638000	999 Ball
638001-639000	926
B638001-639000	999 Ball
639001-640000	925
B639001-640000	999 Ball
640001-642000	924
B640001-644400	999 Ball
644401-645000	940
645001-645500	927
B645001-645500	999 Ball
645501-646000	925
B645501-646000	999 Ball
646001-647000	926
B646001-647000	999 Ball
647001-648000	940
B647001-648000	999 Ball
648001-649000	940
B648001-649000	998 Ball
649001-650000	998
B649001-650000	998 Ball
650001-651000	999
B650001-651000	999 Ball
651001-652000	940
B651001-652000	998 Ball
652001-652700	924
B652001-652700	998 Ball
652701-652800	924
652801-652900	927
652901-653000	937
653001-655000	940
B653001-655000	999 Ball
655001-655200	925
B655001-655200	999 Ball
655201-656000	924
656001-657000	926
657001-659000	927
659001-660000	925
660001-661000	927
661001-662000	924
662001-664000	940
664001-666000	924
666001-667000	940
667001-668000	941
668001-669000	926
669001-670000	999
670001-100	937
670101-100	
670501-673000	925
673001-675000	926
675001-677000	940
677001-678000	924
678001-679200	927
679201-680000	926
680001-685000	924
685001-687000	940
687001-688000	925
688001-689000	946
689001-694000	940
694001-696000	924
696001-697000	941
697001-700000	924
700001-702000	974
702001-703800	992
703801-704000	990
704001-400	992
704401-705000	990
705001-700	972
705701-706000	974
706001-707000	990
707001-800	972
707801-708000	990
708001-709500	975
709501-710000	973
710001-800	993
710801-711000	991
711001-300	973
711301-712000	975
712001-600	993
712601-713000	991
713001-714900	975
714901-715000	991
715001-716000	993
716001-100	972
716101-717000	974
717001-200	991
717201-718000	975L
718001-721500	974
721501-722000	992
722001-724000	974
724001-725000	972
725001-726000	974
726001-727000	992
727001-728000	974
728001-729000	992
729001-730000	975
730001-731000	992
731001-732000	975
732001-734000	992
734001-735000	975
735001-736000	974
736001-738000	975
738001-739000	974
739001-740000	975
740001-100	972
740101-200	974
740201-900	974
740901-741000	975
741001-742000	992
742001-743000	974
743001-300	975
743301-400	993
743401-744000	975
744001-500	974
744501-745000	992
745001-747000	975
747001-700	974
747701-748000	972
748001-749500	992
749501-750000	974
750001-100	961
750101-200	961
750201-700	950
750701-751000	952
751001-752000	960
752001-500	952
752501-753000	950
753001-500	952
753501-754000	975
754001-100	960
754101-500	952
754501-755000	960
755001-400	992
755401-500	974
755501-700	972
755701-900	974
755901-756000	992
756001-757000	974
757001-300	975
757301-500	993
757501-758000	975
758001-100	972
758101-759000	992
759001-760000	975
760001-400	992
760401-600	972
760601-800	974
760801-761000	992

Serial	Grade	Serial	Grade	Serial	Grade	Serial	Grade
761001-400	975	826001-500	975L	898001-899100	992	1051001-200	975
761401-600	993	826501-827000	993	899101-500	978	1051201-1052000	993
761601-762000	975	827001-828000	975P	899501-900000	974	1052001-500	972P
762001-200	992	828001-829000	974L	900001-902000	940	1052501-900	954
762201-300	972	829001-830000	974P	902001-904000	926	1052901-1053000	974
762301-763000	974	830001-500	990L	904001-906000	924	1053001-1054000	992
763001-300	993	830501-831000	992L	906001-914000	940	1054001-1056000	974
763301-600	973	831001-100	954P	914001-916000	926	1056001-1057000	975
763601-764000	975	831101-200	972P	916001-917000	927	1057001-1061300	992
764001-300	992	831201-500	954P	917001-919000	925	1061301-1062300	972
764301-400	972	831501-832000	974P	919001-921000	940	1062301-1066000	992
764401-765000	974	832001-400	974L	921001-923000	924	1066001-1068000	974
765001-300	992	832401-833000	992L	923001-500	999	1068001-1069000	975
765301-767000	974	833001-834000	990L	923501-924000	925	1069001-1070000	974
767001-600	992	834001-600	974P	924001-926000	940	1070001-1071000	992L
767601-800	972	834601-800	974L	926001-100	927	1071001-1073000	975P
767801-768000	974	834801-835000	974P	927001-929000	926	1073001-1075000	992
768001-769000	975	835001-600	992L	929001-933000	924	1075001-1076200	974L
769001-700	992	835601-800	990L	933001-935000	925	1076201-700	972L
769701-770000	972	835801-836000	974L	935001-937000	926	1076701-1077000	978L
770001-100	974	836001-500	974P	937001-939000	940	1077001-1079000	974P
770101-771200	992	836501-900	954P	939001-941000	924	1079001-1080000	992L
771201-400	972	836901-837000	974P	941001-944000	940	1080001-100	952L
771401-772000	974	837001-838000	975P	944001-949000	926	1080101-200	960L
772001-773000	975	838001-839000	975L	949001-952000	925	1080201-400	994L
773001-800	992	839001-400	974L	952001-958000	924	1080401-1081000	950L
773801-774000	972	839401-700	992L	958001-960000	926	1081001-1082000	978L
774001-775000	975	839701-840000	990L	960001-968000	940	1082001-400	993L
775001-500	952	840001-400	952L	968001-970000	926	1082401-1083000	973L
775501-776000	950	840401-900	950L	970001-971700	924	1083001-1084000	990L
776001-300	973	840901-841000	952L	971701-972000	948	1084001-1085000	992L
776301-700	993	841001-842000	975P	972001-973000	924	1085001-1086000	992L
776701-777000	975	842001-843000	974L	973001-974000	936	1086001-1088000	974P
777001-300	972	843001-844000	974P	974001-975400	924	1088001-1091000	992L
777301-778300	974	844001-200	993	975401-25 Spec.	926	1091001-200	978L
778301-800	992	844201-845000	975	975426-976000	924	1091201-1092000	974L
778801-900	972	845001-200	992	976001-979000	940	1092001-1093000	992L
778901-779300	974	845201-400	972	979001-100	942	1093001-1095000	974P
779301-780100	992	845401-700	954	979101-981000	940	1095001-1096000	992P
780101-300	972	845701-846000	972	981001-982000	948	1096001-400	974L
780301-781300	992	846001-500	952	982001-984000	924	1096401-1097000	974P
781301-400	972	846501-847000	950	984001-986000	940	1097001-1098000	992L
781401-500	974	847001-200	972	986001-987000	946	1098001-400	975P
781501-782000	992	847201-849000	974	987001-988000	936	1098401-1099000	975L
782001-783000	975	849001-850000	975	988001-992000	940	1099001-600	993L
783001-600	992	850001-300	992	992001-996000	924	1099601-1100000	975P
783601-784000	974	850301-800	990	996001-999998	940	1100001-1104000	992L
784001-785000	992	850801-851000	972	999999-1000000	947	1104001-1105000	974P
785001-500	952	851001-400	993	1000001-1000300	972	1105001-1106000	992L
785501-786000	950	851401-852000	975	1000301-1003000	992	1106001-500	978L
786001-787000	992	852001-853000	992	1003001-1004000	974	1106501-1107000	972L
787001-300	974	853001-854000	974	1004001-900	992	1107001-1109000	992L
787401-788000	972	854001-600	950	1004901-1007100	974	1109001-1111000	972L
788001-791300	992	854601-900	952	1007101-1008300	992	1111001-1112000	974L
791301-792600	974	854901-855100	960L	1008301-1009500	974	1112001-1113000	974P
792601-900	972	855101-856000	950L	1009501-1010700	992	1113001-1116000	992L
792901-793700	992	856001-857840	975	1010701-1011200	972	1116001-900	974P
793701-900	990	857841-858000	975L	1011201-1012700	974	1116901-1117000	974L
793901-794000	992	858001-500	974	1012701-1013000	992	1117001-1119000	992L
794001-200	972	858501-859000	972	1013001-1015000	978	1119001-1120000	978L
794201-795000	974	859001-860000	974	1015001-300	974	1120001-1122000	992L
795001-796400	992	860001-862300	992	1015301-1016000	992	1122001-1123000	974P
796401-800	972	862301-400	954	1016001-300	975	1123001-500	972P
796801-797200	974	862401-500	972	1016301-600	973	1123501-1125000	974P
797201-500	954	862501-600	954	1016601-1018000	993	1125001-1127000	992L
797501-799000	974	862601-800	972	1018001-1020000	992	1127001-1128000	972L
798001-500	990	862801-863000	974	1020001-1022600	950	1128001-1129000	974L
798501-800	972	863001-864000	992	1022601-1023000	952	1129001-1130500	974P
798801-799000	974	864001-865000	975	1023001-700	992	1130501-1131000	956P
799001-200	954	865001-866000	992	1023701-1024500	974	1131001-1132000	992L
799201-600	992	866001-600	974	1024501-600	974	1132001-1133000	990L
799601-800000	954	866601-700	954	1024601-1025000	972	1133001-1134000	978L
800001-802000	974	866701-867000	972	1025001-1027000	975	1134001-1135000	972L
802001-200	954	867001-868000	975	1027001-400	993	1135001-1137000	992L
802201-2	972	868001-869000	992	1027401-1029600	975	1137001-1138000	956P
802203-300	954	869001-870000	975	1029601-1030000	973	1138001-1139000	956P
802301-500	972	870001-872000	992	1030001-1032000	992	1139001-1140000	978L
802501-803700	974	872001-200	993	1032001-1033000	974	1140001-1141000	972L
803701-804200	954	872201-874000	975	1033001-200	972	1141001-1142000	956P
804201-806000	974	874001-800	974	1033201-800	954	1142001-500	974P
806001-807000	975	874801-875000	975	1033801-1035300	974	1142501-1145000	974L
807001-500	993	875001-300	952	1035301-600	972	1145001-1146000	975P
807501-808800	975	875301-876000	975	1035601-1036000	974	1146001-500	956P
808801-809000	993	876001-600	993	1036001-300	972	1146501-1149000	974P
809001-500	974	876601-877000	975	1036301-800	954	1149001-1150000	974L
809501-600	972	877001-400	992	1036801-1037000	992L	1150001-600	950L
809601-810000	974	877401-700	975	1037001-1038000	974	1150601-1151800	952L
810001-300	990	877701-878000	993	1038001-1039000	992	1151801-1152000	952P
810301-812000	974	878001-879400	975	1039001-200	972	1152001-900	950P
812001-700	992	879401-880000	992	1039201-500	978	1152901-1153200	952P
812701-813000	974	880001-600	992	1039501-1040300	974	1153201-300	
813001-814000	974P	880601-882400	974	1040301-1041000	992	1153301-500	994P
814001-800	974L	882401-883400	992	1041001-1042000	974	1153501-800	994L
814801-815900	992	883401-884100	974	1042001-700	992	1153801-1154000	960L
815901-816000	974L	884101-885300	992	1042701-1043000	972	1154001-500	950L
816001-817000	974P	885301-886000	974	1043001-700	978	1154501-1155000	950P
817001-819000	974L	886001-887000	992	1043701-1044000	992	1155001-200	994P
819001-820000	974P	887001-300	974	1044001-1045000	974	1155201-500	994L
820001-821500	974L	887301-890300	992	1045001-1046000	992	1156001-1158000	996L
821501-822000	990L	890301-891000	974	1046001-1047000	975	1158001-1160000	974P
822001-700	992L	891001-600	992	1047001-1048000	974L	1160001-1162000	992L
822701-823000	974L	891601-892200	978	1048001-1049000	992	1162001-500	993L
823001-824000	974P	892201-896200	992	1049001-500	990	1162501-1164000	992L
824001-826000	975P	896201-897800	974	1049501-1051000	992	1164001-1166000	974P
		897801-898000	972				

Serial Numbers	Grade
1166001-1167000	974L
1167001-1168000	956P
1168001-1169000	975P
1169001-1170000	974P
1170001-1174000	956P
1174001-1176000	974P
1176001-1177000	992L
1177001-1178000	956P
1178001-1179000	974P
1179001-1181000	996L
1181001-1182000	992L
1182001-1183000	996L
1183001-1184400	974P
1184401-1185400	956P
1185401-1186000	974P
1186001-1187000	992L
1187001-1188000	996L
1188001-1189000	992L
1189001-1190000	974P
1190001-1192000	996L
1192001-1193000	975P
1193001-1194000	974P
1194001-1195000	956P
1195001-1196000	974P
1196001-1199000	992L
1199001-1201000	974P
1201001-1202000	975P
1202001-1203000	992L
1203001-1204000	974P
1204001-500	956P
1204501-1206000	974P
1206001-1207000	992L
1207001-1210000	974P
1210001-1212000	992L
1212001-1213000	974P
1213001-500	996L
1213501-1214000	992L
1214001-1214600	993L
1214601-1215000	975P
1215001-1216000	974L
1216001-1219000	992L
1219001-1220000	974P
1220001-1221000	992L
1221001-1223500	974P
1223501-1224000	956P
1224001-1227000	992L
1227001-1228000	972L
1228001-700	992L
1228701-1229000	990L
1229001-500	956P
1229501-1230000	974P
1230001-1231000	974L
1231001-1232000	992L
1232001-1233000	974P
1233001-1236000	992L
1236001-500	974P
1236501-1237000	956P
1237001-500	996L
1237501-1238000	992L
1238001-1239000	956P
1239001-1241000	992L
1241001-1242000	975P
1242001-400	974L
1242401-1243000	972L
1243001-500	996L
1243501-1244000	992L
1244001-1245000	974P
1245001-1246000	992L
1246001-300	974P
1246301-800	956P
1246801-1247000	974L
1247001-1248000	992L
1248001-1249700	974P
1249701-1250000	956P
1250001-1252000	983
1252001-1253000	985
1253001-1257000	983
1257001-900	985
1260001-970	Chro.*
1260971-1265000	956P
1265001-1266000	974P
1266001-1267000	978L
1267001-1268200	992L
1268201-1269000	978L
1269001-600	992L
1269601-1270000	956P
1270001-1271700	956P
1271701-1272000	974P
1272001-1274000	996L
1274001-500	993L
1274501-700	956P
1274701-1275000	992L
1275001-1276000	972L
1276001-1277000	974L
1277001-1278000	992L
1278001-1279000	975P
1279001-1280000	974P
1280001-1281000	992L
1281001-800	992L
1281801-1282000	956P
1282001-1284000	992L
1284001-1285000	992L
1285001-1286000	992L
1286001-1288000	978L
1288001-500	993L
1288501-1289100	992L
1289101-700	990L
1289701-1290000	992L
1290001-1291500	974P
1291501-1292000	992P
1292001-1297000	992L
1297001-1298000	974P
1298001-1299000	992L
1299001-1300000	975P
1300001-1301000	974P
1301001-1302000	974L
1302001-500	992L
1302501-1303000	990L
1303001-500	972L
1303501-1304000	972P
1304001-1305000	978L
1305001-1306000	956P
1306001-1307000	974P
1307001-1308500	992L
1308501-1309000	993L
1309001-1310000	974L
1310001-1311000	972L
1311001-1312000	992L
1312001-800	974P
1312801-1313000	956P
1313001-1317000	992L
1317001-1318000	956P
1318001-1321000	992L
1321001-300	990L
1321301-1322000	992L
1322001-700	974L
1322701-1323000	972L
1323001-1324000	992L
1324001-1325000	996L
1325001-1326500	975P
1326501-1327000	993L
1327001-300	956P
1327301-1329000	974P
1329001-1330000	992L
1330001-1331300	974L
1331301-800	972L
1331801-1332000	978L
1332001-1334000	992L
1334001-400	974P
1334401-1335000	956P
1335001-300	978L
1335301-1336000	972L
1336001-1337000	992L
1337001-1338200	996L
1338201-1339000	996L
1339001-1340000	956P
1340001-1341000	992L
1341001-300	972L
1341301-500	974L
1341501-1342000	978L
1342001-1343000	992L
1343001-400	956P
1343401-1344000	974P
1344001-1345000	992L
1345001-600	974L
1345601-1346000	972L
1346001-1348000	975P
1348001-1349000	974P
1349001-1350000	992L
1350001-600	972L
1350601-1351000	974L
1351001-1352000	993L
1352001-1352300	974L
1352301-800	978L
1352801-1353000	974L
1353001-500	972P
1353501-1354200	956P
1354201-700	992P
1354701-1355000	974P
1355001-1356000	992L
1356001-1357000	974P
1357001-1359800	992L
1359801-1361000	992L
1361001-1362000	996L
1362001-600	974P
1362601-1363000	956P
1363001-1364000	992L
1364001-1365000	975P
1365001-800	956P
1365801-1367000	974P
1367001-1369400	992L
1369401-1370000	996L
1370001-1371000	974L
1371001-600	996L
1371601-1373000	992L
1373001-1374000	975P
1374001-1375000	992L
1375001-1376000	950L
1376001-1377000	992L
1377001-1378300	974P
1378301-1379000	956P
1379001-1380200	992L
1380201-1381000	978L
1381001-500	956P
1381501-1383000	974P
1383001-1384000	992L
1384001-1386100	974P
1386101-1387000	956P
1387001-1388000	992L
1388001-400	978L
1388401-1389000	978L
1389001-300	956P
1389301-1390000	956P
1390001-1391000	992L
1391001-500	956P
1391501-1392000	974P
1392001-1393000	992L
1393001-1394000	974P
1394001-1396000	992L
1396001-500	972L
1396501-1398000	974L
1398001-400	974P
1398401-1399000	956P
1399001-1400000	992L
1400001-1401000	936
1401001-1403000	924
1403001-1409000	940
1409001-500	946
1409501-1410000	940
1410001-1414000	924
1414001-300	941
1414501-1415000	925
1415001-1417000	924
1417001-1419000	940
1419001-1420000	924
1420001-1421000	940
1421001-1422000	924
1422001-1424000	940
1424001-1428000	924
1428001-1430000	940
1430001-200	924
1430201-400	948
1430401-1431000	924
1431001-1433000	940
1433001-1438000	924
1438001-500	926
1438501-1439500	924
1439501-1440000	926
1440001-1441000	940
1441001-1442000	924
1442001-500	926
1442501-1444000	924
1444001-1445000	940
1445001-1447000	924
1447001-1448200	940
1448201-1450500	924
1500001-600	974P
1500601-1501200	956P
1501201-1502000	974P
1502001-1503000	993L
1503001-1504000	996L
1504001-500	974L
1504501-1505200	972L
1505201-700	978L
1505701-1506000	974L
1506001-1507000	975P
1507001-1508000	992L
1508001-400	974P
1508401-1509000	956P
1509001-1510000	992L
1510001-1511000	974P
1511001-1512000	975P
1512001-1513200	992L
1513201-600	992P
1513601-1514000	992L
1514001-200	956P
1514201-1515000	974P
1515001-1516000	992L
1516001-1517000	974P
1517001-1520000	992L
1520001-1521200	974L
1521201-1522000	978L
1522001-600	974P
1522601-1525000	956P
1525001-1527000	996L
1527001-1528000	992L
1528001-1531000	974P
1531001-1533000	992L
1533001-600	974P
1533601-1534000	975P
1534001-100	975P
1535101-200	975P
1535201-400	975P
1535601-1536000	993L
1536001-1537000	972L
1537001-1538000	992L
1538001-800	956P
1538801-1539000	974P
1539001-1540000	992L
1540001-500	992P
1540501-1541000	992L
1541001-1542200	974P
1542201-800	956P
1542801-1543000	974P
1543001-1544000	996L
1544001-1545000	992L
1545001-400	978L
1545401-1546000	974L
1546001-1548000	992L
1548001-600	974L
1548601-1549000	992L
1549001-1550000	974P
1550001-500	972P
1550501-1552000	974P
1552001-1555000	992L
1555001-1557000	993P
1557001-800	972L
1557801-1558000	974L
1558001-500	956
1558501-1559700	956P
1559701-1560000	974P
1560001-1561000	975P
1561001-1563000	992L
1563001-1565000	978L
1565001-1567000	992L
1567001-1568000	974L
1568001-1569000	992L
1569001-1571000	972L
1571001-1572000	974P
1572001-1573000	975P
1573001-1575000	974P
1575001-400	950L
1575401-1576000	950P
1576001-1577000	950L
1577001-1578000	975P
1578001-1580000	992L
1580001-1581200	974L
1581201-1582000	956P
1582001-1583000	974P
1583001-1584000	992L
1584001-1585000	978L
1585001-1586000	972L
1586001-1587000	992L
1587001-500	992P
1587501-1589000	992L
1589001-500	956P
1589501-1590000	974P
1590001-1591000	974L
1591001-1592000	992L
1592001-1593000	974P
1593001-1595000	992L
1595001-200	974P
1595201-900	956P
1595901-1596000	974P
1596001-1611000	992L
1611001-1612100	974P
1612101-1613000	956P
1613001-600	996L
1614001-900	956P
1614901-1615000	974P
1615001-1625000	992L
1625001-200	950L
1625201-1626000	952L
1626001-1627000	974P
1627001-1633000	992L
1633001-1635000	950L
1635001-1636000	992L
1636001-1637000	956P
1637001-1638000	974P
1638001-1642800	992L
1642801-1643000	992P
1643001-1644000	992L
1644001-1646000	974L
1646001-1648000	972L
1648001-1649000	992L
1649001-1652000	974P
1652001-1653000	950L
1653001-1654000	956P
1654001-1657000	974P
1657001-1660000	992L
1660001-1661000	978L
1661001-1663000	974P
1663001-1664000	974L
1664001-1665000	950L
1665001-1666000	974P
1666001-1667000	956P
1667001-1669000	974P
1669001-1670000	978L
1670001-1671000	974P
1671001-300	992L
1671301-900	992P
1671901-1672000	992L
1672001-1676000	974P
1676001-1678000	992L
1678001-1679000	974P
1679001-1681000	974L
1681001-1682000	974P
1682001-1683000	956P
1683001-1685000	974P
1685001-1686000	992L
1686001-1688000	974P
1688001-500	978L
1689001-600	975P
1690001-1691000	956
1691001-1693000	992L
1693001-1696000	956P
1696001-1699000	992L
1699001-1703000	974P
1703001-1704000	992L
1704001-1705000	956P
1705001-1706000	974P
1706001-1707100	992L
1708001-1714000	992L
1714001-1715000	974P
1715001-1717000	992L
1717001-800	956
1718001-1750000	992L
1750001-1761000	900
1761001-1765000	914
1765001-1767000	920
1767001-1768000	914
1768001-1769000	900
1769001-1770000	920
1770001-1778200	914
1778201-1779000	910
1779001-1780000	920
1780001-1782000	910
1782001-500	920
1782501-1783000	900
1783001-1808000	910
1808001-1810000	914
1810001-1811000	910
1811001-1813000	900
1813001-1818000	910
1818001-1819000	914
1819001-1821000	910

1821001-1822000	914	1989001-400	914	2475001-2476000	992L
1822001-1827000	910	2000001-2001700	988	2476001-2477000	974P
1827001-600	914	2001701-2002400	986	2477001-2490000	992L
1827601-1829100	910	2002401-800	988	2490001-2492000	974L
1829101-500	914	2002801-2003100	986	2492001-2504000	992L
1829501-1830000	910	2004001-2035000	986	2504001-2505000	950L
1830001-1831000	900	2035001-2037200	981	2505001-300	950L
1831001-1832000	920	2040001-2064900	986	2506001-2526000	992L
1832001-700	910	2100001-2191300	986A	2526001-2528000	974P
1832701-1833300	914	2200001-2248000	987	2528001-2533000	992L
1833301-1834500	910	2248001-2300000	987F	2533001-2534000	974P
1834501-1835400	914	2300001-2311000	992L	2534001-2535000	992L
1835401-1836900	910	2311001-2312000	974L	2535001-2536000	974P
1836901-1837400	914	2312001-2321700	992L	2536001-2537000	974L
1837401-1839000	910	2321701-2323000	974L	2537001-2538000	974P
1839001-500	914	2323001-2326000	992L	2538001-2539000	974L
1839501-1844700	910	2326001-2327000	974P	2539001-2542000	974P
1844701-1845700	914	2327001-2333000	992L	2542001-2543000	992L
1845701-1848300	910	2333001-2336000	974P	2543001-2545000	974P
1848301-1849500	914	2336001-2338000	992L	2545001-2547000	992L
1849501-1851900	910	2338001-2339000	974P	2547001-2548400	974P
1851901-1853100	914	2339001-2340000	974L	2548401-2548600	974L
1853101-1856800	910	2340001-2341000	974P	2548601-2548700	974P
1856801-1857900	914	2341001-2346000	992L	2548701-2550000	974L
1857901-1860300	910	2346001-2347000	974P	2550001-2551000	992L
1860301-1861000	914	2347001-2356000	992L	2551001-2552000	974L
1861001-1863000	900	2356001-2358000	974P	2552001-2555000	992L
1863001-700	920	2358001-2364000	992L	2555001-2555600	974L
1863701-1864300	900	2364001-2365000	974P	2555701-2557000	974L
1864301-1865000	920	2365001-2374000	992L	2558001-2560000	992L
1865001-500	914	2374001-2375000	974P	2560001-2561000	974L
1865501-1870300	910	2375001-2378000	992L	2561001-2563000	992L
1870301-1871500	914	2378001-2380000	974L	2563001-2564000	974L
1871501-1875100	910	2380001-2383000	992L	2564001-2566000	992L
1875101-400	914	2383001-2384000	950L	2566001-2566800	974L
1875601-1876500	910	2384001-2385000	992L	2567001-2581000	992L
1876501-1877500	914	2385001-2396000	974P	2581001-2583900	992E
1877501-1878700	910	2386001-2390000	992L	2583901-2584300	992L
1878701-1880000	914	2390001-2391000	974P	2584301-2596000	992E
1880001-300	920	2391001-2393000	992L	2596001-2597000	974L
1880301-1881500	900	2393001-2395000	974P	2597001-2608000	992E
1881501-700	920	2395001-2397000	992L	2608001-2608800	974L
1881701-900	900	2397001-2398000	974L	2609001-2611000	992E
1881901-1882900	920	2398001-2401000	992L	2611001-2611400	950L
1882901-1885000	900	2401001-2402000	974P	2611401-2613000	950E
1885001-1887400	910	2402001-2407000	992L	2613001-2618000	992E
1887401-1888600	914	2407001-2409000	974P	2618001-2619000	950E
1888601-1891000	910	2409001-2413000	992L	2619001-2631000	992E
1891001-1892200	914	2413001-2414000	974P	2631001-2631600	950E
1892201-1894600	910	2414001-2415000	974L	2631801-2632000	950E
1894601-1895800	914	2415001-2418000	992L	2632001-2639000	992E
1895801-1899000	910	2418001-2420000	974P	2639001-2641000	950E
1899001-300	900	2420001-2422000	992L	2641001-2649000	992E
1899301-1900000	920	2422001-2423000	974P	2649001-2650600	950E
1900001-400	910	2423001-2432000	992L	2651001-2655300	992E
1900401-1902100	914	2432001-2433000	974P	2900001-2911500	979
1902101-1907000	910	2433001-2434000	992L	2911601-2931900	979F
1907001-1909000	914	2434001-2435000	974P	3000001-3002300	922
1909001-1910000	910	2435001-2437000	992L	3002301-3002500	922 M.P.
1910001-500	920	2437001-2438000	974P	3002501-3003800	922
1910501-1911000	900	2438001-2442000	992L	3003801-3004000	922 M.P.
1911001-1913000	920	2442001-2445000	974P	3004001-3006100	922
1913001-1914000	900	2445001-2451000	992L	3006101-3006300	922 M.P.
1914001-1920000	910	2451001-2453000	974P	3006301-3008000	922
1920001-1922000	920	2453001-2455000	992L	3008001-3008600	922 M.P.
1922001-1924000	910	2455001-2456000	974P	3008601-3010000	922
1924001-1925000	900	2456001-2457000	992L	3010001-3010500	922
1925001-1936000	910	2457001-2458000	950L	3010501-3010700	922 M.P.
1936001-1937000	920	2458001-2459000	974L	3010701-3011900	922
1937001-900	900	2459001-2461000	992L	3011901-3012500	922 M.P.
1940001-1941000	914	2461001-2462000	974L	3012501-3013100	922
1941001-1949000	910	2462001-2464000	992L	3013101-3013700	922 M.P.
1949001-1950000	914	2464001-2466000	974P	3013701-3015700	922
1950001-1962000	910	2466001-2468000	992L	3050001-3054800	902
1962001-1963000	914	2468001-2469000	974P	3054801-3056000	922
1963001-1975000	910	2469001-2472000	992L	3056001-3060600	902
1975001-1976000	914	2472001-2473000	974P	3061001-3065100	904
1976001-1980000	910	2473001-2474000	992L	3100001-3135900	916
1980001-1981000	914	2474001-2475000	974P	3135001-3152700	918
1981001-1988500	910			3200001-3460900	912
				4000001-4447201	987F
				4447301-4523000	987E

A-001 to A-8900	980B
1B-001 to 1B-25300	999B
2B-001 to 2B-700	999B
2B-701 to 2B-800	950B
C-001 to C-396300	992B
E-001 to E-114000	989
E-114001 to E-140400	
	989E
F-101 to F-57600	995
F-57601 to F-59850	995A
F-59851 to F-62000	995
F-62001 to F-63000	995A
F-63001 to F-63800	995
F-63801 to F-286200	995A
G-001 to G-13600	980
G-13601 to G-14600	
	980 & 980A
G-14601 to G-44500	980
G-44501 to G-45000	980A
G-45001 to G-47400	980
G-47401 to G-48400	980A
G-48401 to G-58200	980
G-58201 to G-58700	980A
G-58701 to G-61600	980
G-61601 to G-62500	980A
G-62501 to G-67500	980
G-67501 to G-68600	980A
G-68601- to G-651700	980
H-001 to H-1000	921
H-1001 to H-1800	
	400 & 921
H-1801 to H-2000	921
H-2001 to H-2800	921
	400 & 921
H-2801 to H-3500	400
H-3501 to H-51700	921
H-50001 to H-57500	401
J-001 to J-670600	982
L-001 to L-165000	997
M-001 to M-201900	982M
N-001 to N-532200	721
O-1 to O-486300	987A
R-001 to R-3600	923
8-001 to 8-18700	950B
SS-001 to SS-87400	987S
T-001 to T-783000	911
V-001 to V-127200	911M
X-001 to X-197600	917
Y-001 to Y-396200	747
CY-001 to CY-176700	748
O-01A to 622700-A	750
O-01C to 126000-C	751
001E to 47400E	752
001F to 63700F	753
001H to 26800H	754

*Hamilton 36 size chronometer watch

* Hayden W. Wheeler model

NOTE: The above serial number and grade listing is an actual Hamilton factory list and is accurate in most cases. However, it has been brought to our attention that in rare cases the serial number and grade number do not match the list. One example is the Hayden W. Wheeler model.

(See Hamilton Watch Co. **Serial Numbers and Grades** section located at the end of the Hamilton Watch price section to identify the movement, size and grade of your watch.)

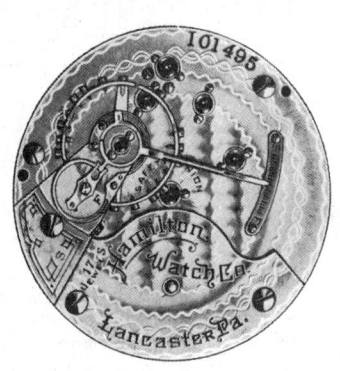 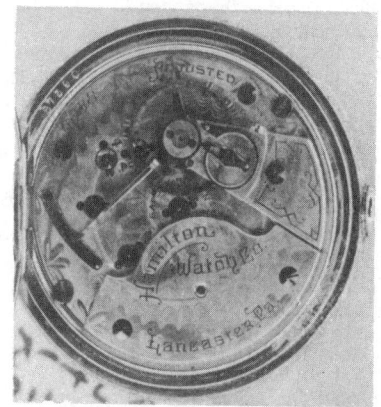

Grade 925, 18 size, 17 jewels, hunting case, serial number 101,495.

Grade 932, 18 size, 16 jewels, open face, serial number 6,888.

HAMILTON
18 SIZE

Grade or Name — Description		Avg	Ex-Fn	Mint
7J, OF, LS, FULL	★★	$1,200	$1,500	$2,000
11J, HC, LS, FULL	★★★	1,400	1,700	2,100
11J, OF, LS, FULL	★★★★	1,600	1,900	2,300
922, 15J, OF	★★	500	600	750
923, 15J, HC	★★	550	650	800
924, 17J, NI, OF, DMK		100	125	150
925, 17J, NI, HC, DMK		125	150	200
926, 17J, NI, OF, DMK, ADJ		100	125	150
927, 17J, NI, HC, DMK, ADJ		125	150	200
928, 15J, NI, OF		150	175	235
929, 15J, NI, HC, 14K		625	725	825
929, 15J, NI, HC		200	250	325
930, 16J, NI, OF		175	225	300
931, 16J, NI, HC		225	285	350
932 or 936, serial #s less than 50, OF	★★★	1,700	1,900	2,500
932, 16J, NI, OF	★★	425	485	550
932 (S#s less than 400 up to $1,200 to $2,000)				
933, 16J, NI, HC	★★	525	585	650
933 ((Serial #s started at 1021, S#s less than 1,500 up to $1,900)				
934, 17J, NI, OF, DMK, ADJ		125	150	200
934, 17J, NI, OF, ADJ, Coin		100	135	175
934 & 935 & 937, 17J, MARKED (**Main Line**)		225	265	325
935, 17J, NI, HC, DMK, ADJ.	★	275	325	400
936, 17J, NI, OF, DMK, SR & DR		100	135	175
936 (S#s less than 400 up to $1,200)				
937, 17J, NI, HC, DMK, MARKED on Mvt. (**Official Standard**)		300	350	425
937, 17J, NI, HC, DMK, SR & DR		175	225	300
937, 17J, serial # 1001 to 1020 = 1st run HC		1,700	1,900	2,500
937, 17J, serial # 1601 to 2000 = 2nd run HC		1,000	1,200	1,500

FIRST Hunting Case serial was **1001**.

937 *(Serial #s started at* **1001,** *S#s less than 1,300 up to $1,200)*

🕐 Watches listed in this book are priced at the collectable retail level, as **Complete** watches having an original 14k gold-filled case for Stem Wind and *Key Wind* with silver case, an original white enamel single sunk dial, and with the entire original movement in good working order with no repairs needed.

Grade or Name — Description	Avg	Ex-Fn	Mint
938, 17J, NI, OF, DMK, DR .... ★★	$535	$650	$800
939, 17J, NI, HC, DMK, DR.. ★★	635	750	900
940, 21J, NI, OF, Mermod Jaccards St. Louis Paragon			
Time Keeper & a hour glass on mvt.	375	475	585
940, 21J, NI, OF, DMK, SR & DR, Adj.5P, GJS............................	225	250	300
940, 21J, NI, OF, GF or Coin..	225	250	295
940, 21J, NI, OF, SR & DR, 2-Tone	325	350	400
940, 21J, NI, OF, DR, Marked Extra...★	375	435	600
940, 21J, NI, OF, DR, Marked Special..★	375	435	600
940, 21J, NI, OF, DR, Marked Special for R R Service........ ★★	600	700	850
940, 21J, NI, OF, DR, Marked			
Pennsylvania Special	850	900	1,000
941, 21J, NI, HC, DR, GJS, ...	275	335	375
941, 21J, NI, HC, DR, GJS, Marked Special ....★	450	500	575
941, 21J, NI, HC, DMK, SR & DR, Adj.5P, GJS	285	375	425
942, 21J, NI, OF, DMK, DR, Adj.5P, GJS	275	350	400
942, 21J, NI, OF, DMK, DR, Adj.5P, GJS			
Marked For Railroad Service.. ★★	1,000	1,100	1,250
943, 21J, NI, HC, DMK, DR, Adj.5P, GJS ....★	425	475	525
943, 21J, Marked Burlington Special...............................★	585	675	825
944, 19J, NI, OF, DMK, DR, Adj.5P, GJS	275	300	350
946, Anderson (jobber name on movement), 14K..........................	900	1,100	1,400
946, 23J, Marked Extra, OF, GJS ....★	650	700	775
946, 23J, Marked "Loaner" on case ....★	625	675	735
946, 23J, NI, OF, DMK, DR, Adj.5P, GJS	600	650	725
946, 23J, NI, OF, DMK, Adj.5P, GJS, unmarked	600	650	725
947, 23J, NI, DMK, DR, Adj.5P, GJS, 14K, HC,			
NOT MARKED "947"................................ ★★★	5,000	6,000	7,000
947, 23J, NI, DMK, DR, Adj.5P, GJS, 14K, HC,			
MARKED "947"..................................... ★★★★	7,000	8,000	9,000
947, 23J, NI, DMK, DR, Adj.5P, GJS, 14K, HC,			
MARKED "947" EXTRA................................. ★★★★★	7,500	8,500	9,500

MOVEMENTS WITH ODD GRADE NUMBERS ARE HUNTING CASE.
MOVEMENTS WITH EVEN GRADE NUMBERS ARE OPEN FACE.
Note: Some 18 size movements are **marked** with grade numbers, some are not. Collectors prefer marked movement.

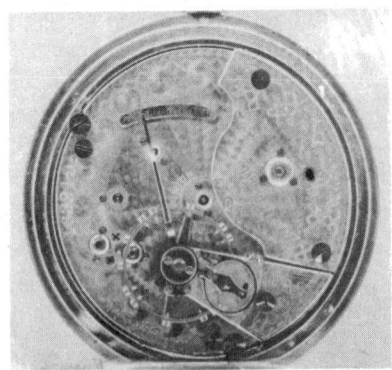

Grade 947 (marked), 18 size, 23 jewels, gold jewel settings, hunting case, Adj6p, serial number 163,219.

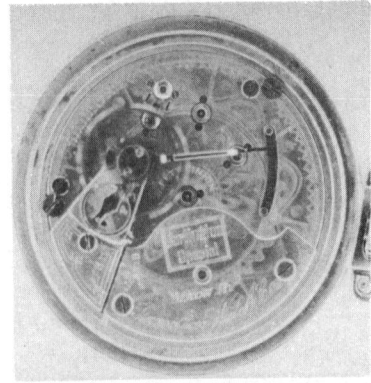

Burlington Special, 18 size, 21 jewels, Grade 943, open face, serial number 121,614.

Grade or Name — Description	Avg	Ex-Fn	Mint
948, 17J, NI, OF, DMK, DR, Adj.5P, GJS ....★	$325	$375	$450
948, 17J, NI, DMK, DR, Adj.5P, GJS, OF, Coin ....★	325	375	450
The Banner, 928, 15J, NI, OF	150	175	225
The Banner, 940, 21J, NI, OF	275	325	395
The Banner, 940 **special**, 21J, NI, OF...................................	375	425	525
The Banner, 941, 21J, NI, HC..	325	375	425
The Banner, 17J, M#927, HC, ADJ	150	175	225
Burlington Special, 17J, Adj.5P, OF.....................................	800	900	1,000
Burlington Special, 17J, Adj.5P, HC	900	1,000	1,200
Burlington Special, 21J, Adj.5P, OF.....................................	1,000	1,100	1,300
Burlington Special, 21J, Adj.5P, HC	1,100	1,200	1,400
Imperial Canada, GRADE 922, OF ....★	635	700	850
Imperial Canada, GRADE 923, HC......................................★	750	850	1,000
Inspectors Standard, 21J, OF...	325	385	500
RAILROAD watches with R.R. names as			
Chesapeake & Ohio, Special, (936)	1,000	1,100	1,300
Chesapeake & Ohio, Railway Special, (936).........................	800	900	1,000
Chesapeake & Ohio, Railway Special, (937).........................	1,000	1,100	1,300
The Union, 17J..	150	185	225
The Union Special, 17J...	150	185	225
The Union, 17J, G#925, HC..	225	250	300

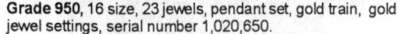

Grade 950, 16 size, 23 jewels, pendant set, gold train, gold jewel settings, serial number 1,020,650.

Grade 961, 16 size, 21 jewels, gold train, gold jewel settings, serial number 81,848.

16 SIZE

Grade or Name — Description	Avg	Ex-Fn	Mint
950, 23J, LS, BRG, DR, GT, **14K, OF**...	$800	$900	$1,000
950, 23J, **LS**, DR, OF, BRG, GJS, Adj.5P, NI, GT........................	525	575	625
950, 23J, **PS**, DR, OF, GJS, BRG, Adj.5P, NI, GT........................	525	575	625
950B, 23J, LS, OF, Adj.6P, NI, DR, BRG	550	600	650
950B, 23J, LS, OF, Adj.6P, NI, DR, BRG, **Gold Train**.................	575	625	675
950E, 23J, LS, OF, Adj.6P, NI, DR, BRG, marked **Elinvar**..........	625	675	750
951, 23J, LS, BRG, Adj.5P, NI, GT, GJS, DR, HC .... ★★★	6,000	6,500	7,000
951, 23J, PS, BRG, Adj.5P, NI, GT, GJS, DR, HC.............. ★★★	6,000	6,500	7,000
951, 23J, PS, BRG, Adj.5P, NI, GT, GJS, DR, HC,**14K** ..... ★★★	6,500	7,000	7,500
952, 19J, LS or PS, OF, BRG, Adj.5P, NI, GJS, DR	235	275	325
952, 19J, LS or PS, BRG, Adj.5P, OF, **14K**................................	500	535	600

🕒 Watches listed in this book are priced at the collectable retail level, as **Complete** watches having an original 14k gold-filled case for Stem Wind and Key Wind with silver case, an original white enamel single sunk dial, and with the entire original movement in good working order with no repairs needed.

Grade or Name — Description	Avg	Ex-Fn	Mint
954, 17J, LS or PS, OF, 3/4, DR, Adj.5P..........................	$100	$125	$175
956, 17J, PS, OF, 3/4, DR, Adj.5P......................	100	125	175
960, 21J, PS, OF, BRG, GJS, GT, DR, Adj.5P .... ★	375	400	450
960, 21J, LS, OF, BRG, GJS, GT, DR, Adj.5P .... ★	400	425	475
961, 21J, PS & LS, HC, BRG, GJS, GT, DR, Adj.5P .... ★	425	475	550
962, 17J, PS, OF, BRG.. ★★	525	625	725
963, 17J, PS, HC, BRG .... ★★	575	675	775
964, 17J, PS, OF, BRG.. ★★	675	725	825
965, 17J, PS, HC, BRG .... ★★	525	575	675
966, 17J, PS, OF, 3/4.. ★★	625	675	775
967, 17J, PS, HC, 3/4.. ★★	650	700	800
968, 17J, PS, OF, 3/4.. ★	350	400	500
969, 17J, PS, HC, 3/4.. ★	450	475	525
970, 21J, PS, OF, 3/4..	300	350	400
971, 23J, Adj.5P, **SWISS MADE**...............	75	100	135
971, 21J, PS, HC, 3/4..	250	300	350
972, 17J, PS & LS, OF, 3/4, NI, GJS, DR, Adj.5P, DMK	175	200	225
973, 17J, PS & LS, HC, 3/4, NI, DR, Adj.5P	200	225	275
974, 17J, LS, OF, 3/4, NI, Adj.3P.............	100	125	150
974, 17J, OF, PS, Adj.3P....................	100	125	150
974, 17J, OF, 2-tone............................	175	200	275
2974B, 17J, OF, Adj.3P, **hacking, U.S. GOV.**............................ ★	250	285	325
975, 17J, PS & LS, HC, 3/4, NI, Adj.3P............................	125	150	175
976, 16J, PS, OF, 3/4..	175	200	250
977, 16J, PS, HC, 3/4..	175	200	250
978, 17J, LS, OF, 3/4, NI, DMK..................................	100	125	150
990, 21J, LS, OF, GJS, DR, Adj.5P, DMK, NI, 3/4, GT	275	300	325
991, 21J, LS, HC, 3/4, GJS, Adj.5P, DMK, NI, GT..................	300	325	350

Grade 992B, 16 size, 21 jewels, Adj.6p.   Grade 4992B, 16 size, 22 jewels, Adj.6p.

Note: Prefix before serial no. was Hamilton's method of I.D.,(C & serial no.= 992B railroad watch), (2B & serial no. = 950B railroad watch also S), (3C & serial no. = 4992B G.T.C. Canada Gov't), (4C & serial no.= 4992B for U.S.A. Gov't), (2K & serial no.= 2974B used for comparing watch).

IMPORTANT NOTE: Railroad Standards, Railroad Approved & Railroad Grade **terminology,** as defined and used in this *BOOK*.
1. **RAILROAD STANDARDS** = A commission or board appointed by the railroad companies outlined a set of **guidelines** to be accepted or approved by each railroad line.
2. **RAILROAD APPROVED** = A **LIST** of watches each railroad line would approve if purchased by their employee's. (this list changed through the years).
3. **RAILROAD GRADE** = A watch made by manufactures to met or exceed the guidelines set by the railroad **standards**. Grade such as 992, Vanguard and B.W. Raymond etc.
☉ Some GRADES **exceeded** the R.R. standards such as 23 jewels, diamond end stone, gold train, raised gold jewel settings, double sunk dial and the list goes on. Examples: such as Veritas, Sangamo, 950 & Riverside Maximus and many others.

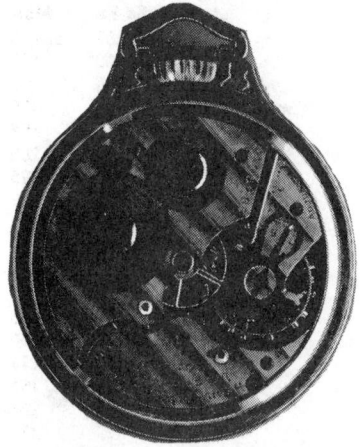

Grade 992E, 21jewels, gold center wheel, gold jewel settings, Adj.5P, marked Elinvar under balance wheel, Note the wide striped style Damaskeening, serial #2,595,787.

Grade 3992B, 22J, Adj.6P, "Navigation Master", note outside chapter on dial 1--10.

Grade or Name — Description	Avg	Ex-Fn	Mint
992, 21J, OF, 3/4, Adj.5P, SR & DR, NI	$200	$235	$275
992, 21J, OF, 3/4, **gold center wheel**,GJS, Adj.5P, SR & DR, NI.	225	250	295
992, 21J, OF, 3/4, PS & LS, GJS, Adj.5P, DR, NI, DMK, **2 -Tone**	300	325	375
992, 21J, **Extra**, OF, 3/4, PS & LS, GJS, Adj.5P, DR, NI, DMK ...	325	350	400
992, 21J, marked **Special,** OF, 3/4, PS & LS, GJS, Adj.5P, DR, NI, DMK, Adj. for RR Service' on dial	425	475	550
992E, 21J, marked **Elinvar, gold center wheel,** 3/4, GJS, Adj.5P .	325	350	400
992B, 21J, LS, Adj.6P, OF, 3/4	325	365	425
992B, 21J, Adj.6P, **2-Tone**	425	475	525
992B, 21J, OF, Adj.6P, 3/4, military silver case	295	325	375
3992B, 22J, Adj.6P, 12 hr. dial, (Canadian), silver case .... ★	450	500	585
3992B, 22J, Adj.6P, "Navigation Master", Silver case .... ★	475	525	595
4992B, 22J, LS, OF, 3/4, 24-hr. dial, Greenwich Civil Time	235	285	325
993, 21J, PS, HC, GJS, Adj.5P, DR, NI, DMK	350	375	425
993, 21J, LS, HC, GJS, Adj.5P, DMK, DR, NI	350	375	425
993, 21J, marked **Special,** tu-tone, HC, GJS, Adj.5P, DMK, DR ★	375	400	475
993, 21J, LS, HC, GJS, Adj.5P, DMK, DR, NI, **14K**	750	800	875
993, 21J, LS, HC, GJS, Adj.5P, DMK, DR, (GF multi color case)	500	550	600

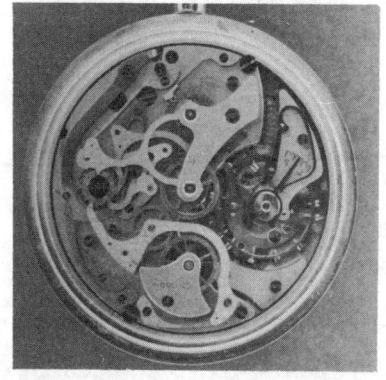

ADMIRAL,16 size, 16 jewels, Damaskeened on nickel 3/4 plate, serial no. 57821.

Chronograph, Grade 23, 16 size, 19 jewels, start-stop-reset to 0.

Grade or Name — Description	Avg	Ex-Fn	Mint
994, 21J, BRG, OF, GJS, GT, DR, Adj.5P, DMK, PS .... ★	$1,000	$1,200	$1,500
994, 21J, BRG, OF, GJS, GT, DR, Adj.5P, DMK, LS .... ★	1,100	1,300	1,600
996, 19J, LS, OF, 3/4 GJS, DR, Adj.5P, DMK	225	250	300
Admiral, 16J., Grade 977, 3/4 plate, OF, ... ★ ★ ★	135	155	175
Admiral,16J,NI, ADJ., DMK, HC...	135	155	175
DeLong Escapement, 21J, 992-B .... ★ ★ ★ ★	1,700	1,900	2,200
Electric Interurban, 17J, G#974, OF	150	175	225
Official Standard, 17J, OF..	200	225	300
Union Special, 17J...	125	150	225
Hayden W. Wheeler, 17J, OF...★	425	500	600
Hayden W. Wheeler, 17J, HC ....★	450	535	650
Hayden W. Wheeler, 21J..★	525	625	725
Hayden W. Wheeler, 21J, **14K** H.W.W. case............................★	900	1,000	1,100
Limited, 17J, G#974	150	175	250
Swiss Mfg., 17J, Adj.2P, GF case.....................................	85	100	125
Swiss Mfg., 23J, Adj.3P, (by Buren W. Co. G# 917), Ca. 1969-70s	95	110	145

CHRONOGRAPH
Grade 23

Grade or Name — Description	Avg	Ex-Fn	Mint
16S, 19J, start-stop-reset to 0	$300	$350	$400

12 SIZE
(Some cases were octagon, decagon, cushion, etc.)

Grade or Name — Description	Avg	Ex-Fn	Mint
900, 19J, BRG, DR, Adj.5P, GJS, OF, **14K**	$300	$325	$400
900, 19J, BRG, DR, Adj.5P, GJS, OF	125	150	200
902, 19J, BRG, DR, Adj.5P, GJS..	125	150	200

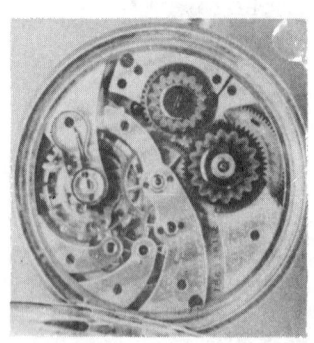

Grade **918**, 12 size, 19 jewels, Adj3p, serial number 3,136,257.

Grade **920**, 12 size, 23 jewels, gold train, gold jewel settings, serial number 1,863,381.

 Watches listed in this book are priced at the collectable retail level, as **Complete** watches having an original 14k gold-filled case for Stem Wind and *Key Wind* with silver case, an original white enamel single sunk dial, and with the entire original movement in good working order with no repairs needed.

MOVEMENTS WITH ODD GRADE NUMBERS ARE HUNTING CASE.
MOVEMENTS WITH EVEN GRADE NUMBERS ARE OPEN FACE.

Grade or Name — Description	Avg	Ex-Fn	Mint
902, 19J, BRG, DR, Adj.5P, GJS, **14K**	$325	$350	$400
904, 21J, BRG, DR, Adj.5P, GJS, GT	125	150	200
910, 17J, 3/4, DR, ADJ	75	95	100
912, 17J, **Digital model, rotating seconds,** OF	95	125	150
912, 17J, 3/4, DR, ADJ	60	75	100
914, 17J, 3/4, DR, Adj.3P, GJS	60	75	100
914, 17J, 3/4, DR, Adj.3P, GJS, **14K**	250	275	325
916, 17J, 3/4, DR, Adj.3P	60	75	100
916, 17J, Adj.3P, silver case	60	75	100
918, 19J, Adj.3P, WGF	100	125	175
918, 19J, 3/4, DR, Adj.3P, GJS, OF	100	125	175
920, 23J, BRG, DR, Adj.5P, GJS, GT, OF	225	275	350
920, 23J, BRG, DR, Adj.5P, GJS, GT, **14K**	425	475	550
922, 23J, BRG, DR, Adj.5P, GJS, GT, **14K**	425	475	550
922, 23J, BRG, DR, Adj.5P, GJS, GT, OF	225	275	350
922 MP, 23J, marked (MASTERPIECE), **18K case** ★	800	900	1,100
922 MP, 23J, marked (MASTERPIECE), **Platinum case** ★	850	950	1,200
922 MP, GF, Hamilton case	325	425	575
400, 21J, (Illinois 12 size M#2, 5 tooth click) **Hamilton on dial.** ★	325	425	575

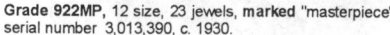

Grade **922MP**, 12 size, 23 jewels, marked "masterpiece" serial number 3,013,390, c. 1930.

Grade **912**, 12 size, 17 jewels, with Secometer dial, originally sold for $88.70.

10 SIZE

Grade or Name — Description	Avg	Ex-Fn	Mint
917, 17J, 3/4, DR, Adj.3P	$75	$95	$125
917, 17J, 3/4, DR, Adj.3P, **14K**	225	250	325
921, 21J, BRG, DR, Adj.5P	100	125	150
923, 23J, BRG, DR, Adj.5P, **G.F.**	275	300	375
923, 23J, **18K, and box**	500	600	700
945, 23J, Adj.5P, Masterpiece on DIAL	150	175	250

🕐 Watches listed in this book are priced at the collectable retail level, as complete watches having an original 14k goldfilled case & KW with a Silver case, an original white enamel single sunk dial, and with the entire original movement in good working order with no repairs needed, unless otherwise noted.

0 SIZE

Grade or Name — Description	Avg	Ex-Fn	Mint
981, 17J, 3/4, Adj.3P, DR, **18K, HC**	$300	$325	$375
982, 17-19J, open face same as 981 & 983 HC but no seconds bit	100	125	150
983, 17J, Adj.3P, DR, GJS, **18K, HC**	300	325	375
985, 19J, BRG, Adj.3P, DR, GJS, GT, **18K, HC**	325	350	400
Lady Hamilton, 14K case, OF	225	250	325
Lady Hamilton, 23J, GJS, **gold filled OF**	150	175	225

**Above:** model 22, 21 jewels, 70mm, wind indicator, adjusted to 6 positions, base metal case.

Right: Chronometer in gimbals and box, 36 size, wind indicator.

CHRONOMETER

Grade or Name — Description	Avg	Ex-Fn	Mint
35S, M#22, 21J, Wind Indicator, Adj.6P, in gimbals and box, lever	$150	$750	$850
35S, M#22, 21J, Wind Indicator, Adj.6P, in a large base metal OF case	575	650	775
36S, M#36, 21J, Wind Indicator, in gimbals and box	1,300	1,500	1,700
36S, M#36, 21J, 56 hr.W. Ind.,"SID" (sidereal), chrome case ..... ★	1,300	1,500	1,700
36S, M#36, 21J, Wind Indicator, in Hamilton sterling pocket watch case with bow (s# 1,260,001 to 1,260,970) .... ★ ★ ★	2,000	2,400	3,000
37S, 21J, 940 movement S# range= 420,001 to 421,000, ONLY 220 made for U.S. Navy, true 24 hour black dial .... ★ ★ ★ ★	1,400	1,500	1,700
85S, M#21, 14J, KW, KS, Fusee, Detent Escapement with helical hairspring, gimbals and box	1,400	1,600	1,900

CASE MODEL # A
gold filled : $100 - $125 - $140

CASE MODEL #2
gold filled : $100- $125 - $150
14K Gold : $350 - $400 - $500

CASE MODEL #3
gold filled : $95- $115 - $130

This Tag Identifies
The Improved
992

CASE MODEL # 4
gold filled : $90 - $115 - $130

CASE MODEL #5
gold filled : $100- $115 - $130

CASE MODEL #6
gold filled : $110- $130 - $150

CASE MODEL # 7
White gold filled : $90 -$100 - $125

CASE MODEL #8
gold filled : $110- $130 - $150

CASE MODEL #10
gold filled : $100- $125 - $150

Model "A" was advertised in a Gold-filled Case & advertised with a grade 950 movement.
Models 2 & 17 came in 14K solid GOLD or gold-filled, model 2 advertised with 992 or 950.
Models 3, 4, 5, 6, (7 white G.F.), 8, 10, 11, Cross Bar, & Traffic Special II all gold-filled.
Model "16" gold plate and Model "15" & Traffic Special I was stainless steel case.

⊕ NOTE: Factory Advertised as a **complete** watch and was fitted with a certain matched, timed
and rated movement and sold in the factory designed case style as a complete watch. The factory
also sold _uncased_ movements to **JOBBERS** such as Jewelry stores & they cased the movement in
a case styles the **CUSTOMER requested.** All the factory advertised complete watches came with
the dial **SHOWN or CHOICE** of other **Railroad** dials.

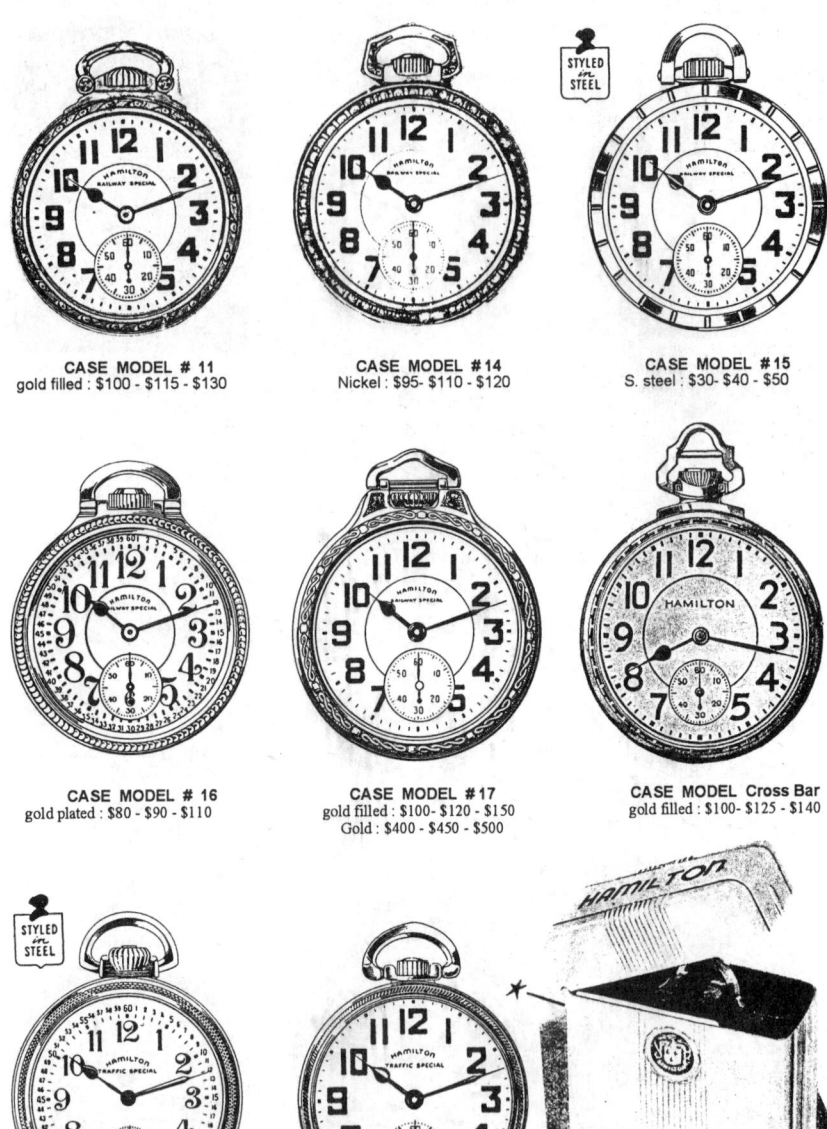

CASE MODEL # 11
gold filled : $100 - $115 - $130

CASE MODEL #14
Nickel : $95- $110 - $120

CASE MODEL #15
S. steel : $30- $40 - $50

CASE MODEL # 16
gold plated : $80 - $90 - $110

CASE MODEL #17
gold filled : $100- $120 - $150
Gold : $400 - $450 - $500

CASE MODEL Cross Bar
gold filled : $100- $125 - $140

TRAFFIC SPECIAL I
S. Steel : $25 - $35 - $45

TRAFFIC SPECIAL II
gold plated : $45- $55 - $65

Railway Specials were packed & shipped in a plastic ivory cigarette style box and were sealed with a ribbon. To remove the watch break seal by cutting the ribbon which holds the watch in box.

Model "A" was advertised in a Gold-filled Case & advertised with a grade 950 movement.
Models 2 & 17 came in 14K solid GOLD or gold-filled, model 2 advertised with 992 or 950.
Models 3, 4, 5, 6, 8, 10, 11, & Cross Bar gold-filled.
Model "16" gold plate and Model "15" & Traffic Special I was stainless steel case.
Case Model 14 = Nickel-Chrome.

HAMILTON W. CO. IDENTIFICATION OF MOVEMENTS

How To Identify Your Watch: Compare the movement with the illustration in this section. While comparing, note the location of the balance, jewels, screws, gears, and back plate (Full, 3/4, Bridge) which will be clues in identifying the movement you have. Having determined the size, the **GRADE** can also be found by looking up the serial number of your watch in the Hamilton Serial Number & Grades List. Illustrations of selected grades of the different size movements are shown to assist you in identifying movements. Hamilton movements which do not have grade numbers engraved on them <u>do</u> carry serial numbers which can be checked against the serial number list to secure the *grade number.*

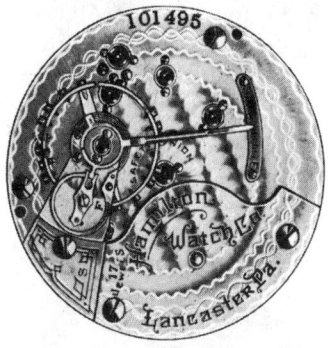

Grade 936, <u>18 SIZE,</u> **Full Plate, OPEN FACE** SHOWN. Also grades 922, 924, 926, 928, 930, 932, 934, 938, 940, 942, 944, 946, & 948 All look SIMILAR to the above.

Grade 925, <u>18 SIZE,</u> **Full Plate, Hunting Case** SHOWN. Also grades 923, 927, 929, 931, 933, 935, 937, 939, 941, 943, 945, and 947 All look SIMILAR to the above.

NOTE: 18 Size Grades 924, 925, 926, 927, 928, 929, 930, 931, 932, 933, 934, & 935 use 90% same parts but not plates. 18 Size Grades 936, 937, 938, 939, & 948 use 90% same parts but not plates. Grades 940, 941, 942, & 943 use 90% same parts but not plates. 18 Size Grades 944 & 946 use 90% same parts.

Grade 971, <u>16 SIZE,</u> **Hunting Case,** 3/4 Plate, 21 jewels, Shown. Note; Crown Wheel with 2 Screws this movement uses a 4 Footed Dial. Also grades 969, 973, 975, 991, & 993 all look SIMILAR to the above. Note location of the larger ratchet wheel next to balance cock.

Grade 992, <u>16 SIZE,</u> **Open Face,** 3/4 Plate, 21 jewels, Shown. Note; Crown Wheel with 2 Screws this movement uses a 4 Footed Dial. Also grades 954, 968, 970, 972, 974, & 990 all look SIMILAR to the above. Note location of the smaller Crown wheel next to balance cock.

NOTE: 16 Size Grades 950, 952, & 996 use 90% same parts. 16 Size Grades 954, 962, 963, 966, 967, 972, & 973 use 90% same parts but not plates. 16 Size Grades 956, 964, 965, 968, 969, 974, 975, 976, 977, & 978 use 90% same parts. 16 Size Grades 960, 961, 970, 971, 990,991, 992, 993, & 994 use 90% same parts but not plates. Grades 950E & 950B differ from grade 950. Grades 992E & 992B differ from grade 992.

Grade 992 Note: with narrow stripes, 16 size, 3/4 plate, 21 jewels, 5 positions. Note: Crown Wheel with 1 Screw.

Grade 992 E = wide stripes Damaskeening with ELINVAR under balance wheel. 16 size, 3/4 plate, 21J., 5 positions.

Grade 992 B, 16 size, 3/4 plate, 21J., **6 POSITIONS.**

Grade 950 16 size, BRIDGE, 23J., 5 positions. Note: with narrow stripes,

Grade 950 E = wide stripes Damaskeening with ELINVAR under balance wheel. 16 size, BRIDGE, 23J., 5 positions.

Grade 950 B, 16 size, BRIDGE, 23J., **6 POSITIONS.**

Grade 960, 16 SIZE, BRIDGE, OPEN FACE SHOWN. Also GRADES 950, 952, 962, 964, 994 all look SIMILAR to the above. Note location of the smaller Crown wheel next to balance cock.

Grade 961, 16 SIZE, BRIDGE, Hunting Case SHOWN. Also GRADES 951, 963, 965 all look SIMILAR to the above. Note location of the larger ratchet wheel next to balance cock.

SWISS MADE, 16 size, open face, 17 to 23 jewels, 3/4 plate.

Grade 902, 12 size
Open face, bridge movt., 19 jewels, double roller

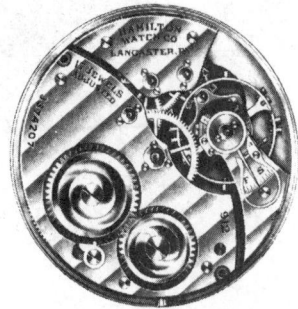

Grade 912, 12 size
Open face, ¼ plate movt., 17 jewels, double roller

Grade 918, 12 size
Open face, ¼ plate movt., 19 jewels, double roller

Grade 922, 12 size
Open face, bridge movt., 23 jewels, double roller

Grade 917, 10 size
Open face, ¾ plate movt., 17 jewels, double roller

Grade 921, 10 size
Open face, bridge movt., 21 jewels, double roller

Grade 923, 10 size
Open face, bridge movt., 23 jewels, double roller

Grade 983, 0 size
Hunting, bridge movt., 17 jewels, double roller

Grade 979, 6/0 size
Hunting, ¾ plate movt., 19 jewels, double roller

Grade 986, 6/0 size
Open face, ¾ plate movt., 17 jewels, double roller

HAMPDEN WATCH CO.
(DUEBER WATCH CO.)
Springfield, Massachusetts
Canton, Ohio
1876 - 1930

The New York Watch Co. preceded Hampden, and before that Don J. Mozart (1864) produced his three-wheel watch. Mozart was assisted by George Samuel Rice of New York and, as a result of their joint efforts, the New York Watch Co. was formed in 1866 in Providence, Rhode Island. It was moved in 1867 to Springfield, Massachusetts. Two grades of watches were decided on, and the company started with a 18S, 3/4 plate engraved "Springfield." They were sold for $60 to $75. The 18S, 3/4 plate were standard production, and the highest grade was a "George Walker" that sold for about $200 and a 16S, 3/4 plate "State Street" which had steel parts and exposed balance and escape wheels that were gold plated.

John C. Dueber started manufacturing watch cases in 1864 and bought a controlling interest in a company in 1886. At about this time a disagreement arose between Elgin, Waltham, and the Illinois Watch companies. Also, at this time, an anti-trust law was passed, and the watch case manufacturers formed a boycott against Dueber. Dueber was faced with a major decision, whether to stay in business, surrender to the watch case companies or buy a watch company. He decided to buy the Hampden Watch Co. of Springfield, Mass. By 1889 the operation had moved to Canton, Ohio. By the end of the year the company was turning out 600 watches a day. The first 16 size watch was produced in 1890. In 1894 Hampden introduced the first 23J movement made in America. Hampden assigned serial numbers at random to the New York Watch Co. movements for years after they purchased the N.Y.W.Co.

HAMPDEN ESTIMATED SERIAL NUMBER
AND PRODUCTION DATES

DATE-SERIAL NO.	DATE-SERIAL NO.	DATE-SERIAL NO.	DATE-SERIAL NO.
1877--- 60,000	1889--- 555,500	1901---1,512,000	1913---3,048,000
1878--- 91,000	1890--- 611,000	1902---1,642,000	1914---3,176,000
1879---122,000	1891--- 666,500	1903---1,768,000	1915---3,304,000
1880---153,000	1892--- 722,000	1904---1,896,000	1916---3,432,000
1881---184,000	1893--- 775,000	1905---2,024,000	1917---3,560,000
1882---215,000	1894--- 833,000	1906---2,152,000	1918---3,680,000
1883---250,000	1895--- 888,500	1907---2,280,000	1919---3,816,000
1884---300,000	1896--- 944,000	1908---2,408,000	1920---3,944,000
1885---350,000	1897---1,000,000	1909---2,536,000	1921---4,072,000
1886---400,000	1898---1,128,000	1910---2,664,000	1922---4,200,000
1887---450,000	1899---1,256,000	1911---2,792,000	1923---4,400,000
1888---500,000	1900---1,384,000	1912---2,920,000	1924---4,600,000

The above list is provided for determining the **APPROXIMATE** age of your watch. Match serial number with date. Watches were not necessarily sold in the exact order of manufactured date.

Chronology of the Development of Hampden Watch Co.:
The Mozart Watch Co., Providence, R. I. (1864-1866)
New York Watch Co., Providence, R. I. (1866-1867)
New York Watch Co., Springfield, Mass. (1867-1875)
New York Watch Mfg. Co., Springfield, Mass. (1875-1876)
Hampden Watch Co., Springfield, Mass. (1877-1886)
Hampden-Dueber Watch Co., Springfield, Mass. (1886-1888)
Hampden Watch Co., Canton, Ohio. (1888–1923)
Dueber Watch Co., Canton, Ohio. (1888–1923)
Dueber-Hampden Watch Co., Canton, Ohio. (1923–1931)
Amtorg, U.S.S.R (1930–Present)

Issued 1890

Issued 1892

Issued 1895

NR inside flag =New Railway and SR inside flag =Special Railway
D & ★ D & anchor inside flag =Duber and H inside flag =Hampden

Dueber Watch Co., 18 size, 15 jewels, nickel movement. Model 3, hunting case.

Dueber Grand, 18 size, 17 jewels, open face, originally sold for $20.00.

HAMPDEN
18 SIZE

Grade or Name — Description	Avg	Ex-Fn	Mint
America, 7J, KW KS	$85	$110	$135
Anchor (inside flag), 17J, ADJ, GJS, DMK, OF	100	125	175
"3" Ball, 17J, ADJ, NI, DMK, OF	175	200	225
Canadian Pacific R.W., 17J, Adj., M# 4, OF ....★	300	400	550
Champion, 7-11J, ADJ, FULL, gilded, or, NI, OF	85	110	125
Champion, 7-11J, ADJ, FULL, gilded, or, NI, HC	125	150	175
Champion, 15-17J, ADJ, FULL, gilded, or, NI, OF	95	110	135
Champion, 15-17J, ADJ, FULL, gilded, or, NI, HC	150	165	195
Correct Time, 15J, HC	150	175	225
Dueber, 16J, gilded, DMK, OF	100	125	150
Dueber, 17J, gilded, DMK, OF	100	125	150
John C. Dueber, 15J, gilded, DMK, OF	100	125	150
John C. Dueber, 17J, gilded, ADJ, DMK, OF	100	125	150
John C. Dueber, Special, 17J, ADJ, DMK, OF	125	150	175
John C. Dueber, Special, 17J, ADJ, DMK, HC	150	175	225
John C. Dueber, 17J, HC	135	150	200
John C. Dueber, 21J, HC	275	325	400
Dueber Grand, 17J, OF	100	125	150
Dueber Grand, 17J, ADJ, HC	135	150	200
Dueber Grand, 21J, ADJ, DMK, NI, HC	275	325	400

🕐 Generic, nameless or unmarked grades for watch movements are listed under the Company name or initials of the Company, etc. by size, jewel count and description.

Dueber W. Co., 7-11J, OF	$100	$125	$150
Dueber W. Co., 15J, DMK, OF	100	125	150
Dueber W. Co., 15J, DMK, HC	125	150	200
Dueber W. Co., 16J, OF	100	125	150
Dueber W. Co., 16J, HC	125	150	200
Dueber W. Co., 17J, DMK, ADJ, OF	100	125	150
Dueber W. Co., 17J, Gilded	100	125	150
Dueber W. Co., 17J, DMK, ADJ, HC	125	150	200
Dueber W. Co., 19J, ADJ, GJS, HC ....★	400	475	575
Dueber W. Co., 21J, Adj.5P, GJS, OF	225	250	295
Dueber W. Co., 21J, GJS, Adj.5P, HC	275	300	375

John C. Dueber Special, 18 size, 17 jewels, serial number 949,097.

Oriental, 18 size, 15 jewels, open face, serial number 117,825.

Grade or Name — Description	Avg	Ex-Fn	Mint
Homer Foot, gilded, KW, OF (Early)	$225	$250	$300
Gladiator, KW, OF	100	125	175
Gladiator, 11J, NI, DMK, OF	100	125	175
Gulf Stream Sp., 21J, R.R. grade, OF, LS ★	425	525	650

🕐 Generic, nameless or unmarked grades for watch movements are listed under the Company name or initials of the Company, etc. by size, jewel count and description.

	Avg	Ex-Fn	Mint
Hampden W. Co., 7J, KW, KS, coin silver OF	$100	$125	$175
Hampden W. Co., 7J, SW, OF	75	100	135
Hampden W. Co., 11J, OF, KW	75	100	135
Hampden W. Co., 11J, HC, KW	100	125	150
Hampden W. Co., 11J, OF, SW	75	100	135
Hampden W. Co., 11J, HC, SW	100	125	175
Hampden W. Co., 15J, OF, KW	85	100	150
Hampden W. Co., 15J, HC, KW	100	125	175
Hampden W. Co., 15J, HC, SW	100	125	175
Hampden W. Co., 15J, SW, Gilded, OF	75	100	135
Hampden W. Co., 15J, SW, NI, OF	85	100	150
Hampden W. Co., 15J, **Multi-color, 14K, HC**	1,600	1,800	2,200
Hampden W. Co., 16J, OF	100	125	175
Hampden W. Co., 17J, SW, Gilded	100	125	175
Hampden W. Co., 17J, SW, NI, OF	100	125	175
Hampden W. Co., 17J, SW, HC	135	150	200
Hampden W. Co., 17J, LS, HC, **14K**	525	575	650
Hampden W. Co., 17J, LS, HC, **10K**	375	425	500
Hampden W. Co., 21J, OF, SW	225	250	300
Hampden W. Co., 21J, HC, SW	250	275	335
John Hancock, 7J, Adj., OF	75	95	125
John Hancock, 15J, Adj.3P, OF	100	125	150
John Hancock, 17J, GJS, Adj.3P, OF	125	135	175
John Hancock, 17J, GJS, Adj.3P, HC	150	175	225
John Hancock, 21J, GJS, Adj.3P, OF	225	250	300
John Hancock, 23J, GJS, Adj.5P, OF	275	300	350
Hayward, 15J, KW	125	150	225
Hayward, 11J, SW	100	125	150

🕐 Watches listed in this book are priced at the **collectable fair market value** at the RETAIL level, as complete watches having an original 14k gold filled case, KEY WIND with silver, an original white enamel single sunk dial, and with the entire original movement in good working order with no repairs needed, unless otherwise noted.

Menlo Park, 18 size, 17 jewels, serial number 1,184,116.

New Railway, 18 size, 23 jewels, open face only, gold jewel settings, originally sold for $50.00, Model 2.

Grade or Name — Description	Avg	Ex-Fn	Mint
Lafayette, 11J, NI	$100	$125	$150
Lafayette, 15J, NI, KW	150	175	225
Lafayette, 15J, NI	125	150	200
Lakeside, 15J, NI, SW	125	150	200
M. J. & Co. Railroad Watch Co., 15J, HC ★	325	425	550
Menlo Park, 15-17J, NI, ADJ, OF	125	150	200
Mermod, Jaccard & Co., 15J, KW, HC	150	175	225
Metropolis, 15J, NI, SW, OF	100	125	175
Wm. McKinley, 17J, Adj.3P, OF	100	125	175
Wm. McKinley, 21J, GJS, Adj.5P	225	250	295
New Railway, 17J, GJS, Adj.5P, OF	100	125	175
New Railway, 19J, GJS, Adj.5P, OF	175	200	250
New Railway, 19J, GJS, Adj.5P, HC	200	250	300

Railway, 18 size, 17 jewels, key wind & set; early railroad watch.

Special Railway, 18 size, 23 jewels, Adj5p, serial number 3,357,284.

🕐 Watches listed in this book are priced at the collectable retail level, as **complete** watches having an original 14k gold-filled case and *Key Wind* with silver, an original white enamel single sunk dial, and with the entire original movement in good working order with no repairs needed.

NR inside flag = New Railway and SR inside flag = Special Railway
D & ★ D & anchor inside flag = Duber and H inside flag = Hampden

Grade or Name — Description	Avg	Ex-Fn	Mint
New Railway, 21J, GJS, Adj.5P, OF	$225	$250	$295
New Railway, 21J, GJS, Adj.5P, HC	250	275	325
New Railway, 23J, GJS, Adj.5P	300	335	375
New Railway, 23J, GJS, Adj.5P, **14K**, OF	700	750	800
North Am. RR, 21J, GJS, Adj.5P, OF, LS	225	250	275
North Am. RR, 21J, GJS, Adj.3P, HC, PS	225	300	350
Order of Railroad Conductors, 17J, ADJ, OF	200	225	250
Pennsylvania Special, 17J, GJS, Adj.5P, DR, NI ★★	700	900	1,200
J. C. Perry, 15J, KW, gilded, HC	150	175	225
J. C. Perry, 15J, NI, SW, OF	125	150	175
J. C. Perry, 15J, gilded, SW, OF	100	125	150
Railway, 11J, gilded, OF	100	125	150
Railway, 15-17J, NI, OF	125	150	175
Railway, 15-17J, **KW**, marked on mvt., HC ★★	500	600	800
Railroad with R.R. names on dial and movement:			
Canadian Pacific RR, 17J, OF ★	500	600	800
Canadian Pacific RR, 21J, OF ★	550	700	900
Private Label R.R. 17J, OF ★	300	350	400
Special Railway, 17J, GJS, Adj.5P, NI, DR, OF	100	125	150
Special Railway, 21J, GJS, Adj.5P, NI, DR, 2-Tone, OF	225	250	275
Special Railway, 21J, GJS, Adj.5P, NI, DR, HC	250	275	300
Special Railway, 23J, GJS, Adj.5P, NI, DR, OF	300	335	400
Special Railway, 23J, GJS, Adj.5P, NI, DR, 2-Tone, OF	325	350	425
Special Railway, 23J, GJS, Adj.5P, NI, DR, HC	350	400	500
Special Railway, 23J, **14K, HC**	800	850	950
Springfield, 7-11J, KW, gilded, HC	125	150	200
Springfield, 7-11J, SW, NI, HC	125	150	200
Standard, 15J, gilded, HC	125	150	200
State Street, 15J, NI, LS, (Early KW)	200	225	275
Train Service Standard, 17J, LS, M# 2, NI, HC	200	225	275
Theo. Studley, 15J, KW, KS, HC	125	150	200
Tramway Special, 17J, NI	175	200	250
Wisconsin Central R W, 17J, LS, OF	200	225	275
Woolworth, 11-15J, KW	125	150	175
Grade 31,45,46,49,65,66,69, 70,71, ALL =11J	75	95	110
Grade 32,33,34,35,36,40,41,55,56,58,59,60, All =15J	85	100	135
Grade, 43,44,47,48,63,64,67,68,80,81, ALL =16-17J	100	125	150
Grade 85, **19J**, GJS, 2-Tone, HC ★★	500	600	750
Grade 95, **21J**, GJS, OF	225	250	275
Grade 125, **21J**, Adj.3P, OF	200	225	250

16 SIZE

Grade or Name — Description	Avg	Ex-Fn	Mint
Beacon, 7J, OF	$65	$70	$95
Champion, 7J, NI, 3/4, gilded, coin, OF	70	85	125
Champion, 7J, NI, 3/4, gilded, OF	70	85	125
Champion, 7J, NI, 3/4, gilded, HC	125	150	200
Chronometer, 21J, **detent escapement**, NI, Adj.3P, GJS	600	750	950
John C. Dueber, 17J, GJS, NI, Adj.5P, 3/4	100	125	175
John C. Dueber, 21J, GJS, NI, Adj.5P, 3/4 ★	325	400	475
John C. Dueber, 21J, GJS, NI, Adj.5P, DR, BRG	225	250	275
Dueber Watch Co., 17J, ADJ, 3/4	100	125	165

IMPORTANT NOTE: Railroad Standards, Railroad Approved & Railroad Grade **terminology,** as defined and used in this *BOOK*.
1. **RAILROAD STANDARDS** = A commission or board appointed by the railroad companies outlined a set of **guidelines** to be accepted or approved by each railroad line.
2. **RAILROAD APPROVED** = A **LIST** of watches each railroad line would approve if purchased by their employee's. (this list changed through the years).
3. **RAILROAD GRADE** = A watch made by manufactures to met or exceed the guidelines set by the railroad **standards**. Grade such as 992, Vanguard and B.W. Raymond etc.
☉ Some GRADES **exceeded** the R.R. standards such as 23 jewels, diamond end stone, gold train, raised gold jewel settings, double sunk dial and the list goes on. Examples: such as Veritas, Sangamo, 950 & Riverside Maximus and many others.

Hampden W. Co., Bridge Model, 16 size, 23 jewels, 2-tone movement, serial number 1,899,430.

Hampden W. Co., 16 size, 17 jewels, gold jewel settings, serial number 3,075,235.

🕐 Generic, nameless or unmarked grades for watch movements are listed under the Company name or initials of the Company, etc. by size, jewel count and description.

Grade or Name — Description	Av	Ex-Fn	Mint
Hampden W. Co., 7J, SW, OF	$70	$85	$125
Hampden W. Co., 7J, SW, HC	85	125	150
Hampden W. Co., 11J, SW, OF	70	85	125
Hampden W. Co., 11J, SW, HC	85	125	150
Hampden W. Co., 15J, SW, OF	60	85	125
Hampden W. Co., 15J, SW, HC	85	125	150
Hampden W. Co., 17J, SW, OF	70	85	125
Hampden W. Co., 17J, **14K, Multi-color,** HC	1,500	1,600	1,800
Hampden W. Co., 17J, SW, HC	85	125	150
Hampden W. Co., 21J, SW, HC	275	325	400
Hampden W. Co., 21J, SW, OF	225	250	275
Hampden W. Co., 23J, Adj.5P, GJS, 3/4	350	400	450
Hampden W. Co., 23J, Series 2, **Freesprung,** GJS GT, HC ★★★	500	650	800
Masonic Dial, 23J, GJS, 2-Tone **porcelain dial**	450	525	650

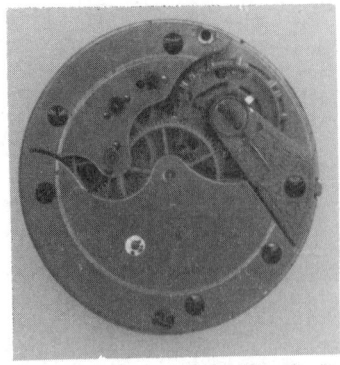
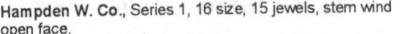
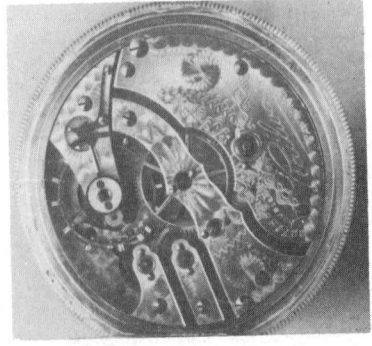

Hampden W. Co., Series 1, 16 size, 15 jewels, stem wind open face.

Railway, 16 size, 17 jewels, Adj.5P, gold jewel settings, serial number 2,271,866.

NR inside flag = New Railway and SR inside flag = Special Railway
D & ★ D & anchor inside flag = Duber and H inside flag = Hampden

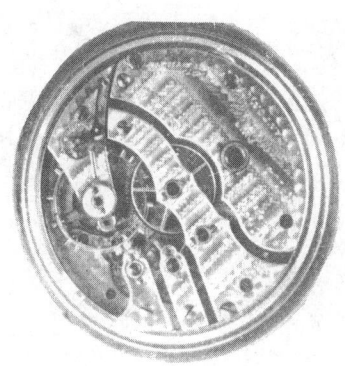

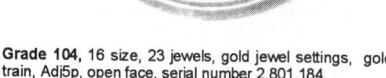

Grade 104, 16 size, 23 jewels, gold jewel settings, gold train, Adj5p, open face, serial number 2,801,184.

Hampden style watch produced in Russia with the machinery purchased by the Russian factory. This watch is a 16 size 7 jewel movement Ca. 1935

Grade or Name — Description	Avg	Ex-Fn	Mint
Wm. McKinley, 17J, GJS, Adj.5P, NI, DR, 3/4	$100	$125	$175
Wm. McKinley, 21J, GJS, Adj.5P, NI, DR, 3/4	250	295	375
Wm. McKinley, 21J, GJS, Adj.5P, NI, DR, 3/4, Coin	225	250	300
Wm. McKinley, 21J, GJS, Adj.5P, NI, DR, BRG	225	250	275
New Railway, 21J, GJS, Adj.5P	275	300	350
New Railway, 23J, GJS, Adj.5P, LS, HC	400	425	475
Ohioan, 21J, Adj.5P, GJS, 3/4	275	325	400
Railway, 17-19J, GJS, Adj.5P, BRG, DR	225	250	295
Special Railway, 17J, Adj, NI, BRG, DR, OF	125	150	185
Special Railway, 17J, Adj, NI, BRG, DR, HC	150	195	225
Special Railway, 23J, Adj.5P, NI, BRG, DR	300	335	400
Russian made model, 7J, 16 size, 3/4 plate	75	85	95
Garfield, 21J., Adj.5P, OF	225	250	275
Gen'l Stark, 15J, DMK, BRG	100	125	150
Gen'l Stark, 17J, DMK, BRG	110	135	175
95, 21J, marked "95", GJS, Adj.5P,	250	275	300
97 HC, 98 HC, 107 OF, 108 OF, ALL = 17J, Adj.3P, NI, 3/4	100	125	175
99, 15J, 3/4, HC	125	150	200
103, 21J, GJS, Adj.5P, NI, BRG, DR	250	275	325
104, 23J, GJS, Adj.5P, NI, 3\4 or BRG, DR, DMK, OF	300	350	425
104, 23J, GJS, Adj.5P, NI, BRG, DR, DMK, HC	350	400	475
105, 21J, GJS, Adj.5P, NI, 3/4, DR, DMK	225	250	275
106, 107 OF, & 108, 17J, SW, NI	100	125	175
109, 15J, 3/4, OF	100	125	175
110, 11J, 3/4	70	80	95
115, 21J, SW, NI, OF	225	250	275
120, 21J, SW, NI, OF, Chronometer on dial	250	275	300
340, 17J, SW, NI	100	125	175
440, 15J, 2-tone	125	150	200
555, 21J, GT, GJS, Chronometer on dial & mvt.	325	375	425
555, 21J, GT, GJS, Chronometer on dial ONLY	225	250	300
600, 17J, SW, NI	100	125	175

🕐 Generic, nameless or unmarked grades for watch movements are listed under the Company name or initials of the Company, etc. by size, jewel count and description.

🕐 Some watch manufacturers personalize watches for jobbers or jewelry firms, with exclusive private signed or marked movements. The valuable collectable watches are listed under the signed or marked movement. Other exclusive private signed or marked movements will have equivalent value are only slightly higher value and should be compared to Generic or Nameless movements. Railroad signed or marked (dials & movements) are usually more collectable & higher in value.

Dueber Grand, 12 size, 17 jewels, gold jewel settings, hunting case, serial number 1,737,354.

Dueber Grand, 12 size, 17 jewels, gold jewel settings, open face, pin set, serial number 1,732,255.

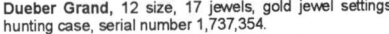

12 SIZE
(SEE ALSO "12 SIZE " THIN MODEL)

Grade or Name — Description	Avg	Ex-Fn	Mint
Champion, 7J, SW	$40	$50	$75
Dueber Grand, 17J, BRG, OF	50	75	100
Dueber Grand, 17J, BRG, HC	50	75	100
Dueber Grand, 17J, 3/4 plate	50	75	100
Hampden W. Co., 7J, SW, OF	50	75	100
Hampden W. Co., 17J, **14K, Multi-color, HC**	700	800	1,000
John Hancock, 21J, BRG	125	150	175
Gen'l Stark, 15J, BRG	50	75	100
Gen'l Stark, 15J, pin set	50	75	100
207-300 HC & 302 OF, 7J, 3/4 (add $35 for HC)	50	75	100
304 HC & 306 OF, 15J, 3/4 (add $35 for HC)	50	75	100
305-308 HC & 310 OF, 17J, 3/4 (add $35 for HC)	50	75	100
307, 17J	50	75	100
310, 17J, gold filled OF case	50	75	100
310, 17J, **14K** OF case	175	195	225
312, 21J, 3/4, Adj.5P, DMK, OF	125	150	175
314, 21J, DR, Adj. 5P, DMK, HC	135	165	195
31 OF, 17J, SW, **14K**	275	325	400

Paul Revere, Example of Hampden Watch Co.'s **thin series** showing face and movement, 12 size, 17-19 jewels, Adj5p.

12 SIZE (THIN MODEL)

Grade or Name — Description	Avg	Ex-Fn	Mint
Aviator, 17J, Adj.4P	$65	$75	$95
Aviator, 19J, Adj.4P	75	95	125
Beacon, 17J	75	90	125
Nathan Hale, 15J ★	85	100	135
Minuteman, 17J ★	85	100	135
Ohioan, 21J, Adj.3P, GJS, 3/4	95	125	150
Paul Revere, 17J, OF, **14K**	275	325	400
Paul Revere, 17J	75	90	125
Paul Revere, 19J	100	125	150

Note: Some 12 Sizes came in cases of octagon, decagon, hexagon, triad, and cushion shapes.

6 SIZE

Grade or Name — Description	Avg	Ex-Fn	Mint
200, 7J (add $25 for HC)	$50	$75	$100
206, 11J (add $25 for HC)	50	75	100
213, 15J (add $25 for HC)	50	75	100
220, 17J (add $25 for HC)	50	75	100
Hampden W. Co., 15J, **multi-color Gold Filled, HC**	225	275	325
Hampden W. Co., 15J, **multi-color, 14K, HC**	435	550	650

Molly Stark, 000 size, 7 jewels, hunting or open face, originally sold for $12.00.

000 SIZE

Grade or Name — Description	Avg	Ex-Fn	Mint
Diadem, 11-15J, **14K**, OF Case	$125	$150	$225
Diadem, 11-15J, **14K**, HC Case	225	275	350
Diadem, 11-15J, **Gold Filled**, HC Case	100	150	200
Molly Stark, 7J, **Gold Filled**, HC Case	100	150	200
Molly Stark, 7J, **14K**, HC Case	225	275	350
Molly Stark, 7J, Pin Set, OF	75	100	150
Four Hundred, 11, 15, 16, & 17J, HC	100	150	200
14K Multi-color, HC	450	550	700

🕐 Watches listed in this book are priced at the collectable retail level, as **complete** watches having an original 14k gold-filled case and *Key Wind* with silver, an original white enamel single sunk dial, and with the entire original movement in good working order with no repairs needed.

HAMPDEN WATCH CO.
IDENTIFICATION OF MOVEMENTS

How to Identify Your Watch Size & Model: Compare the movement of your watch with the illustrations in this section. While comparing, note the location of the balance, jewels, screws, gears, and type of back plate (Full, 3/4, Bridge) which will be clues in identifying the movement you have.

Series I, 18 size
Hunting or open face, key wind & set

Series II, 18 size
Hunting, stem wind, pendant or lever set

Series III, 18 size
Hunting, stem wind, pendant or lever set

Series IV, 18 size
Open face, stem wind, lever set

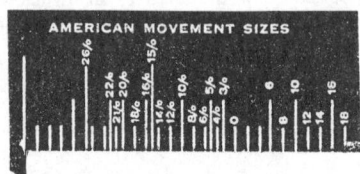

Series 1, 16 size
Open face, stem wind, pendant or lever set

Series II, 16 size
Hunting, stem wind, pendant or lever set

Series III, 16 size
Open face, stem wind, pendant set

Series IV, 16 size
Hunting, stem wind, pendant or lever set

Series V, 16 size
Open face, stem wind, pendant or lever set

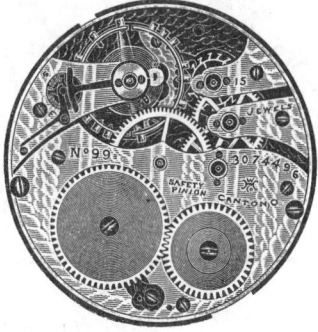

Series VI, 16 size
Hunting, stem wind, pendant set

Series VII, 16 size
Open face, stem wind, pendant set

Series III, 12 size
Open face, stem wind, pendant set

Series I, 12 size
Hunting, stem wind, lever set

Series II, 12 size
Open face, stem wind, lever set

Series IV, 12 size
Open face, stem wind, pendant

Series V, 12 size
Open face, stem wind, pendant set

Series I, 6 size
Open face, stem wind

Series I, 3/0 size
Hunting, stem wind

⏱ Characteristics of watches differ for the same age of both case and movement, because these features vary it may not be accurate to date a watch by one single influence. Example: the second hand was _not_ commonly found on watches before 1750, but common about 1800. The first second hand appeared in 1665 and another in 1690. Therefore statements are broad rather than accurate.

Series II, 3/0 size
Open face, stem wind, pendant

Series III, 3/0 size
Hunting, lever or pendant

Series IV, 3/0 size
Hunting, stem wind, pendant

HERMAN VON DER HEYDT
CHICAGO SELF–WINDING WATCH CO.
Chicago, Illinois
1883- 1895

Herman von der Heydt patented a self-winding watch on Feb. 19, 1884. A total of 35 watches were hand-made by von der Heydt. The watches were 18S, full plate, lever escapement and fully-jeweled. The wind mechanism was a gravity type made of heavy steel and shaped like a crescent. The body motion let the heavy crescent move which was connected to a ratchet on the winding arbor, resulting in self-winding. Five movements were nickel and sold for about $90; the gilded model sold for about $75.

Grade or Name — Description		Avg	Ex-Fn	Mint
18S, 19J, FULL, NI	★ ★ ★ ★	$12,000	$14,000	$16,000
18S, 19J, FULL, gilded	★ ★ ★ ★	10,000	12,000	14,000

Herman Von Der Heydt, 18 size self winding watch. "Chicago S. W. Co." on dial. H. VON DER HEYDT, PATENTED, FEB.19, 84 on auxiliary dial.

Herman Von Der Heydt, 18 size, 19 jewels; America's only self winding pocket watch. Note crescent shaped winding weight serial number 19.

E. HOWARD & CO.
Boston (Roxbury), Massachusetts
December 11, 1858 - 1903

After the failure of the Boston Watch Company (1853-57), Edward Howard decided to personally attempt the successful production of watches using the interchangeable machine-made parts system. He and Charles Rice, his financial backer, were unable to buy out the defunct watch company in Waltham, however, they did remove (per a prior claim) the watches in progress, the tools and the machinery to Howard and Davis' Roxbury factory (first watch factory in America), in late 1857. During their first year, the machinery was retooled for the production of a revolutionary new watch of Howard's design. Also, the remaining Boston Watch Co. movements were completed (E. Howard & Co. dials, Howard & Rice on the movement). By the summer of 1858, Edward Howard had produced his first watch. On December 11, 1858 the firm of E. Howard & Co. was formed for the manufacture of high-grade watches. Howard's first model was entirely different from any watch previously made. It introduced the more accurate "quick beat" train to American watchmaking. The top plate was in two sections and had six pillars instead of the usual four pillars in a full plate. The balance was gold or steel at first, then later it was a compensation balance loaded with gold screws. Reed's patented barrel was used for the first time. The size, based on the Dennison system, was a little larger than the regular 18 size. In 1861, a 3/4 plate model was put on the market. Most movements were being stamped with "N" to designate Howard's 18 size. On February 4, 1868 Howard patented a new steel motor barrel which was to supersede the Reed's, but not before some 28,000 had been produced. Also, in 1868 Howard introduced the stemwinding movement and was probably the first company to market such a watch in the U. S. By 1869, Howard was producing their "L" or 16 size as well as their first nickel movements. In 1870, G. P. Reed's micrometer regulator was patented for use by E. Howard & Co. The Reed style "whiplash" regulator has been used in more pocket watches, worldwide, than any other type. In 1878, the manufacturing of keywind movements was discontinued. Mr. Howard retired in 1882, but the company continued to sell watch movements of the grade and style set by him until 1903 and beyond. This company was the first to adjust to all six positions. Their dials were always a hard enamel and always bore the name "E. Howard & Co., Boston." In 1902, the company transferred all rights to use the name "Edward Howard," in conjunction with the production of watches, to the Keystone Watch Case Co. Most of their models were stamped "Howard" on the dial and "E. Howard Watch Co., Boston. U.S.A." on the movement. Edward Howard's company never produced its own watch cases, the great majority of which were solid gold or silver. Keystone, however, produced complete watches, many of which were gold filled.

CHRONOLOGICAL DEVELOPMENT OF E. HOWARD & CO.:

Howard, Davis & Dennison, Roxbury, Mass., (1850)
American Horologue Company, Roxbury, Mass., (1851)
Warren Manufacturing Company, Roxbury, Mass., (1851-53)
Boston Watch Co., Roxbury, Mass., (1853-54) & Waltham, Mass., (1854-57)
Howard & Rice, Roxbury, Mass., (1857-58) with (E. Howard & Co. on dials)
E. Howard & Co., Roxbury, Mass., (1858-1903)
Keystone Watch Case Co. (Howard line), Jersey City, N. J., (1902-30)

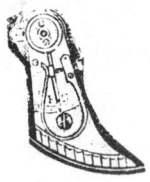 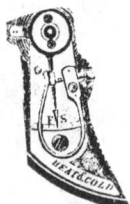 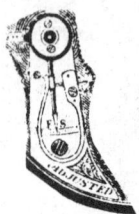

LEFT: Balance cock unmarked =UNADJUSTED
CENTER: Balance cock marked heat &cold =adjusted to TEMPERATURE
RIGHT: Balance cock marked adjusted =FULLY ADJUSTED

A List of initials for most of the Solid Gold watch case companies used with E. Howard & Co.

A.W.C. Co.=American Watch Case Co.
B & T = Booz & Thomas
B.W.C. Co.=Brooklyn Watch Case Co.
C & M =Crosby & Mathewson
C.E.H. & Co. = C.E. Hale & Co.
C.W. Mfg. Co. = Courvoisier Wilcox Mfg. Co.
D T W & Co.= D.T. Warren & Co.
E.H. & Co. = E. Hale & Co.
F & Co. = Fellows & Co.
F & S = Fellows & Shell
J M H = J.M. Harper
J S (intertwined)= Jeannot & Shiebler

K (inside) U = Keller & Untermeyer
K E & F. Co.= Keller, Ettinger & Fink N.Y.
M B = Margot Bros.
M & B = Mathey Bros.
N.Y.G.W.C.Co =New York Gold Watch Case Co.
P & B = Peters & Boss
S & D = Serex & Desmaison
S & M B = Serex Maitre Bros.
S & R = Serex & Robert
W & S = Warren & Spadone
W P & Co = Wheeler Parsons & Co.
W W C Mfg. Co =Western Watch Case Co.

Crescent Watch Case Co.
Dueber Watch Case Co.
Keystone Watch Case Co.

Ladd Watch Case Co.
Marsh= Marsh Watch Case Co.
Muhr Watch Case Co.

Roy = Roy Watch Case Co.

E. HOWARD & CO., Series I, helical hair-spring, detent escapement, KW KS, N (18)size, serial # 1120

E. HOWARD & CO., N (18) size, 15 jewels, chronometer escapement engraved on balance cock, Robin's escapement, serial # 3126.

E. HOWARD & CO., İ (10) size, KW KS, note compensating balance above center wheel, serial # 3363.

E. HOWARD & CO., İ (10) size, KW KS, **note** solid balance wheel below center wheel, serial # 3406.

E. HOWARD & CO.
APPROXIMATE DATES, SERIAL NOS., AND TOTAL PRODUCTION

Serial No.	Date	Series	Total Prod.
131-1,900—	1858-1860—	I (18S)—	1,800
1,901-3,000—	1860-1861—	II (18S)—	1,100
3,001-3,100—	1861—	K (14S)—	100
3,101-3,250—	1861—	III (18S)—	150
3,401-3,500—	1861—	i (10S)—	100
3,501-28,000—	1861-1871—	III (18S)—	4,500
30,001-50,000—	1868-1883—	IV (18S)—	20,000
50,001-71,000—	1869-1899 —	V (16S)—	21,000
100,001-105,500—	1869-1899—	VI (6S)—	5,500
200,001-227,000—	1880-1899—	VII (18S)—	27,000
*228,001-231,000—	1895—	VII (18S)—	3,000
300,001-309,000—	1884-1899—	VIII (18S)—	9,000
*309,001-310,000—	1895—	VIII (18S)—	1,000
400,001-405,000—	1890-1895—	IX (18S)—	5,000
500,001-501,500—	1890-1899—	X (12S)—	1,500
*600,001-601,500—	1896—1903—	XI (16S)—	1,500
*700,001-701,500—	1896—1903—	XII (16S)—	1,500

(*) = 3/4 Split Plates with 17 Jewels. Total about- 100,000

The above list is provided for determining the APPROXIMATE age of your watch. Match serial number with date. Watches were not necessarily sold in the exact order of manufactured date.

E. HOWARD & CO. WATCH SIZES

Letter	Inches	Approx. Size
N	1 13/16	18
L	1 11/16	16
K	1 10/16	14
J	1 9/16	12
I	1 8/16	10
H	1 7/16	8
G	1 6/16	6
F	1 5/16	4
E	1 4/16	2
D	1 3/16	0

Below Mershon's Patent center wheel rack regulator (April 26 1859),

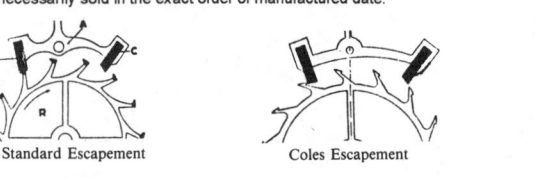

Standard Escapement

Coles Escapement

Deer
Adjusted to
Hcl6P

Horse
Adjusted to
HCl-No positions

Hound
Unadjusted

NOTE: E. Howard & Co. movements will not fit standard cases properly.

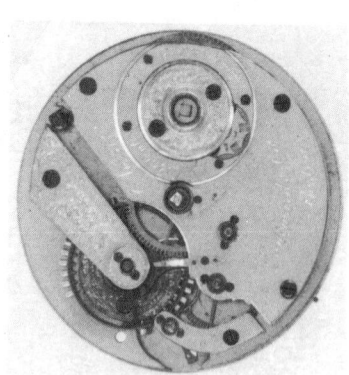
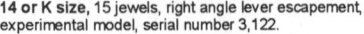

14 or K size, 15 jewels, right angle lever escapement, experimental model, serial number 3,122.

10 or I size, 15 jewels; note cut-out to view escape wheel, experimental model, serial number 3,472.

E. HOWARD & CO.
N SIZE (18) (In Original Cases)

Series or Name — Description	Avg	Ex-Fn	Mint
E. Howard & Co. on dial and movement, 15-16J, 1857 Model, (Howard & Rice style), KW & KS, silver case .... ★★★	$1,600	$2,000	$2,500
I, II or III, Isochronism, 15J, gilded, KW, helical hairspring .... ★★★★	5,000	6,000	8,000

Series 1, 18 size, 15 jewels, note the compensating balance on this early movement, serial number 133.

Series II, 18 size, 15 jewels, key wind & set, serial number 2,477.

Grade or Name — Description	Avg	Ex-Fn	Mint
I, 15J, with serial # below 100	$5,000	$6,000	$7,500
I, 15J, with serial # below 200	2,000	3,000	4,500
I, 15J, with serial # below 300	1,000	2,000	3,000
I, 15J, gilded, KW, 18K, HC or OF, upright pallets ....★★	3,000	4,000	5,000
I, 15J, gilded, KW, 18K, HC or OF, horizontal pallets ....★	2,200	2,500	3,000
I, 15J, gilded, KW, silver HC ....★	1,500	1,900	2,400
I, 15J, (movement only) ....★	500	600	700
II, 15J, gilded, KW, 18K, HC or OF ....★	2,000	2,500	3,000
II, 15J, gilded, KW, silver HC ....★	1,200	1,500	2,000
II, 15J, (movement only) ....★	450	550	650
III, 15J, gilded, KW, 18K, HC	1,300	1,500	1,800
III, 15J, gilded, KW, silver case	600	800	1,000
III, 15J, nickel, KW, silver case	700	900	1,100
III, 15J, gilded, KW, 18K, Mershon's Patent	1,500	1,800	2,000
III, 15J, gilded, KW, 18K, Coles Escapement ....★★	1,600	1,900	2,300
III, 15J, NI, Private label	800	1,000	1,200
III, 15J, (movement only)	150	175	225
IV, 15J, gilded or nickel, KW, 18K, HC	1,200	1,400	1,700
IV, 15J, gilded or nickel, SW, 18K, HC	1,000	1,200	1,400

Series III, 18 size, 15 jewels, note **Mershon's Patent** center wheel rack regulator (April 26 1859), serial number 22,693.

Series III, 18 size, 15 jewels, note high balance wheel over center wheel, serial number 7,000.

Series IV, 18 size, 15 jewels, key wind and set, serial number 37,893.

Series VII, 18 size, 15 jewels, nickel movement, note running deer on movement, "adjusted" on bridge, serial number 219,304.

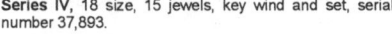

Series or Name — Description		Avg	Ex-Fn	Mint
IV, personalized with jobber's name, silver	★ ★	$500	$600	$800
IV, 15J, gilded, Cole's Escapement	★ ★ ★ ★	1,500	1,600	1,700
IV, 15J (movement only)		90	110	150
VII, 15J, gilded or nickel, SW, 14K, HC		1,000	1,200	1,500
VII, 17J, nickel, split plate, SW, 14K, HC	★ ★ ★ ★	1,200	1,400	1,700
VII, 17J, nickel, split plate, SW, silver, HC	★	600	700	900
VII, 19J, nickel, split plate, SW, 14K, HC	★ ★ ★	2,500	3,000	4,000
VII, 15J (movement only)		95	100	115
VII, Ball, 17J, nickel, SW, 14K, HC	★ ★ ★	3,500	4,000	6,000
VII, Ball, 17J, nickel, SW, GF, HC	★ ★ ★	2,200	2,800	3,500
VIII, 15J, gilded or nickel, SW, 14K, OF		900	1,000	1,400
VIII, 17J, nickel, split plate, SW, 14K, OF	★	1,200	1,400	1,700
VIII, 17J, nickel, split plate, SW, silver, OF	★	425	525	650
VIII, 15J (movement only)		85	90	100
VIII, Ball, 17J, nickel, SW, 14K, OF	★ ★	3,000	3,500	4,000
VIII, Ball, 17J, nickel, SW, GF, OF	★ ★	1,000	1,500	2,000

Series VII, 18 size, 17J, nickel, split plate, adjusted, Stem Wind, serial number 228,055.

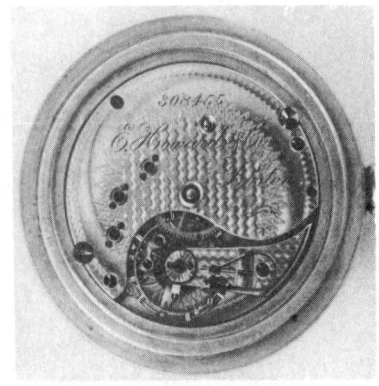

Series VIII, 18 size, 15 jewels, serial number 308,455.

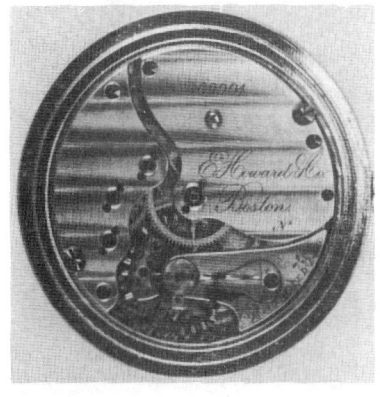

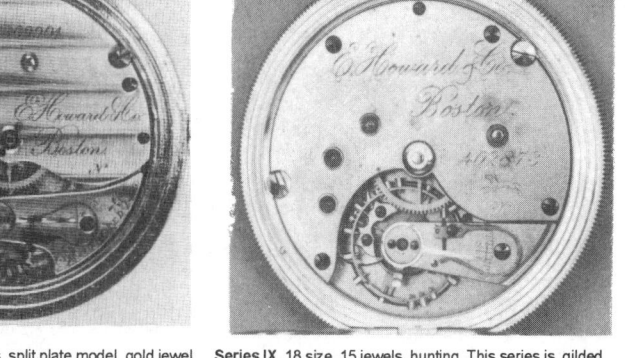

Series VIII, 18 size, 17 jewels, split plate model, gold jewel settings, serial number 309,904.

Series IX, 18 size, 15 jewels, hunting. This series is gilded only and hound grade exclusively, S # 402,873.

Series or Name — Description	Avg	Ex-Fn	Mint
IX, 15J, gilded, SW, 14K, HC	$900	$1,100	$1,400
IX, 15J, gilded, SW, silver, HC	425	525	650
IX, 15J (movement only)	80	85	100

L SIZE (16)

(In Original Cases)

Series or Name — Description		Avg	Ex-Fn	Mint
V, 15J, gilded, KW, 18K, HC		$1,000	$1,200	$1,500
V, 15J, gilded, KW, 18K, Coles Escapement	★ ★ ★ ★	1,300	1,500	1,800
V, 15J, gilded or nickel, SW, 14K, HC		800	1,000	1,300
V, 15J, gilded, SW, 14K, Coles Escapement	★ ★ ★ ★	1,100	1,300	1,600
Prescott, 15J., gilded, SW, (Series V movement only)	★ ★	1,000	1,500	2,000

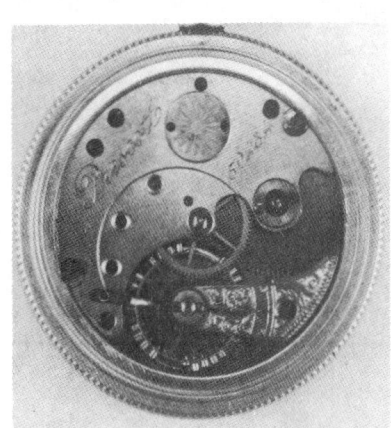

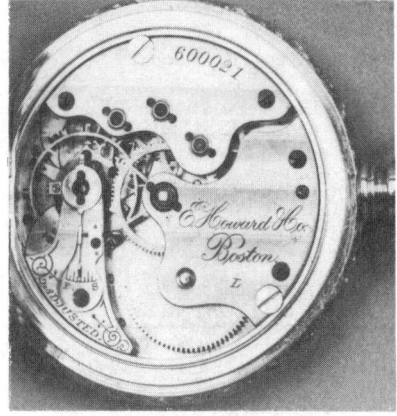

Series V, 16 or L size, Prescott Model, 15 jewels, hunting, serial number 50,434.

Series XI, 16 size, 17 jewels, split plate model, nickel movement, gold jewel settings, serial number 600,021.

🕐 Watches listed in this book are priced at the collectable retail level, as **complete** watches having an original 14k gold-filled case and *Key Wind* with silver, an original white enamel single sunk dial, and with the entire original movement in good working order with no repairs needed.

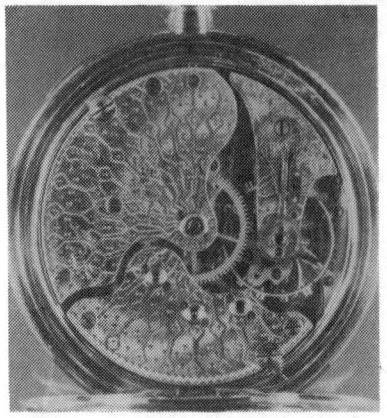

Series XII, L-16 size, 21 jewels, split plate model, nickel movement, gold lettering, gold jewel settings, serial number 700,899.

Series K, 14 or K size, 15 jewels, key wind & set, serial number 3,004.

Series or Name — Description		Avg	Ex-Fn	Mint
V, 15J (movement only)		$90	$100	$125
XI, 17J, nickel, split plate, SW, 14K, HC .... ★		1,100	1,300	1,600
XI, 17J, nickel, split plate, SW, silver, HC .... ★		400	500	650
XI, 17J (movement only)...		200	300	450
XII, 17J, nickel, split plate, SW, 14K, OF .... ★		1,000	1,200	1,500
XII, 17J, nickel, split plate, SW, silver, OF .... ★		375	475	625
XII, 17J (movement only)		100	150	175
XII, 21J, nickel, split plate, SW, 14K OF .... ★ ★ ★		2,500	3,000	4,000

K SIZE (14)
(In Original Cases)

Series or Name — Description		Avg	Ex-Fn	Mint
K, 15J, gilded, KW, 18K, HC .... ★ ★ ★ ★		$4,000	$5,000	$6,500

J SIZE (12)
(In Original Cases)

Series or Name – Description		Avg	Ex-Fn	Mint
X, 15J, nickel, hound, SW, 14K, OF.. ★		$700	$900	$1,200
X, 15J, nickel, horse, SW, 14K, OF... ★		800	1,000	1,300
X, 15J, nickel, deer, SW, 14K, OF... ★		900	1,100	1,400
X, 15J, hound (movement only)... ★		200	250	300

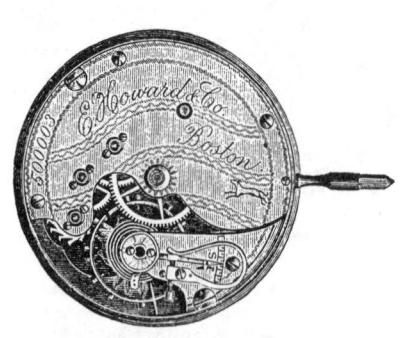

X, 15J, nickel, hound, SW, serial # 500,003

Series X, 12 or J size, 15 jewels, note deer on movement, serial number 501,361.

I size (10 size), 15 jewels, gilded, key wind, serial number 3,404.

I SIZE (10)
(In Original Cases)

Series or Name — Description	Avg	Ex-Fn	Mint
I, 15J, gilded, KW, 18K HC .... ★ ★ ★	$2,800	$3,400	$4,200

G SIZE (6)
(In Original Cases)

Series or Name — Description	Avg	Ex-Fn	Mint
VI, 15J, gilded, KW, 18K, HC .... ★ ★	$1,400	$1,800	$2,400
VI, 15J, gilded or nickel, SW, 18K, HC	1,000	1,200	1,500
VI, 15J, gilded or nickel, SW, 14K, HC	700	850	1,000
VI, 15J (movement only)...	175	200	300

Series VI, 6 or G size, 15 jewels, stem wind.

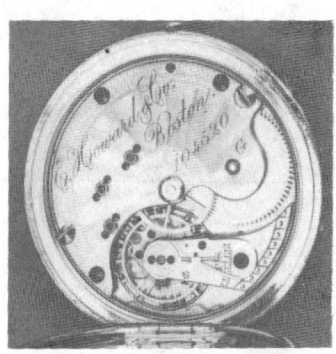

Series VI, 6 or G size, 15 jewels, stem wind, serial number 104,520.

🕐 Generic, nameless or unmarked grades for watch movements are listed under the Company name or initials of the Company, etc. by size, jewel count and description.

E. HOWARD WATCH CO. (KEYSTONE)
Waltham, Massachusetts
1902 - 1930

The Howard name was purchased by the Keystone Watch Case Co. in 1902. The watches are marked "E. Howard Watch Co. Boston, U. S. A." There were no patent rights transferred, just the Howard name. The "Edward Howard" chronometer was the highest grade, 16 size, and was introduced in 1912 for $350. All watches cased & timed at factory as a complete watch only.

Keystone Howard also gained control of U. S. Watch Co. of Waltham and New York Standard Watch Company. 16 size 21 jewel hunting case watches not made, 21 jewel were in open- face only.

ESTIMATED SERIAL NUMBERS
AND PRODUCTION DATES

Date	Serial No.
1902—	850,000
1903—	900,000
1909—	980,000
1912—	1,100,000
1915—	1,285,000
1917—	1,340,000
1921—	1,400,000
1930—	1,500,000

The arrows denote number of jewels and adjustments in each grade.

Cross =23 jewel, 5 positions

Star =21 jewel, Adj.5P, & 19J with V under star

Triangle =19 jewel, 5 positions

Circle =17 jewel, 3 positions

SERIES 1905, 16 size, 17 jewels, open face. This 3/4 model can be identified by the slant parallel damaskeening. This represents the 3/4 **top** grade with raised gold jewel settings double, roller, Adj.5P and sold for $115.00 in 1910.

1907 Brige Model, Series 0, 23 jewels, HUNTING CASE, Serial # 953,481. NOTE: The escape wheel bridge & the fourth wheel bridge is not notched out as is the Series 0 movement .

SERIES 9, 16 size, 17 jewels, open face. This 3/4 model can be identified by the checkerboard damaskeening. This represents the 3/4 **mid** grade, GJS, double roller, Adj.3P and sold for $105.00 in 1910.

SERIES 3, 16 size, 17 jewels open face. This 3/4 model can be identified by the circular damaskeening. This represents the 3/4 **lowest** grade of the three with single roller, Adj.3P and sold for $100.00 in 1910.

E. Howard Watch Co., Series 0, 16 size, 23 jewels, in original E. Howard Watch Co. swing-out movement Keystone Extra gold filled Open Face case.

E. HOWARD WATCH CO. Series 0 (not marked), 16S, 23J., Hunting Case,

⊕ unmarked Series, No., 0, 1, 2, 5 & 10 , also 1907 look the same as the 2 above illustrations, 1907 & Series or No. 0=23J, Series or No.1&10=21J, Series2=17J, 1905 & Series or No.=19J.

E. HOWARD WATCH CO. (KEYSTONE)
16 SIZE

Series or Name — Description	Avg	Ex-Fn	Mint
No. 0, & 1907, 23J, BRG, Adj.5P, DR, OF	$600	$650	$750
1907 model & No.0, 23J, BRG, Adj.5P, DR, HC	650	700	785
Unmarked, 23J, BRG, Adj.5P, DR, OF	525	550	600
Series 0, 23J, BRG, Adj.5P, DR, **Ruby banking pins**	650	700	750
Series 0, 23J, BRG, Adj.5P, DR, **jeweled barrel**	650	700	750
Series 0, 23J, BRG, Adj.5P, DR, **OF, 14K**	950	1,000	1,200
Series 0, 23J, BRG, Adj.5P, DR, **HC, 14K**	1,100	1,300	1,600
No. 1, 21J, BRG, Adj.5P, DR ★	400	445	500
Series 1, 21J, BRG, Adj.5P, DR	400	445	500
Series 2, 17J, BRG, Adj.5P, DR, HC	200	245	300

Series II, Railroad Chronometer, 16 size, 21 jewels, Adj5p, serial number 1,217,534.

Edward Howard Model, 16 size, 23 blue sapphire jewels, frosted gold bridge, wolfteeth wind, serial # 77.

⊕ Watches listed in this book are priced at the **collectable fair market value** at the RETAIL level, as complete watches having an original 14k gold filled case, KEY WIND with silver, an original white enamel single sunk dial, and with the entire original movement in good working order with no repairs needed, unless otherwise noted.

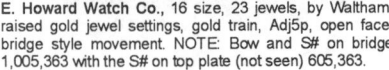

E. Howard Watch Co., 16 size, 23 jewels, by Waltham, raised gold jewel settings, gold train, Adj5p, open face, bridge style movement. NOTE: Bow and S# on bridge 1,005,363 with the S# on top plate (not seen) 605,363.

E. Howard Watch Co., 16 size 19 jewels, by Waltham, gold jewel settings, Adj3p, hunting case, 3/4 plate movement.

Series or Name — Description	Avg	Ex-Fn	Mint
Series 2, 17J, BRG, Adj.5P, DR, OF	$125	$145	$175
Series 3, 17J, 3/4, Adj.3P, circular DMK	100	120	150
Series 3, 17J, OF, Adj.3P, 14K, circular DMK	500	525	560
No. 5, 19J, GJS, BRG, HC ★	400	425	475
Series 5, 19J, BRG, Adj.5P, DR, 14K	550	575	625
Series 5, 19J, BRG, Adj.5P, DR, 1907 Model	225	250	300
1905, 17J, 3/4, Adj.5P, DR, RGJS, slant parallel DMK, OF	125	145	175
1905, 17J, 3/4, Adj.5P, DR, RGJS, slant parallel DMK, HC	175	200	250
Series 9, 17J, 3/4, Adj.5P, DR, LS, checkerboard DMK	175	200	250
Series 9, 17J, 3/4, Adj.5P, DR, 14K, checkerboard DMK (railroad grade)	475	500	550
Series 10, 21J, BRG, Adj.5P, DR Marked Non–Magnetic ★	400	425	500
Series 10, 21J, BRG, Adj.5P, DR	375	450	475
No. 10, 21J, BRG, Adj.5P, DR	350	375	400
Series 11, 21J, R.R. Chrono., Adj.5P, DR	400	450	550
Edward Howard, 23 blue sapphire pressed J, Free Sprung, Adj.5P, DR, Serial numbers below 300, without box ★★	6,000	7,000	8,000
Edward Howard, 23 blue sapphire pressed J, Free Sprung, Adj.5P, DR, Serial numbers below 300, with original box and papers, 18K Edward Howard case ★★★	8,000	9,000	10,000
23J, E. Howard W. Co. on movement (mfg. by Waltham), 14K, Brg model ★★	1,200	1,400	1,700
23J, E. Howard W. Co. on movement (mfg. by Waltham), OF, gold filled	550	650	750
23J, E. Howard W. Co. on movement (mfg. by Waltham), HC, gold filled	650	750	900
21J, Waltham Model, Bridge model, HC	400	450	550
21J, Waltham Model, 3/4, OF	275	300	350
19J, Waltham Model, Bridge model, HC	275	300	375
19J, Waltham Model, 3/4, OF	275	300	350
17J, Waltham Model, Bridge model, HC	250	300	375
17J, Waltham Model, 3/4, OF	225	250	300
Climax,7J., (made for export), gilded, OF	60	70	90

12 SIZE

Series or Name — Description	Avg	Ex-Fn	Mint
Series 6, 19J, BRG, DR, Adj.5P, 1908 Model, 14K, HC	$300	$350	$425
Series 6, 19J, BRG, DR, Adj.5P, 14K, OF	200	250	325
Series 6, 19J, BRG, DR, Adj.5P, OF	100	120	150
Series 7, 17J, BRG, DR, Adj.3P, 14K, OF	200	250	325
Series 7, 17J, BRG, DR, Adj.3P, OF	70	90	125
Series 8, 21J, BRG, DR, Adj.5P, OF	175	200	250
Series 8, 23J, BRG, DR, Adj.5P, **14K, OF**	425	475	525
Series 8, 23J, BRG, DR, Adj.5P, OF	225	275	300
Series 8, 23J, BRG, DR, Adj.5P, **14K, HC**	525	625	725
23J, Waltham Model, BRG, HC	275	325	375
23J, Waltham Model, BRG, OF	225	275	325
21J, Waltham Model, BRG, HC	225	275	325
21J, Waltham Model, BRG, OF	225	250	275
17J, Waltham Model, BRG, HC	150	175	200
17J, Waltham Model, BRG, OF	125	150	175
17J, Waltham Model, 3/4, HC	125	150	175
17J, Waltham Model, 3/4, OF	100	125	150

NOTE: First Serial # for 12 size with 17J.=977,001; 19J.=977,451; 21J.=1,055,851.

Series 8, 12 size, 21 jewels, open face, stop works, extra thin.

E. Howard Watch Co., 10 size, 17J, Adj3p, serial # 61,230. (Serial # started at about 1,001 on this model.)

SERIES 8 GOING BARREL =21J.   SERIES 6 GOING BARREL =19J.   SERIES 7 GOING BARREL =17J.

10 SIZE

NOTE: 10 Size Serial numbers start at about 1,001 on this model.

Series or Name — Description	Avg	Ex-Fn	Mint
Thin Model, 21J, ADJ, 14K case, OF	$250	$275	$325
Thin Model, 19J, ADJ, 14K case, OF	225	250	300
Thin Model, 17J, ADJ, 14K case, OF	200	225	275

STYLE R.R. Chronometer
gold filled: $110 - $135 - $160

STYLE R.R. Antique Bow
note: Jointed- Inside Cap
gold filled: $100 - $125 - $150

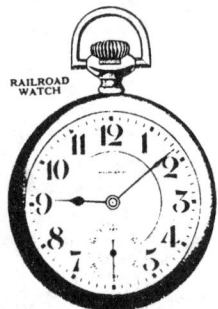

STYLE R.R. Plain swing out
gold filled: $100 - $125 - $150

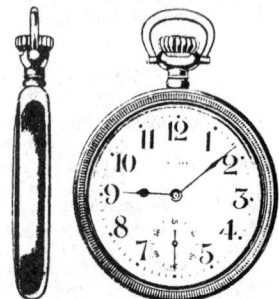

STYLE R.R. Engine Turned swing out
gold filled: $100 - $125 - $150

STYLE R.R. SWING OUT
gold filled: $100 - $125 - $150
14K GOLD: $300 - $325 - $365

Rail Road Chronometer = Gold Filled
Rail Road Antique Bow= solid 18K gold, 14K gold heavy, 14K gold, & 25 year **Gold Filled**
SWING OUT = Gold Filled and the swing out **Plain** also came 14K solid gold

🕐 NOTE: Factory Advertised as a **complete** watch and was fitted with a certain matched, timed and rated movement and sold in the factory designed case style as a **complete** watch. The factory advertised as *"Howard movements and cases are not sold separately"*. All the factory advertised **complete** watches came with a enamel dial **SHOWN** or **CHOICE** of other **Railroad** dials.

ILLINOIS WATCH CO.
Springfield, Illinois
1869 - 1927

The Illinois Watch Company was organized mainly through the efforts of J. C. Adams. The first directors were J. T. Stuart, W. B. Miller, John Williams, John W. Bunn, George Black and George Passfield. In 1879 the company changed all its watches to a quick train movement by changing the number of teeth in the fourth wheel. The first mainspring made by the company was used in 1882. The next year soft enamel dials were used.

The Illinois Watch Co. used more names on its movements than any other watch manufacturer. To identify all of them requires extensive knowledge by the collector plus a good working knowledge of watch mechanics. Engraved on some early movements, for example, are "S. W. Co." or "I. W. Co., Springfield, Ill." To the novice these abbreviations might be hard to understand, thus making Illinois watches difficult to identify. But one saving clue is that the location "Springfield, Illinois" appears on most of these watches. It is important to learn how to identify these type watches because some of them are extremely collectible. Examples of some of the more valuable of these are: the Benjamin Franklin (size 18 or 16, 25 or 26 jewels), Paillard's Non-Magnetic, Pennsylvania Special, C & O, and B & O railroad models.

The earliest movements made by the Illinois Watch Co. are listed below. They made the first watch in early 1872, but the company really didn't get off the ground until 1875. Going by the serial number, the first watch made was the Stuart. Next was the Mason, followed by the Bunn, the Miller, and finally the Currier. The first stem-wind was made in 1875.

> **STUART, FIRST** Run was serial numbers .... 1 to 100.
> **MASON, FIRST** Run was serial numbers .... 101 to 200.
> **BUNN, FIRST** Run was serial numbers .... 201 to 300.
> **MILLER, FIRST** Run was serial numbers .... 301 to 400.
> **CURRIER, FIRST** Run was serial numbers .... 401 to 500.

The Illinois Watch Company was sold to Hamilton Watch Co. in 1927. The Illinois factory continued to produce Illinois watches under the new management until 1932. After 1933 Hamilton produced watches bearing the Illinois name in their own factory until 1939.

CHRONOLOGY OF THE DEVELOPMENT OF ILLINOIS WATCH CO.:
> Illinois Springfield Watch Co. 1869-1879
> Springfield Illinois Watch Co. 1879-1885
> Illinois Watch Co. 1885-1927
> Illinois Watch Co. sold to Hamilton Watch Co. 1927

ILLINOIS WATCH CO., Bates Model, 18 size, 7 jewels, key wind & set, serial number 43,876, c.1874.

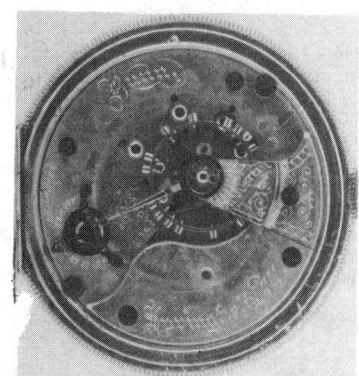

BUNN, 18 size, 16 jewels, hunting case, NOTE: Chalmer patented regulator, serial number 1,185,809.

🕐 NOTE: Numerous model 2 & 3 movements have <u>key-wind style barrel arbors</u> and stem wind *capabilities* they are referred to as **transition** Models. When model 2 & 3 were introduced the factory must have had a large supply of key-wind style barrel arbors so being frugal they were used.

ILLINOIS ESTIMATED SERIAL NUMBERS AND PRODUCTION DATES

DATE – SERIAL NO.	DATE – SERIAL NO.	DATE – SERIAL NO.
1872 – 5,000	1893 – 1,120,000	1914 – 2,600,000
1873 – 20,000	1894 – 1,160,000	1915 – 2,700,000
1874 – 50,000	1895 – 1,220,000	1916 – 2,800,000
1875 – 75,000	1896 – 1,250,000	1917 – 3,000,000
1876 – 100,000	1897 – 1,290,000	1918 – 3,200,000
1877 – 145,000	1898 – 1,330,000	1919 – 3,400,000
1878 – 210,000	1899 – 1,370,000	1920 – 3,600,000
1879 – 250,000	1900 – 1,410,000	1921 – 3,750,000
1880 – 300,000	1901 – 1,450,000	1922 – 3,900,000
1881 – 350,000	1902 – 1,500,000	1923 – 4,000,000
1882 – 400,000	1903 – 1,650,000	1924 – 4,500,000
1883 – 450,000	1904 – 1,700,000	1925 – 4,700,000
1884 – 500,000	1905 – 1,800,000	1926 – 4,800,000
1885 – 550,000	1906 – 1,840,000	1927 – 5,000,000
1886 – 600,000	1907 – 1,900,000	(Sold to Hamilton)
1887 – 700,000	1908 – 2,100,000	1928 – 5,200,000
1888 – 800,000	1909 – 2,150,000	1929 – 5,350,000
1889 – 900,000	1910 – 2,200,000	1930 – 5,400,000
1890 – 1,000,000	1911 – 2,300,000	1931 – 5,500,000
1891 – 1,040,000	1912 – 2,400,000	1932 – 5,600,000
1892 – 1,080,000	1913 – 2,500,000	

The above list is provided for determining the **APPROXIMATE** age of your watch. Match serial number with date. Watches were not necessarily sold in the exact order of manufactured date.

NOTE: It required several months for raw material to emerge as a finished movement. All the while the factory is producing all sizes, models and grades. The numbering system was basically "consecutive", due to demand a batch of movements could be side tracked, thus allowing a different size and model to move ahead to meet this demand. Therefore, the dates some movements were sold and delivered to the trade, may not be "consecutive".

(See Illinois Identification of Movements section located at the end of the Illinois price section to identify the movement, size and model number of your watch.)

ILLINOIS
18 SIZE (ALL FULL PLATE)

Grade or Name — Description	Avg	Ex-Fn	Mint
Alleghany, 11J, KW, gilded, OF	$125	$150	$175
Alleghany, 11J, M#1, NI, KW	150	175	200
Alleghany, 11J, M#2, NI, Transition	125	150	200
America, 7J, M#3, Silveroid	75	95	125
America, 7J, M#1-2, KW	125	150	200
America Special, 7J, M#1-2, KW	175	200	250
Army & Navy, 19J, GJS, Adj.5P, OF	250	275	325
Army & Navy, 19J, GJS, Adj.5P, HC	275	300	350
Army & Navy, 21J, GJS, Adj.5P, OF	300	325	375
Army & Navy, 21J, GJS, Adj.5P, HC	325	350	400
Baltimore & Ohio R.R. Special, 17J, GJS, ADJ	550	700	900
Baltimore & Ohio R.R. Special, 21J, GJS, NI, ADJ	1,100	1,250	1,400
Baltimore & Ohio R.R. Standard, 24J, GJS, ADJ	1,500	1,700	2,000
Bates, 7J, M#1-2, KW	150	175	200

🕐 Watches listed in this book are priced at the **collectable fair market value** at the **retail** level, as **complete** watches having an original 14k gold filled case, *KEY WIND* with silver, an original white enamel single sunk dial, and with the entire original movement in good working order with no repairs needed, unless otherwise noted.

🕐 GENERIC, NAMELESS OR **UNMARKED GRADES** FOR WATCH MOVEMENTS ARE LISTED UNDER THE COMPANY NAME OR INITIALS OF THE COMPANY, ETC. BY SIZE, JEWEL COUNT AND DESCRIPTION.

🕐 Some watch manufacturers personalize watches for jobbers or jewelry firms, with exclusive private signed or marked movements. The valuable collectable watches are listed under the signed or marked movement. Other exclusive private signed or marked movements will have equivalent value are only slightly higher value and should be compared to Generic or Nameless movements. Railroad signed or marked (dials & movements) are usually more collectable & higher in value.

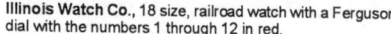

Illinois Watch Co., 18 size, railroad watch with a Ferguson dial with the numbers 1 through 12 in red.

Army and Navy, 18 size, 19 jewels, engraved on movement "Washington Watch Co.," serial number 1,606,612.

Grade or Name — Description	Avg	Ex-Fn	Mint
Benjamin Franklin U.S.A., 17J, ADJ, NI	$600	$675	$750
Benjamin Franklin U.S.A., 21J, GJS, **Adj.6P**, NI ★	1,000	1,200	1,400
Benjamin Franklin U.S.A., 21J, GJS, Adj.5P, NI ★	900	1,100	1,300
Benjamin Franklin U.S.A., 24J, GJS, Adj.6P, NI ★	2,500	2,800	3,250
Benjamin Franklin U.S.A., 25J, GJS, Adj.6P, NI ★	6,000	6,500	7,500
Benjamin Franklin U.S.A., 26J, GJS, Adj.6P, NI, ★★★★★	6,500	7,000	7,500
Bunn, 15J, M#1, KW, KS, **1st. run S# 201 to 300**, OF ★★★	2,000	2,400	3,000
Bunn, 15J, M#1, KW, KS, OF ★	525	625	800
Bunn, 15J, M#1, KW, KS, **"ADJUSTED"**,	575	675	850
Bunn, 15J, KW/SW transition	450	525	675
Bunn, 15J, M#1, KW, Coin	525	625	800
Bunn, 15J, KW, M#1, HC	575	675	850
Bunn, 16J, KW, (not marked 16J.), OF	525	625	800
Bunn, 16J, KW, (not marked 16J.), HC	575	675	850
Bunn, 16J, SW, (not marked 16J.), HC	575	675	850
Bunn, 16J, SW, ADJ, (not marked 16J.), HC	575	675	850
Bunn, 17J, SW, M#1, HC ★	675	775	950
Bunn, 17J, M#2, SW, NI, ADJ, Chalmers patent reg., HC ★	575	625	725
Bunn, 17J, SW, NI, Coin	150	175	225
Bunn, 17J, SW, M#3, 5th pinion, gilded, OF	375	425	500
Bunn, 17J, M#4, SW, NI, OF	150	175	225
Bunn, 17J, M#5, SW, NI, HC	175	225	300
Bunn, 17J, M#6, SW, NI, OF	150	175	225
Bunn, 18J, SW, NI, ADJ., (not marked 18J.), OF ★★★★	1,000	1,100	1,250
Bunn, 19J, SW, NI, DR, LS, GJS, Adj.5P, **J. barrel**, OF	275	325	350
Bunn, 19J, SW, Adj.6P, DR, **J. barrel**, OF	325	375	450
Bunn, 19J, SW, GJS, DR, Adj.5P, **J. barrel**, HC ★	375	425	525

IMPORTANT NOTE: Railroad Standards, Railroad Approved & Railroad Grade **terminology**, as defined and used in this *BOOK*.
1. **RAILROAD STANDARDS** = A commission or board appointed by the railroad companies outlined a set of **guidelines** to be accepted or approved by each railroad line.
2. **RAILROAD APPROVED** = A **LIST** of watches each railroad line would approve if purchased by their employee's. (this list changed through the years)
3. **RAILROAD GRADE** = A watch made by manufactures to met or exceed the guidelines set by the railroad **standards**. Grade such as 992, Vanguard and B.W. Raymond etc.
☉ Some GRADES **exceeded** the R.R. standards such as 23 jewels, diamond end stone, gold train, raised gold jewel settings, double sunk dial and the list goes on. Examples: such as Veritas, Sangamo, 950 & Riverside Maximus and many others.

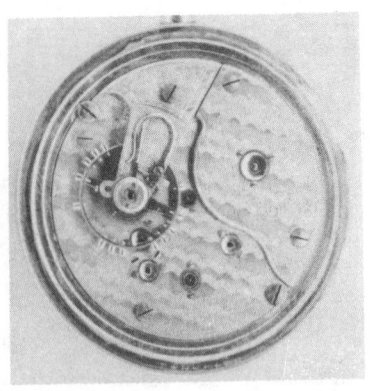

Bunn Special, 18 size, 24 jewels, adjusted, serial number 1,413,435

Bunn Special, 18 size, 26 Ruby jewels, "J. Home & Co." on dial, adjusted to six positions, gold jewel settings, serial number 2,019,415.

Grade or Name — Description	Avg	Ex-Fn	Mint
Bunn Special, 21J, SW, **Coin**	$225	$250	$275
Bunn Special, 21J, GJS, ADJ, HC	425	475	525
Bunn Special, 21J, GJS, ADJ, DR, OF	225	250	300
Bunn Special, 21J, GJS, DR, Adj.5P, OF	225	250	300
Bunn Special, 21J, GJS, DR, Adj.6P, OF	250	275	325
Bunn Special, 21J, GJS, Adj.5P, **HC, 14K**	750	800	900
Bunn Special, 21J, GJS, ADJ, 2-Tone	275	300	350
Bunn Special, 21J, GJS, Adj.5P, DR	250	275	325
Bunn Special, 21J," EXTRA", GJS ★	400	525	650
Bunn Special, 23J, GJS, ADJ, DR, OF	525	575	650
Bunn Special, 23J, GJS, Adj.6P, DR, OF	550	600	675
Bunn Special, 23J, GJS, Adj.6P, DR, 2-Tone, OF ★★★	600	700	850
Bunn Special, 23J, GJS, ADJ, DR, HC ★★	2,200	2,500	3,000
Bunn Special, 24J, GJS, Adj.5P, DR, HC	825	925	1,100
Bunn Special, 24J, GJS, Adj.5P, DR, **14K, HC**	1,450	1,600	1,800
Bunn Special, 24J, GJS, Adj.5P, DR, OF	725	800	875
Bunn Special, 24J, GJS, Adj.6P, DR, OF	750	825	900
Bunn Special, 24J, GJS, Adj.6P, DR, HC	825	925	1,200
Bunn Special, 25J, GJS, Adj.6P, DR ★★★	5,000	5,500	6,500
Bunn Special, 26J, GJS, Adj.6P, DR ★★	4,500	5,000	6,000
Central Truck Railroad, 15J, KW, KS ★	375	425	500
Chesapeake & Ohio, 17J, ADJ, OF ★	700	800	900
Chesapeake & Ohio Special, 21J, GJS, 2-Tone ★	1,000	1,200	1,500
Chesapeake & Ohio Special, 24J, NI, ADJ, GJS ★	1,700	1,900	2,200
Chronometer, 11-15J, KW, OF	150	175	200
Chronometer, 15J, M#2, HC	175	200	250
Columbia, 11J, M#3, 5th Pinion	125	150	200
Columbia, 11J, M#1 & 2, KW	125	150	200
Columbia, 11J, M#1 & 2, Silveroid	100	125	175
Columbia Special, 11J, M#1-2-3, HC	125	150	200
Columbia Special, 11J, M#1-2-3, KW, transition	100	125	150
Comet, 11J, M#3, OF, LS, SW	100	125	150
Commodore Perry, 15-16J, HC	175	200	250
Criterion, 11-15J, HC	125	150	175

🕛 Some watch manufacturers personalize watches for jobbers or jewelry firms, with exclusive private signed or marked movements. The valuable collectable watches are listed under the signed or marked movement. Other exclusive private signed or marked movements will have equivalent value are only slightly higher value and should be compared to Generic or Nameless movements. Railroad signed or marked (dials & movements) are usually more collectable & higher in value.

Diurnal, 18 size, 7 jewels, key wind & set, only one run, total production 2,000, serial number 86,757.

Emperor, 18 size, 21 jewels, Adj3p, serial number 2,396,628.

Grade or Name — Description	Avg	Ex-Fn	Mint
Currier, 11-12J, KW, OF	$125	$150	$200
Currier, 11-12J, KW, HC	150	200	250
Currier, 11-12J, **1st run S# 401 to 500** ★★★	400	500	650
Currier, 11-12J, transition, OF	100	125	150
Currier, 13–15J, M#3, OF	100	125	150
Currier, 13–15J, M#3, HC	125	150	195
Dauntless, 11J	100	125	150
Dean, 15J, M#1, KW, HC ★	275	375	475
Diurnal, 7J, KW, KS, HC, Coin ★	225	275	350
Dominion Railway, with train on dial ★	900	1,000	1,300
Eastlake, 11J, SW, KW, Transition	125	150	200
Emperor, 21J, M#6, LS, SW, ADJ	225	250	300
Enterprise, M#2, ADJ	125	150	200
Eureka, 11J	125	150	200
Favorite, 16J, LS, OF	125	150	175
Forest City, 7–11J, SW, LS, HC	150	175	200
Forest City, 17J, KW/SW, gilted,	150	175	225
General Grant or General Lee, 11J, M#1, KW	225	250	300
Hoyt, 7-9-11J, M#1-2, KW	100	125	150

🕐 Generic, nameless, Personalized Jobber Watches or unmarked grades for watch movements are listed under the Company name or initials of the Company, etc. by size, jewel count and description.

	Avg	Ex-Fn	Mint
Illinois Watch Co., 7-9J,	$100	$125	$150
Illinois Watch Co., 11J, M#1-2, KW,	100	125	150
Illinois Watch Co., 11J, M#3	75	100	125
Illinois Watch Co., 13J, M#1-2, KW,	125	150	200
Illinois Watch Co., 15J, M#1-2, KW,	125	150	200
Illinois Watch Co., 15J, KW, ADJ, NI	150	175	225
Illinois Watch Co., 15J, SW, ADJ, DMK, NI	100	125	150
Illinois Watch Co., 15J, transition	85	110	135
Illinois Watch Co., 15J, SW, **Silveroid**	75	95	125
Illinois Watch Co., 15J, SW, **9K, HC**	325	425	575
Illinois Watch Co., 16J, SW, ADJ, DMK, NI	100	125	150
Illinois Watch Co., 16J, SW, ADJ, DMK, NI, marked **ADJ** ★	225	250	325
Illinois Watch Co., 17J, SW, **Silveroid**	85	95	125
Illinois Watch Co., 17J, M#3, **5th Pinion**	225	250	275
Illinois Watch Co., 17J, SW, 2 tone mvt,	100	125	150

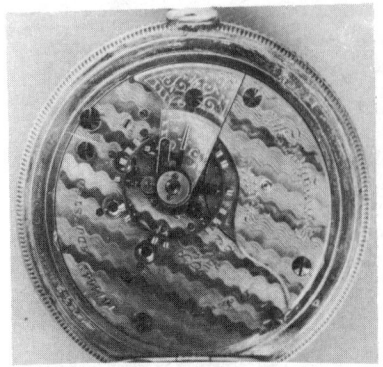
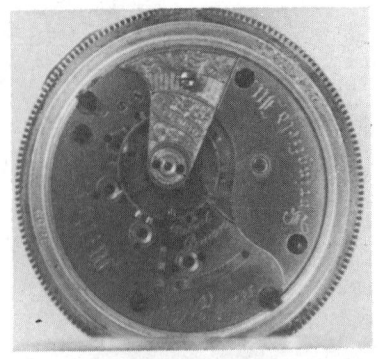

Ill. W. Co., 18 size, 17 jewels, adjusted, 2-tone movement, serial number 1,404,442.

Miller, 18 size, 17 jewels, 5th pinion model which changed hunting case to open face.

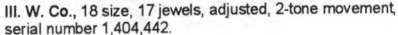 Generic, nameless, Personalized Jobber Watches or unmarked grades for watch movements are listed under the Company name or initials of the Company, etc. by size, jewel count and description.

Grade or Name — Description	Avg	Ex-Fn	Mint
Illinois Watch Co., 17J, SW, ADJ	$100	$125	$150
Illinois Watch Co., 17J, SW, "EXTRA", Adj.4P	100	125	150
Illinois Watch Co., 17J, transition	100	125	150
Illinois Watch Co., 19J, ADJ. J. Barrel, OF	225	250	275
Illinois Watch Co., 21J, Adj.3P, OF	200	225	250
Illinois Watch Co., 21J, ADJ5-6P,	350	375	425
Illinois Watch Co., 23J, ADJ6P, OF ★★★★	1,500	1,700	2,000
Illinois Watch Co., 24J, ADJ,	525	575	650
Interior, 7J, KW & SW, OF	125	150	200
Interstate Chronometer, 17J, HC	425	525	675
Interstate Chronometer, 17J, OF	325	425	575
Interstate Chronometer, 23J, Adj.5P, GJS, NI, OF ★	900	950	1,200
Interstate Chronometer, 23J, Adj.5P, GJS, NI, HC ★★	1,200	1,400	1,650
Iowa W. Co., 7-11J, M#1-2, KW,	200	225	275
King of the Road, 16 &17J, NI, OF & HC, LS, ADJ ★	400	500	625
King Special, 17J, 2-tone, OF	125	150	200
King Philip Sp., 17J, (RR spur line)	300	375	450
Lafayette, 24J, GJS, Adj.6P, NI, SW, OF	950	1,050	1,250
Lafayette, 24J, GJS, Adj.6P, NI, SW, single roller, HC	1,200	1,400	1,600
Lafayette, 24J, GJS, Adj.6P, NI, SW, double roller, HC ★★	1,500	1,600	1,800
Lakeshore, 17J, OF, LS, NI, SW	125	150	200
Landis W. Co., 15-17J	100	125	175
Liberty Bell, 17J, LS, NI, SW, OF	100	125	150
Liberty Bell, 17J, LS, NI, SW, HC	125	150	200
Lightning Express, 11-13J, KWKS,	100	125	150
A. Lincoln, 21J, Adj.5P, NI, DR, GJS, HC	375	400	425
A. Lincoln, 21J, Adj.5P, NI, DR, GJS,OF	250	275	325
Lincoln Park, 15-17J, LS, OF	100	125	175
Majestic Special, 17J, 2-tone, OF	125	150	175
Locomotive, 11J, M# 2 grade 4, Locomotive engraved on Mvt.	195	225	275
Maiden Lane, 16-17J, 5th Pinion	375	425	500
Manhattan, 11-13J, NI, KW, LS, HC or OF	150	175	200
Manhattan, 15-17J, NI, KW, LS,HC or OF	175	200	250
Mason, 7J, KW, KS, HC	150	175	225
Mason, 7J, KW, KS, HC, 1st run S# 101 to 200 ★★★	425	525	675
Miller, 15J,1st run S# 301 to 400 ★★★	400	450	575
Miller, 15J, M#1, HC, KW	175	200	250
Miller, 15J, M#1, HC, KW, ADJ	200	225	275
Miller, 15J, KW, OF	150	175	225
Miller, 17J, 5th Pinion, ADJ	300	325	400
Monarch W. Co., 17J, NI, ADJ, SW	150	175	225

Paillard Non-Magnetic W. Co., 18 size, 24 jewels, gold jewel settings, serial number 1,397,812.

Pennsylvania Special, 18 size, 26 jewels, Adj6p, 2-tone movement, serial number 1,742,913.

Grade or Name — Description	Avg	Ex-Fn	Mint
Montgomery Ward, 15-17-19J, OF, GJS	$150	$175	$225
Montgomery Ward, 21J	200	225	300
Montgomery Ward Timer, 21J, ★	200	225	300
Montgomery Ward, 24J, OF	950	1,050	1,250
Montgomery Ward, 24J, HC ★	1,200	1,400	1,700
Montgomery Ward, 24J, marked double roller, HC ★	1,300	1,500	1,800
Muscatine W. Co., 15J, LS, NI, HC	175	200	250
The National, 11J, SW, LS, OF	100	125	150
Non-Magnetic W. Co., 21J, OF ★	250	300	375
A.Norton,7J, KW, KS,	125	150	175
Paillard Non-Magnetic W. Co., 15J, NI, OF	100	125	175
Paillard Non-Magnetic W. Co., 17J, GJS, NI, Adj.5P, OF	125	150	200
Paillard Non-Magnetic W. Co., 21J, GJS, NI, Adj.5P, OF	225	275	350
Paillard Non-Magnetic W. Co., 23J, GJS, NI, Adj.5P, OF	850	900	1,150
Paillard Non-Magnetic W. Co., 24J, GJS, NI, Adj.5P, OF	950	1,050	1,250
Pennsylvania Special, 17J, GJS, ADJ ★	600	750	900
Pennsylvania Special, 21J, DR, Adj.5P ★	1,200	1,400	1,800
Pennsylvania Special, 24J, DR, GJS, ADJ ★	1,800	2,000	2,400
Pennsylvania Special, 25J, DR, GJS, ADJ, NI ★★★★	5,000	5,500	6,500
Pennsylvania Special, 26J, DR, GJS, ADJ, NI ★★	4,500	5,000	6,000
Pierce Arrow, 17J, "automaker logo" ★	375	450	600
Plymouth W. Co., 15-17J, SW	95	125	150
Potomac, 17J, ADJ, NI, OF	150	175	225
Potomac, 17J, ADJ, NI, HC ★★★	225	275	325
The President, 15J, NI, OF	150	175	225
The President, 17J, DMK, **14K gold case**	600	700	850
Rail Road Construction, 17J, OF	225	275	350
Rail Road Dispatcher Extra or Special, 15-17J, OF	225	250	325
Rail Road Dispatcher Extra, 15-17J, HC	225	275	350
Rail Road Employee's Special, 17J, NI, LS, HC	275	325	375
Rail Road Timer Extra, 17-21J, (Montgomery Ward), OF ★	325	375	475
Rail Road King, 15J, NI, ADJ, OF	250	275	300
Rail Road King, 15J, NI, ADJ, HC	275	300	325
Rail Road King, 16J, NI, ADJ, OF ★	325	375	450
Rail Road King, 16J, NI, ADJ, HC	350	400	475
Rail Road King, 17J, NI, ADJ, OF ★	325	375	450
Rail Road King, 17J, NI, ADJ, HC	350	400	475
The Railroader, 15J, OF, ADJ, NI	250	300	375
Railway , 11J, KW, KS, gilt ★	100	125	150
Railway Engineer, 15J	275	325	400
Railway Regulator, 11-15J, LS, (R.W.Sears Watch Co.) ★★	425	525	695

The President, 18 size, 17 jewels, Chalmer patented regulator, serial number 1,240,909.

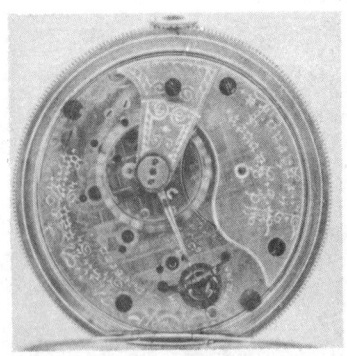

Railroad King, 18 size, 17 jewels, Fifth Pinion Model, adjusted. Note Chalmer patented regulator, S# 1,160,836.

Grade or Name — Description	Avg	Ex-Fn	Mint
Remington W.Co. 17J, OF ....★	$200	$225	$325
Remington W.Co. 17J, HC...★	225	275	400
Remington Special, 21J, Adj.6P, OF	500	600	700
Standard W. Co., 15J, several models..	150	175	225
S. W. Co., 15J, M#1, KW, HC...	150	175	225
R.W. Sears Watch Co. Chicago,"Defiance" model, **14K,HC**.........	650	750	900
Sears & Roebuck Special, 17J, GJS, NI, DMK, Adj......................	150	175	225
Senate, 17J, NI, DMK, Washington W. Co.	150	175	225
Southern R.R. Special, 21J, LS, ADJ, OF ....★	1,200	1,400	1,700
Southern R.R. Special, 21J, M#5, LS, Adj., HC ....★	1,600	1,850	2,200
Star Light, 17J, 5th pinion, Chalmers Reg. OF...............................	200	250	325
Stewart Special, 11-15J, Adj.	100	125	150
Stewart Special, 17J, Adj..	150	175	200
Stewart Special, 21J, Adj.	200	225	250
Stuart, 15J, M#1, KW, KS..	500	600	750
Stuart, 15J, M#1, KW, KS, transition ....★	300	350	450
Stuart, 15J, M#1, KW, KS, marked Adj. ....★ ★	500	650	825
Stuart, 15J, ADJ, KW, Abbotts Conversion, **18K, HC** ....★ ★	1,500	1,700	2,000
Stuart, 15J, M#1, KW, KS, Coin ....★	500	600	775
Stuart, 15J, M#1, KW, KS, **1st run** S# 1 to 10" ....★ ★ ★ ★	5,000	6,500	8,500
Stuart, 15J, M#1, KW, KS, **1st run** S# 11 to 100" ....★ ★ ★ ★	3,000	3,500	4,500

Sears & Roebuck Special, 18 size, 17 jewels, serial number 1,481,879.

Washington W. Co., Lafayette model, 18 size, 24 Ruby jewels, gold jewel settings, adjusted, serial # 3,392,897.

Grade or Name — Description	Avg	Ex-Fn	Mint
Stuart, 17J, M#3, 5th Pinion .... ★ ★	$300	$400	$475
Stuart, 17J, M#3, 5th Pinion, ADJ .... ★ ★	375	425	500
Transition Models, 17J, OF..	125	150	175
Train Dispatcher Special, 17J, (Montgomery Ward), Adj, OF ..... ★	425	475	550
Time King, 17J, OF, LS, NI..	175	200	275
Time King, 21J, OF, LS, ...	200	225	300
Union Pacific Sp., 17J; OF.................................... ★	300	375	475
Vault Time Lock for Mosler, 15J, 72 hr..................	100	125	175
Ward's Special, 15J, NI, FULL, LS, ...	100	125	150
George Washington,11J, HC...................................	125	150	185
Washington,11-17J, also (U.S.A)............................	100	125	150
⊕ **Washington W. Co.** (See Army & Navy, Liberty Bell, Lafayette, Senate)			
Wathiers Railway Watch, 15-17J, Adj., NI	200	250	350
N0. 5, 11J, KW KS, (**marked** No.5), HC..................	175	225	295
65, 15J, HC, LS, M#2..	100	125	150
89, 17J, nickel, ADJ, OF	95	125	150
89, 21J, nickel, ADJ, HC...	175	200	265
101, 11J, SW, KW, OF...	100	125	150
101, 11J, SW, KW, Silveroid	75	100	125
101, 11J, SW, KW, HC	100	125	175
102, 13J, SW, KW, Silveroid	60	85	125
102, 13J, SW, KW, OF...	100	125	150
102, 13J, SW, KW, HC	125	150	195
103, 15-16J, ADJ..	100	125	150
104, 15J, M#2, HC.................................... ★ ★	375	450	600
104, 17J, M#3, early high grade for RR, Ca. 1885, OF....... ★ ★ ★	450	550	700
105, 17J, M#3, early high grade for RR, Ca. 1885, OF....... ★ ★ ★	750	850	1,000
105, 15J, M#2, GJS, ADJ, KW, KS, HC .... ★ ★	700	775	895
106, 15J, ADJ, KW, KS	125	150	175
444, 17J, NI, ADJ, OF..	100	125	150
445, 19J, GJS, 2-Tone, HC....................................... ★ ★	1,000	1,200	1,500
1908 Special, 21J, NI, Adj.5P,(**marked** 1908 special), OF	325	425	575

STUART, 17 jewels, Model #3, 5th Pinion, Transition Model.

First Model in 14K white or green gold
filled Wadsworth case, showing
Montgomery numerical dial.

⊕ Watches listed in this book are priced at the collectable RETAIL level, **as complete** watches having an original 1 4k gold filled case, *KEY WIND* with silver, an original white enamel single sunk dial, and with the entire original movement in good working order with no repairs needed, unless otherwise noted.

ILLINOIS
16 SIZE

Grade or Name — Description	Avg	Ex-Fx	Mint
Adams Street, 17J, 3/4, SW, NI, DMK	$200	$250	$325
Adams Street, 21J, 3F brg, NI, DMK	325	375	450
Ak-Sar-Ben (Nebraska backward), 17J, OF, GCW	175	200	250
Ariston, 11J, OF	75	100	150
Ariston, 15J, OF	75	100	150
Ariston, 17J, 3F brg, HC	200	250	325
Ariston, 17J, Adj.3P, OF	175	200	250
Ariston, 19J, Adj.3P, OF	200	225	265
Ariston, 21J, GJS, Adj.6P, OF	350	400	500
Ariston, 23J, GJS, Adj.6P, OF	500	600	750
Ariston, 23J, GJS, Adj.6P, HC ★★	700	800	1,000
Arlington Special, 17J, OF	100	125	150
Arlington Special, 17J, OF, Silveroid	85	100	135
Army & Navy, 19J, GJS, Adj.3P, NI, 1F brg, OF	175	200	225
Army & Navy, 19J, GJS, Adj.3P, NI, 1F brg, HC	200	250	325
Army & Navy, 21J, GJS, Adj.3P, 1F brg, OF	200	250	325
Army & Navy, 21J, GJS, Adj.3P, 1F brg, HC	300	350	400
B & M Special, 17J, BRG, Adj.4P	225	275	350
B & O Standard, 21J	450	500	625
Benjamin Franklin, 17J, ADJ, DMK,	300	325	400
Benjamin Franklin, 21J, GJS, Adj.5P, DR, GT,	550	625	700
Benjamin Franklin, 25J, GJS, Adj.6P, DR, GT, OF ★★	3,000	3,500	4,000
Benjamin Franklin, 25J, GJS, Adj.6P, DR, GT, HC ★★★	3,500	4,000	4,500

Ben Franklin, 16 size, 25 jewels, gold jewel settings, gold train, **Getty Model**, serial number 2,242,138.

Bunn Special, Model 163, 16 size, 23J., gold jewel settings, gold train, 60 hour movement, serial # 5,421,504.

Note: Bunn Special original cases were marked Bunn Special except for Elinvars (Hamilton cased). also GRADES 161 & 163 were made by Hamilton W. Co.

🕐 Generic, nameless or **unmarked grades** for watch movements are listed under the Company name or initials of the Company, etc. by size, jewel count and description.

🕐 Watches listed in this book are priced at the **collectable fair market value** at the RETAIL level, as complete watches having an original 14k gold filled case, KEY WIND with silver, an original white enamel single sunk dial, and with the entire original movement in good working order with no repairs needed, unless otherwise noted.

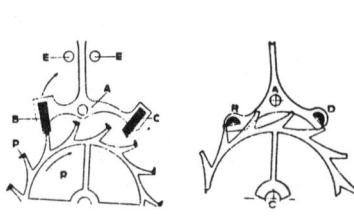

Left: Standard style escapement. Right: DeLong style escapement.

Illinois Watch Co., 16 size, 25J., 3 fingered bridge Getty Model, gold train, HC, note serial number S731,870.

Grade or Name — Description	Avg	Ex-Fn	Mint
Bunn, 17J, LS, OF, NI, 3/4, GJS, Adj.5P	$175	$200	$225
Bunn, 17J, LS, NI, 3/4, Adj.5P, HC............................... ★★★	650	800	1,000
Bunn, 19J, LS, OF, NI, 3/4, GJS, Adj.5P	200	250	275
Bunn, 19J, LS, NI, 3/4, Adj.5P, HC .... ★★★	800	1,000	1,500
Bunn, 19J, LS, OF, NI, 3/4, GJS, Adj.5P, 60 hour..........................	325	375	450
Bunn, 19J, **marked Jeweled Barrel**................................	225	250	300
Bunn Special, 19J, LS, OF, NI, 3/4, Adj.6P, GT............................	200	225	250
Bunn Special, 19J, LS, OF, NI, 3/4, Adj.5P, GT, 60 hour	325	375	450
Bunn Special, 21J, NI, GJS, Adj.6P, GT, HC............................ ★	525	600	725
Bunn Special, 21J, LS, OF, NI, 3/4, GJS, Adj.6P, GT	275	300	350
Bunn Special, 21J, LS, GJS, Adj.6P, GT, **gold plated Mvt.**.... ★★	500	600	800
Bunn Special, 21J, LS,OF, NI, 3/4, GJS, Adj.6P, GT, 60 hour	350	425	450
Bunn Special, 21J, LS, OF, NI, 3/4, GJS, Adj.6P, GT, 60 hr.			
Elinvar..	425	525	575
Bunn Special, 21J, 60 hr., 14K, OF, Bunn Special case .... ★	850	900	1,100
Bunn Special, 23J, LS, OF, NI, 3/4, GJS, Adj.6P, GT	450	500	575
Bunn Special, 23J, LS, OF, NI, 3/4, GJS, Adj.6P, GT, 60 hour	500	575	625
Bunn Special, 23J, LS, OF, NI, 3/4, GJS, Adj.6P, GT,			
with 23J, 60-hour on dial...	725	775	825
Bunn Special, 23J, LS, NI, GJS, GT, Adj.6P, HC........... ★★★★	1,700	2,000	2,500
161 Bunn Special, 21J, 3/4, Adj.6P, 60 hour..............................	575	625	675
161A Bunn Special, 21J, 3/4, Adj.6P, 60 hour (**Elinvar**			
signed under balance or on top plate)	650	700	800
161 Elinvar Bunn Special, 21J, 3/4, Adj.6P, 60 hour			
(**Elinvar** signed at bottom of bridge)....................................	650	700	800
161B, Bunn Special, 21J, 60 hour, pressed jewels .... ★★★★	4,000	5,000	6,500
163 Bunn Special, 23J, GJS, Adj.6P, 3/4, 60 hour.........................	850	950	1,200
163 Elinvar Bunn Special, 23J, GJS, Adj.6P, 60 hour			
(**Elinvar** signed at bottom of cock, uncut balance).............★	1,100	1,250	1,400
163A Elinvar Bunn Special, 23J, GJS, Adj.6P, 3/4, 60 hour			
(**Elinvar** signed under balance)..	1,100	1,250	1,400
163A Elinvar Bunn Special, 23J, Adj.6P, 3/4, 60 hour			
(**Elinvar** signed on train bridge)	1,100	1,250	1,400

🕐 Generic, nameless or unmarked grades for watch movements are listed under the Company name or initials of the Company, etc. by size, jewel count and description.

🕐 Some grades are not included. Their values can be determined by comparing with **similar** age, size, metal content, style, models and grades listed.

Grade or Name — Description	Avg	Ex-Fn	Mint
Burlington W. Co., 15J, OF	$75	$100	$135
Burlington W. Co., 15J, HC	125	150	200
Burlington W. Co., 17J, OF	85	125	150
Burlington W. Co., 17J, HC	150	175	225
Burlington W. Co., 19J, 3/4, NI, Adj.3P	125	150	185
Burlington W. Co., 19J, BRG, NI, Adj.3P	125	150	185
Burlington W. Co., 19J, 3/4, HC	175	200	250
Burlington W. Co., 19J, 3F brg, NI, Adj.3P	125	150	185
Burlington W. Co., 21J, 3/4, NI, Adj.3P	200	225	250
Burlington W. Co., 21J, Adj.6P, GJS ★★	300	350	450
Burlington, Bull Dog- on dial, 21J, SW, LS, GJS, GT	325	375	425
C & O Special, 21J, 3/4, NI, ADJ ★	900	1,100	1,250
Capitol, 19J, OF, 3/4, NI, Adj.3P	125	150	185
Central, 17J, SW, PS, OF	75	100	150
Commodore Perry Special, 21J, Adj.6P, GT, OF	350	375	425
Craftsman, 17J, OF	85	100	150
DeLong Escapement, 21J, GJS, (Bunn Sp. or A. Lincoln) Adj.6P, 14K OF ★★★★★	2,000	2,200	2,500
Dependon, 17J, (J.V.Farwell)	150	175	250
Dependon, 21J, (J.V.Farwell)	200	245	300
Diamond, Ruby, Sapphire, 21J, GJS, GT, Adj.6P, BRG, OF ★	1,000	1,200	1,400
Diamond, Ruby, Sapphire, 23J, GJS, GT, Adj.6P, BRG, OF ★★★	2,200	2,400	2,700
Diamond, Ruby, Sapphire, 23J, GJS, GT, Adj.6P, grade # 310, tall Arabic # on dial, BRG, DR, HC ★★★	3,500	4,000	4,800
Diamond, Ruby, Sapphire, 23J, GJS, GT, Adj.6P, BRG, OF also marked Greenwich (Washington W.Co.) ★★★	2,500	3,000	3,500
Diamond, Ruby, Sapphire, 23J, GJS, GT, Adj.6P, 3/4 plate, OF ★★★	1,600	1,800	2,200
Dispatcher, 19J, Adj.3P	200	225	250
Fifth Ave., 19J, Adj.3P,GT,OF	110	130	150
Fifth Ave., 21J, Adj.3P,GT,OF	175	200	225
Franklin Street, 15J, 3/4, NI, ADJ	100	125	175
Grant, 17J, ADJ, LS, Getty Model, OF	100	125	150
Getty Model # 4 &5, 17J	100	125	150
Getty Model # 4 &5, 21J	275	325	375

Interstate Chronometer, 16 size, 23 jewels, one-fingered bridge, Getty Model, serial number 2,327,614.

A. Lincoln, 16 size, 21 jewels, gold jewel settings, gold train, Adj5p, Getty Model, serial number 2,237,406.

Grade or Name — Description	Avg	Ex-Fn	Mint
Great Northern Special, 17J, BRG, ADJ	$275	$300	$350
Great Northern Special, 19J, BRG, ADJ	300	325	375
Great Northern Special, 21J, BRG, ADJ, Adj.3P	350	375	450
Illinois Central, 17-21J, 2-Tone, Adj.3P, GT	125	150	175
⊕ GENERIC, NAMELESS OR **UNMARKED GRADES** FOR WATCH MOVEMENTS ARE LISTED UNDER THE COMPANY NAME OR INITIALS OF THE COMPANY, ETC. BY SIZE, JEWEL COUNT AND DESCRIPTION.			
Illinois Watch Co., 7-9J, M#1-2-3	$65	$85	$125
Illinois Watch Co., 11-17J, (Rockland)	100	125	150
Illinois Watch Co., 11-13J, 3/4, OF	65	85	135
Illinois Watch Co., 11-13J, M#7, 3/4, OF	65	85	135
Illinois Watch Co., 11-13, M#6, 3/4, HC	100	125	175
Illinois Watch Co., 15J, M#2, OF	65	85	135
Illinois Watch Co., 15J, M#1, HC	125	150	200
Illinois Watch Co., 15J, M#3, OF	65	85	135
Illinois Watch Co., 15J, 3/4, ADJ	65	85	135
Illinois Watch Co., 15J, 3F brg, GJS	65	85	135
Illinois Watch Co., 16-17J, **14K, HC**	425	475	550
Illinois Watch Co., 16-17J, Adj.3P, OF	85	100	150
Illinois Watch Co., 16-17J, M#2-3, SW, OF	85	100	150
Illinois Watch Co., 17J, M#6, SW, HC	125	150	200
Illinois Watch Co., 17J, M#7, OF	100	125	150
Illinois Watch Co., 17J, M#5, 3/4, ADJ, HC	125	150	175
Illinois Watch Co., 17J, M#4, 3F brg, GJS, Adj.5P, HC	150	175	250
Illinois Watch Co., 19J, 3/4, GJS, Adj.5P , **jeweled barrel**	150	175	200
Illinois Watch Co., 19J, 3/4, BRG, Adj.3-4P	100	125	175
Illinois Watch Co., 21J, Adj.3P, OF ★	200	225	275
Illinois Watch Co., 21J, ADJ, OF ★	200	225	275
Illinois Watch Co., 21J, GJS, HC ★	225	250	300
Illinois Watch Co., 21J, 3/4, GJS, Adj.5P ★	200	225	250
Illinois Watch Co., 21J, 3F brg, GJS, Adj.4P ★	175	195	225
Illinois Watch Co., 21J, 3F brg, GJS, Adj.5P ★	225	275	295
Illinois Watch Co., 23J, GJS, Adj.5P, OF ★★	400	500	650
Illinois Watch Co., 23J, GJS, Adj.5P, HC ★★	500	600	750
Illinois Watch Co., 25J, 4th model,3F brg, GJS, Adj.5P, HC ★★★	3,000	3,500	4,000
Imperial Sp., 17J, SW, LS, Adj.4P, OF	125	150	175
Interstate Chronometer, 17J, GCW, Adj.3P, HC	300	325	350
Interstate Chronometer, 17J, GCW, Adj.3P, OF	275	300	325
Interstate Chronometer, 23J, 1F brg, ADJ, OF	700	800	950
Interstate Chronometer, 23J, 1F brg, ADJ, HC ★★	1,000	1,100	1,300
Lafayette, 23J, Washington W.Co., GJS, Adj.5P, GT, OF ★★	850	950	1,100
Lafayette, 23J, Washington W.Co., GJS, Adj.5P, GT, HC ★★★	1,200	1,400	1,700
Lakeshore, 17J, OF	100	125	150
Lakeshore, 17J, HC	175	200	250
Landis W. Co., 15-17J	100	125	150
Liberty Bell, 15-17J, OF	125	150	175
Liberty Bell, 17J, HC ★★★	600	700	800
A. Lincoln, 21J,3/4, GJS, Adj.5P, OF	250	275	325
A. Lincoln, 21J,3/4, GJS, Adj.5P, HC	325	375	450
The Lincoln, 15J, 3F brg,	125	150	175
Logan, 15, OF	65	85	125
Marvel, 19J, GT, GJS, Adj.3P, Of	85	100	125
Marine Special, 21J, 3/4, Adj.3P	250	275	325
Monarch W. Co., 17J, NI, ADJ, SW	150	175	200
Monroe, 17J, NI,3/4, OF (Washington W. Co.)	100	120	150
Monroe, 15J, 3/4, OF (Washington W. Co.)	85	100	150
Montgomery Ward, 17J, LS, Thin Model , OF	85	95	135
Our No. 1, 15J, HC, M#1	150	200	275
Overland Special, 19J, Adj., OF	150	175	225

Sangamo, 16 size, 23 jewels, Adj.6p, gold jewel settings, gold train, Getty Model, serial number 2,307,867.

Sangamo Special, 16 S, 23J., marked 60 hr. movement, Adj.6p, gold jewel settings, gold train, S# 4,758,199.

Grade or Name Description	Avg	Ex-Fn	Mint
Pennsylvania Special, 17J, Adj.3P, HC	$225	$250	$325
Pennsylvania Special, 19J, OF	250	275	350
Pennsylvania Special, 21J, Getty model, GT, GJS, 2-tone, Adj.5P★	1,000	1,200	1,500
Pennsylvania Special, 23J, 3/4, GJS, Adj.5P ★	1,300	1,500	1,700
Plymouth W. Co., 15-17J, OF (Add $25 for HC)	85	100	125
Precise, 21J, OF, LS, Adj.3P	175	200	225
Quincy Street, 17J, 3/4, NI, DMK, ADJ	85	100	125
Railroad Dispatcher, 11-17J, DMK, 3/4	175	200	250
Railroad Dispatcher Extra or Special, 15-17J, DMK, 3/4	225	275	325
Railroad Employee's, 17J,	125	175	200
Railroad King, 16-17J, M#2 or 5 (Getty model), NI, PS, OF	275	300	375
Railroad Official, 23J, 3 Finger bridge ★★★★★	1,600	2,000	2,500
Railway King, 17J, OF	175	200	250
Remington W.Co. 11-15J, OF	125	150	175
Remington W.Co. 17J, OF ★	200	225	325
Remington W.Co. 17J, HC ★★	250	300	400
Rockland, 17J, GJS, GT, 7th model, grade 305, OF	65	85	125
Sangamo, 19J, model # 4, GJS, GT, ADJ., HC ★★★	4,000	5,000	6,000
Sangamo, 21J, GJS, Adj.6P, HC	350	400	425
Sangamo, 21J, GJS, Adj.6P, EXTRA or SPECIAL, HC ★	525	625	775
Sangamo, 21J, GJS, Adj.6P, EXTRA or SPECIAL, OF ★	525	625	775
Sangamo, 21J, GJS, Adj., 2-tone Mvt., Adj.6P, OF ★	475	500	550
Sangamo, 21J, GJS, Adj., OF	225	275	350
Sangamo, 21J, 3/4, GJS, DR, Adj.6P, OF	250	300	355
Sangamo, 23J,3/4, GJS, DR, Adj.6P, OF	350	400	450
Sangamo, 23J, 3/4, GJS, DR, Adj.6P, HC	525	575	625
Sangamo, 25J, M#5, 3/4, GJS, DR, Adj.6P ★★★	4,000	5,000	6,500
Sangamo, 26J, M#5, 3/4, GJS, DR, Adj.6P ★★★	5,000	6,000	7,500
Sangamo Special, 19J, BRG, GJS, GT, Adj.6P, OF	350	375	425
Sangamo Special, 19J, BRG, GJS, GT, Adj.6P, HC ★★★	1,200	1,500	1,800
Sangamo, Extra, 21J, Adj.6P, gold train, Of	425	475	550
Sangamo Special, 21J, M#7, OF	350	400	475
Sangamo Special, 21J, M#8, BRG, HC ★★★	1,400	1,600	1,900
Sangamo Special, 21J, M#9, BRG, GJS, GT, Adj.6P, OF	350	400	475
Sangamo Special, 21J, BRG, GJS, GT, Diamond end cap	375	425	500

Grade or Name — Description	Avg	Ex-Fn	Mint
Sangamo Special, 23J, M#9-10, BRG, GJS, GT, Adj.6P,			
Sangamo Special **HINGED** case	$700	$750	$850
Sangamo Special, 23J, BRG, GJS, GT, Adj.6P, Diamond			
end stone, **screw back,** Sangamo Special case	650	700	750
Sangamo Special, 23J, M#8, GJS, GT, Adj.6P, **HC** ★★★	1,500	1,800	2,000
Sangamo Special, 23J, BRG, GJS, GT, Adj.6P, **not marked**			
60 hour, rigid bow, Sangamo Special case	650	700	750
Sangamo Special, 23J, BRG, GJS, GT, Adj.6P,			
marked 60 hour, Sangamo Special case ★★★★	1,000	1,200	1,500
Sangamo Special, 23J, BRG, GJS, GT, Adj.6P, 60 hour,			
rigid bow, Sangamo Special case **14K gold case**	1,400	1,600	1,800
Santa Fe Special, 17J, BRG, Adj.3P	225	250	300
Santa Fe Special, 21J, 3/4, Adj.5P, OF	275	325	400
Santa Fe Special, 21J, 3/4, Adj.5P, HC	400	425	475
Sears, Roebuck & Co. Special, 15-17J, ADJ	85	100	135
Senate, 17J, (Washington W. Co.), NI, 3/4, ADJ	85	100	135
Standard, 15J	75	100	125
Sterling, 17J, SW, PS, Adj.3P, OF	75	100	125
Sterling, 19-21J, SW, PS, Adj.3P, OF	175	200	225
Stewart, 17J	75	100	125
Stewart Special, 21J, Adj.,	175	200	225
Stewart Special, 19J, Adj.3P	100	125	150
Stewart Special, 15-17J,	75	100	125
The General, 15J, OF	75	100	125
Time King, 17J, OF	75	100	135
Time King, 19J, Adj.3P, OF	100	125	150
Trainmen's Special, 17J, HC	75	100	125
Union Pacific,17J, Adj.,DR, 2-tone, DMK, OF ★	325	375	425
Victor, 21J, 3/4, Adj.3P	150	175	200

☺ **Washington W. Co.** (See Army & Navy, Liberty Bell, Lafayette, Senate)

Grade 163, 16 size, 23 jewels, adjusted to 6 positions, motor barrel, 60 hour model, serial number 5,421,504.

LAFAYETTE, 23J, 16 size, WASHINGTON W.CO., GJS, Adj.5P, GT, HC.

161 through 163A —See Bunn Special

Grade or Name — Description	Avg	Ex-Fn	Mint
167L, 17J, marked	$150	$175	$200
167, 17J	100	125	150
169, 19J, Adj.3P, OF	125	150	175
174, 23J, LS, GJS, Adj., OF, marked ★★	675	725	800
175, 17J, RR grade & a (RR inspectors name on dial &mvt.)	200	245	300
177, 19J, SW, LS, 60 hour, Adj.5P, OF ★	425	500	650

🕐 Generic, nameless or unmarked grades for watch movements are listed under the Company name or initials of the Company, etc. by size, jewel count and description.

Grade or Name — Description	Avg	Ex-Fn	Mint
179, 21J, HC, 3F brg, **marked** Ruby Jewels ....★	$325	$425	$575
184, 19J, 3F brg, LS, OF	125	150	200
187, 17J, 3F brg, Adj.5P, GJS, GT, **marked** 187, HC..................	250	300	375
181-189, 21J, 3F brg, Adj.6P, GJS, GT, **marked** Ruby Jewels, HC	400	450	525
333, 15J, HC	125	150	185
555, 17J, 3/4, ...	85	100	135
777, 17J, 3/4, ADJ	85	100	135
805, 17J, BRG, GJS, GT, DR, OF	85	100	135
809, 23J, Adj.6P, GT, **marked 809** ....★★★	300	350	400
900, 19J, LS, Adj.3P..	125	150	175

Illinois Watch Co., 14 size, 16 jewels, Adj5p.

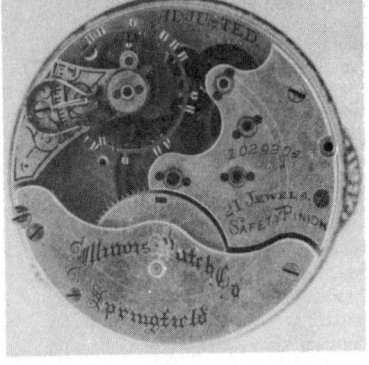

Illinois Watch Co., 14 size, 21J., adjusted, nickel movement, gold jewel settings, serial number 1,029,204.

ILLINOIS
14 SIZE

Grade or Name — Description	Avg	Ex-Fn	Mint
Illinois Watch Co., 7J, M#1-2-3, SW, OF	$75	$80	$115
Illinois Watch Co., 11J, M#1-2-3, SW, OF	75	80	115
Illinois Watch Co., 15J, M#1-2-3, SW, OF	75	80	115
Illinois Watch Co., 16J, M#1-2-3, SW, OF	85	100	125
Illinois Watch Co., 21J, M#1-2-3, SW, OF ....★	175	195	225
Illinois Watch Co., 22J, ...★	200	275	375

NOTE: Add $25 for above watches in hunting case.

ILLINOIS
12 SIZE and 13 SIZE

Grade or Name — Description	Avg	Ex-Fn	Mint
Accurate, 21J, GJS, OF	$100	$125	$150
Aristocrat, 19J, OF..	75	100	125
Ariston, 11-17J, OF	60	70	85
Ariston, 19J, OF..	75	100	135
Ariston, 21J, OF..	100	125	175
Ariston, 23J, OF..★	225	275	325
Aluminum Watch, 17J, model #3, G#525, **made of aluminum**			
S# 3,869,251 to S# 3,869,300 ....★★★★	2,200	2,500	3,000

Characteristics of watches differ for the same age of both case and movement, because these features vary it may not be accurate to date a watch by one single influence. Example: the second hand was not commonly found on watches before 1750, but common about 1800. The first second hand appeared in 1665 and another in 1690. Therefore statements are broad rather than accurate.

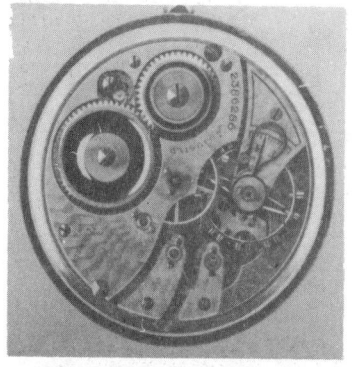

Ben Franklin, 12 size, 17 jewels, open face, gold train, serial number 2,366,286.

Illini, 13 size, 21 jewels, bridge model, serial number 3,650,129. Note five tooth click.

Grade or Name — Description	Avg	Ex-Fn	Mint
Autocrat, 17J, Adj.3P, 3/4	$70	$80	$95
Autocrat, 19J, Adj.3P, 3/4	85	100	135
Banker, 17J, Adj.3P, OF	75	100	135
Banker, 21J, Adj.3P, OF	100	135	175
Benjamin Franklin, 17J, OF	200	250	325
Bunn Special, 21J, Adj 3P, (by Hamilton), OF ★★	200	250	325
Burlington Special, 19J, GT, OF	85	100	135
Burlington Special, 19J, GT, HC	125	150	175
Burlington W. Co., 21J, GT, OF	100	125	165
Burlington W. Co., 21J, GT, HC	125	150	195
Central, 17J, OF, 2-Tone	70	80	95
Commodore Perry Special, 17J., adj.3P	80	100	125
Criterion, 21J, OF	100	125	150
Dependon, 17, (J.V.Farwell), HC,	100	125	185
Diamond Ruby Sapphire, 21J, Adj.5P, GJS ★	300	350	425
Elite, 19J, OF	75	100	135
Garland, 17J, Adj.,GT, OF	70	80	95
Gold Metal, 17J, OF	70	80	90

Example of Illinois Thin Model, 12 size, 17 jewels, adjusted to 3 positions.

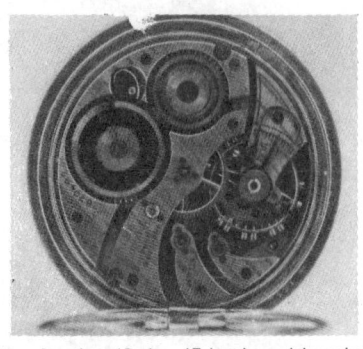

Maiden America, 12 size, 17 jewels, serial number 2,820,499.

Santa Fe Special, 12 size, 21 jewels, three-quarter plate, serial number 3,414,422.

Grade or Name — Description	Avg	Ex-Fn	Mint
Illini, 13 Size, 21J, Adj.5P, BRG, GJS, five tooth click, OF	$100	$125	$150
Illini **Extra,** 13 Size, 21J, Adj.5P, five tooth click, OF..................	100	125	175
Illini, 13 Size, 23J, Adj.5P, BRG, GJS, five tooth click, ...	150	175	225
Illini, 13 Size, 23J, Adj.6P, BRG, GJS,five tooth click, **14K**	300	350	425
Illinois Watch Co., 7-11J...	60	75	85
Illinois Watch Co., 15J..	50	75	85
Illinois Watch Co., 16-17J, OF, **14K**....................................	275	300	350
Illinois Watch Co., 16-17J,OF, GF	75	100	125
Illinois Watch Co., 17J, GF, HC	125	150	175
Illinois Watch Co., 19J..	95	125	150
Illinois Watch Co., 21J, OF..	100	125	175
Illinois Watch Co., 21J, marked (21 SPECIAL), OF	125	150	200
Illinois Watch Co., 21J, HC..	150	175	225
Illinois Watch Co., 23J, OF..	185	225	265
Illinois Watch Co., 19J, OF, EXTRA THIN MODEL.....................	75	95	125
Illinois Watch Co., 21J, OF, EXTRA THIN MODEL.....................	125	150	175
Interstate Chronometer, 21J, GJS, OF	175	200	225
Interstate Chronometer, 21J, GJS, HC...........................★	225	250	275
A. Lincoln, 19J, Adj.5P, GJS, DR, 3/4, marked on mvt.	125	150	175
A. Lincoln, 21J, Adj.5P, DR, GJS...	125	150	175
Maiden America, 17J, ADJ...	70	85	95
Marquis Autocrat, 17J, OF	70	85	95
Master, 21J, GT, GJS, OF	100	125	150
Masterpiece, 19J, Adj.3P, OF...	85	100	125
A. Norton, 21J, OF	100	125	150
Plymouth Watch Co., 15-17J, HC...	75	100	125
Railroad Dispatch , 11-15J, ...	55	75	95
Railroad Dispatch , 17-19J, SW, GT.....................................	80	95	125
Rockland, 17J, ...	65	80	95
Roosevelt, 19J, Adj.3P, OF	80	95	125
Santa Fe Special, 21J..	125	150	175
Sterling, 17J, OF..	60	75	95
Sterling, 19-21J, OF..	100	125	150
Stewart Special, 17J, SW, Adj.3P..	60	75	95
Stewart Special, 19J, SW, OF, GT..	65	80	100
Time King, 19J, SW, Adj.3P...	75	100	125
Time King, 21J, SW, Adj.3P...	100	125	150
Transit, 19J, OF, PS..	75	100	125

ILLINOIS WATCH CO., 12 & 13 SIZE (continued)

Grade or Name — Description	Avg	Ex-Fn	Mint
Vim, 17J, ADJ, BRG, GJS, DR, OF	$60	$75	$95
Washington W. Co., **Monroe,** 11J	125	150	175
Washington W. Co., **Army & Navy,** 19J	135	170	185
Washington W. Co., **Senate,** 17J, M#2, PS,	80	95	125
121, 21J, Adj.3P	100	125	150
127, 17J, ADJ	65	75	95
129, 19J, Adj.3P	95	100	125
219, 11J, M#1	50	60	75
403, 15J, BRG	60	70	85
405, 17J, BRG, ADJ, OF	70	85	95
409, 21J, BRG, Diamond, Ruby, Sapphire, Adj.5P, GJS ★	275	325	450
410, 23J, BRG, GJS, Adj.6P, DR,	175	200	275
410, 23J, BRG, GJS, Adj.6P, DR, **14K, OF**	275	300	375

ILLINOIS
8 SIZE

Grade or Name — Description	Avg	Ex-Fn	Mint
Arlington, 7J, ★	$150	$175	$225
Rose LeLand, 13J, ★ ★	225	250	300
Stanley, 7J, ★ ★ ★	250	300	350
Mary Stuart, 15J, ★ ★	200	250	300
Sunnyside, 11J, ★	150	200	250
151, 7J, 3/4	50	60	75
152, 11J, 3/4	60	70	85
155, 11J, 3/4	70	80	95
Illinois W. Co. , 11-15J, (nameless unmarked grades)	60	75	100
Illinois W. Co. , 16-17J, (nameless unmarked grades)	75	100	125

Note: Add $10 to $20 more for above watches in hunting case.

Illinois Watch Co., 8 size, 7 jewels   Grade 144, 6 size, 15 jewels, serial number 5,902,290.

ILLINOIS
6 SIZE

Grade or Name — Description	Avg	Ex-Fn	Mint
Illinois W. Co., 7J, LS, HC, **14K**	$225	$250	$325
Illinois W. Co., 7J, HC	75	100	150
Illinois W. Co., 7J, OF, Coin	50	75	100
Illinois W. Co., 11-12-13J, OF, HC	75	100	125
Illinois W. Co., 15J, OF, HC, **14K**	225	275	350
Illinois W. Co., 17J, OF, HC	75	100	125
Illinois W. Co., 19J, OF, HC	85	110	150
Plymouth Watch Co., 17J, OF, HC	75	100	125
Washington W. Co., 15J, Liberty Bell, HC	135	170	225
Washington W. Co., 11J, Martha Washington, HC	225	275	325

ILLINOIS
4 SIZE

Grade or Name — Description	Avg	Ex-Fn	Mint
Illinois W. Co., 7J, LS, HC	$75	$100	$125
Illinois W. Co., 11J, LS, HC	75	100	125
Illinois W. Co., 15-16J, LS, HC	75	100	125

ILLINOIS
0 SIZE

Grade or Name — Description	Avg	Ex-Fn	Mint
Accuratus, 17J, OF	$95	$125	$150
Burlington Special, 15-17J, 3/4, OF	95	125	150
Illinois W. Co., 7 to 17J, LS, HC, 14K	200	250	300
201, 11J, BRG, NI	95	100	150
203, 15J, BRG, NI	95	100	150
204, 17J, BRG, NI	95	100	150
Interstate Chronometer, 15J, HC, SW	175	200	275
Interstate Chronometer, 17J, HC, SW	185	210	285
Plymouth Watch Co., 15-17J, HC	95	100	125
Santa Fe Special, 15-17J	75	100	125
Washington W. Co., Liberty Bell, 15J, ADJ	150	175	250
Washington W. Co., Mt. Vernon, 17J, ADJ	160	185	275

Washington W. Co., Mt. Vernon, 0 size, 17J, hunting case.

Grade 203, 0 size, 15 jewels, originally sold for $10.40.

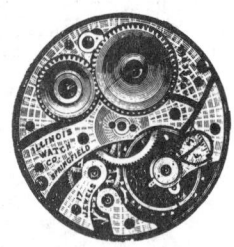

Grade 204, 0 size, 17 jewels, originally sold for $12.83.

ILLINOIS
CAPRICE

Grade or Name — Description	Avg	Ex-Fn	Mint
Caprice, 17J, handbag, pocket or desk watch, snake or ostrich	$150	$175	$225

Ca. 1929 AD

The CAPRICE
Just the watch for the handbag, pocket or desk; for sports wear or dress. It's an entirely practical timekeeper, too. In genuine coverings of snake or ostrich. 17 jewels, 14K gold filled inner case **$50**

ILLINOIS SPRINGFIELD WATCH CO.
IDENTIFICATION OF MOVEMENTS
BY MODEL NUMBER

How to Identify Your Watch: Compare the movement of your watch with the illustrations in this section. Upon matching the movement exactly, the model number and size can be determined. While comparing, note the location of the balance, jewels, screws, gears, and type of back plate (Full, 3/4, Bridge) which will be clues in identifying the movement you have. Having determined the size and model number, you can now find your watch in the main price listing by name or number (which is engraved on the movement).

THE ILLINOIS WATCH CO. GRADE AND MODEL CHART

Size	Model	Plate Design	Setting	Hunting or Open Face	Type Barrel	Started w/ Serial No.	Remarks
18	1	Full	Key	Htg	Reg	1	Course train
	2	Full	Lever	Htg	Reg	38,901	Course train
	3	Full	Lever	OF	Reg	46,201	Course train, 5th pinion
	4	Full	Pendant	OF	Reg	1,050,001	Fast train
	5	Full	Lever	Htg	Reg	1,256,101	Fast train, RR Grade
	6	Full	Lever	OF	Reg	1,144,401	Fast train, RR Grade
16	1	Full	Lever	Htg	Reg	1,030,001	Thick model
	2	Full	Pendant	OF	Reg	1,037,001	Thick model
	3	Full	Lever	OF	Reg	1,038,001	Thick model
	4	¾ & brg	Lever	Htg	Reg	1,300,001	Getty model
	5	¾ & brg	Lever	OF	Reg	1,300,601	Getty model
	6	¾ & brg	Pendant	Htg	Reg	2,160,111	DR & Improved RR model
	7	¾ & brg	Pendant	OF	Reg	2,160,011	DR & Improved RR model
	8	¾ & brg	Lever	Htg	Reg	2,523,101	DR & Improved RR model
	9	¾ & brg	Lever	OF	Reg	2,522,001	DR & Improved model
	10	Cent brg	Lever	OF	Motor	3,178,901	Also 17S Ex Thin RR gr 48 hr
	11	¾	Lever & Pen	OF	Motor	4,001,001	RR grade 48 hr
	12	¾	Lever & Pen	Htg	Motor	4,002,001	RR grade 48 hr
	13	Cent brg	Lever	OF	Motor	4,166,801	Also 17S RR grade 60 hr
	14	¾	Lever	OF	Motor	4,492,501	RR grade 60 hr
	15	¾	Lever	OF	Motor	5,488,301	RR grade 60 hr Elinvar
14	1	Full	Lever	Htg	Reg	1,009,501	Thick model
	2	Full	Pendant	OF	Reg	1,000,001	Thick model
	3	Full	Lever	OF	Reg	1,001,001	Thick model
13	1	brg	Pendant	OF	Motor		Ex Thin gr 538 & 539
12 Thin	1	¾	Pendant	OF	Reg	1,685,001	
	2	¾	Pendant	Htg	Reg	1,748,751	
	3	Cent brg	Pendant	OF	Reg	2,337,011	Center bridge
	4	Cent brg	Pendant	Htg	Reg	2,337,001	Center bridge
	5	Cent brg	Pendant	OF	Motor	3,742,201	Center bridge
	6	Cent brg	Pendant	Htg	Motor	4,395,301	Center bridge
12T	1	True Ctr brg	Pendant	OF	Motor	3,700,001	1 tooth click, Also 13S
	2	True Ctr brg	Pendant	OF	Motor	3,869,301	5 tooth click
	3	¾	Pendant	OF	Motor	3,869,201	2 tooth click
8	1	Full	Key or lever	Htg	Reg	100,001	Plate not recessed
	2	Full	Lever	Htg	Reg	100,101	Plate is recessed
6	1	¾	Lever	Htg	Reg	552,001	
4	1	¾	Lever	Htg	Reg	551,501	
0	1	¾	Pendant	OF	Reg	1,815,901	
	2	¾	Pendant	Htg	Reg	1,749,801	
	3	Cent brg	Pendant	OF	Reg	2,644,001	
	4	Cent brg	Pendant	Htg	Reg	2,637,001	

Rigid bow 60 HR. MODEL
gold filled: $175 - $225 - $275
14K gold: $400 - $475 - $550

Antique bow MODEL
gold filled: $100 - $120 - $135
14K gold: $350 - $400 - $465

FIRST MODEL
gold filled: $110 - $135 - $160

Stiff bow 60 HR. MODEL
gold filled: $200 - $250 - $275
14K gold: $410 - $485 - $560

Empire bow MODEL
gold filled: $100 - $120 - $140
14K gold: $350 - $400 - $465

MODEL 29
gold filled: $110 - $135 - $160

MODEL 28
gold filled: $135 - $160 - $185
gold filled **2 tone**: $150 - $175 - $200

MODEL 107
gold filled: $110 - $125 - $140

MODEL 28, 173 & 206=combination white & yellow gold-filled
models Solid Gold cases= rigid bow
Gold-filled cases (1st. model), (antique), (rigid bow), 28, 29, 107, 108, 128, 173, 181, 193, & 206

🕐 NOTE: Factory Advertised as a **complete** watch and was fitted with a certain matched, timed
and rated movement and sold in the factory designed case style as a **complete** watch. The factory
also sold _uncased_ movements to **JOBBERS** such as Jewelry stores & they cased the movement in
a case styles the **CUSTOMER requested**. All the factory advertised **complete** watches came with
the dial **SHOWN** or **CHOICE** of other **Railroad** dials.

MODEL 108
gold filled: $110 - $125 - $140

MODEL 128
gold **plated**: $75 - $85 - $100

MODEL 173
gold filled: $110 - $135 - $160
gold filled **2 tone**: $150 - $175 - $200

MODEL 181
gold filled: $110 - $125 - $140

MODEL 193
gold filled: $110 - $135 - $160

MODEL 206
gold filled: $100 - $120 - $150
gold filled **2 tone**: $110 - $140 - $160

BUNN SPECIALS were packed & shipped
in a ALUMINUM cigarette style box.

MODEL 28, 173 & 206=combination white & yellow gold-filled
models Solid Gold cases= rigid bow
Gold-filled cases (1st. model), (antique), (rigid bow), 28, 29, 107, 108, 128, 173, 181, 193, & 206

🕒 NOTE: Factory Advertised as a **complete** watch and was fitted with a certain matched, timed and rated movement and sold in the factory designed case style as a **complete** watch. The factory also sold _uncased_ movements to **JOBBERS** such as Jewelry stores & they cased the movement in a case styles the **CUSTOMER requested.** All the factory advertised **complete** watches came with the dial **SHOWN or <u>CHOICE</u>** of other **Railroad** dials.

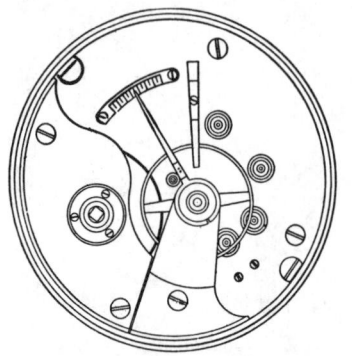

Model 1, 18 size, hunting, key wind & set.

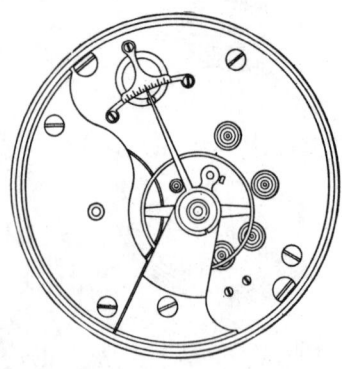

Model 2, 18 size, hunting, lever set, coarse train.

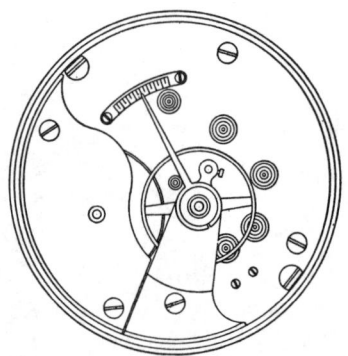

Model 3, 18 size, open face, lever set, coarse train, with fifth pinion.

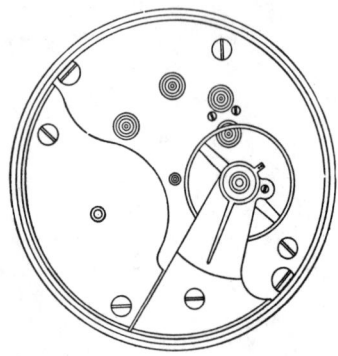

Model 4, 18 size, open face, pendant set, fine train.

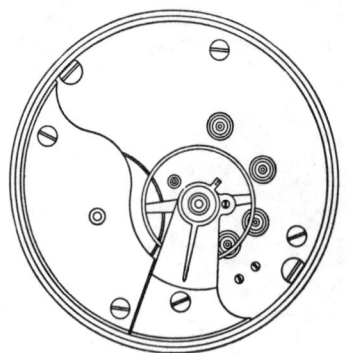

Model 5, 18 size, hunting, lever set, fine train.

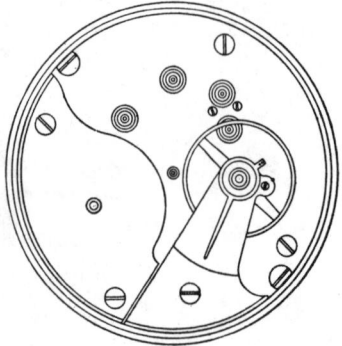

Model 6, 18 size, open face, lever set, fine train.

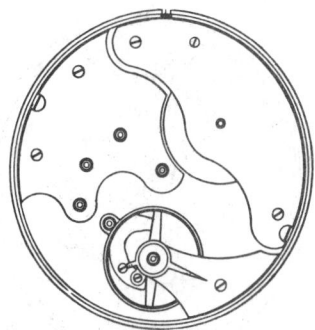

Model 1, 16 size, hunting, lever set.

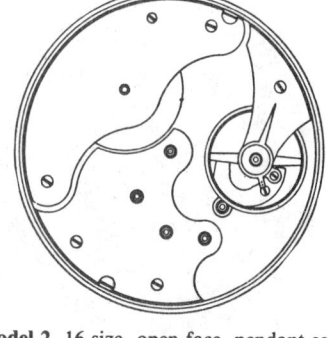

Model 2, 16 size, open face, pendant set.

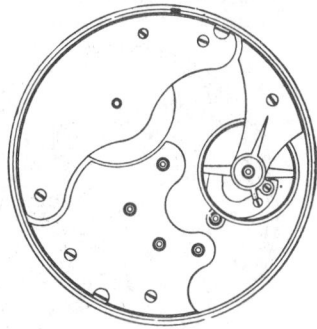

Model 3, 16 size, open face, lever set

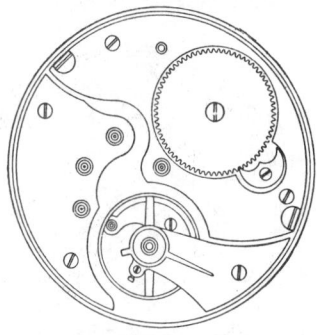

Model 4, 16 size, three-quarter plate, hunting, lever set.

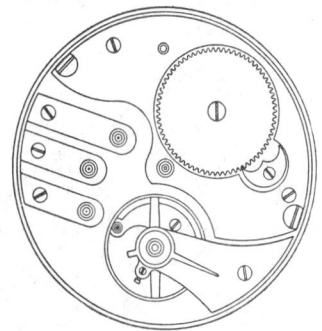

Model 4, 16 size, three-quarter plate, bridge, hunting, lever set.

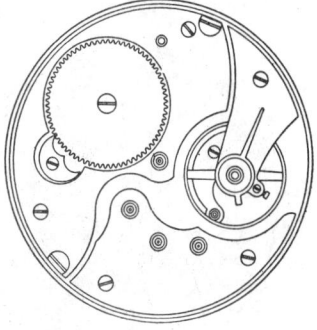

Model 5, 16 size, three-quarter plate, open face, lever set.

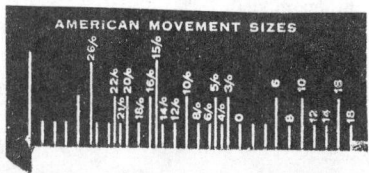

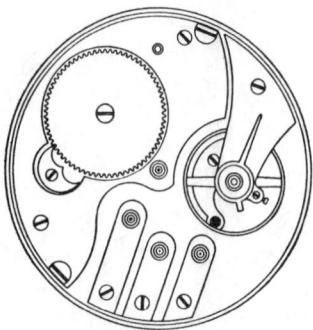

Model 5, 16 size, three-quarter plate, bridge, open face, lever set.

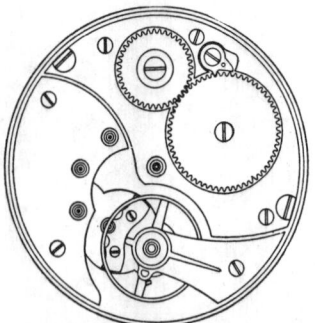

Model 6, 16 size - Pendant set
Model 8, 16 size - Lever set
hunting, three-quarter plate

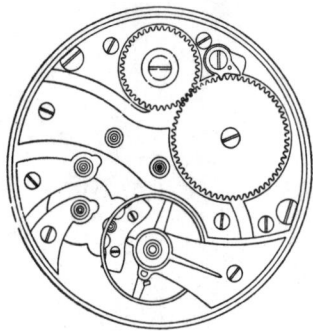

Model 6, 16 size - Pendant set
Model 8, 16 size - Lever set
hunting, bridge model

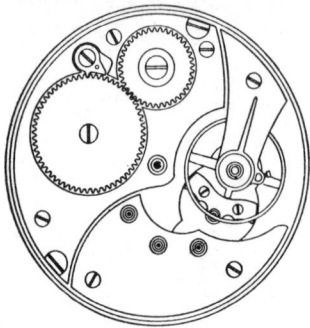

Model 7, 16 size - Pendant set
Model 9, 16 size - Lever set
open face, three-quarter plate

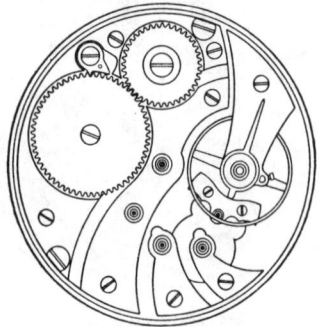

Model 7, 16 size - Pendant set
Model 9, 16 size - Lever set
open face, bridge model

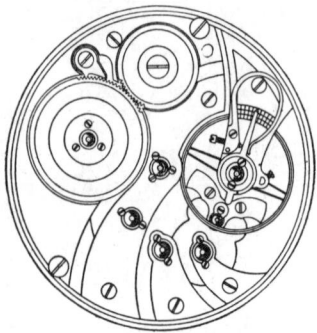

Model 10, 16 size, bridge, extra thin, open face, lever set, motor barrel.

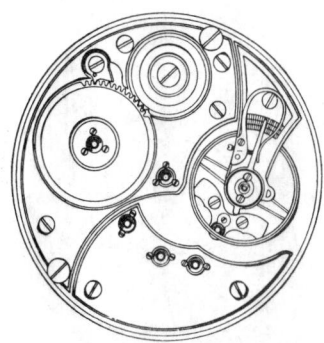

Model 11, 16 size, three-quarter plate, open face, pendant set, motor barrel.

Model 12, 16 size, three-quarter plate, hunting, pendant set, motor barrel.

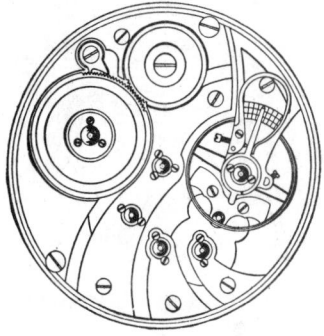

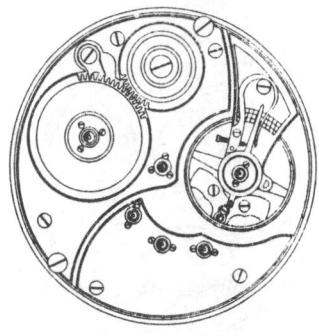

Model 13, 16 size, bridge, open face, lever set, motor barrel.

Model 14, 16 size, three-quarter plate, open face, lever set, 60-hour motor barrel.

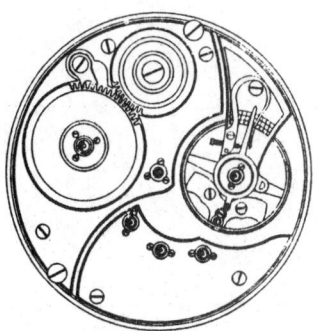

Model 15, 60 Hr. Elinvar.

Model B, 16 size, hunting case.

Model C, 16 size, open face

Model D, 16 size, open face

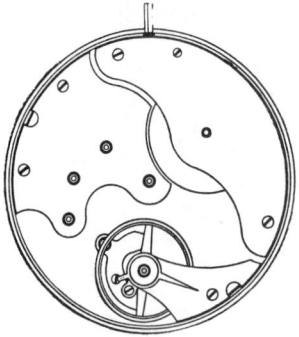

Model 1, 14 size, hunting, lever set.

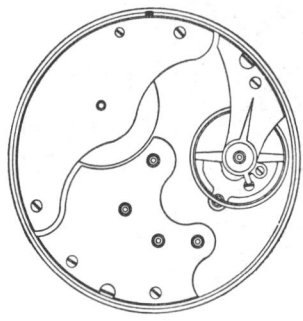

Model 2, 14 size, open face, pendant set.

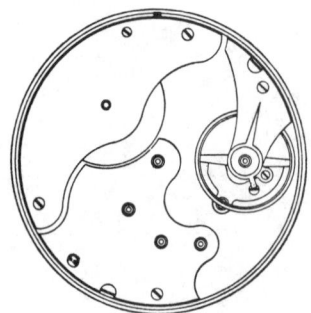

Model 3, 14 size, open face, lever set.

Model 1, 13 size, bridge, extra thin, open face, pendant set, motor barrel.

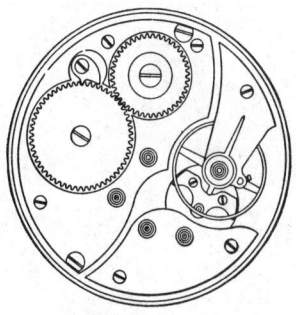

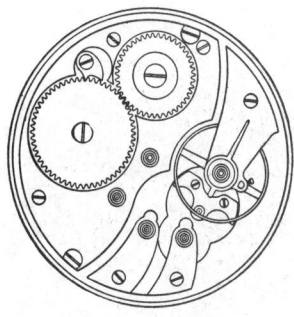

Model 1, 12 size, three-quarter plate, open face, pendant set.

Model 1, 12 size, three-quarter plate, bridge, open face, pendant set.

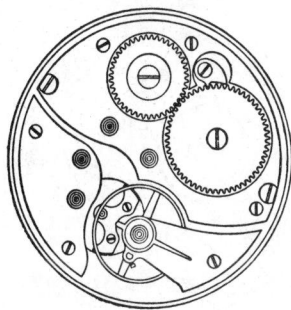

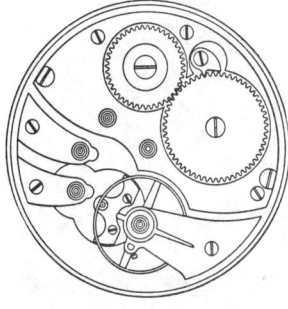

Model 2, 12 size, three-quarter plate, hunting, pendant set.

Model 2, 12 size, three-quarter plate, bridge, hunting, pendant set.

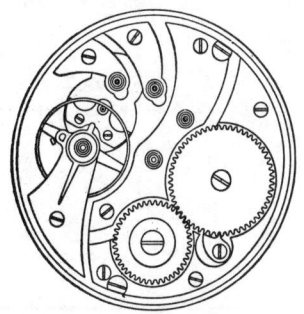

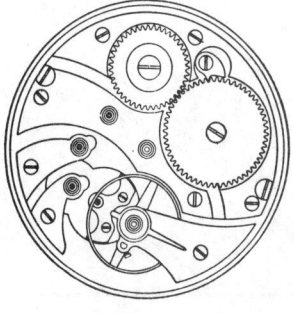

Model 3, 12 size, **Model 4,** 12 & 14 size, bridge, open face, pendant set.

Model 4, 12 size, bridge, hunting, pendant set.

Model 5, 12 size, bridge, open face, pendant set, motor barrel.

Model 1, 12 size, extra thin, bridge, open face, pendant set, motor barrel.

Model 2, 12 size, extra thin, bridge, open face, pendant set, motor barrel.

Model 3, 12 size, extra thin, three-quarter plate, open face, pendant set, motor barrel.

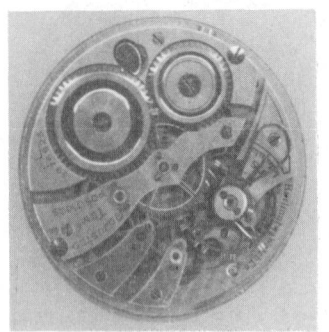

Model A, 12 size, bridge, open face.

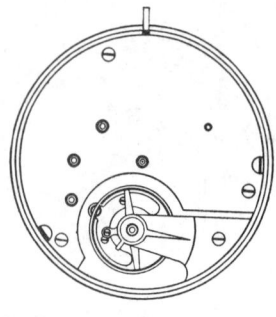

Model 1, 8 size, hunting, key or lever set.

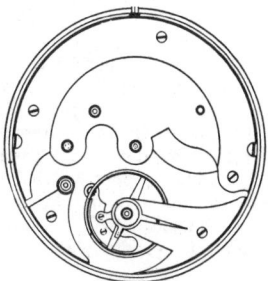

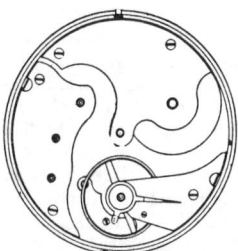

Model 2, 8 size, hunting, lever set.

Model 1, 6 size, hunting, lever set.

Model 1, 4 size, hunting, lever set.

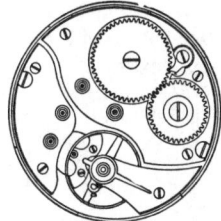

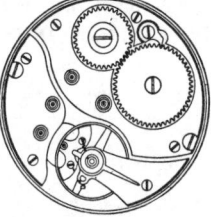

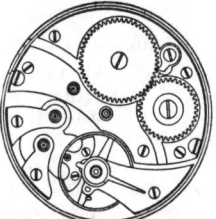

Model 1, 0 size, three-quarter plate, open face, pendant set.

Model 2, 0 size, three-quarter plate, hunting, pendant set.

Model 3, 0 size, bridge, open face, pendant set.

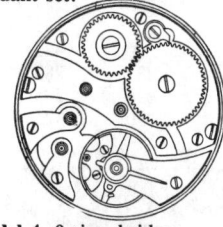

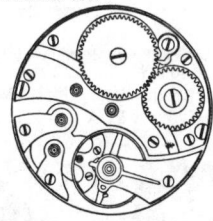

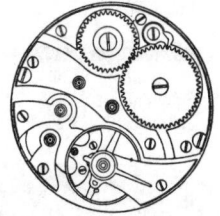

Model 4, 0 size, bridge, hunting, pendant set.

Model 3, 3/0 size, bridge, open face, pendant set.

Model 4, 3/0 size, bridge, hunting, pendant set.

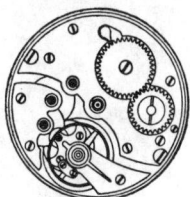

Model 1, 6/0 size, three-quarter plate, open face, pendant set.

Model 2, 6/0 size, bridge, open face, pendant set.

INDEPENDENT WATCH CO.

Fredonia, New York

1875 - 1881

The California Watch Company was idle for two years before it was purchased by brothers E. W. Howard and C. M. Howard. They had been selling watches by mail for sometime and started engraving the Howard Bros. name on them and using American-made watches. Their chief supply came from Hampden Watch Co., Illinois W. Co., U. S. Watch Co. of Marion. The brothers formed the Independent Watch Co. in 1880, but it was not a watch factory in the true sense. They had other manufacturers engrave the Independent Watch Co. name on the top plates and on the dials of their watches. These watches were sold by mail order and sent to the buyer C. O. D. The names used on the movements were "Howard Bros.," "Independent Watch Co.," "Fredonia Watch Co.," and "Lakeshore Watch Co., Fredonia, N. Y."

The company later decided to manufacture watches and used the name Fredonia Watch Co., but they found that selling watches two different ways was not very good.The business survived until 1881 at which time the owners decided to move the plant to a new location at Peoria, Illinois. Approximately180,000 watches were made that sold for $16.00.

CHRONOLOGY OF THE DEVELOPMENT OF INDEPENDENT WATCH CO.

Independent Watch Co.	1875–1881
Fredonia Watch Co.	1881–1885
Peoria Watch Co.	1885–1889

18 SIZE

Grade or Name — Description	Avg	Ex-Fn	Mint
18S, 7J, KW, KS, OF, made by U.S. W. Co. Marion, with expanded butterfly cutout ★	$450	$550	$675
18S, 11J, KW, KS, by Hampden	250	325	375
18S, 11J, KW, KS, Coin	235	285	350
18S, 11J, KW, KS	235	285	350
18S, 15J, KW, KS	235	285	350
18S, Howard Bros., 11J, KW, KS	350	425	475
18S, Independent W. Co., 11J, by Illinois W. Co.	235	285	350
18S, Independent W. Co., 15J, transition model by Illinois W. Co.	250	295	375
18S, Lakeshore W. Co., 15J, KW, HC, by N.Y. W. Co.	250	325	375

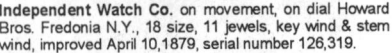

Independent Watch Co. on movement, on dial Howard Bros. Fredonia N.Y., 18 size, 11 jewels, key wind & stem wind, improved April 10,1879, serial number 126,319.

Independent Watch Co., 18 size, 15 jewels, key wind, made by U.S. Marion Watch Co., note expanded butterfly cutout, serial number 192,661.

🕐 Watches listed in this book are priced at the **collectable fair market value** at the RETAIL level, as complete watches having an original 14k gold filled case, KEY WIND with silver, an original white enamel single sunk dial, and with the entire original movement in good working order with no repairs needed, unless otherwise noted.

ROBERT H. INGERSOLL & BROS.

New York, New York

1892 - 1922

In 1892 this company published a catalog for the mail order trade. It listed men's watch chains and a "silverine" watch for $3.95. It was not a true Ingersoll but a "Universal," introduced that same year to the dealers. The first $1 watches were jeweled; "Reliance" had seven jewels. By 1899 the output was 8,000 per day and in 1901 Ingersoll advertised for sale by 10,000 dealers at $1.00 in U.S.A. and Canada. In 1916, Ingersoll's production was 16,000 a day. The slogan was "The Watch that Made the Dollar Famous." The first 1,000 watches were made by Waterbury Clock Co. By 1922 the Ingersoll line was completely taken over by Waterbury. U. S. Time Corp. acquired Waterbury in 1944 and continued to use the Ingersoll name on certain watches.

ESTIMATED SERIAL NUMBERS
AND PRODUCTION DATES

DATE—SERIAL NO.	DATE—SERIAL NO.	DATE—SERIAL NO.	DATE—SERIAL NO.
1892 – 150,000	1902 – 7,200,000	1912 – 38,500,000	1922 – 60,500,000
1893 – 310,000	1903 – 7,900,000	1913 – 40,000,000	1923 – 62,000,000
1894 – 650,000	1904 – 8,100,000	1914 – 41,500,000	1924 – 65,000,000
1895 – 1,000,000	1905 –10,000,000	1915 – 42,500,000	1925 – 67,500,000
1896 – 2,000,000	1906 –12,500,000	1916 – 45,500,000	1926 – 69,000,000
1897 – 2,900,000	1907 –15,000,000	1917 – 47,000,000	1927 – 70,500,000
1898 – 3,500,000	1908 –17,500,000	1918 – 47,500,000	1928 – 71,500,000
1899 – 3,750,000	1909 –20,000,000	1919 – 50,000,000	1929 – 73,500,000
1900 – 6,000,000	1910 –25,000,000	1920 – 55,000,000	1930 – 75,000,000
1901 – 6,700,000	1911 –30,000,000	1921 – 58,000,000	1944 – 95,000,000

The above list is provided for determining the APPROXIMATE age of your watch. Match serial number with date. Watches were not necessarily sold in the exact order of manufactured date.

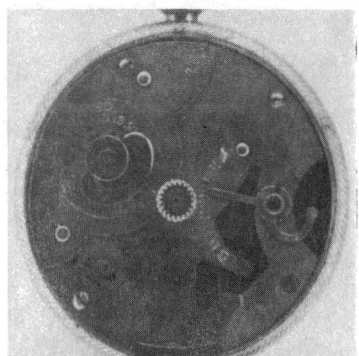

Ingersoll Back Wind & Set, patent date Dec. 23, 1890 and Jan. 13, 1891, c. late 1890s.

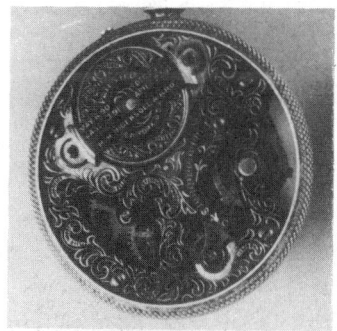

Ingersoll , engraved movement also pin set..

Ingersoll , Celluloid Case in Black or White.

Ingersoll, Blind Man's Watch.

INGERSOLL DOLLAR TYPE

NOTE: Prices are for complete watch in **good running order**. In some specialty markets, the comic character watches may bring higher prices in top condition.

Grade or Name — Description	Avg	Ex-Fn	Mint
Ingersoll All **Back Wind** Models	$100	$125	$175
Admiral Dewey, "Flagship Olympia" on back of case	150	175	250
American Pride	75	100	125
Are U My Neighbor	40	45	65
B. B. H. Special, Backwind	65	75	95
Blind Man Pocket Watch	50	75	95
Boer War, on dial **Souvenier of South African War 1900** ★★★★	900	1,100	1,400
Buck	40	45	65
Calendar (on moveable calendar on back of case)	75	85	125
Celluloid Case in Black or White	100	135	185
Champion (many models)	50	75	125
Chancery	50	75	125
Chicago Expo. 1933	200	250	325
Climax	40	45	65
Clock Watch, pat. 1878-90-91	75	85	125
Cloverine	60	70	85
Colby	40	45	65
Columbus	45	60	85
Columbus (3 ships on back of case), 1893 ★	250	300	450
Connecticut W. Co.	40	45	65
Cord	40	45	65
Crown	40	45	65
Dan Dee	40	45	65
Defiance	40	45	65
Delaware W. Co.	40	45	65
Devon Mfg. Co.	40	45	65
Eclipse (many models)	40	45	65
Eclipse Radiolite	45	65	75
Endura	40	45	65
Ensign	40	45	65
Escort	40	45	65

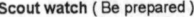

Scout watch (Be prepared)

Yankee watch with bicycle on dial.

NOTE : ADD $25 to $75 for original BOX and PAPERS

Ingersoll Premium, early back wind & set.

Ingersoll Triumph, note pin or rim setting.

Grade or Name — Description	Avg	Ex-Fn	Mint
Fancy Dials (unfaded to be mint)...	$125	$150	$200
Freedom	40	45	65
Gotham...	40	45	65
Graceline	45	50	65
Gregg..	40	45	65
Junior (several models)...	40	45	65
Junior Radiolite...	40	45	65
Kelton..	40	45	65
Lapel Watches..	30	45	65
Leader..	30	45	65
Leeds	30	45	65
Leonard Watch Co..	30	45	65
Liberty U.S.A., backwind..	75	100	150
Liberty Watch Co...	35	45	75
Limited, LEVER SET ON CASE RIM OF WATCH	50	60	80
Major..	45	50	65
Maple Leaf...	45	50	65
Master Craft	45	50	65
Midget (several models)...	40	50	75
Midget , 6 size, "patd. Jan. 29 -01," Damaskeened, fancy case......	75	100	150
Monarch	45	50	65
New West..	45	50	65
New York World's Fair, 1939...	150	175	200
Overland...	40	50	65
Pan American Expo., Buffalo, 1901	200	275	350
Paris World Expo., 1900..	150	175	225
Patrol	45	50	65
Perfection	40	45	55
Pilgram	45	55	65
Premier, back wind, eagle on back, c. 1894...................★	95	125	200

NOTE : ADD $25 to $75 for original BOX and PAPERS

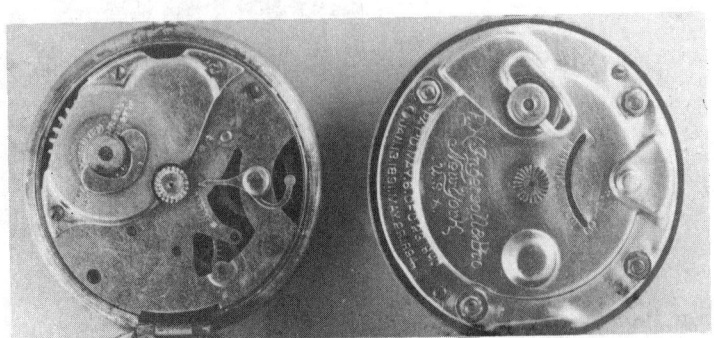

Left: Ingersoll Back Wind, c. 1895.   Right: Yankee Back Wind, c. 1893.

Grade or Name — Description	Avg	Ex-Fn	Mint
Premium Back Wind and Set	$60	$75	$125
Progress, 1933 World's Fair Chicago	200	275	350
Puritan	40	50	75
Quaker	40	45	65
Radiolite	45	65	75
Reliance, 7J	60	75	95
Remington W. Co. USA	60	75	95
Rotary International, c. 1920	50	65	80
Royal	45	50	65
St. Louis World's Fair (two models)	250	300	400
St. Louis World's Fair, 1904	150	200	275
The Saturday Post	150	175	225
Senator	40	50	65
Senior	45	50	65
Sir Leeds	35	40	50
Solar	35	40	50
Souvenir Special	50	75	100
Sterling	35	40	50
Ten Hune	60	70	85
The Yankee Bicycle Watch	50	65	75
Traveler with Bed Side Stand	35	45	65
Triumph	100	125	150
Triumph Pin set or rim set, large crown, engine turned case (early model) with engraved barrel or movement	150	185	235
True Test	35	45	55
Trump	35	45	55
USA (two models)	50	75	100
Universal, 1st model	200	250	300
Uncle Sam	45	55	65
George Washington	150	175	225
Waterbury (several models)	40	60	90

NOTE : ADD $25 to $75 for original BOX and PAPERS

Grade or Name — Description	Avg	Ex-Fn	Mint
Waterbury Back Wind, 35 Size	$100	$150	$200
Winner	40	45	55
Winner , with Screw Back & Bezel.	65	75	100
Yankee Backwind	85	95	150
Yankee Bicycle Watch (sold for $1.00 in 1896)	175	195	250
Yankee Radiolite	55	65	75
Yankee Radiolite with Screw Back & Bezel.	75	100	135
Yankee Special (many models)	75	100	150
Yankee, Perpetual calendar on back of case	100	125	165

Ingersoll moveable calendar for years 1929-1951 located on back of case.

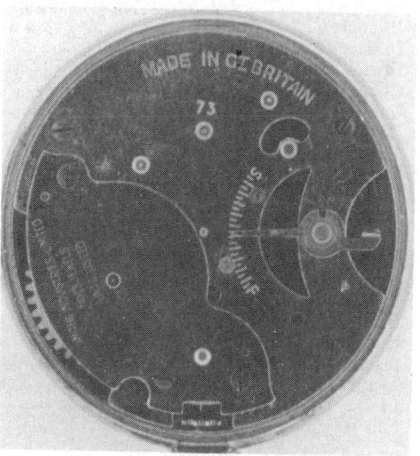

Ingersoll movement made in Great Britain.

INGERSOLL LTD.
(GREAT BRITAIN)

Grade or Name — Description	Avg	Ex-Fn	Mint
Ingersoll Ltd. (many models)	$65	$75	$100
Coronation, Elizabeth II on watch	175	200	250
Coronation, June 2, 1953 on dial	175	200	250
16S, 7J, 3F Brg	65	75	95
16S, 15J, 3F Brg	85	95	125
16S, 17J, 3F Brg, ADJ	125	145	175
16S, 19J, 3F Brg, Adj 5P	250	300	375
12S, 4J	45	65	85

🕐 Some grades are not included. Their values can be determined by comparing with **similar** age, size, metal content, style, models and grades listed.

E. INGRAHAM CO.
Bristol, Connecticut 1912 - 1968

The E. Ingraham Co. purchased the Bannatyne Co. in 1912. They produced their first pocket watch in 1913. A total of about 65 million pocket watches and over 12 million wrist watches were produced before they started to import watches in 1968.

Grade or Name — Description	Avg	Ex-Fn	Mint
Ingraham W. Co. (many models)	$30	$40	$55
Allure	30	40	55
Aristocrat Railroad Special	50	65	75
Autocrat	30	45	65
Basket Ball Foot Ball Timer	40	45	65
Beacon	30	40	55
Biltmore	30	40	55
Biltmore Radium dial	50	65	85
Bristol	30	40	55
Clipper	30	40	55
Co-Ed	30	40	55
Comet	30	40	55
Companion, sweep second hand	50	65	85
Cub	25	30	45
Dale	30	40	55
Demi–hunter style cover	65	75	95
Digital seconds dial, (no second hand but a digital seconds on dial)	50	60	75
Dixie	30	45	50
Dot	30	45	50
Endura	30	45	50
Everbrite (all models)	40	50	65
Graceline,	30	45	50
Ingraham USA	30	45	50
Jockey	30	45	50
Laddie	25	30	40
Laddie Athlete	40	45	55
Lady's Purse Watch, with fancy bezel	45	50	65
Lendix Extra	30	45	50
Master	25	30	40
Master Craft	30	45	50
Miss Ingraham	25	30	40
New York to Paris(with box for mint)	225	275	350
Overland	45	50	65
The Pal	30	45	50

INGRAHAM, Seven Seas, shows standard time, & Nautical time.

New York to Paris, with airplane model on dial, engraved bezel, commemorating Lindbergh's famous flight.

🕐 Prices are for complete watch in **good running order.** In some specialty markets, the comic character watches may bring higher prices in top condition.

NOTE : ADD $25 to $75 for original BOX and PAPERS

 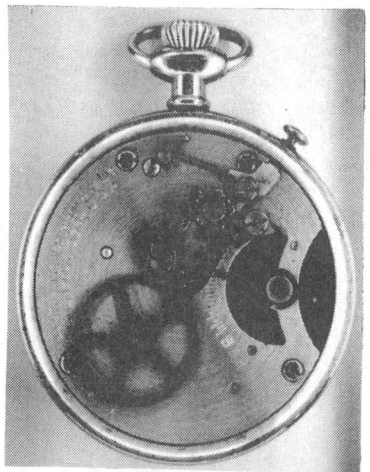

Pastor Stop Watch, Sterling W. Co. printed on dial, with start stop & fly back to zero function. The Sterling Watch Company. Inc. Waterbury, Conn. U.S.A. on movement

Grade or Name — Description	Avg	Ex-Fn	Mint
Pastor Stop Watch, (Sterling W. Co), fly back to zero......... ★★★	$200	$225	$295
Pathfinder, compass on pendant...	85	100	135

Path Finder showing compass in crown.   Printed on dial, "Unbreakable crystal," ca. 1924.

Grade or Name — Description	Avg	Ex-Fn	Mint
Patriot...	$125	$150	$250
Peerless..	30	35	55
Pilot...	40	50	65
Pocket Pal...	30	45	50
Pony...	30	45	50
Pride..	30	45	50
Princess	30	45	50
Prince..	30	45	50
Professional..	30	35	45
Pup..	30	45	50
Reliance..	45	50	65
Rex	30	45	50
Rite Time..	30	45	50
St. Regis	30	45	50
Secometer..	40	50	65
Sentinel...	30	45	50
Sentinel Click...	30	45	50
Sentinel Fold Up Travel	50	65	75
Sentry	30	45	50
Seven Seas, 24 hr. dial & nautical dial..	75	100	150
Silver Star...	30	45	50

Grade or Name — Description	Avg	Ex-Fn	Mint
Sturdy	30	45	50
Target	30	45	50
The Best	30	45	50
The Pal	30	45	50
Time Ball	40	50	65
Time & Time	30	40	55
Top Flight	35	45	55
Top Notch	35	45	55
Tower	30	45	50

Trail Blazer, Commemorating Byrd's Antarctic Expedition.

Showing back side of **Trail Blazer**, also depicted on box.

FOB

BOX: Same as depicted on BACK of watch.

Grade or Name — Description	Avg	Ex-Fn	Mint
Trail Blazer, Commemorating BYRD'S Antarctic Expedition	$200	$235	$300
Trail Blazer **watch**, with **fob** (wings over the pole), + **box** . ★ ★ ★	400	500	750
Treasure	15	20	25
Unbreakable Crystal	45	50	65
Uncle Sam (all models)	50	75	95
Uncle Sam Backwind & Set	125	150	190
United	30	35	40
Viceroy	30	45	50
Victory	30	45	50
Wings	40	50	65

NOTE : ADD $25 to $75 for original BOX and PAPERS

Left: Example of a basic International Watch Co. movement with patent dates of Aug. 19, 1902, Jan. 27, 1903 & Aug. 11, 1903.

ABOVE & Right: Example of a **Highland.**

INTERNATIONAL WATCH CO.

Newark City, New Jersey

1902 - 1907

This company produced only non-jeweled or low-cost production type watches that were inexpensive and nickel plated. Names on their watches include: Berkshire, Madison, and Mascot.

Grade or Name — Description		Avg	Ex-Fn	Mint
18 Size, skeletonized, pinlever escape., first model	★★	$150	$175	$225
Berkshire, OF	★	95	125	165
Highland	★	95	125	165
Madison, 18S, OF	★	95	125	165
Mascot, OF	★	95	125	165

KANKAKEE WATCH CO.

Kankakee, Illinois

1900

This company reportedly became the McIntyre Watch Co. Little other information is available.

Grade or Name — Description		Avg	Ex-Fn	Mint
16S, BRG, NI	★★★★	$5,500	$6,000	$7,000

🕐 Watches listed in this book are priced at the **collectable fair market value** at the RETAIL level, as complete watches having an original 14k gold filled case, KEY WIND with silver, an original white enamel single sunk dial, and with the entire original movement in good working order with no repairs needed, unless otherwise noted.

KELLY WATCH CO.

Chicago, Illinois
c. 1900

Grade or Name — Description	Avg	Ex-Fn	Mint
16S, aluminum movement and OF case............................ ★★★★	$300	$350	$450

Kelly Watch Co., 16 size, aluminum movement, straight line lever, quick train, porcelain dial, stem set, reversible ratchet stem wind, originally sold for $2.20, Ca. 1900.

KEYSTONE STANDARD WATCH CO.

Lancaster, Pennsylvania
1886 - 1890

Abram Bitner agreed to buy a large number of stockholders' shares of the Lancaster Watch Co. at 10 cents on the dollar; he ended up with 5,625 shares out of the 8,000 that were available. Some 8,900 movements had been completed but not sold at the time of the shares purchase. The company Bitner formed assumed the name of Keystone Standard Watch Co. as the trademark but in reality existed as the Lancaster Watch Co. The business was sold to **Hamilton Watch Co.** in 1891. Total production was 48,000.

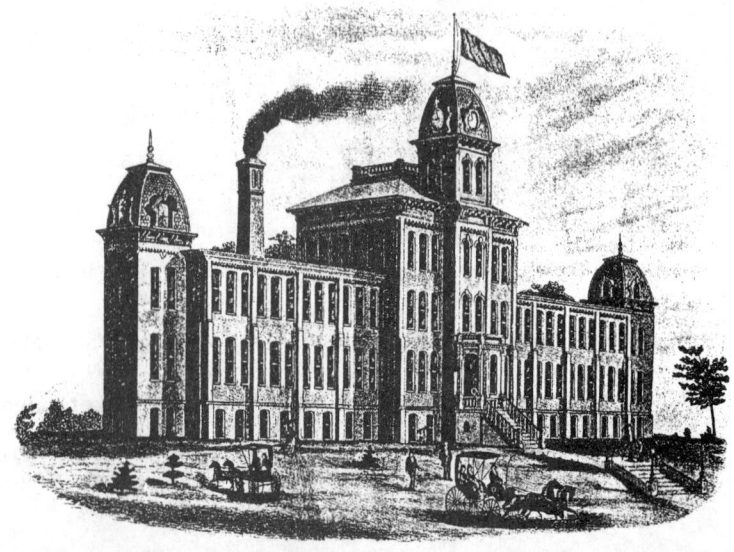

Grade or Name — Description	Avg	Ex-Fn	Mint
18S, 7-15J, OF, KW	$100	$120	$150
18S, 7-15J, OF, SW, 3/4, LS	85	100	150
18S, 15J, dust proof, ADJ..	150	175	225
18S, 11-15J, dust proof, OF...	100	125	175
18S, 11-15J, dust proof, HC	150	175	225
18S, 17J, dust proof, HC..	150	175	225
18S, 20J, dust proof, HC... ★ ★	225	250	300
18S, West End, 15J, HC	85	125	175
8S, 11J, dust proof	100	125	175
6S, 7-10J, HC...★	175	200	250

Keystone Watch Co., dust proof model, 18 size, 15 jewels, serial number 352,766.

Knickerbocker movement, 16-18 size, 7 jewels, duplex escapement.

KNICKERBOCKER WATCH CO.

New York, New York
1890 - 1930

This company imported and sold Swiss and low-cost production American watches.

Grade or Name — Description	Avg	Ex-Fn	Mint
18S, 7J, OF, PS, NI, duplex escapement...........................	$75	$85	$100
16S, 7J..	50	65	75
12S, 7J, OF...	45	55	85
10S, Barkley "8 Day" .... ★ ★	100	125	165
6S, Duplex..	50	60	75

🕐 Some grades are not included. Their values can be determined by comparing with **similar** age, size, metal content, style, models and grades listed.

🕐 Watches listed in this book are priced at the **collectable fair market value** at the RETAIL level, as complete watches having an original 14k gold filled case, KEY WIND with silver, an original white enamel single sunk dial, and with the entire original movement in good working order with no repairs needed, unless otherwise noted.

LANCASTER WATCH CO.

Lancaster, Pennsylvania

1877 - 1886

Work commenced on Sept. 1, 1877, at the Lancaster Watch Co. The watches produced there were designed to sell at a cheaper price than normal. They had a solid top, 3/4 plate, and a pillar plate that was fully ruby-jeweled (4 pairs). They had a gilt and nickel movement and a new stem-wind device, modeled by Mosly & Todd. By mid-1878 the Lancaster Watch Co. had produced 150 movements. Four grades of watches were made: Keystone, Fulton, Franklin, and Melrose. In September 1879 the company had made 334 movements. In 1880 the total was up to 1,250 movements, and by mid-1882 about 17,000 movements had been produced. All totaled, about 20,000 watch movements were made.

About 75, 8-size ladies' watches were also made.

CHRONOLOGY OF THE DEVELOPMENT OF THE LANCASTER WATCH CO.

Adams and Perry Watch Mfg. Co.	1874-1876
Lancaster Watch Co.	1877-1878
Lancaster Pa. Watch Co.	1878-1879
Lancaster Watch Co.	1879-1886
Keystone Standard Co.	1886-1890
Hamilton Watch Co.	1892 to present

LANCASTER

18 SIZE

(All 3/4 Plate)

Grade or Name — Description	Avg	Ex-Fn	Mint
Chester, 7-11J, KW, dust proof, gilded	$125	$150	$200
Comet, 7J, NI	125	150	200
Delaware, 20J, ADJ, SW, dust proof, gilded	300	375	450
Denver, 7J, dust proof, gilded	85	100	135
Denver, 7J, gilded, dust proof, Silveroid	65	75	95
Elberon, 7J, dust proof	125	150	200
Ben Franklin, 7J, KW, gilded	250	300	375
Ben Franklin, 11J, KW, gilded	300	350	425
Fulton, 7J, ADJ, KW, gilded	125	150	200
Fulton, 11J, ADJ, KW, gilded	125	150	200
Girard, 15J, ADJ, dust proof, gilded	100	145	200
Hoosac, 11J, OF	125	175	225
Keystone, 15J, ADJ, gilded, GJS, dust proof	100	125	175
Keystone, 15J, ADJ, gilded, GJS, Silveroid	85	95	125
Lancaster, 7J, SW	85	95	120
Lancaster, 15J, SW, Silveroid	65	75	100
Lancaster, 15J, OF	75	100	150
Lancaster Pa., 20J, ADJ, NI, ★★★	400	500	650

🕐 Some grades are not included. Their values can be determined by comparing with similar age, size, metal content, style, models and grades listed.

🕐 Watches listed in this book are priced at the **collectable fair market value** at the RETAIL level, as complete watches having an original 14k gold filled case, KEY WIND with silver, an original white enamel single sunk dial, and with the entire original movement in good working order with no repairs needed, unless otherwise noted.

Lancaster Watch Co., 18 size, 20 jewels, gold jeweled settings, This is referred to as Adams & Perry S# 1747.

Stevens Model, 18 size, 15 jewels, adjusted, dust proof model, swing-out movement, c.1886.

Grade or Name — Description	Avg	Ex-Fn	Mint
Lancaster Watch Co., 20J, ADJ, GJS, about 19 or 20 size			
Referred to as (Adams & Perry) model .... ★★★	$1,000	$1,500	$2,200
Malvern, 7J, dust proof, gilded..	95	110	130
Melrose, 15J, NI, ADJ, GJS	100	125	175
Nation Standard American Watch Co., 7J, HC	200	225	275
New Era, 7J, gilded, KW, HC	75	100	150
New Era, 7J, gilded, KW, Silveroid......................................	65	80	100
Paoli, 7J, NI, dust proof, ...	75	100	150
Wm. Penn, 20J, ADJ, NI, dust proof	400	500	650
Radnor, 7J, dust proof, gilded	100	125	175
Record, 7J, dust proof, Silveroid..	75	95	125
Record, 15J, NI..	75	100	150

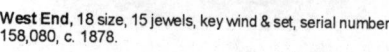

West End, 18 size, 15 jewels, key wind & set, serial number 158,080, c. 1878.

Lancaster movement, 8-10 size, 15 jewels, serial number 317,812.

🕐 Watches listed in this book are priced at the **collectable fair market value** at the RETAIL level, as complete watches having an original 14k gold filled case, KEY WIND with silver, an original white enamel single sunk dial, and with the entire original movement in good working order with no repairs needed, unless otherwise noted.

Grade or Name — Description	Avg	Ex-Fn	Mint
Ruby, 7-16J, NI	$275	$325	$400
Sidney, 15J, NI, dust proof,	100	125	150
Stevens, 15J, ADJ, NI, dust proof	150	175	225
West End, 19J, HC, KW, gilded	450	500	550
West End, 15J, HC, KW, KS	175	200	250
West End, 15J, SW	175	200	250
West End, 15J, SW, Silveroid	85	100	125

8 SIZE

Grade or Name — Description	Avg	Ex-Fn	Mint
Cricket, 11J	$65	$70	$80
Diamond, 15J	70	80	90
Echo, 11J	65	70	75
Flora, 7-11J, gilded	75	100	150
Iris, 13J	65	70	80
Lady Penn, 20J, GJS, ADJ, NI ★	300	350	425
Lancaster W. Co., 7J	75	100	125
Pearl, 7J	55	60	65
Red Rose, of Lancaster, 15J	75	80	90
Ruby, 15J	75	80	90

MANHATTAN WATCH CO.

New York, New York
1883 - 1891

The Manhattan Watch Co. made mainly low cost production watches. A complete and full line of watches was made, and most were cased and styled to be sold as a **complete** watch. The watches were generally 16S with full plate movements. The patented winding mechanism was different. These watches were in both in hunter and open-face cases and later had a sweep second hand. Total production was 160,000 or more watches.

Manhattan Watch Co., stop watch, 16 size, note the escapement uses upright "D"—shaped pallets (steel), serial number 117,480.

Manhattan Watch Co., 16 size, stop watch. Note the two buttons on top; the right (at 2 o'clock) one sets the hands, the left (at 10 o'clock) starts and stops the watch.

16 SIZE

Grade or Name — Description		Avg	Ex-Fn	Mint
OF, with back wind, base metal case	★	$250	$300	$400
OF, 2 button stop watch, screw back & bezel, enamel dial, gold-filled case	★★	200	250	350
OF, 2 button stop watch, snap back & bezel, paper dial, base metal case	★	100	125	150
HC, 2 button stop watch, snap back & bezel, paper dial, base metal case	★	200	250	300
OF, 1 button, sweep sec., base metal case , paper dial	★	125	175	225
HC, 1 button, sweep sec., base metal case, paper dial	★	200	250	300
Ship's Bell Time Dial, OF or HC	★★★★	325	425	550
Twenty-Four Hour Dial, OF or HC	★★★★	325	425	550
Stallcup, 7J, OF	★	150	200	250

12 SIZE

Grade or Name — Description		Avg	Ex-Fn	Mint
12S	★	$125	$200	$275

Manhattan Watch Co., **16 size**, time only watch & note no second hand, the button at Right sets the hands.

Manhattan Watch Co., **16 size,** time only with Sweep-Second hand, the button at Right sets the hands.

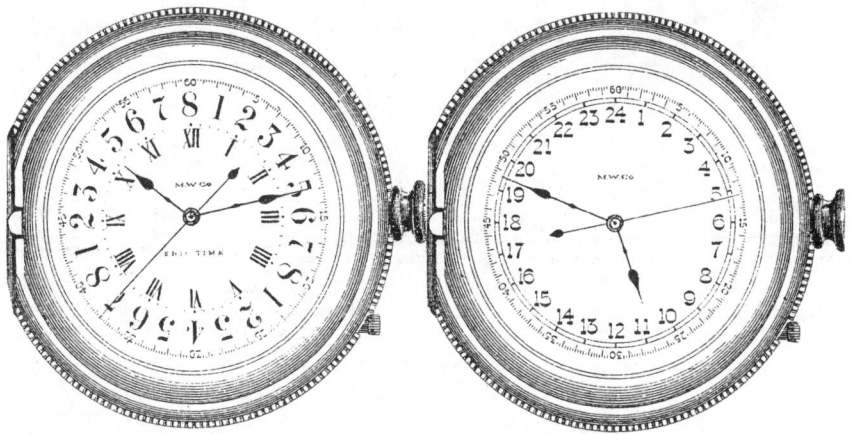

Manhattan Watch Co., **16 size,** Ship's Bell Time DIAL for NAUTICAL USES & sweep second hand, Hunting Case.

Manhattan Watch Co., **16 size,** with a 24-HOUR DIAL.& sweep second hand, Hunting Case.

MANISTEE WATCH CO.

Manistee, Michigan
1908 - 1912

The Manistee watches, first marketed in 1909, were designed to compete with the low-cost production watches. Dials, jewels, and hairsprings were not produced at the factory. The first movement was 18S, 7J, and sold for about $5. Manistee also made 5J, 15J, 17J, and 21J watches in cheap cases in sizes 16 and 12. Estimated total production was 60,000. Most were sold by Star Watch Case Co.

18 SIZE

Grade or Name —Description		Avg	Ex-Fn	Mint
18S, 7J, 3/4, LS, HC	★	$325	$375	$425
18S, 7J, 3/4, LS, OF	★	275	325	375
18S, 7J, 3/4, LS, OF, gold train	★★	375	400	450

16 TO 12 SIZE

Grade or Name —Description		Avg	Ex-Fn	Mint
16S, 7J, OF	★	$200	$250	$325
16S, 15J, OF	★	225	250	325
16S, 15J, HC	★	250	275	350
16S, 17J, OF	★	225	250	325
16S, 19J, HC	★	300	350	425
16S, 21J, OF	★	325	375	450
12S, 15J	★	150	175	225

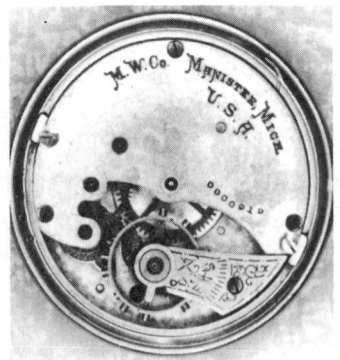

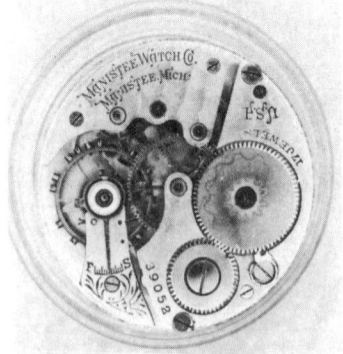

Manistee movement, 18 size, 7 jewels, 3/4 plate, open face, serial number 919.

Manistee movement, 16 size, 17 jewels, three-quarter plate, open face, serial number 39,052.

🕐 Watches listed in this book are priced at the collectable retail level, as **complete** watches having an original 14k gold-filled case and *Key Wind* with silver, an original white enamel single sunk dial, and with the entire original movement in good working order with no repairs needed.

🕐 Some grades are not included. Their values can be determined by comparing with **similar** age, size, metal content, style, models and grades listed.

McINTYRE WATCH CO.

Kankakee, Illinois

1905 - 1911

This company probably bought the factory from Kankakee Watch Co. In 1908 Charles DeLong was made master watchmaker, and he designed and improved the railroad watches. Only a few watches were made, estimated total production being about **eight watches**.

Grade or Name — Description		Avg	Ex-Fn	Mint
16S, 21J, BRG, NI, WI.. ★★★★		$4,500	$5,000	$6,500
16S, 25J, BRG, NI, WI, Adj.5P, equidistant escapement .. ★★★★		5,500	6,000	7,500
12S, 19J, BRG.. ★★★★		2,000	2,500	3,500

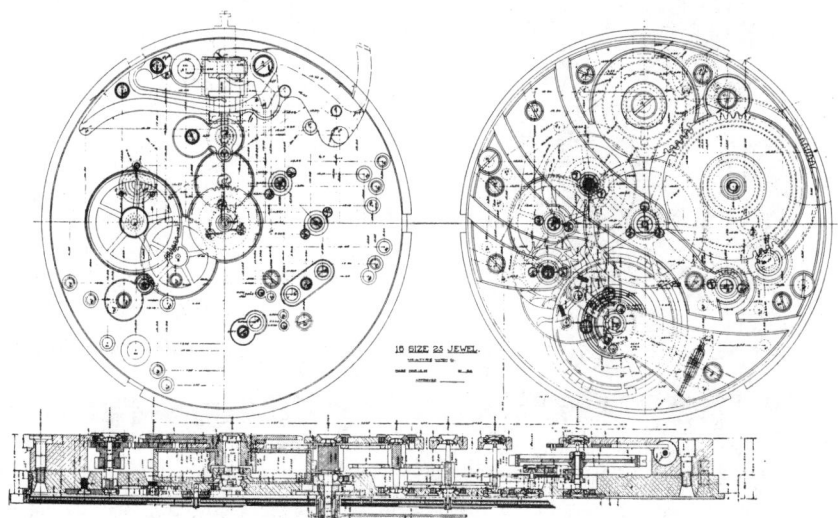

McIntyre Watch Co., 16 size, 25 jewels, adjusted to 5 positions with wind indicator, with equidistant escapement, manufactured about 1909. Above illustration taken from a blue print.

EXAMPLE OF A BREGUET STYLE DIAL

EXAMPLE OF A BOX CAR STYLE DIAL

MELROSE WATCH CO.

Melrose, Massachusetts
1866 - 1868

Melrose Watch Co. began as Tremont Watch Co. and imported the expansion balances and escapements. In 1866 the Tremont Watch Co. moved, changed its name to Melrose Watch Co., and started making complete watch movements, including a new style 18S movement engraved "Melrose Watch Co." About 3,000 were produced. Some watches are found with "Melrose" on the dial and "Tremont" on the movement. Serial numbers start at about 30,000.

Example of a basic **Melrose Watch Co.** movement, 18 size, 15 jewels, key wind & set.

Grade or Name — Description		Avg	Ex-Fn	Mint
18S, 7J, KW, KS	★ ★	$300	$350	$375
18S, 11J, KW, KS, OF	★ ★	325	370	450
18S, 15J, KW, KS	★ ★	350	400	475
18S, 15J, KW, KS, Silveroid	★ ★	250	300	375

Note: Add $25.00 - $50.00 to values of above watches in hunting case.

MOZART WATCH CO.
Providence, Rhode Island
Ann Arbor, Michigan
1864 - 1870

In 1864 Don J. Mozart started out to produce a less expensive three-wheel watch in Providence, R. I. Despite his best efforts, the venture was declared a failure by 1866. Mozart left Providence and moved to Ann Arbor, Mich. There, again, he started on a three-wheel watch and succeeded in producing thirty. The three-wheel watch was not a new idea except to American manufacturers. Three-wheel watches were made many decades before Mozart's first effort, but credit for the first American-made three-wheel watch must go to him. The size was about 18 and could be called a 3/4 or full plate movement. The balance bridge was screwed on the top plate, as was customary. The round bridge partially covered the opening in the top plate and was just large enough for the balance to oscillate. The balance was compensated and somewhat smaller in diameter than usual. Mozart called it a chronolever, and it was to function so perfectly it would be free from friction. That sounded good but was in no way true.

The watch was of the usual thickness for the American 18 size with a train that had a main wheel with the usual number of teeth and a ten-leaf center pinion, but it had a large center wheel of 108 teeth and a third wheel of 90 teeth, with a six-leaf third (escape) pinion. The escape wheel had 30 teeth and received its impulse directly from the roller on the staff, while the escape tooth locked on the intermediate lever pallet. The escape pinion had a long pivot that carried the second hand, which made a circuit of the dial, once in 12 seconds. The total number of Mozart watches produced was 165, and about 30 of these were the three-wheel type.

Grade or Name — Description		Avg	Ex-Fn	Mint
18S, 3/4, KW, KS, 3-wheel	★★★★★	$11,000	$15,000	$20,000
18S, 3/4, KW, KS	★★★★	6,000	7,000	8,000

Mozart Watch Co. movement, 18 size, three-quarter plate, key wind & set, three-wheel train, "Patent Dec. 24th, 1868" engraved on back plate.

NASHUA WATCH CO. (marked), 20 size, 19 jewels, gold jewel settings, key wind & set from back, stop work, serial number 1,219.

NASHUA WATCH CO.

Nashua, New Hampshire

1859 - 1862

One of the most important contributions to the American Watch industry was made by the Nashua Watch Co. of Nashua, New Hampshire. Founded in 1859 by B. D. Bingham, the company hired some of the most innovative and creative watchmakers in America and produced an extremely high grade American pocket watch.

His company included N. P. Stratton, C. V. Woerd, Charles Moseley, James H. Gerry, and James Gooding, among others. Most of the people connected with the Nashua Watch Company became famous for various advances in watch manufacture, at one time or another. Many had extremely important American patents on various inventions that came to be regarded as a benchmark of the best watches America was capable of making at the time.

The Nashua Watch Co. is important for many reasons. It was the first American company to produce a truly superior high grade movement; the 3/4 plate design used by Nashua became the standard for over 40 years in the American marketplace. Perhaps most importantly, the watches designed by the Nashua Watch Co., and later by the Nashua division of the American Watch Co., became the leaders in the production of the highest quality watches made in America and forced the entire Swiss watch industry to change their technology to compete with the Nashua designs.

Nashua continually won awards for their various models of watches both here and in Europe. By virtue of their sheer technical superiority and classical elegance, Nashua became known universally as the most innovative producer of watches America ever knew.

The original Nashua company produced material for about 1,000 movements but, except for a handful, almost the entire production was finished by the American Watch Company at Waltham, Mass., after R. E. Robbins took over Nashua in 1862 when the company was in grave financial difficulty. Robbins was very happy about the arrangement since he got back almost all the watchmaking geniuses who had left him in 1859 to join Nashua. Robbins incorporated the Nashua Division into the American Watch Company as its high grade experimental division.

Over the years, many of the major advances were made by the Nashua division of Waltham, including the 1860 model 16-size keywind keyset, the 1862 model 20-size key wind keyset, the 1870 model 18-size keywind keyset, pin set, and lever set (which became the first American advertised Railroad watch), the 1868 model 16-size stem wind, and the 1872 model 17-size stemwind. The Nashua division also greatly influenced the 1888 model and the 1892 model by Waltham.

Since almost all the production material made by Nashua from 1859 until its incorporation into the American Watch Co. in 1862 was unfinished by Nashua, only about four examples of the 20-size keywind keyset from the back signed Nashua Watch Co. are known to exist.

20-size keywind keyset from the back signed Nashua Watch Co.

Grade or Name — Description	Avg	Ex-Fn	Mint
Nashua (marked), 19J, KW, KS, 3/4, 18K .... ★★★★★	$18,000	$22,000	$28,000
Nashua (marked), 15J, KW, KS, 3/4, silver case .... ★★★★	9,000	11,000	13,000

NEWARK WATCH CO.

Newark, New Jersey

1864 - 1870

Arthur Wadsworth, one of the designers for Newark Watch Co., patented an 18 Size full plate movement. The first movements reached the market in 1867. This company produced only about 8,000 watches before it was sold to the Cornell Watch Co.

CHRONOLOGY OF THE DEVELOPMENT OF NEWARK WATCH CO.

Newark Watch Co. 1864-1870; S#s 6,501 to 12,000;

Cornell Watch Co., Chicago, Ill. 1870-1874; S#s 12,001 to 25,000;

Cornell Watch Co., San Francisco, Calif. 1874-Jan. 1876; S#s 25,001 to 35,000;

California Watch Co., Jan. 1876-mid 1876.

🕓 Watches listed in this book are priced at the **collectable fair market value** at the RETAIL level, as complete watches having an original 14k gold filled case, KEY WIND with silver, an original white enamel single sunk dial, and with the entire original movement in good working order with no repairs needed, unless otherwise noted.

Newark Watch Co. Robert Fellows movement, 18 size, 15 jewels, key wind & set, serial number 12, 044.

Grade or Name — Description	Avg	Ex-Fn	Mint
18S, 15J, KW, KS, HC ★★	$375	$425	$525
18S, 15J, KW, KS, OF ★★	325	375	450
18S, 7J, KW, KS ★★'	300	350	435
J. C. Adams, 11J, KW, KS ★★	375	425	500
J. C. Adams, 11J, KW, KS, Coin ★★	350	400	475
Edward Biven, 11-15J, KW, KS ★★	375	425	500
Robert Fellows, KW, KS ★★	400	450	535
Keyless Watch Co., 15J, LS, SW ★★	300	350	435
Newark Watch Co., 7-15J, KW, KS ★★	350	400	475
Arthur Wadsworth, SW ★★★	425	525	650
Arthur Wadsworth, 18S, 15J, 18K, HC ("Arthur Wadsworth, New York" on dial; "Keyless Watch, Patent #3655, June 19, 1866" engraved on movement) ★★★	1,000	1,200	1,500

NEW ENGLAND WATCH CO.

Waterbury, Connecticut
1898 - 1914

The New England Watch Co., formerly the Waterbury Watch Co., made a watch with a duplex escapement, gilt, 16S, open faced. Watches with the skeletonized movement are very desirable. The company later became Timex Watch Co.

Grade or Name — Description	Avg	Ex-Fn	Mint
16S, OF, duplex, SKELETON, good running order ★	$250	$295	$350
12S, 16S, 18S, OF, pictures on dial: ladies, dogs, horses, trains, flags, ships, cards, etc.	150	175	225
12S, 16S, 18S, OF, duplex escapement, good running order	65	75	95
12S, 16S, 18S, OF, pin lever escapement, good running order	45	55	65

Front and back view of a **skeletonized** New England Watch Co. movement. This watch is fitted with a glass back and front, making the entire movement and wheels visible, 4 jewels, silver hands, black numbers, originally sold for $10-13.

Grade or Name — Description	Avg	Ex-Fn	Mint
6S, duplex..	$40	$50	$65
0 S, 15-17 J, lever escapement..	50	65	85
Addison, (all sizes)..	55	65	75
Alden..	40	55	65
Ambassador, 12S, duplex...	40	55	65
Americus, duplex...	40	55	65
Avour, duplex escapement...	40	55	65
Berkshire, duplex, 14K, **GF**..	65	75	95

New England Watch Co., 16 size, 7 jewels, open face, double roller, Dan Patch stop watch.

New England Watch Co., Scout, about 16 size, 4 jewels, duplex escapement, New England base metal case.

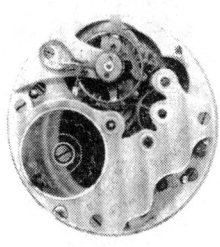

New England Watch Co., multi-colored paper dials, showing poker style playing cards. Watches complete with these type dials bring $150 - $400.00.

New England Watch Co., 0 size, 17 jewels, serial # 1,000,283.

Grade or Name — Description	Avg	Ex-Fn	Mint
Cadish, duplex escapement	$40	$50	$65
Cavour, duplex escapement	45	50	60
Columbian	45	55	65
Chronograph, 7J, Start, Stop & Reset	135	150	200
Cruiser, duplex	45	50	65
Dan Patch, 7J ★	275	350	425
Dominion, **0 size**	35	40	55
Excelsior, 7J	65	70	95
Enamel, full enamel cased watches back and bezel, blue red green, sizes from 6 size to 0 size	95	125	175
Embossed, base metal cases with duplex escapement	65	95	125
Fancy, **"unfaded dial"**	100	145	200
Gabour	65	70	85
General	45	50	65
Hale, 7J	45	50	65
Jockey, duplex	55	60	75
Oxford	45	50	65
Padishah, duplex	45	50	75
Putnam	65	70	85
Queen Mab, duplex escapement - **0 size**, 4J	40	50	65
Rugby, stop watch	65	70	85
Scout, 12 Size, duplex escapement, HC	40	45	60
Senator, duplex escapement	40	45	55
Trump, duplex	40	45	65
Tuxedo	45	50	65
Tuxedo, DUPLEX ESCAPEMENT	55	65	85

🕐 Some grades are not included. Their values can be determined by comparing with **similar** age, size, metal content, style, models and grades listed.

NEW HAVEN CLOCK AND WATCH CO.

New Haven, Connecticut

1853 - 1956

The company started making watches in early 1880 in New Haven and produced the regular 16S, lever watch. These sold for $3.75. The company soon reached a production of about 200 watches per day, making a total of some 40 million watches.

NEW HAVEN Clock & Watch Co., Angelus, with rotating dials, patented Jan 23, 1900.

NEW HAVEN, Ships Time, Ben Franklin dial , Note this watch uses only one hand.

Grade or Name – Description	Avg	Ex-Fn	Mint
Always Right	$45	$55	$75
Angelus, 2 rotating dials ★	135	200	265
Beardsley Radiant	65	75	95
Buddy	45	50	65
Bull Dog	40	45	60
Compensated	45	50	65
Captain Scout	85	100	150
Celluloid case (bold colors)	95	125	175
Chronometer	65	85	100
Earl	45	50	65
Elite	40	50	65
Elm City	45	50	65
Fancy dials, no fading	100	145	200
Football Timer	65	75	95
Ford Special	75	85	100
Hamilton	45	50	65
Handy Andy	50	60	75
Jerome USA	45	50	65

🕐 Note: Some styles, models and grades are not included. Their values can be determined by comparing with **similar** styles, size, age, models and grades listed.

NOTE : ADD $25 to $50 for original BOX and PAPERS

Example of Kaiser Wilhelm.

Example of Traveler.

Grade or Name – Description	Avg	Ex-Fn	Mint
Kaiser Wilhelm .... ★ ★	$225	$275	$350
Kermit	40	45	55
Laddie.......................	25	30	40
Lady Clare.................	25	30	40
Leonard Watch Co.	25	40	50
Leonard	45	50	65
Mastercraft Rayolite ...	75	85	95
Miracle	45	50	65
Nehi...........................	50	70	85
New Haven, pin lever, SW	65	75	100
New Haven, back wind..............................	100	135	200
Panama Official Souvenir, 1915	200	250	350
Pastor Stop Watch......................................	100	125	150
Paul Pry, 14 size with a Locomotive on back of case	35	45	65
Pedometer, 14 size, OF...............................	45	50	65
Pentagon-shaped case.................................	45	50	65
Playing cards on dial...................................	150	200	300
Service..	30	35	40
Ships Time & Franklin dial	75	95	125
Sports Timer...	65	75	95
Surity...	45	50	65
Tip Top...	20	30	50
Tip Top Jr...	20	30	50
The American...	45	50	60
Tommy Ticker	30	35	40
Tourist..	45	50	65
Traveler, with travel case	40	45	60
True Time Teller Tip Top..............................	40	45	60
United...	30	35	40
USA..	30	35	40
Victor..	30	35	45

NOTE : ADD $25 to $50 for original BOX and PAPERS

NEW HAVEN WATCH CO.

New Haven, Connecticut
1883 - 1887

This company was organized October 16, 1883 with the intention of producing W. E. Doolittle's patented watch; however, this plan was soon abandoned. They did produce a "Model A" watch, the first was marketed in the spring of 1884. Estimated total production is 200 and only **5 known to exist.** The original capital became absorbed by Trenton W. Co.

New Haven Watch Co., on movement "Alpha, 149, Pat. Dec. 27-81," lever escapement, open face, very rare watch.

Grade or Name – Description		Avg	Ex-Fn	Mint
"A" Model, about 18S, pat. Dec. 27, '81 .... ★★★★		$625	$750	$950
Alpha Model, pat. Dec. 27, '81 .... ★★★★		625	750	950

NEW YORK CITY WATCH CO.

New York, New York
1890 - 1897

This company manufactured the Dollar-type watches, which had a pendant-type crank. The watch is wound by **cranking the pendant,** and has a pin lever escapement. The hands are set from the back of the watch movement. The" **patent number 526,871",** is engraved on movement, patent is dated October 1894, and was held by S. Schisgall. The New York City Watch Co., 20 size watch has the words "Lever Winder" printed on the paper dial.

🕐 Watches listed in this book are priced at the **collectable fair market value** at the RETAIL level, as complete watches having an original 14k gold filled case, KEY WIND with silver, an original white enamel single sunk dial, and with the entire original movement in good working order with no repairs needed, unless otherwise noted.

Grade or Name – Description	Avg	Ex-Fn	Mint
18-20S, no jewels, "Lever Winder on dial" .... ★★★★★	$700	$800	$1,000
18-20S, no jewels, "SUN DIAL on dial" .... ★★★★	$700	$800	$1,000

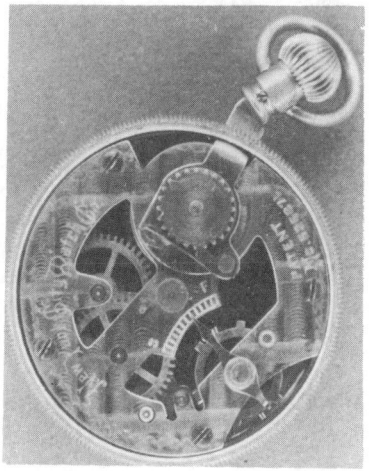

New York City Watch Co., about 18-20 size, "Lever Winder" printed on paper dial. This watch is **WOUND** by cranking the pendant back and forth , pin lever escapement, also **back set**, & "*New York City Watch Co., patent No. 526,871*" engraved on movement.

NEW YORK CHRONOGRAPH WATCH CO.

NEW YORK, NEW YORK

1880 -1885

This company sold about 800 watches marked ''New York Chronograph Watch Co.'' The 18 size stop watch was manufactured by Manhattan Watch Co.

Grade or Name –Description	Avg	Ex-Fn	Mint
18S, 7J, stop watch, HC .... ★	$125	$150	$200
18S, 7J, stop watch, OF .... ★	100	125	175
16S, 7J, SW, time only, OF .... ★	100	175	250
16S, 9-11J, SW, time only, OF .... ★	100	175	250
16S, 7-11J, SW, time only sweep sec., OF .... ★	125	200	275
16S, 7-11J, SW, **true CHRONOGRAPH**, OF .... ★★★★	300	375	450

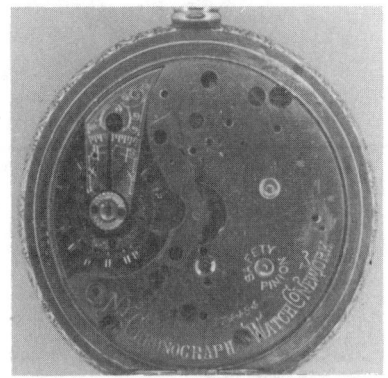

N.Y. Chronograph Watch Co., dial and movement, 16 size, 7 jewels, open face, time only, sweep second hand.

 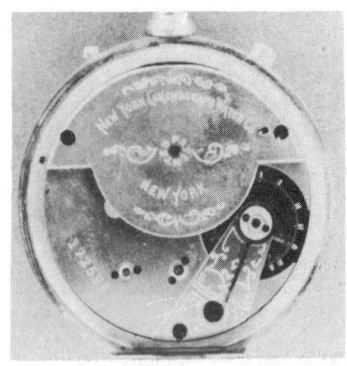

New York Chronograph Watch Co. dial and movement, 7 jewels, open face, buttons at the top of case set hands and stop watch.

NEW YORK STANDARD WATCH CO.

Jersey City, New Jersey
1885 - 1929

The first watch reached the market in early 1888 and was a 18S. The most interesting feature was a straight line lever with a "worm gear escapement." This was patented by R. J. Clay. All watches were quick train and open-faced. The company also made its own cases and sold a complete watch. A prefix number was added to the serial number after the first 10,000 watches were made. Estimated total production was 7,000,000.

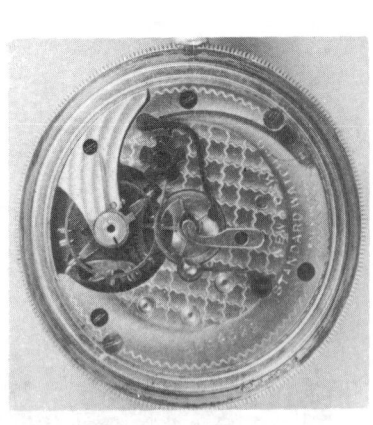 

New York Standard, Chronograph, 18 size, 7 jewels, stem wind, second hand start-stop and fly back, three-quarter plate, serial number 5,334,322.

New York Standard, converts to a hunting case movement or a open face movement, serial number 602,506.

N. Y. STANDARD
16 AND 18 SIZE

Grade or Name – Description	Avg	Ex-Fn	Mint
18S, 7J, N. Y. Standard, KW, KS	$250	$300	$375
18S, 7J, N. Y. Standard, SW	50	60	75
18S, 15J, N. Y. Standard, SW, LS, HC	100	125	175
Chronograph, 7J, 3/4, NI, DMK, SW, fly back hand	150	200	275
Chronograph, 10J, (marked 10J), fly back hand ★	195	235	295
Chronograph, 13J, sweep sec., stop & fly back hand	150	200	275
Chronograph, 15J, 3/4, NI, DMK, SW,fly back hand,	150	200	275
Columbus, 7J	50	60	75
Convertible,15J.,16 Size, HC or OF ★ ★ ★ ★	300	425	600
Crown W. Co., 7J, OF or HC	50	60	65
Crown W. Co., 15J, HC	60	75	100
Dan Patch, 7J, stop watch(pat. DEC. 22 '08) ★	275	350	425
Dan Patch, 17J, stop watch(pat. DEC. 22 '08) ★ ★	375	450	525
Edgemere, 7J, OF & HC	50	60	75
Excelsior, 7J, OF or HC	50	60	75

New York Standard, with WORM GEAR (located under cutout star), 18 size, 7 jewels, there was two runs of the worm-drive model 52,000 made, serial number 31,138.

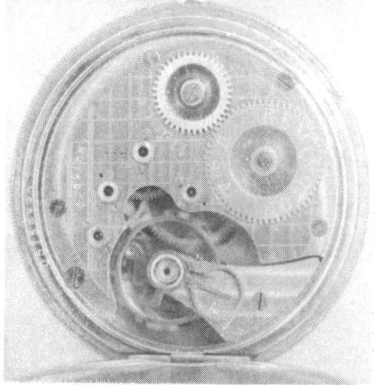

Remington W. Co. (marked on movement & case), 16 size, 11 jewels, 2-tone damaskeening, NOTE crown wheel & ratchet (no click), serial # CC021,331.

Grade or Name – Description	Avg	Ex-Fn	Mint
Harvard W. CO., 7–11J.,	$40	$50	$65
Hi Grade	50	60	75
Ideal	50	60	75
Jefferson, 7J.,	50	60	70
La Salle, 7J.,	35	45	55
New Era, 7J., OF or HC, skeletonized (Poor Man's Dudley)	250	275	325
New Era,7–11J.	40	50	65
New York Standard W. Co., 11J, 3/4	60	85	100
New York Standard, 7J, 3/4	60	85	100
New York Standard, 15J, BRG	75	100	125
N. Y. Standard, with (" WORM GEAR") ★	400	450	500

🕐 Note: Some styles, models and grades are not included. Their values can be determined by comparing with **similar** styles, size, age, models and grades listed.

Grade or Name – Description	Avg	Ex-Fn	Mint
Pan American, 7J, OF	$60	$85	$100
Perfection, 7J, OF or HC	50	60	75
Perfection, 15J, OF or HC, NI	60	85	100
Remington W. Co., 11J, marked mvt. & case.	75	100	135
Solar W. Co., 7J	50	60	75
Special USA, 7J.	45	55	65
18S Tribune USA, **23J**, HC or OF, Pat. Reg. Adj.	150	175	225
Washington, 7-11J.,	50	60	75
William Penn, 7-11J.,	50	60	75
Wilmington	50	60	75

For watches with **O'Hara Multi-Color Dials**, add $75 to value in **mint condition**; add $5 for Hunting Cases.

12 SIZE

Grade or Name – Description	Avg	Ex-Fn	Mint
N. Y. Standard, 7J-11J, OF	$25	$30	$45
N. Y. Standard, 7J-11J, HC	40	55	60
N. Y. Standard, 7J, HC, Multi-Color dial	125	150	195
N. Y. Standard, 15J, OF	35	40	45
N. Y. Standard, 15J, HC	45	55	70
Crown W. Co., 7J, OF or HC	30	40	55

 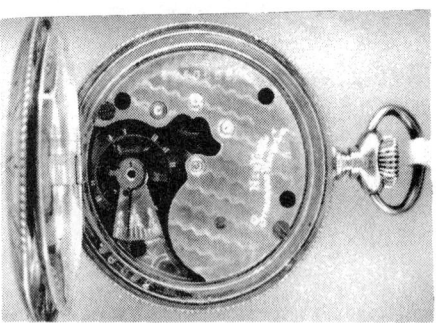

New York Standard Watch Co., 12 size, 7 jewels, open face, serial number 1021224.

New York Standard W.Co., 6 size G# 144, Hunting Case.

6 SIZE AND 0 SIZE

Grade or Name – Description	Avg	Ex-Fn	Mint
Alton, 7-15J.	$35	$40	$55
American,7J.,	35	40	55
Empire State W. Co., 7J	40	50	65
Standard USA, 7J.	40	50	65
6S, Columbia, 7J, HC	60	70	85
6S, N. Y. Standard, 7J, HC	60	70	85
6S, Orient, SW	30	40	55
6S, Progress, 7J, YGF	40	50	65
6S or 0S, Crown W. Co., 7J, OF or HC	20	30	45
0S, Ideal, 7J, HC	60	70	85
0S, N. Y. Standard, 7J, HC	60	70	85

NEW YORK STANDARD WATCH CO.
IDENTIFICATION OF MOVEMENTS

How to Identify Your Watch: Compare the movement of your watch with the illustrations in this section. Upon matching the movement exactly, the model number and size can be determined. While comparing, note the location of the balance, jewels, screws, gears, and type of back plate (Full, 3/4, Bridge) which will be clues in identifying the movement you have. Having determined the size and model number, you can now find your watch in the main price listing by name or number (which is engraved on the movement).

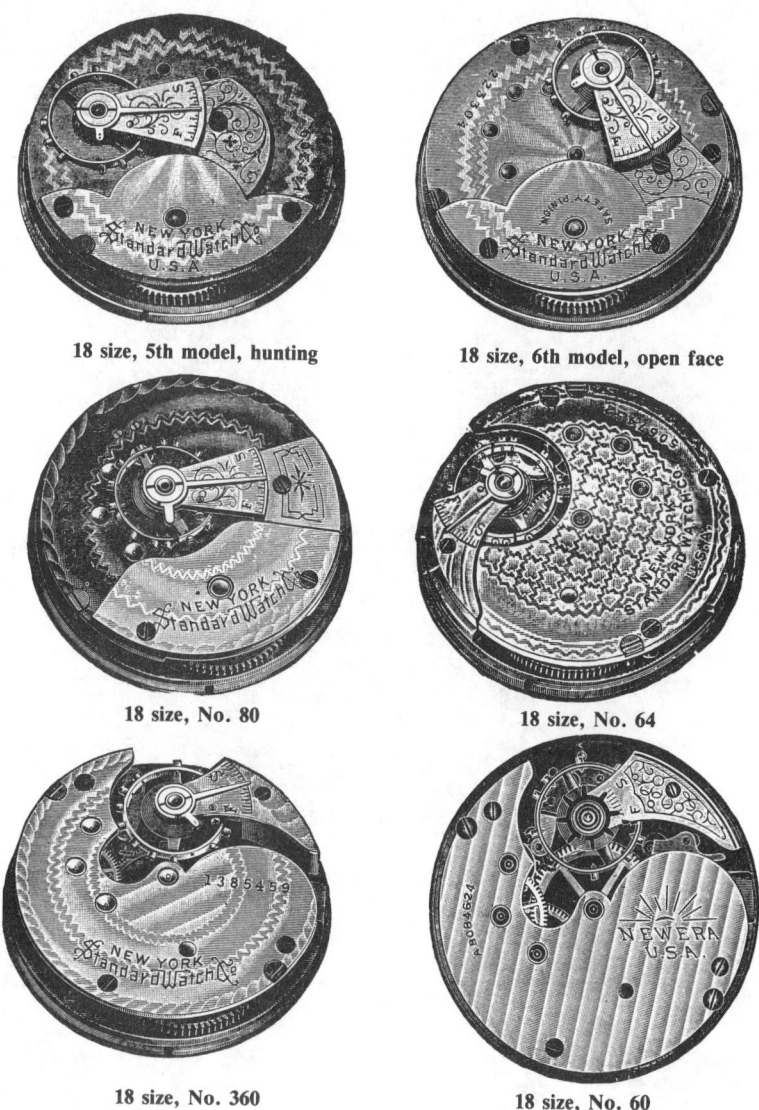

| 18 size, 5th model, hunting | 18 size, 6th model, open face |

18 size, No. 80   18 size, No. 64

18 size, No. 360   18 size, No. 60

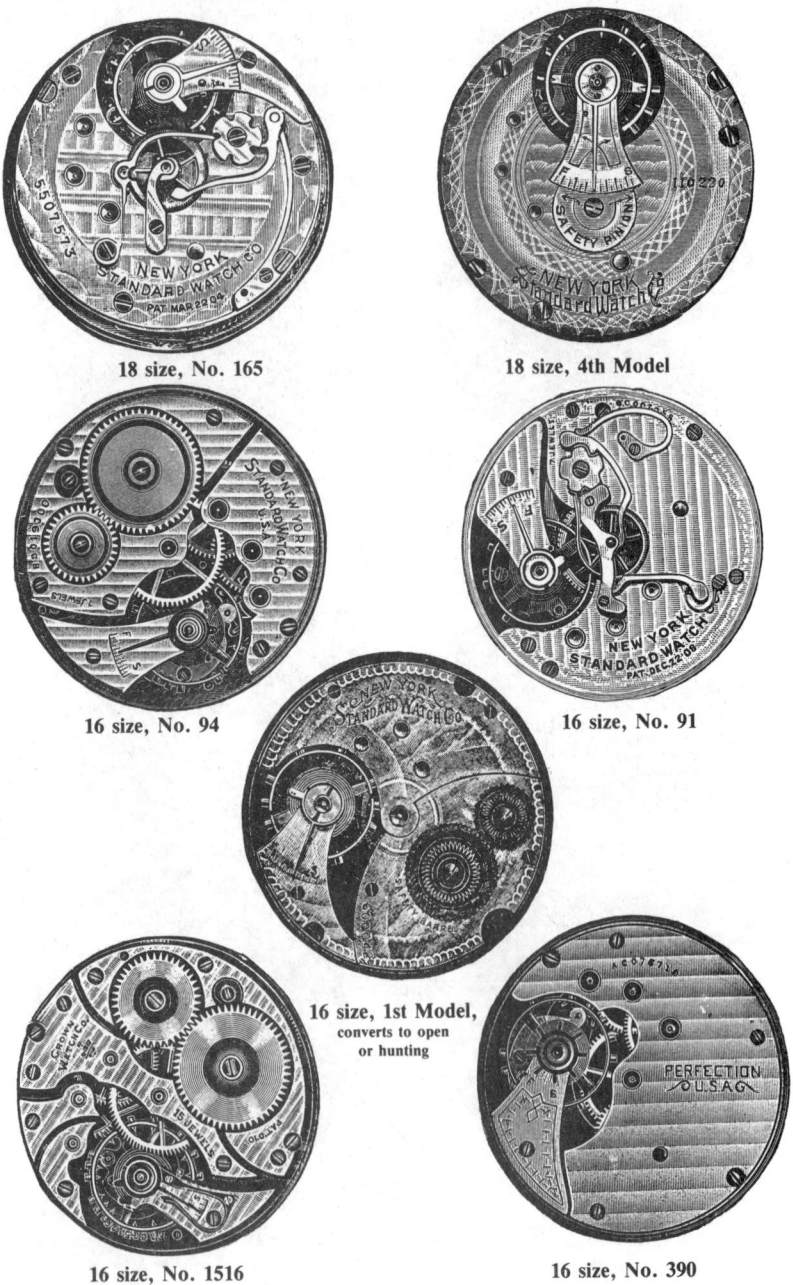

18 size, No. 165

18 size, 4th Model

16 size, No. 94

16 size, No. 91

16 size, 1st Model,
converts to open
or hunting

16 size, No. 1516

16 size, No. 390

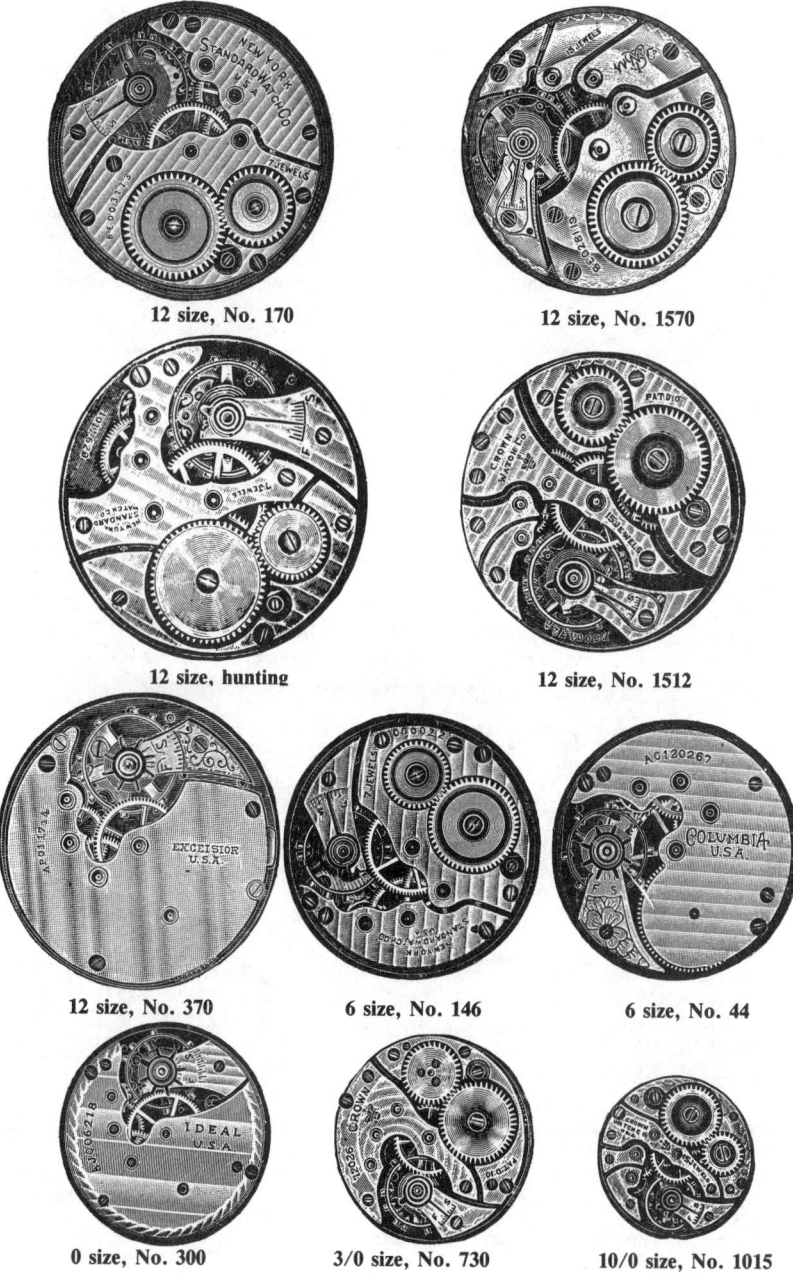

12 size, No. 170

12 size, No. 1570

12 size, hunting

12 size, No. 1512

12 size, No. 370

6 size, No. 146

6 size, No. 44

0 size, No. 300

3/0 size, No. 730

10/0 size, No. 1015

NEW YORK SPRINGFIELD WATCH CO.

Springfield, Massachusetts

1866 - 1876

The New York Watch Co. had a rather difficult time getting started. The name of the company was changed from the Mozart Watch Co. to the New York Watch Co., and it was located in Rhode Island. Before any watches had been produced, they moved to Springfield, Mass., in 1867. A factory was built there, but only about 100 watches were produced before a fire occurred on April 23, 1870. Shortly after the fire, in 1870, a newly-designed watch was introduced. The first movements reached the market in 1871, and the first grade was a fully-jeweled adjusted movement called "Frederick Billings." The standard 18S and the Swiss Ligne systems were both used in gauging the size of these watches. The New York Watch Co. used full signatures on its movements. The doors closed in the summer of 1876.

In January 1877, the Hampden Watch Co. was organized and commenced active operation in June 1877.

CHRONOLOGY OF THE DEVELOPMENT OF NEW YORK WATCH CO.

The Mozart Watch Co., Providence, R. I. 1864-1866
New York Watch Co., Providence, R. I. 1866-1867
New York Watch Co., Springfield, Mass. 1867-1875
New York Watch Mfg. Co., Springfield, Mass. 1875-1876
Hampden Watch Co., Springfield, Mass. 1877-1886
Hampden-Dueber Watch Co., Springfield, Mass. 1886-1888
Hampden Watch Co. Works, Canton, Ohio 1888-1923
Dueber-Hampden Watch Co., Canton, Ohio 1923-1930
Amtorg, U.S.S.R. 1930

NEW YORK WATCH CO. SPRINGFIELD
ESTIMATED SERIAL NUMBERS
AND PRODUCTION DATES

DATE – SERIAL NO.	DATE – SERIAL NO.
1866 – 1,000	1871 – 20,000
1867 – 3,000	1872 – 30,000
1868 – 5,000	1873 – 40,000
1869 – 7,000	1874 – 50,000
1870 – 10,000	1875 – 60,000

The above list is provided for determining the APPROXIMATE age of your watch. Match serial number with date. Watches were not necessarily sold in the exact order of manufactured date.

N. Y. W. SPRINGFIELD

18 TO 20 SIZE

Grade or Name – Description		Avg	Ex-Fn	Mint
Aaron Bagg, 7J, KW, KS .... ★		$225	$275	$350
Frederick Billings, 15J, KW, KS... ★		225	275	350
E. W. Bond, 15J, 3/4... ★ ★ ★		500	600	700
J. A. Briggs, 11J, KW, KS, from back.................................. ★ ★		325	350	425

🕐 Some grades are not included. Their values can be determined by comparing with **similar** age, size, metal content, style, models and grades listed.

🕐 Watches listed in this book are priced at the collectable retail level, as **complete** watches having an original 14k gold-filled case and *Key Wind* with silver, an original white enamel single sunk dial, and with the entire original movement in good working order with no repairs needed.

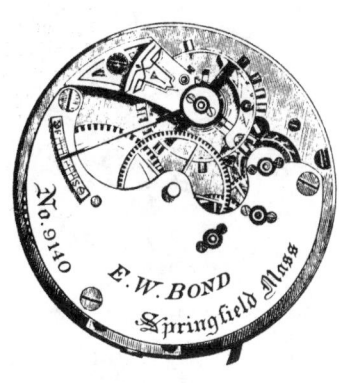

E.W. Bond movement, 18 size, 7 jewels, three-quarter plate.

Chas. E. Hayward, 18 size, 15 jewels, key wind & set, note the hidden key, serial number 18,733.

Grade or Name – Description

Grade or Name – Description		Avg	Ex-Fn	Mint
Albert Clark, 15J, KW, KS, from back, 3/4	★ ★	$300	$350	$425
Homer Foot, 15J, KW, KS, from back, 3/4	★	300	350	425
Herman Gerz, 11J, KW, KS	★	200	250	325
John Hancock, 7J, KW, KS		100	200	275
John Hancock, 7J, KW, KS, Silveroid		95	125	150
John Hancock, 7J, KW, KS, Coin		150	200	275
Chas. E. Hayward, 15J, KW, KS, long balance cock		150	200	275
Chas. E. Hayward, 15J, KW, KS, Coin		150	200	275
J. L. King, 15J, KW, KS, from back, 3/4	★	400	500	600
New York Watch Co., 7J, KW, KS	★	150	200	275
New York Watch Co., 15-19J, KW, KS, Wolf's Teeth winding, (Serial #s below 75)	★ ★ ★ ★	1,300	1,500	2,000
New York Watch Co., 15-19J, KW, KS, Wolf's Teeth winding, all original	★ ★ ★	1,000	1,200	1,500
New York Watch Co., 11J, KW, KS	★ ★	300	350	375
H. G. Norton, 15J, KW, KS, from back, 3/4	★	300	350	425
H. G. Norton, 17J, KW, KS, from back, 3/4	★	300	350	425
H. G. Norton, 19J, KW, KS, from back, 3/4	★ ★ ★	500	600	700

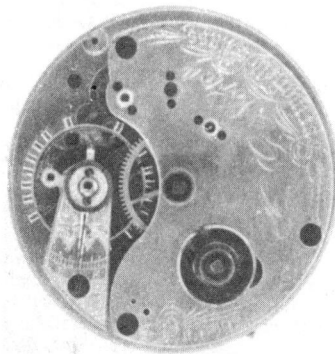

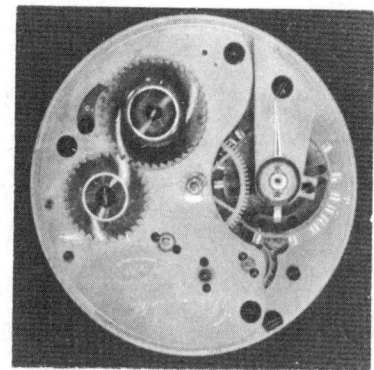

H.G. Norton, 18 size, 15 jewels, three-quarter plate, gold escape wheel, serial number 6592.

New York Watch Co., 18 size, 15-19 jewels, stem wind, hunting case, note wolf teeth winding, serial number 978.

State Street movement, 18 size, 11 jewels, three-quarter plate.

Theo E. Studley movement, 18 size, 15 jewels, key wind & set, full plate.

Grade or Name – Description		Avg	Ex-Fn	Mint
J. C. Perry, 15J.. ★		$150	$200	$275
J. C. Perry, 15J, Silveroid.. ★		125	150	175
Railway, 15J, KW, FULL, Coin............................ ★ ★		600	650	725
Railway, 15J, KW, KS, FULL .... ★ ★		600	650	725
William Romp,15J,KW,KS from back,3/4 .... ★ ★		500	650	950
Geo. Sam Rice, 7J, KW, KS................................... ★		300	350	425
Springfield, 15J, KW, KS, from back, ADJ, Wolf teeth wind, serial Nos. below 1,000 .... ★ ★ ★		1,000	1,200	1,500
Springfield, 19J, KW, KS, from back, ADJ, Wolf teeth wind, serial Nos. below 1,000 .... ★ ★ ★		1,300	1,500	1,800
State Street, 11J, 3/4, SW .... ★ ★		325	400	500
State Street, 11J, 3/4, SW, Silveroid .... ★ ★		325	425	550
Theo E. Studley, 15J, KW, Coin............................		125	150	175
Theo E. Studley, 15J, KW, KS...............................		125	150	175
George Walker, 17J, KW, 3/4, ADJ........................ ★		300	400	500
Chester Woolworth, 15J, KW, KS		125	150	175
Chester Woolworth, 11J, KW, KS		125	150	175
Chester Woolworth, 11J, KW, KS, Silveroid		95	125	150
Chester Woolworth, 11J, KW, KS, ADJ..................		150	175	225
#4, 15J, ADJ, KW, KS		125	150	200
#5, 15J, KW, KS...		100	125	175
#6, 11J, KW, KS...		100	125	175
#6, 11J, KW, KS, Silveroid..................................		85	95	125

🕐 Some KW, KS watches made by the New York Watch Co. have a hidden key. If you unscrew the crown, and the crown comes out as a key, add $100 to the listed value.

🕐 Watches listed in this book are priced at the collectable retail level, as **complete** watches having an original 14k gold-filled case and *Key Wind* with silver, an original white enamel single sunk dial, and with the entire original movement in good working order with no repairs needed.

🕐 This book endeavours to be a GUIDE or helpful manual and offers a wealth of material to be used as a tool not as a absolute document. Price Guides are like watches the worst may be better than none at all, but at best cannot be expected to be 100% accurate.

🕐 Characteristics of watches differ for the same age of both case and movement, because these features vary it may not be accurate to date a watch by one single influence. Example: the second hand was not commonly found on watches before 1750, but common about 1800. The first second hand appeared in 1665 and another in 1690. Therefore statements are broad rather than accurate.

NON-MAGNETIC WATCH CO.

Geneva and America
1887 - 1905

The Non-Magnetic Watch Co. sold and imported watches from the Swiss as well as contracted watches made in America. Geneva Non-Magnetic marked watches appear to be the oldest type of movement. This company sold a full line of watches, high grade to low grade, as well as repeaters and ladies watches. An advertisement appeared in the monthly journal of "Locomotive Engineers" in 1887. The ad states that the "Paillard's patent non-magnetic watches are uninfluenced by magnetism of electricity." Each watch contains the Paillard's patent non-magnetic, inoxidizable compensation balance and hairspring. An ad in 1888 shows prices for 16 size Swiss style watches as low as $15 for 7 jewels and as high as $135 for 20 jewels.

18 SIZE
(must be marked Paillard's Patent)

Grade or Name – Description	Avg	Ex-Fn	Mint
Elgin, 17J, FULL, SW, LS, OF	$125	$150	$200
Elgin, 17J, FULL, SW, LS, HC	150	175	250
Elgin, 15J, FULL, SW, LS, OF	100	125	175
Elgin, 15-17J, FULL, SW, LS, HC	125	150	200
Illinois, 24J, GJS, NI, Adj.5P, OF	900	1,000	1,200
Illinois, 24J, GJS, NI, Adj.5P, HC ★★	1,100	1,200	1,500
Illinois, 23J, GJS, NI, Adj.5P, OF	700	750	925
Illinois, 23J, GJS, NI, Adj.5P, HC ★★★	1,600	1,800	2,100
Illinois, 21J, GJS, NI, Adj.5P, OF	225	275	350
Illinois, 21J, GJS, NI, Adj.5P, HC	300	400	500
Illinois, 17J, NI, ADJ, OF	125	150	200
Illinois, 17J, NI, ADJ, HC	175	225	300
Illinois, 15J, NI, OF	100	125	175
Illinois, 15J, NI, HC	125	150	200
Illinois, 11J, OF	100	125	175
Illinois, 11J, HC	125	150	200

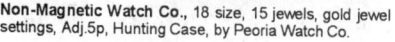

Non-Magnetic Watch Co., 18 size, 15 jewels, gold jewel settings, Adj.5p, Hunting Case, by Peoria Watch Co.

Non-Magnetic Watch Co., 18 size, 21 Ruby jewels, Adj.5p, note "Paillard' engraved on movement.

🕐 Watches listed in this book are priced at the collectable retail level, as **complete** watches having an original 14k gold-filled case and *Key Wind* with silver, an original white enamel single sunk dial, and with the entire original movement in good working order with no repairs needed.

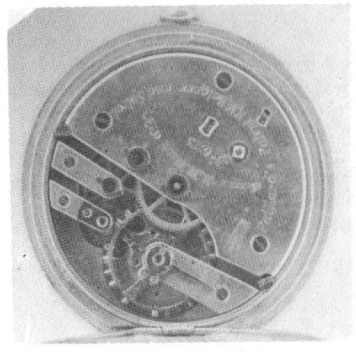
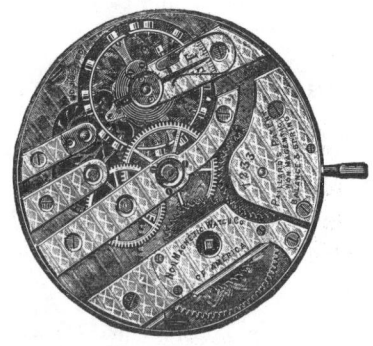

Non-Magnetic Watch Co., 18 size, 16J., 3/4 plate, hunting, note "Geneva" engraved on movement, serial # 6113.

Non-Magnetic Watch Co., 18 size, 16 jewels, Bar bridge model, example of a Swiss Ebauche.

Grade or Name – Description	Avg	Ex-Fn	Mint
Peoria, 17J, FULL, SW, LS, Adj., OF	$325	$350	$400
Peoria, 15J, FULL, SW, LS, Adj., OF	300	325	375
Peoria, 15J, FULL, SW, LS, Adj., HC	400	425	475
Peoria, 11J, FULL, SW, LS, OF	125	150	175
Peoria, 11J, FULL, SW, LS, HC	175	200	250
Swiss, 16J, 3/4 plate, SW, LS, Adj., OF	95	125	150
Swiss, 16J, 3/4 plate, SW, LS, Adj., HC	125	150	175
Swiss, 15-16J, bar bridge, SW, LS, Adj., OF	100	125	165
Swiss, 15-16J, bar bridge, SW, LS, Adj., HC	125	150	175
Swiss, 11J, 3/4 plate, SW, LS, OF, HC	85	100	150
Swiss, 11J, bar bridge, SW, LS, OF, HC	85	100	150

Non-Magnetic Watch Co., 16 size, 21 Ruby jewels, adjusted, made by Illinois Watch Co.

Non-Magnetic Watch Co., 16 size, 20J., in gold jewel settings, stem wind, open or hunting. Swiss made.

🕑 Watches listed in this book are priced at the **collectable fair market value** at the RETAIL level, as complete watches having an original 14k gold filled case, KEY WIND with silver, an original white enamel single sunk dial, and with the entire original movement in good working order with no repairs needed, unless otherwise noted.

Non-Magnetic Watch Co., 16 size, 1/2 plate, 16 jewels, hunting case, adjusted. Swiss made.

Non-Magnetic Watch Co., 16 size, 1/2 plate, 15 jewels, note "Paillard's Patent, Balance And Spring" engraved on movement. Swiss made.

16 SIZE
(must be marked Paillard's Patent)

Grade or Name – Description	Avg	Ex-Fn	Mint
Elgin, 21J, ADJ 5P, OF	$175	$200	$250
Elgin, 21J, ADJ 5P, HC	225	250	300
Illinois, 21J, GJS, 3/4, DR, Adj.6P, OF	250	300	400
Illinois, 21J, GJS, 3/4, DR, Adj.6P, HC	350	450	600
Illinois, 17J, 3/4, DR, ADJ, OF	125	150	175
Illinois, 17J, 3/4, DR, ADJ, HC	150	175	225
Illinois, 15J, HC	125	150	175
Illinois, 15J, OF	95	125	150
Illinois, 11J, OF	85	95	125
Illinois, 11J, HC	95	125	150
Swiss, 20J, GJS, DR, Adj.6P, NI, 1/2 ,OF	95	125	150
Swiss, 20J, GJS, DR, Adj.6P, NI, 1/2, HC	100	125	175
Swiss, 18J, GJS, DR, Adj.6P, NI, 1/2, OF	95	125	150
Swiss, 18J, GJS, DR, Adj.6P, NI, 1/2, HC	125	150	175
Swiss, 16J, GJS, DR, Adj.6P, NI, 1/2, OF	85	110	150
Swiss, 16J, GJS, DR, Adj.6P, NI, 1/2, HC	95	125	175
Swiss, 15J, DR, NI, 3/4, OF	75	100	150
Swiss, 15J, DR, NI, 3/4, HC	100	125	175
Swiss, 11J, NI, 3/4, OF	70	80	95
Swiss, 11J, NI, 3/4, HC	100	125	175
Swiss, 7J, OF & 3/4, HC	65	75	85

🕐 Generic, nameless or unmarked grades for watch movements are listed under the Company name or initials of the Company, etc. by size, jewel count and description.

🕐 Some watch manufacturers personalize watches for jobbers or jewelry firms, with exclusive private signed or marked movements. The valuable collectable watches are listed under the signed or marked movement. Other exclusive private signed or marked movements will have equivalent value are only slightly higher value and should be compared to Generic or Nameless movements. Railroad signed or marked (dials & movements) are usually more collectable & higher in value.

🕐 Some grades are not included. Their values can be determined by comparing with **similar** age, size, metal content, style, models and grades listed.

OTAY WATCH CO.

Otay, California

1889 - 1894

This company produced about 1,000 watches with a serial number range of 1,000 to 1,500 and 30,000 to 31,000. The company was purchased by a Japanese manufacturer in 1894. Names on Otay movements include: Golden Gate, F. A. Kimball, Native Sun, Overland Mail, R. D. Perry, and P. H. Wheeler.

Otay Watch Co. Dial; note hunting case style and lever for setting hands.

Otay Watch Co., F.A. Kimball, 18 size, 15 jewels, lever set, hunting, serial number 1,264.

18 SIZE

Grade or Name – Description		Avg	Ex-Fn	Mint
California, 15J., LS, HC, NI	★★★	$2,200	$2,400	$2,700
Golden Gate, 15J, LS, HC, OF, NI	★★★	2,200	2,400	2,800
F. A. Kimball, 15J, LS, HC, Gilt	★★	1,400	1,600	1,900
Native Son, 15J, LS, HC, NI	★★	1,800	2,000	2,300
Overland Mail, 15J, LS, HC, NI	★★★	2,400	2,800	3,000
R. D. Perry, 15J, LS, HC, Gilt	★★	1,400	1,600	1,900
P. H. Wheeler, 15J, LS, HC, Gilt	★★	1,400	1,600	1,900
Sunset, 7J, Gilt, HC	★★	1,400	1,600	1,900

D. D. PALMER WATCH CO.

Waltham, Massachusetts

1864 - 1875

In 1858, at age 20, Mr. Palmer opened a small jewelry store in Waltham, Mass. Here he became interested in pocket chronometers. At first he bought the balance and jewels from Swiss manufacturers. In 1864 he took a position with the American Watch Co. and made the chronometers in his spare time (only about 25 produced). They were, 18S, 3/4 plate, gilded, key wind, and some were nickel. At first they were fusee driven, but he mainly used going barrels. About 1870, Palmer started making lever watches and by 1875 he left the American Watch Co. and started making a 10S keywind, gilded movement, and a 16S, 3/4 plate, gilt and nickel, and a stem wind of his own invention (a vibrating crown wheel). In all he made about 1,500 watches. The signature appearing on the watches was "Palmer W. Co. Wal., Mass."

He basically had three grades of watches: Fine-Solid Nickel; Medium-Nickel Plated; and Medium-Gold Gilt. They were made in open-face and hunter cases.

D. D. Palmer Watch Co., 18 size, 15 jewels, Palmer's Pat.
Stem Winder on movement, serial number 1,098.

Grade or name – Description	Avg	Ex-Fn	Mint
10-14S, 15-17J, 3/4 plate, KW, spring detent chronometer. ★★★★	$4,000	$4,500	$6,000
16-18S, 17J, NI, OF, 18K.. ★★★	1,800	2,100	2,500

PEORIA WATCH CO.

Peoria, Illinois

1885 - 1895

The roots of this company began with the Independent Watch Co. (1880 - 1883). These watches marked Marion and Mark Twain were made by the Fredonia Watch Co. (1883 - 1885) Peoria Watch Co. opened Dec. 19, 1885, and made one model of railroad watches in about 1887.

Peoria watches were 18S, quick train, 15 jewel, and all stem wind. These watches are hard to find, as only about 3,000 were made. Peoria also made railroad watches for A. C. Smith's Non-Magnetic Watch Co. of America, from 1884-1888. The 18 Size watches were full plate, adjusted, and had a whiplash regulator.

The Peoria Watch Co. closed in 1889, having produced about 47,000 watches.

Peoria Watch Co., 18 size, 15 jewels, nickel damaskeening plates, hunting, note patented regulator, serial number 11,532.

⏰ Watches listed in this book are priced at the **collectable fair market value** at the RETAIL level, as complete watches having an original 14k gold filled case, KEY WIND with silver, an original white enamel single sunk dial, and with the entire original movement in good working order with no repairs needed, unless otherwise noted.

Grade or Name – Description	Avg	Ex-Fn	Mint
18S, 9-11J, SW, OF	$200	$250	$300
18S, 15J, SW, personalized name	225	275	325
18S, Peoria W. Co., 15J, SW, OF	225	275	325
18S, Peoria W. Co., 15J, SW, HC	250	275	350
18S, Peoria W. Co., 15J, SW, low S#	375	425	500
18S, Anti-Magnetic, 15J, OF	300	325	365
18S, Anti-Magnetic, 15J, HC	350	375	425
18S, Anti-Magnetic, 15J, Made for Railway Service, OF	350	400	450
18S, Anti-Magnetic, 15J, Made for Railway Servic, HC	375	435	500
18S, Superior Quality Anti-Magnetic, 15J, NI, SW, GJS, Adj.5P, OF	425	525	625
18S, Superior Quality Anti-Magnetic, 15J, NI, SW, GJS, Adj.5P, HC ★★	525	625	725
18S, Made for Railway Service, 15J, NI, GJS, Adj.5P, OF	325	350	400
18S, Made for Railway Service, 15J, NI, GJS, Adj.5P, HC	350	385	465

PHILADELPHIA WATCH CO.

Philadelphia, Pennsylvania

1874 - 1886

Eugene Paulus organized the Philadelphia Watch Co. about 1874. Most all the parts were made in Switzerland, and finished and cased in this country. The International Watch Co. is believed to have manufactured the movements for Philadelphia Watch Co. Estimated total production of the company is 12,000 watches.

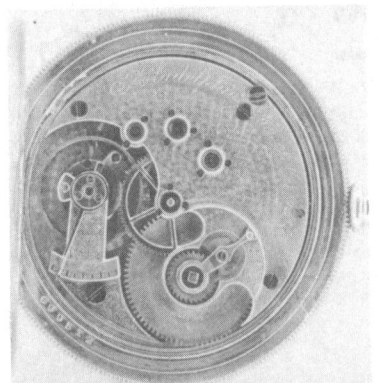

Philadelphia Watch Co., 16 size, 15 jewels, gold jewel settings, hunting case model. "Paulus Patents 1868. Aug. 25th, Nov. 3rd" on movement, serial number 5,751.

Grade or Name – Description		Avg	Ex-Fn	Mint
18S, 15J, SW, HC	★	$350	$450	$575
18S, 15J, KW, KS	★	275	375	500
18S, 15J, SW, OF	★	325	425	525
18S, HC, KW, KS, **18K** original case marked Philadelphia Watch Co.	★★	1,200	1,400	1,800
18S, 11J, KW, KS	★	150	175	225
16S, 15J, KW, KS	★	150	175	225
16S, 19J, KW, KS, GJS	★	375	475	600
8S-6S, 11J, HC	★	150	175	225
8S-6S, 15J, HC	★	150	175	225
8S-6S, Paulus, 19J, KW, KS	★	225	300	400
000/S, 7J, HC, PS	★	125	200	300

JAMES & HENRY PITKIN

Hartford, Connecticut
New York, New York
1838 - 1852

Henry Pitkin was the first to attempt to manufacture watches by machinery. The machines were of Pitkin's own design and very crude, but he had some brilliant ideas. His first four workers were paid $30 a year plus their board. After much hardship, the first watches were produced in the fall of 1838. The watches had going barrels, not the fusee and chain, and the American flag was engraved on the plates to denote they were American made and to exemplify the true spirit of American independence in watchmaking.

The first 50 watches were stamped with the name "Henry Pitkin." Others bore the firm name "H. & J. F. Pitkin." The movements were about 16S and 3/4 plate. The plates were rolled brass and stamped out with dies. The pinions were lantern style with eight leaves. The movement had a slow train of 14,400 beats per hour. Pitkin's first plan was to make the ends of the pinions conical and let them run in the ends of hardened steel screws, similar to the Marine clock balances. A large brass setting was put in the plates and extended above the surface. Three screws, with small jewels set in their ends, were inserted so that they closed about the pivot with very small end shake. This proved to be too expensive and was used in only a few movements. Next, he tried to make standard type movements extend above the plates with the end shake controlled by means of a screw running down into the end of the pivots, reducing friction. This "capped jewel train" was used for a while before he adopted the standard ways of jeweling. The escape wheels were the star type, English style. The balance was made of gold and steel. These movements were fire gilded and not interchangeable. The dials, hands, mainsprings and hairsprings were imported. The rounded pallets were manufactured by Pitkin, and the cases for his watches were made on the premises. As many as 900 watches could have been made by Pitkin.

Grade or Name – Description		Avg	Ex-Fn	Mint
Henry Pitkin S#1-50 .... ★ ★ ★ ★ ★		$15,000	$20,000	$25,000
H. & J. F. Pitkin, S#50-377 .... ★ ★ ★ ★		10,000	15,000	20,000
Pitkin & Co., New York, S#378-900 .... ★ ★ ★		4,500	6,000	7,500
W. Pitkin, Hartford, Conn., S# approx. 40,000, fusee lever, KW, Coin .... ★ ★		600	700	800

H. & J. F. Pitkin, about 16 size, engraved on movement
"H. & J. F. PITKIN DETACHED LEVER", key wind & set.

Movements marked with New York are English made imports.

ALBERT H. POTTER WATCH CO.

New York, New York
1855 - 1875

Albert Potter started his apprenticeship in 1852. When this was completed he moved to New York to take up watchmaking on his own. He made about 35 watches in all that sold for $225 to $350. Some were chronometers, some were lever escapements, key wind, gilded movements, some were fusee driven, both bridge and 3/4 plate. Potter was a contemporary of Charles Fasoldt and John Mulford, both horological inventors from Albany, N. Y. Potter moved to Cuba in 1861 but returned to New York in 1868. In 1872 he worked in Chicago and formed the Potter Brothers Company with his brother William. He moved to Geneva about 1876. His company produced a total of about 600 watches, but only about 40 of those were made in the U. S.

Grade or Name – Description		Avg	Ex-Fn	Mint
18S, 29J, 18K HC, 1 min. repeater, Geneva	★ ★ ★	$8,500	$10,000	$13,000
18S, BRG lever, Chronometer, signed A. H. Potter, New York, 18K Potter case, U.S. mfg.	★ ★ ★ ★ ★	10,000	12,000	16,000
18S, BRG lever with wind indicator, 18K Potter case	★ ★ ★	6,500	8,500	9,500
18S-20S, Tourbillion, signed A. H. Potter, Boston, gilded, 18K Potter case, U.S. mfg.	★ ★ ★ ★	15,000	17,000	20,000
16S-18S, 22J, helical spring, detent chronometer escapement, Geneva, 18K		4,000	5,000	6,500
4S, 21J, hour repeater, Geneva, 18K Potter HC		3,000	3,500	4,500

Albert H. Potter, 18 size, 22 jewels, pat. Oct. 11, 1875 & June 4, 1876, helical hairspring, detent escapement, made in **GENEVA**, serial number 14.

A.H. Potter Watch Co., BOSTON, 18 size, about 6 jewels, detent escapement, note similarity to E.H. Howard & Co. early watches, serial number 5.

GEORGE P. REED
Boston, Massachusetts 1865 - 1885

In 1854, George P. Reed entered the employment of Dennison, Howard and Davis, in Roxbury, Mass., and moved with the company to Waltham, Mass. Here he was placed in charge of the pinion finishing room. While there he invented and received a patent for the mainspring barrel and maintiming power combination. This patent was dated February 18, 1857. Reed returned to Roxbury with Howard who purchased his patented barrel. He stayed with the Howard factory as foreman and adjuster until 1865, when he left for Boston to start his own account.

He obtained a patent on April 7, 1868, for an improved chronometer escapement which featured simplified construction. He made about 100 chronometers with his improved escapement, to which he added a stem-wind device. His company turned out about 100 watches the first three years. Most, if not all, of his watches run for two days and have up and down indicators on the dial. They are both 18S and 16S, 3/4 plate, nickel, and are artistically designed. Reed experimented with various combinations of lever and chronometer escapements. One was a watch he made in 1862 and called the "Monitor." In all, Reed made a total of about 350 watches, and these are valuable to collectors.

Grade or Name – Description		Avg	Ex-Fn	Mint
18S, 15J, LS, OF or HC, Wind Indicator, chronometer escapement, 18K case	★★★★	$10,000	$12,000	$15,000
16S, 15J, LS, OF or HC, not chronometer, 18K case	★★★	7,500	8,000	10,000
16S, 15J, LS, OF, 31 day calendar, 18K case	★★★	7,500	8,000	10,000
16S, 15-17J, Wind Indicator, "Monitor", 14K, OF	★★	6,500	7,000	9,000

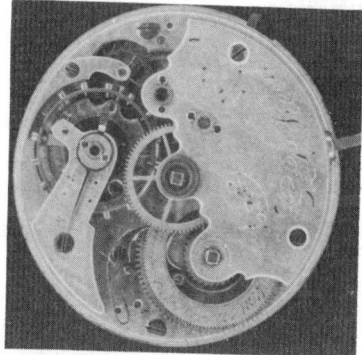

George P. Reed, 18 size, 15 jewels, key & stem wind, key & lever set, lever escapement, 48 hour up and down wind indicator, serial number 262.

George P. Reed, 18 size, 15 jewels, key & stem wind, key & lever set, lever escapement, 48 hour up and down wind indicator, serial number 5.

George P. Reed Boston, 18-16 size, 15 jewels, key wind, with key & lever set, lever escapement, serial # 282.

George P. Reed Boston, Monitor, 18-16 size, 15 jewels, wind indicator, serial # 322.

ROCKFORD WATCH CO.

Rockford, Illinois
1873 - 1915

The Rockford Watch Company's equipment was bought from the Cornell Watch Co., and two of Cornell's employees, C. W. Parker and P. H. Wheeler, went to work for Rockford. The factory was located 93 miles from Chicago on the Rock River. The first watch was placed on the market on May 1, 1876. They were key wind, 18S, full plate expansion balance & dials made by outside contract. By 1877 the company was making 3/4 plate nickel movements that fit standard size cases. Three railroads came through Rockford, and the company always advertised to the railroad and the demand was very popular with them. The company had some problems in 1896, and the name changed to Rockford Watch Co. Ltd. It closed in 1915.

ROCKFORD ESTIMATED SERIAL NUMBERS AND PRODUCTION DATES

DATE–SERIAL #	DATE–SERIAL #	DATE–SERIAL #	DATE–SERIAL #
1874 – 22,200	1884 – 226,000	1895 – 450,000	1906 – 670,000
1875 – 42,600	1885 – 247,000	1896 – 470,000	1907 – 690,000
1876 – 63,000	1886 – 267,000	1897 – 490,000	1908 – 734,000
1877 – 83,000	1887 – 287,500	1898 – 510,000	1909 – 790,000
1878 – 103,000	1888 – 308,000	1899 – 530,000	1910 – 824,000
1879 – 124,000	1889 – 328,500	1900 – 550,000	1911 – 880,000
1880 – 144,000	1890 – 349,000	1901 – 570,000	1912 – 936,000
1881 – 165,000	1891 – 369,500	1902 – 590,000	1913 – 958,000
1882 – 185,000	1892 – 390,000	1903 – 610,000	1914 – 980,000
1883 – 206,000	1893 – 410,000	1904 – 630,000	1915-1,000,000
	1894 – 430,000	1905 – 650,000	

The above list is provided for determining the APPROXIMATE age of your watch. Match serial number with date. Watches were not necessarily sold in the exact order of manufactured date.

ROCKFORD
18 SIZE

Grade or Name – Description	Avg	Ex-Fn	Mint
Belmont USA, 21J, LS, OF, NI, M#7	$275	$325	$400
Chronometer, 17J, ADJ, OF, G925	300	375	500
Dome Model, 9J, brass plates ★	175	200	250

Rockfork Watch Co., Enamel **Railroad** double sunk dial, with two hour hands for a second time zone the hour hand at 2 O'clock is **BLUE**, the hour hand at 3 O'clock is **RED**.

Watches listed in this book are priced at the collectable retail level, as **complete** watches having an original 14k gold-filled case and *Key Wind* with silver, an original white enamel single sunk dial, and with the entire original movement in good working order with no repairs needed.

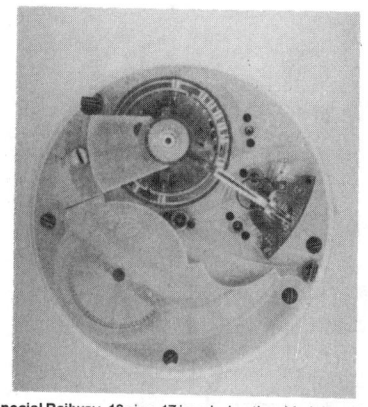

Rockford Watch Co., 18 size, 11 jewels, hunting, Model number 3, exposed escapement, serial number 190,564.

Special Railway, 18 size, 17 jewels, hunting, Model number 8, serial number 344,551.

Grade or Name – Description	Avg	Ex-Fn	Mint
King Edward, 21J, **Plymouth W. Co.**, 14K HC	$850	$950	$1,100
King Edward, 21J, **(Sears)**, Plymouth W. Co. GJS, ADJ, NI, OF.	375	500	550
King Edward, 21J, **(Sears)**, Plymouth W. Co.GJS, ADJ, NI, HC .	425	600	700
Paxton's, 21J, **(Special on dial)**, OF	350	400	450
Pennsylvania Special, 25J, LS, Adj.6P, tu-tone, OF .... ★★★	3,000	4,000	6,000
Railway King, 21J, OF	575	675	800
The Ramsey Watch, 11J, NI, KW or SW	125	150	175
The Ramsey Watch, 15J, NI, KW or SW	125	150	175
The Ramsey Watch, M#7, 21J, OF, NI, ADJ	425	500	575

🕐 Generic, nameless or **unmarked** grades for watch movements are listed under the Company name or initials of the Company, etc. by size, jewel count and description.

Rockford Early KW-KS, M#1-2, with low Serial #s			
less than 500...★	$600	$700	$850
Rockford Early KW-KS, M#1-2, with low Serial #s			
from 500-1,000 ....★	400	500	600
Rockford Early KW-KS, M#1-2, with **reversible case**	300	400	500
Rockford Early,**19J,** KW-KS, M#1-2, S# less than 100 .... ★★	1,000	1,400	2,000
Rockford, 7-9J, SW, FULL, OF...	95	125	150
Rockford, 7J, KW, FULL, OF..	95	125	150
Rockford, 7J, KW, FULL, Silveroid...................................	95	125	150
Rockford, 9J, SW, FULL, HC..	125	150	200
Rockford, M#1, 9J, KW, FULL, HC	175	200	250
Rockford, 11J, SW, FULL, OF	100	125	175
Rockford, 11-13J, M#6, exposed escape wheel, FULL, HC...........	200	250	325
Rockford, M#1-2, 11J, KW, FULL......................................	175	200	250
Rockford, M#1-2, 11J, transition case, FULL	125	150	200
Rockford, 11J, KW, Coin HC	175	200	250
Rockford, 9J, KW, M#5, 3/4 Plate, HC Coin ....★	250	325	475
Rockford, 11J, KW, M#5, 3/4 Plate, HC Coin ....★	275	350	525
Rockford, 15J, KW, M#5, 3/4 Plate, HC Coin ....★	300	375	575
Rockford, 13J, HC...	125	150	200
Rockford, 15J, SW, FULL	100	125	175
Rockford, 15J, KW, FULL, **multi-color dial**.......................	300	375	450
Rockford, 15J, SW, 2-Tone movement..................................	125	150	200

NOTE: For hunting cased models add $25 to $50.

🕐   Watches listed in this book are priced at the collectable retail level, as **complete** watches having an original 14k gold-filled case and *Key Wind* with silver, an original white enamel single sunk dial, and with the entire original movement in good working order with no repairs needed.

Rockford movement, 18 size, 7 jewels, model 5, hunting, lever set, three-quarter plate.

Grade 900, 18 size, 24J., Adj5p. Warning: 24J. fakes have been made from 21J movements. The fakes are missing the eliptical jewel setting on the barrel bridge.

Grade or Name – Description	Avg	Ex-Fn	Mint
Rockford, 15J, KW, FULL, marked- **ADJ**	$185	$225	$250
Rockford, 15J, KW/SW	125	175	225
Rockford, 15J, KW/SW, Silveroid	125	150	195
Rockford, 15J, M#6, exposed escapement wheel, FULL, HC, LS, nickel mvt.	285	310	365
Rockford, 15J, M#6, exposed escapement wheel, FULL, HC, LS, gilded mvt.	185	210	265
Rockford, 15J, M#6, exposed wheel, nickel mvt., Coin	175	200	250
Rockford, M#1, 15J, KW, FULL	125	150	185
Rockford, 16J, GJS, NI, DMK, SW	125	150	185
Rockford, 16J, GJS, NI, DMK, SW, Silveroid	125	150	185
Rockford, 16J, GJS, NI, DMK, SW, Coin	125	150	185
Rockford, 17J, NI, DMK, SW, OF	125	150	185
Rockford, 17J, GJS, NI, DMK, SW, Adj.5P	150	165	200
Rockford, 17J, GJS, NI, SW, 2-Tone, OF	165	175	225
Rockford, M#1-2, 19J, KW, **gilt,** ADJ, HC ★★	1,700	1,900	2,200
Rockford, M#1-2, 19J, KW, **nickel,** GJS, ADJ, HC ★★★★	2,400	2,600	3,000
Rockford, 21J, SW, Silveroid	250	275	325
Rockford, 21J, GJS, OF, Adj.5P, **wind indicator** ★★	2,500	3,000	3,500
Rockford, 21J, SW, DMK, ADJ, HC	400	470	500
Rockford, 21J, NI, DMK, ADJ, OF	325	375	425
Rockford, 21J, GJS, NI, DMK, Adj.5P, marked "RG" OF	325	375	425
Rockford,(**"22J", marked,)** GJS, NI, **Adj.5P, 2 tone, HC** . ★★	1,400	1,600	1,800
Rockford, 24J, GJS, SW, LS, Adj.5P, G# 900 or G# 918 marked "RG," OF	1,200	1,400	1,700
Rockford, 24J, GJS, SW, LS, Adj.5P, G# 800 marked "RG," HC ★	1,400	1,750	1,950
Rockford, 25J, GJS, SW, LS, Adj.5P, NI, DMK ★★	3,500	5,000	6,500
Rockford, 26J, GJS, SW, LS, Adj.5P, NI, DMK ★★★	8,000	10,000	16,000

🕐 Generic, nameless or **unmarked** grades for watch movements are listed under the Company name or initials of the Company, etc. by size, jewel count and description.

R.W. Co., 7-9-11J, NI or Gilded	$75	$85	$100
R.W. Co., 15J, NI or Gilded, OF	100	125	150
R.W. Co., 15J, NI or Gilded, HC	125	150	175
R.W. Co., 16-17J, Adj, NI, OF	125	150	175
R.W. Co., 16-17J, Adj, NI, HC	150	175	200
R.W. Co., 21J, Adj, NI, SW, OF	200	250	300
R.W. Co., 21J, Adj, NI, SW, HC	200	250	300
R.W. Co., **22J,** Adj, NI, SW, "RG," OF	475	575	675

Rockford Watch Co., 18 size, 15 jewels, model # 5, 3/4 plate, key & stem wind.

Rockford Watch Co., 18 size, 15 jewels, model 4, open face, lever set, serial number 227,430.

Grade or Name – Description	Avg	Ex-Fn	Mint
Railway Special, 17J, ADJ, 2-tone, SW, HC	$425	$525	$675
The Syndicate Watch Co., M#7, 15J, LS, NI, HC	175	225	300
Winnebago, 17J, LS, GJS, Adj.5P, DR, NI, DMK, HC	175	200	250
Winnebago, 17J, LS, GJS, Adj.5P, DR, NI, DMK, OF	125	150	200
24 Hour Dial, 15J, SW or KW	175	200	250
40, 15J, M#3, HC ★★	275	325	400
43, 15J, M#3, HC, 2-Tone	125	150	200
66, 11J, M#7, OF	100	125	175
66, 11J, M#7, OF, Silveroid	95	100	150
66, 11J, M#7, HC	100	125	175
72, 15J, KW-SW, exposed escapement, HC ★	600	700	850
81, 9J, M#3, HC, Gilt	125	150	200
82, Special, 21J, SW ★★	425	525	650
83, 15J, M#8, HC, 2-Tone	150	175	225
86, 15J, M#7, OF, NI	95	125	150
93, 9J, M#8, HC, Gilt	100	125	175
94, 9J, M#7, OF	75	125	150
200-205, 17J, M#9, OF, NI, LS	100	150	175
800, 24J, GJS, DR, Adj.5P, DMK, HC ★	1,200	1,400	1,600
805, 21J, GJS, Adj.5P, NI, DMK, HC, marked "RG"	350	400	500
810, 21J, NI, DMK, ADJ, HC	335	385	450
820, 17J, HC, SW ★★	300	350	425
825, 17J, HC, FULL	150	175	225
830, 17J, HC, FULL	125	150	200
835, 17J, HC, FULL	125	150	200
835, 17J, HC, FULL, Silveroid	100	125	175
845, 21J, HC, GJS, FULL ★	425	500	575
870, 7J, HC, FULL	85	110	150

IMPORTANT NOTE: Railroad Standards, Railroad Approved & Railroad Grade **terminology,** as defined and used in this **_BOOK_**.
1. **RAILROAD STANDARDS** = A commission or board appointed by the railroad companies outlined a set of **guidelines** to be accepted or approved by each railroad line.
2. **RAILROAD APPROVED** = A LIST of watches each railroad line would approve if purchased by their employee's. (this list changed through the years).
3. **RAILROAD GRADE** = A watch made by manufactures to met or exceed the guidelines set by the railroad **standards**. Grade such as 992, Vanguard and B.W. Raymond etc.
☉ Some GRADES **exceeded** the R.R. standards such as 23 jewels, diamond end stone, gold train, raised gold jewel settings, double sunk dial and the list goes on. Examples: such as Veritas, Sangamo, 950 & Riverside Maximus and many others.

Grade or Name – Description	Avg.	Ex-Fn	Mint
890, 24J, GJS, DR, Adj.5P, **HC**, NI, DMK .... ★★	$1,500	$1,700	$1,950
900, 24J, GJS, DR, Adj.5P, OF, NI, DMK .... ★★	1,400	1,550	1,800
900, 24J, GJS, DR, Adj.5P, 14K, OF case .... ★★	2,000	2,400	3,000
905, 21J, GJS, DR, Adj.5P, OF, NI, DMK	325	375	425
910, 21J, NI, DMK, ADJ, OF	175	200	275
912, 21J, Adj. 5P, LS, OF... ★★	475	600	750
915, 17J, M#9, OF, SW .... ★★★	450	500	625
918, 24J, GJS, DR, Adj.5P, OF, NI, DMK .... ★★	1,400	1,600	1,850
918, 21J, OF, NI, GJS, Adj.5P, DR	300	350	400
918, 21J, OF, NI, GJS, Adj.5P, DR, Coin................................	275	325	375
920 & 930 , 17J, OF..	175	225	275
925 & 935, 17J, OF...	100	135	150
945, 21J, M#9, OF, SW	225	275	325
950, 21J, OF, NI, GJS, Adj.5P, DR, **Wind Indicator** .... ★★	2,500	3,000	4,000
970, 7J, OF...	70	90	125
970, 7J, OF, Silveroid	70	85	100

16 SIZE

Grade or Name – Description	Avg	Ex-Fn	Mint
Commodore Perry, 21J, OF, GJS, GT, marked "RG" ....★	$300	$350	$425
Commodore Perry, 15-17J, ADJ	125	150	175
Cosmos, 17J, OF, GJS, LS, DMK, marked dial & mvt.	250	325	425
Cosmos, 17J, **HC**, GJS, LS, DMK, marked dial & mvt.	300	350	475
Doll Watch Co., 17J, marked dial & mvt. ....★	250	325	425
Doll Watch Co., 21J, marked dial & mvt. ....★	325	425	575
Doll Watch Co., 23J, marked dial & mvt. .... ★★★	1,000	1,200	1,500
Dome Model, 15J..	75	100	125
Dome Model, 17J..	75	100	125
Dome Model, 17J, 2-tone, HC..	225	275	350
Herald Square, 7J, 3/4, OF	100	125	150
Iroquois, 17J, DR, **14K, HC**..	550	585	675
Iroquois, 17J, DR, OF..	175	200	250
Peerless, 17J, OF, NI, LS, DMK	100	125	150
Pocahontas, 17-21J, GJS, Adj.5P, DR ....★	250	275	400
Prince of Wales (Sears), 21J, Plymouth W. Co........................	325	375	425
Prince of Wales (Sears), 21J, Plymouth W. Co.**14K**.....................	625	685	750

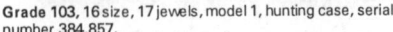

Grade 103, 16 size, 17 jewels, model 1, hunting case, serial number 384,857.

Cosmos movement, 16 size, 17 jewels, open face, gold jewel settings, grade 565, model 2.

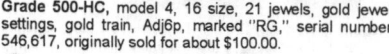

Grade 500-HC, model 4, 16 size, 21 jewels, gold jewel settings, gold train, Adj6p, marked "RG," serial number 546,617, originally sold for about $100.00.

Grade 505-OF, model 5, 16 size, 21 jewels, gold jewel settings, gold train, Adj6p, marked "RG," serial number 593,929, originally sold for about $100.00.

🕐 Generic, **nameless** or **unmarked** grades for watch movements are listed under the Company name or initials of the Company, etc. by size, jewel count and description.

Grade or Name – Description	Avg	Ex-Fn	Mint
Rockford, 7J, 3/4, HC	$125	$150	$200
Rockford, 9J, 3/4, SW, OF	75	100	135
Rockford, 9J, SW, Silveroid	75	100	135
Rockford, 9J, SW, HC	125	150	200
Rockford, 11J, SW, Silveroid	75	100	135
Rockford, 11J, 3/4, HC	125	150	200
Rockford, 15J, 3/4, ADJ, OF	100	125	150
Rockford, 15J, 3/4, ADJ, Silveroid	85	100	125
Rockford, 15J, 3/4, ADJ, HC	125	150	200
Rockford, 16J, 3/4, SW, Silveroid	85	100	125
Rockford, 16J, 3/4, ADJ, NI, DMK	100	125	150
Rockford, 17J, 3/4	100	125	150
Rockford, 17J, 3/4, 2-Tone, marked "RG"	150	175	225
Rockford, 17J, BRG, Adj.3P, DR	125	150	200
Rockford, 17J, GJS, Adj.5P, DR, **Wind Indicator**	825	895	1,000
Rockford, 17J, BRG, Silveroid	90	110	150
Rockford, 17J, 3/4, Silveroid	85	100	135
Rockford, 21J, 3/4, SW, Silveroid	225	250	300
Rockford, 21J, BRG, SW, Silveroid	225	250	300
Rockford, 21J, 3/4, GJS, Adj.5P	275	300	350
Rockford, 21J, BRG, GJS, Adj.5P, GT, DR	300	325	400
Rockford, 21J, GJS, Adj.5P, DR, **Wind Indicator**	1,000	1,100	1,250
Winnebago, 17J, BRG, GJS, Adj.5P, NI, OF	200	250	300
Winnebago, 17J, BRG, GJS, Adj.5P, NI, HC	225	275	325
Winnebago, 21J, BRG, GJS, Adj.5P, NI ⋯⋯⋯⋯★	400	450	525
100, 16J, M#1, HC, 3/4, 2-Tone	225	275	325
100S, 21J, Special, HC, 3/4, LS	300	375	400
102, 15J, HC, M#1	150	175	225
103, 15-17J, HC, M#1 ⋯⋯⋯⋯★★	275	325	400
104, 11J, HC, M#1	75	100	135
110, 17J, 2 tone dome style mvt.,HC	325	350	425
115-125, 17J, Special, HC ⋯⋯⋯★★★	525	625	775
120-130, 17J, HC ⋯⋯⋯★★★	425	525	675

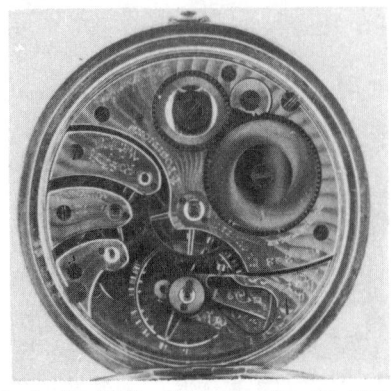

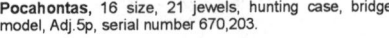

Pocahontas, 16 size, 21 jewels, hunting case, bridge model, Adj.5p, serial number 670,203.

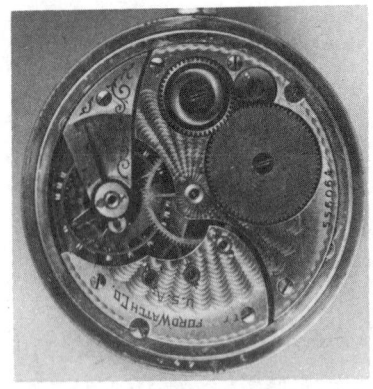

Rockford movement, 16 size, 17 jewels, 3/4 plate, open face, grade 575, model 2, serial number 556,064.

Grade or Name – Description	Avg	Ex-Fn	Mint
400 & 405, 17J, NI, Adj.5P, GJS, DR, BRG	$125	$150	$200
445, 19J, HC, GJS, BRG ★★	850	1,000	1,200
500, 21J, BRG, NI, GJS, Adj.5P, GT, HC ★★	500	550	625
501, 21J, GJS, HC ★★★	900	1,100	1,250
505, 21J, BRG, NI, GJS, Adj.5P, GT, OF ★★	425	525	675
510, 21J, BRG, NI, GJS, Adj.5P, GT, HC ★	400	475	575
515 & 525, 21J, OF, 3/4	225	275	300
520, 21J, HC, 3/4	300	375	425
520, 21J, BRG, NI, GJS, Adj.5P, HC	425	475	550
525, 21J. M#5, GT, Adj.5P ★	300	375	425
530, 21J, HC, GJS, Adj.5P, marked "RG" ★	325	375	450
535, 21J, OF, 3/4 ★	250	300	375
537, 21J, OF, GJS, Adj.5P ★★	525	600	775
545, 21J,GT,BRG, Adj.5P, OF	275	325	375
561, 17J, BRG	150	175	225
566, 17J, BRG	150	175	225
572, 17J, BRG, NI, GJS, Adj.5P	150	175	225
573, 17J, BRG, NI	150	175	225
578-579, 17J, PS, GJS ★★	300	350	475
584 & 585, 15J, 3/4 NI	85	100	125
620-625, 21J, HC, 3/4 ★	325	425	550
655, 21J, OF, **Wind Indicator,** marked 655 ★	875	925	1,000

🕐 Watches listed in this book are priced at the collectable retail level, as **complete** watches having an original 14k gold-filled case and *Key Wind* with silver, an original white enamel single sunk dial, and with the entire original movement in good working order with no repairs needed.

🕐 This book endeavours to be a GUIDE or helpful manual and offers a wealth of material to be used as a tool not as a absolute document. Price Guides are like watches the worst may be better than none at all, but at best cannot be expected to be 100% accurate

Rockford Watch Co., 12 size, 15 jewels, model 1, hunting, pendant set.

Rockford Watch Co., 12 size, 15 jewels, model 2, open face, pendant set.

12 SIZE
All 3/4 Bridge

Grade or Name – Description	Avg	Ex-Fn	Mint
Commodore Perry, 15-17J, ADJ.	$65	$80	$100
Doll Watch Co., 21J, marked on dial & movement, OF ★	325	375	450
Iroquois, 17J, BRG, DR, ADJ	75	100	125
Pocahontas, 21J, GJS, Adj.5P, BRG, DR	175	200	225
Rockford, 15J, BRG	60	70	100
Rockford, 17J, BRG, NI, DR, ADJ	60	70	100
Rockford, 21J, BRG, NI, DR, ADJ	125	150	175
Rockford, 21J, BRG, NI, DR, ADJ, Silveroid	100	125	150
Winona, 15J, BRG	60	70	100
300, 23J, 3/4, GJS, Adj.5P, HC ★★★	325	375	450
305, 23J, BRG, NI, GJS, Adj.5P, GT, OF ★★★	325	375	450
310(HC)-315(OF), 21J, BRG, NI, GJS, Adj.5P	100	125	175
320(HC)-325(OF), 17J, BRG, NI, ADJ, DR	60	70	100
330, 17J, BRG, NI, DR, OF	60	70	100
335, 17J, BRG, NI, DR, HC	70	100	125
340(HC)-345(OF), 21J, M#1 ★	225	250	325
350, 17J, OF	60	70	100
355, 17J, HC	70	100	125

Note: Add $10 to $25 to above watches with hunting case.

8 SIZE

Grade or Name – Description	Avg	Ex-Fn	Mint
15J, 3/4, HC, LS, 14K, 40 DWT	$385	$425	$485
9–15J, 3/4, KW or SW, LS, OF or HC,	125	150	200

Rockford movement, 6 size, 17 jewels, quick train, straight line escapement, compensating balance, adjusted to temperature, micrometric regulator, three-quarter damaskeened plates.

6 SIZE

Grade or Name – Description	Avg	Ex-Fn	Mint
9J, NI, HC	$90	$125	$150
15J, 3/4, NI	80	100	125
16J, 3/4, NI	80	100	125
17J, 3/4, ADJ, NI	100	125	150

0 SIZE

Grade or Name – Description	Avg	Ex-Fn	Mint
Iroquois, 17J., HC	$225	$250	$300
Plymouth Watch Co., 15-17J, HC	225	250	300
7J, BRG, NI, DR, HC	125	140	175
11J, BRG, NI, DR, HC	125	140	175
15J, BRG, NI, DR, HC	150	175	200
17J, BRG, NI, DR, HC	175	200	250
17J, BRG, NI, DR, marked Rockford, HC ★	325	350	375

🕐 Watches listed in this book are priced at the collectable retail level, as **complete** watches having an original 14k gold-filled case and *Key Wind* with silver, an original white enamel single sunk dial, and with the entire original movement in good working order with no repairs needed.

🕐 This book endeavours to be a GUIDE or helpful manual and offers a wealth of material to be used as a tool not as a absolute document. Price Guides are like watches the worst may be better than none at all, but at best cannot be expected to be 100% accurate.

🕐 Characteristics of watches differ for the same age of both case and movement, because these features vary it may not be accurate to date a watch by one single influence. Example: the second hand was not commonly found on watches before 1750, but common about 1800. The first second hand appeared in 1665 and another in 1690. Therefore statements are broad rather than accurate.

ROCKFORD WATCH CO.
IDENTIFICATION OF MOVEMENTS
BY MODEL NUMBER

How to Identify Your Watch: Compare the movement of your watch with the illustrations in this section. Upon matching the movement exactly, the model number and size can be determined. While comparing, note the location of the balance, jewels, screws, gears, and type of back plate (Full, 3/4, Bridge) which will be clues in identifying the movement you have. Having determined the size and model number, you can now find your watch in the main price listing by name or number (which is engraved on the movement).

The Rockford Watch Company, Ltd.

NUMBER AND GRADE

WITH

DESCRIPTION OF MOVEMENTS MANUFACTURED TO DATE

Number and Grade of Movement	GRADE	Size	Style (case)	Style (plate)	Style (finish)	Jewels	Wind	Sett	Model
1 to 114,000		18	Htg.	F. Pl.			Key	Key	1
114,001 " 115,000		"	"	¾ Pl.			Stem	Lever	5
115,001 " 126,000		"	"	F. Pl.			"	"	2
126,001 " 127,000		"	"	¾ Pl.			"	"	5
127,001 " 130,000		"	"	F. Pl.			"	"	2
130,001 " 131,000		"	"	¾ Pl.			"	"	5
131,001 " 133,000		"	"	F. Pl.			"	"	3
133,001 " 134,000		"	"	¾ Pl.			"	"	5
134,001 " 138,000		"	"	F. Pl.			"	"	3
138,001 " 139,000		"	"	¾ Pl.			"	"	5
139,001 " 143,000		"	"	F. Pl.			"	"	3
143,001 " 144,000		"	"	¾ Pl.			"	"	5
144,001 " 145,000		"	"	F. Pl.			"	"	3
145,001 " 146,000		"	"	¾ Pl.			"	"	5
146,001 " 149,000		"	"	F. Pl.			"	"	3
149,001 " 151,000		"	"	¾ Pl.			"	"	5
151,001 " 153,000		"	"	F. Pl.			"	"	3
153,001 " 154,000		"	"	¾ Pl.			"	"	5
154,001 " 158,000		"	"	F. Pl.			"	"	3
158,001 " 159,000		"	'	¾ Pl.			"	"	5
159,001 " 169,000		"	"	F. Pl.			"	"	3
170,001 " 170,100		"	"	¾ Pl.			"	"	5
170,101 " 177,000		"	"	F. Pl.		15	"	"	3
177,001 " 177,800		"	"	"			"	"	6
177,901 " 189,500		"	"	"			"	"	3
189,601 " 190,900		"	"	"			"	"	6
191,001 " 191,100		"	"	"			"	"	3
191,101 " 196,400		"	O. F.	"			"	"	4
196,501 " 197,000		"	Htg.	"			"	"	6
197,101 " 197,500		"	"	"			"	"	3
197,601 " 198,000		"	"	"			"	"	6
198,101 " 199,100		"	O. F.	"			"	"	4
199,201 " 199,500		"	Htg.	"			"	"	6
199,600 " 200,000		"	"	¾ Pl.			"	"	5
200,001 " 213,100		8	"	"			"	"	1
213,101 " 218,900		6	"	"			"	"	..
219,001 " 219,500		18	"	"			"	"	5
219,501 " 224,500		"	"	F. Pl.			"	"	3
224,501 " 228,900		"	O. F.	"			"	"	4
229,001 " 232,000		"	Htg.	"			"	"	3
232,001 " 233,000		"	"	¾ Pl.			"	"	5
233,001 " 234,000	47	"	O. F.	F. Pl.	Nickel	15	"	"	4
234,001 " 235,000	45	"	"	"	"	"	"	"	..
235,001 " 236,000	43	"	Htg.	F. Pl.		"	"	"	3
236,001 " 237,000	44	"	"	"	Gilt	"	"	"	..
237,001 " 238,000	45	"	O. F.	F. Pl.	"	"	"	"	4
238,001 " 239,000		"	"	"	"	9	"	"	..
239,001 " 240,000	45	"	"	"	"	15	"	"	..
240,001 " 241,000	46	"	"	"	"	11	"	"	..
241,001 " 241,800	47	"	"	"	Nickel	15	"	"	..
241,801 " 242,000	40	"	Htg.	"	"	"	"	"	3
242,001 " 243,000	43	"	"	"	"	"	"	"	..
243,001 " 244,000	44	"	"	"	Gilt	"	"	"	..
244,001 " 244,300	49	"	"	"	Nickel	"	"	"	6
244,301 " 244,400	72	"	"	"	"	"	"	"	..
244,401 " 245,000	62	"	"	"	"	11	"	"	8
245,001 " 246,000	81	"	"	"	Gilt	9	"	"	3
246,001 " 247,000	44	"	"	"	"	15	"	"	..
247,001 " 248,000	64	"	O. F.	"	"	11	"	"	4
248,001 " 249,000	46	"	Htg.	"	"	15	"	"	6
249,001 " 250,000	49	"	"	"	Nickel	"	"	"	..
250,001 " 250,500	62	"	"	"	"	11	"	"	..
250,501 " 251,000	60	"	O. F.	"	"	"	"	"	7
251,001 " 252,000	66	"	"	"	"	"	"	"	..
252,001 " 253,000	67	"	"	"	Gilt	"	"	"	..
253,001 " 253,500	83	"	Htg.	"	Nickel	15	"	"	8
253,501 " 253,700	77	"	"	"	"	"	"	"	..
253,701 " 254,000	68	"	"	"	Gilt	11	"	"	..
254,001 " 254,600	86	"	O. F.	"	Nickel	15	"	"	7
254,601 " 254,800	76	"	"	"	"	"	"	"	..
254,801 " 255,000	78	"	"	"	Gilt	"	"	"	..
255,001 " 256,000	89	"	"	"	"	"	"	"	..
256,001 " 257,000	68	"	Htg.	"	"	11	"	"	8
257,001 " 258,000	93	"	"	"	"	9	"	"	..
258,001 " 259,000	69	"	"	"	Nickel	11	"	"	..

The Rockford Watch Company, Ltd.

Number and Grade of Movement	GRADE	Size		F. Pl.	Style	Jewels	Wind	Sett	Model
259,001 to 260,000	66	18	O. F.	F. Pl.	Nickel	11	Stem	Lever	7
260,001 " 261,000	68	"	Htg.	"	Gilt	"	"	"	8
261,001 " 262,000	86	"	O. F.	"	Nickel	15	"	"	7
262,001 " 263,000	67	"	"	"	Gilt	11	"	"	"
263,001 " 264,000	83	"	Htg.	"	Nickel	15	"	"	8
264,001 " 265,000	69	"	"	"	"	"	"	"	"
265,001 " 266,000	68	"	"	"	Gilt	11	"	"	"
266,001 " 267,000	93	"	"	"	"	9	"	"	8
267,001 " 267,800	83	"	"	"	Nickel	15	"	"	"
267,801 " 268,000	77	"	"	"	"	"	"	"	"
268,001 " 269,000	68	"	"	"	Gilt	11	"	"	7
269,001 " 270,000	67	"	O. F.	"	"	"	"	"	7
270,001 " 270,800	85	"	Htg.	"	"	15	"	"	8
270,801 " 271,000	79	"	"	"	"	"	"	"	"
271,001 " 272,000	66	"	O. F.	"	Nickel	11	"	"	7
272,001 " 272,100	77	"	Htg.	"	"	15	"	"	8
272,101 " 272,200	83	"	"	"	"	"	"	"	"
272,201 " 272,300	77	"	"	"	"	"	"	"	"
272,301 " 272,600	83	"	"	"	"	"	"	"	"
272,601 " 272,700	77	"	"	"	"	"	"	"	"
272,701 " 272,900	83	"	"	"	"	"	"	"	"
272,901 " 273,000	77	"	"	"	"	"	"	"	"
273,001 " 274,000	69	"	"	"	"	"	"	"	"
274,001 " 275,000	83	"	"	"	"	"	"	"	"
275,001 " 276,000	69	"	"	"	"	11	"	"	"
276,001 " 277,000	83	"	"	"	"	15	"	"	"
277,001 " 278,000	85	"	"	"	Gilt	"	"	"	"
278,001 " 279,000	66	"	O. F.	"	Nickel	11	"	"	7
279,001 " 279,200	76	"	"	"	"	15	"	"	"
279,201 " 280,000	86	"	"	"	"	"	"	"	"
280,001 " 281,000	66	"	"	"	"	11	"	"	"
281,001 " 282,000	85	"	Htg.	"	Gilt	15	"	"	8
282,001 " 283,000	83	"	"	"	Nickel	"	"	"	"
283,001 " 284,000	93	"	"	"	Gilt	9	"	"	"
284,001 " 285,000	89	"	O. F.	"	"	15	"	"	7
285,001 " 286,000	69	"	Htg.	"	Hickel	11	"	"	8
286,001 " 286,200	83	"	"	"	Nick.& Gilt	15	"	"	"
286,201 " 286,500	84	"	"	"	"	"	"	"	"
286,501 " 287,000	83	"	"	"	Nickel	"	"	"	"
287,001 " 288,000	66	"	O. F.	"	"	11	"	"	7
288,001 " 289,000	67	"	"	"	Gilt	"	"	"	"
289,001 " 289,500	84	"	Htg.	"	Spot Gilt	15	"	"	8
289,501 " 291,000	83	"	"	"	Nickel	"	"	"	"
291,001 " 292,000	69	"	"	"	"	11	"	"	"
292,001 " 293,000	67	"	O. F.	"	Gilt	"	"	"	7
293,001 " 294,000	85	"	Htg.	"	"	15	"	"	8
294,001 " 295,000	93	"	"	"	"	9	"	"	"
295,001 " 296,000	66	"	O. F.	"	Nickel	11	"	"	7
296,001 " 297,000	89	"	"	"	Gilt	15	"	"	"
297,001 " 298,000	69	"	Htg.	"	Nickel	11	"	"	8
298,001 " 299,000	67	"	O. F.	"	Gilt	"	"	"	7
299,001 " 300,000	93	"	Htg.	"	"	9	"	"	8
300,001 " 300,500	84	"	"	"	Nick.& Gilt	15	"	"	"
300,501 " 300,700	83	"	"	"	Nickel	"	"	"	"
300,701 " 301,000	70	"	"	"	Nick.& Gilt	16	"	"	"
301,001 " 302,000	66	"	O. F.	"	Nickel	11	"	"	7
302,001 " 303,000	93	"	Htg.	"	Gilt	9	"	"	8
303,001 " 304,000	69	"	"	"	Nickel	11	"	"	"
304,001 " 304,500	84	"	"	"	Nick.& Gilt	15	"	"	"
304,501 " 305,000	83	"	"	"	Nickel	"	"	"	"
305,001 " 305,500	84	"	"	"	Nick.&Gilt	"	"	"	"
305,501 " 306,000	83	"	"	"	Nickel	"	"	"	"
306,001 " 307,000	66	"	O. F.	"	"	11	"	"	7
307,001 " 308,000	83	"	Htg.	"	"	15	"	"	8
308,001 " 309,000	93	"	"	"	Gilt	9	"	"	"
309,001 " 310,000	83	"	"	"	Nickel	15	"	"	"
310,001 " 310,500	87	"	O. F.	"	Nick.& Gilt	"	"	"	7
310,501 " 310,700	88	"	"	"	Nickel	16	"	"	"
310,701 " 311,000	86	"	"	"	"	15	"	"	"
311,001 " 312,000	69	"	Htg.	"	"	11	"	"	8
312,001 " 313,000	93	"	"	"	Gilt	9	"	"	"
313,001 " 314,000	83	"	"	"	Nickel	15	"	"	"
314,001 " 317,000	93	"	"	"	Gilt	9	"	"	"
317,001 " 318,000	85	"	"	"	"	15	"	"	"
318,001 " 319,000	93	"	"	"	"	9	"	"	"
319,001 " 320,000	85	"	"	"	"	15	"	"	"
320,001 " 321,000	84	"	"	"	Nick.& Gilt	"	"	"	"
321,001 " 322,000	83	"	"	"	Nickel	"	"	"	"
322,001 " 323,000	84	"	"	"	Nick.& Gilt	"	"	"	"
323,001 " 325,000	83	"	"	"	Nickel	"	"	"	"
325,001 " 326,000	85	"	"	"	Gilt	"	"	"	"
326,001 " 327,000	93	"	"	"	"	9	"	"	"
327,001 " 328,000	83	"	"	"	Nickel	15	"	"	"
328,001 " 329,000	89	"	O. F.	"	Gilt	"	"	"	7
329,001 " 329,100	84	"	Htg.	"	Nick.& Gilt	"	"	"	8
329,101 " 329,200	83	"	"	"	Special	.....	"	"	"
329,201 " 329,700	84	"	"	"	Nick.& Gilt	15	"	"	"
329,701 " 330,000	70	"	"	"	"	16	"	"	"
330,001 " 330,800	87	"	O. F.	"	Nickel	15	"	"	7

The Rockford Watch Company, Ltd.

Number and Grade of Movement	GRADE	Size		Style		Jewels	Wind	Sett	Model
330,801 to 331,000	88	18	O. F.	F. Pl.	Nick.& Gilt	16	Stem	Lever	7
331,001 " 332,000	68	"	Htg.	"	Gilt	11	"	"	8
332,001 " 333,000	86	"	O. F.	"	Nickel	15	"	"	7
333,001 " 334,000	69	"	Htg.	"	"	11	"	"	8
334,001 " 335,000	66	"	O. F.	"	"	"	"	"	7
335,001 " 336,000	94	"	O. F.,	"	Gilt	9	"	"	"
336,001 " 337,000	68	"	Htg.	"	"	11	"	"	8
337,001 " 338,000	94	"	O. F.	"	"	9	"	"	7
338,001 " 338,500	88	"	"	"	Nick.& Gilt	16	"	"	"
338,501 " 339,000	86	"	"	"	Nickel	"	"	"	"
339,001 " 339,500	70	"	Htg.	"	Nick.& Gilt	"	"	"	8
339,501 " 340,000	84	"	"	"	"	15	"	"	"
340,001 " 341,000	66	"	O. F.	"	Nickel	11	"	"	7
341,001 " 342,000	85	"	Htg.	"	Gilt	15	"	"	8
342,001 " 343,000	89	"	O. F.	"	"		"	"	7
343,001 " 344,000	94	"	"	"	"	9	"	"	"
344,001 " 345,000	84	"	Htg.	"	Nick.& Gilt	15	"	"	8
345,001 " 346,000	68	"	"	"	Gilt	11	"	"	"
346,001 " 347,000	87	"	O. F.	"	Nick.& Gilt	15	"	"	7
347,001 " 348,000	94	"	"	"	Gilt	9	"	"	"
348,001 " 348,300	88	"	"	"	Nick.& Gilt	16	"	"	"
348,301 " 348,500	87	"	"	"	"	15	"	"	"
348,501 " 349,000	86	"	"	"	Nickel		"	"	"
349,001 " 349,500	67	"	"	"	Gilt	11	"	"	"
349,501 " 350,000	89	"	"	"	"	15	"	"	"
350,001 " 350,500	70	"	Htg.	"	Nick.& Gilt	16	"	"	8
350,501 " 351,000	85	"	"	"	Gilt	15	"	"	"
351,001 " 352,000	87	"	O. F.	"	Nick & Gilt		"	"	7
352,001 " 352,500	88	"	"	"	"	16	"	"	"
352,501 " 353,000	67	"	"	"	Gilt	11	"	"	"
353,001 " 353,500	100	16	Htg.	¾ Pl.	Nick.& Gilt	16	"	"	1
353,501 " 353,800	101	"	"	"	Nickel	15	"	"	"
353,801 " 354,000	102	"	"	"	"		"	"	"
354,001 " 354,500	103	"	"	"	"		"	"	"
354,501 " 355,000	104	"	"	"	"	11	"	"	"
355,001 " 355,500	111	"	"	"	"	15	"	"	"
355,501 " 356,000	112	"	"	"	Gilt		"	"	"
356,001 " 356,500	113	"	"	"	"	11	"	"	"
356,501 " 357,000	114	"	"	"	"	9	"	"	"
357,001 " 358,500	68	18	"	F. Pl.	"	11	"	"	8
358,501 " 359,000	67	"	O. F.	"	"		"	"	7
359,001 " 359,500	87	"	"	"	Nick.& Gilt	15	"	"	"
359,501 " 360,000	86	"	"	"	Nickel		"	"	"
360,001 " 360,500	101	16	Htg.	¾ Pl.	Nick.& Gilt		"	"	1
360,501 " 361,000	102	"	"	"	Nickel		"	"	"
361,001 " 361,500	103	"	"	"	"		"	"	"
361,501 " 362,000	104	"	"	"	"	11	"	"	"
362,001 " 364,000	67	18	O. F.	F. Pl.	Gilt	"	"	"	7
364,001 " 365,000	112	16	Htg.	¾ Pl.	"	15	"	"	1
365,001 " 366,000	102	"	"	"	Nickel		"	"	"
366,001 " 367,000	103	"	"	"	"		"	"	"
367,001 " 368,000	67	18	O. F.	F. Pl.	Gilt	11	"	"	7
368,001 " 368,500	112	16	Htg.	¾ Pl.	"	15	"	"	1
368,501 " 369,000	101	"	"	"	Nick.& Gilt		"	"	"
369,001 " 370,000	104	"	"	"	Nickel	11	"	"	"
370,001 " 370,500	86	18	O. F.	F. Pl.	"	15	"	"	7
370,501 " 371,000	87	"	"	"	Nick.& Gilt		"	"	"
371,001 " 371,500	89	"	"	"	Gilt		"	"	"
371,501 " 372,000	94	"	"	"	"	9	"	"	"
372,001 " 372,500	113	16	Htg.	¾ Pl.	"	11	"	"	1
372,501 " 373,000	114	"	"	"	"	9	"	"	"
373,001 " 374,000	113	"	"	"	"	11	"	"	"
374,001 " 374,500	68	18	"	F. Pl.	"		"	"	8
374,501 " 375,000	94	"	O. F.	"	"	9	"	"	7
375,001 " 376,000	87	"	"	"	Nick.& Gilt	15	"	"	"
376,001 " 376,200	100	16	Htg.	¾ Pl.	"	16	"	"	1
376,201 " 376,700	101	"	"	"	"	15	"	"	"
376,701 " 377,000	102	"	"	"	Nickel	15	"	"	"
377,001 " 377,500	104	"	"	"	"	11	"	"	"
377,501 " 378,000	103	"	"	"	"	15	"	"	"
378,001 " 379,000	94	18	O. F.	F. Pl.	Gilt	9	"	"	7
379,001 " 379,500	86	"	"	"	Nickel	15	"	"	"
379,501 " 380,000	84	"	Htg.	"	Nick.& Gilt		"	"	8
380,001 " 380,500	101	16	"	¾ Pl.	"		"	"	1
380,501 " 381,000	104	"	"	"	Nickel	11	"	"	"
381,001 " 381,300	102	"	"	"	"	15	"	"	"
381,301 " 382,000	103	"	"	"	"		"	"	"
382,001 " 382,200	111	"	"	"	Gilt		"	"	"
382,201 " 383,000	112	"	"	"	"		"	"	"
383,001 " 383,500	113	"	"	"	"	11	"	"	"
383,501 " 384,000	114	"	"	"	"	9	"	"	"
384,001 " 384,500	100	"	"	"	Nick.& Gilt	16	"	"	"
384,501 " 385,000	103	"	"	"	Nickel	15	"	"	"
385,001 " 385,500	104	"	"	"	"	11	"	"	"
385,501 " 386,000	103	"	"	"	"	15	"	"	"
386,001 " 387,000	112	"	"	"	Gilt		"	"	"
387,001 " 387,500	93	18	"	F. Pl.	"	9	"	"	8
387,501 " 388,000	68	"	"	"	"	11	"	"	"

The Rockford Watch Company, Ltd.

Number and Grade of Movement	GRADE	Size		Style	Jewels	Wind	Sett	Model
				Description of Movement				
388,001 to 388,500	94	18	O. F.	F. Pl. Gilt	9	Stem	Lever	7
388,501 " 389,000	89	"	"	" "	15	"	"	"
389,001 " 389,100	76	"	"	" Nickel	"	"	"	"
389,101 " 390,000	86	"	"	" "	"	"	"	"
390,001 " 391,000	69	"	Htg.	" "	11	"	"	8
391,001 " 391,400	162	6	"	¾ Pl. Gilt	9	"	"	2
391,401 " 391,700	161	"	"	" "	11	"	"	"
391,701 " 392,000	160	"	"	" "	15	"	"	"
392,001 " 392,300	154	"	"	" Nickel	9	"	"	"
392,301 " 392,500	153	"	"	" "	11	"	"	"
392,501 " 392,700	152	"	"	" "	15	"	"	"
392,701 " 392,900	151	"	"	" Nick.& Gilt	"	"	"	"
392,901 " 393,000	150	"	"	" "	16	"	"	"
393,001 " 393,500	154	"	"	" Nickel	9	"	"	"
393,501 " 394,000	153	"	"	" "	11	"	"	"
394,001 " 394,500	152	"	"	" "	15	"	"	"
394,501 " 394,800	151	"	"	" Nick.& Gilt	"	"	"	"
394,801 " 395,000	150	"	"	" "	16	"	"	"
395,001 " 396,000	162	"	"	" Gilt	9	"	"	"
396,001 " 396,500	161	"	"	" "	11	"	"	"
396,501 " 397,000	160	"	"	" "	15	"	"	"
397,001 " 397,800	162	"	"	" "	9	"	"	"
397,801 " 398,600	161	"	"	" "	11	"	"	"
398,601 " 399,000	160	"	"	" "	15	"	"	"
399,001 " 400,200	153	"	"	" Nickel	11	"	"	"
400,201 " 400,700	152	"	"	" "	15	"	"	"
400,701 " 401,000	152	"	"	" Nick.& Gilt	"	"	"	"
401,001 " 401,500	93	18	"	F. Pl. Gilt	9	"	"	8
401,501 " 402,000	68	"	"	" "	11	"	"	"
402,001 " 402,500	69	"	"	" Nickel	"	"	"	"
402,501 " 403,000	85	"	"	" Gilt	15	"	"	"
403,001 " 403,500	94	"	O. F.	" "	9	"	"	7
403,501 " 404,000	86	"	"	" Nickel	15	"	"	"
404,001 " 404,300	60	"	"	" Nick.& Gilt	11	"	"	"
404,301 " 405,000	66	"	"	" Nickel	17	"	"	"
405,001 " 405,500	86	"	"	" "	15	"	"	"
405,501 " 406,000	83	"	Htg.	" "	"	"	"	8
406,001 " 407,000	69	"	"	" "	11	"	"	"
407,001 " 407,500	68	"	"	" Gilt	"	"	"	"
407,501 " 408,000	85	"	"	" "	15	"	"	"
408,001 " 408,500	93	"	"	" "	9	"	"	"
408,501 " 409,000	94	"	O. F.	" "	"	"	"	7
409,001 " 410,000	69	"	Htg.	" Nickel	11	"	"	8
410,001 " 410,500	93	"	"	" Gilt	9	"	"	"
410,501 " 411,000	68	"	"	" "	11	"	"	"
411,001 " 411,500	94	"	O. F.	" "	9	"	"	7
411,501 " 412,000	67	"	"	" "	11	"	"	"
412,001 " 412,500	86	"	"	" Nickel	15	"	"	"
412,501 " 413,000	69	"	Htg.	" "	11	"	"	8
413,001 " 414,000	93	"	"	" Gilt	9	"	"	"
414,001 " 415,000	94	"	O. F.	" "	"	"	"	7
415,001 " 415,200	81	"	Htg.	" Plain	17	"	"	8
415,201 " 415,500	83	"	"	" Nickel	15	"	"	"
415,501 " 415,600	80	"	"	" Spot Gilt	17	"	"	"
415,601 " 416,000	82	"	"	" Plain	"	"	"	"
416,001 " 416,100	61	"	O. F.	"	"	"	"	7
416,101 " 416,500	86	"	"	" Nickel	15	"	"	"
416,501 " 417,000	62	"	"	" Plain	17	"	"	"
417,001 " 417,500	66	"	"	" Nickel	11	"	"	"
417,501 " 418,000	83	"	Htg.	" "	17	"	"	8
418,001 " 419,000	93	"	"	" Gilt	9	"	"	"
419,001 " 419,500	94	"	"	" "	"	"	"	"
419,501 " 420,500	153	6	"	¾ Pl. Nickel	11	"	"	2
420,501 " 421,500	161	"	"	" Gilt	"	"	"	"
421,501 " 422,500	162	"	"	" "	9	"	"	"
422,501 " 423,000	66	18	O. F.	F. Pl. Nickel	11	"	"	7
423,001 " 424,000	93	"	Htg.	" Gilt	9	"	"	8
424,001 " 425,000	69	"	"	" Nickel	11	"	"	"
425,001 " 425,500	94	"	O. F.	" Gilt	9	"	"	7
425,501 " 426,000	66	"	"	" Nickel	11	"	"	"
426,001 " 427,000	83	"	Htg.	" "	15	"	"	8
427,001 " 428,000	69	"	"	" "	11	"	"	"
428,001 " 429,000	66	"	O. F.	" "	"	"	"	7
429,001 " 430,000	83	"	Htg.	" "	15	"	"	8
430,001 " 431,000	68	"	"	" Gilt	11	"	"	"
431,001 " 431,500	66	"	O. F.	" Nickel	"	"	"	7
431,501 " 432,000	82	"	Htg.	" Plain	17	"	"	8
432,001 " 433,000	67	"	O. F.	" Gilt	11	"	"	7
433,001 " 433,100	83	"	Htg.	" Nickel	15	"	"	8
433,101 " 433,140	82a	"	"	" "	"	"	"	"
433,141 " 433,400	82	"	"	" "	"	"	"	"
433,401 " 433,500	82	"	"	" "	17	"	"	"
433,501 " 433,600	83	"	"	" "	15	"	"	"
433,601 " 433,700	82	"	"	" Plain	17	"	"	"
433,701 " 433,750	80	"	"	" Spot Gilt	"	"	"	"
433,751 " 433,800	81	"	"	" Plain	"	"	"	"
433,801 " 434,000	83	"	"	" Nickel	15	"	"	"
434,001 " 434,500	69	"	"	" "	"	"	"	"

The Rockford Watch Company, Ltd.

Number and Grade of Movement	GRADE	Size		Style	Jewels	Wind	Sett	Model
434,501 to 434,600	86	18	O. F.	F. Pl.	Nickel	15	Stem	Lever	7
434,601 " 434,700	62	"	"	"	Plain	17	"	"	"
434,701 " 435,000	86	"	O. F.	"	Nickel	15	"	"	"
435,001 " 435,500	85	"	Htg.	"	Gilt	"	"	"	8
435,501 " 436,000	94	"	O. F.	"	"	9	"	"	7
436,001 " 436,100	67	"	"	"	"	11	"	"	"
436,101 " 436,200	89	"	"	"	"	15	"	"	"
436,201 " 436,300	67	"	"	"	"	11	"	"	"
436,301 " 437,000	89	"	"	"	"	"	"	"	"
437,001 " 437,800	82	"	Htg.	"	Nickel	17	"	"	8
437,801 " 438,000	81	"	"	"	Plain	"	"	"	"
438,001 " 438,500	83	"	"	"	"	15	"	"	"
438,501 " 438,900	62	"	O. F.	"	"	17	"	"	7
438,901 " 439,000	86	"	"	"	Nickel	15	"	"	"
439,001 " 439,500	82	"	Htg.	"	"	17	"	"	8
439,501 " 439,550	80	"	"	"	Nick.& Gilt	"	"	"	"
439,551 " 439,650	82a	"	"	"	"	"	"	"	"
439,651 " 439,700	81	"	"	"	Nickel	"	"	"	"
439,701 " 439,750	62a	"	O. F.	"	"	"	"	"	7
439,751 " 439,850	62	"	"	"	"	"	"	"	"
439,851 " 439,900	61	"	"	"	"	"	"	"	"
439,901 " 439,950	86	"	"	"	"	15	"	"	"
439,951 " 440,000	62a	"	"	"	"	17	"	"	"
440,001 " 441,000	93	"	Htg.	"	Gilt	9	"	"	8
441,001 " 441,500	62	"	O. F.	"	Nickel	17	"	"	7
441,501 " 442,000	83	"	Htg.	"	Plain	15	"	"	8
442,001 " 442,050	80	"	"	"	Nick.& Gilt	17	"	"	"
424,051 " 442,150	81	"	"	"	Plain	"	"	"	"
442,151 " 442,500	82	"	"	"	Nickel	"	"	"	"
500,001 " 500,054	930	"	O. F.	"	"	"	"	"	9
500,055	935	"	"	"	"	"	"	"	"
500,056 to 500,250	930	"	"	"	"	"	"	"	"
500,251 " 500,260	920	"	"	"	"	"	"	"	7
500,261 " 500,300	930	"	"	"	"	"	"	"	9
500,301 " 500,400	935	"	"	"	"	"	"	"	"
500,401 " 500,800	830	"	Htg.	"	"	"	"	"	10
500,801 " 500,900	835	"	"	"	"	"	"	"	"
500,901 " 501,100	830	"	"	"	"	"	"	"	"
501,101 " 501,900	835	"	"	"	"	"	"	"	"
501,901 " 502,400	830	"	"	"	"	"	"	"	"
502,401 " 502,481	930	"	O. F.	"	"	"	"	"	9
502,482 " 502,489	935	"	"	"	"	"	"	"	"
502,490 " 502 592	930	"	"	"	"	"	"	"	"
502,593	935	"	"	"	"	"	"	"	"
502,594 to 502,700	930	"	"	"	"	"	"	"	"
502,701 " 503,200	935	"	"	"	"	"	"	"	"
503,201 " 503,460	830	"	Htg.	"	"	"	"	"	10
503,461 " 503,470	820	"	"	"	"	"	"	"	8
503,471 " 503,483	830	"	"	"	"	"	"	"	10
503,484 " 503,489	820	"	"	"	"	"	"	"	8
503,490 " 503,520	830	"	"	"	"	"	"	"	10
503,521 " 503,531	820	"	"	"	"	"	"	"	8
503,532 " 503,536	830	"	"	"	"	"	"	"	10
503,537 " 503,540	820	"	"	"	"	"	"	"	8
503,541 " 503,550	825	"	"	"	"	"	"	"	10
503,551 " 503,610	830	"	"	"	"	"	"	"	"
503,611 " 503,620	820	"	"	"	"	"	"	"	8
503,621 " 503,700	830	"	"	"	"	"	"	"	10
503,701 " 504,000	835	"	"	"	"	"	"	"	"
504,001 " 504,100	830	"	"	"	"	"	"	"	"
504,101 " 505,150	835	"	"	"	"	"	"	"	"
505,151 " 505,200	830	"	"	"	"	"	"	"	"
505,201 " 505,300	835	"	"	"	"	"	"	"	"
505,301 " 505,350	830	"	"	"	"	"	"	"	"
505,351 " 505,360	835	"	"	"	"	"	"	"	"
505,361 " 505,370	830	"	"	"	"	"	"	"	"
505,371 " 505,398	835	"	"	"	"	"	"	"	"
505,399 " 505,400	830	"	"	"	"	"	"	"	"
505,401 " 505,700	835	"	"	"	"	"	"	"	"
505,701 " 506,000	830	"	"	"	"	"	"	"	"
506,001 " 506,800	935	"	O. F.	"	"	"	"	"	9
506,801 " 506,810	910	"	"	"	"	21	"	"	"
506,811 " 507,600	930	"	"	"	"	17	"	"	"
507,601 " 507,900	830	"	Htg.	"	"	"	"	"	10
507,901 " 508,500	835	"	"	"	"	"	"	"	"
508,501 " 509,000	830	"	"	"	"	"	"	"	"
509,001 " 509,100	820	"	"	"	"	"	"	"	8
509,101 " 509,700	925	"	O. F.	"	"	"	"	"	9
509,701 " 509,729	920	"	"	"	"	"	"	"	7
509,730	915	"	"	"	"	"	"	"	"
509,731 to 509,759	920	"	"	"	"	"	"	"	"
509,760	915	"	"	"	"	"	"	"	"
509,761 to 509,791	920	"	"	"	"	"	"	"	"
509,792	915	"	"	"	"	"	"	"	"
509,793 to 509,900	920	"	"	"	"	"	"	"	"
509,901 " 510,200	810	"	Htg.	"	"	21	"	"	10
510,201 " 510,700	825	"	"	"	"	17	"	"	"
510,701 " 511,300	830	"	"	"	"	"	"	"	"
511,301 " 511,600	835	"	"	"	"	"	"	"	"

The Rockford Watch Company, Ltd.

Number and Grade of Movement	GRADE	Size	Style		Jewels	Wind	Sett	Model
511,601 to 512,500	935	18	O. F.	F. Pl. Nickel	17	Stem	Lever	9
512,501 " 512,600	910	"	"	" "	21	"	"	"
512,601 " 512,700	920	"	"	" "	17	"	"	7
512,701 " 512,800	930	"	"	" "	"	"	"	9
512,801 " 512,850	920	"	"	" "	"	"	"	7
512,851 " 512,872	830	"	Htg.	" "	"	"	"	10
512,873	915	"	O. F.	" "	"	"	"	7
512,874 to 512,875	920	"	"	" "	"	"	"	"
512,876	915	"	"	" "	"	"	"	"
512,877 " 512,900	920	"	"	" "	"	"	"	"
512,901 " 513,101	830	"	Htg.	" "	"	"	"	10
513,102 " 513,181	820	"	"	" "	"	"	"	8
513,182	815	"	"	" "	"	"	"	"
513,183 to 513,251	820	"	"	" "	"	"	"	"
513,252 " 513,259	810	"	"	" "	21	"	"	10
513,260 " 513,300	820	"	"	" "	17	"	"	8
513,301 " 513,400	830	"	"	" "	"	"	"	10
513,401 " 513,500	835	"	"	" "	"	"	"	"
513,501 " 513,600	830	"	"	" "	"	"	"	"
513,601 " 513,900	835	"	"	" "	"	"	"	"
513,901 " 514,000	930	"	O. F.	" "	"	"	"	9
514,001 " 514,100	935	"	"	" "	"	"	"	"
514,101 " 514,150	825	"	Htg.	" "	"	"	"	10
514,151 " 514,500	835	"	"	" "	"	"	"	"
514,501 " 514,600	930	"	O. F.	" "	"	"	"	9
514,601 " 514,900	935	"	"	" "	"	"	"	"
514,901 " 515,100	835	"	Htg.	" "	"	"	"	10
515,101 " 515,400	935	"	O. F.	" "	"	"	"	9
515,401 " 515,500	810	"	Htg.	" "	21	"	"	10
515,501 " 515,600	910	"	O. F.	" "	"	"	"	9
515,601 " 516,000	935	"	"	" "	17	"	"	"
516,001 " 516,300	925	"	"	" "	"	"	"	"
516,301 " 516,400	935	"	"	" "	"	"	"	"
516,401 " 516,500	925	"	"	" "	"	"	"	"
516,501 " 517,200	825	"	Htg.	" "	"	"	"	10
517,201 " 519,300	910	"	O. F.	" "	21	"	"	9
519,301 " 519,400	900	"	"	" "	24	"	"	"
519,401 " 519,500	800	"	Htg.	" "	"	"	"	10
519,501 " 519,600	805	"	"	" "	21	"	"	"
519,601 " 519,700	905	"	O. F.	" "	"	"	"	9
519,701 " 520,000	835	"	Htg.	" "	17	"	"	10
520,001 " 521,000	935	"	O. F.	" "	"	"	"	9
521,001 " 522,000	870	"	Htg.	" "	7	"	"	10
522,001 " 522,400	970	"	O. F.	" "	"	"	"	9
522,401 " 523,500	870	"	Htg.	" "	"	"	"	10
523,501 " 524,800	970	"	O. F.	" "	"	"	"	9
524,801 " 525,000	935	"	"	" "	17	"	"	"
525,001 " 525,100	900	"	"	" "	24	"	"	"
525,101 " 525,400	935	"	"	" "	17	"	"	"
525,401 " 525,900	925	"	"	" "	"	"	"	"
525,901 " 526,700	825	"	Htg.	" "	"	"	"	10
526,701 " 526,900	930	"	O. F.	" "	"	"	"	9
526,901 " 527,900	935	"	"	" "	"	"	"	"
527,901 " 528,800	930	"	"	" "	"	"	"	"
528,801 " 529,800	935	"	"	" "	"	"	"	"
529,801 " 530,800	925	"	"	" "	"	"	"	"
530,801 " 531,800	835	"	Htg.	" "	"	"	"	10
531,801 " 532,450	825	"	"	" "	"	"	"	"
532,451 " 532,500	835	"	"	" "	"	"	"	"
532,501 " 533,400	925	"	O. F.	" "	"	"	"	9
533,401 " 534,000	935	"	"	" "	"	"	"	"
534,001 " 534,012	920	"	"	" "	"	"	"	7
534,013	915	"	"	" "	"	"	"	"
534,014 to 534,035	920	"	"	" "	"	"	"	"
534,036	915	"	"	" "	"	"	"	"
534,037 to 534,039	920	"	"	" "	"	"	"	"
534,040	915	"	"	" "	"	"	"	"
534,041 to 534,064	920	"	"	" "	"	"	"	"
534,065	915	"	"	" "	"	"	"	"
534,066 to 534,112	920	"	"	" "	"	"	"	"
534,113 " 534,115	915	"	"	" "	"	"	"	"
534,116 " 534,119	920	"	"	" "	"	"	"	"
534,120	915	"	"	" "	"	"	"	"
534,121	920	"	"	" "	"	"	"	"
534,122 to 534,123	915	"	"	" "	"	"	"	"
534,124 " 534,127	920	"	"	" "	"	"	"	"
534,128	915	"	"	" "	"	"	"	"
534,129 to 534,130	920	"	"	" "	"	"	"	"
534,131	915	"	"	" "	"	"	"	"
534,132	920	"	"	" "	"	"	"	"
534,133	915	"	"	" "	"	"	"	"
534,134	920	"	"	" "	"	"	"	"
534,135	915	"	"	" "	"	"	"	"
534,136 to 534,138	920	"	"	" "	"	"	"	"
534,139	915	"	"	" "	"	"	"	"
534,140 to 534,144	920	"	"	" "	"	"	"	"
534,145	915	"	"	" "	"	"	"	"
534,146 to 534,147	920	"	"	" "	"	"	"	"
534,148	915	"	"	" "	"	"	"	"

The Rockford Watch Company, Ltd.

Number and Grade of Movement	GRADE	Description of Movement						
		Size		Style	Jewels	Wind	Sett	Model
534,149..	920	18	O. F.	F. Pl.	Nickel	17	Stem	Lever	7
534,150..	915	"	"	"	"	"	"	"	7
534,151 to 534,155	920	"	"	"	"	"	"	"	"
534,156 " 534,157	915	"	"	"	"	"	"	"	"
534,158 " 534,163	920	"	"	"	"	"	"	"	"
534,164..	915	"	"	"	"	"	"	"	"
534,165 to 534,171	920	"	"	"	"	"	"	..	"
534,172..	915	"	"	"	"	"	"	"	"
534,173..	920	"	"	"	"	"	"	"	"
534,174..	915	"	"	"	"	"	"	"	"
534,175..	920	"	"	"	"	"	"	"	"
534,176 to 534,179	915	'	"	"	"	"	"	"	"
534,180 " 534,182	920	"	"	"	"	"	"	"	"
534,183..	915	"	"	"	"	"	"	"	"
534,184..	920	"	"	"	"	"	"	"	"
534,185..	915	"	"	"	"	"	"	"	"
534,186 to 534,188	920	"	"	"	"	"	"	"	"
534,189..	915	"	"	"	"	"	"	"	"
534,190 to 534,196	920	"	"	"	"	"	"	"	"
534,197..	915	"	"	"	"	"	"	"	"
534,198..	920	"	"	"	"	"	"	"	"
534,199..	915	"	"	"	"	"	"	"	"
534,200..	920	"	"	"	"	"	"	"	"
534,401 to 534,600	930	"	"	"	"	"	"	"	9
534,601 " 535,200	910	"	"	"	"	21	"	"	"
535,201 " 535,400	900	"	"	"	"	24	"	"	"
535,401 " 535,600	910	"	"	"	"	21	"	"	"
535,601 " 535,700	800	"	Htg.	"	"	24	"	"	10
535,701 " 535,800	805	"	"	"	"	21	"	"	"
535,801 " 536,300	910	"	O. F.	"	"	"	"	"	9
536,301 " 536,600	930	"	"	"	"	17	"	"	"
536,601 " 536,700	945	"	"	"	"	21	"	"	Special
536,701 " 537,400	910	"	"	"	"	"	"	"	9
537,401 " 539,400	935	"	"	"	"	17	"	"	"
539,401 " 540,400	910	"	"	"	"	21	"	"	"
540,401 " 541,400	935	"	"	"	"	17	"	"	"
541,401 " 541,500	905	"	"	"	"	21	"	"	"
541,501 " 542,000	835	"	Htg.	"	"	17	"	"	10
542,001 " 542,300	800	"	"	"	"	24	"	"	"
542,301 " 542,500	810	"	"	"	"	21	"	"	"
542,501 " 542,700	900	"	O. F.	"	"	24	"	"	9
542,701 " 542,800	905	"	"	"	"	21	"	"	"
542,801 " 543,300	805	"	Htg.	"	"	"	"	"	10
543,301 " 543,500	905	"	O. F.	"	"	"	"	"	9
543,501 " 544,000	835	"	Htg.	"	"	17	"	"	10
544,001 " 544,100	560	16	O. F.	¾ Pl.	"	"	"	"	3
544,101 " 544,200	570	"	"	"	"	"	"	"	"
544,201 " 544,400	560	"	"	"	"	"	"	"	"
544,401 " 544,500	530	"	"	"	"	21	"	"	"
544,501 " 544,800	550	"	"	"	"	17	"	"	4
544,801 " 545,000	540	"	"	"	"	21	"	"	2
545,001 " 545,500	535	"	O. F.	"	"	"	"	"	2
545,501 " 546,500	570	"	Htg.	"	"	17	"	"	3
546,501 " 546,600	540	"	"	"	"	21	"	"	4
546,601 " 546,700	500	"	"	"	"	"	"	"	"
546,701 " 546,800	510	"	"	"	"	"	"	"	"
546,801 " 546,900	520	"	"	"	"	"	"	"	"
546,901 " 547,000	530	"	"	"	"	"	"	"	3
547,001 " 548,000	560	"	"	"	"	17	"	"	"
548,001 " 549,000	565	"	O. F.	"	"	"	"	"	2
549,001 " 550,000	575	"	"	"	"	"	"	"	"
550,001 " 550,500	560	"	Htg.	"	"	"	"	"	3
550,501 " 550,600	515	"	O. F.	"	"	"	"	"	5
550,601 " 550,700	525	"	"	"	"	21	"	"	"
550,701 " 550,900	545	"	"	"	"	"	"	"	"
550,901 " 551,200	555	"	"	"	"	17	"	"	"
551,201 " 551,700	530	"	Htg.	"	"	21	"	"	3
551,701 " 552,700	575	"	O. F.	"	"	17	"	"	2
552,701 " 553,200	565	"	"	"	"	"	"	"	3
553,201 " 554,200	570	"	Htg.	"	"	"	"	"	3
554,201 " 554,700	565	"	O. F.	"	"	"	"	"	2
554,701 " 554,900	555	"	"	"	"	"	"	"	2
554,901 " 554,920	535	"	"	"	"	21	"	"	2
554,921 " 554,927	570	"	Htg.	"	"	"	"	"	2
554,928 " 554,930	575	"	O. F.	"	"	17	"	"	2
554,931 " 554,940	560	"	Htg.	"	"	"	"	"	3
554,941 " 554,960	605	"	O. F.	"	"	11	"	Pend.	Special
554,961..	......	"	"	"	Gilt	"	"	"	"
554,962..	......	"	"	"	"	"	"	"	"
554,963..	......	"	"	"	"	"	"	"	"
554,964..	......	"	Htg.	"	Nickel	17	"	"	"
554,965..	......	"	"	"	Gilt	"	"	"	"
554,966..	......	"	"	"	"	"	"	"	"
554,967..	......	"	"	"	Nickel	"	"	"	"
554,968..	......	"	"	"	Gilt	15	"	"	"
554,699..	......	"	O. F.	"	....	"	"	"	"
554,970..	......	"	"	"	....	"	"	"	"
554,971..	......	"	Htg.	"	....	"	"	"	"
554,972..	......	"	"	"	....	"	"	"	"

The Rockford Watch Company, Ltd.

Number and Grade of Movement	GRADE	Size		Style		Jewels	Wind	Sett	Model
554,973..........		16	Htg.	¾ Pl.	Gilt	11	Stem	Pend.	Special
554,974..........	935	18	O. F.	F. Pl.	Nickel	17	"	Lever	9
554,975..........		16	Htg.	¾ Pl.	Nickel	11	"	Pend.	Special
554,976..........		"	"	"	....	"	"	"	"
554,977..........		"	O. F.	"	Nickel	17	"	"	"
554,978..........		"	"	"	"	"	"	"	"
554,979..........		"	"	"	"	"	"	"	"
554,981 to 554,992	25	18	"	F. Pl.	"	25	"	Lever	"
555,001 " 556 000	560	16	Htg.	¾ Pl.	"	17	"	"	3
556,001 " 558,000	575	"	O. F.	"	"	"	"	"	2
558,001 " 558,000	550	"	Htg.	"	"	"	"	"	4
558,501 " 559,000	540	"	"	"	"	21	"	"	"
559,001 " 560,000	560	"	"	"	"	17	"	"	3
560,001 " 560,500	545	"	O. F.	"	"	21	"	"	5
560,501 " 561,000	555	"	"	"	"	17	"	"	"
561,001 " 562,000	835	18	Htg.	F. Pl.	"	"	"	"	10
562,001 " 563,000	935	"	O. F.	"	"	"	"	"	9
563,001 " 565,000	570	16	Htg.	¾ Pl.	"	"	"	"	3
565,001 " 566,000	575	"	O. F.	"	"	"	"	"	2
566,001 " 566,500	918	18	"	F. Pl.	"	24	"	"	9
566,501 " 566,600	930	"	"	"	"	17	"	"	"
566,601 " 566,800	935	"	"	"	"	"	"	"	10
566,801 " 566,900	830	"	Htg.	"	"	"	"	"	
566,901 " 566,940	500	16	"	¾ Pl.	"	21	"	"	4
566,941 " 567,000	501	"	"	"	"	"	"	"	
567,001 " 568,000	575	"	O. F.	"	"	17	"	"	2
568,001 " 570,000	570	"	Htg.	"	"	"	"	"	3
570,001 " 571,000	575	"	O. F.	"	"	"	"	"	2
571,001 " 571,300	545	"	"	"	"	21	"	"	5
571,301 " 571,500	575	"	"	"	"	17	"	"	2
571,501 " 571,530	505	"	"	"	"	21	"	"	5
571,531 " 571,600	515	"	"	"	"	"	"	"	"
571,601 " 571,700	570	"	Htg.	"	"	17	"	"	3
571,701 " 571,900	575	"	O. F.	"	"	"	"	"	2
571,901 " 572,000	585	"	"	"	"	15	"	"	"
572,001 " 572,700	565	"	"	"	"	17	"	"	
572,701 " 573,000	560	"	Htg.	"	"	"	"	"	3
573,001 " 573,500	810	18	"	F. Pl.	"	21	"	"	10
573,501 " 573,510	590	16	"	¾ Pl.	"	11	"	"	3
573,511 " 574,000	584	"	"	"	"	15	"	"	"
574,001 " 574,500	905	18	O. F.	F. Pl.	"	21	"	"	9
574,501 " 575,000	835	"	Htg.	"	"	17	"	"	10
575,001 " 577,000	570	16	"	¾ Pl.	"	"	"	"	3
577,001 " 577,500	584	"	"	"	"	15	"	"	
577,501 " 577,800	565	"	O. F.	"	"	17	"	"	2
577,801 " 577,900	520	"	Htg.	"	"	21	"	"	4
577,901 " 578,000	525	"	O. F.	"	"	"	"	"	5
578,001 " 579,150	835	18	Htg.	F. Pl.	"	17	"	"	10
579,201 " 579,370	935	"	O. F.	"	"	"	"	"	9
579,401 " 579,500	570	16	Htg.	¾ Pl.	"	"	"	"	3
579,501 " 579,600	575	"	O. F.	"	"	"	"	"	2
579,601 " 579,700	560	"	Htg.	"	"	"	;	"	3
579,701 " 579,735	565	"	O. F.	"	"	"	"	"	2
579,801 " 579,900	830	18	Htg.	F. Pl.	"	"	"	"	10
579,901 " 580,000	930	"	O. F.	"	"	"	"	"	9
580,001 " 580,200	560	16	Htg.	¾ Pl.	"	"	"	"	3
580,201 " 580,300	565	"	O. F.	"	"	"	"	"	2
580,301 " 580,500	570	"	Htg.	"	"	"	"	"	3
580,501 " 580,600	575	"	O. F.	"	"	"	"	"	2
580,601 " 581,000	930	18	"	F. Pl.	"	"	"	"	9
581,001 " 582,000	585	16	"	¾ Pl.	"	15	"	"	2
582,001 " 583,000	584	"	Htg.	"	"	"	"	"	3
583,001 " 584,000	560	"	"	"	"	17	"	"	"
584,001 " 585,000	584	"	"	"	"	15	"	"	"
585,001 " 585,500	935	18	O. F.	F. Pl.	"	17	"	"	9
585,501 " 585,600	515	16	"	¾ Pl.	"	21	"	"	5
585,601 " 585,700	525	"	"	"	"	"	"	"	"
585,701 " 585,800	830	18	Htg.	F. Pl.	"	17	"	"	10
585,801 " 585,900	930	"	O. F.	"	"	"	"	"	9
585,901 " 586,000	835	"	Htg.	"	"	"	"	"	10
586,001 " 588,000	584	16	"	¾ Pl.	"	15	"	"	3
588,001 " 590,000	835	18	"	F. Pl.	"	17	"	"	10
590,001 " 591,000	570	16	"	¾ Pl.	"	"	"	"	3
591,001 " 592,000	584	"	"	"	"	15.	"	"	"
592,001 " 593,000	835	18	"	F. Pl.	"	17	"	"	10
593,001 " 593,100	560	16	"	¾ Pl.	"	"	"	"	3
593,101 " 593,200	570	"	"	"	"	"	"	"	
593,201 " 593,300	100	"	"	"	"	21	"	Pend.	Special
593,301 " 593,400	101	"	O. F.	"	"	"	"	"	
593,401 " 593,600	925	18	"	F. Pl.	"	17	"	Lever	9
593,601 " 593,700	835	"	Htg.	"	"	"	"	"	10
593,701 " 593,800	825	"	"	"	"	"	"	"	
593,801 " 593,900	520	16	"	¾ Pl.	"	21	"	"	4
593,901 " 594,000	505	"	O. F.	"	"	"	"	"	5
594,001 " 596,000	590	"	Htg.	"	"	11	"	Pend.	3
596,001 " 597,000	595	"	O. F.	"	"	"	"	"	2
597,001 " 598,000	590	"	Htg.	"	"	"	"	"	3
598,001 " 599,000	586	"	"	"	"	15	"	"	5
599,001 " 599,500	587	"	O. F.	"	"	"	"	"	2

The Rockford Watch Company, Ltd.

Number and Grade of Movement	GRADE	Size		Style		Jewels	Wind	Sett	Model
599,501 to 599,502	575	16	O. F.	¾ Pl.	Nickel	17	Stem	Lever	2
599,503 " 599,504	565	"	"	"	"	"	"	"	"
599,505	575	"	"	"	"	"	"	"	"
599,506 to 600,000	587	"	"	"	"	15	"	Pend.	"
600,001 " 601,000	935	18	"	F. Pl.	"	17	"	"	9
601,001 " 602,000	590	16	Htg.	¾ Pl.	"	11	"	Lever	9
602,001 " 603,000	595	"	O. F.	"	"	"	"	Pend.	3
603,001 " 605,000	561	"	Htg.	"	"	17	"	"	2
605,001 " 605,700	573	"	O. F.	"	"	"	"	"	4
605,701 " 605,850	845	18	Htg.	F. Pl.	"	21	"	Lever	Special
605,851 " 605,900	945	"	O. F.	"	"	"	"	"	Special
605,901 " 605,950	540	16	Htg.	¾ Pl.	"	"	"	"	4
606,001 " 608,000	935	18	O. F.	F. Pl.	"	17	"	"	9
608,001 " 609,000	572	16	Htg.	¾ Pl.	"	"	"	Pend.	4
609,001 " 610,000	566	"	O. F.	"	"	"	"	"	5
610,001 " 613,000	605	"	"	"	"	11	"	"	2
613,001 " 614,000	587	"	"	"	"	15	"	"	
614,001 " 615,000	600	"	Htg.	"	"	11	"	"	3
615,001 " 617,000	605	"	O. F.	"	"	"	"	"	2
617,001 " 617,500	586	"	Htg.	"	"	15	"	"	3
617,501 " 617,800	845	18	"	F. Pl.	"	21	"	Lever	Special
617,801 " 618,000	810	"	"	"	"	"	"	"	10
618,001 " 618,500	587	16	O. F.	¾ Pl.	"	15	"	Pend.	2
618,501 " 618,600	578	"	Htg.	"	"	17	"	"	3
618,601 " 618,700	579	"	O. F.	"	"	"	"	"	2
618,701 " 618,800	600	"	Htg.	"	"	11	"	"	3
618,801 " 618,900	586	"	"	"	"	15	"	"	
618,901 " 618,950	120	"	"	"	"	17	"	"	Special
618,951 " 619,000	125	"	O. F.	"	"	"	"	"	"
619,001 " 619,300	525	"	"	"	"	21	"	Lever	5
619,301 " 619,700	600	"	Htg.	"	"	11	"	Pend.	3
619,701 " 619,900	565	"	O. F.	"	"	17	"	Lever	"
619,901 " 620,000	101	"	"	"	"	21	"	Pend.	Special
620,001 " 621,000	545	"	"	'	"	"	"	Lever	5
621,001 " 622,000	935	18	"	F. Pl.	"	17	"	"	9
622,001 " 622,300	160	0	Htg.	¾ Pl.	"	15	"	Pend.	1
622,301 " 622,350	140	"	"	"	"	17	"	"	"
622,351 " 622,500	150	"	"	"	"	"	"	"	"
622,501 " 623,000	160	"	"	"	"	15	"	"	"
623,001 " 623,100	200	18	O. F.	F. Pl.	"	17	"	Lever	10
623,101 " 623,500	605	16	"	¾ Pl.	"	11	"	Pend.	2
623,501 " 624,000	160	0	Htg.	"	"	15	"	"	1
624,001 " 624,200	205	18	O. F.	F. Pl.	"	17	"	Lever	10
624,201 " 624,300	945	"	"	"	"	21	"	"	Special
624,301 " 624,400	930	"	"	"	"	17	"	"	9
624,401 " 624,450	110	16	Htg.	¾ Pl.	"	"	"	"	Special
624,451 " 624,500	115	"	O. F.	"	"	"	"	Pend.	Special
624,501 " 624,525	130	"	Htg.	"	"	"	"	"	"
624,526 " 624,550	135	"	O. F.	"	Gilt	"	"	"	"
624,601 " 624,800	540	"	Htg.	"	Nickel	21	"	Lever	4
625,001 " 625,400	400	"	"	"	"	17	"	Pend.	"
626,001 " 626,200	405	"	"	"	"	21	"	"	5
626,201 " 626,400	510	"	"	"	"	"	"	Lever	4
626,401 " 626,600	515	"	O. F.	"	"	"	"	"	5
626,601 " 626,700	520	"	Htg.	"	"	"	"	"	4
626,701 " 626,900	525	"	O. F.	"	"	"	"	"	5
626,901 " 627,000	845	18	Htg.	F. Pl.	"	"	"	"	Special
627,001 " 627,300	572	16	"	¾ Pl.	"	17	"	Pend.	4
628,001 " 628,100	500	"	"	"	"	21	"	Lever	"
628,101 " 628,300	520	"	O. F.	"	"	"	"	"	"
628,301 " 628,500	515	"	"	"	"	"	"	"	5
628,501 " 628,600	505	"	"	"	"	"	"	"	5
628,601 " 628,800	510	"	Htg.	"	"	"	"	"	4
628,801 " 628,950	100	"	"	"	"	"	"	Pend.	Special
628,951 " 629,000	101	"	O. F.	"	"	"	"	"	"
629,001 " 630,000	935	18	"	F. Pl.	"	17	"	Lever	9
630,001 " 630,600	835	"	Htg.	"	"	"	"	"	10
630,601 " 630,700	162	0	"	¾ Pl.	"	"	"	Pend.	1
630,701 " 630,800	150	"	"	"	"	"	"	"	"
630,801 " 631,000	160	"	"	"	"	15	"	"	"
631,001 " 632,000	586	16	"	"	"	"	"	"	3
632,001 " 632,500	825	18	"	F. Pl.	"	17	"	Lever	10
633,001 " 633,500	925	"	O. F.	"	"	"	"	"	9
634,001 " 635,000	587	16	"	¾ Pl.	"	15	"	Pend.	2
635,001 " 636,000	935	18	"	F. Pl.	"	17	"	Lever	9
636,001 " 636,500	160	0	Htg.	¾ Pl.	"	15	"	Pend.	1
636,501 " 636,600	150	"	"	"	"	17	"	"	1
636,601 " 638,000	160	"	"	"	"	15	"	"	"
638,001 " 639,000	600	16	"	"	"	11	"	"	"
639,001 " 640,000	160	0	"	"	"	15	"	Pend.	1
640,001 " 641,000	162	"	"	"	"	"	"	"	1
641,001 " 642,000	610	16	"	"	"	7	"	"	Special
642,001 " 643,000	615	"	O. F.	"	"	"	"	"	3
643,001 " 644,000	587	"	"	"	"	15	"	"	2
644,001 " 644,500	142	0	Htg.	"	"	17	"	"	2
645,001 " 646,600	162	"	"	"	"	15	"	"	1
646,001 " 647,000	610	16	"	"	"	7	"	"	Special
647,001 " 648,000	615	"	O. F.	"	"	"	"	"	3
648,001 " 649,000	160	0	Htg.	"	"	15	"	Pend.	1
649,001 " 650,000	605	16	O. F.	"	"	11	"	"	2

The Rockford Watch Company, Ltd.

Number and Grade of Movement	GRADE	Size	Style		Jewels	Wind	Sett	Model
				Description of Movement				
650,001 " 651,000	573	16	O. F.	¾ Pl. Nickel	17	Stem	Pend.	5
651,001 to 656,000	160	0	Htg.	" "	15	"	"	1
656,001 " 656,100	152	"	"	" "	17	"	"	Special
657,001 " 657,200	182	"	"	" "	7	"	"	
658,001 " 659,000	600	16	O. F.	F. Pl. "	11	"	"	3
659,001 " 659,200	930	18	"	" "	17	"	Lever	9
660,001 " 660,100	910	"	"	" "	21	"	"	10
661,101 " 661,200	810	"	Htg.	" "	"	"	Pend.	Special
662,001 " 662,600	100	16	O. F.	¾ Pl. "	"	"	"	"
663,001 " 663,100	101	"	"	" "	"	"	Lever	"
664,001 " 664,100	845	18	Htg.	F. Pl. "	17	"	"	10
665,001 " 665,100	830	"	O. F.	" "	24	"	"	9
666,001 " 666,100	900	"	"	" "	21	"	"	"
667,001 " 667,100	905	"	"	" "	11	"	Pend.	2
668,001 " 669,000	605	16	"	¾ Pl. "	21	"	Lever	9
669,001 " 669,100	912	18	"	F. Pl. Spot Gilt	"	"	"	2
670,001 " 670,100	537	16	"	¾ Pl. Nickel	17	"	"	10
671,001 " 671,300	200	18	"	F. Pl. "	"	"	"	"
672,001 " 673,000	205	"	"	" "	"	"	Pend.	5
674,001 " 675,000	405	16	"	¾ Pl. "	"	"	Lever	"
675,001 " 675,500	525	"	"	" "	21	"	Pend.	"
676,001 " 677,000	566	"	"	" "	17	"	"	"
677,001 " 678,000	573	"	"	" "	"	"	"	3
678,001 " 678,500	586	"	"	" "	15	"	"	2
679,001 " 680,500	587	"	"	" "	"	"	"	3
681,001 " 682,000	600	"	Htg.	" "	11	"	"	2
682,001 " 686,000	605	"	O. F.	" "	"	"	"	"
686,001 " 693,000	615	"	"	" "	7	"	"	3
693,001 " 694,000	610	"	Htg.	" "	"	"	"	"
694,001 " 694,500	935	18	O. F.	F. Pl. "	17	"	Lever	9
695,001 " 695,500	945	"	"	" "	21	"	"	Special

STYLE & NAMES OF U.S.A. HANDS

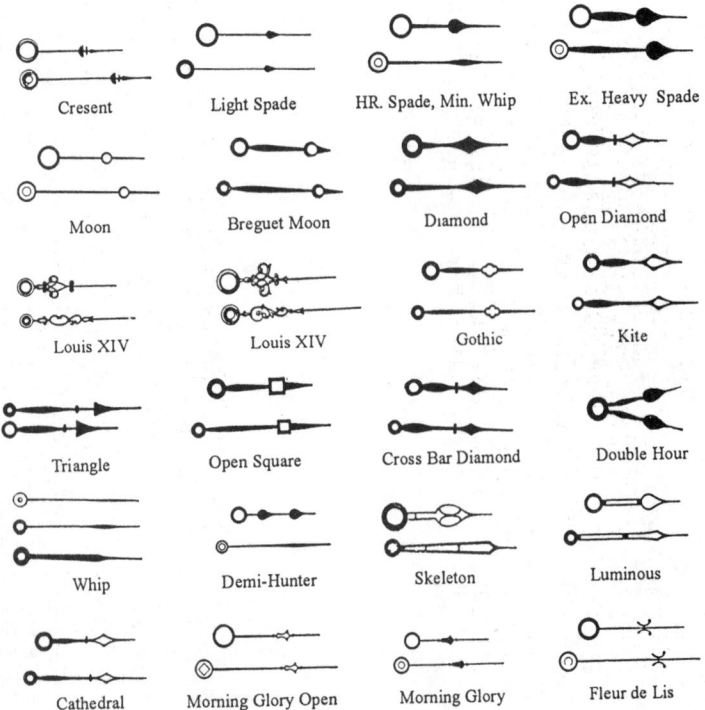

Cresent   Light Spade   HR. Spade, Min. Whip   Ex. Heavy Spade

Moon   Breguet Moon   Diamond   Open Diamond

Louis XIV   Louis XIV   Gothic   Kite

Triangle   Open Square   Cross Bar Diamond   Double Hour

Whip   Demi-Hunter   Skeleton   Luminous

Cathedral   Morning Glory Open   Morning Glory   Fleur de Lis

SERIAL NUMBER - GRADE, Size, Style, Jewels,MODEL

695501-696000=945,18S.O.F.21J,M#SP.
696001-697000=838,18S.H.C.17J,M#10
697001-698000=938,18S.O.F.17J,M# 9
698001-699000=150, 0S. H.C.17J,M# 1
699001-700000=140, 0S. H.C.17J,M# 1
700001-702100=180, 0S. H.C. 7J,M# 1
702101-703000=160, 0S. H.C.15J,M# 1
703001-703500=170, 0S. H.C.11J,M# 1
703501-704000=160, 0S. H.C.15J,M# 1
704001-704300=935,18S.O.F.17J,M# 9
704301-704400=930,18S.O.F.17J,M# 9
704401-704500=935,18S.O.F.17J,M# 9
704501-704600=930,18S.O.F.17J,M# 9
704601-705000=935,18S.O.F.17J,M# 9
705001-706000=572,16S.H.C.17J,M# 4
706001-707000=600,16S.H.C.11J,M# 3
707001-708000=918,18S.H.C.21J,M# 9
708001-709000=586,16S.H.C.15J,M# 4
709001-710000=587,16S.O.F.15J,M# 3
710001-710100=930,18S.O.F.17J,M# 9
710101-710600=935,18S.O.F.17J,M# 9
710601-710700=930,18S.O.F.17J,M# 9
710701-711000=935,18S.O.F.17J,M# 9
711001-711100=830,18S.H.C.17J,M# 9
711101-711500=835,18S.H.C.17J,M#10
711501-711600=830,18S.H.C.17J,M#10
711601-712000=835,18S.H.C.17J,M#10
712001-712700=573,16S.O.F.17J,M# 5
712701-713000=635,16S.O.F.17J,M# 5
713001-714000=610,16S.O.F. 7J,M#SP.
714001-715000=572,16S.H.C.17J,M# 4
715001-716000=586,16S.O.F.15J,M# 3
716001-717000=587,16S.O.F.15J,M# 2
717001-718000=600,16S.O.F.11J,M# 3
718001-719000=605,16S.O.F.11J,M# 2
719001-720000=615,16S.O.F. 7J,M# 3
720001-721000=610,16S.O.F. 7J,M#SP.
721001-721500=600,16S.H.C.11J,M# 3
721501-722000=586,16S.H.C.15J,M# 3
722501-722700=573,16S.O.F.17J,M# 5
722701-722800=635,16S.O.F.17J,M# 5
722801-722900=573,16S.O.F.17J,M# 5
722901-723000=635,16S.O.F.17J,M# 5
723001-724000=935,18S.O.F.17J,M#10
724001-725000=205,18S.O.F.17J,M# 9
725001-725100=930,18S.O.F.17J,M# 9
725101-726000=935,18S.O.F.17J,M# 9
726001-727000=405,16S.O.F.17J,M# 5
727001-728000=587,16S.O.F.15J,M# 2
728001-728500=573,16S.O.F.17J,M# 5
728501-728600=635,16S.O.F.17J,M# 5
728601-728800=573,16S.O.F.17J,M# 5
728801-729000=635,16S.O.F.17J,M# 5
729001-729800=600,16S.H.C.11J,M# 3
729801-730000=586,16S.O.F.15J,M# 3
730001-730700=610,16S.O.F. 7J,M#SP.
730701-731000=586,16S.O.F.15J,M# 3
731001-732000=615,16S.O.F. 7J,M# 3
732001-732500=162, 0S.H.C.17J,M# 1
732501-733000=150, 0S.H.C.17J,M# 1
733001-734000=572, 6S.H.C.17J,M# 4
734001-735000=586,16S.O.F.15J,M# 2
735001-735200=610,16S.H.C. 7J,M#SP.
735201-736000=586,16S.O.F.15J,M# 2
736001-738000=935,18S.O.F.17J,M# 9
738001-739000=938,18S.O.F.17J,M#10
739001-740000=925,18S.O.F.17J,M# 9
740001-740200=830,18S.H.C.17J,M#10
740201-741000=835,18S.H.C.17J,M#10
741001-741100=600,16S.H.C.11J,M# 3
741101-742000=586,16S.H.C.15J,M# 3
742001-742500=605,16S.O.F.11J,M# 2
742501-743000=587,16S,O,F.15J,M# 2
743001-745000=935,18S.O.F.17J,M# 9
745001-746000=930,18S.O.F.17J,M# 9
746001-747000=586,16S.O.F.15J,M# 2
747001-748000=935,18S.O.F.17J,M# 9
748001-749000=938,18S.O.F.17J,M#10
749001-749600=572,16S.H.C.17J,M# 4
749601-750000=630,16S.H.C.17J,M# 4
750001-750200=573,16S.O.F.17J,M# 5
750201-750600=635,16S.O.F.17J,M# 5
750601-751000=573,16S.O.F.17J,M# 5
751001-751200=605,16S.O.F.15J,M# 2
752001-752100=572,16S.H.C.17J,M# 4
752101-752200=630,16S.H.C.17J,M# 4
752201-753000=572,16S.H.C.17J,M# 4
753001-754000=573,16S.O.F.17J,M# 5
754001-755000=586,16S.H.C.15J,M# 3
755001-756000=587,16S.O.F.15J,M# 2
756001-757000=935,18S.O.F.17J,M# 9
757001-758000=925,18S.O.F.17J,M# 9
758001-759000=150, 0S.H.C.17J,M# 1
759001-759500=572,16S.H.C.17J,M# 4

759501-756000=620,16S.H.C.21J,M# 5
760001-760500=573,16S.O.F.21J,M# 5
760501-761000=625,16S.O.F.21J,M# 5
761001-762000=160, 0S.H.C.15J,M# 1
762001-762500=400,16S.H.C.17J,M# 4
762501-764000=405,16S.O.F.17J,M#10
764001-765000=205,16S.O.F.17J,M#10
765001-765500=515,16S.O.F.21J,M# 5
765501-766000=545,16S.O.F.21J,M# 5
760010-767000=930,18S.O.F.17J,M# 9
767001-768000=572,16S.H.C.17J,M# 4
768001-769000=935,18S.O.F.17J,M# 9
769001-770000=918,18S.O.F.21J,M#10
770001-770500=938,18S.O.F.17J,M#10
770501-771000=835,18S.H.C.17J,M#10
771001-772000=586,16S.O.F.15J,M# 3
772001-772100=320,12S.H.C.17J,M# 1
772101-772200=330,12S.H.C.17J,M# 1
772201-772300=310,12S.H.C.21J,M# 1
772301-772400=300,12S.H.C.23J,M# 1
772401-772600=325,12S.O.F.17J,M# 2
772601-772800=335,12S.O.F.17J,M# 2
772801-772900=315,12S.O.F.21J,M# 2
772901-773000=305,12S.O.F.23J,M# 2
773001-773100=300,12S.H.C.23J,M# 1
773101-773200=310,12S.H.C.21J,M# 1
773201-773400=320,12S.H.C.17J,M# 1
773401-773500=305,12S.O.F.23J,M# 2
773501-773600=315,12S.O.F.21J,M# 2
773601-773800=325,12S.O.F.17J,M# 2
773801-774000=330,12S.H.C.17J,M# 1
774001-774500=335,12S.O.F.17J,M# 2
774501-774700=325,12S.O.F.17J,M# 2
774701-774000=330,12S.H.C.17J,M# 1
774701-775000=320,12S.H.C.17J,M# 1
775001-776000=587,16S.O.F.15J,M# 2
776001-777000=630,16S.H.C.17J,M# 5
777001-778000=635,16S.O.F.17J,M# 5
778001-779000=838,18S.H.C.17J,M#10
779001-779500=938,18S.H.C.17J,M#10
779501-780000=935,18S.O.F.17J,M# 9
780001-781000=835,18S.H.C.17J,M#10
781001-782000=545,16S.O.F.21J,M# 5
782001-783000=404,16S.O.F.17J,M# 5
783001-784000=561,16S.H.C.17J,M# 4
784001-785000=930,18S.O.F.17J,M# 9
785001-786000=205,18S.O.F.17J,M# 9
786001-787000=935,18S.O.F.17J,M# 9
787001-787200=310,12S.H.C.21J,M# 1
787201-788000=335,12S.O.F.17J,M# 2
788001-788100=315,12S.O.F.21J,M# 2
788101-789000=335,12S.O.F.17J,M# 2
788901-789100=320,12S.H.C.17J,M# 1
789001-789500=320,12S.O.F.17J,M# 1
789501-790000=330,12S.H.C.17J,M3 1
790001-791000=325,12S.O.F.17J,M# 2
791001-792000=330,12S.H.C.17J,M# 1
792001-792900=335,12S.O.F.17J,M# 2
722901-793000=355,12S.O.F.17J,M# 2
793001-796000=935,18S.O.F.17J,M# 9
796001-797000=930,18S.O.F.17J,M# 9
797001-798000=938,18S.O.F.17J,M# 9
798001-799000=830,18S.H.C.17J,M# 8
799001-800000=587,16S.O.F.15J,M# 2
800001-801000=572,16S.H.C.17J,M# 4
801001-802000=573,16S.O.F.17J,M# 5
802001-802500=573,16S.O.F.17J,M# 5
802501-803000=566,16S.O.F.17J,M# 5
803001-804000=573,16S.O.F.17J,M# 5
804001-805000=150, 0S.H.C.17J,M# 1
805001-806000=335,12S.O.F.17J,M# 2
806001-806100=300,12S.H.C.23J,M# 1
806101-807000=335,12S.O.F.17J,M# 2
807001-807100=305,12S.O.F.23J,M# 2
807101-808000=335,12S.O.F.17J,M# 2
808001-810000=573,16S.O.F.17J,M# 5
810001-811000=572,16S.H.C.17J,M# 4
811001-812000=160, 0S.H.C.15J,M# 1
812001-813000=330,12S.H.C.17J,M# 1
813001-814000=355,12S.O.F.17J,M# 2
814001-814500=350,12S.H.C.21J,M# 1
814501-814600=345,12S.H.C.21J,M# 2
814601-814700=340,12S.O.F.21J,M# 2
814701-815000=350,12S.H.C.17J,M# 1
815001-816000=335,12S.O.F.17J,M# 2
816001-817000=190, 0S.H.C.15J,M# 1
817001-818000=185 0S.H.C.17J,M# 1
818001-819000=335,12S.O.F.17J,M# 2
819001-820000=355,12S.O.F.17J,M# 2
820001-821000=190, 0S.H.C.15J,M# 1
821001-822000=335,12S.H.C.17J,M# 1
822001-823000=350,12S.H.C.17J,M# 1
823001-824000=330,12S.H.C.17J,M# 1

SERIAL NUMBER - GRADE, Size, Style, Jewels,MODEL

695505-696000=945,18S.O.F.21J.
696001-697000=838,18S.H.C.17J.
697001-698000=938,18S.O.F.17J.
698001-699000=150, 0S. H.C.17J.
699001-700000=140, 0S. H.C.17J.
700001-702100=180, 0S. H.C. 7J.
702101-703000=160, 0S. H.C.15J.
703001-703500=170, 0S. H.C.11J.
703501-704000=160, 0S. H.C.15J.
704001-704300=935,18S.O.F.17J.
704301-704400=930,18S.O.F.17J.
704401-704500=935,18S.O.F.17J.
704501-704600=930,18S.O.F.17J.
704601-705000=935,18S.O.F.17J.
705001-706000=572,16S.H.C.17J.
706001-707000=600,16S.H.C.11J.
707001-708000=918,18S.O.F.21J.
708001-709000=586,16S.H.C.15J.
709001-710000=587,16S.O.F.15J.
710001-710100=930,18S.O.F.17J.
710101-710600=935,18S.O.F.17J.
710601-710700=935,18S.O.F.17J.
710701-711000=935,18S.O.F.17J.
711001-711100=830,18S.H.C.17J.
711101-711500=835,18S.H.C.17J.
711501-711600=830,18S.H.C.17J.
711601-712000=835,18S.H.C.17J.
712001-712700=573,16S.O.F.17J.
712701-713000=635,16S.O.F.17J.
713001-714000=610,16S.O.F. 7J.
714001-715000=572,16S.H.C.17J.
715001-716000=586,16S.O.F.15J.
716001-717000=587,16S.O.F.15J.
717001-718000=600,16S.O.F.11J.
718001-719000=605,16S.O.F.11J.
719001-720000=615,16S.O.F. 7J.
720001-721000=610,16S.O.F. 7J.
721001-721500=600,16S.H.C.11J.
721501-722000=586,16S.H.C.15J.
722501-722700=573,16S.O.F.17J.
722701-722800=635,16S.O.F.17J.
722801-722900=573,16S.O.F.17J.
722901-723000=635,16S.O.F.17J.
723001-724000=935,18S.O.F.17J.
724001-725000=205,18S.O.F.17J.
725001-725100=930,18S.O.F.17J.
725101-726000=935,18S.O.F.17J.
726001-727000=405,16S.O.F.17J.
727001-728000=587,16S.O.F.15J.
728001-728500=573,16S.O.F.17J.
728501-728600=635,16S.O.F.17J.
728601-728800=573,16S.O.F.17J.
728801-729000=635,16S.O.F.17J.
729001-729800=600,16S.H.C.11J.
729801-730000=586,16S.O.F.15J.
730001-730700=610,16S.O.F. 7J.
730701-731000=586,16S.O.F.15J.
731001-732000=615,16S.O.F. 7J.
732001-732500=162, 0S.H.C.17J.
732501-733000=150, 0S.H.C.17J.
733001-734000=572, 6S.H.C.17J.
734001-735000=586,16S.O.F.15J.
735001-735200=610,16S.H.C. 7J.
735201-736000=586,16S.O.F.15J.
736001-738000=935,18S.O.F.17J.
738001-739000=938,18S.O.F.17J.
739001-740000=925,18S.O.F.17J.
740001-740200=830,18S.H.C.17J.
740201-741000=835,18S.H.C.17J.
741001-741100=600,16S.H.C.11J.
741101-742000=586,16S.H.C.15J.
742001-742500=605,16S.O.F.11J.
742501-743000=587,16S.O,F.15J.
743001-745000=935,18S.O.F.17J.
745001-746000=930,18S.O.F.17J.
746001-747000=586,16S.O.F.15J.
747001-748000=935,18S.O.F.17J.
748001-749000=938,18S.O.F.17J.
749001-749600=572,16S.H.C.17J.
749601-750000=630,16S.H.C.17J.
750001-750200=573,16S.O.F.17J.
750201-750600=635,16S.O.F.17J.
750601-751000=573,16S.O.F.17J.
751001-751200=605,16S.O.F.17J.
752001-752100=572,16S.H.C.17J.
752101-752200=630,16S.H.C.17J.
752201-753000=572,16S.H.C.17J.
753001-754000=573,16S.O.F.17J.
754001-755000=586,16S.H.C.15J.
755001-756000=587,16S.O.F.15J.
756001-757000=935,18S.O.F.17J.
757001-758000=925,18S.O.F.17J.
758001-759000=150, 0S.H.C.17J.
759001-759500=572,16S.H.C.17J.

SERIAL NUMBER - GRADE, Size, Style, Jewels,MODEL

759501-756000=620,16S.H.C.21J.
760001-760500=573,16S.O.F.17J.
760501-761000=625,16S.O.F.21J.
761001-762000=160, 0S.H.C.15J.
762001-762500=400,16S.H.C.17J.
762501-764000=405,16S.O.F.17J.
764001-765000=205,18S.O.F.17J.
765001-765500=515,16S.O.F.21J.
765501-766000=545,16S.O.F.21J.
760010-767000=930,18S.O.F.17J.
767001-768000=572,16S.H.C.17J.
768001-769000=935,18S.O.F.17J.
769001-770000=918,18S.O.F.21J.
770001-770500=938,18S.O.F.17J.
770501-771000=835,18S.H.C.17J.
771001-772000=586,16S.O.F.15J.
772001-772100=320,12S.H.C.17J.
772101-772200=330,12S.H.C.17J.
772201-772300=310,12S.H.C.21J.
772301-772400=300,12S.H.C.23J.
772401-772600=325,12S.O.F.17J.
772601-772800=335,12S.O.F.17J.
772801-772900=315,12S.O.F.21J.
772901-773000=305,12S.O.F.23J.
773001-773100=300,12S.H.C.23J.
773101-773200=310,12S.H.C.21J.
773201-773400=320,12S.H.C.17J.
773401-773500=305,12S.O.F.23J.
773501-773600=315,12S.O.F.21J.
773601-773800=325,12S.O.F.17J.
773801-774000=330,12S.H.C.17J.
774001-774500=335,12S.H.C.17J.
774501-774700=325,12S.O.F.17J.
774701-774000=330,12S.H.C.17J.
774901-775000=320,12S.H.C.17J.
775001-776000=587,16S.O.F.15J.
776001-777000=630,16S.H.C.17J.
777001-778000=635,16S.O.F.17J.
778001-779000=838,18S.H.C.17J.
779001-779500=938,18S.H.C.17J.
779501-780000=935,18S.O.F.17J.
780001-781000=835,18S.H.C.17J.
781001-782000=545,16S.O.F.21J.
782001-783000=404,16S.O.F.17J.
783001-784000=561,16S.H.C.17J.
784001-785000=930,18S.O.F.17J.
785001-786000=205,18S.O.F.17J.
786001-787000=935,18S.O.F.17J.
787001-787200=310,12S.H.C.21J.
787201-788000=335,12S.O.F.17J.
788001-788100=315,12S.O.F.21J.
788101-789000=335,12S.O.F.17J.
789001-789100=330,12S.H.C.21J.
789001-789500=320,12S.H.C.17J.
789501-790000=330,12S.H.C.17J.
790001-791000=325,12S.O.F.17J.
791001-792000=330,12S.H.C.17J.
792001-792900=335,12S.O.F.17J.
722901-793000=355,12S.O.F.17J.
793001-796000=935,18S.O.F.17J.
796001-797000=930,18S.O.F.17J.
797001-798000=938,18S.O.F.17J.
798001-799000=830,18S.H.C.17J.
799001-800000=587,16S.O.F.15J.
800001-801000=572,16S.H.C.17J.
801001-802000=573,16S.O.F.17J.
802001-802500=573,16S.O.F.17J.
802501-803000=566,16S.O.F.17J.
803001-804000=573,16S.O.F.17J.
804001-805000=150, 0S.H.C.17J.
805001-806000=335,12S.O.F.17J.
806001-806100=300,12S.H.C.23J.
806101-807000=335,12S.O.F.17J.
807001-807100=305,12S.O.F.23J.
807101-808000=335,12S.O.F.17J.
808001-810000=573,16S.O.F.17J.
810001-811000=572,16S.H.C.17J.
811001-812000=160, 0S.H.C.15J.
812001-813000=330,12S.H.C.17J.
813001-814000=355,12S.O.F.17J.
814001-814500=350,12S.H.C.17J.
814501-814600=345,12S.H.C.21J.
814601-814700=340,12S.O.F.21J.
814701-815000=350,12S.H.C.17J.
815001-816000=335,12S.O.F.17J.
816001-817000=190, 0S.H.C.15J.
817001-818000=185 0S.H.C.17J.
818001-819000=335,12S.O.F.17J.
819001-820000=355,12S.O.F.17J.
820001-821000=190, 0S.H.C.15J.
821001-822000=335,12S.H.C.17J.
822001-823000=350,12S.H.C.17J.
823001-824000=330,12S.H.C.17J.

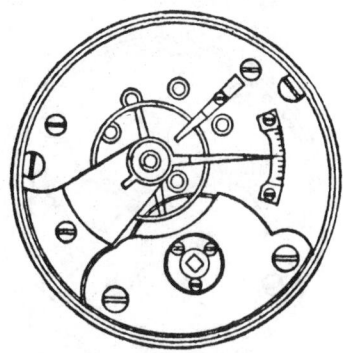

Model 1, 18 size, full plate, hunting, key wind & set.

Model 2, 18 size, full plate, hunting, lever set.

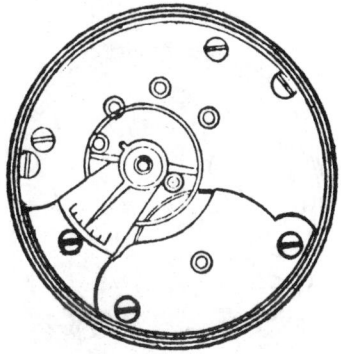

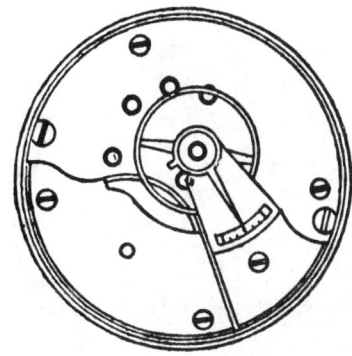

Model 3, 18 size, full plate, hunting, lever set.

Model 4, 18 size, full plate, open face, lever set.

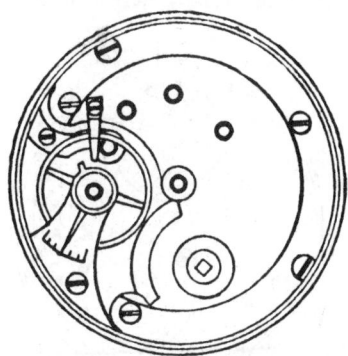

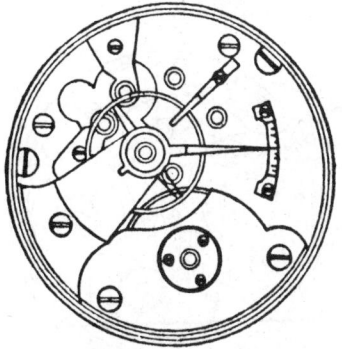

Model 5, 18 size, three-quarter plate, hunting, lever set.

Model 6, 18 size, full plate, hunting, lever set, exposed escapement.

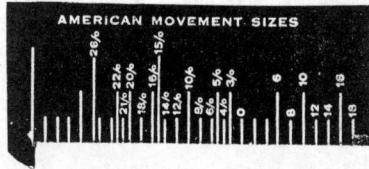

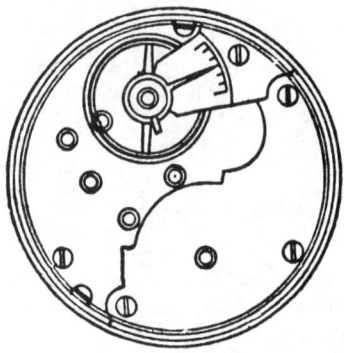

Model 7, 18 size, full plate, open face, lever set.

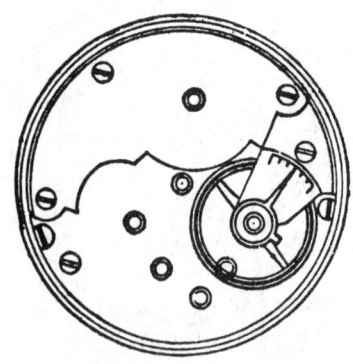

Model 8, 18 size, full plate, hunting, lever set.

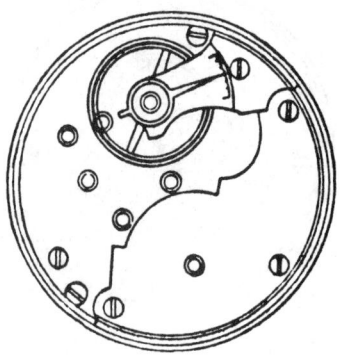

Model 9, 18 size, full plate, open face, lever set.

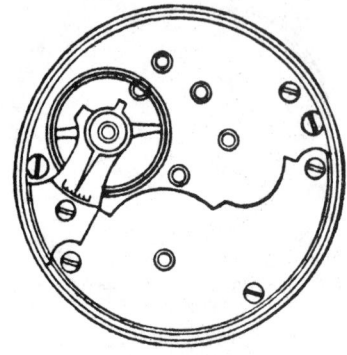

Model 10, 18 size, full plate, hunting, lever set.

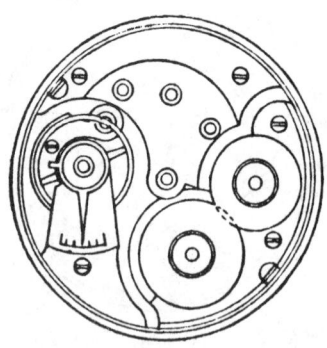

Model 1, 16 size, three-quarter plate, hunting, lever set.

Model 2, 16 size, three-quarter plate, open face, pendant & lever set.

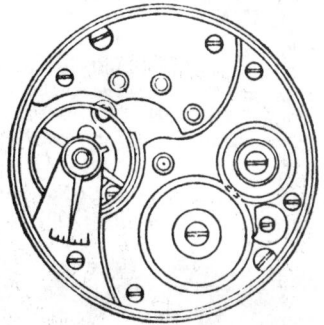

Model 3, 16 size, three-quarter plate, hunting, pendant & lever set.

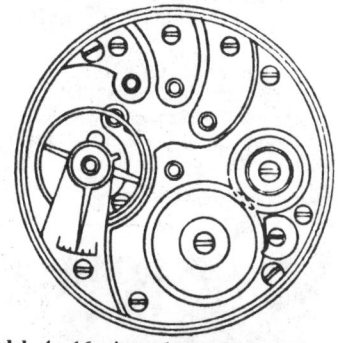

Model 4, 16 size, three-quarter plate, bridge, hunting, pendant & lever set.

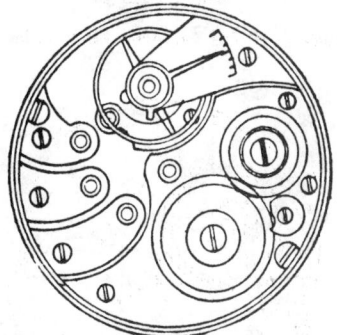

Model 5, 16 size, three-quarter plate, bridge, open face, pendant & lever set.

Model 1, 12 size, three-quarter plate bridge, hunting, pendant set.

Model 2, 12 size, three-quarter plate bridge, open face, pendant set.

Model 1, 6 & 8 size, three-quarter plate, hunting, lever set.

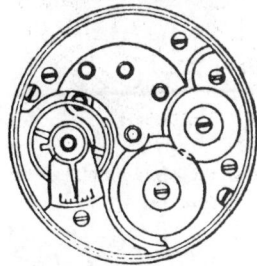

Model 2, 6 size, three-quarter plate, hunting, lever set.

Model 1, 0 size, three-quarter plate, bridge, hunting, pendant set.

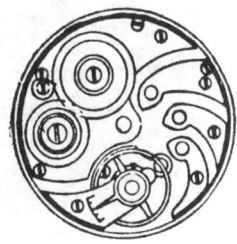

Model 2, 0 size, three-quarter plate, bridge, open face, pendant set.

SAN JOSE WATCH CO.

California 1891

Very few watches were made by the San Jose Watch Co., and very little is known about them. The company purchased the Otay Watch Company and machinery and remaining watch movements. The San Jose Watch Co. produced about a dozen watches. Engraved on a San Jose Watch Co. movement S# 30,656 (First watch manufactured by San Jose Watch Co. November 1891).

Grade or Name – Description		Avg	Ex-Fn	Mint
18S, 15J, LS, SW	★ ★ ★ ★	$2,800	$3,000	$3,500

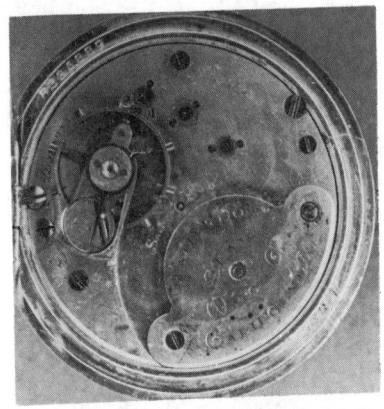

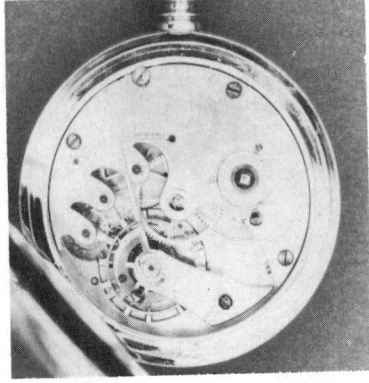

SAN JOSE WATCH CO. movement 18 size 15 jewels, Otay W. Co. material & machinery used to produce movement.

M.S. Smith & Co. movement, 18 size, 19 jewels, three-quarter plate, key wind & set.

M. S. SMITH & CO.

Detroit, Michigan 1870 - 1874

Eber B. Ward purchased the M. S. Smith & Co. which was a large jewelry firm. These watches carried the Smith name on them. A Mr. Hoyt was engaged to produce these watches and about 100 were produced before the Freeport Watch Co. purchased the firm. These watches are very similar to the "J.H. Allison" movements.

Grade or Name – Description		Avg	Ex-Fn	Mint
18S, 19J, 3/4, KW, KS, Freeport Model, 18K case	★ ★ ★	$2,500	$3,000	$3,600
18S, 19J, 3/4, KW, KS, Freeport Model	★ ★ ★	1,200	1,500	2,300
18S, 15J, 3/4, wolf 's tooth -wind, Swiss, 14K HC	★	800	900	1,100
6S, 15J, KW, KS, HC 18K case	★	700	800	1,000
6S, 15J, SW	★	400	500	700

M. S. Smith & Co., 18S, 15J, 3/4, wolf's tooth -wind, Swiss, Ca. 1874.

M. S. Smith, 6-8 size, 15 jewels, KW KS, Swiss, 18K HC, Ca. 1870.

SOUTH BEND WATCH CO.

South Bend, Indiana
March 1903 - December 1929

Three brothers, George, Clement and J. M. Studebaker, purchased the successful Columbus Watch Co. The first South Bend watches were full plate and similar to the Columbus watches. The serial numbers started at 380,501 where as the Columbus serial numbers stopped at about 500,000. The highest grade watch was a "Polaris," a 16S, 3/4 plate, 21 jewels, and with an open face. This watch sold for about $100. The 227 and 229 were also high grade. The company identified its movements by model numbers 1, 2, and 3, and had grades from 100 to 431. The even numbers were hunting cases, and the odd numbers were open-faced cases. The lowest grade was a 203, 7J, that sold for about $6.75. The company closed on Dec. 31, 1929.

SOUTH BEND ESTIMATED SERIAL NUMBERS
AND PRODUCTION DATES

DATE – SERIAL NO.	DATE – SERIAL NO.	DATE – SERIAL NO.	DATE – SERIAL NO.
1903 – 380,501	1910 – 620,000	1917 – 865,000	1924 – 1,110,000
1904 – 410,000	1911 – 655,000	1918 – 900,000	1925 – 1,145,000
1905 – 445,000	1912 – 690,000	1919 – 935,000	1926 – 1,180,000
1906 – 480,000	1913 – 725,000	1920 – 970,000	1927 – 1,215,000
1907 – 515,000	1914 – 760,000	1921 – 1,005,000	1928 – 1,250,000
1908 – 550,000	1915 – 795,000	1922 – 1,040,000	1929 – 1,275,000
1909 – 585,000	1916 – 825,000	1923 – 1,075,000	

The above list is provided for determining the APPROXIMATE age of your watch. Match serial number with date. Watches were not necessarily sold in the exact order of manufactured date.

SOUTH BEND
18 SIZE (Lever set)

Grade or Name – Description	Avg	Ex-Fn	Mint
South Bend, 15J, OF	$100	$125	$175
South Bend, 15J, HC	125	150	200
South Bend, 17J, OF	100	125	175
South Bend, 17J, HC	125	150	200
South Bend, 21J, OF	250	275	325
South Bend, 21J, HC, **14K**	725	800	900
South Bend, 21J, OF, HC, Silveroid	250	275	300
South Bend, 21J, SW, HC	400	450	500
The Studebaker, G#323, 17J, GJS, NI, Adj.5P, OF	300	375	450
The Studebaker, G#328, 21J, GJS, NI, FULL, Adj.5P, HC .... ★	550	700	875
The Studebaker, G#329, 21J, GJS, NI, FULL, Adj.5P, OF	450	525	575
304, 15J, HC	125	150	200

IMPORTANT NOTE: Railroad Standards, Railroad Approved & Railroad Grade **terminology**, as defined and used in this _**BOOK**_.
1. **RAILROAD STANDARDS** = A commission or board appointed by the railroad companies outlined a set of **guidelines** to be accepted or approved by each railroad line.
2. **RAILROAD APPROVED** = A LIST of watches each railroad line would approve if purchased by their employee's. (this list changed through the years).
3. **RAILROAD GRADE** = A watch made by manufactures to met or exceed the guidelines set by the railroad **standards**. Grade such as 992, Vanguard and B.W. Raymond etc.
🕐 Some GRADES **exceeded** the R.R. standards such as 23 jewels, diamond end stone, gold train, raised gold jewel settings, double sunk dial and the list goes on. Examples: such as Veritas, Sangamo, 950 & Riverside Maximus and many others.

🕐 Generic, nameless or **unmarked** grades for watch movements are listed under the Company name or initials of the Company, etc. by size, jewel count and description.

🕐 Watches listed in this book are priced at the collectable retail level, as **complete** watches having an original 14k gold-filled case and _Key Wind_ with silver, an original white enamel single sunk dial, and with the entire original movement in good working order with no repairs needed.

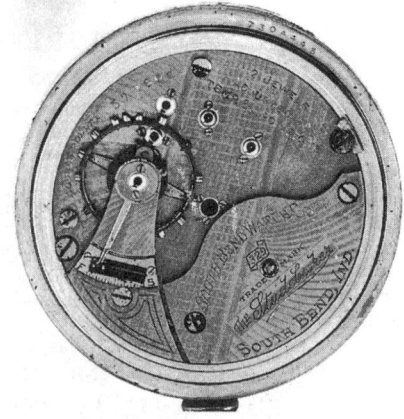

South Bend movement, 18 size, 17 jewels, stem wind, hunting, serial number 426,726.

The Studebaker in (SCRIPT), 18 size, 21 jewels, gold jewel settings, marked 329, stem wind.

Grade or Name – Description		Avg	Ex-Fn	Mint
305, 15J, OF		$100	$125	$175
305, 15J, OF, Silveroid		75	100	125
309, 17J, OF		100	125	175
312, 17J, HC, NI, ADJ		125	150	200
313, 17J, OF, NI, ADJ, **marked 313**	★	225	275	350
315, 17J, OF, NI, Adj.3P		100	125	175
G#s 323, 328 & 329 see "The Studebaker"				
327, 21J, OF, Adj.5P, marked 327	★	300	350	450
327, 21J, OF, Adj.5P, marked 327, Silveroid	★	225	250	300
330, 15J, M#1, LS, HC		125	150	225
331, 15J, M#1, LS, OF		100	125	175
332, 15J, HC		200	250	325
333, 15J, OF		100	125	175
337, 17J, OF		100	125	175
340, 17J, M#1, Adj.3P, NI, HC		150	175	225
341, 17J, M#1, ADJ, NI, Adj.3P, OF		125	150	200
342, 17J, M#1, LS		100	125	175
343, 17J, M#1, LS, OF		100	125	175
344, 17J, HC, NI, Adj.3P	★★	325	375	450
345, 17J, OF, NI, Adj.3P	★★	300	350	425
346, 17J, HC, NI	★★	325	375	450
347, 17J, OF, NI		100	125	150
355, 19J, GJS, 2-Tone, HC	★★	1,000	1,200	1,500

🕘 Generic, nameless or **unmarked** grades for watch movements are listed under the Company name or initials of the Company, etc. by size, jewel count and description.

🕘 Watches listed in this book are priced at the collectable retail level, as **complete** watches having an original 14k gold-filled case and *Key Wind* with silver, an original white enamel single sunk dial, and with the entire original movement in good working order with no repairs needed.

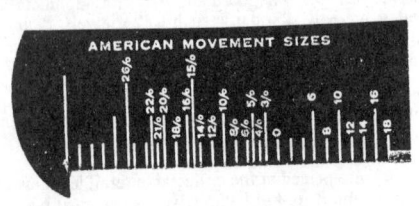

AMERICAN MOVEMENT SIZES

Grade 211, 16 size, 17 jewels, three-quarter plate, serial number 703,389.

Grade 295, 16 size, 21 jewels, first model, gold jewel settings, gold train, open face, serial number 518,022.

16 SIZE
M#1 Lever set

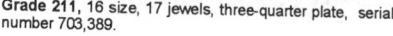

Grade or Name – Description	Avg	Ex-Fn	Mint
Polaris, 21J, M#1, Adj.5P, 3/4, NI, DR, GJS, GT, 14K South Bend case with Polaris dial ★★	$1,800	$2,000	$2,400
South Bend, 7J, OF	75	100	125
South Bend, 7J, HC	100	125	175
South Bend, 9J, OF	75	100	125
South Bend, 9J, HC	100	125	175
South Bend, 15J, OF	75	100	125
South Bend, 15J, HC	100	125	175
South Bend, 15J, OF, Silveroid	75	100	125
South Bend, 17J, OF	75	100	125
South Bend, 17J, HC, ADJ	125	150	200
South Bend, 17J, **14K HC**	485	500	575
South Bend, 21J, OF, Adj, 5P	250	275	325
South Bend, 21J, HC, ADJ	325	375	425
The Studebaker 223, 17J, M#2, Adj.5P, GJS, DR, GT ★★	350	400	475
The Studebaker 229, 21J, M#2, Adj.5P, GJS, DR, GT ★★	450	500	575
Studebaker, 21J, OF, PS, Adj.5P	325	375	425
203, 7J, 3/4, NI, OF	75	100	125
204, 15J, 3/4, NI, HC	100	125	175
207, 15J, OF, PS	75	100	125
209, 9J, M#2, OF, PS	75	100	125
211, 17J, M#2, 3/4, NI, OF	75	100	125
212, 17J, M#2, HC, LS, heat & cold	125	150	200
215, 17J, M#2, OF, LS, heat & cold	75	100	125
215, 17J, M#2, OF, SILVEROID	75	100	125
217, 17J, M#2, OF, NI, BRG, DR, GT, ADJ.3P	100	125	175
219, 19J, OF, NI, PS, BRG, DR, ADJ.4P	150	175	225

🕐 Generic, nameless or unmarked grades for watch movements are listed under the Company name or initials of the Company, etc. by size, jewel count and description.

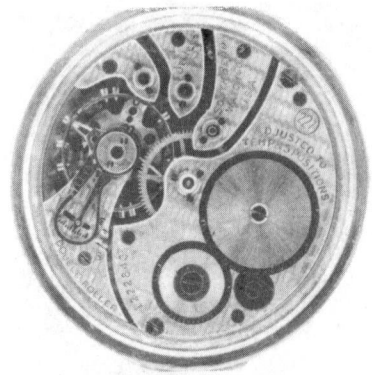

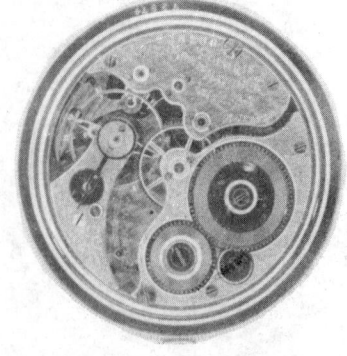

South Bend Watch Co. Polaris, 16 size, 21 jewels, model number 1, Adj5p, gold jewel setting, gold train, open face, serial number 518,236.

Grade 227, 16 size, 21 jewels, RR approved, gold jewel settings, Adj5p, serial number 1,222,843.

Grade or Name – Description		Avg	Ex-Fn	Mint
223, 17J, M#2, OF, LS, ADJ.5P		$75	$100	$125
227, 21J, M#2, BRG, NI, LS, DR, ADJ.5P, OF		225	250	300
260, 7J, M#1, HC		100	125	150
261, 7J, M#1, OF		75	100	125
280, 15J, M#1, HC		125	135	150
281, 15J, M#1, OF		85	100	135
290, 17J, M#1, LS, ADJ.3P, HC	★★	225	275	350
291, 17J, M#1, OF, ADJ.3P	★★	200	225	300
292, 19J, M#1, HC, 3/4, GJS, NI, DR, Adj,5P	★	275	325	400
293, 19J, M#1, OF, 3/4, GJS, NI, DR, Adj,5P	★	200	250	300
294, 21J, M#1, ADJ.5P, GJS, GT, HC, marked 294	★★	325	375	500
295, 21J, M#1 OF, LS, ADJ.5P, GJS, GT, marked 295	★	375	425	500
298, 17J, M#1, HC, ADJ.3P	★★	225	275	350
299, 17J, M#1, OF, ADJ.3P	★★	200	250	300

12 SIZE
(OF Only)

Grade or Name – Description		Avg	Ex-Fn	Mint
Chesterfield, 15J, BRG, NI, DR, G#407		$75	$100	$125
Chesterfield, 17J, BRG, NI, DR, GJS, ADJ.3P,G#419		75	100	125
Chesterfield, 21J, BRG, NI, DR, GJS, ADJ.5P,G#431	★	125	135	150
Digital,Studebaker, 21J, BRG, NI, DR, GJS, ADJ.5P,	★★	225	275	350
South Bend, 15J		75	100	125
South Bend, 17J		75	100	125
South Bend, 17J, Silveroid		75	100	125
South Bend, 19J		95	125	150
South Bend, 21J		125	150	185
Studebaker, 21J, PS, 3/4, NI, Adj.5P, GJS		175	200	225
407, 15J, Silveroid		75	100	125
407, 15J		75	100	125
411, 17J, DR, GJS		100	125	150
415, 17J, ADJ to temp.	★★	125	150	200
419, 17J, Adj.3P	★★	135	165	225
429, 19J, Adj.4P, GT, GJS	★	100	125	150
431, 21J, Adj.5P, DR, GJS	★★	150	175	225
431, 21J, Adj.5P, Silveroid		125	150	200

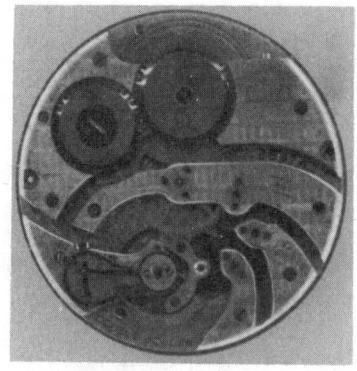

Grade 411, 12 size, 17 jewels, open face, double roller.

Chesterfield, 12 size, 21 jewels, open face only, bridge, gold jewel settings, pendant set, double roller, Adj5p.

6 SIZE

Grade or Name – Description		Avg	Ex-Fn	Mint
South Bend, 11J, G#160, HC	★	$100	$125	$150
South Bend, 15J, G#170, HC	★	125	150	225
South Bend, 17J, G#180, HC	★ ★	125	150	225
South Bend, 17J, G#180, **14K,HC**	★ ★	225	275	325

South Bend, 6 size, grade # 170, 15 jewels.

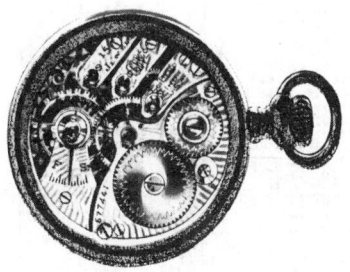

Grade 120-HC, 121-OF, 0 size, 17 jewels, bridge, nickel, double roller, pendant set.

0 SIZE

Grade or Name – Description		Avg	Ex-Fn	Mint
South Bend, 15J, M# 1 & 2, OF, PS		$75	$100	$150
Grade 100 HC & 101 OF, 7J, PS		100	125	175
Grade 110 HC & 111 OF, 15J, 3F Brg, DR	★	125	150	175
Grade 120 HC & 121 OF, 17J, BRG, NI, DR, PS	★ ★	150	175	225
Grade 150 HC & 151 OF, 17J, M# 3, BRG, NI, PS	★ ★	150	175	225

Record of Serial and Grade Numbers of South Bend Watch Movements

Serial Number	Grade	Size	Model	Jewels	Serial Number	Grade	Size	Model	Jewels
1000 to 4000...	Htg.	18	1	7	400001 to 401200...	331	18	1	15
4001 to 7000...	"	18	1	7	401201 to 403200...	330	18	1	15
7001 to 10000...	"	16	1	15	403201 to 407200...	341	18	1	17
10001 to 21000...	"	18	1	15	407201 to 408500...	340	18	1	17
21001 to 29500...	"	16	1	7	408501 to 408700...	342	18	1	17
29501 to 37000...	"	18	1	7	408701 to 409200...	342	18	1	17
37001 to 41000...	"	16	1	15	409201 to 412200...	330	18	1	15
41001 to 52000...	"	18	1	15	412201 to 413800...	290	16	1	17
52001 to 61000...	"	18	1	7	413801 to 414800...	342	18	1	17
61001 to 76000...	"	18	1	15	414801 to 415800...	291	16	1	17
76001 to 83000...	"	16	1	15	415801 to 417700...	331	18	1	15
83001 to 92000...	"	16	1	7	417701 to 418700...	342	18	1	17
92001 to 97000...	"	18	1	7	418701 to 419700...	343	18	1	17
97001 to 105000...	"	18	1	15	419701 to 420600...	290	16	1	17
105001 to 114000...	"	16	1	17	420601 to 421900...	291	16	1	17
114001 to 127000...	"	18	1	15	421901 to 422400...	281	16	1	15
127501 to 138000...	"	18	1	17	422401 to 423200...	280	16	1	15
138001 to 156000...	"	16	1	7	423201 to 423800...	343	18	1	17
156001 to 165000...	"	18	1	15	423801 to 425800...	261	16	1	7
165001 to 171000...	"	16	1	7	425801 to 426100...	281	16	1	15
171001 to 196000...	"	16	1	17	426101 to 428100...	342	18	1	17
196001 to 201000...	"	18	1	7	428101 to 431100...	260	16	1	7
201001 to 214000...	"	18	1	15	431101 to 431600...	280	16	1	15
214001 to 218000...	"	16	1	7	431601 to 432100...	281	16	1	15
218001 to 220000...	"	18	1	15	432101 to 433100...	342	18	1	17
220001 to 232000...	"	16	1	15	433101 to 435100...	340	18	1	17
232001 to 250000...	"	18	1	7	435101 to 436600...	280	16	1	15
250001 to 261000...	"	16	1	7	436601 to 437900...	281	16	1	15
261001 to 267000...	"	16	1	15	437901 to 438200...	280	16	1	15
267001 to 271000...	"	18	1	15	438201 to 438500...	290	16	1	17
271001 to 274000...	"	16	1	15	438501 to 439500...	293	16	1	19
274001 to 281000...	"	16	1	7	439501 to 440500...	280	16	1	15
281001 to 292000...	"	18	1	7	440501 to 441500...	290	16	1	17
292001 to 294000...	"	16	1	17	441501 to 441600...	260	16	1	7
294001 to 295500...	"	18	1	17	441601 to 441700...	261	16	1	7
295501 to 299100...	"	16	1	7	441701 to 441800...	290	16	1	17
299101 to 302000...	"	18	1	7	441801 to 441850...	293	16	1	17
302001 to 311000...	"	16	1	7	441901 to 445900...	280	16	1	15
311001 to 314000...	"	16	1	15	445901 to 446000...	Htg.	16	1	21
314001 to 321000...	"	18	1	15	446001 to 447000...	261	16	1	7
321001 to 329000...	"	18	1	7	447001 to 450000...	260	16	1	7
329001 to 334000...	"	18	1	7	450001 to 451000...	261	16	1	7
334001 to 341000...	"	16	1	15	451001 to 453000...	260	16	1	7
341001 to 347000...	"	16	1	7	453001 to 455000...	261	16	1	7
347001 to 349500...	"	16	1	17	455001 to 457000...	343	18	1	17
349501 to 354000...	"	16	1	15	457001 to 461000...	260	16	1	7
354001 to 361000...	"	18	1	7	461001 to 462500...	331	18	1	15
361001 to 366000...	"	16	1	7	462501 to 464000...	281	16	1	15
366001 to 368000...	"	18	1	17	464001 to 465300...	331	18	1	15
368001 to 371000...	"	16	1	15	465301 to 467300...	261	16	1	7
371001 to 374000...	"	18	1	15	467301 to 468800...	331	18	1	15
374001 to 376000...	"	16	1	17	468801 to 469300...	290	16	1	17
376001 to 377000...	"	16	1	15	469301 to 469800...	294	16	1	21
377001 to 378000...	"	18	1	17	469801 to 470100...	295	16	1	21
378001 to 379500...	"	18	1	15	*470101 to 470200...	295	16	1	21
379501 to 380500...	"	16	1	15	470201 to 470300...	295	16	1	21
380501 to 381000...	160	6	1	11	470301 to 471300...	281	16	1	15
381001 to 381500...	170	6	1	15	471301 to 472300...	280	16	1	15
381501 to 382500...	330	18	1	15	472301 to 473300...	281	16	1	15
382501 to 383000...	160	6	1	11	473301 to 474800...	330	18	1	15
383001 to 383500...	170	6	1	15	474801 to 475800...	331	18	1	15
*383501 to 384000...	302	18	1	15	475801 to 476800...	290	16	1	17
384001 to 384500...	160	6	1	11	477001 to 478000...	261	16	1	7
384501 to 384900...	291	16	1	17	478001 to 479000...	330	18	1	15
384901 to 385200...	281	16	1	15	479001 to 480000...	261	16	1	7
385201 to 385500...	291	16	1	17	480001 to 480200...	295	16	1	21
385501 to 386400...	290	16	1	17	*480201 to 480500...	295	16	1	21
386401 to 386900...	280	16	1	15	480501 to 481500...	290	16	1	17
386901 to 387400...	170	6	1	15	481501 to 483500...	291	16	1	17
387401 to 387900...	330	18	1	15	483501 to 485000...	280	16	1	15
387901 to 388400...	331	18	1	15	485001 to 486000...	331	18	1	15
388401 to 389400...	180	6	1	17	486001 to 487000...	330	18	1	15
389401 to 389900...	170	6	1	15	487001 to 489000...	331	18	1	15
389901 to 390400...	341	18	1	17	489001 to 490000...	341	18	1	17
390401 to 390900...	331	18	1	15	*490001 to 490500...	294	16	1	21
390901 to 391200...	330	18	1	15	490501 to 490800...	293	16	1	19
391201 to 391700...	341	18	1	17	*490801 to 490900...	293	16	1	19
391701 to 392600...	330	18	1	15	490901 to 491000...	293	16	1	19
392601 to 394100...	331	18	1	15	491001 to 492000...	281	16	1	15
394101 to 396000...	330	18	1	15	492001 to 493000...	330	18	1	15
396001 to 400000...	340	18	1	17	493001 to 494000...	340	18	1	17

Although grade numbers appear in this list some of the earlier watches did not have grade numbers stamped upon them. In all instances odd grade numbers indicate open face movement, even grade numbers indicate hunting movement.

*Watches with these serial numbers have double roller.

Serial Number	Grade	Size	Model	Jewels	Serial Number	Grade	Size	Model	Jewels
494001 to 495000...	290	16	1	17	570001 to 571000...	261	16	1	7
495001 to 497000...	331	18	1	15	*571001 to 572000...	313	18	2	17
497001 to 498000...	261	16	1	7	572001 to 573000...	280	16	1	15
498001 to 499000...	291	16	1	17	573001 to 574000...	347	18	2	17
499001 to 500000...	261	16	1	7	*574001 to 575000...	323	18	2	17
500001 to 501000...	281	16	1	15	*575001 to 576000...	217	16	2	17
501001 to 502000...	290	16	1	17	576001 to 577000...	333	18	2	15
502001 to 503000...	331	18	1	15	577001 to 578000...	281	16	1	15
503001 to 503500...	341	18	1	17	*578001 to 579000...	223	16	2	17
503501 to 504000...	343	18	1	17	*579001 to 580000...	329	18	2	21
504001 to 505000...	290	16	1	17	*580001 to 581000...	212	16	2	17
505001 to 505100...	293	16	1	19	*581001 to 582000...	333	18	2	15
505101 to 505500...	293	16	1	19	582001 to 583000...	261	16	1	7
505501 to 506500...	261	16	1	7	*583001 to 584000...	227	16	2	21
506501 to 507500...	280	16	1	15	*584001 to 585000...	229	16	2	21
507501 to 508500...	261	16	1	7	585001 to 586000...	207	16	2	15
508501 to 509500...	280	16	1	15	586001 to 587000...	211	16	2	17
509501 to 510500...	281	16	1	15	*587001 to 588000...	215	16	2	17
510501 to 511400...	291	16	1	17	588001 to 589000...	260	16	1	7
511401 to 511500...	299	16	1	17	*589001 to 590000...	217	16	2	17
511501 to 511900...	292	16	1	19	590001 to 591000...	204	16	2	15
511901 to 512000...	292	16	1	19	591001 to 592000...	203	16	2	7
512001 to 513000...	333	18	2	15	592001 to 593000...	207	16	2	15
513001 to 514000...	280	16	1	15	*593001 to 594000...	212	16	2	17
514001 to 515000...	261	16	1	7	594001 to 595000...	203	16	2	7
515001 to 516000...	260	16	1	7	595001 to 596000...	332	18	2	15
516001 to 516500...	298	16	1	17	*596001 to 597000...	215	16	2	17
516501 to 516600...	298	16	1	17	*597001 to 598000...	223	16	2	17
516601 to 516800...	298	16	1	17	*598001 to 599000...	229	16	2	21
516801 to 516900...	298	16	1	17	599001 to 600000...	260	16	1	7
516901 to 517000...	298	16	1	17	600001 to 601000...	211	16	2	17
517001 to 517700...	345	18	2	17	*601001 to 602000...	313	18	2	17
517701 to 518000...	345	18	2	17	602001 to 603000...	203	16	2	7
518001 to 518500...	295	16	1	21	603001 to 604000...	204	16	2	15
518501 to 519000...	294	16	1	21	604001 to 605000...	207	16	2	15
519001 to 520000...	347	18	2	17	605001 to 606000...	333	18	2	15
520001 to 521000...	332	18	2	15	606001 to 607000...	347	18	2	17
521001 to 522000...	329	18	2	21	*607001 to 608000...	215	16	2	17
522001 to 523000...	293	16	1	19	608001 to 609000...	211	16	2	17
523001 to 523400...	299	16	1	17	609001 to 610000...	203	16	2	7
523401 to 524000...	299	16	1	17	*610001 to 611000...	215	16	2	17
524001 to 524300...	344	18	2	17	611001 to 612000...	207	16	2	15
524301 to 524800...	344	18	2	17	612001 to 613000...	203	16	2	7
524801 to 525000...	344	18	2	17	*613001 to 614000...	212	16	2	17
525001 to 526000...	346	18	2	17	614001 to 615000...	305	18	2	15
526001 to 527000...	333	18	2	15	615001 to 616000...	204	16	2	15
527001 to 528000...	347	18	2	17	616001 to 617000...	207	16	2	15
528001 to 529000...	345	18	2	17	617001 to 618000...	203	16	2	7
529001 to 530000...	292	16	1	19	*618001 to 619000...	415	12	1	17
530001 to 531000...	260	16	1	7	*619001 to 620000...	431	12	1	21
531001 to 532000...	281	16	1	15	620001 to 621000...	211	16	2	17
532001 to 533000...	333	18	2	15	*621001 to 622000...	223	16	2	17
533001 to 534000...	323	18	2	17	*622001 to 623000...	229	16	2	21
534001 to 535000...	345	18	2	17	*623001 to 624000...	411	12	1	17
535001 to 536000...	347	18	2	17	*624001 to 625000...	215	16	2	17
536001 to 537000...	333	18	2	15	625001 to 626000...	203	16	2	7
537001 to 538000...	312	18	2	17	626001 to 627000...	305	18	2	15
538001 to 539000...	332	18	2	15	627001 to 628000...	207	16	2	15
539001 to 539500...	298	16	1	17	*628001 to 629000...	419	12	1	17
539501 to 539700...	298	16	1	17	629001 to 630000...	260	16	1	7
539701 to 540000...	298	16	1	17	*630001 to 631000...	407	12	1	15
540001 to 540400...	299	16	1	17	*631001 to 632000...	217	16	2	17
540401 to 541000...	299	16	1	17	632001 to 633000...	204	16	2	15
541001 to 542000...	328	18	2	21	633001 to 634000...	347	16	2	17
542001 to 543000...	313	18	2	17	*634001 to 635000...	329	18	2	21
543001 to 544000...	261	16	1	7	635001 to 636000...	203	16	2	7
544001 to 545000...	260	16	1	7	*636001 to 637000...	217	16	2	17
545001 to 546000...	333	18	2	15	*637001 to 638000...	411	12	1	17
546001 to 547000...	332	18	2	15	638001 to 639000...	211	16	2	17
547001 to 548000...	333	18	2	15	*639001 to 640000...	212	16	2	17
548001 to 549000...	346	18	2	17	*640001 to 641000...	217	16	2	17
549001 to 550000...	261	16	1	7	*641001 to 642000...	415	12	1	17
550001 to 551000...	280	16	1	15	642001 to 643000...	203	16	2	7
551001 to 552000...	281	16	1	15	*643001 to 644000...	229	16	2	21
552001 to 553000...	347	18	2	17	644001 to 645000...	260	16	1	7
553001 to 554000...	313	18	2	17	*645001 to 646000...	215	16	2	17
554001 to 555000...	323	18	2	17	646001 to 647000...	207	16	2	15
555001 to 556000...	327	18	2	21	*647001 to 648000...	407	12	1	15
556001 to 557000...	298	16	1	17	*648001 to 649000...	419	12	1	17
557001 to 558000...	299	16	1	17	649001 to 650000...	207	16	2	15
558001 to 559000...	347	18	2	17	650181 to 655200...	Htg.	0	1	7
559001 to 560000...	346	16	2	17	655201 to 656200...	"	0	1	15
560001 to 561000...	313	18	2	17	656201 to 659700...	"	0	1	7
561001 to 562000...	333	18	2	15	659701 to 662400...	"	0	1	7
562001 to 563000...	332	18	2	15	662401 to 662500...	O.F.	0	2	7
563001 to 564000...	261	16	2	7	662501 to 665400...	Htg.	0	2	7
564001 to 565000...	347	18	2	17	665401 to 665500...	O.F.	0	2	7
565001 to 566000...	260	16	1	7	665501 to 666000...	Htg.	0	2	7
566001 to 567000...	211	16	2	17	666001 to 666500...	"	0	2	17
567001 to 569000...	333	18	2	15	666501 to 666600...	"	0	2	15
569001 to 570000...	215	16	2	17	666601 to 666650...	O. F.	0	2	15

Although grade numbers appear in this list some of the earlier watches did not have grade numbers stamped upon them. In all instances odd grade numbers indicate open face movement, even grade numbers indicate hunting movement.
*Watches with these serial numbers have double roller.

Serial Number	Grade	Size	Model	Jewels
666651 to 667500...	Htg.	0	2	15
667501 to 671500...	"	0	2	7
671501 to 671600...	O. F.	0	2	7
671601 to 672800...	Htg.	0	2	7
672801 to 672900...	O. F.	0	2	7
672901 to 673000...	Htg.	0	2	15
673001 to 674000...	"	0	2	17
674001 to 675000...	"	0	2	7
675001 to 676000...	"	0	2	15
676001 to 679400...	"	0	2	15
679401 to 679500...	O. F.	0	2	15
679501 to 680400...	Htg.	0	2	15
680401 to 680500...	O. F.	0	2	15
680501 to 681000...	Htg.	0	2	15
681001 to 682000...	"	0	2	17
682001 to 682800...	"	0	2	15
682801 to 682900...	O. F.	0	2	15
682901 to 683000...	Htg.	0	2	15
683001 to 684000...	"	0	2	17
684001 to 684600...	"	0	2	7
684601 to 684700...	O. F.	0	2	7
684701 to 685000...	Htg.	0	2	7
685001 to 686000...	"	0	2	15
686001 to 686100...	101	0	2	7
686101 to 687000...	100	0	2	7
687001 to 687100...	111	0	2	15
687101 to 688000...	110	0	2	15
688001 to 688100...	101	0	2	7
688101 to 689000...	100	0	2	7
689001 to 689100...	111	0	2	15
689101 to 690000...	110	0	2	15
690001 to 690100...	101	0	2	7
690101 to 691000...	100	0	2	7
691001 to 691100...	101	0	2	7
691101 to 692000...	100	0	2	7
692001 to 692100...	111	0	2	15
692101 to 693000...	110	0	2	15
693001 to 693100...	101	0	2	7
693101 to 694000...	100	0	2	7
•694001 to 695000...	217	16	2	17
695001 to 696000...	305	18	2	15
696001 to 696100...	111	0	2	15
696101 to 697000...	110	0	2	15
697001 to 697100...	101	0	2	7
697101 to 698000...	100	0	2	7
•698001 to 699000...	215	16	2	17
•699001 to 700000...	415	12	1	17
•700001 to 701000...	431	12	1	21
•701001 to 702000...	313	18	2	17
702001 to 702100...	111	0	2	15
702101 to 703000...	110	0	2	15
703001 to 704000...	211	16	2	17
•704001 to 705000...	212	16	2	17
705001 to 706000...	305	18	2	15
•706001 to 707000...	215	16	2	17
707001 to 708000...	203	16	2	7
•708001 to 709000...	407	12	1	15
709001 to 710000...	204	16	2	15
710001 to 711000...	305	18	2	15
711001 to 712000...	260	16	1	7
712001 to 713000...	207	16	2	15
•713001 to 713000...	111	0	2	15
•713101 to 714000...	110	0	2	15
•714001 to 715000...	227	16	2	21
715001 to 716000...	211	16	2	17
•716001 to 717000...	411	12	1	17
•717001 to 717100...	101	0	2	7
•717101 to 718000...	100	0	2	7
•718001 to 719000...	215	16	2	17
719001 to 720000...	309	18	2	17
720001 to 721000...	203	16	2	7
•721001 to 722000...	227	16	2	21
722001 to 723000...	204	16	2	15
723001 to 724000...	207	16	2	15
724001 to 725000...	211	16	2	17
•725001 to 726000...	217	16	2	17
726001 to 727000...	227	16	2	21
•727001 to 728000...	223	16	2	17
•728001 to 729000...	212	16	2	15
729001 to 730000...	305	18	2	15
730001 to 731000...	304	18	2	15
•731001 to 732000...	313	18	2	17
732001 to 733000...	309	18	2	17
733001 to 734000...	211	16	2	17
•734001 to 735000...	215	16	2	17
•735001 to 736000...	217	16	2	17
736001 to 737000...		0	2	17
•737001 to 738000...	227	16	2	21
•738001 to 739000...	215	16	2	17

Serial Number	Grade	Size	Model	Jewels
•739001 to 740000...	217	16	2	17
•740001 to 740200...	101	0	2	7
•740201 to 741000...	100	0	2	7
•741001 to 741200...	111	0	2	15
•741201 to 742000...	110	0	2	15
742001 to 743000...	207	16	2	15
743001 to 744000...	203	16	2	7
•744001 to 745000...	212	16	2	17
•745001 to 746000...	227	16	2	21
•746001 to 746100...	111	0	2	15
•746101 to 747000...	110	0	2	15
747001 to 748000...	305	18	2	15
748001 to 749600...	309	18	2	17
•749601 to 750000...	223	16	2	17
750001 to 751000...	207	16	2	15
•751001 to 751100...	101	0	2	7
•751101 to 752000...	100	0	2	7
752001 to 753000...	211	16	2	17
•753001 to 754000...	229	16	2	21
754001 to 755000...	203	16	2	7
•755001 to 756000...	215	16	2	17
•756001 to 757000...	313	18	2	17
•757001 to 758000...	323	18	2	17
758001 to 759000...	204	16	2	15
•759001 to 759500...	Htg.	0	2	17
759501 to 759510...	150	0	3	17
759511 to 759520...	103	0	3	7
759521 to 759530...	102	0	3	7
759531 to 759540...	151	0	3	17
759541 to 760000...	Htg.	0	2	17
760001 to 761000...	305	18	2	15
761001 to 762000...	207	16	2	15
•762001 to 762100...	111	0	2	15
762101 to 763000...	110	0	2	17
763001 to 764000...	203	16	2	7
•764001 to 765000...	215	16	2	17
•765001 to 766000...	217	16	2	17
766001 to 767000...	211	16	2	17
•767001 to 768000...	217	16	2	17
•768001 to 769000...	212	16	2	17
•769001 to 770000...	217	16	2	17
•770001 to 771000...	151	0	3	17
•771001 to 772000...	217	16	2	17
•772001 to 773000...	150	0	2	17
•773001 to 774000...	215	16	2	17
•774001 to 775000...	107	0	3	15
•775001 to 776000...	106	0	3	15
776001 to 777000...	207	16	2	15
•777001 to 778000...	102	0	3	15
•778001 to 779000...	103	0	3	17
779001 to 780000...	211	16	2	17
780001 to 781000...	203	16	2	17
781001 to 782000...	305	18	2	15
•782001 to 783000...	217	16	2	17
•783001 to 784000...	215	16	2	17
784001 to 785000...	207	16	2	15
•785001 to 786000...	215	16	2	17
•786001 to 787000...	227	16	2	21
•787001 to 788000...	407	12	1	17
•788001 to 789000...	217	16	2	17
789001 to 790000...	211	16	2	17
•790001 to 791000...	215	16	2	17
•791001 to 792000...	217	16	2	17
•792001 to 793000...	407	12	1	17
•793001 to 794000...	215	16	2	17
•794001 to 795000...	212	16	2	17
•795001 to 796000...	411	12	1	17
796001 to 797000...	203	16	2	7
•797001 to 798000...	407	12	1	17
•798001 to 799000...	429	12	1	17
•799001 to 800000...	411	12	1	17
•800001 to 801000...	219	16	2	17
•801001 to 802000...	429	12	1	17
•802001 to 804000...	219	16	2	17
•804001 to 805000...	411	12	1	17
•805001 to 806000...	407	12	1	17
•806001 to 808000...	429	12	1	17
•808001 to 809000...	219	16	2	17
•809001 to 810000...	411	12	1	17
•810001 to 811000...	429	12	1	17
•811001 to 812000...	211	16	2	17
•812001 to 814000...	219	16	2	17
•814001 to 815000...	429	12	1	17
•815001 to 816000...	407	12	1	17
•816001 to 817000...	219	16	2	17
•817001 to 818000...	429	12	1	17
•818001 to 819000...	219	16	2	17
•819001 to 820000...	429	12	1	17

Although grade numbers appear in this list some of the earlier watches did not have grade numbers stamped upon them. In all instances odd grade numbers indicate open face movement, even grade numbers indicate hunting movement.

•Watches with these serial numbers have double roller.

A-

18 SIZE—MODEL 1
Open Face and Hunting Lever Set

No. 341—Open Face, 17 Jewels, Lever Set, Adjusted to Temperature & 3 Positions.
No. 340—Hunting, 17 Jewels, Lever Set, Adjusted to Temperature & 3 Positions.
No. 343—Open Face, 17 Jewels, Lever Set.
No. 342—Hunting, 17 Jewels, Lever Set.
No. 331—Open Face, 15 Jewels, Lever Set.
No. 330—Hunting, 15 Jewels, Lever Set.

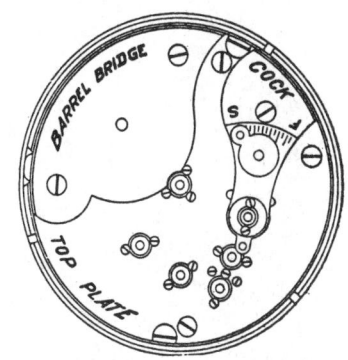

Model 1, Full Plate, Open face.   Model 1 , Full Plate, Hunting

18 SIZE—MODEL 2
Open Face and Hunting, Lever Set

No. 329—21J, Open Face, "Studebaker," Adjusted to Temperature and 5 Positions.
No. 328—21J, Hunting, "Studebaker," Adjusted to Temperature and 5 Positions.
No. 327—21J, Open Face, Adjusted to Temperature and 5 Positions.
No. 323—17J, Open Face, "Studebaker," Adjusted to Temperature and 5 Positions.
No. 345—17J, Open Face, Adjusted to Temperature and 3 Positions.
No. 344—17J, Hunting, Adjusted to Temperature and 3 Positions.
No. 313—17J, Open Face, Adjusted to Temperature.
No. 312—17J, Hunting, Adjusted to Temperature.
Nos. 309, 337, 347—17J, Open Face.
No. 346—17J, Hunting.
Nos. 333, 305—15J, Open Face.
Nos. 332, 304—15J, Hunting.

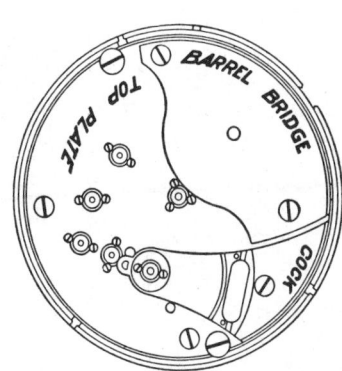
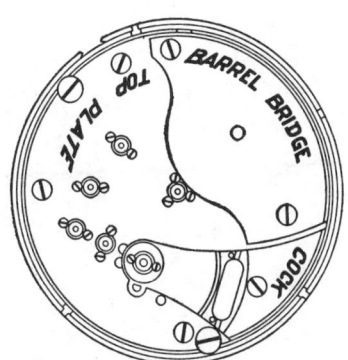

Model 2, Full Plate, Open face.   Model 2, Full Plate, Hunting.

16 SIZE—MODEL 1
Open Face and Hunting, Lever Set

No. 295—Open Face, 21 Jewels, Adjusted to Temperature and 5 Positions.
No. 294—Hunting, 21 Jewels, Adjusted to Temperature and 5 Positions.
No. 293—Open Face, 19 Jewels, Adjusted to Temperature and 5 Positions.
No. 292—Hunting, 19 Jewels, Adjusted to Temperature and 5 Positions.
No. 299—Open Face, 17 Jewels, Adjusted to Temperature and 3 Positions.
No. 298—Hunting, 17 Jewels, Adjusted to Temperature and 3 Positions.
No. 291—Open Face, 17 Jewels, Adjusted to Temperature and 3 Positions.
No. 290—Hunting, 17 Jewels, Adjusted to Temperature and 3 Positions.
No. 281—Open Face, 15 Jewels, & No. 280—Hunting, 15 Jewels.
No. 261—Open Face, 7 Jewels, & No. 260—Hunting, 7 Jewels.

Model 1, 3/4 Plate, Open Face.   Model 1, 3/4 Plate, Hunting.

16 SIZE—MODEL 2
Open Face and Hunting, Pendant and Lever Set.

No. 229—21J, Open Face, Lever Set, "Studebaker," Adjust. to Temp. and 5 Positions.
No. 227—21J, Open Face, Lever Set, Adjusted to Temperature and 5 Positions.
No. 219—19J, Open Face, Pendant Set, Adjusted to Temperature and 4 Positions.
No. 223—17J, Open Face, Lever Set, "Studebaker," Adjust. to Temp. and 5 Positions.
No. 217—17J, Open Face, Lever Set, Adjusted to Temperature and 3 Positions.
No. 215—17J, Open Face, Pendant Set, Adjusted to Temperature.
No. 212—17J, Hunting, Lever Set, Adjusted to Temperature.
No. 211—17J, Open Face, Pendant Set
No. 207—15J, Open Face, Pendant Set, & No. 204—15J, Hunting, Lever Set.
No. 209—9J, Open Face, Pendant Set, & No. 203—7J, Open Face, Pendant Set.

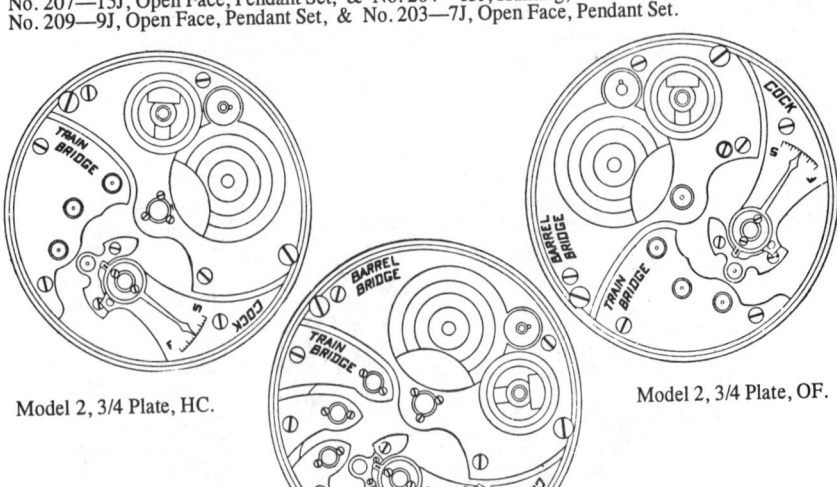

Model 2, 3/4 Plate, HC.   Model 2, 3/4 Plate, OF.

Model 2, Bridges, Open Face.

12 SIZE—MODEL 1
Chesterfield Series and Grade 429 Special
Made in Pendant Set, Open Face Only

No. 431—21J, Adjusted to Temperature and 5 Positions.
No. 429—19J, Adjusted to Temperature and 4 Positions.
No. 419—17J, Adjusted to Temperature and 3 Positions.
No. 415—17J, Adjusted to Temperature.
No. 411—17J.
No. 407—15J.

Model 1, Bridges, Open Face.

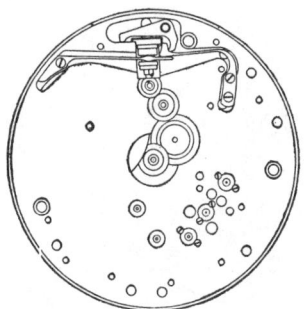

Model 1, Lower Plate, Dial Side.

6 SIZE— MODEL 1
Hunting

Grade No. 180, 17 Jewels
Grade No. 170, 15 Jewels
Grade No. 160, 11 Jewels

Serial Number Range
380,501 to 389,900

Model 1, 3/4 Plate, 6 size

0 SIZE—MODEL 1
Open Face, No second hand, Hunting has second hand

Model numbers 1 & 2 serial numbers under 659,700. All open face and hunting parts for this model except dial and fourth pinion are interchangeable.

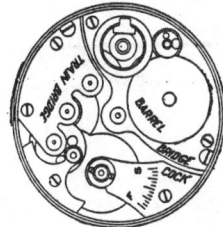

Model 1, Open Face, 3/4 Plate, 7 jewels.

Model 1, Hunting, Bridges, 15-17 jewels.

0 SIZE—MODEL 2
Open Face, No second hand, Hunting has second hand

No. 100— 7 Jewels, Hunting, 3/4 Bridge.
No. 101— 7 Jewels, Open Face, 3/4 Plate.
No. 110— 15 Jewels, Hunting, 3/4 Bridge.
No. 111— 15 Jewels, Open Face, 3/4 Plate.
No. 120— 17 Jewels, Hunting, 3/4 Bridge.
No. 121— 17 Jewels, Open Face, 3/4 Plate.

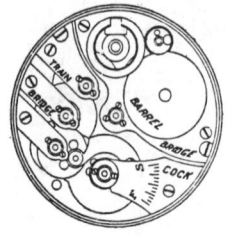

Model 2, Open Face, 3/4 Plate.   Model 2, Hunting, 3/4 Bridge.

Model numbers 1 & 2 serial numbers under 659,700. All open face and hunting parts for this model except dial and fourth pinion are interchangeable.

0 SIZE—MODEL 3
Both Open Face and Hunting have second hand

No. 151— 21J, Open Face, Bridge Model.
No. 150— 21J, Hunting, Bridge Model.
No. 121— 17J, Open Face, Bridge Model.
No. 120— 17J, Hunting, Bridge Model.

Model 3, Open Face, Bridges.   Model 3, Hunting, Bridges.

J. P. STEVENS & CO.

J. P. STEVENS & BRO.
J. P. STEVENS WATCH CO.
Atlanta, Georgia
1882 - 1887

In mid-1881 J. P. Stevens bought part of the Springfield Watch Co. of Massachusetts; and some unfinished watch components from E. F. Bowman. He set up his watchmaking firm above his jewelry store in Atlanta, Ga., and started to produce the Bowman unfinished watches which were 16 size and 18 size, to which was added the "Stevens Patent Regulator." This regulator is best described as a simple disc attached to the plate which has an eccentric groove cut for the arm of the regulator to move in. This regulator is a prominent feature of the J. P. Stevens, and only the top is jeweled. These watches were 16S, 3/4 plate, stem wind and had a nickel plate with damaskeening. The pallets were equidistant locking and needed greater accuracy in manufacturing. About 50 of these watches were made. A line of gilt movements was added. The pallet and fork are made of one piece aluminum. The aluminum was combined with 1/10 copper and formed an exceedingly tough metal which will not rust or become magnetized. The lever of this watch is only one-third the weight of a steel lever. The aluminum lever affords the least possible resistance for overcoming inertia in transmitting power from the escape wheel to the balance. In 1884, the company was turning out about ten watches a day at a price of $20 to $100 each. In the spring of 1887 the company failed. Only 174 true Stevens watches were made, but other watches carried the J. P. Stevens name.

Original J. P. Stevens movement, 16-18 size, 15 jewels, note patented eccentric style regulator, serial number 65.

J.P. Stevens Watch Co. movement by Columbus Watch Co., 18 size, 11-15 jewels.

16 TO 18 SIZE

Grade or Name – Description		Avg	Ex-Fn	Mint
Original Model, Serial Nos. 1 to 174, (recased)	★★★	$2,000	$2,500	$3,000
Original Model, Serial Nos. 1 to 174 with original J. P. Stevens dial & 18K case	★★★★	7,000	8,000	9,500
Aurora, 15-17J	★	350	400	525
Chronograph, 17J, Swiss made, fly back hand	★	500	600	750
Columbus W. Co., 15-17J	★	400	450	575

J. P. Stevens & Bro., on movement & dial, made by **Aurora**, 18 size, 15 jewels, Hunting Case, S # 39806.

J.P. Stevens & Bro., Swiss chronograph movement, about 18 size, with fly back hand.

Grade or Name – Description		Avg	Ex-Fn	Mint
Elgin, 15-17J	★	$300	$350	$425
Hamilton, 17J	★	400	450	525
Hampden, 15-17J		300	350	425
Illinois, 15-17J	★	600	650	725
N. Y. W. Co., 17J, Full Plate, S#s range in 500s	★	700	750	825
N. Y. W. Co. "Bond" Model, S#s range in 500s	★★	850	950	1,100
A. Potter, 14K case, Swiss made	★★	2,000	3,000	4,000
Rockford, 15J, Full Plate, HC	★	400	450	625
18S Swiss, 15-17J, bar style movement, wolf teeth winding		400	500	650
16S Swiss, 15-17J, Longines	★	175	200	250
16S Swiss, 15-17J, 3/4 plate	★	175	200	250
Waltham, 11-15-17J	★	400	450	625

J.P. Stevens & Bro., about 18 size, 17 jewels, wolf teeth winding, Ca. about 1889.

J.P. Stevens Watch Co. movement by **Waltham**, 18 size, 11 jewels, serial number 1,240,058.

J.P. **Stevens** movement made by Hampden, 18 size, 17 jewels, note eccentric style regulator, serial # 1695.

J.P. **Stevens & Bro.**, movement made by Hampden, model 4, 18 size, 17jewels, model 4, S#732,085.

6 SIZE

Grade or Name – Description	Avg	Ex-Fn	Mint
Ladies Model, 15J, LS, HC, 14K	$500	$575	$650
Ladies Model, 15J, LS, GF case, HC	225	275	350
Ladies Model, 15J, LS, GF cases, OF	200	250	325
Ladies Model, 15J, LS, GF cases, Swiss made	175	225	325

J.P. **Stevens Watch Co.**, 16 size, 15 jewels, Adjusted to temperature & positions, serial number 21,814.

J.P. **Stevens Watch Co.**, 6 size, 11 jewels, exposed winding gears.

🕐 Generic, nameless or **unmarked** grades for watch movements are listed under the Company name or initials of the Company, etc. by size, jewel count and description.

🕐 Watches listed in this book are priced at the collectable retail level, as **complete** watches having an original 14k gold-filled case and *Key Wind* with silver, an original white enamel single sunk dial, and with the entire original movement in good working order with no repairs needed.

SUFFOLK WATCH CO.

Waltham, Massachusetts 1899 - 1901

The Suffolk Watch Company officially succeeded the Columbia Watch Company in March 1901. However, the Suffolk 0-size, 7-jewel nickel movement with lever escapement was being manufactured in the Columbia factory before the end of 1899. More than 25,000 movements were made. The factory was closed after it was purchased by the Keystone Watch Case Company on May 17, 1901. The machinery was moved to the nearby factory of the United States Watch Company (purchased by Keystone in April 1901), where it was used to make the United States Watch Company's 0-size movement, introduced in April 1902. Both the Columbia Watch Company and the Suffolk Watch Company made 0-size movements only.

Grade or Name – Description		Avg	Ex-Fn	Mint
0S, 7J, NI, HC ....★		$100	$135	$175

Suffolk Watch Co., 0 Size, 7 jewels, serial number 216,841.   Seth Thomas, *Colonia U.S.A.* on movement, 18 size, 7 jewels, model # 11.

SETH THOMAS WATCH CO.

Thomaston, Connecticut

1883 - 1915

Seth Thomas is a very prominent clock manufacturer, but in early 1883, the company made a decision to manufacture watches. The watches were first placed on the market in 1885. They were 18S, open face, stem wind, 3/4 plate, and the escapement was between the plates. The compensating balance was set well below the normal. They were 11J, 16,000 beats per minute train, but soon went to 18,000 or quick train. In 1886, the company started to make higher grade watches and produced four grades: 7J, 11J, 15J, and 17J. That year the output was 100 watches a day.

SETH THOMAS ESTIMATED SERIAL NUMBERS AND PRODUCTION DATES

DATE – SERIAL NO.	DATE – SERIAL NO	DATE–SERIAL NO.	DATE – SERIAL NO.
1885 – 5,000	1893 – 510,000	1901 – 1,230,000	1909 – 2,500,000
1886 – 20,000	1894 – 600,000	1902 – 1,320,000	1910 – 2,725,000
1887 – 40,000	1895 – 690,000	1903 – 1,410,000	1911 – 2,950,000
1888 – 80,000	1896 – 780,000	1904 – 1,500,000	1912 – 3,175,000
1889 – 150,000	1897 – 870,000	1905 – 1,700,000	1913 – 3,490,000
1890 – 235,000	1898 – 960,000	1906 – 1,900,000	1914 – 3,600,000
1891 – 330,000	1899 – 1,050,000	1907 – 2,100,000	
1892 – 420,000	1900 – 1,140,000	1908 – 2,300,000	

The above list is provided for determining the APPROXIMATE age of your watch. Match serial number with date. Watches were not necessarily sold in the exact order of manufactured date.

Seth Thomas movement, 18 size,17 jewels, Molineux model, 2 tone yellow gold, heavy damaskeening, H. C.

Seth Thomas 18 size,"Molineux" 17 J., 2 tone yellow gold gilt & nickel heavy damaskeening model #2 ,HC

18 SIZE

Grade or Name – Description	Avg	Ex-Fn	Mint
Century, 7J, OF	$75	$100	$150
Century, 7J, HC	100	125	175
Century, 15J, OF	75	100	150
Century, 15J, HC	100	125	175
Chautauqua, 15J, GJS, M#5	150	175	250
Colonia U.S.A., 7J, model # 11	75	100	125
Early model # 1, low serial # under **1,000**	250	300	400
Eagle Series, No. 36, 7J, OF	100	125	150
Eagle Series, No. 37, 7J, HC	125	150	175
Eagle Series, No. 106, 11J, OF	100	125	150
Eagle Series, No. 107, 11J, HC	125	150	175
Eagle Series, No. 206, 15J, OF	100	125	150

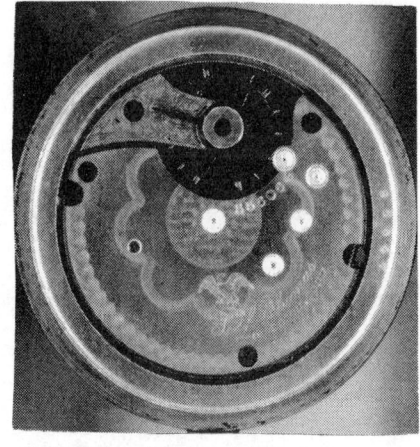

Liberty, Eagle Series,18 size, 7 jewels, hunting or open face, eagle on movement.

Maiden Lane, 18 size, 28 jewels, gold jewel settings, Adj5p, engraved dated as =8,1,99. No serial number.

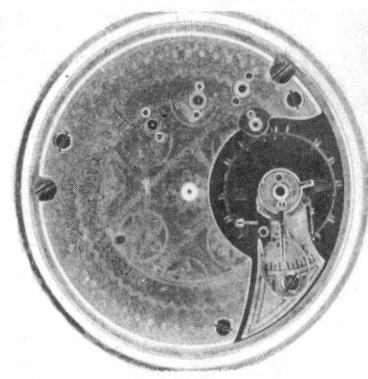
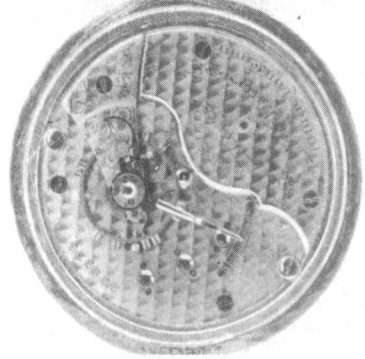

Henry Molineux, 18 size, 17 jewels, "Corona W. Co. USA" on dial, open face, serial number 54,951.

Seth Thomas, 18 size, 23 jewels, gold jewel settings, adjusted, serial number 298,333.

Grade or Name – Description	Avg	Ex-Fn	Mint
Eagle Series, No. 207, 15J, HC	$150	$175	$200
Eagle Series, 15J, M# 2, HC	125	150	200
Eagle Series, No. 210, 17J, OF	125	150	175
Eagle Series, No. 211, 17J, HC	175	200	250
Eagle Series, 17J, NI, 3/4, OF	125	150	175
Edgemere, 11J	100	125	150
Edgemere, 17J	100	125	175
Keywind M#2, 7J, 11J, & 15J, 3/4	175	225	325
Keywind M#4, 7J, 11J, & 15J, 3/4	175	225	325
Lakeshore, 17J, GJS, ADJ, NI	225	275	325
Liberty, 7J, 3/4, eagle on back plate	100	125	150
Maiden Lane, 17J, GJS, DR, Adj.6P, NI, marked ★★	1,200	1,400	1,700
Maiden Lane, 19J, GJS, DR, Adj.6P, NI, marked ★★★	1,300	1,500	1,800
Maiden Lane, 21J, GJS, DR, Adj.6P, NI, marked ★	1,500	1,800	2,000
Maiden Lane, 24J, GJS, DR, Adj.6P, marked ★★★	2,000	2,300	2,500
Maiden Lane, 25J, GJS, DR, Adj.6P, NI, marked ★★	2,800	3,100	3,500
Maiden Lane, 28J, GJS, DR, Adj.5P, NI, marked ★★★★★	15,000	18,000	25,000
Henry Molineux, M#3, 17J, 3/4, GJS, ADJ ★★	575	625	725
Henry Molineux, M#2, 17J, GJS, ADJ ★★	575	625	750
Henry Molineux, M#2, 20-21J, GJS, ADJ ★★★	1,000	1,200	1,500
Monarch Watch Co., 7-15J, 2-tone	100	125	175
R. R. Special USA, 7J, with a locomotive on dial	125	150	195
Republic USA, 7J, OF	75	100	125

🕐 Generic, nameless or **unmarked** grades for watch movements are listed under the Company name or initials of the Company, etc. by size, jewel count and description.

	Avg	Ex-Fn	Mint
S. Thomas, 7J, 3/4, **multi-color dial**	175	225	300
S. Thomas, 7J, 3/4	100	125	150
S. Thomas, 11J, 3/4, HC	100	125	175
S. Thomas, 11J, 3/4, OF	100	125	150
S. Thomas, 15J, 3/4, HC	125	150	200
S. Thomas, 15J, 3/4, gilded, OF	100	125	150
S. Thomas, 15J, 3/4 , OF	100	125	150
S. Thomas, 16J, 3/4	100	125	175
S. Thomas, 17J, 3/4, OF, nickel	125	150	200

Grade or Name – Description	Avg	Ex-Fn	Mint
S. Thomas, 17J, 3/4, 2-Tone	$150	$175	$225
S. Thomas, 17J, 3/4, OF, gilded	100	125	175
S. Thomas, 17J, 3/4, HC	150	175	200
S. Thomas, 19J, GJS, DR, Adj.5P, OF ★★	600	700	950
S. Thomas, 21J, GJS, DR, Adj.5P	350	425	500
S. Thomas, 23J, GJS, DR, Adj.5P ★★	1,000	1,300	1,500
Special Motor Service, 17J, 2 tone, LS, OF	300	325	375
20th Century (Wards), 11J	100	125	175
20th Century (Wards), 11J, 2-Tone	125	150	200
Wyoming Watch Co., 7J, OF	150	175	225
S. Thomas, G# 33, 7J, 3/4, gilded, OF	100	125	150
S. Thomas, G# 37, 7J, 3/4, NI, HC	95	110	150
S. Thomas, G# 44, 11J, 3/4, gilded, OF	100	125	150
S. Thomas, G# 47, 7J, gilded, FULL, OF	100	125	150
S. Thomas, G# 58, 11J, FULL, gilt, OF	100	125	150
S. Thomas, G# 70, 15J, 3/4, gilded, OF	100	125	150
S. Thomas, G# 80, 17J, 3/4, gilded, ADJ, HC	125	150	175
S. Thomas, G# 101, 15J, 3/4, gilded, ADJ, OF	100	125	150
S. Thomas, G# 149, 15J, gilded, FULL, OF	100	125	150
S. Thomas, G# 159, 15J, NI, FULL, OF	100	125	150
S. Thomas, G# 169, 17J, NI, FULL, OF	100	125	150
S. Thomas, G# 170, 15J, 3/4, NI, OF	100	125	150
S. Thomas, G# 179, 17J, 3/4, NI, ADJ, OF	125	150	175
S. Thomas, G# 180, 17J, 3/4, NI, HC	150	175	200
S. Thomas, G# 182, 17J, DR, NI, FULL, OF	100	125	175
S. Thomas, G# 201, 15J, 3/4, NI, ADJ, OF	100	130	175
S. Thomas, G# 245, 19J, GJS, 2-Tone, HC ★★	1,000	1,200	1,500
S. Thomas, G# 260, 21J, DR, Adj.6P, NI, FULL, OF	375	425	475
S. Thomas, G# 281-282, 17J, FULL, DR, Adj.3P, OF, 2-tone	200	250	300
S. Thomas, G# 382, 17J, FULL, DR, Adj.5P, OF, 2-tone	200	250	300
Trainsman Special, **fake "23"J Adj**, seen in model 10 or 12	95	125	165

Trainsman Special, fake 23 jewels, Adjusted, Chicago U.S.A., jewels made of glass, seen in model 10 or 12.

Grade 36, 16 size, 7 jewels, open face, three-quarter nickel plate.

🕐 Generic, nameless or **unmarked** grades for watch movements are listed under the Company name or initials of the Company, etc. by size, jewel count and description.

🕐 Watches listed in this book are priced at the collectable retail level, as **complete** watches having an original 14k gold-filled case and *Key Wind* with silver, an original white enamel single sunk dial, and with the entire original movement in good working order with no repairs needed.

16 SIZE
(OF Only)

Grade or Name – Description	Avg	Ex-Fn	Mint
Centennial, 7J, 3/4, NI, OF...	$75	$95	$125
Locust, 7J, NI, 3/4, OF	75	95	125
Locust, 17J, NI, ADJ, 3/4, OF.....................................	125	150	200
Republic USA, 7J, OF	75	95	125

🕐 Generic, nameless or **unmarked** grades for watch movements are listed under the Company name or initials of the Company, etc. by size, jewel count and description.

	Avg	Ex-Fn	Mint
S. Thomas, G# 25, 7J, BRG, OF.....................................	$75	$95	$125
S. Thomas, G# 26, 15J, BRG, GJS, OF	75	95	125
S. Thomas, G# 27, 17J, BRG, GJS, OF	75	95	125
S. Thomas, G# 28, 17J, BRG, Adj.3P, GJS, OF................	125	150	175
S. Thomas, G# 326, 7J, 3/4, NI, OF................................	75	95	125
S. Thomas, G# 328, 15J, 3/4, NI, OF..............................	75	95	125
S. Thomas, G# 332, 7J, 3/4, NI, OF................................	75	95	125
S. Thomas, G# 334, 15J, NI, ADJ,3/4, DMK, OF............	75	100	150
S. Thomas, G# 336, 17J, ADJ, 3/4, DMK, OF	125	150	175

Seth Thomas, 12 size, 7 jewels, open face, pendant set.   **Seth Thomas**, 12 size, 17 jewels, gold jewel settings, gold center wheel, open face, Adj3p.

12 SIZE
(OF Only)

Grade or Name – Description	Avg	Ex-Fn	Mint
Centennial, 7J..	$75	$80	$95
Republic USA, 7J, OF	75	80	95
S. Thomas, G# 25, 7J, BRG, OF.....................................	75	80	95
S. Thomas, G# 26, 15J, BRG, GJS, OF	75	80	95
S. Thomas, G# 27, 17J, BRG, GJS, OF	75	80	95
S. Thomas, G# 28, 17J, OF, BRG, Adj.3P, GJS..............	95	100	125
S. Thomas, G# 326, 7J, OF, 3/4, NI...............................	75	80	95
S. Thomas, G# 328, 15J, OF, 3/4, NI..............................	75	80	95

🕐 Watches listed in this book are priced at the collectable retail level, as complete watches having an original 14k gold-filled case and Key Wind with silver, an original white enamel single sunk dial, and with the entire original movement in good working order with no repairs needed.

🕐 Generic, nameless or unmarked grades for watch movements are listed under the Company name or initials of the Company, etc. by size, jewel count and description.

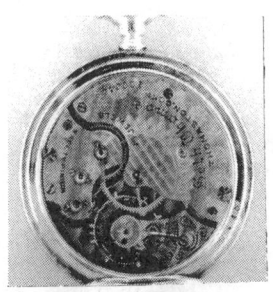

Seth Thomas movement, 6 size, 7 jewels, serial number 441,839. Sometimes appears in a 12 size case.

SETH THOMAS, 0 size, 15 jewels, pendant set, hunting case, serial number 200,449.

6 SIZE

(Some 6 Size were used to fit 12 Size cases)

Grade or Name – Description	Avg	Ex-Fn	Mint
Century, 7J, NI, 3/4	$65	$85	$100
Countess Janet, 17J, Adj., HC	100	125	150
Eagle Series, 7J, No. 45, 3/4, NI, DMK, OF	65	85	100
Eagle Series, 7J, No. 205, 3/4, HC	100	125	150
Eagle Series, 15J, No. 35, 3/4, NI, DMK, OF	65	85	100
Eagle Series, 15J, No. 245, 3/4, HC	100	125	150
Edgemere, 7-11J,	65	85	100
Republic USA, 7J	65	85	100
Seth Thomas, 7J, 3/4, HC, **14K, 26 DWT**	250	275	325
Seth Thomas, 11J, 3/4, HC	100	125	150
Seth Thomas, 11J, 3/4, OF	65	85	100
S. Thomas, G# 35, 7J, HC, NI, DMK, 3/4	65	85	100
S. Thomas, G# 119, 16J, HC, GJS, NI, DMK, 3/4	100	125	175
S. Thomas, G# 205, 15J, HC	100	125	150
S. Thomas, G# 320, 7J, OF, NI, DMK, 3/4	65	85	100
S. Thomas, G# 322, 15J, OF	65	85	100

NOTE: Add $25 to $50 for HC.

0 SIZE

Grade or Name – Description	Avg	Ex-Fn	Mint
Seth Thomas, 7J, OF, No. 1	$80	$90	$125
Seth Thomas, 7J, HC, No. 1	100	125	175
Seth Thomas, 15J, OF, GJS, No. 3	75	100	150
Seth Thomas, 15J, HC, No. 3	75	100	150
Seth Thomas, 17J, GJS, PS, No. 9, OF	75	100	150
Seth Thomas, 17J, GJS, PS, No. 9, HC	100	125	175

NOTE: Add $25 to $50 for HC.

SETH THOMAS WATCH CO.
IDENTIFICATION OF MOVEMENTS
BY MODEL NUMBER

How to Identify Your Watch: Compare the movement of your watch with the illustrations in this section. Upon matching the movement exactly, the model number and size can be determined. While comparing, note the location of the balance, jewels, screws, gears, and type of back plate (Full, 3/4, Bridge) which will be clues in identifying the movement you have. Having determined the size and model number, you can now find your watch in the main price listing by name or number (which is engraved on the movement).

Model 1, 18 size, Open Face

Model 2, 18 size, Hunting

Model 3, 18 size, Open Face

Model 4, 18 size, Key Wind

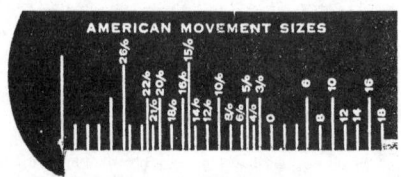

Model 5, 18 size, Maiden Lane Series, Open Face.

Model 6, 18 Size, Open Face

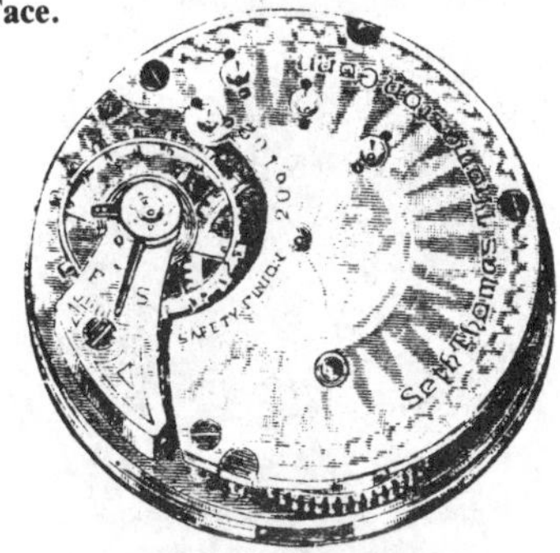

Model 7 & 9, 18 size

Model 8, 18 size

Model 10, 18 size, Open Face

Model 11, 18 size, Hunting

🕐 This book endeavours to be a GUIDE or helpful manual and offers a wealth of material to be used as a tool not as a absolute document. Price Guides are like watches the worst may be better than none at all, but at best cannot be expected to be 100% accurate.

🕐 Characteristics of watches differ for the same age of both case and movement, because these features vary it may not be accurate to date a watch by one single influence. Example: the second hand was _not_ commonly found on watches before 1750, but common about 1800. The first second hand appeared in 1665 and another in 1690. Therefore statements are broad rather than accurate.

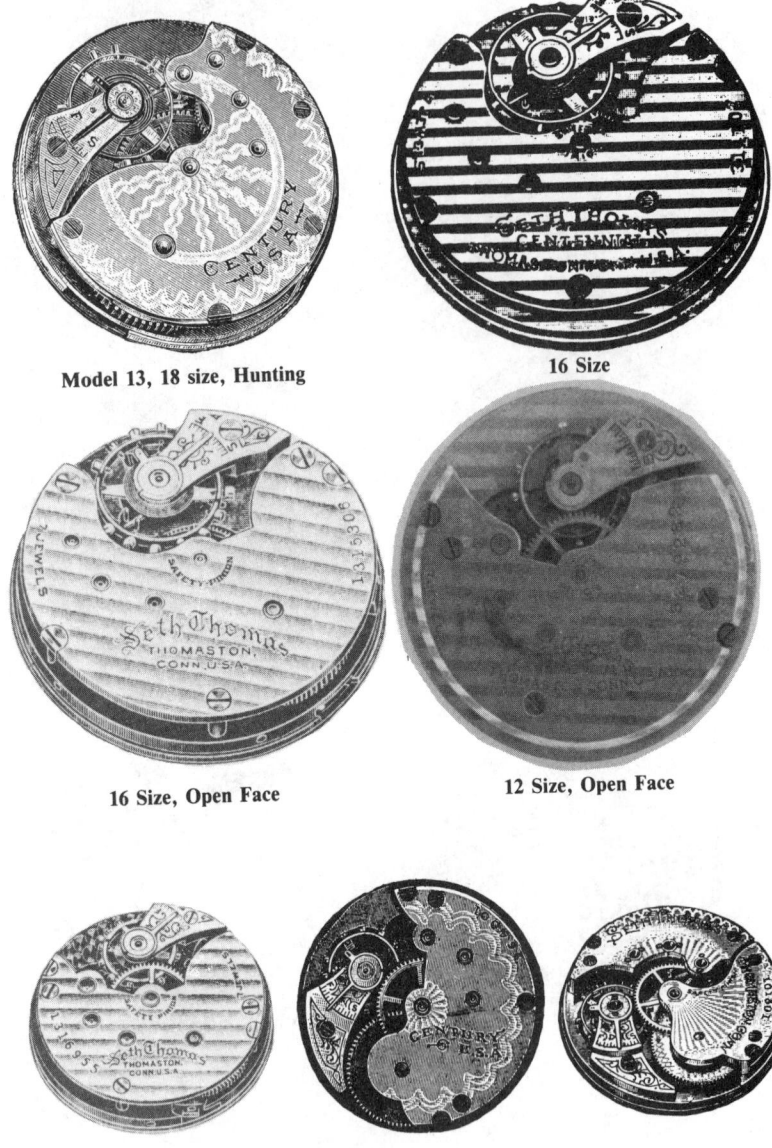

Model 13, 18 size, Hunting

16 Size

16 Size, Open Face

12 Size, Open Face

6 Size, Open face

Model 14, 6 size

Model 16 & 17, 6 size

TREMONT WATCH CO.

Boston, Massachusetts
1864 - 1866

In 1864 A. L. Dennison thought that if he could produce a good movement at a reasonable price, there would be a ready market for it. Dennison went to Switzerland to find a supplier of cheap parts, as arbors were too high in America. He found a source for parts, mainly the train and escapement and the balance. About 600 sets were to be furnished. Dials were first made by Mr. Gold and Mr. Spurr, then later by Mr. Hull and Mr. Carpenter. Tremont had hoped to produce 600 sets of trains per month. In 1865, the first movements were ready for the market. They were 18S, key wind, fully jeweled, and were engraved "Tremont Watch Co." In 1886, the company moved from Boston to Melrose. The Tremont Watch Co. produced about 5,000 watches before being sold to the English Watch Co.

Tremont Watch Co., with "Washington Street Boston" engraved on movement, 18 size, 15 jewels, key wind and set, serial number 5,264.

Tremont movement, 18 size, 15 jewels, key wind & set, serial number 8,875.

Grade or Name – Description	Avg	Ex-Fn	Mint
18S, 7J, KW, KS .... ★	$250	$275	$350
18S, 11J, KW, KS	250	275	350
18S, 7-11-15J, KW, KS, gilded Silveroid	200	235	275
18S, 7-11-15J, KW, KS, gilded, marked LONDON	200	235	275
18S, 15J, KW, KS, gilded	250	275	350
18S, 15J, KW, KS, HC, **14K**	650	675	750
18S, 15J, KW, KS, gilded, Washington Street .... ★ ★	450	550	700
18S, 17J, KW, KS, gilded	300	325	400
18S, 15J, KW, **Key Set from back**, 3/4 plate ...... ★ ★ ★	1,500	1,700	2,000

🕑 Watches listed in this book are priced at the collectable retail level, as **complete** watches having an original 14k gold-filled case and *Key Wind* with silver, an original white enamel single sunk dial, and with the entire original movement in good working order with no repairs needed.

TRENTON WATCH CO.
Trenton, New Jersey
1885 - 1908

Trenton watches were marketed under the following labels: Trenton, Ingersoll, Fortuna, Illinois Watch Case Company, Calumet U.S.A., Locomotives Special, Marvel Watch Co., and Reliance Watch Co.

Serial numbers started at 2,001 and ended at 4,100,000. Total production was about 1,934,000.

CHRONOLOGY OF THE DEVELOPMENT OF TRENTON WATCH CO.:

New Haven Watch Co., New Haven, Conn. 1883-1887
Trenton Watch Co., Trenton, N. J. .... 1887 -1908
Sold to Ingersoll 1908-1922

TRENTON MODELS AND GRADES
With Years of Manufacture and Serial Numbers

Date	Numbers	Size	Model	Date	Numbers	Size	Model
				1900-1903	2,000,001-2,075,000	6	2
1887-1889	2,001- 61,000	18	1	1902-1905	2,075,001-2,160,000	6	3 LS
1889-1891	64,001- 135,000	18	2			12	2 LS
1891-1898	135,001- 201,000 *¹	18	3	1905-1907	2,160,001-2,250,000	6	3 PS
1899-1904	201,001- 300,000	18	6			12	2 PS
1891-1900	300,001- 500,000	18	4	1899-1902	2,500,001-2,600,000	3/0	1
1892-1897	500,001- 600,000	6	1	ca. 1906	2,800,001-2,850,000	6	3 PS
1894-1899	650,001- 700,000	16	1			12	2 PS
1898-1900	700,001- 750,000	6	2	1900-1904	3,000,001-3,139,000	16	2
1900-1904	750,001- 800,000 *²	18	4	1903-1907	3,139,001-3,238,000	16	3 OF
1896-1900	850,001- 900,000	12	1	1903-1907	3,500,001-3,600,000	16	3 HC
1898-1903	900,001-1,100,000	18	5	1905-1907	4,000,001-4,100,000	0	1
1902-1907	1,300,001-1,400,000	18	6				

1—7 jewel grades made only during 1891; 9 jewel chronograph Pat. Mar. 17, 1891, made 1891-1898.
2—A few examples are KWKS for export to England.

Trenton movement, 18 size, 4 jewels, model # 1, serial number 4,744.

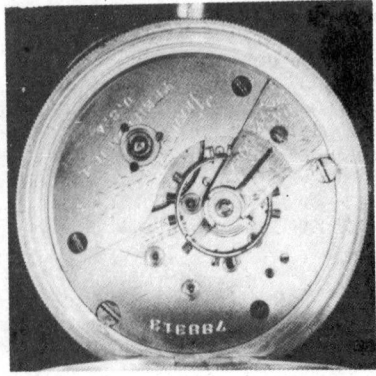

Trenton movement, 18 size, 7 jewels, 4th model, serial number 788,313.

18 SIZE

Grade or Name – Description	Avg	Ex-Fn	Mint
Trenton W. Co., M#1-2, gilded, OF .... ★	$150	$175	$250
Trenton W. Co., M#3, 7J, 3/4..	60	75	125
Trenton W. Co., M#3, 9J, 3/4..	60	75	125
Trenton W. Co., M#4, 7J, FULL...	60	75	125
Trenton W. Co., M#4, 11J, FULL...	60	75	125
Trenton W. Co., M#4, 15J, FULL...	60	75	125
Trenton W. Co., M#4-5, FULL, OF, NI	60	75	125
Marvel W. Co. Fake 23 jewels...	100	125	150
New Haven Watch Co. style, M#1, 4J .... ★★★	250	325	450
Railroad Special, fake 23J, tu-tone, locomotive on dial & mvt. ★★	150	185	235
Trenton, 7J, KW, KS .... ★	225	300	425

Note: Add $25 to value of above watches in hunting case.

Trenton movement, 18 size, 7 jewels, model #3, serial number 148,945.

Chronograph, 16 size, 9 jewels, third model; start, stop & fly back, sweep second hand.

16 SIZE

Grade or Name – Description	Avg	Ex-Fn	Mint
Trenton W. Co., M#1-2, 7J, 3/4, NI, OF..	$50	$75	$125
Trenton W. Co., M#3, 7J, 3F BRG	50	75	125
Trenton W. Co., M#3, 11J, 3F BRG	50	75	125
Trenton W. Co., M#3, 15J, 3F BRG	60	85	135
Trenton W. Co., 7,11,15J, 3F BRG, NI	60	85	135
Chronograph, 9J, start, stop, & fly back, **DMK** .... ★★★★	275	350	475
Chronograph, 9J, start, stop, & fly back, **GILDED** .... ★★★★	275	350	475
Convertible Model, 7J, OF .... ★	100	125	175
Trenton W. Co., Grade #30 & 31, 7J	50	75	125
Trenton W. Co., Grade #35, 36 & 38, 11J....................................	50	75	125
Trenton W. Co., Grade #45, 16J...	85	100	150
Trenton W. Co., Grade #125, 12J..	50	75	125
Ingersoll Trenton, 7J, 3F BRG..	60	75	125

🕐 Generic, nameless or **unmarked** grades for watch movements are listed under the Company name or initials of the Company, etc. by size, jewel count and description.

🕐 Watches listed in this book are priced at the collectable retail level, as **complete** watches having an original 14k gold-filled case and *Key Wind* with silver, an original white enamel single sunk dial, and with the entire original movement in good working order with no repairs needed.

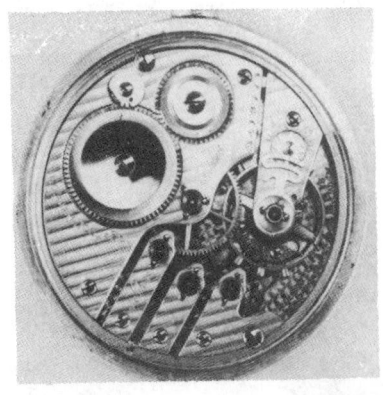

Ingersoll Trenton movement, 16 size, 19 jewels, three fingered bridge, adjusted, serial number 3,419,771.

Ingersoll Trenton movement, 16 size, 12 jewels; "Edgemere" engraved on movement.

Grade or Name – Description	Avg	Ex-Fn	Mint
Ingersoll Trenton, 15J, 3F BRG, NI, ADJ	$75	$100	$150
Ingersoll Trenton, 17J, 3F BRG, NI, ADJ	85	110	160
Ingersoll Trenton, 19J, 3F BRG, NI, Adj.5P ★	165	250	300
Peerless, 7J, SW, LS	50	65	80
Railroad Reliance, 17J, OF ★	100	125	150
Reliance, 7J	50	65	80

Note: Add $25 to value of above watches in hunting case.

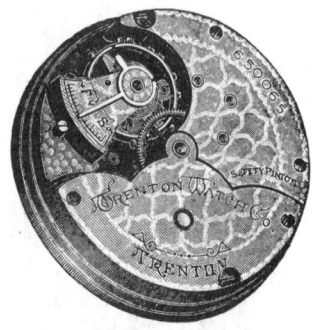

Railroad Special, 18 size, 23 jewels, tu-tone, locomotive on dial & movement, model # 6, S# 1,3660,044.

Trenton movement, convertible model converts to open face or hunting case, 16 size, 7 J.

10 - 12 SIZE

Grade or Name – Description	Avg	Ex-Fn	Mint
''Fortuna,'' 7J, 3 finger BRG	$40	$50	$65
Trenton W. Co., M#1, 7J, 3/4	40	50	65
Monogram, 7J, SW	30	40	55

Note: Add $25 to value of above watches in hunting case.

Trenton Watch Co. movement, 6 size, 7 jewels, open face & hunting, nickel damaskeened.

6 SIZE

Grade or Name – Description	Avg	Ex-Fn	Mint
Trenton W. Co., 7J, 3/4, NI	$30	$40	$55
Trenton W. Co., 7J, 3Finger BRG	30	40	55
Trenton W. Co., 15J, 3Finger BRG	40	50	65
"Fortuna," 7J, 3 Finger Bridge	30	40	55

Note: Add $25 to value of above watches in hunting case.

0 SIZE

Grade or Name – Description	Avg	Ex-Fn	Mint
Trenton W. Co., 7J, 3F BRG	$40	$50	$65
Trenton W. Co., 15J, 3F BRG	50	60	75

Note: Add $25 to value of above watches in hunting case.

Trenton Chronograph, 9J, start, stop, & fly back, **Model # 3.**

UNITED STATES WATCH CO.

Marion, New Jersey
1865 - 1877

The United States Watch Company was chartered in 1865, and the factory building was started in August 1865 and was completed in 1866. The first watch, called the ''Frederic Atherton,'' was not put on the market until July 1867. It was America's first mass produced stem winding watch. This first grade was 18S, 19J, full plate and a gilt finish movement. A distinctive feature of the company's full plate movements was the butterfly shaped patented opening in the plate which allowed escapement inspection. That same year a second grade called the ''Fayette Stratton'' was introduced. It was also a gilt finish, full plate movement.

Most of these were 15J, but some of the very early examples have been noted in 17J. In 1868 the ''George Channing,'' ''Edwin Rollo,'' and ''Marion Watch Co.'' grades were introduced. All were 18S, 15J, full plate movements in a gilt finish. In February 1869 the gilt version of the ''United States Watch Co.'' grade was introduced. It was 18S, 19J, full plate and was the company's first entry into the prestige market. Later that year the company introduced their first nickel grade, a 19J, 18S, full plate movement called the ''A. H. Wallis.'' About this same time, in December 1869, they introduced America's most expensive watch, the first nickel, 19J, 18S, full plate ''United States Watch Co.'' grade. Depending on case weight, these prestige watches retailed between $500 and $600, more than the average man earned in a year at that time. The company also introduced damaskeening to the American market; first on gilt movements and later on the nickel grades. The damaskeening process was later improved by using **IVORY** disc in place of wooden disc. The United States and Wallis 19J prestige grades were beautifully finished with richly enameled engraving including a variety of unique designs on the balance cock. It is significant to note that no solid gold trains have been seen with these prestige items in the extant examples presently known.

NOTE the **PIN** or **NAIL** set feature on top side of this watch example.
This feature is considered more desirable and will bring a **HIGHER** price.

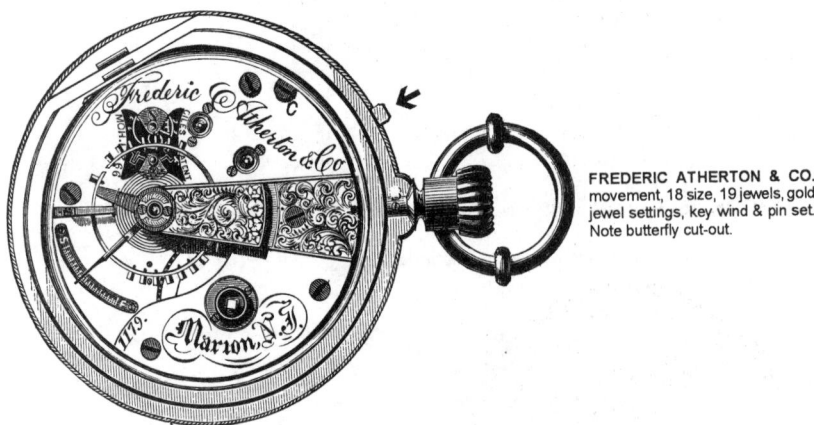

FREDERIC ATHERTON & CO.
movement, 18 size, 19 jewels, gold
jewel settings, key wind & pin set.
Note butterfly cut-out.

In 1870 the company introduced their first watch for ladies, a 10S, 15J, plate, cock & bridge movement which was made to their specifications in Switzerland. This model was first introduced in two grades, the ''R. F. Pratt'' and ''Chas. G. Knapp,'' both in a 15J, gilt finish movement. Later it was offered in a high grade, 19J ''I. H. Wright'' nickel finish movement. During 1870 and 1871 several other full plate grades in both gilt and nickel finish were introduced. In 1871 development on a new line of full plate, 3/4, plate, and plate & bridge was started but not introduced to the market until late in 1872 and early in 1873. The 10S and 16S new grades in plate and bridge were probably delayed well into 1873 and were not available long before the ''Panic of 1873'' started in September; this explains their relative scarcity.

By July 1874 the "Panic" had taken its toll and it was necessary for the company to reorganize as the Marion Watch Company, a name formerly used for one of their grades. At this time jewel count, finish standards, and prices were lowered on the full plate older grades, but this proved to be a mistake. That same year they introduced a cased watch called the "North Star", their cheapest watch at $15 retail.

The year of 1875 hit the watch industry the hardest; price cutting was predatory and the higher priced watches of the United States Watch Co. were particulary vulnerable. Further lowering of finish standards and prices did not help and in 1876 the company was once again reorganized into the Empire City Watch Co. and their products were displayed at the Centennial that year. The Centennial Exhibition was not enough to save the faltering company and they finally closed their doors in 1877. The Howard brothers of Fredonia, New York (Independent and Fredonia Watch Co.) purchased most of the remaining movement stock and machinery. In the ten year period of movement production, current statistical studies indicate an estimated production of only some 60,000 watches, much smaller than the number deduced from the serial numbers assigned up to as high as 289,000.

NOTE: The above historical data and estimated production figures are based on data included in the new NAWCC book **MARION, A History of the United States Watch Company,** by William Muir and Bernard Kraus. This definitive work is available from NAWCC, Inc., 514 Poplar St., Columbia, PA. (Courtesy, Gene Fuller, MARION book editor.) This book is recommended by Mr. Shugart and Mr. Gilbert for your library.

EMPIRE CITY W. CO. & EQUIVALENT U.S.W. CO. GRADES

Empire City W. Co.	United States W. Co.
W. S. Wyse	A. H. Wallis
L. W. Frost	Henry Randel
Cyrus H. Loutrel	Wm. Alexander
J. L. Ogden	S. M. Beard
E. F. C. Young	John W. Lewis
D. C. Wilcox	George Channing
Henry Harper	Asa Fuller
Jesse A. Dodd	Edwin Rollo
E. C. Hine	J. W. Deacon
New York Belle	A. J. Wood
The Champion	G. A. Read
Black Diamond	Young America

NOTE: Courtesy Gene Fuller, NAWCC "MARION" book editor.

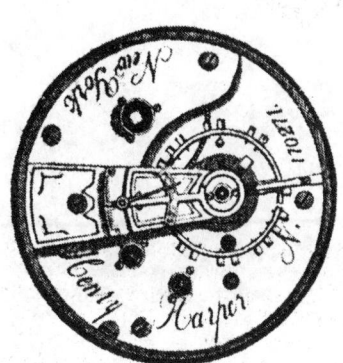

Empire City W. Co., Henry Harper, note:
movement does not have **Butterfly Cut-out**

United States Watch Co. movement, 18 size, 19 jewels, gold jewel settings, key wind. Their highest grade watch.

United States Watch Co., Henry Randel, 15jewels, KWKS, FROSTED plates, S.# 24,944

MARION
18 SIZE
(All with Butterfly Cut-out Except for 3/4 Plate)

Grade or Name – Description	Avg	Ex-Fn	Mint
Wm. Alexander, 15J, NI, KW, HC	$375	$450	$550
Wm. Alexander, 15J, NI, KW, OF	300	350	450
Wm. Alexander, 15J, NI, SW, OF	300	375	485
Frederic Atherton & Co., 15J, SW, gilded	275	325	425
Frederic Atherton & Co., 17J, KW, gilded, HC	300	350	425
Frederic Atherton & Co., 17J, KW, gilded, OF	250	300	375
Frederic Atherton & Co., 17J, SW, gilded, HC	300	350	450
Frederic Atherton & Co., 17J, SW, gilded, OF	275	325	425

U.S. Watch Co., dial and movement, 18 size, 20 jewels, hunting case, 3/4 plate, engraved on movement "N.D. Godfrey," serial number 72,042. Painted on the dial "New York 1873." The dial consists of day-date-month and moon phases.

NOTE: The **PIN** or **NAIL** set feature is considered more desirable & will bring a **HIGHER** price.

Grade or Name – Description	Avg	Ex-Fn	Mint
Frederic Atherton & Co., 19J, SW, gilded, ...★★★★	$1,000	$1,200	$1,500
Frederic Atherton & Co., 19J, KW, gilded ....★★	650	700	900
BC&M R.R., 11J, KW...............................★★★★	1,600	1,800	2,200
BC&M R.R., 15J, gilded, KW ....★★★★	1,600	1,800	2,200
S. M. Beard, 15J, KW, NI, OF..........................	275	300	400
S. M. Beard, 15J, SW, NI, OF...........................	275	300	400
S. M. Beard, 15J, SW or KW, HC	300	350	450
Centennial Phil., 11-15J, SW or KW, NI ....★★★★	1,900	2,200	2,500
George Channing, 15J, KW, NI........................	275	300	400
George Channing, 15J, KW, gilded	250	295	350
George Channing, 15J, KW, NI, 3/4 Plate ....★★	375	425	500
George Channing, 17J, KW, NI........................	300	350	425
J. W. Deacon, 11-13J, KW, gilded......................	175	225	250
J. W. Deacon, 15J, KW, gilded	200	250	325
J. W. Deacon, 11-15J, KW, 3/4 Plate................★	300	350	425
Empire City Watch Co., 11J, SW, **no butterfly cut-out** ..... ★★★	225	300	400
Empire City Watch Co., 15-19J, **no butterfly cut-out**........ ★★★	250	350	450
Empire Combination Timer, 11J, FULL, time & distance on dial.......................................★★★	500	600	800
Empire Combination Timer, 15J, 3/4, time & distance on dial.......................................★★★	850	1,000	1,200
Fellows, 15J, NI, KW	400	450	550
Benjamin Franklin, 15J, KW..........................	400	450	550
Asa Fuller, 7-11J, gilded, KW........................	200	225	300
Asa Fuller, 15J, gilded, KW..........................	200	225	300
Asa Fuller, 15J, gilded, KW, 3/4 Plate................★★	300	325	385
N. D. Godfrey, 20J, NI, 3/4 plate, day date month, moon phases, c. 1873, HC, 18K ....★★★★	4,000	5,000	6,000
John W. Lewis, 15J, NI, KW..........................	225	275	375
John W. Lewis, 15J, NI, SW..........................	250	300	400

Edwin Rollo, 18 size, 15 jewels, gilded, key wind & set, note butterfly cut-out, serial number 110,214.

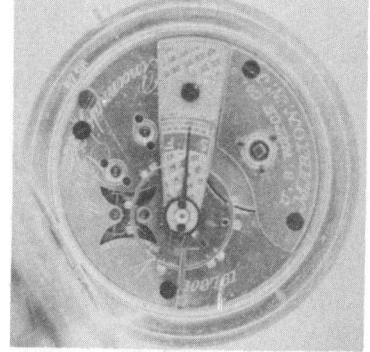

Marion Watch Co. personalized Watch, 18 size, about 15J., pin set, note butterfly cut-out, serial # 106,761.

🕐 Watches listed in this book are priced at the collectable retail level, as **complete** watches having an original 14k gold-filled case and *Key Wind* with silver, an original white enamel single sunk dial, and with the entire original movement in good working order with no repairs needed.

NOTE: The **PIN** or **NAIL** set feature is considered more desirable & will bring a **HIGHER** price.

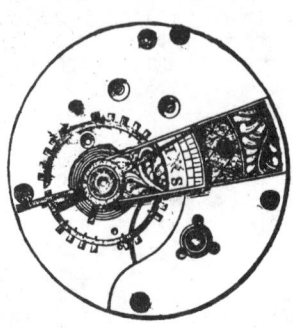

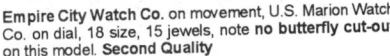

Empire City Watch Co. on movement, U.S. Marion Watch Co. on dial, 18 size, 15 jewels, note no butterfly cut-out on this model. Second Quality

United States Watch Co., 18 size, 19 jewels, gold jewel settings, key wind & pin set, serial number 24,054.

Grade or Name – Description	Avg	Ex-Fn	Mint
John W. Lewis, 15J, NI, 3/4 Plate .... ★★	$375	$425	$525
Marion Watch Co., 11J, KW, gilded..	200	250	375
Marion Watch Co., 15J, KW, gilded..	200	250	375
Marion Watch Co., 15J, SW, gilded, 3/4 Plate .... ★★	300	350	475
Marion Watch Co., 17-19J, KW, gilded .... ★	300	350	475
N.J. R.R.&T. Co., 15J, gilded, KW................................... ★	1,200	1,400	1,700
Newspaper Special Order, 11-15J, gilded, SW or KW	325	375	450
North Star, 7J, KW, NI case..	300	350	425
North Star, 7J, SW, KS...	300	350	425
North Star, 7J, 3/4 Plate...	325	375	450
Pennsylvania R.R., 15J, NI, KW, HC .... ★★★★	2,500	2,700	2,900
Personalized Watches, 7-11J, KW, 3/4 Plate..................... ★	250	300	375
Personalized Watches, 11J, KW, gilded .... ★	250	300	375
Personalized Watches, 15J, KW, gilded .... ★	250	300	375
Personalized Watches, 15J, KW, NI .... ★	275	325	400
Personalized Watches, 15J, KW, 3/4 Plate .... ★	300	350	425
Personalized Watches, 19J, KW, Full Plate...................... ★	400	450	525
Henry Randel, 15J, KW, NI	275	325	425
Henry Randel, 15J, KW, frosted plates...............................	300	350	450
Henry Randel, 15J, SW, NI..	275	325	425
Henry Randel, 15J, 3/4 Plate .... ★★	350	425	525
Henry Randel, 17J, KW, NI .... ★	275	325	450
G. A. Read, 7J, gilded, KW...	200	250	325
G. A. Read, 7J, 3/4 Plate..	300	350	425
Edwin Rollo, 11J, KW, gilded..	200	250	325
Edwin Rollo, 15J, KW, gilded..	200	250	325
Edwin Rollo, 15J, SW, gilded..	200	250	325
Edwin Rollo, 15J, 3/4 Plate .... ★	300	350	425
Royal Gold, 11J, KW..	200	250	300
Royal Gold, 15J, KW..	300	350	425
Royal Gold, 15J, 3/4 Plate... ★★	400	450	525

🕐 Watches listed in this book are priced at the collectable retail level, as **complete** watches having an original 14k gold-filled case and *Key Wind* with silver, an original white enamel single sunk dial, and with the entire original movement in good working order with no repairs needed.

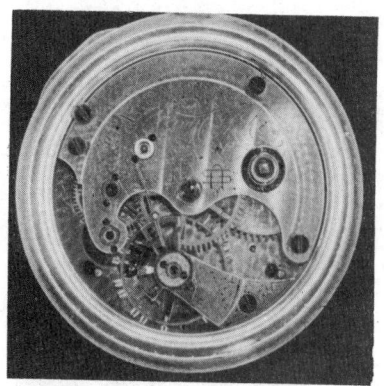

A.H. Wallis on movement, Empire City Watch Co. on dial, 18 size, 19 jewels, three-quarter plate, hunting. This combination timer has listed on the dial, 16 cities showing the time of day and distance in comparison with New York City, serial number 54,409.

Grade or Name – Description	Avg	Ex-Fn	Mint
Rural New York, 15J, gilded	$250	$300	$375
Fayette Stratton, 11J, gilded	250	325	425
Fayette Stratton, 15J, KW, gilded	250	325	425
Fayette Stratton, 15J, SW, gilded	250	325	375
Fayette Stratton, 17J, KW, gilded	275	350	450
Fayette Stratton, 17J, SW, gilded	300	350	475
Union Pacific R.R., 15J, KW, gilded ★★★	1,800	2,000	2,300
United States Watch Co., 15J, NI, KW	700	750	825
United States Watch Co., 15J, NI, SW	800	850	925
United States Watch Co., 15J, 3/4 Plate, NI	800	850	925
United States Watch Co., 15J, 3/4 Plate, gilded	800	850	925
United States Watch Co., 19J, GJS, Adj.5P, 18K HC, dial mvt. & case all marked, Pin Set, SW ★★★	3,500	4,000	4,500
United States Watch Co., 19J, NI, KW ★★	1,200	1,500	2,000
United States Watch Co., 19J, NI, SW ★★	1,350	1,650	2,200
A. H. Wallis, 15J, KW, NI	250	300	400
A. H. Wallis, 15J, SW, NI	250	300	400
A. H. Wallis, 17J, KW, NI	275	325	425
A. H. Wallis, 17J, SW, NI	300	350	450
A. H. Wallis, 19J, KW, NI ★★★	600	650	725
A. H. Wallis, 19J, SW, NI ★★★	650	700	775
D. C. Wilcox, 15J, SW, no butterfly cut-out	250	300	375
I. H. Wright, 11J, KW, gilded	225	275	350
I. H. Wright, 15J, KW, gilded	225	275	350

🕐 Watches listed in this book are priced at the collectable retail level, as **complete** watches having an original 14k gold-filled case and *Key Wind* with silver, an original white enamel single sunk dial, and with the entire original movement in good working order with no repairs needed.

🕐 Some grades are not included. Their values can be determined by comparing with **similar** age, size, metal content, style, models and grades listed.

16 SIZE
1/4 Plate

Grade or Name – Description		Avg	Ex-Fn	Mint
S. M. Beard, 15J, NI, KW,	★★★★	$400	$450	$550
John W. Lewis, 15J, NI, KW	★★★★	400	450	550
Personalized Watches, 15J, NI, SW	★★★★	400	450	550
Edwin Rollo, 15J, KW	★★★★	400	450	550
United States Watch Co., 15J, NI, SW	★★★★	600	700	900
A. H. Wallis, 19J, NI, SW,	★★★★	850	900	1,100

Note: 16S, 1/4 plate are the scarcest of the U.S.W.Co.–Marion watches.

Asa Fuller, 16 size, 15 jewels, stem wind, one-quarter plate, serial number 280,018. Note: 3 screws on barrel bridge.

United States Watch Co., 14 size, 15 jewels, three-quarter plate, engraved on movement "Royal Gold American Watch, New York, Extra Jeweled."

14 SIZE
3/4 Plate

Grade or Name – Description		Avg	Ex-Fn	Mint
Centennial Phil., 11J, KW, gilded		$425	$525	$750
J. W. Deacon, 11J,	★★	275	325	395
Asa Fuller, 15J,	★★	375	425	495
John W. Lewis, 15J, NI	★★	325	375	425
North Star, 15J,		275	325	395
Personalized Watches, 7-11J,	★★	375	425	495
Edwin Rollo, 15J,	★	325	375	450
Royal Gold, 15J,	★	375	425	495
Young America, 7J, gilded		325	375	450

🕐 Watches listed in this book are priced at the collectable retail level, as **complete** watches having an original 14k gold-filled case and *Key Wind* with silver, an original white enamel single sunk dial, and with the entire original movement in good working order with no repairs needed.

🕐 Some grades are not included. Their values can be determined by comparing with **similar** age, size, metal content, style, models and grades listed.

10 SIZE
1/4 Plate

Grade or Name – Description	Avg	Ex-Fn	Mint
Wm. Alexander, 15J, KW, NI	$200	$250	$335
S. M. Beard, 15J, KW, NI, 1/4 Plate	200	250	335
Empire City Watch Co., 15J, KW .... ★	200	250	335
Chas. G. Knapp, 15J, Swiss, 1/4 Plate, KW	100	150	235
Personalized Watches, 11-15J, 1/4 Plate	200	250	335
R. F. Pratt, 15J, Swiss, 1/4 Plate, KW	100	150	235
Edwin Rollo, 11-15J, 1/4 Plate .... ★	250	300	385
A. H. Wallis, 17-19J, KW, 1/4 Plate	225	275	360
A. J. Wood, 15J, 1/4 Plate, KW .... ★★★★	300	350	435
I. H. Wright, 19J, Swiss, NI, Plate, KW .... ★★★	500	550	635

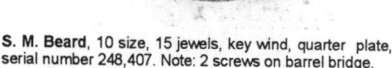
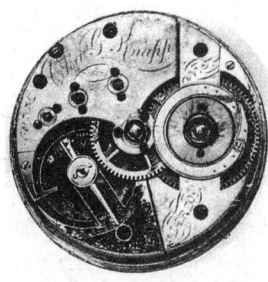

S. M. Beard, 10 size, 15 jewels, key wind, quarter plate, serial number 248,407. Note: 2 screws on barrel bridge.

Chas. G. Knapp, 10 size, 15 jewels, Swiss, quarter plate, key wind.

U. S. WATCH CO.
OF WALTHAM
Waltham, Massachusetts
1884 - 1905

The business was started as the Waltham Watch Tool Co. in 1879. It was organized as the United States Watch Co. in 1884. The first watches were 16S, 3/4 plate pillar movement in three grades. They had a very wide mainspring barrel (the top was thinner than most) which was wedged up in the center to make room for the balance wheel. These watches are called dome watches and are hard to find. The fork was made of an aluminum alloy with a circular slot and a square ruby pin. The balance was gold at first, as was the movement which was a slow train, but the expansion balance was changed when they went to a quick train. The movement required a special case which proved unpopular. By 1887, some 3,000 watches had been made. A new model was then produced, a 16S movement that would fit a standard case. These movements were quick train expansion balance with standard type lever and 3/4 plate pillar movement. This Company reached a top production of 10 watches a day for a **very short period.** The company was sold to the E. Howard Watch Co. (Keystone) in 1903. The United States Watch Co. produced some 890,000 watches total. Its top grade watch movement was the **"President."**

U. S. WATCH CO. OF WALTHAM
ESTIMATED SERIAL NUMBERS AND PRODUCTION DATES

Date	Serial No.	Date	Serial No.
1887	3,000	1896	300,000
1888	6,500	1897	350,000
1889	10,000	1898	400,000
1890	30,000	1899	500,000
1891	60,000	1900	600,000
1892	90,000	1901	700,000
1893	150,000	1902	750,000
1894	200,000	1903	800,000
1895	250,000		

U.S. Watch Co. of Waltham, The President, 18 size, 17 jewels, hunting, serial number 150,000.

U.S. Watch Co. of Waltham, The President, 18 size, 17 jewels, open face, 2-tone, adj., note regulator, serial number 150,350.

18 SIZE

Grade or Name – Description		Avg	Ex-Fn	Mint
Express Train, 15J, ADJ, OF		$300	$350	$425
Express Train, 15J, ADJ, HC		395	450	525
The President, 17J, HC	★★	525	575	650
The President, 17J, GJS, Adj.6P, DR, NI, DMK, OF	★	525	575	650
The President, 21J, GJS, Adj.6P, DR		550	570	650
The President, 21J, GJS, Adj.6P, DR, **14K**	★★	900	950	1,025
U. S. Watch Co., 15J, OF, **2-tone, stem attached**	★	275	325	395
Washington Square, 15J, HCH	★	175	225	295
U. S. Watch Co., 39 (HC) & 79 (OF), 17J, GJS, ADJ, NI, DMK, Adj.5P, BRG		125	150	195
U. S. Watch Co., 40 (HC) & 80 (OF), 17J, GJS		125	150	195
U. S. Watch Co., 48 (HC) & 88 (OF), 7J, gilded, FULL		125	150	195
U. S. Watch Co., 48 (HC) & 88 (OF), 7J, gilded, FULL, Silveroid		70	85	100
U. S. Watch Co., 52 (HC)		135	165	200
U. S. Watch Co., 92 (OF), 17J, Silveroid		80	95	110

⊕ Generic, nameless or unmarked grades for watch movements are listed under the Company name or initials of the Company, etc. by size, jewel count and description.

⊕ Some grades are not included. Their values can be determined by comparing with **similar** age, size, metal content, style, models and grades listed.

Grade or Name – Description	Avg	Ex-Fn	Mint
U. S. Watch Co., 52 (HC) & 92 (OF), 17J..............................	$125	$150	$195
U. S. Watch Co., 53 (HC) & 93 (OF), 15J, NI, FULL, DMK..........	125	150	195
U. S. Watch Co., 54 (HC) & 94 (OF), 15J....................................	125	150	195
U. S. Watch Co., 56 (HC) & 96 (OF), 11J....................................	125	150	195
U. S. Watch Co., 57 (HC) & 97 (OF), 15J....................................	125	150	195
U. S. Watch Co., 58 (HC) & 98 (OF), 11J, NI, FULL, DMK..........	125	150	195

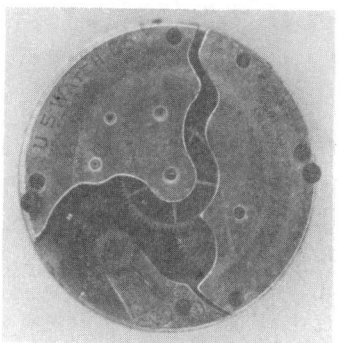

U.S. Watch Co. of Waltham, 16 size, 7 jewels, gilded, note raised dome on center of movement, engraved on movement "Chas. V. Woerd's Patents," serial number 3,564.

U.S. Watch Co. of Waltham, 16 size, 7 jewels, "A New Watch Company At Waltham, Est'd 1885" on movement, serial number 770,771.

16 SIZE

Grade or Name – Description	Avg	Ex-Fn	Mint
Dome Plate Model, 7J, gilded	$150	$175	$225
U. S. Watch Co., Early KW-KS, 7J, S# below 100.........................	500	700	1,000
U. S. Watch Co., 103, 17J, NI, 3/4, ADJ	85	100	135
U. S. Watch Co., 104, 17J, NI, 3/4..	85	100	135
U. S. Watch Co., 104, 17J, NI, 3/4, Silveroid..............................	75	95	120
U. S. Watch Co., 105, 15J, NI, 3/4, HC	135	165	200
U. S. Watch Co., 105, 15J, NI, 3/4, OF	75	95	135
U. S. Watch Co., 105, 15J, NI, 3/4, Silveroid..............................	75	95	125
U. S. Watch Co., 106, 15J, gilded,3/4, Silveroid..........................	75	95	125
U. S. Watch Co., 106, 15J, gilded,3/4..	75	95	135
U. S. Watch Co., 108, 11J, gilded, 3/4..	75	95	135
U. S. Watch Co., 109, 7J, NI, 3/4..	75	95	125
U. S. Watch Co., 110, 7J, 3/4, HC	100	125	150
U. S. Watch Co., 110, 7J, 3/4, OF..	75	95	125

Note: Add $20 - $40 to value of above watches in hunting case.

🕒 Generic, nameless or **unmarked** grades for watch movements are listed under the Company name or initials of the Company, etc. by size, jewel count and description.

🕒 Watches listed in this book are priced at the collectable retail level, as complete watches having an original 14k gold-filled case and Key Wind with silver, an original white enamel single sunk dial, and with the entire original movement in good working order with no repairs needed.

U.S. Watch Co., 16 size, 15 jewels, three-quarter plate.

6 SIZE

Grade or Name – Description	Avg	Ex-Fn	Mint
U. S. Watch Co., 60, 17J, GJS, NI, 3/4, Adj.3P	$50	$70	$95
U. S. Watch Co., 60, 17J, GJS, NI, 3/4, Adj.3P, **HC, 14K**	225	275	350
U. S. Watch Co., 62, 15J, NI, 3/4	50	70	95
U. S. Watch Co., 63, 15J, gilded	50	70	95
U. S. Watch Co., 64, 11J, NI	50	70	95
U. S. Watch Co., 65, 11J, gilded	30	40	65
U. S. Watch Co., 66, 7J, gilded	30	40	65
U. S. Watch Co., 66, 7-11J, NI, 3/4	50	70	95
U. S. Watch Co., 68, 16J, GJS, NI, 3/4	75	100	125
U. S. Watch Co., 69, 7J, NI, HC	85	100	150
U. S. Watch Co., 69, 7J, NI, OF	30	40	65

Grade 64, 6 size, 11 jewels

U.S. Watch Co. of Waltham, 0 size, 7 jewels, serial number 808,231.

0 SIZE

Grade or Name – Description	Avg	Ex-Fn	Mint
Betsy Ross, HC, GF case	$150	$175	$225
U. S. Watch Co., 15J, HC, GF case	125	150	200
U. S. Watch Co., 7-11J, HC, GF case	125	150	200

THE WASHINGTON WATCH CO.

Washington, D. C.

1872 - 1874

J. P. Hopkins, though better known as the inventor of the Auburndale Rotary Watch, was also connected with the Washington Watch Co. they may have produced about 50 watches. They were 18S, key wind, 3/4 plate and had duplex escapements. Before Hopkins came to Washington Watch Co. he had handmade about six fine watches. Most of the materials used to produce the watch movements were purchased from the Illinois Watch Co. The company had a total production of 45 movements with duplex escapements.

Grade or Name – Description	Avg	Ex-Fn	Mint
18S, 15J, 3/4, KW, KS .... ★ ★ ★ ★	$3,500	$4,500	$5,500

WATERBURY WATCH CO.

Waterbury, Connecticut

1880 - 1898

The Waterbury Watch Co. was formed in 1880, and D. A. A. Buck made its first watch. The watches were simple and had only 50 parts. The mainspring was about nine feet long and coiled around the movement. It had a two-wheel train rather than the standard four-wheel train. The Waterbury long wind movement revolved once every hour and had a duplex escapement. The dial was made of paper, and the watch was priced at $3.50 to $4.00. Some of these watches were used as give aways.

Waterbury Watch Co., skeletonized movement; "A poor man's tourbillon," c. 1890.

Waterbury Watch Co., long wind movement. Note six spokes on dial.

CHRONOLOGY OF THE DEVELOPMENT OF THE WATERBURY WATCH CO.:

Waterbury Watch Co., Waterbury, Conn................... 1880-1898
New England Watch Co. 1898-1912
Purchased Ingersoll................ 1914
Became U. S. Time Corp. (maker of Timex) 1944

Waterbury Watch Co. movement, Series C.

Series L, Waterbury W. Co. Duplex Escapement, about 16 size.

18 TO 0 SIZES

Grade or Name – Description	Avg	Ex-Fn	Mint
35S, 1890-1891, back wind.................	$100	$150	$200
Long wind, skeletonized, 3 spokes................................★	350	400	550
Long wind, skeletonized, 4 spokes............................★★	600	750	1,000
Long wind, skeletonized, 6 spokes............................★	400	450	700
Long wind, skeletonized, 6 spokes, **celluloid case**.................★	500	600	750
Series A, long wind, skeletonized ....★	350	400	550
Series B, long wind...	200	225	300
Series C, long wind.............................	200	225	300
Series D, long wind.............................	225	250	350
Series E, long wind (discontinued 1890)	275	300	400
Series F, Duplex escapement........................	85	95	125

🕐 Some grades are not included. Their values can be determined by comparing with **similar** age, size, metal content, style, models and grades listed.

🕐 Watches listed in this book are priced at the collectable retail level, as **complete** watches having an original 14k gold-filled case and *Key Wind* with silver, an original white enamel single sunk dial, and with the entire original movement in good working order with no repairs needed.

🕐 This book endeavours to be a GUIDE or helpful manual and offers a wealth of material to be used as a tool not as a absolute document. Price Guides are like watches the worst may be better than none at all, but at best cannot be expected to be 100% accurate.

🕐 Characteristics of watches differ for the same age of both case and movement, because these features vary it may not be accurate to date a watch by one single influence. Example: the second hand was _not_ commonly found on watches before 1750, but common about 1800. The first second hand appeared in 1665 and another in 1690. Therefore statements are broad rather than accurate.

Series I, The Trump, about 18 size, no jewels, pin lever escapement.

Series T, Oxford Duplex Escapement, about 18 size, no jewels.

Grade or Name – Description	Avg	Ex-Fn	Mint
Series G, 3/4 lever escapement.......................................★	$200	$225	$300
Series H, Columbian Duplex.................................★ ★	250	275	350
Series I, Trump, duplex, ...	85	95	125
Series I, Trump, 3/4	85	95	125
Series J, Americus Duplex	85	95	125
Series K, Charles Benedict Duplex	125	150	200
Series L, Waterbury W. Co. Duplex	85	100	125
Series N, Addison Duplex	75	85	110
Series P, Rugby Duplex..	100	125	150
Series R, Tuxedo Duplex..	80	100	125
Series S, Elfin	65	75	85
Series T, Oxford Duplex...	75	85	100
Series W, Addison	85	125	135
Series Z	65	85	95
Free Press Watch, Series E..	200	225	250
Old Honesty, Series C, longwind, ...	250	300	400
Oxford, ...	65	80	95
The Trump..	60	75	90
Waterbury W. Co., 7J, 3/4, low Serial No.	300	375	500
18size, Waterbury W. Co., KW, LS.........................★	300	325	400

NOTE: Dollar -watches must be in **Running** condition to bring these prices.

🕐 Some grades are not included. Their values can be determined by comparing with **similar** age, size, metal content, style, models and grades listed.

🕐 Watches listed in this book are priced at the collectable retail level, as **complete** watches having an original 14k gold-filled case and *Key Wind* with silver, an original white enamel single sunk dial, and with the entire original movement in good working order with no repairs needed.

🕐 This book endeavours to be a GUIDE or helpful manual and offers a wealth of material to be used as a tool not as a absolute document. Price Guides are like watches the worst may be better than none at all, but at best cannot be expected to be 100% accurate.

E. N. WELCH MFG. CO.

Bristol, Connecticut
1834 - 1897

Elisha Welch founded this company about 1834. His company failed in 1897, and the Sessions Clock Co. took over the business in 1903. E. N. Welch Mfg. Co. produced the large watch which was displayed at the Chicago Exposition in 1893. This watch depicted the landing of Columbus on the back of the case.

E.N. Welch Mfg. Co., 36 size, back wind & set, made for the Chicago Exposition in 1893. Die debossed back depicting the landing of Columbus in America, Oct, 12th, 1492.

Grade or Name – Description	Avg	Ex-Fn	Mint
36S, Columbus Exhibition watch	$400	$450	$550

WESTCLOX

United Clock Co. – Western Clock Mfg. Co.– General Time Corp.
Athens, Georgia
1899 - Present

The first Westclox pocket watch was made about 1899; however, the Westclox name did not appear on their watches until 1906. In 1903 they were making 100 watches a day, and in 1920 production was at 15,000 per day. This company is still in business in Athens, Georgia.

Grade or Name – Description	Avg	Ex-Fn	Mint
M#1, SW, push to set, GRO	$75	$100	$125
M#2, SW, back set, GRO	50	60	75
18S, Westclox M#4, OF, GRO	50	60	75
1910 Models to 1920, GRO	35	45	60
Anniversary	35	45	60
Antique	20	30	45
Boy Proof	45	50	75
Bingo	30	40	55
Bulls Eye (several models)	15	20	25
Campus	15	20	25
Celluloid case, 70mm	30	35	45
Coronado	15	20	25
Country Gentleman	40	50	60

Boy Proof Model, about 16 size, designed to be tamper proof.

Westclox movement, stem wind, back set.

Grade or Name – Description	Avg	Ex-Fn	Mint
Dax (many models)	$10	$15	$20
Dewey	10	15	20
Elite	25	35	40
Everbrite (several models)	30	45	65
Explorer	225	275	325
Farm Bureau	65	85	100
Glo Ben	65	85	100
Glory Be	20	25	30
Johnny Zero (several models)	65	75	95
Ideal	30	35	40
Lighted Dial	25	30	40
Magnetic	20	25	30
Major	25	30	35
Man Time	15	20	25
Mark IV	35	45	55
Mascot	20	25	30
Maxim	30	40	50

Zep, about 16 size with radiant numbers and hands, c. 1929.

Explorer, back of case and dial, "Wings Over The Pole, The Explorer" on back of case.

World's Fair watch & fob, (1982 -Knoxville Tn.){Wagner Time Inc.}, total production for watch 4,200 and 200 for the FOB, Ca. 1982 .

Grade or Name – Description	Avg	Ex-Fn	Mint
Military Style, 24 hour..	$65	$85	$100
Monitor...	15	20	25
Mustang..	40	45	60
NAWCC, TOTAL PRODUCTION = 1,000...................................	65	85	110
Panther...	45	50	60
Pasture Stop Watch, (fly back hand) Sterling Watch Co.	100	145	200
Pocket Ben (many models)...	20	35	60
Ruby...	25	30	45
Scepter..	20	25	30
Scotty (several models)	15	20	25
Silogram	15	20	25
Smile	25	30	40
Solo..	15	20	25
St. Regis	20	25	35
Sterling Watch Co. **(see Pasture Stop Watch)**			
Sun Mark...	30	35	40
Team Mate (various major league teams).....................................	25	35	40
Tele Time..	25	35	45
Texan..	35	45	65
The Airplane	45	55	65
The American, **back SET**	50	60	75
The Conductor	45	55	65
Tiny Tim..	150	200	275
Trail Blazer	40	45	55
Uncle Sam...	40	50	60
Victor..	80	100	130
Vote	25	35	45
Westclox..	15	20	25
World's Fair (1982 -Knoxville Tn.){Wagner Time Inc.}	75	85	100
Zep, (Zepplin)..	225	275	375
Zodiak Time...	35	40	45

WESTERN WATCH CO.

Chicago, Illinois
1880

Albert Trotter purchased the unfinished watches from the California Watch Co. Mr. Trotter finished and sold those watches. Later he moved to Chicago and, with Paul Cornell and others, formed the Western Watch Company. Very few watches were completed by the Western Watch Co.

Grade or Name – Description		Avg	Ex-Fn	Mint
Western Watch Co., 18S, FULL ....★★★★		$2,500	$3,000	$4,000

Western Watch Co. movement, 18 size, 15 jewels, key wind & set.

WICHITA WATCH CO.

Wichita, Kansas
July, 1887 - 1888

This company completed construction of their factory in Wichita, Kansas in June 1888, and only a half dozen watches were produced during the brief period the company was in operation. The president was J. R. Snively. These watches are 18S, half plate, adjusted, 15 jewels.

Grade or Name – Description		Avg	Ex-Fn	Mint
18S, 15J, plate, ADJ ....★★★★		$3,500	$4,500	$5,500

⊕ Watches listed in this book are priced at the collectable retail level, as **complete** watches having an original 14k gold-filled case and *Key Wind* with silver, an original white enamel single sunk dial, and with the entire original movement in good working order with no repairs needed.

COMIC AND CHARACTER WATCHES

When discussing the topic of watches and someone mentions Comic Character Watches, we immediately picture a watch with Mickey Mouse. Isn't Mickey Mouse the most famous of all watches in the world? Before Mickey appeared in the 1930's there were a handful of lesser known comic watches with characters like Skeezix, Smitty and Buster Brown, but it was the Mickey Mouse Watch that paved the way for all other comic character watches. As a collaboration between Walt Disney (the creator of Mickey Mouse) and Robert Ingersoll and his brother the founders of the Ingersoll-Waterbury Watch Company. The Mickey Mouse Watch was one of this century's greatest marketing concepts. In a two year period Ingersoll had sold nearly 2.5 million Mickey Mouse wrist and pocket watches. Throughout the 1930's they also introduced other watches with Disney characters such as Big Bad Wolf in 1934, as well as, the Donald Duck wrist watch. The Donald Duck pocket watch was produced several years later in 1939. The Mickey Lapel and Mickey Deluxe Wrist were produced in the late 1930's.

Ingersoll dominated the character watch market in the early 1930's due to the incredible popularity of the Disney characters, however by the mid 1930's other companies mainly Ingraham and New Haven secured the rights to other popular characters. Throughout the 1930's kids fell in love with these watches featuring their favorite comic character or hero, such as, Popeye, Superman, Buck Rogers, Orphan Annie, Dick Tracy and The Lone Ranger. There was also a couple of other well known characters, Betty Boop and Cowboy Tom Mix produced but for some reason these watches did not become popular like all the others, so very small quantities were produced.

During World War II production of comic watches ceased, but after the war comic watches came back stronger than ever. Once again Disney was the overall leader. The Ingersoll name only appeared on some of the watches to keep the trade name still familiar, as Ingersoll was sold to U.S. Time Watch Company.

The late 1940's was very good to the character watch market and proof being the many character watches produced as the Twentieth Birthday Series for Mickey in 1948 that included with Mickey, Donald Duck, Pinocchio, Pluto, Bambi, Joe Carioca, Jiminy Cricket, Bongo Bear and Daisy Duck. Other watches from this time include Porky Pig, Puss-N-Boots, Joe Palooka, Gene Autry, Captain and Mary Marvel and others featuring characters of the comic and cartoons, space and western heroes.

The early to mid 1950's was also a vibrant time for character watch production with more Disney characters, western heroes and comic characters than ever before, but by 1958 manufacturing of character watches had almost completely stopped as manufacturing costs went up, popularity of some characters faded and many other circumstances led to a complete stop of any of these watches until the late 1960's. The watches were never the same again.

In the 1970's Comic Character Watch once again made it's come back with the Bradley Watch Company (Elgin W. Co.) leading the way just as Ingersoll did in the first years of comic watches.

Today there are hundreds of character watches to choose from, Disney Super Hero movie characters like E.T., and Roger Rabbit and a wealth of others, but today's fascination is not just with the new but with the old as we see in the re-issue of the original Mickey watches. There is a growing awareness and appreciation for all the originals. It is a very unusual attraction that draws people to love and collect the character watches of the past. Collectors appreciate the original boxes (that are fascinating works of art) and the face of the watch that features the character that we love. The manufacturing method of these simple pin lever movements were not the best of timekeepers, but were solidly constructed. All in all, when you put together the watches and boxes they are pieces of functional art and history that brings back memories of our youth. Something that no other kind of watch can do.

LEFT: SNOOPY & WOODSTOCK - CENTER: SNOOP DIAL 1to 12 - RIGHT: SNOOP DIAL 12- 3- 6- 9 (ALL 3 Ca.1968)

Babe Ruth, by Exact Time, ca. 1948.

Betty Boop, by Ingraham, ca. 1934.

Style or Grade – Description	Avg	Ex-Fn	Mint	Mint +Box
Alice in Wonderland, WW, c. 1951, by U.S. Time	$40	$50	$60	$275
Alice, Red Riding Hood, & Marjory Daw, WW, c. 1953, by Bradley	40	50	60	150
Alice in Wonderland, WW, c. 1958, by Timex	40	50	60	300
Alice in Wonderland & Mad Hatter, WW, c. 1948, by New Haven	65	85	125	250
All * Stars, c.1965, autograped by Mickey Mantel, Rodger Maris, Willie Mays, Sandy Koufax, Swiss, GREEN DIAL	100	150	225	350
All * Stars, c.1965, autograped by Mickey Mantel, Rodger Maris, Willie Mays, Sandy Koufax, Swiss, BLACK DIAL	75	100	185	275
Annie Oakley, WW, (Action Gun) c. 1951, by New Haven	150	195	275	425
Archie, WW, c.1970s, Swiss,	50	60	100	150
Babe Ruth, WW, c. 1948, by Exact Time, box baseball pledge card	★175	275	400	1,300
Ballerina, WW, c.1955, Ingraham, Action legs,	40	50	60	75
Bambi, WW, c. 1949, by U.S. Time, Birthday series	100	175	250	450
Barbie, WW, c.1964, by Bradley, facing "3",	40	50	60	85
Barbie, WW, c.1970, by Bradley, action arms	40	50	60	85
Batman, WW, c. 1970 by Gilbert (band in shape of bat)	100	175	225	300
Batman, WW, c. 1978, by Timex	100	125	175	250
Betty Boop, PW, c. 1934, by Ingraham (with diedebossed back)	★★★★350	750	1,000	1,800
Betty Boop, WW, c.1980s, with hearts on dial & band	40	50	60	75
Bert & Ernie, WW, c.1970s, swiss	40	50	60	70
Big Bad Wolf & 3 Pigs, PW, c. 1936, by Ingersoll	300	450	700	1,200
Big Bad Wolf & 3 Pigs, WW, c. 1936, by Ingersoll	300	550	850	1,800
Big Bird, WW, c.1970s, Swiss, action arms, (pop up box)	40	50	60	75
Blondie & Dagwood, WW, c.1950s, Swiss	150	200	250	475
Bongo Bear, WW, c.1946, Ingersoll, Birthday series	100	150	200	300
Boy Scout,PW, c.1937, by Ingersoll, be prepared hands	250	275	350	600
Boy Scout,WW, c.1938, by New Haven.	75	85	100	150
Buck Rogers, PW, c.1935, Ingraham (lightning bolt hands)	300	400	650	1,000
Bud Man, WW, Swiss, c.1970s	40	50	60	75
Bugs Bunny, WW, c. 1951, Swiss, (carrot shaped hands)	100	175	275	550
Bugs Bunny, WW, c. 1951, Swiss, (without carrot hands)	70	100	175	400
Bugs Bunny, WW, c. 1970, Swiss, (standing bugs)	45	50	60	75

🕐 NOTE: Beware (**COLOR COPY DIALS**) are being faked as Buck Rodgers, Babe Ruth, Hopalong Cassidy and others. *BUYER BEWARE*

BIG BAD WOLF & 3 PIGS, + FOB INGERSOLL

BUSTER BROWN, INGERSOLL, Ca. 1925

BUGS BUNNY, EXACT TIME, Ca. 1949

BUCK ROGERS, INGRAHAM, Ca. 1935

BIG BAD WOLF & 3 PIGS

– DICK TRACY, NEW HAVEN, Ca.1948

– DICK TRACY, (six shooter action arm) Ca.1952

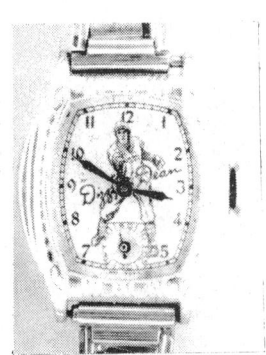

DIZZY DEAN, By Everbright W. Co.

DONALD, with mickey seconds hand, 3 grades.

DONALD DUCK, by INGERSOLL, C. 1942.

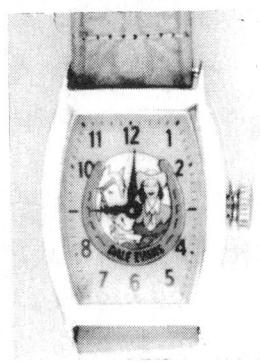

DALE EVANS, INGRAHAM

DAN DARE, INGERSOLL made in England

FROM OUTER SPACE, INGERSOLL made in England

Style or Grade – Description	Avg	Ex-Fn	Mint	Mint +Box
Buster Brown, PW, c. 1928, by Ingersoll	$125	$175	$250	$450
Buster Brown, PW, c. 1928, by Ingersoll (Buster in circle)	125	175	300	450
Buster Brown, WW, c.1930, engraved case	125	145	180	225
Buzz Corey, WW, c. 1952, by U.S. Time	75	125	200	450
Buzzy the Crow, in red hat	40	50	60	75
Captain Liberty, WW, c. 1950, by U.S.Time, multi-color band	50	80	150	450
Captain Marvel, PW, c. 1945, by New Haven	175	250	400	700
Captain Marvel,WW, c.1948, New Haven (small w.w.)	65	95	175	350
Captain Marvel, WW, c. 1948, by New Haven (larger size)	90	125	200	475
Captain Marvel, WW, c. 1948, Swiss made	95	140	225	350
Captain Marvel Jr., c. 1948, Swiss	90	130	200	300
Captain Midnight, PW, c. 1948, by Ingraham	250	300	400	600
Casper, WW, c.1970s, Swiss, action arms	40	50	60	75
Cat In The Hat, WW, c.1970s, Swiss, Action arms	40	50	60	75
Cinderella, WW, c. 1950, by U.S. Time (slipper box)	40	45	65	225
Cinderella, WW, c. 1955, by Timex (box with imitation cel)	40	50	60	225
Cinderella, WW, c. 1958, by Timex (box with plastic statue)	25	30	60	225
Cinderella, WW, c. 1958, by Timex (box & porcelain statue)	40	50	75	225
Coca Cola, PW, c. 1948, by Ingersoll	125	150	200	300
Cowboy, WW, c.1955, by Muros, Swiss, action gun	40	50	60	75
Cowgirl, WW, c.1951, by New Haven, Action Gun	40	45	65	85
Cub Scout, WW, by Timex	40	50	60	75
Daisy Duck, WW, c. 1947, by Ingersoll (tonneau style)	100	175	250	500
Daisy Duck, WW, c. 1948, by U.S. Time (fluted bezel, birthday series)	100	175	250	450
Daisy Duck, WW, c. 1949, by U.S. Time, (grooved bezed)	95	135	175	300
Dale Evans, WW, c.1949,by Ingraham,Dale standing,(tonneau)	80	100	125	250
Dale Evans, WW, c. 1950, by Bradley (western style leather band & necklace &lucky horseshoe), tonneau style case	75	85	100	350
Dale Evans, WW, c. 1960, by Bradley (round)	40	50	65	150
Dan Dare, PW, c. 1950, by Ingersoll Ltd. England, action arm	200	300	400	700
Davy Crockett, WW, c. 1951, by Bradley (round dial)	40	50	90	250
Davy Crockett, WW, c. 1954, Action gun, (round dial)	65	75	100	200
Davy Crockett, WW, c. 1954, Liberty , (round dial)	40	50	85	125
Davy Crockett, WW, c. 1955, by U.S. Time (& powder horn)	75	85	110	350
Davy Crockett, WW, c. 1956, by Bradley (barrel shaped dial)	40	55	100	225
Dennis the Menace, WW, c. 1970, by Bradley	45	55	75	100
Dick Tracy, PW, c. 1948, by Ingersoll	250	350	500	800
Dick Tracy, WW, c. 1948, by New Haven (round dial)	95	110	140	325
Dick Tracy, WW, c. 1948, by New Haven (small tonneau)	75	100	150	275
Dick Tracy, WW, c. 1935, by New Haven (large)	150	225	300	500
Dick Tracy, WW, c. 1951, by New Haven (6 shooter action)	195	275	350	575
Dizzy Dean, PW, c. 1935, by Ingersoll ★★	200	350	500	1,000
Dizzy Dean, WW, c. 1938, by Everbright W.Co. ★★	200	300	500	1,000

🕐Note: To be mint condition, character watches must have **unfaded dials**, and boxes must have ALL inserts. (PW=Pocket Watch; WW=Wrist Watch)

COCA COLA, PW, Ca. 1948, by Ingersoll.

ADOLF HITLER, character wrist watch, Swiss movement "Roskopf" caliber, Ca. 1935.

Dizzy Dean, Ingersoll, ca. 1935

Donald Duck, Ingersoll, ca. 1940. Mickey on back of case.

Style or Grade – Description	Avg	Ex-Fn	Mint	Mint +Box
Donald Duck, PW, c. 1939, by Ingersoll (Mickey on back).. ★	$200	$400	$700	$1,500
Donald Duck, WW, c. 1935, by Ingersoll (Mickey on second hand)............................... ★ ★	500	800	1,200	3,000
Donald Duck, WW, c. 1942, by U.S. Time (tonneau style, silver tone)............................	100	150	250	500
Donald Duck, WW, c. 1948, by U.S. Time (tonneau style, gold tone).............................	150	200	300	500
Donald Duck, PW, , c. 1954, Swiss made	75	150	250	400
Donald Duck, WW, c. 1948, by Ingersoll (fluted bezel, birthday series)..........................	150	175	250	450
Donald Duck, WW, c. 1955, by U.S. Time, (plain bezel, pop-up in box)..........................	65	85	145	420
Dopey, WW, c. 1948, by Ingersoll (fluted bezel, birthday series).................................	100	150	250	450
Dudley Do-Right, WW, 17J (Bullwinkle & Rocky)....................	65	85	150	225
Elmer Fudd, WW, c.1970s, Swiss....................................	55	75	100	150
Elvis, WW, c.1970s, Bradley	55	60	75	125
Flash Gordon, PW, c. 1939, by Ingersoll..........................	350	475	650	950
Flash Gordon,WW, c.1970, Precision................................	100	225	350	500
From Outer Space, PW, Ingersoll G.Britian, ...	100	150	225	350
Fred Flintstone, WW, (Fred on dial)..............................	100	125	150	250
Garfield,WW, (The Cat Jumped Over The Moon)....................	40	45	65	75
Gene Autry, WW, c. 1939, by Ingersoll (Gene and Champion on dial)	100	150	250	400

Donald Duck, Ingersoll, ca.1947.   – Gene Autry, (action gun), by Ingersoll, ca.1950.   – Gene Autry (Swiss made),
ca.1956.

MICKEY MOUSE, by Ingersoll, original band, Ca.1938

MICKEY MOUSE, by Ingersoll,

MICKEY MOUSE by Ingersoll, center LUGS.

MICKEY MOUSE, by Bradley, 1972 -1985

MICKEY MOUSE, made in England by Ingersoll, Ca.1934

Who's afraid of the Big Bad Wolf

Hopalong Cassidy, U.S. Time, ca. 1950s.

Hopalong Cassidy, Ingersoll, ca. 1955.

Style or Grade – Description	Avg	Ex-Fn	Mint	Mint +Box
Gene Autry, WW, c. 1939, by Ingersoll	$95	$125	$200	$400
Gene Autry, WW, c. 1950, by New Haven, (action gun)	200	275	350	425
Gene Autry, WW, c. 1956, Swiss made	65	75	95	225
Girl Scouts, WW, c.1955, by Timex	40	50	60	75
Goofy, WW, c. 1972, by Helbros, 17J (watch runs backward)	385	500	750	950
Hoky Poky, WW, c.1950, **action arm**	35	50	75	150
Hopalong Cassidy, WW, by U.S. Time (metal watch, box with saddle)	40	50	60	225
Hopalong Cassidy, WW, by U.S. Time (plastic watch, box with saddle)	45	55	75	235
Hopalong Cassidy, WW, by U.S. Time (small watch, leather Western band, flat rectangular box)	45	55	75	300
Hopalong Cassidy, WW, by U.S. Time (regular size watch, black leather cowboy strap)	45	55	85	325
Hopalong Cassidy, PW, c. 1955, by U.S. Time (rawhide strap and fob)	125	225	300	450
Hot Wheels, WW, c.1971, Bradlet -Swiss, checkered hands	45	55	75	90
Hot Wheels, WW, c.1971, Bradlet -Swiss, rotating bezel	35	45	65	80
Hot Wheels, WW, c.1983, Swiss, LCD QUARTZ	25	35	45	65
Howdy Doody, WW, c. 1954, by Ingraham (with moving eyes)	100	125	175	400
Howdy Doody, WW, c. 1954, by Ingraham (with friends)	75	100	150	550
Jamboree, PW, c. 1951, by Ingersoll, Ltd.	75	100	250	400

Robin Hood, Swiss, Ca.1950 — BUD MAN Ca.1970s — Li'l Abner (waving flag)

LONE RANGER, New Haven, ca.1939

LONE RANGER, New Haven, ca.1939

MICKEY MOUSE Ingersoll, ca.1933

MICKEY MOUSE Ingersoll, ca.1933

LEFT: Mickey Mouse, Ingersoll, w/ Mickey seconds, ca.1939. **CENTER:** Mickey Mouse, Ingersoll, no seconds, ca.1939.. **RIGHT:** Mickey Mouse, Ingersoll, birthday series, ca.1948

Note: To be **mint** condition, character watches must have unfaded dials, and boxes must have all inserts. (PW=Pocket Watch; WW=Wrist Watch)

Style or Grade – Description	Avg	Ex-Fn	Mint	Mint +Box
James Bond 007, WW, c. 1972, by Gilbert.	$70	$125	$200	$300
Jeff Arnold, PW, c. 1952, by Ingersoll (English watch with moving gun)	150	200	325	550
Jiminy Cricket, WW, c.1948, Ingersoll, Birthday series (fluted)	75	100	200	450
Jiminy Cricket, WW, c.1949, Ingersoll, **Not** Birthday (groved)	75	100	200	450
Joe Carioca, WW, c. 1948, by U.S. Time (fluted bezel, birthday series)	115	165	265	460
Joe Palooka, WW, c. 1948, by New Haven	150	200	300	550
Li'l Abner, WW, c. 1948, by New Haven (waving flag)	150	175	250	500
Li'l Abner, WW, c. 1948, by New Haven (moving mule)	150	175	200	400
Li'l Abner, WW, c. 1955, all black dial	100	135	175	200
Little King, WW, c. 1968, by Timex	55	125	225	425
Little Pig Fiddler, WW, c.1947, by Ingersoll	125	200	300	450
Lone Ranger, PW, c. 1939, by New Haven (with fob)	150	250	400	600
Lone Ranger, WW, c. 1938, by New Haven (large)	95	185	295	475
Lone Ranger, WW, c. 1948, New Haven, (Fluted lugs)	75	125	200	400
Lone Ranger, WW, c. 1950's, round case	65	95	145	200
Louie, WW, c.1940s, by Ingersoll, (Donalds nephew)	100	150	200	400
Mary Marvel, WW, c. 1948, by U.S. Time (paper box)	65	85	125	315
Mary Marvel, WW, c. 1948, by U.S. Time (plastic box)	65	85	125	325
Mickey Mouse, PW, c.1933, by Ingersoll, #1&2 (tall stem)	285	350	450	650
Mickey Mouse, PW, c. 1936, by Ingersoll, #3&4 (short stems)	200	275	400	650
Mickey Mouse, PW, c. 1938, by Ingersoll (Mickey decal on back)	275	400	700	1,000
Mickey Mouse, PW, c. 1933, by Ingersoll Ltd. (English)	300	450	750	1,400
Mickey Mouse, PW, c. 1934, by Ingersoll (Foreign)	275	325	450	650
Mickey Mouse, PW, c.1976, by Bradley (bicentennial model)	40	50	75	125
Mickey Mouse, PW, c. 1974, by Bradley (no second hand)	40	50	60	85
Mickey Mouse, PW, c. 1974, by Bradley ("Bradley" printed at 6)	40	50	60	75

MICKEY MOUSE, Ingersoll, model no.3 on the left.   Right: Model no.4 is shown with lapel button

NOTE: Beware (**COLOR COPY DIALS**) are being **FAKED** as Buck Rodgers, Babe Ruth, Hopalong Cassidy and others. *BUYER BEWARE*

Style or Grade – Description	Avg	Ex-Fn	Mint	Mint +Box
Mickey Mouse, WW, c. 1933, by Ingersoll (metal band with 3 Mickeys' on seconds disc)	$200	$300	$375	$750
Mickey Mouse, WW, c. 1933, by Ingersoll wir lugs, (English Mickey with 3 Mickeys' on seconds disc, 24 hr. outer dial)	200	300	375	750
Mickey Mouse, WW, c. 1938-9, by Ingersoll (one Mickey for second hand)	125	200	295	900
Mickey Mouse, WW, c. 1938-9, by Ingersoll, plain seconds	85	125	200	350
Mickey Mouse, WW, c. 1938-9, by Ingersoll (girl's watch, 1 Mickey for second hand)	175	200	275	900
Mickey Mouse, WW, c. 1948, by Ingersoll (fluted Bezel, birthday series, 2 styles Mickey in a circle & no circle)	150	175	200	450
Mickey Mouse, WW, c. 1949, by Ingersoll, **groved** bezel	125	145	175	250
Mickey Mouse, WW, c. 1946, by U.S. Time (10k gold plated)	100	125	200	300
Mickey Mouse, WW, c. 1946, **Kelton**, 2 Styles	100	125	200	275
Mickey Mouse, WW, c. 1947, by U.S. Time (tonneau, plain, several styles)	75	95	150	325
Mickey Mouse, WW, c. 1947, by U.S. Time (same as above, gold tone)	85	100	160	350
Mickey Mouse, WW, c. 1950s, by U.S. Time (round style)	40	50	60	275
Mickey Mouse, WW, c. 1958, by U.S. Time (statue of Mickey in box)	50	60	75	250
Mickey Mouse, WW, c. 1965 to 1970, by Timex (Mickey Mouse electric)	85	100	150	250
Mickey Mouse, WW, c. 1965-70s, Timex (manual wind)	55	65	90	140
Mickey Mouse, WW, c. 1970s, by Bradley	40	50	60	90
Mickey Mouse, WW, c. 1980, by Bradley (colored min. chapter)	60	70	85	150
Mickey Mouse, WW, c. 1983, by Bradley (limited commemorative model)	60	75	100	150

Mickey Mouse, Bradley, ca. 1969.

Mickey Mouse, with wide bezel, Ingersoll, it is believed dealers have used a Wrist Watch dial in a Hopalong case, ca. 1955.

Note: To be **mint** condition, character watches must have unfaded dials, and boxes must have all inserts. (PW=Pocket Watch; WW=Wrist Watch)

Left: Captain Marvel, Ca. 1948. **Center:** Minnie Mouse, U.S.Time, Ca.196. **Right:** Orphan Annie, New Haven, Ca.1939

ORPHAN ANNIE, New Haven, Ca. 1940   2 styles of POPEYE & friends, New Haven, Ca. 1936

POPEYE, New Haven, (with friends), Ca. 1935   POPEYE, New Haven, Ca. 1940

Note: To be **mint** condition, character watches must have unfaded dials, and boxes must have all inserts. (PW=Pocket Watch; WW=Wrist Watch)

LEFT: GOOFY watch runs backward.   CENTER: Little Pig & fiddle.   RIGHT: Porky Pig

Left: Pluto, Birthday Series, by Ingersoll.   Center: Rocky Jones, Ca.1955.   Right: Speedy Gonzales, Swiss

DONALD DUCK, on face with MICKEY on back side of watch.

Style or Grade – Description	Avg	Ex-Fn	Mint	Mint +Box
Mickey Mouse, WW, c. 1985, by ETA (clear plastic bezel and band)	$40	$50	$65	$85
Mickey Mouse, WW, c.1980s, Bradley, (Tachemeter dial)	45	50	60	75
Mighty Mouse, WW, c.1980s, Swiss, (Plastic case)	25	30	35	40
Minnie Mouse, WW, c. 1958, by U.S. Time (statue of Minnie in box)	40	50	75	225
Moon Mullins, PW, c. 1930, by Ingersoll	★ 200	300	500	750
Orphan Annie, WW, c. 1939, by New Haven (fluted bezel)	75	95	125	350
Orphan Annie, WW, c. 1935, by New Haven (large style)	100	120	155	400
Orphan Annie, WW, c. 1948, by New Haven smaller model)	50	65	100	300
Orphan Annie, WW, c. 1968, by Timex	45	55	75	110
Peter Pan, PW, c. 1948, by Ingraham	150	200	300	600
Pinocchio, WW, c. 1948, by Ingersoll (fluted bezel, birthday series)	125	150	250	400
Pinocchio, WW, c. 1948, by U.S. Time (Happy Birthday cake box)	125	150	250	450
Pluto, WW, c. 1948, by U.S. Time(birthday series)	100	150	250	450
Popeye, PW, c. 1935, by New Haven (with friends on dial)	★ 275	450	650	1,100
Popeye, PW, c. 1936, by New Haven (plain dial)	225	375	500	1,000
Popeye, WW, c. 1936, by New Haven (tonneau style, with friends on dial)	★ 250	375	650	1,200
Popeye, WW, c. 1966, by Bradley (round style)	75	100	125	200
Popeye, WW, c. 1948, Swiss, Olive Oyl at 3	75	150	250	400
Porky Pig, WW, c. 1948, by Ingraham (tonneau)	100	175	250	450
Porky Pig, WW, c. 1949, by U.S. Time (round)	95	185	265	465
Punkin Head, WW, c.1946, Ingraham,	55	65	85	135
Puss-N-Boots, WW, c. 1959, by Bradley	100	175	250	400
Quarterback, WW, c.1965, Swiss, (Football action arm)	65	75	85	125
Red Ryder, WW, c.1949, Swiss, (with Little Beaver)	100	135	175	250
Robin, WW, c. 1978, by Timex	40	45	65	90
Robin Hood, WW, c. 1955, by Bradley (tonneau style)	85	125	195	350
Robin Hood, WW, c. 1958, by Viking (round)	75	150	200	400
Rocky Jones Space Ranger, WW, c. 1955, by Ingraham	125	235	350	700
Roy Rogers, PW, c. 1960, by Ingraham, rim set	70	85	100	150
Roy Rogers, WW, c. 1954, by Ingraham (Roy and rearing Trigger)	75	95	125	250

Joe Palooka, Ca.1948.   — Snow White U.S.Time. —   Roy Rogers, Ingraham, ca. 1954.

ROY ROGERS, Ingraham, note rim set, Ca. 1960.

ROY ROGERS, Ingraham (large), Ca. 1951.

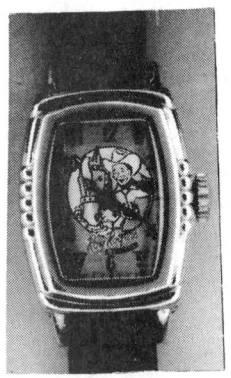

ROY ROGERS, Ingraham, Ca. 1951

SKEEZIX, Ingraham, Ca. 1936.

Left: Smitty, New Haven, Ca.1936. **Center:** Superman, New Haven, Ca.1939. **Right:** Superman, New Haven, Ca.1939.

Style or Grade – Description	Avg	Ex-Fn	Mint	Mint +Box
Roy Rogers, WW, c. 1954, by Ingraham (Roy and Trigger)	$60	$75	$100	$250
Roy Rogers, WW, c. 1954, by Ingraham (expansion band).........	60	75	100	250
Roy Rogers, WW, c. 1956, by Ingraham (round dial).................	60	75	100	200
Rudolf the Red Nose Reindeer, c.1946, Ingersoll	45	55	75	150
Rudy Nebb, PW, c. 1930, by Ingraham	150	200	275	500
Shirley Temple, PW, c.1958, by Westclox.......................★ ★	275	375	450	550
Skeezix, PW, c. 1928, by Ingraham	225	275	350	650
Sky King, WW, (action gun)..	75	100	150	200
Smitty, PW, c. 1928, by New Haven	225	275	350	650
Smitty, WW, c. 1936, by New Haven	150	200	300	550
Smokey Stover, WW, c. 1968, by Timex	75	100	150	225
Snoopy, WW, c. 1958 (tennis racket)	40	50	60	85
Snoopy, WW, c. 1958 (Woodstock)...	40	50	60	85
Snow White, WW, c. 1938, by Ingersoll (tonneau)....................	100	125	200	400
Snow White, WW, c. 1952, by U.S. Time (round)......................	45	50	65	275
Snow White, WW, c. 1956, by U.S. Time (statue in box)	40	45	70	285
Snow White, WW, c. 1962, by U.S. Time (plastic watch)..........	40	45	65	275
Space Explorer, c.1953, COMPASS watch	75	95	135	200
Speedy Gonzales, WW, Swiss	75	95	150	225
Spiro Agnew, WW,c.1970s, Swiss	25	30	35	45
Superman, PW, c. 1956, by Bradley	150	250	350	600
Superman, WW, c. 1938, by New Haven	200	250	325	600
Superman, WW, c.1946, by Ingraham(lightning bolt hands)....	150	175	250	450
Superman, WW, c. 1978, by Timex (large size).........................	50	65	95	150
Superman, WW, c. 1978, by Timex (small size).........................	45	50	75	125
Superman, WW, c.1975, Dabs & Co., yellow min. chapter........	45	50	75	150
Superman, WW, c.1965, Swiss, rotating superman....................	55	75	125	225
Superman, WW, c.1976, Timex, sweep sec. hand......................	60	65	95	150
Texas Ranger, WW, c.1950, by New Haven, action gun	100	125	150	200
Three Little Pigs, PW, c. 1939, by Ingersoll.....................★ ★	400	600	850	1,200
Tom Corbett, WW, c. 1954, by New Haven................................	75	100	150	450
Tom Mix, PW, c. 1936, by Ingersoll (with fob) ....★ ★ ★	450	750	1,000	2,500
Tom Mix, WW, c. 1936, by Ingersoll.............................★ ★ ★	400	600	900	3,000
Winnie the Pooh Bear, c.1970s, Swiss......................................	40	50	60	75
Wizard of Oz, c.1972, swiss, ...	40	55	70	120
Wonder Woman,WW, c.1975, stars at 1,2,4,5,7,8,10,11	65	70	95	160
Wonder Woman,WW, c.1975, Dabs & Co.	50	65	95	150
Woody Woodpecker, WW, c. 1948, by Ingersoll (tonneau)	85	125	250	450
Woody Woodpecker, WW, c. 1952, by Ingraham (round dial)...	100	125	175	400
Yogi Bear, WW, c. 1964, by Bradley	50	55	75	100
Zorro, WW, c. 1956, by U.S. Time..	55	60	85	250

Left: Tom Corbett, Space Cadet, New Haven, ca. 1935. **Center:** Tom Mix, Ingersoll, ca. 1936. **Right:** Woody Woodpecker, U.S. Time, ca. 1948.

Moon Mullins, by Ingersoll, ca. 1928

Rudy Nebb, by Ingersoll, ca. 1928

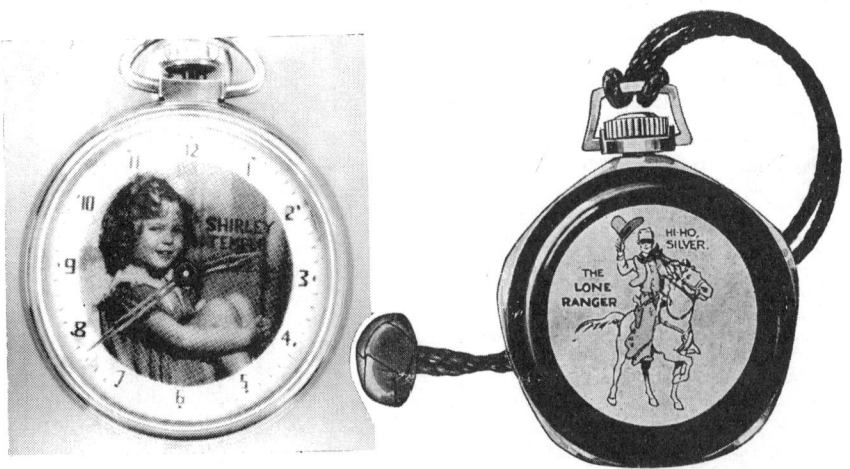

Shirley Temple, by Westclox, ca. 1958

Lone Ranger, New Haven, complete with leather cord.

CUB SCOUT by Timex   BOY SCOUT by New Haven   DAVY CROCKETT, by Ingraham

MICKEY MOUSE WRIST WATCH with
metal or leather strap bearing
Mickey's picture. The watch itself is
smartly styled ... round and therefore entirely practical for a very little girl's wrist. Packed in Mickey
Mouse display carton. Retails $2.75.
List $3.90

MICKEY MOUSE WATCH AND FOB—
a wonderful buy at $1.50 complete.
Mickey on the dial of the watch
pointing out the time—Mickey on
the fob—three little Mickies on the
second-circle chasing each other
around. List $2.20

New Mickey Mouse Lapel Watch. A handsome
lapel model with Mickey's hands telling time on
small dial. Mickey on dial and back of a black
glossy finished case with nickel trim. Black lapel
cord and button. Each in a display box.

No. 1W61. Each.......................$2.10

LONE RANGER FOB WATCH

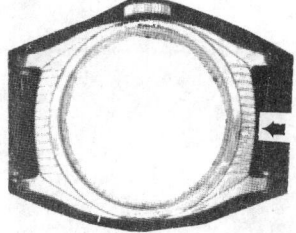

ABOVE: 20th Birthday series style case note **fluted** bezel.
The Birthday series used ten different characters & sold for
$6.95. The TEN CHARACTERS are: Mickey Mouse, Daisy
Duck, Pluto, Bambi, Joe Carioca, Bongo, Donald Duck,
Pinnochio, Dopey, and Jiminy Cricket.

New De Luxe Mickey Mouse Wrist Watch. A
smarter thinner chromium plated rectangular case.
Mickey appears in bright colors on the dial. Fitted
with a perspiration proof leather band. Each in
display box.

No. 11W440. Each.................$5.54

EARLY ANTIQUE WATCHES

The early antique watches looked quite similar to small table clocks. These drum-shaped watches were about two inches in diameter and usually over one-half inch thick. The drum-shaped watch lost popularity in the late 1500s. The earliest portable timepieces did not carry the maker's name, but initials were common. The cases generally had a hinged lid which covered the dial. This lid was pierced with small holes to enable ready identification of the position of the hour hand. They also usually contained a bell. The dial often had the numbers ''I'' to ''XII'' engraved in Roman numerals and the numbers ''13'' to ''24'' in Arabic numbers with the ''2'' engraved in the form of a ''Z.'' Even the earliest of timepieces incorporated striking. The oldest known watch with a date engraved on the case was made in 1548. A drum-shaped watch with the initials ''C. W.,'' it was most likely produced by Casper Werner, a protege of Henlein.

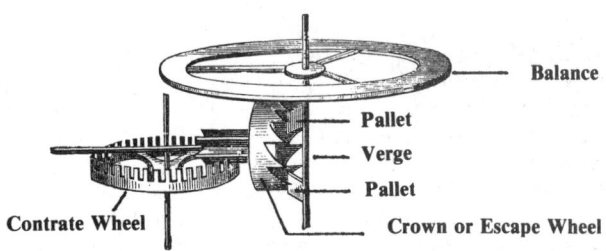

Early pocket watches were designed to run from 12 to 16 hours. The pinions usually bore five leaves, the great wheel 55 teeth, the second wheel 45 teeth, the third wheel 40 teeth, and the escape wheel 15 teeth. With one less pinion and wheel the escape wheel ran reverse to a standard four-wheel watch. During the 1500s, 1600s, and much of the 1700s, it was stylish to decorate not only the case and balance cock but all parts including the clicks, barrel, studs, springs, pillars, hands, and stackfreed. The plates themselves were decorated with pierced and engraved metal scrolls, and in some instances the maker's name was engraved in a style to correspond with the general decoration of the movement. During these periods the most celebrated artists, designers, and engravers were employed. The early watches were decorated by famous artists such as Jean Vauquier 1670, Daniel Marot 1700, Gillis l'Egare 1650, Michel Labon 1630, Pierre Bourdon 1750, and D. Cochin 1750. Most of the artists were employed to design and execute pierced and repousse cases.

Alarm watch made by Bockel of London Ca. 1648.

THE MID-1700s

In the mid-1700s relatively minor changes are noticed. Decoration became less distinctive and less artistic. The newer escapements resulted in better time keeping, and a smaller balance cock was used. The table and foot became smaller. The foot grew more narrow, and as the century and the development of the watch advanced, the decoration on the balance cock became smaller and less elaborate. About 1720 the foot was becoming solid and flat. No longer was it hand pierced; however, some of the pierced ones were produced until about 1770. Thousands of these beautiful hand pierced watch cocks have been made into necklaces and brooches or framed. Sadly, many of the old movements were destroyed in a mad haste to cater to the buyers' fancy.

THE 1800s

As the 1800s approached the balance cocks became less artistic as the decoration on movements gradually diminished. Breguet and Berthoud spent very little time on the beauty or artistic design on their balance cocks or pillars. But the cases were often magnificent in design and beauty, made with enamels in many colors and laden with precious stones. During this period the movements were plain and possessed very little artistic character.

As early as 1820 three-quarter and one-half plate designs were being used with the balance cock lowered to the same level as the other wheels. The result was a slimmer watch.

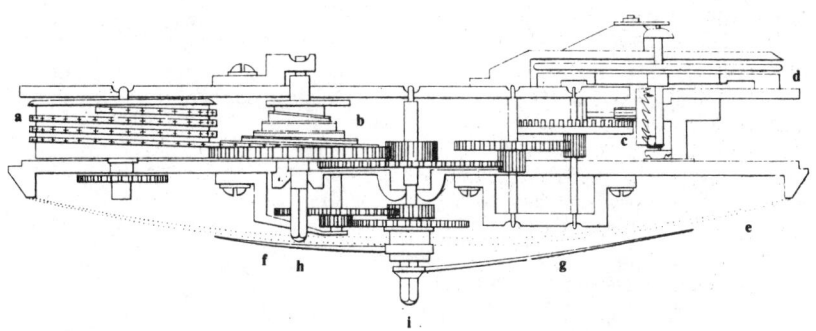

Exposed illustration of an early watch movement, c. 1800-1850. Note that movement is key wind and set from the dial side. The illustrated example is a chain driven fusee with a verge escapement: a- Main spring barrel and chain. b- Fusee. c - Verge escapement. d- Balance wheel. e- Dial. f - Hour hand. g- Minute hand. h- Winding arbor. i- Setting arbor.

🕐 Characteristics of watches differ for the same age of both case and movement, because these features vary it may not be accurate to date a watch by one single influence. Example: the second hand was not commonly found on watches before 1750, but common about 1800. The first second hand appeared in 1665 and another in 1690. Therefore statements are **broad** rather than absolute.

WATCH—MAKER

The term watch-maker might originally denote the *maker* of *watches* from base material or one who manufactures watches. But as we shall see a watch-maker may better be described as the expert in charge of producing watches. One other note before we move on, a watch may be considered as a miniature spring driven clock, so early on many **clock-makers** were also watch-makers.

There are surviving artifacts that make it possible to make certain assumptions. Thomas Tompion (also a clock-maker) born 1639, death 1713, used a production system for making watches. About 1670 Tompion divided and sub-divided laborers into various branches of manufacturing of watches. This meant each craftsman specialized in making single watch parts, thus the division of labor led to a faster rate of production, with higher quality and a lower cost to the ebauche movement. About 1775 John Elliott and John Arnold had much of their work done by other sub-divided workers. The quality of the employees work depends upon the watch-maker. Thus, the **PRICE depends** on the **reputation** of the master (watch-maker). The same holds true for todays prices, the reputation of the maker helps to determine the price they can fetch for the timepieces. The parts and materials are of little value in their original state, but the various pieces requires such delicacy of manipulation and the management of production of watches thus the responsibility for the action of the watch depends on the committee in the house of the maker.

In about 1760 to 1765 Le' Pine introduced the French or Le'Pine style calibre of ebauche movements. The Le'Pine style used separate bridges instead of the single top plate design. Frederic Japy (Japy Freres & Cie.) of Beaucourt, France, later manufactured ebauche Swiss bar style movements in the early 1770's. About 1776, Japy aids in setting up a factory in the LeLocle area and latter in England. Japy Freres & Co. were producing 3,000 movements each year by 1795, 30,000 by 1805, and close to a 50,000 ebauche style movements each year by 1860. Other "BAR" style Ebauche Companies: 1804-Sandoz & Trot of Geneva, 1840-G.A. Leschot with Vacheron & Constantin and about 1850- LeCoultre. These bar style ebauche movements were imported into the U.S.A. about 1850 and were used in the jewelry trade with the jewelers name on the case and dial until about 1875.

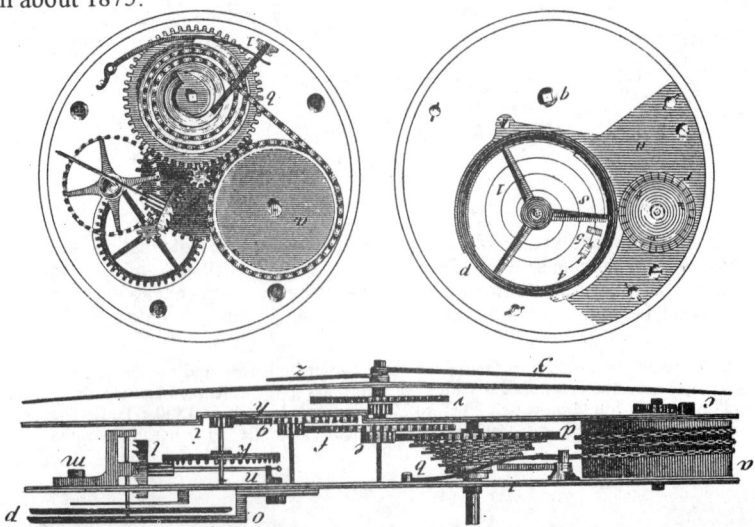

MOVEMENTS " IN THE GRAY "
Movements in an early stage of manufacture.

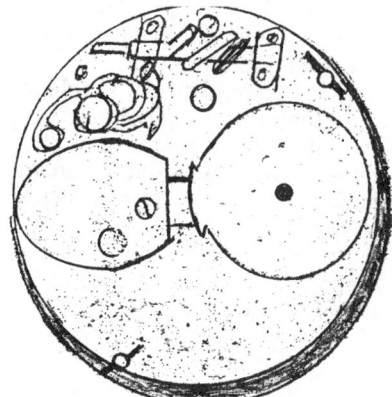

ABOUT MID 1600'S

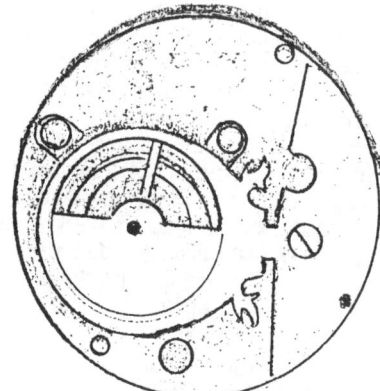

ABOUT 1700'S

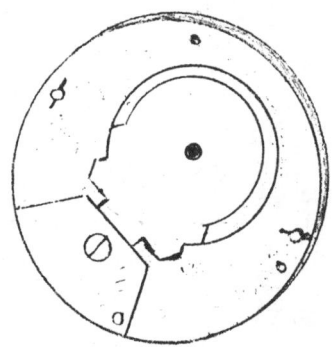

**ABOUT 1790—1830
ENGLISH STYLE**

EBAUCHE style movement with verge,
chain driven fusee, under sprung, KW,
ABOUT 1810 — 1860.

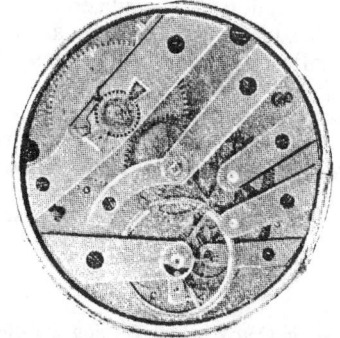

BAR STYLE movement, cylinder, **ABOUT 1840–80.**

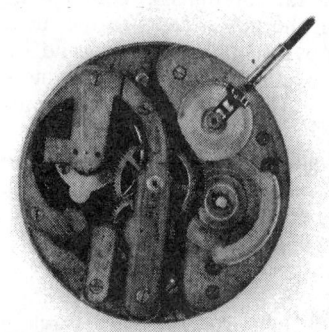

Le Locle style EBAUCHE **ABOUT 1870 to 1890.**

Multi-color cases became popular by 1800, 1st. used in 1760 & **Engine Turning** rarely found before early 1760s. **Tortoise Shell** 1st. used in 1620, but did not become popular till about 1780.

The ebauche makers and the cottage industry made different models designed to conform or answer the needs of each country to which they were trying to do business with such as French style, English style, Chinese style, etc. This makes it hard to determine the origin of the ebauche watch. The case may be made in England, the movement Swiss, and the dial French.

Below are some of the principle workmen employed in the sub-divided production of plain parts or ebauche simple watch movements (in the rough) from about 1800s. Some of these were small family specialist that formed a **cottage industry**, (some being females) they usually produced only one product as: verge-makers, hairspring-makers, fusee-makers, wheel-makers, dial-makers, chain-makers, balance-makers, hand-makers & etc.

1. Cock-maker (made brass blanks)
2. Pillar-maker (turn the pillars, etc.)
3. Frame-maker (two full plates, bars, bridges, etc.)
4. Fusee-maker
5. Verge-makers
6. Chain makers
7. Wheel-maker (small and large)
8. Wheel-cutter (cuts the teeth on the wheels)
9. Pinion- maker
10. Escapement-maker
11. Balance-makers (made of steel or brass)
12. Spring-maker(hair & main springs)
13. Hand-maker
14. Dial-maker

The following is a list of craftsman employed to make the cases.

1. Case-maker (makes cupped lids for cases)
2. Side-maker (makes the side of the case)
3. Cap-maker (makes the lids of the case)
4. The joint-finisher (joints for cases)
5. Glass-maker (made the crystal for the bezels)
6. Bezel-makers
7. Pendant-maker

These blank movements, parts, dials and cases were bought, then shipped on to the final destination. The *watch-maker* or *finisher,* such as, the house of (CARTIER). The Finisher would often house or contract decorators to finish the cases. The Finisher completed, polished, engraved, timed, regulated and made all the adjustments to the movements. They added and fitted the case to the movement. They added and fitted the complications such as repeaters to the movements. The *finished* watch is now ready for sale.

This type of system of producing watches left time for the Master watch-makers or famous watch-makers to invent, design new and better ways to make watches, such as, did Abraham Louis Breguet. In early 1800's Breguet firm received parts and Swiss ebauches from 18 different suppliers. Thus the more famous the maker the higher the price of the watch even though the watch-maker may not have **made** the smallest piece for the *finished* watch.

🕐 **Multi-color** cases became popular by 1800, 1st. used in 1760 & **Engine Turning** rarely found before early 1760s. **Tortoise Shell** 1st. used in 1620, but did not become popular till about 1780.

CLUES TO DATING YOUR WATCH

To establish the age of a watch there are many points to be considered. The dial, hands, pillars, balance cock and pendant, for example, contain important clues in determining the age of your watch. However, no one part alone should be considered sufficient evidence to draw a definite conclusion as to age. The watch as a whole must be considered. For example, an English-made silver-cased watch will have a hallmark inside the case. It is quite simple to refer to the London Hallmark Table for hallmarks after 1697. The hallmark will reveal the age of the case only. This does not fix the age of the movement. Many movements are housed in cases made years before or after the movement was produced.

An informed collector will note that a watch with an **enamel dial**, for instance, could not have been made before 1635. **A pair of cases** indicates it could not have been made prior to 1640. The **minute hand** was introduced in 1687. The presence of a **cylinder escapement** would indicate it was made after 1710. **1750 the duplex escapement** was first used. A **dust cap** first appeared in 1774. *1776 LePine introduced the thin watch.* **Keyless winding** came into being after 1820, but did not gain widespread popularity until *after* about 1860. All of these clues and more must be considered before accurately assessing the age of a watch. *Some watches were also updated such as minute hand added or new style escapement added.*

Example of an early pocket watch with a stackfreed design to equalize power much as a fusee does. Note dumbbell shaped foliot which served as a balance for verge escapement, and the tear shaped cam which is part of the stackfreed.

🕐 **Characteristics of watches differ for the same age of both case and movement, because these features vary it may not be accurate to date a watch by one single influence. Example: the second hand was not commonly found on watches before 1750, but common about 1800. The first second hand appeared in 1665 and another in 1690. Therefore statements are broad rather than absolute.**

PILLARS

Pillars are of interest and should be considered as one of the elements in determining age. Through the years small watches used round pillars, and the larger watches generally used a square type engraved pillar.

(*Illus.* 1) This pillar is one of the earliest types and used in the 1800s as well. This particular pillar came from a watch which dates about 1550. It is known that this type pillar was used in 1675 by Gaspard Girod of France and also in 1835 by James Taylor of England.

(*Illus.* 2) This style pillar is called the tulip pattern. Some watchmakers preferred to omit the vertical divisions. This style was popular between 1660 and 1750 but may be found on later watches. It was common practice to use ornamentation on the tulip pillar.

(*Illus.* 3) The ornament shown was used by Daniel Quare of London from 1665 to 1725 and by the celebrated Tompion, as well as many others.

(*Illus.* 4) This type pillar is referred to as the Egyptian and dates from 1630 to the 1800s. The squared Egyptian pattern was introduced about 1630 and some may be found with a wider division with a head or bust inserted. This style was used by D. Bouquet of London about 1640 and by many other watchmakers.

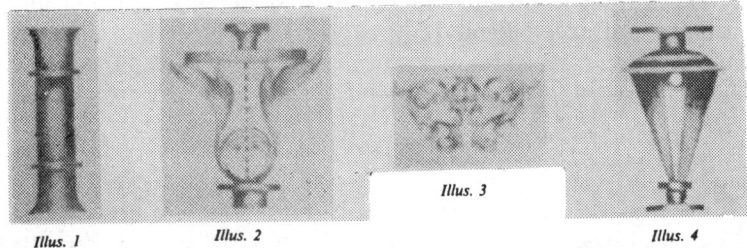

Illus. 1   Illus. 2   Illus. 3   Illus. 4

(*Illus.* 5) This pillar was used by Thomas Earnshaw of London about 1780. The plain style was prominent for close to two hundred years 1650 to 1825.

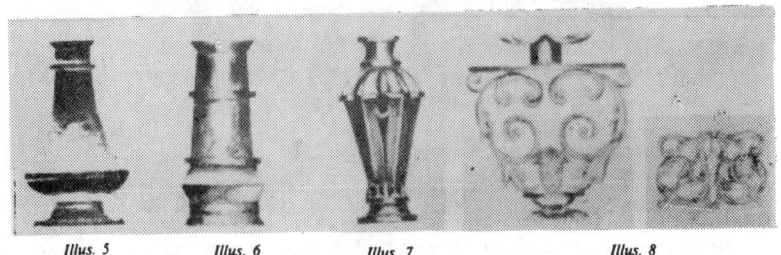

Illus. 5   Illus. 6   Illus. 7   Illus. 8

(Illus. 6) This style was popular and was used by many craftsmen. Nathaniel Barrow of London put this in his watches about 1680.

(Illus. 7) This pillar may be seen in watches made by Pierre Combet of Lyons, France, about 1720. It was also used by many others.

(Illus. 8) This style pillar and the ornament were used by John Ellicott of England and other watchmakers from 1730 to 1770.

These illustrations represent just a few of the basic pillars that were used. Each watchmaker would design and change details to create his own individual identity. This sometimes makes it more difficult to readily determine the age of watches.

Example of a 2 Egyptian pillars left & right also a hand pierced ornament that is not a pillar.

BALANCE COCKS OR BRIDGES

The first balance cocks or bridges used to support the balance staff were a plain "S" shape. The cocks used on the old three-wheel watches were very elaborate; hand-pierced and engraved. At first no screws were used to hold the cock in place. It is noteworthy that on the three wheel watch the regulator was a ratchet and click and was used on these earlier movements to adjust the mainspring. About 1635 the balance cock was screwed to the plate and pinned on its underside, which helped steady the balance. The first cock illustrated is a beautifully decorated example made by Josias Jeubi of Paris about 1580. Note that it is pinned to a stud which passes through a square cut in the foot of the cock. Next is a balance cock made by Bouquet of London about 1640. The third balance cock is one made by Jean Rousseau and dates around 1650. The fourth one dates around 1655.

The next two bridges are supported on both sides of the balance bridge by means of screws or pins. They are strikingly different and usually cover much of the plate of the movement. This style of balance bridge was used around 1675 and was still seen as late as 1765.

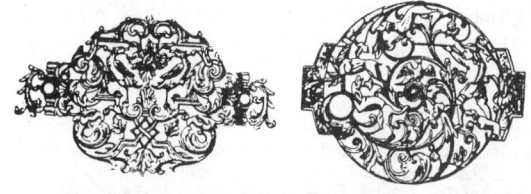

The beautiful balance cock below at left, with the ornate foot, dates about 1660. The next illustrated balance cock with the heavy ornamentation was used from about 1700 to 1720 or longer. By 1720 a face was added to the design. The face shows up where the table terminates on most balance cocks.

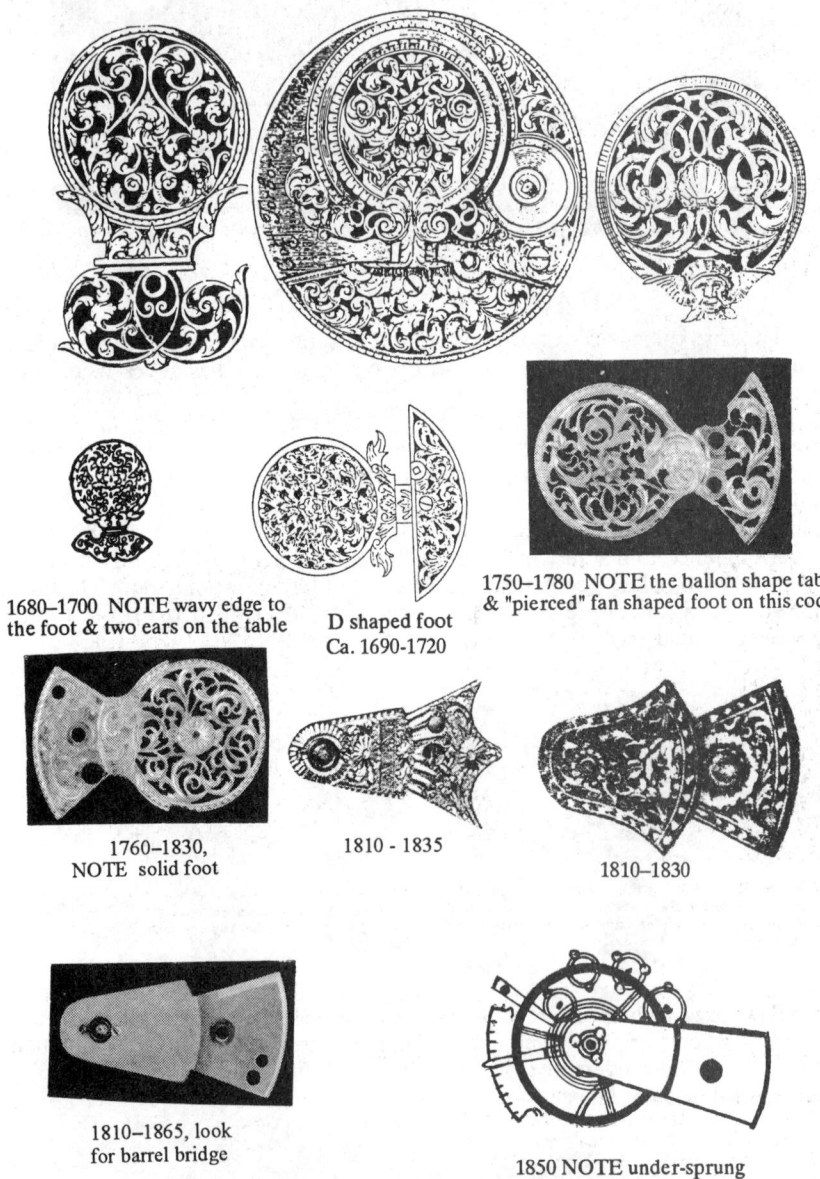

1680–1700 NOTE wavy edge to the foot & two ears on the table

D shaped foot Ca. 1690-1720

1750–1780 NOTE the ballon shape table & "pierced" fan shaped foot on this cock.

1760–1830, NOTE solid foot

1810 - 1835

1810–1830

1810–1865, look for barrel bridge

1850 NOTE under-sprung

🕐 Characteristics of watches differ for the same age of both case and movement, because these features vary it may not be accurate to date a watch by one single influence. Example: the second hand was **not** commonly found on watches before 1750, but common about 1800. The first second hand appeared in 1665 and another in 1690. Therefore statements are **broad** rather than absolute.

LePine style movement Ca. 1790-1820, with free standing barrel, also note the horse shoe shaped bridge, this denotes center seconds.

LePine, or FRENCH style ebauche caliber, NOTE the step shaped and tapered bridges, also note the free standing barrel, Ca. 1800--1825.

LePine, or FRENCH style ebauche caliber, NOTE the step shaped and tapered bridges, also note the COVERED barrel bridge, this style movement was popular from Ca.1820-1835.

LePine, or FRENCH style ebauche caliber, NOTE the step shaped and tapered bridges, also note the CURVED barrel bridge, this style movement was popular from Ca.1830-1845.

🕐 Characteristics of watches differ for the same age of both case and movement, because these features vary it may not be accurate to date a watch by one single influence. Example: the second hand was not commonly found on watches before 1750, but common about 1800. The first second hand appeared in 1665 and another in 1690. Therefore statements are **broad** rather than absolute.

Muti-colored cases became popular by 1800, 1st. used in 1760 & **Engine Turning** rarely found before early 1760s. **Tortoise Shell** 1st. used in 1620, but did not become popular till about 1780. An informed collector will note that a watch with an enamel dial, for instance, could not have been made before 1635. A pair of cases indicates it could not have been made prior to 1640. The minute hand was introduced in 1650. The presence of a cylinder escapement would indicate it was made after 1710. 1750 the duplex escapement was first used. A dust cap first appeared in 1774. 1776 Lepine introduced the thin watch. Keyless winding came into being after 1820 but did not gain widespread popularity until after about 1860. All of these clues and more must be considered before accurately assessing the age of a watch. Some watches were also **updated** such as minute hand added or new style escapement added.

Bar (Le Coultre) SWISS style ebauche caliber, NOTE the flat straight bridges and parallel design, also the CURVED barrel bridge this movement was popular Ca.1830–1850.

Bar (Le Coultre) SWISS style ebauche caliber, NOTE the flat straight bridges and parallel design, also the STRAIGHT barrel bridge this movement was popular Ca.1840–1885.

JULES JURGENSEN Style Bar SWISS La Chaux de Fonds ebauche caliber, Ca.1870–1895.

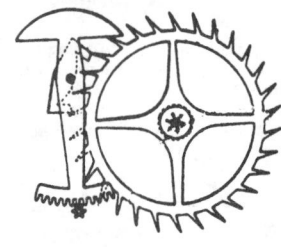

Rack and lever escapement

Invented in 1722

ESCAPEMENTS

Virgule Escapement

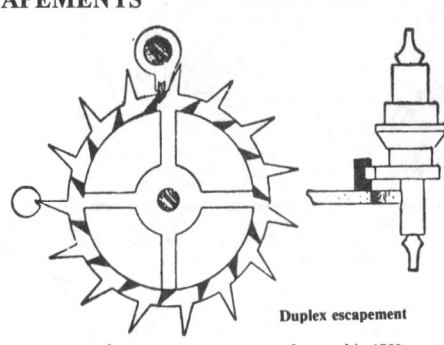

Duplex escapement

Invented in 1750

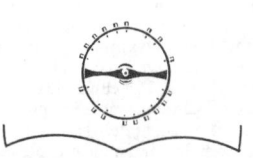

The "Glucydur" Balance can be recognized by the **shape** of its spokes.

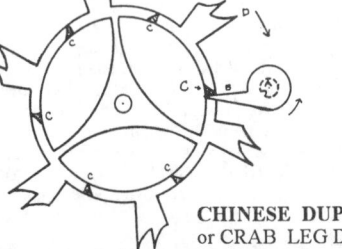

CHINESE DUPLEX or CRAB LEG DUPLEX

EARLY EUROPEAN WATCHMAKERS

NOTE ABBREVIATIONS USED
art = maker used this enamel case painter
enamel = enamel case painter or artist
pat. = patent or inventor
ca. = circa or about
since = founded to present

Achard, J. Francois (Geneva, ca. 1750)
Addison, J. (London, 1760-1780)
Adamson, Gustave (Paris, 1775-1790)
Alfred, W. Humphreys (London, ca. 1905)
Alibut (Paris, ca. 1750s)
Alliez, Buchelard & Teron Co. (French, ca. 1830)
Amabric, Abraham (Geneva, ca. 1750-1800)
Amabric, Freres (Geneva, ca. 1760-1795)
Amon (Paris, 1913)
Andre, Jean (enamel) (Geneva, 1660-1705)
Anthony, Willams (London, 1785-1840)
Antram, J. (London, ca. 1700-1730)
Appleby, Edward (London, ca. 1675)
Appleby, Joshua (London, ca. 1720-1745)
Ardin, Coppet (ca. 1710)
Arlaud, Benjamin (London, c. 1680)
Arlaud, Louis (Geneva, ca. 1750)
Anord & Dent (London) ca. 1839
Arnold & Frodsham, Charles (London, 1845)
Arnold, Henery (London, ca. 1770-1780)
Arnold, John (London, ca. 1760-1790)
Arnold, John Roger, son of (London, ca. 1800-1830)
Arnold, Nicolas (ca. 1850)
Arnold & Lewis, Lote Simmons (Manchester, ca. 1860)
Arnold & Son (London, ca. 1787-1799)
Assman, Julius (Glasshutte, 1850-1885)
Auber, Daniel (London, ca. 1750)
Aubert, D. F. (Geneva, ca. 1825)
Aubert, Ferdinand (1810-1835)
Aubert & Co. (Geneva, ca. 1850)
Aubry, Irenee (Geneva, 1885-1910)
Audebert (Paris, 1810-1820)
Audemars, Freres (Swiss, 1810 until Co. splits in 1885)
Audemars, Louis-Benjamin (Swiss, 1811-1867)
Aureole (Swiss, 1921)
Auricoste, Jules (Paris, ca. 1910)
Bachhofen, Felix (Swiss, 1675-1690)
Badollet, Jean-Jacques (Geneva, 1779-1891)
Baillon, Jean-Hilaire (Paris, ca. 1727)
Baird, Wm. (London, 1815-1825)
Balsiger & Fils (ca. 1825)
Barberet, J. (Paris, ca. 1600)
Barbezat, Bole (Swiss, 1870)
Baronneau, Jean-Louis (France, 1675-1700)
Barnett, John (England) 1690
Barraud & Lunds (England) 1872
Barraud & Lunds (1812-1840)
Barraud, Paul-Philip (London, 1752-1820)
Barrow, Edward (London, ca. 1650-1710)
Barrow, Nathaniel (London, 1653-1689)
Barry, M. (French, ca. 1620)
Bartholony, Abraham (Paris, 1750-1752)
Barton, J. (London, 1760-1780)
Barwise J.(London, 1800)
Bassereau, Jean-Hilaire (Paris, ca. 1800-1810)
Bautte, Jean-Francois (Geneva, 1800-1835)
Bautte & Moynier (Geneva, ca. 1825)
Beaumarchais, Caron (Paris, 1750-1795)
Beauvais, Simon (London, ca. 1690)
Beckman, Daniel (London, 1670-1685)
Beckner, Abraham (London, ca. 1640)
Beliard, Dominique (Paris, ca. 1750)
Bell, Benj. (London, 1650-1668)
Bennett, John (London, 1850-1895)
Benson, J. W. (London, 1825-1890)
Benson, J. W. (London, 1850-1900)
Bergstein, L. (London, ca. 1840)
Bernard, Nicholas (Paris, 1650-1690)
Bernoulli, Daniel (Paris, 1720-1780)

Berrollas, J. A. (Denmark, 1800-1830)
Berthoud, Augusta-Louis (Paris, ca. 1875)
Berthoud, Ferdinand (Paris, 1750-1805)
Beihler & Hartmann (Geneva, ca. 1875)
Blanc, Henri (Geneva, ends 1964)
Blanc, Jules (Geneva, 1929-1940)
Blanc & Fils (Geneva, 1770-1790)
Bock, Johann (German, 1700-1750)
Bockel (London, ca. 1650)
Bolslandon, Metz (ca. 1780)
Bolviller, Moise (Paris, 1840-1870)
Bommelt, Leonhart (Nuremburg, Ger., ca. 1690)
Bonney (London, ca. 1790)
Bonniksen, Bahne (England, 1890-1930) invented karrusel
Booth, Edward (name change to Barlow)
Bordier, Denis (France, ca. 1575)
Bordier, Freres (Geneva, 1787-1810)
Bordier, Jacques (enamel) (ca. 1670)
Bornand, A. (Geneva, 1895-1915)
Boubon (Paris, 1810-1820)
Bouquet, David (London, ca. 1630-1650)
Bovet (England) 1815 (used J.L.Richer Art)
Bovet, Edouard (Swiss, 1820-1918)
Bovier, G. (enamel painter) (Paris, c. 1750)
Brandt, Iacob (Swiss, ca. 1700)
Brandt, Robert & Co. (Geneva, ca. 1820)
Breitling, "Leon" (Swiss, since 1884)
Brookbank (London, 1776)
Brocke (London, ca. 1640)
Brodon, Nicolas (Paris, 1674-1682)
Bronikoff, a Wjatka (Russia, 1850 "watches of wood")
Bruguier, Charles A. (Geneva, 1800-1860)
Bull, Rainulph (one of the first British) (1590-1617)
Burgis, Eduardus (London, 1680-1710)
Burgis, G. (London, 1720-1740)
Burnet, Thomas (London, ca. 1800)
Busch, Abraham (Hamburg, Ger., ca. 1680)
Buz, Johannes (Augsburg, Bavaria, ca. 1625)
Cabrier, Charles (London, ca. 1690-1720)
Capt, Henry Daniel (Geneva, 1802-1880)
Caron, Augustus (Paris, ca. 1750-1760)
Caron, Francois-Modeste (Paris, 1770-1788)
Caron, Pierre (Paris, ca. 1700)
Caron, Pierre Augustin (pat. virgule escap.) (Paris,1750-1795)
Carpenter, William (London, 1750-1800)
Carte, John (England, 1680-1700)
Champod, P. Amedee (enamel) (Geneva, 1850-1910)
Chapeau, Peter (England) 1746
Chapponier, Jean (Geneva, 1780-1800)
Charlton, John (England) 1635
Charman (London, 1780-1800)
Charrot (Paris, 1775-1810)
Chartiere (enamel) (France, ca. 1635)
Chaunes (Paris, ca. 1580-1600)
Chauvel, J. (England) 1720-25
Chavanne & Pompejo (Vienna, 1785-1800)
Cheneviere, Louis (Geneva, 1710-1740)
Cheneviere, Urbain (Geneva, 1730-1760)
Cheriot or Cherioz, Daniel (ca. 1750-1790)
Cheuillard (Blois, France, ca. 1600)
Chevalier & Co. (Geneva, 1795-1810)
Cisin, Charles (Swiss, 1580-1610)
Clark, Geo. (London, 1750-1785)
Clay, Charles (England) 1750
Clerc (Swiss, ca. 1875)
Clouzier, Jacques (Paris, 1690-1750)
Cochin, D. (Paris, ca. 1800)
Cocque, Geo. (ca. 1610)
Cogniat (Paris, ca. 1675)

Coladon, Louis (Geneva, 1780-1850)
Cole, James Ferguson (London, 1820-1875)
Cole, Thomas (London, 1820-1864)
Collins, Clement (London, ca. 1705)
Collins, John (London, ca. 1720)
Collins, R. (London, ca. 1815)
Colondre & Schnee (ca. 1875)
Combret, Pierre (Lyons, France, ca. 1610-1625)
Cooper, T.F. (England) 1842-80 *later* "T.M."
Cotton, John (London, ca. 1695-1715)
Coulin, Jaques & Bry, Amy (Paris & Geneva, 1780-1790)
Court, Jean-Pierre (ca. 1790-1810)
Courvosier, Freres (Swiss, 1810-1852)
Courvoisier & Houriet (Geneva, ca. 1790)
Cox, James (London, 1760-1785)
Crofswell J.N. (London), ca. 1825
Csacher, C. (Prague, Aus., ca. 1725)
Cumming, Alexander (London, 1750-1800)
Cummins, Charles (London, 1820)
Cuper, Barthelemy (French, 1615-1635)
Curtis, John (London, ca. 1720)
Cusin, Charles (Geneva, ca. 1587)
Darling, William (British, ca. 1825)
Dariel, de St. Leu (England) 1815
De Baghyn, Adriaan (Amsterdam, ca. 1750)
Debaufre, Peter (French, 1690-1720) (Debaufre escap.)
Debaufre, Pierre (Paris, London, Geneva, 1675-1722)
De Bry, Theodore (German, 1585-1620)
De Charmes, Simon (London, France, 1690-1730)
De Choudens (Swiss & French, 1760-1790)
Decombaz, Gedeon (Geneva, 1780-1820)
Degeilh & Co. (ca. 1880-1900)
De Heca, Michel (Paris, ca. 1685)
De L Garde, Abraham (Paris, "Blois," ca. 1590)
Delynne, F. L. (Paris, ca. 1775)
"Dent", (Edward John)(London, 1815-1850)
Derham, William (English, ca. 1677-1730)
Deroch, F. (Swiss, 1730-1770)
Des Arts & Co. (Geneva, 1790-1810)
Desquivillons & DeChoudens (Paris, ca. 1785)
Destouches, Jean-Francois-Albert (Holland, ca. 1760)
Devis, John (London, 1770-1785)
Dimier & Co. (Geneva, 1820-1925)
Dinglinger (enamel) (Dresden, Ger., ca. 1675)
Ditisheim & Co. "Maurice" (Swiss, 1894)
Ditisheim, Paul (Swiss, 1892)
Dobson, A. (London, 1660-1680)
Droz, Daniel (Chaux-de-Fonds, Sw., ca. 1760)
Droz, Henri (Chaux-de-Fonds, Sw., ca. 1775)
Droz, Pierre Jacquet (Chaux-de-Fonds, Sw., 1750-1775)
Droz, Pierre (Swiss, 1740-1770)
Droz & Co. (Swiss, ca. 1825)
Dubie (enamel) (Paris, ca. 1635)
Dubois & Fils (Paris, ca. 1810)
Duchene & Co. "Louis" (Geneva, 1790-1820)
Ducommun, Charles (Geneva, ca. 1750)
Duduict, Jacques (Blois, France, ca. 1600)
Dufalga, Philippe (Geneva, 1730-1790)
Dufalga, P. F. (Geneva, ca. 1750)
Dufour, Foll & Co. (Geneva, 1800-1830)
Dufour, J. E. & Co. (ca. 1890)
Dufour & Ceret (Ferney, Fr., ca. 1770-1785)
Dufour & Zentler (ca. 1870)
Duhamel, Pierre (Paris, ca. 1680)
Dunlop, Andrew (England) 1710
Dupin, Paul (London, 1730-1765)
Dupont (Geneva, ca. 1810-1830)
Dupont, Jean (enamel) (Geneva, 1800-1860)
Duru (Paris, ca. 1650)
Dutertre, Baptiste (ca. 1730) (pat. duplex escapement)
Dutton, William (London, 1680-1794)
Dyson, John & Sons (England) 1816
Earnshaw, Thomas (London, 1780-1825)
East, Edward (London, 1630-1670)

Edmonds, James (London to U.S.A., 1720-1766)
Edward, George & Son (London, ca. 1875)
Ekegren, Henri-Robert (Geneva, 1860)
Ellicott, John (London, 1728-1810)
Emanuel, E.& E (England) 1861
Emery, Josiah (Geneva, 1750-1800)
Etherington, George (England) 1700
Esquivillon & De Choudens (Paris, 1710-1780)
Ester, Jean Henry (Geneva, 1610-1665)
Etherington, George (London, 1680-1730)
Etienne Guyot & Co. (Geneva, ca. 1880)
Facio De Duillier, Nicholas (British, 1665-1710)
Fallery, Jacques (Geneva, ca. 1760)
Farmer, G. W. (wooden watches) (Germany, 1650-1675)
Fatio, Alfred (Geneva, 1920-1940)
Fatton, Frederick Louis (London, ca. 1822)
Favre Marius & Fils (Geneva, 1893)
Fenie, M. (ca. 1635)
Ferrero, J. (ca. 1854-1900)
Fiarce, Clement (Paris, ca. 1700)
Fitter, Joseph (London, ca. 1660)
Fontac (London, ca. 1775)
Forfaict, Nicolas (Paris, 1573-1619)
Fowles, Allen (Kilmarnock, Scot., ca. 1770)
French (London, 1810-1840)
Fureur (Swiss, 1910)
Gallopin "Henri Capt" (Geneva, 1875)
Gamod, G. (Paris, ca. 1640)
Garnier, Paul (Paris, 1825) (pat. Garnier escapement)
Garon, Peter (England) 1700
Garrault, Jacobus (Geneva, ca. 1650)
Garty & Constable (London, ca. 1750)
Gaudron, Antoine (Paris, 1675-1707)
Gaudron, Pierre (Paris, 1695-1740)
Geissheim, Smod (Augsburg, Ger., ca. 1625)
Gent, James & Son (London, 1875-1910)
Gerbeau, V. (Paris, 1900-1930)
Gerrard (British, 1790-1820)
Gibs, William (Rotterdam, ca. 1720)
Gibbons Joshua (London), ca. 1825
Gibson & Co., Ltd. (Ireland, ca. 1875-1920)
Gidon (Paris, ca. 1700)
Gillespey, Charles (Ireland, 1774-1171)
Girard, Perregaux (Swiss, 1856)
Girard, Theodore (Paris, 1623-1670)
Girardier, Charles (Geneva, 1780-1815)
Girod, B. (Paris, ca. 1810)
Girod, Gaspard (Paris, ca. 1670-1690)
Godod, E. (Paris, ca. 1790)
Godon, F. L. (Paris, ca. 1787)
Golay, A. Leresche & Fils (Geneva, 1844-1857)
Golay, H. (Swiss, 1969-1911)
Golay, Stahl & Fils (1878-1914)
Gollons (Paris, ca. 1663)
Gould, Christopher (England) 1650
Gounouilhou, P. S. (Geneva, 1815-1840)
Gout, Ralph (London, 1790-1830)
Graham, George (London, 1715-1750)
Grandjean, Henri (Swiss, 1825-1880)
Grandjean, L. C. (Swiss, 1890-1920)
Grant, *John & Son* (English, 1780-1867)
Grantham, William (London, ca. 1850-60)
Grasset, Isaac (Geneva, ca. 1896)
Gray & Constable (London, ca. 1750-90)
Grazioza (Swiss, ca. 1901)
Grebauval, Hierosme (ca. 1575)
Gregory, Jermie (London, ca. 1652-1680)
Gregson, Jean P. (Paris, 1770-1790)
Grendon, Henry (England) 1645
Griblin, Nicolas (French, 1695-1716)
Griessenback, Johann G. (Bavaria, ca. 1660)
Grignion "family" (London, 1690-1825)
Grignion, Daniel & Thomas (London, 1780-1790)
Grinkin, Robert (England) 1625

Grosclaude, Ch. & Co. (Swiss, ca. 1865)
Grosjean, Henry (French, ca. 1865)
Gruber, Hans (Nurnberg, Ger., ca. 1520-1560)
Gruber, Michel (Nurnberg, Ger., ca. 1605)
Gruet (Geneva, Sw., ca. 1664)
Gubelin, E. (Lucern, Switzerland, ca. 1832)
Guillaume, Ch. (pat. Invar, Elinvar)
Haas Nevevx & Co. (founder B. J. Haas) (Swiss, 1828-1925)
Hagen, Johan (German, ca. 1750)
Haley, Charles (London, 1781-1825)
Hallewey (London, 1695-1720)
Hamilton & Co. (London, 1865-1920)
Hamilton G.(London), Ca.1800s
Harper, Henry (London, ca. 1665-1700)
Harrison, John (England, 1710-1775) (pat. comp. balance)
Hasluck Brothers (London, ca. 1695)
Hautefeuille, Jean (Paris, 1670-1722)
Hautefeuille, John (Paris, 1660-1700)
Hawley, John (London, ca. 1850)
Hebert, Juliette (enamel) (Geneva, ca. 1890)
Helbros (Geneva, since 1918)
Hele or Henlein, Peter (Nurnberg, 1510-1540)
Heliger, J. (Zug, Sw., ca. 1575)
Henner, Johann (Wurtzburg, Ger., ca. 1730)
Henry, F. S. (Swiss, ca. 1850)
Hentschel, J. J. (French, ca. 1750)
Hess, L. (Zurich, Sw., ca. 1780)
Hessichti, Dionistus (ca. 1630)
Higgs & Evans (London, 1775-1825)
Hill, Ben. (London, 1640-1670)
Hindley, Henry (England) 1758
Hoddell, James, & Co. (England) 1869
Hoguet, Francois (Paris, ca. 1750)
Hooke, Robert (England, 1650-1700)
Hoseman, Stephen (London, ca. 1710-1740)
Houghton, James (England, ca. 1800-1820)
Houghton, Thomas (Chorley, England, ca. 1820-1840)
Houriet, Jacques Frederic (Paris 1810-1825)
Howells & Pennington (England) 1795
Huaud, Freres (enamel) (Geneva, ca. 1685)
Huber, Peter (German, ca. 1875)
Hubert, David (London, 1714-1747)
Hubert, James (England) 1760
Hubert, Oliver (London, ca. 1740)
Hubert, Etienne (French, 1650-1690)
Hues, Peter (Augsburg, Ger., ca. 1600)
Huguenin, David L. (Swiss, 1780-1835)
Humbert-Droz, David (Swiss, ca. 1790)
Hunt & Roskell (England) 1846
Huygens, Christian (Paris, 1657-1680)
Iaquier or Jacquier, Francois (Geneva, 1690-1720)
Ilbery, *William* (London, 1800-35) (used J.L. Richer art)
Ingold, Pierre-Frederic (Swiss, Paris, London, 1810-1870)
Invicta ("R. Picard") (Swiss, 1896)
Jaccard, E. H. & Co. (Swiss, ca. 1850)
Jacot, Charles-Edouard (Swiss, 1830-1860) (pat. Chinese duplex)
Jaeger, Edmond (Paris, 1875-1920)
Jaeger Le Coultre & Co. (Swiss, since 1833)
Jamison, Geo. (London, 1786-1810)
Janvier, Antide (Paris, 1771-1834)
Japy, Frederic & Sons "family" (French, Swiss, ca. 1776)
Jaquet, Pierre (Swiss, 1750-1790)
Jean Richard, Daniel (Swiss, 1685-1740)
Jean Richard, Edouard (Swiss, 1900-1930)
Jeannot, Paul (ca. 1890)
Jefferys & Gildert (London, 1790)
Jessop, Josias (London, 1780-1794)
Jeubi, Josias (Paris, ca. 1575)
Joly, Jacques (Paris, ca. 1625)
Jovat (London, ca. 1690)
Johnson Josh. Liverpool (English), ca.1810-1850
Jones, Henry (London, ca. 1665-1690)
Jump, Joseph (English, ca. 1827-1850)

Junod, Freres (Geneva, ca. 1850)
Jurgensen, Urban & Jules (Copenhagen, Swiss,1745-1912)
Just & Son (London, 1790-1825)
Juvet, Edouard (Swiss, 1844-1880)
Juvet, Leo (Swiss, 1860-1890)
Keates, William (London, ca. 1780)
Keely, W. (London, ca. 1790)
Kendall, Larcum (London, ca. 1786)
Kendall, James (London, 1740-1780)
Kessels, H. J. (Holland, 1800-1845)
Kirkton, R. (London, ca. 1790)
Klein, Johann Heinr (Copenhagen, Den., ca. 1710)
Klentschi, C. F. (Swiss, 1790-1840)
Koehn, Edward (Geneva, 1860-1908)
Kreizer, Conard (German, 1595-1658)
Kuhn, Jan Hendrik (Amsterdam, 1775-1800)
Kullberg, Victor (Copenhagen to London, 1850-1890)
Lamy, Michel (Paris, 1767-1800)
Lang & Padoux (ca. 1860)
Larcay (Paris, ca. 1725)
Lardy, Francois (Geneva, ca. 1825)
Larpent, Isaac & Jurgensen (Copenhagen, 1748-1811)
Laurier, Francois (Paris, 1654-1675)
Le Baufre (Paris, ca. 1650)
Lebet (Geneva, ca. 1850)
Lebet & Fils (Swiss, 1830-1892)
Le Coultre, Ami (Geneva, ca. 1887)
Le Coultre, Eugene (Geneva, ca. 1850)
Leekey, C. (London, ca. 1750)
Leeky, Gabriel (London, ca. 1775-1820)
Lepaute, Jean-Andre (Paris, 1750-1774)
Le Pine', Jean-Antoine (Paris, 1744-1814)
Le Prevost (Swiss), ca.1810
Le Puisne, Huand (enamel) (Blois, Fr., ca. 1635)
Leroux, John (England, 1758-1805)
Le Roy & Co. (Paris, ca. 1853)
Le Roy, Charles (Paris, 1733-1770)
Le Roy, Julien (Paris, 1705-1750)
Le Roy, Pierre (Frer.ch, 1710-80) (improved duplex escap.)
Levy, Hermanos (Hong Kong, "Swiss," 1880-1890)
L'Hardy, Francois (Geneva, 1790-1825)
Lichtenauer (Wurzberg, Ger., ca. 1725)
Lindesay, G. (London, ca. 1740-1770)
Lindgren, Erik (England, 1735-1775) (pat. rack lever)
Litherland, Peter (English, 1780-1876)
Loehr, (Von) (Swiss, ca. 1880)
Long & Drew (enamel) (London, ca. 1790-1810)
Losada, Jose R. (London, 1835-1890)
Lowndes, Jonathan (London, ca. 1680-1700)
MacCabe, James (London, 1778-1830)
Maillardet & Co. (Swiss, ca. 1800)
Mairet, Sylvain (Swiss, 1825-1885) (London, 1830-1840)
Malignon, A. (Geneva, ca. 1835)
Marchand, Abraham (Geneva, 1690-1725)
Margetts, George (London, 1780-1800)
Markwick Markham, "Perigal" "Recordon" (London, 1780-1825)
Marshall, John (London, ca. 1690)
Martin (Paris, ca. 1780)
Martin, Thomas (London, ca. 1870)
Martineau, Joseph (London, 1765-1790)
Martinot, "family" (Paris, 1570-1770)
Martinot, James (London, ca. 1780)
Mascarone, Gio Batt (London, ca. 1635)
Massey, Edward (England, 1800-1850)
Massey, Henry (London, 1692-1745)
E. Mathey-Tissot & Co. (Swiss, 1886-1896)
Matile, Henry (Swiss, ca. 1825)
Maurer, Johann (Fiessna, Ger., ca. 1640-1650)
May, George (English, 1750-1770)
Mayr, Johann Peter (Augsburg, Ger., ca. 1770)
McCabe, James (London, 1780-1710)
McDowall, Charles (London, ca. 1820-1860)
Meak, John (London, ca. 1825)

Mecke, Daniel (ca. 1760)
Melly, Freres (Geneva, Paris, 1791-1844)
Mercier, A. D. (Swiss, 1790-1820)
Mercier, Francois David (Paris, ca. 1700)
Meuron & Co. (Swiss, ca. 1784)
Meylan, C. H. "Meylan W. Co." (Swiss, ca. 1880)
Michel, Jean-Robert (Paris, ca. 1750)
Miller, Joseph (London, ca. 1728)
Milleret & Tissot (ca. 1835)
Miroir (London, ca. 1700-1725)
Mistral (Swiss, ca. 1902)
Mobilis (Swiss, ca. 1910)
Modernista (Swiss, ca. 1903)
Moillet, Jean-Jacques (Paris, 1776-1789)
Molina, Antonio (Madrid, Spain, ca. 1800)
Molinie (Swiss, ca. 1840)
Molyneux, Robert (London, ca. 1825-1850)
Montandon, Chs. Ad. (Swiss, 1800-1830)
Morand, Pierre (Paris, ca. 1790)
Moricand & Co. (Swiss, ca. 1780)
Moricand & Desgranges (Geneva, 1828-1835)
Moricand, Christ (Geneva, 1745-1790)
Morin, Pierre (English, French & Dutch style, ca. 1700)
Morliere (enamel) (Blois, Fr., ca. 1636-1650)
Moser, George Michael (London, ca. 1716-1730)
Motel, Jean Francois (French, 1800-1850)
Moulineux, Robert (London, 1800-1840)
Moulinier, Aine & Co. (Swiss, 1828-1851)
Moulinier, Freres & Co. (Swiss, ca. 1822)
Mudge, Thomas (London, 1740-1790)
Mulsund (enamel) (Paris, ca. 1700)
Munoz, Blas (Madrid, Spain, ca. 1806-1823)
Mussard, Jean (Geneva, 1699-1727)
Musy Padre & Figlo (Paris, 1710-1760)
Myrmecide (Paris, ca. 1525)
Nardin, Ulysse (Swiss, ca. 1846)
Nelson, W. (London, 1777-1818)
Nocturne (ca. 1920)
Noir, Jean-Baptiste (Paris, 1680-1710)
Norris, J. (Dutch, 1680-1700)
Norton (London), ca.1805
Nouwen, Michael (1st English, 1580-1600)
Noyean (ca. 1850)
Oldnburg, Johan (German, ca. 1648)
Oudin, Charles (Paris, 1807-1900)
Owen, John (English, ca. 1790)
Palmer, Samuel (London, ca. 1790-1810)
Panier, Iosue "Josue" (Paris, ca. 1790)
Papillon (ca. 1690)
Papillon, Francesco (Florence, ca. 1705)
Parr, Thomas (London, ca. 1735-1775)
Payne, H. & John (London, ca. 1735-1775)
Pellaton, Albert (Swiss, ca. 1873)
Pellaton, James (Swiss, 1903) (Tourbillon)
Pendleton, Richard (London, 1780-1805)
Pennington, Robert (English, 1780-1816)
Perigal, Francis (English, 1770-1790)
Pernetti, F. (Swiss, ca. 1850)
Perrelet, Abram (Swiss, 1780) (self wind)
Perret, Edouard (Swiss, 1850)
Perrin, Freres (Swiss, 1810)
Phillips, Edouard (Paris, ca. 1860)
Phleisot (Dijon, Fr., ca. 1540)
Piaget, George (Swiss, ca. 1881)
Picard, James (Geneva, ca. 1850)
Piguet & Capt (Geneva, 1802-1811)
Piguet & Meylan (Geneva, 1811-1828)
Piguet, Victorin-Emile (Geneva, 1870-1935)
Plairas, Solomon (Blois, Fr., ca. 1640)
Plumbe, David (ca. 1730)
Poitevin, B. (Paris, 1850-1935)
Poncet, J. F. (Dresden, 1750)
Poncet, Jean-Francois (Swiss, 1740-1800)
Potter, Harry (London, 1760-1800)

Pouzait, Jean-Moise (Geneva, 1780-1800)
Poy, Gottfrey (London, ca. 1725-1730)
Prest, Thomas (English, 1820-1855)
Prevost, Freres (ca. 1820)
Prior, Edward (London, 1825-1865)
Prior, George (London, 1800-1830) (used J.L. Richer art)
Pyke, John (English, 1750-1780)
Quare, Daniel (London, 1700-1724)
Quarella, Antonio (ca. 1790)
Racine, Cesar (Swiss, ca. 1902)
Racine, C. Frederic (la Chaux-de-Fonds, Swiss, ca.1810-32)
Raillard, Claude (Paris, 1662-1675)
Raiss (1890-1910) (enamel)
Rait, D. C. (German, ca. 1866)
Ramsay, David (Scotland, France, London, 1590-1654)
Ramuz, Humbert U. & Co. (Swiss, ca. 1882)
Ratel, Henri (Paris, 1850-1900)
Recordon, Louis (London, 1778-1824)
Redier, Antoine (Paris, 1835-1883)
Renierhes (London, ca. 1850)
Rey, Jn. Ante, & Fils (Paris, 1790-1810)
Reynaud, P. & Co. (1860)
Rich, John (Geneva, London, 1795-1825)
Richard, Daniel Jean (1685-1740)
Richer, J. L. (outstanding enamel artist) (Geneva, 1786-1840)
Rigaud, Pierre (Geneva, 1750-1800)
Rigot, Francois (Geneva, ca. 1825)
Robert & Courvoisier & Co. (Paris, 1781-1832)
Robin, Robert (Paris, 1765-1805)
Robinet, Charles (Paris, ca. 1640)
Robinson, Olivier & Fredmahn (Naples, 1727-1790)
Robinson William (Liverpool), ca.1850
Rogers, Isaac (London, 1770-1810)
Romilly, Sieur (Geneva, ca. 1750-1775)
Rooker, Richard (London, 1790-1810)
Rose, Joseph (London, 1752-1795)
Rosier, John (Geneva, ca. 1750)
Roskell, Robert (London, 1798-1830) (rack-lever)
Roskopf, G. (German to Swiss, 1835-1885)
Rosselet, Louis (Geneva, 1855-1900) (enamel)
Rousseau, Jean (Paris, 1580-1642)
Roux, Bordier & Co. (Geneva, ca. 1795)
Ruegger, Jacques (ca. 1800-1840)
Ruel, Samuel (Rotterdam, ca. 1750)
Rugendas, Nicholas (Augsburg, Ger., ca. 1700-1750)
Rundell & Bridge (London, ca. 1772-1825)
Russel, Thomas & Son (England) 1898
Sailler, Johann (Vienna, Aus., ca. 1575)
Sanchez, Cayetano (Madrid, Spain, c. 1790-1800)
Sandoz, Henri F. (Tavannes W. Co.) (ca. 1840)
Savage, George (London, 1808-1855) (Inv. pin lever)
Savage, William (London (1800-1850)
Savile, John (London, ca. 1656-1679)
Schatck, Johann Engel (Prague, ca. 1650)
Schultz, Michael (ca. 1600-1650)
Schuster, Caspar (Nunburg, ca. 1570)
Sermand, J. (Geneva, ca. 1640)
Sellar - Reading (England) 1854
Shepherd, Thomas (England) 1632
Sherman De Neilly (Belfort, ca. 1910)
Sherwood, J. (London, ca. 1750-1775)
Sidey, B. (England) 1770
Solson (London, 1750)
Soret (Geneva, ca. 1810)
Soret, Frederic II (1735-1806)
Soret, Isaac & Co. (1690-1760)
Sleightholm & Co. (England) 1800
Smith, C. (England) 1829
Smith, George (England) 1630
Smith, S, & Son (England) 1910
Snelling, J.50
Speakman, Edward (England) 1690
Spencer & Perkins (London, 1770-1808)
Stadlin, Francois (Swiss, 1680-1735)

Staples, James (1755-1795)
Stuffer, M. T. (Swiss, 1830-1855)
Stauffer "Stauffer Son & Co." (London, 1880)
Strasser & Rohde (Glashutte, 1875)
Sudek, J. (ca. 1850)
Sully, Henry (French, London, 1700-1725)
Swift, Thomas (London, ca. 1825-1865)
Tavan, Antoine (Geneva, 1775-1830)
Tavernier, Jean (Paris, 1744-1795)
Tempor Watch Co. (1930) (Masonic watch)
Terond, Allier & Bachelard (ca. 1805-1830)
Terrot & Fazy (ca. 1767-1775)
Terrot, Philippe (Geneva, ca. 1732)
Terroux (ca. 1776)
Theed & Pikett (ca. 1750)
Thierry, J. (London, ca. 1760)
Thierry, Niel (ca. 1810)
Thiout, Antoine (Paris, 1724-1760)
Tobias & Co. M.I. (England) 1805-68 (Michael Isac)
Tobias large family very active in exporting watches
Thomlinson, George (England) 1675
Thorne, Robert (London, 1850)
Thoroton, James (London, 1860)
Thuret, Jacques (Paris, ca. 1695)
Thomason J.N. (Edinburgh), ca.1830
Timing & Repeating W. Co. (Geneva, 1900)
Tompion, Thomas (English, 1671-1715)
Tonkin, Tho. (London, ca. 1760)
Torin, Daniel (England) 1750
Toutaia, Henri (French, 1650) (enamel)
Toutin, Jean (enamel) (Blois, Fr., ca. 1630)
Treffler, Sebastain (ca. 1750)
Tregent, J. (English, 1765-1800)
Truitte, Louis & Mourier (Geneva, ca. 1780)
Tupman (England) 1828
Tyrer, Thomas (London, ca. 1782)
Uhren Fabrik Union (Glashutte, 1893-1970)
Ullman, J. & Co. (Swiss, 1893)
Ulrich, Johann (London, 1820-1870)
Upjohn, W. J. (London, 1815-1824)
Vacheron, Abraham Girod (German, 1760-1843)
Valere (Paris, 1860)
Vallier, Jean (Lyons, Fr., ca. 1630)

Valove, James (London, ca. 1740)
Vanbroff, James (Germany, ca. 1600)
Van Ceule, J. (ca. 1799-1725)
Vandersteen (ca. 1725)
Vaucher, C. H. (Geneva, ca. 1835)
Vaucher, Daniel (Paris, 1767-1790)
Vaucher, Freres (Swiss, 1850)
Vauquer, Robert (French, ca. 1650) (enamel)
Veigneur, F. I. (ca. 1780)
Verdiere A. (Paris), ca.1810
Vernod, Henriette (Paris, ca. 1790)
Vigne, James (London, ca. 1770)
Viner (England) 1834
Vrard, L., & Co. (Pekin, 1860-1872)
Vulliamy, *Justin* (London, ca. 1830-1854)
Vully, Jaques (ca. 1890-1900)
Vuolf (Swiss, ca. 1600)
Waldron, John (London, 1760)
Wales, Giles & Co. (Swiss, ca. 1870)
Walker, Allen (England) 1784
Waltrin (Paris, ca. 1820)
Webb, Benjamin (England) 1799
Weston, D. & Willis (enamel) (London, ca. 1800-1810)
Welldon, I. (England) 1731
Wichcote, Samuel (England) 1733
Widenham (England) 1824
Windmills,J. (England) 1710
Whitthorne, James (Dublin, since 1725)
Willats, John (London, ca. 1860)
Williamson, Timothy (London, 1770-1790)
Wilter, John (London, ca. 1760)
Winckles, John (London, 1770-1790)
Winnerl, Joseph Thaddeus (Paris, 1829-1886)
Wiss, Freres & Menu (Swiss, ca. 1787-1810)
Wiss, G. (Geneva, ca. 1750)
Wood, William (England) 1860
Wright, Charles (London, 1760-1790)
Wright, Thomas (English, ca. 1770-1790)
Yates, Thomas (England) 1855
Young, Richard (London, 1765-1785)
Zech, Jacob (Prague, Aus. 1525-1540)
Zolling, Ferdinand (Frankfurt, Ger. ca. 1750)

Tambour style case, probably Nuremburg, ca. 1575, hinged cover, pierced to reveal engraved Roman chapter I-XII and Arabic 13-24 Central chapter, 60mm.

HALLMARKS OF LONDON

Hallmarks were used on gold and silver cases imported from England. These marks, when interpreted, will give you the age of the case and location of the assay office.

The date-marks used 20 letters of the alphabet, A-U, never using the letters W, X, Y, or Z. The letters J & I or U & V, because of their similarity in shape, were never used together within the same 20-year period. A total of four marks can be found on English cases, which are:

The **MAKER'S MARK** was used to denote the manufacturer of the case.
The **STANDARD MARK** was used to denote a guarantee of the quality of the metal.
The **ASSAY OFFICE MARK** (also known as the town mark) was used to denote the location of the assay office.
The **DATE LETTER MARK** was a letter of the alphabet used to denote the year in which the article was stamped.
The stamp was used on gold and silver cases by the assay office.

The Maker's Mark The Standard Mark

The Assay Office Mark   The Date Letter Mark

1822-up   1478 to 1821

Chester

Birmingham

Edinburgh

Dublin

Glasgow

SWISS HALLMARKS

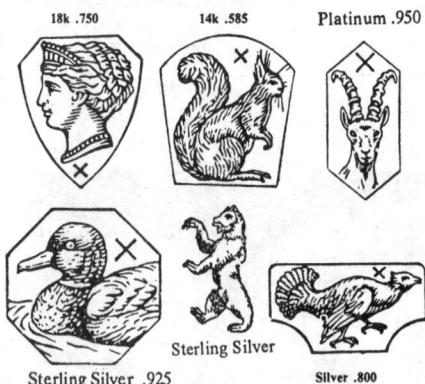

18k .750   14k .585   Platinum .950

Sterling Silver .925

Sterling Silver

Silver .800

Lucerne.

Neuchâtel,
Poinçons d'essai
de décembre 1852.

.800

German
silver mark

German
gold mark

TROY WEIGHT = 24 grains=1dwt., 1 Grain= 0.0648 grams, 20dwt = 1 OZ., 12oz = 1 LB.
NOTE: Gold & Silver Standards Vary from Country to Country. U.S.A. Coin Gold =.900 or 21 3/5K, Silver Coin=.900.
Gold Standards: 24K=1,000%or 1.0, 23K=.958 1/3, 22K=.916 2/3, 21K=.875, 20K=.833 1/3, 19K=.791 2/3, 18K=.750,
17K=.708 1/3, 16K=.666 2/3, 15K=.625, 14K=.583 1/3, 13K=.541 2/3, 12K=.500, 11=.458 1/3, 10K=.416 2/3, 9K= .375.
8K=.333 1/3, 7K=.291 2/3, 6K=.250, 5K=.208 1/3, 4K=.166 2/3, 3K=.125, 2K=.83 1/3, 1K=.41 2/3.

LONDON HALLMARKS

Letter	Year	Letter	Year	Letter	Year
O	1551	M	1589	k	1627
P	1552	N	1590	l	1628
Q	1553	O	1591	m	1629
R	1554	P	1592	n	1630
S	1555	Q	1593	o	1631
T	1556	R	1594	p	1632
V	1557	S	1595	q	1633
a	1558	T	1596	r	1634
b	1559	V	1597	s	1635
C	1560	X	1598	t	1636
D	1561	B	1599	u	1637
E	1562	C	1600	A	1638
F	1563	D	1601	B	1639
G	1564	E	1602	C	1640
h	1565	F	1603	D	1641
I	1566	G	1604	E	1642
k	1567	h	1605	ff	1643
l	1568	I	1606	O	1644
m	1569	K	1607	H	1645
n	1570	L	1608	a	1646
O	1571	M	1609	B	1647
P	1572	N	1610	C	1648
q	1573	O	1611	D	1649
r	1574	P	1612	R	1650
S	1575	Q	1613	b	1651
t	1576	R	1614	P	1652
u	1577	S	1615	O	1653
A	1578	T	1616	U	1654
B	1579	V	1617	O	1655
C	1580	a	1618	d	1656
D	1581	b	1619	B	1657
E	1582	C	1620	F	1658
F	1583	d	1621	B	1659
G	1584	e	1622	C	1660
H	1585	f	1623	D	1661
I	1586	g	1624	C	1662
K	1587	h	1625	F	1663
L	1588	i	1626	G	1664
				H	1665

Letter	Year	Letter	Year	Letter	Year
J	1666	φ	1709	r	1752
R	1667	s	1710	s	1753
l	1668	O	1711	t	1754
m	1669	S	1712	u	1755
n	1670	S	1713	a	1756
o	1671	U	1714	B	1757
p	1672	h	1715	c	1758
q	1673	A	1716	D	1759
R	1674	B	1717	e	1760
S	1675	C	1718	f	1761
T	1676	D	1719	e	1762
a	1677	E	1720	h	1763
a	1678	F	1721	i	1764
b	1679	G	1722	k	1765
c	1680	H	1723	l	1766
d	1681	I	1724	M	1767
e	1682	K	1725	n	1768
f	1683	L	1726	o	1769
g	1684	M	1727	p	1770
h	1685	N	1728	C	1771
i	1686	O	1729	R	1772
B	1687	P	1730	S	1773
j	1688	Q	1731	C	1774
m	1689	R	1732	U	1775
n	1690	S	1733	a	1776
O	1691	T	1734	b	1777
p	1692	V	1735	c	1778
q	1693	a	1736	d	1779
r	1694	b	1737	e	1780
g	1695	c	1738	f	1781
t	1696	d	1739	g	1782
B	1697	d	1739	h	1783
C	1698	e	1740	i	1784
S	1699	f	1741	k	1785
t	1700	g	1742	l	1786
ff	1701	h	1743	m	1787
O	1702	i	1744	n	1788
b	1703	k	1745	o	1789
d	1704	l	1746	p	1790
k	1705	m	1747	q	1791
t	1706	n	1748	r	1792
N	1707	o	1749	s	1793
R	1708	p	1750	t	1794
		q	1751	u	1795
				A	1796

Letter	Year	Letter	Year	Letter	Year
B	1797	f	1841	I	1884
C	1798	G	1842	K	1885
D	1799	H	1843	L	1886
E	1800	J	1844	M	1887
F	1801	k	1845	N	1888
G	1802	l	1846	O	1889
H	1803	M	1847	P	1890
I	1804	N	1848	Q	1891
K	1805	O	1849	R	1892
L	1806	P	1850	S	1893
M	1807	Q	1851	T	1894
N	1808	R	1852	U	1895
O	1809	S	1853	a	1896
P	1810	T	1854	b	1897
Q	1811	U	1855	c	1898
R	1812	a	1856	d	1899
S	1813	b	1857	e	1900
T	1814	c	1858	f	1901
U	1815	d	1859	g	1902
a	1816	e	1860	h	1903
b	1817	f	1861	i	1904
c	1818	g	1862	k	1905
d	1819	h	1863	l	1906
e	1820	t	1864	m	1907
f	1821	k	1865	n	1908
g	1822	l	1866	o	1909
h	1823	m	1867	p	1910
i	1824	n	1868	q	1911
k	1825	o	1869	r	1912
l	1826	p	1870	s	1913
m	1827	q	1871	t	1914
n	1828	r	1872	u	1915
o	1829	s	1873	a	1916
p	1830	t	1874	b	1917
q	1831	u	1875	c	1918
r	1832	A	1876	d	1919
s	1833	B	1877	e	1920
t	1834	C	1878	f	1921
u	1835	D	1879	g	1922
a	1836	E	1880	h	1923
B	1837	F	1881	i	1924
C	1838	G	1882	k	1925
D	1839	U	1883	l	1926
E	1840				

DATE LETTER MARKS FOR
BIRMINGHAM & CHESTER

BIRMINGHAM ASSAY OFFICE DATE LETTERS

A 1773	a 1798	A 1824	A 1849	a 1875
B 1774	b 1799	B 1825	B 1850	b 1876
C 1775	C 1800	C 1826	C 1851	c 1877
D 1776	d 1801	D 1827	D 1852	d 1878
E 1777	e 1802	E 1828	E 1853	e 1879
F 1778	f 1803	F 1829	F 1854	f 1880
G 1779	g 1804	G 1830	G 1855	g 1881
H 1780	h 1805	H 1831	H 1856	h 1882
I 1781	i 1806	I 1832	I 1857	i 1883
K 1782	j 1807	K 1833	J 1858	k 1884
L 1783	k 1808	L 1834	K 1859	l 1885
M 1784	l 1809	M 1835	L 1860	m 1886
N 1785	m 1810	N 1836	M 1861	n 1887
O 1786	n 1811	O 1837	N 1862	o 1888
P 1787	o 1812	P 1838	O 1863	p 1889
Q 1788	p 1813	Q 1839	P 1864	q 1890
R 1789	q 1814	R 1840	Q 1865	r 1891
S 1790	r 1815	S 1841	R 1866	s 1892
T 1791	s 1816	T 1842	S 1867	t 1893
U 1792	t 1817	U 1843	T 1868	u 1894
V 1793	u 1818	W 1844	U 1869	v 1895
W 1794	v 1819	W 1845	V 1870	w 1896
X 1795	w 1820	X 1846	W 1871	x 1897
Y 1796	x 1821	Y 1847	X 1872	y 1898
Z 1797	y 1822	Z 1848	Y 1873	z 1899
	Z 1823		Z 1874	

CHESTER ASSAY OFFICE DATE LETTERS

A 1701	A 1726	a 1751	a 1776	A 1797	A 1818	N 1839	a 1864
B 1702	B 1727	b 1752	b 1777	B 1798	B 1819	B 1840	b 1865
C 1703	C 1728	c 1753	c 1778	C 1799	C 1820	C 1841	c 1866
D 1704	D 1729	d 1754	d 1779	D 1800	D 1821	D 1842	d 1867
E 1705	E 1730	e 1755	e 1780	E 1801	E 1822	E 1843	e 1868
F 1706	F 1731	f 1756	f 1781	F 1802	F 1823	F 1844	f 1869
G 1707	G 1732	G 1757	G 1782	G 1803	G 1824	G 1845	g 1870
H 1708	H 1733	h 1758	h 1783	H 1804	G 1825	H 1846	h 1871
I 1709	I 1734	i 1759	i 1784	I 1805	H 1826	J 1847	i 1872
K 1710	K 1735	k 1760	K 1785	K 1806	I 1827	K 1848	K 1873
L 1711	L 1736	l 1761	l 1786	L 1807	K 1828	L 1849	l 1874
M 1712	M 1737	m 1762	m 1787	M 1808	L 1829	M 1850	m 1875
N 1713	N 1738	n 1763	n 1788	N 1809	M 1830	a 1851	n 1876
O 1714	O 1739	o 1764	o 1789	O 1810	N 1831	o 1852	o 1877
P 1715	P 1740	p 1765	P 1790	P 1811	O 1832	P 1853	p 1878
Q 1716	Q 1741	Q 1766	q 1791	Q 1812	P 1833	Q 1854	q 1879
R 1717	R 1742	R 1767	R 1792	R 1813	Q 1834	R 1855	T 1880
S 1718	S 1743	S 1768	S 1793	S 1814	R 1835	S 1856	s 1881
T 1719	T 1744	T 1769	t 1794	T 1815	S 1836	C 1857	t 1882
U 1720	U 1745	T 1770	U 1795	U 1816	T 1837	a 1858	u 1883
V 1721	V 1746	U 1771	Y 1796	V 1817	U 1838	a 1859	A 1884
W 1722	W 1747	V 1772				a 1860	B 1885
X 1723	X 1748	W 1773				I 1861	C 1886
Y 1724	Y 1749	X 1774				W 1862	D 1887
Z 1725	Z 1750	Y 1775				a 1863	E 1888
							F 1889

REPEATING WATCHES

Repeating watches or repeaters are those watches which will sound the time at the wish of the user. The repeating mechanism is operated by either a slide, plunger, or button in the case of the watch. There are basically five types of repeating mechanisms, some more common than others:

(1). **QUARTER REPEATERS**– The quarter repeater strikes the previous hour and quarter hour. In the older watches usually verge the striking is on a single bell attached to the inside of the case and the hour and quarter striking uses the same tone. There is first a series of hammer blows on the bell to indicate the hours, followed, after a short pause, by up to three twin strikes to denote the number of quarters elapsed. In later watches the striking is on wire gongs attached to the movement itself. The hours are struck on a single deep gong and the quarters on a higher-pitched gong followed by the deeper gong, producing a "ting-tang" sound.

(2). **HALF-QUARTER REPEATERS** -These strike the hours, the last quarter (ting-tang) and the previous half-quarter; i.e., seven and a half minutes. Half-quarter repeaters are mostly all verge escapement watches and are rarely seen by the average collector.

(3). **FIVE-MINUTE REPEATERS**– These fall into two types. One system is similar to the half-quarter repeater but follows the 1/4 "ting-tang" by a single higher-pitched strike for each 5 minute interval elapsed since the last quarter. The other system strikes the hours on a deep gong and follows this with a single higher note for each 5 minute period after the hour, omitting a 1/4 striking.

(4).**MINUTE REPEATERS**– The most complicated of the repeater is similar to the 1/4 repeater with the addition of the minutes. The minute repeater strikes the last recorded hour, quarter and minutes. At 10:52; a minute repeater will strike 10 deep chimes for the hour, 3 double chimes (deep & high) producing a "ting-tang for 3/4 hours & 7 high pitched chimes for 7 minutes (45+7=52).

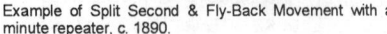

Example of Split Second & Fly-Back Movement with a minute repeater, c. 1890.

Example of English Clock Watch, 20 size, jeweled through hammers, minute repeater.

(5). **CLOCK WATCHES**– The clock watch is essentially a repeater with the features of a striking clock. Where as the above-mentioned repeaters are all operated by a plunger or slide which winds the repeating function and which runs down after the last strike, the clock watch is wound in the same way as the going train usually with a key and is operated by the touch of a button in the case. The repeat function can be operated many times before the watch needs to be rewound. The CLOCK part of the name comes from the watch also striking the hours and sometimes the quarters or half hour in passing. The clock watch is easily recognizable by the two winding holes in either the case or the dial.

In addition to the five types described above, the features of striking are sometimes found with not only two but three and even four gongs, this producing a peal of notes. These repeaters are known as **"CARILLONS."**

At the other end of the scale from the carillon is the ''dumb'' repeater. This strikes on a block of metal in the case or on the movement and is felt rather than heard. It is said that the idea was to produce a watch that would not embarrass its owner when he wished to know when to slip away from boring company. Although the dumb repeater is less desirable for the average collector, it certainly should not be avoided–Breguet himself made dumb repeaters.

Grande Sonnerie and **Petite Sonnerie** have been used since early 1700's. The clock watch striking system at first was called *Dutch Striking* because it was used in clock making in about 1665. The older system used striking on bells and struck the hours of the day. Then came the Dutch Striking which also struck the half-hour. This system later developed into a chiming function called **Grande Sonnerie** (grand strike or tone) which struck <u>both</u> the hour and quarter hours are struck ever 15 minutes (thus the hour is repeated ever 15 minutes). The **Petite Sonnerie** is a simpler variation of *Grande Sonnerie* in which the 1/4 hour are struck, but the hour is struck only at the o'clock (not repeated).

L.Audemars 2 train Grande or Petite Sonnerie minute repeating clock watch. Note: Marked on bezel sonne & silence at 12 o'clock also Petite Sonnerie & Grande Sonnerie at 6 o'clock, Ca. 1870's.

L. Audemars 2 train Grande or Petite Sonnerie 1/4 repeating clock watch. Note: The push button in the pendant that activate the repeating gongs, Ca. 1850.

A BIT OF HISTORY

Now that we have seen what repeaters are supposed to do, it might be in order to look briefly at their origins. Before the days of electric light, it was a major project to tell the time at night, since striking a tinderbox was said to have taken up to fifteen minutes to accomplish. Clocks, of course, had striking mechanisms, but they tended to keep the occupants of the house awake listening for the next strike. The repeating addition to the clock meant that the master of the house could silence the passing strike at night and, at his whim, simply pull a cord over his bed to activate the striking in another part of the house and thus waking everyone. To silence those members of the household who did not appreciate a clock booming out in the early hours of the morning, the horologists of the day turned their thoughts to the idea of a repeating watch.

The first mention of repeating watches is in the contest between Daniel Quare (1649-1724) and the Rev. Edward Barlow (1639-1719) to miniaturize the repeating action of a clock. Barlow, who for some reason had changed his name from Booth, was a theoretical horologist of outstanding ability. Barlow's design made for him by Thomas Tompion and Quare's watch were both submitted to King James II and the Privy Council for a decision as to whom should be granted a patent. The King chose Quare's design because the repeating mechanism was operated by a single push-button, whereas Barlow's required two. Quare was granted a patent in 1687. Barlow had had his share of fame earlier, however, with the invention of rack-striking for clocks in 1676.

Quare went into production with his new repeater watches, but changed the design to replace the push-button in the case with a pendant that could be pushed in. The first of these watches showed a fault that is still found on the cheaper repeaters of this century – that is, if the pendant was not pushed fully in, then the incorrect hours were struck. To overcome this problem, he invented the so-called "all-or-nothing" piece. This is a mechanism whereby if the pendant was not pushed fully home, then the watch would not strike at all.

The half-quarter appeared shortly after the all-or-nothing piece, and then by about 1710 the five-minute repeater was on the market. Some five years after this, a "deaf-piece" was often fitted to the watch. This was a slide or pin fitted to the case which, when activated, caused the hammers to be lifted away from the bell and had the same effect as a dumb repeater.

Sometime around 1730, Joseph Graham decided to dispense with the idea of a bell and arranged for the hammers to strike a dust-cover, thus making the watch slimmer and preventing dust from entering the pierced case.

About the middle of the century, the French master Le Roy carried the idea a stage further and dispensed with both bells and dust covers, and used a metal block which revolutionized the thickness of the repeating watch and introduced the dumb repeater. Breguet used wire gongs around 1789 and the pattern for the modern repeater was set. The minute repeater came into more common use after 1800, and earlier examples are definitely very rare, although it is known that Thomas Mudge made a complicated watch incorporating minute repeating for Ferdinand VI of Spain about 1750.

By the last quarter of the 1700s, Switzerland had gone for the repeater in a big way and the center of fine craftsmanship for complicated watches was in the Valley of Joux. Here the principle of division of labor was highly refined and whole families were hard at work producing parts for repeating and musical watches. Since one person concentrated only on one part of the watch, it is hardly surprising that parts of excellent quality were turned out. The basic movements were then sold to watchmakers/finishers all over the Continent and even to England, where the principle of one man, one watch, among the stubborn majority eventually led to the downfall of what had once been the greatest watchmaking nation in history.

The greatest popularity of the repeater came, however, in the last quarter of the 1800s, when Switzerland turned them out in the tens of thousands. Although there were many different names on the dials of the watches, most seem to have been produced by the company "Le Phare" and only finished by the name on the dial. The production of repeaters in quantity seems to have ground to a finish in about 1921 due to (a) the invention of luminous dials and universal electric or gas lighting, and (b) a lack of watchmakers willing to learn the highly demanding skills. The interest in horology over the past decade has, however, revived the idea of the repeater and several companies in Switzerland are now producing limited editions of expensive models.

BUYING A REPEATER

Since so many repeaters seem to have been repaired at some time in the past by incompetent watchmakers, it is often too expensive a purchase if the buyer does not know what he is doing.

Rule One should be: if it does not work perfectly, avoid it like the plague unless a competent repairer first gives you an estimate which suits your pocket. All too often in the past the repairer was under the impression that metal grows with age and he has filed the teeth of a rack in order to get the full striking to work again. When it dawned on him that the problem was a worn bearing, the tooth was stretched with a punch and refiled, making it weak. It was then goodbye to a fine piece of craftsmanship.

A better quality repeater is usually one which is "jeweled to the hammers." This simply means that the hammers have jeweled bearing which can be seen by searching the movement for the hammers, locating the pivots around which they swing, and looking for the jeweled bearing in which they sit.

All repeaters have some system for regulating the speed of the repeating train. On the older fusee types, there was usually a rather primitive arrangement of a pinion in an eccentric bushing which could be turned to increase or decrease the depth of engagement of the pinion with the next wheel. Another system, a little better, uses an anchor and a toothed wheel as in an alarm clock. This system is usually located under the dial but can be detected by the buzzing sound it makes when the train is operated. The far superior system is the centrifugal governor which can be seen whizzing around in the top plate of the watch when the repeating action is operated. On the whole, the watch with the centrifugal governor is more desirable, although it must be mentioned that the Swiss turned out some inferior watches with this system.

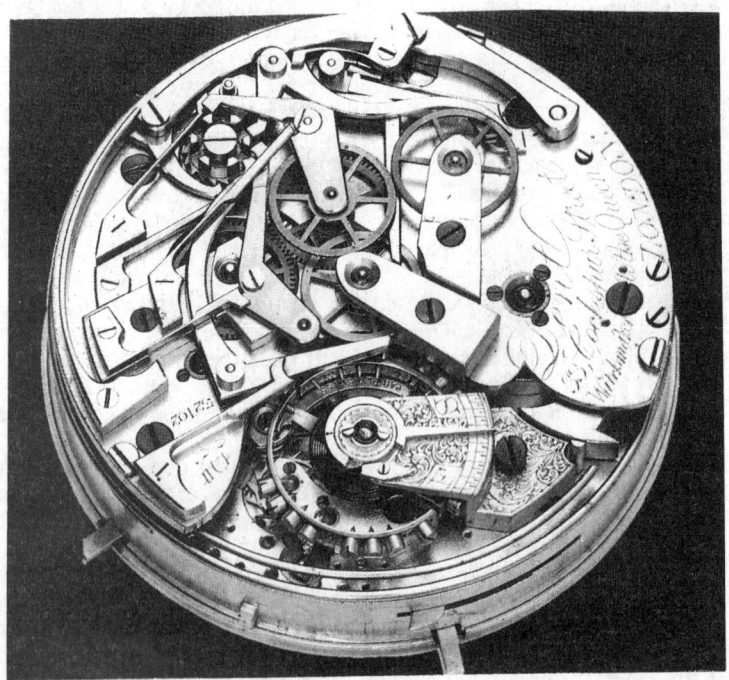

Minute repeating movement by Dent of London. Minute repeating on two gongs and slide activated. Also note the watch has a split second chronograph, Ca. early 1900s.

Test the watch by operating the repeating train over a full hour, seeing that the quarters and minutes function correctly, then test each individual hour. Finally, set the hands to just before 1 o'clock (about 12:45) and test the striking. Any defect due to dirt or worn bearings will show up by the final blow(s), being either sluggish or not striking at all. If there is incorrect striking, have an expert look at it before you buy.

Try a partial operation of the slide or push-piece. If the watch has an all-or-nothing piece (as a reasonable grade movement should have), then the watch will not strike. Partial striking indicates either a low grade watch or a non-functioning all-or-nothing piece.

Note: Additional features such as chronograph functions, calendar, moon phase, etc., and will obviously affect the price of the watch.

Important note: Remember Rule One, if any function does not work, **BUYER BEWARE!**

TOURBILLON

Breguet invented the tourbillon in 1795. A tourbillon is a device designed to reduce the position errors of a watch. This device has the escape wheel, lever and balance wheel all mounted in a **carriage** of light frameworks. The carriage turns 360 degrees at regular intervals (usually once per minute). The fourth wheel is fixed and is concentric with the carriage pinion and arbor. The escape wheel pinion meshes with the fourth wheel and will roll around the fixed fourth wheel. The escape wheel and lever are mounted on the carriage, and the third wheel drives the carriage pinion, turning the carriage once every minute. This rotation of the escapement will help reduce the position errors of a watch. One of the major objections is that the carriage and escapement weight mass must be stopped and started at each release of the escapement. The tourbillon design requires extreme skill to produce and is usually found on watches of high quality. Somewhat similar to the tourbillon is the karrusel, except it rotates about once per hour and the fourth wheel is not fixed. It also takes less skill to produce.

Charles Frodsham, TOURBILLON escapement, minute repeating, split second chronograph, about 600 to 700 tourbillons are known to exist. About 85 % of the English tourbillon movements were made by Albert Pellaton, Favre and Nicole Nielson & Co. as in this watch.

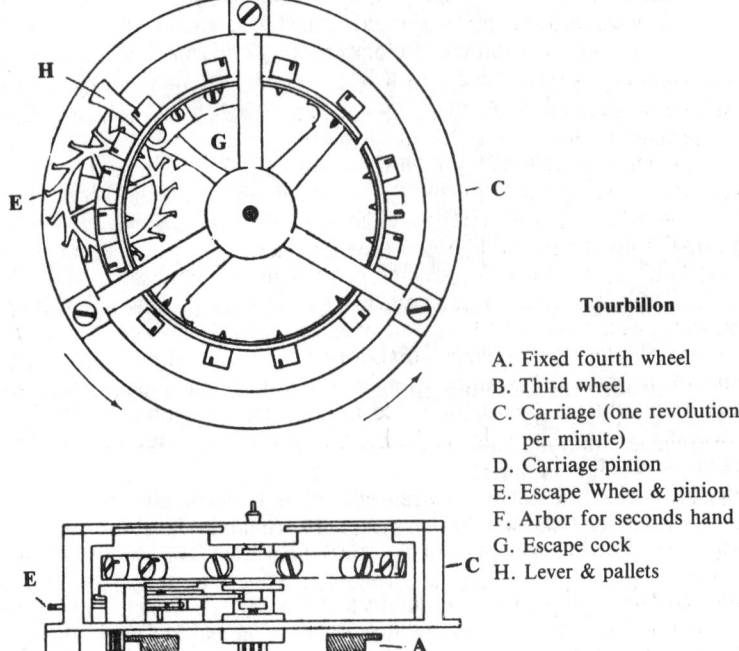

Tourbillon

A. Fixed fourth wheel
B. Third wheel
C. Carriage (one revolution per minute)
D. Carriage pinion
E. Escape Wheel & pinion
F. Arbor for seconds hand
G. Escape cock
H. Lever & pallets

MUSICAL WATCHES
(Three basic types)

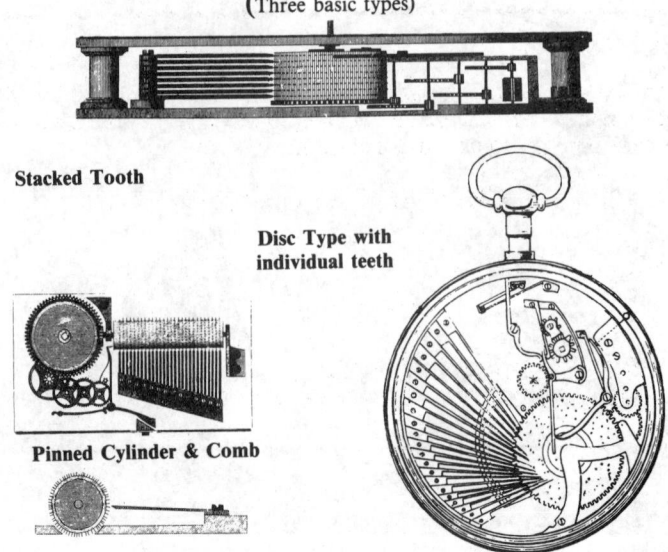

Stacked Tooth

Disc Type with individual teeth

Pinned Cylinder & Comb

EUROPEAN POCKET WATCH LISTINGS
Pricing at Collectable Fair Market Retail Level
(Complete Watches Only)

Unless otherwise noted, watches listed in this section are priced at the collectable **fair market** retail level and as **complete** watches having an original 14k gold-filled case with an original white enamel single sunk dial, and the entire original movement in good working order with no repairs needed. Watches listed as 14k and 18k are solid gold cases. Coin or silveroid type and stainless steel cases will be listed as such. Keywind and keyset pocket watches are listed as having original coin silver cases. Dollar type watches, or low cost production watches, are listed as having a base metal type case and a composition dial.

The prices shown were averaged from dealers' lists just prior to publication and are an indication of the retail level or what collectors will pay. Prices are provided in three categories: average condition, extra fine, and mint condition, and are shown in whole dollar amounts only. The values listed are a guide for the *collectable* retail level and are provided for your information only. Dealers will not necessarily pay FULL RETAIL PRICE. Prices listed are for watches with *original cases* and *dials*.

🕐 Descriptions and serial number ranges listed for early watches cannot be considered 100 percent accurate due to the manner in which records were kept by these companies. Watches were not necessarily sold in the exact order of manufactured date.

Important Notice. All of the information, including valuations, in this book has been compiled from the most reliable sources, and every effort has been made to eliminate errors and questionable data. Nevertheless, the possibility of error, in a work of such immense scope, always exists. The publisher or authors will not be held responsible for losses which may occur in the purchase, sale, statements of its advertisers, or other transaction of items, because of information contained herein. Readers who feel they have discovered errors are invited to write and inform us, so they may be corrected in subsequent editions.

INFORMATION NEEDED

This price guide is interested in any facts and information you might have that should possibly be considered for future editions. Documented facts are needed. Please send photo or sources of information to:

COOKSEY SHUGART
P.O. BOX 3147
CLEVELAND, TENNESSEE
37320-3147

(WHEN CORRESPONDING, PLEASE INCLUDE A ✉ *SELF-ADDRESSED, STAMPED ENVELOPE.)*

AGASSIZ
Swiss

Auguste Agassiz of Saint Imier & Geneva started manufacturing quality watches in 1832. They later became interested in making a flat style watch which proved to be very popular. Some of these movements can be fitted inside a $20 gold piece.

The company was inherited by Ernest Francillion who built a factory called **Longines.** The Longines factory continued the Agassiz line until the Great Depression.

Agassiz, 43mm, 17 jewels, World Time, 42 Cities, ca. 1940.

Agassiz, 40mm, 21 jewels, 8 day with wind indicator.

TYPE – DESCRIPTION	Avg	Ex-Fn	Mint
Early, KW KS, Swiss bar Mvt., time only, Ca. 1870, Silver case ...	$80	$100	$135
Time only, gold, 40–44mm, 10-12 size, OF	225	275	325
HC	375	400	450
Time only, gold, 45- 50mm, OF	275	350	450
Time only, gold & **enamel,** 45- 50mm, OF	1,000	1,200	1,500
HC	425	500	600
Cole's Resilient Escapement, 20J, gold, 45mm, Of	900	1,000	1,200

Agassiz, Time only, gold & **enamel,** 45- 50mm, OF   Agassiz, $20 gold 22 / 18K coin watch, Ca. 1950s.

⏱ Watches listed in this book are priced at the collectable fair market **value** at the retail level, as complete watches having an original case, an original white enamel dial, and with the entire original movement in good working order with no repairs needed, unless otherwise noted.

TYPE – DESCRIPTION

	Avg	Ex-Fn	Mint
8 day, 21J, wind indicator, **18K gold**, 44mm, OF	$900	$1,200	$1,600
14K gold, OF	700	800	1,200
S. S. case, OF	350	450	650
$20 gold 22 to 18K coin watch, 34mm, Ca. 1950s.	1,900	2,000	2,300
World Time, 42 Cities, gold, 43mm, OF	4,800	5,800	7,000
Chronograph, gold, 45-50mm, OF	475	550	650
HC	675	750	850
Split second chronograph, gold, OF	800	900	1,000
HC	900	1,000	1,200
1/4 hr. repeater, gold, 46-52mm, OF	800	900	1,000
HC	1,200	1,400	1,600
Minute repeater, gold, 46-52mm, OF	1,500	1,800	2,500
OF w/chrono.	1,800	2,000	2,800
Minute repeater, gold, 46-52mm, HC	2,000	2,200	3,000
HC w/chrono.	2,500	2,800	3,500

ASSMANN
Glasshute

Julius Assmann began producing watches with the help of Adolf Lange in 1852. His watches are stylistically similar to those produced by Lange. Later on he adopted his own lever style. Assmann made highly decorative watches for the South American market that are highly regarded by some collectors.

Assmann, 50mm, 19 jewels, diamond cap jewels, gold jewel settings, gold lever escapement, serial number 3,086, BRIDGE MODEL, ca. 1875.

Assmann, 50mm, 19 jewels, diamond cap jewels, gold jewel settings, gold lever escapement, serial number 3,739, ca. 1877.

TYPE – DESCRIPTION

	Avg	Ex-Fn	Mint
Time only, gold, 45- 50mm, OF	$1,200	$1,400	$1,600
HC	1,800	2,000	2,200
Chronograph, gold, 45-50mm, OF	2,200	2,500	2,800
HC	3,500	4,000	4,500
Split second chronograph, gold, 45-52mm, OF	3,000	3,500	4,000
HC	3,500	4,000	4,500
1/4 hr. repeater, gold, 46-52mm, OF	2,500	2,800	3,200
HC	3,500	4,000	4,500
Minute repeater, gold, 46-52mm, OF	4,000	4,500	5,000
HC	6,000	6,500	7,500
Perp. moonph. cal. w/min. repeater, gold, HC	40,000	45,000	50,000

Some models and grades are not included. Their values can be determined by comparing with similar age, size, metal content, style, models and grades listed.

AUDEMARS, PIGUET & CIE

Swiss

Audemars, Piguet & Cie was founded in 1875 by Jules Audemars and Edward Piguet, both successors to fine horological families. This company produced many fine high grade and complicated watches, predominantly in nickel and, with a few exceptions, fully jeweled. Their complicated watches are sought after more than the plain timepieces. They also produced some very handsome wristwatches.

Audemars Piguet, 40mm, about 10 size, 19 jewels, cabochon on winding stem, Platinum, OF.

Audemars, Piguet, 43mm., 18 jewels, adj.6P, jumping hour, day-date-month windows, ca. 1925.

TYPE – DESCRIPTION	Avg	Ex-Fn	Mint
Early, KW KS, Swiss bar Mvt., time only, Ca.1870, **Gold case**	$850	$950	$1,200
Time only, gold, 40-44mm, OF	750	900	1,000
HC	1,000	1,200	1,400
Platinum, OF	1,000	1,200	1,400
Time only, gold, 45- 50mm, OF	1,500	1,800	2,000
HC	2,800	3,500	4,000
Jumping hour w/ day-date-month, gold, 43mm., ca. 1925.	6,000	8,000	10,000
Rising Arms (Bras en L'Air), 44mm, one arm points to the hours & the other to the minute, 18K, OF	8,000	10,000	12,000
Chronograph, gold, 45-50mm, OF	3,000	3,500	4,000
HC	3,500	4,000	4,500
OF w/register	3,000	3,500	4,000
HC w/register	5,000	6,000	7,000

Audemars Piguet, (Bras en L'Air) a push-piece on rim of watch, lifts the arms of the bronze, one points to the hour and the other points to the minutes, 44mm, 18K, OF.

Audemars Piguet, Perpetual moon phase calendar, Astronomic watch showing the moon phases, and perpetual calendar showing day, date, & month, Ca.1920s.

AUDEMARS PIGUET, 46mm, 36 jewels, minute repeater, split-second chronograph, serial # 3853, Ca.1888.

AUDEMARS PIGUET, 46mm, Min. repeater, moon-phase, Chronograph, 18K, HC, Ca.1928.

TYPE – DESCRIPTION	Avg	Ex-Fn	Mint
Split second chronograph, gold, 45-52mm, OF	$4,500	$5,000	$5,500
HC	6,000	6,500	7,000
OF w/register	5,000	5,500	6,000
HC w/register	7,000	7,500	8,000
5 minute repeater, gold, 46-52mm, OF	6,000	6,500	7,000
HC	7,000	7,500	8,000
Minute repeater, gold, 46-52mm, OF	8,000	8,500	9,000
HC	10,000	11,000	12,000
OF w/chrono.	10,000	11,000	12,000
HC w/chrono.	11,000	12,000	13,000
OF w/chrono. & register	11,000	12,000	13,000
HC w/chrono. & register	12,000	13,000	14,000
OF w/split chrono. & register	15,000	18,000	20,000
HC w/split chrono. & register	18,000	20,000	22,000
Perpetual moonphase calendar, gold, OF	20,000	25,000	30,000
HC	25,000	30,000	35,000
Perp. moonphase cal. w/min.repeater, chronograph, gold, OF	50,000	55,000	60,000
HC	75,000	85,000	100,000

PRODUCTION TOTALS

Date- Serial #	Date- Serial #	Date- Serial #	Date- Serial #	Date- Serial #
1882 - 2,000	1905 - 9,500	1925-33,000	1945 - 48,000	1965 - 90,000
1890 - 4,000	1910-13,000	1930-40,000	1950 - 55,000	1970-115,000
1895 - 5,350	1915-17,000	1935 - 42,000	1955 - 65,000	1975-160,000
1900 - 6,500	1920-25,000	1940 - 44,000	1960 - 75,000	1980-225,000

REPEATER IDENTIFICATION

Calibre SMV

Calibre SMS

BARRAUD & LUNDS
LONDON (CORNHILL)

The Barraud family (of which) there were several makers, one of them being Paul Philip Barraud. Paul was in the trade at 86 Cornhill from about 1796 to 1813. His sons John and James, traded at 41 Cornhill as Barraud & Sons from 1813 till 1838. After 1838 the firm became known as Barraud & Lunds.

TYPE – DESCRIPTION	Avg	Ex-Fn	Mint
Time only, gold, 45- 50mm, OF	$675	$750	$900
HC	1,000	1,250	1,400
Chronograph, gold, 45-50mm, OF	1,200	1,300	1,450
HC	1,500	1,700	1,850
Split second chronograph, gold, 45-52mm, OF	1,800	2,000	2,300
HC	2,500	2,800	3,250
1/4 hr. repeater, gold, 46-52mm, OF	1,850	2,000	2,300
HC	2,200	2,500	2,800
Minute repeater, gold, 46-52mm, OF	3,000	3,400	4,000
HC	3,800	4,000	4,400
OF w/chrono.	3,500	3,800	4,250
HC w/chrono.	4,250	4,500	4,800

BARWISE
LONDON

John Barwise a leading watchmaker born 1790 died 1843. Dealer at 29 St.Martin's Lane, and with Weston Barwise from 1820 to 1842. John Barwise was also the chairman of British Watch Co. 1842 to 1843. Then Barwise moved back to 29 St.Martin's Lane, 1845 to 1851, and 69 Piccadilly from 1856 to 1875.

TYPE – DESCRIPTION	Avg	Ex-Fn	Mint
Time only, gold, 45- 50mm, OF	$950	$1,250	$1,400
HC	1,200	1,500	1,800
Chronograph, gold, 45-50mm, OF	1,200	1,500	1,800
HC	1,500	1,800	2,000
Split second chronograph, gold, 45-52mm, OF	2,000	2,400	2,700
HC	3,000	3,250	3,500
1/4 hr. repeater, gold, 46-52mm, OF	1,800	2,000	2,300
HC	2,500	2,800	3,200
Minute repeater, gold, 46-52mm, OF	3,500	4,000	4,500
HC	4,250	4,600	5,000
OF w/chrono.	4,000	4,500	5,250
HC w/chrono.	4,500	5,250	5,750
Dent Chronometer, gold, 48-52mm, OF	6,000	6,600	7,500
HC	7,000	8,000	9,000

Some models and grades are not included. Their values can be determined by comparing with similar age, size, metal content, style, models and grades listed.

Watches listed in this book are priced at the collectable fair market value at the retail level, as complete watches having an original case, an original white enamel dial, and with the entire original movement in good working order with no repairs needed, unless otherwise noted.

COMPARISON OF WATCH SIZES

U. S. A.	EUROPEAN
10-12 SIZE	40—44 MM
16 SIZE	45—48 MM
18 SIZE	50—52 MM

J. W. BENSON
London

The Benson signature is found on many medium to high grade gilt movements produced for the English market circa 1870-1900. "Makers to the Admiralty" & "Makers to the Queen" are usually signed on the Benson movements.

TYPE – DESCRIPTION	Avg	Ex-Fn	Mint
KWKS, side lever, Silver hallmarked, 48-52mm, OF, C. 1875	$125	$150	$185
SW, 17J, Silver, 49mm, **Demi-hunter**, C. 1885	150	175	225
Fusee, lever escape., high grade, SW, 18K, 54mm, OF, C.1875	750	900	1,000
Fusee **w/indicator,** KWKS, side lever, Silver, 54mm, OF, C.1870	450	500	575
Fusee, **w/indicator, free spring**, lever escape.,18K, 50mm, OF	1,200	1,300	1,400
Time only, gold, 45-48mm, OF	500	550	600
HC	700	800	900
Split second chronograph, gold, 45-52mm, OF	4,500	5,000	5,500
HC	6,000	6,500	7,000
Minute repeater, gold, 46-52mm, OF	4,000	4,500	5,000
HC	4,500	5,000	5,500

J. W. Benson, 45mm, Split Second Chronograph, 20 jewels, 3/4 plate, free sprung, hunting case, Ca. 1890.

COMPARISON OF WATCH SIZES

U. S. A.	EUROPEAN
10-12 SIZE	40—44 MM
16 SIZE	45—48 MM
18 SIZE	50—54 MM

BOVET
FRENCH & SWISS

Edouard Bovet starts a company in the village of Fleuier Switzerland about 1818 and another firm in Besancon in 1832. The Bovet firm specialized in watches for the chinese market. The Bovet Companies was purchased by Leuba Freres (Cesar & Charles). The new Bovet firm discontinued making watches for the Chinese market. The company was purchased by the Ullmann & Co. in 1918.

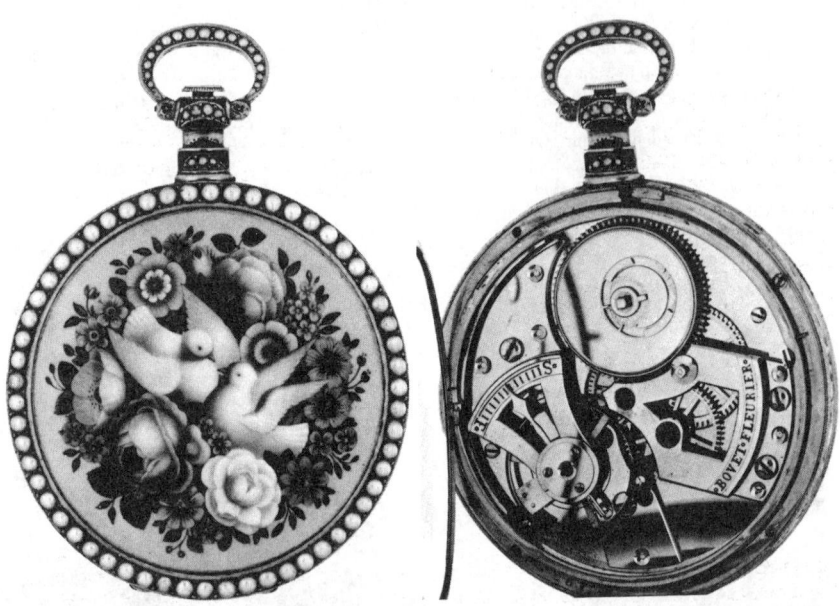

Above: *Superior quality* finely painted turquoise enamel watch set in pearls, 18K, 58mm, time only, Duplex Escapement, signed BOVET, Ca. 1845.

TYPE – DESCRIPTION	Avg	Ex-Fn	Mint
Time only, LEVER escapement, KW, Silver, 58mm, OF	$275	$325	$375
HC	350	395	450
Time only, DUPLEX escapement, KW, Silver, 58mm, OF	300	350	400
HC	395	425	475
Time only, DUPLEX escapement, KW, GOLD, 58mm, OF	1,000	1,200	1,400
HC	1,500	1,600	1,850
Enamel, Time only, DUPLEX escap., KW, Silver, 58mm, OF	900	1,200	1,500
HC	1,200	1,400	1,750
(below *SUPERIOR QUALITY* Gold & Enamel, on OF & HC watches)			
Gold &Enamel, Time only, Duplex escap., KW, 55- 58mm, OF	8,000	15,000	18,000
HC	15,000	20,000	25,000

⊕ Some models and grades are not included. Their values can be determined by comparing with similar age, size, metal content, style, models and grades listed.

⊕ Watches listed in this book are priced at the collectable retail level, as complete watches having an original case, an original dial, and with the entire original movement in good working order with no repairs needed.

ABRAHAM-LOUIS BREGUET
also BREGUET ET FILS
Paris

Abraham-Louis Breguet, one of the worlds most celebrated watchmakers.

ABRAHAM-LOUIS BREGUET was born at Neuchatel in 1747 and died in 1823. He was perhaps the greatest horologist of all time in terms of design, elegance, and innovation. He is responsible for the development of the tourbillion, the perpetual calendar, the shock-proof parachute suspension, the isochronal overcoil, and many other improvements. It is difficult to include him in this section because of the complexity surrounding identification of his work which was frequently forged, and the fact that so many pieces produced by his shop were unique. Suffice it to say that the vast majority of watches one encounters bearing his name were either marketed only by his firm or are outright fakes made by others for the export market. Much study is required for proper identification.

Abraham-Louis Breguet, PRODUCTION TOTALS

Date —	Serial #	Date —	Serial #
1795 —	150	1815 —	2700
1800 —	500	1820 —	3500
1805 —	1500	1825 —	4000
1810 —	2000	1830 —	4500

Abraham-Louis Breguet died on 17th day of September, 1823. The Breguet firm continues today with the tradition started by Abraham-Louis. At first in the hands of his immediate successors and later under the guidance of the "Browns", when the interest of the Breguet family diversified. Today the firm of Breguet continues to produce high quality and exclusive range of watches based on the *classic style* that has made the Breguet name so famous. The Company makes jewelry, wrist watches, clocks, as well as, fine pocket watches. They produce choice examples, with complicated movements and should be signed on dial, case and movement.

🕐 This book endeavors to be a GUIDE or helpful manual and offers a wealth of material to be used as a tool not as a absolute document. Price Guides are like watches the worst may be better than none at all, but at best cannot be expected to be 100% accurate.

🕐 Characteristics of watches differ for the same age of both case and movement, because these features vary it may not be accurate to date a watch by one single influence. Example: the second hand was _not_ commonly found on watches before 1750, but common about 1800. The first second hand appeared in 1665 and another in 1690. Therefore statements are broad rather than absolute.

60 to 62mm. Example of Breguet **SOUSCRIPTION** style face and movement. Gilt movement with central winding arbor, balance with parachute suspension, HANGING ruby cylinder escapement. White enamel dial with secret signature at 12 o'clock. NOTE: Winds from center either front or back, also most had a silver case and gold bezel. "This Example is actual size".

TYPE – DESCRIPTION	Avg	Ex-Fn	Mint
1/4 repeater, Breguet & Fils, silver, OF, KWKS, 54mm C.1820.....	$700	$900	$1,100
1/4 repeater, Breguet & Fils, KWKS, 18K, 54mm, OF, C.1820......	2,000	2,500	3,000
1/4 repeater, Breguet & Fils, verge, automated, 18K, 55mm, OF ...	3,500	4,500	5,500
Ruby cylinder, parachute, KW, 18K, 49mm, OF, C. 1800	5,000	6,500	8,500
Repeater Horologer De La Marine , silver dial, ruby cylinder escapement	17,000	20,000	23,000
Min. repeater, split sec. chrono., min. register 18K, 2 tone case, 53mm, OF, C. 1945	15,000	18,000	23,000
Jump hr.w/ aperture, revolving min.disc, 18K, 46mm, OF, C.1930	11,000	13,000	15,000
Hanging ruby cylinder, enamel "souscription" dial, center wind, all original,18K, 60 to 62mm, OF, C. 1800	17,000	19,000	25,000
Montre'a tact, 6J ruby cylinder, "souscription" , pearl & enamel case, 18K, 36mm, C. 1810	23,000	28,000	33,000

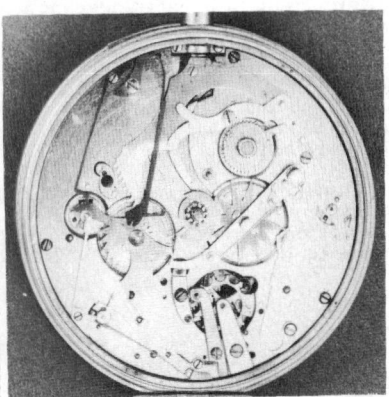

Abraham Louis Breguet, repeating, ruby cylinder watch. Left: gilt movement with standing barrel. Note jeweled parachute suspension. Right: Dial side of movement, repeating train with exposed springs.

Important repeater Horologer De La Marine by Breguet. Left: Guilloche silver dial with roman numerals and typical Breguet hands. Right: Gilt brass movement with ruby cylinder escapement and triple arm balance.

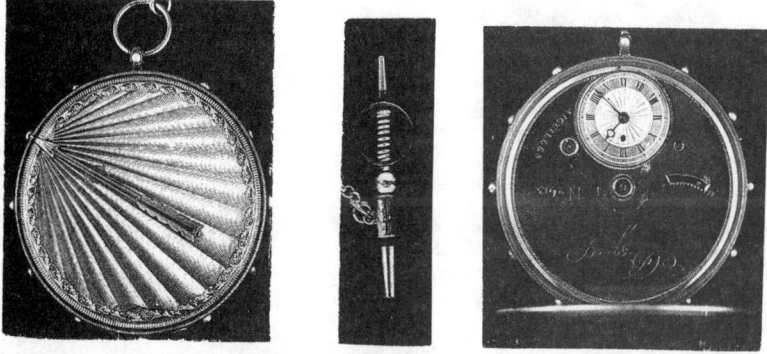

Breguet "montre a tact" or touch time watch, 36mm. Case embellished with 12 pearls for tactile hours (Braille style watch). The arrow on case revolves. Souscription movement with 6 jewels, central barrel, ruby cylinder escapement.

BREGUET, 51mm, chronograph with perpetual calendar and minute repeater. Note sector style wind indicator.

BREGUET, 53mm, minute repeating, split-second chronograph. Chronograph activated by crown and button on band. Repeater activated by slide.

Breguet, 45-48mm, ruby cylinder, KW KS, Swiss bar Mvt., time only, Ca.1830, 18K case

TYPE – DESCRIPTION	Avg	Ex-Fn	Mint
Min. repeater, perpetual calendar chronograph, wind indicator, 18K, OF, 51mm, C. 1932	$43,000	$53,000	$64,000
Min. repeater, split sec. chronograph, two tone gold case, 53mm, C.1948	15,000	19,000	23,000
Perpetual calendar, thin digital watch, 18K case, 45mm	12,000	14,000	17,000
Tactile braille watch, 18K enamel case w/ pearls, 36mm	25,000	30,000	36,000
Small keyless watch, platinum balance, gold case, 18mm	23,000	28,000	35,000
Early, KW / KS, Swiss bar Mvt., time only, Ca.1830, 18K case	3,000	3,500	4,000

BULOVA
U. S. A. & Swiss

Bulova was a leader in the mass production of quality wristwatches; however, their pocket watch output was small and limited to mostly basic time only varieties. The ultra thin "Phantom" was one of their limited production models.

Joseph Bulova started with a wholesale jewelry business in 1875. The first watches were marketed in the early 1920s. Bulova manufactured millions of movements in their own Swiss plant. The company cased these movements in the U.S.A. and imports all production today. The ACCUTRON was introduced in 1960 and sold about 5 million watches.

🕐 Some models and grades are not included. Their values can be determined by comparing with similar age, size, metal content, style, models and grades listed.

🕐 Watches listed in this book are priced at the collectable retail level, as complete watches having an original case, an original dial, and with the entire original movement in good working order with no repairs needed.

TYPE – DESCRIPTION

TYPE – DESCRIPTION	Avg	Ex-Fn	Mint
GF, 17J, 42mm, OF, C. 1940	$50	$60	$85
Rose GF, art deco, 17J, 42mm, OF, C. 1930	70	90	125
14K, 17J, 42mm, OF, C. 1950	200	225	250
Platinum, ultra-thin, "Phantom", 18J, 43mm, OF, C. 1920	600	700	800
Accutron, date, GF, 43mm, HC	135	150	175

BULOVA Accutron, with date, gold filled hunting case, about 43mm, ca. 1970s.

HENRY CAPT, 52mm, 32 jewels, minute repeater, serial number 34,711, ca. 1900.

HENRY CAPT
Geneva

Henry Daniel Capt of Geneva was an associate of Isaac Daniel Piguet for about 10 years from 1802 to 1812. Their firm produced quality watches and specialized in musicals, repeaters and chronometers. By 1844, his son was director of the firm and around 1880 the firm was sold to Gallopin.

TYPE – DESCRIPTION	Avg	Ex-Fn	Mint
Early, KW KS, Swiss bar Mvt., time only, Ca.1870, Silver case	$125	$150	$200
Early, KW KS, Swiss bar Mvt., time only, Ca.1870, Gold	600	750	1,000
Time only, gold, 45- 50mm, OF	700	800	900
HC	900	1,000	1,200
Chronograph, gold, 45-50mm, OF	850	950	1,100
HC	1,000	1,200	1,400
Split second chronograph, gold, 45-52mm, OF	1,200	1,400	1,600
HC	1,500	1,800	2,000
1/4 hr. repeater, gold, 46-52mm, OF	1,800	2,200	2,500
HC	2,500	3,000	3,500
Minute repeater, gold, 46-52mm, OF	2,500	3,500	4,000
HC	3,500	4,000	4,500
OF, w/split chrono.	6,500	7,500	8,500
HC, w/split chrono.	12,000	14,000	16,000
Perpetual moonphase calendar, gold, OF	10,000	12,000	14,000
HC	13,000	15,000	16,000
Perp. moonphase cal., w/min.repeater, gold, OF	25,000	30,000	35,000
Perp. moonphase cal. ,w/min.repeater and chrono., gold, HC	35,000	40,000	45,000

⊕ Characteristics of watches differ for the same age of both case and movement, because these features vary it may not be accurate to date a watch by one single influence. Example: the second hand was not commonly found on watches before 1750, but common about 1800. The first second hand appeared in 1665 and another in 1690. Therefore statements are broad rather than absolute.

CARTIER
Paris

CARTIER was a famous artisan from Paris who first made powder flasks. By the mid-1840s the family became known as the finest goldsmiths of Paris. Around the turn of the century the Cartier firm was designing watches and in 1904 the first wrist watches were being made. In 1917 Cartier created a watch design that was to become known as the tank-style case. The tank-style case was made to look like tank caterpillars of the U. S. A and is still popular today.

Cartier, 52mm, 40 jewels, triple complicated-perpetual calendar, minute repeater, split-second chronograph.

Cartier, 45mm, 18 jewels, flat, astronomic with moon phases triple calendar, platinum watch, Ca. 1930s.

TYPE – DESCRIPTION	Avg	Ex-Fn	Mint
Time only, gold, 40- 44mm, OF	$1,600	$1,800	$2,000
HC	2,000	2,200	2,500
Time only, gold, 45- 50mm, OF	2,500	3,000	3,500
HC	3,500	4,000	4,500
Flat, astronomic w/ moon ph. triple calendar, platinum,OF	10,000	12,000	15,000
Chronograph, gold, 45-50mm, OF	4,500	5,000	5,500
5 minute repeater, gold, 46-52mm, OF	6,000	7,000	8,000
HC	7,000	8,000	9,000
Minute repeater, gold, 46-52mm, OF	10,000	12,000	14,000
HC	12,000	14,000	16,000
Triple complicated, astronomical moon ph. perpetual triple cal., min. repeater, split sec. chron. w/min. recorder, signed European Watch & Clock Co., 18K case, c. 1930	100,000	110,000	120,000

Above: **Cartier,** 43mm, 18 jewels, dial has raised gold Arabic numbers, 18k, OF, Ca.1930s.

T. F. COOPER
Liverpool

The Cooper name is usually marked on inner dust covers which protect Swiss ebauche keywind bar movements. Numerous watches produced from 1850-1890 are found with this Liverpool name. The T.F. Cooper & later the T.W. Cooper firms supplied the U.S. market with low cost silver-cased keywinds.

TYPE – DESCRIPTION	Avg	Ex-Fn	Mint
KWKS, "full-jeweled" , Silver, 44-48mm, OF, Ca.1850-1875......	$75	$90	$125
KWKS, 15J, Silver, 46-50mm, HC, Ca.1850-1870.........................	85	110	150
KW, Fusee, lever, silver, 48mm, OF, C. 1870...............................	130	150	185
KW, 15J, metal dust cover, gilt dial, **18K**, OF, C. 1875	275	325	375
KW, 15J, Lady's , **18K**, 44mm, fancy HC, C. 1875........................	300	350	400
KW, gold dial, bar movement w/side lever escap., parachute shock on balance, **18K,** 50mm, OF, C. 1870.........	285	350	400
Captains double time, 15J, KWKS, silver, 48mm, OF, C.1865.......	400	465	550

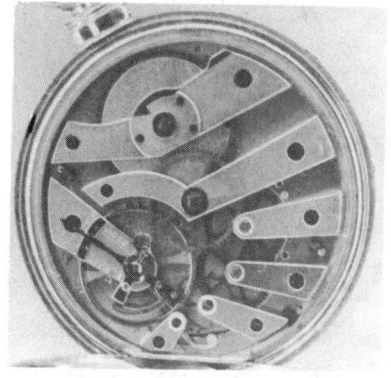  

T.F. Cooper, KW, bar movement with right angle lever escapement, parachute shock on balance, 18K, 50mm, OF, Ca. 1852.

Courvoisier- Freres, 37mm, cylinder escap. with wolf-tooth winding, front & back view, 18K & enamel HC, Ca.1880.

COURVOISIER, Freres
SWISS (La Chaux de Fonds)

Started as Courvoisier & Cie in 1810-11, by 1845 Henri-Louis and Philippe-Auguste became owners. In 1852 name changes to Courvoisier, Freres. The watches circa 1810 are signed with the older signature. They exported very ornate pieces for the Chinese market (LePine bar caliber). They also obtained a Chinese *TRADEMARK* for their signature.

TYPE – DESCRIPTION	Avg	Ex-Fn	Mint
Time only, KW, **SILVER**, 45- 50mm, OF.....................................	$250	$300	$375
HC..	300	375	450
Time only, KW, **Gold**, 45- 50mm, OF..	750	850	1,000
HC..	1,000	1,200	1,500
Captains Watch, **SILVER**, 2 hour dials, 2 trains, Key Wind, center seconds, 50mm, OF......................................	600	700	800
HC, (SAME AS ABOVE)......................................	700	800	1,000
Captains Watch, **GOLD**, 2 hour dials, 2 trains, Key Wind, center seconds, 50mm, OF	1,200	1,500	1,800
HC, (SAME AS ABOVE)......................................	1,800	2,250	2,800
1/4 hr. repeater, **SILVER**, 46-52mm, OF..............................	900	1,000	1,200
1/4 hr. repeater, **GOLD**, 46-52mm, OF	1,600	1,800	2,000
Dent Chronometer, gold, 48-52mm, OF	4,000	4,500	5,000
HC	6,000	6,500	7,000

DENT (M. F. & Co.)
LONDON

Edward John Dent, born in 1790 died in 1853. Edward worked for J.R.Arnold, at 84 Strand, from 1830-1840 and worked alone at 82 Strand from 1841 to 1849. Then moved to 61 Strand 1850 till 1853. The year before his death the Westminster Place gave Dent the contract for making BIG BEN with a big bell weighing over 13 tons. The clock was built by Frederick Rippon Dent. The Dent firm was in business until 1920.

DENT, PIVOTED Detent chronometer, about 15 jewels, fusee, gold, 48-52mm, Ca. 1870, open face.

DENT, 1/4 hr. repeater, marked "Dent Watch Maker to the Queen 61 Strand London", S# 30077, gold, 46-52mm, OF

TYPE – DESCRIPTION	Avg	Ex-Fn	Mint
Time only, gold, 45-50mm, OF	$1,100	$1,200	$1,400
HC	1,400	1,700	2,000
Chronograph, gold, 45-50mm, OF	1,500	1,800	2,200
HC	1,800	2,200	2,600
Split second chronograph, gold, 45-52mm, OF	2,300	2,700	3,200
HC	3,500	4,000	5,000
1/4 hr. repeater, gold, 46-52mm, OF	2,000	2,500	3,000
HC	3,000	3,500	4,250
HC w/chrono., cal. & moonphase	5,700	6,700	8,000
Minute repeater, gold, OF	4,000	5,000	6,000
HC	5,500	6,500	7,500
OF w/chrono.	5,000	5,500	6,750
HC w/split chrono.	12,000	14,000	17,000
HC w/cal. & moonphase	14,000	17,000	20,000
Detent chronometer, gold, 48-52mm, OF	8,000	10,000	12,000
Perpetual moonphase calendar, gold, OF	15,000	20,000	25,000
HC	20,000	25,000	32,500
Perp. moonphase cal. w/min. repeater, OF	35,000	40,000	50,000
HC	50,000	55,000	65,000

🕐 Some models and grades are not included. Their values can be determined by comparing with similar age, size, metal content, style, models and grades listed.

🕐 Watches listed in this book are priced at the collectable fair market value at the retail level, as complete watches having an original case, an original white enamel dial, and with the entire original movement in good working order with no repairs needed, unless otherwise noted.

DUBOIS et FILS
Le Locle (SWISS)

Dealer and Watchmaker, one of the most active in the Le LOCLE region. Founded in 1785 by Philippe (1738-1808). They exported all over the world and specialized in automaton watches, skeleton watches and watches with false pendulums. The company is still in business today.

TYPE – DESCRIPTION	Avg	Ex-Fn	Mint
Verge, KW, pair case, silver, 48-52mm	$475	$525	$575
Verge, enamel w/scene, silver or gilt, 48-52mm	1,500	1,800	2,000
Verge w/mock pendulum, silver, OF, 48-52mm	1,200	1,500	1,800
Verge, KW, GOLD, OF, 50-54mm	1,000	1,250	1,500
Verge, KW, GOLD w/enamel, OF,52mm	2,250	2,500	2,850
1/4 hr. repeater, SILVER, OF, 50-54mm	950	1,100	1,300
1/4 hr. repeater, GOLD, OF, 50-54mm	1,500	1,700	2,000
1/4 hr. repeater w/automaton, 18K, OF, 50-52mm	5,000	5,500	6,000

Dubois et Fils, Verge with mock pendulum, silver, OF, enamel dial, 48-52mm, Ca. 1830.

Dubois et Fils, Verge, enamel w/scene, silver or gilt, OF, painted enamel scene, 48-52mm Ca. 1810.

COMPARISON OF WATCH SIZES

U. S. A.	EUROPEAN
10-12 SIZE	40—44 MM
16 SIZE	45—48 MM
18 SIZE	50—54 MM

DUCHENE L., & Fils
GENEVA

Watchmaker, well known for their large and small pieces, including coach clocks, calendar watches and minute repeater watches. The firm was known also for decorative work with polychrome champleve enamel and painted enamel, and fantasy watches. The movements are classically-designed, with fusee & verge escapements. Cases are in "Empire-style", engraved or guilloche.

TYPE – DESCRIPTION	Avg	Ex-Fn	Mint
KW, cylinder, silver, 46mm, OF	$200	$250	$295
HC	250	300	375
KW, verge fusee, silver, 46-52mm, OF	375	425	500
KW, verge fusee, enamel case ,gilt, 52mm, OF	1,500	1,600	1,700
1/4 hr. repeater, silver, 54mm, OF	1,200	1,350	1,500
1/4 hr. repeater, gold, 52mm, OF	1,500	1,700	2,000
Ball form, KWKS, cylinder, 29mm, OF	1,500	1,650	1,800

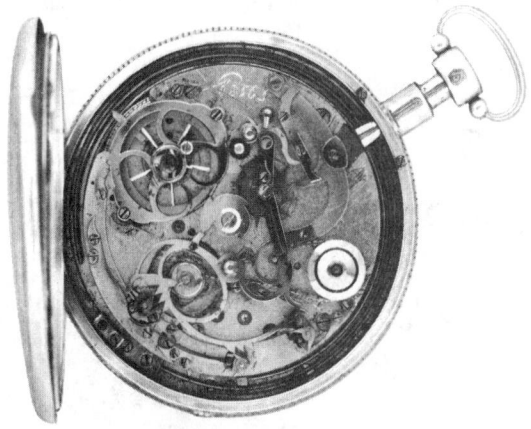

Duchene L. & Fils, 1/4 Hour Repeater, fusee and cylinder escapement, repeats on gongs, 52mm, Ca. 1820.

DUNAND
Swiss

The Dunand factory produced repeaters, timers & chronographs during the 1890-1930 time period. (Also see Timers and Chrono. section.)

TYPE – DESCRIPTION	Avg	Ex-Fn	Mint
Time only, gold, 45-50mm, OF	$350	$400	$500
HC	450	500	600
Chronograph, gold, 45-50mm,OF	500	600	700
HC	700	800	900
Split second chronograph, gold, 45-52mm, OF	900	1,000	1,100
HC	1,000	1,100	1,200
1/4 hr. repeater, gold, 46-52mm, OF	800	900	1,000
HC	1,000	1,200	1,400
OF w/chrono.	1,100	1,200	1,300
HC w/chrono.	1,200	1,400	1,600
Minute repeater, gold, 46-52mm, OF	1,500	1,800	2,200
HC	2,000	2,200	2,500

EARNSHAW, THOMAS
LONDON

Thomas Earnshaw born in 1749 died in 1829. In about 1781 he improves the spring detent. Earnshaw also contributed to the development of the chronometer. He pioneered the method of fusing brass and steel together to form a laminate of the compensation rims as in the modern method of today. Known for his chronometers he also made 1/4 and 1/2 hour repeaters with cylinder and duplex escapements.

THOMAS EARNSHAW, chronometer, KWKS, spring detent, Z or S balance with trapezoidal weights, helical hairspring, serial # 589, silver case, Ca.1810.

TYPE – DESCRIPTION	Avg	Ex-Fn	Mint
Time only, KW, **SILVER**, 45- 48mm, OF	$1,200	$1,500	$2,000
HC	2,000	2,500	3,000
Time only, KW, **GOLD**, 45- 48mm, OF	2,500	3,000	3,500
HC	3,000	3,500	4,000
1/4 hr. repeater, **GOLD**, 46-52mm, OF	6,000	7,000	8,000
HC	7,500	8,500	9,500
Spring detent escapement, chronometer, gold, 48-54mm, OF	7,000	8,000	9,000
HC	10,000	12,000	14,000

H. R. EKEGREN
Copenhagen & Geneva

Henry Robert Ekegren, a Swiss maker of quality watches, started in business around 1870. The firm specialized in flat watches, chronometers and repeaters. Ekegren became associated with F. Koehn in 1891.

TYPE – DESCRIPTION	Avg	Ex-Fn	Mint
Time only, gold, 45- 50mm, OF	$650	$800	$1,000
HC	800	1,200	1,500
Chronograph, gold, 45-50mm, OF	1,000	1,200	1,500
HC	1,200	1,500	1,800
Split second chronograph, gold, 45-52mm, OF	1,500	1,800	2,000
HC	1,800	2,000	2,200
FIVE-Minute repeater, gold, 46-52mm, OF	2,000	2,200	2,500
HC	2,500	3,000	3,500

🕐 Some models and grades are not included. Their values can be determined by comparing with similar age, size, metal content, style, models and grades listed.

🕐 Watches listed in this book are priced at the collectable fair market **value** at the **retail** level, as complete watches having an original case, an original white enamel dial, and with the entire original movement in good working order with no repairs needed, unless otherwise noted.

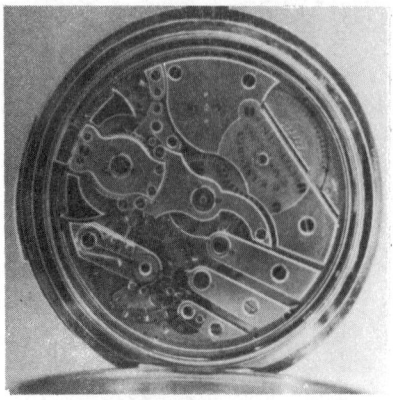

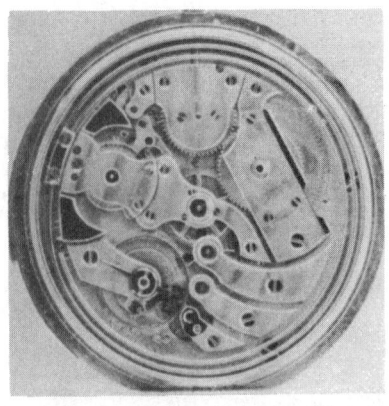

H.R. EKEGREN 46mm, minute repeater, slide activated, jeweled through hammers, open face, serial no. 78,268.

H.R. EKEGREN, 47mm, minute repeater, jeweled through hammers, hunting case.

TYPE – DESCRIPTION	Avg	Ex-Fn	Mint
Minute repeater, gold, 46-52mm, OF	$3,000	$3,200	$4,000
HC	3,500	4,000	4,600
OF w/chrono.	2,500	3,000	3,500
HC w/chrono.	4,000	4,500	5,000
OF w/split chrono.	4,500	5,000	5,500
HC w/split chrono.	7,500	8,500	9,500
Perpetual moonphase calendar, gold, OF	12,000	15,000	18,000
Perpetual moonphase cal. w/ min. repeater, OF	25,000	30,000	35,000
HC	30,000	35,000	40,000
Perp. moonphase cal. w/min. rep. and chrono., OF	40,000	45,000	50,000
HC	45,000	50,000	55,000
Karrusel, gold, 48-55mm, OF	8,000	9,000	10,000
Tourbillion, gold, 48-55mm, OF	40,000	45,000	50,000
Detent chronometer, gold, 48-52mm, OF	6,000	7,000	8,000
World time watch, gold, 48-52mm, OF	15,000	18,000	20,000

FAVRE–LEUBE
Le Locle & Geneva

Founded in 1737, this firm is still active and production has covered more than eight generations of watchmakers. The firm name had a name change when Abraham Favre married Miss Leube. The company has made some very fine quality watches.

FAVER-LEUBE, 53mm, Minute repeater, 15 jewels, slide on rim activates the repeater mechanism, Ca.1895.

TYPE – DESCRIPTION	Avg	Ex-Fn	Mint
Early, KW KS, Swiss bar Mvt., time only, Ca.1870, Silver case ...	$100	$125	$150
KW, Gold w/enamel, 35-40mm, HC	1,700	1,800	2,000
KW, silver w/enamel, 45mm, HC	375	450	500
KW, Gold w/enamel, 45-48mm, OF	1,200	1,500	1,700
Chronograph, gold, 45-50mm, OF	2,200	2,500	2,800
HC	3,500	4,000	4,500
Split second chronograph, gold, 45-52mm, OF	3,000	3,500	4,000
HC	3,500	4,000	4,500
1/4 hr. repeater, gold, 46-52mm, OF	2,500	2,800	3,200
HC	3,500	4,000	4,500
Minute repeater, gold, 46-52mm, OF	4,000	4,500	5,000
HC	6,000	6,500	7,500

CHARLES FRODSHAM
London

Charles Frodsham followed in the footsteps of his father, William, whose father was close with Earnshaw. Charles became the most eminent of the family, producing very fine chronometers and some rare tourbillon and complicated watches. He died in 1871. His quality movements endorse the letters A.D. FMSZ. Originally Arnold & Frodsham was located at 84 Strand, London until 1858. He later moved to New Bond Street, London.

Frodsham, 84 Strand, London engraved on movement, 16-18 jewels, platinum balance screws, Ca. 1850s

Chas. Frodsham, 84 Strand London, 25 jewels, Fusee, Freesprung, Diamond end stone, serial number 3520.

TYPE – DESCRIPTION	Avg	Ex-Fn	Mint
Early, KW KS, Swiss bar Mvt., time only, Silver case	$150	$175	$250
Time only, early mvt. 84 Strand, silver, 45- 48mm, OF, C.1850 ...	350	400	500
Time only, early mvt. 84 Strand, gold, 45- 48mm, OF, C.1850	1,000	1,200	1,500
Time only, gold, 45- 50mm, OF	1,000	1,200	1,500
HC	1,200	1,500	1,800
Chronograph, gold, 45-50mm, OF	1,500	1,800	2,000
HC	1,800	2,000	2,200
Split second chronograph, gold, 45-52m, OF	3,000	3,200	3,500
HC	3,500	4,000	4,500

Frodsham, 46-50mm, jeweled through the center wheel, stem wind, 18K case, Ca. 1895.

Frodsham, 59mm, 60 minute Karrusel, 15 jewels, stem wind, open face, 18K gold case, Ca. 1895.

TYPE – DESCRIPTION	Avg	Ex-Fn	Mint
Minute repeater, gold, 46-52mm,OF	$6,000	$7,000	$8,000
HC	10,000	12,000	14,000
OF w/split chrono.	18,000	20,000	22,000
HC w/split chrono.	20,000	23,000	25,000
Perpetual moonphase calendar, gold, OF	25,000	30,000	35,000
Perp. moonphase cal. w/min. repeater, OF	45,000	55,000	60,000
HC	65,000	70,000	75,000
Karrusel, 16J, 59-60 Min karrusel, 18K, C.1895	4,500	5,000	6,250
Tourbillion, gold, 48-55mm, OF	50,000	55,000	65,000
Marine chronometer, Parkinson-Frodsham, helical hairspring, w/ detent escape., 48 hr. WI, C. 1840, 97mm deck box	2,000	3,000	3,500
Detent chronometer, w/wind ind., silver, OF, KWKS, C. 1850	2,800	3,000	3,300

GIRARD-PERREGAUX
Swiss

In 1856, The Constant Girard and Henry Perregaux families founded the Swiss firm of Girard-Perregaux. About 1880, the firm made a tourbillon with three golden bridges. A replica of this watch was made in 1982. Both were a supreme expression of horological craftsmanship. In 1906, the company purchased the Hecht factory in Geneva. Girard-Perregaux has been recognized many times and still makes prestigious quartz and mechanical watches.

TYPE – DESCRIPTION	Avg	Ex-Fn	Mint
Skeletonized "Shell" (Shell Oil advertising watch), 7 Jewels, Base metal display case, total production =30,000 C.1930	$100	$135	$175
Time only, gold 40-44mm, OF	275	325	375
HC	350	450	575
Time only, gold 45- 50mm, OF	600	850	900
HC	950	1,250	1,500

Skeletonized "Shell Watch" (Golden Shell Oil) advertising a watch filled with Shell car motor oil they wanted to prove even a watch would run on this top quality car motor oil. Most stopped with this heavy car oil, so the oil was removed from some watches. Base metal display case, only 7 jewels, total production was 30,000, Ca. June, 1940.

GIRARD-PERREGAUX, three golden bridges movement patented March 25th, 1884.

GIRARD-PERREGAUX, Chronometer, with pivoted dentent, gold train, 20 jewels, nickel movement, Ca. 1878.

TYPE – DESCRIPTION	Avg	Ex-Fn	Mint
3 gold bridges, with **silver** case, C. 1884,	$4,000	$5,000	$6,000
with **gold** case	4,500	5,500	7,500
Chronometer, pivoted detent, 20J., gold train, 18K, C.1878	13,000	15,000	17,000
Chronograph, gold, 45-50mm, OF	1,200	1,400	1,600
HC	1,500	1,800	2,000
1/4 hr. repeater, gold, 45-52mm, OF	2,000	2,200	2,500
HC	3,000	3,200	3,500
HC w/chrono., cal. & moonphase	6,000	6,500	7,500
Minute repeater, gold, 46-52mm, OF	3,500	4,500	5,000
HC	4,500	5,000	6,000
OF w/chrono.	4,500	5,000	5,500
OF w/split chrono.	6,500	7,000	7,500
HC w/cal. & moonphase	10,000	12,000	15,000
Detent chronometer, gold, 48-54mm, OF	6,000	7,000	8,000
HC	8,000	9,000	10,000

GOLAY A., LERESCHE & Fils
SWISS

Manufactured under the name Golay-Leresche from 1844-1857, then his son changed the name to Golay A., Leresche & Fils, he worked until the beginning of the 20th Century. Watches were primarily exported to U.S.A., he was well known for watches of all kinds and "grande complications".

TYPE – DESCRIPTION	Avg	Ex-Fn	Mint
Time only, gold, 45- 50mm, OF	$900	$1,000	$1,100
HC	1,200	1,500	1,800
Chronograph, gold, 45-50mm, OF	1,200	1,500	1,800
HC	1,500	1,800	2,100
Split second chronograph, gold, 45-52mm, OF	1,800	2,000	2,500
HC	3,000	3,500	4,000

Golay A., Leresche & Fils, 1/4 hour repeater, 47mm, 41 jewels, key wind, Ca. 1855.

Golay A., Leresche & Fils, minute repeater, split seconds chonograph, moon phases, day date month, open face, Ca. 1896.

TYPE – DESCRIPTION	Avg	Ex-Fn	Mint
1/4 hr. repeater, gold, 46-52mm, OF	$1,800	$2,000	$2,200
HC	2,200	2,500	2,800
HC w/chrono., cal. & moonphase	5,500	6,000	6,500
Minute repeater, gold, OF	3,000	3,500	4,000
HC	4,500	5,000	5,500
OF w/chrono.	4,000	4,500	5,000
HC w/split chrono.	10,000	12,000	14,000
HC w/cal. & moonphase	10,000	12,000	15,000
Detent chronometer, gold, 48-52mm, OF	8,000	9,000	10,000
Perpetual moonphase calendar, gold, OF	10,000	15,000	18,000
HC	14,000	17,000	20,000
Perp. moonphase cal. w/min. repeater, OF	25,000	30,000	35,000
HC	45,000	50,000	55,000

🕐 Note: Some models and grades are not included. Their values can be determined by comparing with similar age, size, metal content, style, models and grades listed.

🕐 Watches listed in this book are priced at the collectable fair market **value** at the **retail** level, as complete watches having an original case, an original white enamel dial, and with the entire original movement in good working order with no repairs needed, unless otherwise noted.

H. GRANDJEAN

The son of David-Henri (1774-1845), this respected maker produced high quality complicated watches, chronometers and ornately decorated watches for the South American market. A Grandjean specialty was magnificent enamel and gem set ladies watches.

TYPE – DESCRIPTION	Avg	Ex-Fn	Mint
Time only, gold, 45- 50mm, OF	$900	$1,000	$1,100
HC	1,200	1,500	1,800
Chronograph, gold, 45-50mm, OF	1,200	1,500	1,800
HC	1,500	1,800	2,100
Split second chronograph, gold, 45-52mm, OF	1,800	2,000	2,500
HC	3,000	3,500	4,000
1/4 hr. repeater, gold, 46-52mm, OF	1,800	2,000	2,200
HC	2,200	2,500	2,800
HC w/chrono., cal. & moonphase	4,500	5,000	5,500
Minute repeater, gold, OF	3,000	3,500	4,000
HC	4,500	5,000	5,500
OF w/chrono.	3,500	4,000	4,500
HC w/split chrono.	10,000	12,000	14,000
HC w/cal. & moonphase	10,000	12,000	15,000
Detent chronometer, gold, 48-52mm, OF	8,000	9,000	10,000
Perpetual moonphase calendar, gold, OF	10,000	15,000	18,000
HC	14,000	17,000	20,000
Perp. moonphase cal. w/min. repeater, OF	25,000	30,000	35,000
HC	45,000	50,000	55,000
Grande & Petite Sonnnerie repeating clock watch, 38J, fancy dial, 18k gold, 53mm, HC	35,000	40,000	45,000

H. GRANDJEAN, Grande & Petite Sonnnerie repeating clock watch, 38J, with tandem wind mechanism, fancy dial, 18k gold, 53mm, HC

GRUEN WATCH CO.

Swiss & U. S. A. (1894 - 1953)

The early roots of the Gruen Company are found in Columbus, Ohio where Dietrich Gruen and W.J. Savage formed a partnership in 1876. The D. Gruen & Son legacy began in 1894 and flourished with the introduction of fine quality "Precision" movements. Curvex movements, ultra-thins and the prestigious 50th anniversary model are highlights of this prolific company.

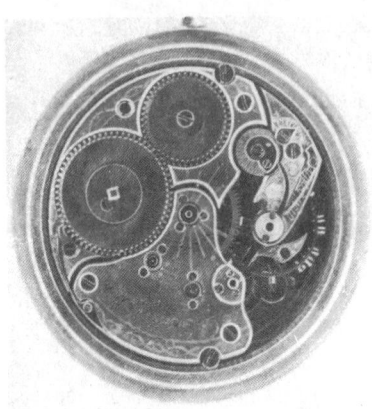

D. Gruen & Son, 44mm, jeweled through center wheel, made for railroad service, serial number 62,428.

Gruen 50th Anniversary Watch, 40mm or 10 size, 21 jewels, (two diamonds) placed in a five-sided pentagon case, solid gold bridges.

TYPE – DESCRIPTION	Avg	Ex-Fn	Mint
17J, veri-thin or precision, GF, 40-43mm, OF, C. 1920's	$75	$95	$125
17J, veri-thin-precision, **14K**, 40-43mm, C.1930	225	275	325
Pentagon case ,17J, GF, 40-43mm, OF, C.1920's	125	150	195
Pentagon case, 17-19J, precision, **14K**, 40-43mm, C. 1930	275	325	395
21-23J, D. Gruen, Swiss, Gold, 45-54mm, OF, C. 1900-20	250	325	450
21J, D. Gruen, (by Assmann),14K, OF, C. 1905	425	500	600
21J, D. Gruen, (by Assmann),14K, HC, C. 1910	750	900	1,100
50th anniversary , 12K gold movement, 21J & 2 diamonds, pentagon case, 18K, 40mm, OF, C. 1924	2,500	3,000	3,500

Gruen W. Co., Swiss made, 23 jewels in screwed settings, 47mm, wind indicator, micrometer regulator, Ca.1900's.

Gruen W. Co., 40mm, Precision V1 1/2 verithin, 21 jewels, 8 positions, serial number 535,203.

E. GUBELIN

Swiss

Jacques Edouard Gubelin joined the firm of Mourice Brithschmid in Lucerne around 1854. By 1919, Edouard Gubelin headed the firm. In 1921 they opened an office in New York & produced fine jewelry and watches for 5 generations.

E. GUBELIN, 50mm, 29J., minute repeater, chronograph, day-date-month-moon phase.

E. GUBELIN, 48mm, world time with 68 cities on outside bezel 24 hour on inter bezel, 18k open face.

TYPE – DESCRIPTION	Avg	Ex-Fn	Mint
Time only, gold, 40- 44mm, OF	$475	$525	$675
HC	525	625	750
Time only, gold, 45- 50mm, OF	835	900	1,000
HC	1,000	1,200	1,500
Chronograph, gold, 45-50mm, OF	1,200	1,300	1,400
HC	1,800	2,000	2,500
Split second chronograph, gold, 45-52mm, OF	2,000	2,200	2,500
HC	2,500	3,000	3,500
1/4 hr. repeater, gold, 46-52mm, OF	2,000	2,500	2,800
HC	2,500	2,800	3,000
OF w/chrono.	2,500	2,800	3,000
HC w/chrono.	2,800	3,000	3,500
HC w/chrono., calendar & moonphase	4,000	4,500	5,000
5 minute repeater, gold, 46-52mm, OF	3,500	3,800	4,000
HC	4,000	4,300	4,500
Minute repeater, gold, 46-52mm, OF	4,000	4,500	5,000
OF w/chrono.	4,500	5,000	5,500
OF w/split chrono.	6,000	6,500	7,500
OF w/chrono., calendar & moonphase	8,500	9,500	11,000
World time watch, gold, 48-52mm, OF	4,500	5,000	5,500
Perpetual moonphase calendar, gold, OF	15,000	18,000	20,000
Perp. moonphase cal. w/min. repeater, OF	40,000	45,000	50,000
Perp. moonphase cal. w/min.rep. and chrono., OF	45,000	50,000	55,000

C. L. GUINAND & CO.
Swiss

TYPE – DESCRIPTION	Avg	Ex-Fn	Mint
Timer, with register, base metal, OF, 46mm	$50	$60	$75
Timer, split second, register, base metal, OF, 46mm	65	75	85
Chronograph, 30 min. register,14K, 50mm, OF, C. 1910	500	600	700
Split sec. chrono., 30 min. register, 14K, OF, 50mm, C. 1915	1,000	1,300	1,600
Minute repeater, split sec. chrono., 18K, OF, 50mm, C. 1915.........	4,000	4,500	5,200

C.L. Guinand, 50mm, split-second chronograph, serial number 44,109.

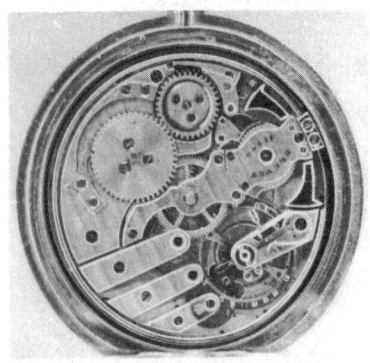

Haas, Neveux & Co., 40mm, 31 jewels, minute repeater, 18k open face case, serial number 11,339.

HAAS, NEVEUX
Swiss

The Haas Neveux factory is one of the oldest in Switzerland, producing from 1828-1925. High grade precision timepieces and chronometers were characteristic of this reputable firm's output.

TYPE – DESCRIPTION	Avg	Ex-Fn	Mint
Time only, gold, 40- 44mm, OF..	$325	$400	$500
HC	450	500	600
Time only, gold, 45- 50mm, OF..	425	500	600
HC	650	800	900
Chronograph, gold, 45-50mm, OF	800	850	900
HC	900	1,000	1,100
Split second chronograph, gold, 45-52mm, OF...............................	1,200	1,800	2,000
HC	1,500	2,000	2,500
1/4 hr. repeater, gold, 46-52mm, OF..	1,500	1,800	2,200
HC	1,200	1,500	1,800
Minute repeater, gold, 46-52mm, OF...	1,500	2,000	2,500
OF w/split chrono.	4,000	4,500	5,000
OF w/cal. & moonphase	4,000	4,500	5,000
Perpetual moonphase calendar, gold, OF..	8,000	9,000	10,000
Perp. moonphase cal. w/min. repeater, OF	25,000	30,000	35,000
HC	28,000	32,000	37,000
Perp. moonphase cal. w/min. rep. and chrono., OF.........................	30,000	35,000	40,000

HEBDOMAS
Swiss

The Hebdomas name is commonly found on imported Swiss novelty "8" day watches. Produced from the early 1900's to the 1960's, these popular timepieces featured fancy colored dials with an opening at the bottom of dial to expose the balance wheel and pallet-fork. This style watch is now being made by Arnex Time Corp. under the name of (Lucien Piccard) & other Co. names.

Hebdomas, 8 day (JOURS) 6 jewels, balance seen from the face of the watch, Ca.1920s. This style watch is now being made by Arnex Time Corp. (Lucien Piccard).

Hebdomas, 8 day (JOURS), 6 jewels, 1 adjustment, exposed balance, day date, center seconds, Ca.1920s

TYPE – DESCRIPTION	Avg	Ex-Fn	Mint
8 day, exposed balance, 7J, gun metal, 50mm, OF, C. 1920............	$125	$135	$150
8 day, exposed balance, 7J, base metal, fancy dial, 50mm, OF, C.1920	135	150	180
8 day, exposed balance, 7J, silver, 50mm, OF, C. 1920...................	150	175	200
8 day, exposed balance, 7J, silver, 50mm, HC, C. 1920's .... ★	250	295	335
8 day, exposed balance, 7J, **day date calendar**, center sec., with fancy dial, silver, 55mm, OF, C. 1920's.......................	250	300	395

🕐 Note: Some models and grades are not included. Their values can be determined by comparing with similar age, size, metal content, style, models and grades listed.

🕐 Watches listed in this book are priced at the collectable fair market **value** at the **retail** level, as complete watches having an original case, an original white enamel dial, and with the entire original movement in good working order with no repairs needed, unless otherwise noted.

COMPARISON OF WATCH SIZES

U. S. A.	EUROPEAN
10-12 SIZE	40—44 MM
16 SIZE	45—48 MM
18 SIZE	50—54 MM

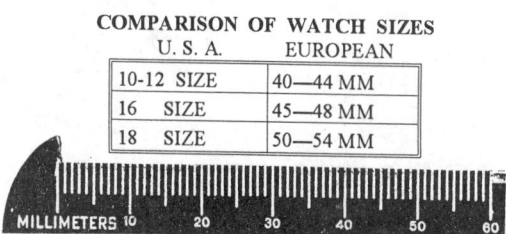

HUGUENIN & CO.
Swiss

Huguenin & Co., 2-Train 1/4 second jump watch, center sweep hand, enamel dial, 54mm, KW KS, 18K, Ca. 1880.

Huguenin & Co., 2-Train 1/4 second jump watch, 2 main barrels & 2 gear trains, 54mm, KW KS, Ca. 1880.

TYPE – DESCRIPTION	Avg	Ex-Fn	Mint
KW, cylinder, silver, 46- 48mm, OF, C. 1870s	$85	$95	$125
KW, silver, 46- 48mm, HC, C. 1870s	125	150	175
KW, cylinder escapement, **18K**, 48mm, OF, C.1870s	250	350	425
KW, fancy engraved, **18K,** 47mm, HC, C. 1870s	400	450	550
1/4 Sec. Jump, 2-train, gold, 50-54mm	2,000	2,400	2,800
Chronograph, gold, 45-52mm, OF	1,000	1,200	1,500
HC	1,300	1,500	1,800
1/4 hr. repeater, gold, 46-52mm, OF	1,500	1,800	2,000
HC	2,000	2,200	2,400
Minute repeater, gold, 46-52mm, OF	2,000	2,500	2,800
HC	3,500	4,000	4,500
OF, w/ chrono.	2,300	2,500	2,800
OF, w/ split chrono.	5,500	6,000	6,500
HC, w/ split chrono.	6,500	7,000	7,500
HC, w/ chrono., cal. & moonphase	6,000	6,500	7,000

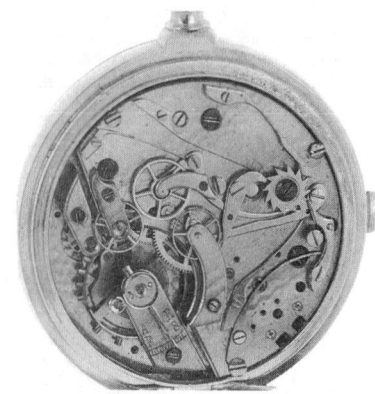

Huguenin & Co., Chronograph, enamel dial, 51mm, 18K, Hunting Case, Ca. 1890.

Huguenin & Co., Chronograph, 3/4 plate movement, 51mm, 18K, Hunting Case, Ca. 1890.

International Watch Co.
Swiss

The founder of the prestigious Swiss International. Watch Co. was an American engineer F. A. Jones from Boston and earlier had worked for E. Howard Watch & Clock company. The company began in 1868 and in 1879 was sold to Mr. J. Rauschenbach. The company today is still making precision, hand crafted watches. IWC is well known for its super-light watch constructed of titanium.

International W. Co., apertures for jump hour and minute disc, 16 jewels, enamel dial,

International Watch Co., 54mm, 17 jewels, adj.6P, serial number 741,073.

TYPE – DESCRIPTION	Avg	Ex-Fn	Mint
Early, KW, Time only, Swiss bar, silver case	$150	$175	$225
Time only, gold, 40-44mm, OF	425	485	550
HC	675	750	850
Time only, gold, 45-50mm, OF	625	700	800
HC	950	1,200	1,500
Jump hour and minute disc, 16 jewels, 14K, HC	1,800	2,000	2,500
Chronograph, gold, 45-50mm, OF	1,800	2,000	2,500
HC	2,000	2,500	3,000
Split second chronograph, gold, 45-52mm, OF	3,000	3,500	4,000
HC	4,000	4,500	5,000
Minute repeater, gold, 46-52mm, OF	3,000	3,200	3,500
HC	3,500	4,500	5,500
OF, w/split chrono.	7,000	7,500	8,500
HC, w/split chrono.	9,000	10,000	11,000
OF, w/cal. & moonphase	8,000	9,000	10,000
HC, w/chrono., cal. & moonphase	9,000	10,000	11,000
Detent chronometer, gold, 48-52mm, OF	7,000	8,000	9,000
World Time watch, gold, 48-52mm, OF	12,000	15,000	18,000
Perpetual moonphase calendar, gold, OF	7,000	8,000	9,000
Perpetual moonphase calendar, w/minute repeater, HC	30,000	35,000	40,000

⊕ Some models and grades are not included. Their values can be determined by comparing with similar age, size, metal content, style, models and grades listed.

⊕ Watches listed in this book are priced at the collectable fair market **value** at the retail level, as complete watches having an original case, an original white enamel dial, and with the entire original movement in good working order with no repairs needed, unless otherwise noted.

INVICTA
Swiss

Invicta trade-mark was registered on May 18, 1896 by Files de R. Picard, of La Chaux-de-Fonds.

TYPE – DESCRIPTION	Avg	Ex-Fn	Mint
1/4 hr. repeater, gun metal ,48mm, OF, C. 1900s............................	$425	$475	$550
1/4 hr. repeater, silver, 48mm, OF, C. 1900s....................................	525	625	750
1/4 hr. repeater, silver, 50mm, HC, C. 1900s	750	850	950
Min. repeater, gun metal, 52mm, HC, C. 1900s	1,000	1,200	1,300
Min. repeater, silver, 52mm, HC, C. 1900s	1,100	1,300	1,400

JACOT, HENRI
PARIS

Henri Jacot settled in Paris in 1820 and developed the carriage clock industry. He also invented and improved watchmaking and clock making tools. Henri Jacot died July 31, 1867.

TYPE – DESCRIPTION	Avg	Ex-Fn	Mint
KW, cylinder, silver, 46mm, OF	$85	$95	$125
HC	125	150	185
KW, LADIES, **18K**, 40-44mm, OF	225	285	350
HC	300	350	425
KW, GENTS, **18K**, 48mm, OF	395	450	495
HC	495	550	650
1/4 hr. repeater, SILVER, 50mm, OF	900	1,000	1,200
1/4 hr. repeater, GOLD, 50mm, OF	1,700	1,800	2,000

JULES JURGENSEN
Swiss

The firm of Jules Jurgensen was an extension of the earlier firm of Urban Jurgensen & Sons, which was located, at various times, in Copenhagen and Le Locle. Jules ultimately established his firm in Le Locle after his father's death in the early 1830's. From that time forward the company produced, generally speaking, very fine watches that were high grade and complicated. It appears that by 1850 the company had already established a strong market in America, offering beautiful heavy 18K gold watches of exemplary quality. Until around 1885, most stem-winding watches exhibited the **bow-setting feature.**

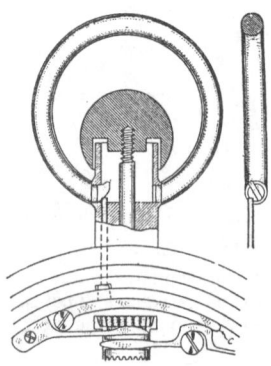

The Jules Jurgensen **famous bow-setting** feature.

Jules Jurgensen, 27 jewels, 1/5 second jump watch, 2 main barrels & 2 gear trains, 54mm, Ca. 1890.

Almost any collectible Jurgensen watch will be fully signed on the dial and movement, with an impressively embossed "JJ" stamping on all covers of the case. Watches not so marked should be examined carefully; and untypical or inelegant stamping should be viewed suspiciously, as there have been some forgeries of these fine watches. Frequently one finds the original box and papers accompanying the watch, which enhances the value. After 1885, as the firm started to buy movements from other companies, we begin to see variations in Jurgensen watches. By 1930, Jurgensen watches barely resembled the quality and aesthetics of the early period, and they are not as desirable to the collector.

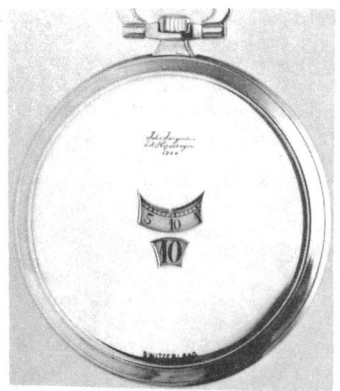

JULES JURGENSEN, 46mm, 21J., hands set by inclination of pendant ring, serial # 14,492, ca.1890.

JULES JURGENSEN, 40mm, flat time only, digital watch, windows for hours and minutes, Ca.1930s.

TYPE – DESCRIPTION	Avg	Ex-Fn	Mint
Time only, gold, 40- 44mm, OF	$250	$300	$375
HC	550	600	650
Time only, gold, 45- 50mm, OF	2,000	2,500	3,000
HC	3,000	3,500	4,000
Flat digital watch, 18J., gold, 40-44mm, OF, C. 1930	5,500	6,000	7,000
1/5 second jump watch, 2 main barrels & 2 gear trains, 18K OF	3,500	4,500	6,000
Chronograph, gold, 45-50mm, OF	2,500	3,000	3,500
HC	4,000	4,500	5,000
HC w/register	4,500	5,000	5,500
Split second chronograph, gold, 45-52mm, OF	5,500	6,000	6,500
HC	6,500	7,000	7,500
5 minute repeater, gold, 46-52mm, OF	6,000	6,500	7,000
HC	7,500	8,500	9,000
Minute repeater, gold, 46-52mm, OF	10,000	11,000	12,000
HC	15,000	18,000	20,000
OF, w/ chrono.	12,000	13,000	14,000
HC, w/ chrono.	16,000	18,000	22,000
OF, w/split chrono.	18,000	20,000	22,000
HC, w/split chrono.	20,000	25,000	30,000
Detent chronometer, gold, 48-52mm, OF	10,000	12,000	15,000
Perpetual moonphase calendar, gold, OF	20,000	25,000	30,000
HC	25,000	30,000	35,000
Perp. moonphase cal. w/min. repeater, OF	45,000	55,000	65,000
HC	55,000	60,000	70,000

478

EDWARD KOEHN

Swiss

Koehn was an innovative watchmaker and a specialist in the design of thin calibre watches. Formerly associated with Patek Phillipe and H. R. Ekegren, he produced watches under his own name from 1891-1930.

TYPE – DESCRIPTION	Avg	Ex-Fn	Mint
Time only, gold, 40- 44mm, OF	$395	$450	$500
HC	550	650	800
Time only, gold, 45- 50mm, OF	800	900	1,000
HC	1,000	1,200	1,500
Chronograph, gold, 45-50mm, OF	1,200	1,500	1,800
HC	1,500	1,800	2,000
Split second chronograph,gold, 45-52mm, OF	1,800	2,000	2,200
HC	2,500	2,800	3,200
5 minute repeater, gold, 45-52mm, OF	3,000	3,500	4,000
HC	3,500	4,000	4,500
Minute repeater, gold, 46-52mm, OF	3,000	3,500	3,800
HC	3,500	4,000	4,500
OF, w/split chrono.	4,500	5,000	5,500
HC, w/split chrono.	6,500	7,000	7,500

E. Koehn, of Geneve, 46mm, 18 jewels, note: **free standing barrel,** lever escapement, Ca. 1900.

🕐 Note: Some models and grades are not included. Their values can be determined by comparing with similar age, size, metal content, style, models and grades listed.

🕐 Watches listed in this book are priced at the collectable fair market **value** at the retail level, as complete watches having an original case, an original white enamel dial, and with the entire original movement in good working order with no repairs needed, unless otherwise noted.

COMPARISON OF WATCH SIZES

U. S. A.	EUROPEAN
10-12 SIZE	40—44 MM
16 SIZE	45—48 MM
18 SIZE	50—54 MM

A. LANGE & SOHNE
Swiss

A. Lange & Sohne was established with the aid of the German government at Glashutte, Germany in 1845. Lange typically produced 3/4 plate lever watches in gilt finish for the domestic market, and in nickel for the export market. High grade and very practical, these watches had a banking system for the pallet that was later used briefly by E. Howard in America. Lange complicated watches are scarce and very desirable.

PRODUCTION TOTALS

DATE– SERIAL #	DATE– SERIAL #	DATE– SERIAL #
1870— 5,000	1895— 35,000	1920— 75,000
1875— 10,000	1900— 40,000	1925— 80,000
1880— 20,000	1905— 50,000	1930— 85,000
1885— 25,000	1910— 60,000	1935— 90,000
1890— 30,000	1915— 70,000	1940—100,000

TYPE – DESCRIPTION	Avg	Ex-Fn	Mint
Time only, **A.L.S.** first. quality , GJS, **18k gold**, 45- 52mm, OF	$2,200	$2,500	$3,000
HC	3,000	3,500	4,000
Time only, **D.U.F.** grade, pressed jewels, **14k gold**, 45- 52mm, OF	1,000	1,500	2,000
HC	2,000	2,500	3,000
World War II model, wind indicator, 52mm, OF	1,500	1,800	2,200
Chronograph, gold, 45-50mm, OF	4,000	4,500	5,000
HC	5,000	5,500	6,000
Split second chronograph, gold, 45-52mm, OF.........	10,000	12,000	15,000
HC	12,000	15,000	18,000
1/4 hr. repeater, gold, 45-52mm, OF.........	8,000	9,000	10,000
HC	10,000	12,000	15,000
Minute repeater, gold, 45-52mm, OF.........	10,000	12,000	15,000
HC	15,000	18,000	20,000
OF, w/split chrono.	15,000	18,000	20,000
HC, w/split chrono.........	20,000	25,000	30,000
Detent chronometer, gold, 48-52mm, OF.........	30,000	35,000	40,000
Perpetual moonphase calendar, gold, OF.........	30,000	35,000	40,000
Perp. moonphase cal. w/min. repeater, OF	45,000	55,000	65,000
Perp. moonphase cal. w/min. rep. and chrono., HC	65,000	75,000	85,000

A. LANGE & SOHNE, 52mm, serial number 87250, hunting case, Ca. 1926. The A.L.S. top grade watches had gold jewel settings which are screwed to the plates, diamond end stone, gold lever, Adj. to 5 positions, a second A.L.S. grade the gold settings are not screwed into plates, and most had no diamond end stone, both A.L.S. grades are in 18K cases.

D. U. F. grade by Lange, 50mm, 3/4 plate, engraved on movement "Deutsche Uhren Fabrikation Glashutte," serial number 58,398. The D. U. F. grade had pressed jewels, brass & nickel balance, adjusted to 3 positions, the D.U.F. grades came in 14K cases and introduced in about 1895 with lower production cost to compete other Companies,

LE COULTRE & CO.
Swiss

Le Coultre and Co. was founded by Antoine Le Coultre in 1833. A fine clock maker, he created a machine to cut pinions from solid steel as well as other machines for manufacturing clocks and watches. By 1900 they were making flat or thin watches. They made parts for Patek Philippe & Co., Tissot, Vacheron & Constantin, Omega, Paul Ditisheim, Agassiz, Longines and others.

TYPE – DESCRIPTION	Avg	Ex-Fn	Mint
Early, KW, Time only, Swiss bar, Pre. 1870, silver case	$125	$150	$225
Time only, gold, 40- 44mm, OF	300	400	500
HC	450	550	650
Time only, gold, 45- 50mm, OF	400	500	600
HC	600	750	900
8 day, 15J, wind indicator, 45mm, 18K, OF	1,000	1,250	1,500
8 day, 14K, OF	700	900	1,200
8 day, S.S., OF	350	450	650
Roulette wheel style bezel, gold, 40mm, OF	800	1,000	1,500
World time watch, gold, 48-52mm, OF	12,000	15,000	17,000
Chronograph, gold, 45-50mm, OF	900	1,200	1,500
HC	1,200	1,500	1,800
OF, w/register	1,000	1,400	1,650
Split second chronograph, gold, 45-52mm, OF	2,000	2,200	2,400
HC	2,500	2,700	3,000

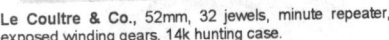

Le Coultre & Co., 52mm, 32 jewels, minute repeater, exposed winding gears, 14k hunting case.

Le Coultre & Co., runs on one winding for **8 DAYS**, wind-indcator at 6 0'clock, 45mm, OF, Ca. 1930.

TYPE – DESCRIPTION	Avg	Ex-Fn	Mint
1/4 hr. repeater, gold, 46-52mm, OF	$1,500	$1,800	$2,000
HC w/chrono., cal. & moonphase	3,000	3,500	4,000
Minute repeater, gold, 46-52mm, OF	2,700	2,900	3,200
HC	3,200	3,400	3,600
OF, w/chrono. & register	3,200	3,400	3,600
HC, w/chrono. & register	3,500	3,800	4,000
HC, w/split chrono.	9,000	10,000	12,000
HC w/chrono., cal. & moonphase	10,000	12,000	15,000
Perpetual moonphase calendar, gold, OF	8,000	9,000	10,000
HC	9,000	10,000	12,000
Perp. moonphase cal. w/min. repeater, OF	15,000	18,000	20,000
HC	18,000	20,000	22,000
Perpetual moonphase cal. w/ min. rep. & chrono., OF	18,000	20,000	22,000
HC	22,000	25,000	30,000

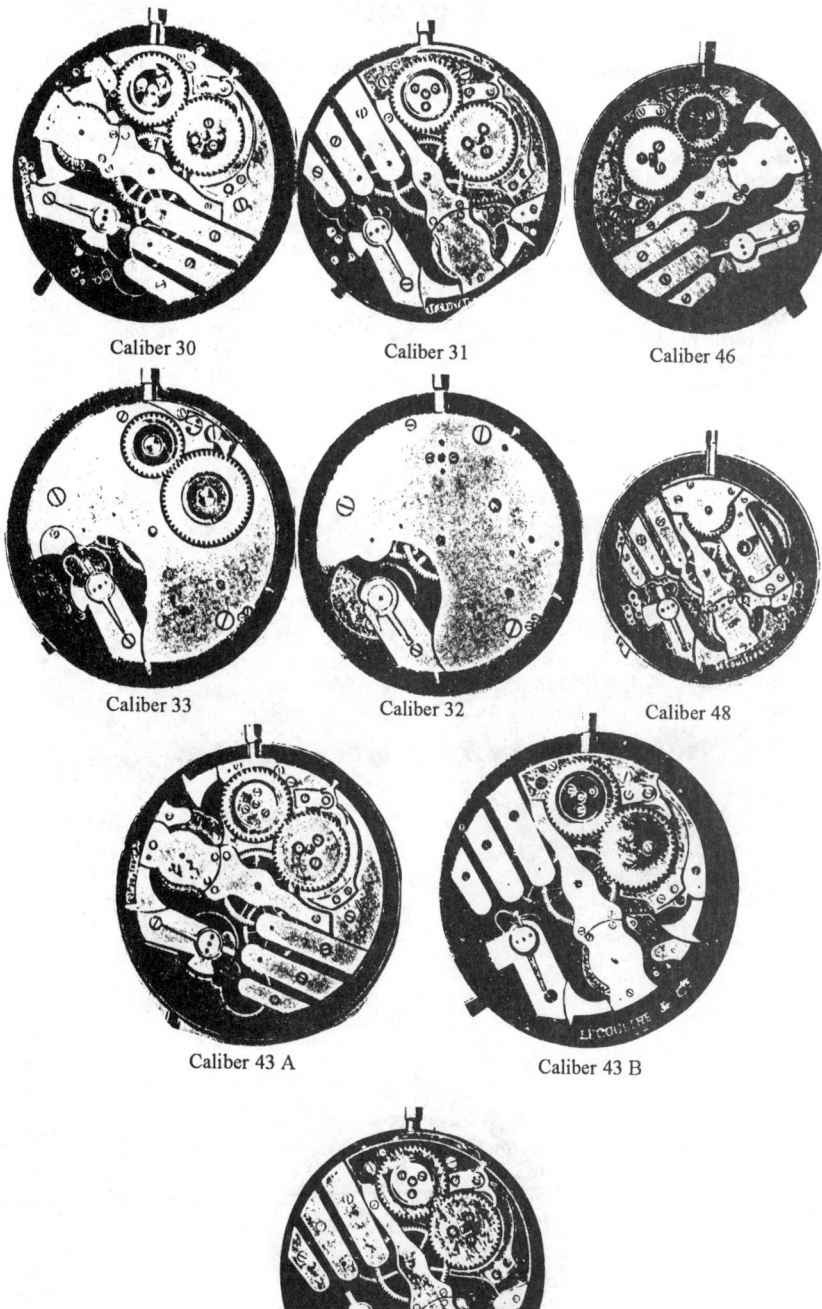

Caliber 30

Caliber 31

Caliber 46

Caliber 33

Caliber 32

Caliber 48

Caliber 43 A

Caliber 43 B

Caliber 49

LE PHARE

Swiss

Le Phare specialized in the production of repeater ebauches from 1880-1940.

TYPE – DESCRIPTION	Avg	Ex-Fn	Mint
Chronograph, gold, 45-50mm, OF	$650	$800	$1,000
HC	750	900	1,100
Split second chronograph, gold, 45-52mm, OF	1,200	1,400	1,600
HC	1,400	1,600	1,800
1/4 hr. repeater, gold, 46-52mm, OF	1,200	1,400	1,500
HC	1,400	1,600	1,800
HC w/chrono., cal. & moonphase	2,500	3,000	3,500
Minute repeater, gold, 46-56mm, OF	1,800	2,000	2,200
HC	2,000	2,200	2,400
OF w/chrono. & register	2,000	2,200	2,400
HC w/chrono.	2,200	2,400	2,600
HC w/chrono., cal. & moonphase	3,500	4,000	4,500

Le Phare, 56mm, minute repeater, chronograph and calendar with moon phases, Note the governor at 6 O'clock..

Le Phare, 57mm, 1/4 repeater, chronograph , Ca. 1905.

Le Phare, Minute repeater, gold, 54mm, HC, 17 jewels, 3/4 plate, push button , Ca. 1895, Note the governor at 6 O'clock.

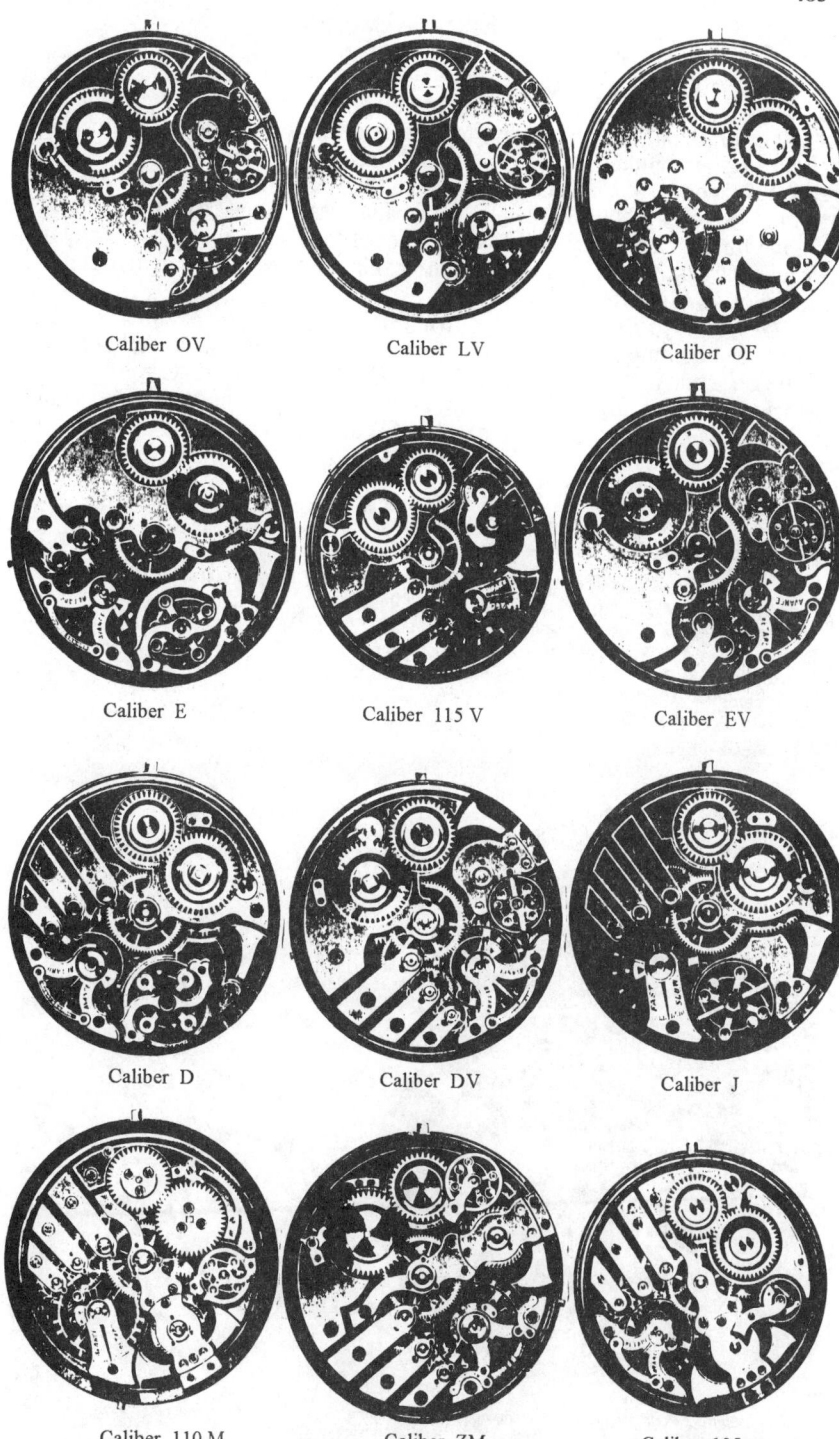

Caliber OV   Caliber LV   Caliber OF

Caliber E   Caliber 115 V   Caliber EV

Caliber D   Caliber DV   Caliber J

Caliber 110 M   Caliber ZM   Caliber 105

L'Epine or Lepine
Paris France (1720 - 1814)

Jean-Antoine L'Epine more than any other one man, revolutionized the **form** of the watch. He developed and first used the following list of improvements in 1770 to 1790, bar bridges, suspended use of the fusee, free-standing barrel, new style virgule, cylinder and lever escapements, stylized arabic numbers, center seconds, moon style hands, wolf's teeth gearing, gongs for repeaters, much thinner watches about 12-13mm, concealed case hinge, cuvette dust cover, engine turned cases, back wind & back set of the hands, pump wind, and open faced style case which is called L'Epine calibre by the Swiss watch makers. The House of Le Pine was sold in 1914.

George Washington was the owner of a L'Epine *Gold Watch*. Governor Morris was commissioned to acquire for his friend, the President, a reliable watch while on a business trip to Paris, France. On April 23, 1789, Governor Morris selected a Le Pine large gold watch with Virgule escapement as the best. Thomas Jefferson was asked to deliver the watch due to the fact the Governor had a delay in Paris. The watch is on exhibit in the Museum of the Historical Society of Pennsylvania, Pittsburgh, Pa.

TYPE – DESCRIPTION	Avg	Ex-Fn	Mint
Time only, **Silver,** KW, verge or cylinder escap., 46-52mm OF	$600	$800	$1,200
Time only, **Silver,** KW, virgule escap., 46-52mm OF	1,000	1,500	2,500
Time only, **Gold,** KW, verge or cylinder escap, , plain, 50mm, OF	1,500	1,800	2,500
Time only, **Gold,** KW, virgule escap., enamel & scene, 50mm, OF	2,000	2,500	3,500
Time only, **Gold,** KW, **"lever"** escap, , plain, 50mm, OF .... ★ ★	2,500	3,500	5,000
1/4 repeater, **SILVER,** 52mm, OF...	2,250	2,750	3,750
1/4 repeater, **GOLD,** 54mm, OF	3,500	4,500	5,500

Signed *L'Epine a Paris*, virgule escapement, open face, standing barrel, note hinged cuvette, key wind key set from back, 50mm, Ca. 1790-95.

Lepine, virgule escapement, note horse-shoe shaped centerbridge for center seconds, Ca. 1790-95.

LE ROY ET CIE
Paris

Le Roy et Cie was the final product of a dynasty of great watchmakers, starting with Julien Le Roy and his son Pierre, whose credits are numerous in the development of horology in the 18th century. There is, however, much confusion and hoopla over "Le Roy" watches. Frequently, you will see watches signed "Le Roy" that have nothing to do with the original family. These watches are unimportant. You have to distinguish between the works of Julien, of Pierre, of Charles, and of their contemporary namesakes. The modern firm, Le Roy et Cie., established in the late 19th century, contracted and finished some very fine and, in some cases, extremely important complicated watches, using imported Swiss ebauches.

TYPE – DESCRIPTION	Avg	Ex-Fn	Mint
Verge, KW, paircase, silver, 49-50mm, C. 1775	$325	$400	$500
Verge, fusee, Enamel w/scene, 18K, 38- 40mm, C. 1760	2,000	2,500	3,000
Miniature, 22mm, diamonds & pearls on enamel, OF	1,000	1,200	1,500
Time only, gold, 45- 50mm, OF	800	900	1,000
1/4 hr. repeater, gold, 46-52mm, OF	1,800	2,200	2,600
Min. repeater, two train, tandem winding wheels, fully jeweled jump center seconds, gold, 50mm	8,000	9,000	10,500

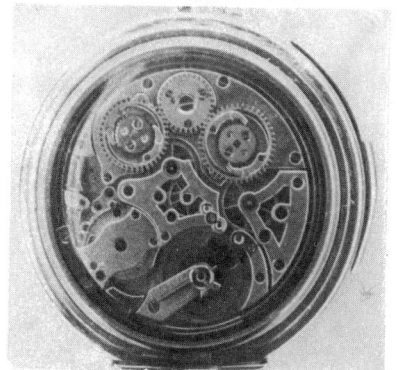

Le Roy, 50mm, minute repeater, two train, tandem winding wheels, jump center seconds.

Le Roy, 22mm, miniature watch with enamel, pearls, with a Diamond on the pin, 18K, OF, Ca. 1910.

🕐 This book endeavours to be a GUIDE or helpful manual and offers a wealth of material to be used as a tool not as a absolute document. Price Guides are like watches the worst may be better than none at all, but at best cannot be expected to be 100% accurate.

🕐 Characteristics of watches differ for the same age of both case and movement, because these features vary it may not be accurate to date a watch by one single influence. Example: the second hand was _not_ commonly found on watches before 1750, but common about 1800. The first second hand appeared in 1665 and another in 1690. Therefore statements are broad rather than accurate.

LONGINES
Swiss

The beautiful Fabrique des Longines is situated in St. Imier, Switzerland. The company was founded by Ernest Francillon in 1866. They manufacture all grades of watches.

PRODUCTION TOTALS
LONGINES DATE OF MOVEMENT MANUFACTURE

DATE– SERIAL #	DATE– SERIAL #	DATE– SERIAL #
1867 — 1	1911 - 2,500,000	1937 - 5,500,000
1870 — 20,000	1912 - 2,750,000	1938 - 5,750,000
1875 — 100,000	1913 - 3,000,000	1940 - 6,000,000
1882 — 250,000	1915 - 3,250,000	1945 - 7,000,000
1888 — 500,000	1917 - 3,500,000	1950 - 8,000,000
1893 — 750,000	1919 - 3,750,000	1953 - 9,000,000
1899 - 1,000,000	1922 - 4,000,000	1956-10,000,000
1901 - 1,250,000	1925 - 4,250,000	1959-11,000,000
1904 - 1,500,000	1926 - 4,500,000	1962-12,000,000
1905 - 1,750,000	1928 - 4,750,000	1966-13,000,000
1907 - 2,000,000	1929 - 5,000,000	1967-14,000,000
1909 - 2,250,000	1934 - 5,250,000	1969-15,000,000

The above list is provided for determining the APPROXIMATE age of your watch. Match serial number with date. Watches were not necessarily sold in the exact order of manufactured date.

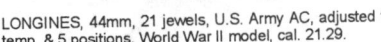

LONGINES, 44mm, 21 jewels, U.S. Army AC, adjusted to temp. & 5 positions, World War II model, cal. 21.29.

LONGINES, 59mm, 21 jewels, Railroad Model , gold filled open face case, Ca. 1910-1925.

TYPE – DESCRIPTION	Avg	Ex-Fn	Mint
15 -17J, GF, 40- 50mm, OF, C. 1930	$55	$65	$85
21J, GF, 40- 50mm, OF, C. 1930	135	165	195
15 -17J, silver, 48- 50mm, HC, C. 1890	100	125	165
15-17J, for Tiffany, Sterling, 45- 50mm OF, C. 1905	135	165	195
KW, for Turkish market, .800 silver, HC, C. 1900	125	150	175
21J, RR "Express Monarch", LS, GF, 48- 50mm, OF, C.1910-20 ..	200	225	265
24J,RR "Express Monarch", LS, GF, 48- 50mm, OF, C.1910-20 ..	250	300	350
21J, Trans-Continental Express, LS, GF, 48- 50mm, OF, C.1910-20	200	225	265
23J, Trans-Continental Express, LS, GF, 48- 50mm, OF, C.1910-20	225	250	295
17J, Rail Road Leader, Adj., LS, GF, 48- 50mm, OF, C.1910-20...	125	150	195
U.S. Army AC, World War II, 21J., silver, 44mm, **WI.**, OF	600	700	850
U.S. Army, World War II, 17-21J., silver, 44mm, OF	350	425	525
Time only, gold, 40- 44mm, OF	250	325	425
HC	350	400	475
Time only, gold, 45- 48mm, OF	300	400	500
HC	450	600	750

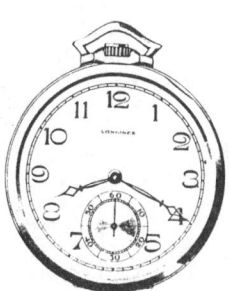

Longines, 21J, Gold Filled, 40- 50mm, OF, C. 1930.

Longines, 46mm, Min. repeater, 24 jewels, 3/4 plate design, open face, Ca. 1915.

TYPE – DESCRIPTION	Avg	Ex-Fn	Mint
World time watch, gold, 48-52mm, OF	$8,000	$9,000	$10,000
Chronograph w/register, silver, OF, 48- 50mm, C. 1905	250	300	400
Chronograph, gold, 45-50mm, OF	500	600	700
HC	700	800	900
Split second chronograph, gold, 45-52mm, OF	1,000	1,200	1,400
HC	1,200	1,500	1,800
Chronograph, Lugrin's Pat., fly back, silver OF case	375	400	475
1/4 hr. repeater, gold, 46-52mm, OF	1,200	1,500	1,800
HC	1,500	1,800	2,000
HC w/chrono., cal. & moonphase	4,000	5,000	6,000
Minute repeater, gold, 46-52mm, OF	2,000	2,200	2,500
HC	2,500	2,800	3,000
OF w/chrono.	2,200	2,500	2,700
HC w/chrono.	3,000	3,500	3,750
OF w/split chrono.	3,500	4,000	4,500
HC w/split chrono.	6,500	7,000	7,500
HC w/cal. & moon- phase	9,000	10,000	12,000
Perpetual moonphase calendar, gold, OF	6,000	8,000	10,000
Perp. moonphase cal. w/min.repeater & chrono., OF	15,000	18,000	20,000
HC	18,000	20,000	22,000

Longines , Chronograph, H.A. Lugrin's Pat. June 13, Oct 3, 1876, Start, Stop, Fly Back.

Longines, 50mm Chronograph, Minute repeater, 18K hunting case, Ca. 1930.

MARKWICK, MARKHAM
LONDON (1725-1825)

He enjoyed selling clocks and watches to the Turkish Market. Watches can be found with his name & that of another maker added, Example: Markwick, Markham "Perigal", or "Recordon". Also watches with the names "Story" Ca.1780, "Borrel" Ca.1813 and "Perigal" Ca.1825 are known.

TYPE – DESCRIPTION	Avg	Ex-Fn	Mint
VERGE, pair case, silver plain, 50mm, OF	$425	$450	$495
VERGE, pair case, silver w/ **repousee**, 50mm, OF	800	1,000	1,200
VERGE, triple cased, **Tortoise shell** on outer case, 56mm, OF	1,200	1,500	2,000
VERGE, GOLD, 48-52mm, OF	1,000	1,200	1,400
VERGE, GOLD, W/ **repousee pair case,** 46-50mm, OF	2,000	2,500	3,000
1/4 hr. repeater, SILVER, 54mm, OF	1,500	2,000	2,500
1/4 hr. repeater, GOLD, 54mm, OF	2,500	3,000	3,500

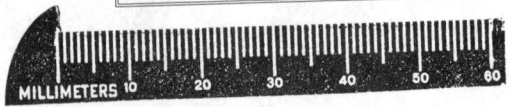

Markwick, Markham, Triple cased , 18K gold cases, Painted enamel on first & second case, made for Turkish Market, Ca. 1800.

COMPARISON OF WATCH SIZES

U. S. A.	EUROPEAN
10-12 SIZE	40—44 MM
16 SIZE	45—48 MM
18 SIZE	50—52 MM

MILLIMETERS 10   20   30   40   50   60

MATHEY – TISSOT

Swiss

TYPE – DESCRIPTION	Avg	Ex-Fn	Mint
Early, KW, Time only, Swiss bar, Pre 1870, silver	$125	$150	$185
Time only, gold, 40- 44mm, OF	285	350	425
HC	425	500	585
Time only, gold, 45- 50mm, OF	435	500	600
HC	600	750	900
1/4 hr. repeater, gold, 46-52mm, OF	1,200	1,400	1,600
HC	1,500	1,800	2,000
OF w/chrono., cal. & moonphase	2,000	2,200	2,400
HC w/chrono., cal. & moonphase	2,500	3,500	4,500

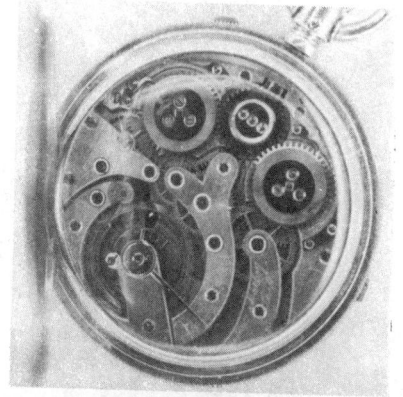

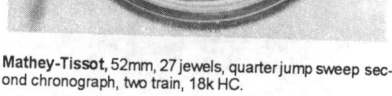

Mathey-Tissot, 52mm, 27 jewels, quarter jump sweep second chronograph, two train, 18k HC.

Mathey-Tissot, min. repeater with chronograph, day date month & moon phases, HC.

TYPE – DESCRIPTION	Avg	Ex-Fn	Mint
Minute repeater, gold, 46-52mm, OF	$2,400	$2,600	$2,800
HC	3,000	3,500	4,000
OF w/chrono. & register	3,000	3,500	4,000
HC w/chrono. & register	3,500	4,000	4,500
HC w/chrono. & moon ph,. day date month,	8,000	9,000	10,000
OF w/split chrono.	6,000	7,000	7,500
HC w/split chrono.	8,000	9,000	10,000
OF w/cal. & moonphase	7,000	8,000	9,000
HC w/cal. & moonphase	9,000	10,000	12,000
World time watch, gold, 48-52mm, OF	12,000	15,000	18,000
Perpetual moonphase calendar, gold, OF	8,000	10,000	12,000
Perp. moonphase cal. w/min. repeater, OF	20,000	25,000	30,000
HC	25,000	30,000	35,000
Perp. moonphase cal. w/min. rep. and chrono., OF	22,000	27,000	32,000
HC	27,000	32,000	37,000

🕐 Note: Some models and grades are not included. Their values can be determined by comparing with **similar** age, size, metal content, style, models and grades listed.

MEYLAN WATCH CO.

Swiss

Meylan Watch Co., founded by C.H. Meylan in 1880, manufactured fine watches, with complications, in Le Brassus, Switzerland.

TYPE – DESCRIPTION	Avg	Ex-Fn	Mint
Time only, gold, 40- 44mm, OF	$395	$435	$500
HC	600	675	750
Time only, gold, 40- 44mm, 18K case & **enamel on bezel**, OF	1,500	1,800	2,200
Time only, gold, 45- 50mm, OF	525	600	700
HC	850	950	1,100
Chronograph, gold, 45-50mm, OF	725	800	900
HC	900	1,000	1,200
Split second chronograph, gold, 45-52mm, OF	1,200	1,400	1,600
HC	1,800	2,000	2,200
1/4 hr. repeater, gold, 46-52mm, OF	1,500	1,800	2,000
HC	2,000	2,200	2,400
HC w/chrono., cal. & moonphase	3,000	3,500	4,000

C. H. Meylan, 42mm, 21 jewels, straight line lever escapement, 18K case with enamel on bezel.

C. H. Meylan, Minute Repeater, split second Chronograph, minute register, 18K gold OF case, Ca. 1895

TYPE – DESCRIPTION	Avg	Ex-Fn	Mint
5 minute repeater, gold, 46-52mm, OF	$2,500	$2,700	$3,000
HC	2,750	3,000	3,250
Minute repeater, gold, OF	3,000	3,200	3,500
HC	4,000	4,500	5,000
OF w/chrono.	3,500	4,000	4,200
HC w/chrono.	4,500	5,000	5,500
OF w/split chrono.	5,000	5,500	6,000
HC w/split chrono.	8,000	9,000	10,000
OF w/cal. & moonphase	8,000	9,000	10,000
HC w/cal. & moonphase	12,000	14,000	15,000
HC w/chrono., cal. & moonphase	13,000	15,000	16,000
Tourbillion, gold, 48-55mm, OF	25,000	30,000	35,000
Detent chronometer, gold, 48-52mm, OF	4,000	5,000	5,500
World time watch, gold, 48-52mm, OF	8,000	9,000	10,000
Perpetual moonphase calendar, gold, OF	12,000	14,000	15,000
HC	13,000	15,000	16,000
Perp. moonphase cal. w/min. rep. and chrono., OF	20,000	22,000	24,000
HC	25,000	30,000	35,000

MORICAND, CH.

GENEVA

Firm specialized in making verge watches with cases highly decorated with stones and enameled portraits. Associates with brother Benjamin and Francois Colladon from 1752 to 1755, with a firm name of Collardon & Moricand. Later, with Jean Delisle then later in 1780 as Moricand.

Delisle & Moricand, 36MM, 1/4 hour repeater pendant activated, two-footed balance bridge, Ca.1775.

Ch. Moricand, 46mm, gilt and enamel with two ladies in a floral garden, KW KS, Ca.1800.

TYPE – DESCRIPTION	Avg	Ex-Fn	Mint
Verge, KW, paircase, **silver**, 50mm, OF	$395	$450	$500
Verge, enamel w/ portrait, **silver/ gilt**, 49-52mm, OF	1,000	1,200	1,400
Verge, KW, **gold**, 50-54mm, OF	1,000	1,250	1,500
Verge, KW, **gold** w/ enamel, 52mm, OF	2,500	3,000	3,500
1/4 hr. repeater, **silver**, 54mm, OF	1,000	1,200	1,500
1/4 hr. repeater, **gold**, 50-54mm, OF	2,000	2,500	3,000
1/4 hr. repeater, **gold** w/ enamel, 54mm, OF	5,000	5,500	6,000

C. MONTANDON

Swiss

This 19th century maker was associated with Perret & Company as well as other Le Locle and Chaux-de-Fonds factories. Montandon specialized in low cost keywind watches for the American market.

TYPE – DESCRIPTION	Avg	Ex-Fn	Mint
KW, cylinder escap., silver, 46mm, OF, C. 1870	$85	$95	$125
KW, silver, 46-48mm, HC, C. 1875	100	125	150
KW, 15J, lady's, **18K**, 40-44mm, OF, C. 1870	175	200	250
KW, 15J, lady's, **18K**, 40-44mm, HC, C. 1870	250	300	385
KW, 15J, gent's, **18K**, 48mm, OF, C. 1875	275	325	395
Chronograph, gold, 45-50mm, OF	1,000	1,200	1,400
HC	1,800	2,000	2,200
1/4 hr. repeater, gold, 46-52mm, OF	2,000	2,200	2,600
HC	2,500	3,000	3,500
Minute repeater, gold, 46-52mm, OF	2,500	3,000	3,500
OF w/cal. & moonphase	3,500	4,000	4,500
HC	3,000	3,500	4,000
HC w/cal. & moonphase	5,500	6,000	6,500
HC w/chrono., cal. & moonphase	6,000	6,500	7,000

MOVADO
Swiss

L. A. I. Ditesheim & Freres (L.A.I. the initials of the 3 Ditesheim brothers) formed their company in 1881. The name Movado ("always in motion") was adopted in 1905. The Swiss company invented a system of watch making which they called "Polyplan." This was an arrangement of three different angles to the watch movement which produced a curve effect to the case so as to fit the curvature of the arm. Another unusual watch produced by this company in 1926 was the "Ermeto." This watch was designed to be protected while inside a purse or pocket and each time the cover was opened to view the time, the watch was partially wound.

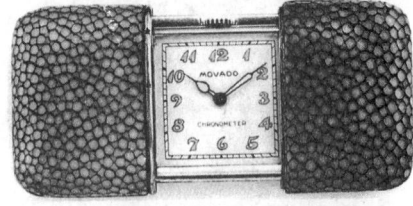

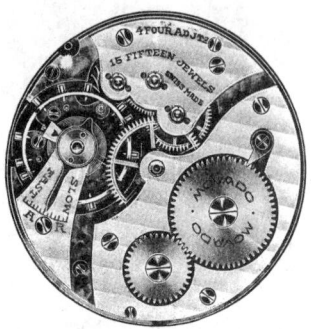

Movado, 44mm, 15J., with jewel settings, Adjusted to 4 Positions, calibre # 800M.

Top: **Movado**, Purse watch, **Sting Ray** leather, 17 jewels.
Bottom: **Movado**, Purse watch, silver case, 17 jewels.

TYPE – DESCRIPTION	Avg	Ex-Fn	Mint
SW, 17J, LS, Silver, 43mm, OF, C. 1920	$125	$150	$175
SW, 15J, LS, Silver, 47mm, HC, C. 1920	150	175	200
Time only, gold, 40-44mm, OF	225	250	325
HC	350	425	500
Time only, gold, 45-50mm, OF	425	500	600
HC	800	900	1,000
Purse watch, black leather, 50 x 33mm, C. 1930's	200	235	275
Purse watch, silver, 50 x 33mm, C. 1930's	225	250	295
Purse watch, Sting Ray leather, 50 x 33mm, C. 1930's	275	300	350
Purse watch with moonph. & calendar, 50 x 33mm, leather	1,000	1,200	1,500
Coin form, 17J, St. Christopher coin, 18K, closed case, 29mm	800	900	1,000
Chronograph, gold, 45-50mm, OF	1,500	1,800	2,000
Minute repeater, gold, 46-52mm, OF	3,500	4,000	4,500
HC	4,000	4,500	5,000
HC w/split chrono. & register	8,000	8,500	9,000

Movado, Purse watch with moonph. & calendar, auto-wind by opening & closing case, leather.

ULYSSE NARDIN
Swiss

Ulysse Nardin was born in 1823. The company he started in 1846 produced many fine timepieces and chronometers, as well as repeaters and more complicated watches. This firm, as did Assmann, found a strong market in South America as well as other countries. Ulysse's son, Paul David Nardin, succeeded him, as did Paul David's sons after him.

Ulysse Nardin, Key wind, 18 jewels, pivoted detent, bridge movement, 48mm, Ca. 1860.

Ulysse Nardin, pocket chronometer with date, 19J. pivoted detent, gold jewel settings, Ca.1890.

TYPE – DESCRIPTION

	Avg	Ex-Fn	Mint
Early KW, 18J., pivoted detent, bar style mvt., gold, HC, C.1860 ..	$3,000	$3,500	$4,000
Time only, gold, 40-44mm, OF	300	400	500
HC	450	550	650
Time only, gold, 45- 50mm, OF	600	650	700
HC	750	800	850
Chronograph, gold, 45-50mm, OF	1,200	1,300	1,400
HC	1,500	1,700	1,900
Deck chronometer w/box, detent chronometer, C. 1905	1,500	1,800	2,000
Pocket chronometer, lever escape., 21J., GJS, 18K, HC, C.1910....	1,200	1,500	1,800
Pocket chronometer, pivoted detent, with date, gold, 57mm	4,000	4,500	5,000
World time watch, gold, 48-52mm, OF	12,000	15,000	18,000
Karrusel, 52 Min. karrusel, free sprung balance, silver case	6,000	7,000	8,000

Ulysse Nardin, 53mm, 52 minute karrusel, free sprung balance, ca. 1905.

Ulysse Nardin, pocket chronometer, lever escapement, 21 jewels, gold jewel settings, Ca. 1910

TYPE – DESCRIPTION	Avg	Ex-Fn	Mint
1/4 hr. repeater, gold, 46-52mm, OF	$1,500	$2,000	$2,500
OF w/chrono., cal. moonphase	2,000	2,200	2,500
HC	1,800	2,300	2,850
HC w/chrono., cal. & moonphase	3,500	4,000	4,500
Minute repeater, gold, 46-52mm, OF	3,000	3,200	3,500
HC	4,000	4,200	4,500
OF w/split chrono.	4,500	4,800	5,500
HC w/split chrono.	7,000	8,000	9,000
OF w/cal. & moonphase	10,000	12,000	15,000
HC w/cal. & moonphase	10,000	12,000	14,000
HC w/chrono., cal. & moonphase	12,000	13,000	15,000
Perpetual moonphase calendar, gold, OF	12,000	14,000	15,000
HC	13,000	15,000	17,000
Perp. moonphase cal. w/min . repeater, OF	25,000	28,000	30,000
HC	27,000	30,000	32,000
Perp. moonphase cal. w/min. rep. and chrono. , OF	28,000	30,000	32,000
HC	30,000	32,000	35,000

NICOLE, NIELSEN & CO.
London

Adolphe Nicole in 1840 came to London from Switzerland and joined Henry Capt. In 1876 Emil Nielsen became a partner in the firm. The company was purchased by S. Smith & Sons in 1904. Tourbillons were made by V. Kullberg and Nicole, Nielsen for the England market.Last watches made Ca. 1933.

(Made ebauche for Dent, Frodsham, and Smith)

Nicole, Nielsen, 50mm, chronograph, 15 jewels, 3/4 plate, gilded movement, Ca. 1890.

Nicole, Nielsen, 64mm, min. repeater, split-second chronograph, tourbillon, free sprung escapement.

TYPE – DESCRIPTION	Avg	Ex-Fn	Mint
Time only, gold, 45- 50mm, OF	$900	$1,000	$1,200
HC	1,200	1,500	1,800
Chronograph, gold, 45-50mm, HC	2,000	2,400	2,900
Minute repeater, gold, 46-52mm, OF	2,700	3,000	3,500
HC	3,500	3,800	4,000
OF w/chrono. & register	3,850	4,250	4,750
HC w/chrono. & register	4,000	4,400	5,000

TYPE – DESCRIPTION	Avg	Ex-Fn	Mint
Minute repeater, tourbillon, split-second chronograph,			
free sprung escapement, gold, 64mm, ...$100,000	$100,000	$125,000	$150,000
Karrusel, gold, 48-55mm, OF.........................	9,000	10,000	12,000
Tourbillion, gold, 48-55mm, OF......................	25,000	30,000	35,000
Perpetual moon phase calendar, gold, OF.......................	22,000	24,000	26,000
HC	25,000	26,000	28,000
Perp. moonphase cal. w/min.rep. and chrono., OF............	35,000	38,000	40,000
HC	38,000	40,000	42,000

NON–MAGNETIC WATCH CO.
Swiss

TYPE – DESCRIPTION	Avg	Ex-Fn	Mint
Time only, gold, 45- 50mm, OF......................	$425	$500	$600
HC	635	800	1,000
Chronograph, gold, 45-50mm, OF	900	1,000	1,200
HC	1,000	1,200	1,400
Split second chronograph, gold, 45-52mm, OF............	1,100	1,200	1,500
HC	1,350	1,500	1,750
1/4 hr. repeater, gold, 46-52mm, OF....................	1,500	1,800	2,200
HC	1,800	2,000	2,400
Minute repeater, gold, 46-52mm, OF....................	2,500	2,800	3,000
HC	2,800	3,200	3,500
OF w/split chrono.	4,500	5,000	5,500
HC w/split chrono.	5,000	5,500	6,000
HC w/chrono., cal. & moonphase	8,000	9,000	10,000

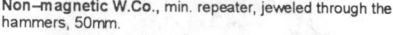

Non–magnetic W.Co., min. repeater, jeweled through the hammers, 50mm.

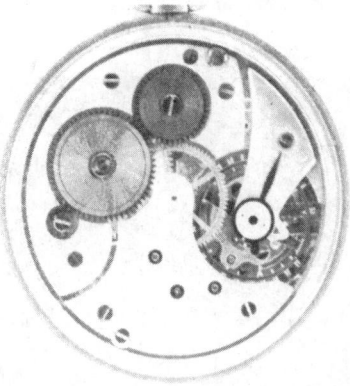

Omega pocket watch movement, 45-48mm, 15 jewels, serial number 9,888,934.

Watches listed in this book are priced at the collectable fair market **value** at the retail level, as complete watches having an original case, an original white enamel dial, and with the entire original movement in good working order with no repairs needed, unless otherwise noted.

OMEGA WATCH CO.

Swiss

Omega Watch Co. was founded by Louis Brandt in 1848. They produced watches of different grades. In 1930, they began to produce different lines with Tissot under the name Societe Sussie pour l'Industrie Horlogere. The firm has been part of the ESTH group since 1971.

PRODUCTION TOTALS

DATE– SERIAL #	DATE– SERIAL #
1895 – 50,000	1940-12,500,000
1900 – 500,000	1945-14,000,000
1905 -1,000,000	1950-15,500,000
1910 -2,500,000	1955-16,500,000
1915 -4,500,000	1960-18,000,000
1920 -6,000,000	1965-23,000,000
1925 -7,500,000	1970-28,000,000
1930 -9,500,000	1975-35,000,000
1935-11,000,000	

The above list is provided for determining the APPROXIMATE age of your watch. Match serial number with date. Watches were not necessarily sold in the exact order of manufactured date.

TYPE – DESCRIPTION	Avg	Ex-Fn	Mint
15J, gilt, silver, 48mm, OF, C. 1905	$75	$95	$125
15J, SW, silver 47mm, HC, C. 1910	100	125	150
21J, **R.R. model**, GF, 52mm, OF, C. 1915	185	225	275
Time only, gold, 45- 48mm, OF	400	500	600
HC	500	600	700
Chronograph, gold, 45-50mm, OF	900	1,000	1,100
HC	1,200	1,400	1,600
Chronograph, gold, 45-50mm, **Double-Dial**, OF	3,000	4,000	4,500
Minute repeater, gold, 46-52mm, OF	2,200	2,500	2,750
HC	2,750	3,000	3,250
OF w/split chrono.	4,200	4,700	5,000
HC w/split chrono.	4,500	5,000	5,250
HC w/chrono., cal. & moonphase	7,500	8,000	8,500

Omega, **Chronograph**, gold, 45-50mm, **Double-Dial**, open face, Multi-color enamel dials.

CHARLES OUDIN
PARIS

Oudin was a pupil of Breguet and became a talented maker from 1807-1830. He produced quality timepieces and invented an early "keyless" watch.

Charles Oudin, Dial & Movement, 51mm, 32J., Minute repeater with Chronograph, Ca.1910.

TYPE – DESCRIPTION	Avg	Ex-Fn	Mint
Verge, KW, silver single case, 45mm, OF, C. 1865	$325	$400	$500
Early, KW, Time only, Swiss bar, silver , OF	85	95	125
GOLD, OF	400	500	700
Split sec. chrono., 29J, w/ register,18K, 51mm, HC, C. 1900	1,800	2,000	2,500
Minute repeater, gold, 46-52mm, OF	3,000	3,500	3,700
HC	3,500	3,750	4,000
OF w/chrono. & register	4,000	4,250	4,500
HC w/chrono. & register	4,700	4,900	5,000

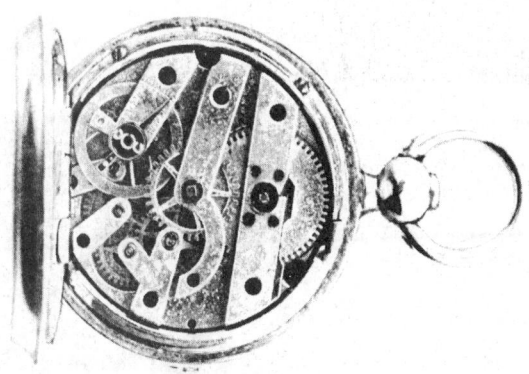

"CHs. OUDIN, Paris," engraved on movement, Key Wind, cylinder escapement, Swiss bar, Ca. 1865.

PATEK, PHILIPPE & CIE.
Swiss

Patek, Philippe & Cie. has produced some of the world's most desirable factory-made watches. Antoine Norbert de Patek began contracting and selling watches in the 1830's, later became partners with Francois Czapek and generally produced lovely decorative watches for a high class of clientele. In 1845 Adrien Philippe, inventor of the modern stem-winding system, joined the firm of Patek & Cie., and in 1851, the firm established its present name. Between Philippe's talent as a watchmaker and Patek's talent as a businessman with a taste for the impeccable, the firm rapidly established an international reputation which lasts to this day. Early Patek, Philippe & Cie. watches are generally signed only on the dust cover, but some are signed on the dial and cuvette. It was not until the 1880's that the practice began of fully signing the dial, movement and case-perhaps in response to some contemporary forgery but more likely a necessity to conform to customs' regulations for their growing international market. Many early and totally original Patek watches have suffered from the misconception that all products of the company are fully signed. Never the less, collectors find such pieces more desirable. It requires more experience, however, to determine the originality of the earlier pieces. As with Vacheron & Constantin, some watches were originally cased in U.S.A., but this lowers their value in general.

PRODUCTION TOTALS

DATE—SERIAL #	DATE—SERIAL #	DATE—SERIAL #
1840--- 100	1950---700,000	1940--- 900,000
1845--- 1,200	1955---725,000	1945--- 915,000
1850--- 3,000	1960---750,000	1950--- 930,000
1855--- 8,000	1965---775,000	1955--- 940,000
1860--- 15,000	1970---795,000	1960--- 960,000
1865--- 22,000		1965--- 975,000
1870--- 35,000		1970--- 995,000
1875--- 45,000	DATE—SERIAL #	
1880--- 55,000	1920--- 800,000	
1885--- 70,000	1925--- 805,000	DATE—SERIAL #
1890--- 85,000	1930--- 820,000	1960---1,100,000
1895---100,000	1935--- 824,000	1965---1,130,000
1900---110,000	1940--- 835,000	1970---1,250,000
1905---125,000	1945--- 850,000	1975---1,350,000
1910---150,000	1950--- 860,000	1980---1,450,000
1915---175,000	1955--- 870,000	1985---1,600,000
1920---190,000	1960--- 880,000	1990---1,850,000
1925---200,000	1965--- 890,000	
	1970--- 895,000	

The above list is provided for determining the APPROXIMATE age of your watch. Match serial number with date. Watches were not necessarily sold in the exact order of manufactured date.

NOTE: Watches signed *PATEK & CIE.* usually have serial numbers from about 1,129 to 3,729, Ca. 1845 to 1850. Usually signed on cuvette with serial number & Patek & Cie. and not on the movement. *"Patek et Czapek"* found signed on cuvette for earlier watches.

1854 Tiffany & Co. became a official customer of the Patek firm.

Patek, Philippe & Cie. 43mm, time only, 18K, open face.

Patek, Philippe & Cie., 18 jewels, engraved gold dial with enamel center, 18K, 43mm, Ca. 1920's.

Patek, Philippe & Cie. , KWKS, lever escapement, gilt movement, signed on 18K case, 47mm, Ca. 1865.

Patek, Philippe & Co., Perpetual calendar, moonphase, min. repeater & split second chronograph, 18K, OF.

Patek, Philippe & Co., "Chronometro Gondolo", 19 jewels, signed, lever escapement, 51mm, Ca. 1908.

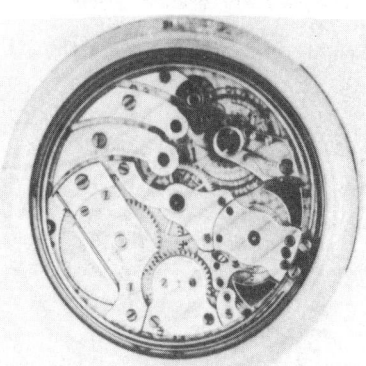

Patek, Philippe & Co., dial & movement, min. repeater, 29J, perpetual calendar, day, date, month, moon-phases, 18K.

TYPE – DESCRIPTION	Avg	Ex-Fn	Mint
Time only, gold, 25- 30mm, ladies, OF	$800	$900	$1,100
HC	1,000	1,500	1,800
Time only, gold, 32- 44mm, OF	1,800	2,000	2,500
HC	2,500	3,000	3,500
Time only, **enameled bezel,** gold, 32- 44mm, OF	2,000	2,500	3,200
Time only, gold, 45- 50mm, OF	2,000	2,200	2,500
HC	3,000	3,200	3,500
EARLY Time only, KWKS, gilt mvt., lever or cylinder escapement pre 1865, signed on gold case, 40-45mm,	1,500	1,800	2,000
Time only, Chronometre Gondolo, gold, 38mm, OF	2,000	2,500	3,000
Time only, Chronometre Gondolo, gold, 50mm, OF	2,500	3,000	3,500

Patek, Philippe & Co., enameled bezel, 18K OF, 42mm

Patek, Philippe & Co., perpetual calendar with moon phases, signed, 18 jewels, 49mm, Ca. 1949

TYPE – DESCRIPTION	Avg	Ex-Fn	Mint
Chronograph, gold, 45-50mm, OF	$3,500	$4,000	$4,500
HC	5,000	5,250	5,500
OF w/register	4,000	4,250	4,750
HC w/register	5,500	5,750	6,000
Split second chronograph, gold, 45-52mm, OF	7,000	7,500	8,000
HC	9,000	9,500	10,000
OF w/register	7,500	8,000	8,500
HC w/register	9,500	10,000	11,000
1/4 hr. repeater, gold, 46-52mm, OF	4,500	4,750	5,000
HC	5,500	6,000	6,500
5 minute repeater, gold, 46-52mm, OF	6,000	6,500	7,000
HC	8,500	9,500	10,000
OF w/split chrono.	12,000	14,000	16,000
HC w/split chrono.	15,000	18,000	20,000
Minute repeater, gold, 46-52mm, OF	9,000	10,000	11,000
HC	12,000	15,000	18,000
OF w/chrono.	14,000	16,000	18,000
HC w/chrono.	18,000	20,000	22,000
OF w/chrono. & register	15,000	18,000	20,000
HC w/chrono. & register	20,000	22,000	24,000

TYPE – DESCRIPTION

	Avg	Ex-Fn	Mint
Minute repeater, w/split chrono., gold, 46-52mm, OF	$15,000	$18,000	$20,000
HC w/split chrono.	20,000	22,000	24,000
OF w/split chrono. & register	18,000	20,000	23,000
HC w/split chrono. & register	25,000	30,000	32,000
OF w/cal. & moonphase	20,000	25,000	30,000
HC w/cal. & moon phase	25,000	30,000	35,000
OF w/chrono., cal. & moonphase	22,000	27,000	32,000
HC w/chrono., cal. & moonphase	30,000	35,000	40,000
Perpetual moonphase calendar, gold, OF	35,000	40,000	45,000
HC	45,000	50,000	55,000
Perp. moonphase cal. w/min. repeater, OF	60,000	65,000	70,000
HC	70,000	75,000	80,000
Perpetual moonphase cal. w/ min. rep. & chrono. , OF	80,000	85,000	90,000
HC	90,000	95,000	100,000
Perpetual moonphase cal. w/ min. rep. & split sec. chrono. , OF	100,000	110,000	125,000
HC	150,000	175,000	200,000

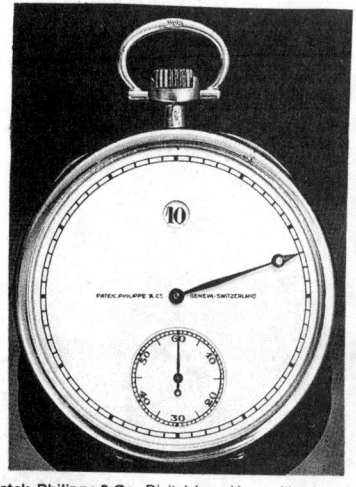

Patek, Philippe & Co., Digital Jump Hour, with minute hand & second hand, 18 jewels, 45mm, 18K.

Patek, Philippe & Co., gold coin watch, 100 pesetas, secret push-piece opens lid to disclose dial, 35mm, Ca.1928.

TYPE – DESCRIPTION

	Avg	Ex-Fn	Mint
Lady's pendant watch w/ brooch,18K & small diamonds, 27mm	$2,400	$2,800	$3,300
Gold Coin, 100 pesetas 18K, 18J., coin opens to disclose dial	4,000	4,500	5,000
Digital Jump Hour, W/minute hand & sec. hand, 45mm, 18K	30,000	40,000	50,000
Karrusel, gold, 48-55mm, OF	90,000	95,000	100,000
Tourbillion, gold, 48-55mm, OF	125,000	130,000	135,000
HC	140,000	145,000	150,000
Detent chronometer, gold, 48-52mm, OF	65,000	70,000	75,000
HC	75,000	80,000	85,000
World time watch, gold, 48-52mm, OF	90,000	95,000	100,000

COMPARISON OF WATCH SIZES

U. S. A.	EUROPEAN
10-12 SIZE	40—44 MM
16 SIZE	45—48 MM
18 SIZE	50—54 MM

PICARD, JAMES
GENEVA

Watch dealer and finisher in the latter part of the 19th Century. Known for his complicated watches and pocket chronometers of high quality.

TYPE – DESCRIPTION	Avg	Ex-Fn	Mint
Time only, gold, 45- 50mm, OF	$500	$600	$700
HC	650	750	850
Chronograph, gold, 45-50mm, OF	800	850	900
Split second chronograph, gold, 45-52mm, OF	1,800	2,000	2,200
HC w/register	2,850	3,250	3,500
5 minute repeater, gold, 45-52mm, OF	3,250	3,500	3,750
HC	3,500	3,750	4,000
Minute repeater, gold, 45-52mm, OF	3,500	3,750	4,000
HC	3,750	4,000	4,250
OF w/split chrono.	5,000	5,500	6,000
HC w/split chrono.	7,500	8,000	8,500
OF w/cal. & moonphase	9,000	9,500	10,000
HC w/chrono., cal. & moonphase	10,000	12,000	14,000
Tourbillion, gold, 48-55mm, OF	30,000	35,000	40,000
Detent chronometer, gold, 48-52mm , OF	4,000	5,000	6,000
HC	5,500	6,500	7,500
Perp. moonphase cal. w/min.rep. and chrono, OF	20,000	25,000	30,000
HC	30,000	35,000	40,000

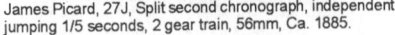

James Picard, 27J, Split second chronograph, independent jumping 1/5 seconds, 2 gear train, 56mm, Ca. 1885.

Albert Potter, 22 jewels, hunting case, helical hair spring, detent escapement.

ALBERT H. POTTER & CO.
(Note: For further information on Potter timepieces, see U.S. Watch Section.)

TYPE – DESCRIPTION	Avg	Ex-Fn	Mint
Time only, gold, 45- 48mm, OF	$4,000	$5,000	$6,000
HC	5,000	6,000	7,000
Pocket chronometer, pivoted detent ,free-spring balance, porcelain dial, bridge mvt., re-cased (silver), 58mm, C.1879.	5,500	6,500	7,500
Calendar, nickel, offset seconds and days of week dials, SW, 18K, 50mm, OF, C.1800	8,000	9,000	10,000
Rare lever, SW, 19J, nickel mvt., 1/2 moon-shaped plate for barrel & train, white enamel dial, triple signed, lever with counterpoise on pallet,18k, 52mm, HC, C.1882	100,000	120,000	140,000

TYPE – DESCRIPTION	Avg	Ex-Fn	Mint
Regulator dial (center minute hand, offset hours, offset seconds),			
half moon- shaped nickel mvt., 18K, 50mm, OF, C.1880	$18,000	$23,000	$30,000
Minute repeater, gold, 46-52mm, OF	15,000	18,000	20,000
HC	20,000	22,000	25,000
Detent chronometer, gold, 48-52mm, OF	15,000	18,000	20,000
HC	18,000	20,000	22,000
Perp. moonphase cal. w/min. repeater, HC	28,000	35,000	40,000
Perp. moonphase cal. w/min. rep. & chrono.,HC	32,000	35,000	38,000

PRIOR, GEORGE
PRIOR, EDWARD
LONDON

George Prior born in 1793 and died in 1830. He was a recipient of two prestigious awards and well known for his pieces for the turkish market. He also produced tortoise shell and triple-case watches with the outer case featuring wood with silver inlay. He made gold watches with Oriental chased cases, watches with pierced outer cases and triple-cased enamel engraved and repeaters.

Edward Prior born in 1800 and died in 1868. Well known for his pieces for the turkish market.

TYPE – DESCRIPTION	Avg	Ex-Fn	Mint
Verge, pair case, plain silver, 50mm, OF	$500	$550	$600
Verge, pair case w/ repousee, silver, 50mm, OF	1,000	1,200	1,500
Verge, triple case w/ tortoise shell, silver, 56mm, OF	1,500	1,800	2,000
Verge, pair case, GOLD, 48-52mm, OF	2,000	2,300	2,800
Verge, pair case, GOLD & enamel, 48-54mm, OF	2,800	3,000	3,500
1/4 hr. repeater, pair case, GOLD & enamel, 50mm, OF	6,000	7,000	8,000

George Prior, 52mm, white porcelain signed dial, and engine turned silver hunter's case, verge with fusee, KW KS, Ca. 1830.

Edward Prior, outer case made of tortoise shell, leather travel case, verge escapement, note the stag beetle hour hand and poker minute hand, Ca. 1830.

ROLEX WATCH CO.
Swiss

Rolex was founded by Hans Wilsdorf in 1905 & in <u>1908</u> the trade-mark **"Rolex"** was officially registered. In 1926, they made the first real waterproof wrist watch and called it the **"Oyster."** In 1931, Rolex introduced a self-wind movement which they called **"Perpetual"**. In 1945, they introduced the **"Date-Just"** which showed the day of the month. The **"Submariner"** was introduced in 1953 and in 1954 the **"GMT Master"** model. In 1956, a "Day-Date" model was released which indicates the day of the month (in numbers) and the day of the week (in letters.)

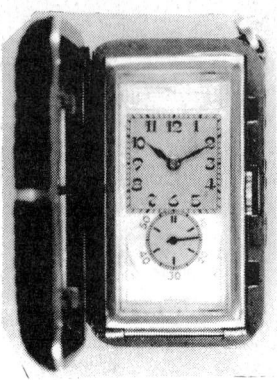

Rolex, **SPORTING PRINCE**, 17 jewels, Adjusted to six positions, silver & leather case,

Rolex, 42-43mm, 17 jewels, three adjustments, cam regulator, exposed winding gears.

ROLEX ESTIMATED PRODUCTION DATES

DATE–SERIAL #	DATE–SERIAL #	DATE–SERIAL #
1925 — 25,000	1949 — 608,000	1973— 3,741,000
1926 — 27,500	1950 — 673,500	1974— 4,000,000
1927 — 30,500	1951 — 735,500	1975— 4,260,000
1928 — 33,000	1952 — 804,000	1976— 4,530,000
1929 — 35,500	1953 — 869,000	1977— 5,000,000
1930 — 38,000	1954 — 935,000	1978— 5,480,000
1931 — 40,000	1955—1,010,000	1979— 5,960,000
1932 — 43,000	1956—1,095,000	1980— 6,430,000
1933 — 49,000	1957—1,167,000	1981— 6,910,000
1934 — 55,000	1958—1,245,000	1982— 7,380,000
1935 — 62,000	1959—1,323,000	1983— 7,860,000
1936 — 82,000	1960—1,401,000	1984— 8,340,000
1937 — 98,000	1961—1,485,000	1985— 8,810,000
1938—118,000	1962—1,557,000	1986— 9,300,000
1939—136,000	1963—1,635,000	1987— 9,760,000
1940—165,000	1964—1,713,000	1987 1/2-9,999,999
1941—194,000	1965—1,791,000	1987 3/4-R000,001
1942—224,000	1966—1,870,000	1988 — R999,999
1943—253,000	1967—2,164,000	1989 — L000,001
1944—284,000	1968—2,426,000	1990 — L999,999
1945—348,000	1969—2,689,000	1990 1/2-E000,001
1946—413,000	1970—2,952,000	1991 1/4-E999,999
1947—478,000	1971—3,215,000	1991 1/2-X000,001
1948—543,000	1972—3,478,000	1991 3/4-N000,001
		1992 1/4-C000,001

The above list is provided for determining the APPROXIMATE age of your watch. Match serial number with date. Watches were not necessarily sold in the exact order of manufactured date.The above list was furnished with the help of TOM ENGLE.

Hans Wilsdorf started in 1905 with his brother-in-law using the name of Wilsdorf & Davis. They used movement supplier Aegler in Bienne and bought cases in London. In 1919 Wilsdorf started the "Manufacture des Montres Rolex", the movements were manufactured in Bienne but finished in Geneva. 1950 the **Turn-o-graph** was used, the forerunner of the **SUBMARINER.**

ROLEX, split seconds Chronograph, register, S.S. case.

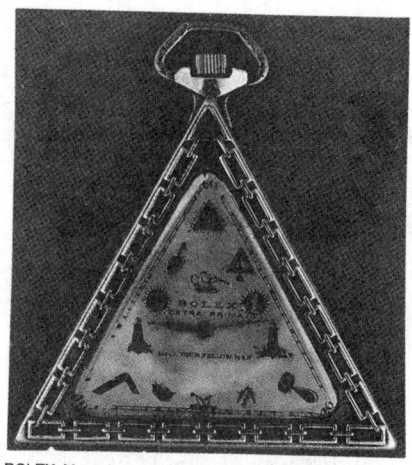

ROLEX, Masonic watch, mother of pearl dial, 15J.

TYPE – DESCRIPTION	Avg	Ex-Fn	Mint
17J, silver, 45mm, OF, C. 1920's	$225	$250	$325
17J, 3 adj., CAM regulator, **14K**, 43mm, OF, C. 1920	500	600	750
1/4 Century Club, 17J, 14K, 41mm, OF, C. 1940	700	800	900
Thin line, 17J, 18K, 42mm, OF, C. 1940	700	800	950
Time only, gold, 40-44mm, 18K, OF	500	700	900
HC	700	900	1,000
Time only, gold, 45-50mm, 18K, OF	800	900	1,000
HC	1,200	1,400	1,600
Rolex, **SPORTING PRINCE**, 17J, Adj. 6P ★★	3,000	3,500	4,000
Duo dial, fancy-shaped, 17J, 18K/WG, OF, 41mm, C. 1930	2,000	2,500	3,000
$20 dollar coin watch in closed case, triple signed, C.1950	2,500	3,000	3,500
World time watch, gold, 45-52mm	9,000	10,000	11,000
Chronograph, split seconds, register, S.S. case, 50mm	3,000	4,000	5,000
Masonic, mother of pearl dial, silver triangler case, Ca.1930s	3,500	4,000	4,500

Romilly, Gold , verge, pair case with polychrome enamel & scene, 52mm, OF, Ca.1730.

ROMILLY, JEAN
PARIS

Became a master Watchmaker in 1752 after studying in Geneva and Paris. In 1755, he completed a repeater with beating seconds and a large balance (at one oscillation per second). He also made watches with a 8 day power reserve. Also known for his very ornate paintings on enamel.

TYPE – DESCRIPTION	Avg	Ex-Fn	Mint
Time only, KW, verge, silver, 46-52mm OF	$700	$900	$1,200
Time & Calendar, verge, silver, 50mm, OF	1,500	1,650	1,800
Gold , verge, pair case, plain, 48mm, OF	2,000	2,200	2,400
Gold , verge, pair case w/ enamel & scene, Ca.1730, 52mm, OF....	4,000	4,500	5,500
1/4 repeater, SILVER, 52mm, OF	2,500	2,800	3,500
1/4 repeater, GOLD, 54mm, OF	3,500	4,000	4,500

ROBERT ROSKELL
Liverpool

Roskell was active from 1798-1830 and worked in both Liverpool and London. He made fine rack lever fusees and gold dial watches. Other family members also produced watches for many years in Liverpool.

R. Roskell, 47mm, bar style movement, cylinder escapement, Ca. 1850.

Roskell, fusee, table pierced & "engraved" & note the foot of balance cock is not pierced ,KW KS, Ca. 1830.

TYPE – DESCRIPTION	Avg	Ex-Fn	Mint
KW, (Swiss ebauche) 15J, silver, 48mm, OF, C. 1830-70	$75	$95	$125
KW, (Swiss) 15J, silver, 46-48mm, HC, C. 1830-70	100	125	150
KW, 13J, dust cover, fancy gold dial, 18K, 47mm, OF, C.1830-70	275	325	375

Roskell, 48mm, lever escapement, KW KS, Ca.1830.

Roskell, 55mm, KW KS, Ca. 1825

TYPE – DESCRIPTION	Avg	Ex-Fn	Mint
Rack lever fusee, porcelain dial, silver, hallmarked, OF, C.1870....	$395	$450	$500
2 day marine chronometer fusee, spring detent escapement, helical hairspring, 54 hr. wind ind., gimbal & box	1,800	2,000	2,500
Debaufre escapement, KW KS, silver, 55mm, OF .... ★ ★	3,000	3,200	3,500

Debaufre escapement,
D-shaped & inclined pallet.

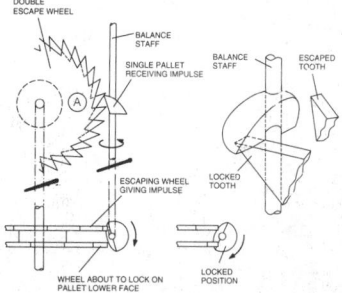

Roskell, 55mm, movement with **Debaufre escapement,** D-shaped and inclined pallet, KW KS, Ca. 1840.

Robert Roskell, 52mm, London, fusee, spring detent escapement, helical hairspring, 54 hr. wind ind., KW KS.

ROSKOPF
Swiss

Maker of pin lever, early low cost stem wind watches, often found with fancy dials. A **true** Roskopf watch has only *3 wheels* in its train of gears.

Roskopf, multi-colored blue enamel dial, nail set.

Roskopf, 45mm, pin lever escapement, 3 wheel train.

TYPE – DESCRIPTION	Avg	Ex-Fn	Mint
4J, pin lever, 3 wheel train, nail set, base metal, OF, Ca. 1885	$65	$85	$95
Fancy dial, oversize plain case, 55mm, OF, Ca. 1880	75	95	125
Fancy enamel dial, **fancy enamel case**, 55mm, OF, Ca. 1880	125	150	195

Roskopf, multi-colored enamel with blue & purple Butterflies & silver case, nail set.

SANDOZ & FILS
SWISS

Large family of watchmakers in the La Chaux-de-Fonds area. Known for repeating watches and pocket chronometers of fine quality.

TYPE – DESCRIPTION	Avg	Ex-Fn	Mint
Time only, gold, 40- 44mm, OF	$325	$375	$450
HC	450	500	600
Time only, gold, 45- 50mm, OF	525	600	700
HC	650	750	850
Chronograph, gold, 45-50mm, OF	700	750	800
Split second chronograph, gold, 45-52mm, OF	1,600	1,800	2,000
HC w/register	2,250	2,500	2,750
5 minute repeater, gold, 45-52mm, OF	2,500	2,650	2,850
HC	3,000	3,300	3,750
Minute repeater, gold, 45-52mm, OF	2,500	2,800	3,000
HC	3,000	3,500	4,000
OF w/split chrono.	5,000	5,500	6,000
HC w/split chrono.	7,500	8,000	8,500
OF w/cal. & moonphase	9,000	9,500	10,000
HC w/chrono., cal. & moonphase	10,000	12,000	14,000
Tourbillion, gold, 48-55mm, OF	25,000	30,000	35,000
Detent chronometer, gold, 48-52mm , OF	5,000	6,000	7,000
HC	5,500	6,500	7,500
World time watch, gold, 48-52mm, OF	8,000	10,000	12,000
Perp. moonphase cal. w/min.rep. and chrono, OF	25,000	30,000	35,000
HC	30,000	35,000	40,000

Sandoz, 52mm, KW, nickel bridge, gold train, Ca.1880.

THOMAS RUSSELL & SONS
London

Thomas Russell & Sons produced quality early keyless watches including Karrusels and chronometers. (Circa 1870-1910)

TYPE – DESCRIPTION	Avg	Ex-Fn	Mint
Time only, gold, 45-48mm, OF	$600	$800	$900
Chronograph, gold, 45-50mm, OF	1,250	1,400	1,650
Split second chronograph, gold, 45-52mm, OF	1,800	2,000	2,500
Minute repeater, gold, 46-52mm, OF	3,500	3,800	4,000
HC	3,850	4,250	4,500
Karrusel, 18K, 51mm, OF, C. 1890	4,000	4,500	5,000

TAVANNES
Swiss
Creates watches in 1895, other names used Dvina, La Tavanes, Obi, Lena Azow, and Kawa.

TYPE – DESCRIPTION	Avg	Ex-Fn	Mint
15J, GF, 35mm, HC, C. 1910	$90	$100	$125
15J, 14K, 35mm, HC, C. 1910	225	250	300
17J, 14K, 45mm, OF, C. 1915	225	250	300
21J, 14K, 45mm, OF, C. 1920	250	275	325
Enamel Bezel & gold, 14K, 40mm, OF	400	575	650
Enamel Scene & gold, 18K, 45mm, OF, C. 1925	5,000	6,000	7,000

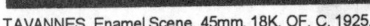

TAVANNES, Enamel Scene, 45mm, 18K, OF, C. 1925.   Tiffany & Co., P.P.Co., 43mm, enamel on bezel, 18K.

TIFFANY & CO.

In 1837 Charles Lewis Tiffany opened a store with John P. Young. They enlarged this operation in 1841, with the help of J.L. Eliss, and imported fine jewelry, watches and clocks from Europe. They incorporated as Tiffany & Co. in 1853. Tiffany made clocks, on special order, in New York around the mid-1800's. About 1874 Tiffany & Co. started a watch factory in Geneva but with little success. Four years later Patek, Philippe & Co. assumed the management of their Geneva watch business. The watch machinery was returned to America. Tiffany, Young & Ellis had been a client of Patek, Philippe & Co. since 1849. Tiffany & Co. introduced Patek, Philippe to the American market in 1885. Audemars, Piguet and International Watch Co. also made watches for this esteemed company. Tiffany & Co. sells watches of simple elegance as well as watches with complications such as chronographs, moon phases, repeaters, etc.

TYPE – DESCRIPTION	Avg	Ex-Fn	Mint
Time only, gold, 40- 44mm, OF	$375	$425	$500
HC	525	625	700
Time only, gold, 40-44mm, (P.P.Co.), 18K, **enamel on bezel**, OF.	1,500	1,800	2,200
Time only, gold, 45- 50mm, OF	800	850	900
HC	900	950	1,000
Chronograph, gold, 45-50mm, OF	1,450	1,600	1,800
HC	1,800	1,900	2,000
OF w/register	1,600	1,700	1,900
Split second chronograph, gold, 45-52mm, OF	2,800	3,000	3,250
HC	3,500	3,800	4,000

Tiffany & Co., 50mm, 25J., split-second chronograph, made by Ekegren.

Tiffany & Co., flat minute repeater, 45mm, 29 jewels, made by Patek, Philippe & Co., ca. 1911.

TYPE – DESCRIPTION	Avg	Ex-Fn	Mint
5 minute repeater, gold, 46-52mm, OF	$3,500	$4,000	$4,500
HC	4,000	4,500	5,000
OF w/split chrono.	6,000	6,500	7,000
HC w/split chrono.	6,850	7,250	7,500
Minute repeater, gold, 46-52mm, OF	3,500	3,750	4,000
HC	4,500	5,000	5,500
by **P. P. & Co.**, flat, 29J., gold, 45mm, OF, C.1912	9,000	12,000	15,000
OF w/split chrono. & register	8,000	9,000	10,000
HC w/split chrono. & register	9,000	10,000	12,000
HC w/chrono., cal. & moonphase	12,000	14,000	16,000
World time watch, gold, 48-52mm, OF	12,000	14,000	16,000
Perpetual moonphase calendar, gold, OF	9,000	10,000	12,000
Perp. moonphase cal. w/min. rep. and chrono, OF	35,000	40,000	45,000
HC	40,000	45,000	50,000

TIMING & REPEATING WATCH CO.
Geneva

Timing & Repeating W. Co., chronograph movement Patented Sept. 23, 1880 - England Pat. # 3224.

Timing & Repeating W. Co., chronograph movement Patented Sept. 23, 1880 - England Pat. # 3224.

TYPE – DESCRIPTION	Avg	Ex-Fn	Mint
Chronograph, 17J, GF, 48mm, OF, C. 1900	$165	$185	$250
Chronograph w/register, 17J, GF, 48mm, OF, C. 1900	200	250	275
Chronograph, 17J, gilt mvt., silver, 49mm, HC, C. 1900	250	300	325

TISSOT
Swiss

The firm of Chs. Tissot & Fils was founded in 1853 in Le Locle by Charles Tissot. This skilled watchmaker worked from his home and in 1907 a factory was started. In 1971 the worlds first plastic wrist watch was made.

TYPE – DESCRIPTION	Avg	Ex-Fn	Mint
Time only, gold, 40- 44mm, OF	$365	$435	$500
HC	485	550	650
Time only, gold, 45- 50mm, OF	525	600	700
HC	650	750	850
2-Train 1/4 second jump watch, silver, 50mm,	700	800	900
2-Train 1/4 second jump watch, gold, 50mm,	1,700	2,000	2,500
Chronograph, gold, 45-50mm, OF	800	850	900
Split second chronograph, gold, 45-52mm, OF	1,800	2,000	2,200
HC w/register	2,850	3,250	3,500
5 minute repeater, gold, 45-52mm, OF	3,250	3,500	3,750
HC	3,500	3,750	4,000
Minute repeater, gold, 45-52mm, OF	3,500	3,750	4,000
HC	3,750	4,000	4,250
OF w/split chrono.	5,000	5,500	6,000
HC w/split chrono.	7,500	8,000	8,500
OF w/cal. & moonphase	9,000	9,500	10,000
HC w/chrono., cal. & moonphase	10,000	12,000	14,000
Tourbillion, gold, 48-55mm, OF	38,000	45,000	50,000
Detent chronometer, gold, 48-52mm , OF	5,000	6,000	7,000
HC	5,500	6,500	7,500
World time watch, gold, 48-52mm, OF	12,000	14,000	15,000
Perp. moonphase cal. w/min.rep. and chrono, OF	25,000	30,000	35,000
HC	30,000	35,000	40,000

Tissot, 2-Train 1/4 second jump watch, center sweep hand, enamel dial, 28 J., gold train, 54mm, KWKS, 18K, Ca. 1880.

Tissot, Minute repeater, with chronograph, day date month, moonphase, 27 jewels, 18K, HC, Ca. 1910.

🕐 Watches listed in this book are priced at the collectable fair market **value** at the retail level, as complete watches having an original case, an original white enamel dial, and with the entire original movement in good working order with no repairs needed, unless otherwise noted.

TOBIAS & CO.

M. I. Tobias started a watchmaking career in Liverpool, about 1805. He specialized in exporting watches to U.S.A. About 1820 the company started using movements made in Switzerland the watches were engraved, *Liverpool*. The script M.I.Tobias can be misleading the script letter (I) may look like a **(J)**. The watches with a (J style) are made in the Swiss manner with a club-tooth escape-wheel made of steel and straight line lever, the Liverpool or English style watches used a (I) & a "ratchet" (sharp-pointed) escape wheel made of brass and right angle lever. The Tobias family activity extends from about 1805 to 1868.

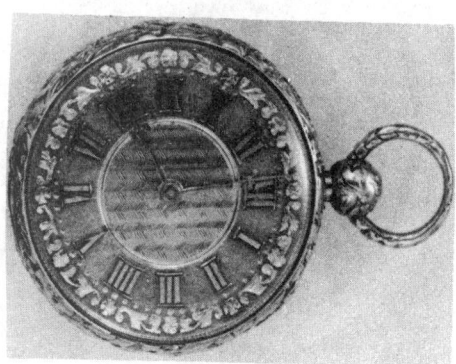

M. I. Tobias, Liverpool, Fusee, Right angle lever, 15 jewels, diamond end stone, S # 41,383, Ca. 1855.

M. I. Tobias, multi-color gold dial & thin gold case, 52mm.

TYPE – DESCRIPTION	Avg	Ex-Fn	Mint
KW, 7-15J, silver, 47mm, OF	$85	$95	$125
KW,7- 15J, silver, 47mm, HC	100	125	175
KW,7-15J, swiss, **gilt dial**, fancy case, **18K**, 48mm,OF	265	300	375
KW, lever, fusee, **gold dial**, Heavy 18K, 52mm, HC	900	1,200	1,500
KW, rack lever escapement, **Silver**, 56mm, OF	400	500	600
HC	500	600	700
KW, rack lever escapement, **Gold**, 56mm, OF	900	1,000	1,200
HC	1,100	1,300	1,500
KW, verge fusee, **multi-color gold dial & THIN case**, 52mm, OF	500	600	700
HC	700	800	950
Captain's watch, center sec., sub-sec., gold dial, **18K**, 51mm, OF..	1,500	1,800	2,000
18K, 51mm, HC	1,800	2,200	2,500

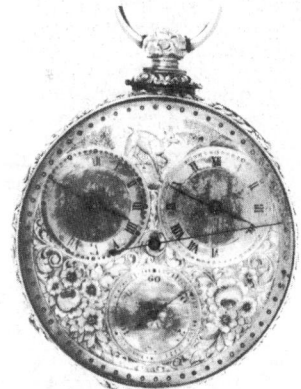

Tobias, (Liverpool), 51mm, OF, 18K, Captain's watch, center sec., subseconds, gold dial.

TOUCHON & CO.

Swiss

Touchon & Co. started using this name as a trade mark in 1907. They manufactured complex and simple watches. In 1921 they associated with the firm of Wittnauer & Co.

Touchon & Co., 47mm, 29 jewels, minute repeater, open face, jeweled through hammers.

Touchon & Co., 47mm, 29 jewels, split-second chronograph and minute repeater, ca. 1910.

TYPE – DESCRIPTION	Avg	Ex-Fn	Mint
Time only, gold, 45- 50mm, OF	$465	$500	$600
HC	565	650	750
1/4 hr. repeater, gold, 46-52mm, OF	1,000	1,200	1,400
HC	1,500	1,800	2,000
OF w/chrono.	1,200	1,400	1,500
HC w/chrono.	1,700	2,000	2,200
OF w/chrono., cal. & moonphase	3,000	3,500	4,000
HC w/chrono., cal. & moonphase	4,500	5,500	6,500
5 minute repeater, gold, 46-52mm, OF	3,000	3,500	4,000
HC	3,500	4,000	4,500
Minute repeater, gold, 46-52mm, OF	3,500	4,000	4,500
HC	4,500	5,000	5,500
OF w/chrono. & register	3,750	4,250	4,750
HC w/chrono. & register	5,000	5,500	6,000
OF w/split chrono.	4,750	5,500	5,750
HC w/split chrono. & register	9,000	9,500	10,000
HC w/chrono., cal. & moonphase	10,000	12,000	13,000
World time watch, gold, 48-52mm, OF	12,000	14,000	16,000
Perpetual moonphase calendar, gold, OF	10,000	11,000	12,000
Perp. moonphase cal. w/min.repeater, HC	25,000	30,000	35,000
Perp. moonphase cal. w/min.rep. and chrono., HC	35,000	38,000	40,000

COMPARISON OF WATCH SIZES

U. S. A.	EUROPEAN
10-12 SIZE	40—44 MM
16 SIZE	45—48 MM
18 SIZE	50—52 MM

VACHERON & CONSTANTIN

Swiss

The firm of Vacheron & Constantin was officially founded by Abraham Vacheron in 1785, but the association bearing the name today did not come into being until 1819. In these early periods, different grades of watches produced by Vacheron & Constantin bore different names.

ESTIMATED PRODUCTION DATES

DATE–SERIAL #	DATE–SERIAL #	DATE–SERIAL #
1830 - 30,000	1880-170,000	1930-410,000
1835 - 40,000	1885-180,000	1935-420,000
1840 - 50,000	1890-190,000	1940-440,000
1845 - 60,000	1895-223,000	1945-464,000
1850 - 75,000	1900-256,000	1950-488,000
1855 - 95,000	1905-289,000	1955-512,000
1860 -110,000	1910-322,000	1960-536,000
1865-125,000	1915-355,000	1965-560,000
1870-140,000	1920-385,000	1970-585,000
1875-155,000	1925-400,000	

The above list is provided for determining the APPROXIMATE age of your watch. Match serial number with date. Watches were not necessarily sold in the exact order of manufactured date.

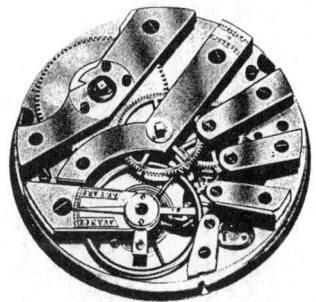

Early movements manufactured with the machines invented by George-Auguste Leschot. The machines were built in the Vacheron Constantin factory Ca. 1839 to 1940. In about 1863 to 1865 V. & C. manufactured a inexpensive watch using the names Abraham Vacheron or Abm. Vacheron also the name of Chossat & Cie.

The association with Leschot, around 1840, catapulted the firm into its position as a top quality manufacturer. Before that time, their watches were typical of Genevese production. Vacheron & Constantin exported many movements to the United States to firms such as Bigelow, Kennard & Co., which were cased domestically, typically in the period 1900-1935. In its early period the firm produced some lovely ladies' enameled watches, later it produced high grade timepieces and complicated watches, & to this day produces fine watches.

Vacheron & Constantin, 44mm, 18 jewels, enamel bezel, 18K, Ca. 1930.

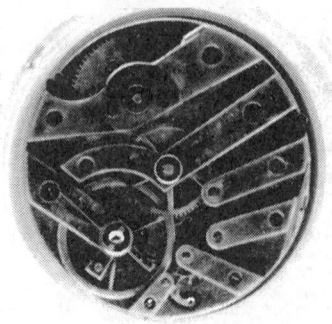

Early bar movement, lever escap., **signed "VACHERON & CONSTANTIN"** time only, KW KS, silver case, Ca.1840-1875.

TYPE – DESCRIPTION	Avg	Ex-Fn	Mint
Early bar movement, lever escap., **signed Vacheron & Constantin**			
time only, KW KS, silver case, 30-39mm, OF	$135	$165	$225
(same as above) 40-44mm, OF	185	235	265
(same as above) 45-48mm, OF	225	250	325
(same as above) 45-48mm, **HC**	250	300	350
Early Le-Pine bar movement, duplex escap., GOLD & ENAMEL			
KW KS, **signed Vacheron & Constantin**, 49mm, OF	4,500	5,000	5,500
Time only, 18K gold & **enamel bezel**, 40-44mm, OF	1,200	1,300	1,500

Vacheron & Constantin, 49mm, Early Le-Pine bar style movement, duplex escapement, GOLD & ENAMEL, KW KS, **signed Vacheron & Constantin**, 49mm, OF, Ca. 1840.

Vacheron & Constantin, Gold coin 50 pesos 900 fine, coin hollowed out to receive watch, LEFT view shows dial & movement.

TYPE – DESCRIPTION

	Avg	Ex-Fn	Mint
Time only, 18K gold, 40-44mm, OF	$700	$800	$900
HC	1,000	1,200	1,500
Time only, gold, 45-50mm, OF	1,200	1,500	1,800
HC	1,800	2,000	2,200
X-thin, 17J., **Aluminum,** weight =20 grains, OF, C. 1940	2,500	3,000	3,500
Desk chronometer, wooden box, 21J., silver, 60mm,OF, C.1943	2,200	2,500	2,800
Gold coin 50 pesos 900 fine, coin hollowed out to receive watch	3,000	3,500	4,000

V. & C., Chronograph, for the corps of engineers USA, 20 jewels, enamel dial, nail set, 50mm, Ca.1919.

V. & C., Astronomic with moon phases, perpetual calendar, minute repeater, split-second chronograph, 1905.

TYPE – DESCRIPTION

	Avg	Ex-Fn	Mint
Chronograph, **SILVER**, 45-50mm, OF	$1,200	$1,500	$1,800
Chronograph, **GOLD**, 45-50mm, presented to officers, OF ..... ★ ★	3,000	3,500	4,000
HC	3,000	3,500	4,000
OF w/register	2,750	3,000	3,250
HC w/register	3,500	4,000	4,500

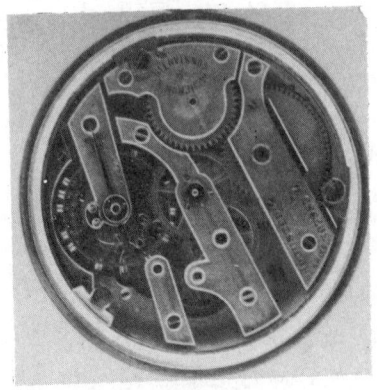

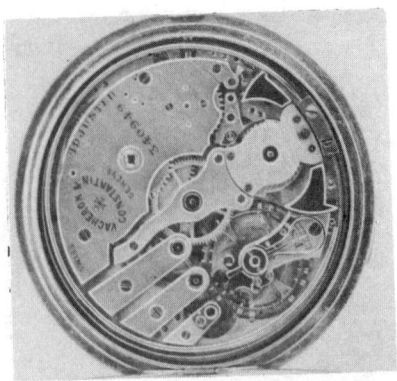

V. & C., 40mm, wolf tooth winding, open face.

V. & C., 40mm, 31J., Min. repeater, slide activated, OF.

TYPE – DESCRIPTION	Avg	Ex-Fn	Mint
Split second chronograph, gold, 45-52mm, OF	$5,500	$5,750	$6,000
HC	6,500	7,000	7,500
OF w/register	6,000	6,500	7,000
HC w/register	7,500	7,750	8,000
Minute repeater, gold, 46-52mm, OF	6,500	7,500	8,000
HC	12,000	14,000	16,000
OF w/chrono.	8,000	9,000	10,000
HC w/chrono.	13,000	15,000	17,000
OF w/chrono. & register	8,500	9,500	10,500
HC w/chrono. & register	14,000	16,000	18,000
OF w/split chrono.	11,000	12,000	13,000
HC w/split chrono.	16,000	18,000	20,000
OF w/split chrono. & register	12,000	14,000	15,000
HC w/split chrono. & register	17,000	19,000	22,000
OF w/chrono., cal. & moonphase	18,000	20,000	22,000
Tourbillion, gold, 48-55mm, OF	65,000	75,000	85,000
World time watch, gold, 48-52mm, OF	55,000	65,000	75,000
Perp. moonphase cal. w/min. repeater, OF	65,000	75,000	85,000
HC	70,000	80,000	90,000
Perp. moonphase cal. w/min. rep. and split sec. chrono., OF	70,000	80,000	90,000
Perp. moonphase cal. w/min. rep. and split sec. chrono., HC	100,000	110,000	120,000

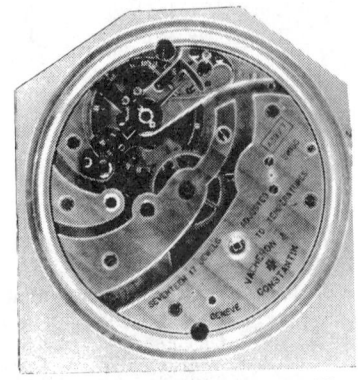

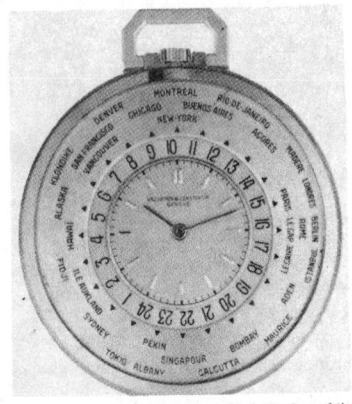

V. & C., extra thin and light weight **Aluminum.** (20 grains), about 12 size, 44mm, OF, 17 jewels, Ca. 1940.

V. & C., World time, revolving 24 hour dial, 31 citys of the world, 18 jewels, 45mm, Ca. 1945

ZENITH
Swiss

Zenith watch and clock factory was founded in 1865 by George Farvre Jacot. They mass produced watches of different grades in large quantities. By 1920 they had manufactured 2,000,000 watches.

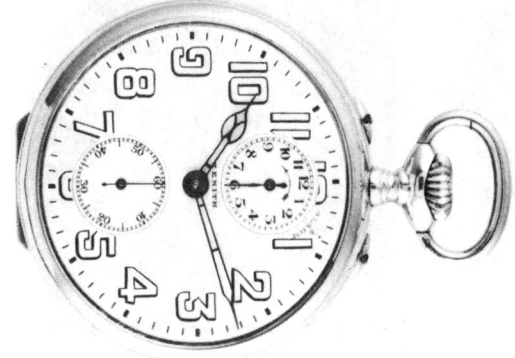

ZENITH, Gold alarm watch, enamel dial, 17 jewels, 50mm, Ca. 1930

TYPE – DESCRIPTION	Avg	Ex-Fn	Mint
Time only, gold, 40-44mm, OF	$285	$335	$400
HC	425	450	500
Time only, gold, 40-44mm, with **enamel** on bezel, **18K**, OF	625	700	800
Time only, gold, 45-50mm, OF	425	500	600
HC	550	600	700
Alarm watch, 17J., nail set, two barrels, gold, 50mm, C.1930	1,500	1,600	1,750
Chronograph, gold, 45-50mm, OF	900	1,000	1,100
HC	1,000	1,100	1,200
Minute repeater, gold, 46-52mm, OF	2,800	3,000	3,200
HC	3,500	3,750	4,000
OF w/split chrono.	4,500	5,000	5,500
HC w/split chrono.	7,000	7,500	8,000
OF w/chrono., cal. & moonphase	6,500	7,000	7,500
HC w/chrono., cal. & moonphase	9,000	9,500	10,000
Perp. moonphase cal. w/min. rep. and chrono., OF	22,000	25,000	27,000
HC	25,000	28,000	30,000

ZENITH, 44mm, 18K, enamel on case, open face, 17 jewels, signed ZENITH, Ca. 1930's.

Swiss 1/4 hr. repeater, verge or cylinder, silver, 55mm, Ca. 1820, OF. Note: Parachute (illo.1)

Swiss 1/4 hr. rep., pump, verge or cylinder, 18K, 52mm, OF, Ca.1800s. (illo.2)

PRE–1850 REPEATERS

TYPE – DESCRIPTION	Avg	Ex-Fn	Mint
Swiss 1/4 hr. rep., verge or cylinder, silver, 55mm, OF (illo.1)......	$1,000	$1,200	$1,500
Swiss 1/4 hr. rep., pump, verge or cylinder, 18K, 52mm, OF, C.1800s (illo.2)	1,500	2,000	2,500
Swiss 1/4 hr., automaton on dial (2 figures), gilt, verge, KW, 55mm, OF, early 1800s	2,500	3,000	3,500
Swiss 1/4 hr. musical repeater disc-driven, KW KS, cylinder,18k, 57mm, OF, C. 1825, (illo.3)............	4,000	5,500	6,000
Swiss 1/4 hr. repeater, 32-35mm, KW KS, gold, Ca. 1850, (illo.4)	1,800	2,000	2,500

Swiss 1/4 hr. musical repeater disc-driven, cylinder, Kw KS, 18k, 57mm, OF, C. 1825, (illo.3)

Swiss 1/4 hr. repeater, 32-35mm, cylinder escapement, Swiss bar movement, KW KS, gold, Ca. 1850, (illo.4)

French, 1/4 hr. repeater, gold and enamel superior quality, enameled scene, outer case with pearls, verge, 20K, 52mm, OF, C.1785. (illo.5)

1/4 hr. repeater, Virgule escap., KW, 18K, 46mm, OF, Ca. 1840. (illo.6)

TYPE – DESCRIPTION

	Avg	Ex-Fn	Mint
Skeletonized 1/4 hr., cylinder, Swiss, 18K, 58mm, OF, C.1810......	$4,000	$4,500	$5,000
French 1/4 hr. repeater, 18K gold and enamel, verge, enameled scene, superior quality, outer pearls, 52mm, OF, C.1785 (illo.5)......	6,000	7,000	7,500
1/4 hr. repeater, Virgule escap., KW, 18K, 46mm, OF (illo.6)........	3,000	3,200	3,500
1/4 hr. rep., erotic scene (concealed in cuvette), automated, multi-color gold figures, verge, pump 1/4 hr., 18K, 54mm, OF, C.1800...	3,500	4,000	4,250
French or Swiss pump 1/4 hr. repeater, free standing barrel, **Thin gold** case, cylinder escape., tapered bridges , Ca.1790-1835, (illo.7).....	2,000	3,000	3,500
1/4 hr. repeater, repousse pair case, verge, 22K, 49mm (illo.8)	5,500	6,000	7,000
1/4 hr. repeater, musical, 25 musical tines, cylinder, center seconds, KW, 18K, 58mm,OF, C. 1820 (illo.9)	5,000	6,000	7,500

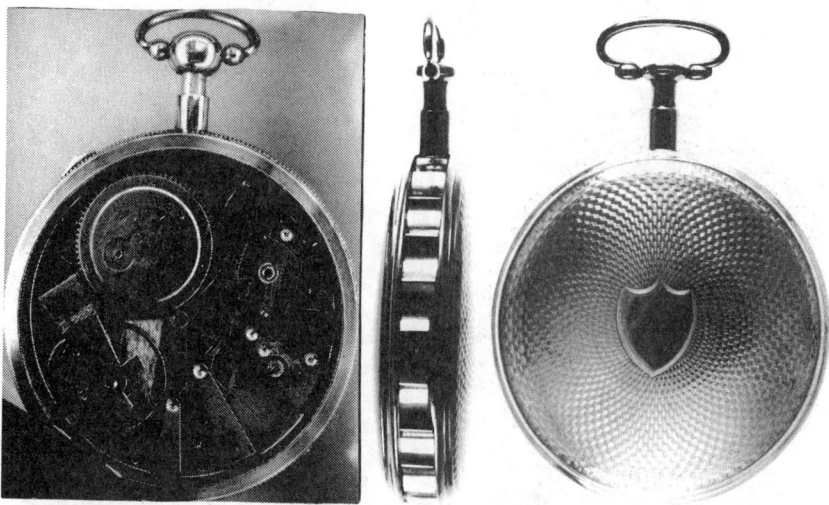

French **or Swiss** pump 1/4 hr. repeater, free standing barrel, cylinder escapement, tapered bridges, **Thin** gold engine turned case, Ca. 1790-1835. (illo.7)

1/4 hour verge repeater, 49mm, 22K gold repousse pair case, repeating on an inner bell, repeat mechanism is activated from the pendant. ca. 1750-1780, **(illo.8)**

1/4 hour repeater, musical, 25 musical tines, cylinder, center seconds, KW, 18K, 58mm, OF, Ca.1820, **(illo.9)**

1/4 hour repeater, verge (London, Dutch), pierced inner case, repousee outer case, gold, 49mm, C.1750, **(illo.10)**

1/4 Hr. repeating coach watch, with alarm,120mm diameter, verge fusee, silver repousse case, ca.1730-40. **(illo. 11)**

TYPE – DESCRIPTION	Avg	Ex-Fn	Mint
Early 1/4 hr. rep., Paris (Clouzier) gilt dial w/ enamel hour cartouches, verge, gilt & shagreen case, 58mm, OF, C.1700	$7,000	$8,000	$8,500
1/4 hr. rep., verge (London, Dutch), pierced inner case, repousee outer case, gold, 49mm, C.1750 (illo.10)	5,500	6,000	7,000
1/4 hr. repeating coach watch w/alarm, verge, fusee, silver repousee case, 120mm, C. 1730 (illo. 11)	8,000	9,000	11,000
1/4 hr. repeater with automaton dial, verge, Swiss, KW, 3 automated figures on dial and carillon chimes, silver, 52mm, OF, C. 1790.	2,500	3,000	3,250
1/4 hr. repeater, London, gilt & shagreen paircase, verge, extremely fine, 56mm, OF, C.1700s	4,000	4,250	4,500
Gold & enamel, 1/4 hr. repeater, London, cylinder, Fusee, paircase, enamel on outer case, 18K, 48mm, C. 1790	4,000	4,500	5,000
Swiss, 1/4 hr. pump repeater, w/ automaton, verge, 18K, 54mm, OF, C. 1800	4,500	5,500	6,000
Virgule escapement, 1/4 hr. repeater, fancy gold & multi-dial, London, KW, 18K, OF, C. 1840	2,800	3,000	3,500

REPEATERS

1/4 hour repeater, 17 jewels, nail set, gun metal case, 49mm, C. 1910. (illo.12)

1/4 hour repeater with chronograph, gun metal base-metal or gold filled, 49-50mm, (illo.13)

TYPE – DESCRIPTION	Avg	Ex-Fn	Mint
1/4 hr. repeater, 17J, gun metal, 49-50mm, C. 1910 (illo.12)	$450	$500	$600
1/4 hr. repeater, 17J, silver, 49-50mm, OF, C. 1910	550	600	700
1/4 hr. repeater, 17J, silver, 49-50mm, HC, C. 1910	650	700	900
1/4 hr. rep. w/chrono.,17J, base metal gun metal or GF, OF 49-50mm, C.1910 (illo.13)	650	750	950
1/4 hr. rep. w/chrono.,17J, base metal, gun metal or GF, HC 49-50mm, C.1910	750	800	1,000

1/4 hr. repeater with Calendar, 17J, gold filled, 3/4 plate, open face, 50mm, C. 1910 (illo.14)

1/4 hour repeater, 55mm, 2 Jacquemarts, gilt case. (illo.15)

TYPE – DESCRIPTION	Avg	Ex-Fn	Mint
1/4 hr. repeater with Calendar, 17J, gun metal or gold filled, 3/4 plate, OF, 49-50mm, C. 1910 (illo.14)	$600	$700	$800
Swiss 1/4 hr. repeater w/moonphase & calendar, 17J, 18K, 53mm, HC, C. 1900...	3,000	3,500	4,000
55mm, 1/4 repeater, 2 Jacquemarts, gilt case, (illo.15)...................	2,000	2,300	2,800
Swiss 1/4 hr. repeater, **Erotic Scene**, 14K, HC, 50-54mm, ALL ORIGINAL, (note: beware of fakes), (illo.16)...........	4,000	6,000	9,000

Swiss 1/4 hour repeater, **Erotic Scene** with automaton action dial, 14K, HC, 50-54mm, **all original,** (illo.16)

COMPARISON OF WATCH SIZES

U. S. A.	EUROPEAN
10-12 SIZE	40—44 MM
16 SIZE	45—48 MM
18 SIZE	50—54 MM

Minute Repeater, 20J, Swiss, gilt mvt., gun metal, 52mm, HC, C.1910. (illo.17)

Swiss minute repeater, 54mm, jeweled through hammers, 14k case. (illo.18)

TYPE – DESCRIPTION	Avg	Ex-Fn	Mint
Min. rep., 20J, Swiss, gilt mvt., gun metal, 52mm, **OF**, 1910	$1,000	$1,100	$1,200
Min. rep., 20J, Swiss, gilt mvt., gun metal, 52mm, **HC**, Ca.1910 (illo.17)	1,200	1,300	1,500
Min. rep., 17J, Swiss, gilt, 18K, 52mm, HC, C. 1910	2,000	2,300	2,500
Min. rep., 32 J, Swiss, gilt, 18K, 54mm, HC, C. 1910	2,400	2,800	3,000
Min. rep., 32 J, Swiss, porcelain dial, 14K, OF, C. 1905 (illo.18)	2,200	2,500	2,800
Min. rep., 32 J, Swiss, porcelain dial, 18K, OF, C. 1905 (illo.19)	2,500	2,700	3,200
Min. repeater, Self contained, (activated from button on crown) 25J, 14K, OF, C. 1915	3,500	4,000	4,500
Min. repeater, Swiss, ultra thin,32J, 18K, OF, C. 1930	4,000	5,000	6,000
Min. repeater, automated Father & Baby Time, 18K, 54mm,(illo.20)	5,000	5,500	6,000

Minute Repeater, 32 J, Swiss, porcelain dial, wolf tooth winding, 18K, OF, C. 1905. (illo.19)

Father & Baby Time, automated min. repeater, 54mm, note father and baby striking bell, 18K. (illo.20)

Minute repeating **Clock Watch**, 3/4 plate, a on or off strike activated mechanism, three gongs, tandem-winding barrels, 18K, 48-50mm, HC, Ca.1900 (illo.21)

Minute repeater, split second chronograph, Swiss, 18K, 47-50mm, OF, Ca.1900 . (illo.22)

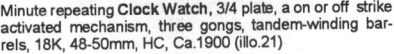

TYPE – DESCRIPTION	Avg	Ex-Fn	Mint
Min. repeating Clock Watch, 18K, 48-50mm, HC, Ca.1900 (illo.21)	$7,500	$8,500	$9,500
Min.rep. w/ chrono, Swiss ,SW, 18K, large 58mm, OF, C.1900.....	3,000	3,500	4,000
Min. repeater w/chrono. register, 32J, nickel, very high quality, 18K, 50mm, OF, C. 1900	3,500	4,000	4,500
Min. rep.w/chrono, 30 min. register, Swiss, 36J, 18K ,HC, C.1895	4,000	4,500	5,000
Min. rep., split sec. chrono, Swiss, 18K, 47-50mm, OF, C.1900 (illo.22)	5,500	7,000	7,500
Min. rep., split sec. chrono, Swiss, 18K, 47-50mm, HC,C.1900	6,500	7,500	9,000
Swiss min. repeater, chrono, moonphase and calendar, 30J or more, 18K, 60mm, HC, C. 1895 (illo.23)..........................	5,500	6,500	7,500
Swiss min. repeater, chrono, moonphase and **perpetual calendar**, 30J or more, 18K, 60mm, HC, C. 1895 (illo.24).................★	12,500	14,500	18,500
Swiss min. rep., Grand Sonnerie, clockwatch w/ carillon chimes, 2 train, nickel, tandem wind, 30J, 3 hammers, ornate case, 18K, 55mm, HC, C. 1900.........................	10,500	12,500	15,500

Swiss minute repeater, chronograph, start - stop - return to zero, moonphase and calendar, 30J or more, 18K, 60mm, HC, C. 1895. (illo.23)

Swiss minute repeater, chronograph, moonphase and **perpetual calendar**, 30J or more, 18K, 60mm, HC, C. 1895. (illo.24)

PRE–1850 ALARMS

TYPE – DESCRIPTION	Avg	Ex-Fn	Mint
Alarm, (**Blois, France**), double silver case pierced and engraved, gilt mvt., cut gut cord fusee, 2 wheel train + verge escape. w/foliot, silver balance cock, 44mm, Ca. 1640, (illo.25)	$15,000	$17,000	$20,000
Alarm, 2 cases pierced, 3 wheel train, Egyptian pierced pillers, verge & foliot, 51mm, Ca. 1675 (illo.26)	7,000	9,000	12,000

ALARM, **from BLOIS**, FRANCE, double silver case pierced and engraved, silver crown dial with roman numbers, alarm center dial with arabic numbers, gilt movement, cut gut cord fusee, 2 wheel train plus verge escapement with foliot, silver balance cock, 44mm, Ca. 1640. It is believed French watch-making started in the town of **Blois, France.** (illo.25)

ALARM, 2 cases pierced & engraved, roman outer dial, alarm center dial, blued hands , 3 wheel train, Egyptian pierced pillers, verge & foliot, endless screw adjustment, Paris, 51mm, Ca. 1675. (illo.26)

ALARM, strikes on bell, pair cased, verge, C. 1650. (illo.27)

Alarm, pair cased, first case pique nailed skin, second case pierced, 4 wheel train, verge, amphora pillers, 56mm, Ca. 1680. (illo.28)

TYPE – DESCRIPTION	Avg	Ex-Fn	Mint
Alarm, strikes on bell, pair cased, verge, C. 1650. (illo.27).............	$6,000	$6,500	$7,000
Alarm, pair cased, first case pique nailed skin, 4 wheel train, verge, 56mm, Ca. 1680. (illo.28)	9,000	11,000	13,000
Alarm, Rotterdam, silver pierced case, gilt, tulip pillars, verge, fusee, 48mm, Ca. 1685 (illo.29)..	6,000	6,500	7,000
Alarm, "oignon", verge, fusee, large pierced bal. bridge (illo.30)...	6,000	7,000	8,000

ALARM, Rotterdam, silver pierced case, gilt, tulip pillars, verge, fusee, 48mm, Ca. 1685. (illo.29)

ALARM, "oignon", verge, fusee, large pierced balance bridge. (illo.30)

ALARM, nailed pique shagreen skin, second case pierced silver, balance cock has short feet, 4 wheel train verge, 60mm, London, Ca. 1685. (illo.31)

ALARM, nailed pique shagreen (**Sting-Ray**) skin, triple cases, entirely pierced throughout, richly decorated, 4 wheel train, verge, fusee, English-Swiss, Ca. 1700. (illo.32)

TYPE – DESCRIPTION	Avg	Ex-Fn	Mint
Alarm, nailed pique shagreen skin, second case pierced silver, 4 wheel train verge, 60mm, London, Ca. 1685 (illo.31)	$6,500	$7,500	$8,500
Alarm, nailed pique shagreen (**Sting-Ray**) skin, English-Swiss, verge, fusee, Ca.1700s, (illo.32)...	6,000	6,500	7,500
Oignon alarm, verge, French, silver and animal skin cover, movement wound from center arbor on dial, silver champleve dial, 60mm, OF, C. 1760	5,000	5,500	6,000

ALARMS

The most common Swiss and German alarms are usually in base metal or gun metal cases. Early makes with porcelain dials are more desirable than later (post 1920's) metal dial alarms.

TYPE – DESCRIPTION	Avg	Ex-Fn	Mint
Swiss alarm sounding on bell,7J, base metal, 49mm,OF, C.1915 ...	$95	$110	$135
Swiss alarm sounding on gongs, 15J, tandem wind, gun metal, 50mm, OF, C. 1900	175	200	275
Cricket alarm, w/cricket design, Swiss , SW, silver case, 48mm, OF, C.1890...	500	700	800

COMPARISON OF WATCH SIZES

U. S. A.	EUROPEAN
10-12 SIZE	40—44 MM
16 SIZE	45—48 MM
18 SIZE	50—54 MM

TIMERS & CHRONOGRAPHS

Gallet, Racine & other names are commonly found on timers & chronographs.

Timer, 1/5 sec., 7J, register, base metal, 48mm, OF.

Timer, **split second**, register, base metal, 46mm, OF.

TYPE – DESCRIPTION	Avg	Ex-Fn	Mint
Timer, 1/5 sec., register,7J, base metal, 48mm, OF, C. 1940	$45	$55	$75
Timer, 1/5 sec. register, **17J**, base metal, 48mm, OF, C. 1940	65	75	95
Timer, **split sec.**, register, base metal, 46mm, OF, C. 1940	75	100	125
Timer or Stop Watch, **silver,** 48mm, **HC,** 1925	135	165	195
Chronograph, **7J, GF or silver,** 48mm, OF, C. 1905......................	130	150	185
HC	165	175	200
Chronograph, **15-17J, porcelain** dial, GF or silver, 50mm, OF, ...	225	250	300
HC, ...	250	300	350
Chronograph, **20J, 18K,** 52mm, OF, C. 1895	500	600	700
HC	600	700	850

Timer or Stop Watch, **silver,** 48mm, HC.

Chronograph, 7-17J, GF, 48mm, OF, C. 1905.

Chronograph, w/register, porc. dial, **20J, 14K**, 52mm, HC, Ca. 1890.

Chronograph, Split Seconds, w/register, porc. dial, **20J, 18K**, 52mm, OF, Ca. 1910.

TYPE – DESCRIPTION	Avg	Ex-Fn	Mint
Chronog. w/register, porc. dial, **15J, silver,** 52mm, OF, C. 1890....	$250	$300	$350
HC	300	325	375
Chronog. w/register, porc. dial, **20J, 14K**, 52mm, OF, C. 1890......	400	500	600
HC	500	600	750
Chronog. w/register, porc. dial, **20J, 18K,** 52mm, OF, C. 1890......	600	700	800
HC	800	900	1,200
Split sec. chronograph, 15-17J, **.800 silver,** 52mm, OF, C. 1900..	300	325	365
Split sec. chronograph, 19-32J, **18K,** 52mm, OF, C. 1900	800	900	1,200
HC	1,000	1,200	1,500
Double dial (time on front, chrono. on back), Swiss , 17J, **14K** display case , 51mm, OF, Ca. 1885	900	1,100	1,250
1/4 second jump watch, 26J, two gear train, KW , **18K**, HC, C.1880	2,200	2,500	3,000

Double dial (time on front, chrono. on back), Swiss , 17J, 14K display case , 51mm, OF, Ca. 1885.

1/4 second jump watch, 26J, two gear train, two main spring barrels, KW , 18K, 53mm, HC, C.1880.

POCKET CHRONOMETER

JOHN ARNOLD, chronometer, KWKS, spring detent, Z balance with adjustable weights, helical hair spring, 18K case, serial # 14, upright escape wheel, "INV ET FECT" engraved on movement (made by), his chronometer factory was located in Chigwell (London), #36 pocket chronometers sold for about $500.00 in 1776. (illo.33)

TYPE – DESCRIPTION	Avg	Ex-Fn	Mint
Chronometer, KWKS, spring detent, Z bal., helical hair-spring, "JOHN ARNOLD", 18K case, C. 1776 (illo.33)	$10,000	$12,000	$15,000
Chronometer, KWKS, spring detent, Z bal., helical hair-spring, silver case, C. 1795 (illo.34)	5,000	6,000	7,000
Chronometer, KWKS, spring detent, Z bal., helical hair-spring, "R. ARNOLD", 18K case, C. 1805 (illo.35)	8,000	10,000	12,000

Chronometer,13 jewels, KWKS, spring detent, Z balance with screw counterpoise on terminal curves, helical hair-spring, silver case, Ca. 1795. (illo.34)

R. ARNOLD, chronometer, KWKS, spring detent, Z balance with screw counterpoise on terminal curves, helical hair-spring, 18K case, 58mm, C. 1805. (illo.35)

JOHANNES KESSELS "ALTON", deck chronometer, KWKS, spring detent, fusee, silver case, C. 1830 . (illo.36)

Detent chronometer, Helical hairspring, Swiss, SW, 18K, 56mm, HC, C. 1900. (illo.37)

TYPE – DESCRIPTION	Avg	Ex-Fn	Mint
Chronometer, KWKS, spring detent, Z bal., helical hair-spring, "KESSELS", **silver case**, C. 1830. (illo.36)	$2,000	$3,000	$4,000
Chronometer, KW, spring detent, **coin**, OF, C. 1875	600	700	900
Detent chronometer, Swiss, SW, **18K**, 56mm, HC, Ca.1900 (ill0.37)	1,500	1,700	2,000
Detent chronometer, English, w/ wind indicator, **18K**, 48mm, OF .	3,500	4,000	5,000
Chronometer, pivoted detent, helical hairspring, (French), SW, **silver**, 56mm, OF, (illo.38)	300	400	550
Pocket chronometer, Swiss, 20 jewel, fancy case, silver and gilt dial, detent, w/ helical spring, **18K**, 49mm, HC, C. 1890	8,000	9,000	10,000

Engraved on movement "*Chronome'tre*" (French), 16 jewels, pivoted detent, helical hairspring, stem wind, manufactured by **LIP** in **Besancon France**, silver, 56mm, OF, Ca. 1910-30. (illo.38)

Detent chronometer, English, w/ fusee, helical hairspring, note: Trapezoidal weights on balance.

⊕ Note: Some models and grades are not included. Their values can be determined by comparing with **similar** age, size, metal content, style, models and grades listed.

⊕ Note: Watches listed in this book are priced at the **collectable retail** level, as **complete** watches having an original case, an original dial, and with the entire original movement in good working order with no repairs needed.

TOURBILLON, KARRUSEL, RARE & UNUSUAL MOVEMENTS

One minute so called "Poor Man's Tourbillon", center seconds silver watch with centered dial & visible system. Swiss, 54mm. (illo.39)

Visible Tourbillon, 53mm, 13 jewels, tourbillon system is visible from dial side, ca. 1913. (illo.40)

TYPE – DESCRIPTION	Avg	Ex-Fn	Mint
Tourbillon, Swiss, base metal, 54mm, OF (illo.39)	$1,700	$2,000	$2,300
Tourbillon, 53mm, 13J, visible from dial, Ca. 1913 (illo.40)	2,100	2,200	2,500
Tourbillon, In 4 min., 15J, enamel dial, silver, C.1930 (illo.41)	3,500	3,700	4,000
Karrusel, in 52 min., English, 3/4, gilt, 16J, SW, silver case, 56mm, OF, C.1885, (illo.42)	3,800	4,200	4,700
Helicoil mainspring, Swiss, 15J, cylinder esc., base metal, 51mm, OF, C. 1910 (illo.43)	1,500	1,700	2,000

TOURBILLON, in 4 minutes, 15 jewels, enamel dial, silver case, Ca.1930. (illo.41)

52 minute KARRUSEL, 57mm, 14J., English, silver case, Ca.1885. (illo.42)

COMPARISON OF WATCH SIZES

U. S. A.		EUROPEAN
10-12 SIZE		40—44 MM
16	SIZE	45—48 MM
18	SIZE	50—54 MM

Helicoil Mainspring, 51mm, 15J., rare winding system, cylindrical spring replaces standard mainspring. (illo.43)

Lever with Fusee, KW KS, (Liverpool), hallmarked, silver, **undersprung**, 46mm, OF, Ca. 1850-70.(illo.44)

EARLY PRE–1850 NON—GOLD

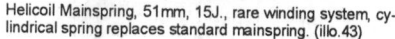

TYPE – DESCRIPTION	Avg	Ex-Fn	Mint
Lever, Fusee, (Liverpool), silver, 46mm, OF, Ca. 1850-70 (illo.44)	$150	$200	$250
Lever or cylinder, BAR, KW KS, silver, 46-52mm,OF(illo.45)	125	150	175
Lever or cylinder, BAR, KW KS, silver, 46-52mm, OF, Ca. 1840-85	125	150	175
Lever or cylinder, **engraved** BAR, KW KS, silver, 46-52mm, OF, Ca. 1840-85 (illo.46)	150	200	250
Lever or cylinder, **Le-PINE,** KW KS, silver, 46-52mm (illo.46)	150	200	250
Rack & pinion lever escap., KW KS, silver, 46-52mm, OF (illo.48)	250	300	350

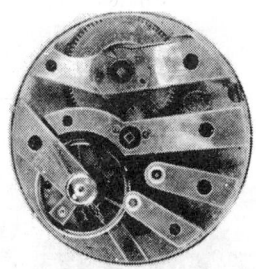

Lever, KW KS, bar style movement, note **curved barrel bridge**, silver, 46-52mm, OF, C. 1830-50. (illo.45)

Lever, **Le-PINE style bar, engraved,** KW KS, silver, 46-52mm, OF, Ca. 1840-85. (illo.46)

Lever, **Le-PINE style tapered bar movement,** KW KS, silver, 46-52mm, OF, Ca. 1820-35. (illo.47)

Rack & pinion lever escapement, KW KS, silver, 46-52mm, Ca. 1830. (illo.48)

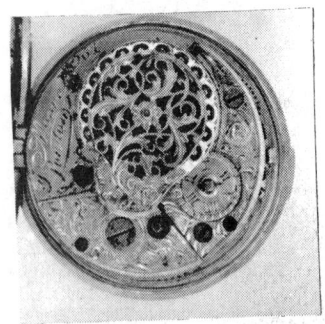

Verge, chain driven fusee, (English) paircase, 52mm, OF, C.1800- 40. (illo.49)

Verge, fusee, (English) paircase, hallmarked, KW, 52mm, OF, Ca. 1780-90. (illo.50)

TYPE – DESCRIPTION	Avg	Ex-Fn	Mint
Verge, Fusee (Swiss), KW, (unmarked) single case, silver, 49mm, OF, C. 1810-40	$300	$350	$400
Verge (English) paircase, 52mm, OF, C.1800- 40 (illo.49)	300	350	400
Painted "farmer's dial," verge, Swiss / London, silver, 52-55m, OF	500	600	700
Rack &lever, Fusee, silver, 52mm, OF, C. 1830-50	400	500	600
Cylinder, Fusee, silver, 48-52mm, OF, C. 1830s	400	500	600
Verge, Fusee (Swiss), KW, silver single case, 49mm OF, C. 1810-1840	400	450	500
Verge (English) paircase, hallmarked, KW, 52mm, OF, C. 1780-90-(illo.50)	400	450	500
Miniature, verge, lady's, plain, porcelain dial, hallmarked silver, 24mm, OF, C. 1810	900	1,000	1,100
Gilt & enamel, verge, Swiss or French, 46mm, OF, C. 1800	1,000	1,200	1,400
Skeletonized, verge, Swiss, double case, hand-carved movement, case silver & horn, 53mm,OF, C. 1800	700	800	900
Repousee paircase, fancy dial, verge, London, hallmarked silver, 49mm, OF, C. 1800, (illo.51)	1,300	1,500	1,700
Erotic Repousee paircase, Swan & Lady, verge, London, (illo.52).	1,400	1,600	2,100

Repousee paircase, fancy dial, verge, English hallmarked silver case, 49mm, OF, C. 1800. (illo.51)

Erotic Repousee silver paircase, Swan & Lady, verge, Fusee, London. (illo.52)

OIGNON watch with mock pendulum, 58mm, Ca. 1700-1720. (illo.53)

Lady & mock pendulum, mock pendulum can be seen at top of Ladies head , 58mm, Ca. 1690 (illo.54)

TYPE – DESCRIPTION	Avg	Ex-Fn	Mint
Oignon watch with mock pendulum, 58mm, ca. 1700-20 (illo.53) .	$3,800	$4,800	$5,300
Lady & mock pendulum, enamel Lady, 58mm, Ca. 1690 (illo.54) .	4,000	5,000	6,000
Verge w/ calendar, repousee paircase, London hallmarked, 51mm, OF, C. 1690	3,800	4,300	4,800
Dublin, early verge, silver paircase, champleve silver dial (signed), 54mm, OF, C. 1720.........................	2,800	3,300	3,800
Early verge, large winged cock, signed silver dial, London, Egyptian pillars, silver, 55mm, OF, C. 1700 (illo.55).............	2,800	3,300	3,500
Viennese enamel on gilt, verge, fusee, multi-scenes on case, KW, 55mm, HC, C. 1780...	3,100	3,800	4,100
English, verge w/ calendar, signed champleve dial, silver & horn, 54mm OF, C. 1680...	3,800	4,300	4,800

Early verge, large D shaped foot on the cock, London, signed silver dial, Egyptian pillars, silver, 55mm, OF, C. 1700 . (illo.55)

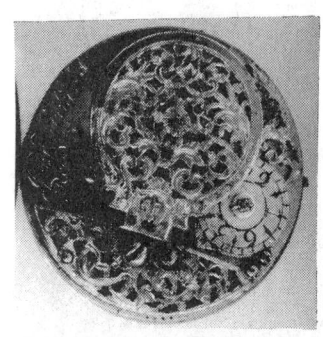

Tortoise shell case, verge with chain driven fusee, calendar, D shaped foot balance cock, C. 1700, (illo.56)

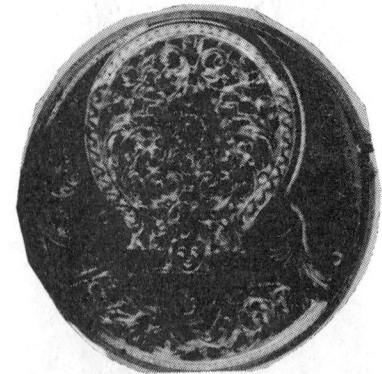

English, verge, hand pierced cock, fusee, silver, note face on balance cock, C. 1720, (illo.57)

TYPE – DESCRIPTION	Avg	Ex-Fn	Mint
Tortoise shell, verge, calendar, Ca. 1700, (illo.56)..........................	$3,300	$3,800	$4,800
English, verge, hand pierced cock, fusee, silver, Ca. 1720, (illo.57)	2,800	3,300	3,800
Pumpkin Form Case, verge, silver, 40mm, Ca. 1775 (illo.58).......	3,300	3,800	4,300
Garooned Case, verge, fusee, 44mm, silver, Ca. 1650 (illp.59).......	9,300	10,300	12,300
Painted scene on horn, verge, gilt, 57mm, OF, Ca. 1780, (illo.60)..	2,300	2,800	3,800

Pumpkin Form Case, verge, silver, Ca. 1775. (illo.58)

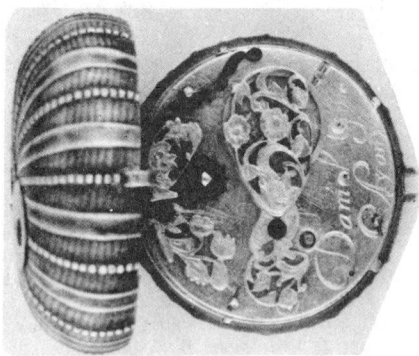

Garooned Case, verge, fusee, 44mm, Ca. 1650. (illp.59)

Painted horn (full scene in color) London, verge, gilt, 57mm, OF, C. 1780. (illo.60)

EARLY NON—GOLD

Early Astronomic watch with day date month calendar, lunar calendar, 57mm, Ca. 1680. (illo.61)

TYPE – DESCRIPTION	Avg	Ex-Fn	Mint
Early Astronomic watch with day date month calendar, lunar calendar, 57mm, Ca. 1680. (illo.61)	$10,000	$15,000	$18,000
Early Astronomic watch with moon phases and triple date, fusee with cut-gut cord, 3 gear train, foliot, Ca.1660. (illo.62)	15,000	17,000	20,000

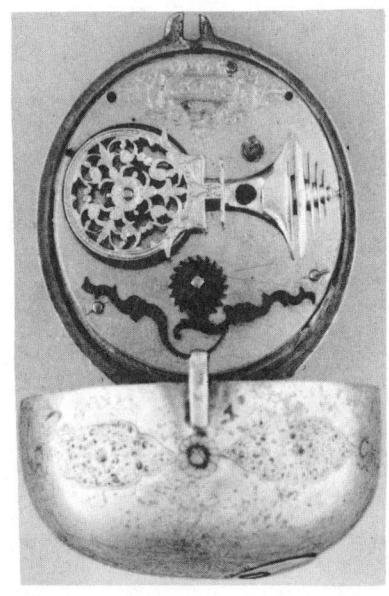

Early Astronomic watch with moon phases and triple date, fusee with cut-gut cord, 3 gear train, 6 armed foliot, Ca.1660. (illo.62)

Early German made silver watch, verge and foliot, silver pierced dial, "Hamburg", Ca. 1660. (illo.63)

TYPE – DESCRIPTION	Avg	Ex-Fn	Mint
Early German made silver watch, verge and foliot, silver pierced dial, "Hamburg", Ca. 1660 (illo.63)	$8,000	$9,000	$10,000
Early silver watch, blued steel hand, cut-gut fusee, foliot, rosette for adj., 53mm, Ca.1660 (illo.64)	16,000	18,000	20,000

Early silver watch, silver dial with blued steel hand, cut gut fusee, 3 wheel train, foliot, rosette for adjustment of the motor-spring tension, 53mm, Ca.1660. (illo.64)

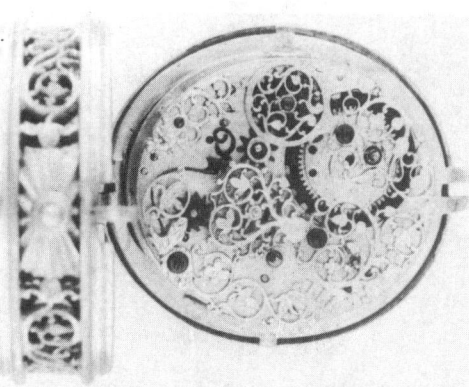

Pair cased, first case silver covered with nailed skin, verge, cut-gut cord fusee, 3 wheel train, foliot, pierced cock, endless screw adjustment for main spring tension, 45mm, Ca. 1660. (illo.65)

Early French watch movement with hour and minute hand, striking bell each hour, hand pierced case & gilt brass movement, cut-gut fusee, c. 1600s. (illo.66)

TYPE – DESCRIPTION

	Avg	Ex-Fn	Mint
Pair cased, first case silver & nailed skin, verge, fusee, 3 wheel train, foliot, pierced cock, 45mm, Ca. 1660 (illo.65)	$5,500	$6,500	$7,500
Early French watch hour and minute hand, striking on bell, cut-gut fusee, c. 1600s (illo.66)	15,000	18,000	20,000
Early Drum Clock, iron plates, 4 wheel train, brass fusee on a steel great wheel, steel contrate wheel with brass teeth, steel verge and foliot balance w/ T-shaped ends, 34mm high (illo.67)	28,000	35,000	45,000

43mm, Early Drum Clock, iron plates, 4 wheel train, brass fusee on a steel great wheel, steel contrate wheel with brass teeth, steel verge and foliot balance with T-shaped ends . The cylindrical gilt brass case is finely engraved and is 34mm high, Ca. 1550—1560. (illo.67)

PRE–1850 *GOLD*

Lever or verge, (Liverpool), 18K, multi-colored gold dial, 52mm, OF, C.1845-75. (illo.68).

Lever or cylinder, BAR style movement, GOLD, 45-52mm, OF, 1840-1865. (illo.69)

TYPE – DESCRIPTION	Avg	Ex-Fn	Mint
Lever or verge, (Liverpool), **18K**, 52mm, OF, C.1845-75 (illo.68).	$600	$700	$800
Lever or verge, (Liverpool), 15J, **18K**, 52mm, HC, C. 1845-75......	700	900	1,100
Lever or cylinder, BAR, GOLD, 45-52mm, OF(illo.69)...................	325	375	450
(same as above) w / skeletonized movement,**18K,** (illo.70) ...	600	700	800
Lever or cylinder, Le-Pine style, GOLD, 45-52mm, OF(illo.71)	325	375	450
Cylinder Fusee, paircase, London, plain case, porcelain dial,18K, 48mm, OF, C. 1880..............................	1,600	1,800	1,900
Verge, multi-color case, Swiss/ French, porcelain dial, 18K, 42mm,OF, Ca. 1770-1800...	1,500	1,800	2,000
Verge, French, gold & enamel patterns on case, KWKS, OF, C. 1805...	1,800	2,200	2,500
Verge, (Swiss), 18K, 52-54mm, plain case, OF, C. 1790-1820.......	750	950	1,200
Verge ,Swiss, gold scene, high quality ,18K, 50mm, OF, C.1790...	2,000	2,200	2,500

Lever or cylinder, skeletonized & engraved bar movement, Swiss, 45-52mm, OF,18K. (illo.70)

Lever or cylinder escapement, Le-Pine style movement, Ca. 1820-1835, GOLD, 45-52mm, OF. (illo.71)

Verge, repousee paircase, 20K gold case, 43mm, Open Face, Ca.1780, (illo.72)

Early verge, D shaped balance cock, signed dial, London, Egyptian pillars, gold, 55mm, OF, Ca. 1760. (illo.73)

TYPE – DESCRIPTION

TYPE – DESCRIPTION	Avg	Ex-Fn	Mint
Verge, repousee paircase, 20K, 43mm, OF, C.1780 (illo.72)	$2,700	$3,200	$3,700
Early verge, large winged cock, signed dial, London,Egyptian pillars, gold, 55mm, OF, C. 1760 (illo.73)	3,000	3,400	3,900
Virgule, Fusee, Swiss or French, 18K, 50-55mm, OF, C. 1790	1,400	1,700	1,800
Fusee, made in HOLLAND, Ca. 1800, GOLD case	500	600	700
Skeletonized French, diamonds on bezel, 39mm, C.1780 (illo.75)	2,200	2,600	3,000
Rack & Pinion lever escapement, 18K, OF, Ca. 1830 (illo.76)	650	700	850

Fusee, made in HOLLAND, GOLD case, note the bridge style, 60mm, OF, Ca. 1800 (illo.74)

Skeletonized French watch, diamonds on bezel, 39mm, C.1780 (illo.75)

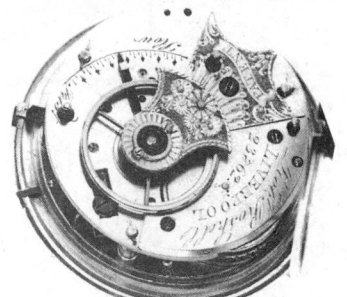

Rack and Lever Escapement, 18K, OF, Ca. 1830 (illo.76)

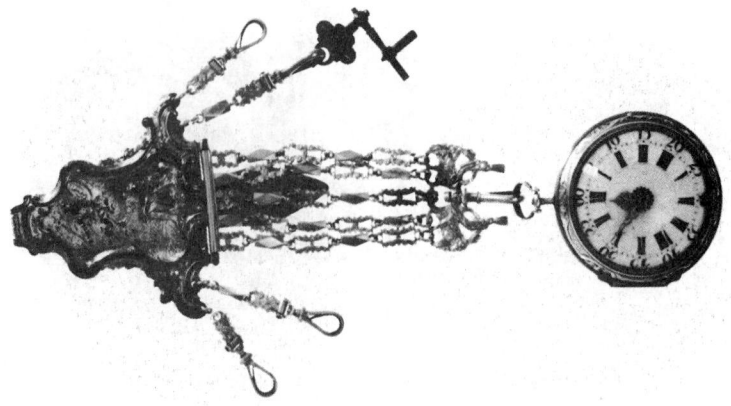

CHATELAINE, verge, fusee, 22k pair case, 45mm, (illo.76)

TYPE – DESCRIPTION	Avg	Ex-Fn	Mint
Chatelaine, verge, fusee, 22k pair case, (illo.76)	$3,500	$4,000	$4,500
Early gold & nailed double case watch, foliot, C.1670 (illo.77)	22,000	25,000	28,000

Early gold & nailed double case watch, Champleve gold dial, 3 wheel train, verge, foliot, rosette adjustment and endless screw, 50mm, C.1670 (illo.77)

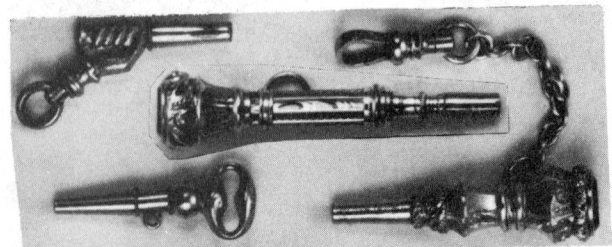

GOLD KEYS, the tops are all gold and the bottom key shaft is base metal, PRICES= **$85 to $150** each.

MISC. MEN'S GF / SILVER / BASE METAL

Dollar watch **German**, base metal ,OF, C.1895. (illo.78)

Dollar watch **German**, with camera, back wind, **waterproof style model**, base metal, OF, C.1885. (illo.79)

TYPE – DESCRIPTION	Avg	Ex-Fn	Mint
Dollar watch **German,** base metal ,OF, C.1895 (illo.78)	$45	$65	$85
Dollar watch **German,** back wind, **waterproof,** OF, C.1885 (illo.79)	325	350	400
Base metal, 7-17J, SW, 43-48mm, OF, C. 1900-1930	45	65	75
GF or silver, 7-17J, SW, 43-48mm, OF, C. 1895-1940	65	75	95
GF or silver, 7-17J, SW, 43-52mm, **HC,** C. 1895-1940..................	100	125	150
Swiss Fakes , 7J, KW, base metal, OF, 52mm, C. 1870-90.............	65	85	100
Non-magnetic, pat.# 7546/780, **Moeris,** base metal, (illo.80)	100	125	150
Cylinder, (Liverpool), 1/2 plate design, (illo.81)............................	100	125	150

Non-magnetic, pat.#7546/780, **Moeris**, base metal, thumb-nail set, SW, OF. (illo.80)

Cylinder escapement, (Liverpool), 1/2 plate design, marked 4 hole jeweled=8 jewels. (illo.81)

COMPARISON OF WATCH SIZES

U. S. A.	EUROPEAN
10-12 SIZE	40—44 MM
16 SIZE	45—48 MM
18 SIZE	50—54 MM

KW KS, **Chinese Duplex** escapement, 3/4 plate design, OF. (illo.82)

KW KS, with a **Compass** on movement, lever escapement. (illo.83)

TYPE – DESCRIPTION	Avg	Ex-Fn	Mint
KWKS, **Chinese Duplex,** 3/4 plate design, OF, (illo.82)	$300	$350	$400
KWKS, **Compass** on movement, lever escap., (illo.83)	125	150	195
KWKS, 6-15J, silver, 45-52mm, OF, C. 1860-85	65	90	100
KWKS, 8-17J, silver, 45-52mm, HC, C. 1860-85	75	100	130
Engraved movement, KWKS, 15J, silver, 46mm, HC, C.1870	100	130	150
KWKS, marked railway, pin lever, Swiss, (illo.84)	45	65	85
21J, RR type, GF, 48mm, OF, C. 1910-30	80	100	130
25J, Waltham (Swiss made), GF, 48mm, OF, C. 1950	100	150	175
Niello enamel, 17J, SW, silver, 45mm, HC, C. 1940	125	175	225
Niello enamel & **embossed** hunting scene on case, enamel dial, 3/4 plate, made in **Beaucourt France,** OF, (illo.85)	200	225	265

KWKS, marked railway, pin lever, Swiss. (illo.84)

Niello enamel & embossed hunting scene on case, enamel dial, 3/4 plate, made in Beaucourt France, OF, Ca. 1890. (illo.85)

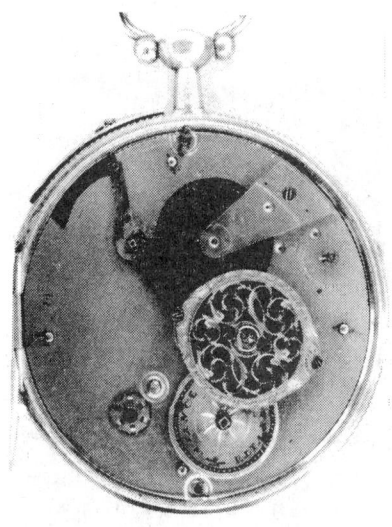

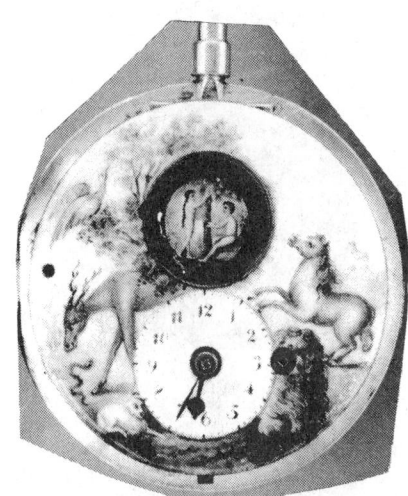

1/4 repeater early rim activated, Swiss or French, silver, OF, Ca. 1820. (illo.86)

Automaton, **Adam & Eve**, note snake circles Adam & Eve, hand painted enamel dial, KW KS, OF. (illo. 87)

TYPE – DESCRIPTION

TYPE – DESCRIPTION	Avg	Ex-Fn	Mint
1/4 repeater early rim activated, silver, OF, Ca.1820 (illo.86)	$900	$1,000	$1,200
Automaton, **Adam & Eve**, w/ snake, KW KS, OF (illo. 87)	5,000	6,000	7,000
Spring detent chronometer w/Tandem wind, fusee, 56mm, Ca.1875 (illo.88)	700	800	900
Gamblers playing cards on dial porcelain, Swiss, silver, OF (illo.89)	425	465	500

Spring Detent chronometer with Tandem wind, chain driven fusee, Helical hair spring, 56mm, Ca.1875. (illo.88)

Gamblers playing cards on porcelain dial, Swiss, silver, OF. (illo.89)

Exposed Skeletonized Balance from dial, enamel painted dial, verge, fusee, KW KS, large advance-retard index, Ca.1790. (illo.90)

TYPE – DESCRIPTION	Avg	Ex-Fn	Mint
Exposed Balance from dial, enamel painted dial, Ca.1790 (illo.90)	$1,500	$2,000	$2,400
Wandering Digital Jump Hour Hand, 45mm, Ca. 1880 (illo.91)....	6,000	7,000	8,000
Jump Digital Hour, W/ Date, at 6, sec. hand at 3, Ca. 1820 (illo.92)	3,000	3,500	4,000

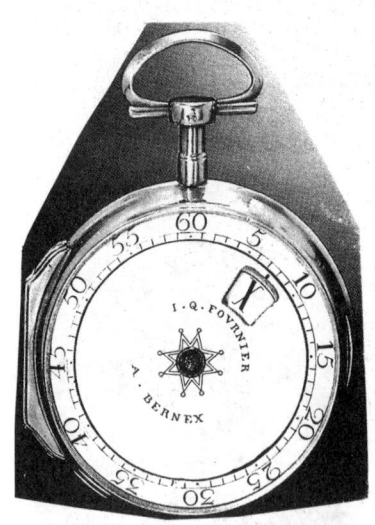

Wandering Digital Jump Hour Hand, Fusee, Cylinder Escapement, 45mm, silver, OF, Ca. 1880, (illo.91)

Jump Digital Hour, W/ Date, at 6, sec. hand at 3, silver, engine turned dial, OF, Ca. 1820 (illo.92)

COMPARISON OF WATCH SIZES

U. S. A.	EUROPEAN
10-12 SIZE	40—44 MM
16 SIZE	45—48 MM
18 SIZE	50—54 MM

Day, date, moon phases, Swiss, fancy dial GF, 46mm lever set at rim of case. (illo.93)

Day, date, Swiss, fancy dial, base metal, 46mm. (illo.94)

TYPE – DESCRIPTION	Avg	Ex-Fn	Mint
Day, date, moon phases, Swiss, fancy dial, **GF**, 46mm (illo.93).....	$300	$350	$425
Day, date, moon phases, Swiss, fancy dial, **gun metal**, 46mm	200	250	300
Day, date, Swiss, fancy dial, **base metal**, 46mm (illo.94)	125	150	175
Self winding, (Loehr patent), KW, set from back, (illo.95).............	450	500	575
Mock pendulum (seen from face side), duplex escap. (illo.96).......	400	500	600

Self winding, (Loehr patent), KW, set from back. (illo.95)

Mock pendulum (seen from face side), duplex escap. Multi-color dial. (illo.96)

MISC. MEN'S *GOLD* / PLATINUM

TYPE – DESCRIPTION	Avg	Ex-Fn	Mint
SW, 17J, **14K**, 43-46mm, OF, C. 1910-1940	$195	$225	$275
SW, 17J-19J, **18K**, 43-46mm, OF, C. 1910-1940	250	275	350
SW, 17J, **14K**, 48mm, HC, C. 1910-1940	375	425	500
SW, 17J, **Platinum**, 42mm, OF, C. 1940's	495	550	650
KWKS, 15J, lever, fancy ,gilt dial, **18K**, 45mm, C. 1870................	275	300	400
KWKS, 15-20J, lever **18K**, 49-53mm, C. 1870-1885	400	500	650
Lever, Fusee, (Liverpool), 15J, porcelain dial, **18K**, 52mm, C.1860	450	550	700

UNUSUAL NON—GOLD

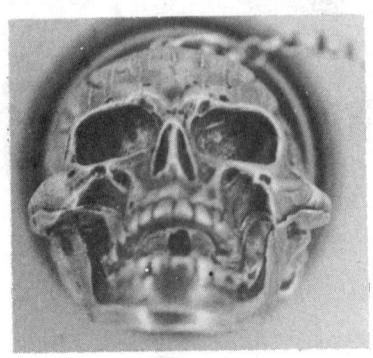

Skull (miniature) form watch, fusee, cylinder escapement, 25mm. (illo.97)

Blinking Eyes, pin set animated eyes, 46mm. (illo.98)

TYPE – DESCRIPTION	Avg	Ex-Fn	Mint
Skull (miniature) form, fusee, cylinder escape., 25mm, (illo.97)	$550	$700	$950
Blinking Eyes, pin set animated eyes, 46mm, (illo.98)	200	250	300
8 day, exposed balance, 7J, gun metal, 50mm, C. 1920s (illo.99)...	100	125	150
8 day, exposed balance, 7J, Swiss, **DAY & DATE,** gun metal, 50mm, C. 1920s	150	175	225
Roulette wheel dial, 7J, SW, base metal, 46mm, OF, C.1915	130	150	200
Game spin wheel novelty watch, 6 horses, gun metal, (illo.100).....	300	350	400

8 DAY, exposed balance, 7J, by Hebdomas but with other name, gun metal, 50mm, C. 1920s. (illo.99)

Game spin wheel novelty watch, 6 horses, gun metal. (illo.100)

🕐 Note: Some models and grades are not included. Their values can be determined by comparing with **similar** age, size, metal content, style, models and grades listed.

🕐 Note: Watches listed in this book are priced at the collectable retail level, as **complete** watches having an original case, an original dial, and with the entire original movement in good working order with no repairs needed.

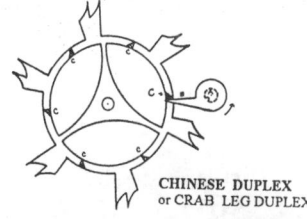

CHINESE DUPLEX
or CRAB LEG DUPLEX

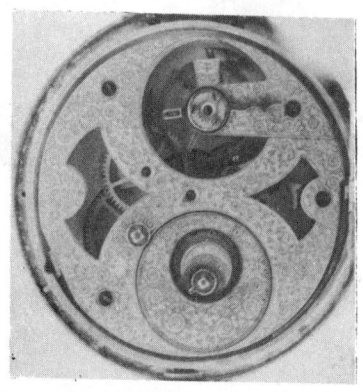

Chinese market, KWKS, duplex esc. silver, 58mm, OF, C.1870. (illo.101)

Chinese market, KW, duplex esc. silver, 58mm, OF, C.1870. (illo.102)

TYPE – DESCRIPTION	Avg	Ex-Fn	Mint
For Chinese market, lever esc., 12J, KWKS, silver, 55mm, OF, C. 1880	$250	$300	$325
Chinese market, KW, duplex esc. silver, 58mm, OF, C.1870 (illo.101)	300	350	400
Chinese market, KW, duplex esc. silver, 58mm, OF, C.1870 (illo.102)	300	350	425
same as above with a **GOLD CASE**	600	700	850
Chinese market, KW, duplex esc. silver, carved movement, 58mm, OF, C.1870 (illo.103)	375	425	475
Carved movement, lever escap., KWKS, silver, 58mm, OF(illo.104)	135	160	185
KW, for Turkish market, 15J, .800 silver, 47mm, HC, C. 1880	125	150	175

Chinese market, KW, duplex esc. silver, carved movement,58mm, OF, C.1870. (illo.103)

Carved movement, lever escap., KWKS, silver, 58mm, OF. (illo.104)

Oversize, moon phase & calendar, silver, 65-70mm, Ca.1900. (illo.105)

Moonphase triple cal., Swiss, gun metal , 50mm, OF, C.1905. (illo.106)

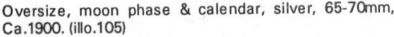

TYPE – DESCRIPTION	Avg	Ex-Fn	Mint
Oversize PW, 15J, base metal, 65-70mm, C. 1900-1915	$200	$250	$275
Oversize, moon ph. & calendar, silver,65-70mm, Ca.1900 (illo.105)	900	1,200	1,500
Moonphase triple cal., Swiss, gun metal , 50mm, OF, C.1905(illo.106)	300	400	450
Moonphase triple cal., Swiss, silver or GF, 50mm, OF, C.1905......	350	450	550
Moonphase triple cal., Swiss, silver, 52-54mm, **HC**, C. 1905.........	750	850	900
Moonphase calendar, sterling, , oversize 65mm, OF, C. 1895.........	650	800	850
Verge (Swiss) skeletonized KW movement, silver & horn paircase, 61mm, C. 1800..	650	750	850
Captain's watch, 2 hour dials, 1 train, KW KS, center second, silver, 50mm, HC, C. 1870 (illo.107)	650	750	850
Digital dial (porcelain), 15J, SW, Swiss, jump hr. & min. discs, silver,HC, C. 1900 (illo.108)	450	550	700

Captain's watch, 2 hour dials, 1 train, KW KS, center second, silver, 50mm, HC, C. 1870. (illo.107)

Digital dial (porcelain), 15J, SW, Swiss, jump hr. & min. discs, silver,HC, C. 1900. (illo.108)

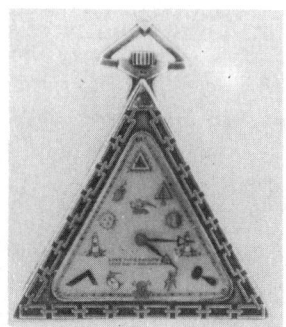

Automated with moving windmill on dial, Swiss, colored scene, exposed balance, 8 day , base metal, OF, C.1910. (illo.109)

Masonic triangular watch, Swiss ,17J, **mother of pearl** masonic dial, sterling, C. 1920's. (illo.110)

TYPE – DESCRIPTION	Avg	Ex-Fn	Mint
Automated w/moving windmill on dial, Swiss, colored scene, exposed balance, 8 day , base metal, OF, C.1910 (illo.109)...	$475	$500	$575
Masonic triangular watch, Swiss ,17J, **mother of pearl** masonic dial, sterling, C. 1920's (illo.110)................................	1,800	2,500	2,800
World time w/ 6 zones, Swiss, **Gun Metal**, OF, C. 1900 (illo.111)	500	650	800
World time w/ 6 zones, Swiss, **silver**, 52mm, OF, C. 1900	700	800	1,000
World time, 24 Cities, w/ coded color rotating dial, 61mm(illo.112)	3,000	3,500	4,000

World time, with 6 zones, Swiss, GUN METAL, 52mm, OF, Ca.1900. (illo.111)

World time, 24 Cities, with coded color rotating dial, Ca. 1895, 61mm. (illo.112)

🕐 Note: Some models and grades are not included. Their values can be determined by comparing with **similar** age, size, metal content, style, models and grades listed.

🕐 Note: Watches listed in this book are priced at the collectable retail level, as **complete** watches having an original case, an original dial, and with the entire original movement in good working order with no repairs needed.

TYPE – DESCRIPTION	Avg	Ex-Fn	Mint
Sector watch, fan-shaped, fly back hour & min. hands, 17J, "Record Watch Co.," silver, 49x34mm, Ca. 1900 (illo.113)..	$1,800	$2,500	$3,000
Mysterieuse watch, Swiss, see-through dial, hidden movement silver, 52mm, OF, Ca. 1895 (illo.114)......................................	2,000	2,500	2,850
Wooden works, wooden wheels, wooden case, 50mm (illo.115)....	1,400	1,800	2,400
Self-wind, Swiss, cylinder escape., self-wind, gun metal (illo.116)	300	350	400
Musical, play's 2 tunes, silver, HC, 50mm, Ca. 1900 (illo.117)......	3,000	3,500	4,000

Sector watch, fan-shaped, fly back hour & min. hands, 17J, "Record Watch Co.," silver, 49x34mm, Ca. 1900. (illo.113)

Mysterieuse watch, Swiss, see-through dial, hidden movement silver, 52mm, OF, Ca. 1895. (illo.114)

Wooden works, wooden wheels, wooden case, all wooden watch, 50mm, made in Russia in, Ca. 1860. (illo.115)

Self-wind, Swiss, cylinder escapement, self-wind, gun metal. (illo.116)

Musical, play's 2 tunes, silver, 30 Tynes, HC, 50mm, 1900. (illo.117)

Rock crystal & enamel, star shape case, champleve enameled dial, verge, French, gilt & crystal
case, 57x27mm, original French form Ca. 1600-1660, Viennese form Ca. 1780-1800. (illo.118)

TYPE – DESCRIPTION	Avg	Ex-Fn	Mint
Rock crystal & enamel, star shape case, champleve enameled dial, verge, French, gilt & crystal case, 57x27mm, C.1800 (illo.118)	$5,000	$5,500	$6,000
Crucifix form 1/4 hr. repeater & musical, crystal & silver form case, (illo.119)	10,000	13,000	15,000

Crucifix form 1/4 hr. repeater & musical, crystal & silver form case, original French form Ca. 1600-
1660, Viennese form Ca. 1780-1800. (illo.119)

MEN'S UNUSUAL *"GOLD"*

Extra flat watch, **1.5mm thick,** Swiss, 18K, HC, <u>ACTUAL SIZE</u>,50mm. (illo.120)

TYPE – DESCRIPTION	Avg	Ex-Fn	Mint
Extra flat watch, 1.5mm thick, Swiss, 18K, HC, 50mm (illo.120) ..	$7,000	$8,000	$9,000
Jump 1/4 seconds, 2 train, 30J, KW, nickel, by August Saltzman (Swiss), 18K, 56mm, HC, C. 1870	2,000	2,500	3,000
Captain's watch, enameled portraits on case, Maharaja & Queen Victoria, KW, lever movement, 18K, 44mm, HC, C.1870	2,500	3,000	3,500
Captain's watch, KW, 15J, engraved case & gold dial, 18K, 52-58mm, OF, C. 1870 (illo.121)....................................	1,200	1,400	1,500
1776-1876 centennial watch, H.O. Stauffer, bridges in 1776 form, 17J, 18K, 53mm, HC, C. 1876, (illo.122)..............................	2,500	2,800	3,000

Captain's watch, KW, 15J, engraved case & gold dial, 18K, 52-58mm, OF, Ca. 1870. (illo.121)

1776-1876 centennial watch, H.O. Stauffer, bridges in 1776 form, 17J, 18K, 53mm, HC, Ca. 1876. (illo.122)

Double dials double lids, back side cal., front time & moon phases, 18K, HC, Ca. 1910. (illo.123)

TYPE – DESCRIPTION	Avg	Ex-Fn	Mint
Captain's watch, KW KS, 15J, ornate case, Swiss, 18K, 52mm, HC, C. 1870	$1,500	$1,700	$2,000
Digital dial, hrs. & min. on digital jump discs, Swiss, 15J, SW, 18K, 51mm, HC, C. 1905	1,500	1,600	1,900
Moonphase, double dial, calendar, Swiss, 17J, back lid opens to reveal full moon w/cal. dial, 14K, HC, C.1890 (illo.123)	3,000	3,500	3,750
Two train, center independent sec.,2 going barrels, lever escap., KW KS, GOLD, 42mm, Ca. 1880, HC (illo. 124)	1,800	2,000	2,500
Art Deco dial, Swiss, 18K, 45mm,OF (illo.125)	1,000	1,200	1,500

Two train, center independent sec.,2 going barrels, lever escap.,KW KS, GOLD, 42mm, Ca. 1880, HC. (illo. 124)   Art Deco dial, Swiss, 18K, 45mm,OF. (illo.125)

TYPE – DESCRIPTION	Avg	Ex-Fn	Mint
Double dials, world time & moon ph. triple date,18K, (illo.126)	$8,000	$9,000	$10,000
Perpetual calendar with moonphase and chrono., Swiss , 20J, porcelain dial, 3/4 plate, 18K, 51mm, OF, C.1890-1900	8,000	9,000	10,000
Rare verge, w/ automaton "Serpent, Adam & Eve" on dial with moving serpent, verge, French , 18K, OF, C. 1800	5,000	6,000	6,500
Musical, two train of gears, pin cylinder & 24 blades, one tune, 18K, (illo.127)	6,500	7,000	7,500
Waterproof watch w/wind ind. 17J., C.1885, (illo.128)	1,875	2,000	2,300
Cigarette lighter & Swiss watch, Dunhill, Silver, C.1926, (illo.129)	300	400	500
9K case	1,200	1,400	1,500
14K case	1,700	1,800	2,000
$20.00 U.S. gold coin, 17J, mvt. in coin, 35mm, Ca.1920's (illo.130)	2,000	2,500	3,000

Double dials, world time & moon ph. triple date,18K. (illo.126)

Musical, two train of gears, pin cylinder & 24 blades, one tune, 18K. (illo.127)

Waterproof watch w/wind ind. 17J., C.1885. (illo.128)

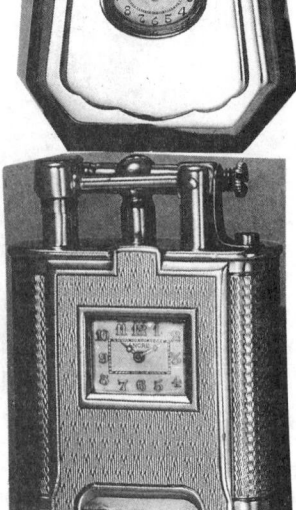

Cigarette lighter & Swiss watch, Dunhill, Silver, Ca.1926. (illo.129)

$20.00 U.S. gold coin, 17J, Swiss mvt. in coin, 35mm, Ca.1920's. (illo.130)

MISC. SWISS LADY'S Ca. 1850–1950 SILVER or GOLD FILLED

TYPE – DESCRIPTION	Avg	Ex-Fn	Mint
GF or silver, 7-17J, SW, 35mm, OF, C. 1900-1930	$45	$55	$75
GF or silver, 10-15J, SW, 35mm, fancy dial, OF, C. 1910	65	75	100
GF or silver, 7-17J, SW, 35- 40mm, HC, C. 1890-1930	75	95	125
Enamel or silver, cylinder, pinset, 35mm, OF, C. 1910	85	90	125
KWKS, silver, 40- 45mm, OF, C. 1865-1885	75	90	125
KWKS, silver, 37- 45mm, **HC**, C. 1865-1885	100	125	150
Ball shaped, 17J, 35mm, SW, GF or silver with chain	100	135	195

MISC. LADYS Ca. 1850–1950 *GOLD* (NO ENAMEL)

TYPE – DESCRIPTION	Avg	Ex-Fn	Mint
SW, 7-15J, 14K, 35- 40mm, OF, C. 1910-1930	$100	$135	$195
SW, 7-15J, 14K, 35- 40mm, HC, C. 1910-1930	235	300	325
KWKS, 10J, cylinder, 18K, 34- 40mm, OF, C.1865-90	165	225	275
KWKS, 10J, cylinder, 18K, 38- 43mm, HC, C. 1865-85	300	350	400
Fusee, lever, fancy dial, 18K, 38- 43mm, OF, C. 1845-75	350	450	550
Fusee, lever, fancy dial, 18K, 38- 43mm, HC, C. 1850s	400	500	600
Ball shaped w/pin, 10J, 14K, 25mm, OF, C. 1890	500	600	650

MISC. LADYS Ca. 1850–1950 ENAMEL ON *GOLD*

TYPE – DESCRIPTION	Avg	Ex-Fn	Mint
KW, enamel (black outlines) 18K, 40- 42mm HC, C. 1860	$450	$550	$650
KW, enamel & dia., Swiss, 10J, 18K, OF, C. 1860	450	550	650
Pattern enamel & demi-hunter, 15J, 18K , 35mm, HC, C.1885	500	650	800
Portrait enamel, KWKS, Swiss, 14K, 34- 42mm, HC, C. 1870	550	700	850
Enamel , with pearls and/ or dia., 10-17J,			
w/ matching pin, 18K, 23-26mm, OF	900	1,100	1,300
Enamel, w/dia. or pearls, w/ pin, 18K, 26-30mm, HC, C. 1895	1,400	1,500	1,700
Miniature verge, gold & enamel w/ pearls, superior enamel,			
Swiss, KW, gold case, 27mm, OF, C. 1770,	4,000	4,500	5,000
Miniature HC enamel & dia., 17J, Swiss, with orig. pin,			
18K, 23mm, HC, C. 1890	1,500	2,000	2,300
Ball-shaped (Duchene) Geneva, verge, KW,			
enamel and gold, 25mm, C. 1800	1,800	2,200	2,500

Note: Some models and grades are not included. Their values can be determined by comparing with similar age, size, metal content, style, models and grades listed.

Note: Watches listed in this book are priced at the collectable retail level, as complete watches having an original case, an original dial, and with the entire original movement in good working order with no repairs needed.

COMPARISON OF WATCH SIZES

U. S. A.	EUROPEAN
10-12 SIZE	40—44 MM
16 SIZE	45—48 MM
18 SIZE	50—54 MM

LADY'S UNUSUAL *GOLD* & ENAMEL

LEFT; Ball-shaped, bezel wind, 18K, enamel & diamonds, Swiss, 16mm, OF, C. 1920. (illo.131) CENTER: Ring watch w/enamel & dia., Swiss, 18K, 18mm, C.1910. (illo.132) RIGHT: Padlock form enamel and gold, Swiss, KW. (illo.133)

TYPE – DESCRIPTION	Avg	Ex-Fn	Mint
Ball-shaped, bezel wind, Swiss, enamel & diamonds on 18K case, 16mm, OF, C. 1920 (illo.131)	$1,200	$1,400	$1,600
Ring watch w/enamel & dia., Swiss, 18K, 18mm, C.1910 (illo.132)	1,200	1,800	2,000
Cherry form enamel & 18K, 17J, closed case, bezel wind, Swiss, 22mm,	2,500	3,000	3,500
Flower basket form, enamel and 18K, Swiss, KWKS, with heart form movement, 10J, 18K, 30x24mm, HC, C. 1860	3,000	3,500	4,000
Padlock form enamel and gold, Swiss, KW (illo.133)	2,000	2,250	2,500
Padlock form enamel and gold (cover over dial,) Swiss, KW, diamonds on case, heart shaped mvt.,18K, 28x51mm, HC, C.1870	3,000	3,500	4,000
Form watch in shape of **leaf**, gold & enamel, Bar mvt. (illo.134)	3,000	3,250	3,500

 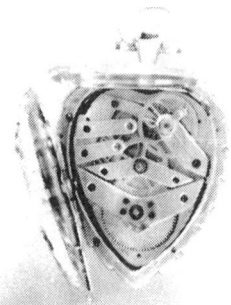

Form watch in shape of **leaf**, gold & enamel, cylinder escapement, Bar movement., KW KS, Ca.1865. (illo.134)

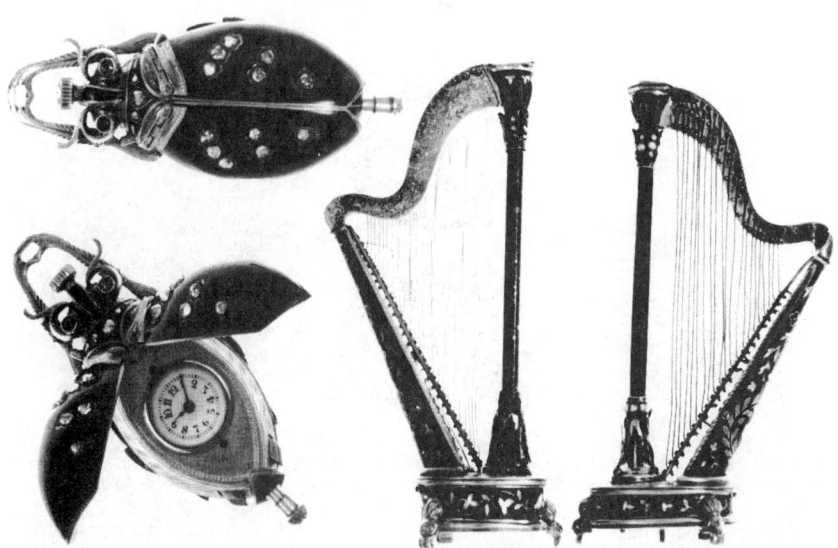

Scarab form gold & enamel, 10J, cylinder, diamonds, closed case w/wings that open, 18K, 54x23mm, C.1885. (illo.135)

Rare enamel & gold harps, matched pair w/ music, verge, diamonds, lapis and enameled scenes, 3 3/4 high, C.1830. (illo.136)

TYPE – DESCRIPTION	Avg	Ex-Fn	Mint
Scarab form gold & enamel, 10J, cylinder, diamonds, closed case w/wings that open, 18K, 54x23mm, C.1885 (illo.135)	$5,000	$6,000	$7,000
Lorgnette with enamel & gold, KW, 10J, Swiss, 3 1/4" x 1" cover ornamented w/dia., 18K	4,000	5,000	6,000
Rare enamel & gold harps, matched pair w/ music, verge, diamonds, lapis and enameled scenes, 3 3/4 high, C.1830 (illo.136)	25,000	30,000	35,000
Rock crystal case, silver dial, Viennese made, C. 1730 (illo.137)	10,000	12,000	15,000

Rock crystal case, silver dial, Viennese made, C. 1830. (illo.137)

ENAMEL WATCHES

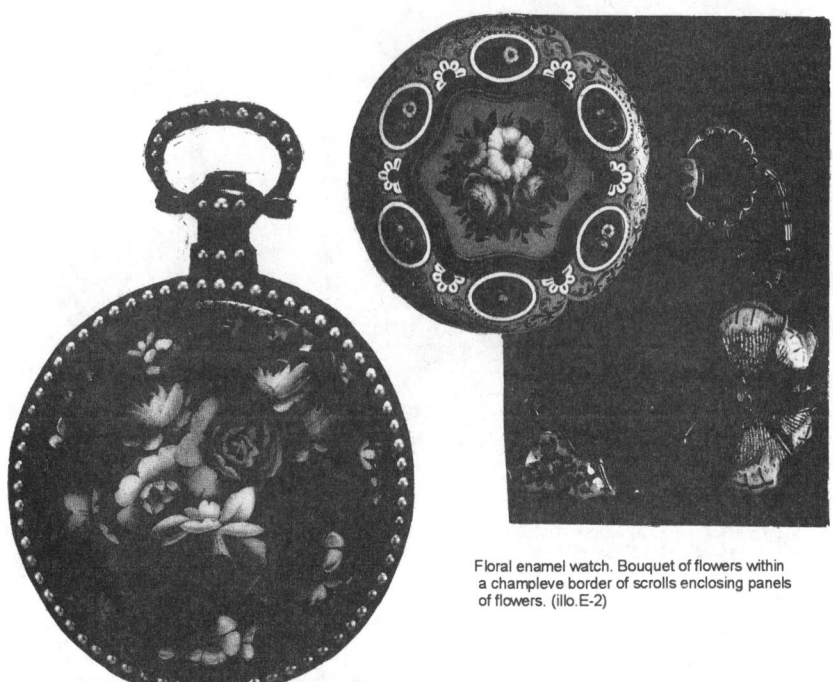

Floral enamel watch. Bouquet of flowers within a champleve border of scrolls enclosing panels of flowers. (illo.E-2)

Floral enamel watch. Finely painted floral enamel panel within border of seed pearls. (illo.E-1)

SIZE AND DESCRIPTION	Avg	Ex-Fn	Mint
55mm, finely painted floral, seed pearls, (Bovet also Ilbery),18K (illo.E.1)	$6,000	$7,500	$9,000
47mm, gold enamel repeater, with chatelaine of pierced gold links & enamel plaques with enamel key & fob seals (illo.E.2)	3,500	4,500	5,500
Enamel & pearls, hunting scene of lion, for China market, duplex escapement, 62mm, Ca. 1845 (illo.E.3)	5,000	6,000	7,000
Enamel and 18K case, automated horseman and windmill also fountain, horse drinks water (illo.E-4)	35,000	37,500	40,000
Enamel floral scene, enamel and pearls on gold case, finely painted floral bouquet, 55mm (illo.E-5)	30,000	35,000	40,000
Enamel and 18K case, MINUTE- REPEATER, HC, surrounded with pearls, 55mm, (illo.E-5A)	22,000	25,500	28,000
VIENNESE enamel watch, the front cover shows a lady and gentleman in a scene, the back cover pictures three boys in a scene, 55mm (illo.E-6 & E-6A)	2,000	2,500	3,000
54mm, 29J., 1/4 repeater, pearls & enamel, silver case (illo.E-8)	2,200	2,800	3,500
VIENNESE Lapis Lazuli enamel watch, verge fusee, top and bottom covers are finely cut solid lapis stone, champleve enamel dial, Ca. 1800 (illo.E-9)	3,500	4,500	5,000

🕐 French watch-making believed to have started in town of Blois, France. French Enamel Watches also believed to have started in Blois, in early 1600's.

Enamel & pearls, hunting scene of lion, for China market, duplex escapement, 62mm, Ca. 1845. (illo.E-3)

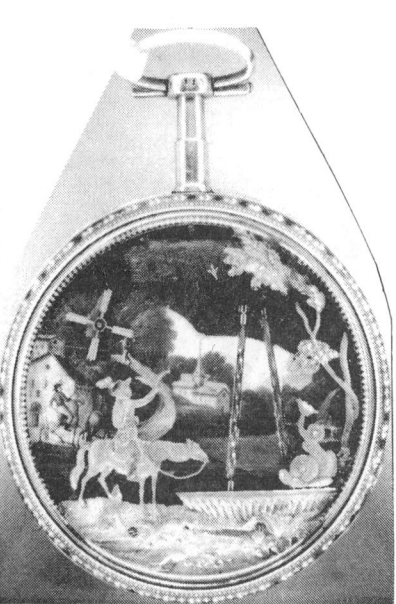

Enamel and 18K case, automated horseman and windmill also fountain, horse drinks water. (illo.E-4)

Enamel floral scene, enamel and pearls on gold case, finely painted floral bouquet, 55mm (illo.E-5)

Enamel and 18K case, MINUTE- REPEATER, Hunting Case, surrounded with pearls, 55mm, Ca.1890. (illo.E-5A)

VIENNESE enamel watch, the front cover shows a lady and gentleman in a scene, the back cover pictures three boys in a scene, 55mm. (illo.E-6)

VIENNESE enamel watch, same watch as above, two-footed balance bridge, the inner lids are decorated with polychrome enamelled scenes. (illo.E-6A)

54mm, 29J, 1/4 hour repeater, Pearls and enamel on a silver case, ca. 1885. (illo.E-8)

VIENNESE Lapis Lazuli enamel watch, verge fusee, top and bottom covers are finely cut solid lapis stone, champleve enamel dial, ca. 1800. (illo.E-9)

Floral enamel watch, 57mm, bouquet of flowers within a gold case set with split pearls. (illo.E-10)

Enamel scene watch, 58mm, finely painted scene of ships in harbor. (illo.E-11)

SIZE AND DESCRIPTION	Avg	Ex-Fn	Mint
57mm, floral enamel, duplex, (Bovet), pearls, 18K, (illo.E-10)	$8,000	$9,000	$10,000
58mm, harbor scene enamel, duplex, 18k, Ca. 1790 (illo.E-11)	20,000	26,000	32,000
43mm, basket form champleve enamel, 18k, Ca. 1800 (illo.E.12)...	3,000	3,500	4,000
42mm, champleve border, finely painted flowers, (Le Roy), gold case & chain..	2,500	3,000	3,500
37mm, rose gold guilloche enamel demi-hunter..............................	400	500	600
36mm, gold enamel & champleve enamel, verge, Ca. 1800	1,800	2,200	2,800
35mm, gold champleve enamel, (L'Epine), cylinder	800	1,000	1,200
35mm, gold enamel & seed pearls, rose cut diamonds	400	500	600
34mm, gold egg-shaped form enamel, verge, (Austrian)	2,000	2,200	2,500
30mm, gold miniature enamel, verge, seed pearls, Ca. 1800	2,000	2,400	2,800
27mm, gold enamel lapel brooch with seed pearls & rose cut diamonds, Ca. 1890	700	800	900
27mm, gold fine enamel lapel brooch with cut diamonds by C. H. Meylan (illo.E.13)	1,500	2,000	2,500

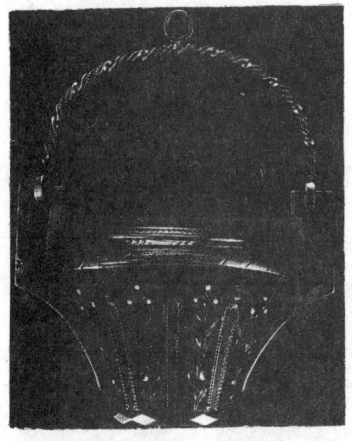

Enamel form tapered oval basket with rising rope handle, enhanced with panels of flowers, 18K case. (illo.E-12)

A chased enamel gold lady's pendant watch. Enamel portrait of a lady. (illo.E-13)

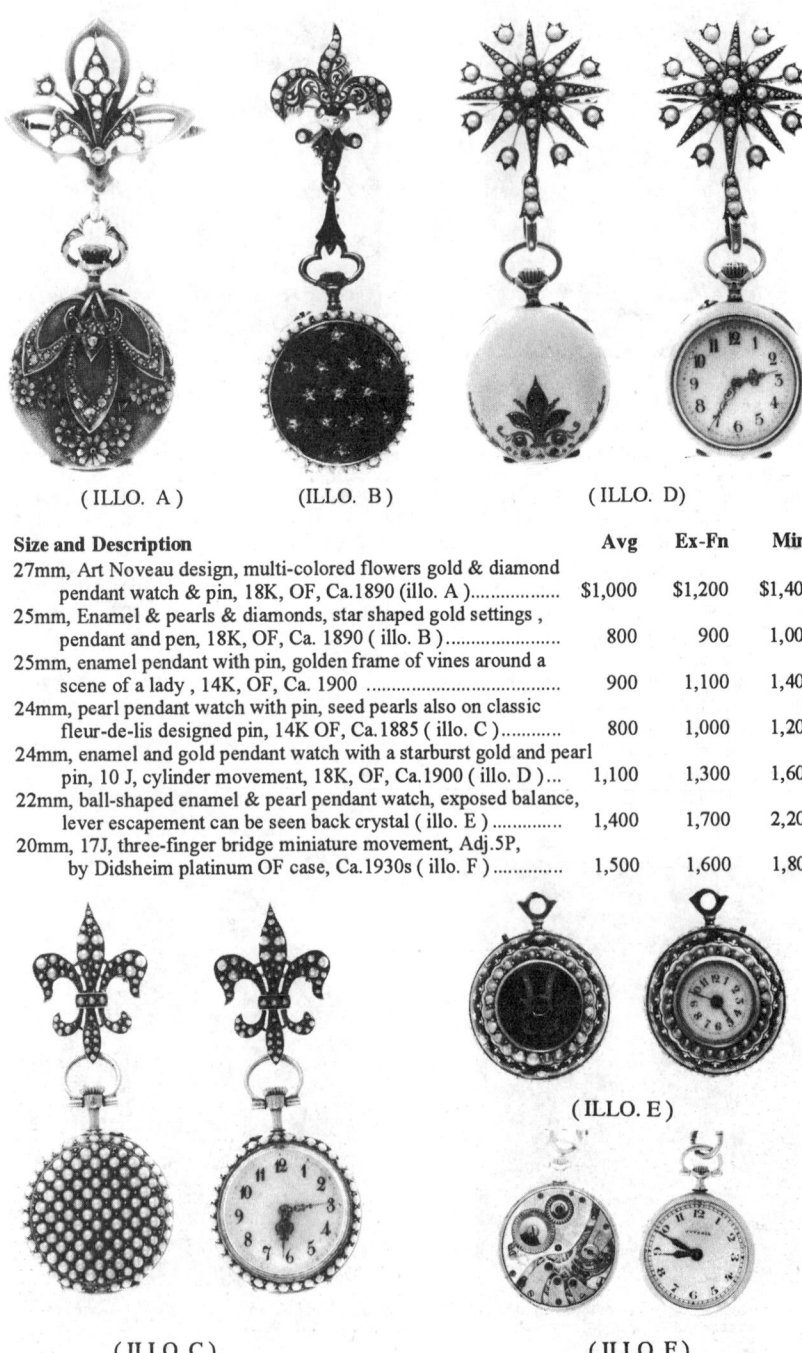

(ILLO. A)   (ILLO. B)   (ILLO. D)

Size and Description	Avg	Ex-Fn	Mint
27mm, Art Noveau design, multi-colored flowers gold & diamond pendant watch & pin, 18K, OF, Ca.1890 (illo. A)	$1,000	$1,200	$1,400
25mm, Enamel & pearls & diamonds, star shaped gold settings , pendant and pen, 18K, OF, Ca. 1890 (illo. B)	800	900	1,000
25mm, enamel pendant with pin, golden frame of vines around a scene of a lady , 14K, OF, Ca. 1900	900	1,100	1,400
24mm, pearl pendant watch with pin, seed pearls also on classic fleur-de-lis designed pin, 14K OF, Ca.1885 (illo. C)	800	1,000	1,200
24mm, enamel and gold pendant watch with a starburst gold and pearl pin, 10 J, cylinder movement, 18K, OF, Ca.1900 (illo. D)	1,100	1,300	1,600
22mm, ball-shaped enamel & pearl pendant watch, exposed balance, lever escapement can be seen back crystal (illo. E)	1,400	1,700	2,200
20mm, 17J, three-finger bridge miniature movement, Adj.5P, by Didsheim platinum OF case, Ca.1930s (illo. F)	1,500	1,600	1,800

(ILLO. C)   (ILLO. E)   (ILLO. F)

ABOUT THE COVER

Since the inception of wearable timepieces, watchmakers have been faced with the problem of gravity and its effects on the escapement and hence upon the time keeping quality of the watch itself. It must therefore be considered one of the most difficult horological complications to overcome in watchmaking. The Pocket Watch was made by **Derek Pratt** and the Wrist Watch by **Philippe Dufour**, using two different approaches to the difficult escapement *"errors"*.

Philippe Dufour's *"DUALITY"* a **Double Escapement** wrist watch. The technical aspect of the **double escapement** may be deceptive at first glance. A complicated differential system is essential for the operation of the two balances and the *mutual compensation of the error*, also reduces by half the errors caused by the escapements. The **double escapement** wrist watch technical characteristics include 2 levers escapements, 2 Gulucydur balances with timing screws, 2 hairsprings and 40 jewels. The movement is 30MM in diameter and 4MM thick. Mr. Dufour was awarded a prize in 1992 at the Basel Watch Fair with his "Grande et Petite Sonnerie Minute Repeater" wrist watch and again last year with the worlds first **double escapement** wrist watch. Mr.Dufour is established in Le Sentier Switzerland and the *Vallee de Joux*, a strip of of land wedged between the Alps and Jura mountains and is synonymous to the connoisseurs of watches.

Derek Pratt a senior watchmaker of Urban Jurgensen & Sonner completed the pocket watch in 4300 hours of work between 1981 and 1982. This example of a individual made pocket watch indicating full seconds (jumping seconds) with a carriage-mounted tourbillon incorporating a **one second remontoir** also a twin mainspring barrels and a state of wind indicator. The skeletonized variant of the tourbillon offers maximum visibility of the tourbillon carriage and the twin barrels. Mr. Pratt lives in Balm, Switzerland which is near Solothurn.

The *author* was privileged to have lunch with Philippe Dufour and dinner with Derek Pratt while on a recent trip to Switzerland.

LEFT: A view of **Derek Pratt's** one-minute tourbillon with a one-second remontoire mounted in the carriage and twin barrels. (photographed by Tony Baggentos).

RIGHT: A view of **Philippe Dufour's** *"DUALITY"* the worlds first wrist watch with a double escapement and 40 jewels.

Am. Waltham W. Co.

Date	Serial #
1852	50
1853	400
1854	1,000
1855	2,500
1856	4,000
1857	6,000
1858	10,000
1859	15,000
1860	20,000
1861	30,000
1862	45,000
1863	65,000
1864	110,000
1865	180,000
1866	260,000
1867	330,000
1868	410,000
1869	460,000
1870	500,000
1871	540,000
1872	590,000
1873	680,000
1874	730,000
1875	810,000
1876	910,000
1877	1,000,000
1878	1,150,000
1879	1,350,000
1880	1,500,000
1881	1,670,000
1882	1,835,000
1883	2,000,000
1884	2,350,000
1885	2,650,000
1886	3,000,000
1887	3,400,000
1888	3,800,000
1889	4,200,000
1890	4,700,000
1891	5,200,000
1892	5,800,000
1893	6,300,000
1894	6,700,000
1895	7,100,000
1896	7,450,000
1897	8,100,000
1898	8,400,000
1899	9,000,000
1900	9,500,000
1901	10,200,000
1902	11,100,000
1903	12,100,000
1904	13,500,000
1905	14,300,000
1906	14,700,000
1907	15,500,000
1908	16,400,000
1909	17,600,000
1910	17,900,000
1911	18,100,000
1912	18,200,000
1913	18,900,000
1914	19,500,000
1915	20,000,000
1916	20,500,000
1917	20,900,000
1918	21,800,000
1919	22,500,000
1920	23,400,000
1921	23,900,000
1922	24,100,000
1923	24,300,000
1924	24,550,000
1925	24,800,000
1926	25,200,000
1927	26,100,000
1928	26,400,000
1929	26,900,000
1930	27,100,000
1931	27,300,000
1932	27,550,000
1933	27,750,000
1934	28,100,000
1935	28,600,000
1936	29,100,000
1937	29,400,000
1938	29,750,000
1939	30,050,000
1940	30,250,000
1941	30,750,000
1942	31,050,000
1943	31,400,000
1944	31,700,000
1945	32,100,000
1946	32,350,000
1947	32,750,000
1948	33,100,000
1949	33,500,000
1950	33,560,000
1951	33,600,000
1952	33,700,000
1953	33,800,000
1954	34,100,000
1955	34,450,000
1956	34,700,000
1957	35,000,000

AURORA W. CO.

Date	Serial #
1884	10,001
1885	60,000
1886	101,000
1887	160,000
1888	200,000
1889	215,000
1891	230,901

COLUMBUS W. CO.

Date	Serial #
1875	1,000
1876	3,000
1877	6,000
1878	9,000
1879	12,000
1880	15,000
1881	18,000
1882	21,000
1883	25,000
1884	30,000
1885	40,000
1886	53,000
1887	75,000
1888	97,000
1889	119,000
1890	141,000
1891	163,000
1892	185,000
1893	207,000
1894	229,000
1895	251,000
1896	273,000
1897	295,000
1898	317,000
1899	339,000
1900	361,000
1901	383,000

SPECIAL BLOCK OF SERIAL NOS.

Date	Serial #
1894	500,001
1896	501,500
1898	503,000
1900	504,500
1902	506,000

ELGIN WATCH CO.

Date	Serial #	
1867	10,000	
1868	25,001	Nov,20th
1869	40,001	May, 20th
1870	50,001	Aug. 24th
1871	185,001	Sep. 8th
1872	201,001	Dec. 20th
1873	325,001	
1874	400,001	Aug 28th
1875	430,000	
1876	480,000	
1877	520,000	
1878	550,000	
1879	625,001	Feb.8th
1880	750,000	
1881	900,000	
1882	1,000,000	March,9th
1883	1,250,000	
1884	1,500,000	
1885	1,855,001	May,28th
1886	2,000,000	Aug 4th
1887	2,500,000	
1888	3,000,000	June 20th
1889	3,500,000	
1890	4,000,000	Aug 16th
1891	4,449,001	Mar.26th
1892	4,600,000	
1893	5,000,000	July 1st
1894	5,500,000	
1895	6,000,000	Nov. 26th
1896	6,500,000	
1897	7,000,000	Oct. 28th
1898	7,494,001	May,14th
1899	8,000,000	Jan. 18th
1900	9,000,000	Nov. 14th
1901	9,300,000	
1902	9,600,000	
1903	10,000,000	May 15th
1904	11,000,000	April 4th
1905	12,000,000	Oct.6th
1906	12,500,000	
1907	13,000,000	April 4th
1908	13,500,000	
1909	14,000,000	Feb.9th
1910	15,000,000	April 2nd
1911	16,000,000	July 11th
1912	17,000,000	Nov.6th
1913	17,339,001	Apr.14th
1914	18,000,000	
1915	18,587,001	Feb.11th
1916	19,000,000	
1917	20,031,001	June,27th
1918	21,000,000	
1919	22,000,000	
1920	23,000,000	
1921	24,321,001	July,6th
1922	25,100,000	
1923	26,050,000	
1924	27,000,000	
1925	28,421,001	July,14th
1926	29,100,000	
1927	30,050,000	
1928	31,500,000	
1929	32,000,000	
1930	32,599,001	July
1931	33,000,000	
1932	33,700,000	
1933	34,558,001	July,24th
1934	35,000,000	
1935	35,650,000	
1936	36,200,000	
1937	36,978,001	July,24th
1938	37,900,000	
1939	38,200,000	
1940	39,100,000	
1941	40,200,000	
1942	41,100,000	
1943	42,200,000	
1944	42,600,000	
1945	43,200,000	
1946	44,000,000	
1947	45,000,000	
1948	46,000,000	
1949	47,000,000	
1950	48,000,000	
1951	50,000,000	
1952	52,000,000	
1953	53,500,000	
1954	54,000,000	
1955	54,500,000	
1956	55,000,000	

HAMILTON WATCH CO.

Date	Serial No.
1893	1-2,000
1894	5,000
1895	11,500
1896	16,000
1897	27,000
1898	50,000
1899	74,000
1900	104,000
1901	143,000
1902	196,000
1903	260,000
1904	340,000
1905	425,000
1906	590,000
1907	756,000
1908	921,000
1909	1,087,000
1910	1,150,500
1911	1,290,500
1912	1,331,000
1913	1,370,000
1914	1,410,500
1915	1,450,500
1916	1,517,000
1917	1,580,000
1918	1,650,000
1919	1,700,000
1920	1,790,000
1921	1,860,000
1922	1,900,000
1923	1,950,000
1924	2,000,000
1925	2,100,000
1926	2,200,000
1927	2,250,000
1928	2,300,000
1929	2,350,000
1930	2,400,000
1931	2,450,000
1932	2,500,000
1933	2,600,000
1934	2,700,000
1935	2,800,000
1936	2,900,000
1937	3,000,000
1938	3,200,000
1939	3,400,000
1940	3,600,000
1941	3,800,000
1942	4,025,000

DATE LETTERS
B on 950B=1942-50
C on 992B=1942-50
S on 950B=1950-55
OTHER DATE LETTERS = 1930s to 1950s

HAMPDEN W. CO.

Date	Serial #
1877	60,000
1878	91,000
1879	122,000
1880	153,000
1881	184,000
1882	215,000
1883	250,000
1884	300,000
1885	350,000
1886	400,000
1887	450,000
1888	500,000
1889	555,500
1890	611,000
1891	666,500
1892	722,000
1893	775,000
1894	833,000
1895	888,500
1896	944,000
1897	1,000,000
1898	1,128,000
1899	1,256,000
1900	1,384,000
1901	1,512,000
1902	1,642,000
1903	1,768,000
1904	1,896,000
1905	2,024,000
1906	2,152,000
1907	2,280,000
1908	2,408,000
1909	2,536,000
1910	2,664,000
1911	2,792,000
1912	2,920,000
1913	3,048,000
1914	3,176,000
1915	3,304,000
1916	3,432,000
1917	3,560,000
1918	3,680,000
1919	3,816,000
1920	3,944,000
1921	4,072,000
1922	4,200,000
1923	4,400,000
1924	4,600,000

E. HOWARD & CO.

Date	Serial #
1858-60)	131-1,900
1860-61)	1,901-3,000
1861)	3,001-3,100
1861)	3,101-3,250
1861)	3,401- 3,500
1861-71)	3,501-28,000
1868-83)	30,001-50,000
1869-99)	50,001-71,000
1869-90)	100,001-105,000
1880-99)	200,001-227,000
1895)	228,001-231,000
1884-99)	300,001-309,000
1895)	309,001-310,000
1890-95)	400,001-405,000
1890-99)	500,001-501,500
1896-1903)	600,001-601,500
1896-1903)	700,001-701,500

HOWARD WATCH CO. (KEYSTONE)

Date	Serial #
1902	850,000
1903	900,000
1909	980,000
1912	1,100,000
1915	1,285,000
1917	1,340,000
1921	1,400,000
1930	1,500,000

ILLINOIS WATCH CO.

Date	Serial #
1872	5,000
1873	20,000
1874	50,000
1875	75,000
1876	100,000
1877	145,000
1878	210,000
1879	250,000
1880	300,000
1881	350,000
1882	400,000
1883	450,000
1884	500,000
1885	550,000
1886	600,000
1887	700,000
1888	800,000
1889	900,000
1890	1,000,000
1891	1,040,000
1892	1,080,000
1893	1,120,000
1894	1,160,000
1895	1,220,000
1896	1,250,000
1897	1,290,000
1898	1,330,000
1899	1,370,000
1900	1,410,000
1901	1,450,000
1902	1,500,000
1903	1,650,000
1904	1,700,000
1905	1,800,000
1906	1,840,000
1907	1,900,000
1908	2,100,000
1909	2,150,000
1910	2,200,000
1911	2,300,000
1912	2,400,000
1913	2,500,000
1914	2,600,000
1915	2,700,000
1916	2,800,000
1917	3,000,000
1918	3,200,000
1919	3,400,000
1920	3,600,000
1921	3,750,000
1922	3,900,000
1923	4,000,000
1924	4,500,000
1925	4,700,000
1926	4,800,000
1927	5,000,000
(Sold to Hamilton)	
1928	5,200,000
1929	5,350,000
1930	5,400,000
1931	5,500,000
1932	5,600,000

ROCKFORD W.Co.

Date	Serial #
1874	22,200
1875	42,600
1876	63,000
1877	83,000
1878	103,000
1879	124,000
1880	144,000
1881	165,000
1882	185,000
1883	206,000
1884	226,000
1885	247,000
1886	267,000
1887	287,500
1888	308,000
1889	328,500
1890	349,000
1891	369,500
1892	390,000
1893	410,000
1894	430,000
1895	450,000
1896	470,000
1897	490,000
1898	510,000
1899	530,000
1900	550,000
1901	570,000
1902	590,000
1903	610,000
1904	630,000
1905	650,000
1906	670,000
1907	690,000
1908	734,000
1909	790,000
1910	824,000
1911	880,000
1912	936,000
1913	958,000
1914	980,000
1915	1,000,000

SOUTH BEND W. CO.

Date	Serial #
1903	380,501
1904	410,000
1905	445,000
1906	480,000
1907	515,000
1908	550,000
1909	585,000
1910	620,000
1911	655,000
1912	690,000
1913	725,000
1914	760,000
1915	795,000
1916	825,000
1917	865,000
1918	900,000
1919	935,000
1920	970,000
1921	1,005,000
1922	1,040,000
1923	1,075,000
1924	1,110,000
1925	1,145,000
1926	1,180,000
1927	1,215,000
1928	1,250,000
1929	1,275,000

SETH THOMAS W. Co.

Date	Serial #
1885	5,000
1886	20,000
1887	40,000
1888	80,000
1889	150,000
1890	235,000
1891	330,000
1892	420,000
1893	510,000
1894	600,000
1895	690,000
1896	780,000
1897	870,000
1898	960,000
1899	1,050,000
1900	1,140,000
1901	1,230,000
1902	1,320,000
1903	1,410,000
1904	1,500,000
1905	1,700,000
1906	1,900,000
1907	2,100,000
1908	2,300,000
1909	2,500,000
1910	2,725,000
1911	2,950,000
1912	3,175,000
1913	3,490,000
1914	3,600,000

BALL WATCH CO.

Date	Serial #
(Hamilton)	
1895	13,000
1897	20,500
1900	42,000
1902	170,000
1905	462,000
1910	600,000
1915	603,000
1920	610,000
1925	620,000
1930	637,000
1935	641,000
1938	647,000
1939	650,000
1940	651,000
1941	652,000
1942	654,000
(Waltham)	
1900	060,700
1905	202,000
1910	216,000
1915	250,000
1920	260,000
1925	270,000
(Illinois)	
1929	800,000
1930	801,000
1931	803,000
1932	804,000
(Elgin)	
1904-1906	S # range 11,853,000-12,282,000
(E. Howard & CO.)	
1893-1895	S # range 226,000-308,000
(Hampden)	
1890-1892	S # range 626,750-657,960-759,720

Audemars Piguet

DATE	SERIAL #
1882	2,000
1890	4,000
1895	5,350
1900	6,500
1905	9,500
1910	13,000
1915	17,000
1920	25,000
1925	33,000
1930	40,000
1935	42,000
1940	44,000
1945	48,000
1950	55,000
1955	65,000
1960	75,000
1965	90,000
1970	115,000
1975	160,000
1980	225,000

International W.Co. (Schaffhausen)

DATE	SERIAL #
1875	4,000
1885	10,000
1900	150,000
1905	300,000
1910	500,000
1915	600,000
1920	700,000
1925	750,000
1930	800,000
1935	850,000
1940	900,000
1945	955,000
1950	1,000,000
1955	1,200,000
1960	1,500,000

A. Lange & Sohne

DATE	SERIAL #
1870	5,000
1875	10,000
1880	20,000
1885	25,000
1890	30,000
1895	35,000
1900	40,000
1905	50,000
1910	60,000
1915	70,000
1920	75,000
1925	80,000
1930	85,000
1935	90,000
1940	100,000

LONGINES

DATE	SERIAL #
1867	1
1870	20,000
1875	100,000
1882	250,000
1888	500,000
1893	750,000
1899	1,000,000
1901	1,250,000
1904	1,500,000
1905	1,750,000
1907	2,000,000
1909	2,250,000
1911	2,500,000
1912	2,750,000
1913	3,000,000
1915	3,250,000
1917	3,500,000
1919	3,750,000
1922	4,000,000
1925	4,250,000
1926	4,500,000
1928	4,750,000
1929	5,000,000
1934	5,250,000
1937	5,500,000
1938	5,750,000
1940	6,000,000
1945	7,000,000
1950	8,000,000
1953	9,000,000
1956	10,000,000
1959	11,000,000
1962	12,000,000
1966	13,000,000
1967	14,000,000
1969	15,000,000

OMEGA

DATE	SERIAL #
1895	50,000
1900	500,000
1905	1,000,000
1910	2,500,000
1915	4,500,000
1920	6,000,000
1925	7,500,000
1930	9,500,000
1935	11,000,000
1940	12,500,000
1945	14,000,000
1950	15,500,000
1955	16,500,000
1960	18,000,000
1965	23,000,000
1970	28,000,000
1975	35,000,000

PATEK PHILIPPE & CO.

DATE	SERIAL #
1840	100
1845	1,200
1850	3,000
1855	8,000
1860	15,000
1865	22,000
1870	35,000
1875	45,000
1880	55,000
1885	70,000
1890	85,000
1895	100,000
1900	110,000
1905	125,000
1910	150,000
1915	175,000
1920	190,000
1925	200,000
1950	700,000
1955	725,000
1960	750,000
1965	775,000
1970	795,000
1920	800,000
1925	805,000
1930	820,000
1935	824,000
1940	835,000
1945	850,000
1950	860,000
1955	870,000
1960	880,000
1965	890,000
1970	895,000
1940	900,000
1945	915,000
1950	930,000
1955	940,000
1960	960,000
1965	975,000
1970	995,000
1960	1,100,000
1965	1,130,000
1970	1,250,000
1975	1,350,000
1980	1,450,000
1985	1,600,000
1990	1,850,000

ROLEX (Case S #)

DATE	SERIAL #
1925	25,000
1926	27,500
1927	30,500
1928	33,000
1929	35,500
1930	38,000
1931	40,000
1932	43,000
1933	49,000
1934	55,000
1935	62,000
1936	82,000
1937	98,000
1938	118,000
1939	136,000
1940	165,000
1941	194,000
1942	224,000
1943	253,000
1944	284,000
1945	348,000
1946	413,000
1947	478,000
1948	543,000
1949	608,000
1950	673,500
1951	735,500
1952	804,000
1953	869,000
1954	935,000
1955	1,010,000
1956	1,095,000
1957	1,167,000
1958	1,245,000
1959	1,323,000
1960	1,401,000
1961	1,485,000
1962	1,557,000
1963	1,635,000
1964	1,713,000
1965	1,791,000
1966	1,870,000
1967	2,164,000
1968	2,426,000
1969	2,689,000
1970	2,952,000
1971	3,215,000
1972	3,478,000
1973	3,741,000
1974	4,000,000
1975	4,260,000
1976	4,530,000
1977	5,000,000
1978	5,480,000
1979	5,960,000
1980	6,430,000
1981	6,910,000
1982	7,380,000
1983	7,860,000
1984	8,340,000
1985	8,810,000
1986	9,300,000
1987	9,760,000
1987 1/2	9,999,999
1987 3/4	R000,001
1988	R999,999
1989	L000,001
1990	L999,999
1990 1/2	E000,001
1991 1/4	E999,999
1991 1/2	X000,001

VACHERON

DATE	SERIAL #
1830	30,000
1835	40,000
1840	50,000
1845	60,000
1850	75,000
1855	95,000
1860	110,000
1865	125,000
1870	140,000
1875	155,000
1880	170,000
1885	180,000
1890	190,000
1895	223,000
1900	256,000
1905	289,000
1910	322,000
1915	355,000
1920	385,000
1925	400,000
1930	410,000
1935	420,000
1940	440,000
1945	464,000
1950	488,000
1955	512,000
1960	536,000
1965	560,000
1970	585,000

The above list is provided for determining the **approximate** age of your watch. Match serial number with date. Watches were not necessarily sold in the exact order of manufactured date.

ROMANCING THE WRIST WATCH

The wrist watch is considered by many watch collectors to be "today's collectable." This phenomenon is due, in part, to the development of the quartz movement which began in the 1970's and virtually revolutionized the watch market. Although these quartz watches are quiet, accurate timekeepers, and are inexpensive to manufacture, the watches of the past hold a special fascination in the heart of the collector. They enjoy collecting the timepieces with jeweled and moving parts that produce a rhythmic heartbeat inside their gold cases.

The watch collector has seen the prices of wrist watches soar in the past years, as wrist watches have become more and more in demand as an object of fashion, function and jewelry. A Patek, Philippe man's platinum minute repeater wrist watch sold for the record price of 345,000 Swiss francs, about $250,000 U.S. Not far behind this record setting sale was a Patek - Philippe "Calatrava" that brought $198,000. A Patek - Philippe enameled white gold "World Time" man's wrist watch sold for about $130,000. Some collectors have seen the values of their wrist watches double and, in many cases, triple in recent years. For example, in the early 1980s, a Patek, Philippe perpetual calendar chronograph watch would have sold for $10,000. In 1987, the same watch would have sold for $50,000, and in 1988 for $80,000. In 1989, the price was up to $100,000. Such dramatic increases in values have brought about a feverish demand for wrist watches. The Swiss wrist watch has the attention of the wealthiest collectors, with Patek, Philippe & Co. at the top of their list and Audemars Piguet, Cartier, Rolex, and Vacheron & Constantin close behind. Other wrist watches showing appreciable value are Ebel, A. Lange, Gubelin, International Watch Co., Le Coultre, Ulysse Nardin, and Piaget. Next are Jules Jurgensen, Baume & Mercier, Gerard Perregaux, Movado, and Omega; then Benrus, Bulova, Agassiz, Elgin, Gruen, Hamilton, Illinois, Longines, and Waltham, the character watches, chronographs, and complicated watches.

Many wrist watch collectors have focused on fashion and take pride in wearing their unique watches. Women have been buying high fashion men's watches to wear, making women candidates for collecting. Young men appear to enjoy collecting wrist watches rather than pocket watches. The intense competition within their increasing numbers has influenced the rising prices.

*   *   *

European and Japanese collectors are making the biggest impact on the wrist watch market with their volume of buying, as well as the higher prices being paid. The American collector has been inspired by the heated market which has been, in part, fueled by the weakened U.S. dollar. The general appearance of a wrist watch seems to be the main factor in the price of the watch, but high mechanical standards, along with the various functions of the watch, also determine the price. Some of these features include repeaters, chronographs, duo-dials, bubble backs, curvex, flip-up tops, reverso, day-date-month moon phase, jump hour, diamond dial, world time, sector, skeletonized, character, first versions as early auto winds, very early electronics, unusual shapes, and enamel bezels.

EBEL WATCH CO., chronograph with triple day & moon phases, outside chapter shows tachymetre, 18k gold.

Today's watches are a "mixed bag," ranging from gold luxury watches priced at $10,000, and mid-priced watches at $1,000, to the low-end plastic quartz watches at $30, and all keep time equally well. The gold watch is still a status symbol today; a mark of affluence and of appreciation for the finer things in life. The Swiss control about 85 percent of the luxury watch market, while the Japanese have about the same percentage of the market for more moderately-priced watches. The predominant companies producing the "top of the line" watches are Patek, Philippe & Co., Cartier, Gubelin, Audemars Piguet, Piaget, Vacheron Constantin. Just below in price, but higher in volume, are names like Rolex, International Watch Co., Girard Perregaux, and Le Coultre. Collectors are also wearing high grade new watches by Ebel, Blancpain, Gerald Genta, Hublot, Raymond Weil, and watches produced for and bearing the names of Chanel, Christian Dior, and Dunhill. Prices of Ebel watches start at about $1,000 and go upward to $24,000. This company also manufactures watches for Cartier. Patek, Philippe watches range in price from $3,000 to $100,000.

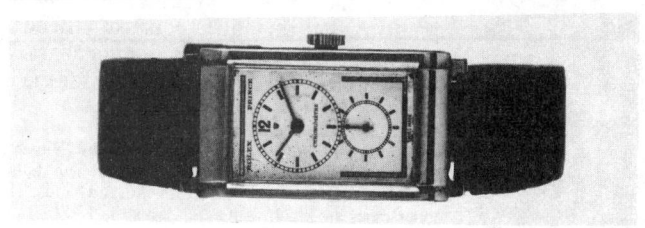

Audemars Piguet produces a tourbillon wrist watch that retails for about $28,000. Blancpain, owned by Omega, produces only about 100 ultra-thin handmade watches per year. Rolex is the most recognizable name in today's luxury wrist watch market. The Rolex 18k gold President with fluted bezel, champagne cabochon dial, and 18k gold bracelet, sells for $9,400, while the same watch with diamond bezel and dial sells for $14,400. Rolex makes the Oyster Quartz day-date, 18k gold, pave diamond dial with sapphire, bezel case, and bracelet set with 107 diamonds totaling 8.06 carats, which bears a price tag of $100,000.

The Warhol collection, which included about 200 watches, was sold on April 27, 1988 at Sotheby's for a reported price of $461,000. The artist collected watches of various styles and types. A set of three vinyl quartz character watches brought the price of $2,400. A stainless steel Gene Autry watch listed and pre-determined to bring about $100 sold for $1,700. The so-called "heavy weight" wrist watches such as Patek Philippe, Cartier, Rolex, and Vacheron Constantin sold for two to three times the estimated prices.

The trend or vogue for older watches has motivated some watch companies to reproduce favorite watches from their past models. Companies have searched their archives to find older models that sold well, and are now marketing replicas of those watches. Hamilton Classics Authentic Reproductions From America's Past include the Ventura (1957), Wilshire City (1939), Cabot (1935), and Ardmore (1934). Jaeger LeCoultre's Reverso has been reintroduced, as well as Longines' hour angle watch developed and worn by Charles Lindbergh. Also, the Lorus Company has marketed a close look-a-like to the Mickey Mouse wrist watch first sold by Ingersoll in the early 1930s.

The romancing of the wrist watch is moving at a steady upward pace. Price adjustments may be needed, but should hold for a few more years. The quality American movements may still be undervalued, and the novelty or comic character wrist watches may still be a good value for the investor.

Left: Movado designed by Andy Warhol the "Times Five" were made in Quartz and limited to 205 pieces. The dials have New York scenes are in black and white with red hands. The five time zones cases are black with black links Ca. 1987.

A SHORT HISTORY OF WRIST WATCHES

While no one is sure who invented the first wrist watch or when the first wrist watch was ever worn. Watch-bracelets were created by great makers for ladies of great wealth and a few ladies wrist watches began to appear around 1790. Small miniature watches had been made earlier than this, however. David Rosseau made a watch which was about 18mm in diameter (the size of a dime) in the late 1600s.

Early BRACELET that holds a small pendant-watch, a lid opens on this 18K & enamel case to view the watch, Ca.1840.

Miniaturization was a great challenge to many of the famous watch makers including Louis Jaquet, Paul Ditisheim, John Arnold and Henri Capt. The smallest watch in semi-mass production was 12mm by 5mm. In early 1930, the American Waltham Watch Co. made a 9mm by 20mm Model 400 watch.

Wrist watches were at first thought to be too small and delicate to be practical for men to wear. However, during World War I a German officer was said to have strapped a small pocket watch to his wrist with a leather webbed cup. This arrangement freed both hands and proved to be most useful. After the war, the wrist watch gained in popularity. Mass production of wrist watches was started around 1880 by the **Girard - Perregaux** factory which were designed to be used by officers of the German Navy. The Swiss introduced wrist watches to the United States around 1895, but they did not prove to be very popular at first. Around 1907 the Elgin and Illinois watch companies were manufacturing wrist watches and by 1912 Hampden and Waltham had started.

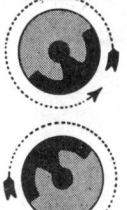

Miniaturized wrist watch by Waltham model # 400. Note size comparison to dime.

ROTOR for self winding wrist watch.

HARWOOD self-winding wrist watch, RIM SET, Ca.1928.

By 1920 the round styles were being replaced with square, rectangular and tonneau shapes and decorated with gems. By 1928 wrist watches were outselling pocket watches, and, by 1935, over 85 percent of the watches being produced were wrist watches.

Self-wind pocket watches were first developed by Abraham Louis Perrelet in 1770 and by Abraham Louis Breguet about 1777. Louis Recordon made improvements in 1780, but is was not until 1923 that the principle of self-winding was adapted to the wrist watch by John Harwood, an Englishman who set up factories to make his patented self-wind wrist watches in Switzerland, London, France, and the United States. His watches first reached the market about 1929. The firm A. Schild manufactured about 15,000 watches in Switzerland. Mr. Harwood's watch company removed the traditional stem or crown to wind the mainspring, but in order to set the hands it was necessary to turn the bezel. The Harwood Watch Co. failed around 1931 and the patent expired.

Snap on protector used on some early Wrist Watches.   Rolex Oyster Perpetual, BUBBLE BACK, Ca. 1940.

Early in 1930 the Rolex Watch Co. introduced the Rolex Oyster Perpetual, the first waterproof and self-winding wrist watch. In 1933 the first "Incabloc" shock protection device was used. By 1940 wrist watches came in all shapes and types including complicated chronographs, calendars, and repeaters. Novelties, digital jump hour and multi-dial were very popular, as well.

A dramatic change occurred in 1957 when the Hamilton Watch Co. eliminated the mainspring and replaced it with a small battery that lasted well over one year. In 1960 the balance wheel was removed in the Accutron by Bulova and replaced by a tuning fork with miniature pawls.

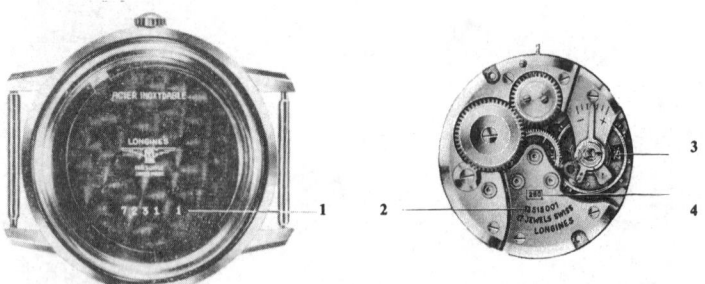

1. Case number.   2. Movement serial number.   3. Caliber number.   4. Caliber number.

NOTE: Some wrist watches have a grade or caliber number engraved on the movement. For example, Patek, Phillipe & Co. has a caliber number 27-460Q. The '27' stands for 27mm; the '460Q' is the grade; the 'Q' designates Quantieme (Perpetual calendar and moon phases).

AUTOMATIC WINDING

The self-winding watch uses the movements of the body in order to wind up the mainspring slowly and nearly continuously. The first pocket self-winding watches were executed by a watchmaker from Le Locle, Abraham-Louis Perrelet, around 1770.

Early self wind pocket watch by Breguet Ca. 1785.

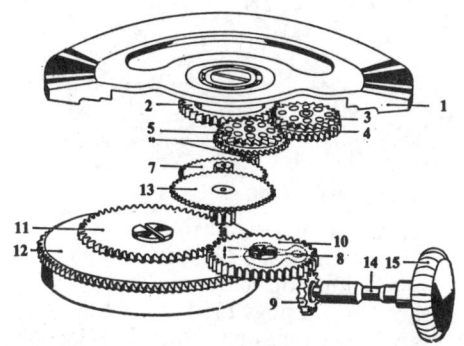

ETERNA-MATIC automatic winding mechanism with rotor oscillating on *5 ball bearings 1st introduced in 1949.* 1.–Oscillating weight. 2. –Oscillating gear. 3. –Upper wheel of auxiliary pawl-wheel. 4. –Lower wheel of auxiliary pawl-wheel. 5. –Pawl-wheel with pinion. 6. –Lower wheel of pawl wheel with pinion. 7. –Transmission-wheel with pinion. 8. –Crown-wheel yoke. 9. –Winding pinion. 10. –Crown-wheel. 11. –Ratchet-wheel. 12. –Barrel. 13. –Driving runner for ratchet-wheel. 14. –Winding stem. 15. –Winding button.

They were improved soon after by Abraham-Louis Breguet. In the case of the pocket watch, the movements causing the winding of the watch were essentially the result of walking. This system of winding was never widely adopted. The watch was a fancy model and not a really useful one. Herman von der Heydt was the only maker in America to work with the self-winding pocket watch. However, inventors always kept the idea of the self-winding watch in mind.

In 1923, the British firm Harwood took up once again the solution of the problem of automatic winding, for wrist watches. This was the spark which rapidly resulted in research to improve and simplify this type of mechanism. A company was formed in London to manufacture Harwood's watch, and before long over 500 jewelers in the United Kingdom were selling his automatic watch. A second company was formed in France, and a third in the United States. The business flourished about two and one-half years. Then, in 1931, these companies were liquidated.

Early self-winding wrist watch by FREY W. Co., Ca. 1930's.
NOTE: The pendulum style weight for self-winding.

Early self-winding wrist watch by AUTORIST W. Co. Ca.1930's. Winding by moving flexible lugs.

CHRONOGRAPH with ONE push piece.

CHRONOGRAPH with TWO push pieces.

Chronograph with two push pieces:

Action and movement of hands : The pusher No .1 sets the hands in action and second action stops the same hands.

Pusher No. 2 brings the hands back to zero. During their movement this pusher is a fixture, thus preventing the accidental return of the hands to zero. The double pusher chronograph permits an interruption in the reading, the hands are set going again from the position they stopped, thus indispensable for any time lost during a control of any description.

HOW TO READ THE TACHY-TELEMETER DIAL

Tachometer

The spiral scale around center of dial indicates miles per hour, based on a trial over one mile. It indicates speeds from 400 to 20 miles per hour on three turns. Each turn of spiral corresponds to one minute (scale for first 8 seconds being omitted), the outer turn from 400 to 60 (0 to 1 minute) and the center turn from 30 to 20 miles per hour (2 to 3 minutes).

When passing the first marker of mile zone, start chronograph hand by pressing push piece. When passing following mile marker, press push piece again. The chronograph hand now indicates the speed in miles per hour on the spiral. If a mile has been made in less than one minute the speed will be indicated on outside turn of spiral; from 1 to 2 minutes on middle turn and 2 to 3 minutes on center turn.

EXAMPLE: If a mile has been made in 1 minute and 15 seconds the chronograph hand indicates 48 miles per hour on middle turn of spiral.

Telemeter

The Telemeter scale around margin of dial is based on the speed of sound compared with the speed of light. Each small division is 100 meters. The scale is read in kilometers and hundreds of meters. Approximately 16 divisions equal 1 mile.

To determine the distance of a storm: When you see the flash of lightning press push piece of chronograph. When hearing thunder press again, the chronograph hand will indicate on the Telemeter scale the distance in kilometers and hundreds of meters. One kilometer equals 5/8 of a mile.

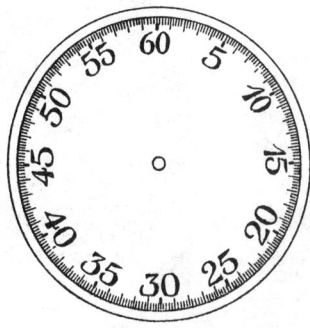

Dial No. 1 is a simple stop watch and chronograph dial. Graduated into fifths of seconds.

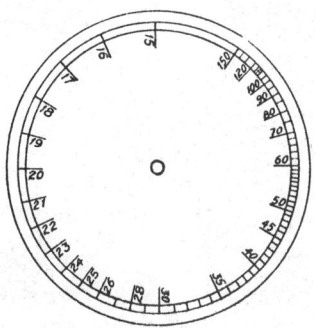

Dial No. 2 is used to time a car over a quarter-mile track and read the numbers of miles per hour directly from dial.

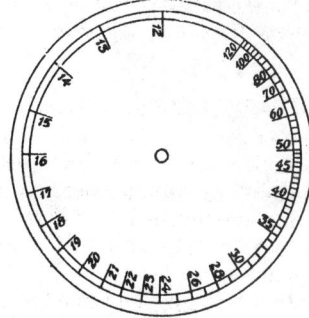

Dial No. 3 is used to measure speed in kilometers per hour over a course of one fifth of a kilometer.

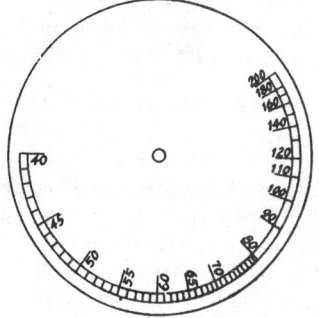

Dial No. 4 used by physicians to count the pulse beats of a patient.

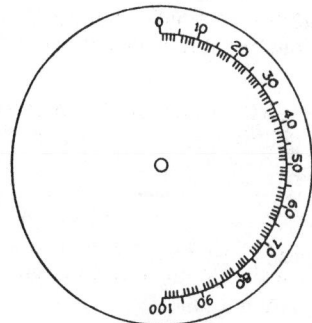

Dial No. 5 is used by artillery officers for determining distance by means of sound in kilometers.

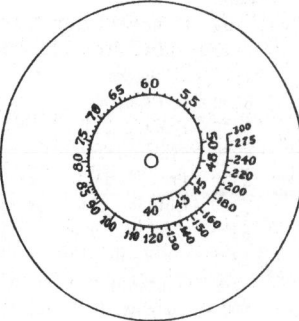

Dial No. 6 shows a tachometer: many watches are made with several scales on the same dial in order to cover a greater range of functions. The figures are sometimes grouped in a spiral form or in several circles, thus the hand may make more than one complete revolution.

CHRONOGRAPH MECHANISM
NUMBERS & NAMES USED IN THE EBAUCHE BOOK
" TECHNOLOGICAL DICTIONARY OF WATCH PARTS " Ca. 1953

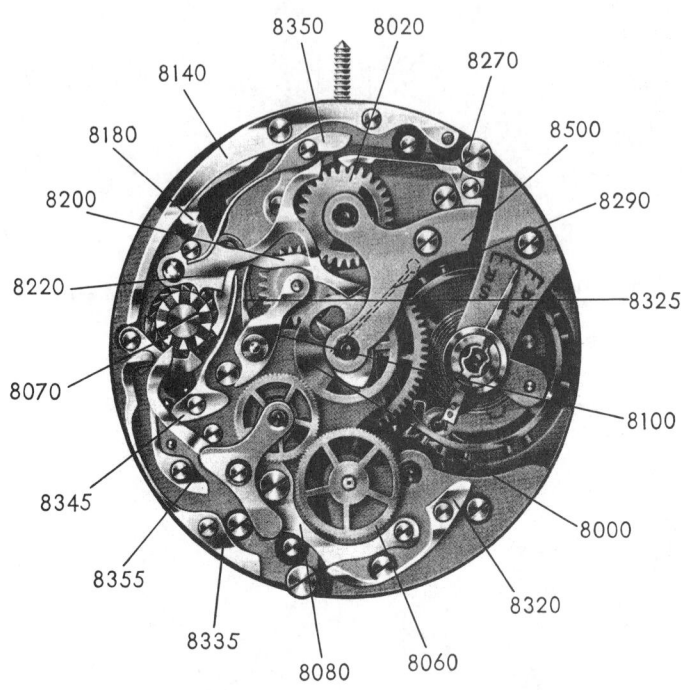

8000 Chronograph central wheel, w/ finger
8020 = Minute-recording wheel, register
8060 = Driving wheel
8070 = Pillar or Crown wheel, 3 functions
8080 = Coupling clutch w/ transmission wheel, 2 functions
8100 = Sliding or star gear, 2 functions
8140 = Operating or starting lever, 2 functions
8180 = Fly-back lever, reset to zero
8200 = Blocking lever, 2 functions
8220 = Hammer or heart piece striker, 2 functions
8270 = Minute-recording jumper spring
8290 = Friction spring , for chronograph central wheel
8320 = Coupling clutch spring
8325 = Sliding gear spring, 2 functions
8335 = Operating or starting lever spring
8345 = Blocking lever spring
8350 = Hammer or heartpiece lever spring, 2 functions
8355 = Pillar or crown wheel jumper or block
8500 = Chronograph bridge, for center & min. recording wheels

CHRONOGRAPH

The term chronograph is derived from the Greek words chronos which means "time" and grapho which means "to write." The first recording of intervals of time was around 1822 by the inventor Rieussec. His chronograph made dots of ink on a dial as a measure of time. Around 1862 Adolph Nicole introduced the first chronograph with a hand that returned to zero. The split second chronograph made its appearance around 1879. Today a chronograph can be described as a timepiece that starts at will, stops at will, and can return to zero at will. A mechanical chronograph had a sweep or center second hand that will start, stop, and fly back to zero. The term chronometer should not be confused with chronograph. A chronometer is a timepiece that has superior time keeping qualities at the time it is made. The CHRONOGRAPH **1 button** wrist watch was 1st. advertised in 1910 & a 2 **button** CHRONOGRAPH in 1939 by Breitling.

A. Day window. B. Split second hand. C. Calendar pusher. D. Register for seconds. E. Calendar pusher. F. Date hand. G. Register for total hours. H. Sweep center second hand. I. Month window. J. Start/stop pusher. K. Register for total minutes. L. Return pusher. M. Day of month.

TRADE MARK	MANUFACTURER	TRADE MARK	MANUFACTURER
	VALJOUX Now part of the ETA group		LANDERON
	VENUS		FONTAINEMELON

WRIST WATCH CASE AND DIAL STYLES

Barrel

Maxine

Square

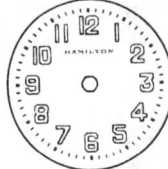
Round

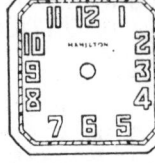
Square Cut Corner

Cushion

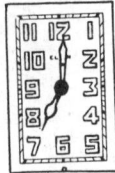
Rectangle

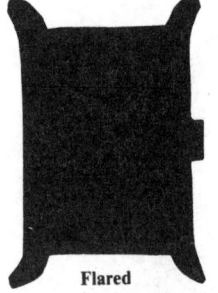
Flared

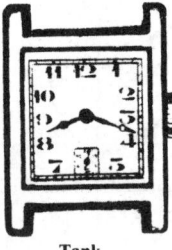
Tank

Round
(Ladies style; converts to lapel or wrist)

Curved or Curvex

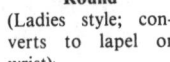

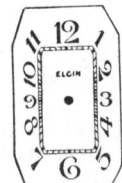
Rectangle Cut Corner

Tonneau

Baguette

Oval

EXAGGERATED

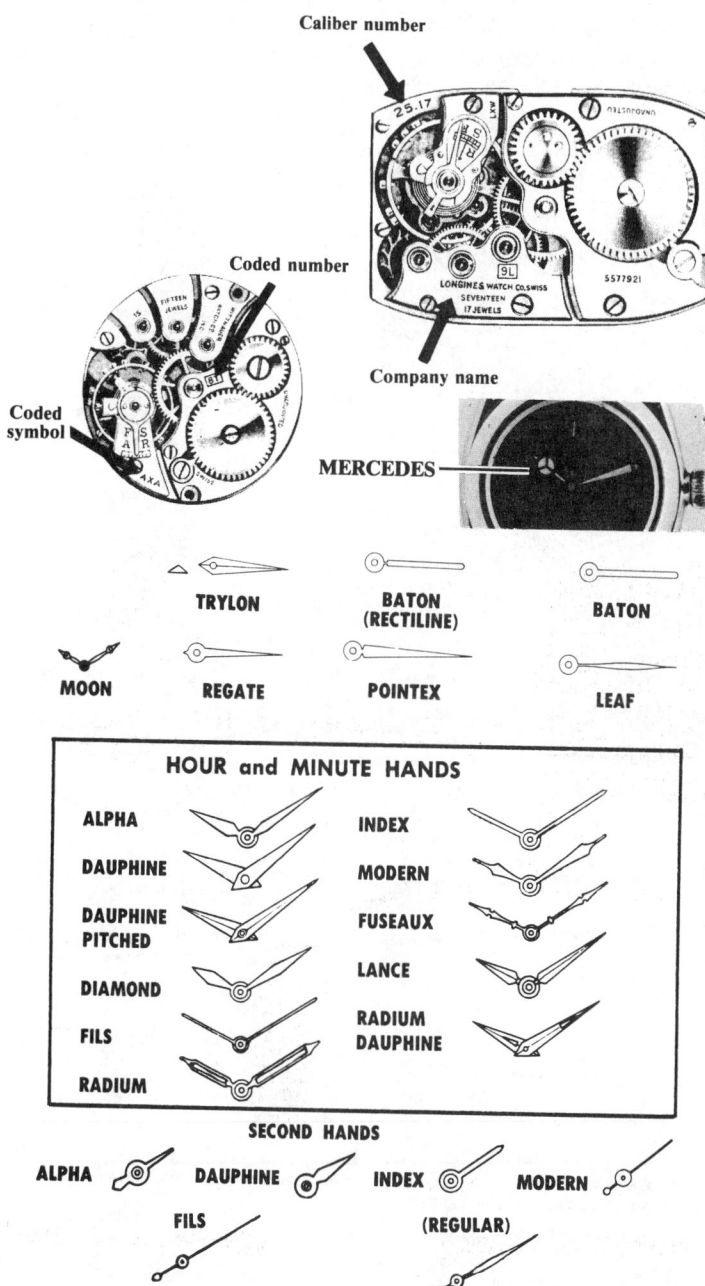

Caliber number

Coded number

Coded symbol

Company name

MERCEDES

TRYLON

BATON
(RECTILINE)

BATON

MOON

REGATE

POINTEX

LEAF

HOUR and MINUTE HANDS

ALPHA

INDEX

DAUPHINE

MODERN

DAUPHINE
PITCHED

FUSEAUX

DIAMOND

LANCE

FILS

RADIUM
DAUPHINE

RADIUM

SECOND HANDS

ALPHA

DAUPHINE

INDEX

MODERN

FILS

(REGULAR)

SWISS CODE INITIALS

Some Swiss watches have three initials on the balance bridge. These initials are not model identification but are for house identification. Following is a list of import initials with the name of the Swiss company maker.

AOC–Roamer
AOL–Adolph Schwarcz & Son
AOX–Alstate W. Co.
AXA–Wittnauer
AXZ–Benrus
AYP-Audemars Piguet
BOL–Lemania
BXC–Avia
BXJ–Midland
BXN–Benrus
BXP–Imperial, Bayer, Pretzfelder & Mills
BXW–Bulova
COC–Crawford
COW–Croton
CXC–Concord
CXD–Cypres
CXH–Clinton
CXV–Cort
CXW–Central; Benrus
DOB–Dreffa W. Co.
DOW–Deauville
EOE–Elrex
EON–Avalon
EOP–Harvel
EOT–Lavina
EXC–Everbrite
FXE–Provis
FXU–Louis Aisenstein & Bros.
FXW–Louis
GXC–Gruen
GXI–Gotham (Ollendorff)
GXM–Girard-Perregaux
GXR–Grant
GXW–Gothic
HOM–Homis
HON–Tissot; A. Hirsch
HOR–Lanco; Langendorf

HOU–Oris
HXF–Harman
HXM–R. H. Macy & Co.
HXN–Harvel
HXO–Harold K. Oleet
HXW–Helbros
HYL– Hamilton
HYO–Hilton W Co.
JXE–Normandie
JXJ–Jules Jurgensen
JXR–Gallet
KOT–Landau
KXJ–Wm. J. Kappel
KXV–Louis
KXZ–Kelton; Benrus, Central
LOA–Emil Langer
LOD–Latham
LOE–Packard
LXA–Laco, Winton, Elbon
LXE–Evkob
LXJ–LeCoultre
LXW–Longines
MOG–Mead & Co.; Boulevard
MOU–Tower; Delbana
MXE–Monarch
MXH–Seeland
MXI–Movado
MXT–Mathey-Tissot
NOA–U.Nardin
NOS–Heritage
NOU–Louvic
NXJ–National Jewelers Co.
NXO–Oris
OXG–Omega
OXL–Wyler
OYT–Shriro (Sandoz)
POY–Camy; Copley
PXA–Pierce
PXP–Patek, Philippe

PXT–Paul Breguette
PXW–Parker
PYS–Langel
QXO–Kelbert
ROC–Raleigh
ROL–Ribaux
ROP–Rodania
ROR-Audemars Piguet
ROW–Rolex
RXG–R. Gsell & Co.
RXM–Galmor
RXW–Rima
RXY–Liengme
RYW–Ritex
SOA–Felca
SOE–Semca
SOW–Seeland
SOX–Cortebert, Orvin
SXE–Savoy; Banner
SXK–S. Kocher & Co.
SXS–Franco
UOA–Actua
UOB–Aero
UOW–Universal
UXM–Medana
UXN–Marsh
UYW–Stanley W. Co.
VOS–Sheffield
VXN–Vacheron & Constantin
VXT–Kingston
WOA–Tower
WOB–Wyler
WOG–Breitling
WOR–Creston
WXC–Buren
WXE–Welsbro
WXW–Westfield
ZFX–Zenith W.Co.
ZOV–Titus
ZYV–Hampden (new company)

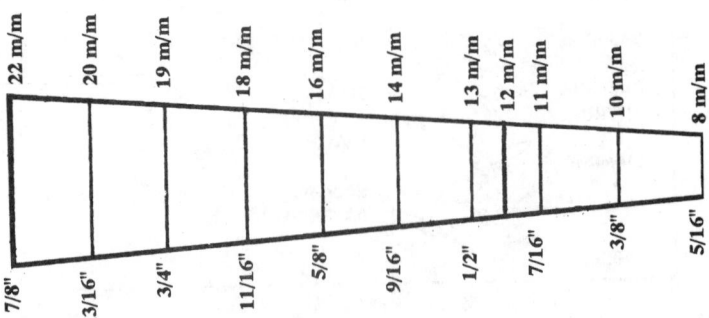

To determine your wrist watch band size use the above gauge and measure between the lugs. The band sizes are listed on each side of the gauge.

When performing any underwater activity, the dynamic pressure generated through movement is greater than the static pressure. Below a ranking of water resistance for most watches.

1 **meter** = 3.28 ft., 330 ft. =about 100 **meters.**

33.89 ft. =1 **atmosphere**, 100 ft. = about 3 **atmospheres**.

50M = shower only, rain, sweat-resistant (1 AT.)
100M = swimming (**no diving**) -330 ft.
200M = snorkeling, skin diving -600 ft.
1000M =scuba diving -3,300 ft.

WRIST WATCH LISTINGS

Pricing At Collectable Fair Market <u>Value</u> At Retail Level
(Complete Watches Only)

Unless otherwise noted, wrist watches listed in this section are priced at the *collectable* fair market RETAIL level (What a <u>**collector**</u> may expect to pay for a watch from a watch dealer) and as **complete** watches having an original gold-filled case and stainless steel back, also with original dial, and the entire original movement in good working order with no repairs needed. They are also priced as having a watch band made of **leather** except where a bracelet is described. Watches listed as 14k and 18k are solid gold cases. Coin or silveroid type and stainless steel cases will be listed as such. Dollar-type watches, or low cost production watches, are listed as having a base metal type case and a composition dial.

Many of the watch manufacturers were commissioned to put jewelers' or jobbers' **names** on their movements in place of their own. Because of this practice, the true manufacturers of these movements are difficult to identify.

The prices shown were averaged from dealers' lists just prior to publication and are an indication of the retail level or what collectors will pay. **Prices** are provided in three categories: **average condition, extra fine, and mint condition,** and are shown in whole dollar amounts only. The values listed are a guide for the *collectable* retail level and are provided for your information only. **Dealers** will not necessarily <u>pay full retail</u> price. Prices listed are for watches with **original** cases, movement and dials and in good running order.

Warning: There are currently fake wrist watches being sold on the world-wide market. These watches have the appearance of authenticity but are merely cheap imitations of prestigious companies such as Rolex (all types), Gucci, Cartier, & Piaget.

Important Notice. All of the information, including valuations, in this book has been compiled from the most reliable sources, and every effort has been made to eliminate errors and questionable data. Nevertheless, the possibility of error, in a work of such immense scope, always exists. The publisher or authors will not be held responsible for losses which may occur in the purchase, sale, statements of its advertisers, or other transaction of items, because of information contained herein. Readers who feel they have discovered errors are invited to write and inform us, so they may be corrected in subsequent editions.

<u>**INFORMATION**</u> **NEEDED** — The authors are interested in any facts and information you might have that should possibly be considered for future editions. Documented facts are needed, so please send photo or sources of information. Send to:

COOKSEY SHUGART
P.O. BOX 3147
CLEVELAND, TN. 37320-3147

When **CORRESPONDING**, Please send a self addressed, stamped **ENVELOPE**.

ABERCROMBIE & FITCH, 17J., chronog.by Valj.,3 reg.

14K.	$1,000	$1,100	$1,200
s.steel	$400	$475	$575

Abercrombie & Fitch, 17J., **Sea Farer,** chronog., waterproof

18k	$1,200	$1,400	$1,600
s. steel	$375	$475	$575

Abercrombie & Fitch, 17J., chronog.by Valj.,3 reg., Ca.1950

s.steel	$350	$400	$500

ABRA, 17J., step case, c.1930s

base metal	$45	$55	$65

🕐 Some grades are not included. Their values can be determined by comparing with similar age, size, metal content, style, grades, or models such as time only, chronograph, repeater etc. listed.

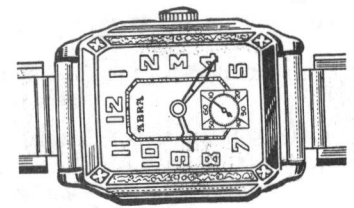

ABRA,17J., carved case, c.1930s

base metal	$40	$50	$65

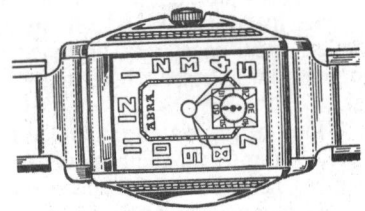

ABRA, 17J., engraved case

base metal	$45	$55	$65

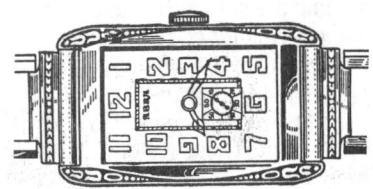

ABRA,15J., curved case, c.1930s

base metal	$50	$65	$75

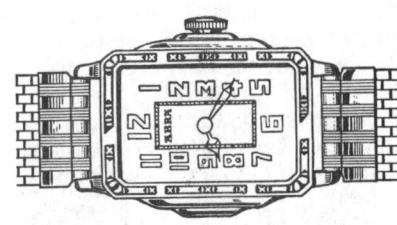

ABRA,15J., engraved case, c.1930s

gold plate	$50	$60	$75

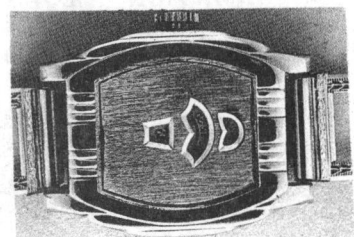

ABRA, 17J., **jump hour**

s. steel	$300	$350	$400

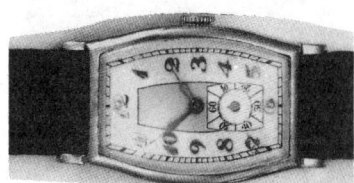

ACRO W. CO., 17 jewels, **hinged back**
18k $250 $300 $350

ADMES, 17 jewels, self wind, waterproof, center sec.,
14K..$85 $100 $135
gold filled................................. $35 $40 $55

AGASSIZ, 17 jewels, **World Time**
18k $5,000 $6,000 $7,000

AGASSIZ, 17 jewels, fancy bezel,
18k $600 $700 $800

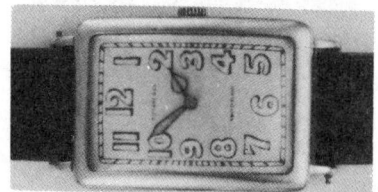

AGASSIZ, 18 jewels, for Tiffany & Co., 48mm, oversize
18k $800 $900 $1,000

AGASSIZ,17J., C. 1940s
18K(W).................................. $600 $700 $800

AGASSIZ, 18 jewels, barrel shaped dial, 40mm,
18k $400 $500 $600

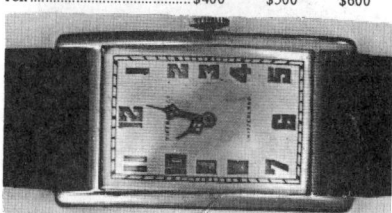

AGASSIZ, 17 jewels, for Tiffany & Co., 45mm
18k $700 $800 $950

ALPHA, 17J., chrono. 2 reg., cal.48, c.1950s
14K $400 $450 $550
s.steel $150 $175 $225

ALPHA, 17J., **Fancy lugs**, sweep sec., c. 1948
18k $250 $275 $300

ALPHA, 17J, autowind, c.1950s
18K..$175 $200 $250

ALPINA, 15 jewels, automatic, water proof, center sec.
gold filled..................................$50 $60 $75

ALPINA, 17 jewels, automatic, water proof, aux. sec.
18k...$175 $200 $250

ALSTA, 17J., **chronograph**, 3 reg.
14K..$425 $475 $525
base metal $200 $250 $325

ALSTA, 17 jewels, **wrist alarm**
gold filled $95 $125 $150

ALTON, 17J., fancy lugs, c.1950s
14K $150 $175 $225

ALTUS, 17 jewels, ref. 827
18k $150 $175 $200

AM. WALTHAM, 17J.,c.1930s
14k $150 $175 $250

AM. WALTHAM, 17J., aux, sec. c.1930s
14k $150 $175 $250

AM. WALTHAM, 17J., aux.sec., c.1930s
14k $140 $165 $240

AM. WALTHAM, 21J., cal.750B, GJS, c.1950s
14k $150 $175 $250

AM. WALTHAM, 17J., cal.750B, c.1951
gold filled.................................$75 $100 $125

AM. WALTHAM, 15J., "Masonic" model, c.1925
14k $500 $600 $700

AM. WALTHAM, 15-17J, **solid lugs**, c.1920s
sterling silver $200 $250 $325

AM. WALTHAM, 15-17J, "Ruby"model, c.1920s
gold filled $125 $150 $175

AM. WALTHAM, 17 J, barrel shaped dial, c. 1920
14k $175 $200 $250

AM. WALTHAM, 17 jewels, "Cromwell"
gold filled $50 $65 $95

AM. WALTHAM, 17 jewels, "Oberlin"
gold filled $50 $65 $95

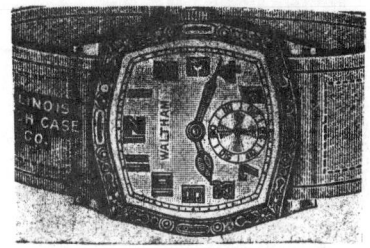

AM. WALTHAM, 15 jewels, engraved bezel
gold filled $100 $125 $175

AM. WALTHAM, 17J., for Tiffany & Co.
14k $300 $350 $400

AM.WALTHAM, 19J., **enamel dial**, C. 1905
silver $135 $165 $225

AM. WALTHAM, 17 jewels, wire lugs
14k $450 $500 $600

AM. WALTHAM, 17 jewels, "Duxbury"
gold filled.................................. $65 $75 $100

AM. WALTHAM, 21 jewels, curved back
14k $225 $275 $300

AM. WALTHAM, 7-15 jewels, wandering sec., c. 1930
gold filled $150 $200 $275

AM. WALTHAM, 17 jewels, **wandering sec.**, c. 1930
gold filled $175 $225 $295

AM. WALTHAM, 17 jewels, "Fairmont"
gold filled $75 $100 $135

AM. WALTHAM, 17 jewels, "Stan Hope"
gold filled $50 $75 $100

AM. WALTHAM, 17 jewels, "Winfield"
gold filled $65 $75 $100

AM. WALTHAM, wandering min., **jumping hour.**, c. 1933
gold filled $500 $600 $750

AM. WALTHAM, 15J., aux. sec.
gold filled.................................$45 $55 $75

AM. WALTHAM, 21 jewels, "Albright"
14k $125 $150 $175

AM. WALTHAM, 21 jewels, "Sheraton"
14k $125 $150 $175

AM. WALTHAM, 17 jewels, center sec.
gold filled.................................$45 $55 $75

AM. WALTHAM, 15 jewels, **winds at 12,** wire lugs, c. 1916
silver $250 $300 $400

AM. WALTHAM, 15 J., case by Rolland Fischer
silver $300 $350 $450

AM. WALTHAM, 15J., **enamel dial, center lugs,** c.1915
silver $300 $350 $400

AM. WALTHAM, 15J., **wire lugs,** engraved, S#16,952,060
14K $250 $300 $350

AM. WALTHAM, 15 jewels, **multi-color enamel dial,**
Ca. 1920
base metal................................$250 $300 $375

AM. WALTHAM, 7-15J., **pulsations**, solid lugs, c.1925
silver $300 $350 $450

AM. WALTHAM, 17J.,**"Riverside"**, GJS, c.1918
silver $450 $500 $600

AM. WALTHAM, 15 jewels, c. 1930
gold filled.................................. $60 $70 $85

AM. WALTHAM, 7J., **oxidized case**, c.1930s
gold filled.................................$75 $100 $125

AM. WALTHAM, 7-15J., **cut corner dial**, c.1930s
gold filled.................................$75 $100 $125

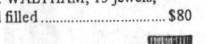

AM. WALTHAM, 15 jewels,
gold filled.................................$80 $90 $100

AM. WALTHAM, 15J., **engraved oxidized case**,c.1930s
gold filled $75 $100 $125

AM. WALTHAM, 15J.,engraved case
gold filled $75 $85 $100

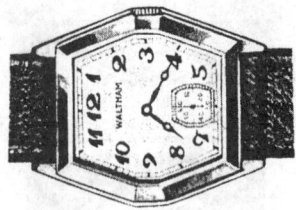

AM. WALTHAM, 17 jewels, 18K applied #s
silver $175 $200 $235

AM. WALTHAM, 7-15 jewels, engraved case
gold filled $75 $100 $135

AM. WALTHAM, 7-15 jewels, **carved** case
gold filled $80 $95 $125

AM. WALTHAM, 15 jewels, **curved back**
14k $200 $225 $250

AM. WALTHAM, 7-15 jewels, engraved case
gold filled.................................$80 $100 $125

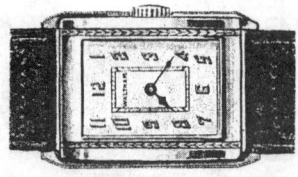

AM. WALTHAM, 17 jewels, tank style, **18K applied #s**
14kw $200 $225 $250

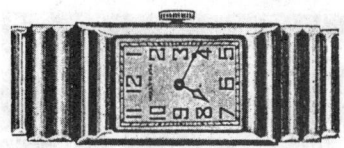

AM. WALTHAM, 15-17 jewels,
gold filled.................................$60 $70 $85

AM. WALTHAM, 7-15 jewels,
gold filled.................................$80 $90 $100

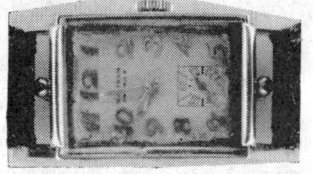

AM. WALTHAM, 15-17J, Premier, note **screwed on case**
water-resistant, Ca. 1920
14K...$300 $350 $400

AM. WALTHAM, 15J., case by Rolland Fischer,
silver $400 $500 $625

AM. WALTHAM, 15 jewels, "Depollier," **early water proof, (Canteen style)**, c. 1917
silver $500 $600 $750

AM. WALTHAM, 15 jewels, protective grill, c. 1907
gold filled $250 $300 $365
14k $750 $850 $1,000

AM. WALTHAM, 17 jewels, military with **hack setting**
s. steel $85 $100 $135

AM. WALTHAM, 17 jewels, **cut-corner dial**
14k $200 $250 $300

🕐 Some grades are not included. Their values can be
determined by comparing with **similar** age, size, metal
content, style, grades, or models such as **time only**,
chronograph, repeater etc. listed.

AM. WALTHAM, 17 jewels, luminous dial
14k $175 $225 $275

AM. WALTHAM, 17 jewels, **WINDS at 12,** wire lugs
gold filled................................$150 $175 $200

AM. WALTHAM, 17 jewels, **center lugs**
14k $185 $225 $275

AM. WALTHAM, 17 jewels, **"Allen"**
gold filled...................................$60 $75 $100

AM. WALTHAM, 17 jewels, **"Penton"**
gold filled...............................$50 $75 $100

AM. WALTHAM, 9-17 jewels, **"Side-wrist"**
gold filled...............................$125 $150 $200

AM. WALTHAM, 17 jewels, **curvex, 42mm**
14k $300 $350 $400

AM. WALTHAM, 17 jewels, **curvex, 52mm**
14k $500 $600 $750

AM. WALTHAM, 17 jewels, **curvex, 42mm**
gold filled...............................$100 $150 $175

🕐 Some grades are not included. Their values can be
determined by comparing with **similar** age, size, metal
content, style, grades, or models such as **time only**,
chronograph, repeater etc. listed.

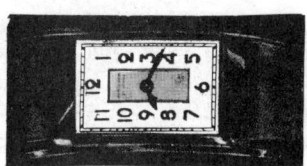

AM. WALTHAM, 17-21 jewels, curved
14k $175 $225 $300
gold filled............................$65 $75 $100

AM. WALTHAM, 17 jewels, curved, aux. sec.
gold filled............................$65 $80 $100

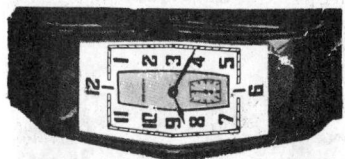

AM. WALTHAM, 17 jewels, curved
gold filled............................$65 $75 $120

AM. WALTHAM, 21 jewels, C.1938
14K....................................$150 $200 $250

AM. WALTHAM, 17 jewels, curved
gold filled............................$75 $85 $125

AM. WALTHAM, 17 jewels, curved
gold filled............................$65 $75 $100

AM. WALTHAM, 15J., **note bow swings, screw back case, solid lugs, enamel dial, early water proof** , c. 1920s
14K .... ★★$450 $550 $750

AM. WALTHAM, 17 jewels, enamel bezel
14k $650 $750 $950
14k (w) $500 $600 $800
gold filled $150 $200 $250

AM. WALTHAM,17J., enamel bezel,**"ruby"** model,c.1928
14k(w)................................. $550 $650 $800

AM. WALTHAM,17J., **stepped case**
gold filled $75 $100 $125

AM. WALTHAM, 17 jewels, **"Jeffrey"**
gold filled $75 $100 $125

AM. WALTHAM, 21 jewels, "**Tulane**"
gold filled................................$40 $50 $80

AM. WALTHAM, 7J., luminous dial, c.1928
base metal $60 $70 $90

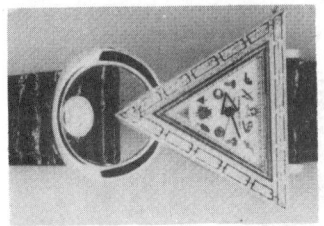

AM. WALTHAM, 17J., triangular, masonic symbols
fancy hands, **mother of pearl dial**, Ca. 1950
gold filled............................$1,000 $1,200 $1,500

AM. WALTHAM, 7J., luminous dial, c. 1928
gold filled $75 $100 $125

AM. WALTHAM, 7-15J., luminous dial, c.1928
base metal $40 $50 $75

AM. WALTHAM, 17J., luminous dial, c.1929
gold filled $60 $70 $80
14k(w)..................................$175 $200 $275

AM. WALTHAM, 7-15J., cushion case, c.1928
gold filled................................$50 $75 $100

AM. WALTHAM, 17J., aux. sec., c. 1928
14k(w)..................................$175 $200 $275

AM. WALTHAM, 7-15J., tonneau case, c. 1928
gold filled................................$50 $75 $100

AM. WALTHAM,7-15J., **lugless case**, c.1928
gold filled $60 $75 $125

AM. WALTHAM,15J., luminous dial, c.1928
14k $175 $225 $300

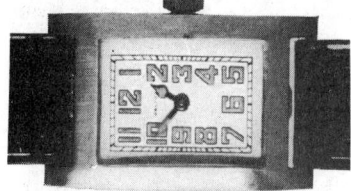

AM. WALTHAM,15J., brush finish, c.1928
14k $175 $225 $300

AM. WALTHAM,7J., luminous dial, c.1928
gold plate $75 $85 $125

AM. WALTHAM,17J.,GJS, ca.1940
14K...$150 $175 $200

AM. WALTHAM,7-15J., cut corner case, c.1929
gold filled..................................$75 $85 $95

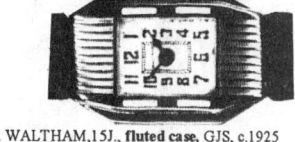

AM. WALTHAM,15J., fluted case, GJS, c.1925
14k(w)+enamel..........................$95 $110 $150

AM. WALTHAM,7-15J., **Butler finish** = (smooth), c.1928
gold filled $75 $100 $125

AM. WALTHAM, 7-15J., GJS, Ca.1927
14K(w)....................................$175 $225 $300

AM. WALTHAM,7-15J., engraved case, etched dial, c.1929
14k(w)....................................$60 $70 $100
gold filled $30 $40 $65

AM. WALTHAM,15J., engraved case, etched dial, c.1928
14K(W)....................................$50 $65 $75
gold filled $30 $45 $65

AM. WALTHAM,7-15J., enamel case, c. 1928
14k(w)....................................$75 $90 $120

AM. WALTHAM,15J., enamel case, c.1929
gold filled (w)..........................$45 $55 $75

AMERICAN WALTHAM WATCH CO. IDENTIFICATION BY MOVEMENT

Model 1900, 0 size    Model 1907, 0 size    Jewel Series

Model 1900, 0/3 size, open face

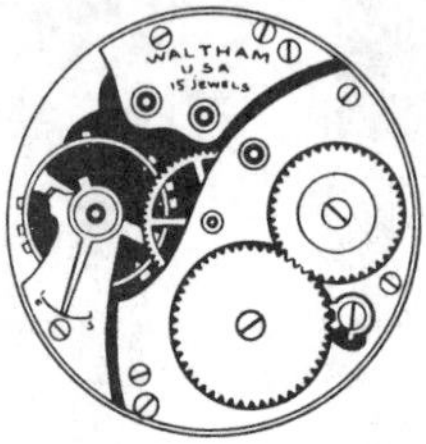

Model 1907, 0/3 size, hunting

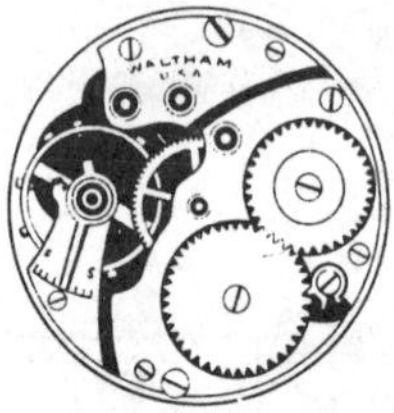

Model 1898 & 1912, 0/6 size, hunting

Model 1898 & 1912, 0/6 size, open face

10½ ligne

10 ligne

7½ ligne 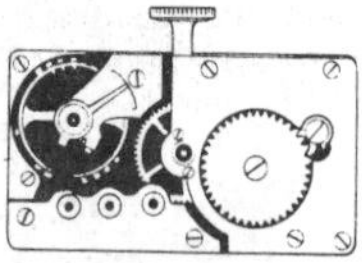   5¼ ligne    Model 400    Model 450

Model 650    Model 675   Model 750

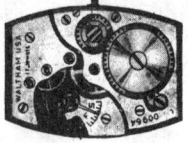

AMERICUS, 17 jewels, **8 day** movement, c. 1933
18k ....$1,000 $1,200$ $1,500
gold filled.............................$400 $500 $600
s. steel $300 $400 $500

ANGELUS, 17J., day, date, moon ph.,C. 1949
s. steel....................................$300 $365 $450

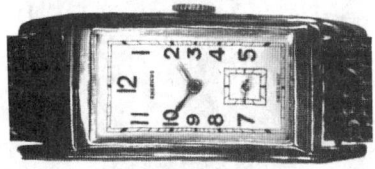

AMERICUS, 7 jewels, curved, c.1935
gold filled..............................$100 $125 $150

ANGELUS, 17 jewels, chronograph, 2 reg., water proof
14k...$500 $600 $700
18k...$700 $800 $900
s. steel....................................$200 $250 $300

ANGELUS, 17 jewels, chronograph, 2 reg., c. 1943
18k $600 $700 $800
14k $400 $500 $600
gold filled..............................$150 $200 $250

ANGELUS, 17J., **date and alarm**, c.1955
s. steel....................................$175 $200 $250

ANGELUS, 17J., chronograph, **triple date**, C. 1949
s. steel $350 $400 $500
14k $700 $900 $1,000
18k $1,300 $1,400 $1,500

ANGELUS, 27 jewels, **1/4 hour repeater**
s. steel..................................$2,700 $3,000 $3,500

ARAMIS, 15 jewels, **early self wind, lug action winding by back & forth motion of watch case**, c. 1933
s. steel $600 $700 $900

ARBU, 17 jewels, triple date, moon phase
18k $800 $1,000 $1,200
s. steel $300 $350 $400

ARBU, 17 jewels, chronograph, 3 reg., day-date-month
18k $700 $850 $1,000
s. steel $350 $400 $450

ARBU, 17 jewels, **split second chronograph**
18k $3,000 $3,300 $3,700

ARCTOS, 17J., "PARAT", world map on dial, c.1955
base metal................................$100 $125 $150

ARDATH, 17J., chronograph, triple date, c.1947
s. steel....................................$250 $300 $350

ARISTO, 17 jewels, chronog., water proof
14k...$500 $600 $750
s. steel....................................$150 $175 $225

ARISTO, 17J., chronog., 3 reg., **triple date**
14k...$1,500 $1,750 $2,000
s. steel....................................$400 $500 $625

ARISTO, 17 jewels, day-date-month, moon phase
s. steel $300 $350 $425

ARMADILLO, by DAVE WALDO, flip top, coin
silver coin $450 $550 $650
18k plate $500 $600 $700

ARSA, 17 jewels, day-date-month, moon phase
18k $800 $900 $1,000
s. steel $300 $350 $425

ARSA, 15 jewels, day-date-month, moon phase
18k $800 $900 $1,000
s. steel $300 $350 $425

ASPREY, 16 jewels, **curved hinged back**
9k..$175 $225 $350

ASPREY, 17J., **date**, ca. 1930s
14k..$375 $425 $475
gold filled..............................$150 $200 $275

ASPREY, 15 jewels, **duo dial**
18k......................................$1,700 $2,000 $2,500

ASPREY, 17 jewels, **enamel dial, center lugs**
9k..$200 $250 $300

AUDAX, 15J., Ca.1938
9k..$100 $135 $185

🕐 Some grades are not included. Their values can be
determined by comparing with similar age, size, metal
content, style, grades, or models such as time only,
chronograph, repeater etc. listed.

AUDEMARS PIGUET, 33J., **minute** repeater, gold train, platinum & 18K with **40** diamond bezel, diamond dial & diamonds on band
18K & platinum.................$70,000 $80,000 $90,000

AUDEMARS PIGUET, 29 J., **minute repeater**, c. 1907
18k $70,000 $80,000 $90,000

AUDEMARS PIGUET, 29 J., **minute repeater**, c. 1925
platinum $70,000 $80,000 $90,000

AUDEMARS PIGUET, 19 J., **tourbillon,** self-winding tourbillon can be seen from dial side
18k $9,000 $10,000 $12,000

AUDEMARS PIGUET, 36 J., octogonal shaped case, triple date, moon phase, perpetual
18k C&B $10,000 $11,000 $13,000

AUDEMARS PIGUET, 33J., day date, moon ph., c.1989
18k..$2,500 $3,000 $3,500

AUDEMARS PIGUET, day date, moon ph., C. 1980s
18k..$2,500 $3,000 $3,500

AUDEMARS PIGUET, chronograph, triple date, moon ph., tear drop lugs, Ca. 1940s
18k..$25,000 $35,000 $45,000

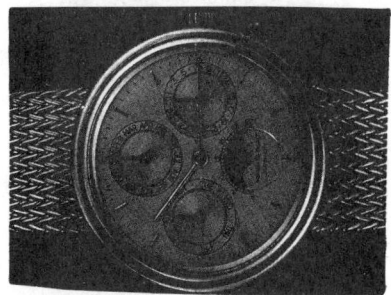

AUDEMARS PIGUET, 36 jewels, gold rotor, day-date
month, moon phase, perpetual
18 k C&B............................$9,000 $10,000 $11,000

AUDEMARS PIGUET, skeletonized, triple date,
moon phase, perpetual , C. 1980s
platinum.............................$14,000 $16,000 $18,000

AUDEMARS PIGUET, 17 J., chronog., 3 reg., c. 1945
s.steel $12,000 $14,000 $16,000
18k $15,000 $17,000 $20,000

AUDEMARS PIGUET, 18 J., "Le Brassus," chronog.
skeletonized
18k C&B...........................$20,000 $22,000 $25,000

AUDEMARS PIGUET, 22 jewels, chronog., 2 reg.,
s.steel $9,000 $12,000 $15,000
18k $13,000 $15,000 $18,000

AUDEMARS PIGUET, 18 jewels, skeletonized
18k $5,000 $6,000 $7,000

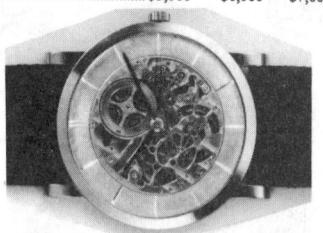

AUDEMARS PIGUET, 17 jewels, thin skeletonized
18k $5,000 $6,000 $7,000

🕐 Some grades are not included. Their values can be
determined by comparing with similar age, size, metal
content, style, grades, or models such as time only,
chronograph, repeater etc. listed.

AUDEMARS PIGUET, 18 J., triple date, moonphase
18k $5,500 $7,000 $8,500

AUDEMARS PIGUET, 36 jewels, skeletonized
18k $5,500 $6,500 $8,000

AUDEMARS PIGUET, 17 J., center lugs, skeletonized
18k $7,000 $7,500 $8,500

AUDEMARS PIGUET, 17J., Dodecagonal, black dial
18k $1,200 $1,400 $1,600

AUDEMARS PIGUET, 17J., diamond dial, c. 1970
18k $2,000 $2,200 $2,500

AUDEMARS PIGUET, 12 diamond dial c.1960
platinum $2,000 $2,200 $2,500

AUDEMARS PIGUET, 11 diamond dial
18k $1,600 $1,800 $2,000

AUDEMARS PIGUET, 12 sapphire dial, c.1950
18k $2,500 $2,700 $3,000

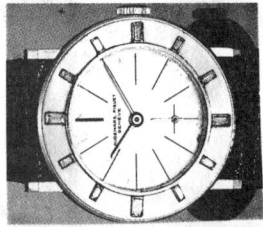

AUDEMARS PIGUET, 17 jewels, 12 diamond dial
18k (w) $2,500 $2,700 $3,000

AUDEMARS PIGUET, 36 jewels, self-winding
18k $1,400 $1,600 $1,900

AUDEMARS PIGUET, 17 jewels, adj. to 5 positions
18k C&B..............................$1,200 $1,400 $1,600

AUDEMARS PIGUET, 17 jewels, rope style bezel
18k C&B............................$1,500 $1,800 $2,000

AUDEMARS PIGUET, 36 jewels, self-winding
18k $1,800 $2,000 $2,400

AUDEMARS PIGUET, 17J., diamond bezel, center lugs
18k $2,000 $2,200 $2,400

AUDEMARS PIGUET, 36 jewels, lazuli dial
18k C&B............................$2,200 $2,400 $2,800

AUDEMARS PIGUET, 20J., rope style bezel, c. 1980s
18k case, 14k band $1,000 $1,100 $1,200

AUDEMARS PIGUET, 17 jewels, thin style
18k C&B............................$2,000 $2,200 $2,500

AUDEMARS PIGUET, 20J., "Le Brassus," c. 1970
18k C&B............................$2,000 $2,200 $2,400

AUDEMARS PIGUET, 17 jewels, fancy bezel, c. 1950
18k $2,000 $2,400 $2,800

AUDEMARS PIGUET, fancy shaped, c.1960s
18k $2,500 $3,000 $3,500

AUDEMARS PIGUET, 17J., "Philosopher", hour hand
18k $2,200 $2,500 $2,800

AUDEMARS PIGUET, 20 jewels, thin model
18k $1,100 $1,200 $1,300

AUDEMARS PIGUET, **world time**, fancy lugs
s. steel $10,000 $12,000 $15,000

AUDEMARS PIGUET, 17J., engraved bezel, c. 1963
18k $1,500 $2,000 $2,200

AUDEMARS PIGUET, **world time**, c. 1940s
14k $12,000 $14,000 $17,000

AUDEMARS PIGUET, 17J., wide bezel, thin model
14k C&B..............................$1,500 $1,600 $1,800

AUDEMARS PIGUET, 18 jewels, gold train
18k $2,500 $3,000 $3,500

AUDEMARS PIGUET, 18J., **hidden lugs**, Ca. 1950
18k $1,200 $1,400 $1,700

AUDEMARS PIGUET, 21J., auto wind, center sec.
18k $1,600 $1,800 $2,000

🕐 Some grades are not included. Their values can be
determined by comparing with similar age, size, metal
content, style, grades, or models such as time only,
chronograph, repeater etc. listed.

AUDEMARS PIGUET, 18 jewels, aux. sec. c. 1940
18k $2,000 $2,200 $2,500

AUDEMARS PIGUET, 17 jewels, for Tiffany & Co.
18k C&B.............................$2,000 $2,200 $2,400

AUDEMARS PIGUET, 18J., no second hand, Ca. 1965
18k $800 $950 $1,100

AUDEMARS PIGUET, 18 jewels, aux. sec.
18k $2,000 $2,100 $2,300

AUDEMARS PIGUET, 18 jewels, center sec., c. 1950
18k $1,500 $1,800 $2,200

AUDEMARS PIGUET, 18 jewels, tank style, c. 1960
18k (w)................................$1,500 $1,600 $1,800

AUDEMARS PIGUET,18J., straight line lever escape.
18k $1,200 $1,400 $1,700

AUDEMARS PIGUET, 18 jewels, hooded lugs
18k $1,500 $1,600 $1,800

AUDEMARS PIGUET, 17 jewels, mid-size
18k $500 $600 $750

AUDEMARS PIGUET, 17J., engraved bezel, c.1966
18k $1,400 $1,600 $1,800

AUDEMARS PIGUET, 18J., mid size, **flat bezel**, Ca. 1969
18k $1,200 $1,400 $1,700

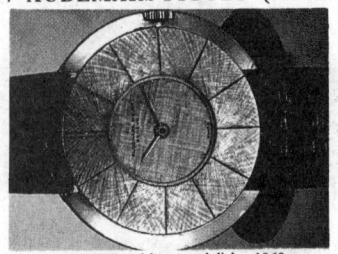

AUDEMARS PIGUET, gold textured dial, c.1960s
18k $1,000 $1,100 $1,200

AUDEMARS PIGUET,18J., aux. sec., c. 1950s
18k $1,200 $1,500 $1,800

AUDEMARS PIGUET, 18J., auto wind, waterproof
18k $1,600 $1,800 $2,000

AUDEMARS PIGUET, 18 jewels, **painted dial**, c. 1970
18k $1,000 $1,100 $1,300

AUDEMARS PIGUET, 21 jewels, 18k gold rotor
18k $1,700 $1,900 $2,300

AUDEMARS PIGUET, 19J., center sec.
18k $1,500 $2,000 $2,500

AUDEMARS PIGUET, 18J., screw back, waterproof
18k $1,600 $1,800 $2,000

AUDEMARS PIGUET, 17 jewels, gold train
18k $1,000 $1,200 $1,500

AUDEMARS PIGUET, **triple date, moon ph.**, c.1930s
18k $35,000 $40,000 $45,000

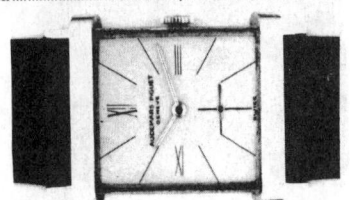

AUDEMARS PIGUET, 18 J.," **top hat**", aux. sec., c. 1950
platinum...............................$3,000 $3,500 $4,000

🕐 Some grades are not included. Their values can be determined by comparing with **similar** age, size, metal content, style, grades, or models such as **time only,** chronograph, repeater etc. listed.

AUDEMARS PIGUET, 17J., gold train, 2 tone case in platinum & gold
18k (w) C&B $2,500 $2,700 $3,000

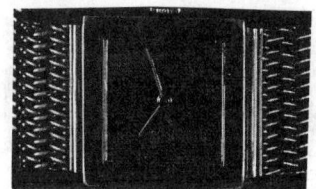

AUDEMARS PIGUET, large bezel, c.1940s
18k C&B............................$3,000 $3,500 $4,000

AUDEMARS PIGUET, 17 jewels, gold train
14k C&B............................$1,600 $1,800 $2,200

AUDEMARS PIGUET, 18 J., textured bezel, c. 1950
18k $1,700 $1,900 $2,000

AUDEMARS PIGUET, 2 tone dial, c.1930s
18k $2,500 $3,000 $3,500

🕐 Some grades are not included. Their values can be determined by comparing with **similar** age, size, metal content, style, grades, or models such as **time only**, chronograph, repeater etc. listed.

AUDEMARS PIGUET, 17 jewels, gold train, c. 1940
18k (w) $2,200 $2,500 $2,800

AUDEMARS PIGUET, 18J, curvex, large bezel, c. 1950
18k $2,000 $2,200 $2,500

AUDEMARS PIGUET, 18 jewels, tank style, c. 1950's
18k $2,000 $2,200 $2,500

AUDEMARS PIGUET, Royal Oak, **date,** auto wind, c.1973
s.steel & Quartz...................$1,500 $1,700 $2,000
18k C&B............................$6,000 $7,000 $8,000

AUDEMARS PIGUET, quartz, 12 diamonds, c. 1981
s. steel $1,200 $1,400 $1,600

AUDEMARS PIGUET, ladys, 72 small diamonds, c.1930s
plat.case & band $1,500 $1,700 $2,000

AUSTIN, 17J., fancy bezel,
gold filled................................... $75 $80 $95

AUTOMATIQUE, 17J., cal.F699, c. 1955
s. steel $55 $60 $75

AUTORIST, 15 jewels, **lug action wind**, enamel dial
s. steel $400 $500 $600

AUTORIST, 15 jewels, **lug action wind**, c. 1930
s. steel $400 $500 $600

🕐 Some grades are not included. Their values can be
determined by comparing with similar age, size, metal
content, style, grades, or models such as time only,
chronograph, repeater etc. listed.

AUTORIST, 15 jewels, **lug action wind**, c. 1930
gold filled $500 $600 $700

AUTORIST, 15 jewels, **lug action wind**, (lady's)
s. steel $200 $300 $400

AVALON, 17J., aux.sec.
gold filled $35 $40 $50

AVALON, 17J., aux.sec.
gold filled $50 $60 $70

BALL W. CO., 25 jewels, auto wind, adj. to 5 pos., E.T.A.
10k $375 $400 $450

BALL W. CO., 25 jewels, auto wind, adj. to 5 pos., E.T.A.
gold filled...............................$250 $275 $325

BALL W. CO., 25 jewels, auto wind, adj. to 5 pos., E.T.A.
s. steel $250 $275 $325

BAUME & MERCIER, 18J., triple date, moon phase
s. steel $400 $500 $600

BAUME & MERCIER, 17J., chronog., 2 reg., c.1949
gold filled...............................$250 $300 $400

BAUME & MERCIER, 17J., chronog., 2 reg.,c.1950s
18k $500 $600 $700

BAUME & MERCIER, 18J., chronog., 3 reg. & dates
s. steel $400 $500 $625

BAUME & MERCIER, 18 J., chronog., 3 reg. & dates
18k $1,200 $1,400 $1,700

BAUME & MERCIER, 18 jewels, tachymeter, c. 1940
s. steel, original black dial $400 $450 $500

BAUME & MERCIER, 17J., triple date, chronog.
moon ph., c.1950s
18k $1,500 $1,700 $2,000

BAUME & MERCIER, 17J., 2 dials, 2 time zones &
2 movements
18k $700 $800 $900

BAUME & MERCIER, 18 J., chronog., fancy lugs
18k $1,800 $2,200 $2,600

BAUME & MERCIER, 18 jewels, gold dial, date
14k C&B..................................$400 $450 $500

BAUME & MERCIER, 17J., chronog., triple date
18k $1,200 $1,400 $1,600

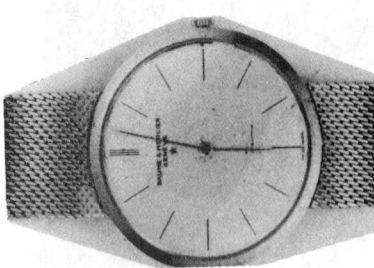

BAUME & MERCIER, 18 jewels, thin model
14k C&B..................................$400 $450 $500

BAUME & MERCIER, 18J., triple date, moon phase
18k $1,000 $1,100 $1,300

BAUME & MERCIER, 17 jewels, center sec., c. 1956
14k $200 $250 $325

BAUME & MERCIER, 17 jewels, aux. sec., c. 1955
14k $225 $250 $275

BAUME & MERCIER, 17J., RF#49300, c. 1965
14k $150 $175 $225

BAUME & MERCIER, 18 J., "Riviera", date, c. 1980s
18k & s. steel $500 $600 $700

BAUME & MERCIER, quartz, enamel dial, tank, c.1990s
14k $300 $350 $400

BAUME & MERCIER, 17J., curved, c. 1990s
14k C&B.................................$500 $600 $700

BAUME & MERCIER,17J., sec. window, auto-w., c.1950s
base metal..............................$100 $125 $150

BAUME & MERCIER, 17J.,diam. dial, cal#1080, c.1950s
14k(W)....................................$500 $600 $750

BAYLOR, 17J., hidden lugs
gold filled $40 $55 $75
14k $125 $150 $175

BAYLOR, 17J., diamond on bezel & dial, c.1948
14k $300 $350 $400

BELTONE, 17J., fancy hidden lugs
14k $175 $200 $250

BEMONTOIR, 15J., enamel dial, c.1920
14k $125 $150 $175

BENRUS,17J., day date
base metal $25 $35 $50

BENRUS, 18J., mystery-diamond dial
18k $400 $475 $550
gold filled $100 $150 $200

BENRUS, 15 jewels, day, date, c. 1948
s. steel $75 $90 $110

⏲ Some grades are not included. Their values can be
determined by comparing with **similar** age, size, metal
content, style, grades, or models such as **time only**,
chronograph, repeater etc. listed.

BENRUS, 15 jewels, quick change date
gold filled $80 $100 $125

BENRUS,17J.,"Sky Chief", chronog., c.1945
s. steel $300 $350 $425

BENRUS,17J., "Sky Chief", chronog., center lugs, c.1945
gold filled $325 $375 $450

BENRUS,17J.,"Sky Chief",triple date,chronog.,c.1940s
s. steel $400 $475 $575

BENRUS, 15 jewels, auto wind, fancy lugs, c. 1950
14k $150 $200 $250
gold filled...............................$60 $75 $90

BENRUS, 15 jewels, jumping hour, wandering min.
gold filled $125 $150 $175
s. steel $100 $125 $140

BENRUS, 15J., auto wind, fancy bezel, by ETA, c. 1950
gold filled...............................$60 $75 $90
14k $115 $135 $200

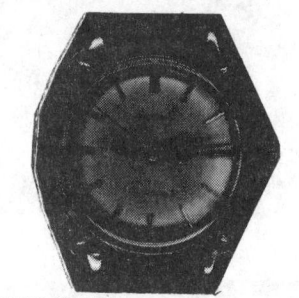

BENRUS,17J., fancy lugs
gold filled $55 $65 $80

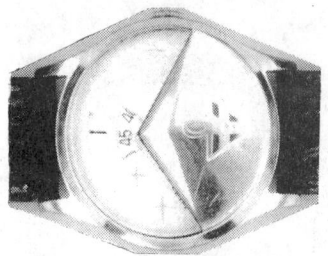

BENRUS,17J., jumping hour, wandering min.
gold filled...............................$150 $175 $225

BENRUS,17J., fancy lugs
gold filled $45 $50 $70

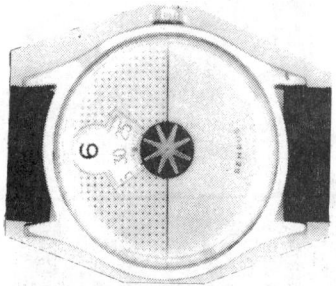

BENRUS,17J., dial-0-rama, direct read, c. 1958
gold filled...............................$150 $175 $225

BENRUS,17J., center sec., heavy lugs,
gold filled $45 $50 $70

🕐 Some grades are not included. Their values can be determined by comparing with **similar** age, size, metal content, style, grades, or models such as **time only**, chronograph, repeater etc. listed.

🕐 Some grades are not included. Their values can be determined by comparing with **similar** age, size, metal content, style, grades, or models such as **time only**, chronograph, repeater etc. listed.

BENRUS, 15 jewels, fancy lugs, c. 1948
14k $325 $375 $425
gold filled............................$125 $150 $175

BENRUS, 15 J., auto-wind, **water-proof**
gold filled.................................$35 $40 $60

BENRUS, 15 jewels, fancy bezel, cal. BB14
14k $250 $300 $375
gold filled............................$100 $135 $175

BENRUS, 21J., aux. sec., c. 1950s
14k $125 $150 $175

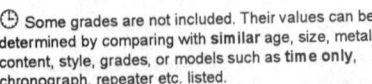

⊕ Some grades are not included. Their values can be
determined by comparing with similar age, size, metal
content, style, grades, or models such as time only,
chronograph, repeater etc. listed.

BENRUS, 17J., **wind indicator**, c.1955
gold filled $100 $125 $155

BENRUS, 21J., aux. sec., fancy lugs, c.1950
gold filled $60 $70 $95

BENRUS, 17J., hidden lugs
14K $125 $150 $185

BENRUS, 17J., cadillac logo, c.1950s
gold plate $80 $90 $100

BENRUS, 17J., by ETA, c.1955
gold filled $65 $75 $85

BENRUS, 15J., engraved bezel, c.1935
14k $175 $200 $250

BENRUS, 17J., Rhinestone dial, c. 1945
gold filled..................................$75 $85 $100

BENRUS, 17J., date, fancy lugs, c.1950
gold filled............................$100 $125 $150

BENRUS, 17J., aux. sec., c.1940
14k $100 $125 $150

BENRUS, 15J.,aux sec.
gold filled..................................$55 $70 $90

BENRUS,17J., **flared case**, cal.180, c. 1951
gold filled $85 $100 $135

BENRUS, 7J., rhinestone dial, fancy lugs, c. 1948
base metal..................................$50 $60 $85

BENRUS,17J., rhinestone dial, cal. bb1, c. 1945
gold plate $60 $70 $90

BENRUS, 15J.,stepped case
gold filled $50 $60 $80

BENRUS, 15J.,fancy lugs
14kC&B................................$500 $550 $650

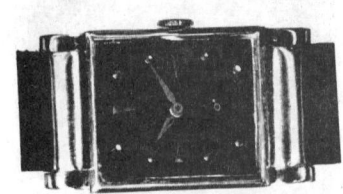

BENRUS, 17J., hidden lugs, cal.11ax, Ca.1951
14k $250 $275 $325

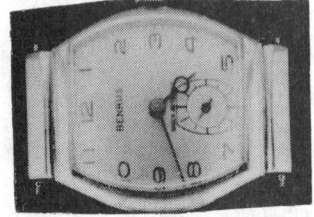

BENRUS, 15J., hooded lugs, cal#bb3
gold filled...................................$60 $75 $100

BENRUS, 15J., **enamel bezel**, c. 1930
14k (w)....................................$350 $450 $525

BENRUS, 15 jewels, 26 diamond bezel
14k (w)....................................$350 $450 $550

BENRUS,17J., aux sec., Ca.1935
gold filled..................................$60 $75 $100

BENRUS, 15 jewels, **flip-top case,** c. 1940
gold filled $275 $325 $400

BENRUS,17J., hooded lugs, c.1948
14k $150 $175 $225

BENRUS,17J., hooded lugs, cal.AX11, c. 1950
14k $225 $250 $300

BENRUS, 15 jewels, hooded lugs
gold filled $60 $70 $100

BENRUS, 15 jewels, cal. AX, fancy bezel
14k $175 $200 $275

🕐 Some grades are not included. Their values can be
determined by comparing with **similar** age, size, metal
content, style, grades, or models such as **time only,**
chronograph, repeater etc. listed.

BENRUS, 17 jewels, curved, rhinestones , hooded lugs
14k $225 $300 $375

BENRUS, 15 jewels, curved back, c. 1942
gold filled..................................$60 $75 $90

BENSON, 15 jewels, of London, aux sec. c.1930s
9k $175 $200 $250

BENSON, 15J., of London, Ca.1938
9k $150 $175 $200

BENSON, 15 jewels, enamel dial, tank style case
9k $200 $250 $300

🕐 Some grades are not included. Their values can be
determined by comparing with similar age, size, metal
content, style, grades, or models such as time only,
chronograph, repeater etc. listed.

BENSON, 15 jewels, enamel dial, flared case
9k $200 $250 $300

BENSON, 15 jewels, enamel dial, 2-tone flared case
9k $275 $325 $375

BERG, 25J., auto-wind, c.1959
14k $125 $150 $175

BLANCPAIN, 23J, day-date-month, moon ph., auto-wind
18k $2,000 $2,500 $3,000
18K—perpetual $6,000 $7,000 $8,000

BLANCPAIN, 17J.,hooded lugs, c.1945
14k $200 $250 $300

BLANCPAIN, 16J., c.1925
silver $100 $125 $150

BOILLAT FRERES, 17 jewels, "Blita," waterproof
s. steel $35 $45 $60

E. BOREL, 17 jewels, chronometer, aux. sec.
18k $200 $300 $375
gold filled..................................$50 $60 $75

E. BOREL, 17J., cocktail style, c.1960s
gold filled..............................$100 $150 $200
s. steel $85 $100 $130

E. BOREL, 17J., cocktail dial, date, c. 1969
base metal $75 $95 $125

E. BOREL, 15J., hour dial, min. dial, center sec., c.1940
s. steel $250 $325 $375

E. BOREL, 17 jewels, auto wind, date
gold filled $70 $80 $110

BOUCHERON, 17J., c.1930s
18k $500 $600 $750

🕐 Some grades are not included. Their values can be determined by comparing with similar age, size, metal content, style, grades, or models such as time only, chronograph, repeater etc. listed.

🕐 Some grades are not included. Their values can be determined by comparing with similar age, size, metal content, style, grades, or models such as time only, chronograph, repeater etc. listed.

BOULEVARD, 17J., "STOP", c.1950s
s. steel $75 $100 $125

BREGUET, 17J., chronog., triple date, Ca.1950
s. steel $6,000 $7,000 $8,000

BOVET, 17 jewels, chronog., 2 reg., c. 1940
s. steel $150 $175 $225

BREGUET, auto-w., triple date, moon ph., **leap year**
18k $16,000 $18,000 $22,000

BOVET, 17 jewels, chronog., triple date & 3 reg.
14k $700 $800 $1,000
gold filled...............................$375 $450 $500

BREGUET, jump hour, c.1980s, **total made =50**
18k $9,000 $10,000 $12,000

BREGUET, 21 jewels, skeletonized
18k C&B..............................$8,000 $9,000 $10,000

BREGUET, 37J., auto-w., date, moon ph., 60 hr.wind ind.
18k $12,000 $13,000 $14,000

BREGUET, 17 jewels, silver dial, thin model
18k $1,200 $1,400 $1,600

BREGUET, 17 jewels, curvex
platinum...............................$3,000 $4,000 $5,000

P. BREGUETTE, 17J., gold jewel settings, Ca.1948
14k $150 $175 $225

P. BREGUETTE, 17J., gold jewel settings, flared case
14k $200 $225 $250

P. BREGUETTE, 17J., gold jewel settings, date, Ca.1948
gold filled...................................$60 $80 $100

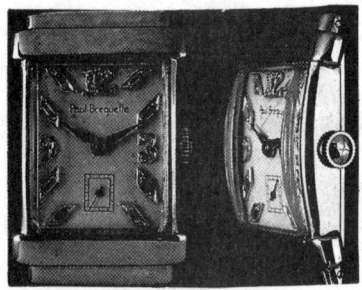

P. BREGUETTE, 17 jewels, diamond dial, c. 1940
14k $500 $600 $700

P. BREGUETTE, 17J., triple date, c.1960s
gold filled $125 $165 $200
s. steel $100 $125 $175

Breitling, 17 J., "Chronomat," slide rule bezel
18k $2,000 $2,250 $2,500
gold filled $900 $1,000 $1,200
s. steel $800 $900 $1,100

Breitling, 17 J., **Navitimer,** date, slide rule bezel, RF 7806
s. steel $1,300 $1,400 $1,650

BREITLING, 17J., **Chronomat.**, RF 808, c.1950
gold filled...............................$900 $1,000 $1,200

BREITLING, 18J., date, moon ph., split chronog. 3 reg.
18k $8,000 $9,000 $10,000

BREITLING, 17J., chronog., RF#1199, sq. button, c.1958
s. steel $400 $450 $525

BREITLING, 17 J, chronog., "Navitimer," RF 806
18K C&B...........................$5,000 $5,500 $6,000
18K case only $4,500 $5,000 $5,500
gold filled $1,100 $1,300 $1,500
s. steel $1,000 $1,200 $1,400

BREITLING, 17J., chronog., "Navitimer," **24 hour,** 3 reg.
18k $4,500 $5,000 $5,500
s. steel $1,000 $1,200 $1,400

BREITLING, 17 J., chronog., "Cosmonaute," 24 HR.
s. steel $1,200 $1,300 $1,550

🕐 Some grades are not included. Their values can be
determined by comparing with **similar** age, size, metal
content, style, grades, or models such as **time only**,
chronograph, repeater etc. listed.

BREITLING, 17 jewels, split sec. chronog., 2 reg.
s. steel $3,000 $4,000 $5,000

BREITLING, 17 J., chronog., "Chronomat," 3 reg.
s. steel $500 $550 $625

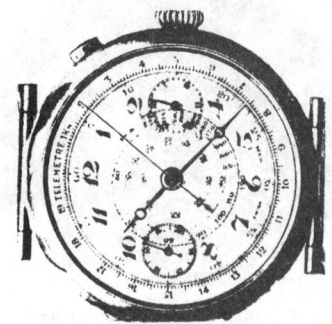

BREITLING, 17 J., telemeter, 1 button, hinged lugs
s. steel- 44mm.........................$850 $950 $1,100

BREITLING, 17 J., chronog., Navitimer, Ca. 1952
s. steel $1,000 $1,200 $1,400

BREITLING, 17 jewels, tachymeter, Ca.1925
s. steel $1,200 $1,300 $1,400

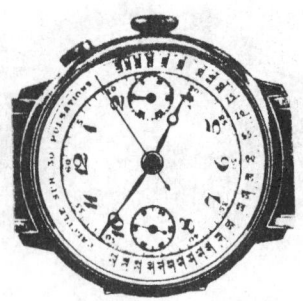

BREITLING, 17 jewels, chronog., pulsations
s. steel $600 $700 $800

BREITLING, 17 jewels, chronog., 2 reg.
s. steel $1,200 $1,300 $1,400

BREITLING, 17 jewels, tachymeter, center hinged lugs
s. steel - 35mm $800 $1,000 $1,200

BREITLING, 17J., chronog., RF#765, c.1960
14k $1,000 $1,200 $1,500
s. steel $400 $500 $600

BREITLING, 17 jewels, chronog., Toptime, 24 HR.
s. steel $425 $525 $650

BREITLING, 17 jewels, chronog., "Premier," 3 reg.
s. steel $500 $600 $700

BREITLING, 17 jewels, chronog., 2 reg. RF#790
18K **refinished dial**............$1,000 $1,200 $1,400
18K original dial.................$1,200 $1,400 $1,700

BREITLING, 17 J., chronog., day-date-month, 3 reg.
18k $2,000 $2,250 $2,500
s. steel $800 $900 $1,000

BREITLING, 17J., chronog., 2 reg., "Premier", RF#790
18k $1,300 $1,500 $1,800

BREITLING, 17 jewels, chronog., 2 reg. RF 178
s. steel $375 $450 $525

BREITLING, 17J., chronog., 3 reg., RF#787, c.1942
14k C&B..............................$1,200 $1,400 $1,600

BREITLING, 17 jewels, chronog., 2 reg.
18k $1,250 $1,400 $1,650
s. steel $275 $325 $400

BREITLING, 17 J., split sec. chronog., "Duograph"
18k $6,000 $7,000 $8,000
s. steel $3,000 $4,000 $5,000

BREITLING, 17J., **Super Ocean,** RF 2005, c.1960
s. steel $1,000 $1,250 $1,500

BREITLING, 17J., chronog., 3 reg., RF#815, c.1968
gold filled..............................$450 $500 $600

BREITLING, 17J., chronog., RF#2110, c.1970
s. steel $400 $450 $500

BREITLING, 17J., chronog., Toptime, RF#810, c.1968
s. steel $400 $475 $575

BREITLING, 17J., chronog., RF#2009-33, c. 1975
s. steel $325 $375 $400

BREITLING, 17J., **Tour de France,** c. 1945
18K..............................$1,200 $1,450 $1,650

BREITLING, 17J., **Co-Pilot,** enamel bezel, RF 765, c. 1960
s. steel $900 $1,000 $1,200

BREITLING, 17J., **Cosmonaute II**, 24 hr., Ca.1990
s.steel C&B...........................$1,100 $1,200 $1,400

BREITLING, 17J., **Old Navitimer II**, gold bezel, Ca.1990
s.steel & G-B $1,200 $1,350 $1,600

BREITLING, 17J., **Navitimer 92**, self-wind, Ca.1992
s.steel case $1,200 $1,300 $1,550
18K case $3,500 $4,000 $4,500

BREITLING, 17J., **Chronomat**, date, self-wind, Ca.1990
s.steel $1,200 $1,400 $1,600
18K & s.steel C&B..............$2,300 $2,400 $2,600

BREITLING, 17J., **Chronomat Yachting**, date, Ca.1990
s.steel C&B...........................$1,100 $1,200 $1,400

BREITLING, 17J., **Chrono Cockpit**, date, Ca.1990
18K & s.steel C&B..............$2,500 $2,700 $3,000

BREITLING, **UTC** (Universal Time Coordinated), Quartz
second time zone with a totally self contained quartz watch
s.steel gold bezel $300 $350 $400

BREITLING, 17J., **Corono QP**, day date moon ph., Ca.1990
18K C&B...........................$10,000 $11,000 $12,000

BREITLING, 17J., **Corono 1461**, day date moon ph., c.1990
s.steel C&B.........................$2,100 $2,300 $2,500

BREITLING, 17J., **Chrono Longitude**, date, Ca.1990
s.steel & gold C&B $1,500 $1,600 $1,800

BREITLING, 17J., **Navitimer Airborne**, date, Ca.1990
s.steel case $1,300 $1,500 $1,800

BREITLING, 17J., **Navitimer AVI**, date, Ca.1990
s.steel case $700 $800 $1,000

Nautical mile guide mark

Statute mile guide mark

Hour guide mark

Kilometer guide mark

Seconds totalizer

Chronograph start-and-stop pushpiece

Analogue calendar

Unit guide mark

Setting crown

Minute totalizer

Hour totalizer

Chronograph reset pushpiece

BEZEL

ROTATING BEZEL: bi-directional bezel, with type 52 aviation slide rule.

Complex functions

A mechanical chronograph incorporates an amazing amount and variety of horological knowhow and resourcefulness. Chronographs usually begin with a standard movement to which talented watchmakers add one or more often complex auxiliary mechanisms. Driven by the basic movement's own power, the chronograph mechanism will measure short times without affecting in the least the permanent indication of the time.

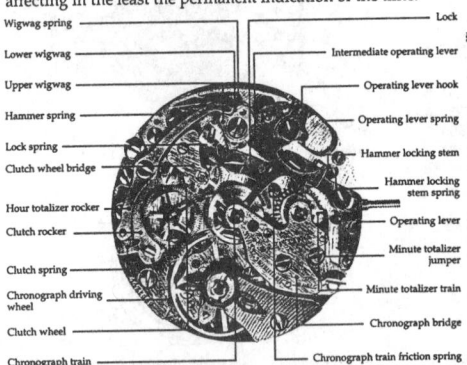

Wigwag spring

Lower wigwag

Upper wigwag

Hammer spring

Lock spring

Clutch wheel bridge

Hour totalizer rocker

Clutch rocker

Clutch spring

Chronograph driving wheel

Clutch wheel

Chronograph train

Lock

Intermediate operating lever

Operating lever hook

Operating lever spring

Hammer locking stem

Hammer locking stem spring

Operating lever

Minute totalizer jumper

Minute totalizer train

Chronograph bridge

Chronograph train friction spring

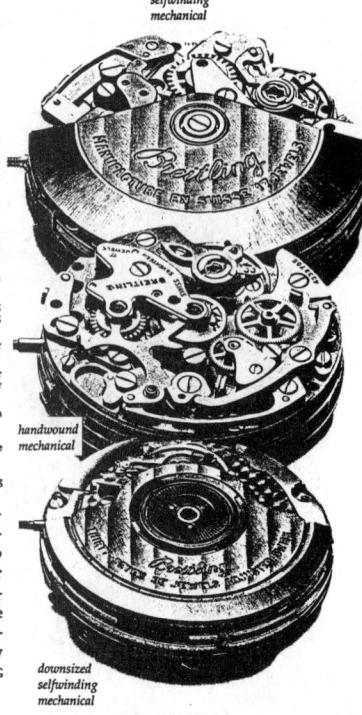

selfwinding mechanical

handwound mechanical

downsized selfwinding mechanical

NAVITIMER movements comprise up to 250 parts, some no larger than a human hair. Unaffected by marked temperature differences, its balance spring can withstand accelerations of up to 10 G's. Three movement generations reflect, each in their own way, BREITLING's ongoing mastery of mechanical chronograph design. First, the handwound version, which alone is able to run in weightless space, for the COSMONAUTE. Then the self-winding version developed in 1969 for the NAVITIMER. Now comes the compact model, made possible by the BREITLING caliber's modular construction.

BREITLING, 17J., chronog., RF#1450, 3 reg., c.1970
s. steel $400 $465 $525

BUCHERER,17 jewels, **note day date in lugs**
18k $900 $1,200 $1,400

BREITLING, 17J., day date month,
18k $400 $450 $500

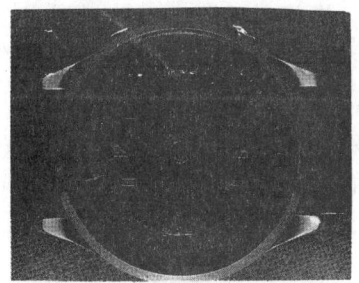

BUCHERER,17 jewels, chronog., 2 reg.
18k $475 $500 $550

BREITLING, 21J., "UNITIME", date, 24 hour, c.1958
gold filled................................$800 $1,000 $1,250
18k $1,650 $1,850 $2,250

BUCHERER, 17J., chronog., 2 reg., C.1959
18k $500 $600 $750
s. steel $275 $325 $375

BREITLING, 21J., auto-wind, rf#2528, c.1959
s. steel $150 $200 $250

BUCHERER, 25 J., triple date moon ph., cal.693, c.1950
18k $1,200 $1,350 $1,550

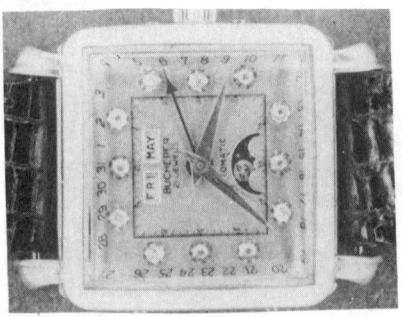

BUCHERER, 21J., 3 dates, moon ph., diamond dial
18k $2,400 $2,600 $2,800

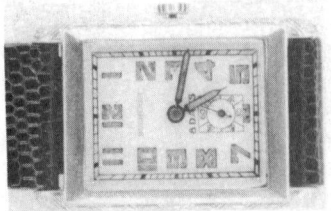

BUCHERER, 15 jewels, 8 day movement
18k $1,000 $1,200 $1,400
gold filled................................$500 $600 $700

BUECHE-GIROD, 17 J., day-date-month, moon ph.
s. steel $325 $375 $425

BUECHE-GIROD, 17J., by Piguet, cal.99, c.1975
18k $400 $500 $600

⊕ Some grades are not included. Their values can be
determined by comparing with similar age, size, metal
content, style, grades, or models such as time only,
chronograph, repeater etc. listed.

BUECHE-GIROD, 17J., dual time movements,
18k $500 $600 $700

BUECHE-GIROD, 17 jewels, tank style case
18k $500 $550 $600

BUECHE-GIROD, 17 jewels
18k C&B................................$600 $700 $800

P. BUHRE, 17 jewels, aux. sec.
gold filled $40 $50 $65

P. BUHRE, 17J., alarm, C.1956
s. steel $90 $120 $155

BULOVA, Accutron, "Spaceview Alpha" Ca. 1960
Accutron the first transistorized watch was sold Oct. 26, 1960.
14k $500 $600 $750

BULOVA, Accutron, "Spaceview B"
s.steel $150 $200 $250

BULOVA, Accutron, "Spaceview H"
gold filled................................$175 $225 $275

BULOVA, Accutron, "RF # 202"
gold filled................................$175 $225 $275

BULOVA, Accutron, "RF # 210" **gold bezel** & s.steel case
s.steel & **14k**..........................$250 $285 $375

BULOVA, Accutron, "RF # 213"
s.steel $150 $200 $250

BULOVA, Accutron, "RF # 214"
s.steel $150 $200 $250

BULOVA, Accutron, "RF # 216"
s.steel $150 $200 $250

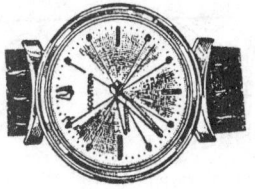

BULOVA, Accutron, "RF # 218" center lugs
s.steel $175 $225 $275

BULOVA, Accutron, "RF # 223"
s.steel $175 $225 $275
14k $425 $475 $575

BULOVA, Accutron, "RF # 412" gold filled bezel & s.steel
gold filled & s.steel case $175 $225 $275

BULOVA, Accutron, "RF # 400"
gold filled................................$175 $225 $275

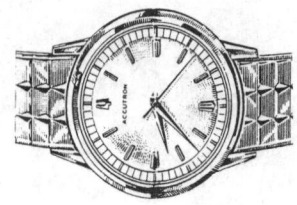

BULOVA, Accutron, "RF # 413" gold filled bezel & s.steel
gold filled & s.steel case $175 $225 $275

BULOVA, Accutron, "RF # 401"
s.steel $150 $200 $250

BULOVA, Accutron, "RF # 417"
gold filled $175 $225 $275

BULOVA, Accutron, "RF # 403"
gold filled................................$175 $225 $275

BULOVA, Accutron, "RF # 420"
gold filled $175 $225 $275

BULOVA, Accutron, "RF # 411"
gold filled................................$175 $225 $275

BULOVA, Accutron, "RF # 500" center lugs
14k $400 $450 $550

BULOVA, Accutron, "RF # 505" Ca. 1960
14k yellow or white................$425 $475 $585

BULOVA, Accutron, "RF # 513"
14k $400 $450 $550

BULOVA, Accutron, "RF # 514" Florentine engraved case
14k $425 $475 $585

BULOVA, Accutron, "RF # 560"
14k $400 $450 $550

BULOVA, Accutron, "RF # 602"
18k $500 $550 $650

🕐 NOTE: Some Bulova cases are stamped with a year date
code letter & number .L=1950s, M=1960s, N=1970s
example: L3=1953, M4=1964, N5=1975, etc.

Note: A small **predictable** position error can be taken into
consideration in the daily regulation of your Accutron. In the 12
- down **vertical** position the rate is about 5 seconds per day faster
conversely in the 6-down **vertical** position a rate of 5 seconds
per day slower. You can take advantage of this, if slow place it
in the 12-down vertical position at night and it will gain back
lost time, if fast use the 6-down vertical position to slow it down.

BULOVA, Accutron, "Mickey" day & date, **RARE**
14k C&B.............................$550 $650 $775

BULOVA, Accutron, date, "M 8" on back - Ca. 1968
14k $400 $425 $475

BULOVA, Accutron, "Spaceview"
s. steel $150 $200 $250

BULOVA, Accutron, **"converted dial"**, cal. 214, c.1963
gold filled $125 $150 $225
Note Below: Bulova Accutron regulator, to regulate use a
tooth pick and move regulator up or down.

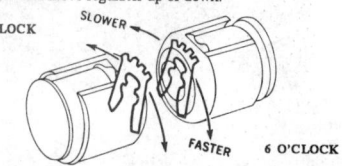

12 O'CLOCK   SLOWER

FASTER   6 O'CLOCK

🕐 NOTE: Some Bulova cases are stamped with a year date code letter & number .L=1950s, M=1960s, N=1970s example: L3=1953, M4=1964, N5=1975, etc.

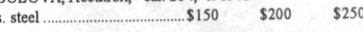

BULOVA, Accutron, cal. 214, c. 1963
s. steel $150 $200 $250

BULOVA, Accutron, "Spaceview," c. 1960
14k $400 $450 $600
gold filled $175 $225 $275
s. steel $150 $200 $250

BULOVA, Accutron, "Spaceview"
s. steel $150 $200 $250

BULOVA, Accutron, "Spaceview"
18k $600 $700 $800
14k $400 $500 $600
s. steel $150 $200 $250

BULOVA, Accutron, "Spaceview," c. 1965
gold filled $175 $225 $275

BULOVA, Accutron, "Spaceview," c. 1961
gold filled $175 $225 $275

BULOVA, Accutron, "Spaceview," c. 1967
gold filled $225 $275 $350
s. steel $175 $225 $275
14k $500 $600 $700

BULOVA, Accutron, **converted dial,** Alpha, waterproof
14k $250 $300 $375

Accutron, reached 1/2 million in sales by 1966, 3/4 by 1968, by 1970 1 million watches, and by 1976, 2 million watches.

BULOVA, Accutron, "Spaceview," center lugs
gold filled..............................$200 $225 $300

BULOVA, Accutron, "Spaceview," center lugs
s. steel $200 $235 $275

BULOVA, Accutron, center lugs
gold filled...............................$200 $225 $300

BULOVA, Accutron, "Spaceview," center lugs
14k C & B.............................$500 $600 $700

BULOVA, Accutron, **converted** dial, date, cal.218
14k 2 tone $200 $250 $300

BULOVA, Accutron, 2 tone, Ca. 1967
gold filled $200 $250 $300

BULOVA, Accutron, Skeletonized, date, cal.218, Ca.1967
14k $350 $400 $500

BULOVA, Accutron, oval, "Spaceview"
s. steel $150 $200 $250

⏱ Some grades are not included. Their values can be
determined by comparing with **similar** age, size, metal
content, style, grades, or models such as **time only**,
chronograph, repeater etc. listed.

BULOVA, Accutron, two tone, date
14k 2 tone $225 $250 $350

BULOVA, Accutron, "Spaceview,"
s. steel $150 $200 $250

BULOVA, Accutron, M# 218, RR approved, red 24 hr. dial
gold filled $175 $200 $235

BULOVA, Accutron, "Spaceview,"
s. steel $150 $200 $250

BULOVA, Accutron, **quartz**, RR approved, day date
gold plate $75 $85 $150

BULOVA, Accutron, "Spaceview," gold bezel
14k $400 $500 $650
gold bezel & s. steel case $200 $250 $300

BULOVA, Accutron, RR approved
s. steel $125 $145 $200

BULOVA, Accutron, M# 214, railroad approved, C. 1960s
gold filled................................$150 $185 $225
s. steel $125 $150 $200

⏱ NOTE: Some Bulova cases are stamped with a year date
code letter & number. L=1950s, M=1960s, N=1970s
example: L3=1953, M4=1964, N5=1975, etc.

BULOVA, Accutron," **Mark IV" / RR approved,** date
Crown at 2 sets the hour hand, Crown at 4 sets Time & Date
two hour hands for two time zones
s. steel $200 $250 $350

BULOVA, Accutron, cal. 214," Pulsation", c. 1966
gold filled..............................$125 $150 $195
14k $500 $550 $600

BULOVA, Accutron, masonic dial
NOTE: This dial can be printed for about $35.00.
14k $235 $265 $325

BULOVA, Accutron, cal. 214," Pulsation", c. 1966
14k $500 $550 $600

BULOVA, Accutron, asymmetric
14k $450 $500 $575

BULOVA, Accutron, cal. 214, diamond dial
14k $450 $550 $700
18K...$500 $600 $800

BULOVA, Accutron, asymmetric, 2- tone dial, Ca.1963
14k $500 $575 $650

BULOVA, Accutron, sweep sec. hand
gold filled.................................$75 $95 $100

BULOVA, Accutron, "ASTRONAUT A", 24 hour dial
18kC&B.............................$1,200 $1,400 $1,800
14k $800 $1,000 $1,200
gold filled $250 $300 $375
s. steel $175 $225 $300

BULOVA, Accutron, "ASTRONAUT B", rotating bezel
s. steel $195 $250 $295

BULOVA, Accutron, "ASTRONAUT C", 18k case & band,
retail price in June, 1964 was $1,000.00.
18k C & B $1,400 $1,600 $2,000

BULOVA, Accutron, "Astronaut Mark II", time zone, window
at six o'clock, date at 12, note: red dial, on back N2 = 1972
14k $400 $495 $600
s. steel $150 $175 $240

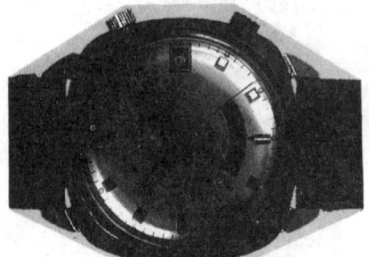

BULOVA, Accutron, "Astronaut Mark II", time zone, original sales price was $275.00 in S. Steel.
14k $400 $495 $600
gold filled.............................. $200 $275 $350
s. steel $195 $235 $275

BULOVA, Accutron, "Astronaut Mark II", auxiliary time
zone window at 6-o'clock & date at 12-o'clock.
14k $475 $525 $600

BULOVA, Accutron, "Astronaut Mark II", time zone with a
extra red hour hand, date at 3 o'clock, on back M9 = 1969
gold filled $200 $275 $350

BULOVA, Accutron
gold filled $100 $125 $150

BULOVA, Accutron, Ca. 1966
gold filled $75 $100 $135

BULOVA, Accutron, fancy lugs
gold filled.............................$100 $125 $150

BULOVA, Accutron, date, gold filled bezel
s. steel $65 $75 $95

BULOVA, Accutron
gold filled...............................$175 $200 $250

BULOVA, Accutron, date, Ca.1967
s. steel $85 $100 $135

BULOVA, Accutron, 4 diamond dial, Ca. 1967
gold filled...............................$150 $200 $250

BULOVA, Accutron, date
gold filled $125 $150 $200

BULOVA, Accutron, day date
14k $175 $225 $300

BULOVA, Accutron, **Spaceview Anniversary**, model 214
14k $400 $425 $475

BULOVA, (Accu- quartz), quartz & tuning fork, day date
gold filled...................................$75 $100 $125

BULOVA, Accutron, cushion spaceview, Ca. 1970
s. steel $150 $200 $250

BULOVA, Accutron, model 2183,
s. steel $60 $70 $80

BULOVA, Accutron, **wood bezel**, day date
gold filled $75 $100 $150

BULOVA, Accutron, date, Ca.1972
base metal $65 $75 $85

BULOVA, Accutron, red dial, date
gold filled $75 $100 $125

BULOVA, Accutron, gold filled bezel, day date
gold filled.................................$75 $85 $100

BULOVA, Accutron, numbered bezel, day date
14k $350 $400 $475

BULOVA, Accuquartz, diamond bezel, day date
14k $350 $400 $450

BULOVA, Accuquartz, note band with **accutron symbol**
18k C&B...............................$600 $700 $850

BULOVA, Accutron, day date
gold filled.................................$100 $125 $150

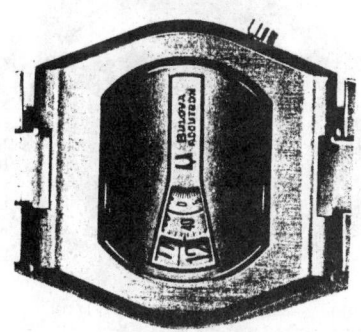

BULOVA, Accutron, day date, c. 1970
s. steel $50 $60 $70

BULOVA, Accutron, day date, Ca.1972
gold filled.................................$100 $125 $150

BULOVA, Accutron, model 2186, direct read
gold filled $75 $100 $150

BULOVA, Accutron, date
gold plate $65 $75 $90

BULOVA, Accutron, **Accutron 14k Gold Band**, Ca.1972
14k C & B.............................$500 $600 $700

BULOVA, Accutron, diamond on bezel
14k(w) C&B $400 $500 $600

BULOVA, Accutron, date
gold filled.................................$100 $125 $150

BULOVA, Accutron, divers 660 ft.depth, 24 hr.dial,
rotating outside chapter, day date, Ca. 1970
s. steel $175 $200 $275

BULOVA, Accutron, DEEP SEA, 666 feet, date
enamel rotating bezel
s. steel $250 $300 $350

BULOVA, Accutron, day of week at 12 & date at 6 0'clock
s. steel $165 $195 $225

BULOVA, Accutron, fancy bezel
14k C&B.................................$400 $450 $525

BULOVA, Accutron, lady accutron
14k $100 $110 $120

BULOVA, Accutron, note links in accutron band
gold plate $60 $75 $95

BULOVA, Accutron, date, Ca. 1968
gold filled $100 $125 $150

⏱ NOTE: Some Bulova cases are stamped with a year date code letter & number .L=1950s, M=1960s, N=1970s example: L3=1953, M4=1964, N5=1975, etc.

BULOVA, Accutron, wide oval bezel
gold filled.................................$40 $50 $60

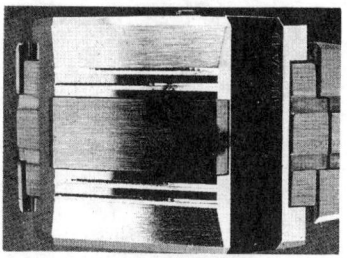

BULOVA, digital,
s. steel $95 $125 $165

BULOVA, Accutron, 32 small diamond bezel
14k(w)....................................$250 $275 $300

BULOVA, enamel bezel
s. steel $100 $125 $150

BULOVA, Accutron, cal. #221, textured bezel
sterling & 14k...........................$75 $100 $125

BULOVA, 15J., one button chronog.,1/5 sec.,C.1946
14k $500 $550 $600
gold filled $300 $335 $375

BULOVA, Accutron, pendant style watch
14k $100 $125 $150

BULOVA, 17J., one button chronog., cal.10BK, c.1947
gold filled $300 $325 $375

BULOVA, 17J., chronog., "660 feet" dive watch, c.1972
s. steel $100 $125 $150

BULOVA, 16 jewels, military style
s. steel $250 $300 $350

BULOVA, 17J., Alarm, cal.11aerc, c.1967
s. steel $100 $125 $150

BULOVA, self winding, c. 1960
14k $100 $125 $150
gold filled................................$50 $60 $75

BULOVA, 17J., fancy lugs
gold filled $75 $90 $125

BULOVA, 23 jewels, waterproof
14k $175 $200 $250

BULOVA, 23 jewels, date, 6 adj., c. 1951
gold filled $100 $125 $175

BULOVA, 17J., cal.11 af, ca.1959
gold filled $60 $70 $95
14K $175 $200 $250

BULOVA, fancy long lugs, c. 1942
gold filled...................................$65 $80 $100

BULOVA, 17J., fancy lugs, c.1958
14k $275 $325 $375

BULOVA, 21J., fancy lugs, c.1950
gold filled...................................$65 $80 $100

BULOVA, 17J., center sec., c.1942
gold filled...................................$45 $55 $65

BULOVA, 15J., military style, c.1940
s. steel $75 $85 $120

BULOVA, cal. 700, canteen style, c. 1946
s. steel $375 $475 $575

BULOVA, 15J., military style, cal.10 bnch, c.1940
s. steel $95 $125 $150

BULOVA, 17J., U.S.A. military, c.1945
s. steel $90 $110 $130

BULOVA, 17J., 20 diamond dial
14k(w).....................................$250 $300 $375

BULOVA, 23J., 12 diamond dial, c. 1959
14k(w)....................................$250 $300 $375

BULOVA, 30J., diam. dial, cal#10B2AC, C.1960s
14k(w)....................................$200 $250 $300

BULOVA, early auto wind movement by Champ

BULOVA, early auto wind, by Champ, c. 1930
gold filled................................$400 $500 $600

BULOVA, diamond dial, c. 1939
platinum...................................$900 $1,100 $1,250
14k (w)....................................$600 $700 $800

BULOVA, 21 jewels, hidden lugs, diamond dial, c. 1935
14k...$600 $700 $800

BULOVA, hidden lugs, diamond dial, c. 1945
14k...$500 $600 $700

BULOVA, 21 jewels, diamond dial, long lugs, c. 1941
14k (w) $250 $300 $375

BULOVA, 17J., 3 diamond dial, cal.8ae, c.1949
14k...$200 $250 $325

BULOVA, 17 jewels, curved, cal. 7AP, c. 1939
14k...$250 $300 $375

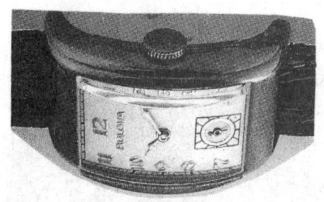

BULOVA, 17J., drivers watch, c.1935
gold filled.............................$300 $350 $400

BULOVA, 17J., engraved, Ca. 1928
gold filled.............................$80 $90 $110

BULOVA, 17J., 5th ave., cal.6am, engraved bezel, c.1935
gold filled.............................$90 $110 $150

BULOVA, 21J., stepped bezel, curved,
gold filled.............................$100 $125 $165

BULOVA, 21J., plain bezel, curved,
gold filled.............................$100 $125 $165

BULOVA, 17J., cal. 7ap, c.1937
gold filled.............................$100 $125 $165

BULOVA, 17J., curved, cal.7ap, c.1936
gold filled.............................$75 $100 $150

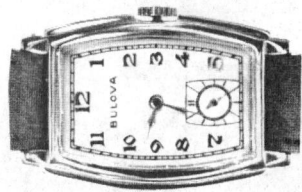

BULOVA, 17J., cal.13al,c.1935
14k.............................$165 $185 $225

BULOVA, 17J., cal.9af, c.1929
s. steel.............................$65 $75 $100

BULOVA, 17J., cal.7ap, c.1934
gold filled.............................$100 $125 $175

BULOVA, 15J., cal.10ae, c.1938
gold filled.............................$65 $75 $90

BULOVA, 17 jewels, curved, c. 1939
gold filled.............................$75 $100 $125

BULOVA, 21 jewels, curved, c. 1939
gold filled..................................$75 $100 $125

BULOVA, 21J., cal# 6AE,
14k $175 $225 $300

BULOVA, 17 jewels, duo dial, c. 1935
gold filled..............................$475 $550 $625
s. steel $375 $425 $475

BULOVA, 17 jewels, 2 tone duo dial
s. steel $400 $450 $500

BULOVA, 17 jewels, 2 tone dial, **flexable lugs**, fancy bezel
s. steel $75 $85 $100

🕐 Some grades are not included. Their values can be determined by comparing with **similar** age, size, metal content,
style, models and grades listed.

BULOVA, 21 J., **President, wandering sec.**, c. 1932
gold filled $150 $200 $250

BULOVA, 17 jewels, cal. 10GM, fancy lugs, c. 1953
gold filled $80 $90 $100
14k $250 $300 $350

BULOVA, 15J., fancy lugs, c.1952
gold filled $80 $90 $100

BULOVA, 21J., fancy lugs, c.1952
14k $225 $250 $325
gold filled $80 $90 $100

BULOVA, 17J., fancy lugs, cal.8an, c.1951
14k $375 $425 $475
gold filled $150 $175 $225

BULOVA, 17J., cal.8ad, fancy lugs, c.1939
gold plate $80 $90 $100

BULOVA, 17J., fancy lugs, c.1950 code on case=(LO)
gold filled $50 $60 $70

BULOVA, 21J., cal. 7ak, c.1945
gold filled.................................. $60 $70 $80

BULOVA, 17J., gold jewel settings, Ca.1923
gold filled $100 $125 $150

BULOVA, 21J., c.1950s
gold filled.................................. $80 $100 $130

BULOVA, 21J., **carved case**, c.1948
14k $165 $185 $235

BULOVA, 21J., scalloped case, c.1950s
gold filled $100 $125 $150

BULOVA, 21J., cal.7ak, c.1945
gold filled $60 $70 $80

BULOVA, 7J., c.1945
gold filled.................................. $45 $55 $75

BULOVA, 17J., cal.8ae, fancy hidden lugs, c.1941
gold filled $75 $100 $125

BULOVA, 21J., hooded lugs, c.1945
14k $175 $200 $250

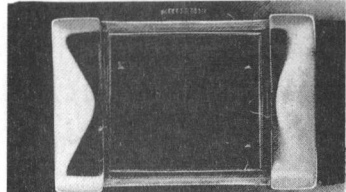

BULOVA, 21 jewels, hooded lugs, cal. 8AC, c. 1952
14k $300 $350 $400

BULOVA, 17 jewels, fancy long lugs, c. 1942
14k $200 $250 $300

BULOVA, 15 jewels, 2 tone engraved bezel, flexable lugs,
Ca. 1925
gold filled...............................$100 $125 $150

BULOVA, 17J., cal. 8AC, flip top, photo watch, c. 1940
gold filled...............................$225 $300 $375
14k $350 $400 $525

🕐 Some grades are not included. Their values can be determined by comparing with similar age, size, metal content,
style, models and grades listed.

BULOVA, 15 jewels, wandering hr. min. sec., c. 1928
s. steel $200 $235 $275

BULOVA, 17J., right angle, cal. 8AZ, c. 1938
gold filled $125 $150 $175
14k $300 $350 $400

BULOVA, 17 jewels, aux. sec.
14k $175 $200 $250

BULOVA, 17 jewels, fancy bezel
gold filled $100 $120 $140

BULOVA, 17 jewels, bell shaped lugs
14k $225 $275 $300

BULOVA, 17 jewels, fancy lugs
14k $200 $250 $300

BULOVA, 21J., hidden lugs, c.1950s
14k $250 $300 $350

BULOVA, 17J., center sec., cal.10bac, c.1935
gold filled...................................$75 $100 $125

BULOVA, 21J., hidden lugs, c.1945
gold filled $75 $85 $125

BULOVA, 17J., cal.8ac, fancy lugs, c.1940
gold plate $60 $70 $85

BULOVA, 17J., BMW- logo, c.1957
gold filled $90 $110 $135

BULOVA, 17J., flared top of case & sides,
gold filled...................................$70 $80 $90

BULOVA, 17J., FORD logo, c.1947
base metal $70 $80 $90

BULOVA, 21J., hidden lugs, c.1961
gold filled...................................$65 $80 $125

BULOVA, 17J., engraved lugs & bezel, cal.10an, c.1928
s. steel $50 $60 $75

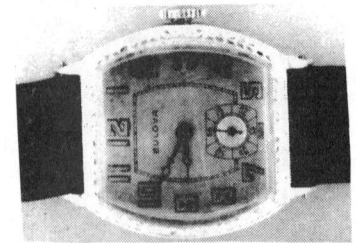

BULOVA, 17J., engraved bezel only
base metal $45 $50 $60

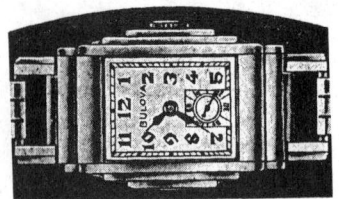

BULOVA, 15 jewels, **Senator,**
gold filled $55 $65 $75

BULOVA, 15J., cal.11ac, c.1958
gold filled...................................$90 $110 $135

BULOVA, 17 jewels, **Oakley,**
gold filled $75 $85 $95

BULOVA, 15J., cal.10ae, c.1935
gold filled...................................$50 $60 $70

BULOVA, 17 jewels, **LONE EAGLE,** stepped style case
gold filled $125 $150 $175

BULOVA, 7J., cal.10bc, c.1949
gold filled...................................$45 $55 $70

BULOVA, 15 jewels, **LONE EAGLE,** tonneau style case
gold filled $125 $150 $175

BULOVA, 15J., cal.10an, c.1929
base metal $40 $50 $60

BULOVA, 17J., **LONE EAGLE,** radium & cut corner dial
gold filled $125 $150 $175

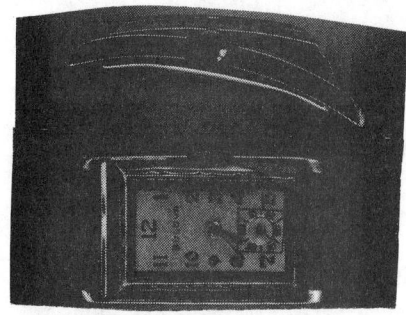

BULOVA, 17J., right angle case
gold filled..............................$175 $225 $275

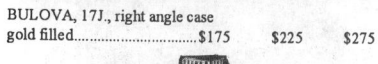

BULOVA, 17 jewels, "The Ambassador"
gold filled..................................$40 $50 $60

BULOVA, 17 jewels, "The Curtis," tank style
gold filled..............................$100 $125 $150

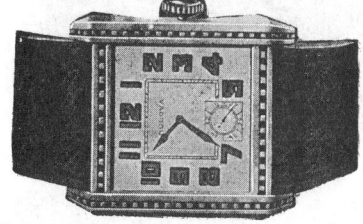

BULOVA, 15 jewels, "The Athelete"
gold filled..............................$100 $115 $125

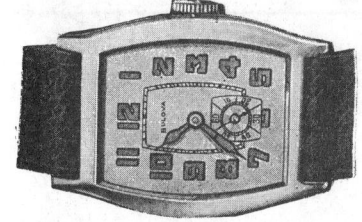

BULOVA, 17 jewels, "The Governor,"
14K..$200 $225 $275

BUREN, 17 jewels, day-date-month, moon phase
s. steel....................................$225 $275 $325

BUREN, 17 jewels, long lugs
14k..$150 $170 $200

BUREN, 17 jewels, center lugs, c.1940
9k..$250 $275 $325

BUTEX, 17J., triple date, moon ph.
gold filled..............................$250 $300 $375

CARLTON, 15 jewels, stepped case, c. 1939
gold filled..............................$100 $125 $175
14k..$275 $325 $375

CARTIER, 18 J., 8 day Mvt., tank style, by E. W. Co.
18k $30,000 $35,000 $40,000

CARTIER, 18 J., sapphire crown & bezel, c. 1970
18k $2,500 $3,000 $3,500

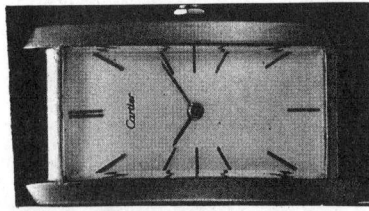

CARTIER, 18 jewels, curved, tank style
18k $7,000 $8,000 $9,000

CARTIER, 18 jewels, curved, signed E. W. Co., c.1930s
18k $6,000 $7,000 $8,000

CARTIER, 18 J., tank style, platinum case & band
platinum C&B....................$10,000 $12,000 $14,000

CARTIER, 18 jewels, tank style case, c. 1970s
18k $1,200 $1,400 $1,600

CARTIER, 20 jewels, tank style case, c. 1950
18k $1,800 $2,000 $2,200

CARTIER, Must de, **quartz**, tank style case, c.1980s
Vermeil =(gold over sterling)
G.P. vermeil............................$200 $250 $300
SAME STYLE CASE AS ABOVE
CARTIER, Must de, **Mechanical**, tank style case, c.1980s
Vermeil =(gold over sterling)
G.P. vermeil............................$200 $250 $300

CARTIER, 18 jewels, tank style, European W. Co.
platinum...............................$4,000 $5,000 $6,000

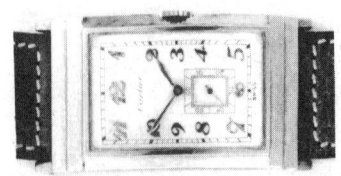

CARTIER, 18 jewels, by Movado
14k $1,000 $1,200 $1,400

CARTIER, 18 jewels, duo plan, European W. Co.
18k C&B...........................$2,500　$3,000　$3,500

CARTIER, 18J., by Le Coultre, long lugs
18k ....$1,200　$1,400　$1,600

CARTIER, 18 jewels, curved, hidden lugs
18k ....$3,500　$4,000　$4,500

CARTIER, 18 jewels, by Universal, c. 1960
18k ....$800　$1,000　$1,200

CARTIER, 18 jewels, center lugs, c. 1930
18k ....$2,800　$3,200　$3,600

CARTIER, 18 J., Prince, by Le Coultre, C.1930
18k ....$30,000　$40,000　$50,000

CARTIER, 18 J., reversible to view 2nd dial & 2nd
time zone
18k ....$25,000　$30,000　$35,000

CARTIER, 18 jewels, by European W. Co. c. 1927
18k ....$2,000　$2,500　$3,000

CARTIER, 18 J., early E.W.Co., C. 1928
18k ....$4,000　$5,000　$6,000

CARTIER, 18 J., lady's watch by European W. Co.
18kC&B...............................$2,000　$2,500　$3,000

CARTIER, 18 J., sovonnette H.C.style, C. 1928
18k ....$10,000　$11,000　$12,000

CARTIER, 18 J., tank for Chinese mkt., E.W.Co., Ca. 1925
18k ....$3,500　$4,000　$4,500

CARTIER, 18 J., guichet tank, jump hr. & min. by E.W.Co.
18k $30,000 $35,000 $40,000

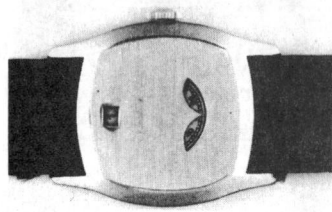

CARTIER, 18 J., jump hr. & min., E. W. Co. c. 1930
platinum.............................$35,000 $40,000 $45,000

CARTIER, 18 J.,"Santos", cal.21
mens18k.............................$1,800 $2,000 $2,200
ladies 18k.............................$1,600 $1,800 $2,000

CARTIER, 18 J., "Santos," 18k & s. steel case, band
platinum & 18k C&B $12,000 $14,000 $16,000
18k & s. steel C&B.................$800 $1,000 $1,200

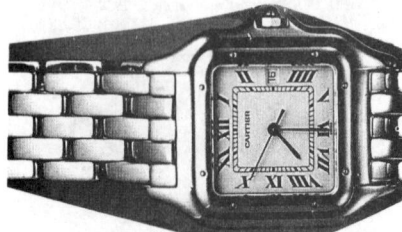

CARTIER, Panthere, large, date, water resistant
18k C & B............................$4,000 $5,000 $6,500

CARTIER, 18 jewels, "Santos," date
18k & s. steel C&B $800 $1,000 $1,200

CARTIER, 18 jewels, "Santos," octagonal, date
18k & s. steel C&B $600 $800 $1,000

CARTIER, 18 jewels, "Santos," lady's, date
18k & s. steel C&B $500 $600 $700

CARTIER, 25 jewels, chronog., European W. Co.
18k $60,000 $70,000 $80,000

CARTIER, 29 jewels, min. repeater, c. 1925
18k $100,000 $125,000 $150,000

CARTIER, 18 jewels, c. 1925
18k $3,500 $4,000 $4,500

CARTIER, 18 jewels, asymmetric, E. W. Co., c. 1928
18k $8,000 $9,000 $10,000

CARTIER, 18 J., oval maxi, C. 1968
18k $10,000 $12,000 $14,000

CARTIER, 18 jewels, by Le Coultre
18k $2,000 $2,500 $3,000

CARTIER, 18 J., bamboo style bezel, C.1970s
18k $4,000 $4,500 $5,000

CARTIER, 18 J., large cut corner bezel, C.1970s
18k $3,000 $3,500 $4,000

CARTIER, 18 J., "Helm", single lug, C. 1950s
18k $20,000 $25,000 $30,000
platinum $60,000 $70,000 $80,000

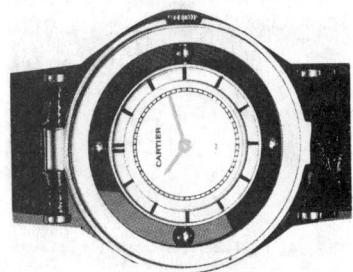

CARTIER, 18 J., by E.W.CO., single lug, C. 1949
18k $15,000 $18,000 $22,000

CARTIER, 29 J., min. repeater, by Le Coultre, c. 1930
platinum $80,000 $90,000 $100,000

CARTIER, 18 J., **triple date, moon ph.**, tear-drop lugs, marked European Watch & clock Co., Ca.1945
s. steel $6,000 $6,500 $7,500
18K..$8,000 $9,000 $10,000

CARTIER, 18 J., **triple date**, tear-drop lugs, marked European Watch & clock Co., Ca.1945
s. steel $1,500 $2,000 $2,500
18K..$3,500 $4,000 $4,500

CARTIER, 18J, day of week & date chapter, by Le Coultre
14k $1,000 $1,200 $1,400

CARTIER,Quartz, 296 diamonds on bezel & 18k Band
18k $12,000 $13,000 $14,000

CARTIER, 18 J., lady's, back wind, E.W.CO., c.1940s
18k $2,000 $2,500 $3,000

CARTIER, 18J., tonneau, Ca. 1920
platinum...............................$4,000 $5,000 $6,000

CARTIER, 18 J., lady's, E.W.Co., C.1949
14k(w) C&B $400 $500 $600

CERTINA, 17J., "NEWART", auto-wind, date, c.1965
14k $150 $175 $200

CENTRAL, 7J., cal.39, c.1937
gold filled $60 $70 $80

CHEVROLET, 6J., in form of car radiator, C. 1927
silver $400 $500 $650

CHOPARD, 18 J., 2 dial , 2 time zones, diam.bezel
18k C&B.............................$2,000 $2,500 $3,000

CHOPARD, 18 J., skeletonized, diamond dial &hands
18k $3,500 $4,000 $4,500

CHOPARD, 28J., triple date moon ph., cal.900, c.1980
18k $800 $900 $1,000

CHOPARD, 20 J., RF#2113, c.1978
18k $300 $400 $500

CHOPARD, 17J., RF#2134, c.1978
18k ....,....................$300 $400 $500

CLEBAR, 17 jewels, chronog., 2 reg., cal.2248, c.1952
gold filled $250 $275 $325
base metal $200 $250 $300

CLEBAR, 17 jewels, chronog., 3 reg. c.1950s
gold filled $275 $325 $375
s. steel $250 $300 $350

CLEBAR, 17J., chronog.,triple date, moon ph.
gold filled $550 $650 $800
s. steel $500 $600 $750

CLEBAR, 17 jewels, center lugs, chronog., c. 1938
s. steel $350 $400 $475

CONCORD, 17J., aux. sec., ca. 1947
14k $200 $250 $300

CONCORD, 17 jewels, center sec.
14k $200 $250 $325

CONCORD, 17 jewels, chronog. 2 reg., c.1940s
s. steel $250 $300 $350

CONDAL,15J. hunter style, flip top, C.1928
silver $400 $500 $600

CONTINENTAL, 17J., 3 diamond dial
14k $150 $175 $200

CORNAVIN, 17J., day date, c. 1960
gold filled $100 $125 $150

CORNAVIN, 17J., date, auto, RF#1243, C.1963
gold filled $60 $75 $110
s. steel $50 $65 $100

CORONET, 17J., chronog.
s. steel $175 $200 $250

CORTEBERT, 15 jewels, c. 1940s
gold filled $40 $50 $60

CORTEBERT, 15 jewels, c. 1941
gold filled $50 $60 $75

CORTEBERT, 17 J., "Sport," triple date, moon phase
18k $600 $700 $800
gold filled..........................$200 $250 $350

CORTEBERT, 17 jewels, center sec.
s. steel $35 $45 $65

CORTEBERT, **quartz**, U.K. military, (CWC)
s. steel $75 $100 $125

CORTEBERT, (CWC), chronog., by Valjoux, c.1971
s. steel $300 $350 $400

CORUM, 17 J., twenty dollar gold piece
18k & 22k $3,000 $3,500 $4,000

CORUM, 24k gold ingot, GR.15
24k $1,200 $1,400 $1,600

CORUM, 17 J., in form of Rolls-Royce car radiator
18k $3,000 $3,250 $3,500

CORUM, 17 jewels, peacock feather dial
18k $800 $900 $1,000

CORUM, 17 jewels, rope style bezel
18k C&B.............................$1,000 $1,200 $1,500

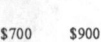

CORUM, 17 jewels, in form of book
18k $600 $700 $900

CRAWFORD, 17J., hooded lugs, c. 1940
14k $150 $175 $225

CORUM, 21 jewels, "pave" diamond dial, c.1990
18k C&B $2,200 $2,500 $3,000

CRAWFORD, 17J., pendant watch
base metal $65 $75 $100

CORUM, 21 jewels, gold dial
18k $400 $500 $600

CROTON, 17 jewels, day date
gold filled $45 $55 $65

CRAWFORD, 17J., triple date, c. 1942
s. steel $80 $110 $150

CROTON, 17 jewels, diamond bezel & dial
14k (w) $300 $375 $500

CRAWFORD, 17J., chronog.engraved bezel
base metal $125 $150 $175

CROTON, 17 jewels, chronog., c. 1948
s. steel $175 $200 $250

CROTON, 17 jewels, chronog., c. 1946
s. steel $185 $225 $275

CROTON, 17 jewels, cal.630, c.1943
gold filled..................................$40 $50 $65

CROTON, 17 jewels, fancy lugs
14k $175 $225 $275

CROTON, 17 jewels, fancy lugs
14k $250 $300 $375

CROTON, 7 jewels, drivers style, c.1938
gold filled..................................$175 $225 $275

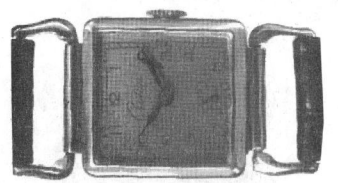

CROTON, 17 jewels, swinging lugs, cal.f3x, c.1940
14k $125 $150 $175

CROWN, 7J., luminous dial
base metal..................................$35 $45 $65

CROWN, 7J., luminous dial
gold filled $50 $75 $100

CRYSLER, 17J., aux. sec., ca. 1950s
gold filled $50 $70 $90

CYMA,7J.,enamel dial, wire lugs,(signal corp.USA),c.1928
silver $250 $300 $350

CYMA, 17 jewels, aux. sec.
18k	$200	$250	$300
14k	$175	$200	$250
gold filled	$65	$75	$85

CYMA, 15J., enamel dial, (Tacy W. Co.), c. 1925
silver $65 $75 $100

CYMA, 15J., military style, cal.234, Ca.1945
s. steel $100 $125 $150

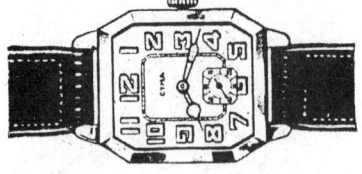

CYMA, 15J.,
base metal $40 $50 $60

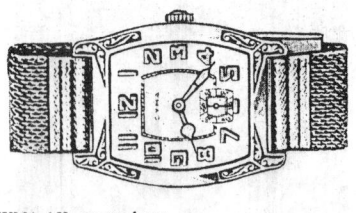

CYMA, 15J., engraved case
chromium................................ $50 $60 $70

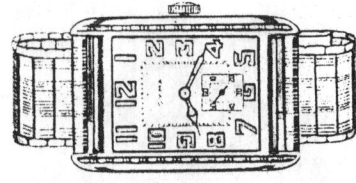

CYMA, 15J., engraved case
chromium................................ $50 $60 $70

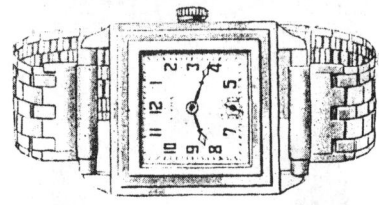

CYMA, 15J., 2-tone case
chromium................................ $60 $70 $80

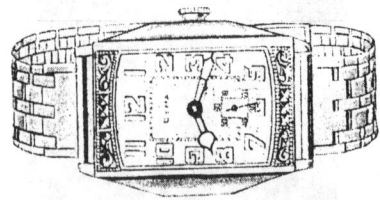

CYMA, 15J., engraved case
chromium................................ $60 $70 $80

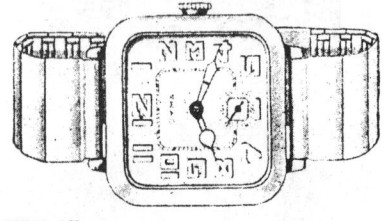

CYMA, 15J.,
chromium................................ $50 $60 $70

🕐 Some grades are not included. Their values can be determined by comparing with **similar** age, size, metal content, style, models and grades listed.

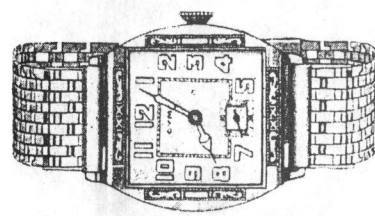

CYMA, 15J., engraved case
chromium.................................$60 $70 $80

DAU, 15J., wire lugs, c.1915
14k $80 $90 $100

DAYNITE, 7J., **8 day movement by Hebdomas**, Ca. 1920
s. steel $250 $300 $400

DELBANA, 17J., fancy hooded lugs, c.1951
14k $150 $175 $225

DIDISHEIM, 15J., "Winton", enamel art deco bezel, c.1927
14k(w)...................................$250 $300 $350

P. DITISHEIM, 17 J., "Solvil," diamond dial, c. 1947
18k $300 $350 $400

P. DITISHEIM, 17 J., "Solvil," diamond dial, c. 1947
platinum...................................$600 $700 $800

P. DITISHEIM, 17 J., "Solvil," diamond dial, c. 1948
platinum...................................$600 $700 $800

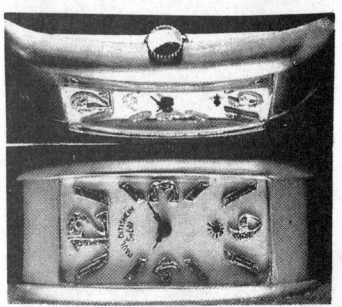

P. DITISHEIM, 17 J., "Solvil," curved, diamond dial
platinum...............................$1,000 $1,200 $1,400

P. DITISHEIM, 17 jewels, diamond dial, curved
platinum...............................$1,000 $1,200 $1,400

P. DITISHEIM, 17 J., baguette diamonds, fancy bezel
platinum................................$1,400 $1,600 $1,800

P. DITISHEIM, 17 jewels, hinged lugs, enameled bezel
14k $700 $800 $900

DOME, 25 jewels, triple dates, moon ph., auto wind
18k $450 $550 $650

DORIC, 17J., fancy lugs, two tone case, c.1935
gold filled...................................$60 $70 $85

DOXA, 17 jewels, aux sec.
gold filled...................................$40 $50 $60

DOXA, 17 jewels, center sec., fancy lugs
14k $150 $200 $250

DOXA, 17 jewels, chronog., fluted lugs
14k $350 $400 $475

DOXA, 17J., chronog., date, 3 reg., by Valjoux
gold filled $325 $375 $450
14k $600 $700 $800

DOXA, 17 jewels, chronog., triple dates, moon phase
14k $1,100 $1,200 $1,500

DOXA, 17 jewels, chronog., 2 reg., c. 1942
gold filled..................................$300 $400 $500

DOXA, 17 jewels, chronog., cal. 1220, c. 1940
gold filled..................................$225 $275 $325
s. steel $175 $225 $275

DOXA, 17 jewels, center sec
s. steel $55 $65 $85

DOXA, 17 jewels, center sec., c. 1949
gold filled..................................$70 $85 $125

DOXA, 17J., "Grafic" date,
14k $200 $250 $300

DOXA, 17J., cal. 1361, c.1948
14k $200 $250 $300

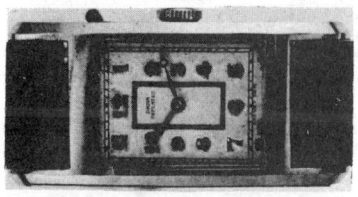

DRIVA, 15 jewels, repeater, repeats on gong, repeater
wound by bolt above hand, c. 1930
s. steel $3,500 $4,000 $4,500

DRIVA, 15 jewels, 5 min. repeater
14k $3,000 $3,500 $4,000

DRIVA, 17 jewels, double teardrop lugs, c.1945
14k $300 $350 $400

DUGENA, 17J., cal.985, c.1960
14k $150 $200 $250

DUNHILL, 17J., date, alarm by Le Coultre, c. 1965
s. steel $400 $450 $500

DUNHILL, 15J., by Bulwark W.Co., engraved bezel,c.1930
gold filled..................................$75 $125 $185

DUODIAL, 15 jewels, c. 1934
9k $900 $1,000 $1,200

EBEL, 21 jewels, chronog., self winding, perpetual cal.
18k $8,000 $9,000 $10,000

EBEL, 18 jewels, Ca.1959
18k $200 $250 $300

EBEL, 18 jewels, applied gold numbers, c. 1950
18k $400 $450 $500

EBEL, 17 jewels, slide open to wind
leather $200 $250 $300

EBEL, 17 jewels, chronog., 2 reg., enamel dial
s. steel $200 $250 $300

🕐 Some grades are not included. Their values can be
determined by comparing with similar age, size, metal
content, style, grades, or models such as time only,
chronograph, repeater etc. listed.

EBEL, 17 jewels, chronog., c. 1955
14k $400 $500 $550
gold filled.................................$200 $250 $325

EBEL, 17 jewels, chronog., "pulsation", c. 1943
s. steel $300 $350 $400

EBEL, 17 jewels, chronog., 3 reg., c. 1941
14k $500 $575 $650
s. steel $300 $350 $400

EBEL, 17J., "sport", c.1949
gold filled................................$100 $125 $150

EBEL, 17J., cal.119, auto-wind, c.1950
s. steel $125 $150 $175

EBEL, 17J., cal.93, center sec., c.1950
18k $300 $350 $400

EBEL, 17J., lady's watch, c.1948
14k C&B.................................$200 $225 $250

EBERHARD, 18 jewels, split sec. chronog., 3 reg.
18k $5,500 $6,500 $7,500

🕐 Some grades are not included. Their values can be determined by comparing with **similar** age, size, metal content, style, grades, or models such as **time only**, chronograph, repeater etc. listed.

EBERHARD, 17 J., tele-tachymeter, enamel dial, c. 1930
18k $1,500 $1,700 $2,000

EBERHARD, 17J., water proof, auto wind, triple date, moon phases
18k rose $3,000 $3,200 $3,500

EBERHARD, 17 jewels, chronog., 2 reg.
18k $800 $900 $1,000

EKEGREN, 18 jewels, **jumping hr.**, c. 1920
platinum.................................$8,000 $9,000 $10,000
18k $6,000 $7,000 $8,000

EBERHARD, 17 J., chronog., center lugs, 1 button, enamel dial
s. steel $550 $650 $800

ELECTRA W. Co., 17J, chronog., 1 button, hinged back, enamel dial
silver $600 $700 $850

EBERHARD, 17 J., wire lugs, enamel dial, c.1928
early waterproof case
silver $700 $800 $900

ELECTRA W. Co., 17J, chronog., 1 button, hinged back, wire lugs, enamel dial
silver $600 $700 $850

ELECTION, 17J., cal. 4019, c.1940
s. steel $60 $70 $80

ELGIN, 21J., Lord Elgin, extended lugs, Ca.1955
14k $200 $225 $275

ELGIN, 21J., Lord Elgin, extended lugs,
gold filled...................................$125 $150 $175

ELGIN, 21J., hooded bezel, Lord Elgin, Ca. 1953
14K..$225 $250 $300

ELGIN, 19J., fancy bezel, c.1950s
gold filled...................................$150 $200 $250

⊕ Some grades are not included. Their values can be
determined by comparing with similar age, size, metal
content, style, grades, or models such as time only,
chronograph, repeater etc. listed.

ELGIN, 17J., 7 diamonds & 8 baguettes, Ca. 1950
14K $500 $600 $700

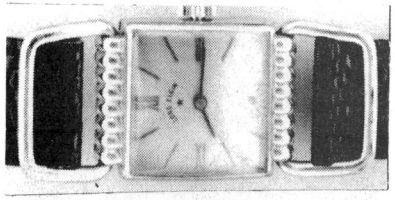

ELGIN, 21J., Lord Elgin, hinged lugs
gold filled...............................$100 $125 $150

ELGIN, 15-17J., hooded lugs, gold jewel settings, Ca. 1925
gold filled $175 $200 $250
14k(w)....................................$700 $800 $1,000

ELGIN, 21J., Lord Elgin, Ca. 1948
14K $165 $175 $225

ELGIN, 21J., Lord Elgin, 3 diamonds, cal.626, c.1950
14k(w)......................................$175 $200 $250

ELGIN, 21J., cal.626, Ca.1950's
14k $175 $225 $285

ELGIN, 17J., stepped case, Ca. 1935
gold filled...................................$75 $100 $120

ELGIN, 15J., cal. 554, Ca. 1950's
gold filled...................................$65 $100 $115

ELGIN, 15J., spur lugs, embossed dial, Ca.1929
gold filled...................................$60 $75 $100

ELGIN, 15J., Crown Guard, Ca.1929
gold filled...................................$50 $65 $85

ELGIN, 17J., stepped hooded lugs, c.1925
gold filled $100 $125 $175

ELGIN, 17J., side lugs, Ca. 1958
gold filled $150 $175 $200

ELGIN, 15J., stepped case,
gold filled $40 $50 $60

ELGIN, 15J., hinged case, engraved bezel, c.1928
gold filled(w)........................... $60 $70 $80

ELGIN, 17J., **Dollar markers**, Ca. 1955
gold filled $75 $95 $125

ELGIN, 19J., cal. 626, Ca. 1946
14k $200 $225 $250

ELGIN, 7J., tear drop lugs,
gold filled.............................. $50 $60 $90

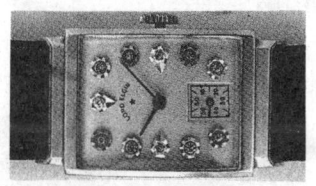

ELGIN, 21J., Lord Elgin, **11 diamonds,** Ca. 1946
14K.. $300 $350 $400

ELGIN, 21J., Lord Elgin,
gold filled.............................. $60 $70 $100

ELGIN, 15J., Legionnaire, Ca. 1929
gold filled.............................. $60 $70 $100

ELGIN, engraved case, Ca. 1924
14k $200 $225 $250

ELGIN, 21J., Lord Elgin, cal.625, c.1950
14k $175 $225 $275

ELGIN, 21J., Lord Elgin, cal. 713, GJS, c.1958
14k $225 $250 $300

ELGIN, 17J., carved case,
gold filled $50 $60 $70

ELGIN, 21J., Lord Elgin, cal.559, c.1942
gold filled $60 $70 $95

🕐 Some grades are not included. Their values can be
determined by comparing with similar age, size, metal
content, style, grades, or models such as time only,
chronograph, repeater etc. listed.

ELGIN, 21J., Lord Elgin, GJS, c. 1936
14k $175 $200 $250

ELGIN, 21J., Lord Elgin, GJS, cal.626, c.1940
14k $175 $200 $250

ELGIN, 17J., **Adonis**, engraved, Ca. 1929
gold filled...................................$75 $85 $110

ELGIN, 17J., "Dura Power" mainspring LOGO,
gold plate $70 $80 $90

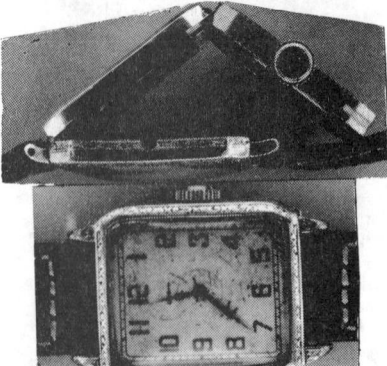

ELGIN, 7J., hinged case, engraved case, c.1920s
gold filled...................................$75 $95 $125

ELGIN,15J., fancy bezel, G#554
gold filled $60 $70 $85

ELGIN, 17 jewels, raised numbers
14k $150 $175 $225

LORD ELGIN, 21 jewels, curved, raised numbers
14k $175 $200 $250

ELGIN, 17 jewels, embossed dial
14k $175 $225 $250

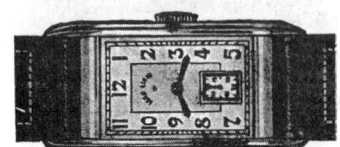

LORD ELGIN, 21 jewels, curved
gold filled $75 $100 $125

ELGIN, 17 jewels, curved, "Streamlined"
gold filled $100 $120 $140

🕒 Some grades are not included. Their values can be
determined by comparing with **similar** age, size, metal
content, style, grades, or models such as **time only**,
chronograph, repeater etc. listed.

ELGIN, 17 jewels, raised numbers
gold filled..............................$65 $75 $85

ELGIN, 15 jewels, curved, fancy bezel
gold filled..............................$100 $120 $140

LORD ELGIN, 21 jewels, curved
platinum...................................$400 $500 $600

LORD ELGIN, 21 jewels, curved
14k $225 $275 $350

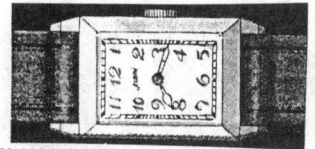

ELGIN, 15 jewels, Ca. 1929
Sterling......................................$75 $100 $125

ELGIN, 17 jewels, curved
gold filled..............................$65 $75 $90

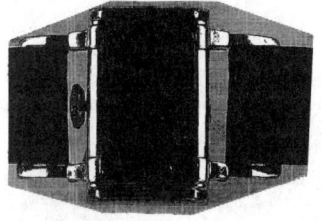

ELGIN, 15 jewels, drivers style
gold filled $175 $200 $250

ELGIN, 17 jewels, "Ristflo"
gold filled $150 $175 $225

ELGIN, 17 jewels
gold filled $80 $90 $100

ELGIN, 17 jewels, hidden lugs
gold filled $80 $90 $100

ELGIN, 17 jewels, embossed dial
gold filled $70 $80 $95

Ⓛ Some grades are not included. Their values can be
determined by comparing with similar age, size, metal
content, style, grades, or models such as time only,
chronograph, repeater etc. listed.

ELGIN, 17 jewels, curved, thin model
gold filled.................................$65 $75 $90

ELGIN, 17 jewels, stepped case
gold filled...................................$75 $90 $120

ELGIN, 17J., center sec., cal.11553, c.1928
gold filled................................$200 $250 $300

ELGIN, 15 jewels, "William Osler" recess crown
gold filled................................$225 $275 $350

ELGIN, 7 jewels, center sec., recess crown
gold filled................................$225 $275 $350

ELGIN, 17J., engraved case, c.1928
gold filled................................$100 $125 $175

ELGIN, 15J., 2 tone case, recessed crown
gold filled.............................$100 $125 $150

ELGIN, 7-15J., engraved case, c. 1928
14K $200 $250 $325
gold filled $70 $90 $110

ELGIN, 15J., engraved **Mermaid** design case, c.1928
gold filled $200 $275 $350

ELGIN, 15J., engraved case, c. 1928
gold filled $100 $125 $150

ELGIN, 15J., curved engraved case, c. 1928
gold filled $90 $100 $125

ELGIN, 17J., cal. 555, Ca. 1950
gold filled..................................$75 $100 $125

ELGIN, 17 jewels, "Crusade"
gold filled $100 $120 $140

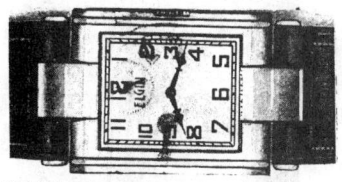

ELGIN, 15 jewels, center lugs
gold filled..................................$100 $120 $150

ELGIN, 7 jewels
gold filled $40 $50 $60

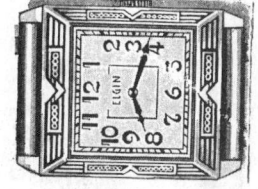

ELGIN, 7 jewels, fancy bezel
s. steel $55 $65 $75

ELGIN, 7 jewels, stepped bezel
s. steel $50 $60 $70

ELGIN, 7 jewels, fancy bezel
gold filled..................................$90 $100 $125

ELGIN, 15J., wire lugs, stem at "12", c.1920s
silver $150 $200 $275

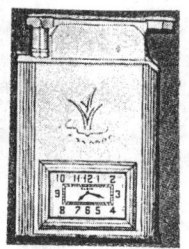

ELGIN, 15J.,combination lighter and Elgin Watch
Sterling....................................$150 $200 $275

ELGIN, 7J., **"Recased"**, left hand wind c.1920s
base metal $45 $55 $75

ELGIN, 15J., engraved case, c.1925
gold filled..................................$90 $100 $125

ELGIN, 21J., Lord Elgin, stepped case, c.1930
gold filled..................................$75 $85 $95

ELGIN, 21J., Lord Elgin, stepped case, c.1930
gold filled..................................$70 $80 $90

ELGIN, 7J., stepped case, c.1925
gold filled..................................$60 $70 $80

ELGIN, 17J., **BMW** logo, Ca.1955
gold filled..................................$70 $80 $100

ELGIN, 21J., Lord Elgin, GJS, c.1937
14k $175 $225 $275

ELGIN, 17J., stepped case, c.1930
gold filled $65 $75 $90

ELGIN, 17J., curved, stepped case, c.1927
gold filled $70 $80 $90

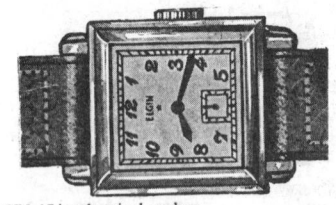

ELGIN, 17 jewels, raised numbers
gold filled $55 $65 $75

ELGIN, 17 jewels, c. 1927
14k $150 $175 $225

⊕ Some grades are not included. Their values can be determined by comparing with **similar** age, size, metal content, style, models and grades listed.

LORD ELGIN, 21 jewels, diamond dial
14k (w)....................................$200 $275 $325

ELGIN, 19 jewels, c. 1947
14k $175 $225 $275
gold filled..................................$70 $80 $90

LORD ELGIN, 21 jewels, diamond dial
14k (w)....................................$235 $300 $365

LORD ELGIN, 21 jewels, aux. sec., fancy lugs
14k $250 $300 $325

ELGIN, 21J., Lord Elgin, cal.670, c.1948
14k $225 $250 $300

🕐 Some grades are not included. Their values can be determined by comparing with **similar** age, size, metal content, style, models and grades listed.

LORD ELGIN, 21 jewels, flared case
14k $250 $300 $350

ELGIN, 19 jewels, flared case, fancy lugs
14k $250 $300 $350

ELGIN, 7J., cushion case, c.1930
gold filled $100 $125 $175

ELGIN, 7-15J., cushion case, c.1930
chromium....................................$50 $60 $90

ELGIN, 7-15J., solid lugs, Ca. 1925
s. steel $100 $125 $150

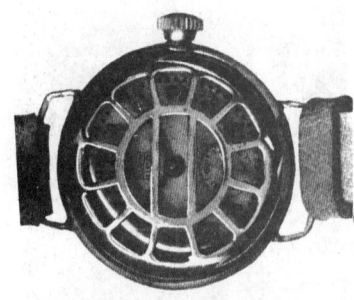

ELGIN, 15J., pierced shield, wire lugs, c.1918
silver $400 $450 $500

ELGIN, 15J., pierced shield, c.1918
silver $500 $550 $600

ELGIN, 15J., canteen style case, wire lugs, c.1919
nickel....................................$400 $450 $525

ELGIN, 16J., canteen style case, U.S.N.234C, c.1930s
s. steel $475 $500 $575

ELGIN, 15J., U.S.GOV'T grade II, c.1960s
s. steel $75 $100 $125

ELGIN, 15J., military style, 24 hr. dial, c.1942
s. steel $125 $150 $175

ELGIN, 15J., military style, cal.539, c.1940
s. steel $100 $125 $175

ELGIN, 15 jewels, "Official Boy Scout" model
s. steel $175 $250 $300

🕐 Some grades are not included. Their values can be
determined by comparing with similar age, size, metal
content, style, grades, or models such as time only,
chronograph, repeater etc. listed.

ELGIN, 7 jewels, "Official Boy Scout" model
s. steel $70 $85 $120

ELGIN, 15 jewels, enamel dial, wire lugs, c. 1915
silver $125 $150 $175

ELGIN, 15 jewels, enamel dial, wire lugs, c. 1915
silver $125 $150 $200

ELGIN, 15 jewels, center lugs
gold filled $100 $125 $150

ELGIN, 15J., case by Rolland Fischer, c. 1928
silver $250 $300 $375

ELGIN, 17J., center sec., c.1950
base metal $40 $45 $50

ELGIN, 21 jewels, "Black Knight"
14k $175 $200 $250

ELGIN, 7 jewels, "Avigo ", Ca. 1929
base metal $75 $95 $125

⌚ Some grades are not included. Their values can be
determined by comparing with **similar** age, size, metal
content, style, grades, or models such as **time only**,
chronograph, repeater etc. listed.

ELGIN, 15 jewels, center lugs, c. 1922
silver $125 $150 $200

ELGIN, 21J., center sec., wire lugs, cal. 680, c.1952
gold filled..................................$50 $60 $70

ELGIN, 30J., auto-wind, grade 760,
gold filled $65 $75 $85

ELGIN, 17 jewels, **Alarm**, Ca. 1960
gold filled..................................$175 $200 $275

ELGIN, 19J.,cal. 681 , c.1959
gold filled $45 $55 $65

ELGIN, 21J., Lord Elgin, **enamel bezel**, cal.688, c.1948
gold filled $75 $100 $125

ELGIN, 21J., water-proof, c.1952
s. steel $50 $60 $70

ELGIN, 23 J., "B. W. Raymond," R.R. approved
14k $400 $450 $500
gold filled $200 $275 $325
s. steel $175 $200 $250

🕐 Some grades are not included. Their values can be determined by comparing with **similar** age, size, metal content, style, grades, or models such as **time only**, chronograph, repeater etc. listed.

ELGIN, 21J., Lord Elgin, **shockmaster**, aux. sec., ca. 1955
14K..$175 $200 $250

LORD ELGIN, 21 jewels, diamond dial, c. 1958
14k (w)....................................$325 $375 $450

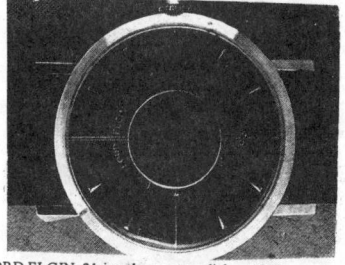

LORD ELGIN, 21 jewels, mystery dial, c. 1957
14k (w)....................................$190 $240 $275

LORD ELGIN, 21J., direct reading, cal#719, C.1957
gold filled................................$325 $400 $475

ELGIN, 17 J., in form of golf ball, rotating hr. & min.
gold filled................................$400 $450 $500

LORD ELGIN, 21 jewels, applied numbers, c. 1946
14k $175 $200 $300

LORD ELGIN, 21 jewels, curved, applied numbers
14k $200 $250 $300

LORD ELGIN, 21 jewels, diamond dial, faceted crystal
14k $300 $350 $400

ELGIN, 17 jewels, hinged back
14k (w) $150 $175 $250

ELGIN, 17 jewels, enamel bezel, Ca. 1930
14k (w) $600 $700 $775

ELGIN, 15 jewels, Art Deco bezel, c. 1935
gold filled................................$125 $150 $175

⊕ Some grades are not included. Their values can be
determined by comparing with **similar** age, size, metal
content, style, grades, or models such as **time only**,
chronograph, repeater etc. listed.

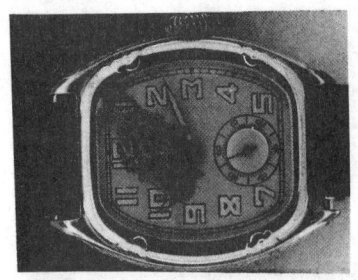

ELGIN, 15 jewels, 2 tone, c. 1930
gold filled..............................$100 $125 $150

ELGIN, 15 jewels, enamel bezel, c. 1920
14k (w)..................................$550 $650 $800

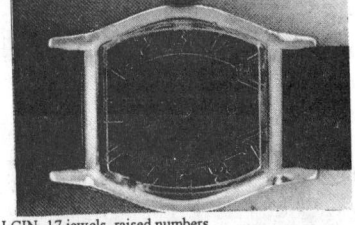

ELGIN, 17 jewels, raised numbers
gold filled..............................$60 $70 $80

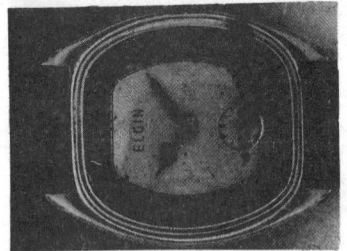

ELGIN, 21 jewels, enamel bezel, 2 tone, c. 1931
14k.......................................$600 $700 $800
   gold filled..........................$150 $200 $300

ELGIN, 7 jewels, fancy bezel
s. steel $50 $60 $70

ELGIN, 7 jewels, engraved bezel
s. steel $45 $55 $65

ELGIN, 17 jewels, aux. sec., curved
gold filled $75 $95 $120

ELGIN, 17 jewels, curved
gold filled $75 $90 $125

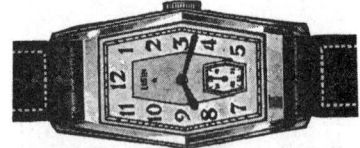

ELGIN, 17 jewels, curved
gold filled $90 $100 $110

ELGIN, 21 jewels, blue enamel bezel, c. 1920
14k $1,200 $1,400 $1,800

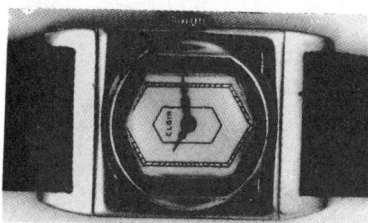

ELGIN, 21 jewels, enamel bezel
18k $1,200 $1,450 $1,850

LORD ELGIN, 21J, model 670, large lugs, anniversary of
50,000,000th watch (small run of watches),
gold plated movement, Ca. 1951
18k $1,300 $1,600 $1,850

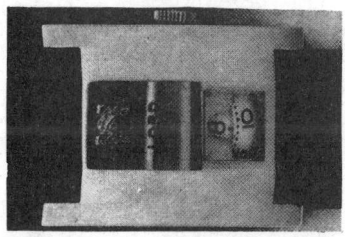

LORD ELGIN, 21 jewels, wandering hr. & min., curved
gold filled................................$425 $500 $600

ELGIN, 17 jewels, double dial
gold filled................................$600 $675 $750

LORD ELGIN, 21 jewels, hooded lugs, c. 1952
14k $275 $325 $375

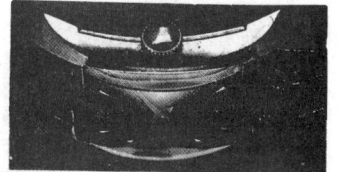

LORD ELGIN, 21 jewels, curved, c. 1957
14k $225 $275 $325

LORD ELGIN, 21 jewels, hooded lugs, c. 1950s
14k $200 $250 $300

ELGIN, 15 jewels, waterproof
s. steel $35 $45 $55

ELGIN, 15 jewels, center sec.
gold filled $40 $50 $65

ELGIN, 7 jewels, aux. sec.
gold filled $35 $45 $60

LORD ELGIN, 21 jewels, stepped case
18k $375 $425 $500

LORD ELGIN, 21 jewels, stepped case, curved
14k $200 $250 $350

ELGIN, 17 jewels, stepped case
14k $200 $250 $300

LORD ELGIN, 21 jewels, curved
gold filled..................................$70 $80 $90

ELGIN, 17 jewels, curved, fancy bezel
gold filled..................................$90 $125 $150

ELGIN, 17 jewels, curved, stepped case
gold filled..................................$90 $100 $120

ELGIN, 17 jewels, curved, stepped case
gold filled..................................$90 $100 $120

ELGIN, 17 jewels, curved
gold filled $90 $100 $120

ELGIN, 19 jewels, stepped case
gold filled $100 $125 $150

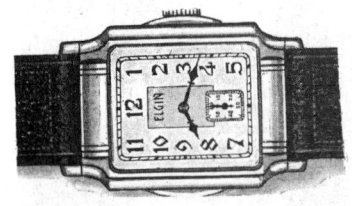

ELGIN, 15 jewels
gold filled $60 $70 $80

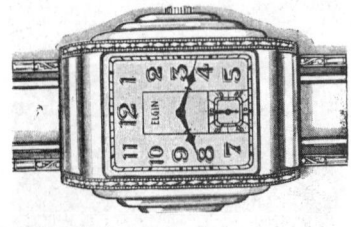

ELGIN, 7 jewels, fancy bezel
s. steel $40 $50 $60

ELGIN, 7 jewels, fancy bezel
gold filled $60 $70 $80

LORD ELGIN, 21 jewels, curved, c. 1938
14k $200 $250 $350

ELGIN, 15 jewels, fancy bezel
gold filled..................................$80 $90 $100

ELGIN, 21 jewels, curved
gold filled..................................$50 $60 $70

LORD ELGIN, 21 jewels, raised numbers
14k $175 $200 $275

LORD ELGIN, 21 jewels, curved
14k $175 $200 $275

LORD ELGIN, 21 jewels, curved
14k $200 $250 $300

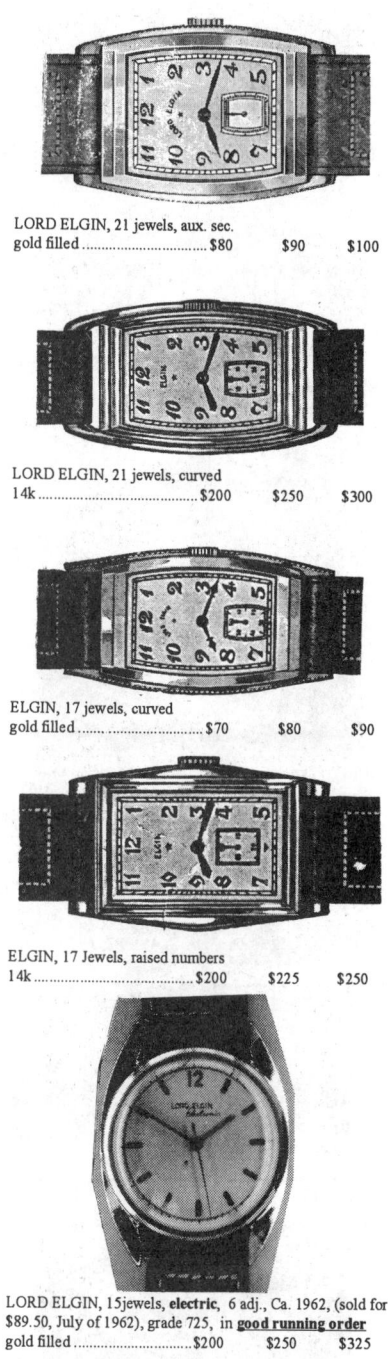

LORD ELGIN, 21 jewels, aux. sec.
gold filled $80 $90 $100

LORD ELGIN, 21 jewels, curved
14k $200 $250 $300

ELGIN, 17 jewels, curved
gold filled $70 $80 $90

ELGIN, 17 Jewels, raised numbers
14k $200 $225 $250

LORD ELGIN, 15jewels, **electric**, 6 adj., Ca. 1962, (sold for
$89.50, July of 1962), grade 725, in **good running order**
gold filled $200 $250 $325

**Elgin pioneering effort in electric watches
started in 1955.**

LORD ELGIN, 15 jewels, **electric**, c. 1962
(back–set)
s. steel $200 $250 $325

LORD ELGIN, 15 jewels, **electric**, c.1962
(grade 725, 6 adj.)
gold filled................................$200 $250 $325

ELGIN, 17 Jewels, Lady Elgin, flared case, cal. 650, c.1950
14k $100 $125 $150

ELGIN, 15 Jewels, art deco, c.1925
gold filled................................$40 $50 $60

ELGIN, 15 Jewels, art deco, c.1928
14k $60 $70 $90

ELGIN, 17 Jewels, art deco, c.1928
18k(w)......................................$75 $90 $110

ELGIN, 15 jewels, art deco, Ca. 1929
14K(W) $65 $75 $95

ELGIN, 15 jewels, art deco, Ca. 1928
gold filled................................$25 $30 $45

ELGIN, 15 jewels, art deco, Ca. 1928
gold filled................................$25 $30 $45

ELGIN, 15 jewels, art deco, Ca. 1928
gold filled................................$25 $30 $45

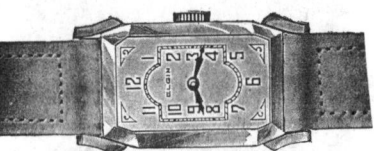

ELGIN, 15 jewels, sports model, Ca. 1928
14k...$60 $70 $85

ELGIN, 17J., 20 diamonds, art deco, Ca. 1928
18k..$225 $250 $350

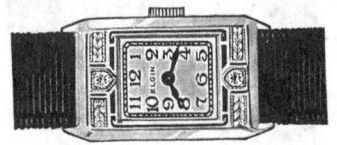

ELGIN, 15 jewels, 2 diamonds, art deco, Ca. 1928
gold filled................................$75 $85 $125

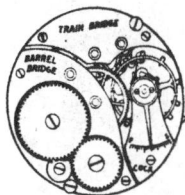

Model 3, 3-0 size, three-quarter plate, open face, pendant set, first serial number 18,179,001, Grade 414, March, 1915.

Model 1, 5-0 size, three-quarter plate, hunting, pendant set, first serial number 14,699,001, Grade 380, Feb., 1910.

Model 2, 5-0 size, three-quarter plate, open face, pendant set, first serial number 17,890,001, Grade 399, Feb., 1914.

Model 2, 8-0 size, Grade 532, 539, sweep second.

Model 7, 8-0 size, Grades 554, 555,

Model 20, 8-0 size, Grades 681, 682.

Model 1, 10-0 size, three-quarter plate,

Model 2, 15-0 size, Grades 623, 624, 626.

15-0 Size, movement, Grades 670, 672, 673.

15-0 size, movement. Grade 674.

15-0 size, movement, Grades 557, 558, 559.

Model 2, 21-0 size, Grade 541, 533, 535.

Model 3, 21-0 size, Grade 547, sweep second.

Model 4, 21-0 size, Grades 617, 617L, 619, 619L.

Model 9, 21-0 size, Grades 650, 651.

Model 9, 21-0 size, Grades 655, 656.

GRADE 725, 15 jewels, "electric" model movement

"ELECTRIC", case showing back—set

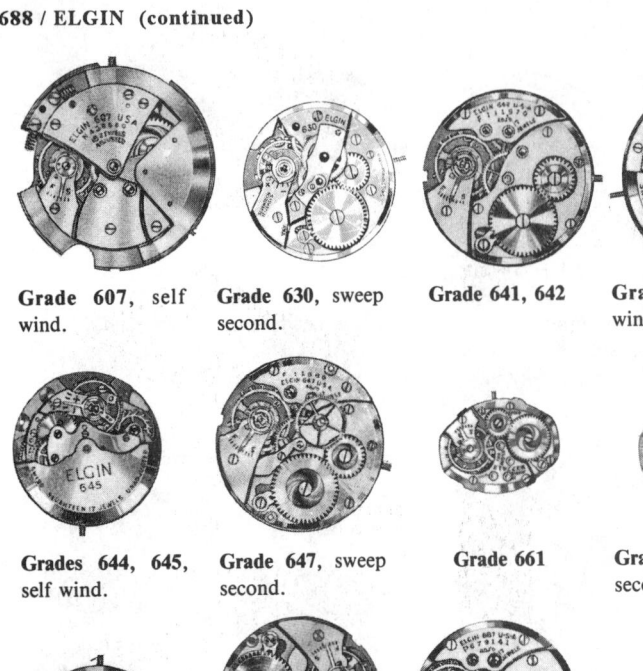

Grade 607, self wind.

Grade 630, sweep second.

Grade 641, 642

Grade 643, self wind.

Grades 644, 645, self wind.

Grade 647, sweep second.

Grade 661

Grade 666, sweep second.

Grade 668, sweep second.

Grade 685

Grade 687

Grade 700

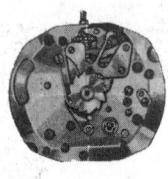

GRADE 710 & 719
719 = DIRECT READ TRAIN SIDE

719 = DIAL SIDE OF MOVEMENT

Grade 716

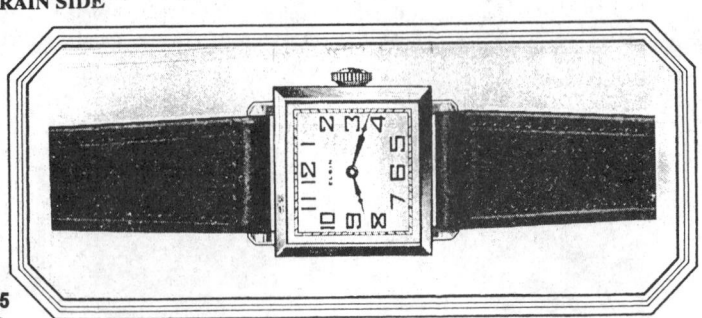

ELOGA, triple calendar,
base metal $50 $65 $85

EMERSON, 17J., hooded lugs,
gold filled................................$50 $60 $70

ENICAR, 17 jewels, center sec.
18k $200 $250 $300

ENICAR, 17J., chronograph, 2 reg. Ca. 1955
s. steel $200 $250 $300

ENICAR, 17 jewels, center sec.
s. steel......................................$30 $40 $60

ENICAR, 17 jewels, triple date, moon phase
gold filled...............................$250 $300 $350

ENICAR, 15 jewels, egg shaped with compass, c. 1918
silver..$400 $450 $500

ENICAR, 17J., autow., date, 24 hour dial, C.1970
s. steel.....................................$100 $125 $150

ESKA, 17J.,chronog., triple date, moon phase
14k...$1,500 $1,700 $2,000

ESKA, 17 jewels, chronog., 2 reg., C. 1950s
s. steel $200 $250 $300

ESKA, 17 jewels, chronog., 2 reg., c. 1940
s. steel $1,200 $1,400 $1,600

ESKA, 17 jewels, multi-colored enamel dial
18k $2,500 $2,700 $3,000

ETERNA, quartz, date, by ETA, cal#954, C.1975
s. steel $65 $75 $100

🕐 Some grades are not included. Their values can be
determined by comparing with similar age, size, metal
content, style, grades, or models such as time only,
chronograph, repeater etc. listed.

ETERNA, 19 jewels, day-date-month
18k..$250 $300 $350

ETERNA, 17 jewels, chronog., triple date, 3 reg.
s.steel...................................... $375 $425 $500
18k..$800 $900 $1,000

ETERNA, 21 jewels, date, cal. 14390, c.1960
18k..$250 $300 $350

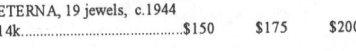

ETERNA, 19 jewels, c.1944
14k..$150 $175 $200

ETERNA, 16 jewels, aux. sec., c.1945
gold filled.................................$80 $90 $100

ETERNA, 19 jewels, c.1938
gold filled.................................$55 $65 $75

ETERNA, 17 jewels, gold jewel settings, c.1935
14k $175 $225 $275

EVANS, 17 jewels, rhinestones on bezel, c. 1948
gold plate $70 $80 $125

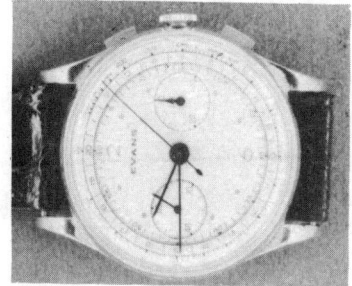

EVANS, 17 jewels, chronog., 2 reg., c. 1940
18k $350 $400 $475

EXACTUS, 17 J., chronog.,triple-date, moon ph.
s. steel.....................................$500 $600 $700

EXCELSIOR, 17 jewels, chronog., 2 reg.
14k...$375 $450 $500
gold filled................................$175 $200 $235

EXCELSIOR, 17 jewels, chronog.
gold filled.............................. $200 $225 $275
s. steel.....................................$175 $200 $250

EXCELSIOR PARK, 17 jewels, chronog.
s. steel.....................................$175 $225 $275

FAIRFAX, 6J, engraved case, c.1929
base metal $45 $55 $65

FAIRFAX, 6J, engraved case, c.1929
base metal $50 $60 $70

FAIRFAX, 6J, butler finish case, c.1929
base metal $45 $55 $65

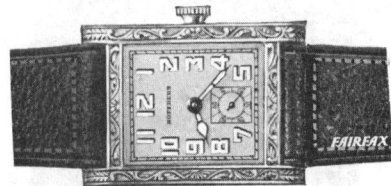

FAIRFAX, 6J, engraved case, c.1929
gold filled $50 $60 $70

FAITH, 17J, flip top case, by Hyde Park, c.1950
gold filled $150 $175 $225

⊕ Some grades are not included. Their values can be
determined by comparing with **similar** age, size, metal
content, style, grades, or models such as **time only**,
chronograph, repeater etc. listed.

FAVRE LEUBA, 17J., altimeter or aneroid barometer
s. steel $200 $250 $300

FAVRE LEUBA, 17J., triple date, cal. Valj.89, c.1948
s. steel $150 $175 $200

FERRARI, quartz, chronog., c.1988
base metal $200 $250 $300

FELCA, 17 jewels, auto wind
gold filled $50 $60 $75
14k $125 $150 $200
18k $175 $225 $275

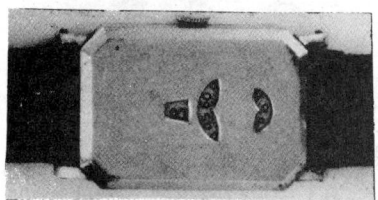

FONTAINEMELON, S. A., 17 J., gold train, digital
14k $1,500 $1,700 $2,000

FREY,15J., engraved case, c.1933
base metal..................................$40 $50 $65

FRAMONT, 17J, timer, date, cal. 290, c.1970
s. steel $100 $125 $150

FREY,15J., engraved stepped case, c.1933
base metal..................................$40 $50 $65

FREY, 25J., rotating outside chapter, c.1970
s. steel $75 $100 $125

FREY,15J., engraved case, c.1933
base metal..................................$50 $60 $70

FRIEDLI, 17 jewels, auto wind, center sec.
gold filled................................. $45 $50 $65
18k..$175 $225 $275

FREY,17J., GJS, c.1970
s. steel $40 $50 $65

🕐 Note: Some models and grades are not included. Their
values can be determined by comparing with **similar** age,
size, metal content, style, models and grades listed.

FRODSHAM, 17J., Ca. 1935
18k(w)...................................... $400 $500 $600

GALLET, 15 jewels, wire lugs, Ca. 1925
silver $100 $150 $200

GALLET, 15 jewels, waterproof, auto wind
s. steel $55 $65 $75

GALLET, 17 jewels, chronog., single button, c. 1950
s. steel $350 $400 $465

GALLET, 17J., chronog., by Racine, US air force, c. 1978
s. steel $150 $200 $250

GALLET, 17 jewels, chronog., 3 reg., c. 1945
s. steel......................................$300 $350 $400

GALLET, 17 jewels, chronog., 3 reg., c. 1942
gold filled...............................$350 $400 $475

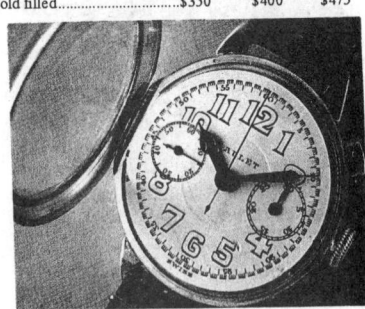

GALLET, 17J., chronog., 2 reg.,single button, C.1925,
silver"small size" $800 $1,000 $1,200

GALLET, 17J., chronog., 3 reg.,triple date, moon ph.
18k...$2,000 $2,500 $3,000

GALLET, 17J., chronog., 3 reg.,triple date,
14k $700 $800 $900
s. steel $400 $500 $600

GALLET, 17 jewels, chronog., 3 reg., c. 1955
s. steel $300 $350 $400

GALLET, 17 jewels, day-date-month, c. 1941
gold filled.............................$400 $500 $600

GALLET, 17 jewels, chronog., 2 reg.
14k $425 $525 $575
s. steel $200 $235 $275

GALLET, 17 jewels, chronog., mid size, c. 1940
s. steel.................................. $300 $350 $400

GALLET, 17J., chronog., flying officer, cal.149, c. 1958
s. steel..................................... $400 $500 $600

GALLET, 17 jewels, chronog., waterproof
s. steel.....................................$300 $400 $500

GALLET, 17 jewels, chronog., 2 reg.
s. steel..................................... $200 $250 $300

🕐 Some grades are not included. Their values can be
determined by comparing with similar age, size, metal
content, style, grades, or models such as time only,
chronograph, repeater etc. listed.

GALLET, 17 jewels, oval, chronog., 2 reg.
s.steel $300 $400 $500

GALLET, 17 jewels, chronog., 2 reg.
gold filled................................$200 $225 $275

GALLET, 17 jewels, chronog., 2 reg.
s. steel $175 $225 $275

GALLET, 17 jewels, chronog., 2 reg., c. 1939
s. steel $200 $300 $350

GALLET, 17 jewels, time dial at 12 , chronog.
s. steel..................................$300 $350 $400

P. GARNIER, 17 jewels, minu-stop, c. 1965
s. steel.................................. $90 $125 $150

P. GARNIER, 17 jewels, world time, c. 1968
s. steel................................. $100 $125 $150

GARLAND, 17J., center sec., water-proof.
s. steel.................................. $35 $45 $55

🕐 Some grades are not included. Their values can be
determined by comparing with similar age, size, metal
content, style, grades, or models such as time only,
chronograph, repeater etc. listed.

GENEVE, 15 jewels, dual dial, c. 1939
s. steel $400 $550 $650

GENEVE, 15 jewels, dual dial, c. 1937
s. steel $350 $400 $550

GENEVE, 17 jewels, curly lugs, c.1950
14k $250 $325 $375

GERMINAL, 17 J., "Voltaire"
14k $150 $175 $200

GERMINAL, 15 J., early auto wind, lug action, c. 1933
s. steel $500 $600 $700

GERALD GENTA, 29J., skeletonized, auto wind,
perpetual calendar
18k C&B $15,000 $17,000 $20,000

GIRARD-PERREGAUX, 17J., auto wind, C.1951
s. steel $65 $80 $100

GIRARD-PERREGAUX, 17J., alarm, c.1960
gold filled...............................$100 $125 $150

GIRARD-PERREGAUX, 39J., center sec. c.1955
14k...$200 $225 $275

🕐 Some grades are not included. Their values can be
determined by comparing with similar age, size, metal
content, style, grades, or models such as time only,
chronograph, repeater etc. listed.

GIRARD-PERREGAUX, 17J., center sec., c.1948
18k $250 $275 $300

GIRARD-PERREGAUX, 17J., aux. sec., c.1958
gold filled...............................$55 $65 $85

GIRARD-PERREGAUX, 17J., center sec., c.1960
s. steel $65 $75 $95

GIRARD-PERREGAUX, 17J., aux. sec., c.1950
s. steel.......................................$80 $90 $125

GIRARD-PERREGAUX, 17J., cal.47ae, c.1953
14k $200 $235 $300

GIRARD-PERREGAUX, 17J., date, c.1960
gold filled...............................$55 $65 $85

GIRARD-PERREGAUX, 17J., Sea Hawk., c.1960
gold filled...................................$55 $65 $85

GIRARD-PERREGAUX, 39J., auto-matic, date, c.1960
18k.. $225 $275 $325

🕐 Some grades are not included. Their values can be determined by comparing with similar age, size, metal content, style, grades, or models such as time only, chronograph, repeater etc. listed.

GIRARD-PERREGAUX, 39J., chronometre "HF", c.1970
s. steel $75 $85 $100

GIRARD-PERREGAUX, 39 jewels, center sec.
14k..$175 $200 $300

GIRARD-PERREGAUX,17J.,"Gyromatic",date
gold filled...................................$65 $75 $90

GIRARD-PERREGAUX, 17J., chronog., 2 reg.
s. steel.....................................$300 $350 $400

GIRARD-PERREGAUX, 39J.,"Gyromatic",date, Ca. 1960
18k $200 $225 $275

GIRARD-PERREGAUX, 17J., by Valjoux cal.72, c.1955
s. steel.....................................$475 $550 $600

GIRARD-PERREGAUX, 17J., triple date, autow.
s. steel $150 $175 $200

GIRARD-PERREGAUX, 17J., chronog cal.285, c.1940
gold filled...............................$350 $400 $475

GIRARD-PERREGAUX, 17J., pulsations, c.1948
14k $500 $550 $600

GIRARD-PERREGAUX, 17 J., chronog., 3 reg., c. 1952
s. steel $400 $500 $600

GIRARD-PERREGAUX, 17J, chronog., triple date, moon
phase
18k $2,000 $2,200 $2,500

GIRARD-PERREGAUX, 39 J., Ca. 1955
14k $200 $225 $300
18k $250 $300 $375

GIRARD-PERREGAUX, 17J., aux. sec., Ca.1960
14k $200 $225 $265

GIRARD-PERREGAUX, 17J., "gyromatic",
14k $200 $225 $250

GIRARD-PERREGAUX, 17J., RF#2459, c.1970
14k $150 $175 $200

GIRARD-PERREGAUX, 17J., cal.a6 3606, GJS, c.1955
14k $150 $175 $200

GIRARD-PERREGAUX, 17J., recess crown, GJS, c.1954
14k $200 $225 $250

GIRARD-PERREGAUX, 17J., cal.86, GJS, c.1948
14k $100 $125 $165

GIRARD-PERREGAUX, 17J., cal.86ae, GJS, c.1940
s. steel $50 $60 $75

GIRARD-PERREGAUX, 17J., two tone case,GJS, c.1942
14k $250 $275 $350

GIRARD-PERREGAUX, 17J., GJS, c.1953
14k $150 $175 $200

GIRARD-PERREGAUX, 17J., cal. 86ae, GJS, c.1942
s. steel $55 $65 $85

🕐 Some grades are not included. Their values can be
determined by comparing with similar age, size, metal
content, style, grades, or models such as time only,
chronograph, repeater etc. listed.

GIRARD-PERREGAUX, 17J., recess crown, GJS, c.1947
gold filled.................................$55 $65 $85

GIRARD-PERREGAUX, 17J., "1791", GJS, c.1942
s. steel...................................$100 $125 $150

GIRARD-PERREGAUX, 17J., cal.91ae220, GJS, c.1948
gold filled.................................$65 $75 $95

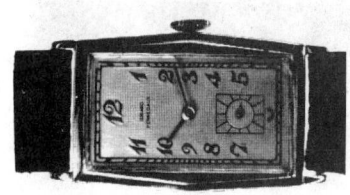

GIRARD-PERREGAUX, 17J., GJS, c.1936
gold filled.................................$80 $90 $110

GIRARD-PERREGAUX, 17J., cal.86ae, GJS, c.1942
14k...$150 $175 $200

GIRARD-PERREGAUX, 39 jewels, aux. sec.
14k $200 $225 $300

GIRARD-PERREGAUX, 17 jewels, aux. sec.
gold filled....................................$65 $75 $85

GIRARD-PERREGAUX, 17 jewels, tank style, c. 1948
14k $200 $250 $300

GIRARD-PERREGAUX, 17 J., C. 1948
14k $200 $225 $300

GIRARD-PERREGAUX, 17 J., date, stepped case,
18k $600 $700 $850
14k $450 $525 $650

GLASHUTTE, 17J., 2 reg., fluted bezel, c.1942
s. steel....................................$800 $900 $1,100

GLASHUTTE, 17J., signed Uhrenfabrik Glashutte, c.1935
18k..$600 $750 $950

GLASHUTTE, 15J., signed "GUB", Ca.1950's
gold filled................................$300 $350 $400

GLYCINE, 17J., **Airman**, auto-wind, 24hr., date, c.1970
s. steel....................................$200 $250 $275

GLYCINE, 17J., 15 diamond dial, cal.4645, c.1945
14k..$700 $800 $900

GLYCINE, 17J., 3 diamond dial, c.1950
14k(w).....................................$175 $200 $275

GLYCINE, 17 jewels, airman, 24 hr. dial, date, C.1960s
s. steel $250 $300 $375

GLYCINE, 17 jewels, **curved,** c. 1938
18k $350 $400 $500

GLYCINE, 17 jewels, aux. sec., c. 1934
14k (w)..................................$200 $250 $275

GLYCINE, 18 jewels, faceted crystal & bezel
gold filled...............................$80 $90 $100

GOERING W. Co.,jump hr., wandering sec.,C.1935
14k......................................$1,000 $1,300 $1,700

GOERING W. Co.,jump hr., wandering sec.,C.1935
chrome...................................$200 $250 $300

GOERING W. Co., 15J., center sec., C.1935
base metal...............................$50 $60 $75

GOERING W. Co., 15J., engraved case, C.1935
gold filled...............................$50 $60 $75

GOERING W. Co., 15J., engraved case, C.1935
gold filled...............................$80 $90 $110

GOERING W. Co., 15J., engraved case, C.1935
gold filled...............................$80 $90 $110

GOERING W. Co., 15J., rectangular, C.1935
gold filled....................................$70 $80 $95

GOERING W. Co., 15J., ladies engraved case, C.1935
gold filled....................................$35 $45 $60

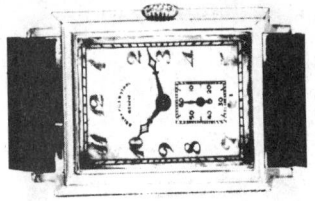

GOLAY, 18 jewels, aux. sec., c. 1928
18k & platinum....................$1,500 $1,800 $2,200

GOLAY, 32 jewels, min. repeater, adj. to 5 positions
18k $20,000 $25,000 $30,000

GRANA, 16J., **Masonic dial**, GJS, ca. 1948
14k $175 $225 $250

GRUEN, 17J., curved, precision, cal. 330, Ca. 1937
platinum..................................$900 $1,000 $1,200

GRUEN, 15J., enamel dial, wire lugs, c. 1915
silver $150 $175 $250

GRUEN, 17J., driver's watch, winds at 12, cal.400, c.1938
gold filled $250 $300 $350

GRUEN,17J., curved, drivers, cal.401, RF#352, c.1932
gold filled $450 $500 $650

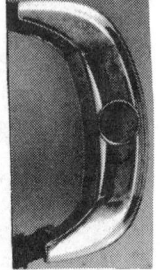

GRUEN, 17J., extremely curved, drivers, c. 1932 , and
side view of watch
gold filled $600 $700 $850

GRUEN, 17 J., extremely curved, driver's watch
gold filled.............................$600 $700 $850

GRUEN, 17J., driver's watch , flexible long lugs
gold filled.............................$700 $800 $950

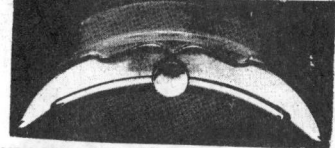

GRUEN, 17 jewels, curvex, c. 1949
gold filled.............................$250 $300 $350

GRUEN, 17 jewels, curvex, 35mm long
gold filled.............................$250 $300 $400

GRUEN, 17 jewels, curvex, 55mm long, C.1937
14k $900 $1,000 $1,200

GRUEN, 17J.,curvex, precision, C. 1936
14k $500 $600 $700

GRUEN, 17 jewels, curvex, c. 1937
gold filled.............................$250 $300 $350

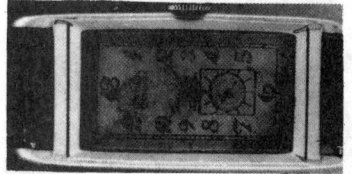

GRUEN, 17 jewels, curvex, c. 1945
gold filled.............................$300 $350 $400

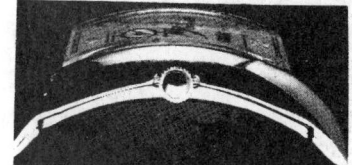

GRUEN, 17 jewels, curvex, 50mm long, c. 1937
gold filled $400 $500 $650

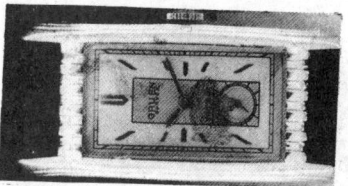

GRUEN, 17 jewels, curvex, c. 1937
s. steel $175 $200 $250

GRUEN, 17 jewels, curvex, aux. sec.
gold filled $275 $350 $400

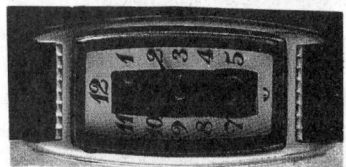

GRUEN, 17J., note bezel,curvex, ca.1936
gold filled $250 $300 $350

GRUEN, 17 jewels, curvex
gold filled $250 $300 $350

🕐 First **CURVEX** was introduced on October 26, 1935 it
was series # 311, the 2nd. series was 330 in 1939 and in 1940
series # 440 was issued.

GRUEN, 17 jewels, curvex
gold filled.............................$175 $200 $250

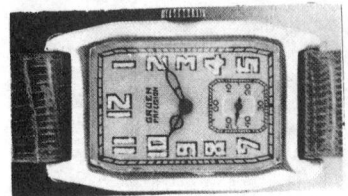

GRUEN, 17 jewels, curvex
gold filled.............................$175 $200 $250

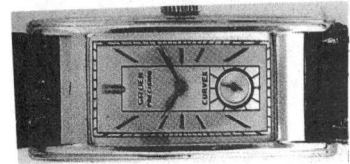

GRUEN, 17J., curvex, RF#202, cal.311, c. 1936
gold filled.............................. $250 $300 $350

GRUEN, 15J., curvex, RF#226, c. 1936
gold filled.............................. $175 $200 $300

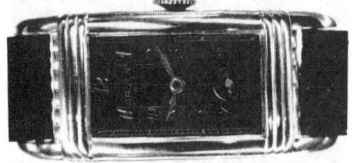

GRUEN, 15J., curvex, stepped case, RF#278, c. 1936
s. steel $250 $300 $350

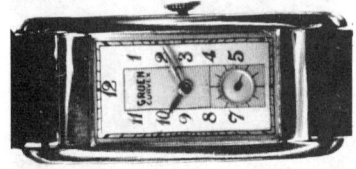

GRUEN, 15J., curvex, RF#255, cal.500, c. 1936
gold filled.............................. $250 $300 $350

GRUEN, 17J., curvex, RF#266, cal.165, c. 1935
gold filled $100 $150 $200

GRUEN, 17J., curvex, RF#280, cal.330, c. 1936
gold filled $250 $300 $350

GRUEN, 17J., curvex, stepped case, RF#280, c. 1937
14k $550 $650 $750
gold filled $250 $300 $350

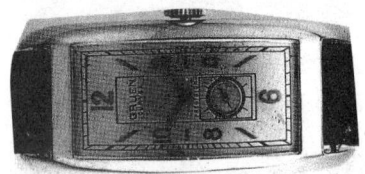

GRUEN, 17J., curvex, precision, RF#292, cal.330, c. 1937
gold filled $350 $400 $450

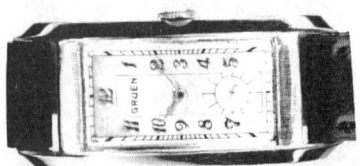

GRUEN, 15J., curvex, RF#324, cal.500, c. 1936
gold filled $275 $325 $400

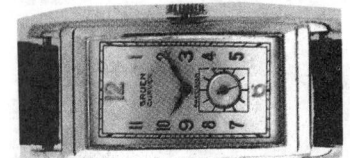

GRUEN, 17J., curvex, RF#308, cal.330, c. 1936
14k $550 $650 $750
gold filled $250 $300 $350

GRUEN, 17J., curvex, RF#339, cal.330, c. 1939
gold filled................................. $250 $300 $350

GRUEN, 17J., curvex, aux. sec.
gold filled.................................$100 $150 $200

GRUEN, 17J., curvex, cal#440, hooded lugs, ca.1943
14k $200 $250 $300

GRUEN, 17 jewels, curvex, fancy lugs
14k $300 $350 $400

GRUEN, 17 jewels, curvex, long lugs
14k $300 $350 $450

GRUEN, 15 jewels, **tu-tone case**, double dial, Ca. 1937
14k W & Y $3,000 $3,500 $4,000

GRUEN, 17 jewels, **jumping hr.**, double dial
14k $4,000 $4,500 $5,000

GRUEN, 17 jewels, double dial
gold filled $900 $1,100 $1,300

GRUEN, 17 jewels, double dial, curved, c.1930s
gold filled $400 $450 $500

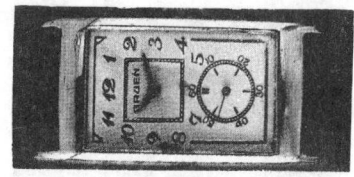

GRUEN, 17 jewels, double dial, curved, c. 1938
gold filled $900 $1,100 $1,300

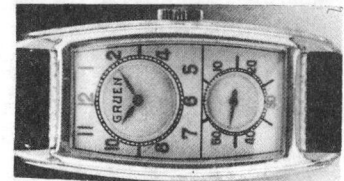

GRUEN, 17 jewels, double dial
gold filled $900 $1,000 $1,100

GRUEN, 17 jewels, double dial, c. 1932
gold filled $900 $1,000 $1,200

GRUEN, 15 jewels, in form of car radiator, curved
nickel...$800 $1,000 $1,250

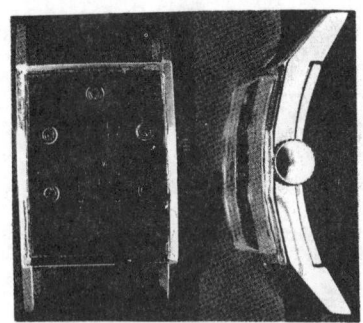

GRUEN, 17J., curvex, diamond dial, faceted crystal
14k $450 $500 $550

GRUEN, 17 jewels, curvex, diamond dial, c. 1946
14k $400 $450 $500

GRUEN, 17 jewels, veri thin model, fancy lugs
14k $350 $425 $500

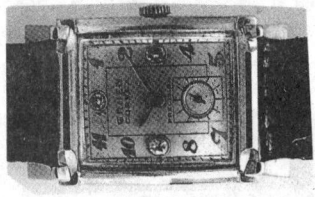

GRUEN, 17J., curvex, 3 diam., RF#568, cal.440, c. 1945
14k(w)...................................... $325 $375 $450

GRUEN, 17 jewels, auto wind, cal. 840, c. 1952
18k $300 $350 $400

GRUEN, 17J., curvex, 5 diam., RF#615, cal.370c. 1945
14k(w)...................................... $275 $375 $400

GRUEN, 17 jewels, curvex, fancy lugs
gold filled $150 $175 $200

GRUEN, 17J., stepped case, 3 diam., RF#798, c. 1950
14k(w)...................................... $300 $350 $425

GRUEN, 17 jewels, curvex, diamond dial, fancy lugs
14k (w) $250 $300 $375

GRUEN, 21 jewels, diamond dial, fancy center lugs
14k $425 $500 $575

GRUEN, 21 jewels, fancy lugs, c. 1945
14k $350 $400 $500

GRUEN, 17 jewels, curvex, fancy lugs, c. 1943
gold filled................................$90 $125 $150
14k $300 $350 $450

GRUEN, 17 jewels, curvex, diamond dial, c. 1945
14k $350 $400 $450

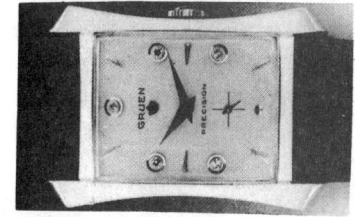

GRUEN, 17J., flared, diamond dial,
14k(w)....................................$400 $450 $500

GRUEN, 17 jewels, curvex, diamond dial, c.1945
14k $250 $300 $375

GRUEN, 17 jewels, curvex, diamond dial, c. 1951
14k(w)C&B $650 $750 $850

GRUEN, 17J., so called **50th Anniversary, with a engraved**
quadron precision extra **mvt. G# 119**, Adj., also used **G# 123.**
14k(w)....................................$400 $450 $500

GRUEN, 17 jewels, curvex, c.1951
14k $275 $325 $450

GRUEN, 17 jewels, curvex
14k $400 $500 $600

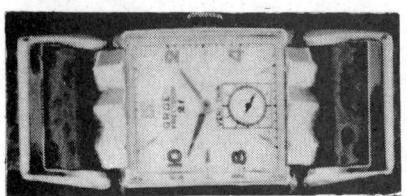

GRUEN, 21J., veri-thin, precision, swinging lugs
gold filled.................................$150 $175 $200

GRUEN, 15J., RF#467, cal.431, c. 1948
gold filled $60 $70 $95

GRUEN, 15J., RF#93, cal.179, c. 1925
gold filled................................. $75 $100 $125

GRUEN, 17J., precision, RF#498, cal.440, c. 1945
gold filled $60 $70 $95

GRUEN, 17J., stepped lugs, RF#449, cal.440, c. 1945
gold filled................................. $100 $125 $150

GRUEN, 17J., curvex, RF#498, cal.440, c. 1945
gold filled $100 $125 $175

GRUEN, 17J., large lugs, RF#449, cal.440, c. 1945
gold filled................................. $125 $150 $200

GRUEN, 17J., curvex, RF#530, cal.335, c. 1948
gold filled $60 $70 $95

GRUEN, 17J., veri-thin, RF#530, cal.430, c. 1945
14k $200 $250 $300

GRUEN, 17J., RF#449, cal.440, c. 1943
gold filled................................. $100 $125 $175

GRUEN, 17J., curvex, RF#544, cal.440, c. 1942
gold filled............................... $100 $125 $150

GRUEN, 17J., veri-thin 3 diam., RF#558, cal.335, c. 1945
14k(w)................................... $200 $275 $325

GRUEN, 17J., curvex, RF#576, cal.440, c. 1942
gold filled...............................$125 $150 $185
14k $250 $300 $375

GRUEN, 17J., 3 diam.curvex, RF#587, cal.430, c. 1948
gold filled............................... $125 $150 $225

GRUEN, 17J., curvex, RF#607, cal.370, c. 1943
gold filled............................... $125 $150 $200

GRUEN, 17J., fancy lugs, curvex, RF#610, c. 1945
14k $550 $600 $675

GRUEN, 17J., curvex, RF#610, cal.1370, c. 1945
14k $475 $550 $650

GRUEN, 17J., 3 diam., curvex, RF#615, cal.370, c. 1945
14k $200 $250 $350

GRUEN, 17J., curvex, RF#642, cal.370, c. 1945
gold filled $100 $125 $150

GRUEN, 17J., curvex, RF#650, cal.370, c. 1948
gold filled $100 $125 $150

GRUEN, 17J., twisted bezel, RF#657, cal.335, c. 1953
gold filled.............................. $150 $175 $225

GRUEN, 17J., curvex, faceted crystal, cal.440, c. 1947
14k $250 $300 $375

GRUEN, 21J., precision, RF#674, cal.430, c. 1947
gold filled................................ $60 $70 $95

GRUEN, 21J., precision, RF#801, cal335., c. 1953
14k $200 $250 $300

GRUEN, 21J., precision, RF#738, cal.335, c. 1948
14k $225 $275 $325

GRUEN, 17J., veri-thin, large lugs, c. 1950
14k $200 $235 $300

GRUEN, 17J., curvex, RF#750, cal.370, c. 1940
gold filled.............................. $100 $135 $175

GRUEN, 17J., center wheel not jeweled, c. 1938
gold filled $90 $110 $150

GRUEN, 17J., curvex, RF#773, cal.370, c. 1945
gold filled..............................$100 $125 $165

GRUEN, 17J., stepped case, ca.1930
gold filled $80 $90 $110

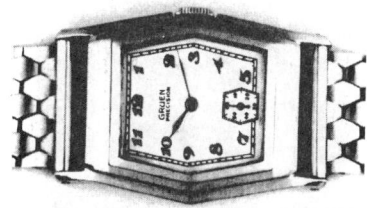

GRUEN, 19 jewels, precision, c. 1920
14k $300 $400 $500

GRUEN, 17 jewels, curvex
14k $300 $350 $400

GRUEN, 17J., curvex, cal#440, ca.1940s
gold filled $100 $125 $175

GRUEN, 17 jewels, curvex, c. 1943
14k $400 $450 $500

GRUEN, 17 jewels, cal. 440, RF#449, Ca. 1945
gold filled $150 $175 $200

🕐 Some grades are not included. Their values can be determined by comparing with **similar** age, size, metal content, style, grades, or models such as **time only**, chronograph, repeater etc. listed.

GRUEN, 17 jewels, Curvex, RF#610, 3 diam.dial, Ca.1945
14k(w) 6 diam.case $400 $450 $500

GRUEN, 21J., "Precision", RF#709, cal.335, Ca.1945
gold filled $75 $85 $125

GRUEN, 15 jewels, RF#8w, cal.157, Ca. 1929
gold filled $75 $100 $150

GRUEN, 15 jewels, 3 Adj., Ca.1930
gold filled $60 $70 $95

GRUEN, 17J., veri-thin, cal.405, c. 1946
gold filled $70 $90 $125

GRUEN, 17J., curvex, RF#450, cal.440, c. 1938
gold filled.............................. $150 $200 $275

GRUEN, 17J., curvex, RF#448, cal.440, c. 1941
gold filled.............................. $150 $200 $250

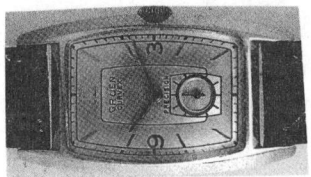

GRUEN, 17J., curvex, RF#450, cal.440, c. 1938
14k $250 $300 $375

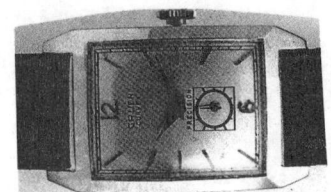

GRUEN, 17J., curvex, RF#879, cal.370, c. 1942
14k $300 $350 $400

GRUEN, 17J., curvex, RF#450, cal.440, c. 1942
14k .... $ 225 $265 $350

GRUEN, 17J., curvex, RF#448, cal.440, c. 1944
14k $350 $400 $450

GRUEN, 17J., curvex, RF#364, cal.400, c. 1935
gold filled.............................. $150 $175 $225

GRUEN, 17J., curvex, RF#293, cal.330, c. 1940
gold filled.............................. $150 $175 $225

GRUEN, 17J., precision, RF#271, cal., c. 1936
gold filled.............................. $125 $150 $200

GRUEN, 17J., fluted bezel, RF#240, cal.335, c. 1935
14k $200 $250 $325

GRUEN, 17J., curvex, RF#602, cal.370, c. 1943
14k $300 $350 $400

GRUEN, 17J., curvex, RF#449, cal.440, c. 1945
14k $250 $300 $350

GRUEN, 17J., veri-thin, cal.420, c. 1948
gold filled.................................. $65 $75 $95

GRUEN, 17 jewels, curvex, c. 1936
gold filled...............................$200 $250 $300

GRUEN, 17 jewels, precision, fancy lugs
14k $300 $400 $500

🕐 Some grades are not included. Their values can be
determined by comparing with similar age, size, metal
content, style, grades, or models such as time only,
chronograph, repeater etc. listed.

GRUEN, 17 jewels, curvex, c. 1947
14k $300 $350 $450

GRUEN, 17 jewels, curvex, c. 1937
gold filled $185 $225 $275

GRUEN, 17 jewels, curvex, fancy lugs
14k $250 $300 $350

GRUEN, 17 jewels, curvex, c. 1939
14k $400 $450 $500
gold filled $300 $350 $400

GRUEN, 17 jewels, curvex, fancy lugs, c. 1961
14k $400 $500 $600

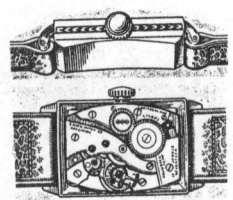

Gruen Quadron rectangular movement

GRUEN, 15-17J., enamel on nickel, mvt.# 158, Ca. 1927
nickel...$200 $225 $275

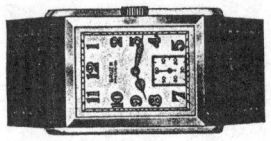

GRUEN, 17J., crown-guard, quadron mvt.# 59, Ca. 1927
18k $225 $300 $350

GRUEN, 15-17J., enamel art Deco, Ca. 1927
gold filled................................$250 $275 $300

GRUEN, 15-17J., inlaid enamel case, quadron mvt., Ca. 1927
gold filled................................$100 $125 $175

GRUEN, 15-17J., center sec., radium dial, Ca. 1927
14k..$200 $225 $275

GRUEN, 15-17J., engraved case, quadron mvt.# 47, Ca. 1927
gold filled................................$65 $80 $100

GRUEN, 15-17J., engraved case, radium dial, Ca. 1927
nickel.......................................$75 $95 $125

GRUEN, 15-17J., crown-guard, quadron mvt., Ca. 1927
14k $200 $225 $275

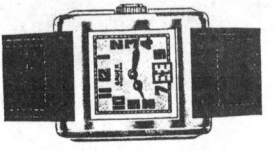

GRUEN, 15-17J., tank w/crown guard, Ca. 1927
14k..$200 $250 $325

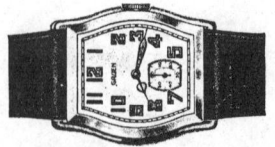

GRUEN, 15-17J., crown-guard, quadron mvt., Ca. 1927
gold filled................................$125 $150 $175

GRUEN, 15-17J., tank engraved, mvt.# 13, Ca. 1927
14k.. $200 $225 $275

GRUEN, 17J., pulsemeter,
s. steel $500 $600 $750

GRUEN, 17J., triple date, cal.415, c. 1953
gold filled............................... $150 $175 $225

GRUEN, 17 jewels, physicians chronog., screw back
18k $1,700 $2,000 $2,500

GRUEN, 17 jewels, rope style bezel with diamonds
14k...$250 $300 $375

GRUEN, 17J., jump 24 hour, c. 1970
s. steel $100 $130 $175

GRUEN, 17J., center sec., cal.n510, waterproof, c. 1960
base metal.................................. $50 $60 $75

GRUEN, 17 jewels, day-date-month, c. 1948
s. steel.....................................$150 $175 $225

GRUEN, 17J., alarm, date, c. 1964
s. steel $125 $150 $175

GRUEN, 17 jewels, veri thin model, fancy lugs
14k $250 $300 $350

GRUEN, 17J., mystery dial, cal#215, ca.1965
gold filled................................. $200 $250 $300

GRUEN, 17J., veri thin model, fancy lugs, 24 hr. dial
14k $225 $300 $400

GRUEN, 17J., **Airflight**, jumping hours, c. 1960
gold filled................................. $235 $300 $375

GRUEN, 17J., engraved case, cal.117, c. 1929
14k(w)................................... $250 $325 $375

GRUEN, 15J., cushion, luminous dial, c. 1930s
gold filled.................................$85 $95 $150

GRUEN, 15-17J., barrel shaped, Ca. 1939
gold filled............................... $100 $150 $175

GRUEN, 17J., veri-thin, fancy bezel, Ca. 1948
gold filled................................ $125 $150 $175

GRUEN, 15-17J., RF# 544, Ca. 1949
gold filled............................... $125 $150 $175

GRUEN, 17J., fluted center lugs, cal.343, c. 1936
gold filled............................ $100 $125 $150

GRUEN, 17J., nurse style double dial, ca.1937
s. steel $225 $275 $350

E. GUBELIN, 17 jewels, chronog. 3 reg., Valj.72, c. 1950
18k $1,000 $1,100 $1,200

E. GUBELIN, 19 jewels, chronog., day-date-month
18k $1,250 $1,500 $1,800

E. GUBELIN, 19J., chronog.by Valjoux, waterpf, 3 reg.
18k $1,200 $1,300 $1,500

E. GUBELIN, 29 jewels, min. repeater
18k C&B $25,000 $30,000 $35,000

E. GUBELIN, 25J., ipso-matic, triple date, moon ph.
14k & steel back $1,250 $1,350 $1,550
18k.......................................$2,000 $2,250 $2,500

E. GUBELIN, 15J., triple date, c.1945
s. steel....................................$300 $350 $400

E. GUBELIN, 19 jewels, 18k case, 14k band
18k & 14k C&B......................$600 $700 $900

E. GUBELIN, 17J., ca. 1970s
18k $200 $250 $300

E. GUBELIN,17J., cal#F690, center sec., ca. 1950s
18k $250 $300 $350
s. steel $100 $125 $175

E. GUBELIN, 17J., ca. 1952
s. steel $150 $200 $250

E. GUBELIN, 25J., ipso-matic, c.1955
14k $300 $350 $400

E. GUBELIN, 17J., alarm, ipso-vox, c.1960
18k.......................................$1,000 $1,100 $1,300

E. GUBELIN, 17J., ipso-vox, date, alarm, c.1960
s. steel...................................$350 $400 $450

E. GUBELIN, 17J., carved lugs, center sec., c.1944
18k.......................................$400 $450 $500

E. GUBELIN, 17J., 8 baguettes, 3 diamonds, c.1948
platinum $500 $550 $600

E. GUBELIN, 15J., **back wind duoplan**, c.1935
s. steel...................................$300 $350 $400

E. GUBELIN, 15J., ca. 1935
18k(W).....................................$700 $800 $900

E. GUBELIN, 19 J., hunter style pop-up lid, c. 1930
18k (w).................................$4,500 $5,500 $6,000

E. GUBELIN, 17jewels, jumping hr., c. 1924
14k $8,000 $9,000 $10,000

E. GUBELIN, 25J., triple date, moon phase, c. 1950
18k $2,500 $3,000 $3,500

E. GUBELIN, triple date & moon ph., by Audemars-Piguet,
Ca. 1930
18k ....,...$30,000 $35,000 $40,000

E. GUBELIN, 19 jewels, fancy lugs, center sec.
18k...$500 $600 $700

E. GUBELIN, 19 jewels, fancy hooded lugs
18k...$800 $1,000 $1,200

E. GUBELIN, 19 jewels, curvex, 2 tone
18k..$1,000 $1,100 $1,200

E. GUBELIN, 19J., center sec., flared case, c. 1950
18k...$350 $450 $550

E. GUBELIN, 21 jewels, center sec.
18k...$300 $350 $425

E. GUBELIN, 17 jewels, by Vacheron & Constantin
18k $2,000 $2,500 $3,000

E. GUBELIN, 18 jewels, curved, stepped case, c. 1940
18k $900 $1,000 $1,200

GUINAND, 17J., chronog., day-date-month, 3 reg.
18k $800 $900 $1,100
s. steel $350 $400 $475

GUINAND, 17 J., chronog., triple date, moon phase
18k $1,000 $1,200 $1,400
s. steel $600 $700 $800

HAFIS, 15J., center sec., cushion style
gold plate $50 $60 $75

HAFIS, 15J., luminous dial
gold plate..................................$50 $60 $75

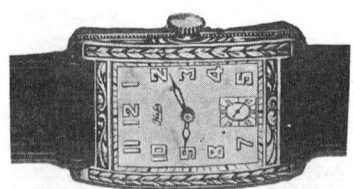

HAFIS, 15J., engraved case
gold plate..................................$70 $80 $95
14k..$150 $200 $275

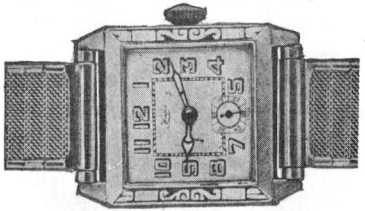

HAFIS, 15J., engraved case
gold plate..................................$50 $60 $75

HAFIS, 15J., engraved case
gold plate..................................$60 $70 $85

HAFIS, 15J., engraved case
gold plate..................................$50 $60 $75

HAFIS, 15J., engraved case
gold plate $60 $70 $85

HAFIS, 15J., engraved case
gold plate $60 $70 $85

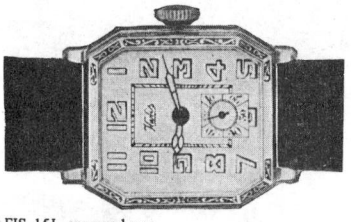

HAFIS, 15J., engraved case
gold plate $60 $70 $85

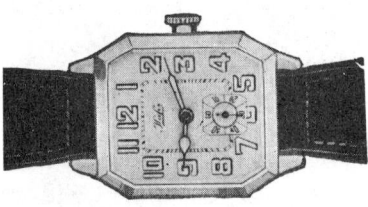

HAFIS, 15J., luminous dial
gold plate $50 $55 $65

HAFIS, 15J., curved case
gold plate $50 $60 $75
14k $125 $150 $200

HAFIS, 17 jewels, carved lugs
14k $150 $175 $200

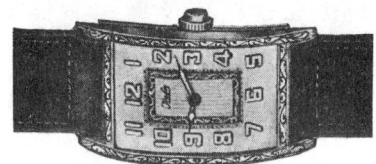

HAFIS, 15J., engraved case, curved
gold plate $60 $70 $85
14k $150 $175 $200

HAFIS, 17J., 'Queen Druga', 52 diamonds
Platinum....................................$350 $400 $450

HAFIS, 15J., "Queen Marie", 26 diamonds
18k $200 $250 $300

HAFIS, 15J., "Queen Charlotte", 22 diamonds
18k $175 $200 $225

HALLMARK, 17 jewels, day-date-month, auto wind
gold filled $150 $175 $200

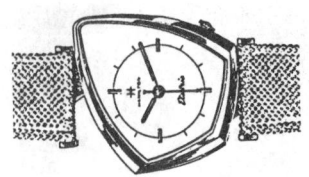

HAMILTON, electric, "Altair"
gold filled...............................$800 $1,000 $1,300

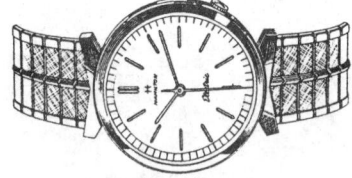

HAMILTON, electric, "Aquatel"
gold filled...............................$100 $125 $200

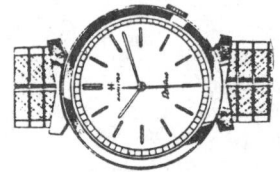

HAMILTON, electric, "Aquatel B"
gold filled...............................$100 $125 $200

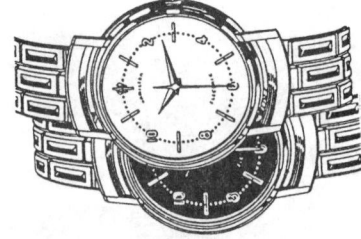

HAMILTON, electric, "Atlantis"
gold filled...............................$100 $125 $200

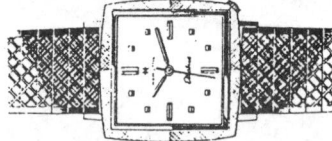

HAMILTON, electric, "Centaur"
gold filled...............................$125 $175 $225

HAMILTON, electric, "Clearview" , **display back**
gold filled...............................$200 $250 $300

HAMILTON, electric, "Converta I", 18k bezel & s.s. case
18k &S.S. $175 $225 $275

HAMILTON, electric, "Converta II", 14k bezel & s.s. case
14k &S.S. $150 $175 $225

HAMILTON, electric, "Converta III", 10k bezel & s.s. case
10k &S.S. $100 $125 $200

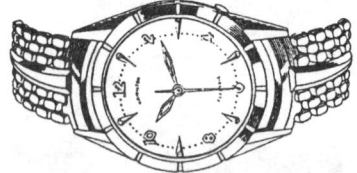

HAMILTON, electric, "Converta IV", S.S. bezel & case
s. steel $100 $125 $150

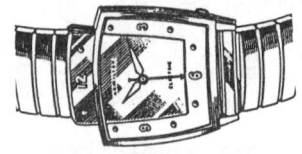

HAMILTON, electric, "Everest"
gold filled $175 $225 $275

HAMILTON, electric, "Everest II"
gold filled $125 $165 $235

HAMILTON, electric, "Gemini" Ca.1963
gold filled...................................$85 $100 $150

HAMILTON, electric, "Gemini II" Ca.1965
gold filled...................................$85 $100 $150

HAMILTON, electric, "Lord Lancaster E," 12 diamonds
14k $450 $500 $600

HAMILTON, electric, "Lord Lancaster J," 8 diamonds
gold filled...................................$225 $275 $350

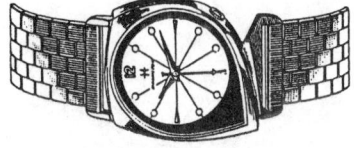

HAMILTON, electric, "Meteor," c. 1959
gold filled...................................$275 $325 $400

HAMILTON, electric, "Nautilus" 200, single lugs
14k $200 $250 $325

HAMILTON, electric, "Nautilus" 201
14k $175 $200 $225

HAMILTON, electric, "Nautilus" 202
14k $225 $250 $275

HAMILTON, electric, "Nautilus" 400
gold filled $80 $90 $100

HAMILTON, electric, "Nautilus" 401
gold filled $80 $90 $100

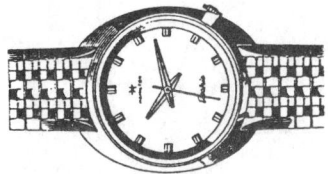

HAMILTON, electric, "Nautilus" 402
gold filled $80 $90 $100

HAMILTON, electric, "Nautilus" 403, pocket watch
gold filled $150 $200 $275

HAMILTON, electric, "Nautilus" 404
gold filled.....................................$80 $90 $100

HAMILTON, electric, "Nautilus" 405
gold filled.....................................$60 $70 $80

HAMILTON, electric, "Nautilus" 450, gold filled bezel
gold filled.................................$60 $70 $80

HAMILTON, electric, "Nautilus" 500
s. steel $60 $70 $80

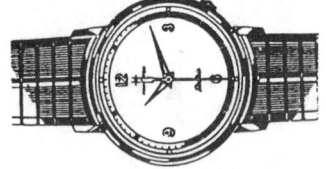

HAMILTON, electric, "Nautilus" 501
s. steel $60 $70 $80

HAMILTON, electric, "Nautilus" 502
s. steel $60 $70 $80

HAMILTON, electric, "Nautilus" 503
s. steel $60 $70 $80

HAMILTON, electric, "Nautilus" 506
s. steel $70 $80 $90

HAMILTON, electric, "Nautilus" 507
s. steel $70 $80 $90

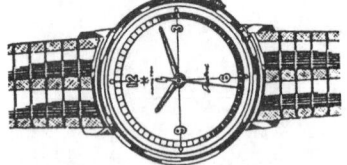

HAMILTON, electric, "Nautilus" 508
s. steel $60 $70 $80

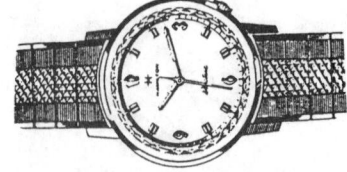

HAMILTON, electric, "Nautilus" 509
s. steel $70 $80 $90

HAMILTON, electric, "Nautilus" 600
gold plate $60 $70 $80

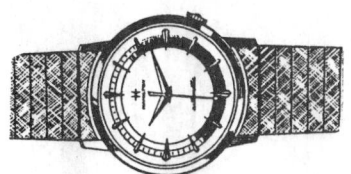

HAMILTON, electric, "Nautilus" 601
gold plate $60 $70 $80

HAMILTON, electric, "Nautilus" 602
gold plate $60 $70 $80

HAMILTON, electric, "Nautilus" 604
gold plate $70 $80 $90

HAMILTON, electric, "Nautilus" 605
gold plate $60 $70 $80

HAMILTON, electric, "Pacer," 2 tone
14k $700 $950 $1,100
gold filled...............................$275 $300 $350

HAMILTON, electric, "Pegasus", engraved bezel
gold filled $100 $135 $200

HAMILTON, electric, "Polaris"
14k $300 $350 $400

HAMILTON, electric,"Polaris", diamond dial
14k $400 $450 $500

HAMILTON, electric,"Polaris II"
14k $300 $350 $400

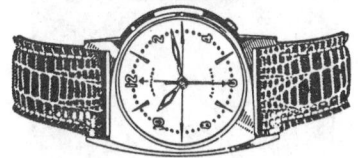

HAMILTON, electric, "Regulus"
s. steel $200 $300 $400

HAMILTON, electric, "Regulus" II
s. steel $80 $90 $125

HAMILTON, electric, "R. R. Special"
model#52 =10k GF case.........$150 $200 $250
model#51 =GF bezel $100 $150 $200
model#50 =s. steel....................$90 $125 $150

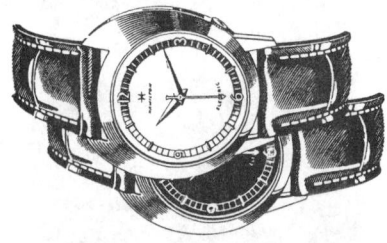

HAMILTON, electric, "Saturn"
gold filled...............................$175 $225 $300

HAMILTON, electric, "Savitar"
14k $350 $400 $450

HAMILTON, electric, "Savitar 11", ca.1966
gold filled...............................$175 $200 $250

HAMILTON, electric, "Sea-Lectric I", GF bezel
s. steel $100 $125 $175

HAMILTON, electric, "Sea-Lectric II"
s. steel $100 $125 $150

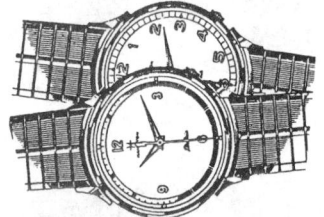

HAMILTON, electric, "Skip Jack"
s. steel $70 $80 $100

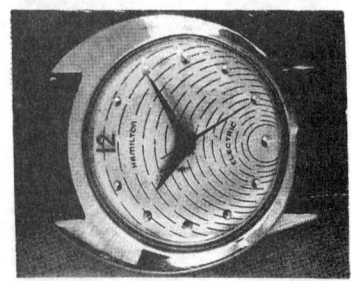

HAMILTON, electric, "Spectra"
18k **Rose gold** $1,000 $1,100 $1,250
14k $550 $650 $750

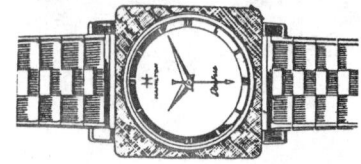

HAMILTON, electric, "Spectra" II
gold filled $100 $125 $175

HAMILTON, electric, "Summit"
14k $150 $175 $225

HAMILTON, electric, "Summit" II
gold filled.............................. $125 $150 $200

HAMILTON, electric, "Taurus"
gold filled.............................. $100 $125 $175

HAMILTON, electric, "Titan"
gold filled.............................. $100 $125 $175

HAMILTON, electric, "Titan II"
gold filled.............................. $125 $150 $200

🕐 Some grades are not included. Their values can be determined by comparing with similar age, size, metal content, style, grades, or models such as time only, chronograph, repeater etc. listed.

HAMILTON, electric, "Titan III"
gold filled.............................. $125 $150 $200

HAMILTON, electric, "Titan IV-B"
14kC&B.................................. $350 $400 $500

HAMILTON, electric, "Uranus"
gold filled.............................. $125 $150 $175

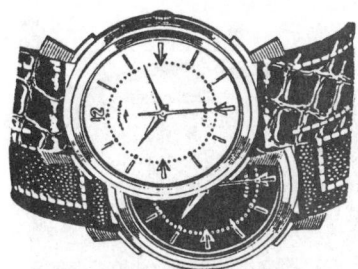

HAMILTON, electric, "Van Horn", Ca.1957
14k $200 $250 $350
14k +diam. dial...................... $250 $300 $400

HAMILTON, electric, Vantage , ca.1959
gold filled.............................. $125 $150 $200

HAMILTON, electric, "Vega"
gold filled................................$325 $400 $475

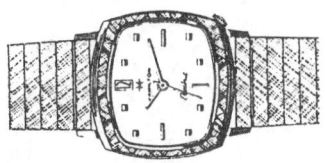

HAMILTON, electric, "Vela"
gold filled................................$100 $125 $175

HAMILTON electric, "Ventura"
18k $1,500 $1,700 $2,000
14k $1,000 $1,200 $1,400

HAMILTON electric, "Ventura", 6 diamond dial
14K..$1,100 $1,250 $1,450

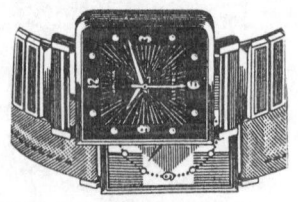

HAMILTON, electric,"Victor", ca.1958
gold filled................................$125 $150 $200

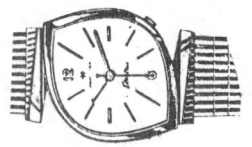

Hamilton, electric, "Victor II"
gold filled................................$150 $200 $250

HAMILTON, 17 jewels, "Seckron," dual dial, c. 1935
gold filled................................$900 $1,000 $1,250

HAMILTON, 17 jewels, dual dial
gold filled................................$900 $1,000 $1,250

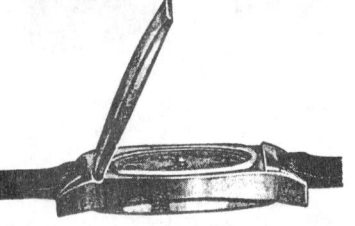

HAMILTON, "Flint Ridge," flip top is lug activated Grade
987=17J., Grade 979=19J.
14k $2,500 $2,800 $3,200

HAMILTON, 17 jewels, "Cross Country," c. 1962
14k $250 $300 $400
gold filled................................$150 $200 $250

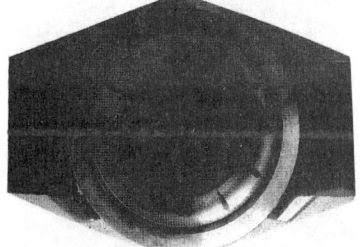

HAMILTON, 17J., "Transcontinental," auto-wind, Ca. 1963
14k $350 $400 $500
gold filled................................$175 $225 $300

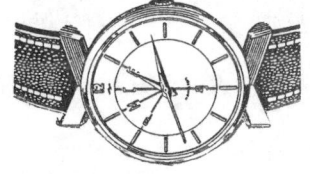

HAMILTON, Golden Tempus, 18J., time zones, Ca. 1961
14k $400 $450 $550
14k +diamonds $450 $500 $650

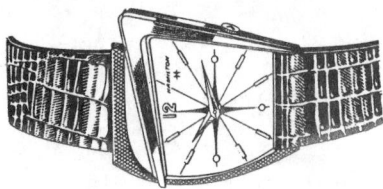

HAMILTON, 22J., above Flight I =14k MARKERS & # 12
14k case $1,600 $2,000 $2,500

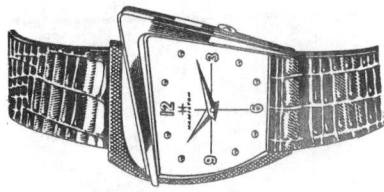

HAMILTON, 22J., above Flight II =14k dots & #s 12,3,6,9
gold filled case.....................$700 $850 $1,000

HAMILTON, 17J., chronog., by Valjoux cal.7733, c.1971
s. steel $275 $300 $350

HAMILTON, 17J., chronog., DATE, by Valjoux cal.7732,
s. steel $200 $250 $350

HAMILTON, 17J., chronog., screw -back,
s. steel $100 $125 $175

HAMILTON, 22J., auto-wind, Ca. 1970
gold filled $50 $65 $95
s. steel $40 $50 $80

HAMILTON, 17J., auto-wind,day date, c.1971
s. steel $40 $50 $75

HAMILTON, 17J., hinged lugs, "Tuxedo", cal., c.1940
gold filled................................$125 $150 $200

HAMILTON, 17J., hinged lugs, cal., c.1940
gold filled................................$125 $150 $200

HAMILTON, 17J., drivers, cal.907, c.1938
gold filled................................$125 $150 $200

HAMILTON,17J., drivers, **winds at 12**, ca. 1938
gold filled................................$400 $450 $500

HAMILTON, 19 jewels, "Otis," reversible, c. 1946
gold filled $1,000 $1,150 $1,300

HAMILTON, 19 J., "Coronado," black enamel bezel
14k $1,100 $1,300 $1,500

HAMILTON, 19 jewels, "Piping Rock," enamel bezel
14k yellow or white................$900 $1,000 $1,200

HAMILTON, 19 jewels, "Spur," enamel bezel
14k $2,000 $2,500 $3,000
14k(w)...................................$1,800 $2,200 $2,750

HAMILTON, 17J., enamel on white gold bezel & case yellow
14k $900 $1,000 $1,200

HAMILTON, 15J., "Oval", c. 1920s
14k $500 $575 $650

HAMILTON, 17 jewels, cal. 987, GJS, ca. 1932
gold filled................................ $175 $200 $225

HAMILTON, 17 jewels, "Alan"
gold filled.................................... $90 $125 $175

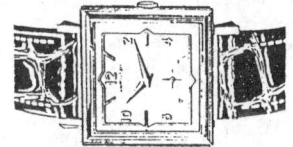

HAMILTON, 22 jewels, " Aldrich", Ca, 1961
14k $150 $185 $250

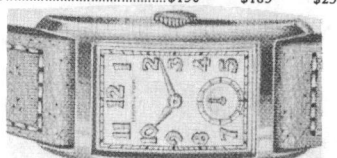

HAMILTON, 19 jewels, "Allison" , Ca. 1940
14k $300 $350 $450

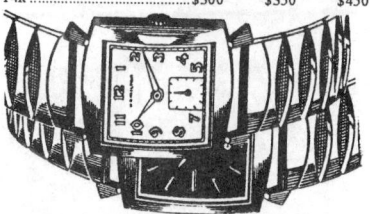

HAMILTON,17J., " Amherst", 14k markers
gold filled................................ $80 $90 $100

HAMILTON, 19 jewels, "Andrews"
14k $300 $375 $500

HAMILTON, 22J., " Ansley" , 14k markers
gold filled $80 $90 $100

HAMILTON, 17J., "Aqualine ", 14k markers, Ca. 1961
gold filled $55 $65 $85

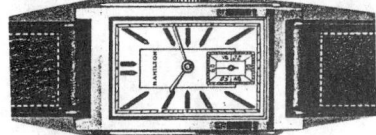

HAMILTON, 17J., " Ardmore", Ca. 1935
14k $300 $375 $475

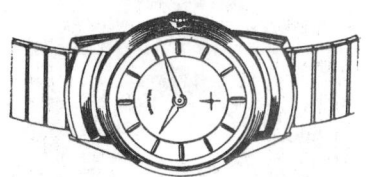

HAMILTON, 17J., " Arnold", Ca. 1961
gold plate $50 $60 $75

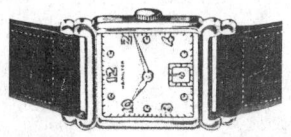

HAMILTON, 19J., " Ashley", Ca. 1951
gold plate $60 $75 $95

HAMILTON, 22J., "Attache", 14k markers, c.1961
gold filled..............................$150 $175 $225

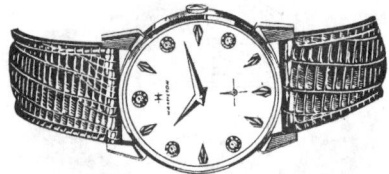

HAMILTON, 22J., " Baron II" , 5 diamond dial, c. 1961
14k $200 $225 $275

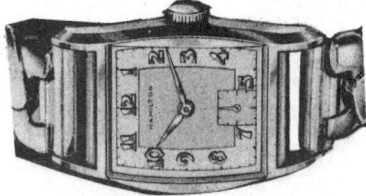

HAMILTON, 17J.," Austin ", c. 1951
gold filled.................................$100 $125 $175

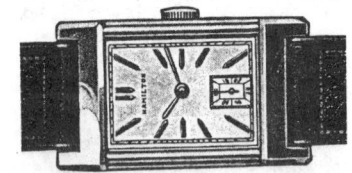

HAMILTON, 17J.," Bartley", Ca.1936
gold filled $100 $125 $175

HAMILTON, 17J, "Bagley," applied numbers, c. 1941
gold filled...............................$125 $150 $200

HAMILTON, 19J.,"Barton", tu tone dial, c.1951
14k $275 $350 $425

HAMILTON, 19J.," Bailey ", c.1951
gold filled................................$100 $125 $175

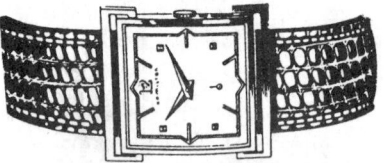

HAMILTON, 22J., "Baton", 14k markers
14k $250 $300 $350

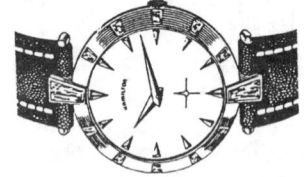

HAMILTON, 22J., " Barbizon", diam. bezel, Ca.1957
18k(w)......................................$500 $600 $800

HAMILTON,17J.,"Beldon", 2 tone dial, sealed case, c.1951
gold filled $80 $100 $150

HAMILTON, 22J., " Baron", 5 diam. dial, BIG lugs, c.1961
14k $225 $275 $325

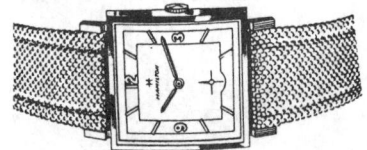

HAMILTON, 22J., " Bentley", 14k markers, c. 1961
gold filled $80 $100 $150

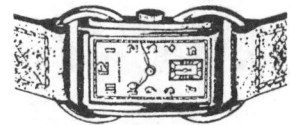

HAMILTON, 19J., " Bentley", 14k markers, Ca. 1938
14k $400 $450 $575

HAMILTON, 17J., " Benton", 14k markers, c. 1954
10k $200 $250 $300

HAMILTON, 17J., " Berkshire", 14k markers, Ca. 1952
gold filled...............................$100 $125 $175

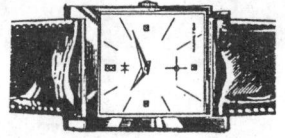

HAMILTON, 17J.," Blake ", 4 diam. dial, Ca.1961
gold filled...............................$125 $150 $200

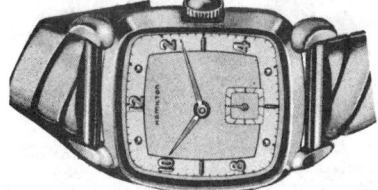

HAMILTON, 17-21J.," Blake ", c.1951
gold filled...............................$90 $100 $150

HAMILTON, 17J., " Boatswain", center sec., c. 1961
gold plate $50 $60 $75

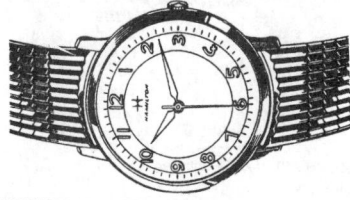

HAMILTON, 17J., " Boatswain II" , c.1961
gold plate $60 $70 $85

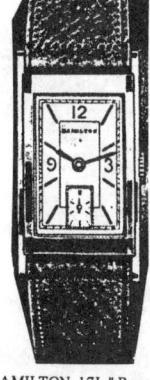

HAMILTON, 17J.," Boone ", Curved, Ca.1937
gold filled $100 $125 $175

HAMILTON, 19 jewels, "Boulton" , Ca. 1941
gold filled $100 $125 $175

HAMILTON, 22J., " Boulton II" , 14k markers, c. 1961
gold filled $90 $100 $150

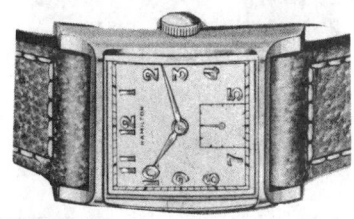

HAMILTON, 17J.,"Boyd", c.1951
gold filled $100 $135 $185

HAMILTON, 22J., "Bradford B" , 14k markers, c. 1961
14k $125 $150 $200

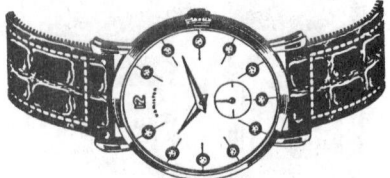

HAMILTON, 22J., "Bradford B" , **11 diam. dial,** c. 1961
14k $225 $250 $300

HAMILTON, 17J., "Brandon", swing lugs, c. 1951
gold filled................................$100 $125 $165

HAMILTON, 17 jewels, "Brandon", Ca. 1951
gold filled................................$100 $125 $175

HAMILTON, 19J.,"Brent ", **faceted** crystal, c.1951
gold filled................................$100 $135 $185

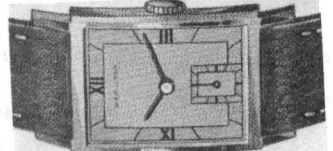

HAMILTON, 19 jewels, "Brock", c. 1941
14k $250 $300 $350

HAMILTON, 19 jewels, "Brock", c. 1951
14k $250 $300 $350

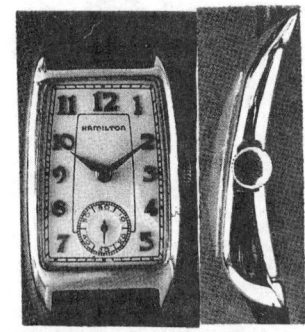

HAMILTON, 19J.," Brooke ", Curved, Ca.1951
gold filled................................$250 $300 $400

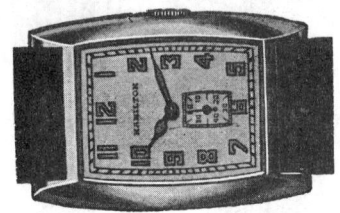

HAMILTON, 19 jewels, "Byrd"
18k $550 $650 $800
14k $400 $500 $650

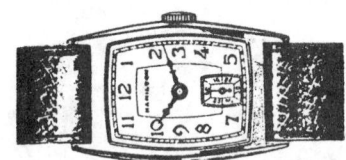

HAMILTON, 17J.,"Cabot", cal.960, Ca. 1938
gold filled $90 $100 $150

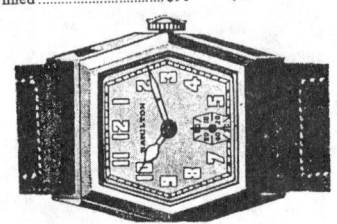

HAMILTON, 17J.,"Cambridge"
14k $450 $550 $700

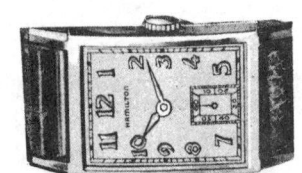

HAMILTON, 19J.," Cambridge ", c.1951
platinum...................................$700 $800 $1,000

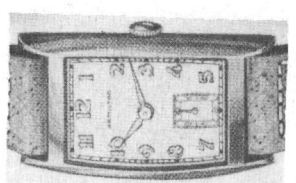

HAMILTON, 19 jewels, "Cameron" , c. 1941
14k $250 $300 $400

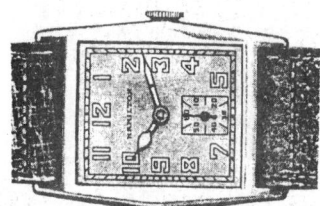

HAMILTON, 17J.,"Captain Rice"
14k $250 $300 $375

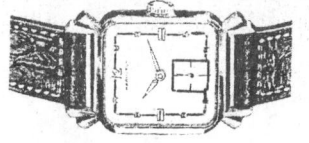

HAMILTON, 17J.," Carl ", Ca.1953
gold filled................................$90 $100 $135

HAMILTON, 17J.," Carlisle ", cal. 937, Ca.1937
gold filled................................$150 $200 $250

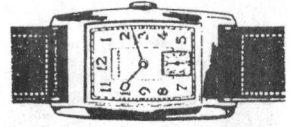

HAMILTON, 17J.," Carson ", Ca.1935
gold filled................................$125 $150 $175

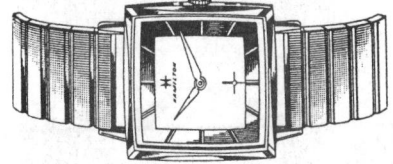

HAMILTON, 17J., " Carson", c. 1961
gold plate $80 $100 $125

HAMILTON, 17J.," Carlton ", c.1951
gold filled................................$100 $125 $165

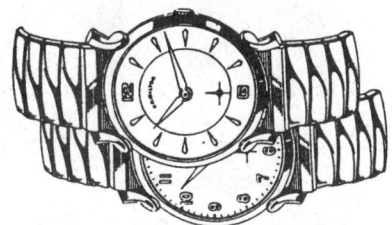

HAMILTON, 17J., " Carlyle", c. 1961
gold plate................................$50 $60 $75

HAMILTON, 17J., " Carteret"   14k markers
14k $175 $200 $250

HAMILTON, 19J.," Cedric ", c.1951
gold filled $100 $125 $165

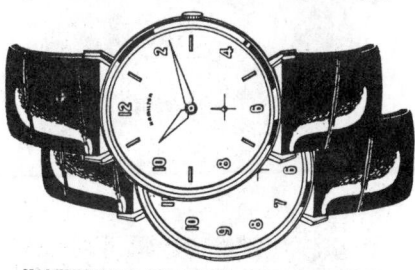

HAMILTON, 22J., "Chadwick ", 14k markers, c. 1961
14k $125 $150 $185

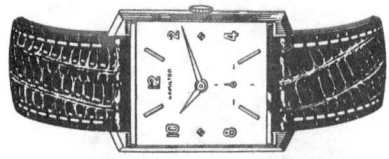

HAMILTON, 22J., "Chapman ", 14k markers, c. 1961
gold filled..............................$90 $100 $135

HAMILTON, 17J., " Chattam",Ca. 1953
gold filled..............................$100 $125 $175
14k $250 $300 $375

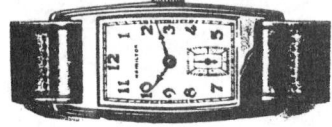

HAMILTON, 17J., " Clark", Ca. 1937
gold filled..............................$150 $200 $275

HAMILTON, 18J., "Clearview ", 14k markers, c. 1961
14k $175 $200 $235

HAMILTON, 17J.," Clinton ", c.1951
s. steel $50 $60 $75

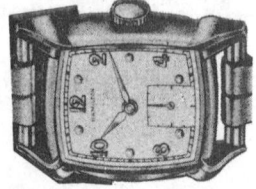

HAMILTON, 17J.," Clyde ", c.1951
gold filled..............................$90 $115 $150

HAMILTON, 17J., "Coburn ", c. 1961
gold plate $60 $70 $85

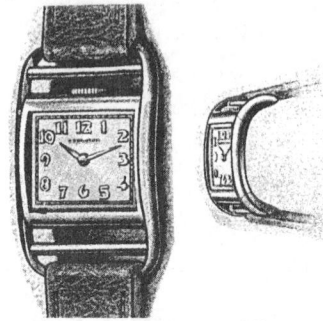

HAMILTON, 17J., "Contour ", c. 1937
gold filled $350 $400 $450

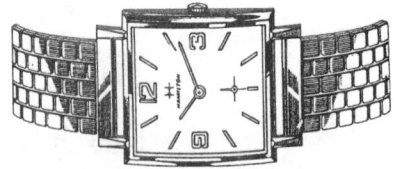

HAMILTON, 17J., "Conway ", c. 1961
gold plate $70 $85 $120

HAMILTON, 17J., " Cordell", Ca. 1961
14k C&B................................$275 $300 $325

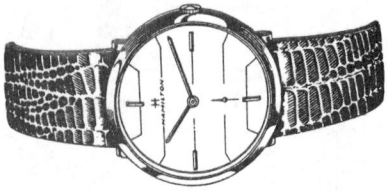

HAMILTON, 22J., "Corvet ", 14k markers, c. 1961
gold filled $100 $125 $165

HAMILTON, 17J., "Courtney", 14k markers, c. 1961
gold filled..............................$80 $90 $125

HAMILTON, 22J., "Courtney", 6 diamond dial, c. 1961
14k $200 $225 $250

HAMILTON, 17J.," Craig ", c.1951
gold filled..............................$90 $100 $135

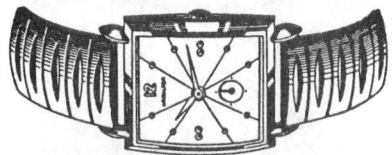

HAMILTON, 22J., " Cullen", 14k markers, c. 1961
gold filled..............................$80 $90 $100

HAMILTON, 22J., " Curtiss", Ca. 1956
14k $200 $250 $350

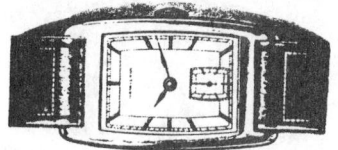

HAMILTON, 19J., " Custer", Ca. 1937
14k $200 $250 $350

HAMILTON, 17J., "Darrell", cal#747, c. 1951
gold filled..............................$120 $160 $180

HAMILTON, 17J., "Dawson ", c. 1961
gold filled..............................$80 $90 $110

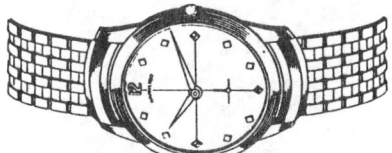

HAMILTON, 17J., "Dean ", c. 1961
gold filled..............................$50 $60 $75

HAMILTON, 17J., "Deauville ", c. 1961
gold plate..............................$60 $70 $80

HAMILTON, 17J.," Dennis ", Ca.1961
14k $150 $175 $200

HAMILTON, 17J.," Dennis ", Ca.1951
gold filled..............................$100 $150 $200

HAMILTON, 17J.," Dewitt ", c.1951
gold filled..............................$100 $125 $150

HAMILTON, 17J., " Dexter", c. 1961
gold plate $80 $90 $100

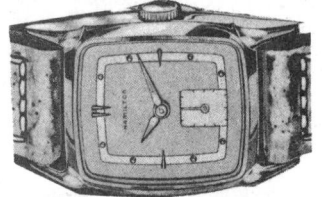

HAMILTON, 17J.," Dexter ", c.1951
gold filled..............................$100 $125 $175

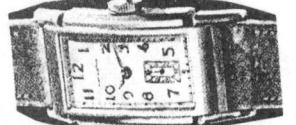

HAMILTON, 17J.," Dickens ", Ca.1937
Note: Also see **Gilman** = 14k (**look-a-like**)
gold filled..............................$175 $200 $250

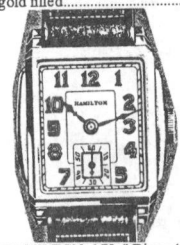

HAMILTON, 17J.," Dixon ", Ca.1937
gold filled..............................$100 $135 $200

HAMILTON, 17 jewels, "Dodson" , c. 1937
gold filled..............................$150 $175 $225

HAMILTON, 19J.," Donald ", c.1951
14k $275 $325 $400

HAMILTON, 17J.," Donavan ", center lugs
14k $350 $450 $550

HAMILTON, 22J.," Donavan II", Ca.1961
14k $200 $225 $275

HAMILTON, 17J.," Dorsey ", Ca.1937
14k $200 $250 $325

HAMILTON, 17J.," Doublet ", Ca.1961
14k $125 $150 $200

HAMILTON, 17J.," Drake ", Ca.1951
gold filled $100 $125 $175

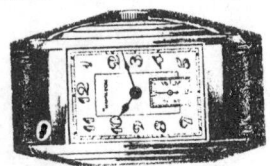

HAMILTON, 17J.," Drake ", Ca.1935
gold filled $125 $150 $195

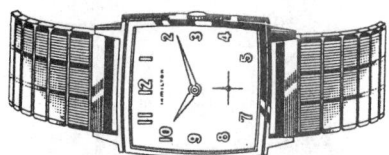

HAMILTON, 17J., "Drummond ", 14k markers, c. 1961
gold filled..............................$75 $85 $120

HAMILTON, 17J.," Dunham ", c.1951
gold filled..............................$100 $125 $175

HAMILTON, 19 jewels, "Dunkirk", c. 1941
14k $250 $300 $400

HAMILTON, 17 jewels, "Dyson", c. 1951
gold filled..............................$95 $125 $165

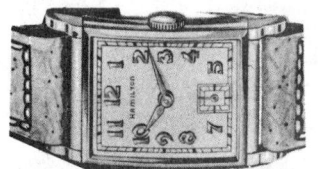

HAMILTON, 17J.," Eaton ", c.1951
gold filled..............................$100 $135 $200

HAMILTON, 17J.," Eliott ", Cal.980
gold filled..............................$100 $125 $150

HAMILTON, 17J.," Emery ", c.1951
gold filled $90 $100 $135

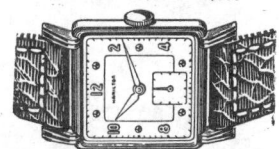

HAMILTON, 17 jewels, "Eric", c. 1951
gold filled $85 $95 $125

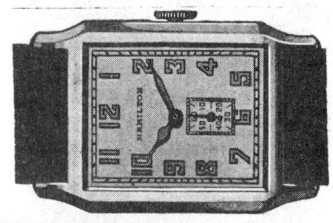

HAMILTON, 17 jewels, "Ericsson"
14k $275 $350 $450

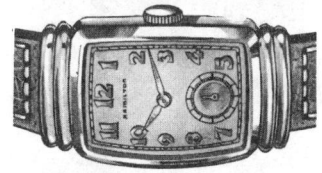

HAMILTON, 17 jewels, "Emerson", c. 1941
gold filled $100 $125 $175

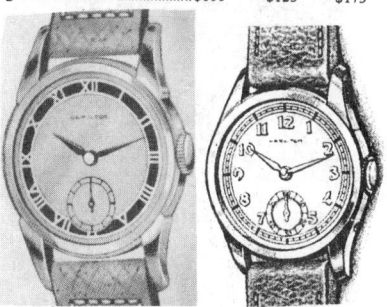

HAMILTON, 17 jewels, "Endicott", c. 1941
gold filled $80 $125 $150

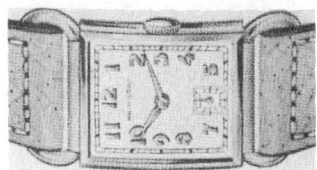

HAMILTON, 17 jewels, "Essex", c. 1941
gold filled $125 $150 $175

HAMILTON, 17J., " Farrell", 14k # s, c.1961
gold plate $60 $70 $80

HAMILTON, 17J., " First Mate", c.1961
gold plate $60 $70 $80

HAMILTON, 18J.,"Fleetwood ", c.1951
14k $125 $175 $200

HAMILTON, 17 jewels, "Forbes", c. 1951
gold filled...............................$100 $125 $175

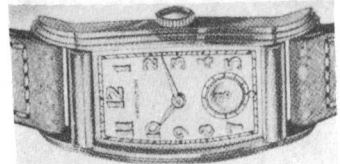

HAMILTON, 19 jewels, "Foster" , c. 1941
14k $325 $400 $475

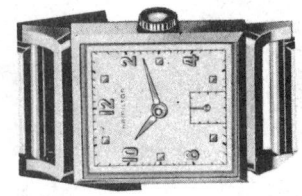

HAMILTON, 17J.," Franklin ", c.1951
gold filled $90 $120 $165

HAMILTON, 17J., " Gardner", c.1961
gold plate $60 $75 $90

HAMILTON, 17J.," Gary ", c.1951
gold filled $100 $125 $165

HAMILTON, 17J.," Gary ", fluted lugs, Ca.1951
gold filled $80 $95 $125

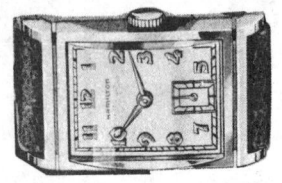

HAMILTON, 19J.," Gilbert ", c.1951
14k $225 $275 $350

🕐 Some grades are not included. Their values can be
determined by comparing with similar age, size, metal
content, style, grades, or models such as time only,
chronograph, repeater etc. listed.

HAMILTON, 19 jewels, "Gilman" , c. 1941
Note: Also see **Dickens** = *Gold Filled* (**look-a-like**)
14k $350 $400 $450

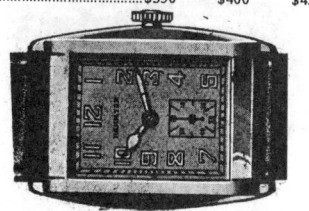

HAMILTON, 17J.,"Gladstone", cal.981, c.1951
gold filled................................$100 $125 $175

HAMILTON, 17J.," Glendale ", engraved case,
14K..$600 $750 $900

HAMILTON, 17J., " Glendon", c.1961
gold plate $70 $80 $90

HAMILTON, 17J.," Glenn ", c.1951
14k $200 $250 $300

HAMILTON, 19 jewels, "Glenn Curtis"
14k $300 $350 $450

HAMILTON, 18J., " Golden Tempus II", 14k #s, c.1961
gold filled $70 $80 $95

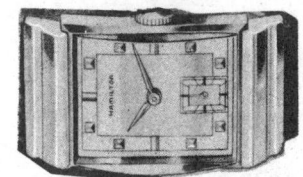

HAMILTON, 19J.," Gordon ", c.1951
18k $400 $500 $600

HAMILTON, 22J., " Gramercy", 14k #s, c.1961
gold filled $80 $90 $120

HAMILTON, 17 jewels, "Grant"
sterling....................................$200 $250 $300

HAMILTON, 17 jewels, "Greenwich"
gold filled $100 $125 $175

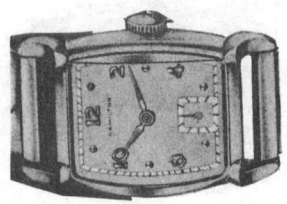

HAMILTON, 17J.," Grover ", c.1951
gold filled..................................$90 $100 $135

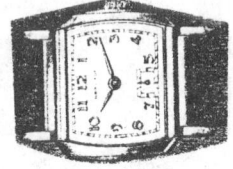

HAMILTON, 17J.," Harris ", Ca.1937
gold filled..................................$60 $80 $100

HAMILTON, 17J.," Hastings ", cal.987
gold filled..................................$125 $150 $200

HAMILTON, 19J.," Hayden ", c.1951
gold filled..................................$100 $125 $175

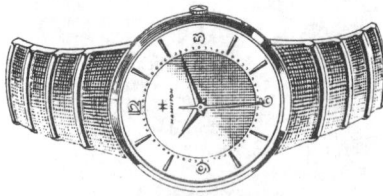

HAMILTON, 18J., " Holden", c.1961
gold filled..................................$70 $80 $90

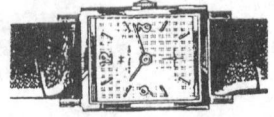

HAMILTON, 17J.," Huntley ", Ca.1961
gold filled..................................$100 $120 $150

HAMILTON, 17J., " Howard", on dial & movement
gold filled..................................$425 $525 $675

HAMILTON, 17J.," Jeffrey ", c.1951
gold filled..................................$100 $125 $175

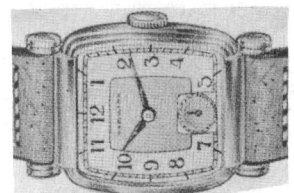

HAMILTON, 19 jewels, "Judson"
gold filled..................................$100 $125 $150

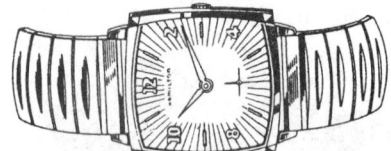

HAMILTON, 17J., " Keane", c.1961
gold plate..................................$60 $75 $100

HAMILTON, 19J.," Keith ", c.1951
14k..................................$250 $275 $350

HAMILTON, 22J.," Kevin ", hidden lugs, Ca.1951
14k..................................$350 $400 $500

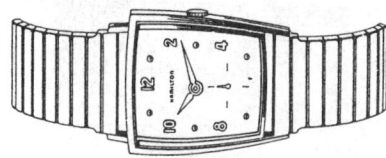

HAMILTON, 17J., " Khyber", 14k #s, c.1961
gold filled................................$120 $140 $165

HAMILTON, 17J.," Kinematic II ", Ca.1961
gold plate $60 $70 $95

HAMILTON, 19J.," Kirby ", c.1951
gold filled...................................$90 $100 $135

HAMILTON, 17J.," Kirk ", c.1951
14k $125 $150 $200

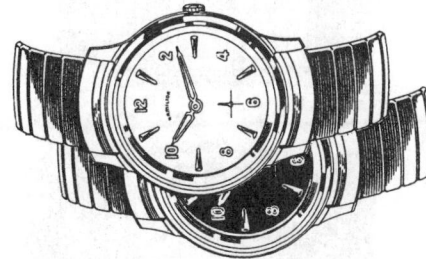

HAMILTON, 17J., " Lakeland", c.1961
s. steel $50 $60 $75

HAMILTON, 17J.,"Lambert ", c.1951
gold filled $90 $100 $135

HAMILTON, 17J.,(Lange is =14k), Langdon is =G. filled
14k $150 $175 $200
gold filled $75 $100 $150

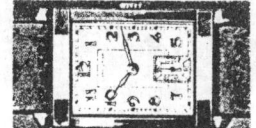

HAMILTON, 17J.," Langford ", Ca.1937
14k $200 $250 $350

HAMILTON, 17 jewels, "Langley"
18k $425 $525 $675

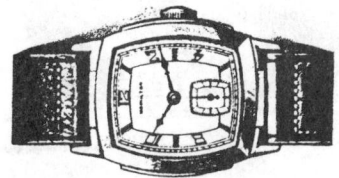

HAMILTON, 17J.," Lawrence ", Ca.1937
gold filled $100 $125 $165

⊕ Some grades are not included. Their values can be determined by comparing with similar age, size, metal content, style, grades, or models such as time only, chronograph, repeater etc. listed.

HAMILTON, 17 jewels, "Lee"
gold filled.................................$125 $150 $200

HAMILTON, 17 & 19 jewels, "Linwood" Ca. 1937
gold filled.................................$150 $200 $250

HAMILTON, 19 jewels, "Livingston"
14k $250 $300 $375

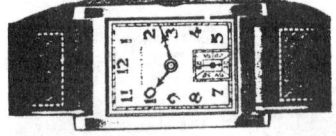

HAMILTON, 17J., " Lord Lancaster", Ca.1965
14k W.....................................$300 $400 $500

HAMILTON, 19J., " Lowell", Ca.1935
14k $200 $250 $300

HAMILTON, 17J., " Lowell", Ca.1961
gold plate $50 $60 $75

HAMILTON, 17 jewels, "Martin"
gold filled.................................$80 $95 $125

HAMILTON, 17J., "Masterpiece", Ca.1955
14k $175 $200 $275

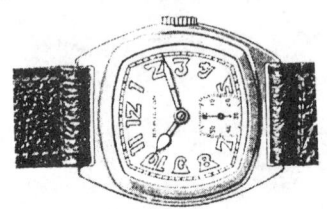

HAMILTON, 17J.,"Meadowbrook"
14k $600 $700 $800
18k $800 $900 $1,100
Platinum..................................$1,400 $1,600 $1,800

HAMILTON, 17J., " Merritt", Ca.1937
gold filled $100 $125 $150

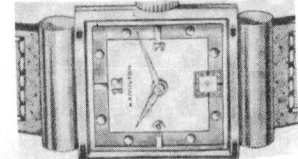

HAMILTON, 19 jewels, "Midas," hidden lugs , c. 1941
14k rose $250 $300 $375

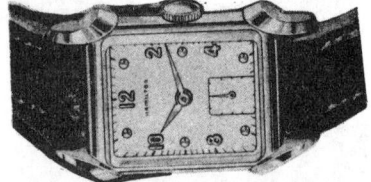

HAMILTON, 19J.," Milton ", c.1951
gold filled $100 $125 $165

HAMILTON, 17J., " Montclair", 14k #s, c.1961
gold filled...................................$75 $100 $125

HAMILTON, 17J.," Morley ", c.1937
gold filled...................................$90 $125 $150

HAMILTON, 17J., " Mount Vernon", Ca.1932
gold filled...................................$200 $250 $325

HAMILTON, 17J.," Myron ", c.1951
gold filled...................................$90 $125 $150

HAMILTON, 22J., " Newlin", 14k #s, c.1961
gold filled...................................$60 $75 $90

HAMILTON, 17J.," Neil ", c.1951
gold filled $80 $90 $100

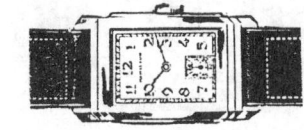

HAMILTON, 17J., " Nelson", Ca.1937
gold filled $100 $125 $175

HAMILTON, 17J., " Newton", cal.747, Ca.1951
gold filled $100 $125 $175

HAMILTON, 17J, Norde is 14k, Nordon,18J, is gold filled
14k $175 $200 $250
gold filled $75 $100 $125

HAMILTON, 19 jewels, "Norman" , c. 1951
14k $175 $225 $275
gold filled $100 $125 $175

HAMILTON, 17J., " Norman", 14k #s, c.1961
gold filled................................$70 $80 $95

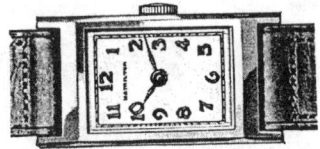

HAMILTON, 17 jewels, "Norfolk"
14k $450 $550 $700

HAMILTON, 22J., " Norton", 14k #s, c.1961
gold filled................................$100 $125 $150

HAMILTON, 19 jewels, "Oakmont"
14k $450 $550 $700

HAMILTON, 17J., "Orson ", c.1961
gold filled................................$50 $60 $75

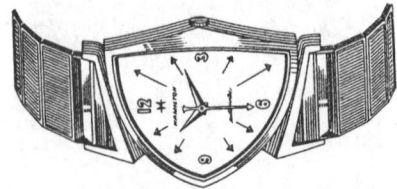

HAMILTON,17J., " Pacermatic", auto-wind,14k #s, c.1961
gold filled................................$500 $575 $700

HAMILTON, 19 jewels, "Paige", c. 1941
gold filled................................$100 $135 $175

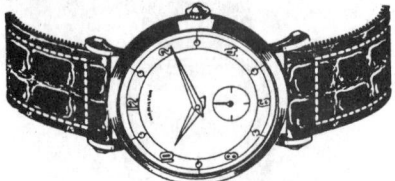

HAMILTON, 22J., " Parker B", 14k #s, c.1961
gold filled................................$100 $125 $150

HAMILTON, 17 jewels, "Perry"
gold filled................................$125 $150 $175

HAMILTON, 19J.," Perry ", c.1951
gold filled................................$85 $100 $135

HAMILTON, 22J., "Peyton ", c.1961
gold filled................................$60 $70 $80

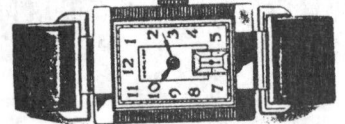

HAMILTON, 19 jewels, "Pierre" Ca. 1937
14k $400 $500 $600

HAMILTON, 17J.," Pinehurst "
14k $900 $1,000 $1,200

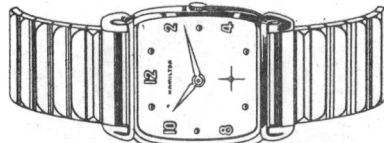

HAMILTON, 17J., " Prentice", c.1961
gold plate $60 $75 $100

HAMILTON, 17J., "Prescott ", Ca. 1937
gold filled..............................$100 $135 $175

HAMILTON, 17 jewels, "Putnam"
14k $400 $450 $525

HAMILTON, 17 jewels, "Putnam"
gold filled...............................$200 $275 $325

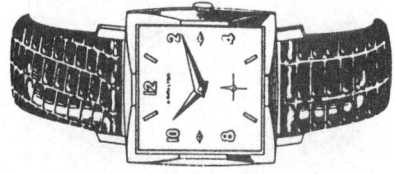

HAMILTON, 22J., " Radburn", 14k #s, c.1961
14k $175 $200 $225

HAMILTON, 17J.," Raleigh ", Plain
14k $300 $350 $425

HAMILTON, 17J., "Raleigh", Engraved
gold filled $150 $175 $225

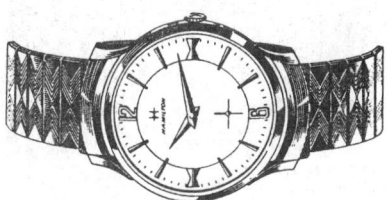

HAMILTON, 17J., " Ramsey", c.1961
gold plate $50 $60 $75

HAMILTON, 17 jewels, "Randolph" , c. 1937
gold filled $90 $125 $155

HAMILTON, 18J., " Randolph", 14k #s, c.1961
14k $150 $175 $200

HAMILTON, 17 jewels, "Reagan", c. 1941
gold filled $90 $125 $155

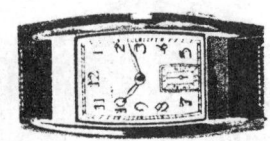

HAMILTON, 17J., " Richman", 14k #s, Ca.1935
18k $300 $350 $450

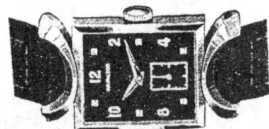

HAMILTON, 17J., " Robert", Ca.1953
14k $250 $300 $400

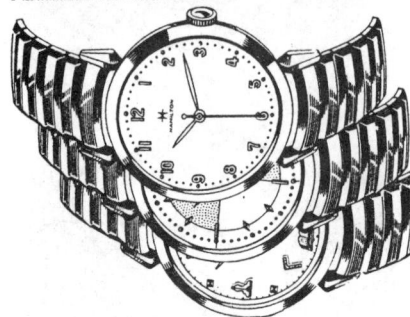

HAMILTON, 18J., " Rodney", 14k #s, Ca.1961
gold filled.................................$60 $70 $80

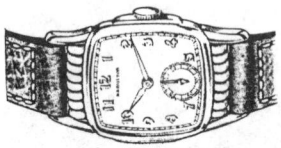

HAMILTON, 17J., "Roland", Ca.1937
gold filled.............................$100 $125 $175

HAMILTON, 22J., " Romanesque M", c.1961
14k $150 $175 $225

HAMILTON, 17J., "Romanesque N ", c.1961
gold filled.................................$50 $60 $75

HAMILTON, 22J., " Romanesque R", c.1961
gold filled $50 $60 $75

HAMILTON, 22J., "Romanesque S ", c.1961
gold filled $75 $80 $100

HAMILTON, 17J., " Romanesque T", c.1961
gold plate $75 $80 $100

HAMILTON, 19 jewels, "Ross" , c. 1941
gold filled $75 $95 $150

HAMILTON, 17 jewels, "Russell", hinged lugs , c. 1941
gold filled $125 $150 $175

HAMILTON, 19 jewels, "Rutledge" , c. 1941
platinum...................................$700 $800 $1,000

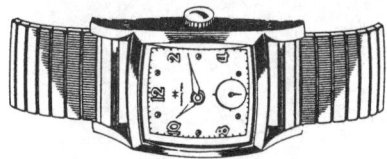

HAMILTON, 17J., " Sawyer", 14k #s, c.1961
gold filled...................................$80 $100 $120

HAMILTON, 17J.," Scott ", GJS, Ca..1935
gold filled...................................$70 $80 $100

HAMILTON, 19J.," Scott ", GJS, 982, Ca.1951
14k $300 $400 $500

HAMILTON, 17J., " Sea Breeze", c.1961
gold plate $60 $70 $80

HAMILTON, 17J., " Seabrook", c.1961
gold plate $60 $70 $80

🕐 Some grades are not included. Their values can be
determined by comparing with similar age, size, metal
content, style, grades, or models such as time only,
chronograph, repeater etc. listed.

HAMILTON, 17J., " Sea-cap ", c.1961
gold plate $70 $80 $90

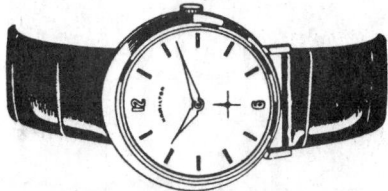

HAMILTON, 22J., " Sea Cliff ", 14k #s, c.1961
gold filled $80 $90 $100

HAMILTON, 17J., " Sea - crest", c.1961
s. steel $40 $50 $65

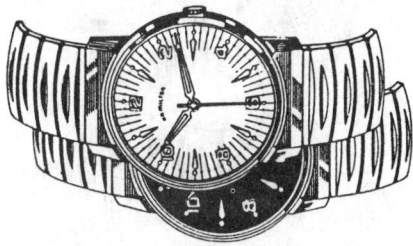

HAMILTON, 17J., " Sea- glo ", c.1961
s. steel $50 $60 $75

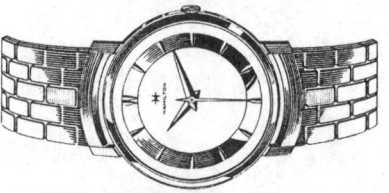

HAMILTON, 17J., " Sea - guard", c.1962
s. steel $50 $60 $75

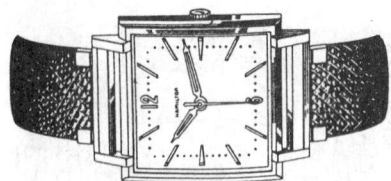

HAMILTON, 17J., " Sea - mate", c.1961
gold plate $60 $80 $100

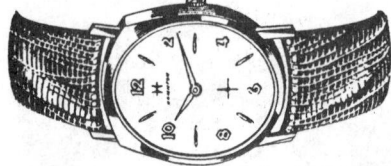

HAMILTON, 22J., " Sea Ranger" , 14K #s, c.1961
gold filled..................................$ 80 $90 $100

HAMILTON, 17J., " Sea Rover B", c.1961
s. steel ....,............................$60 $70 $80

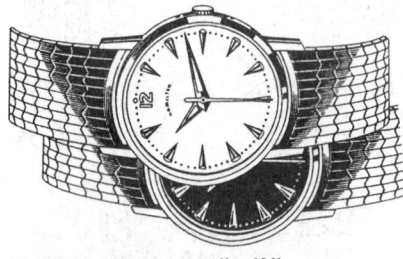

HAMILTON, 17J., " Sea- scape ", c.1961
gold plate $60 $70 $80

HAMILTON, 17J., " Sea- scout B ", c.1961
s. steel $70 $80 $90

HAMILTON, 17J., " Sea - skip", c.1962
s. steel $60 $70 $80

HAMILTON, 17J., " Seaview", 14k #s, c.1961
14k $125 $150 $175

HAMILTON, 18J.,"Sectometer B ", c.1951
gold filled $70 $80 $90

HAMILTON, 18J.," Sectometer C ", c.1951
14k $150 $175 $225

HAMILTON, 17J., " Sedgman", Ca. 1952
gold filled $65 $75 $95

HAMILTON, 17 jewels, "Sentinel," hack setting , Ca. 1941
gold filled.................................$100 $120 $140

HAMILTON, 18J., " Seville", c.1961
gold filled.................................$60 $75 $90

HAMILTON, 19J., " Sherwood", Ca.1935
14k $200 $250 $300

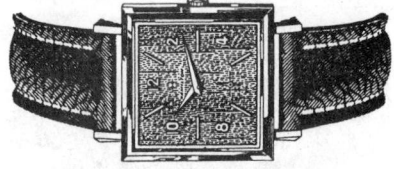

HAMILTON, 22J., " Sherwood M", 14k #s, wood dial,
American walnut wood dial, c.1961
14k $500 $600 $900

HAMILTON, 17J., " Sherwood N", 14k #s, wood dial,
Mexican Mahogany wood dial, c.1961
14k $500 $600 $850

HAMILTON, 22J.," Sherwood R", dial is made of wood,
(dial is American walnut) c.1961
14k $600 $700 $1,000

HAMILTON, 19J.," Sherwood", c.1951
gold filled $90 $100 $150

HAMILTON, 17J.," Sheryll ", small size, c.1951, also
matched styling to the Sherwood, ladies watch
gold filled $80 $90 $125

HAMILTON, 17 jewels, "Sidney" , c. 1941
gold filled $125 $175 $225

HAMILTON, 22J., " Sir Echo" ,14K #s, 6 diamond, c.1961
14k $225 $250 $300

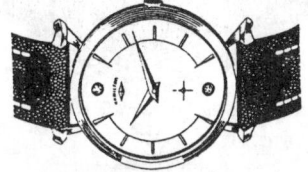

HAMILTON, 22J., " Sir Echo", 2 diamonds, 14K #s, c.1961
14k $200 $225 $250

HAMILTON, 22J., " Sir Echo" , 14K #s, c.1961
14k $150 $175 $200

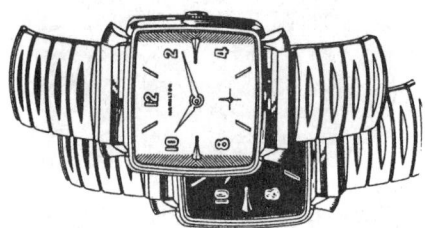

HAMILTON, 17J., "Sloane ", c.1961
gold plate $60 $70 $95

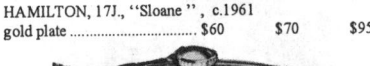

HAMILTON, 17J.," Spencer ", c.1951
10k $140 $160 $200

HAMILTON, 22J., " Stafford" , 14K #s, c.1961
14k $225 $250 $300

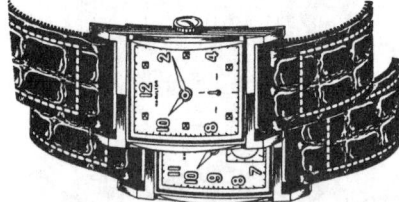

HAMILTON, 18 jewels, "Steeldon" , c. 1951
s. steel $50 $60 $95

HAMILTON, 17 jewels, "Stanford" , c. 1941
gold filled...................................$90 $100 $135

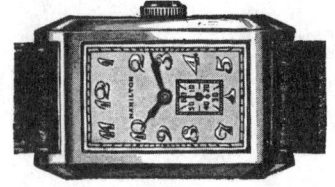

HAMILTON, 19 jewels, "Stanley"
gold filled $125 $165 $225

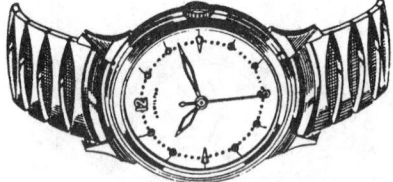

HAMILTON, 18J., " Stormking IV" , 14K #s, c.1961
gold filled $70 $80 $90

HAMILTON, 18J., " Stormking VI" , c.1961
gold filled $80 $90 $100

HAMILTON, 18J., " Stormking VII" , c.1961
gold filled $60 $70 $80

HAMILTON, 18J., " Stormking VIII" , 14K #s, c.1961
10k $100 $120 $150

HAMILTON, 17J., " Stormking IX", 14K #s, c.1961
14k $150 $175 $200

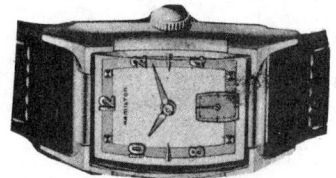

HAMILTON, 19J.," Stuart ", c.1951
gold filled................................$90 $100 $135

HAMILTON, 17-19 jewels, "Sutton", Ca. 1941
gold filled................................$125 $165 $200

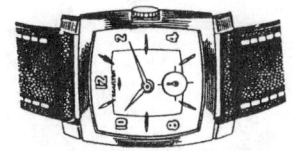

HAMILTON, 22 jewels, "Sutton II" , Ca. 1961
14k $150 $175 $200

HAMILTON, 17J., " Talbot", Ca.1937
gold filled................................$90 $120 $165

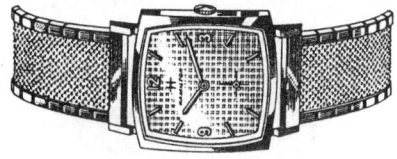

HAMILTON, 17J., " Talbot", c.1961
gold filled................................ $80 $100 $120

HAMILTON, 17J., " Taylor", Ca.1936
gold filled $150 $175 $200

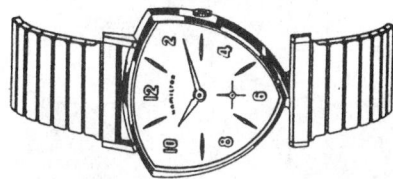

HAMILTON, 22J., " Thor", 14K #s, c.1961
gold filled $175 $200 $250

HAMILTON, 22J., " Trent", 14K #s, c.1961
gold filled $90 $100 $125

HAMILTON, 18J.," Todd ", c.1951
gold filled $75 $90 $110

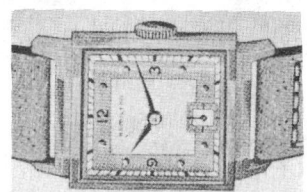

HAMILTON, 19 jewels, "Touraine", c. 1941
14k rose $200 $245 $295

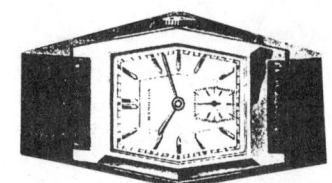

HAMILTON, 17J., " Turner", Ca.1937
gold filled $90 $120 $165

HAMILTON,22J., "Tuxedo B ", 44 diamonds,14K #s,
14k(w).. $350 $400 $525

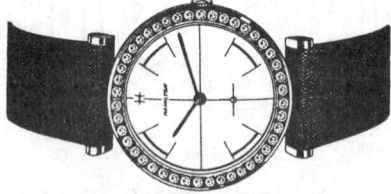

HAMILTON, 22J., " Tuxedo II " , 44 diamonds,14K #s,
14k(w).. $350 $400 $525

HAMILTON, 17J.," Raymon ", c.1951
s. steel $60 $70 $80

HAMILTON, 17J.," Vardon ", sealed. c.1951
s. steel $50 $60 $70

HAMILTON, 22J., " Valiant" , 14K #s, c.1961
gold filled............................... $150 $175 $200

HAMILTON, 17J., " Viking", c.1961
gold plate................................. $70 $80 $90

HAMILTON, 17J., " Viking II" , c.1961
gold plate................................. $60 $70 $80

HAMILTON, 17 jewels, "Vincent" , c. 1941
gold filled $125 $150 $175

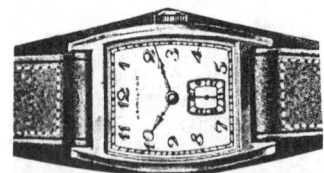

HAMILTON, 17 jewels, "Watson", Ca. 1930
gold filled $100 $125 $175

HAMILTON, 19 jewels, "Wayne", Ca. 1935
14k $200 $250 $300

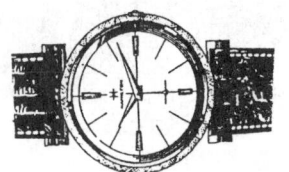

HAMILTON, 17 jewels, "Whitford", Ca. 1960
14k $175 $200 $250

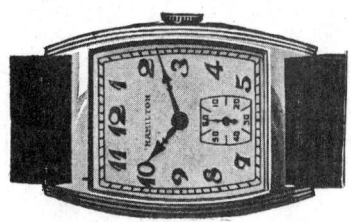

HAMILTON, 17 jewels, "Webster"
gold filled..............................$125 $150 $200

HAMILTON, 19J.," Wesley ", c.1951
14k $200 $250 $300

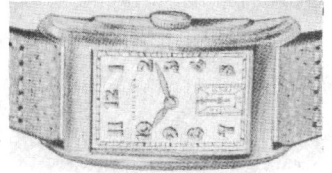

HAMILTON, 17 jewels, "Whitman" , c. 1941
gold filled...............................$100 $125 $150

HAMILTON, 17 jewels, "Wilson", flared, Ca. 1956
gold filled...............................$125 $150 $175

HAMILTON, 17 jewels, "Whitney"
gold filled.................... ★ ★ $200 $265 $350

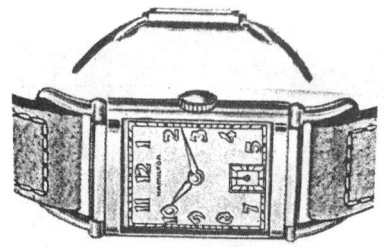

HAMILTON, 19 jewels, "Wilshire" , c. 1941
gold filled $125 $150 $175

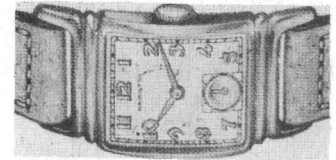

HAMILTON, 19 jewels, "Winthrop" , c. 1941
gold filled $100 $125 $150

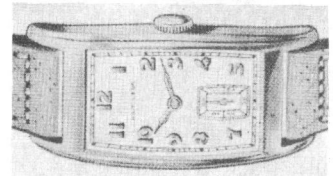

HAMILTON, 17 jewels, "Yorktown" , c. 1941
gold filled $100 $125 $175

HAMILTON,18J., cal.735 , c.1960
gold filled $100 $125 $165

HAMILTON,18J., cal.748 , c.1950
gold filled $85 $95 $125

HAMILTON,17J., pierced lugs
14k $200 $225 $250

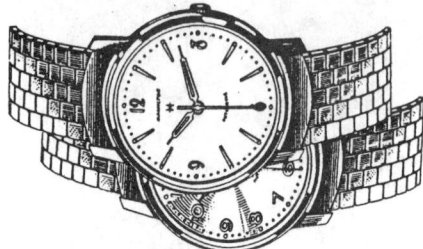

HAMILTON, 17 jewels, "Accumatic X"
s. steel $50 $60 $75

HAMILTON, 17 jewels, "Accumatic XI"
s. steel $50 $60 $75

HAMILTON, 17 jewels, "Accumatic A-575", date
s. steel $50 $60 $75

HAMILTON, 17 jewels, "Accumatic A-600"
gold plate $50 $60 $75

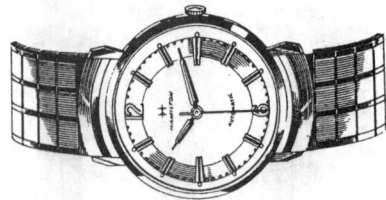

HAMILTON, 17 jewels, "Accumatic A-650"
gold plate $50 $60 $75

HAMILTON, 17 jewels, "Accumatic A-651"
gold plate $50 $60 $75

HAMILTON, 17 jewels, "Automatic K-203"
14k $150 $175 $200

HAMILTON, 17 jewels, "Automatic K-303"
10k $100 $125 $150

HAMILTON, 17 jewels, "Automatic K-304"
10k $100 $125 $150

Note: Hamilton acquired the Buren
Watch Factory of Switzerland in 1966
and adapted a ultra thin self-winding
movement for the **Thin-o-matic.**

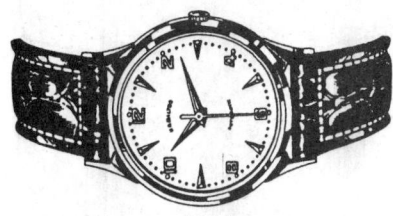

HAMILTON, 17 jewels, ''Automatic **K-414**''
gold filled.................................$60 $75 $95

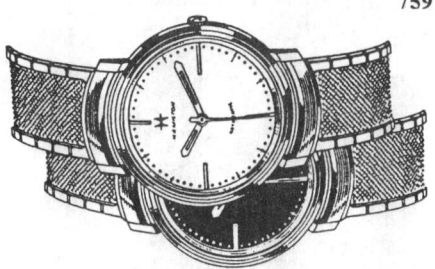

HAMILTON, 17 jewels, ''Automatic **K-417**''
gold filled.................................$60 $75 $95

HAMILTON, 17 jewels, ''Accumatic **VII**''
gold plate $50 $60 $75

HAMILTON, 17 jewels, ''Automatic **K-418**''
gold filled.................................$60 $75 $95

HAMILTON, 17 jewels, ''Automatic **K-415**''
gold filled.................................$60 $75 $95

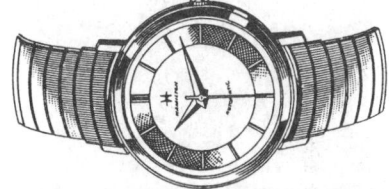

HAMILTON, 17 jewels, ''Automatic **K-419**''
gold filled.................................$60 $75 $95

HAMILTON, 17 jewels, ''Automatic **K-416**''
gold filled.................................$60 $75 $95

HAMILTON, 17 jewels, ''Automatic **K-420**''
gold filled.................................$60 $75 $95

HAMILTON, 17 jewels, ''**Kinematic II**''
gold plate $50 $60 $75

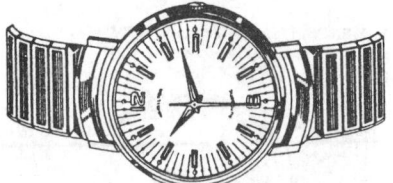

HAMILTON, 17 jewels, ''Automatic **K-458**''
gold filled.................................$60 $75 $95

🕐 Some grades are not included. Their values can be
determined by comparing with similar age, size, metal
content, style, grades, or models such as time only,
chronograph, repeater etc. listed.

HAMILTON, 17 jewels, "Automatic **K-459**"
gold filled..................................$60 $75 $95

HAMILTON, 17 jewels, "Automatic **K-650**"
gold plate..................................$50 $60 $75

HAMILTON, 17 jewels, "Automatic **K-460**"
gold filled..................................$60 $75 $95

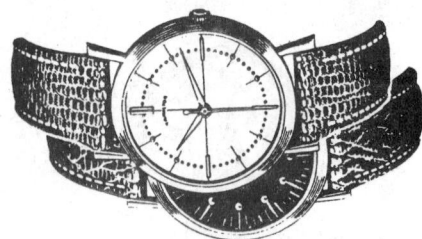

HAMILTON, 18 jewels, "Thincraft **II**"
gold filled..................................$60 $75 $95

HAMILTON, 17 jewels, "Automatic **K-475**", DATE
gold filled..................................$225 $275 $350

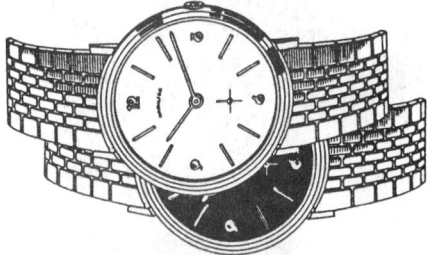

HAMILTON, 17 jewels, "Thinline **2000**"
14k..$125 $150 $185

HAMILTON, 17 jewels, "Automatic **K-503**" Ca.1962
s. steel.....................................$60 $75 $85

HAMILTON, 17 jewels, "Thinline **2001**"
14k..$125 $150 $185

HAMILTON, 17 jewels, "Automatic **K-507**"
s. steel.....................................$50 $60 $75

HAMILTON, 17 jewels, "Thinline **3000**"
10k..$100 $125 $150

HAMILTON, 17 jewels, "Thinline **4000**"
gold filled.................................$60　$70　$85

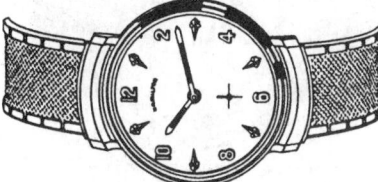

HAMILTON, 17 jewels, "Thinline **4001**"
gold filled.................................$60　$70　$85

HAMILTON, 17 jewels, "Thin-o-matic", **date**
gold plate ....$70　$80　$95

HAMILTON, 17 jewels, "Thin-o-matic", **Masterpiece**
14k ....$150　$175　$200

HAMILTON, 17 jewels, "Thin-o-matic **T-200**"
14k ....$125　$150　$200

HAMILTON, 17 jewels, "Thin-o-matic **T-201**", 6- diamonds
14k ....$150　$200　$250

HAMILTON, 17 jewels, "Thin-o-matic **T-201**"
14k ....$125　$150　$200

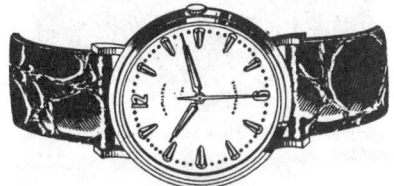

HAMILTON, 17 jewels, "Thin-o-matic **T-202**"
14k ....$125　$150　$200

HAMILTON, 17 jewels, "Thin-o-matic **T-300**"
10k ....$100　$125　$165

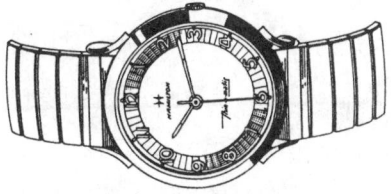

HAMILTON, 17 jewels, "Thin-o-matic **T-400**"
gold filled ....$60　$70　$95

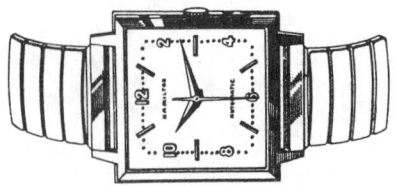

HAMILTON, 17 jewels, "Thin-o-matic **T-401**"
gold filled..................................$90 $100 $125

HAMILTON, 17 jewels, "Thin-o-matic **T-402**"
gold filled..................................$60 $70 $95

HAMILTON, 17 jewels, "Thin-o-matic **T-403**"
gold filled...............................$195 $225 $265

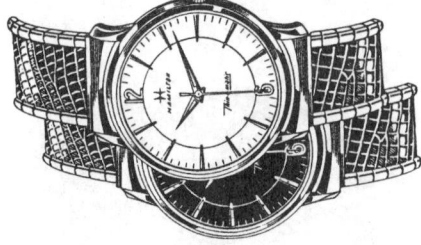

HAMILTON, 17 jewels, "Thin-o-matic **T-404**"
gold filled..................................$60 $70 $95

HAMILTON, 17 jewels, "Thin-o-matic **T-405**"
gold filled..................................$60 $70 $95

HAMILTON, 17 jewels, "Thin-o-matic **T-450**"
gold filled $60 $70 $95

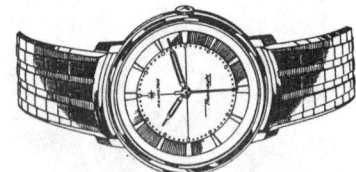

HAMILTON, 17 jewels, "Thin-o-matic **T-451**"
gold filled $60 $70 $95

HAMILTON, 17 jewels, "Thin-o-matic **T-475**"
gold filled $60 $70 $95

HAMILTON, 17 jewels, "Thin-o-matic **T-476**", date
gold filled $70 $80 $100

HAMILTON, 17 jewels, "Thin-o-matic **T-500**"
s. steel $50 $60 $75

🕐 Some grades are not included. Their values can be
determined by comparing with **similar** age, size, metal
content, style, grades, or models such as **time only**,
chronograph, repeater etc. listed.

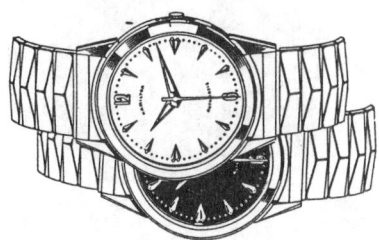

HAMILTON, 17 jewels, "Thin-o-matic **T-501**"
s. steel $50 $60 $75

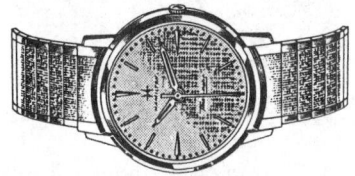

HAMILTON, 17 jewels, "Thin-o-matic **T-502**"
s. steel $50 $60 $75

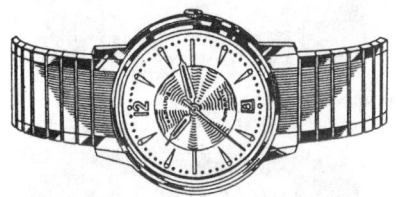

HAMILTON, 17 jewels, "Thin-o-matic **T-575**" date
s. steel $55 $65 $75

HAMILTON, 17 jewels, "Thin-o-matic **T-650**"
gold plate $50 $60 $75

HAMILTON, 17 jewels, "Thinline **5000**"
s. steel $50 $60 $75

HAMILTON, 17 jewels, "Cushion B"
gold filled $80 $100 $120

HAMILTON, 17 jewels, " Cushion " plain or engraved
14k $225 $250 $275
gold filled $80 $100 $125

HAMILTON, 17 jewels, tonneau engraved
14k $225 $275 $350
gold filled $85 $100 $125

HAMILTON, 17J.,"Tonneau" plain
14k $200 $250 $300
gold filled $100 $125 $165

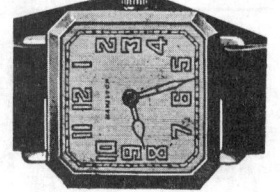

HAMILTON, 17J., " Square " cal.986 cut corner
gold filled $90 $100 $135
14k $150 $200 $250

HAMILTON, 17J., Square cut corner, engraved lugs
gold filled.................................$100 $125 $150

HAMILTON, 17 jewels, 2 tone dial, engraved fancy
14k $250 $300 $350
gold filled................................$100 $125 $150

HAMILTON, 17 jewels, 2 tone dial, aux. sec.
14k $200 $250 $295

HAMILTON, 17J., cal.986, c.1928
gold filled..................................$90 $100 $135

HAMILTON, 19J., gold jewel settings, cal.982, c.1943
platinum..................................$700 $800 $1,000

HAMILTON, 17J., cal.987, enamel on case, c.1930
gold filled $100 $125 $165

HAMILTON, 17J., GJS, Ca.1940
gold filled $125 $150 $185

HAMILTON, 17J., aux. sec.,
14k $225 $250 $300

HAMILTON, 19J., gold seal on movement, cal.982
14k $235 $265 $325

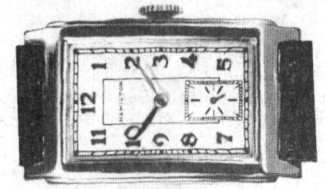

HAMILTON, 19J., cal.982, c.1938
14k $250 $300 $350

HAMILTON, 17J., curvex style, Ca. 1935
14k $300 $350 $400

HAMILTON,17J., cal.980 , c.1938
gold filled...............................$175 $225 $265

HAMILTON,17J., cal.989E , c.1936
gold filled...............................$90 $100 $135

HAMILTON,17J., cal. 989E, c.1938
gold filled...............................$90 $100 $135

HAMILTON, 17 jewels, engraved bezel, hinged back
14k(w).....................................$400 $500 $600

HAMILTON, 22J., "Viscount", cal.770, Ca.1959
14k $300 $350 $450

HAMILTON, 17J., cal. 980, Ca.1937
gold filled...............................$125 $150 $185

HAMILTON, 17J., Ca.1950
gold filled $125 $150 $185

HAMILTON, 17 jewels, hidden lugs
14k $325 $375 $425

HAMILTON, 17 jewels, long lugs
14k $225 $250 $285

HAMILTON, 17 jewels, engraved bezel, c. 1920
14k $300 $350 $400

HAMILTON, 17J, *Hamilton Illinois* on dial, sold by Hamilton & Illinois marked on case with Illinois mvt. (**crossover**).
gold filled $100 $150 $175

HAMILTON, 19 jewels
platinum.................................$650 $750 $850

HAMILTON, 19 jewels
platinum C&B.....................$1,100 $1,200 $1,300

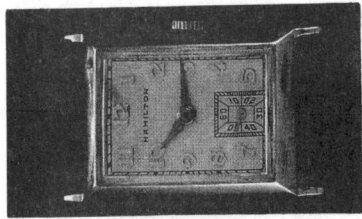

HAMILTON, 19 jewels, applied numbers
platinum.................................$700 $800 $1,000

HAMILTON, 17J., cal.987, Ca.1932
gold filled...............................$100 $125 $150

HAMILTON, 19J.,"bomb timer", c.1944
base metal $300 $350 $400

HAMILTON, 15 J., military frogman style, waterproof
(USN BU SHIPS on dial), canteen style
s. steel....................................$450 $525 $625

HAMILTON, 21 J., military issue, hack setting, c.1960s
base metal...............................$80 $95 $140

HAMILTON, 17-19 jewels, top hat, diamond dial
14k $800 $950 $1,100

HAMILTON, 17-19 jewels, Top Hat, diamond dial
14k...$800 $950 $1,100

HAMILTON, 17-19 jewels, diamond dial, hooded lugs
14k $800 $950 $1,100

HAMILTON, 17-19 jewels, diamond dial
14k(w).....................................$800 $950 $1,100

HAMILTON, 17-19 jewels, diamond dial , curved
14k $1,000 $1,100 $1,250

HAMILTON, 17-19 jewels, diamond dial, c. 1940
14k $1,000 $1,100 $1,250

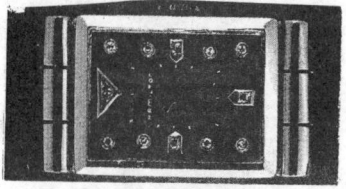

HAMILTON, 17-19 jewels, diamond dial
14k $600 $700 $800

HAMILTON, 17-19 jewels, diamond dial, hooded lugs
14k $800 $900 $1,000

HAMILTON, 17-19 jewels,diamond dial
14k...$800 $900 $1,000

HAMILTON, 17-19 jewels, diam. dial, c.1948, top hat
platinum $1,200 $1,300 $1,400
14k (w) $1,100 $1,200 $1,300

HAMILTON, 17-19 jewels, diamond dial
14k (w) $700 $800 $900

HAMILTON, 17-19 jewels, diamond dial, hooded lugs
14k...$600 $700 $800

HAMILTON, 17-19 jewels, diamond dial
platinum $1,100 $1,200 $1,300
14k (w) $900 $1,000 $1,100

HAMILTON, 17-19J., mystery dial with diamonds & **bezel**
18k $550 $650 $800
14k $450 $550 $650

HAMILTON, 17-19 jewels, diamond dial
14k $300 $350 $400

HAMILTON, 17-19 jewels, diamond dial
14k (w)......................................$300 $350 $400

HAMILTON, 19 jewels, diamond dial, fancy *knoted* lugs
14k (w)......................................$300 $350 $400

HAMILTON,17J., " Belmont ", cal.955 , c.1933
gold filled...................................$30 $40 $50

HAMILTON,17J., " Ladies Tonneau "cal.987 , c.1933
gold filled...................................$40 $50 $60

HAMILTON,17J., "Bianca", diamond & sapphire, c.1933
18k(w)......................................$150 $175 $250

HAMILTON,17J., " Bryn Mawr ", c.1933
14k...$60 $80 $100

HAMILTON,17J., " Briarcliffe ", c.1933
gold filled...................................$30 $40 $50

HAMILTON,17J., " Caroline ", cal.955, c.1933
gold filled...................................$20 $30 $40

HAMILTON,17J., " Cedarcrest ", cal.955, c.1933
14k...$50 $60 $70

HAMILTON,17J., " Chevy Chase A ", cal. , c.1933
14k(w)......................................$60 $70 $85

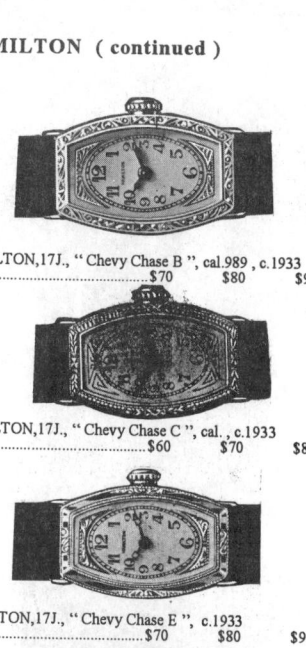

HAMILTON,17J., " Chevy Chase B ", cal.989 , c.1933
14k $70 $80 $90

HAMILTON,17J., " Chevy Chase C ", cal. , c.1933
14k(w)....................................$60 $70 $80

HAMILTON,17J., " Chevy Chase E ", c.1933
14k(w)....................................$70 $80 $90

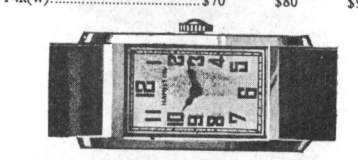

HAMILTON,17J., " Diane ", c.1933
14k $60 $70 $85

HAMILTON,17J., " Drexel ", cal.955 , c.1933
14k $70 $95 $135

HAMILTON,17J., " Edgewood ", c.1933
gold filled................................$30 $40 $45

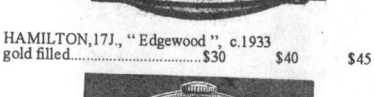

HAMILTON,17J., " Eugenie ", 44 diamonds, c.1933
platinum..................................$350 $400   . $550

HAMILTON,17J., " Glenwood ", cal.955, c.1933
gold filled................................$30 $40 $50

HAMILTON,17J., " Linden Hall ", c.1933
gold filled................................$30 $40 $50

HAMILTON,17J.," Maritza ", 8 diamonds, cal.955 , c.1933
18k(w) $95 $125 $150

HAMILTON,17J., " Mayfield ", cal.955 , c.1933
gold filled................................$40 $45 $60

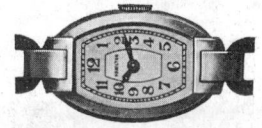

HAMILTON,17J., " Newcomb ", cal.989, c.1933
gold filled................................$40 $45 $60

HAMILTON,17J., " Nightingale ", 40 diamonds, c.1933
18k(w) $300 $350 $450

HAMILTON,17J., " Portia ", 8 diamonds, c.1933
18k(w) $200 $250 $350

HAMILTON,17J., " Trudy ", c.1948
14k...$75 $100 $135

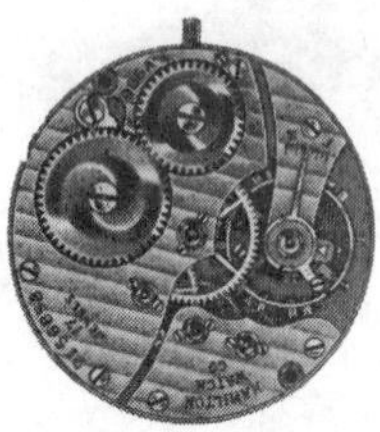

Grade 986A, 6/0 size
Open face, ¾ plate movt., 17 jewels, double roller

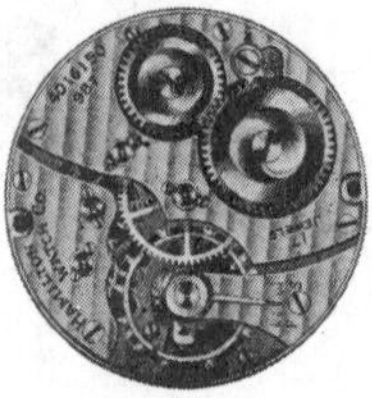

Grade 987, 6/0 size
Hunting, ¾ plate movt., 17 jewels, double roller

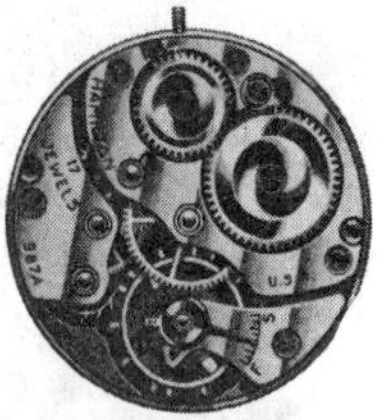

Grade 987A, 6/0 size
Open face, ¾ plate movt., 17 jewels, double roller

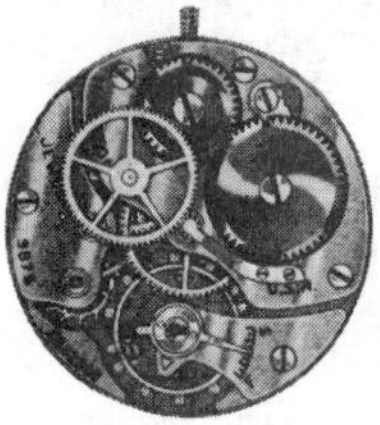

Grade 987S, 6/0 size
Hunting, ¾ plate movt., 17 jewels, double roller

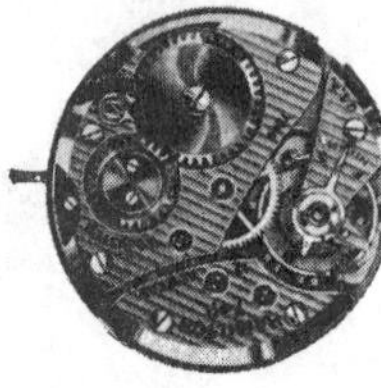

Grade 747, 8/0 size
Open face, ¾ plate movt., 17 jewels, double roller

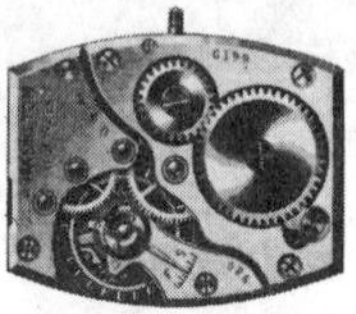

Grade 980, 14/0 size
Open face, ¾ plate movt., 17 jewels, double roller

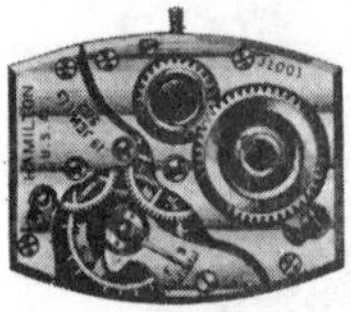

Grade 982, 14/0 size
Open face, ¾ plate movt., 19 jewels, double roller

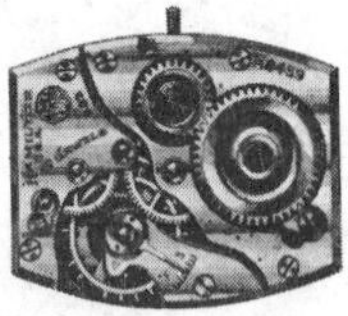

Grade 982M, 14/0 size
Open face, ¾ plate movt., 19 jewels, double roller

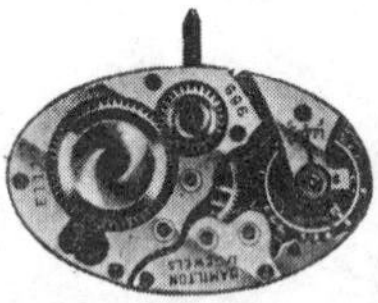

Grade 989, 18/0 size
Open face, ¾ plate movt., 17 jewels, double roller

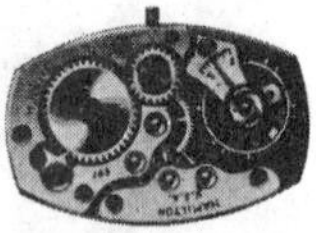

Grade 997, 20/0 size
Open face, ¾ plate movt., 17 jewels, double roller

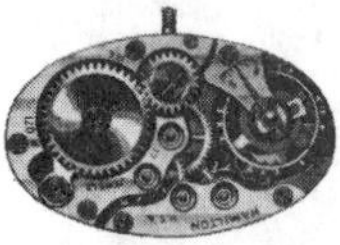

Grade 721, 21/0 size
Open face, ¾ plate movt., 17 jewels, double roller

Grade 995, 21/0 size
Open face, ¾ plate movt., 17 jewels, double roller

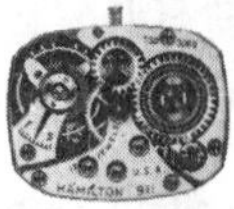

Grade 911, 22/0 size
Open face, ¾ plate movt., 17 jewels, double roller

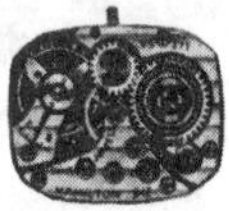

Grade 911M, 22/0 size
Open face, ¾ plate movt., 17 jewels, double roller

Grade 780, 21/0 size
17 jewels

Grade 770, 12/0 size
22 jewels

Grade 761, 21/0 size
22 jewels

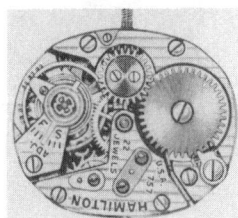

Grade 757, 21/0 size
22 jewels

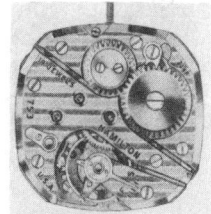

Grade 753, 12/0 size, 19 jewels
Grade 752, 12/0 size, 17 jewels

Grade 754, 12/0 size, 19 jewels
Grade 770, 12/0 size, 17 jewels

Grade 750 & 751, 21/0 size
17 jewels

Grade 748, 8/0 size
18 jewels

Grade 747, 8/0 size
17 jewels

LIGNE GAUGE

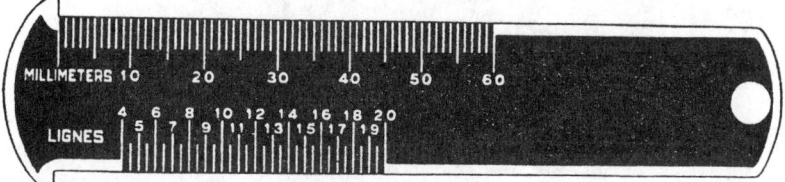

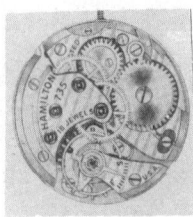

Grade 735, 8/0 size
18 jewels

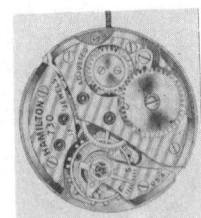

Grade 730, 8/0 size
17 jewels

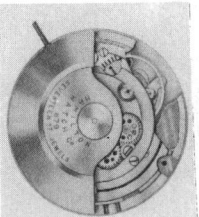

Grade 679, 17 jewels
Grade 692, 694 - calendar

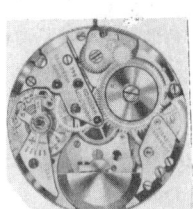

Grade 666 & 663, 17 jewels
Grade 668 - calendar

Grade 658, 661, 667, 17 jewels
Grade 665, 23J, **Grade 664**, 25J
Grade 662, 690 - calendar, 17J

Grade 623 & 624, 17 jewels

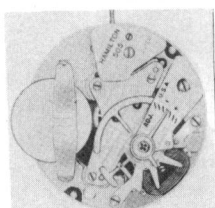

Grade 505, electric, 11 jewels

THE SPUR

**1930
AD**

A Hamilton the true Sportsman will
love. In either 14K yellow or white
gold with numerals of gold in a black
enamel circlet on the outside of the
case—19 jewel movement, $125

HAMPDEN, 15J., engraved case, c.1925
gold filled..............................$125 $150 $175

HAMPDEN, 17 jewels., c. 1936
14k $175 $200 $235

HAMPDEN, 17J., by Lonville W. Co., c. 1936
gold filled..............................$175 $200 $250

HAMPDEN, 17 jewels, double dial, c. 1930
gold filled..............................$175 $225 $275

HAMPDEN, 15 jewels, c. 1928
14k $175 $200 $250
gold filled..............................$60 $70 $80

🕐 Some grades are not included. Their values can be
determined by comparing with similar age, size, metal
content, style, grades, or models such as time only,
chronograph, repeater etc. listed.

HAMPDEN,11J., "LEVER SET", 3/0 size, c.1928
silver.....................................$200 $250 $300

HAMPDEN, 15 jewels, c. 1928
14k...$175 $200 $225
gold filled..............................$50 $60 $70

HAMPDEN, 11J., Molly Stark, c. 1928
base metal..............................$60 $70 $80

HAMPDEN, 7J., tonneau shaped, c. 1928
gold filled..............................$40 $60 $70

HARMAN,7J.,doctor style duo-dial,
gold filled..............................$450 $500 $550

HARMAN, 17J., one button chronog., mid size, c.1940s
s. steel $250 $300 $350

HARVARD, 17 jewels, chronog., tach-telemeter
s. steel $250 $300 $350

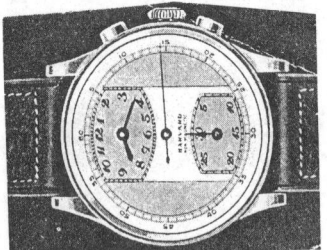

HARVARD, 17 jewels, 1/5 sec. chronog.
s. steel $275 $325 $400

HARVEL, 17 jewels, date-o-graph
s. steel $150 $175 $200

🕐 Some grades are not included. Their values can be determined by comparing with similar age, size, metal content, style, grades, or models such as time only, chronograph, repeater etc. listed.

HARVEL, 17J., center sec.
gold filled.............................$20 $30 $45

HARWOOD, 15 jewels, early self winding, c. 1928
18k (w)................................... $800 $900 $1,100
14k.. $650 $700 $800
gold filled.............................. $350 $400 $450
s. steel.................................... $250 $300 $400

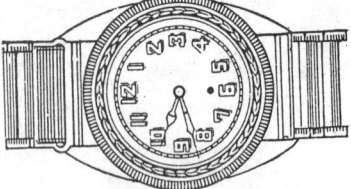

HARWOOD, 15 J., rim set by turning bezel clockwise
9k...$500 $550 $600

HARWOOD, 15 jewels, back set, c. 1925
18k...$500 $600 $700

HASTE, 17J., triple calendar moon ph.
gold filled.............................$250 $300 $375

HAYDEN, 7J., by Solomax W.Co., hinged case
gold filled....................................$60 $70 $85

HEBDOMAS, 7 J., visible escapement, 8 day movement
s. steel $400 $500 $600

HELBROS, 17 jewels, aux.sec., alarm
gold filled................................$100 $125 $150

HELBROS, 7 jewels, fancy bezel, curvex
gold filled................................$100 $120 $140

HELBROS, 7 jewels, aux. sec., ca. 1962
gold filled....................................$40 $50 $65

HELBROS, 17 jewels, aux. sec.
gold filled................................$40 $50 $65

HELBROS, 17 jewels,
14k..$175 $200 $225

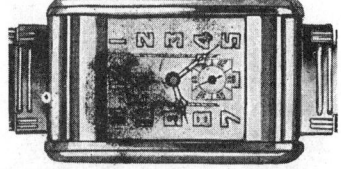

HELBROS, 7J., " Falcon ", c. 1929
base metal................................$40 $50 $65

HELBROS, 7J., " Fairfax ", c. 1929
base metal................................$40 $50 $65

HELBROS, 7J., " Federal ", c. 1929
base metal................................$40 $50 $65

HELBROS, 7J., " Filmore ", c. 1929
base metal................................$40 $50 $65

HELBROS, 7J., " Fletcher ", c. 1929
base metal $40 $50 $65

HELBROS, 7J., " Franklin ", c. 1929
base metal................................$40 $50 $65

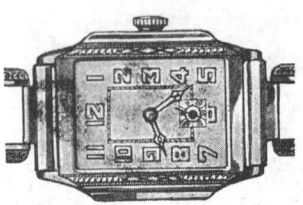

HELBROS, 7J., " Flint ", c. 1929
gold plate $50 $60 $75

HELBROS, 7J., " Frigate ", c. 1929
base metal................................$40 $50 $65

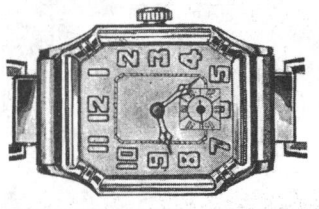

HELBROS, 7J., " Forbes ", c. 1929
base metal $40 $50 $65

HELBROS, 7J., " Fulton ", c. 1929
base metal................................$40 $50 $65

HELBROS, 7J., " Forrest ", c. 1929
base metal $40 $50 $65

HELBROS,17J., 24 hour dial
base metal................................$50 $60 $75

HELBROS, 7J., " Fortress ", c. 1929
gold plate $40 $50 $65

HENDA, 15J., direct read, c. 1930
nickel..$250 $300 $350

HERMES, 17J., big wire lugs, enamel dial
14k $350 $400 $450

HELVETIA, 15 jewels, Ca. 1935
9k $100 $125 $150

HELVETIA, 21 jewels, auto wind
gold filled.................................$30 $40 $50

HEUER, 15 jewels, chronog., 2 reg., one button,
14k $1,300 $1,600 $1,850

⏱ Some grades are not included. Their values can be determined by comparing with similar age, size, metal content, style, grades, or models such as time only, chronograph, repeater etc. listed.

HEUER, 17J., chronog., 3 reg., 3 dates, moon phase
18k......................................$1,800 $2,100 $2,500
s. steel...................................$700 $950 $1,200

HEUER, 17 J., chronog., 3 reg., "Carrera, c.1960
s. steel.....................................$375 $450 $525

HEUER, 17 jewels, chronog., 3 dates, 3 reg. c.1948
14k...$800 $1,000 $1,250
s. steel....................................$400 $500 $600

HEUER, 17 jewels, "Carrera," chronog., 2 reg., c.1960s
14k...$500 $600 $700
s. steel....................................$275 $325 $400

HEUER,17J., " Seafarer ", by Valjoux # 72, c. 1972
14k $800 $950 $1,100
s. steel $450 $500 $600

HEUER,17J., "Camro ", by Valjoux #7730, c. 1965
14k $450 $485 $575
s. steel $200 $250 $325

HEUER,17J., " Autavia ", cal.72, micro rotor, c. 1972
s. steel $250 $325 $375

🕐 Some grades are not included. Their values can be
determined by comparing with similar age, size, metal
content, style, grades, or models such as time only,
chronograph, repeater etc. listed.

HEUER,17J., " Monaco ", date, c. 1974
base metal.............................$225 $275 $325

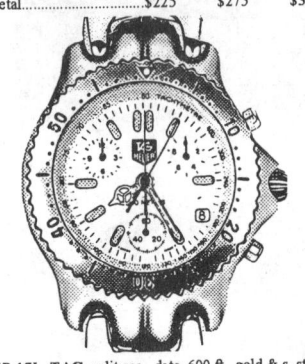

HEUER,17J., TAG, split sec., date, 600 ft., gold & s. steel,
sold new for $1,895.00 in Ca.1991
14k...$900 $1,000 $1,200
s. steel & 14k $600 $700 $850

HEUER, 17 jewels, day-date-month, moon phase
s. steel...................................$325 $400 $475

HEUER, 17 jewels, day-date-month
14k..$500 $600 $700
s. steel...................................$125 $150 $175

HILTON W. Co.,17J., chronog. by Venius W.Co.
18k $375 $450 $500

HIRCO, 17J., center sec. auto-w.
gold filled....................................$30 $40 $50

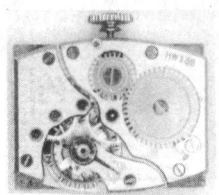

HOWARD, 17J. engraved on movement, (Howard
Watch USA, Lancaster, PA, HW138, 17J. H980)
⊕ ..(see HAMILTON W. CO.)

E. HUGUENIN, 17 jewels, "Black Star," c. 1940
14k $500 $600 $700

⊕ Some grades are not included. Their values can be
determined by comparing with similar age, size, metal
content, style, grades, or models such as time only,
chronograph, repeater etc. listed.

HYDEPARK, 17 jewels, flip up top
14k $500 $600 $750

ILLINOIS, 17J., GJS, model 207 on Mvt., model 250 on case
14K $400 $450 $500

ILLINOIS, 17J., **Aluminum** case & band, direct read
Aluminum......... ★ ★ ★ ★ ★ $2,000 $2,200 $2,500

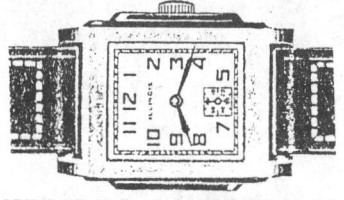

ILLINOIS, 15J., "Arlington also Hawthorne", Ca. 1929
gold filled $175 $200 $250

ILLINOIS, 17J., "Ardsley also Hudson", Ca. 1929
gold filled $150 $175 $200

ILLINOIS, 17 jewels, "Aviator"
gold filled..............................$225 $250 $300

ILLINOIS, 17J., " Beau Monde also Beau Gest = WGF"
gold filled $225 $275 $350

ILLINOIS, 21J., " BARONET ", GJS, cal.601, c.1925
gold filled................................$400 $450 $500

ILLINOIS, 15J., "Beau Royal "
gold filled $225 $275 $350

ILLINOIS, 19J., " Beau Brummel"
18k $700 $800 $950

ILLINOIS, 17J., " Blackstone"
gold filled $125 $150 $195

ILLINOIS, 19 jewels, "Beau Brummel"
gold filled..............................$275 $325 $400

ILLINOIS, 15J., " Bostonian also Commodore"
gold filled $150 $175 $225

ILLINOIS, 17J., " Beau Brummel ", c.1929
gold filled..............................$250 $325 $400

ILLINOIS, 17J., " Cavalier "
gold filled $195 $235 $295

ILLINOIS, 17 jewels, "Champion"
gold filled................................$150 $175 $250

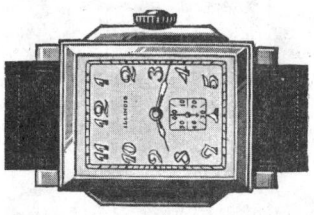

ILLINOIS, 15 jewels, "Chatham"
gold filled................................$150 $175 $225

ILLINOIS, 17J., " The Chief's", chased bezel
gold filled (w)........................$185 $225 $275

ILLINOIS, 17 jewels, "Chieftain"
gold filled................................$350 $450 $575

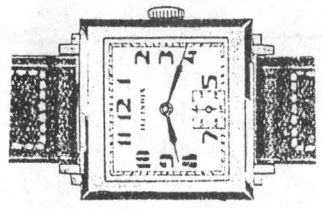

ILLINOIS, 17J., " Commodore also Bostonian"
gold filled................................$150 $175 $225

ILLINOIS, 19 jewels, "Consul"
14k $400 $485 $600

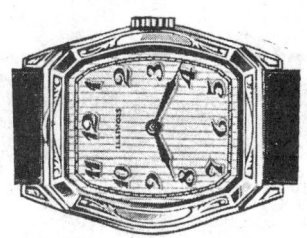

ILLINOIS, 21 jewels, "Consul"
14k $400 $485 $600

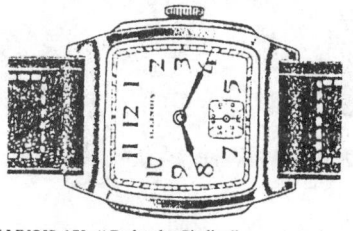

ILLINOIS, 17J., " Derby also Pimlico"
gold filled..............................$125 $150 $200

ILLINOIS, 15 jewels, "Ensign"
gold filled..............................$225 $300 $395

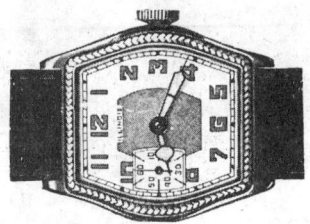

ILLINOIS, 15 jewels, "Ensign"
gold filled $225 $300 $395

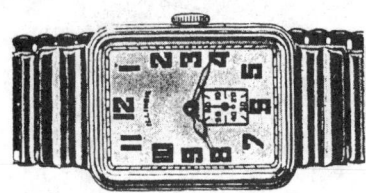

ILLINOIS, 17J., " Fontenac "
gold filled..............................$175 $200 $250

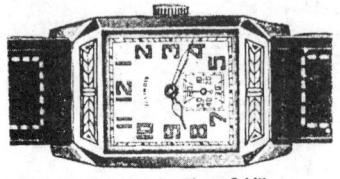

ILLINOIS, 17J., " Finalist also Chesterfield"
gold filled..............................$225 $250 $275

ILLINOIS, 17J., " Futura "
gold filled..............................$200 $225 $250

ILLINOIS, 17J., " Guardsman ", plain, rotor second dial
gold filled..............................$350 $400 $450

ILLINOIS, 17J., "Guardsman ", engraved, cal.307, c.1929
gold filled..............................$350 $400 $450

ILLINOIS, 17 jewels, "Jolly Roger"
gold filled..............................$300 $400 $550

ILLINOIS, 17J., " Kenilworth "
gold filled..............................$175 $225 $275

ILLINOIS, 19 jewels, "Major"
gold filled..............................$250 $325 $400

ILLINOIS, 17 jewels, "Major",
gold filled..............................$250 $325 $400

ILLINOIS, 17 jewels, "Major"
gold filled..............................$250 $325 $400

ILLINOIS, 17-21J., " Manhattan ", aux. sec. at 9
14k $375 $450 $525

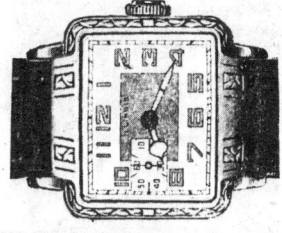

ILLINOIS, 17-21 jewels, "New Yorker", aux. sec. at 9
also "Yorktown in smooth bezel
gold filled................................$250 $300 $350

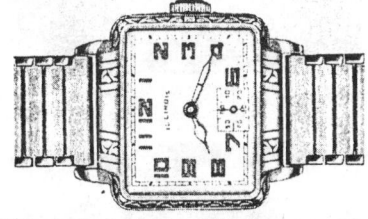

ILLINOIS, 17-21J., " Manhattan ", aux. sec. at 6
14k $375 $450 $525

ILLINOIS, 17-21 jewels, "New Yorker", aux. sec. at 6
gold filled................................$250 $300 $350

ILLINOIS, 19 jewels, "Marquis", engraved, curved case
gold filled................................$250 $300 $375

ILLINOIS, 17J., " Marquis ", plain, curved case
gold filled $200 $235 $350

ILLINOIS, 17J., " Mate ", engraved
gold filled $175 $200 $275

ILLINOIS, 17J., "Mate" , plain
gold filled $150 $175 $225

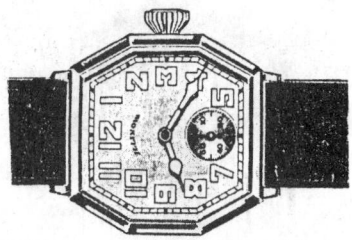

ILLINOIS, 17J., engraved case in Maxine, plain, ladies
gold filled $100 $125 $150

ILLINOIS, 17 jewels, "Maxine", wire lugs, ladies
14k $150 $175 $200

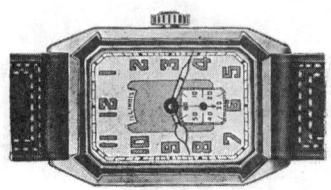

ILLINOIS, 17J., " Medalist also Wembley", c.1929
gold filled...............................$150 $175 $250

ILLINOIS, 17 jewels, "Piccadilly" in white or yellow G.F.
came with Luminous or Modern as a option
gold filled plain.......................$750 $900 $1,150
gold filled engraved...............$875 $1,000 $1,250

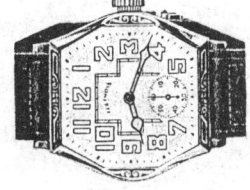

ILLINOIS, 17 jewels, "Pilot"
gold filled...............................$200 $250 $300

ILLINOIS, 17 jewels, "Prince"
gold filled...............................$175 $200 $225

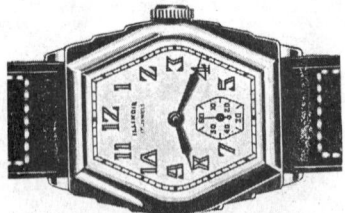

ILLINOIS, 17J., "Ritz", white bezel & yellow center case
also called "Valedictorian"
gold filled...............................$375 $450 $550

ILLINOIS, 15 jewels, "Rockingham also Potomac"
gold filled...............................$200 $250 $325

ILLINOIS, 17J., " Rockliffe ", cal.805, c.1925
14k $350 $400 $495

ILLINOIS, 15 jewels, "Sangamo"
gold filled $100 $150 $200

ILLINOIS, 17J., " Skyway ", engraved case, G#307
gold filled $400 $500 $600

ILLINOIS, 17J., " Special ", c.1929
silver $250 $300 $450

ILLINOIS, 17 jewels, "Speedway"
gold filled $225 $275 $375

ILLINOIS, 15 jewels, "Urbana"
gold filled $125 $150 $200

ILLINOIS, 15 jewels, "Standish"
gold filled $150 $195 $250

ILLINOIS, 17J., " Viking "
gold filled $200 $250 $300

ILLINOIS, 17J., " Sterling ", direct read, c.1929
sterling silver $225 $275 $350

ILLINOIS, 17J., GENERIC, engraved side of case
base metal $100 $135 $175

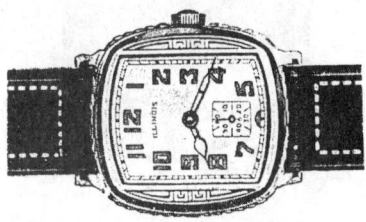

ILLINOIS, 17J., " Townsman also Metropolitan", carved
case
gold filled $175 $225 $275

ILLINOIS, 17J., "Tuxedo", engraved bezel, c. 1920
14k $300 $350 $450

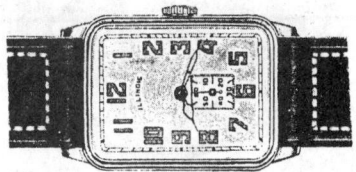

ILLINOIS, 17J., " Trophy also Westchester"
gold filled $125 $175 $250

ILLINOIS, 17 jewels, "Off Duty", stars on bezel, Ca. 1927
gold filled $200 $250 $300

ILLINOIS, 15J., GENERIC, Square cut corner
gold filled..............................$150 $195 $275

ILLINOIS, 19 jewels, GENERIC, aux. sec at 9
14k(W)...................................$400 $450 $550

ILLINOIS, 17 jewels, GENERIC, hand engraved, wire lugs
14k (W)...................................$150 $200 $250

ILLINOIS, 17J., GENERIC, maxine style, hand engraved,
14k (W)...................................$150 $200 $250

ILLINOIS, 15J., GENERIC, seconds at "9" c.1929
gold filled..............................$200 $250 $300

ILLINOIS, 17J., GENERIC, engraved case, c.1929
gold filled $150 $200 $275

ILLINOIS, 17J., GENERIC, art deco, cal.207, c.1925
gold filled $135 $175 $250

ILLINOIS, 17J., GENERIC, double hinged, GJS, c.1929
gold filled $150 $175 $250

ILLINOIS, 15J., GENERIC, contract case, gold train, c.1929
14k $100 $125 $175

ILLINOIS, 17J., GENERIC, engraved bezel, Ca.1929
gold filled $150 $175 $225

ILLINOIS, 17J., GENERIC, Shock-Proof Model,
nickel.................................$100 $125 $175

ILLINOIS, 17J., GENERIC, engraved case
gold filled.............................$125 $150 $200

ILLINOIS, 15J., GENERIC, engraved bezel, GJS, c.1926
14k (w)...................................$275 $300 $350

ILLINOIS, 15J., GENERIC, winds at 12:00 o'clock
silver $250 $300 $400

ILLINOIS, 15-17J., lady's watch, black enamel on bezel
14k $100 $120 $140
gold filled................................$30 $40 $50

6-0 SIZE OR ELEVEN LIGNE

Only delivered fitted in cases supplied by Jobbers

Illustrations simply indicate some of the different styles of cases, made by various watch case manufacturers, for these movements.

No. 907, 19 Jewels   No. 903, 15 Jewels
$35.00 *Movements Only* $26.50

19 and 15 ruby and sapphire jewels; compensating balance with timing screws; double roller escapement; Breguet hairspring; steel escape wheel; polished winding wheels; recoil click; silvered or gilt metal dials; full or three-quarter open.

No. 1045   The Ace $37.30
3/0 Illinois 17 Jewel
White Engraved Stellar Quality Star Case
Silver Dial Luminous Figures and Hands
Established retail price with each

No. 1047   The Whippet $36.20
3/0 Illinois 17 Jewel
Stellar White Plain Barrel Case
Silver Dial Luminous Figures and Hands
Established retail price with each

ILLINOIS, 17J., " Eliza ", c.1929
gold filled.................................$65 $75 $90

ILLINOIS, 17J., " Long Beach ", c.1929
gold filled.................................$55 $65 $80

ILLINOIS, 17J., " Lynette ", c.1929
gold filled.................................$50 $60 $75

ILLINOIS, 17J., " Mariette ", c.1929
gold filled.................................$50 $60 $75

ILLINOIS, 17J., " Marionette ", c.1929
gold filled.................................$50 $60 $75

ILLINOIS, 17J., " Marlette ", c.1929
gold filled.................................$50 $60 $75

ILLINOIS, 16J., " Mary Todd ", c.1929
18k(w).................................$150 $200 $250

ILLINOIS, 16J., " Mary Todd ", black enamel bezel, c.1929
18k(w).................................$150 $200 $250

ILLINOIS, 16J., " Mary Todd ", c.1929
18k $150 $200 $250

ILLINOIS, 17J., " Mateel ", c.1929
14k(w).................................$90 $100 $140

ILLINOIS, 17J., " Miami ", c.1929
gold filled $55 $65 $85

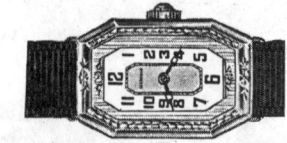

ILLINOIS, 17J., " Narragansett ", c.1929
14k $85 $95 $110

ILLINOIS, 17J., " Newport ", engraved case, c.1929
gold filled $55 $65 $80

ILLINOIS, 16J., " Queen Wilhelmina ", 22 diamonds and
8 synthetic sapphires
18k(w).................................$200 $275 $350

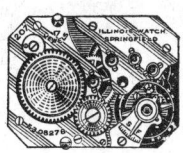

ILLINOIS, rectangular, Grade 207, 17 jewels

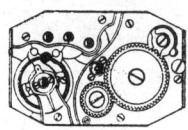

ILLINOIS, rectangular, 1st, 2nd & 3rd model

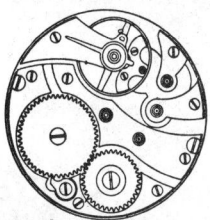

ILLINOIS, Model #4, 3/0 size, bridge, hunting, movement.

IMPERIAL, 17J., fancy lugs
14k(W).....................................$250 $300 $350

IMPERIAL, 17J., center sec.
s. steel $30 $40 $55

🕐 Some grades are not included. Their values can be determined by comparing with similar age, size, metal content, style, grades, or models such as time only, chronograph, repeater etc. listed.

INGERSOLL, 2 J.," Rist-Arch", stepped case
base metal $30 $40 $60

INGERSOLL, "Swagger",
base metal $30 $45 $75

INGERSOLL, 7 jewels
base metal $20 $25 $35

INGERSOLL, 7 jewels, radiolite dial wire lugs
W/ original band $40 $55 $75
base metal $25 $35 $55

INGERSOLL, 7 J., military style, **protective grill cover wire lugs, all original band and cover**
base metal $75 $100 $150

INTERNATIONAL W. CO., 17J., Ca. 1926
18k $500 $600 $750

INTERNATIONAL W. CO., 17 jewels, c. 1925
18k $500 $600 $700

INTERNATIONAL W. CO., 16J., enamel dial, c. 1920
silver $400 $450 $500

INTERNATIONAL W. CO., 17 jewels
14k $500 $550 $600

INTERNATIONAL W. CO., 16J., cal.53, c. 1920
18k $500 $600 $750

INTERNATIONAL W. CO., 21 J., center sec., c. 1940
18k $600 $700 $800

INTERNATIONAL W. CO., 17 jewels, c. 1920
18k $500 $600 $700

INTERNATIONAL W. CO., 17J., "Art Deco", Ca. 1925
TU-TONE case w/ enamel on bezel
18k $1,200 $1,400 $1,850

INTERNATIONAL W. CO., **17 jewels, curved**
14k **$800**   **$900**   **$1,000**

INTERNATIONAL W. CO., 17 jewels
14k C&B $800 $850 $950

INTERNATIONAL W. CO., 17 jewels, c. 1940
18k $500 $600 $700

INTERNATIONAL W. CO., 17J., c. 1945
14k $400 $450 $500

INTERNATIONAL W. CO., 17J., Tiffany on dial, c. 1942
14k $600 $650 $700

INTERNATIONAL W. CO., 17 jewels, hidden lugs
14k $700 $800 $900

INTERNATIONAL W. CO., 17J., aux. sec.
14k $400 $500 $600

🕐 Some grades are not included. Their values can be determined by comparing with similar age, size, metal content, style, grades, or models such as time only, chronograph, repeater etc. listed.

INTERNATIONAL W. CO., 17J., c. 1946
18k $400 $450 $500

INTERNATIONAL W. CO., 17J., tank style, c. 1937
18k $700 $800 $900

INTERNATIONAL W. CO., 17J., c. 1926
s. steel $350 $400 $475

INTERNATIONAL W. CO., 17 J., on dial "Yard"
18k $1,000 $1,200 $1,400

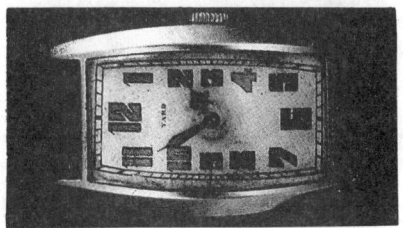

INTERNATIONAL W. CO., 17 J., curved, on dial, "Yard"
platinum $1,800 $2,000 $2,200

INTERNATIONAL W. CO., 17 jewels, **hinged back**
14k $700 $800 $900

INTERNATIONAL W. CO., 17 jewels, curved
14k $700 $800 $900

INTERNATIONAL W. CO., 17J, date, auto-wind, water-proof
18k $850 $1,000 $1,200

INTERNATIONAL W. CO., 21 jewels, auto wind, date
18k $900 $1,000 $1,100

INTERNATIONAL W. CO., 17 jewels, center sec.
18k $600 $700 $800

INTERNATIONAL W. CO., 17 jewels, center sec.
18k $600 $700 $800

INTERNATIONAL W. CO., 17J., cen. sec., date, platinum $1,400 $1,600 $1,800

INTERNATIONAL W. CO., 17J., RF# 802a, cal.8541, c.1920
s. steel $300 $350 $400

INTERNATIONAL W. CO., 21J., "Ingeneur", date, c.1976
non-magnetic.................. ★ $500 $600 $750

🕐 Some grades are not included. Their values can be determined by comparing with **similar** age, size, metal content, style, grades, or models such as **time only**, chronograph, repeater etc. listed.

INTERNATIONAL W. CO., 21J., date, c. 1960
18k $900 $1,000 $1,100

INTERNATIONAL W. CO., 17J., center sec.cal.89, c.1957
18k $500 $600 $700

INTERNATIONAL W. CO., 21J., cal.853, c. 1961
18k $600 $700 $800

INTERNATIONAL W. CO., 17J., wide lugs, c. 1960
18k $600 $700 $800

INTERNATIONAL W. CO.,17J.,fancy lugs,cal.C89, c.1952
18k $700 $800 $900

INTERNATIONAL W. CO., 21J., cal.C852, c. 1952
18k $600 $700 $800

INTERNATIONAL W. CO., 21J., cal.853, c. 1958
18k $600 $700 $800

INTERNATIONAL W. CO., 17J., cal.89, c. 1962
s. steel $300 $350 $400

INTERNATIONAL W. CO., 17J., ca.1960s
18k C & B $1,100 $1,200 $1,400

INTERNATIONAL W. CO., 17J., auto wind, Ca. 1960
18k..$650 $750 $850

INTERNATIONAL W. CO., 17J., center sec.
18k $800 $900 $1,000

INTERNATIONAL W. CO., 17 jewels, center sec.
18k..$600 $700 $800

INTERNATIONAL W. CO., 17J., fancy lugs, cen. sec.
18k $700 $800 $900

INTERNATIONAL W. CO., 17 jewels, center sec., cal.402
18k..$600 $700 $800

INTERNATIONAL W. Co., 18 jewels, center sec.
18k $600 $700 $800

INTERNATIONAL W. CO., 17 jewels, center sec., cal. 89
18k..$600 $700 $800

🕐 Some grades are not included. Their values can be
determined by comparing with similar age, size, metal
content, style, grades, or models such as time only,
chronograph, repeater etc. listed.

INTERNATIONAL W. CO., 17 jewels, center sec., cal.89
14k $450 $500 $600

INTERNATIONAL W. CO., 36J., "Da Vinci," chronog.
auto wind, triple date, moon ph., center lugs
18k C & B.........................$10,250 $11,000 $12,500
18k $8,000 $9,000 $9,500

INTERNATIONAL W. CO., "Porsche Design", date, auto-
wind, compass, sapphire mirror, RF#3510-LMW, Ca.1988
Titanium....................................$700 $800 $950

INTERNATIONAL W. CO., 17J, for Royal Navy, ca.1950
s. steel.......................................$400 $500 $600

INTERNATIONAL W. CO., 17J., winds at 12 o'clock
s. steel.......................................$600 $700 $800

INTERNATIONAL W. CO., 17 jewels, c. 1953
18k..$500 $600 $700

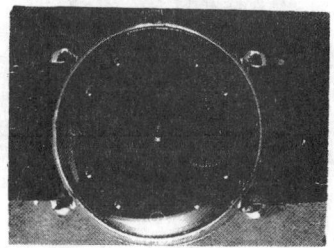

INTERNATIONAL W. CO., 17 jewels, aux. sec.
18k..$600 $700 $800

INTERNATIONAL W. CO., 17 jewels, c. 1948
18k $600 $700 $800

INTERNATIONAL W. CO., 17J.,date, 30 ATM=1,000 ft.
s. steel $300 $400 $450

INTERNATIONAL W. CO., 17J., aux sec., cal.83, c.1938
14k $500 $550 $600

INTERNATIONAL W. CO., 17J., ca.1940s
18k..$500 $600 $750

INTERNATIONAL W. CO., 17J., aux. sec., cal., c.1948
s. steel $275 $300 $350

INTERNATIONAL W. CO., 15J., cal. 83, ca.1945
14k..$400 $450 $500

INTERNATIONAL W. CO., 17J., cal.461, c.1962
18k $600 $700 $800

INTERNATIONAL W. CO., 21J., cal.44, mid-size, ca.1962
18k..$400 $450 $500

INTERNATIONAL W. CO., 17J., 36 small diamonds
platinum $600 $700 $800

INTERNATIONAL WATCH CO.
MOVEMENT IDENTIFICATION

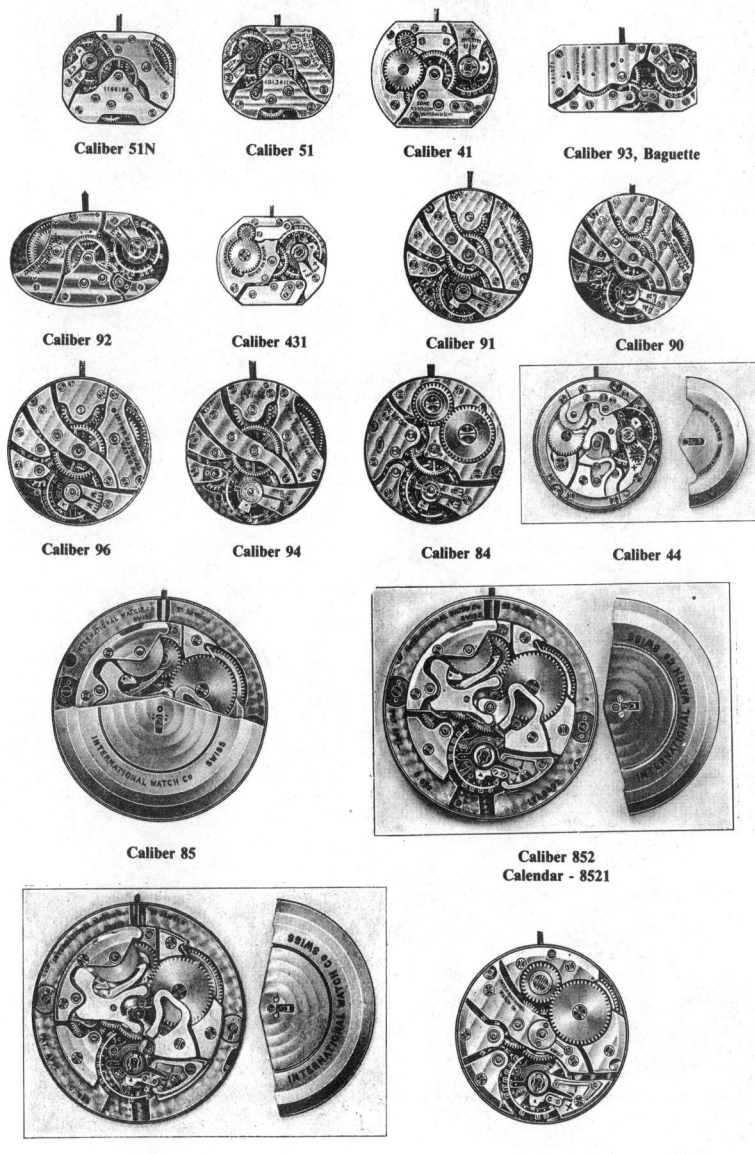

Caliber 51N

Caliber 51

Caliber 41

Caliber 93, Baguette

Caliber 92

Caliber 431

Caliber 91

Caliber 90

Caliber 96

Caliber 94

Caliber 84

Caliber 44

Caliber 85

Caliber 852
Calendar - 8521

Caliber 853
Calendar - 8531

Caliber 401

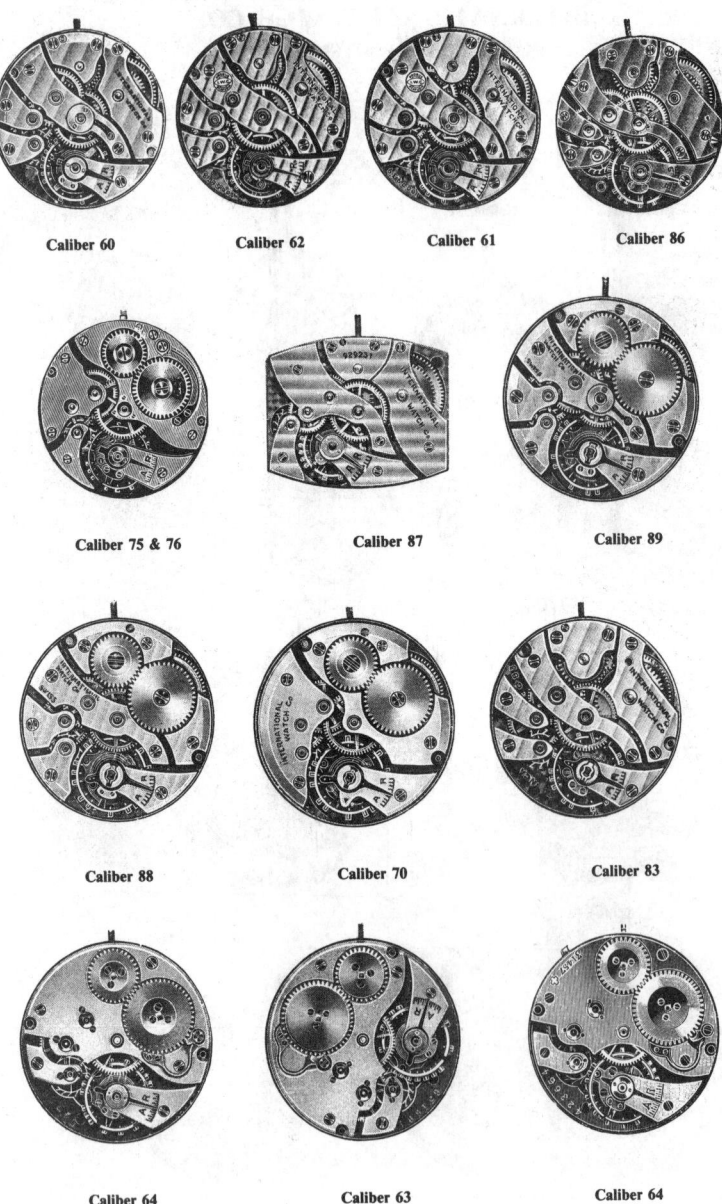

Caliber 60   Caliber 62   Caliber 61   Caliber 86

Caliber 75 & 76   Caliber 87   Caliber 89

Caliber 88   Caliber 70   Caliber 83

Caliber 64   Caliber 63   Caliber 64

INVICTA, 15 jewels, chronograph, min. reg. at 6 o'clock,
decimal aperture for sec. at 12 o'clock
18k $7,000 $8,000 $9,500

INVICTA, 17 jewels, date, center sec.
18k $200 $250 $300
s. steel $50 $75 $100

INVICTA, 17 jewels, day-date, waterproof
18k $150 $175 $225
s. steel $60 $70 $80

INVICTA, 17 jewels, day-date-month
18k $200 $250 $300
s. steel $70 $80 $95

🕐 Some grades are not included. Their values can be
determined by comparing with similar age, size, metal
content, style, grades, or models such as time only,
chronograph, repeater etc. listed.

INVICTA, 17 jewels, day-date-month, moon phase
18k $450 $550 $650
s. steel $225 $300 $350

INVICTA, 17 jewels, waterproof
18k $150 $200 $250
s. steel $40 $50 $60

INVICTA, 17 jewels, auto wind, waterproof
18k $150 $200 $250
s. steel $50 $60 $70

JAEGER W. CO., 17J., RF#5184, chronog., Ca.1942
s.steel $500 $600 $700

JAEGER W. CO., 15J., **duoplan, backwind,** c.1935
s steel $400 $450 $500

JARDUR W. CO., 17J., RF#29840, c.1950
s. steel $300 $350 $425

JEAN LOUIS, 17 jewels, double dial, c. 1930
14k $350 $400 $475

J. E. Watch Co., 17J., tank style, c.1950
gold plate $100 $125 $150

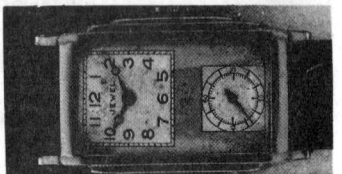

JEWEL, 15 jewels, dual dial, c. 1938
gold filled $400 $500 $600

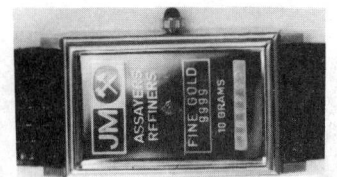

JOHNSON-MATTHEY, 15 J., 5 gram ingot 24k gold
24k $200 $250 $300

JUNGHANS, 16J., chronometer, c.1965
14k $135 $165 $200

JUNGHANS, electronic "Ato Chron" , C.1978
14k $125 $150 $185

JUNGHANS , 17J., cal.J88, c.1980
s. steel $150 $225 $275

🕒 Some grades are not included. Their values can be
determined by comparing with **similar** age, size, metal
content, style, grades, or models such as **time only,**
chronograph, repeater etc. listed.

J. JURGENSEN, 31J, 5 min. repeater, enamel bezel, c.1906
18k $25,000 $30,000 $35,000

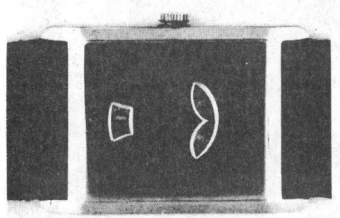

J. JURGENSEN, 15J, jumping hr., revolving min., c.1930s
18k $4,000 $5,000 $6,000

J. JURGENSEN,17J., large lugs, recess crown, c.1950
14k $300 $350 $400

J. JURGENSEN,17J., long lugs, c.1948
18k $175 $200 $275

J. JURGENSEN,17J., recess crown, fancy lugs, c.1952
14k $200 $225 $250

J. JURGENSEN,17J., 2 tone, center lugs, c.1940
14k $400 $450 $500

J. JURGENSEN, 17 jewels, fancy lugs, ca.1949
14k $300 $350 $450

J. JURGENSEN, 17 jewels, fancy lugs
14k $300 $350 $400

J. JURGENSEN, 17 jewels, extra fancy lugs, c. 1946
18k $500 $575 $650

J. JURGENSEN, 17 jewels, c. 1950
18k $250 $300 $350

J. JURGENSEN, 17 jewels
18k $175 $200 $225

J. JURGENSEN,17J., center sec., c.1946
14k $150 $175 $200

J. JURGENSEN,17J., aux. sec., c.1948
14k $150 $175 $200

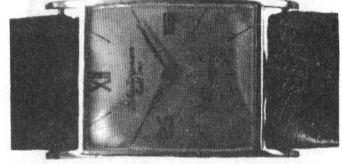

J. JURGENSEN,17J., aux. sec., c.1940
14k $150 $175 $200

J. JURGENSEN,17J., textured bezel, c.1960
14k $125 $150 $175

J. JURGENSEN,17J., hidden lugs, c.1948
14k $175 $200 $225

J. JURGENSEN,17J., hidden lugs, c.1940
14k.......................................$150 $175 $200

J. JURGENSEN,17J., hidden lugs, c.1952
14k.......................................$300 $350 $400

J. JURGENSEN,17J., hidden lugs, c.1950
14k.......................................$300 $350 $400

J. JURGENSEN,17J., hidden lugs, c.1948
14k.......................................$150 $175 $200

J. JURGENSEN, 17 J., small size chronog., ca. 1945
14k.......................................$1,200 $1,400 $1,800

🕐 Some grades are not included. Their values can be determined by comparing with similar age, size, metal content, style, grades, or models such as time only, chronograph, repeater etc. listed.

J. JURGENSEN (continued)

J. JURGENSEN,17J., by Valjoux, cal. 69, c.1944
s. steel $700 $800 $900

J. JURGENSEN, 17 J., auto-w., cen. sec., ca. 1954
14k $250 $300 $350

J. JURGENSEN,17J., cal.8273, extended lugs, c.1958
i4k $250 $275 $300

J. JURGENSEN,17J., aux, sec., c.1968
14k $125 $150 $175

J. JURGENSEN,17J., extended bezel, c.1950
14k $350 $375 $400

J. JURGENSEN,17J., cal.1139, c.1950
18k...$225 $250 $300

J. JURGENSEN,17J., center sec., date, c.1960
14k...$150 $175 $200

J. JURGENSEN,17J., center sec., mid size, c.1940
14k... $175 $200 $225

⏱ Some grades are not included. Their values can be
determined by comparing with **similar** age, size, metal
content, style, grades, or models such as **time only**,
chronograph, repeater etc. listed.

J. JURGENSEN,17J., 12 diamond dial, date, c.1960
14k(w)....................................$200 $250 $300

J. JURGENSEN,17J., 40 diamond bezel, c.1960
14k(w)....................................$350 $375 $400

J. JURGENSEN, 17 J., 12 diamond dial, ca. 1960s
14k(W)....................................$200 $250 $300

JUVENIA,17J.,3 dates, moon ph., screw on back c. 1950s
18k $500 $600 $700

JUVENIA, 21 jewels, **gold movement**
18k...$350 $400 $450

JUVENIA, 17J.,
s. steel.......................................$50 $60 $75

JUVENIA, 17J.,
s. steel.......................................$55 $65 $85

JUVENIA, 17J.,
s. steel.......................................$75 $85 $110

🕐 Some grades are not included. Their values can be
determined by comparing with similar age, size, metal
content, style, grades, or models such as time only,
chronograph, repeater etc. listed.

JUVENIA, 17J.,
s. steel $100 $125 $150

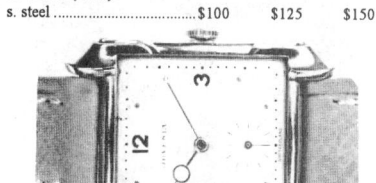

JUVENIA, 17J.,
s. steel $85 $100 $125

JUVENIA, 17J.,
s. steel $80 $100 $120

KELBERT, 17J., triple date, moon ph., ca.1945
s. steel $325 $365 $400

KELBERT, 17 jewels, fancy lugs, c. 1949
gold filled.................................$70 $80 $100

KELEK,17J., tachymeter, auto-wind, c.1970
s. steel $175 $225 $275

Kelton, 7 jewels, curved, stepped case
gold filled $30 $35 $40

KELTON, 7 jewels, "Drake"
gold filled $30 $35 $40

KENT W. CO.,17J., Continental W.Co.(french),chronog.
s. steel $100 $125 $150

KINGSTON, 17 jewels, day-date-month, moon phase
gold filled $225 $275 $325

KINGSTON, 17J., cal. G10, hidden lugs, c.1943
gold filled..................................$60 $70 $85

KORD, day date month, moon ph.
s. steel $250 $300 $350

KURTH, 17 jewels, "Certina"
gold filled...................................$20 $30 $40

LACO, 17J., center sec., c.1955
gold plate $25 $35 $50

🕐 Some grades are not included. Their values can be
determined by comparing with similar age, size, metal
content, style, grades, or models such as time only,
chronograph, repeater etc. listed.

LANCEL (Paris), 17J., one button chronog. by Nicolet, c.1960
gold filled $225 $250 $285

A.LANGE & SOHNE, 17J., 55mm., c.1940
s. steel $1,200 $1,400 $1,600

A.LANGE & SOHNE, 17J, (Glashutte), c.1936
14k $1,400 $1,600 $1,850

LANGE "UHR" (Glashutte), 15J., c.1936
14k $800 $900 $1,000

LANGE "UHR" (Glashutte), 17J., c.1937
s. steel $600 $700 $800

LANGE, 17J, (Glashutte), date, auto wind, waterproof
18k $800 $900 $1,000

LAVINA, 17J., ca.1937
9K...$125 $150 $175

LE COULTRE, 15 jewels, wire lugs, c. 1919
silver $200 $225 $250

LE COULTRE, 18J., skeletonized,
18k $1,400 $1,600 $2,000

LE COULTRE, 19 jewels, alarm
18k $1,000 $1,200 $1,500
gold filled...............................$300 $375 $475
s. steel $275 $350 $450

LE COULTRE, 19 jewels, alarm, c. 1950
18k $1,000 $1,200 $1,500
gold filled $350 $425 $475
s. steel $300 $350 $450

LE COULTRE, 17J., , alarm, cal.815, c.1960
gold filled $300 $350 $400

LE COULTRE, 17J., ruby dial, alarm, c.1960
gold filled $350 $400 $500

LE COULTRE, 17J.,cal.814, memovox, alarm, c.1960
14k $1,000 $1,150 $1,250
gold filled $275 $350 $450

LE COULTRE, 17J., cal.p815, alarm, c.1960
gold filled..............................$350 $375 $425

LE COULTRE, 17J.,memvox , alarm, auto wind,c.1973
14k & s.s................................$500 $550 $600

LE COULTRE, 17J., RF#3025, wrist-alarm, c.1948
gold filled..............................$350 $400 $450

LE COULTRE, 17J., RF#2676, cal.911, memvox, c.1960
gold filled $350 $400 $450

LE COULTRE, 17J., wrist alarm, Ca.1949
gold filled..............................$350 $400 $450

LE COULTRE, 17J., date, memvox, c.1975
s. steel $200 $250 $300

LE COULTRE, 17J., "Polaris", underwater alarm tested to
600 feet, date, Ca. 1968
s. steel $400 $450 $500

LE COULTRE, 17J., auto wind, date, memvox, c.1976
gold filled $300 $350 $400

LE COULTRE, 19J., date, Memovox, ca. 1959
18k $1,000 $1,200 $1,400
gold filled.............................$350 $400 $475
s. steel $225 $300 $375

LE COULTRE, 17J., powermatic, auto-wind, c.1950
gold filled $225 $250 $300

LE COULTRE, 19J., alarm, date, autowind
14k $1,000 $1,100 $1,200

LE COULTRE, 17J., cal 481, auto-wind, c.1954
gold filled $200 $225 $275

LE COULTRE, 19 jewels, alarm, date, autowind, ca. 1950
18k $1,200 $1,400 $1,600
gold filled.............................$325 $400 $475
s. steel $300 $350 $400

LE COULTRE, 17J., auto wind, wind indicator
14k $550 $625 $700

LE COULTRE, 17 jewels, screw back
18k $350 $400 $450

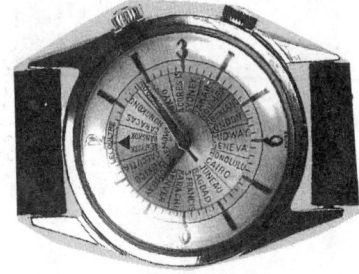

LE COULTRE, 17-19J., **World Time,** Memovox, ca. 1956
s. steel $400 $475 $550

LE COULTRE, 17J., "Master Mariner, c.1960
14k $300 $350 $400

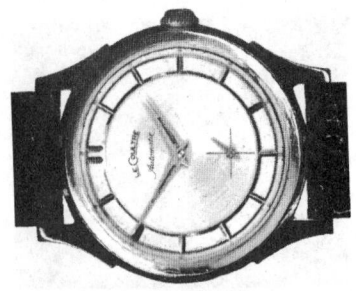

LE COULTRE, 17J., auto-wind, cal.p812, c.1955
gold filled $100 $125 $150

LE COULTRE, 17J., cal.p478, center sec.c.1947
s. steel $225 $250 $300

LE COULTRE, 17J., cal.818, aux. sec., c.1962
gold filled $100 $125 $150

LE COULTRE, 17J., "Master Mariner", c.1952
14k $300 $375 $475

LE COULTRE, 17J., RF#2013, cal.480cw, c.1950
14k $250 $275 $325

LE COULTRE, 17J., "Master Mariner", auto-wind, c.1960
s. steel $125 $150 $200

LE COULTRE, 17J., RF#555-149, c.1955
14k $350 $400 $475

LE COULTRE, 17J., cal812, auto-wind, c.1952
s. steel $125 $150 $200

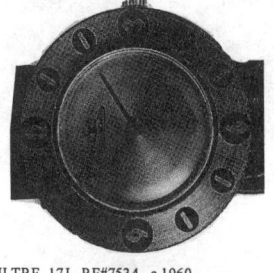

LE COULTRE, 17J., RF#7534, c.1960
14k $400 $500 $600

LE COULTRE, 17J.,"Coronet", cal.480cw, c.1951
gold filled................................$350 $400 $475

LE COULTRE, 17J., 11 diamond dial, RF#197, c.1955
14k(w)....................................$300 $350 $400

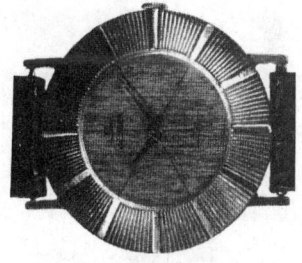

LE COULTRE, 17J., cal.480, wide bezel, c.1958
gold filled................................$125 $150 $200

LE COULTRE, 17 jewels, center lugs, c. 1960
18k $400 $450 $500

LE COULTRE, 17J., cal.480, c.1955
14k $250 $300 $350

LE COULTRE, 17 jewels, fancy lugs, c. 1950
14k $400 $450 $500

🕐 Some grades are not included. Their values can be
determined by comparing with **similar** age, size, metal
content, style, grades, or models such as **time only**,
chronograph, repeater etc. listed.

LE COULTRE, 17J., fancy lugs
14k $400 $450 $500

LE COULTRE, 17J., fancy lugs, ca. 1950s
18k $500 $600 $700

LE COULTRE, 17 jewels, fancy lugs, c. 1952
14k $300 $400 $500

LE COULTRE, 17 jewels, fancy bezel & lugs
14k $600 $650 $700

LE COULTRE, 17J., fancy bezel, Ca.1952
gold filled $150 $175 $225

LE COULTRE, 17J., auto wind, textured bezel, c. 1950
18k $250 $350 $450

LE COULTRE, 17 jewels, center sec., c. 1949
18k $400 $500 $600
s. steel $125 $150 $200

LE COULTRE, 17J., cen. sec., 24 hr dial, c. 1940
s. steel $275 $325 $375

This book endeavours to be a GUIDE or helpful manual and offers a wealth of material to be used as a tool not as a absolute document. Price Guides are like watches the worst may be better than none at all, but at best cannot be expected to be 100% accurate.

LE COULTRE, 17 jewels, fancy bezel & lugs, Ca.1953
14k $400 $450 $500

LE COULTRE, 17J., "Quartermaster", 24 hr dial, RF#114
s.steel $400 $450 $525

LE COULTRE, 17J., cal.813, RF#388-870, Ca.1959
gold filled.............................$100 $125 $150

LE COULTRE, 17J., center sec., Ca.1959
s.steel $125 $150 $200

LE COULTRE, 17J., center sec., ca. 1930s
silver $350 $400 $450

LE COULTRE, 17J., alarm, date, ca.1964
s. steel $200 $225 $250

LE COULTRE, 17J., quartz, cal.352, c.1970
gold filled $50 $60 $75

LE COULTRE, 17J., date alarm, c.1975
gold filled $225 $250 $285

LE COULTRE, 17 jewels, alarm, date, auto wind
14k $400 $450 $500

LE COULTRE, 17J., chronog., 2 reg.
14k $1,200 $1,350 $1,550
s. steel $500 $600 $700

LE COULTRE, 17J., chronog., cal.281, c.1940
s. steel $450 $500 $550

LE COULTRE, 17J., chronog., FR#2644, blue dial,
s. steel $500 $550 $600

LE COULTRE, 17J., chronog. 3 reg., ca. 1958
14k $1,800 $2,000 $2,200
s. steel $900 $1,000 $1,200

LE COULTRE, 17 jewels, chronog., 3 reg.
18k $3,000 $3,500 $4,000

LE COULTRE, 17 jewels, mystery dial, c. 1955
14k $400 $500 $600

LE COULTRE, 17J., diamond mystery dial & bezel
platinum...................................$1,500 $1,750 $2,000
14k(W) C&B $1,200 $1,400 $1,600

LE COULTRE, 17J., diamond mystery dial,
14k $500 $575 $650

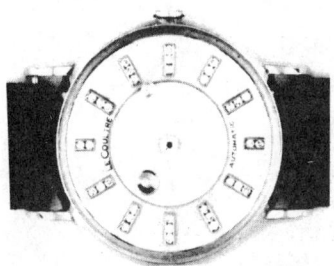

LE COULTRE, 17J., diamond mystery dial, waterp.
platinum $1,200 $1,400 $1,650
14k $900 $1,000 $1,200

LE COULTRE, 17J, diamond dial, textured bezel, c. 1960s
14k (w)....................................$350 $400 $450

LE COULTRE, 17J., date, cal.810, c.1952
14k $450 $500 $550

LE COULTRE, 17J., date, center sec., c.1950
14k $450 $500 $550

LE COULTRE, 15 jewels, triple-date, c. 1945
s. steel $400 $500 $600
14k $1,000 $1,100 $1,300
18k $1,300 $1,500 $1,800

LE COULTRE, 17J, astronomic ,moon ph., c. 1940s
18k $2,000 $2,200 $2,500
gold filled $700 $800 $900

LE COULTRE, 17J., triple date, moon ph., fancy lugs
gold filled $800 $900 $1,000

LE COULTRE, 17J., auto-w., Memovox, world time, c.1960
14k $1,500 $1,750 $2,000

⏱ Some grades are not included. Their values can be
determined by comparing with similar age, size, metal
content, style, grades, or models such as time only,
chronograph, repeater etc. listed.

LE COULTRE, 17J., weems style, cal.450, c.1942
s. steel $800 $900 $1,000

LE COULTRE, 17J., "Futurematic", auto- w., W. Ind.
gold filled $400 $475 $525
s. steel .... ★ $450 $500 $575

LE COULTRE, 17J., rotating chapters, date, c.1960
s. steel $700 $750 $800

LE COULTRE, 23 J., auto-w., date cen. sec.
14k $300 $350 $400

LE COULTRE, 17J., "Futurematic", cal.817, c.1952
14k $850 $950 $1,150

LE COULTRE, 17J., auto-w., date
14k $300 $350 $400

LE COULTRE, 17 jewels, "Futurematic"
18k $1,200 $1,400 $1,650
14k $1,000 $1,200 $1,350

LE COULTRE, 17J., day date, mid size, ca. 1940s
gold filled $300 $350 $400

🕐 Some grades are not included. Their values can be determined by comparing with **similar** age, size, metal content, style, grades, or models such as **time only**, chronograph, repeater etc. listed.

LE COULTRE, 17J., fancy lugs, aux. sec., ca. 1948
14k $500 $550 $600

LE COULTRE, 17J., auto-w., ca. 1950s
14k $300 $350 $400

LE COULTRE, 17J., fancy lugs
14k $350 $400 $450

LE COULTRE, 17J., aux. sec. ca.1950s
14k $200 $250 $300

LE COULTRE, 17 jewels, fancy wide bezel, ca.1955
14k (W)................................. $400 $500 $600

LE COULTRE, 17J., alarm, date,
14k $400 $500 $600

LE COULTRE, 15J., drivers style wind at 12, c.1960s
s. steel $350 $400 $500

LE COULTRE,17J.,drivers style crown at 6, RF#9041
s. steel $350 $400 $500

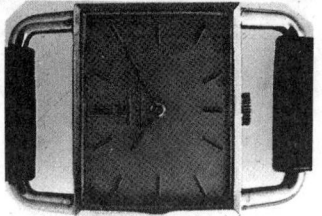

LE COULTRE, 17J.,RF#9041, cal.818, c.1960s
18k $500 $700 $800

LE COULTRE, 17J, "Reverso," center sec., c. 1930
18k $5,500 $6,500 $7,500
s. steel $1,500 $1,700 $2,200

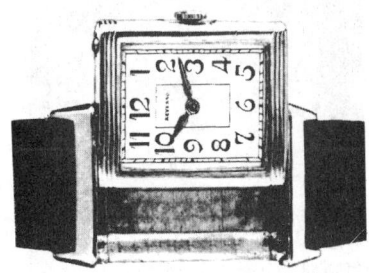

LE COULTRE, 17J., "Reverso," c. 1940s
18k $5,500 $6,500 $7,500
s. steel $1,500 $1,700 $2,200

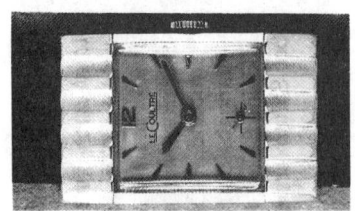

LE COULTRE, 17 jewels, fancy hooded lugs, c. 1952
14k $650 $700 $750

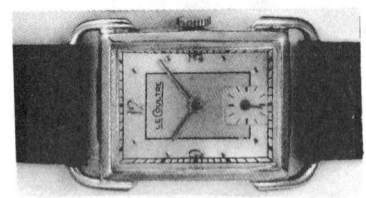

LE COULTRE, 17 jewels, fancy lugs
14k $600 $650 $750

LE COULTRE, 17 jewels, fancy lugs
14k $800 $900 $1,100

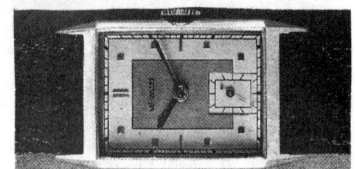

LE COULTRE, 17J., curvex,
14k $450 $550 $650

LE COULTRE, 17J., curvex, ca. 1940s
14k $550 $650 $750

LE COULTRE, 17J., stepped lugs, ca. 1944
gold filled $200 $225 $250

LE COULTRE, 17J., aux. sec., ca. 1940s
gold filled $200 $225 $250

LE COULTRE, 17J., square lugs, ca. 1948
14k $550 $650 $750

LE COULTRE, 17J., extended lugs, c.1938
gold filled..................................$150 $175 $200

LE COULTRE, 17J., aux. sec., c.1940
14k $300 $350 $400

LE COULTRE, 17J., tu tone dial, c.1940
gold filled..................................$150 $175 $200

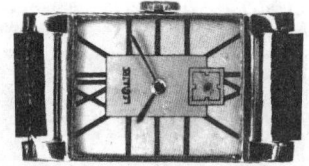

LE COULTRE, 17J., large lugs, c.1938
gold filled..................................$175 $200 $250

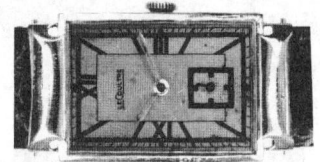

LE COULTRE, 17J.,hidden lugs, c.1942
14k $450 $500 $550
gold filled..................................$225 $250 $350

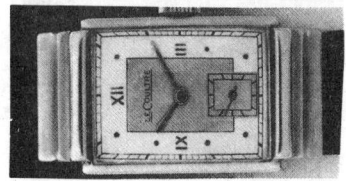

LE COULTRE, 17J., hooded lugs, ca. 1940s
14k $550 $650 $750

LE COULTRE, 17J., swing lugs, cen. sec.
s. steel $350 $400 $450

LE COULTRE, 17J., fancy bezel, ca. 1940s
14k $800 $900 $1,000

LE COULTRE, 17J., Asymmetric, Ca. 1960s
gold filled $250 $275 $325

LE COULTRE, 17J., Asymmetric, cal.438.4cw, Ca.1957
gold filled $250 $275 $325

LE COULTRE, 17J., Asymmetric, diamond dial, RF#2406,
Ca.1960
14k $375 $425 $500

LE COULTRE, 15J., **Duoplan, back-wind,** c. 1930
18k $1,000 $1,100 $1,250

LE COULTRE, 17 jewels, **uniplan,** c. 1938
14k (w)..................................$400 $450 $550

LE COULTRE, 15J., **Duoplan, back-wind,** c. 1930
14k $900 $1,000 $1,100

LE COULTRE, 17 jewels, fancy lugs, c. 1948
14k $450 $500 $650

LE COULTRE, 17J., fancy lugs, cal.438-4cw, c.1951
18k $550 $650 $750

LE COULTRE, 17 jewels, fancy lugs
14k $650 $725 $800

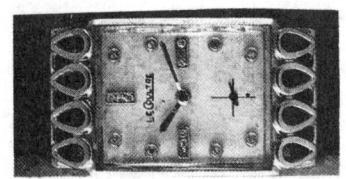

LE COULTRE, 17 jewels, diamond dial, fancy lugs
14k $750 $900 $1,100

LE COULTRE, 17J., diamond dial, ca. 1940s
14k $450 $550 $650

LE COULTRE, 17J., 12 diamond dial, cal.4870cw, c.1958
14k(w)..................................$300 $325 $375

LE COULTRE, 17J., diamond mystery dial ca.1940s
14k $850 $950 $1,100

LE COULTRE, 15J., hinged case, c.1920
14k $450 $500 $550

LE COULTRE, 17J., stepped case & lugs, cal., c.1950
gold filled.................................$150 $175 $200

LE COULTRE, 17J., aux. sec., c.1940
14k $250 $300 $350

LE COULTRE, 17J., cal.493, c.1955
10k $225 $250 $285

LE COULTRE, 17J., cal.438-4cw, wide bezel, c.1950
14k $450 $500 $550

LE COULTRE, 17J., textured bezel, c.1952
14k $450 $500 $550

LE COULTRE, 17J., textured bezel, c.1950
14k $450 $500 $550

LE COULTRE, 17J., RF#7540,engraved bezel, cal., c.1960
14k $450 $500 $550

LE COULTRE, 17J., cal.p812, c.1948
gold filled $200 $250 $300

LE COULTRE, 17 jewels, tank style, c.1958
18k $450 $550 $650

LE COULTRE, 17J., textured bezel, cen. sec.
18k $550 $675 $800

LE COULTRE, 17J., aux. sec., ca. 1930s
14k $350 $450 $550

LE COULTRE, 17J, triple date, moon ph., fancy bezel
18k .... ★ ★ ★ $3,000 $4,000 $5,000
gold filled............................$2,000 $2,200 $2,500

LE COULTRE, 17 jewels, c. 1945
18k $350 $400 $450

LE COULTRE, 17 jewels, fancy lugs, c. 1948
14k $450 $550 $650

LE COULTRE, 17 jewels, center lugs, c. 1945
14k $450 $550 $650

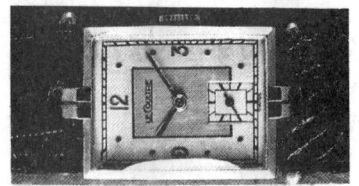

LE COULTRE, 17 jewels, center lugs, c. 1945
14k $450 $550 $650

LE COULTRE, 17 jewels, c. 1950s
14k $450 $550 $650

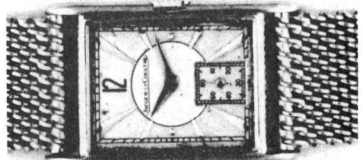

LE COULTRE, 17 jewels, 18k case & band
18k C&B............................ $1,000 $1,200 $1,500

LE COULTRE, 17 jewels, date cal. 810, c. 1952
14k $650 $750 $850

LE COULTRE, 17 jewels, two tone dial
14k $350 $450 $550
18k $450 $550 $650

🕒 Some grades are not included. Their values can be
determined by comparing with similar age, size, metal
content, style, grades, or models such as time only,
chronograph, repeater etc. listed.

LE COULTRE, 15 jewels, by Blancpain, c.1925
gold filled..............................$100 $125 $175

LE COULTRE, quartz, date, waterproof, c. 1960s
18k $300 $350 $400

LE COULTRE, electric, digital calendar
silver & gold...........................$300 $400 $500

LE COULTRE, 17 jewels, Asymmetric, c. 1953
gold filled..............................$350 $425 $550

LE COULTRE, 17 jewels, small, Asymmetric, c. 1953
gold filled..............................$200 $250 $300

LE COULTRE, 15J., lady's
14k(W)..................................$200 $250 $300

LE COULTRE, 15J., lady's art deco, by Blancpain, c.1925
silver $300 $350 $400

LE COULTRE, 15J., lady's REVERSO, c.1940
s. steel $800 $900 $1,000

LE COULTRE, 15J., **Duoplan, back-wind,** c. 1930
silver $550 $625 $725

LE COULTRE, 17J., lady's MYSTERY dial, c.1959
gold filled $100 $125 $150

LE JOUR, 17J., by Valjoux, cal.7750, c.1973
s. steel $150 $200 $250

LEMANIA, 17 jewels, auto wind
s. steel $50 $60 $70

LEMANIA, 17 jewels, chronog., military, ca.1970s
s. steel $350 $400 $450

LEMANIA,17J., chronog., 3 reg., c.1946
14k $500 $600 $700

LEONIDAS,17J., chronog., triple date, c.1945
gold filled $400 $450 $500

LEMANIA, 17 jewels, chronog., c. 1950
18k $500 $600 $700

LEONIDAS, 17 jewels, triple date, 3 reg.
18k $1,200 $1,300 $1,500
s. steel $350 $400 $450

LEMANIA, 17 jewels, chronog., waterproof
s. steel $300 $350 $400

LEONIDAS, 17 jewels, auto wind, triple date, moon phase
s. steel $300 $350 $400

LEONIDAS, 17 jewels, chronog., 2 reg.
s. steel $150 $200 $275

LEVRETTE,17J., chronog., (fly back), center lugs, c.1935
18k $1,500 $1,600 $1,800

LE PHARE, 17 jewels, chronog., triple date, 3 reg.
18k $900 $1,000 $1,250

LIBELA,7J., direct read, c.1952
base metal...............................$150 $200 $250

LE PHARE, 17 jewels, chronog., 2 reg.
18k $375 $450 $500
14k $275 $325 $375
s. steel $100 $150 $200

LIP,15J., chronog., tu-tone, center lugs, (French), c.1940
gold filled & s.steel. $550 $650 $750

LIP, electric, bulbous crown, (French)
s. steel $200 $250 $350

LE PHARE, 17J., triple date, moon ph., waterproof
18k $800 $1,100 $1,250
gold filled...............................$400 $475 $550

🕐 Some grades are not included. Their values can be determined by comparing with similar age, size, metal content, style, grades, or models such as time only, chronograph, repeater etc. listed.

LONGINES, 15J., center lugs, enamel dial, ca.1923
silver $325 $400 $475

LONGINES,15J., enamel dial, pierced shield , c.1923
silver $325 $375 $475

LONGINES,15J., enamel dial, GJS, c.1925
14k $250 $300 $400

LONGINES, 18J.,wire lugs, ca.1928
14k $400 $500 $600

⊕ Some grades are not included. Their values can be
determined by comparing with **similar** age, size, metal
content, style, grades, or models such as **time only**,
chronograph, repeater etc. listed.

LONGINES, 15J., wire lugs, enamel dial, c.1927
silver $250 $300 $375

LONGINES, 15J., wire lugs, ca. 1930s
silver $250 $300 $375

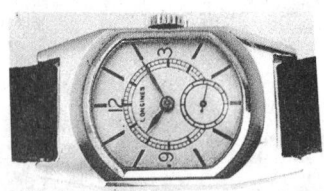

LONGINES,17J., tu-tone, GJS, c.1936
14k & s.s................................$175 $200 $325

LONGINES,17J., double dial, cal.932, c.1937
s. steel $700 $800 $1,000

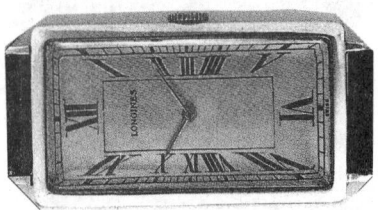

LONGINES,17J., large & curved, GJS,
gold filled $175 $225 $325

LONGINES, 15J., GJS, c.1922
silver $250 $300 $375

LONGINES, 17J., GJS, cal.940, c.1931
18k $500 $550 $700

LONGINES, 17J., GJS, cal.1086, c.1928
14k $400 $500 $700

LONGINES, 17J., cal.101, c.1947
14k $200 $225 $325

LONGINES, 17J., large Lindberg model 47mm., movable bezel & center dial (weem's second setting), Ca. 1930s

18k .... ★★★	$20,000	$25,000	$30,000
silver	$3,000	$4,000	$5,000
nickel................................	$2,000	$3,000	$4,400

LONGINES, 17J., small Lindberg model, original retail price $97.50, Ca. 1930s

18k .... ★★	$8,000	$9,000	$10,000
14k	$7,000	$8,000	$9,000
gold filled	$1,200	$1,400	$1,700
s. steel	$1,200	$1,400	$1,700

LONGINES, 17J., Weems U.S. Patent 2008734 on dial

s. steel	$450	$550	$650
14k	$800	$900	$1,000

LONGINES, 17J., "Weems", revolving bezel, Ca. 1940s
s. steel $475 $550 $650

LONGINES, 17J., "Weems", revolving bezel, Ca. 1940s
s. steel $475 $550 $650

LONGINES,17J., 1 button, fly back hand, c.1945
center recording
s. steel $400 $500 $600

LONGINES, 17 jewels, chronog., 1 button, c. 1923
silver $1,400 $1,600 $1,800

LONGINES,17J., 1 button chronog., c.1946
14k $2,000 $2,200 $2,400

LONGINES, 17J., chronog., one button
14k $1,000 $1,100 $1,200

LONGINES,17J., 1 button, fly back hand, center recording,
RF# 5034, Ca. 1940
s. steel $400 $500 $600

LONGINES, 17J. chronog., ref. 1333, enamel dial
silver $1,300 $1,500 $1,800

LONGINES, 17J., chronog. 2 reg., tach.,
14k $2,200 $2,400 $2,800

LONGINES, 17 jewels, chronog., 2 reg.
18k $2,000 $2,200 $2,400

LONGINES,17J., chronog., c.1942
s. steel $700 $800 $900

LONGINES,17J., RF#6474, c.1955
s. steel $800 $1,000 $1,200

LONGINES, 17 jewels, chronog., 2 reg.
18k $1,500 $1,700 $2,000

LONGINES, 17 jewels, chronog., 2 reg.
14k $1,200 $1,400 $1,650
s. steel $800 $900 $1,000

LONGINES, 17J., chronog., ca. 1945
gold filled $300 $350 $400

LONGINES, 17 jewels, chronog. 1 button
14k $1,000 $1,200 $1,300

LONGINES,17J., chronog., cal.539, c.1969
s steel $200 $225 $275

LONGINES,17J., Valjoux 726, cal.332, c.1972
s. steel $225 $275 $325

LONGINES, 16J., military issue, waterpr., ca. 1940s
s. steel $400 $500 $600

LONGINES,17J., GJS, c.1965
18k $225 $250 $275

LONGINES,17J., GJS, cal.23z, c.1958
gold filled....................................$75 $100 $125

LONGINES, 17J., GJS, cal.194, c.1963
gold filled....................................$75 $100 $125

LONGINES,17J., GJS, cal.352, c.1960
14k $225 $250 $350

LONGINES,17J., GJS, cal., c.1960
14k $225 $250 $350

LONGINES,17J., aux. seconds, Ca. 1960
gold filled $75 $100 $125

LONGINES,17J., Aux. seconds, gold jewel settings, Ca. 1957
14k $200 $235 $300

🕘 Some grades are not included. Their values can be determined by comparing with similar age, size, metal content, style, grades, or models such as time only, chronograph, repeater etc. listed.

LONGINES,17J., RF#2033p, GJS, cal., c.1958
14k $225 $250 $300

LONGINES,17J., RF#2021, GJS, cal.23z, c.1955
14k $400 $500 $600

LONGINES,17J., GJS, cal.23z, c.1955
14k $250 $275 $300

LONGINES,17J., large fluted lugs, GJS, c.1940
14k $300 $375 $475

LONGINES,17J., large lugs, GJS, c.1952
18k $350 $400 $450

LONGINES,17J., GJS, cal.18LN, c.1952
14k $250 $300 $350

LONGINES,17J., one lug at 11 & one at 5, GJS, 1955
14k $350 $400 $450

LONGINES,17J., GJS, cal.22a, auto-wind, c.1958
14k $275 $350 $400

🕒 Some grades are not included. Their values can be
determined by comparing with **similar** age, size, metal
content, style, grades, or models such as **time only**,
chronograph, repeater etc. listed.

🕒 Some grades are not included. Their values can be
determined by comparing with **similar** age, size, metal
content, style, grades, or models such as **time only**,
chronograph, repeater etc. listed.

LONGINES,17J., GJS, cal.10L, c.1952
14k $200 $250 $300

LONGINES, 17 jewels, fancy lugs, c. 1954
14k $450 $550 $600

LONGINES,17J., GJS, cal.23z, c.1954
18k $250 $300 $350

LONGINES, 17 jewels, fancy lugs, c. 1949
14k $350 $400 $450

LONGINES, 15 jewels, c. 1940s
18k $400 $450 $500
14k $300 $350 $400
s. steel $100 $125 $150

LONGINES, 19J.,"Conquest", auto-wind,
14k $500 $600 $700

LONGINES,17J., GJS, cal.22ls, c.1950
14k $250 $300 $350

LONGINES, 17J., fancy lugs, diamond dial,
14k $500 $600 $700

⏱ Some grades are not included. Their values can be
determined by comparing with **similar** age, size, metal
content, style, grades, or models such as **time only**,
chronograph, repeater etc. listed.

LONGINES,17J., "Flagship", GJS, cal.340, c.1960
18k $200 $250 $300

LONGINES,17J., RF#3759, GJS, cal.22as, c.1949
14k $225 $275 $350

LONGINES,17J., center sec., GJS c.1948
14k $150 $200 $250

LONGINES,17J., GJS, center sec., c.1958
gold filled $100 $125 $175

LONGINES,17J., GJS, cal.19as, c.1955
gold filled..................................$75 $100 $125

LONGINES,17J., center sec., GJS, cal., c.1940
14k $200 $250 $300

LONGINES,17J., GJS, cal.340, c.1960
14k $150 $200 $250

LONGINES,17J., GJS, center sec., c.1943
14k $180 $230 $300

🕐 Some grades are not included. Their values can be
determined by comparing with **similar** age, size, metal
content, style, grades, or models such as **time only**,
chronograph, repeater etc. listed.

LONGINES,17J., a-wind, "Grand Prize", date, Ca.1960
gold filled $60 $80 $100

LONGINES, 17J., military, Ca.1942
s. steel $150 $175 $200

LONGINES,17J., oval textured bezel, cal.506, c.1965
14k $200 $250 $300

LONGINES,17J., GJS, "Flagship", date, c.1964
gold filled................................. $80 $90 $100

LONGINES,17J., high frequency, date, c.1972
s. steel $60 $70 $90

LONGINES,17J., 36,000 (beat), auto-wind, "Ultra-Chron"
14k $200 $250 $300

LONGINES, 17 jewels, ''Flagship''
14k $200 $250 $300

LONGINES,17J., RF#9003, GJS, "Conquest", c.1958
18k $450 $525 $600

LONGINES, 17 jewels, gold jewel settings, Ca. 1950
s. steel $75 $100 $135

LONGINES, 17J., "Grand Prize", auto-w., date
14k $400 $450 $500

LONGINES, 17 jewels, center seconds
14k $200 $250 $350

LONGINES, 17J., "Conquest", auto-w., date, w.-indicator
s. steel $300 $350 $400

LONGINES, 17J., aux. seconds, large lugs
14k $150 $200 $250

LONGINES, 17J., date, ca. 1940s
14k $275 $325 $375

LONGINES, 17J., auto wind
14k $150 $200 $250

LONGINES,17J., mystery dial, cal.232 c.1960
gold filled $125 $150 $175

LONGINES, 19J., "Conquest", auto-w., date, ca.1962
s. steel $125 $175 $225

LONGINES,17J., mystery dial,
gold filled..............................$125 $150 $175

LONGINES, 17 jewels, mystery hand, ca.1962
gold filled..............................$100 $125 $150

LONGINES, 17 jewels, mystery hand,
14k $300 $375 $475

LONGINES, 17 jewels, mystery hand, 12 diamond dial
14k $500 $600 $750

LONGINES,17J., mystery 39 diamond dial, RF#1017
14k(w)...................................$650 $750 $850

LONGINES, 17 jewels, diamond dial, center lugs
14k $600 $700 $800

LONGINES, 17 jewels, "Ultra Chrono," diamond dial
14k $350 $375 $425

LONGINES, 17 jewels, "Ultra Chrono," date, c.1949
14k $200 $250 $300

LONGINES, 17J., auto-w., aux. sec.
14k $200 $250 $300

🕐 Some grades are not included. Their values can be
determined by comparing with **similar** age, size, metal
content, style, grades, or models such as **time only**,
chronograph, repeater etc. listed.

LONGINES, 17J., auto-w., aux. sec.
14k $175 $200 $250

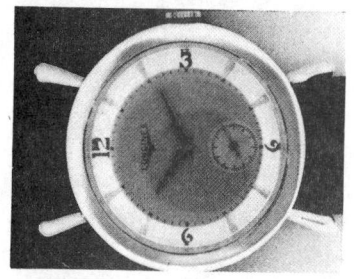

LONGINES, 17J., aux sec.
14k $175 $200 $250

LONGINES, 17J., diamond dial
14k(W) $200 $225 $300

LONGINES, 17J., diamond bezel
gold filled $150 $200 $250

LONGINES, 17J., 3 diamond dial
gold filled $150 $175 $200

LONGINES, 17J., diamond dial,
14k(W) $250 $300 $350

LONGINES, 17 jewels, cocktail style, 36 diamond dial
14k(W) $275 $325 $375

LONGINES, 17 jewels, 12 diamond dial
14k (w) $300 $350 $425

LONGINES, 17J., GJS, 34 diamond dial, date, c.1962
14k $300 $350 $400

LONGINES,17J., 36 diamonds, GJS, cal.194, c.1955
14k(w)..................................$300 $350 $400

LONGINES, 17J., 14 diamond dial, Ca. 1960
14k $275 $350 $400

LONGINES,17J., 14 diamonds,GJS, cal.370, c.1960
14k $250 $300 $350

LONGINES,17J., "Admiral", GJS, auto-wind, Ca. 1960
14k $325 $350 $450

LONGINES,17J., 4 diamonds, cal.194, c.1958
gold filled................................$150 $175 $200

LONGINES, 17J., GJS, tank style
14k C&B...............................$550 $600 $650

LONGINES, 17J., GJS, faceted crystal, Ca.1951
gold filled $125 $150 $185

LONGINES,17J., 37 diamonds on bezel 24 on dial, c.1958
14k(w)...................................$400 $450 $500

LONGINES, 17J., GJS, cal.9L, Ca.1939
gold filled $100 $125 $150

LONGINES, 17J., 4 diamonds, GJS, cal.23z, c.1948
14k $250 $300 $350

LONGINES, 17J., 5 diamonds, GJS, c.1953
gold filled $150 $175 $200

LONGINES, 17J., 5 diamonds, GJS, cal.8ln, c.1940
14k(w)...................................$200 $250 $300

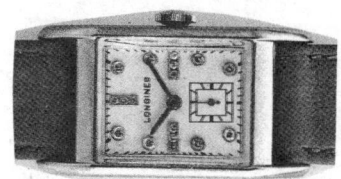

LONGINES, 17J., 17 diamonds, GJS, c.1951
14k $350 $400 $500

LONGINES, 17J., 8 diamonds, GJS, cal.22L, c.1958
14k $275 $300 $350

LONGINES, 17J., 15 diamonds, GJS, cal.9L, c.1945
platinum...................................$675 $775 $925
14k $350 $400 $500

LONGINES,17J.,4 diamonds, textured bezel,cal.194, c.1955
gold filled................................$125 $150 $175

LONGINES, 17J., 18 diamonds, RF#176, GJS, c.1950
14k(w)...................................$400 $500 $600

LONGINES, 17J., 6 diamonds, GJS
14k $250 $300 $350

LONGINES, 17J., 16 diamonds, cal.9LT, c.1958
14k(w)...................................$300 $400 $450

LONGINES, 17J., 4 diamonds, GJS, cal.L8474, c.1960
gold filled..............................$100 $125 $175

LONGINES, 17J., 6 diamonds, RF#2763, GJS, c.1955
14k $250 $300 $350

LONGINES, 17J., 8 diamonds, GJS, cal.9LT, c.1958
14k(w)...................................$250 $300 $350

LONGINES, 17J., 5 diamonds, GJS, c.1945
14k C&B...............................$450 $500 $550

LONGINES, 17J., 5 diamonds, GJS, cal.9L, c.1952
14k $250 $300 $375

LONGINES, 17 jewels, diamond dial, c. 1944
14k $400 $500 $600

LONGINES, 17 jewels, diamond dial, hidden lugs, c. 1938
s. steel $125 $150 $225

LONGINES, 17 jewels, fancy hidden lugs, diamond dial
14k (w) $600 $700 $800

LONGINES, 17 jewels, diamond dial, c. 1944
14k $400 $450 $500

LONGINES, 17 jewels, diamond dial, c. 1949
14k $350 $400 $450

LONGINES, 17 jewels, diamond dial, c. 1935
platinum.............................$1,100 $1,200 $1,400
14k $750 $850 $1,000

LONGINES, 17 jewels, 18 diamond dial
14k (w) $250 $300 $375

LONGINES, 17 jewels, flared, 6 diamond dial
14k $500 $600 $700

LONGINES, 17 jewels, 4 diamond dial
14k $225 $275 $325

LONGINES, 17 jewels, 12 diamond dial
s.steel $250 $300 $400

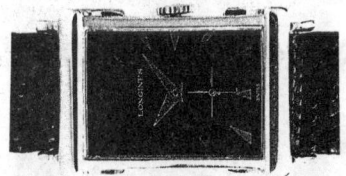

LONGINES, 17 jewels, "Advocat", fancy lugs, Ca. 1951
14k $300 $350 $400

LONGINES, 17 jewels, c. 1923
gold filled...............................$125 $150 $175

LONGINES, 17 jewels, flared, c. 1959
14k $450 $500 $600

LONGINES, 17 jewels, flared
14k C&B................................$750 $850 $950

LONGINES, 17 jewels, fancy lugs, c. 1943
14k $350 $400 $450

LONGINES, 17 jewels, torpedo shaped numbers
14k $250 $300 $350

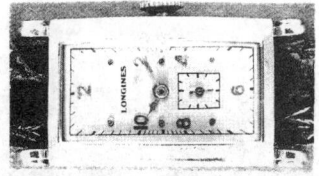

LONGINES, 17 jewels, curved, fancy lugs, c. 1939
14k $350 $400 $500

LONGINES, 17 jewels, center lugs, c. 1937
14k $250 $275 $350

LONGINES, 17 jewels, hooded lugs, diamond dial
14k(w)....................................$700 $800 $950

LONGINES, 17 jewels, hooded lugs
14k $200 $250 $275

LONGINES, 17 jewels, diamond dial, fancy lugs
14k $675 $750 $850

LONGINES, 17 jewels, diamond dial, c. 1944
14k $250 $300 $350

LONGINES, 17 jewels, fancy lugs
14k $250 $300 $350

LONGINES, 17 jewels, c. 1930
18k $800 $900 $1,000
14k $450 $550 $700
gold filled.........................$150 $175 $200

LONGINES, 17 jewels, 20 diamond dial, Ca. 1932
platinum...................................$800 $900 $1,100

LONGINES, 17 jewels, diamond dial
14k(W).................................$400 $450 $500

LONGINES, 17J.,curved,
14k $300 $350 $400

LONGINES, 17J., stepped case,
14k $300 $350 $400

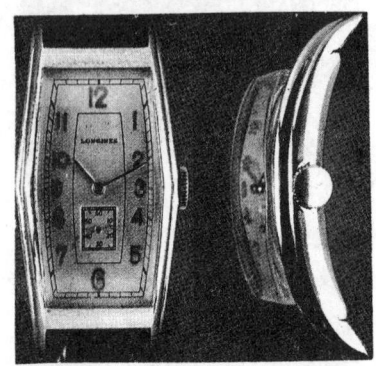

LONGINES, 17J., curvex, 52mm, ca. 1930
gold filled $500 $600 $700

LONGINES, 15J., tonneau, GJS, c.1925
silver $350 $400 $450

LONGINES, 17J., stepped case, GJS, cal.9L, c.1939
14k $275 $300 $325

LONGINES, 17J., extended lugs, GJS, cal.9L, c.1942
14k $250 $300 $350

LONGINES, 17J., cut corner, cal.94w, c.1929
gold filled................................$100 $125 $150

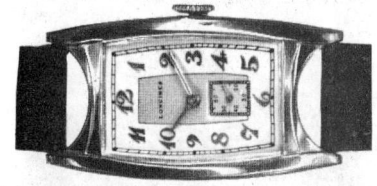

LONGINES, 17J., tonneau, cal.9L, c.1948
gold filled................................$150 $175 $200

LONGINES, 17J., carved bezel, GJS, cal.9LT, c.1950
gold filled $100 $125 $150

LONGINES, 17J., butler finish, GJS, cal., c.1951
gold filled $100 $125 $150

LONGINES, 17J., beveled bezel, GJS, cal., c.1935
gold filled $100 $125 $150

LONGINES, 17J., aux. sec., GJS, cal.9L, c.1948
gold filled $100 $125 $150

LONGINES, 17J., carved case, GJS, cal.9LT, c.1950s
14k $225 $275 $325

⊕ Some grades are not included. Their values can be
determined by comparing with **similar** age, size, metal
content, style, grades, or models such as **time only**,
chronograph, repeater etc. listed.

LONGINES, 17J., butler finish, GJS, cal.9LT, c.1957
14k $200 $250 $300

LONGINES, 17J., fluted lugs, GJS, cal.9L, c.1949
gold filled $125 $150 $185

LONGINES, 15J., butler finish, c.1926
gold filled.................................$100 $125 $150

LONGINES, 17J., carved case, GJS, cal.9LT, c.1959
gold filled $125 $150 $185

LONGINES, 17J., stepped case, GJS, cal.9LT, c.1958
14k $250 $300 $350

LONGINES, 17J., spur lugs, GJS, cal., c.1948
gold filled $125 $150 $185

LONGINES, 17J., stepped case, GJS, curved, c.1938
gold filled.................................$125 $150 $200
s. steel $100 $125 $175
14k $275 $300 $350

LONGINES, 17J., extended lugs, GJS, cal.9LT, c.1955
14k $300 $350 $400

LONGINES, 17J., fancy bezel, GJS, Ca. 1950
14k $450 $500 $550

LONGINES, 17J., fancy lugs, GJS, cal.9LT, c.1957
14k $225 $275 $325

LONGINES, 17J., fluted sides, GJS, cal.9LT, c.1950
gold filled................................$125 $150 $185

LONGINES,17J., GJS, c.1958
14k $175 $225 $275

LONGINES, 17J., carved case, GJS, cal.9LT, c.1955
14k $300 $350 $400

LONGINES, 17J., RF#3327, GJS, cal.,10L c.1948
14k $250 $300 $350

LONGINES, 17J., U shaped lugs, GJS
14k $400 $450 $500

LONGINES, 17J., extended lugs, GJS, cal.9LT, c.1951
14k $250 $300 $350

LONGINES, 17J., gold jewel settings, Ca. 1951
gold filled..............................$100 $125 $150
14k (w)...................................$175 $200 $250

LONGINES, 17J., aux. sec., GJS, Ca.1951
14k $175 $200 $275

LONGINES, 17J., RF#8475, GJS, cal.10L, c.1948
14k $250 $300 $350

LONGINES, 17J., butler finish, GJS, cal.9L, c.1955
14k $175 $200 $275

⊕ Some grades are not included. Their values can be
determined by comparing with **similar** age, size, metal
content, style, grades, or models such as **time only**,
chronograph, repeater etc. listed.

LONGINES, 17J., aux. sec., GJS, cal.9LT, c.1950
14k $225 $275 $325

LONGINES, 17J., butler finish, GJS, cal.8LN, c.1942
14k $200 $250 $350

LONGINES, 17J., beveled lugs, GJS, cal.8LN, c.1947
14k $150 $200 $250

LONGINES, 17J., wide bezel, GJS, cal.23z, c.1950
gold filled..............................$125 $150 $175

LONGINES, 17J., tank style, GJS, cal.23z, c.1957
14k $200 $250 $300

LONGINES, 17J., crab leg lugs, GJS, cal.10L, c.1951
gold filled $75 $100 $125

LONGINES, 17J., GJS, cal. 23Z, Ca. 1950
gold filled $70 $80 $90

LONGINES, 17J., bezeled case, GJS, cal.9LT, c.1955
gold filled $75 $100 $125

LONGINES, 17J., curly lugs, GJS, cal.23z, c.1950
gold filled $100 $135 $200

LONGINES, 17J., checked dial, GJS, cal.22L, c.1957
14k $225 $275 $325

LONGINES, 17J., RF#1050, mystery dial, cal.23z, c.1960
14k $300 $350 $400

LONGINES, 17J., stepped lugs, GJS, cal.10L, c.1948
gold filled................................$125 $150 $185

LONGINES, 17J., textured bezel, GJS, cal.22L, c.1950
14k $300 $350 $400

LONGINES, 17J., stepped case, GJS, cal.23z, c.1955
14k $250 $300 $350
gold filled................................$100 $125 $150

LONGINES, 17J., carved case, GJS,
gold filled................................$100 $125 $150

LONGINES, 17J., hooded lugs, GJS, cal.8LN, c.1942
gold filled................................$100 $125 $150

LONGINES, 17J., RF#2288, hidden lugs, GJS, c.1955
14k $400 $450 $500

LONGINES, 17J., hidden lugs
14k $600 $700 $800

LONGINES, 17J., contract case or recent case,
14k $400 $450 $500

LONGINES, 17 jewels, 42mm
14k (w) $275 $300 $400

Some grades are not included. Their values can be determined by comparing with **similar** age, size, metal content, style, grades, or models such as **time only**, chronograph, repeater etc. listed.

LONGINES, 17 jewels, fancy lugs
14k $300 $350 $400

LONGINES, 17 jewels, c. 1939
14k $350 $400 $500

LONGINES, 17 jewels, curvex, slanted lugs
14k (w).....................................$250 $300 $350

LONGINES, 17 jewels, fancy lugs, c. 1942
14k $300 $350 $375

LONGINES, 17 jewels, fancy lugs, c. 1947
14k $275 $325 $375

LONGINES, 17 jewels, curved, flared
14k $275 $300 $350

LONGINES, 15 jewels, chased bezel
14k $700 $800 $900

LONGINES, 15 jewels, engraved bezel, c. 1928
14k (w) $450 $500 $650

LONGINES, 17J., faceted crystal,
14k $150 $200 $250

LONGINES, 17J., fancy lugs & diamond bezel
14k(W)......................................$500 $600 $700

LONGINES, 17J., curved case, Ca. 1930s
14k $250 $300 $350

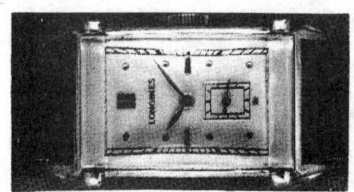

LONGINES, 17J., fancy lugs
14k $400 $450 $500

LONGINES, 17J., fancy lugs,
14k $325 $350 $400

LONGINES, 17J., cal#232, ca. 1948
14k $250 $300 $350

LONGINES, 17J., aux. sec.
14k $250 $300 $350

LONGINES, 17J., ca. 1952
14k $200 $250 $300

⊕ Some grades are not included. Their values can be
determined by comparing with similar age, size, metal
content, style, grades, or models such as time only,
chronograph, repeater etc. listed.

LONGINES, 17J., cal#10L, center sec.,
14k $250 $300 $350

LONGINES, 17J., center sec., fancy lugs, ca.1946
14k $250 $300 $350

LONGINES, 17J., fancy lugs, cal#10L
14k $200 $250 $300

LONGINES, 17J., aux. sec.
14k $200 $250 $275

LONGINES, 17J., offset lugs
14k $250 $300 $350

LONGINES, 17J., fancy lugs, ca. 1951
14k $400 $500 $600

LONGINES, 17J., fancy bezel
14k $200 $250 $300

LONGINES, 17J., flared case, GJS, c.1955
gold filled..............................$175 $200 $275

LONGINES, 17J., flared case, GJS, cal.9LT, c.1950
gold filled..............................$150 $200 $250

LONGINES, 17J., flared, textured dial
14k $400 $450 $550

LONGINES, 17J., Flared
14k $400 $450 $500

LONGINES, 17 jewels, enameled bezel, c. 1928
14k $400 $450 $500

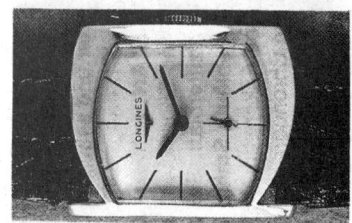

LONGINES, 17 jewels, formed case
14k $350 $400 $475

LONGINES, 17J.,antimagnetic
s. steel $150 $200 $250

🕐 Some grades are not included. Their values can be determined by comparing with similar age, size, metal content, style, grades, or models such as **time only**, chronograph, repeater etc. listed.

LONGINES MOVEMENT IDENTIFICATION

Cal. No. 4.21, Ca.1930

Cal. No. 5.16, Ca.1922

Cal. No. 6.22, Ca.1932

Cal. No. 7.45, Ca.1916

Cal. No. 7.48, Ca.1925

Cal. No. 8.23, Ca.1931

Cal. No. 8.47, Ca.1916

Cal. No. 9.32, Ca.1932

Cal. No. 9.47, Ca.1922

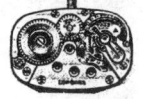
Cal. No. 12.19, Ca.1934

Cal. No. 13.15, Ca.1936

Cal. No. 25.17, Ca.1935

PRODUCTION TOTALS
LONGINES DATE OF MOVEMENT MANUFACTURE

DATE– SERIAL #	DATE– SERIAL #	DATE– SERIAL #
1867 --- 1	1911 - 2,500,000	1937 - 5,500,000
1870 --- 20,000	1912 - 2,750,000	1938 - 5,750,000
1875 --- 100,000	1913 - 3,000,000	1940 - 6,000,000
1882 --- 250,000	1915 - 3,250,000	1945 - 7,000,000
1888 --- 500,000	1917 - 3,500,000	1950 - 8,000,000
1893 --- 750,000	1919 - 3,750,000	1953 - 9,000,000
1899 - 1,000,000	1922 - 4,000,000	1956-10,000,000
1901 - 1,250,000	1925 - 4,250,000	1959-11,000,000
1904 - 1,500,000	1926 - 4,500,000	1962-12,000,000
1905 - 1,750,000	1928 - 4,750,000	1966-13,000,000
1907 - 2,000,000	1929 - 5,000,000	1967-14,000,000
1909 - 2,250,000	1934 - 5,250,000	1969-15,000,000

The above list is provided for determining the APPROXIMATE age of your watch. Match serial number with date. Watches were not necessarily sold in the exact order of manufactured date.
LONGINES date of movement manufacture

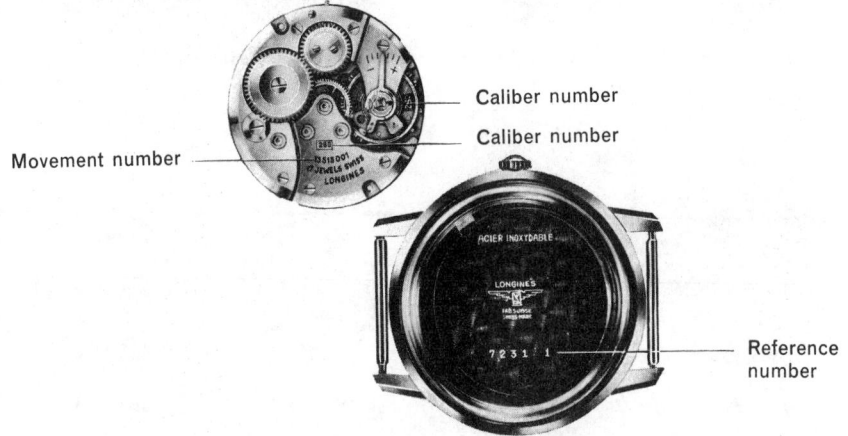

Caliber number

Caliber number

Movement number

Reference number

Cal. No. 10.68, Ca.1932

Cal. No. 10.68, Lindburg

Cal. No. 12.68, Ca.1938

Cal. No. 12.68 Z, Ca.1939

Cal. No. 14.16, Ca.1951

Cal. No. 14.16 S, Ca.1954

Cal. No. 14.17, Ca.1952

Cal. No. 15.18, Ca.1941

Cal. No. 19 A, Ca.1952

Cal. No. 19.4, Ca.1953

Cal. No. 19.4 S, Ca.1953

Cal. No. 22 A, Ca.1945

Cal. No. 22 L, Ca.1946

Cal. No. 23 Z, Ca.1948

Cal. No. 23 ZD, Ca.1954

Cal. No. 25.17, Ca.1935

Cal. No. RR 280, Ca.1963

Cal. No. 290, Ca.1958

Cal. No. 310

Cal. No. 312

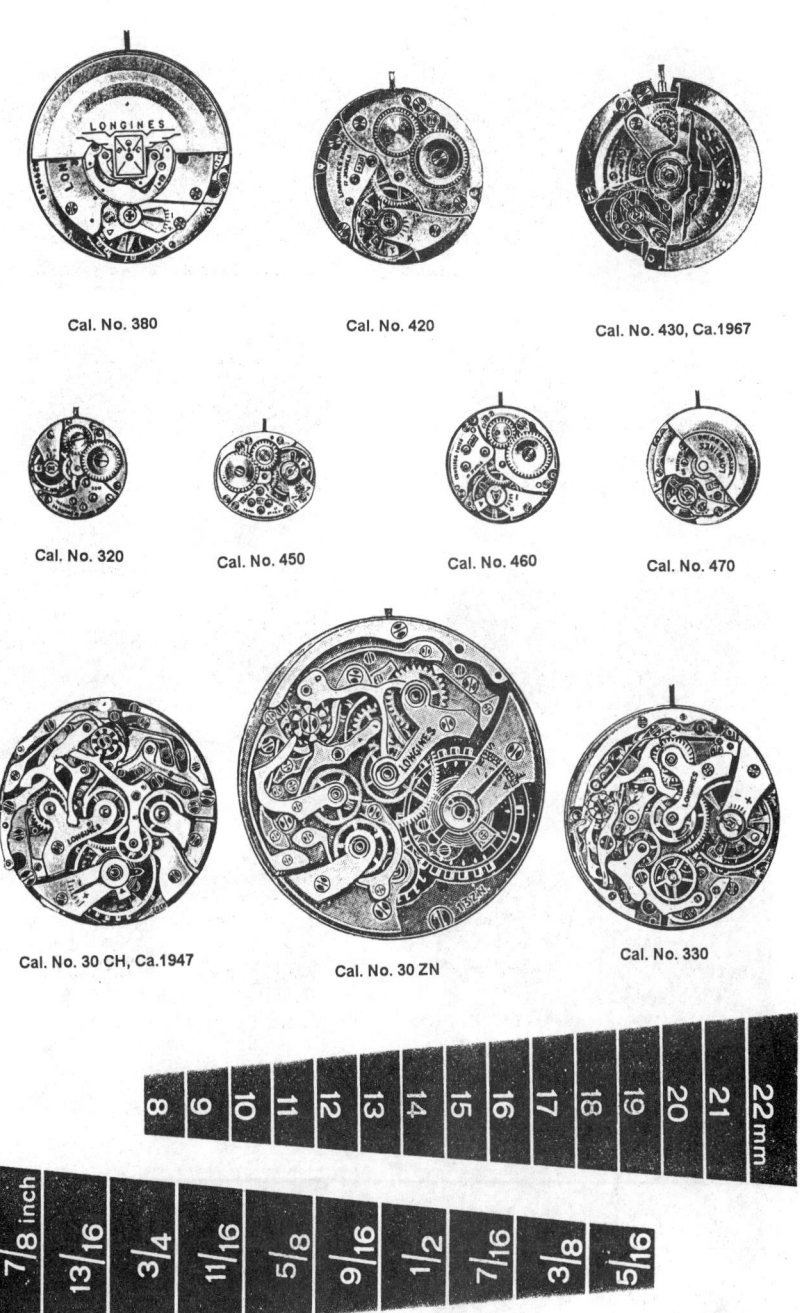

Cal. No. 380

Cal. No. 420

Cal. No. 430, Ca.1967

Cal. No. 320

Cal. No. 450

Cal. No. 460

Cal. No. 470

Cal. No. 30 CH, Ca.1947

Cal. No. 30 ZN

Cal. No. 330

LONGINES, 17J., "COMET", cal.702, c.1972
s. steel $100 $135 $175

LONGINES, 17J., lady's style, center lugs, c.1948
14k C&B.................................$200 $250 $275

LONGINES, 15J., lady's style,
14k C&B.................................$200 $250 $300

LORTON, 17 jewels, chronog., c. 1950
s. steel $150 $175 $200

LOUIS, 17J., center sec.,
14k $100 $125 $150

LOUVIC, 17J., mystery dial, long triangular case, c.1950
base metal $95 $125 $165

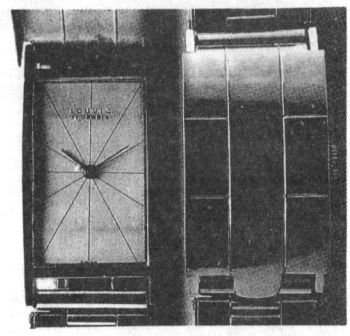

LOUVIC, 17J., hunter style case, ca. 1965
s. steel $125 $150 $200

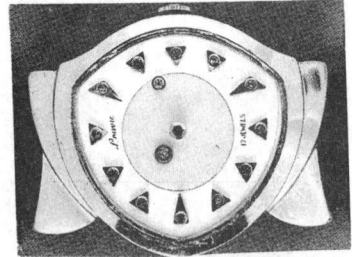

LOUVIC, 17J., mystery diamond dial, ca.1960
s. steel $60 $70 $80

LUCERNE, 17 jewels, 14k case & band
14k C&B.................................$350 $400 $450

LUCIEN PICCARD, 17J., movement by Ditisheim
14k $200 $250 $325

LUCIEN PICCARD, 17 jewels, gem set bezel
gold filled.................................$200 $250 $300

LUCIEN PICCARD, 17 jewels, "Seahawk," auto wind
18k C&B................................$400 $450 $550

LUCIEN PICCARD, 17 jewels, wind indicator, c. 1958
s. steel $100 $125 $175

LUCIEN PICCARD, 17 jewels, skeletonized
18k $800 $900 $1,000

🕐 Some grades are not included. Their values can be
determined by comparing with **similar** age, size, metal
content, style, grades, or models such as **time only**,
chronograph, repeater etc. listed.

LUSINA, 17 jewels, aux. sec., fancy lugs
gold filled $65 $80 $95

LYCEUM, 17J., beveled case, aux. sec.
14k $125 $150 $175

MARLYS, 15J., G.J.S., c.1935
14k $200 $225 $250

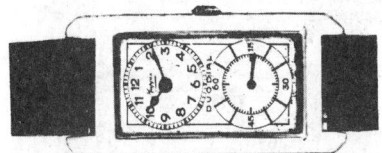

MAPPIN, 15 jewels, duo dial, c. 1930
9k $1,000 $1,150 $1,350

MARS, 17 jewels, "Dateur," hinged back, c. 1934
gold filled $350 $400 $500

MARVIN, 17J., center sec., cal.520s, c.1943
14k $100 $125 $150

MARVIN, 17J., non magnetic,
gold filled..................................$40 $50 $75

MASTER, 17J., engraved case, c.1943
gold plate $40 $45 $55

MASTER, 17J., tonneau case, c.1943
gold plate $40 $45 $55

MASTER, 17J., stepped case, c.1943
gold plate $50 $55 $65

C.H. MEYLAN, 17 jewels, c. 1940s
18k $700 $800 $900

C.H. MEYLAN, 18 jewels, jumping hr., c. 1920
18k $8,000 $9,000 $10,000

C.H. MEYLAN, 16 jewels, wire lugs
14k $700 $800 $900

C.H. MEYLAN, 27 jewels, 1 button chronog., 2 reg.
18k $2,500 $3,000 $3,500

C.H. MEYLAN, 18J., ladies , Octagon case, c.1917
platinum...................................$300 $350 $400

J.E. MEYLAN, 17J., chronograph, 2 reg., ca. 1937
14k $1,000 $1,200 $1,400
s. steel $300 $350 $400

J.E. MEYLAN,17J., stop watch,
s. steel $175 $200 $250

MIDO, 15 jewels, in form of car radiator, c. 1940s
silver $1,700 $2,000 $2,500

MIDO, 17 jewels, chronog., "Multi-centerchrono", c. 1952
s. steel $300 $375 $450

🕐 Some grades are not included. Their values can be
determined by comparing with similar age, size, metal
content, style, grades, or models such as time only,
chronograph, repeater etc. listed.

MIDO, 17 jewels, chronog., "Multi-centerchrono"
s. steel $400 $450 $500
with telemeter dial.................$425 $475 $525

MIDO, 17J., choronog., cal.1300, c.1954
gold filled $250 $300 $375
14k $650 $750 $800
18k $1,000 $1,250 $1,500

MIDO, 17J., choronog., pulsations, c.1955
18k $1,100 $1,300 $1,600

MIDO, 17J., carved case, cal.2m, c.1947
14k $150 $200 $250

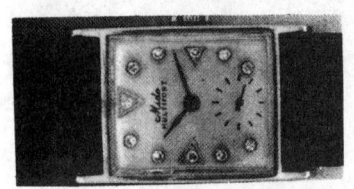

MIDO, 17 jewels, diamond dial
platinum.................................$500 $600 $675
14k $250 $300 $350

MIDO, 17 jewels "Multifort," diamond dial
s. steel $125 $150 $225

MIDO, 17 jewels, fancy lugs, c. 1945
14k $250 $300 $350

MIDO, 15 jewels, mystery dial, c. 1935
s. steel $500 $550 $650

MIDO, 17J., multifort grand luxe, date, ca. 1950s
18k C&B................................$600 $700 $800

MIDO, 17J., RF#7204, cal.d917b, c.1958
s. steel $100 $125 $175

MIDO, 17J., RF#228, mid size case, c.1943
s. steel $100 $125 $150

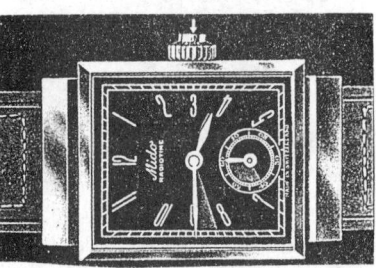

MIDO, 17J., "Radiotime", to correct time push button on
crown advances minutes & seconds hand, Ca. 1939
gold filled $100 $125 $175

MIDO, 17J., mid size case, cal.917r, c.1949
s. steel $100 $125 $150

⊕ Some grades are not included. Their values can be
determined by comparing with similar age, size, metal
content, style, grades, or models such as time only,
chronograph, repeater etc. listed.

MIDO, 17J., super auto-wind, muiltfort extra,
14k $175 $225 $300
s. steel ....,.....................$85 $100 $125

MIDO, 17J., "power wind", c.1955
s. steel $60 $80 $100

MIDO, 17J., rotating bezel, c.1960
s. steel $250 $300 $350

MIDO, 17J., multifort grand luxe, extra-flat
s. steel $100 $125 $150

MILDIA, 17 jewels
s. steel $30 $40 $50

MIMO, 15 jewels, date
gold filled $200 $225 $250

MIMO, 17J., "De Frece", date, c.1935
14k(w)....................................$300 $350 $400

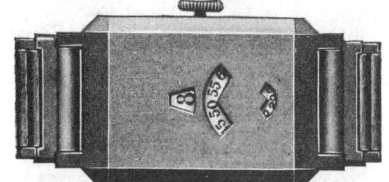

MIMO, 17 jewels, jumping hr., wandering min. & sec.
gold filled $300 $350 $450

MIMO, 17 jewels, 8 day, 6 gear train, c. 1950s
gold filled $800 $900 $1,000

MIMO, 17 jewels, duo dial
s. steel $400 $465 $575

MIMO, 15 jewels, engraved bezel
gold filled..................................$40 $50 $60

MIMO, 15 jewels, "Mimomatic," c. 1932
s. steel $75 $90 $110

MINERVA, 29J., min. repeater, repeats on 2 gongs
18k $20,000 $25,000 $30,000

MINERVA, 17 jewels, chronog., 2 reg.
18k $900 $1,000 $1,400
s. steel $275 $350 $450

MINERVA, 17 jewels, 2 reg.
18k $500 $600 $700

MINERVA, 17 jewels, waterproof, c. 1950s
14k $400 $450 $575
s. steel $250 $300 $350

MINERVA, 17J., Valjoux cal.723, c.1955
14k $750 $850 $1,000
s. steel $500 $600 $700

MINERVA, 19 jewels, chronog., 3 reg.
s. steel $300 $350 $400

MINERVA, 17 jewels, one button chronog., c. 1942
s. steel $275 $325 $365

MINERVA, 17J., chronog., day-date-month, 3 reg.
18k $1,000 $1,200 $1,400

MINERVA, 17 jewels, center sec., auto wind
gold filled..................................$70 $80 $100

MISC. SWISS, 15J., hunter style, wire lugs, ca. 1926
silver $450 $525 $600

MISC. SWISS. 15J., shield cover, enamel dial, ca. 1927
silver $500 $600 $700

MISC. SWISS,15J., rim wind, wire lugs, cal., c.1920
s. steel $250 $300 $375

MISC. SWISS,15J., enamel dial, c.1925
s. steel $300 $350 $400

MISC. SWISS,15J., wire lugs, c.1925
silver $250 $325 $400

🕐 Some grades are not included. Their values can be
determined by comparing with similar age, size, metal
content, style, grades, or models such as time only,
chronograph, repeater etc. listed.

MISC. SWISS, 15J., wire lugs, Ca. 1918
silver $150 $200 $250

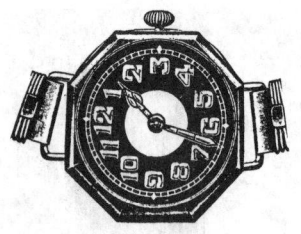

MISC. SWISS, 15J., wire lugs, Ca. 1917
silver $75 $100 $125

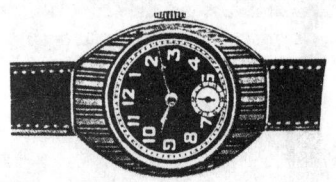

MISC. SWISS, 15J., wire lugs, Ca. 1918
silver $200 $250 $300

MISC. SWISS, 15J., wire lugs, Ca. 1917
silver $100 $125 $150

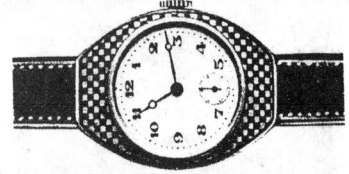

MISC. SWISS, 15J., wire lugs, Ca. 1917
base metal $100 $200 $300

MISC. SWISS, 15J., wire lugs, Ca. 1917
silver $100 $200 $300

MISC. SWISS, 15J., wire lugs, Ca. 1917
silver $100 $200 $300

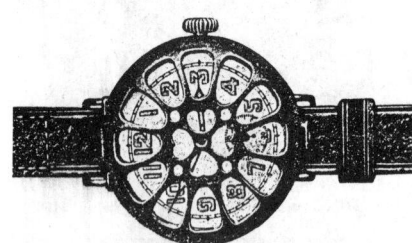

MISC. SWISS, 15J., wire lugs, Ca. 1917
silver $800 $900 $1,000

MISC. SWISS, 15J., wire lugs, Ca. 1917
base metal $150 $250 $350

🕐 Some grades are not included. Their values can be
determined by comparing with **similar** age, size, metal
content, style, grades, or models such as **time only**,
chronograph, repeater etc. listed.

MISC. SWISS, 15J., wire lugs, Ca. 1919
base metal $300 $400 $500

MISC. SWISS, 15J., wire lugs, Ca. 1917
silver $100 $150 $200

MISC. SWISS, 15J., wire lugs, Ca. 1917
14K...$100 $150 $200

MISC. SWISS, 15J., wire lugs, Ca. 1917
14K...$200 $300 $400

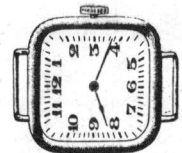

MISC. SWISS, 15J., wire lugs, Ca. 1917
14K...$100 $200 $300

MISC. SWISS, 15J., wire lugs, Ca. 1917
14K...$100 $200 $300

MISC. SWISS, 15J., wire lugs, Ca. 1917
14K...$100 $200 $300

MISC. SWISS, 15J., wire lugs, Ca. 1917
14k $100 $200 $300

MISC. SWISS, 15J., wire lugs, Ca. 1917
14K $200 $300 $400

MISC. SWISS, 15J., Ca. 1935
base metal $150 $200 $250

MISC. SWISS, 17J., nail set, 31 X 43mm, ca.1915
14k $1,200 $1,400 $1,600

MISC. SWISS, 15J., ca.1916
18k $1,200 $1,400 $1,600

MISC. SWISS, 15J., Ca.1916
18K.....................................$1,200 $1,400 $1,600

MISC. SWISS, 15J., Ca.1916
18K.....................................$500 $600 $800

MISC. SWISS, 15J., Ca.1916
18K.....................................$800 $900 $1,200

MISC. SWISS, 15J., Ca.1916
18K.....................................$1,400 $1,600 $1,800

MISC. SWISS, 15J., Ca.1916
14K.....................................$300 $400 $500

MISC. SWISS, 15J., wire lugs, Ca.1916
silver.....................................$100 $200 $300

MISC. SWISS, 15J., Ca.1916
18K.....................................$800 $1,000 $1,200

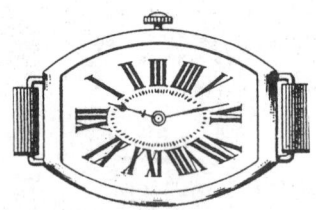

MISC. SWISS, 15J., wire lugs, Ca.1916
silver.....................................$100 $200 $300

MISC. SWISS, 15J., wire lugs, Ca.1916
14K.....................................$200 $300 $400

MISC. SWISS, 15J., Ca.1916
silver.....................................$100 $150 $200

MISC. SWISS, 15J., wire lugs, Ca.1917
silver.....................................$100 $200 $300

MISC. SWISS, 15J., wire lugs, Ca.1917
silver \$100   \$200   \$300

MISC. SWISS, 15J., wire lugs, Ca.1917
silver \$100   \$200   \$300

MISC. SWISS, 15J., wire lugs, Ca.1917
silver \$150   \$250   \$350

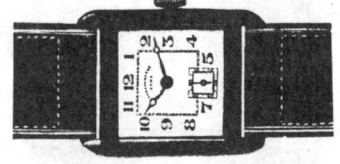

MISC. SWISS, 15J., Ca.1925
14K...\$250   \$350   \$450

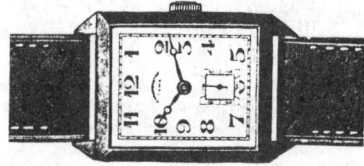

MISC. SWISS, 15J., Ca.1925
14K...\$275   \$375   \$475

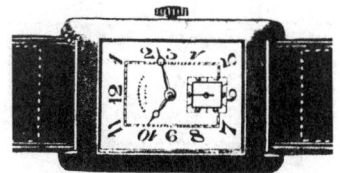

MISC. SWISS, 15J., Ca.1925
14K \$250   \$350   \$450

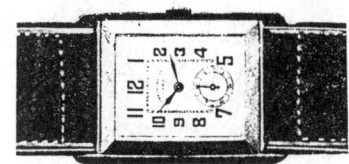

MISC. SWISS, 15J., Ca.1925
14K \$250   \$350   \$450

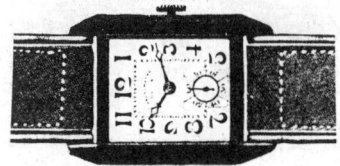

MISC. SWISS, 15J., Ca.1925
14K \$250   \$350   \$450

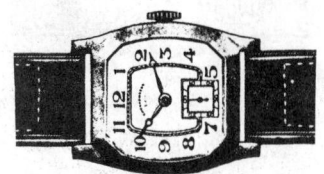

MISC. SWISS, 15J., Ca.1925
14K \$200   \$300   \$400

MISC. SWISS, 15J., Ca.1925
14K \$200   \$300   \$400

🕐 Some grades are not included. Their values can be
determined by comparing with **similar** age, size, metal
content, style, grades, or models such as **time only**,
chronograph, repeater etc. listed.

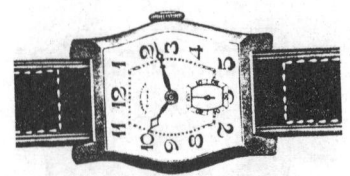

MISC. SWISS, 15J., Ca.1925
14K..............................$300 $400 $500

MISC. SWISS, 15J., Ca.1930
18K..............................$400 $600 $800

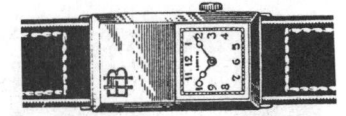

MISC. SWISS, 15J., Ca.1925
14K..............................$200 $300 $400

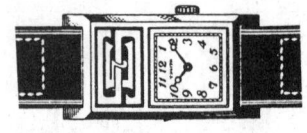

MISC. SWISS, 15J., Ca.1930
14K..............................$300 $400 $500

MISC. SWISS, 15J., Ca.1930
14K..............................$400 $600 $800

MISC. SWISS, 15J., Ca.1930
18K..............................$400 $600 $800

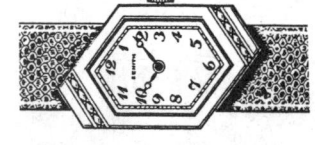

MISC. SWISS, 15J., Ca.1930
18K..............................$400 $600 $800

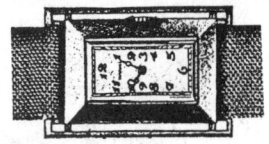

MISC. SWISS, 15J., Ca.1930
18K..............................$300 $400 $500

MISC. SWISS, 15J., Ca.1930
18K..............................$300 $400 $500

MISC. SWISS, 15J., flex lugs, Ca.1930
18K..............................$750 $850 $950

🕐 Some grades are not included. Their values can be
determined by comparing with similar age, size, metal
content, style, grades, or models such as time only,
chronograph, repeater etc. listed.

MISC. SWISS, 15J., Ca.1930
18K..............................$600 $800 $1,000

MISC. SWISS, 15J., wire lugs, ca. 1925
silver $150 $175 $225

MISC. SWISS, 15J., wire lugs, nail set, ca.1925
silver $200 $250 $300

MISC. SWISS, 15J., aux. sec., ca. 1930s
gold filled................................$75 $100 $125

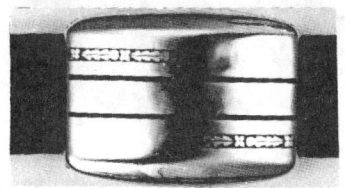

MISC. SWISS, 17 jewels, picture watch "Flip up"
gold filled................................$250 $300 $400

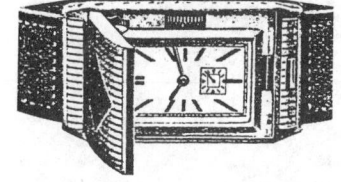

MISC. SWISS, 17J, **Flip Top** winds by opening lid, Ca.1932
base metal $1,000 $1,200 $1,500

MISC. SWISS, 17J., watch top flips up to view photo, c.1950
gold filled $200 $250 $300

MISC. SWISS, 17J., day date month moon phase, Ca. 1955
gold filled $500 $600 $700
14K $1,000 $1,200 $1,450

MISC. SWISS, 17J., jump hr., wandering min., c. 1930
9k $700 $900 $1,100

MISC. SWISS, 17J., wandering min., hr. by red mark
s. steel $250 $300 $350

MISC. SWISS, 17 jewels, fancy bezel
14k $275 $300 $350

MISC. SWISS, 17 jewels, masonic symbols, c. 1950s
s. steel & gold filled $900 $1,100 $1,200

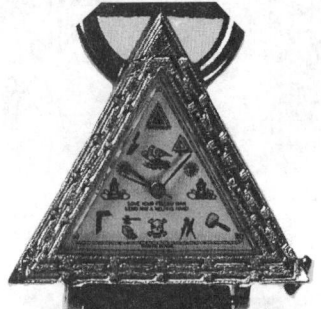

MISC. SWISS, 17 jewels, masonic symbols, c. 1975
base metal $200 $350 $450

MISC. SWISS, 15 jewels, early auto wind, c. 1930s
s. steel $400 $500 $650

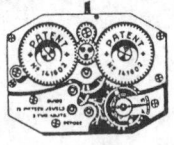

MISC. SWISS, 15 jewels, 8 day movement , (8 JOURS)

MISC. SWISS, 15 jewels, 8 day watch, Ca. 1935
base metal $200 $300 $400
silver $300 $400 $500

MISC. SWISS, 17 jewels, digital hr., min., sec.
gold filled $325 $375 $450
s. steel $300 $350 $400

MISC. SWISS, 15 jewels, double dial, c.1935
9K $575 $675 $825

MISC. SWISS, 15 jewels, center lugs, c.1936
9K $150 $175 $200

MISC. SWISS, 1 jewel, "Chevrolet Corvette", c.1970
base metal $150 $200 $250

MISC. SWISS, 1 jewel, "Mercedes Benz", c.1970
base metal $150 $200 $250

MISC. SWISS, 29 jewels, repeater, 2 jacquemart
18k $4,000 $4,500 $5,000

MISC. SWISS, 17J., silver coin, Ca. 1960
silver $300 $400 $500

MISC. SWISS, 17J., world time, date, Ca. 1965
s. steel $150 $175 $225

MISC. SWISS, 17J., golfers scorer, Ca. 1950
base metal $75 $100 $125

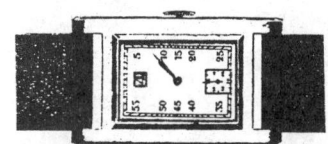

MISC. SWISS, 17J., jump hour at 12:00, Ca. 1930
14K $2,500 $3,500 $4,500

MISC. SWISS,15J., one button chronog. wind and sets at 12,
center hinged lugs, enamel dial, c.1920s
silver $1,200 $1,400 $1,700

MISC. SWISS,15J., 1 button chronog., enamel dial, wire
lugs, Ca.1923
silver $1,000 $1,200 $1,500

MISC. SWISS, 15-17J, enamel dial, one button chronog.
s. steel $900 $1,100 $1,350

MISC. SWISS, 17J.,early chronog., ca.1929
18k $1,600 $1,800 $2,000

MISC. SWISS, 15J., one button chronog., ca. 1925
silver $700 $800 $1,000

MISC. SWISS,15-17J., enamel dial, 1 button chronog., 2 reg.
s. steel $600 $700 $900

MISC. SWISS, 17J., one button, chronog., ca. 1950
gold filled..............................$400 $475 $550

MISC. SWISS, 17J., 2 reg., chronograph
s. steel $175 $200 $225

MISC. SWISS, 17J, chronog., 2 reg.
gold filled $225 $275 $350

MISC. SWISS,17J., "chronographe" on dial, c.1940
base metal $125 $150 $175

MISC. SWISS,17J., by Venus
s. steel $150 $175 $200
14k $325 $375 $425
18K $375 $425 $500

MISC. SWISS, 17J., triple date, chronog., 2 reg., c.1955
s. steel $350 $400 $500

MISC. SWISS, 17J., chronog., triple date, moon ph., c. 1945
14k $1,600 $1,700 $1,900
s. steel $600 $700 $850

MISC. SWISS, 17 jewels, **split sec.** chronog., 2 reg.
18k $3,250 $4,250 $5,250
s. steel $2,000 $2,200 $2,500

MISC. SWISS, 18 jewels, Jaeger,chronog., c. 1930s
18k $600 $700 $900

MISC. SWISS, 17J., triple date, moon ph., ca. 1967
gold filled $300 $350 $400

MISC. SWISS, 17 jewels, early auto wind, c. 1930s
14k $400 $500 $600

MISC. SWISS, 17J., diamond dial, Ca. 1945
14K $450 $550 $650

MISC. SWISS, 17J., diamond dial, top hat, Ca. 1945
platinum..............................$1,200 $1,400 $1,600

MISC. SWISS, 17J., mystery diamond dial, Ca. 1960
gold filled $200 $250 $300

MISC. SWISS, 17J., Rhinestone dial & bezel, Ca. 1950
gold filled.................................$300 $350 $400

MISC. SWISS, 17J., Rhinestone dial & bezel, Ca. 1950
gold filled.................................$200 $250 $300

MISC. SWISS, 17J., hidden lugs, Ca. 1934
gold filled.................................$150 $175 $200

MISC. SWISS, 17J., fancy lugs, Ca. 1945
14K..$550 $650 $750

MISC. SWISS, 17J., fancy lugs, Ca. 1940
gold filled.................................$100 $150 $200

MISC. SWISS, 17J., fancy bezel, Ca. 1938
14K..$350 $450 $550

MISC. SWISS, 17J., fancy bezel, Ca. 1947
gold filled $200 $250 $300
14K $600 $700 $800

MISC. SWISS, 17J., fancy bezel, Ca. 1930
18K (W)...............................$1,250 $1,500 $1,800

MISC. SWISS, 7J., stepped case, Ca. 1935
gold filled $100 $175 $250

MISC. SWISS, 17J., wandering hour, Ca. 1938
base metal................................$250 $350 $450

MISC. SWISS, 15J., Ca. 1938
14K..$250 $300 $350

MISC. SWISS, 15J., Ca. 1925
silver $100 $150 $200

MISC. SWISS, 21J., curved, Ca. 1938
gold filled...............................$200 $250 $300

MISC. SWISS, 17J., Fancy lugs, Chronometer, Ca. 1950
14K...$350 $400 $450

MISC. SWISS, 17J., Fancy lugs & bezel, Ca. 1950
gold filled...............................$200 $250 $300

MISC. SWISS, 17J., Fancy lugs, Ca. 1950
gold filled $175 $250 $300

MISC. SWISS, 17J., Fancy lugs, Ca. 1950
14K $600 $650 $700

MISC. SWISS, 21J., Fancy lugs, Ca. 1955
18K $1,000 $1,400 $1,800

MISC. SWISS, 17J., Fancy lugs, Ca. 1948
gold filled $175 $200 $225

🕐 Some grades are not included. Their values can be
determined by comparing with **similar** age, size, metal
content, style, grades, or models such as **time only**,
chronograph, repeater etc. listed.

MISC. SWISS, 17J., enamel & gold bezel, pin set, c. 1925
18k $275 $300 $350

MISC. SWISS, 22J., Military, Ca. 1941
base metal $400 $450 $550

MISC. SWISS, 15J., wire lugs, Ca. 1930
14K rose $100 $150 $200

MISC. SWISS, 15J., ,Ruby on case, Ca. 1950
14K $100 $200 $300

MISC. SWISS, 15J., Military, Ca. 1942
s. steel $150 $200 $250

MISC. SWISS, 15J., Ca. 1930
14K case & band...................$200 $300 $400

MISC. SWISS, 15J., Ring watch, Ca. 1955
14K $200 $300 $400

MISC. SWISS, 16J., Military, Ca. 1940
base metal $150 $200 $250

MISC. SWISS, 21J., horseshoe shaped, Ca. 1939
gold filled $200 $250 $300

MONARCH, 7 jewels, stepped case
gold filled..................................$40 $50 $60

MONTE, 16J., "ancre", ca.1938
14k $150 $175 $200

MONARCH, 7 jewels,
gold filled..................................$40 $50 $60

MORIVA,17J., auto-w. with wind indicator,
s. steel $100 $125 $150

MONARCH, 7 jewels, engraved bezel, curved
gold filled..................................$50 $60 $70

MONARCH, 7 jewels , curved
14k $275 $325 $400
gold filled..................................$95 $135 $200

HY. MOSER & CIE., 14J., "Signal Corps USA", ctr. lugs
silver $350 $425 $500

MONTBRILLANT, 15J., one button chronog. ca 1925
18k $1,500 $2,000 $2,500

HY. MOSER & CIE., 14-18J., one button chronograph, wind
and set at 12, center lugs, 2 reg. Ca. 1920s
silver $2,000 $2,250 $2,500

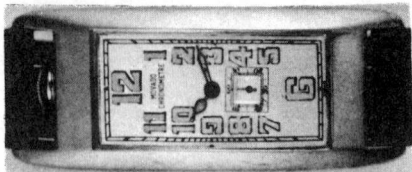

MOVADO, 15J., polyplan, winds at 12 o'clock, 46mm, curved, c. 1910
18k $4,000 $5,000 $6,000

MOVADO, 15J., polyplan, winds at 12 o'clock,
14k $3,000 $4,000 $5,000

MOVADO, 15J., polyplan, winds at 12 o'clock,
silver $2,000 $2,500 $3,000

Movado, Purse Watches See P.W. section Movado

ABOVE:
MOVADO, side view of movement with three inclined plans.

MOVADO, 15J., "Chronometre", c.1930
14k $250 $300 $350

MOVADO, 17J., day date month, "Sportsman"
14k $300 $400 $500

MOVADO, 17J., day date month, snap back
18k $500 $600 $700

MOVADO, 17J., triple date, snap back ," calendomatic"
18k $700 $800 $900

MOVADO, 28J., date, "Kingmatic", c.1950
s. steel $80 $100 $120
14k(w) $250 $300 $350

MOVADO, 17J., month date, ca. 1950s
14k $250 $300 $450

MOVADO, 17J., 1 button chronog., c.1948
s. steel $400 $500 $600

MOVADO, 17 jewels, day-date-month, c. 1945
18k $700 $800 $900
gold filled...............................$350 $400 $500
s. steel $300 $350 $400

MOVADO, 17J., chronog., 2 reg., c.1940
14k $1,200 $1,400 $1,600

MOVADO, 17J, triple date, moon phases, Ca. 1950
s. steel $900 $1,000 $1,200

MOVADO, 17J., 3 reg. chronog.
s. steel $850 $1,100 $1,200

MOVADO, 17J., 3 reg. chronog.,
18k $2,500 $3,000 $3,500
14k $2,000 $2,500 $3,000
s. steel $800 $900 $1,200

MOVADO, 17J., "tempograf, chronog., 2 reg., c.1935
s. steel $750 $850 $950

MOVADO, 17J., 3 reg. chronog., date
s. steel $300 $375 $450

MOVADO, 17J., El Primero date at 5, c.1972
s. steel $300 $375 $450

MOVADO,17J., RF#2652, rotating chapter,cal.352, c.1958
s. steel $250 $300 $400

MOVADO, 17J., center sec., cal.261, c.1948
18k $300 $350 $400

MOVADO, 17J., center sec., c.1942
14k $250 $300 $350

MOVADO, 17J., center sec., c.1948
14k $275 $300 $350

MOVADO, 17J., "Cronoplan", Ca. 1940s
s. steel $250 $300 $400

MOVADO, 15J., aux. sec., cal.75, c.1946
s. steel $100 $150 $200

⊕ Some grades are not included. Their values can be
determined by comparing with similar age, size, metal
content, style, grades, or models such as **time only**,
chronograph, repeater etc. listed.

MOVADO, 17J., aux. sec., cal.135, c.1955
s. steel $100 $125 $150

MOVADO, 17J., auto-wind, cal.8577, c.1957
14k $250 $300 $350

MOVADO, 17J., Tiffany & Co. on dial, center sec.,
14k $300 $350 $400

MOVADO, 15J., 2 colors of gold, tonneau, Ca. 1940
18k $500 $600 $700

MOVADO, 17J., center sec.
14k $250 $300 $350

MOVADO, 17., center sec.
s. steel $100 $150 $200

MOVADO, 20J., auto-wind,
14k $250 $300 $350

MOVADO, 28J., center sec.," Kingmatic",
14k $250 $300 $350

🕐 Some grades are not included. Their values can be determined by comparing with **similar** age, size, metal content,
style, models and grades listed.

MOVADO, 17J., aux. sec.
18k $300 $400 $500

MOVADO, 15 jewels, aux. sec.
14k C&B............................... $300 $400 $500

MOVADO, 17J., auto-w., ca. 1949
14k $300 $350 $400

MOVADO, 17 jewels, aux. sec., center lugs
14k $300 $350 $400

MOVADO, 17J., nonmagnetic
s. steel $150 $200 $250

MOVADO, 17J., cal. 7025, GJS, c.1964
18k $250 $300 $350

MOVADO, 15 jewels, center lugs, c. 1930
18k $500 $600 $700

MOVADO, 17J., hidden lugs, tu-tone dial, c.1960
18k $450 $550 $600

MOVADO, 17J., textured 18k dial
18k $300 $400 $500

MOVADO, 17 jewels, date at 12 o'clock
14k C&B............................... $400 $500 $600

MOVADO, 15 jewels, fancy lugs
18k $400 $450 $500

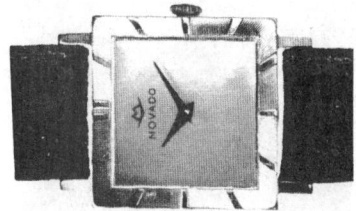

MOVADO, 17J., wide bezel, c.1958
gold filled.............................. $100 $125 $150

MOVADO, 17J., diamond bezel,
18k $250 $300 $350

MOVADO, 17J., RF#621, c.1932
gold filled.............................. $150 $175 $225

MOVADO, 17J., stepped case, "Curviplan", GJS, c.1942
14k $600 $700 $800

MOVADO, 17J., aux. sec., c.1940
14k $300 $350 $400

MOVADO, 17J., extended lugs, c.1945
14k $400 $450 $500

MOVADO, 17J., aux. sec., c.1945
14k $300 $350 $425

MOVADO, 17J., extended lugs, GJS, c.1940
14k $300 $350 $400

MOVADO, 17J., tu-tone case, RF#13906, Ca.1948
14k $300 $350 $400

🕒 Some grades are not included. Their values can be
determined by comparing with **similar** age, size, metal
content, style, grades, or models such as **time only**,
chronograph, repeater etc. listed.

MOVADO, 15 jewels, curved, chronometre
14k $600 $650 $700

MOVADO, 15 jewels, c. 1929
18k $400 $500 $600

MOVADO, 17J., cal#510, ca.1941
14k $400 $450 $500

MOVADO, 17 jewels
14k $250 $300 $375

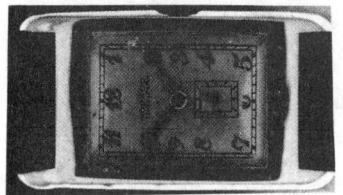

MOVADO, 17J., curviplan,
gold filled..............................$300 $400 $500

MOVADO, 17 jewels, automatic, tank style
18k $400 $500 $600

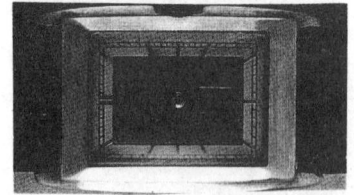

MOVADO, 17J., curviplan, ca.1941
14k $500 $600 $700

MOVADO, 17 jewels, fancy lugs, c. 1947
14k $300 $350 $400

MOVADO, 17J., fancy lugs, ca.1942
14k $500 $550 $600

⏲ Some grades are not included. Their values can be
determined by comparing with **similar** age, size, metal
content, style, grades, or models such as **time only**,
chronograph, repeater etc. listed.

MOVADO, 17J., Ca. 1940s
14k $250 $300 $375

MOVADO, 17 jewels
18k $400 $500 $600

MOVADO, 17 jewels, day date, Ca.1948
18k $400 $500 $600

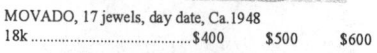

MOVADO, 17 jewels, hidden lugs, Ca.1940
14k $425 $500 $600

MOVADO,17 jewels, stepped & hidden lugs, GJS, Ca.1937
14k $450 $500 $600

MOVADO, 17 jewels, ladies, alarm, Ca.1950
18k $400 $500 $600

SIDE VIEW

Mt. VERNON, 15 & 21 jewels, curvex style
gold plate.................................. $60 $70 $85

Mt. VERNON, 15 jewels, curvex style
gold plate.................................. $60 $70 $85

Mt. VERNON, 15 jewels, stepped case
s. steel.................................... $60 $70 $85

Mt. VERNON, 17 jewels
gold filled................................ $60 $70 $85

Mt. VERNON, 15 jewels
gold filled................................ $35 $40 $55

MOVADO MOVEMENT IDENTIFICATION

Caliber 35  Caliber 65  Caliber 575  Caliber25, 27-Sweep Second

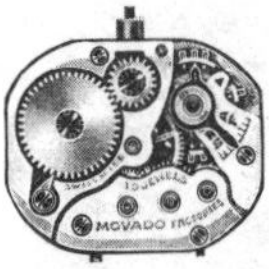

Caliber 28 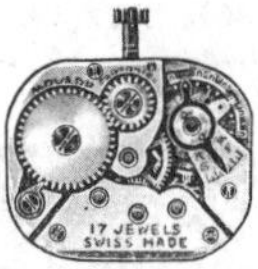 Caliber 575, Ermeto-Baby  Caliber 578, Ermeto Calendine 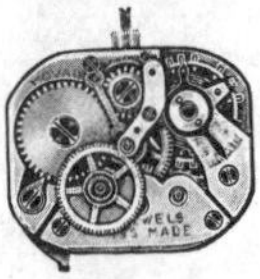 579, Calendoplan Baby

Caliber 5  Caliber 15  Caliber 50SP  Caliber 105, 107-Center Second

Caliber 190 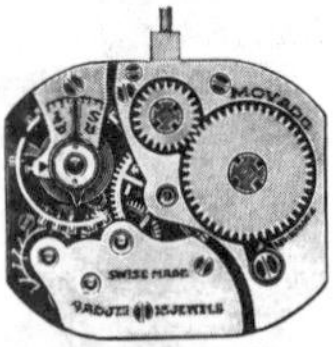 Caliber 375, 377-Center Second  Caliber 440, 443-Center Second

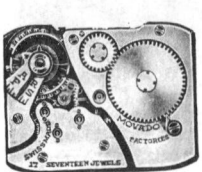

Caliber 510

Caliber 260M, 261

Caliber 150MN, 157-Sweep Second

Caliber 155, Calendermeto

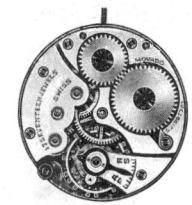

Caliber 470, 477-Center Second

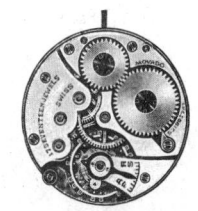

Caliber 473, 473SC-Calendar/Moon phase

Caliber 475, 475SC-Center Second

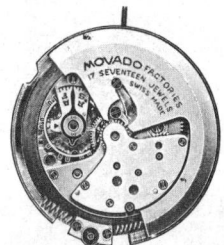

Caliber 225, 255M

Caliber 115

Caliber 118

Caliber 220, 220M

Caliber 221, 226

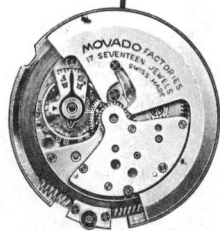

Caliber 223, 228

Caliber 224, 224A

U. NARDIN, 29 J., "Astrolabium," self wind, waterproof, local time, equinoctial time, months, signs of zodiac, elevation & azimuth of sun & moon, aspect in which sun & moon stand to each other
18k $10,000 $12,000 $15,000

U. NARDIN, 17J., one button pulsations. ca.1920
18k $2,000 $2,200 $2,500

U. NARDIN, 17J., chronog., "Pulsations," c. 1920
18k $3,000 $3,500 $4,000

🕐 Some grades are not included. Their values can be determined by comparing with similar age, size, metal content, style, grades, or models such as time only, chronograph, repeater etc. listed.

U. NARDIN, 17 jewels, chronog., c. 1950s
18k...$2,500 $2,700 $3,000

U. NARDIN, 17 jewels, split sec. chronog., c. 1910
silver.....................................$8,000 $9,000 $10,000

U. NARDIN, 17 jewels, chronog., 3 reg. c. 1940s
18k...$2,500 $3,000 $3,500

U. NARDIN, 25 jewels, date
14k...$450 $550 $650

U. NARDIN, 17 jewels, auto wind, c. 1952
14k $350 $400 $475

U. NARDIN,21J.,auto-wind
18k...$400 $500 $600

U. NARDIN, 17J., center sec., chronometer, c.1950
gold filled...............................$150 $200 $250

U. NARDIN, 17J., aux sec.
s. steel....................................$200 $250 $300

U. NARDIN, 17J., center sec., auto-wind, c.1950
14k $300 $375 $450

U. NARDIN, 17J., aux. sec.
18k...$375 $435 $500

U. NARDIN, 17J., center sec., auto-wind, c.1950
18k $400 $500 $625

U. NARDIN, 17J., fancy lugs
18k...$450 $500 $600

U. NARDIN, 17J., aux. sec., carved lugs, c.1950
14k $400 $450 $500

U. NARDIN, 17J., aux. sec., chronometer, c.1950
14k $300 $350 $425

U. NARDIN, 17J., aux. sec., chronometer, c.1947
18k $400 $450 $500

U. NARDIN, 17J., aux. sec., chronometer, C.1951
14k $300 $350 $400

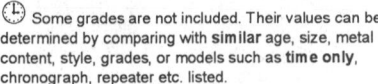

Some grades are not included. Their values can be
determined by comparing with similar age, size, metal
content, style, grades, or models such as time only,
chronograph, repeater etc. listed.

U. NARDIN, 17J., aux. sec., chronometer, c.1964
gold plate..................................$185 $225 $275

U. NARDIN, 17J., aux. sec., chronometer, c.1948
gold filled..............................$175 $200 $250

U. NARDIN, 17J., fancy lugs
14k...$400 $450 $500

U. NARDIN, 25J., chronometer, date, c.1975
s. steel....................................$175 $200 $275

U. NARDIN, 17J., fluted case
14k $400 $450 $500

U. NARDIN, 17J., aux. sec., chronometer, c.1949
14k $300 $350 $400

U. NARDIN, 17J., aux. sec., chronometer, c.1950
18k $350 $400 $500

U. NARDIN, 17J., extended side lugs, chronometer, c.1951
14k $300 $350 $400

U. NARDIN, 17 jewels, faceted crystal & bezel
s. steel $175 $225 $300

🕐 Some grades are not included. Their values can be determined by comparing with similar age, size, metal content, style, grades, or models such as time only, chronograph, repeater etc. listed.

U. NARDIN, 17 jewels, c. 1920
18k.......................................$550 $600 $700

U. NARDIN, 17 jewels, WW I military style
s. steel...................................$450 $525 $600

U. NARDIN, 17J., lady's chronometer, c.1947
14k C&B $400 $450 $500

NATIONAL, 17 jewels,
gold filled...............................$40 $50 $65

NATIONAL, 15 jewels, day-date-month
gold filled...............................$50 $60 $85

NATIONAL, 17 jewels, center sec., waterproof
s. steel $25 $35 $50

NATIONAL, 17 J., auto wind, center sec., waterproof
gold filled...................................$25 $35 $50

NEW ENGLAND W. Co., 7J., Addison, Alden, Cavour,
Hale, and other models, Ca.1915, colored dial add ($25)
14k $100 $125 $150
gold filled.................................$50 $70 $90

NEW HAVEN, 7 jewels, engraved bezel
base metal $20 $25 $35

NEW HAVEN, 7 jewels, stepped case
base metal $20 $25 $35

NEW HAVEN, 7 jewels
base metal..................................$15 $20 $30

NEW HAVEN,2 jewels, "Elf" ladies, etched case
base metal.................................. $10 $15 $20

NEW HAVEN, 7 jewels, "Duchess" ladies, etched case
gold plate.................................... $5 $10 $15

NEWMARK, 17J., military chronog., c.1979
s. steel..................................... $150 $200 $250

NEW YORK STANDARD, 7 jewels, wire lugs
gold filled.................................. $25 $35 $50
base metal..................................$15 $20 $30

NICE WATCH Co., 17J., one button chronog., c.1930
base metal $250 $300 $375

NICOLET W. CO., 17J., one button chronog., Ca. 1960
gold filled..............................$325 $375 $450

CHARLES NICOLET, 17J., chronog., ca. 1945
18k $425 $475 $550

MARC NICOLET, 17J., aux. seconds
14k $150 $165 $195

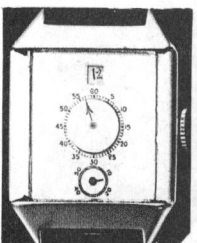

NITON, 18J., jump hr., (showing dial and movement)
(made ebauche for P.P.&CO.)
18k(W) $3,500 $4,500 $5,500

NIVADA, 21J., center sec., c.1960
base metal...................................$50 $65 $80

NIVADA, 21J., center sec., date, auto-w, c.1965
s. steel......................................$40 $60 $85

NIVADA, 25 jewels, waterproof, c. 1940
14k... $500 $550 $625
gold filled...............................$275 $350 $425

NORMANDIE, 17 jewels, compass, c. 1945
s. steel $50 $60 $70

NORMANDIE, 17J., gold train, hidden lugs, cal.4873
14k $150 $175 $200

OCTO, 17J., fluted lugs,
14k $275 $325 $395

OFAIR, 17J., chronog., cal. Valjoux 72c, c.1948
gold filled...............................$300 $350 $400
14k $600 $700 $775
18k $750 $850 $950

⏰ Some grades are not included. Their values can be
determined by comparing with similar age, size, metal
content, style, grades, or models such as time only,
chronograph, repeater etc. listed.

OGIVAL, 17 jewels, auto wind
gold filled...............................$40 $50 $65

OLLENDORFF, 17 jewels, fancy lugs
14k...$300 $350 $425

OLLENDORFF, 17 jewels, movement plates made of gold
14k...$500 $600 $700

OLLENDORFF, 7J., direct read, stepped case, c.1930
base metal...............................$200 $250 $300

OLLENDORFF, 15J., engraved bevel,
chrome plated...........................$50 $55 $65

OLMA, 17J., auto-wind, by Wyler, c.1932
s. steel $150 $175 $200

OLMA, 17J., large crab legs style lugs
gold plate $50 $75 $100

OLYMPIA, 15 jewels, double dial, c. 1938
s. steel $350 $400 $500

OMEGA, 15J., center lugs, enamel dial, Ca. 1930
18k $600 $750 $900

OMEGA, 15J., wire lugs, Ca. 1925
silver $250 $350 $475

OMEGA, 15J., wire lugs, ca. 1930s
18k..$700 $800 $950

OMEGA, 15J., wire lugs,
14k..$350 $400 $450

OMEGA, 17 jewels, center sec.
14k..$225 $250 $300

OMEGA, 17 jewels, chronog., c. 1935
18k...$2,500 $3,000 $3,500

🕐 Some grades are not included. Their values can be
determined by comparing with **similar** age, size, metal
content, style, grades, or models such as **time only**,
chronograph, repeater etc. listed.

OMEGA, 17J., 2 reg. chronog., ca. 1940s
s. steel $400 $475 $550
14k $700 $800 $900
18k $1,000 $1,200 $1,400

OMEGA, 17J., "Speedmaster", chronog., c. 1970
s. steel..................................... $550 $650 $750

OMEGA, 17J., 2 reg., chronog., c. 1958
18k $1,000 $1,200 $1,400

OMEGA, 17J., "Speedmaster Pro.", chronog., c. 1969
"the first watch worn on the moon" on back of watch
18k C&B $3,000 $3,500 $4,000
s. steel..................................... $700 $800 $900

OMEGA, 17 jewels, chronog., "Seamaster," c. 1963
14k $1,250 $1,500 $1,650
s. steel $600 $700 $850

OMEGA, 17J., "Speedmaster Pro. Mark II", c.1975
s. steel..................................... $375 $450 $525

🕐 Some grades are not included. Their values can be
determined by comparing with similar age, size, metal
content, style, grades, or models such as time only,
chronograph, repeater etc. listed.

OMEGA, 17J., "Seamaster", chronog., cal.321, c. 1962
s. steel $600 $725 $850
14k $1,250 $1,450 $1,650
18k $1,600 $1,900 $2,200

OMEGA, 22J., "Seamaster", date, 2 reg., auto-wind, c.1975
s. steel $350 $400 $500

OMEGA, 17J., "Seamaster", chronostop, cal.865, c.1965
s. steel.......................................$150 $200 $250

OMEGA, 17J., Speedmaster Pro. MarkIII,cal.1040,c.1978
s. steel $400 $475 $550

OMEGA, 17J., "Seamaster", chronostop., rotating bezel
s. steel.......................................$175 $225 $350

OMEGA, 17J., Speedmaster, auto-wind, chronog., c.1975
s. steel $375 $450 $550

OMEGA, 17J., "Seamaster", chronog., cal.321, c.1970
s. steel.......................................$300 $350 $425

🕐 Some grades are not included. Their values can be
determined by comparing with **similar** age, size, metal
content, style, grades, or models such as **time only**,
chronograph, repeater etc. listed.

OMEGA, 17 jewels, chronog., "Seamaster," 3 reg.
14k $600 $700 $800

OMEGA, 17 jewels, chronog., "Flightmaster," 3 reg.
18kC&B.............................$3,000 $3,500 $4,500
s. steel $350 $400 $500

OMEGA, 17 jewels, day-date-month, moon phase
18k $1,200 $1,400 $1,600
14k $1,000 $1,100 $1,200

OMEGA, 17J., day-date-month, moon phase, c. 1940
14k $1,000 $1,100 $1,200

OMEGA, 17J., day-date-month, moon phase, c.1950s
18k...$2,500 $3,000 $3,500

OMEGA, 17J.,date, "Constellation", chronometer
18k...$600 $700 $800
14k...$400 $450 $500

OMEGA, 24J., "Constellation", auto-wind, c.1960
14k...$500 $575 $625
s. steel.....................................$225 $250 $300

OMEGA, 24J., "Constellation", auto-wind, c.1968
gold filled................................$225 $250 $300

OMEGA, 24J., "Constellation", auto-wind, c.1969
s. steel $175 $200 $225

OMEGA, 17 jewels, "Constellation," auto wind, date
gold filled................................$225 $275 $350

OMEGA, 7J., "Constellation", quartz, cal.1342, c.1970
18k & s. s. $300 $350 $400

OMEGA, 24 jewels, "Constellation," auto wind
18k C&B $900 $1,000 $1,200

OMEGA, 17J., Chronometre, auto-w.,
14k $400 $450 $500

OMEGA, 24 jewels, "Constellation," c. 1959
18k...$550 $625 $675

OMEGA, electronic, "F300," c. 1950s
18k C&B................................$600 $700 $800

OMEGA, 17 jewels, "Seamaster," date, waterproof
18k...$400 $450 $500

OMEGA, 24J., "Seamaster", auto-wind, c.1962
14k $275 $350 $400
s. steel $100 $125 $150

Omega, 17 jewels, "Seamaster," auto wind
14k..$300 $350 $400

OMEGA, 24J., "Seamaster", auto-wind, cal.562, c.1962
gold filled.................................$100 $125 $150

OMEGA, 17J.,"Seamaster",chronometer
18k..$400 $450 $500

OMEGA, 23J.,"Seamaster", auto-wind, cal.1022, c.1978
s. steel $100 $125 $165

OMEGA, 17J., "Seamaster", c.1953
gold filled.................................$100 $125 $165

OMEGA, 17 jewels, automatic, date
14k $225 $275 $325

OMEGA, 17J., "Seamaster Deluxe",
18k..$400 $450 $500

OMEGA, 20J., "Seamaster", auto-wind, cal.501, c.1957
s. steel $100 $125 $165

OMEGA, 24J., "Constellation", auto-wind, cal.551, c.1962
14k... $400 $450 $525

OMEGA, 17J., "Seamaster", auto-wind, cal.1570, c.1955
gold filled.............................. $100 $125 $165

OMEGA, 16-18J., gold train, center seconds
s. steel.................................... $100 $125 $200

OMEGA, 17J., "Constellation", chronometer
18k $525 $575 $650

OMEGA, 16J., center sec., c.1940
s. steel.................................... $100 $125 $200

OMEGA, 24J., "Constellation", auto-wind, cal.505, c.1958
18k $525 $575 $650

OMEGA, 16J., U.S. Army, cal., c.1948
s. steel.................................... $150 $175 $250

OMEGA, 16J., center sec., c.1948
s. steel $150 $175 $200

OMEGA, 17J., auto-wind, center sec., c.1946
s. steel.....................................$100 $125 $150

OMEGA, 15J., Military (**England**), c.1946
s. steel $200 $235 $300

OMEGA, 17J., Seamaster, diamond dial, cal.563, c.1955
s. steel.....................................$150 $175 $200

OMEGA, 17J., "Railmaster", center sec.
s. steel $225 $275 $325

OMEGA, 17J., 12 diamond dial, center sec.
14k(W) $200 $250 $300

OMEGA, 17J., fancy lugs, ca.1948
14k...$350 $450 $500

OMEGA, 15-17J., 24 hour marked, Ca. 1930
s. steel $250 $300 $350

🕐 Some grades are not included. Their values can be
determined by comparing with **similar** age, size, metal
content, style, grades, or models such as **time only**,
chronograph, repeater etc. listed.

OMEGA, 17J., aux.sec., cal.360, c.1950
14k...$200 $235 $275

OMEGA, 17J., aux.sec., cal.266, c.1956
s. steel $80 $100 $150

OMEGA, 17J., auto-wind, c.1949
18k...$250 $275 $300

OMEGA, 17J., aux. sec., cal.266, c.1945
14k $250 $300 $350

OMEGA, 17J., auto-wind, cal.342, c.1955
gold filled...............................$90 $120 $150

OMEGA, 17J., auto-wind, c.1952
18k $300 $350 $400

OMEGA, 17J., seamaster, auto-wind
s. steel...................................$100 $125 $150

OMEGA, 17J., auto-wind, c.1949
18k $300 $350 $400

OMEGA, 17J., aux. sec., cal.302, c.1948
gold filled..............................$100 $125 $150

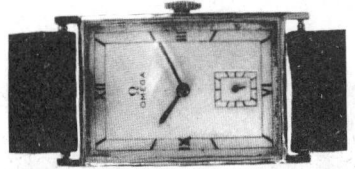

OMEGA, 15J., small lugs, c.1937
s. steel...................................$150 $175 $200

OMEGA, 15J., extended lugs, c.1939
14k $350 $375 $425
gold filled..............................$150 $175 $200

OMEGA, 17J., fancy lugs, ca. 1950s
14k...$350 $385 $425

OMEGA, 15J., aux. sec., c.1937
s. steel $150 $200 $250

OMEGA, 17J., faceted crystal,
14k(W)....................................$300 $335 $375

OMEGA, 15J., small lugs, c.1935
gold filled..............................$150 $175 $250

OMEGA, 17J., fancy lugs, ca. 1948
14k...$400 $450 $500

OMEGA, 17J., beveled case, c.1936
s. steel $150 $175 $225

⏰ Some grades are not included. Their values can be determined by comparing with similar age, size, metal content, style, grades, or models such as time only, chronograph, repeater etc. listed.

OMEGA, 17J., 9 diamond dial, ca. 1955
14k(W)....................................$200 $250 $300

OMEGA, 17 jewels, aux. sec.
14k C&B $700 $750 $800

OMEGA, 17 jewels, curved center lugs
14k...............................$300 $350 $400

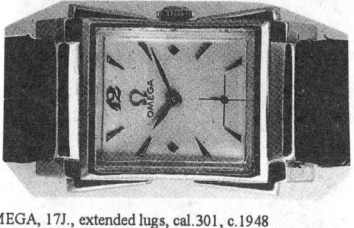

OMEGA, 17J., extended lugs, cal.301, c.1948
14k $350 $400 $475

OMEGA, 17 jewels, sculptured lugs
14k..$600 $700 $800

OMEGA, 17J., sculptured lugs, cal.302, c.1953
14k $300 $350 $400

OMEGA, 17 jewels, c. 1948
14k..$300 $350 $400

OMEGA, 17J., hidden lugs, c.1947
14k $300 $350 $400

OMEGA, 17 jewels, c. 1938
14k..$300 $350 $400

OMEGA, 17 jewels, hidden lugs, asymmetric
14k $600 $700 $800

OMEGA, 15 jewels, c. 1935
14k..$375 $450 $525

OMEGA, 17J., wide bezel, center sec.,cal.470, c.1955
14k $200 $250 $300

OMEGA, 17J., RF#347sc, cal.471, c.1956
18k $250 $300 $350

OMEGA, 17J., wide bezel & lugs, cal.369, c.1947
platinum $1,000 $1,100 $1,200

OMEGA, 17J., "De Ville",
18k $200 $250 $300

OMEGA, 17J., cal.620, c.1960
14k $175 $225 $275

OMEGA, 17 jewels, aux. sec.
18k $300 $350 $400

OMEGA, 17 jewels, c. 1937
s. steel....................................$225 $250 $300

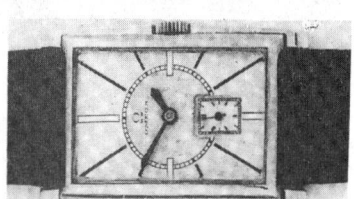

OMEGA, 17 jewels
14k $350 $400 $500

OMEGA, 15J., sliding case, winds at 12, Ca.1930s
18k $1,500 $2,000 $2,500

OMEGA, 15 jewels, hidden winding stem, c. 1930
14k..............................$1,200 $1,400 $1,600
s. steel...........................$800 $900 $1,000

🕐 Some grades are not included. Their values can be
determined by comparing with similar age, size, metal
content, style, grades, or models such as time only,
chronograph, repeater etc. listed.

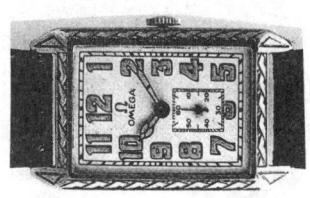

OMEGA, 15J., engraved case, c.1925
14k $275 $325 $400

OMEGA, 15J., ladies, wire lugs, c.1925
silver.................................... $65 $75 $95

OMEGA, 19J., alarm,"Memomatic", c.1975
s. steel $225 $250 $300

OMEGA, 17J., ladies center sec., c.1938
silver.................................... $150 $200 $250

OMEGA, 17J., ladies flip open, 16 diamonds, c.1955
14k C&B $700 $800 $1,000

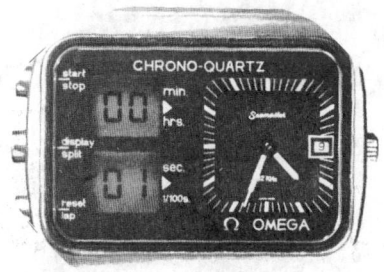

OMEGA, "Chrono-quartz, cal.1611, c.1975
s. steel $175 $200 $250

OMEGA, 15J., ladies, non-magnetic, c.1945
s. steel................................... $55 $65 $85

OMEGA, 17J., ladies, sapphire stones on lugs, c.1950
14k C&B $500 $600 $800

OMEGA, quartz, marine chronometer
s. steel $250 $300 $350

OMEGA, 17J., ladies, RF#8065, c.1965
18k C&B $500 $600 $700

OMEGA BASIC CALIBRE IDENTIFICATION

Cal. No. 100, Ca.1943

Cal. No. 210, Ca.1946

Cal. No. 220, Ca.1941

Cal. No. 230, center second

Cal. No. 240, Ca.1939

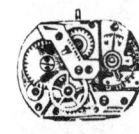

Cal. No. 250, center seconds

Cal. No. 260, Ca.1943

Cal. No. 280, center seconds

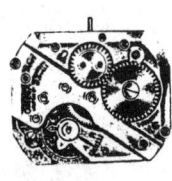

Cal. No. 300, Ca.1944

Cal. No. 310, center seconds

Cai. No. 330, Ca.1943

Cal. No. 360, Ca.1944

Cal. No. 440

Cal. No. 372, jumping seconds

Cal. No. 410, Ca.1951

Cal. No. 420, center seconds

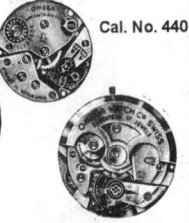

Cal. No. 455, Ca.1955

OMEGA PRODUCTION TOTALS

DATE-SERIAL #	DATE-SERIAL #	DATE-SERIAL #
1895 – 50,000	1920 - 6,000,000	1950-15,500,000
1900 – 500,000	1925 - 7,500,000	1955-16,500,000
1905 - 1,000,000	1930 - 9,500,000	1960-18,000,000
1910 - 2,500,000	1935-11,000,000	1965-23,000,000
1915 - 4,500,000	1940-12,500,000	1970-28,000,000
	1945-14,000,000	1975-35,000,000

🕐 The above list is provided for determining the APPROXIMATE age of your watch. Match serial number with date. Watches were not necessarily sold in the exact order of manufactured date.

Cal. No. 470, Ca.1955

Cal. No. 480, Ca.1955

Cal. No. 490, Ca.1956

Cal. No. 500, Ca.1956

Cal. No. 510, Ca.1956

Cal. No. 520, center seconds

Cal. No. 540, Ca.1957

Cal. No. 550, Ca.1959

Cal. No. 570, Ca.1959

Cal. No. 590, Ca.1960

Cal. No. 600, Ca.1960

Cal. No. 620, Ca.1961

Cal. No. 580, Ca. 1959

Cal. No. 660, Ca.1963

Cal. No. 670, Ca.1963

Cal. No. 690, Ca.1962

Cal. No. 700, Ca.1964

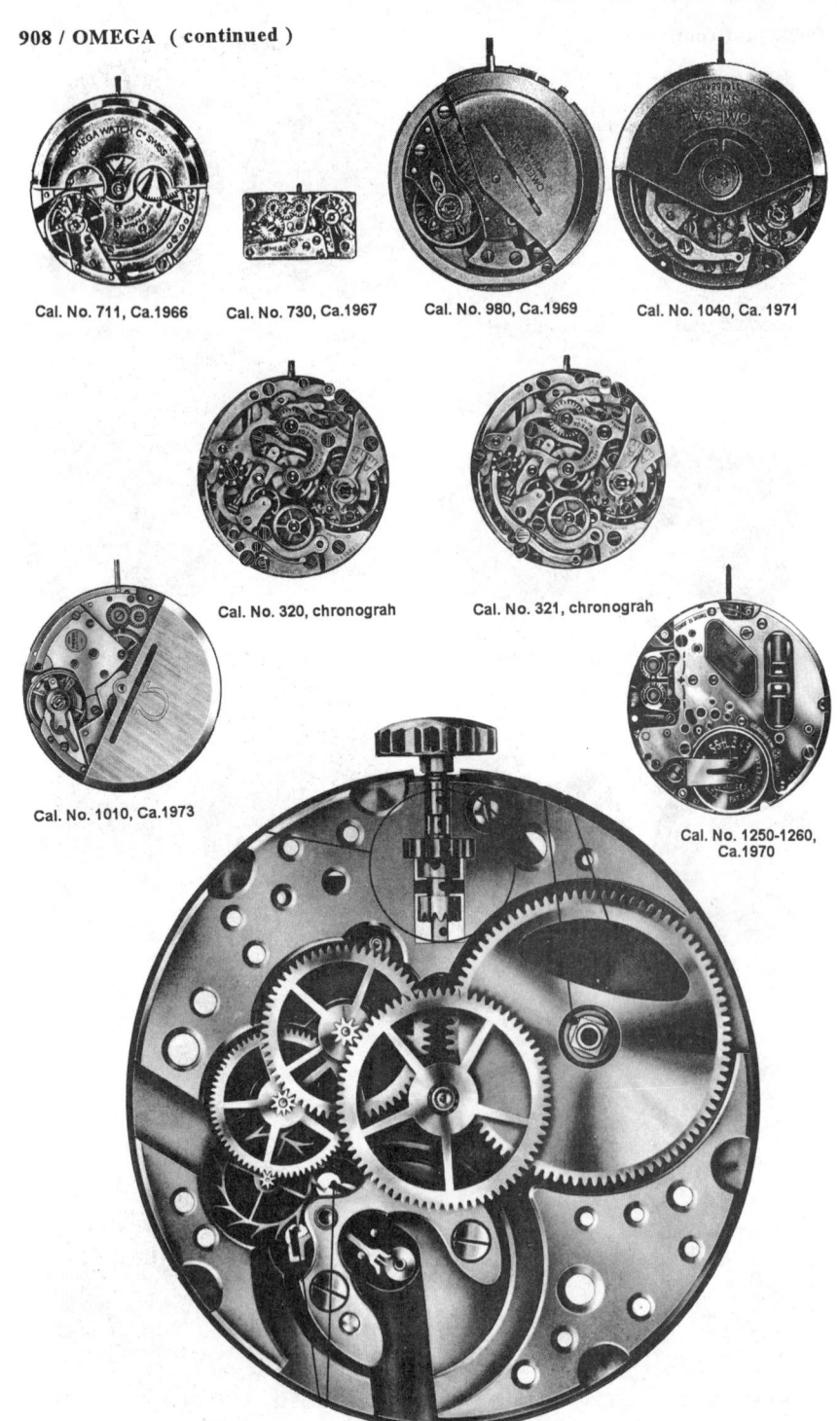

Cal. No. 711, Ca.1966

Cal. No. 730, Ca.1967

Cal. No. 980, Ca.1969

Cal. No. 1040, Ca. 1971

Cal. No. 320, chronograh

Cal. No. 321, chronograh

Cal. No. 1010, Ca.1973

Cal. No. 1250-1260, Ca.1970

OPEL, 21 jewels, waterproof
gold filled $50 $75 $100

ORATOR, 17 jewels, auto wind
s. steel $25 $35 $50

ORFINA, 17 jewels, triple date, moon phase, **bombe' lugs**
gold filled $275 $350 $425

ORFINA, 17 jewels, triple date, moon phase, **carved lugs**
gold filled $275 $350 $425

ORFINA, 17 jewels, day-date-month
gold filled $70 $80 $100

ORFINA, 17 jewels, date
s. steel $50 $60 $70

ORVIN, 17 jewels, day-date, c. 1945
s. steel $70 $80 $90

PABRO, 17J., ladies 76 diamond watch, c.1930
platinum $600 $700 $800

PARKER, 17J., 2 reg. chronog.,ca.1948
s. steel $150 $185 $225

" PATEK PHILIPPE" watches should be signed on the case, dial & movement to bring the prices listed in this book.
(**triple signed P.P.CO.**)

PATEK PHILIPPE, 29 jewels, min. repeater, c. 1920
platinum...........................$125,000 $150,000 $175,000

PATEK PHILIPPE, 29 jewels, min. repeater, six watches finished by E. Gublin, 18k case & band, triple signed
18k C&B........................$130,000 $140,000 $150,000

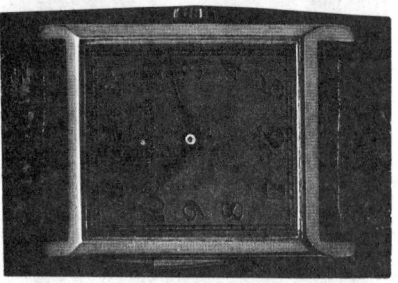

PATEK PHILIPPE, 29J., min. repeater, 30 x 34mm
18k $150,000 $175,000 $200,000

PATEK PHILIPPE, 50 sec. tourbillon, 57 hr. power reserve 5 gear train, 28 x 38mm, RF#3834
18k $150,000 $170,000 $190,000

PATEK PHILIPPE, 39J., auto-wind, min. repeater, perpetual day date month calendars, moon ph., 24 hr. ind., leap year ind., RF#3974, 5 year waiting list, c.1989
18K....................................$225,000 $250,000 $275,000

PATEK PHILIPPE,18J., horizontal case, RF#504, 2 tone
18k $10,000 $11,000 $12,000

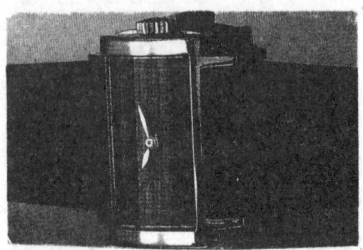

PATEK PHILIPPE,18 J., horizontal case, RF#139
18k $6,000 $7,000 $8,000

" PATEK PHILIPPE" watches should be signed on the case, dial & movement to bring the prices listed in this book.
(**triple signed P.P.CO.**)

PATEK PHILIPPE, 29 jewels, min. repeater, RF#2524
18k $100,000 $120,000 $150,000

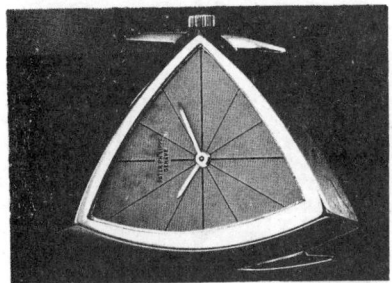

PATEK PHILIPPE, 18J., designed by Gilbert Albert,
RF#3412, c. 1958
18k $18,000 $20,000 $22,000

PATEK PHILIPPE, 18J., asymmetric case designed by
Gilbert Albert, RF#3413, c. 1958
18k $20,000 $22,000 $25,000

PATEK PHILIPPE,18J., fluted hooded lugs, RF#2517
18k $4,000 $5,000 $6,000

PATEK PHILIPPE, 18 J., RF#3497, diamond set case
platinum C&B...................$10,000 $12,000 $14,000

PATEK PHILIPPE, 18J., RF#3424, asymmetric, c. 1960
18k $12,000 $14,000 $17,000

PATEK PHILIPPE, 18J., asymmetric, diamond set
platinum............................$18,000 $20,000 $22,000

PATEK PHILIPPE, 18 J., Cal.# 9, **hinged back**, c. 1920s
18k $4,000 $4,500 $5,000

PATEK PHILIPPE, 18 jewels, Cal.# 9, curved, c. 1926
18k $4,000 $4,500 $5,000

PATEK PHILIPPE, 18 J., Cal.# 10, hinged back, c. 1920s
18k $4,000 $4,500 $5,000

PATEK PHILIPPE, 18 jewels, Cal.# 9, c. 1940s
18k $4,200 $4,800 $5,250

PATEK PHILIPPE, 18 jewels, Cal.. 9, c. 1950s
18k $4,000 $4,500 $5,000

PATEK PHILIPPE,18J., cal.990, c.1936
18K...................................$4,250 $4,500 $4,750

PATEK PHILIPPE,18J., RF#409, cal. c.1934
18K...................................$3,700 $4,000 $4,250

PATEK PHILIPPE, 18 J., stepped case, Cal.# 9, c. 1940s
18k $4,000 $4,400 $4,800

PATEK PHILIPPE, 18 jewels, c. 1950s
18k $3,000 $3,500 $4,000

PATEK PHILIPPE, 18 jewels, Cal.# 9
18k $3,000 $3,500 $4,000

PATEK PHILIPPE, 18 jewels, RF# 1560
18k $4,500 $4,700 $5,000

PATEK PHILIPPE, 18 jewels, c. 1940s
18k $4,000 $4,500 $5,000

PATEK PHILIPPE, 18 jewels, c. 1943
18k $4,000 $4,300 $4,750

PATEK PHILIPPE, 18 jewels, c. 1930s
18k $3,500 $3,800 $4,300

PATEK PHILIPPE, 18 jewels, c. 1945
18k $5,000 $5,500 $6,000

PATEK PHILIPPE, 18 jewels
18k $3,500 $4,000 $4,500

PATEK PHILIPPE, 18 jewels, Cal.# 9, c. 1960s
18k $3,500 $4,000 $4,500

PATEK PHILIPPE, 18 jewels, curved, Cal.# 9
18k $5,500 $6,500 $7,500

PATEK PHILIPPE, 18J., decorated enamel case, c. 1920s
18k $8,000 $9,000 $10,000

PATEK PHILIPPE,18J., RF#2334,
18K....................................$3,500 $3,800 $4,200

PATEK PHILIPPE,18J., extended lugs, **two tone case**,
cal.885, c.1943
18K....................................$5,000 $6,000 $7,000

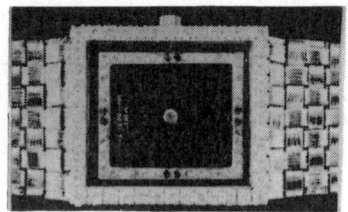

PATEK PHILIPPE,18J., diamond on dial & case
18K C&B............................$3,500 $4,000 $4,700

PATEK PHILIPPE, 18 jewels, hidden lugs, c. 1930s
18k $3,000 $3,600 $4,300

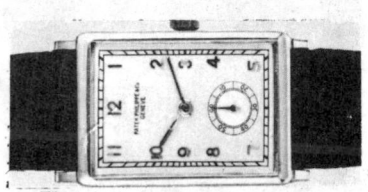

PATEK PHILIPPE, 18 jewels, c. 1940s
18k $4,000 $4,500 $5,000

PATEK PHILIPPE, 18 jewels, hinged back, c. 1920s
18k $4,500 $5,000 $5,500

PATEK PHILIPPE, 18 jewels, applied gold numbers
18K $6,000 $6,500 $7,000

" PATEK PHILIPPE" watches should be signed on the case,
dial & movement to bring the prices listed in this book.
(triple signed P.P.CO.)

PATEK PHILIPPE, 18J., Cal.#9, fancy lugs
18k $6,000 $7,000 $8,000

PATEK PHILIPPE, 18J., curved, hooded satin lugs
18k $8,000 $9,000 $10,000

PATEK PHILIPPE, 18 jewels, "Staybrite," curved case
s. steel $3,000 $3,200 $3,400

PATEK PHILIPPE, 18 jewels, Cal.# 9, hooded lugs
18k $2,500 $3,000 $3,500

PATEK PHILIPPE, 18 jewels, curved
18k $4,000 $4,500 $5,000

PATEK PHILIPPE,18J., engraved bezel,hinged back,c.1920
18k $5,500 $6,500 $7,500

PATEK PHILIPPE, 18J., ribbed case & fancy lugs
18k $3,000 $3,500 $4,000

PATEK PHILIPPE, 18 jewels, large lugs, c. 1960s
18k $4,000 $4,500 $5,000

PATEK PHILIPPE, 18 jewels, M#9, c.1930
18k $4,000 $5,000 $6,000

PATEK PHILIPPE, 18 jewels, c. 1930s
18k $3,000 $3,500 $4,000

PATEK PHILIPPE, 18J., Cal.# 9, center lugs, c. 1940s
18k $3,500 $4,000 $4,500

PATEK PHILIPPE, 18 jewels, c. 1940s
18k $4,000 $4,500 $4,750

PATEK PHILIPPE, 18J., triple lugs, RF#2471, ca.1951
18k $15,000 $20,000 $25,000

PATEK PHILIPPE, 18 jewels, triple lugs, RF#1482
18k $8,000 $9,000 $10,000

PATEK PHILIPPE, 18 jewels, curved, c. 1940s
18k $3,500 $4,000 $4,500

PATEK PHILIPPE, 18 jewels, Cal.#9, c. 1940s
18k $3,500 $4,000 $4,500

PATEK PHILIPPE, 18 jewels, curved, c. 1950s
18k $3,500 $4,000 $5,000

PATEK PHILIPPE, 18 jewels, hinged back, c. 1920s
18k $4,000 $4,500 $5,000

PATEK PHILIPPE, 18J., hinged back, stepped case
18k $4,000 $4,500 $5,000

PATEK PHILIPPE, 18J., RF#2520, M# 9, extended lugs
18k C&B............................$7,000 $8,000 $9,000

PATEK PHILIPPE, 18J., fancy lugs, ca.1949
18k $6,000 $7,000 $8,000

PATEK PHILIPPE, 18 jewels, Cal.# 9, concave lugs
18k $6,000 $7,000 $8,000

PATEK PHILIPPE, 18 jewels, fancy lugs
18k $5,000 $5,500 $6,000

PATEK PHILIPPE, 18 J., Cal.#9, tank model, c.1940
18k $3,500 $3,800 $4,250

PATEK PHILIPPE, 18J., stylized hooded lugs, RF#2441
18k $5,000 $6,000 $7,000

PATEK PHILIPPE, 18 jewels, moveable lugs
18K..$7,000 $8,000 $9,000

PATEK PHILIPPE, 18 jewels, Cal.# 9, c. 1940s
18k $4,000 $4,500 $5,000

PATEK PHILIPPE, 18 jewels, lapidated lugs
18k $4,500 $5,000 $5,500

PATEK PHILIPPE, 18J., 2 tone, hooded & stepped lugs
18k $8,000 $9,000 $10,000

PATEK PHILIPPE, 18 jewels, fancy lugs, RF#1480
18k $4,700 $5,000 $5,300

PATEK PHILIPPE, 18 jewels, ''Reverso''
18k $20,000 $25,000 $30,000
s. steel $6,000 $8,000 $10,000

PATEK PHILIPPE, 18 jewels, top hat style, c. 1940s
18k $5,000 $5,500 $6,500
platinum................................$6,000 $7,000 $8,000

PATEK PHILIPPE, 18 jewels, top hat style
18k C&B................................$5,500 $6,000 $7,000

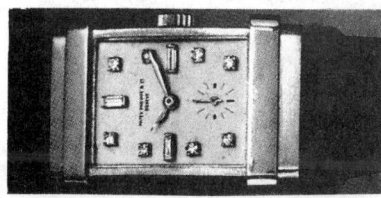

PATEK PHILIPPE, 18 jewels, top hat style, diamond dial
platinum................................$7,000 $8,000 $9,000

PATEK PHILIPPE, 18 jewels, M# 9, curved, tank style
18k $6,000 $6,500 $7,000

PATEK PHILIPPE, 18J., inclined & curved case, Ca.1940s
18k $20,000 $24,000 $28,500

PATEK PHILIPPE, 18 jewels, Adj. to 8 positions
18k $4,000 $4,500 $5,000

PATEK PHILIPPE, 18 jewels, curvex, c. 1940s
18k $4,000 $4,500 $5,000

PATEK PHILIPPE, 18 J., converted to jump hr., recased
18k $4,000 $4,500 $5,000

PATEK PHILIPPE, 18 jewels, flared case, c. 1940s
18k $6,500 $7,000 $8,000

PATEK PHILIPPE, 18 jewels, Cal.# 9, c. 1950s
platinum................................$12,000 $14,000 $16,000

PATEK PHILIPPE, 18J., Cal.# 9, flared case, c. 1950s
18k $6,500 $7,500 $8,500

PATEK PHILIPPE, 18 jewels, massive flared case
18k $14,000 $16,000 $18,000
platinum..............................$18,000 $20,000 $22,000

PATEK PHILIPPE, 18J., RF#2441, curved, flared case
18k $8,000 $9,000 $10,000

PATEK PHILIPPE,18J., RF#2441, Eiffel tower, c. 1945
18k $8,000 $9,000 $10,000

PATEK PHILIPPE, 18 jewels, flared case
18k $5,000 $5,500 $6,500

PATEK PHILIPPE, 18 jewels, flared case, c. 1950s
18k $6,000 $6,500 $7,000

PATEK PHILIPPE, 18 jewels, c. 1950s
18k $6,000 $6,500 $7,000

PATEK PHILIPPE, 18J., 16 diamond on bezel, ca.1960
18k C&B.............................. $6,000 $7,000 $8,000

PATEK PHILIPPE, 18 jewels, diamond dial, c. 1945
18k $5,500 $6,000 $6,500

PATEK PHILIPPE, 18 jewels, diamond dial
platinum............................. $6,000 $6,500 $7,000

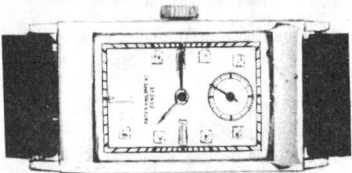

PATEK PHILIPPE, 18 jewels, diamond dial, c. 1935
platinum............................. $6,000 $6,500 $7,000

PATEK PHILIPPE, 18 jewels, diamond dial & bezel
platinum............................. $7,000 $7,500 $8,000

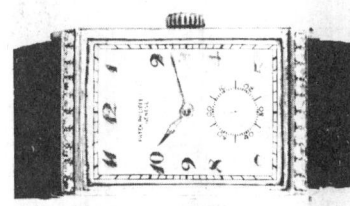

PATEK PHILIPPE, 18J., hinged back, diamond bezel
18k $6,000 $7,000 $8,000

PATEK PHILIPPE,18J., RF#2493, c.1953
18K $2,800 $3,200 $3,800

PATEK PHILIPPE, 18 jewels, c. 1940s
18k $3,500 $4,000 $4,500

PATEK PHILIPPE,18J., RF#1431, cal., c.1940
18K $2,500 $3,000 $3,500

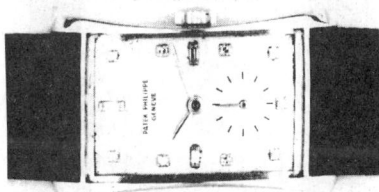

PATEK PHILIPPE, 18J., diamond dial, flared case
18k $7,500 $8,000 $9,000

PATEK PHILIPPE,18J., RF#2447, c.1950
18K $2,500 $2,800 $3,300

PATEK PHILIPPE, 18J, Cal.# 9, diamond dial, starbrite case
s. steel $3,000 $3,500 $4,000

PATEK PHILIPPE,18J., carved lugs, RF#2423, c.1949
18K $3,600 $4,200 $4,750

PATEK PHILIPPE, 18J., RF 3627, **Lapis & 54 Diamonds,**
Ca.1974
18k $9,000 $10,000 $12,000

PATEK PHILIPPE,18J., RF#2424, c.1951
18K $3,600 $4,200 $4,750

PATEK PHILIPPE,18J., stepped lugs, c.1940
18K..................................$3,600 $4,200 $4,750

PATEK PHILIPPE, 18 J., 18k band & case, c. 1950s
18k C&B.............................$4,000 $4,500 $5,000

PATEK PHILIPPE, 18 jewels, textured bezel, c. 1940s
18k $2,500 $2,750 $3,200

PATEK PHILIPPE, 18J., fancy off set lugs, thick crystal
18k $3,000 $3,300 $3,700

PATEK PHILIPPE, 18 jewels
18k $2,500 $3,000 $3,500

PATEK PHILIPPE, 18 jewels, M# 9, c. 1963
18k $2,500 $2,800 $3,300

PATEK PHILIPPE, 18 jewels, c. 1947
18k $3,000 $3,400 $3,900

PATEK PHILIPPE, 18 jewels, c. 1960s
18k $2,000 $2,200 $2,500

PATEK PHILIPPE, 18 jewels, oval lugs
18k $3,500 $4,000 $4,500

PATEK PHILIPPE, 18 jewels
18k $2,000 $2,200 $2,500

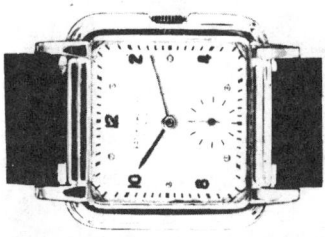

PATEK PHILIPPE, 18 jewels, Cal.# 9, c. 1948
18k $3,500 $3,800 $4,250

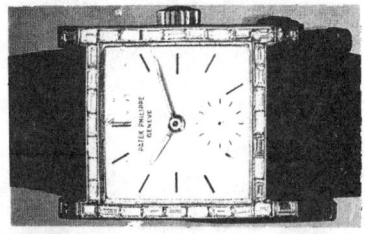

PATEK PHILIPPE, 18 jewels, diamond bezel , tank style
platinum................................$7,500 $8,500 $9,500

PATEK PHILIPPE, 18 J., hooded & fluted lugs
18k $8,000 $9,000 $10,000

PATEK PHILIPPE, 18J., Cal.# 9, hidden dial, gold & plat.
18k & platinum...................$20,000 $22,000 $24,000

PATEK PHILIPPE, 18 jewels, Cal.# 9, c. 1980s
18k C&B..............................$3,000 $3,500 $4,000

PATEK PHILIPPE, 18 jewels, Cal.# 9, c. 1970s
18k C&B..............................$2,500 $3,000 $3,700

PATEK PHILIPPE, 18 jewels
18k (w) $2,000 $2,400 $2,800

PATEK PHILIPPE, 18 jewels
18k C&B..............................$3,200 $3,500 $4,000

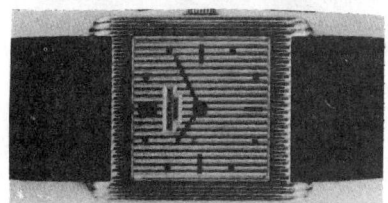

PATEK PHILIPPE, 18 jewels, textured dial & bezel
18k $3,000 $3,500 $4,000

PATEK PHILIPPE, 18 jewels, c. 1950s
18k $3,200 $3,800 $4,500

🕐 Some grades are not included. Their values can be
determined by comparing with similar age, size, metal
content, style, grades, or models such as time only,
chronograph, repeater etc. listed.

PATEK PHILIPPE, 18 jewels, center sec., c. 1960s
18k C&B $4,000 $4,500 $5,000

PATEK PHILIPPE, 18 J., tank, RF#2530-1, Ca. 1959
18k C&B $4,000 $4,500 $5,250

PATEK PHILIPPE, 18J., tank, Cal.# 9, c. early 1910s
18k C&B $4,500 $5,000 $5,500

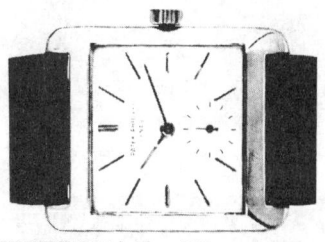

PATEK PHILIPPE, 18 jewels, c. 1950s
18k $2,500 $2,800 $3,250

PATEK PHILIPPE, 18 jewels, c. 1950s
18k $2,800 $3,200 $3,750

PATEK PHILIPPE, 18 jewels, c. 1950s
18k $2,800 $3,100 $3,400

PATEK PHILIPPE, 18 jewels, c. 1960s
18k $3,500 $3,800 $4,250

PATEK PHILIPPE, 18 J., guilloche bezel, thick lugs
18k $3,500 $4,000 $4,500

PATEK PHILIPPE, 18 jewels, hidden lugs, c. 1945
18k $3,000 $3,500 $4,000

PATEK PHILIPPE, 18J., fluted cylindrical hooded lugs
18k $6,000 $7,000 $8,000

PATEK PHILIPPE, 18 jewels, hidden lugs
18k $2,000 $2,300 $2,800

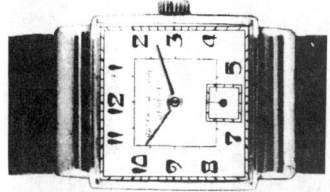

PATEK PHILIPPE, 18 jewels, hooded lugs, c. 1940s
18k $2,800 $3,300 $3,750

PATEK PHILIPPE, 18 jewels, blue sapphire bezel
platinum $8,000 $8,500 $9,500

PATEK PHILIPPE, 18 jewels, overhanging lugs
18k $5,000 $5,500 $6,500

PATEK PHILIPPE, 18 jewels, fluted dropped lugs
18k $4,500 $5,000 $5,500

PATEK PHILIPPE, 18 jewels, c. 1940s
18k $3,000 $3,500 $4,000

PATEK PHILIPPE, 18 jewels, large bezel
18k $2,500 $2,700 $3,200

PATEK PHILIPPE, 18 jewels, c. 1940s
18k $2,200 $2,400 $2,700

PATEK PHILIPPE, 15J.,for Baily,Banks & Biddle, ca.1920
18k $4,000 $4,500 $5,000

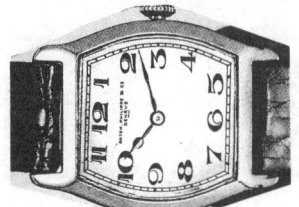

PATEK PHILIPPE, 16J., ca.1923
18k $4,000 $4,800 $5,500

⊕ Some grades are not included. Their values can be
determined by comparing with **similar** age, size, metal
content, style, grades, or models such as **time only**,
chronograph, repeater etc. listed.

PATEK PHILIPPE, 18 jewels, c. 1910
18k $3,500 $4,000 $4,500

PATEK PHILIPPE, 18 jewels, c. 1930s
18k $3,500 $4,000 $5,000

PATEK PHILIPPE, 18 jewels, c. 1920s
18k $4,000 $4,500 $5,000

PATEK PHILIPPE, 18 jewels, c. 1930s
18k $4,000 $4,500 $5,500

PATEK PHILIPPE, 18 jewels, c. 1920s
18k $3,500 $4,000 $4,500

PATEK PHILIPPE, 18 jewels, **contract case, not signed**
18k (w) $1,800 $2,000 $2,500

PATEK PHILIPPE, 18 jewels, enamel dial,c. 1920s
18k $5,500 $6,000 $6,500

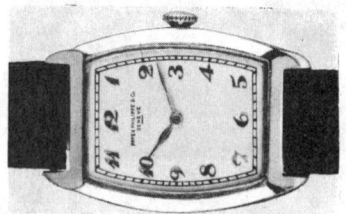

PATEK PHILIPPE, 18 jewels, Cal.# 9, c. 1925
18k $3,500 $4,000 $4,500

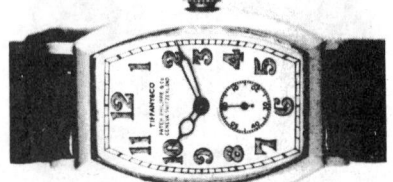

PATEK PHILIPPE, 18 jewels, M# 9, c. 1920s
18k $5,000 $5,500 $6,000

PATEK PHILIPPE, 18 jewels, Cal.# 9, c. 1910
platinum...............................$7,000 $8,000 $9,000

PATEK PHILIPPE, 18J, diamond dial, curved, 42mm, c. 1919
platinum...............................$7,000 $8,000 $9,000

PATEK PHILIPPE, 18 jewels
18k $2,500 $3,000 $3,500

PATEK PHILIPPE, 18 jewels, made for E. Gublin
18k $4,000 $4,500 $5,000

PATEK PHILIPPE, 18 jewels, "Chronometro Gondolo"
18k $5,000 $6,000 $7,000

PATEK PHILIPPE, 18jewels, RF#515, world time zone, 24 hr. rotating outside chapter, **tu-tone** case and band
18K C&B........................$200,000 $250,000 $300,000

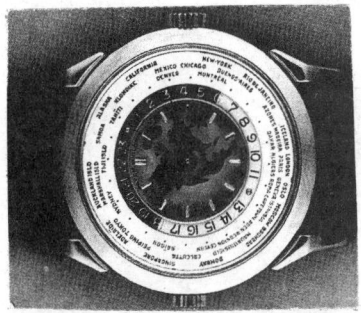

PATEK PHILIPPE, 18 jewels, RF#2523, "World Time," cloisonne polychrome enamel map on dial, **41 cities**
18k $70,000 $80,000 $90,000

PATEK PHILIPPE,18J.,"World Time," **41 cities**, RF#1415
18k $35,000 $40,000 $45,000

PATEK PHILIPPE, 18 jewels, landscape cloisonne polychrome enamel dial
18k $30,000 $35,000 $40,000

PATEK PHILIPPE, 18 jewels, **2 hour hands**, 2 time zones
18k $18,000 $20,000 $24,000

PATEK PHILIPPE, 18J., traveling watch, hr. hand moves forward or backward to time zone, steps 1 hr. at a time
18k $20,000 $25,000 $30,000

PATEK PHILIPPE, 18J., RF#130, chronog., 1940s
18k $15,000 $18,000 $22,000

PATEK PHILIPPE, 18J., RF#530, chronog.
18k $15,000 $18,000 $22,000

PATEK PHILIPPE, 18J., calatrava style,chronog., 2 reg., RF#130, c. 1940s
18k $20,000 $22,000 $25,000

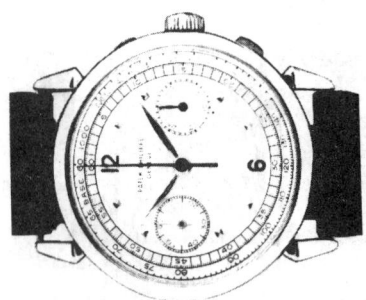

PATEK PHILIPPE,18J.,chronog., RF#1579, fancy lugs
18k $16,000 $18,000 $20,000

PATEK PHILIPPE,18J., chronog., RF#591, 2 reg., c.1943
18k $22,000 $24,000 $26,000

PATEK PHILIPPE,18J., RF#130, chronog.," 2 tone"
18k & s. steel $22,000 $24,000 $26,000

PATEK PHILIPPE, 32J., split sec. chronog.
18k $200,000 $225,000 $250,000

Some grades are not included. Their values can be determined by comparing with **similar** age, size, metal content, style, grades, or models such as **time only**, chronograph, repeater etc. listed.

PATEK PHILIPPE, 26J., split sec. chronog. one button, for Cartier, Sq. button for Rattrapante hand, crown for start stop functions, RF#130, 8 adj., ca.1938
18k $110,000 $130,000 $150,000

PATEK PHILIPPE,18J., RF#130,split sec. chronog.,c.1958
18k $100,000 $115,000 $130,000

PATEK PHILIPPE,18J., RF#1506, chronog., waterproof
18k $24,000 $27,000 $30,000

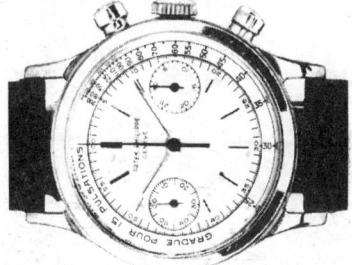

PATEK PHILIPPE, 18J., chronog., pulsometer, c. 1965
18k $26,000 $29,000 $32,000

PATEK PHILIPPE, 18J., rf#3970E, chronog,triple date moon ph., 24 hr. indicator, leap year indicator
18k $38,000 $42,000 $50,000

PATEK PHILIPPE, 18 jewels, chronog., day-date month, moon phase, made for E. Gueblin
18k C&B...........................$60,000 $70,000 $80,000

PATEK PHILIPPE, 23J., chronog., triple date, moon ph. perpetual calendar,RF# 1518, Calatrava case, Ca.1941-54
18k .... ★★ $70,000 $80,000 $90,000

PATEK PHILIPPE, 23 J., chronog., triple date, moon ph. perpetual calendar,ref.2499 (1 series) square button
18K $70,000 $75,000 $85,000

" PATEK PHILIPPE" watches should be signed on the case, dial & movement to bring the prices listed in this book.
(triple signed P.P.CO.)

PATEK PHILIPPE, 23J., chronog., triple date, moon ph. perpetual calendar, ref.2499 (4 series)sapphire crystal
18k....................................$50,000 $55,000 $60,000

PATEK PHILIPPE, 23 J., chronog., triple date, moon ph. perpetual calendar, ref.2499 (2 series)
18K................................$60,000 $65,000 $70,000

PATEK PHILIPPE, 18 jewels, date, mid-sized, auto wind
platinum................................$6,000 $7,000 $8,000

PATEK PHILIPPE, 23J., chronog., triple date, moon ph. perpetual calendar, ref.2499 (3 series)glass crystal
18k $60,000 $65,000 $70,000

PATEK PHILIPPE, 18 jewels, auto wind, date, c. 1970s
18k C&B............................$3,000 $3,500 $4,000

PATEK PHILIPPE, 23J., chronog., triple date, moon ph. perpetual calendar,ref.2499 (3 series)only 2 in platinum
platinum...........................$150,000 $170,000 $200,000

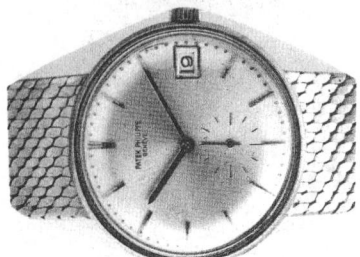

PATEK PHILIPPE,18J., RF#3514/1, date,c.1967
18K C&B............................$2,200 $2,400 $2,800

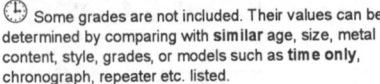
Some grades are not included. Their values can be determined by comparing with **similar** age, size, metal content, style, grades, or models such as **time only**, chronograph, repeater etc. listed.

PATEK PHILIPPE,18J., date, RF#3445, auto-wind, c.1961
18K......................................\$3,200   \$3,500   \$4,000

PATEK PHILIPPE,18J., date, RF#3604, textured dial, c.1977
18K(w)..................................\$2,200   \$2,400   \$3,000

PATEK PHILIPPE,18J., (day, date, month, at 9-12-3),
3 known to exist, manual wind, Ca.1934
18K..................★ ★ ★ ★ ★\$200,000   \$250,000   \$300,000

PATEK PHILIPPE, 18J., RF#96, Calatrava, triple date note
moon phases at 12, Ca.1936
18K....................................\$125,000   \$150,000   \$175,000
platinum............................\$225,000   \$250,000   \$275,000

PATEK PHILIPPE, 18J., RF#3450, day-date-month, moon
phase, waterproof, **perpetual date at 3**
18k \$22,000   \$24,000   \$28,000

PATEK PHILIPPE, 37J., RF#3448, cal.27-460q c.1968
18K \$25,000   \$27,000   \$30,000

PATEK PHILIPPE, 37J., triple date, moon ph. RF #3448
platinum............................\$35,000   \$40,000   \$45,000

PATEK PHILIPPE,18J., triple date, moon ph., RF#2438,
c.1962
18k \$35,000   \$40,000   \$45,000

PATEK PHILIPPE, 15 jewels, enamel dial, c. 1910
18k $7,000 $8,000 $9,000

PATEK PHILIPPE,18J., "Officer", RF#3960, c.1992
18k 2,000 made, 18k(w) 150 made, platinum 50 made
18K.....................................$13,000 $14,000 $15,000
18k(w)..............................$15,000 $16,000 $17,000
platinum $25,000 $27,000 $30,000

PATEK PHILIPPE, 15J., enamel dial, c. 1910
18k $7,000 $8,000 $9,000

PATEK PHILIPPE, 18 jewels, RF#1461
18k $2,500 $3,000 $3,500

PATEK PHILIPPE, 18 jewels
18k $2,000 $2,500 $3,000

PATEK PHILIPPE, 18 jewels, aux. sec.
18k $2,300 $2,700 $3,200

PATEK PHILIPPE, 18J., *Amagnetic* on dial, ca. 1960
18k $3,000 $4,000 $5,000

PATEK PHILIPPE, 18J.,"Calatrava", aux. sec., c. 1940
18k $3,000 $3,200 $3,500

PATEK PHILIPPE, 18 jewels, c. 1955
18k $2,400 $2,600 $3,200

PATEK PHILIPPE, 18 jewels, man's half size, c. 1920
18k $3,000 $4,000 $4,500
s. steel $2,600 $2,800 $3,000

PATEK PHILIPPE, 18 jewels, RF# 2429, Ca. 1950s
18k $4,000 $4,200 $4,500

PATEK PHILIPPE, 18 jewels, aux. sec., c. 1950s
18k $2,800 $3,200 $3,700

PATEK PHILIPPE, 37J., RF#3429, self-winding
18k $3,600 $4,000 $4,500

PATEK PHILIPPE, 18J., aux. sec., RF#2526, ca. 1957
RARE glass enamel dial
18k auto-w.........................$8,000 $9,000 $10,000

PATEK PHILIPPE,18J., **CLASSIC Calatrava,** RF# 96
18k $3,500 $3,800 $4,200
s. steel $2,500 $2,800 $3,200
platinum..............................$7,000 $7,500 $8,000
platinum + diam. dial $7,500 $8,000 $8,500

The **above CLASSIC Calatrava** model 96 was 1st used in
1932. It was designed at a time of transition from pocket watches
to wrist watches. The coin was used as a perfect geometric shape
to design a wrist watch case that has harmony and balance. Many
varations from the classic model 96 have been used, but to most
collectors the **CLASSIC** model 96 is known as the **Calatrava**
model. The original 96 Calatrava model used a flat bezel, 31mm
one piece case (lugs are not soldered on), manual wind, white
dial, barrette-shaped hour markers, dauphine hands and aux.
seconds chapter with a inside and outside circle and long 5 sec.
markers. A Hobnail bezel was added in 1934, a black dial in
1937. To date there are many Calatrava styles and models. The
recent classic Calatrava is RF # 3796.

PATEK PHILIPPE, 18J., "Calatrava," RF#96, c. 1950s
18k $3,300 $4,000 $4,500

PATEK PHILIPPE, 18 J., auto wind, RF#1536, c.1950s
18k $4,000 $4,500 $5,000

PATEK PHILIPPE,18J., auto wind, RF#1516, c.1950
18K...$3,800 $4,000 $4,500

PATEK PHILIPPE,18J., aux. sec., RF#2445,
18K...$2,600 $2,900 $3,300

PATEK PHILIPPE,18J., aux. sec., c.1943
18K $2,700 $2,900 $3,500

PATEK PHILIPPE,37J., auto wind, RF#3429, c.1961
18K $3,700 $4,000 $4,400

PATEK PHILIPPE,18J., aux. sec., RF#96, cal.12-20, c.1937
18K $3,000 $3,200 $3,400

PATEK PHILIPPE,18J., RF#1543, c.1947
18K $2,600 $2,800 $3,000

🕐 Some grades are not included. Their values can be determined by comparing with **similar** age, size, metal content, style, grades, or models such as **time only**, chronograph, repeater etc. listed.

PATEK PHILIPPE,18J., RF#1590, c.1951
18K.....................................$2,800 $3,000 $3,300

PATEK PHILIPPE, 18 jewels, waterproof, c. 1940s
18k $2,800 $3,200 $3,600

PATEK PHILIPPE, 18J., auto-w, extra long lugs, c. 1950
18k $3,000 $3,300 $3,600

PATEK PHILIPPE, 18J.,"Calatrava" waterproof, c. 1950s
18k $4,000 $4,300 $4,700

PATEK PHILIPPE, 18 jewels, aux. sec., c. 1950s
18k $2,200 $2,400 $2,600

PATEK PHILIPPE, 30J.,"Calatrava", auto wind, gold rotor
18k $7,000 $7,500 $8,000

PATEK PHILIPPE, 18 jewels, aux. sec.
18k $2,700 $2,900 $3,200

PATEK PHILIPPE,18J.,"Calatrava,"**enamel dial**, Ca.1940s
18k .... ★ $5,500 $6,000 $6,500

" PATEK PHILIPPE" watches should be signed on the case,
dial & movement to bring the prices listed in this book.
(**triple signed P.P.CO.**)

PATEK PHILIPPE, 18J.,waterproof, "Calatrava," rf#2545
18k $3,500 $4,500 $5,000

PATEK PHILIPPE, 18J., fancy lugs, ca. 1948
18k $7,000 $8,000 $9,000

PATEK PHILIPPE, 18 jewels, "Calatrava," waterproof
platinum $6,000 $7,000 $8,000

PATEK PHILIPPE, 18 jewels, curled lugs
18k $3,800 $4,000 $4,500

PATEK PHILIPPE, 18 jewels, aux. sec.
18k C&B.............................$7,000 $8,000 $9,000

PATEK PHILIPPE, 18 jewels, "Calatrava," c. 1950s
18k $2,800 $3,200 $3,500

PATEK PHILIPPE, 18J., RF#2526, fancy lugs, c. 1940s
18k $4,000 $4,500 $5,000

PATEK PHILIPPE, 18 jewels, "Calatrava," c. 1940s
18k-rose...............................$3,200 $4,000 $4,500

PATEK PHILIPPE, 18J., "Calatrava," black dial, w/proof
18k $3,800 $4,200 $4,700

PATEK PHILIPPE, 18 jewels, center sec., waterproof
s. steel $2,500 $2,800 $3,200

PATEK PHILIPPE, 21J., "Calatrava," **center sec.**, c.1950s
18k $4,000 $4,300 $4,700

PATEK PHILIPPE, 18 jewels, center sec., c. 1950s
18k $3,200 $3,500 $4,000

PATEK PHILIPPE, 18J., center sec., rf#2466, ca.1949
18k $3,500 $3,800 $4,300

PATEK PHILIPPE, 18 jewels, conical lugs, center sec.
18k $3,600 $4,000 $4,500

PATEK PHILIPPE, 18 jewels, center sec., c. 1950s
18k $2,700 $2,900 $3,200

PATEK PHILIPPE, 20 jewels, center sec.
18k $2,700 $3,000 $3,400

PATEK PHILIPPE, 18 jewels, textured dial & bezel
18k $2,600 $2,800 $3,100

PATEK PHILIPPE,18J., center sec., RF#3411, c.1960
18K $2,200 $2,400 $2,700

PATEK PHILIPPE, 18 jewels, center sec., c. 1952
18k $2,800 $3,000 $3,300

PATEK PHILIPPE, 18 jewels, center sec., c. 1950s
18k $2,200 $2,400 $2,700

PATEK PHILIPPE, 18 jewels, center sec., waterproof
18k $3,500 $3,800 $4,200

PATEK PHILIPPE,18J., RF#3495, cal.27sc, c.1969
18K $2,000 $2,200 $2,400

PATEK PHILIPPE, 20 jewels, center sec.
18k $2,200 $2,400 $2,700

PATEK PHILIPPE, 18 jewels, center sec., c. 1960s
18k C&B..............................$3,600 $4,000 $4,400

PATEK PHILIPPE, 18 jewels, auto wind, **back set**
18k $3,200 $3,500 $4,000

PATEK PHILIPPE, 18 jewels
18k C&B.............................$2,500 $3,000 $3,500

PATEK PHILIPPE, 18 jewels
18k $2,000 $2,200 $2,400

PATEK PHILIPPE,18J., RF#2501, c.1954
18K $1,800 $2,000 $2,200

PATEK PHILIPPE, 18 jewels, "Calatrava," c. 1940s
18k $3,500 $4,000 $4,500

PATEK PHILIPPE,18J., RF#2592, c.1956
18K $1,700 $1,900 $2,200

PATEK PHILIPPE, 36 jewels, auto-w.,c. 1970s
18k $2,800 $3,000 $3,200

PATEK PHILIPPE,18J., RF#3574, c.1960
s. steel $1,200 $1,400 $1,600

PATEK PHILIPPE, 18J., ''Calatrava,'', rf#2588, c.1940s
18k $3,500 $3,800 $4,200

PATEK PHILIPPE, 18 jewels, unusual shape, c. 1940s
18k $6,000 $7,000 $8,000

PATEK PHILIPPE, 36J., "Nautilus", date,gold & steel
18K....................................$11,000 $12,000 $13,000
18k&s. steel $5,000 $5,500 $6,000
s. steel $3,000 $3,500 $4,000

PATEK PHILIPPE, **mid size, QUARTZ,** rf#3900/1, date
s. steel $2,600 $2,900 $3,200

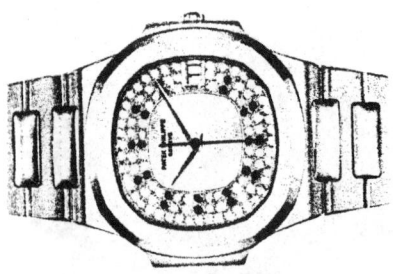

PATEK PHILIPPE, quartz, rf#3900/101, date
paved diamonds=.50ct., ruby hour markers
18k $6,000 $8,000 $10,000

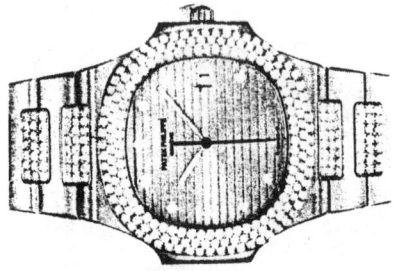

PATEK PHILIPPE, quartz, rf#3900/5, date, dia-
monds=2.27ct.
18k C&B............................ $9,000 $10,000 $13,000

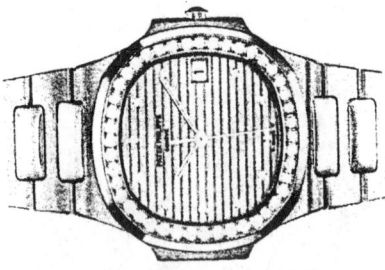

PATEK PHILIPPE, quartz, rf#3900/3, date, Carran dial
diamonds=.68ct.
platinum............................ $20,000 $22,000 $24,000

PATEK PHILIPPE, quartz, rf#3900/103, date
diamonds=.68ct, paved diamonds=.50, ruby markers
18k $7,000 $9,000 $11,000

PATEK PHILIPPE, quartz, rf#3900/105, date,
diamonds=2.27, paved diamonds=.50, ruby markers
18k C&B............................$10,000 $12,000 $14,000

PATEK PHILIPPE, auto wind, rf#3800/103, date
diamonds=.91ct., paved diamonds=63ct., ruby markers
18kC&B............................$17,000 $20,000 $23,000

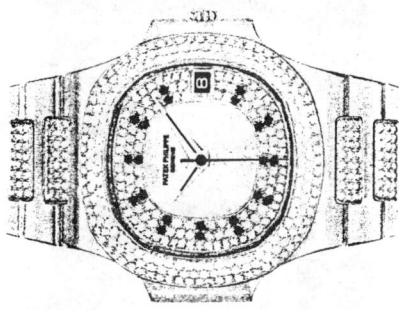

PATEK PHILIPPE, auto wind, rf#3800/105, date
diamonds=2.40ct., paved diam.=.63ct., ruby markers
18kC&B............................$22,000 $24,000 $26,000

" PATEK PHILIPPE" watches should be signed on the case,
dial & movement to bring the prices listed in this book.
            (triple signed P.P.CO.)

🕐 Some grades are not included. Their values can be
determined by comparing with similar age, size, metal
content, style, grades, or models such as time only,
chronograph, repeater etc. listed.

PATEK PHILIPPE, auto wind, rf#3800/108, date,
diamonds=7.46ct.,paved diam.=1.50ct.,sapphire markers
18k C&B............................$30,000 $35,000 $40,000

PATEK PHILIPPE, 36J., "Nautilus," date, large size
s. steel $4,000 $4,500 $5,000

PATEK PHILIPPE, 36 J. "Nautilus," diamond bezel
18k $13,000 $14,000 $15,000

PATEK PHILIPPE, skeleton, rf# 3885
18k $5,000 $6,000 $7,000

PATEK PHILIPPE, skeleton, rf# 3878
18k $6,000 $7,000 $8,000

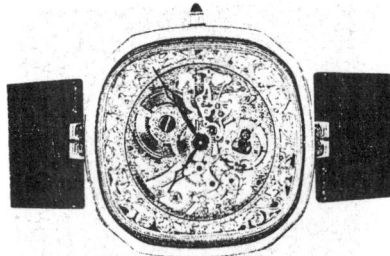

PATEK PHILIPPE, skeleton, rf# 3886
18k $5,000 $6,000 $7,000

PATEK PHILIPPE, skeleton, diamonds=.62ct., rf# 3885
18k $6,000 $7,000 $8,000

PATEK PHILIPPE, skeleton, diamonds=.85ct., rf# 3884
18k $7,000 $8,000 $9,000

PATEK PHILIPPE, 36 jewels, diamond dial & bezel
18k $4,000 $4,500 $5,000

PATEK PHILIPPE, 18J., diamond dial, ca. 1952
platinum..............................$6,000 $7,000 $8,000

PATEK PHILIPPE, 18J., "Calatrava", diamond dial
platinum..............................$8,000 $9,000 $10,000

PATEK PHILIPPE, 18J., ''Calatrava,'' mid-sized, dia. dial
platinum..............................$8,000 $8,500 $9,000

🕐 Some grades are not included. Their values can be
determined by comparing with similar age, size, metal
content, style, grades, or models such as time only,
chronograph, repeater etc. listed.

PATEK PHILIPPE, 18 jewels, c. 1980s
18k C&B...............................$2,800 $3,200 $3,700

PATEK PHILIPPE, quartz, c. 1980s
18k C&B...............................$2,500 $2,800 $3,200

PATEK PHILIPPE, 18 jewels, c. 1960s
18k C&B...............................$4,000 $4,300 $4,800

PATEK PHILIPPE, 18 jewels, c. 1980s
18k C&B...............................$3,200 $3,400 $3,700

PATEK PHILIPPE, 18 jewels, massive lugs
18k.......................................$4,000 $4,500 $5,000

PATEK PHILIPPE, 18 jewels, concave & hooded lugs
18k.......................................$4,300 $4,800 $5,500

PATEK PHILIPPE, 18 jewels, hooded lugs, c.1930s
18K.......................................$4,500 $5,000 $5,500

PATEK PHILIPPE, 18 jewels, mid-sized, 2 tone
18k (y & w).........................$8,000 $9,000 $10,000

⏰ Some grades are not included. Their values can be determined by comparing with similar age, size, metal content, style, grades, or models such as **time only**, chronograph, repeater etc. listed.

⏰ Some grades are not included. Their values can be determined by comparing with similar age, size, metal content, style, grades, or models such as **time only**, chronograph, repeater etc. listed.

PATEK PHILIPPE, 18 J., extended lugs, 2 tone, rf#497
18k (y & w) $8,000 $9,000 $10,000

PATEK PHILIPPE, 18 jewels, lady's watch
18k $1,200 $1,400 $1,700

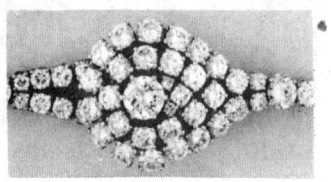

PATEK PHILIPPE,18 J., lady's, hinged lid set in diamonds
18k $3,500 $4,000 $4,500

PATEK PHILIPPE, 18 jewels, lady's watch
18k C&B..............................$2,500 $3,000 $3,500

PATEK PHILIPPE, 18 J., lady's watch, diamond bezel
platinum................................$3,000 $3,500 $4,000

PATEK PHILIPPE, 18 jewels, lady's watch, c. 1950s
18k $3,000 $3,500 $4,000

PATEK PHILIPPE, 18 jewels, lady's watch, c. 1940s
18k C&B $3,500 $4,000 $4,500

PATEK PHILIPPE, 18J., lady's watch, min. repeater
18k.......................................$40,000 $50,000 $60,000

PATEK PHILIPPE, 18 jewels, lady's watch, c. 1950s
18k.......................................$1,800 $2,000 $2,500

PATEK PHILIPPE, 18 jewels, lady's watch, c. 1940s
18k.......................................$1,000 $1,200 $1,400

PATEK PHILIPPE, 18 jewels, lady's watch, c. 1940s
18k.......................................$1,500 $1,700 $2,000

PATEK PHILIPPE, 18 jewels, lady's watch, c. 1950s
18k.......................................$1,000 $1,200 $1,500

PATEK, PHILIPPE
MOVEMENT IDENTIFICATION

Caliber 6¾, no. 60
S.no. 865000-869999
(1940-1955)

Caliber 7, no. 70
S.no. 943300-949999
(1940-1960)

Caliber 8, no. 80
S.no. 840000-849999
(1935-1960)

Caliber 8, no. 85
S.no. 850000-859999
(1935-1968)

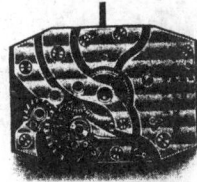

Caliber 9, no. 90
S.no. 833150-839999
S.no. 970000-979999
(1940-1950)

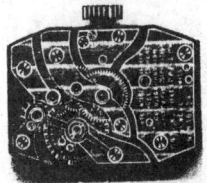

Caliber 9, no. 90a
830000-833149
(1940-1950)

Caliber 10, no. 105
S.no. 900000-909999
(1940-1945)

Caliber 10, no. 110
S.no. 910000-919999
(1940-1950)

Caliber 10, no. 200
S.no. 740000-759999
(1952-1965)
S.no. 950000-959999
(1945-1955)

Caliber 23, no. 300
S.no. 780000-799999
(1955-1965)

Caliber 12, no. 600AT
S.no. 760000-779999
(1952-1960)

Caliber 12, no. 400
S.no. 720000-739999
(1950-1965)

Caliber 12, no. 120
826900-829999 (1935-1940)

Caliber 12, no. 120A
92000-929999 (1940-1950)
960000-969999 (1946-1952)
938000-939999 (1952-1954)

Caliber 12 , center seconds

Caliber 13, no. 130A   **Caliber 13, no. 130B**   **Caliber 13, no. 130C**
Chronograph, no. 862000-863995 (1940-1950); no. 867000-869999 (1950-1970)

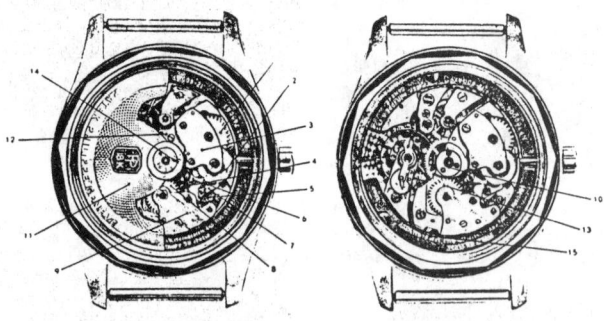

Caliber 12-600 AT, S.no. 760,000-779,999 (1960-1970)

PRODUCTION TOTALS

DATE – SERIAL #	DATE – SERIAL #	DATE – SERIAL #
1840 – 100	1950 – 700,000	1940 – 900,000
1845 – 1,200	1955 – 725,000	1945 – 915,000
1850 – 3,000	1960 – 750,000	1950 – 930,000
1855 – 8,000	1965 – 775,000	1955 – 940,000
1860 – 15,000	1970 – 795,000	1960 – 960,000
1865 – 22,000		1965 – 975,000
1870 – 35,000	DATE – SERIAL #	1970 – 995,000
1875 – 45,000	1920 – 800,000	
1880 – 55,000	1925 – 805,000	DATE – SERIAL #
1885 – 70,000	1930 – 820,000	1960 – 1,100,000
1890 – 85,000	1935 – 824,000	1965 – 1,130,000
1895 – 100,000	1940 – 835,000	1970 – 1,250,000
1900 – 110,000	1945 – 850,000	1975 – 1,350,000
1905 – 125,000	1950 – 860,000	1980 – 1,450,000
1910 – 150,000	1955 – 870,000	1985 – 1,600,000
1915 – 175,000	1960 – 880,000	1990 – 1,850,000
1920 – 190,000	1965 – 890,000	
1925 – 200,000	1970 – 895,000	

The above list is provided for determining the APPROXIMATE age of your watch. Match serial number with date. Watches were not necessarily sold in the exact order of manufactured date.

PATRIA, 7 jewels, enamel dial, compass, Ca. 1920
s. steel $300 $350 $400

PATRIA, 7 jewels, enamel dial,
silver $100 $150 $200

PERFINE, 17 jewels, chronog., 2 reg.
gold filled...............................$150 $175 $195
s. steel $75 $100 $125

PERPETUAL W. CO., 15 jewels, rim wind & set,
original retail price in 1933 was $31.50
14k $800 $900 $1,100
gold filled...............................$350 $400 $450
s. steel $250 $300 $350
base metal $200 $250 $300

PERPETUAL W. CO., 15 jewels, c. 1930s
14k...$600 $700 $800
gold filled...............................$350 $400 $450

PERPETUAL W. CO., 15J., fluted bezel, and sold for
"$37.50" in1933
base metal...............................$150 $200 $250

PERPETUAL W. CO., 15 jewels, fluted bezel
gold filled...............................$300 $350 $400

PERPETUAL W. CO., 15 J., diamond bezel, c. 1930s
platinum $400 $500 $600

PHILLIPE W. CO., 17J., RF#2501, chronog., c.1950
s. steel....................................$175 $200 $250

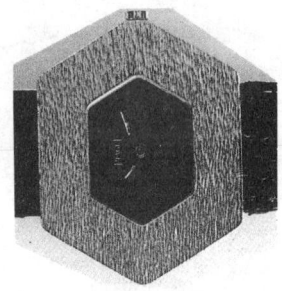

PIAGET,18J., cal.9p2 , c.1980
18k(w)...............................$500 $600 $700

PIAGET,18J., center sec., RF#1176, cal.fl560, c.1952
18k $400 $500 $600

PIAGET,18J., center sec., c.1950
18k $400 $500 $600

PIAGET, 18 jewels, 1904 $20 dollar gold piece, flip top
22k $800 $1,000 $1,400

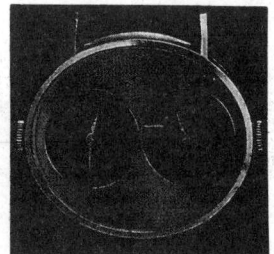

PIAGET, 18 jewels, 2 movements, 2 dials,
18k..$700 $800 $900

PIAGET, 18 jewels, black dial
18k..$500 $600 $700

PIAGET, 18 jewels, center sec., auto wind
18k..$500 $600 $700

PIAGET, 18 jewels, ref. #8177, auto wind
18k..$500 $600 $800

🕐 Some grades are not included. Their values can be
determined by comparing with **similar** age, size, metal
content, style, grades, or models such as **time only**,
chronograph, repeater etc. listed.

PIAGET, 18 jewels
18k $500 $600 $700

PIAGET, 30 jewels, auto wind, gold rotor
18k $500 $600 $700

PIAGET, 18 jewels, 18k case, 14k band
18k & 14k C&B......................$600 $700 $900

PIAGET, 18J., for Van Cleef, center lugs, thin model
18k $500 $600 $700

PIAGET,18J., RF#9821 , c.1975
18k C&B $700 $800 $900

PIAGET, 18 jewels, oval style
18k C&B $400 $450 $550

PIAGET, 18 jewels, oval style
18k.......................................$400 $450 $500

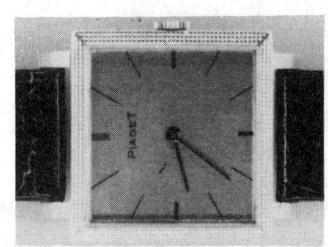

PIAGET, 18 jewels, textured bezel
18k.......................................$700 $800 $900

PIAGET, 18 jewels, textured bezel, classic 90 model
18k.......................................$1,100 $1,200 $1,400

PIAGET, 30 jewels, textured bezel
18k.......................................$500 $600 $700

PIAGET, 18J., rf#9298, c. 1970
18k $1,000 $1,200 $1,400

PIAGET, 18 jewels, tank style
18k $500 $550 $650

PIAGET, 18 jewels, "Executive", rf#7131C516
18k plain dial $4,000 $4,500 $5,500
18k pave dial........................$5,000 $5,500 $6,000

PIAGET, "Polo", rf#7131C701, quartz
18kC&B...............................$4,500 $5,000 $5,500

PIAGET, "Polo", rf#15562C701, quartz
18k $4,000 $4,500 $5,000
NOTE: PIAGET identification # the first 3 to 5 = case design, a letter as A, B, C, =bracelet design. All models beginning with 7, 8,15 may be worn while swimming.

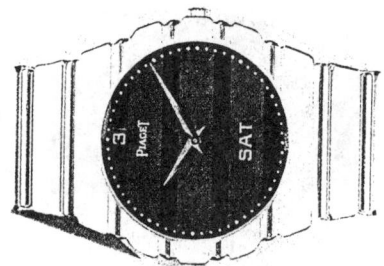

PIAGET, "Polo", rf#15562C701, quartz
18kC&B $4,000 $4,500 $5,000

PIAGET, rf#8065D4
18kC&B $1,500 $1,800 $2,100

PIAGET, 17 jewels, Ca. 1957
18k..$500 $600 $700

PICARD,17J., chronog., reg at 12 ,
base metal...............................$75 $100 $125

⊕ Some grades are not included. Their values can be determined by comparing with similar age, size, metal content, style, grades, or models such as time only, chronograph, repeater etc. listed.

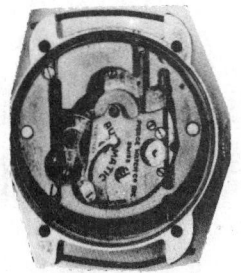

PIERCE, 17J., early auto wind, **"Parashock,"** Ca. 1930s
waterproof, back secured by four screws.
s. steel $400 $550 $750

PIERCE, 17J., triple date, moon ph.
gold filled $275 $350 $425

PIERCE, 17 jewels, auto wind, c. 1948
gold filled....................................$40 $50 $60

POBEDA, 15J., tonneau, Ca. 1930s
14k **rose**...................................$300 $400 $500

PIERCE, 17 jewels, chronog. one button
s. steel $225 $250 $300

PONTIFA, 17 jewels, chronog. day-date-month, 3 reg.
14k $650 $750 $900
s. steel $350 $400 $450

PIERCE, 17 jewels, chronog., c. 1940s
s. steel $135 $175 $225
14k $350 $400 $450
18k $425 $475 $525

PORTA, 17J., antimagnetic, c.1955
gold plate $30 $40 $60

PRAESENT, 17J., triple date, moon ph., mid size, c.1948
gold filled...............................$300 $350 $425

PULSAR, L.E.D. (light emitting diode), ca.1975
14k $300 $350 $400
gold filled $100 $150 $250

PREXA, 17 jewels, auto wind
gold filled...................................$30 $40 $50

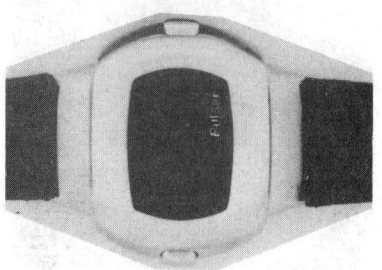

PULSAR, L.E.D. (light emitting diode)
18k $400 $450 $500
14k $300 $375 $450
gold filled $125 $150 $185
s. steel $75 $95 $125

PROVITA, 17J., cal.1525, c.1973
18k $150 $200 $250

RADO, 7J., double dial, c.1938
gold filled $350 $400 $450

PRONTO, 17 jewels, triple date, auto wind, waterproof
s. steel $60 $70 $85

🕐 Some grades are not included. Their values can be
determined by comparing with **similar** age, size, metal
content, style, grades, or models such as **time only**,
chronograph, repeater etc. listed.

RADO, 17J., date, ca.1960
gold plate $40 $50 $60

RAPID, 17J., on mvt. PATHE W. CO.
gold filled.................................$50 $75 $85

RECORD, 17J., split sec. chronog., **date, moon phase**
18k $8,000 $9,000 $10,000

RECORD, 17 jewels, split sec. chronog.
18k $6,000 $7,000 $8,000
s. steel $2,200 $2,500 $3,000

RECORD, 17 J., triple date, moon ph., auto wind,
2 reg. chronograph,
18k $1,500 $1,700 $2,000

RECORD, 17 jewels, triple date, moon phase, c. 1940s
18k $900 $1,000 $1,100

RECORD, 17 jewels, day-date-month, moon phase
s. steel $275 $325 $375

RECORD, 17 J., triple date, moon phase, auto wind
18k $1,000 $1,100 $1,200

REGINA, enamel dial, center lugs, c.1929
silver $150 $175 $200

🕐 Some grades are not included. Their values can be
determined by comparing with **similar** age, size, metal
content, style, grades, or models such as **time only**,
chronograph, repeater etc. listed.

REMBRANT, 17J., chronog., c.1942
18k $425 $475 $550
s. steel $100 $125 $150

REVUE, 17J., beveled case, cal.54, c.1940
nickel......................................$35 $50 $75

RIMA, 17J., aux. sec.,
14k $80 $100 $125

A. RIVALLE, 17J., chronog., c.1970
s. steel $50 $60 $70

ROAMER, 17 jewels, date, auto wind
gold filled $40 $50 $60

ROAMER, 17 jewels, auto wind, aux. sec.
gold filled $25 $30 $35

ROAMER, 23 jewels, ref. #4346
gold filled $30 $40 $50

ROAMER, 17 jewels, hidden lugs
gold filled $30 $40 $50

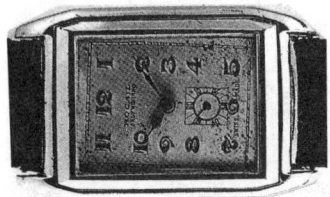

ROCAIL, 15J., auto-wind, c.1930s
s. steel $200 $250 $350

ROLEX,15 jewels, enamel dial, ca.1920
silver $600 $700 $800

ROCKFORD,15J., "Winona", made in USA, S#761074
gold filled...............................$200 $250 $300
s. steel $150 $200 $250

ROLEX, 15 jewels, enamel dial, flip top, c. 1918
silver $1,000 $1,200 $1,500

ROCKFORD, 17J., "Iroquois", gold train
gold filled...............................$200 $250 $300

ROLEX, 17J., RF# 2940, back is flat & tin can shaped
non-magnetic .... ★★★ $1,000 $1,200 $1,400

ROLEX,15 jewels, enamel dial, demi- hunter style, ca.1920
silver $1,500 $1,700 $2,000

ROLEX, 26J., "Milgauss", RF#1019, c.1960s
s.steel $1,600 $2,000 $2,500

ROLEX, 25 jewels, Milgauss, oyster, perpetual, RF#6541
s. steel $1,600 $2,000 $2,600

ROLEX, 17 jewels," Century Club", c. 1960s
18k $1,400 $1,600 $1,800
14k $1,200 $1,400 $1,600

ROLEX, 17 jewels, ''Precision,'' center sec.
18k $1,000 $1,200 $1,500

ROLEX, 26J., **jumping** center sec., RF 6556, cal.# 1040,
Truebeat on dial, also RF 6558 & RF 1020, Ca. 1960
Note: Jumping center sec. must be working to bring prices listed.
s. steel $2,500 $2,700 $3,000
14K.......................................$5,000 $6,000 $7,000
18K.......................................$6,000 $7,000 $8,000

ROLEX, 17J., "Precision"
s. steel $500 $575 $650

ROLEX,17J., center sec., RF#9829, cal.1210
s. steel $400 $450 $500

ROLEX, 17J., rf#3562 , c.1955
14k $800 $900 $1,000

ROLEX,17J., center sec., RF#9659, c.1960
14k $800 $900 $1,000

ROLEX,17J., "Chronometer", RF# 4222, Ca.1945
18k $1,000 $1,200 $1,400

ROLEX, 19J., rf#8443 , c.1965
14k $900 $1,000 $1,100

ROLEX, 17J., "Precision", fancy lugs,
9k $500 $600 $700

ROLEX, 17 jewels, "Precision"
18k $900 $1,000 $1,200

🕐 Some grades are not included. Their values can be
determined by comparing with **similar** age, size, metal
content, style, grades, or models such as **time only**,
chronograph, repeater etc. listed.

ROLEX, 15 jewels, wire lugs
9k $700 $800 $900

ROLEX, 15 jewels, early waterproof, (case within a case)
silver $1,600 $1,800 $2,000

ROLEX, 17 jewels, ref. #9659
14k C&B.............................$1,200 $1,400 $1,600

ROLEX, 17 jewels, "Precision"
gold filled $400 $475 $550

ROLEX,15J., wire lugs, c.1925
silver $500 $600 $700

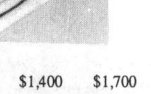

ROLEX, 15J., oyster, royal, c. 1930s
9k $1,200 $1,400 $1,700

ROLEX,15J.,"Aqua", RF#2136, c.1928
s. steel $500 $600 $700

ROLEX, 15J., oyster, ca. 1930
silver $800 $900 $1,000

ROLEX,15J., RF#6071, c.1926
s. steel $500 $600 $700

ROLEX, 15 jewels, oyster, center sec.
18k $3,400 $3,800 $4,200
14k $2,200 $2,600 $3,000
9k $1,400 $1,600 $1,800
silver $1,000 $1,200 $1,400
s. steel $800 $900 $1,000

ROLEX,15J., by OYSTER W. CO., c. 1927
s. steel $500 $600 $800

ROLEX, 17 jewels, oyster, c. 1934
18k $3,200 $3,400 $3,700
14k $2,200 $2,500 $2,800
9k $1,400 $1,600 $1,800
silver $900 $1,000 $1,200
s. steel $700 $750 $800

ROLEX, 15 jewels, oyster, center sec., Ca. 1930
9K $1,500 $1,700 $2,000
14K $2,000 $2,300 $2,700

ROLEX, 17 jewels, oyster, center sec.

18k	$2,500	$2,700	$3,000
14k	$2,000	$2,200	$2,500
9k	$1,400	$1,500	$1,700
s. steel	$600	$700	$800

ROLEX, 18J., center sec. ca. 1937

s. steel $600 $700 $850

ROLEX, 17 jewels, graduated bezel, c. 1928

silver $900 $1,000 $1,200

ROLEX,17J., RF#4647, c.1943

s. steel $550 $650 $750

ROLEX, 18J., note dial top half & bottom, RF#3139

s. steel $600 $725 $950

ROLEX,17J., RF#3139, c.1942

s. steel $550 $650 $750

ROLEX,17J., RF#4647, c.1948

s. steel $600 $700 $900

ROLEX, 17 jewels, oyster, ref. #4547

s. steel $700 $750 $800

ROLEX, 17 jewels, oyster, c. 1930s
18k $2,800 $3,000 $3,500
14k $2,200 $2,400 $2,600

ROLEX, 17J., "Viceroy", RF#3359, c.1943
14k & s. steel.......................$1,400 $1,600 $1,800

ROLEX,17J., "Observatory", RF#3386, c.1940
gold filled................................$650 $750 $850

ROLEX, 17 jewels, oyster, extra prima "Viceroy"
18k $2,500 $2,800 $3,300

ROLEX,17J., RF#3116, c.1942
14k $2,500 $2,800 $3,000

ROLEX, 26 jewels, "Viceroy", center sec.
9k $1,800 $2,000 $2,250

ROLEX, 17 jewels, oyster, "Viceroy," 2 tone, c. 1943
14k & s. steel $1,400 $1,600 $1,900

ROLEX,17J., "Skyrocket", RF#, c.1944
gold filled $500 $600 $700

🕐 Some grades are not included. Their values can be determined by comparing with **similar** age, size, metal content, style, grades, or models such as **time only,** chronograph, repeater etc. listed.

ROLEX,17J., 28mm, small one button chronog., RF# 2303
9k \$20,000   \$22,000   \$25,000

ROLEX, 17J., one button chronog. 2 reg., curved back
18k \$25,000   \$28,000   \$32,000

ROLEX,17J., Chronograph, triple date & **moon-phases**,
about **12 made**, rf# 81806 also rf# 2508, Valjoux caliber 72C,
This chronograph is being **FAKED** so beware.
18k .... ★ ★ ★ ★ \$65,000   \$75,000   \$85,000

ROLEX, 17 J., chronog., center lugs, RF#3233, c. 1940s
18k	\$9,000	\$10,000	\$11,000
14k	\$5,000	\$6,000	\$7,000
9k	\$3,600	\$4,000	\$4,500
s. steel	\$2,500	\$3,000	\$3,500

🕐 **Note: Rolex chronographs must have original dial, deduct 30% for refinished dial.**

ROLEX,17J., rf#3055 , Antimagnetique, 200 made, c.1956
18k \$20,000   \$22,000   \$25,000

ROLEX,17J., split second chronog., RF# 4113, **15 examples**,
large 43mm, Valjoux caliber 55 VBR, Ca.1943
s. steel .... ★ ★ ★ ★ \$30,000   \$40,000   \$50,000

ROLEX, 17 J., chronog., 70-made, flat, tachometer,
rf#8206,c.1940s
18k \$15,000   \$20,000   \$25,000

ROLEX, 17 jewels, chronog., mid-sized, c. 1950s
18k	\$8,000	\$9,000	\$10,000
14k	\$7,000	\$8,000	\$9,000

ROLEX,17J., Valjoux cal.23, RF#4062, c.1940
18k $7,000 $7,500 $8,000

ROLEX, 17 jewels, chronog., 3 reg. oyster, RF#6238
s. steel $3,500 $4,000 $4,500

ROLEX, 17J., chronog., 3 reg., RF#6234, Valjoux 72bc
s. steel $4,000 $4,500 $5,000
14k $8,000 $9,000 $10,000

ROLEX,17J., triple date, RF#4767, c.1948
s. steel $9,000 $10,000 $11,000

ROLEX, 17J., chronog., triple-date, diamond style chapter,
RF# 6036, about 175 made in Y. gold , 144 made pink gold
18k $22,000 $24,000 $26,000
14k $16,000 $18,000 $21,000
s. steel $8,000 $9,000 $10,000

ROLEX, 17J., **pulsation** chronog., 3 reg., rf# 6234, Ca. 1960
s. steel $10,000 $12,000 $14,000

ROLEX,17J., Antimagnetic chronog., 3 reg., rf#6034, about
45 made, Ca.1950s
18k $10,000 $12,000 $14,000

⊕ Some grades are not included. Their values can be
determined by comparing with **similar** age, size, metal
content, style, grades, or models such as **time only**,
chronograph, repeater etc. listed.

ROLEX, 17J., RF#6238, 3 reg., c. 1950s, rect. markers
18k $8,000 $9,000 $10,000

ROLEX, 17J., chronog., 3 reg., tear drop lugs, c. 1940s
18k $10,000 $11,000 $12,000
14k $8,000 $9,000 $10,000
s. steel $4,000 $5,000 $6,000

ROLEX, 17J., triple-date, 3 reg., square markers
s. steel $8,000 $9,000 $10,000

ROLEX, 17J., Daytona, red outside chapter exotic dial
RF# 6241, **"PAUL NEWMAN"**
s. steel $7,000 $8,500 $10,000

ROLEX, 17J., exotic dial, RF#6239, Valjoux 727, c.1965
"PAUL NEWMAN", *(beware of reproduction dials)*
s. steel $7,000 $8,500 $10,000

ROLEX, 17J., "Daytona", RF#6263, c.1978
s. steel $4,400 $4,800 $5,300

ROLEX, 17J., screw down pusher 1st used 1976, RF#6265,
s. steel $4,400 $4,800 $5,300

ROLEX, 17 jewels, "Daytona," chronog., waterproof
18k $8,000 $9,000 $10,000
14k $6,000 $7,000 $8,000
s. steel $4,000 $4,300 $4,700

ROLEX, 17 J., tachometer, 3 reg., RF#6239, c.1960s

18k	$10,000	$12,000	$14,000
14k	$8,000	$9,000	$10,000
s. steel	$4,000	$4,500	$5,000

ROLEX,17J., triple-date, moon ph., RF#8171, **1,000 made**

18k	$12,000	$15,000	$18,000
14k	$9,000	$10,000	$12,000
s. steel	$6,000	$7,000	$8,500

ROLEX,17J., day-date-month, moon ph.,oyster, RF#6062

s. steel C&B	$6,000	$7,000	$8,000

ROLEX,17J., STARS on dial, triple date, rf#6062, about 50 made gold & 350 in s. steel, Ca. 1945

18k	$20,000	$22,000	$25,000

ROLEX,17J., day-date-month, moon ph., RF#6062,c.1945

18k	$12,000	$15,000	$18,000

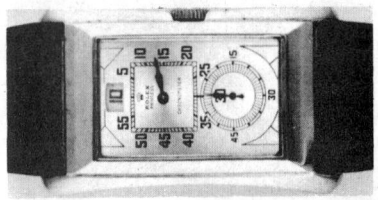

ROLEX, 15J., jumping hr., duo dial, RF#4402, c. 1930s

platinum	$14,000	$16,000	$19,000
18k	$12,000	$14,000	$16,000
14k	$10,000	$11,000	$12,000
9k	$7,000	$8,000	$9,000
silver	$6,000	$7,000	$8,000
gold filled	$4,000	$5,000	$6,500
s. steel	$5,000	$6,000	$7,500

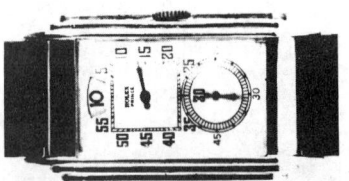

ROLEX,17J.,jump hr., duo dial, stepped case, RF#1521

18k 2 tone	$15,000	$18,000	$22,000
18k	$12,000	$14,000	$16,000
14k	$9,000	$10,000	$12,000
9k	$7,000	$8,000	$10,000
s. steel	$6,000	$7,000	$8,000

ROLEX, 17 jewels, "Prince," duo dial, RF#1490

18k C&B	$6,000	$7,000	$8,000

ROLEX, 17 jewels, flared, duo dial, c. 1930s
9k $3,700 $4,250 $4,800

ROLEX, 17J., 2 tone case tiger stripe, beware of FAKES
18k $12,500 $14,500 $16,500

ROLEX, 17 jewels, "Prince," duo dial, stepped case
18k $6,200 $7,250 $8,300
14k $4,700 $5,250 $6,300
9k $3,700 $4,250 $4,800
silver $3,700 $4,250 $4,800
s. steel $3,200 $3,750 $4,300
gold filled.............................$3,000 $3,450 $3,800

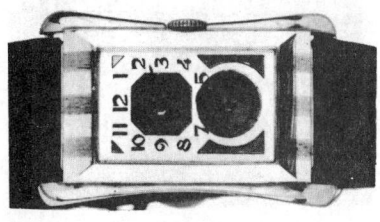

ROLEX, 17J., RF#971, 2 tone stripes, Adj. to 6 pos.
18k $12,500 $14,500 $16,500
14k $10,500 $11,500 $13,000
9k $7,200 $7,750 $8,800

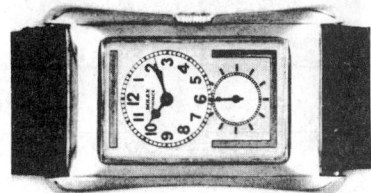

ROLEX, 15 jewels, flared, duo dial, Adj. to 6 pos.
9k $3,700 $4,250 $4,800

ROLEX, 15 jewels, "Prince," duo dial, c. 1930s
s. steel $3,200 $3,700 $4,300

ROLEX, 15 jewels, chronometer, duo dial, c. 1930s
s. steel $3,200 $3,700 $4,300

ROLEX, 15 jewels, "Railway," stepped case, c. 1930s
18k 2 tone $12,000 $14,000 $16,000
18k $10,000 $12,000 $14,000
14k 2 tone $9,000 $10,000 $11,000
14k $7,000 $8,000 $9,000
9k 2 tone $5,000 $6,000 $7,000
9k $4,000 $4,500 $5,500
s. steel $4,000 $4,500 $5,000

ROLEX, 15 jewels, "Prince," center sec., c. 1930s
18k $8,000 $9,000 $10,000

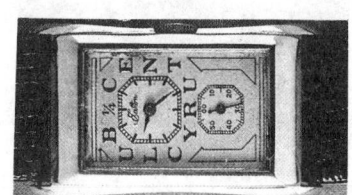

ROLEX, 15 jewels, 1/4 century club, RF#2541
14k $5,000 $5,500 $6,000

ROLEX, 15 jewels, 1/4 century club,
14k $5,000 $5,500 $6,000

ROLEX, 15 jewels, "Prince," RF#1343, c. 1935
platinum.............................$10,000 $11,000 $12,000
18k $6,000 $7,000 $8,000
14k $5,000 $5,500 $6,500
gold filled.............................$3,000 $3,200 $3,500

ROLEX, 17J., "Observatory", c.1938
gold filled.............................$1,200 $1,350 $1,500

ROLEX, 15 jewels, stepped case, RF#1527
18k $8,000 $9,000 $10,000

ROLEX, 17J., date, mid size,
s. steel $400 $450 $550

ROLEX, 25J., rf#6604 , date, c.1958
s. steel $500 $550 $625

ROLEX, 25J., rf#1500 , date, c.1963
s. steel $600 $700 $800

ROLEX, 26J., rf#6694 , date, c.1971
s. steel $400 $450 $500

ROLEX, 17J., rf#6094 , date, Ca.1951
s. steel $400 $450 $550

ROLEX, 26J., rf#1501 , c.1970
s. steel $600 $700 $800

ROLEX,25J., date, **marked gold bezel**, 2 tone case, rf#6305
s. steel/gold bezel $800 $900 $1,000

ROLEX, 17J., date, RF#6964, ca.1953
s. steel $400 $500 $600

ROLEX, 26J., center sec., date just, RF# 1601, Ca.1968
s. steel / gold $1,300 $1,500 $1,600

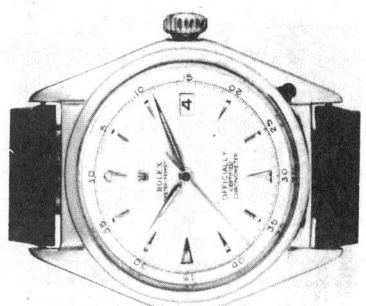

ROLEX, 17 jewels, oyster, perpetual, date, ca.1950s
14k $1,700 $1,900 $2,200

ROLEX, 25J., **Oval Toni,** *about 2,000 made,* RF#6105, auto
wind, oyster, Ca.1953
14k $3,000 $3,200 $3,500

ROLEX, 25J., oyster, perpetual, date, **Oval Toni**, RF#4467,
Ca. 1950s
18k $3,500 $3,700 $4,000

ROLEX, 17 jewels, ''Speed King''
s. steel $500 $550 $600

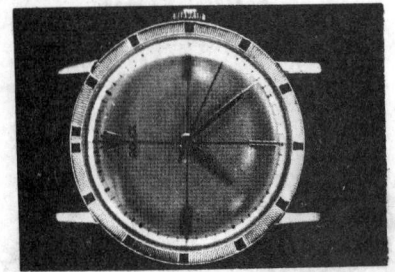

ROLEX, 17 jewels, ref. #4325
14k $900 $1,000 $1,100

ROLEX, 19J., center sec.,gold & s. steel 2 tone case,
Gold & steel...........................$600 $700 $800

ROLEX, 25 jewels, "Explorer", RF#1016
s. steel $1,800 $2,200 $2,500

ROLEX, 17J., marked bezel, rose gold, c.1940s
18k $2,000 $2,200 $2,500

ROLEX, 17 jewels, oyster, manual wind
18k $1,100 $1,250 $1,450
14k $900 $1,000 $1,200
9k $550 $700 $900
gold filled...............................$400 $450 $650
s. steel $350 $400 $600

ROLEX, 17J., marked bezel 2 tone, ca. 1955
gold & s. steel.........................$600 $650 $700

ROLEX, 17J., center sec., precision, rf#6422
s. steel $400 $450 $550

ROLEX, 25J., rf#6202, marked bezel, ca.1962
14k & s.s.............................$1,400 $1,800 $2,200

ROLEX, 26J., RF#1002, c.1965
14k $1,500 $1,600 $1,750

ROLEX, 25J., rf#5500 , Air King, c.1969
s. steel $450 $500 $550

ROLEX, 25J., marked bezel, textured dial, ca. 1949
14k $1,600 $1,800 $2,000

ROLEX, 16J., rf#6082 , c.1950
s. steel $450 $500 $550

ROLEX, 25J., rf#6565 , c.1958
s. steel $800 $850 $950

ROLEX, 25J., RF#1025, c.1960
14k $1,400 $1,600 $1,850

ROLEX, 25J., rf#6024 , c.1953
s. steel $450 $500 $600

ROLEX, 17J., rf#6424 , c.1965
s. steel $450 $500 $550

ROLEX, 25J., rf#6518 , c.1956
s. steel $450 $500 $575

ROLEX, 26J., perpetual oyster, **recent**
s. steel $600 $800 $950

ROLEX, 17J., rf#6284 , c.1955
18k $2,200 $2,400 $2,750

ROLEX, 25J., rf#6098 , star dial, c.1956
18k rose $2,500 $2,700 $3,000

ROLEX, 17J., rf#6024 , c.1952
s. steel $450 $500 $550

ROLEX, 25J., "Air King", RF#5500, c.1962
s. steel $500 $550 $600

ROLEX, 26J., rf#1005 , c.1964
14k & S.S................................$700 $800 $900

ROLEX, 25J., "Air King",RF#5504, c.1959
s. steel $400 $500 $600

ROLEX, 17J., RF#6084, c.1951
14k $1,700 $1,800 $2,000

ROLEX, 25J., RF#6084, c.1953
14k $1,800 $2,000 $2,200

ROLEX, 25J., RF#6564, c.1955
s. steel $450 $500 $550

ROLEX, 25J., marked bezel, RF#6581, c.1954
14k $1,600 $1,800 $2,000

ROLEX, 25J., RF#6568, c.1956
s. steel $450 $500 $550

ROLEX, 18J., RF#8405, c.1950
18k $900 $1,000 $1,100

ROLEX, 17J., center sec.
14k $700 $800 $900

ROLEX, 15J., center sec., ca. 1939
14k $700 $800 $900

ROLEX,17J., RF#6144, c.1948
18k & s.steel $700 $800 $900

ROLEX, 25J., "Bomb'e"12 diamond dial, RF#1030, c.1958
s. steel $700 $800 $900

ROLEX, 17J., Linz 1877, oyster, "Bomb'e", c. 1950s
18k $2,000 $2,200 $2,450

ROLEX, 26 jewels, "Bomb'e", rf#6590, c. 1950
14k $1,600 $1,800 $2,000

ROLEX, 25 jewels, "Bomb'e", rf. #6102, c.1953
14k $1,700 $1,800 $2,000

ROLEX, 26 jewels, "Bomb'e", rf#6102, c. 1950
18k $1,800 $2,000 $2,250

ROLEX, 19 jewels, "Bomb'e", center sec., c. 1950s
18k $1,600 $1,800 $2,000
14k $1,400 $1,600 $1,800
9k $900 $1,000 $1,150
s. steel $600 $700 $800

ROLEX, 17J., precision, center sec.
14k $600 $700 $800

ROLEX, 17 jewels, center sec., gold bezel
18k & s. steel $600 $700 $800

ROLEX, 17 jewels, center sec., c. 1945

18k	$2,000	$2,200	$2,500
14k	$1,200	$1,500	$1,700
9k	$1,000	$1,100	$1,200
s. steel	$450	$525	$600

ROLEX, 18J., center sec.
s. steel $450 $500 $550

ROLEX, 18J., aux. sec.
s. steel $450 $500 $550

ROLEX, 26J., bubble back, hooded lugs, rf#3595

18k	$8,000	$9,000	$10,000
14k	$6,000	$6,500	$7,000
9k	$3,500	$4,000	$4,500
s. steel	★ ★$12,000	$14,000	$16,000

ROLEX, 17J., Pall Mall, manual wind, Ca. 1949

s. steel	★ $1,200	$1,500	$1,750
14k	$600	$700	$800

ROLEX, 17J., "Royal Observatory", RF#3121, c.1937
s. steel $500 $550 $650

ROLEX, 17J., "Record", manual wind, c.1940
s. steel $500 $565 $625

ROLEX, 17J., "Neptune", mid-size, manual wind, c.1939
gold filled.................................$500 $600 $700

ROLEX, 17J., "Victory", mid size, **Tudor**, c.1940
s. steel $475 $550 $650

ROLEX, 17J., sky-rocket, mid size, ca.1949, **steel back**
gold filled & s. steel $500 $575 $650

ROLEX, 26 jewels, bubble back, hooded lugs, 2 tone
18k & s. steel $6,000 $7,000 $8,000

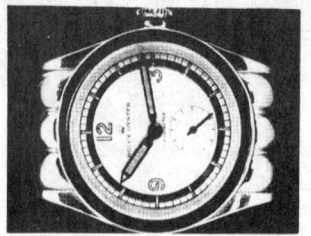

ROLEX, 26 jewels, bubble back, hooded scalloped lugs
18k & s. steel $5,000 $6,500 $8,000

ROLEX, 17J., RF#2280, manual wind, c.1951
s. steel $500 $550 $625

ROLEX, 15J., RF#2574, manual wind, tu-tone dial,
c.1940
s. steel $800 $900 $1,000

ROLEX, 18J., mid size, RF#3767, c.1940
chrome $400 $475 $550

ROLEX, 17J., mid size, RF#3478, c.1940
gold filled $400 $500 $600
s. steel $400 $500 $600

🕐 Some grades are not included. Their values can be
determined by comparing with **similar** age, size, metal
content, style, grades, or models such as **time only**,
chronograph, repeater etc. listed.

ROLEX, 17J., "Speed King", RF#4220, c.1945
s. steel $475 $575 $650

ROLEX, 17J., "Speed King", RF#6056, c.1952
s. steel $500 $550 $600

ROLEX, 17J., mid size, RF#6066, c.1951
s. steel $500 $550 $600

ROLEX, 17J., mid size, RF#6466, c.1957
s. steel $500 $550 $600

ROLEX, 18J., "Royal", mid size, aux. sec.
s. steel $500 $575 $650

ROLEX, 18J., "Speed King", mid size, center sec.
s. steel $500 $575 $650

ROLEX, 18J., B.B., hooded 2 tone yellow gold
Gold & steel..........................$3,500 $4,000 $4,500

ROLEX, 18J., B.B., hooded 2 tone rose gold
Gold & steel..........................$3,800 $4,200 $4,700

🕐 Some grades are not included. Their values can be determined by comparing with **similar** age, size, metal content, style, grades, or models such as **time only**, chronograph, repeater etc. listed.

ROLEX, 18J., B.B., center sec.
s. steel $1,200 $1,350 $1,500

ROLEX, 18J., B.B., not 2 tone, rf#3131
14k $2,850 $3,250 $3,850

ROLEX, 18J., B.B., marked bezel,
s. steel $1,200 $1,350 $1,600

ROLEX, 25J., rf#2764, B.B., marked bezel, 2 tone, c.1945
14k & S.S.............................$1,500 $1,800 $2,300

🕐 Some grades are not included. Their values can be determined by comparing with **similar** age, size, metal content, style, grades, or models such as **time only**, chronograph, repeater etc. listed.

ROLEX, 18J., B.B., marked bezel,
18k $4,000 $5,000 $6,000

ROLEX, 18J., B.B., chronometer, RF#3131, cal#600
14k $3,700 $4,000 $4,500
s. steel $1,200 $1,300 $1,500

ROLEX, 18J., B.B., cal#600, aux. sec., ca. 1945
s. steel $1,200 $1,300 $1,500

ROLEX, 18J., B.B., self winding on dial
14k $3,300 $3,500 $3,900

ROLEX, 17J., BB, RF#3131, c.1948
14k $2,800 $3,000 $3,300

ROLEX, 17J., BB, RF#3725, ROSE GOLD case, c.1945
14k rose $3,500 $4,000 $4,500

ROLEX, 17J., BB, RF#3133, tu-tone, c.1940
14k &s.s................................$1,700 $1,800 $2,000

ROLEX, 17J., RF#3725, B.B., marked bezel, c.1945
12k $3,200 $3,400 $3,600

ROLEX, 17J., BB, RF#3372, marked bezel, c.1954
s. steel $1,250 $1,400 $1,650

ROLEX, 17J., RF#5015, marked bezel, c.1949
s. steel $1,200 $1,400 $1,800

ROLEX, 17J., BB, RF#3372, tu-tone, c.1940
14k & s.s. $1,700 $2,000 $2,300

ROLEX, 18J., B.B., center sec. ca. 1940s
14k $2,800 $3,000 $3,200

ROLEX, 19 J., B.B.,ca. 1940s
14k $3,000 $3,300 $3,600

ROLEX, 26J., bubble back, graduated bezel , aux. sec.
14k $3,000 $3,500 $4,000

ROLEX, 19 jewels, bubble back, 2 tone
18k & s. steel $1,600 $1,800 $2,000

ROLEX, 26 jewels, bubble back, Arabic & Roman no.'s
14k $3,000 $3,500 $4,000

ROLEX, 26 J., bubble back, aux. sec., RF#3458, c1940s

18k $3,500	$4,000	$4,500
14k $3,000	$3,300	$3,600
9k $1,800	$2,000	$2,500
gold filled $1,100	$1,300	$1,500
s. steel $1,000	$1,200	$1,400

ROLEX, 26 J., bubble back, RF#2940, c. 1940s

18k $3,500	$4,000	$4,500
14k $3,000	$3,300	$3,600
9k $1,800	$2,000	$2,200
gold filled $1,100	$1,300	$1,500
s. steel $1,000	$1,200	$1,400

ROLEX, 26 J., bubble back, mercedes hands, c. 1930s

18k $3,500	$4,000	$4,500
14k $3,000	$3,300	$3,600
9k $1,800	$1,900	$2,200
gold filled $1,100	$1,300	$1,500
s. steel $1,000	$1,200	$1,400

Some grades are not included. Their values can be determined by comparing with **similar** age, size, metal content, style, grades, or models such as **time only**, chronograph, repeater etc. listed.

ROLEX, 26J., bubble back, marked bezel, c. 1940s

18k	$4,000	$4,500	$5,000
14k	$3,500	$4,000	$4,500
9k	$3,000	$3,200	$3,500
gold filled	$1,200	$1,400	$1,600
s. steel	$1,200	$1,400	$1,600

ROLEX, 26 jewels, bubble back, c. 1940s

14k	$2,800	$3,200	$3,600

ROLEX, 25J., rare gold #s on black dial, rf#3133, B.B., 14k bezel, c.1945

14k & s. steel.	$3,000	$3,200	$4,000

ROLEX, 26 jewels, bubble back, 2 tone, c. 1940s

18k & s. steel	$1,600	$1,800	$2,000

ROLEX, 26 jewels, bubble back, c. 1940s

s. steel	$1,000	$1,200	$1,400

ROLEX, 19 jewels, bubble back, center sec., rf#1453

18k	$3,800	$4,000	$4,500
14k	$3,000	$3,200	$3,500
s. steel	$1,000	$1,200	$1,400

ROLEX, 26 jewels, bubble back

18k	$4,000	$5,000	$6,000
s. steel	$1,000	$1,200	$1,400

ROLEX, 26 jewels, bubble back, c. 1945

14k	$2,900	$3,200	$3,600

ROLEX, 26 jewels, bubble back, c. 1940s
18k $3,700 $4,000 $4,500
14k $2,800 $3,200 $3,600
s. steel $1,200 $1,350 $1,500

ROLEX, 18 jewels, bubble back, rf# 2940, c. 1940s
s. steel $1,200 $1,350 $1,500

ROLEX, 18 jewels, bubble back, c. 1942
18k $3,700 $4,000 $4,500
14k $2,800 $3,200 $3,600
s. steel $1,200 $1,350 $1,500

ROLEX, 18 jewels, bubble back, gold & s. steel band
14k & s. steel C&B $2,500 $2,700 $3,000

ROLEX, 18 J., date, left hand winds at 9 o'clock
s. steel $1,400 $1,600 $1,800

ROLEX, 30 jewels, ''Presidential,'' 44 diamonds on dial &
bezel, day-date, oyster, perpetual, RF#8038
18k C&B $7,500 $8,500 $9,500

ROLEX, 26 jewels, day-date, 10 diamond dial, old model
RF#1803
18k C&B $5,000 $5,500 $6,000
18k (w) $4,000 $4,500 $5,000

ROLEX, 26 jewels, ''Presidential,'' diamond dial, day-date,
perpetual, oyster, RF#1804, quick set
18k C&B $6,000 $6,500 $7,000

ROLEX, 30 jewels, "Presidential," (Tridor), oyster, daydate, diamond dial, perpetual, oyster
18k (y & w) $8,000 $8,500 $9,000

ROLEX, 26 Jewels, "Presidential," day-date, single quick set model RF#18038, double quick-set RF#18238
18kC&B double quick-set... $6,500	$7,000	$7,500
18k C&B single quick-set... $5,500	$6,000	$6,500
old model 18k.....................$4,000	$4,500	$5,000

ROLEX, 30J., "Presidential," bark finish, RF#1803, c.1971
18k C&B.............................$5,500 $6,000 $6,500

ROLEX, 26J., "Presidential," day-date, perpetual, note textured dial, rose gold, RF#1803 old model
18k C & B $4,500 $5,000 $5,500

ROLEX, 30 jewels, "Presidential," day-date, perpetual, oyster, diamond bezel, bark finish, RF#18078
18k C&B.............................$7,000 $7,500 $8,500

ROLEX, quartz, RF#19018
 diamond dial & diamond bezel add $1,000-$1,200
 18k $4,000 $5,000 $6,000

ROLEX, 26 Jewels, "Presidential," day-date, perpetual, oyster, old model, RF#1803
18k C&B.............................$4,000 $4,500 $5,000

ROLEX, 26 J., jubilee band, 10 diamond dial, date just

18k C&B	$4,500	$5,500	$6,500
14k C&B	$3,500	$4,000	$5,000
gold & s. steel C&B	$2,000	$2,500	$3,000

ROLEX, 26 jewels, date, oyster, mid-size

s. steel C&B	$550	$600	$700

ROLEX, 26 jewels, date, perpetual, oyster

18k	$2,500	$2,700	$3,000
14k	$1,600	$1,800	$2,200
s. steel	$500	$550	$650

ROLEX, 17J., RF#6694, c.1961

s. steel	$500	$550	$650

ROLEX, 26J., quick set, date, Oyster bracelet, c.1965

14k C&B	$2,800	$3,000	$3,200

ROLEX, 17J., RF#6426, c.1961

s. steel	$500	$550	$600

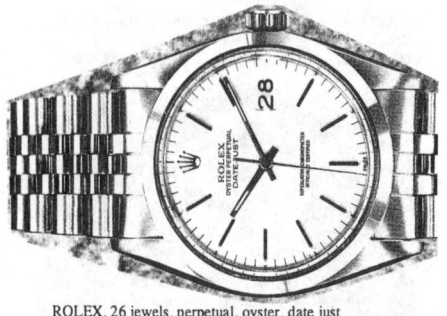

ROLEX, 21 jewels, date just, center sec., c. 1965

18k	$3,000	$3,500	$4,000

ROLEX, 26 jewels, perpetual, oyster, date just

18k	$4,000	$4,500	$5,500
18k & s. steel	$1,400	$1,600	$2,000
14k	$2,800	$3,200	$4,000
14k & s. steel	$1,200	$1,400	$1,600
s. steel	$600	$700	$900

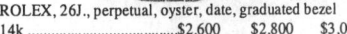

ROLEX, 26J., perpetual, oyster, date, graduated bezel
14k $2,600 $2,800 $3,000
s. steel $700 $850 $1,100

ROLEX, 21 jewels, perpetual, oyster
18k $1,800 $1,900 $2,000
18k & s. steel $800 $900 $1,200
14k $1,400 $1,500 $1,600
14k & s. steel $700 $800 $1,000
s. steel $600 $700 $800

ROLEX, 26 jewels, oyster, date, ref. #1625
18k & s. steel $2,800 $3,200 $3,600
14k & s. steel C&B.............$1,200 $1,500 $1,850

ROLEX, 25J., gold bezel, "Explorer," rf#6610, Ca. 1956
s. steel & gold bezel $2,000 $2,200 $2,500

ROLEX, 21 J., "Thunderbird," perpetual, oyster, date just
18k $4,000 $4,500 $5,000
s. steel $900 $1,100 $1,200

ROLEX, 26 jewels, "Explorer," rf#1016, perpetual, oyster
s. steel $1,850 $2,000 $2,400

ROLEX, 21 jewels, perpetual, oyster date just, 2 tone
Gold & steel $1,200 $1,400 $1,600

ROLEX, 17J., "**Luminor Panerai**," Italian military diving,
RF# 6151-1, Ca. **1940s**, Note: look for reproduction 1992
s. steel $1,700 $1,900 $2,200

ROLEX, 26 jewels, "GMT-Master," perpetual, oyster, date
ruby & diamond dial
18k $5,500 $6,500 $7,500

ROLEX, 26 J., "Submariner," rf#5513
s. steel $1,000 $1,200 $1,500

ROLEX, 26 J., "GMT-Master II," perp., oyster, date
18k $5,000 $6,000 $7,000
s. steel $1,100 $1,300 $1,500

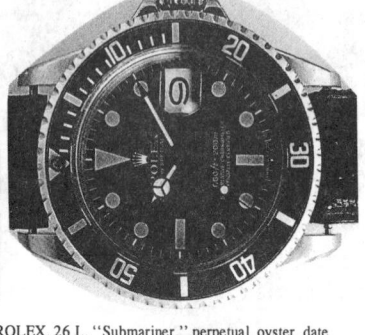

ROLEX, 26 J., "Submariner," perpetual, oyster, date
18k C&B $7,000 $8,000 $9,000
18k & s. steel C&B $2,600 $2,800 $3,400
s. steel $1,000 $1,200 $1,500

ROLEX, 26 J., "GMT-Master", rf#6542, c.1957
s. steel $1,100 $1,250 $1,400
Single quick set Presidential & Jubilee use 6 screws.
Double quick set Presidential & Jubilee use 7 screws.
Presidential or Jubilee gold link $250.00
Jubilee or Oyster s. steel link $40.00
Oyster gold link $200.00
ROLEX first used **HACK** system in Ca. 1972
ROLEX first used the Quick Set feature Ca. 1977
Sapphire crystals were added in U.S.A. Ca.1989=gents $100.
steel screw-on crown=$20., gold screw-on crown=$35.

ROLEX, 26J., "Sea-Dweller," rf#1665, 2,000 ft, date
s. steel $1,200 $1,400 $1,600

ROLEX factory only, mens diamond dials & bezels
Bezel 18k or platinum, W/44 full cut $3,000 $5,000
Dial W/8 brilliants & 2 baguetts for Oyster Perpetual &
DAY DATE................................... $1,000 $1,600
Dial W/ 10 baguettes for Oyster Perpetual &
DAY DATE................................... $2,000 $3,500
Dial W/ 10 brilliants for Oyster Perpetual &
DATEJUST or DATE.................... $700 $1,500

ROLEX, 21J., ''Sea-Dweller,'' up to 4,000 ft., rf# 16660, date
s. steel $1,800 $2,000 $2,300

ROLEX, 26 jewels, ''Explorer II,'' rf# 1665, date
s. steel $1,800 $2,000 $2,400

ROLEX, 26 jewels, ''Submariner,'' rf# 5512, 200M
s. steel $900 $1,100 $1,250

ROLEX, 26J., ''Submariner'', rf# 6536,100M,c.1958
s. steel $1,250 $1,350 $1,550

ROLEX, 15J., ca. 1935
s. steel $750 $850 $950

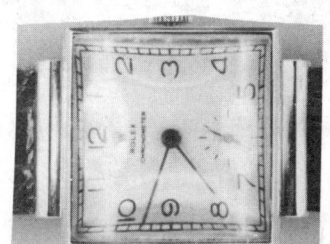

ROLEX,18J., hooded lugs
14k $1,200 $1,400 $1,700

ROLEX, 18J., stepped case, 2 tone, ca. 1940s
G & steel $1,500 $1,700 $2,000

ROLEX, 15J., ca. 1937
s. steel $600 $700 $800

ROLEX, 15J., engraved case, c.1930
s. steel $600 $700 $800

ROLEX, 15J., GJS, c.1935
9K.. $800 $900 $1,100

ROLEX, 18J., rf#4029, c.1945
18k $1,400 $1,800 $2,250

ROLEX, 17J., rf#619, ROSE gold,c.1948
18k $1,200 $1,400 $1,700

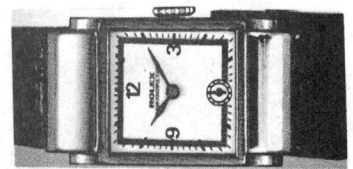

ROLEX, 18J., rf#2537,adj.6 pos. 2 tone,ca. 1940s
gold & steel $2,500 $3,000 $3,500

ROLEX,15J., stepped case, c.1938
18k $1,800 $2,000 $2,200

ROLEX, 17J., center lug "Standard", c.1940
14k & s.s.............................. $1,000 $1,200 $1,400

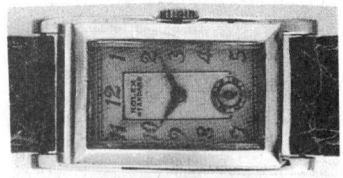

ROLEX, 17J., "Standard", c.1940
gold filled $700 $800 $900

ROLEX, 15J., beveled case, c.1927
s. steel $500 $575 $650

🕐 Some grades are not included. Their values can be
determined by comparing with **similar** age, size, metal
content, style, grades, or models such as **time only**,
chronograph, repeater etc. listed.

ROLEX, 17J., hidden lugs,
14k $1,500 $1,700 $2,000

ROLEX, 17J., "31 Victories",
18k $1,400 $1,600 $1,850

ROLEX, 18J., fluted bezel, rf#3737
18k $1,200 $1,500 $1,800

ROLEX, 18J., 3 diamond dial , ca. 1940s
18kC&B $1,500 $1,800 $2,000

ROLEX, 18J., ca. 1940s
s. steel $500 $650 $800

ROLEX, 18J., round movement, ca. 1947
18k $1,000 $1,200 $1,500

ROLEX, 17 jewels, "Precision"
18k $1,500 $1,700 $1,950

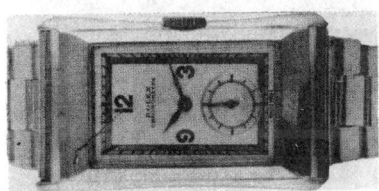

ROLEX, 17 jewels, curvex
18k C&B $3,000 $4,000 $5,000

ROLEX, 17 jewels, curved, c. 1940s
gold filled $500 $600 $800

ROLEX, 17 jewels, "Ultra Prima," gold train
18k $1,800 $2,000 $2,400

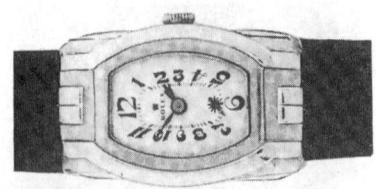

ROLEX, 17 jewels, hooded lugs, 2 tone
rose & white gold $3,000 $4,000 $5,000

ROLEX, 17 jewels, "Standard," c. 1939
14k $2,000 $2,500 $3,000

ROLEX, 17 jewels, "Benvenuto Cellini," thin model
18k $1,000 $1,100 $1,200

ROLEX, 21 jewels, perpetual, oyster, c. 1945
18k $2,200 $2,500 $3,000

ROLEX, 17 jewels, "Precision," c. 1940s
18k $1,200 $1,500 $1,800
14k $1,000 $1,200 $1,400

ROLEX, 17 J. , "Precision," tank style, faceted bezel
18k $1,200 $1,500 $1,800

ROLEX, 17 jewels, extra flat, c. 1950s
18k $1,200 $1,500 $1,800

ROLEX, 21 jewels, "Cellini"
18k $900 $1,000 $1,200

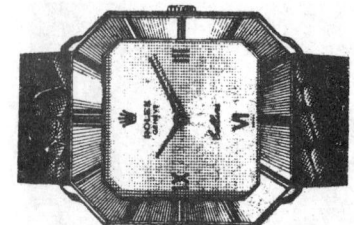

ROLEX, 21 jewels, "Cellini"
18k $1,000 $1,100 $1,300

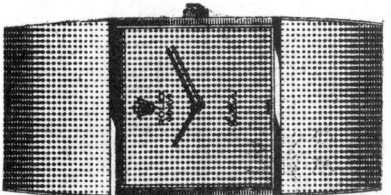

ROLEX, 21 jewels, "Cellini"
18k C&B $1,500 $1,800 $2,200

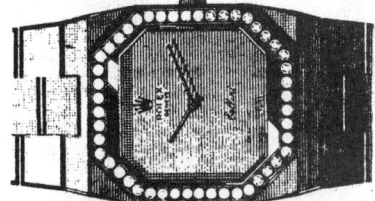

ROLEX, 21 jewels, "Cellini," diamond bezel
18k C&B $2,500 $2,800 $3,200

ROLEX, 17J., "Cellini", Rf#4017, c.1988
18k $1,500 $1,700 $2,000

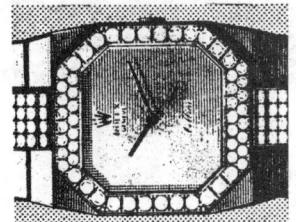

ROLEX, 21 jewels, "Benvenuto Cellini," diamonds on bezel
& band
18k $6,000 $7,000 $8,000

ROLEX, "Tudor," (Prince)
s. steel $250 $300 $400

ROLEX,17J., "Tudor", auto-wind, RF#7909, c.1955
s. steel $125 $150 $195

ROLEX, 25J., "Tudor", rf# 7016, submariner, by ETA
s. steel $275 $325 $400

ROLEX, 25J., "Tudor", submariner, date, by ETA,
rf# 76100, Ca.1985
s. steel $400 $500 $600

ROLEX, 25J., "Tudor", rf#7809, auto-wind, c.1978
s. steel $150 $175 $225

ROLEX, 17J., "Tudor", auto-wind, c.1955
18k $600 $700 $800

ROLEX, "Tudor," chronog., date, rf#9420,
s. steel model sold for $1,200 retail Ca. 1992
s. steel $800 $900 $1,150

ROLEX, 17J., "Tudor", SOLAR, rf4463, c.1955
s. steel $200 $250 $300

ROLEX, 25J., Prince Oyster Date Ranger II, Ca.1973
s. steel $250 $300 $350

ROLEX, 17J., "Tudor", rf#2765, TURTLE, Zell Bros
Gold filled $250 $300 $350

ROLEX, quartz, "Tudor," date, Ca. 1992
s. steel & gold plate................$300 $350 $400

ROLEX, "Tudor," chronog., date, 165 ft., **auto-wind**
s. steel $900 $1,100 $1,250

ROLEX, 17J., **Drivers**, c.1935
gold filled $600 $700 $800

ROLEX, 18J., lady's, Ca. 1948
18k $350 $425 $495
14k $225 $295 $350

ROLEX, 17J., ladies, "Oyster",
14k $1,000 $1,200 $1,400

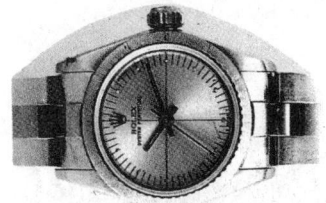

ROLEX, 29J., ladies, "Oyster", RF#67003
s. steel &14k,C&B..............$1,000 $1,100 $1,200

ROLEX, 17J., ladies, "Oyster", RF#4486, c.1957
14k & s.s.case $400 $500 $600

ROLEX, 17J., ladies, "Oyster", c.1948
18k $1,800 $2,000 $2,250

ROLEX, 17J., ladies,"Centergraph"
14k $1,000 $1,100 $1,200

ROLEX, 17J., ladies, "Oyster", RF#3492
s. steel....................................$300 $350 $400

ROLEX, 17J., ladies, RF#4593, c.1954
s. steel....................................$250 $300 $350

ROLEX, 15J., 54 diamonds, 9k band 18k(w) case, c.1930
9k & 18k $1,200 $1,400 $1,600

ROLEX, 17J., ladies, c.1945
gold filled...............................$125 $150 $200

ROLEX, 15J., lady's, curved, ca.1925
9k...$200 $250 $300

ROLEX, 15J., lady's, center lugs, ca.1925
9k...$300 $400 $500

ROLEX, 18J., lady's, ca. 1930s
18k $400 $500 $600

ROLEX, 18J., wire lugs, diamond bezel, ca. 1940s
18k(W).................................$500 $600 $700

ROLEX, 18J., lady's,
14k $300 $350 $400

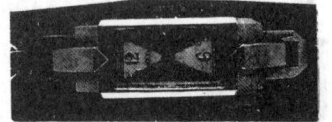

ROLEX, 18J., lady's,
14k(W) C&B $400 $500 $600

ROLEX, 18J., lady's, bubble back
18k $1,600 $1,800 $2,200

ROLEX, 15J., lady's, Ca.1925
18k band..............................$400 $500 $600

ROLEX, Oyster Perpetual Datejust, diamond dial &bezel
18k C&B $6,000 $6,500 $7,000

ROLEX, Oyster Perpetual Datejust
18k C&B $4,000 $4,500 $5,000

ROLEX, Oyster Perpetual Datejust
18k & s. steel $1,700 $2,000 $2,500

ROLEX, Oyster Perpetual
18k & s. steel $1,400 $1,600 $1,800

ROLEX ESTIMATED PRODUCTION DATES

DATE–SERIAL #	DATE–SERIAL #	DATE–SERIAL #	DATE–SERIAL #
1925 --- 25,000	1943 --- 253,000	1961---1,485,000	1979--- 5,960,000
1926 --- 27,500	1944 --- 284,000	1962---1,557,000	1980--- 6,430,000
1927 --- 30,500	1945 --- 348,000	1963---1,635,000	1981--- 6,910,000
1928 --- 33,000	1946 --- 413,000	1964---1,713,000	1982--- 7,380,000
1929 --- 35,500	1947 --- 478,000	1965---1,791,000	1983--- 7,860,000
1930 --- 38,000	1948 --- 543,000	1966---1,870,000	1984--- 8,340,000
1931 --- 40,000	1949 --- 608,000	1967---2,164,000	1985--- 8,810,000
1932 --- 43,000	1950 --- 673,500	1968---2,426,000	1986--- 9,300,000
1933 --- 49,000	1951 --- 735,500	1969---2,689,000	1987--- 9,760,000
1934 --- 55,000	1952 --- 804,000	1970---2,952,000	1987 1/2-9,999,999
1935 --- 62,000	1953 --- 869,000	1971---3,215,000	1987 3/4-R000,001
1936 --- 82,000	1954 --- 935,000	1972---3,478,000	1988 --- R999,999
1937 --- 98,000	1955---1,010,000	1973---3,741,000	1989 --- L000,001
1938---118,000	1956---1,095,000	1974---4,000,000	1990 --- L999,999
1939---136,000	1957---1,167,000	1975---4,260,000	1990 1/2-E000,001
1940---165,000	1958---1,245,000	1976---4,530,000	1991 1/4-E999,999
1941---194,000	1959---1,323,000	1977---5,000,000	1991 1/2-X000,001
1942---224,000	1960---1,401,000	1978---5,480,000	1991 3/4-N000,001
			1992 1/4-C000,001

The above list is provided for determining the APPROXIMATE age of your watch. Match serial number with date. Watches were not necessarily sold in the exact order of manufactured date. The above list was furnished with the help of TOM ENGLE.

6694

Reference number, four figures engraved between the lugs

1705215

Serial number, six or seven figures engraved between the lugs

INSIDE OF BACK
Reference number in four figures

NON-OYSTER CASE

On recent OYSTER models the number is engraved on the outside of the case between the lugs. Reference number of earlier models will be found engraved on the inside of the back of the case.

Reference number for NON-OYSTER models will be found engraved on the inside of the back of the case.

OUTSIDE OF BACK
Serial number in six or seven figures

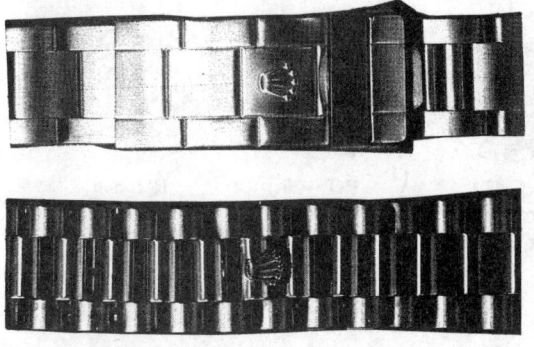

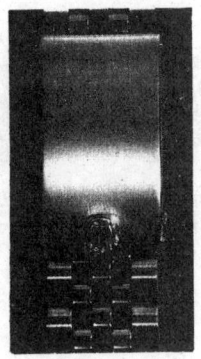

Above: Oyster style bracelet. **Below:** Presidential style band with hidden clasp.
Right: Jubilee style bracelet.

Current *double quick set* Presidential and Jubilee bracelets use **7 screws** for adjustment links.
The older models *Single quick set* Presidential and Jubilee bracelets use **6 screws** for adjustment links.

ROLEX
MOVEMENT IDENTIFICATION

Ref. 90

Ref. 100

Ref. 150

Ref. 160

Ref. 161

(All without seconds)

Ref. 170
without seconds

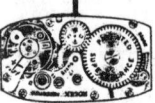
Ref. 180
without seconds

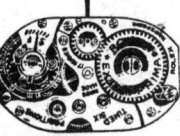
Ref. 200
without seconds

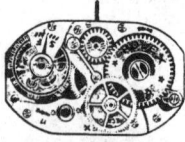
Ref. 210
sweep seconds

Ref. 250
without seconds

Ref. 270
without seconds

Ref. 300
ordinary seconds

Ref. 310
sweep second

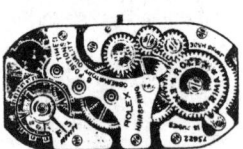
Ref. 350
jump hour

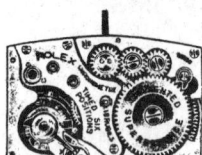
Ref. 360
ordinary second

Ref. 400
ordinary seconds
Ca. 1941

Ref. 420
ordinary seconds
Ca. 1941

Ref. 420
rotor
Ca. 1941

Ref. 500
ordinary seconds
Ca. 1936

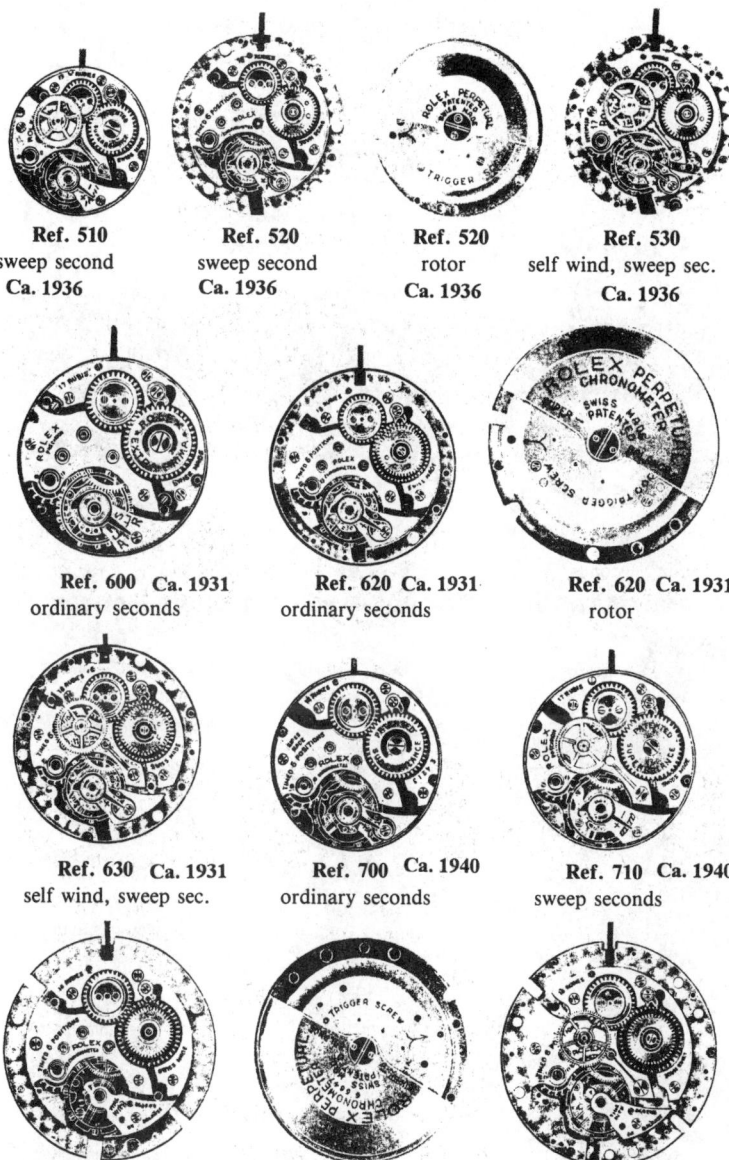

Ref. 510
sweep second
Ca. 1936

Ref. 520
sweep second
Ca. 1936

Ref. 520
rotor
Ca. 1936

Ref. 530
self wind, sweep sec.
Ca. 1936

Ref. 600 Ca. 1931
ordinary seconds

Ref. 620 Ca. 1931
ordinary seconds

Ref. 620 Ca. 1931
rotor

Ref. 630 Ca. 1931
self wind, sweep sec.

Ref. 700 Ca. 1940
ordinary seconds

Ref. 710 Ca. 1940
sweep seconds

Ref. 720 Ca. 1940
ordinary seconds

Ref. 720 Ca. 1940
rotor

Ref. 730 Ca. 1945
self wind, sweep sec.

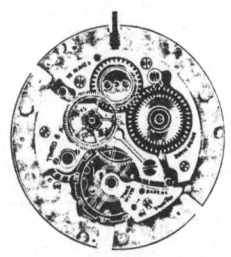

Ref. 740 **Ca. 1945**
self wind, calendar, sweep sec.

Ref. 850
ordinary seconds

Ref. 72
chronograph, 3 registers

Ref. 23
chronograph, 2 registers

POSITIONS OF THE WINDING CROWN FOR CALENDAR MODELS

Pos. 1

Crown fully screwed down.
In this position the Rolex Oyster is warranted pressure-proof to a
depth of 330 feet/100 m.
The watch is ready to be worn.

Pos. 2

Crown unscrewed.
When the crown is free of the screw threads, the watch is in position
for handwinding, if necessary.
In quartz models, this is a neutral position.

Pos. 3

Crown pulled out to the first notch.
When turning the crown from three to six o'clock, the date will
change rapidly.
This position is used to correct the date when months have less
than 31 days.
The timing of the watch will not be altered.

Pos. 4

Crown pulled out to the last notch.
Position for setting the correct time, the date and the day.
The watch stops and enables adjustments to be made, for Day-Date
models, when the hands are turned counter-clockwise, the day of
the week changes while the date remains unchanged.
Change the day before correcting the date.

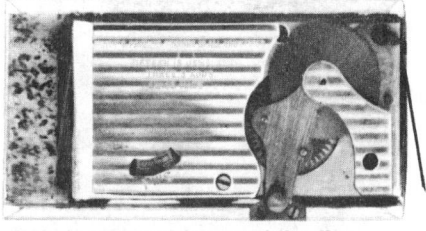

ROLLS, 15J., early auto wind movement, by Leon Hatot, movement moves back & forth inside case to wind, c. 1930s.

RULON, ca. 1940s
gold filled $60 $70 $80

ROLLS, 15 jewels, early auto wind, c. 1920s
s. steel $700 $800 $1,000

RULON, 17J., 3 diamonds on dial
gold plate $100 $125 $150

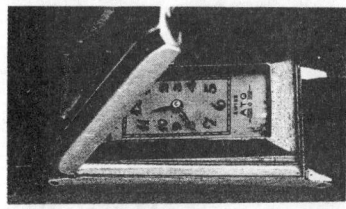

ROLLS, 15 jewels, "ATO," flip top
s. steel $700 $800 $900

ROLLS, 15 jewels, ladies, "ATO," flip top, by Blancpain
18k $800 $900 $1,000

SCHILD, 17J., "Aqua lung", tach.chronog., ca.1972
s. steel $250 $275 $350

ROTARY, 15J., aux. sec., ca.1934
9k $125 $150 $175

SCHULTZ, 17J., diamond dial, c.1930
platinum $1,800 $2,000 $2,200

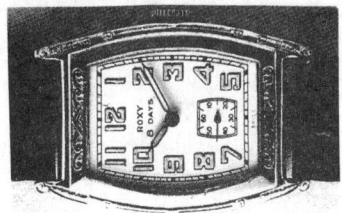

ROXY, 8 day, engraved case, ca. 1930s
s. steel $200 $250 $300

J. SCHULTZ, 17J., enamel hunter style, ca. 1949
18k $1,500 $1,800 $2,000

SEELAND, 17J., aux. sec., Ca. 1955
14k $90 $120 $165

SEELAND, 7J., ca. 1950s
gold filled...................................$50 $60 $70

SEELAND, 17J., "Quadramatic" auto-wind, c.1947
s. steel $25 $30 $40

SEELAND, 17J., manual wind, c.1947
chrome $25 $30 $40

SEIKO, 6J., wire lugs, on dial "LAUREL", ca.1925
s. steel $40 $50 $60

SEIKO, quartz, rope style bezel
14k $175 $200 $225

SEMCA, 17J., day-date-month, moon phase, c. 1950s
18k $1,300 $1,400 $1,600

SEMCA, 17J., day-date-month, moon phase, c. 1950s
14k $800 $1,200 $1,500

SETH THOMAS, day date, moon phases, ca. 1949
s. steel $250 $325 $375

🕐 Some grades are not included. Their values can be determined by comparing with **similar** age, size, metal content, style, grades, or models such as **time only**, chronograph, repeater etc. listed.

SHEFFIELD,17J., chronog., by Venus, cal.189
s. steel $125 $150 $175

SIMGA,17J., textured dial,c.1940
18k $200 $250 $300

SMITH, 17J., military , Ca.1969
s. steel $125 $150 $175

SPERINA, 7 jewels, day & date on lugs
s. steel $100 $125 $165

SOUTH BEND,17J., multi-color dial, made U.S.A.
base metal $250 $300 $400

STANDARD,17J., 24 hr. dial, world time, c.1965
s. steel $100 $125 $165

SUIZO, 17J., one button chronog. ca. 1930s
gold filled $200 $250 $300

SWATCH (see listings at the end of wrist watch section)

TAVANNES, 15J., enamel dial, flip top, c.1915
silver $300 $350 $400

TAVANNES, 17J., chronog., c.1940
s. steel $200 $250 $300

TAVANNES, 17J., extended lugs, c.1955
gold filled.................................$55 $65 $85

TAVANNES, 17J., aux. sec., c.1935
14k $125 $150 $175

TAVANNES, 17J., GJS, cal.365k, c.1938
14k $175 $200 $250

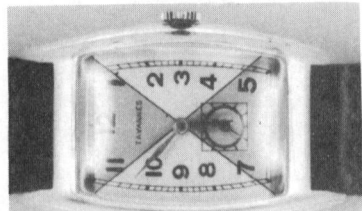

TAVANNES, 17 jewels, hour glass dial, **curved**
14k $200 $250 $300

TAVANNES, 15 jewels, "334," c. 1939
14k (w) $200 $250 $300

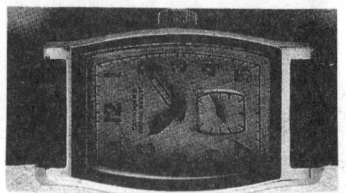

TAVANNES, 17 jewels, aux. sec. ca. 1940s
s. steel $80 $100 $125

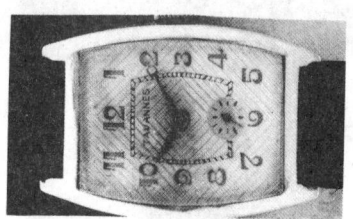

TAVANNES, 17 jewels, aux. sec.
14k $225 $250 $275

TECHNOS, 17J., "Sky Diver", auto-wind, 500m., c.1970
s. steel $50 $60 $75

🕐 Some grades are not included. Their values can be determined by comparing with **similar** age, size, metal content, style, grades, or models such as **time only**, chronograph, repeater etc. listed.

TELDA, 17J., chronog.,3 reg, date, moon ph., c.1980s
s. steel $500 $600 $700

TELDA, 17J., center sec., c.1948
gold filled...................................$40 $50 $65

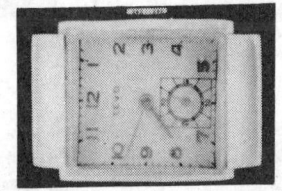

TEVO, 17J., hidden lugs
14k $100 $135 $175

NOTE: Examples of Tiffany made up
watches are listed but were not sold by Tiffany & Co.. These off-brand watches will be
listed but not priced as true Tiffany & Co.
watches. EXAMPLES: *Kingston, Emerson,
Banner*, ETC. were not sold by Tiffany.

TIFFANY & CO.,17J., wire lugs, c.1920
silver $400 $500 $600

TIFFANY & CO., 18J., by P.P.& CO., CA. 1920s
18K $4,000 $5,000 $6,000

TIFFANY & CO., 17J., curved, mvt. by P.P. & Co., c. 1910
18k $6,000 $6,500 $7,000

TIFFANY & CO.,17J., by Banner"?" , c.1926
18k $300 $350 $400

TIFFANY & CO.,17J., by Wheeler "?", c.1930
14k $150 $175 $200

TIFFANY & CO., 26 jewels, min. repeater, slide repeat,
automaton, 40mm
18k $8,000 $9,000 $10,000

TIFFANY & CO., 15J., wire lugs, ca. 1928
silver $300 $350 $400

TIFFANY & CO.,17J., by P.P. & Co., wire lugs, c.1915
18k $3,500 $4,000 $4,500

TIFFANY & CO.,17J., by I.W.C., wire lugs, c.1918
14k $600 $700 $800

TIFFANY & CO., 15J., enamel dial, ca. 1930s
silver $500 $550 $600

TIFFANY & CO., 17J., Concord W. C0.
14k $600 $700 $800

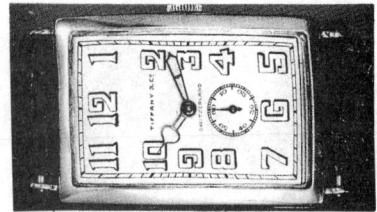

TIFFANY & CO., 18J., by P.P.& CO., Ca. 1930s
platinum...............................$5,000 $6,000 $7,000

TIFFANY & CO., 15 jewels, Swiss, Ca. 1926
18k $500 $600 $700

TIFFANY & CO.,17J., by Longines, c.1928
14k $400 $500 $600

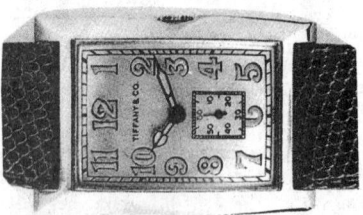

TIFFANY & CO.,17J., aux. sec., Swiss, c.1926
18k(w).....................................$700 $850 $1,000

TIFFANY & CO.,17J., by Fidea "?", c.1930
14k $200 $225 $250

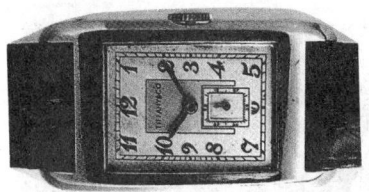

TIFFANY & CO.,17J., GJS, by Movado, c.1940
14k $600 $700 $800

TIFFANY & CO.,17J., by Kingston "?", hidden lugs, c.1943
14k $150 $200 $250

TIFFANY & CO.,17J., by Charlin W. Co. "?", GJS, c.1940
14k $150 $175 $200

TIFFANY & CO.,17J., by Emerson "?", c.1940
14k $100 $125 $150

TIFFANY & CO.,17J., by Hampden "?", c.1949
14k $100 $135 $175

TIFFANY & CO.,17J., by I.W.C., c.1942
14k $600 $650 $750

TIFFANY & CO.,17J., by I.W.C., hidden lugs, c.1942
14k $600 $700 $800

TIFFANY & CO., 17J., top hat, by I. W. C0.
14K $1,000 $1,200 $1,400

TIFFANY & CO.,15J., one button chronog., by Goering,
69 mvt., c.1925
silver $1,000 $1,200 $1,400

TIFFANY & CO.,17J., Valjoux cal.72c., c.1948
s. steel $550 $650 $750
14k $1,200 $1,300 $1,500
18k $1,400 $1,600 $1,750

⊕ Some grades are not included. Their values can be
determined by comparing with similar age, size, metal
content, style, grades, or models such as time only,
chronograph, repeater etc. listed.

TIFFANY & CO.,17J., by Movado, c.1947
14k $2,000 $2,200 $2,500

TIFFANY & CO.,17J., by Bovet"?", c.1940
18k $600 $700 $800

TIFFANY & CO.,17J., by Tourneau , Valjoux 72c, c.1950
s. steel $500 $600 $650

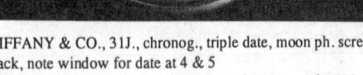

TIFFANY & CO., 31J., chronog., triple date, moon ph. screw-
back, note window for date at 4 & 5
18k $2,500 $2,700 $3,000

TIFFANY & CO., 17J., chronog., day-date-month
14k $1,200 $1,400 $1,600

TIFFANY & CO., 21J., mvt. by P.P. & Co., c. 1950
18k $3,000 $3,500 $4,000

TIFFANY & CO., 17J., curved , ca.1920s
platinum............................$1,000 $1,200 $1,500

TIFFANY & CO.,15J., engraved bezel, c.1919
18k $1,200 $1,500 $1,700

⊕ Some grades are not included. Their values can be
determined by comparing with **similar** age, size, metal
content, style, grades, or models such as **time only**,
chronograph, repeater etc. listed.

TIFFANY & CO., 15J., ca. 1920s
14k $500 $600 $700

TIFFANY & CO.,17J., by Zodiac "?", c.1942
14k $150 $175 $200

TIFFANY & CO.,17J., by Hampden "?", c.1945
gold filled.................................. $75 $100 $125
14k $175 $200 $250

TIFFANY & CO.,17J., by Glycine "?", c.1945
gold filled $75 $100 $125
14k $200 $235 $275

TIFFANY & CO.,17J., by Ollendorf "?", c.1945
14k $200 $250 $300

TIFFANY & CO.,17J., extended bezel, c.1942
14k $400 $500 $600

TIFFANY & CO.,17J., by Crawford "?", c.1947
14k $150 $175 $200

TIFFANY & CO.,17J., by Wyler "?", c.1950
gold filled $100 $125 $150

TIFFANY & CO.,17J., by Tissot, c.1948
14k $300 $350 $400

TIFFANY & CO., 17J., fancy lugs & bezel,ca.1950s
14k $300 $400 $500

TIFFANY & CO., 17J., applied numbers, ca. 1950s
14k $400 $500 $600

TIFFANY & CO., 17J., flared & stepped, ca.1950s
14k $300 $400 $500

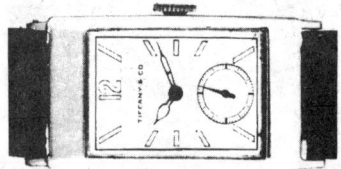

TIFFANY & CO., 17 jewels, Swiss, c. 1935
18k $700 $800 $900

TIFFANY & CO., 17 jewels, fancy bezel, c. 1942
14k $400 $450 $500

TIFFANY & CO., 17 jewels, sculptured lugs, c. 1948
14k $800 $900 $1,000

TIFFANY & CO.,17J., 3 diamond dial, by Lathin "?",
14k(w)..................................... $200 $225 $250

TIFFANY & CO.,15J., rhinestones "?", c.1948
base metal $40 $50 $75

TIFFANY & CO., 17J., "Movado", triple date, center sec.
s. steel $350 $450 $500

TIFFANY & CO.,17J., by Movado, triple date, c.1948
gold filled $400 $450 $500
14k & s.s................................... $500 $600 $700

TIFFANY & CO.,17J.,by Tissot,triple date moon ph.,
14k $1,000 $1,100 $1,200

TIFFANY & CO.,17J., by Helvetia , c.1948
gold filled $100 $125 $150
14k $250 $275 $300

TIFFANY & CO., 17J., triple date, moon ph.
s. steel $400 $450 $500

TIFFANY & CO.,17J., "?", c.1940
gold filled $75 $100 $125

TIFFANY & CO.,17J., by Ardath "?", auto-wind, c.1950
14k $100 $125 $150

TIFFANY & CO.,17J., by Mepa "?", GJS, c.1949
gold filled $50 $65 $80
14k $100 $135 $175

TIFFANY & CO.,17J., by Nicolet "?", c.1955
gold filled.................................$50 $60 $75

TIFFANY & CO.,17J., by Zenith, c.1939
14k $200 $250 $300

TIFFANY & CO.,17J., c.1948
18k $500 $600 $700

TIFFANY & CO.,17J., carved lugs, c.1950
18k $300 $350 $400

TIFFANY & CO.,17J., ladies, by Longines, c.1920
18k $250 $300 $350

TIFFANY & CO.,17J., by I.W.C., c.1948
18k $300 $400 $500

TIFFANY & CO.,17J., I.W.C., c.1955
18k $200 $250 $300

TIFFANY & CO., 15J., 2 tone , ladies, ca. 1939
18k C&B.............................$400 $450 $500

TIFFANY & CO., 15J., early ladies, wire lugs ca.1925
14k $400 $450 $500

TIFFANY & CO., 17J., ladies, aux. sec., Ca.1940
gold filled $40 $45 $55

TIMECRAFT, 17 jewels, chronog., Ca. 1950
s. steel $125 $150 $175

TIMEX,chronog., slide to start, stop & return to zero
base metal $55 $65 $75

TISSOT, 17 jewels, 1898 USA 20 dollar gold piece
24k ....$1,000　　$1,500　　$2,000

TISSOT,17J., military, chronog., Valjoux cal.225, c.1955
s. steel ....$325　　$375　　$425

TISSOT, 21 jewels, world time, 24 hr. dial, 24 cities
s. steel ....$700　　$800　　$900
18k ....$2,000　　$2,500　　$3,000

TISSOT,17J., Valjoux cal.726, c.1965
18k ....$800　　$900　　$1,100
14k ....$700　　$800　　$900

TISSOT, 21J, world time, 24 hr. dial, 24 cities, mid-size
18k ....$2,500　　$3,000　　$3,500

TISSOT,17J., auto-wind,"Navigator", date, c.1972
s. steel ....$150　　$175　　$225

TISSOT, 17J., "Stadium", tachymeter, c.1960
gold plate ....$150　　$175　　$200

TISSOT, 17 jewels, chronog., 3 reg., c. 1956
s. steel ....$325　　$375　　$450

TISSOT, 17 jewels, chronog., 3 reg.
gold filled...............................$325 $450 $500
s. steel $275 $325 $400

TISSOT, 17 jewels, chronog., 3 reg.
14k $700 $800 $900
s. steel $250 $300 $350

TISSOT, 17 jewels, chronog., 3 reg., c. 1940s
18k $1,200 $1,400 $1,600

TISSOT, 17 jewels, chronog., triple date, moon phase
s. steel $900 $1,000 $1,250
14k $2,300 $2,500 $2,900
18k $2,750 $3,000 $3,300

TISSOT, 17J., day-date-month, moon phase, ctr. sec.
18k $1,200 $1,500 $1,800

TISSOT, 17J., "UHF", date, auto-wind, c.1960
14k $200 $250 $300

TISSOT, 17J., auto-wind, date, c.1958
s. steel $60 $70 $80

TISSOT, 17J., hidden lugs, c.1938
14k $300 $350 $425

TISSOT, 17J., 4 diamonds on dial, GJS, hooded lugs
gold filled $125 $150 $200

TISSOT,17J., aux. sec., c.1951
18k ....$300　　$350　　$400

TISSOT,17J., hidden lugs, c.1950
14k ....$400　　$450　　$500

TISSOT,17J., aux. sec., c.1942
s. steel ....$90　　$120　　$150
18k ....$200　　$250　　$300

TISSOT, 17 jewels, large lugs,
14k ....$250　　$300　　$350

TISSOT, 17J., open shutters to reveal dial
base metal ....$200　　$250　　$300

TISSOT, 15 jewels, wire lugs, aux. sec., Ca. 1915
silver ....$250　　$300　　$350

TITUS, 17 jewels, chronog., 2 reg.
18k ....$300　　$350　　$400
14k ....$200　　$250　　$300
s. steel ....$100　　$150　　$200

TORNEX-RAYVILLE,17J., military, "SEAL", auto-wind,
water-proof, 150M or 490 ft., Ca. 1966
s. steel ....$250　　$300　　$350

TOUCHON,17J., tonneau case, c.1928
18k(w)...................................$400　　$500　　$600

TOUCHON, 17J., jump hr., wandering min., c. 1930s
18k $4,000 $4,500 $5,000

TOURNEAU,17J, triple date, 3 reg., moon ph., c. 1952
s. steel $700 $800 $900

TOURNEAU,17J.,chronog. by Valjoux cal.886, c.1965
18k $2,500 $2,700 $3,000

TOURNEAU,17J., day date , c.1945
s. steel $250 $300 $350

TOURNEAU,17J., beveled lugs, c.1945
14k $150 $200 $250

TOURIST, 17J., by MEPA, c.1958
s. steel $50 $60 $70

TREBEX, 15 jewels,cut corner dial, c. 1940
gold filled $40 $50 $60

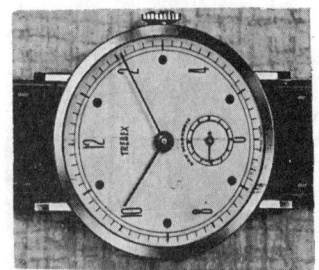

TREBEX, 15 jewels, c. 1940
gold filled $30 $40 $50

TREBEX, 15 jewels, c. 1940s
gold filled $30 $40 $50

TURLER, 15-17J., duo-dial, Ca.1930s
18k $2,000 $2,500 $3,000

UNITAS, 17 jewels, triple date, moon phase, c. 1948
s. steel $250 $300 $375

TURLER, 17 jewels, chronog., triple date, 3 reg.
18k $900 $1,100 $1,300

URANIA, 15 jewels, military style grill, c. 1915
silver $150 $200 $250

UHRENFABRIK GLASHUTTE, 17J., chronog., c. 1940s
s. steel $500 $600 $750

UNIVER, 17J., triple date , moon ph., chronog.
14k $1,400 $1,700 $2,000

ULTIMOR, 17J., chronog., cal.51, c.1945
18k $325 $400 $525

UNIVERSAL,17J.,"medico compax", c.1949
18k $900 $1,000 $1,150

UNIVERSAL,17J., "uni compax", c.1942
s. steel $350 $400 $500

UNIVERSAL,17J., tri-compax, day date moon ph.,c.1955
s. steel $1,300 $1,400 $1,550
14k $2,000 $2,250 $2,550

UNIVERSAL, 17J., chronog., triple date, moon phase
18k $1,800 $2,000 $2,500
14k $1,600 $1,800 $2,000

UNIVERSAL, 17J., chronog., aero compax, diff. meridian,
square pushers
14k $1,800 $2,000 $2,400

UNIVERSAL, 17J. chronog., tri-compax, day date
s. steel $1,100 $1,200 $1,400

UNIVERSAL, 17 jewels, chronog., M. #281, c. 1950s
18k $2,200 $2,500 $2,800

UNIVERSAL, 17J., chronog., tri-compax, moon phase
s. steel $1,200 $1,300 $1,400

UNIVERSAL, 17J., chronog., aero compax, diff. meridian,
round pushers
18k $2,000 $2,200 $2,600

UNIVERSAL, 17J., chronog., compax, massive case
18k $2,500 $2,700 $3,000

UNIVERSAL, 17J., chronog., dato-compax, c. 1950s
14k $1,500 $1,800 $2,000
s. steel $500 $600 $700

UNIVERSAL,17J., compax, RF#885107, Valj.cal.72,c.1965
s. steel $600 $700 $800

UNIVERSAL, 17J. chronog., 10 ligne size,uni-compax
s. steel ....$ 1,000 $1,200 $1,400

UNIVERSAL, 17 jewels, c. 1952
14k $275 $325 $375

UNIVERSAL, 17 jewels, day-date-month
14k $600 $700 $800

UNIVERSAL,17J., "Polerouter Sub", date, auto-w., c.1960
14k $500 $650 $700
s. steel $250 $335 $400

UNIVERSAL,28J.,"Polerouter Sub",rotating bezel, c.1980s
s. steel $300 $350 $425

UNIVERSAL, 17 jewels, "Polerouter", auto wind, day date
18k $600 $675 $750

UNIVERSAL, 23J., auto-wind, date, c.1965
14k $250 $300 $350

UNIVERSAL, 28J., center sec., date, c.1958
18k $400 $450 $500

UNIVERSAL,17J., cal. 138c, date, c.1952
18k $400 $475 $575

UNIVERSAL,17J., Unisonic, cal.52, date, c.1965
18k $250 $300 $350

UNIVERSAL, 17 jewels, day-date-month, moon phase
18k $1,200 $1,350 $1,500

UNIVERSAL,17J., Unisonic chronometer, date, c.1968
s. steel $150 $175 $225

UNIVERSAL,17J., m#264, large lugs, c.1957
gold filled $125 $150 $200

UNIVERSAL,17J., cal.267g, date, center sec. c.1948
18k $450 $500 $550

UNIVERSAL,17J., center sec., cal.263, c.1950
18k $350 $400 $450

UNIVERSAL, 16J., cal#230,ca. 1940s
s. steel $200 $250 $300

UNIVERSAL,17J., center sec., cal.138, c.1950
s. steel $125 $175 $225

UNIVERSAL, 17J., aux. sec. tank style,ca. 1948
14k $400 $450 $500

UNIVERSAL,17J., center sec., cal.236, c.1955
18k $300 $350 $400

UNIVERSAL, 17J., fancy lugs
14k $350 $400 $450

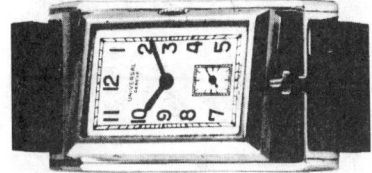

UNIVERSAL,17J., aux. sec., Ca.1955
s. steel $150 $185 $250

UNIVERSAL, 17 jewels, "Cabriolet," reverso, c. 1930s
s. steel $3,500 $3,900 $4,400

UNIVERSAL, 17 jewels, auto wind, c. 1955
14k $300 $350 $400
gold filled................................$100 $120 $140

UNIVERSAL, quartz, day-date, center sec., c. 1960s
18k $400 $500 $600

UNIVERSAL, quartz, , c.1981
18k $300 $350 $400

UNIVERSAL, 17 jewels, auto wind
gold filled................................$80 $90 $100

Some grades are not included. Their values can be determined by comparing with **similar** age, size, metal content, style, models and grades listed.

VACHERON, 36J., skeletonized, triple date, moon phase, leap year, gold rotor
18k $16,000 $17,000 $18,000

VACHERON, 36J., diamond bezel, triple date, moon ph., leap year, gold rotor
18k C&B...........................$12,000 $13,000 $14,000

VACHERON, 17J., triple date, moon phase, c. 1947
18k $12,000 $14,000 $16,000

VACHERON, 17J., triple date, moon phase, c. 1945
18k $8,000 $9,000 $10,000

VACHERON, 17J., triple date, moon phase, c. 1950s
18k $6,000 $7,000 $8,000

VACHERON,17J., triple date, fancy lugs, moon ph.,
c. 1940s
18k $7,000 $8,000 $9,000

VACHERON, 17J., triple date, fancy lugs, c. 1940s
18k $3,000 $3,800 $4,000

VACHERON, 17 jewels, day-date-month, c. 1940s
18k $3,000 $3,500 $4,000

VACHERON, 29 jewels, waterproof, auto-w, c. 1960s
18k $2,200 $2,500 $2,750

VACHERON, 29 jewels, auto wind, c. 1960s
18k $1,800 $2,000 $2,200

VACHERON, 36 jewels, gold rotor, date
18k $1,600 $1,800 $2,000

VACHERON, 29 jewels, center sec., auto wind, date
18k $2,200 $2,500 $2,750

VACHERON, 29 jewels, gold rotor, date
18k $1,800 $2,200 $2,600

VACHERON, 18J., chronog. 2 reg., ca.1942
s. steel $5,000 $6,000 $7,000

VACHERON, 33J., auto-wind 21k rotor, cal.1124, c.1980s
18k & s.s. $1,200 $1,400 $1,600

VACHERON, 17 jewels, chronog., 2 reg. Ca. 1934
18k & 14k band.................$18,000 $20,000 $23,000

VACHERON,17J., enamel dial,1 button chronog.,c. 1910s
18k $25,000 $30,000 $35,000

VACHERON, 19 jewels, chronog., 2 reg., c. 1950s
18k C&B.............................$9,000 $10,000 $11,000

VACHERON, 15J., early chronog.,2 reg.,one button,
ca. 1921, large in size
18k $18,000 $20,000 $22,000

VACHERON, 17 jewels, chronog., 2 reg., c. 1945
18k $8,000 $9,000 $10,000

VACHERON, 29J., min. repeater, slide repeat, c. 1950
18k $60,000 $70,000 $80,000

VACHERON, 29J., min. slide repeater, diamond dial
platinum $80,000 $90,000 $100,000

VACHERON, 29J., min. slide repeater, ca. 1950s
18k $60,000 $70,000 $80,000

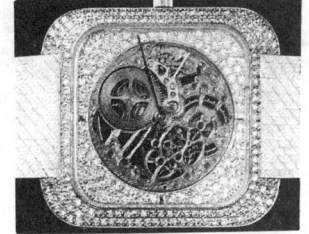

VACHERON, 18J., diamond set case, skeletonized
18k(W)..................................$5,000 $5,500 $6,000

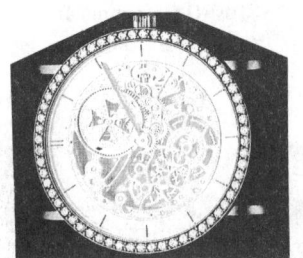

VACHERON, 18J., skeletonized, diamond bezel
18k $3,500 $4,000 $4,500

VACHERON, 17 jewels, skeletonized
18k $3,000 $3,500 $4,000

VACHERON, 17 jewels, skeletonized, c. 1960s
18k $3,000 $3,500 $4,000

VACHERON, 17 jewels, mystery dial with diamonds
18k C&B..............................$1,200 $1,400 $1,600

VACHERON, 17 jewels, textured bezel
18k $1,300 $1,500 $1,800

VACHERON, 18 jewels, center sec., c. 1940s
18k $1,400 $1,600 $2,000

VACHERON, 18 jewels, center sec.
18k $1,300 $1,500 $1,800

VACHERON, 18J., fancy graduated bezel, c. 1950s
18k $4,000 $5,000 $6,000

VACHERON, 18 jewels, center sec.
18k $1,400 $1,600 $2,000

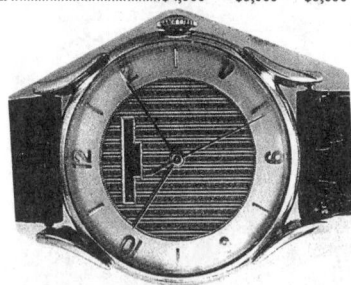

VACHERON, 18 jewels, auto wind, center sec., Ca. 1945
18k $1,700 $1,900 $2,200

VACHERON, 18 J., center sec., waterproof, c. 1950s
18k $1,700 $2,000 $2,200

VACHERON, 18 jewels, center sec., Ca. 1945
18k $1,200 $1,400 $1,700

VACHERON, 21J., auto wind, gold rotor, center sec.
18k $2,200 $2,400 $2,800

VACHERON, 18J., center sec., ca.1940s
18k $1,500 $1,700 $2,000

VACHERON, 17J., center sec., c.1940
s. steel $600 $700 $800

VACHERON, 18J., rf#6903, center sec., ca.1958
18k $1,300 $1,500 $1,900

VACHERON,17J., center sec., large lugs, c.1949
18k $2,400 $2,600 $2,900

VACHERON, 18J., center sec., ca.1953
18k $1,600 $1,800 $2,000

VACHERON,17J., center sec., c.1940
s. steel $600 $700 $800

VACHERON, 18J., textured dial center sec.
18k $1,600 $1,700 $2,000

VACHERON,17J., center sec., c.1940
18k $1,500 $1,700 $2,000

Some grades are not included. Their values can be determined by comparing with **similar** age, size, metal content,
style, models and grades listed.

VACHERON, 18J., center sec.
s. steel $500 $600 $700

VACHERON, 18J., fancy large lugs, center sec., ca.1953
18k $2,200 $2,500 $2,800

VACHERON, 18J., center sec.
18k $1,500 $1,700 $1,900

VACHERON, 18J., rf#4730, fancy lugs, ca. 1950s
18k $1,800 $2,000 $2,400

VACHERON, 18J.,textured dial, center sec.,ca.1947
18k $2,200 $2,400 $2,600

VACHERON, 18J.,textured dial, fancy lugs
18k $1,800 $2,000 $2,400

VACHERON, 18J., rf#4824, ca.1950s
18k(W)..................................$1,400 $1,500 $1,700

VACHERON, 18J., center sec., ca.1944
14k $1,500 $1,700 $1,900

VACHERON, 18J., royal chronometer, ca.1950s
18k $1,500 $1,700 $2,000

VACHERON, 29 jewels, textured dial, c. 1948
18k $1,800 $2,000 $2,200

VACHERON, 17J., center sec.auto-w., ca.1945
18k $1,500 $1,700 $2,000

VACHERON, 29 jewels, 2 tone dial, center sec.
18k $1,500 $1,700 $1,900

VACHERON, 29 jewels, center sec., center lugs,c. 1950s
18k $1,400 $1,600 $1,800

VACHERON, 29J., center sec., auto wind, c. 1950s
18k $2,200 $2,400 $2,700

VACHERON, 29 jewels, center sec.
18k $1,300 $1,500 $1,800

VACHERON, 29 jewels, center sec., auto wind, c. 1949
18k $2,200 $2,500 $3,000

VACHERON,17J., diamond dial, aux. sec., fancy lugs
platinum..............................$2,500 $2,700 $3,000

VACHERON, 17J., aux. sec., c.1945
18k $1,400 $1,600 $1,900

VACHERON, 18J., aux. sec., fancy lugs, ca. 1944
18k $1,600 $1,800 $2,200

VACHERON, 17J., aux. sec., RF#4073, c.1942
s. steel $700 $800 $900

VACHERON, 18J., aux. sec.
18k $1,600 $1,800 $2,200

VACHERON, 17J., aux. sec., tear drop lugs, c.1945
18k $1,600 $1,800 $2,200

VACHERON, 18J., fancy lugs
18k $1,600 $1,900 $2,300

VACHERON, 17J., aux. sec, fluted lugs, c.1950s
18k $2,000 $2,200 $2,500

🕐 Some grades are not included. Their values can be determined by comparing with **similar** age, size, metal content, style, models and grades listed.

VACHERON, 18J., cal#p453/3b, aux. sec.
18k $2,000 $2,200 $2,400

VACHERON, 18J., aux. sec.,
s. steel $600 $700 $850

VACHERON, 18J., aux. sec.
18k(W)..............................$1,500 $1,700 $1,900

VACHERON, 18J., center sec.,fancy lugs, ca.1942
18k $1,500 $1,700 $1,900

VACHERON, 18J., aux. sec., ca.1951
18k $1,600 $1,800 $2,000

VACHERON, 18J., **winds at 12,** ca. 1928
18k $3,000 $3,500 $4,000

VACHERON, 15J., champagne dial, long lugs, ca.1935
18k $1,700 $1,800 $2,000

VACHERON, 17 jewels, aux. sec., fancy lugs
18k $1,600 $1,900 $2,300

VACHERON, 17 jewels, aux. sec., Ca. 1950
18k $1,600 $1,800 $2,200

VACHERON, 17 jewels, aux. sec., stepped lugs
18k $1,800 $2,200 $2,500

VACHERON, 17 jewels, 2 tone dial, aux. sec.
18k $1,500 $1,800 $2,200

VACHERON, 17 jewels, aux. sec., c. 1940s
18k $1,600 $1,800 $2,200

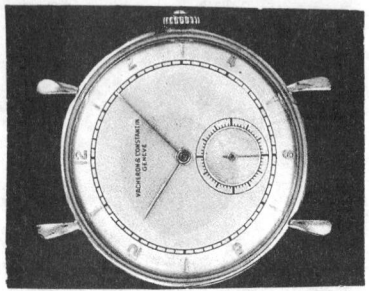

VACHERON, 17 jewels, aux. sec.
18k $1,600 $1,800 $2,200

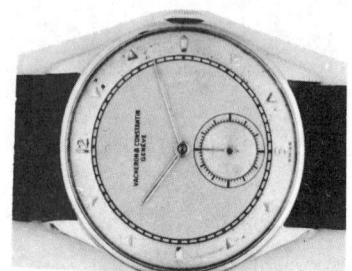

VACHERON, 17 jewels, aux. sec., c. 1940s
18k $1,500 $1,700 $1,900

VACHERON, 17 jewels, aux. sec.
s. steel $500 $600 $700

VACHERON, 17 jewels, aux. sec., large lugs, c. 1950s
18k $2,400 $2,600 $2,800

VACHERON, 17 jewels, aux. sec.
14k C&B.............................$1,000 $1,200 $1,400

VACHERON, 17 jewels, aux. sec.
18k $1,400 $1,600 $1,800

VACHERON, 17 jewels, aux. sec., c. 1940s
18k $1,500 $1,700 $1,900

VACHERON, 17 jewels, aux. sec.
18k $1,500 $1,700 $2,000

VACHERON, 17 jewels
18k C&B $1,800 $2,200 $2,600

VACHERON, 17J., RF# 6498, Ca. 1965
18k $1,500 $1,700 $2,000

VACHERON, 17 jewels
18k $1,400 $1,600 $1,800

VACHERON, 18J., no sec. hand,
18k $1,300 $1,500 $1,700

VACHERON,17J., RF#6099, cal.1003, c.1960
18k $1,200 $1,400 $1,600

VACHERON,17J., 20 dollar gold piece, RF 4928
18k $2,250 $2,500 $3,000

VACHERON, 16J.,barrel shaped silver dial, ca. 1916
18k $3,000 $3,500 $4,000

🕐 Some grades are not included. Their values can be determined by comparing with **similar** age, size, metal content, style, models and grades listed.

VACHERON, 16J., wire lugs, silver dial, ca.1917
14k $3,000 $3,500 $4,000

VACHERON, 18J., tonneau shaped, ca. 1930s
18k $2,500 $3,000 $3,500

VACHERON, 15J., lady's with wire lugs,ca.1920
18k(W)....................................$500 $600 $750

VACHERON, 15 jewels
18k C&B.............................$2,000 $2,200 $2,600

VACHERON, 17 jewels
18k $2,200 $2,400 $2,600

VACHERON, 36 jewels, auto wind
18k C&B.............................$1,500 $1,800 $2,200

VACHERON, 21 J., date, auto-w. ca. 1980s
s. steel $1,000 $1,200 $1,400

VACHERON, 15J., shutters with center slide to view dial, 2 tone case, ca. 1933
18k $10,000 $12,000 $14,000

VACHERON, 17J, with shutters, crowns at 3 & 9
18k $12,000 $14,000 $16,000

🕐 Some grades are not included. Their values can be determined by comparing with **similar** age, size, metal content, style, models and grades listed.

VACHERON, 18J., heavy case, ca.1930s
18k(W).................................$2,500 $3,000 $3,500

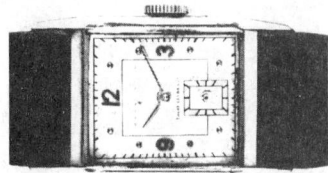

VACHERON, 18J., silver dial, ca.1941
18k $2,000 $2,500 $3,000

VACHERON, 18J., applied numbers, ca.1940
18k $2,000 $2,200 $2,400

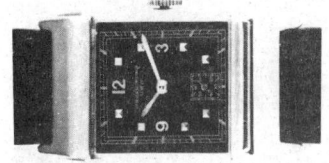

VACHERON, 18J., black dial, aux. sec., ca.1937
18k $2,200 $2,400 $2,600

VACHERON, 18J., silver dial, ca.1942
18k $2,000 $2,500 $3,000

VACHERON, 18J., hidden lugs, ca.1940s
18k $2,200 $2,400 $2,800

VACHERON, 18J., off set lugs,
18k $2,000 $2,200 $2,500

VACHERON, 18J., off set lugs,
18k $2,000 $2,200 $2,500

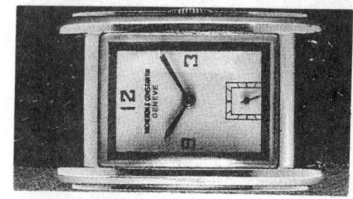

VACHERON, 18J., aux .sec.,
s. steel $1,200 $1,400 $1,600

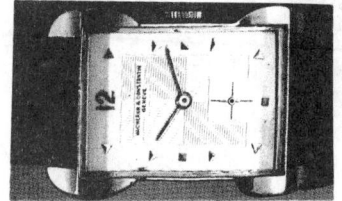

VACHERON, 18J., textured dial, large lugs, ca.1951
18k $4,000 $4,500 $5,000

VACHERON, 18J., fancy lugs,ca.1938
18k $2,800 $3,000 $3,200

VACHERON, 18J., textured bezel,ca.1950s
18k $2,000 $2,200 $2,500

VACHERON, 18 jewels, aux. sec., c. 1950s
18k $1,600 $1,800 $2,000

VACHERON, 18 jewels, aux. sec., c. 1940s
18k $1,600 $1,800 $2,000

VACHERON, 17J., applied gold numbers, c. 1940s
18k $1,600 $1,800 $2,100

VACHERON, 17 jewels, aux. sec., c. 1945
18k $1,600 $1,800 $2,000

VACHERON, 17 jewels, applied gold numbers
18k $1,400 $1,600 $1,800

VACHERON, 17 jewels, fancy lugs
18k $1,800 $2,000 $2,200

VACHERON, 17 jewels, c. 1950s
18k $1,800 $2,000 $2,200

VACHERON, 17 jewels, fancy lugs
14k $1,800 $2,100 $2,400

VACHERON, 17j., stars on dial at, 1-3-5-7-9-11
18k C&B $2,000 $2,300 $2,600

VACHERON, 17 jewels, stepped bezel, fancy lugs, Ca. 1940
18k $2,700 $2,900 $3,200

VACHERON,17J., hidden barrel shaped lugs, c.1943
14k $1,500 $1,700 $2,000

VACHERON,17J., aux. sec., c.1947
18k $1,800 $2,000 $2,400

VACHERON,17J., aux. sec., c.1942
18k $1,700 $1,900 $2,200

VACHERON,17J., RF#6249, aux. sec., c.1963
18k $1,800 $2,000 $2,200

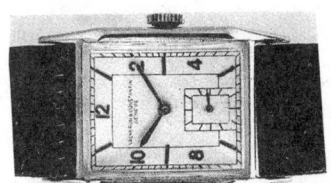

VACHERON,17J., aux. sec., c.1934
18k $2,200 $2,400 $2,600

VACHERON, 17 jewels, aux. sec.
c. 1946
18k $2,200 $2,400 $2,600

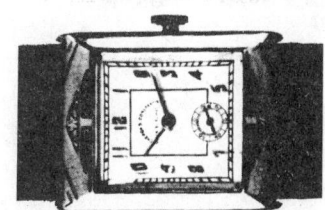

VACHERON, 17 jewels, Art Deco bezel, c. 1925
18k $5,000 $5,500 $6,000

VACHERON, 17 jewels, long lugs, applied numbers
18k $2,200 $2,500 $2,800

VACHERON, 17 jewels, aux. sec.,
18k $2,200 $2,500 $2,800

VACHERON, 18 jewels, aux. sec.
18k C&B $2,300 $2,500 $2,800

VACHERON, 15 jewels, heavy bezel, c.1925
18K C&B $3,500 $3,800 $4,200

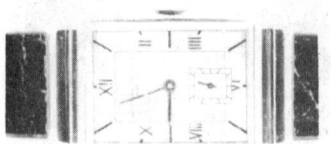

VACHERON, 17 jewels, curved, hooded lugs, c. 1930s
18k $3,000 $3,200 $3,500

VACHERON,15J., curvex,wire lugs,33mm long,ca.1923
18k $2,500 $2,700 $3,000

VACHERON, 15J., hinged back, ca. 1930
18k $2,500 $2,700 $3,000

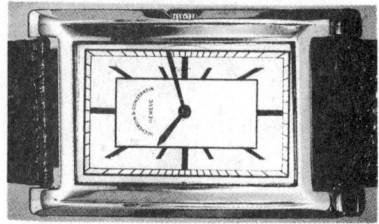

VACHERON, 18J., large 2 tone mans watch, ca.1928
18k $5,000 $6,000 $7,000

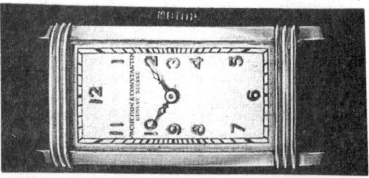

VACHERON, 18J.,long curved case, ca.1929
platinum $4,000 $4,500 $5,000

VACHERON, 18J., ca. 1926
18k $2,000 $2,200 $2,500

VACHERON, 18J., ca. 1950s
18k $1,500 $1,700 $1,900

VACHERON, 15J., early movement, ca.1925
18k $1,500 $1,700 $2,000

VACHERON, 17 jewels, aux. sec.
14k $1,800 $1,900 $2,000

VACHERON, 15J.,2 tone case, ca. 1926
18k $2,000 $2,400 $2,600

VACHERON, 17 jewels, flat & thin model, c. 1960s
18k $1,000 $1,200 $1,500

VACHERON, 18J., tank style, ca.1960s
18k $1,300 $1,500 $1,800

VACHERON, 17 jewels
18k C&B.............................$1,500 $1,600 $1,700

VACHERON, 17 jewels, hinged back
18k $1,400 $1,600 $1,800

VACHERON, 18 jewels, stepped case & beveled lugs
18k $1,600 $1,800 $2,000

VACHERON, 15J., wire lugs, enamel dial, Ca.1920s
18k $2,000 $2,200 $2,500

VACHERON, 15 jewels, c. 1920s
18k $1,200 $1,400 $1,600

VACHERON, 17 jewels, 2 tone, 24mm, c. 1920s
18k $2,000 $2,200 $2,500

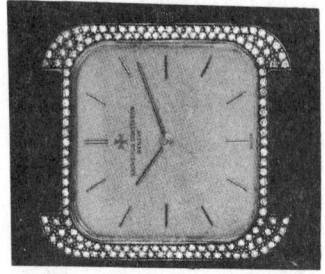

VACHERON, 17 jewels, 68 diamond bezel
18k $1,800 $2,000 $2,500

VACHERON,17J., RF#7252, c.1962
18k $1,200 $1,400 $1,600

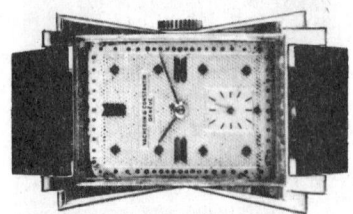

VACHERON, 17 jewels, flared, curvex, c. 1940s
18k $5,000 $5,500 $6,000

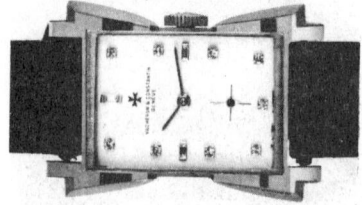

VACHERON, 17J., flared,12 diam. dial, aux. sec., c. 1948
platinum $5,000 $5,500 $6,000

VACHERON, 17 jewels, flared, c. 1948
18k $4,000 $4,500 $5,000

VACHERON, 17 jewels, flared, c. 1940s
18k $4,000 $4,500 $5,000

VACHERON, 17 jewels, "Chronoscope," jumping hr.,
revolving ruby min. indicator, c. 1930s
18k $20,000 $22,000 $24,000

VACHERON, 20 jewels, Adj. to 5 Pos., c. 1970s
18k $2,000 $2,200 $2,500

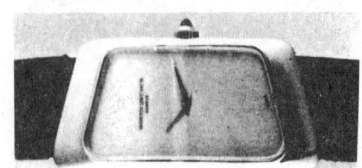

VACHERON, 22 jewels, lady's watch, c. 1970s
18k $1,000 $1,100 $1,200

VACHERON, 17 jewels, aux. sec., ruby dial
18k $2,200 $2,500 $2,800

VACHERON,16J., black star & forrest, wire lugs, c.1919
18k $400 $500 $600

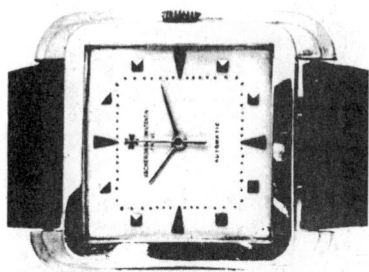

VACHERON, 21 jewels, center sec., c. 1950s
18k $3,000 $3,500 $4,000

VACHERON, 17 jewels, heavy bezel
18k $1,500 $1,700 $2,000

VACHERON, 17 jewels, aux. sec., fancy lugs, c. 1947
18k $2,200 $2,600 $3,000

VACHERON,17J., ladies, c.1948
18k $800 $900 $1,000

VACHERON, 15 J., lady's, wire lugs, ca.1919
18k $400 $500 $600

VACHERON, 17 jewels , swinging lugs
14k $1,200 $1,500 $1,800

VACHERON, 17 jewels, lady's watch, c. 1960s
18k C&B............................ $1,200 $1,400 $1,600

VACHERON, 17J., cased & timed in U.S.A. by Vacheron &
Constantine , heavy 14k gold bracelet, Ca.1950s
14k heavy C&B $1,000 $1,200 $1,400

VAN CLEEF & ARPELS,17J., center lugs, c.1970
18k $500 $600 $700

VULCAIN,17jewels
s. steel $50 $75 $100

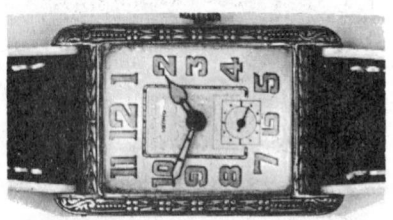

VERNO, 15 jewels, chased bezel
gold filled (w)...........................$75 $100 $125

VULCAIN,17J., "Cricket", alarm, c.1960
base metal................................. $90 $100 $125

VULCAIN, 17 jewels, "Cricket," alarm
s. steel $100 $125 $150

VULCAIN,17J., "Cricket", alarm, c.1948
s. steel $125 $150 $175

VULCAIN, 17 jewels, "Cricket", alarm
14k $225 $275 $325

VULCAIN,17J., center sec., alarm, c.1940
s. steel $120 $135 $165

VULCAIN, 17 jewels, "Cricket," alarm
gold filled.................................$150 $175 $200

WAKMANN,17J., "Gigandet" Valjoux cal.72, c.1955
18k $1,200 $1,400 $1,600

VULCAIN, 17 jewels, "Minstop"
s. steel $90 $125 $145

WAKMANN, 17J., chronog., 3 reg., triple date
14k $500 $600 $700

WAKMANN,17J., 24 hr. dial, c.1955
s. steel $100 $125 $150

WAKMANN,17J., chronog., 3 reg., triple date, sq.buttons
s. steel $200 $250 $325

WAKMANN, 17 jewels, chronog., 3 reg., c. 1958
s. steel $200 $250 $325

WAKMANN,17J., chronog., Valjoux cal.188, c.1960
s. steel $175 $200 $225

WAKMANN,17J., chronog., Valjoux cal.236, c.1968
s. steel $175 $200 $250

WAKMANN,17J., chronog., c.1955
18k $600 $650 $700
s. steel $175 $200 $225

WAKMANN,17J., chronog., c.1970s
s. steel $90 $125 $155

WARWICK, 6J., hinged back, 1930s
gold plate $65 $85 $100

WARWICK, 15J., 1930s
gold plate $40 $50 $60

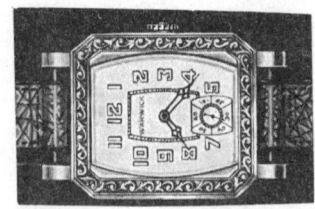

WARWICK, 15J., 1930s
gold plate $40 $50 $60

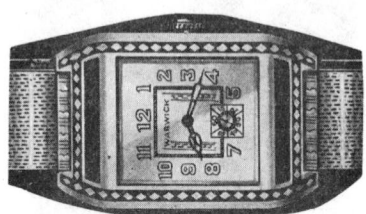

WARWICK, 6-15J., 1930s
gold plate $40 $50 $60

WARWICK, 6-15J., 1930s
gold plate $40 $50 $60

WARWICK, 6-15J., 1930s
gold plate $40 $50 $60

WARWICK, 6-15J., 1930s
gold plate $40 $50 $60

WARWICK, 15J., 1930s
gold plate $40 $50 $60

WARWICK, 15J., 1930s
base metal $25 $35 $55

WATEX, 7J., fluted case, c.1940
gold filled................................$175 $200 $250

WEISCO, 7J., aux. sec., wire lugs, c. 1928
base metal $25 $35 $55

WELDON,17J., aux. sec., large lugs c.1950s
gold filled $75 $100 $125

WELSBRO ,17J., single button chronog., c.1940
s. steel $75 $100 $125

WELTALL W. Co., floral enamel on case, cylinder escp.
wire lugs, Ca. 1910
14k $200 $225 $250

WEST END, 17 jewels, ''Keepsake,'' c. 1925
silver $300 $400 $500

WEST END, 17 jewels, center lugs
18k $300 $350 $400

WHITE STAR, 17J., triple date, moon phase, c. 1948
s. steel $400 $500 $600

WINTON, 17J., hooded lugs
14k $125 $150 $175

WINTON, 16J., curvex, hinged back, c.1930s
silver $125 $150 $200

WITTNAUER, 17 jewels, fancy lugs
14k $175 $200 $225

WITTNAUER, 17 jewels, chronog., day-date-month
s. steel $385 $475 $550

WITTNAUER, 17 jewels, chronog., c. 1948
s. steel $350 $400 $450

WITTNAUER,17J., "Professional", RF#6002, c.1955
18k $600 $650 $725
s. steel $350 $395 $450

WITTNAUER,17J., chronog., waterproof, c.1958
18k $550 $600 $650
s. steel $325 $375 $425

WITTNAUER,17J., chronog., by Venius, **Time Zone Bezel**,
Ca. 1955
s. steel $335 $385 $450

WITTNAUER,17J., chronog., by Valjoux, #72, cal.13w1
s. steel $175 $200 $225

WITTNAUER,7J., "Electronic", day date, c.1968
s. steel $40 $50 $60

WITTNAUER,7J., mid size , stop watch, c.1940
s. steel $150 $185 $225

WITTNAUER,17J., direct read, c.1970
s. steel $60 $70 $85

WITTNAUER, 17 J., day date, set year by button
s. steel $75 $100 $125

WITTNAUER,17J., Zircon on dial, direct read, c.1970
base metal $65 $75 $95

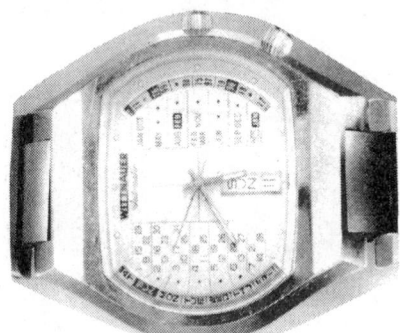

WITTNAUER,17J., perpetual calendar
base metal $125 $150 $200

WITTNAUER, 17 jewels, auto wind, sector, date
s. steel $400 $450 $500

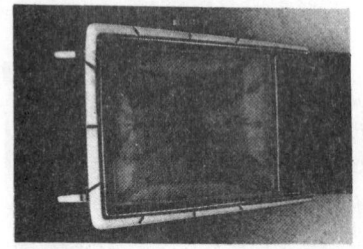

WITTNAUER, 17 jewels, c. 1950s
14k $225 $250 $300

WITTNAUER,17J., aux. sec., c.1958
gold filled................................$100 $125 $150

WITTNAUER,17J., aux. sec., c.1950
14k $175 $200 $275

WITTNAUER,17J., aux. sec., GJS, c.1948
14k $175 $200 $275

WITTNAUER,17J., aux. sec., fancy lugs, c.1955
gold filled................................$70 $80 $95

WITTNAUER, 17 jewels, curved case, c.1950
14k $200 $250 $300

WITTNAUER, 17 jewels, cal.9wn, fancy lugs, c.1954
gold filled............................$100 $125 $150

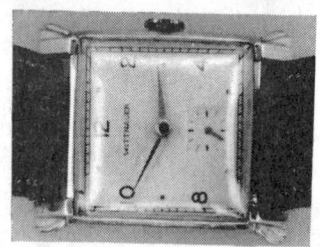

WITTNAUER, 17 jewels, fancy lugs, GJS
14k $175 $200 $275

WITTNAUER,17J., aux. sec., GJS, large lugs, c.1950
14k $200 $225 $250

WITTNAUER,17J., aux. sec., fancy case, c.1950
gold filled $80 $90 $125

WITTNAUER,17J., aux. sec., flared case
14k ....$250　　$275　　$325

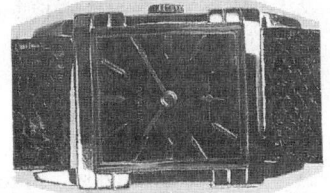

WITTNAUER,17J., aux. sec.
gold filled.................................$75　　$85　　$100

WITTNAUER, 17 jewels, fancy lugs, c. 1950s
14k ....$200　　$250　　$300

WITTNAUER,17J., aux. sec., GJS, c. 1955
14k ....$150　　$200　　$250

WITTNAUER,17J., aux. sec., tu-tone dial, c. 1950
gold filled.................................$70　　$80　　$95

WITTNAUER,17J., aux. sec., c. 1950
gold filled ....$50　　$60　　$70

WITTNAUER,15J., aux. sec., tonneau case, c.1945
gold plate.................................$50　　$60　　$70

WITTNAUER,17J., aux. sec.
gold filled ....$50　　$60　　$70

WITTNAUER,17J., aux. sec.
14k ....$125　　$150　　$175

WITTNAUER,17J., flared case, Ca.1949
14k ....$150　　$175　　$200

🕐 Some grades are not included. Their values can be determined by comparing with **similar** age, size, metal content,
style, models and grades listed.

WITTNAUER,17J., RF#2067, c.1950
gold filled.................................$55 $65 $85

WITTNAUER,17J., auto-wind, c.1960
base metal $40 $50 $60

WITTNAUER,17J., cal.7630, aux. sec., c.1955
14k $140 $160 $180

WITTNAUER,17J., "Alarm", c.1960
gold filled.................................$100 $125 $150

WIG WAG, 15 jewels, early auto wind, c. 1932
s. steel $500 $600 $700

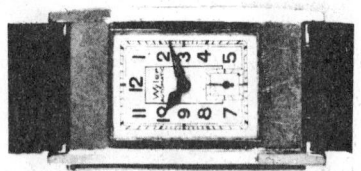

WYLER, 17 jewels, early auto wind, watch winds by using
the muscular movement of the wrist, back set
gold filled $400 $500 $600

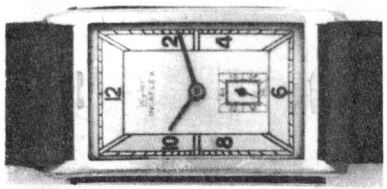

WYLER, 17 jewels, early auto wind, back set
gold filled $400 $500 $600

WYLER, 17 jewels, center sec.
s. steel $50 $60 $75

WYLER, 17 jewels, aux. sec.
s. steel $50 $60 $75

🕐 Some grades are not included. Their values can be determined by comparing with **similar** age, size, metal content, style, models and grades listed.

WYLER, 17 jewels
s. steel $50 $60 $75

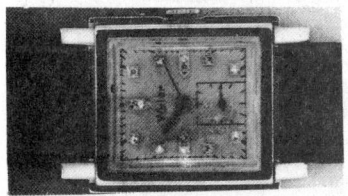

WYLER, 17 jewels, diamond dial, c. 1946
s. steel $60 $70 $80

WYLER,17J., center sec., c.1945
s. steel $50 $60 $75

WYLER,17J., center sec., waterproof, ca.1941
s. steel $50 $60 $80

WYLER,17J., aux. sec., c.1938
s. steel $50 $60 $75

WYLER,17J., auto-wind, c.1932
chrome $50 $60 $70

WYLER,17J., day date month, c.1946
gold filled $100 $125 $175

WYLER, 17 jewels, chronog., c. 1940s
14k $400 $475 $525
s. steel $200 $225 $300

YALE, 15 jewels, calendar, c. 1939
14k $400 $450 $500
gold filled $100 $135 $200

⏱ Some grades are not included. Their values can be determined by comparing with **similar** age, size, metal content,
style, models and grades listed.

ZELIA, 17 jewels, chronog.
18k $375 $425 $475

ZENITH, 19 jewels, 33mm, c. 1950s
gold filled $50 $60 $75

ZENITH,15J., enamel dial, wire lugs, c. 1918
silver $250 $300 $350

ZENITH, 17 jewels, chronog.
18k..$500 $600 $700

ZENITH,15J., signal corps on enamel dial, center lug, 1918
silver $275 $325 $375

ZENITH, 36 jewels, chronog., auto wind, c. 1969
s. steel $225 $275 $325

ZENITH,19J., Date at six, c.1962
s. steel $50 $60 $80

ZENITH,17J., Chronograph 3 reg., Ca.1965
14k $500 $575 $675
s. steel $250 $300 $350

ZENITH, 36J., "El Primero", RF#502,auto wind, c. 1970
18k $1,200 $1,400 $1,600

ZENITH, 36 jewels, "El Primero," chronog., triple date
moon phase, c. 1970s
18k $2,400 $2,600 $2,800

ZENITH,36J., chronog., auto-wind, triple date
base metal $400 $450 $550

ZENITH, 17 jewels, fancy bezel
18k $200 $300 $350

ZENITH, 17J., auto-wind, date at 5, Ca. 1959
18k $200 $250 $300

ZENTRA, 24 jewels, ladies,auto wind, c. 1958
14k $75 $90 $125

ZODIAC, 17J., chronog., 2 reg., c.1948
gold filled $200 $250 $300
14k $425 $475 $525
18k $500 $575 $675

ZODIAC, 17J., chronog., auto-wind, date, c.1971
s. steel $150 $200 $265

ZODIAC, 17J., center sec., auto-wind, c.1959
s. steel $50 $60 $75

ZODIAC, 17 jewels, 24 hour dial
s. steel $150 $175 $225

ZODIAC, 17 jewels, ref. #8088
14k $125 $150 $175

ZODIAC, 17J., auto wind with reserve power indicator
14k $175 $200 $250
gold filled..................................$85 $100 $120

ZODIAC, 17J., day-date-month, moon phase, c. 1957
s. steel $300 $375 $425
14k $700 $800 $900

ZODIAC, 17J., center sec., power reserve, cal. 1094, c. 1959
s. steel $75 $90 $110

ZODIAC, 21J., date, "Olympos", date, auto-wind,c.1965
s. steel $60 $80 $100

ZODIAC, 17J., center sec., Ca.1948
s. steel $50 $60 $75

Some grades are not included. Their values can be determined by comparing with **similar** age, size, metal content, style, grades, or models such as **time only**, chronograph, repeater etc. listed.

TOMORROW'S COLLECTABLE WATCHES

"News about my death was greatly exaggerated" a quote of the famous Mark Twain describes what was once being said about the vanishing mechanical watch. The ability to measure the flow of time is a basic need and is as old as man. The watch has evolved into a necessary adornment and is commonly worn by all. The purchaser of this precision machine believes they would be lost without a watch to confirm the time of day. There are as many people wearing a wrist watch as there are people who wear shoes. This large market is **ever-expanding**, and to satisfy this massive need there are many watchmakers with all types, styles, interesting and unusual timekeepers. Watches were primarily invented to tell time but, in most cases, they are recognized as collectable. The functional watch can also be a piece of jewelry that most men feel at ease wearing and a useful friend.

The Japanese were sure the new ultra-accurate quartz revolution would make the mechanical watch a dinosaur. The mechanical watch amazingly did not die but had a revival that occurred in the late 1980's. Today's mechanical watches with the aid of computers and high tech watchmaking skills make it possible for master watchmakers to make better watches than we could ever have imagined. The World Watch,Clock and Jewelry Trade Fair in BASEL, SWITZERLAND launches it's premier showcase for the world of new collection and new watch models each year in April. Today jewelry and watches go together like champagne and caviar. Unique timepieces, as well as attractive models, are more affordable than ever.

"Everything old is new again," what is popular today may be popular in the future such as mini-skirts, pleats, cuffs and bell bottom pants, long hair versus short hair, etc. With the possible exception of wedding rings the wrist watch is your next favorite form of jewelry. The future of watches is assured with an annual watch sales nearing **one billion** per year. In 1992, over 875 million watches were manufactured. World wide production of watches has more than doubled over the last ten years. The digitals are waning at this time. Europe has the largest market share, U.S.A. number two and Asia number three.

Brand names are just as important as they ever were, the difference is that now there are fewer watch makers that manufacture every part from start to finish to make a complete watch. The traditional manufacturing centers of America & UK make very few of their own watch **parts**. Switzerland and Japan are now the two largest producers of watch parts and complete watches. The watch market is not easy to predict but the market for children will grow and the already "low-priced" and novelty watches may clearly produce new collecting habits. It may be reasonable to say that attitudes to owning more than one watch will continue to grow due to different occasions to wear them such as business, technical, sports, evening dress, casual and fashion statements.

Tomorrow's collectable watch market may be divided into four categories: 1. Quality or Luxury, 2. Complicated, 3. Time only +, Unusual style or shapes and 4. Limited. 1.=Quality would be the amount of Gold or precious metals, Diamond or Gem-stones and workmanship which includes high dollar or Hi-grade watch makers as P.P.&Co., Vacheron, I.W.C., Audemars just to name a few. 2.=Complicated include chronograph, min. repeaters, tourbillon, world-time, and triple calendar with moon phase, etc. 3.=Time only watches list will include Fashion, Famous cartoon characters, Two time zones, Divers, Alarm, Jump hour, Day Date, Unusual shapes and fancy cases, lugs or bezels, Unique materials, Skeleton, Duo-dials, Reverso, Military and so on. 4.=Limited watches will include watches from the category of Quality, Complicated, Time only +, Unusual and also well known designers or artist, but limited in supply.

Audmars Piguet, Automatic, "Dual Time" indicating the time in two Time-zones, date, wind indicator, Ca. 1992.

Audmars Piguet, Automatic Chronograph, the "Royal Oak Offshore" designed for the extremely rugged and durability water-resistant to a depth of 10 atmospheres.

Audmars Piguet, Automatic, Star Wheel shows the passing of time on Sapphire discs bearing the hours and moving over a concentric circular aperture showing the minutes.

Breguet, automatic with perpetual Equation-of-Time, wind indicator and perpetual calendar for day, date and month. Equation-of-Time provides a perpetual indication of the difference between real solar time and mean solar time, as generally indicated on most watches.

Girard-Perregaux, Tourbillon with gold bridge, a hand is attached to the one minute tourbillon carriage to show the passing seconds & at 12 a wind indicator (manual wind).

Mondaine, Official Swiss Railway Watch, with automatic winding and see-through case back.

NEW AGE COLLECTORS

The watch industry responds to the new trends with new creations that range from one of a kind to mass-produced horological marvels from new style tourbillons to twin-rotor self-winding wrist watches. Trends in fashion, unusual, technology, new models and what has made a comeback in the last few years. Crossover watches that mix sport and dress fashion or sport and luxury also sporty railroad or military style and sporty hi-tech watches. First an explanation of what it takes to qualify as a sports watch. Characteristics of a sport watch include water and shock-resistant, as a divers watch 100 meters, one or more sport-related functions for timing and measuring events (chronograph, stop watch, dual time zones, rotatable bezels) and rugged look which include a thicker case, larger hands, sapphire crystal, sub-dials bold numbers and thicker bands. This high-tech sports watch was designed with divers, sport players of all kinds, pilots, race car drivers, explorers, yachting, hiking, running, golfing, fishing, in mind and some are even handy in dark spots. **Sporty railroad or military** watches may include water and shock-resistant, easy to read dials, 24 hour dial, day date dials, dual time zone, stainless steel case, heavy padded band and will take a licking and keep on ticking. **Sport luxury** watches are usually sleeker, dress fashioned and use precious metals and gem stones on the dial, case, band and these functional pieces of jewelry carry a higher price tag. **Hi-tech** sport watches with all those buttons, subdials and functions look great but how do they work. Customized booklets on each sports watch explaining how they function, come with every watch, and should be **saved** to enhance future sales. This a watch designed for rugged versatile active life-styles and can be worn going from business to playing sports or just going out.

Affluent, high end or image luxury watches are very much in demand. Ultra high end expensive complicated timepieces are in a overloaded market. The high end watchmakers are focusing on more affordable (bread & butter) watches and these beauties are increasing. Limited-edition luxury watches are seen as a growing market. Chronometers, precise automatic watches whose precision is certified by the Swiss Official Board, are gaining popularity. Nostalgia is very much on the buyers mind, and designers have up-dated old classics.

Glamour or Fashion watches usually under $100 dollars. This "fashion" watch category include brand names as Anne Klein, Nolan Miller, Joan Rivers, Swatch, Fossil, Guess, Esquire(ESQ), Jaz and Monet, etc. Annually sales of about 20% of the watch market or about $700 million total sales. The "fashion" watch may also be called "Lifestyle" which includes casual, active and dress wear. These watches attract customers to return regularly for more watches and newer styles. New styles are changed every 3 to 4 months, so people change as easily and as often as they change clothes. This lucrative market also use catchy names as Gizmoz, Aviator, Basix, Essentials, and also famous designers.

A new Batteryless Quartz watch by Seiko was introduced at the Basel trade fair. The batteryless watch is call Kinetic Quartz and creates its own electrical power. Battery-free watches and long life batteries (20 years) are expanding. "We have the watch to go with the occasion", this desire to own more than one watch should help boost sales. Today's lifestyle and buying habits to own more than one watch will also influence the **collectable** market.

The 1996 Basel World Watch, Clock and Jewelry Show was one of the highlights of the Henry Fried Memorial 23rd Horological Tour and amazing to see. The Basel Show had 80,000 visitors, 2,433 exhibitors with 249 watch exhibitors. Displaying sought-after sport, offshore chronographs, special time-measuring models, complex, unusual, limited, complicated and luxury watches adorned with Gems for the sophisticated buyer and **New Age Collector**.

Accutron — AC-kew-tron
Agassiz — A-guh-see
Antiquarian — an-tih-KWAIR-ee-un
Art Nouveau — art noo-VOE
Astrolabe — AS-trow-labe
Atelier — a-teh-lee-ay
Audemars, Piguet — aw-dee-MAR, PEE-gay
Automaton — aw-TAW-muh-tahn
Baguette — bah-get
Bannatyne — BAN-uh-tyne
Basse-Taille— boss-tie
Basscine — bah-seen
Basel — BAH-zuhl
Baume & Mercier — bome-MAY & mair-cyay
Beaucourt— boe-koor
Benrus — BEN-rus
Bergeon — BEAR-juhn
Berne — bairn
Berthoud — bair-TWO
Besancon— buh-sahn-son
Bezel — BEZ-EL
Biel — beel
Bienne — by-en
Blancpain — blahnk-PAn
Blois — blu-wah
Bombe' — boom-bay
Bovet — boe-vay
Bras en L'Air— brah on lair
Breguet et Fils — bruh-GAY ay fee
Breitling — BRITE-ling
Brevet — bree-VET (or) bree-VTAY
Bucherer — boo-shay-er
Calibre — KAL-ih-breh
Capt — kapt
Carillon — KARE-il-lahn
Cartier — kar-t-yay
Cartouche — kar-toosh
Champleve — shamp-leh-VAY
Chatelaine — SHATT-e-lane
Chaton — sha-tawn
Chopard — show-par
Chronograph — Kronn-oh-graff
Chronometer — kroe-NOM-meh-tur
Cie — see
Cloisonne' — kloy-zoe-NAY
Cooksey —Cook-see
Cortebert — coh-teh-ber
Courvoisier — koor-voo-see-ya
Corum — Kore-um
Craze — krayze (or) crazing — krayze-ing
Cuvette — koo-vet
Cyma Travannes — SY-ma TA-VA
Damaskeen — dam-us-KEEN
 * damaskeen =A special terminology or American idiom
Detent — dee-TENT
Ditisheim — DI-tish-heim
Doxa — docks-uh
Droz — droze
Dauphine — doug-feen
Ebauche — AY-boesh
Ebel — AY-ble (sounds like **Abel**)
Elinvar — EL-in-var
Ermeto — air-MET-oh
Escapement — es-cape-ment
Escutcheon — es-KUHCH-un
et Fils — AY feece
ETA — EE-ta
Fahys — fah-z
Fasoldt — fa-sole-dt
Favre Leuba — fahv-ruh lew-buh
Fecit — FEE-sit =(made by)
Fleur de lis — flur duh lee
Foliot — FOE-lee-ut
Fontainemelon — fone-ten-meh-loh
Francillon — fran-see-yoh
Freid — freed
Frodsham — FRAHD-shum
Fusee — few-ZEE
Gadroon—ga-drewn
Gallet — gah-lay
Girrard Perregaux — jir-ard per-ay-go
Glashutte — GLASS-hew-tay
Glycine — gly-seen
Gouache — goo-wash
Grande sonnnerie — grawnd   shon-uh-ree
Grenchen — GREN-chun
Gublin — goo-blin
Guilloche — gill-LOWSH
Guinand — gwee-nahnd
Hampden — HAM-dun
Hebdomas — heb-DOM-us
Helical — HEL-ih-kul
Helvetia — hel-VEE-shuh
Henlein — HEN-line

Heuer — HEW-er (the watch Co.)
Heuer —oo-air also eu-air (French for time or hour)
Horology — haw-rahl-uh-gee
Huyghens — hi-guhnz
Illinois—ill-ih-NOY
Ingraham — ing-gram
Invar — in-VAR
Isochronism — eye-SOCK-roe-nism
Jacot— zha-koe
Jaeger — YAY-gur
Japy — zja-pee
Jaquet Droz — zha-KAY droze
Jours — goo-or (French for days)
Jura — joo-rah (moutains on French & Swiss border)
Jurgensen — JUR-gun-sun
Karrusel — kare-us-sell
Kessels — KESS-ulz
La Chaux de Fonds — lah show duh Fawn
A. Lange & Sohne — A. lahng un zoo-nah
Landeron — lan-der-on
Lapis LAZULI — lay-pis laz-you-lye
Lavaliere — la-vahl-yare
Le Coultre — luh-kool-tray
Le Locle — luh LOKEl
Lemania — leh-mahn-yuh
Leonidas — lee-OH-ih-dus
Le Phare — luh-fahr
Le'pine — lay-peen
Le Roy — luh roy
Le Sentier — la sant-ya
Leschot—leh-show
Ligne — line
Longines — LAWNG-jeen
Loupe—loop
Lucien Piccard (Arnex) — lew-see-en pee-kar (ar-nex)
Lyon — lee-OHn
Mathey — ma-tay
Mido — me-DOE
Mollineaux — MOLE-ih-noe
Montre — MON- tru (Swiss name for WATCH)
Moser, Henri & Cie—awn-ree mow-say eh see
Movado — moe-VAH-doe
Mozart — MOE-tsart
Nardin — nar din
Nashua — NASH-U-uh
Neuchatel — noo-sha-TELL
Nicole — nee-kol
Niello — nye-el-oh
Oignon — ohn-yoh
Omega — oh-me-guh
Osaka—oh-sah-kah
Otay — oh-tay
Oudin— oo-dan as in (soon)
Paillard — pay-lar
Pallet — PAL-let
Parachute — PAR-ah-shoot
Patek, Philippe — Pa-tek fee-leep
Patina—pah-teen-ah
Pave' — pah-vay
Piaget — pee-uh-jaay
Piguet — pee-gay
Pique — pee-kay
Quare — kwair
Rado — rah-doe
Remontoire— rem-on-twor
Repousse' — reh-poo-say
Rococo — roe-ko-ko
Roskopf — ROSS-cawf
Sangamo — san-guh-moe
Schaffausen — shaf-HOW-zun
Schild — sheild
Shugart — sugar with a T, or Shug-gart
Sonnerie — shon-uh-ree
Sotheby — SUTH-ee-bee
Souscription — sue-skrip-tshown
Stackfreed — stack-freed
St. Imier — sahnt imm-yay
Tavannes — ta-van
Tempus Fugit — TEM-pus FYOO-jit =(time flies)
Tissot — tee-SOh
Tobias — toe-bye-us
Tonneau — tun-noe
Touchon — too-shahn
Tourbillon — toour-bee-yohn
Vacheron & Constantin — VASH-er-on , CON-stan-teen
Valjoux — val-goo
Vallee de Joux — valley duh Zhoo
Verge — vurj
Veritas — VAIR-ih-tas
Vermeil — vair-may
Vertu — ver-too
Virgule — VIR-gool
Wittnauer — Wit-nower
Woerd — verd

European Terminology — U. S. A. Terminology

AIGUILLES ....Hour Hand
ALARUM ....Alarm
ANCHOR or ANCRE ....Lever Escapement
ATELIER..small workshop
BAGUETTE ....Long & Narrow
BALANCIER..Balance
BOITE-DOUBLE............................ Pair-case
BOMBE ....Convex or Bulges
BRAS EN L'AIR...........................arms in the air
BREVET.. Patented
CALIBRE .... Model
CHASED..Embossing
CHATON...............................Jewel Setting
CHRONOMETRE..............................Chronometer
CIE .... Company
COMPENSE...............................Compensating
CUVETTE or DOME........... Inside Hinged Dust Cover
CUIVRE...copper or brass
DEPOSE ....Register Trademark
DOG SCREW..Case Screw
DOME................................. Inside Hinged Dust Cover
EBAUCHE.............................. Raw Blank Movement
EMPIERRE..Jewelled
ECHAPPEMENT A' ANCRE.........Lever escapement
FAUSSE COTES..............................Damaskeening
FILS .... Sons
FLUTED ....Grooved
GENEVE STRIPES..............................Damaskeening
GUILLOCHE..............................Engine Turned
HOOK .... Pin Lever Escapement
INVENIT ET FECIT...............................Made By
JACQUE-MART .... Figures That Strike Bells
JOURS .... Days As In 8 Days
LE PINE ....Open Face
LIGNE.. Size
MONTRE...Watch
MONTRE A' TACT.......................... Watch by touch
MARQUE DEPOSE (M.D.) ....Register Trademark
OIGNON or TURNIP ..... Large Bulbous French Watch
PARACHUTE ....shock resisting
PAVE... Cover
PIQUE.............................. Pin Work Decoration
PERPETUELLE ....Self-Winding
POLYCHROME...Color
POUSETTE .... Push Piece
REPOUSSE ....Embossing
RATTRAPANTE .... Split seconds
REFERENCE # ....Case # & Style
REMONTOIRE...............Constant Force (also rewind)
RESSORT DE CROCHEMENT .... All-or-nothing
RESSORT SPIRAL...............................Hairspring
ROSKOPH.................................. Dollar Watch
RUBIS ....Ruby Jewel
SAVONETTE...............................Hunting Case
SHAGREEN .... Shark or Ray Fish Skins
SPIRAL BREGUET...................... Overcoil hairspring
TANGENT SCREW............................ Endless Screw
TONNEAU ....Barrel Shaped
TOUT-OU-RIEN................................. All-or-nothing
Vallee de Joux (Swiss - French cradle of watch making)

8 DAYS = 8 DIAS, 8 CIOANI, 8 JOURS, 8 TAGE

ADJUSTED-Adjusted to compensate for temperature, positions, and isochronism.

ALARM WATCH-A watch that will give an audible sound at a pre-set time.

ALL or NOTHING PIECE-A repeating watch mechanism which ensures that ALL the hour & minutes are struck or sounded or nothing is heard.

ANALOGUE-A term used to denote a watch dial with hands rather than digital display.

ANNEALING-Heating and cooling a metal slowly to relieve internal stress.

ANTI-MAGNETIC-Not affected by magnetic field.

ANTIQUARIAN-Of antiques or dealing in, also the study of old and out-of-date items.

Arbor

ARBOR-The mechanical axle of a moving part; on the balance it is called the staff, on the lever it is called the arbor.

ASSAY-Analyzing a metal for its gold or silver content.

AUTOMATON-Automatic working figures moving in conjunction with the movement mechanism. Striking *Jacquemarts* or jacks which are figures (may be humans provided with hammers) striking bells to supply the sound for the hour & quarter hours these hammers take the place of the bells clapper. *Automata* plural of **automaton.**

AUXILIARY COMPENSATION-For middle temperature errors found on marine chronometers.

AUXILIARY DIAL - Any extra dial for information.

BAGUETTE-A French term for oblong shape. A watch having it's length at least 3 times it's width. A long narrow diamond.

Balance Cock

BALANCE COCK-The bridge that holds the upper jewels and the balance and secured at one end only.

Balance Spring

BALANCE SPRING-Also called the hairspring; the spring governing the balance.

Balance Staff

BALANCE STAFF -The shaft of the balance wheel.

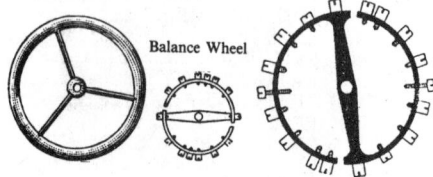
Balance Wheel

BALANCE WHEEL-A device shaped like a wheel that does for a watch what a pendulum does for a clock.

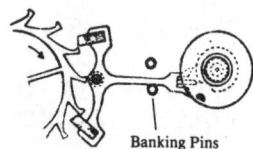
Banking Pins

BANKING PINS-The two pins which limit the angular motion of the pallet.

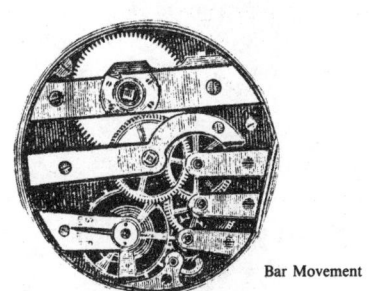

Bar Movement

BAR MOVEMENT-A type of movement employing about six bridges to hold the train. In use by 1840.

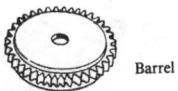

Barrel

BARREL-Drum-shaped container that houses the mainspring.

BEAT-Refers to the tick or sound of a watch; about 1/5 of a second. The sound is produced by the escape wheel striking the pallets.

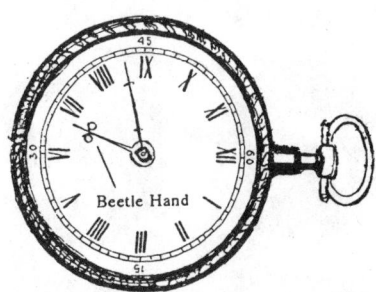

Beetle Hand

BEETLE HAND-Hour hand resembling a stag beetle; usually associated with the poker-type minute hand.

BELL METAL-Four parts copper and one part tin used for metal laps to get a high polish on steel.

O S. Htg. Bezel,

BEZEL-The rim that covers the dial (face) and retains the crystal.

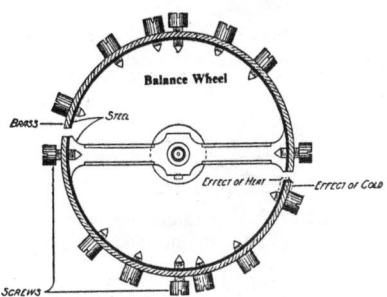

BI-METALLIC BALANCE-A balance composed of brass and steel designed to compensate for temperature changes in the hairspring.

BLIND MAN'S WATCH- A Braille watch; also known as a tact watch.

BLUING or BLUEING-By heating steel to 540 degrees, the color will change to blue.

BOMBE'- Convex on one side.

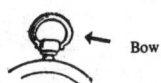

← Bow

BOW-The ring that is looped at the pendant to which a chain or fob is attached

BOX CHRONOMETER-A marine or other type chronometer in gimbals so the movement remains level at sea.

BOX JOINTED CASE-A heavy hinged decorative case with a simulated joint at the top under the pendant. (BOX CASE)

BREGUET KEY-A ratcheting watch key permitting winding in only one direction.

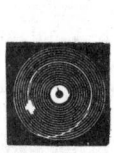 

Overcoil Hairspring

BREGUET SPRING-A type of hairspring that improves time keeping also called overcoil hairspring.

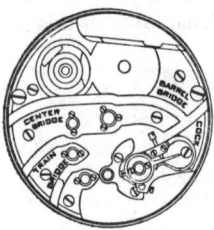

BRIDGE-A metal bar which bear the pivot of wheels and is supported at both ends .(see cock.)

BUBBLE BACK-A Rolex wrist watch which were water proof (Oyster) and auto wind (Perpetual) Ca. 1930 to 1950's.

BULL'S EYE CRYSTAL-Used on old type watches; the center of the crystal was polished which achieved a bull's eye effect.

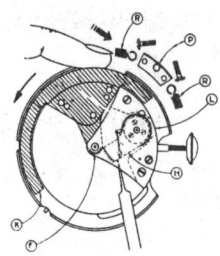

Top Side

BUFFER SPRING - Buffer spring "R" is a stop spring for oscillating weight.

CABOCHON - An unfaceted cut stone of domed form or style. (on some crowns)

CALENDAR WATCH-A watch that shows the date, month and day.

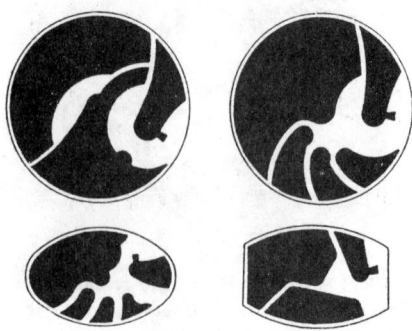

CALIBRE or CALIBER-Size of a watch movement also to describe the model, style or shape of a watch movement.

CAP JEWEL-Also called the end stone, the flat jewel on which the staff rests.

CASE SCREW-A screw with part of the head cut away.

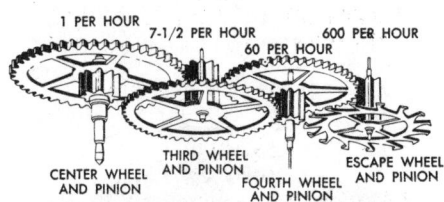

CENTER WHEEL-The second wheel; the arbor for the minute hand; this wheel makes one revolution per hour.

CHAIN (Fusee)-Looks like a miniature bicycle chain connecting the barrel and fusee.

CHAMFER-Sloping or beveled. Removing a sharp edge or edges of holes.

CHAMPLEVE-An area hollowed out and filled with enamel and then baked on.

CHAPTER-The hour, minute & seconds numbers on a dial. The chapter ring is the zone or circle that confines the numbers.

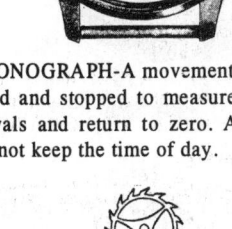

CHRONOGRAPH-A movement that can be started and stopped to measure short time intervals and return to zero. A stopwatch does not keep the time of day.

CHRONOMETER ESCAPEMENT - A detent escapement used in marine chronometers.

CLICK-A pawl that ratchets and permits the winding wheel to move in one direction; a clicking sound can be heard as the watch is wound.

CLOCK WATCH-A watch that strikes the hour but not on demand.

CLOISONNE-Enamel set between strips of metal and baked onto the dial

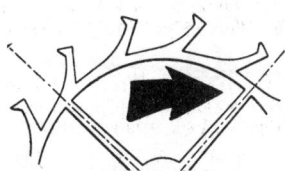

CLUB TOOTH-Some escape wheels have a special design which increases the impulse plane; located at the tip of the tooth of the escape wheel.

COARSE TRAIN-16,000 beats per hour.

COCK -The metal bar which carries the bearing for the balance's upper pivot and is supported at one end.

COMPENSATION BALANCE-A balance wheel designed to correct for temperature.

COMPLICATED WATCH-A watch with complicated works;other than just telling time, it may have a perpetual calendar, moon phases, up and down dial, repeater, musical chimes or alarm.

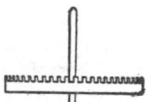

CONTRATE WHEEL-A wheel with its teeth at a right angle to plane of the wheel.

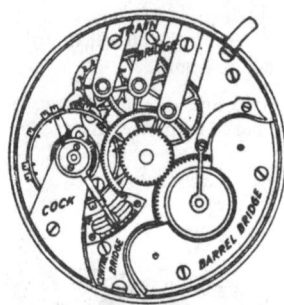

CONVERTIBLE- Movement made by Elgin & other companies; a means of converting from a hunting case to a open-face watch or vice-versa.

CRAZE(crazing)-A minute crack in the glaze of enamel watch dials.

Railroad Style

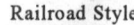

Round Style   Antique Style
CROWN-A winding button.

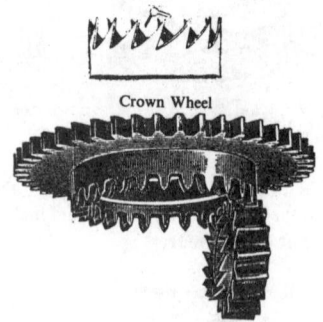

CROWN WHEEL-The escape wheel of a verge escapement; looks like a crown. Also the lower illustration shows a crown wheel used in a stem winding pocket watch.

Curb Pin

CURB PINS-The two pins that change the rate of a watch; the two pins,in effect,change the length of the hairspring.

CUVETTE

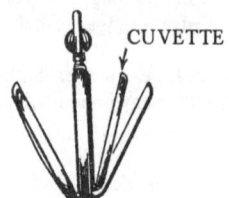

CUVETTE-The inter dust cover of a pocket watch.

CYLINDER ESCAPEMENT-A type of escapement used on some watches.

DAMASKEENING-The art of producing a design, pattern, or wavy appearance on a metal. American idiom or accepted expression of the watch term for damascene.

DEMI-HUNTER-A hunting case with the center designed to allow the position of the hands to be seen without opening the case.

DETENT ESCAPEMENT-A detached escapement . The balance is impulsed in one direction; used on watches to provide greater accuracy. Detent a locking device.

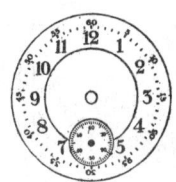

DIAL-The face of a watch. Some are made of enamel.

DISCHARGE PALLET JEWEL-The left jewel.

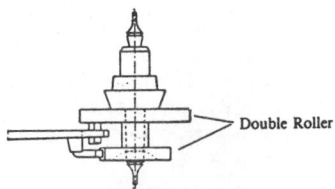

Double Roller

DOUBLE ROLLER-A watch with one impulse roller table and a safety roller, thus two rollers.

DRAW-The angular position of the pallet jewels in the pallet frame which causes those jewels to be drawn deeper into the escape wheel under pressure of the escape wheel's tooth on the locking surface.

DROP-The space between a tooth of the escape wheel and the pallet from which it has just escaped.

DUMB –REPEATER-A repeating watch with hammers that strikes a block instead of a bells or gongs.

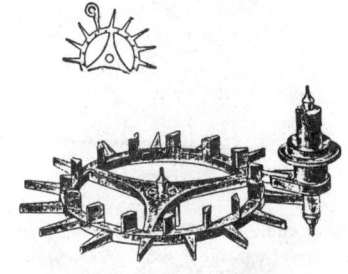

DUPLEX ESCAPEMENT-An escape wheel with two sets of teeth, one for locking and one for impulse.

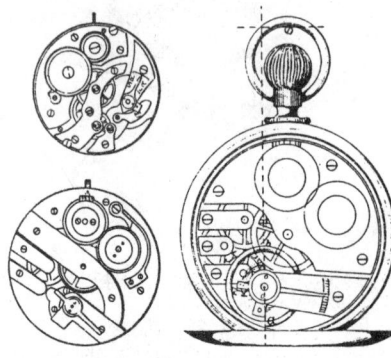

EBAUCHE(ay-boesh)-A movement not completely finished or in the rough; not detailed; a raw movement; a movement made up of two plates ,train, barrel & did not include a dial, case, or escapement.

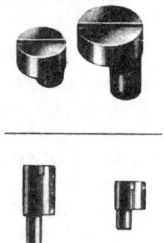

ECCENTRIC-Not exactly circular, *Non-concentric*. A cam with a lobe or egg shape.

ENGINE TURNING-Engraving a watch case with a repetitive design by a machine.

ELECTRONIC WATCH-Newer type watch using quartz and electronics to produce a high degree of accuracy.

ELINVAR-A hairspring composed of a special alloy of nickel, steel, chromium, manganese and tungsten that does not vary at different temperatures.

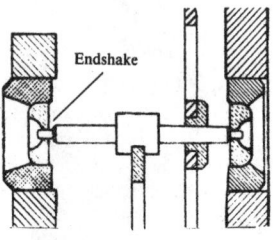

END SHAKE-The up and down play of an arbor between the plates and bridge or between the jewels.

END STONE-The jewel or cap at the end of the staff.

EPHEMEROUS TIME-The time calculated for the Earth to orbit around the sun.

ESCAPE WHEEL-The last wheel in a going train; works with the fork or lever and escapes one pulse at a time.

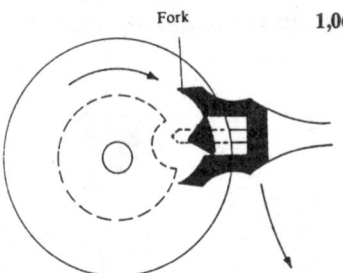

Fork

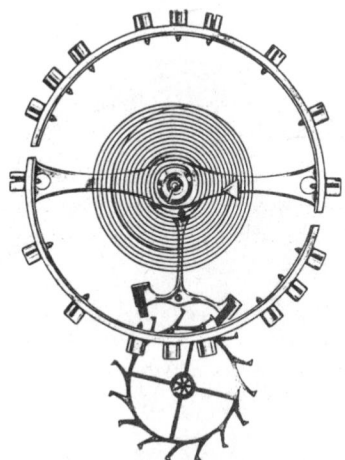

FORK-The part of the pallet lever that engages with the roller jewel.

FREE SPRUNG-A balance spring free from the influence of a regulator.

FULL PLATE -A plate (or disc) that covers the works and supports the wheels pivots. There is a top plate, a bottom plate, half, and 3/4 plate. The top plate has the balance resting on it.

ESCAPEMENT-The device in a watch by which the motion of the train is checked and the energy of the mainspring communicated to the balance. The escapement includes the escape wheel, lever, and balance complete with hairspring.

FUSEE-A spiral grooved, truncated cone used in some watches to equalize the power of the mainspring.

FARMER'S WATCH(OIGNON)-A large pocket watch with a verge escapement and a farm scene on the dial.

GRANDE SONNERIE-(Grand strike) a watch or clock that strikes the hour, 1/4 hours and minutes if minute repeater, a Petite Sonnerie strikes hour only.

FECIT-A Latin word meaning"made by ".

FIVE-MINUTE REPEATER-A watch that denotes the time every five minutes, and on the hour and half hour, by operating a push piece.

FLINQUE-Enameling over hand engraving.

FLY BACK-The hand returns back to zero on a timer.

FOB-A decorative short strap or chain.

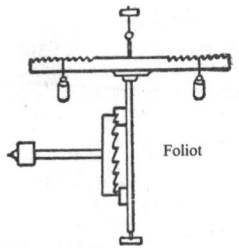

Foliot

GENEVA STOP WORK-A system used to stop the works preventing the barrel from being over wound.

GILT (or GILD)-To coat or plating with gold leaf or a gold color.

GOING BARREL-The barrel houses the mainspring; as the spring uncoils, the barrel turns, and the teeth on the outside of the barrel turn the train of gears as opposed to toothless fusee barrel.

FOLIOT-A straight-armed balance with weights on each end used for regulation; found on the earliest clocks and watches.

GOLD-FILLED-Sandwich-type metal; a layer of gold, a layer of base metal in the middle, another layer of gold-then the layers of metals are soldered to each other to form a sandwich.

GOLD JEWEL SETTINGS-In high-grade watches the jewels were mounted in gold settings.

GREAT WHEEL-The main wheel of a fusee type watch.

GUILLOCHE - A decorative pattern of cross or interlaced lines. (engraving style)

HACK-WATCH-A watch with a balance that can be stopped to allow synchronization with another timepiece.

 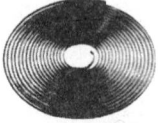

HAIRSPRING-The spring which vibrates the balance.

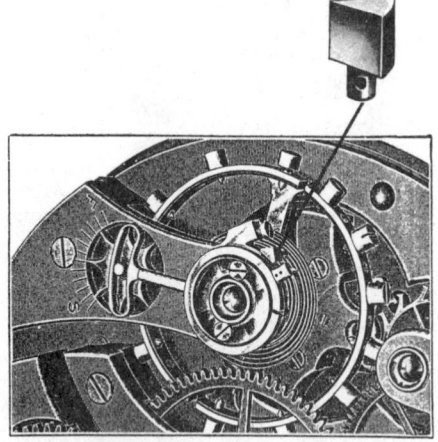

HAIRSPRING STUD-A hairspring stud is used to connect the hairspring to the balance cock.

HALLMARK-The silver or gold or platinum markings of many countries.

HEART CAM-PIECE-A heart-shaped cam which causes the hand on a chronograph to fly back to zero.

HELICAL HAIRSPRING-A cylindrical spring used in chronometers.

HOROLOGY (haw-rahl-uh-jee)-The study of time keeping.

HUNTER CASE-A pocket watch case with a covered face that must be opened to see the watch dial.

IMPULSE-The force transmitted by the escape wheel to the pallet by gliding over the angular or impulse face of the pallet jewel.

IMPULSE PIN(Ruby pin)(roller pin)-A pin on the balance which keeps the balance going .

INCABLOC-A patented shock absorbing device which permits the end stone of the balance to give when the watch is subjected to an impact or jolt. 1st. used in 1933.

INDEX-Another term for the racquet-shaped regulator which lengthens or shortens the effective length of the hairspring.

INDEPENDENT SECONDS-A seconds hand driven independently by a separate train but controlled by the time train.

ISOCHRONISM-"Isos" means equal; chronos means time-occurring at equal intervals of time. The balance and hairspring adjusted will allow the watch to run at the same rate regardless whether the watch is fully wound or almost run down.

JEWEL-A bearing made of a ruby or other type jewel; the four types of jewels include; cap jewel, hole jewel, roller jewel or ruby pin, pallet jewel or stone.

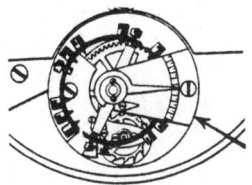

KARRUSEL-An invention of Bonniksen in 1894 which allows the entire escapement to revolve within the watch once in 521/2 minutes (in most karrusels), this unit is supported at one end only as opposed to the tourbillon which is supported at both ends and which most often revolves about once a minute.

KEY SET-Older watch that had to be set with a key.

LEAVES-The teeth of the pinion gears.

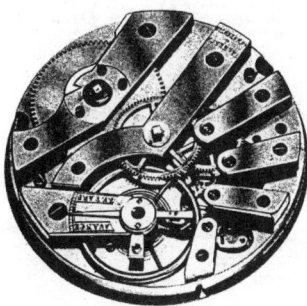

Le PINE' CALIBRE-Introduced by J.A. LePine' about 1770. Swiss for **open face.**

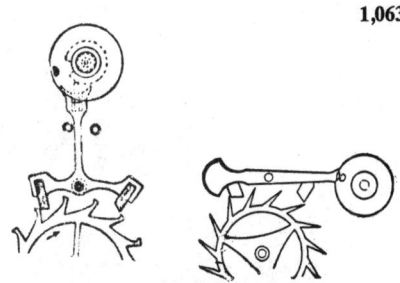

LEVER ESCAPEMENT-Invented by Thomas Mudge in 1760.

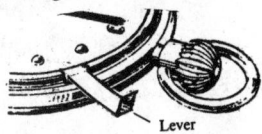

Lever

LEVER SETTING-The lever used to set some watches.

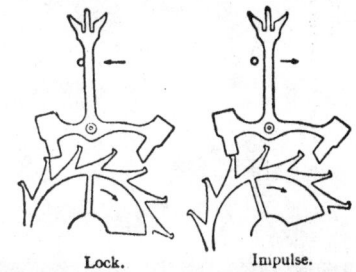

Lock.   Impulse.

LOCKING-Arresting the advance of the escape wheel during the balance's free excursion.

LUGS-The metal extensions of a wrist watch case which the bracelet or band are attached usually with a spring bar.

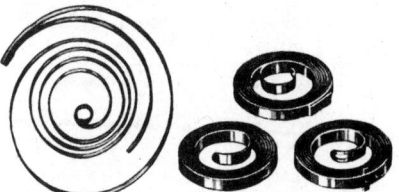

MAIN SPRING-A flat spring coiled or wound to supply power to the watch. The non-magnetic mainspring introduced 1947

MAIN WHEEL-The first driving wheel, part of the barrel.

MALTESE CROSS-The part of the stop works preventing the barrel from being over wound.

MARINE CHRONOMETER- An accurate timepiece; may have a detent escapement and set in a box with gimbals which keep it in a right position.

MEAN TIME- Also equal hours; average mean solar time; the time shown by watches.

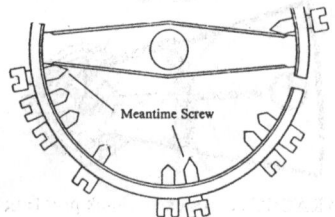

Meantime Screw

MEANTIME SCREWS-Balance screws used for timing, usually longer than other balance screws; when turned away from or toward the balance pin, they cause the balance vibrations to become faster or slower.

MICROMETRIC REGULATOR-A regulator used on railroad grade watches to adjust for gain or loss in a very precise way.

MICRO-SECOND-A millionth of a second.

MINUTE REPEATER -A watch that strikes or sounds the hours , and minutes on demand.

MOVEMENT-The works of a mechanical watch without the case or dial. (quartz watches have modules)

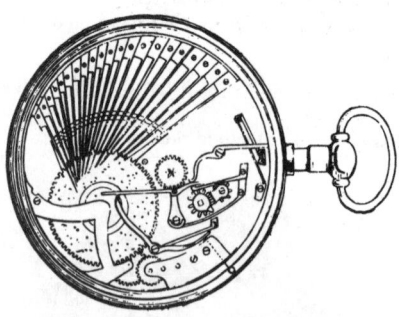

MUSICAL WATCH-A watch that plays a tune on demand or on the hour.

MULTI-GOLD-Different colors of gold-red, green, white, blue, pink, yellow and purple.

NANOSECOND-One billionth of a second.

N.A.W.C.C. - National Association of Watch and Clock Collectors address is P.O. Box 33, Columbia, Pa. 17512. TEL. 1- 717- 684- 8261

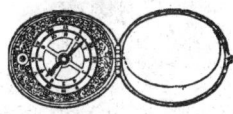

NURENBURG EGG-Nickname for a German watch that was oval-shaped.

OIGNON-Large older (1700s) style watch in the the shape of a onion or *in the shape of a bulb.*

OIL SINK-A small well around a pivot which retains oil.

OVERCOIL-The raised up portion of the balance hairspring, not flat. Also called Breguet hairspring.

PATINA-Oxidation of any surface & change due to age. A natural staining or discoloration due to aging.

PAIR-CASE WATCH-An extra case around a watch-two cases,hence, a pair of cases. The outer case kept out the dust. The inner case could not be dustproof because it provided the access to the winding and setting keyholes in the watch case.

PALLADIUM-One of six platinum metal used watches in place of platinum because it is harder, lighter and cheaper.

PALLET-The part of the lever that works with the escape wheel-jeweled pallet jewels, entry and exit pallets.

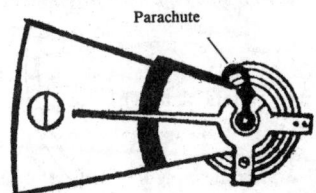

OVERBANKED-A lever escapement error; the roller jewel passes to the wrong side of the lever notch, causing one side of the pallet to rest against the banking pin and the roller jewel to rest against the other side, thus locking the escapement and stopping the motion of the balance.

PARACHUTE-An early shock proofing system designed to fit as a spring on the end stone of balance.

PAVE'- A number of jewels or stone set close together. Paved in diamonds.

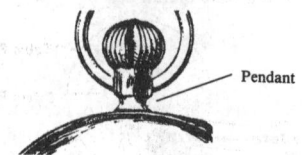

Pendant

PENDANT-The neck of the watch; attached to it is the bow (swing ring) and the crown.

PILLARS-The rods that hold the plates apart. In older watches they were fancy.

PINCHBECK-A metal similar in appearance to gold. Named after the inventor. Alloy of 4 parts copper &3 parts zinc.

PINION-The larger gear is called a wheel. The small solid gear is a pinion. The pinion is made of steel in some watches.

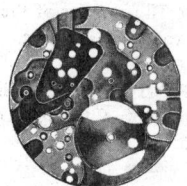 

PLATE-A watch has a front and a back plate or top and bottom plate. The works are in between.

POISE-A term meaning in balance to equalize the weight around the balance.

PONTILLAGE(bull's eye crystal)-The grinding of the center of a crystal to form a concave or so called bull's eye crystal.

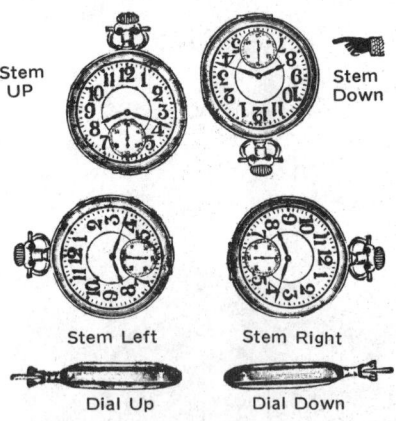

Stem UP

Stem Down

Stem Left

Stem Right

Dial Up

Dial Down

POSITION-As adjusted to five positions; a watch may differ in its time keeping accuracy as it lays in different positions . Due to the lack of poise, changes in the center of gravity, a watch can be adjusted to six positions: dial up, dial down, stem up, stem down, stem left, and stem right.

QUICK TRAIN-A watch with five beats or more per second or 18,000 per hour.

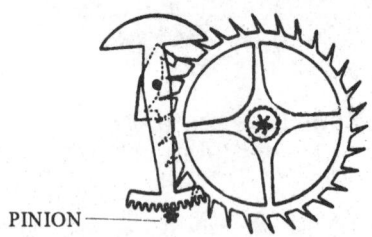

PINION

RACK & PINION LEVER ESCAPEMENT-Developed by Abbe de Huteville in 1722 and by Peter Litherhead in 1791; does not use a roller table, but a pinion.

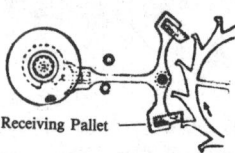

Receiving Pallet

RECEIVING PALLET-Also called left or entrance jewel, the first of two pallet jewels with which a tooth of the escape wheel comes into engagement.

REPEATER WATCH-A complicated watch
that repeats the time on demand with a
sounding device.

REPOUSSE'-A watch with hammered,
raised decoration on the case.

RIGHT ANGLE ESCAPEMENT-Also
called English escapement.

ROLLED GOLD- Thin layer of gold soldered to a base metal.

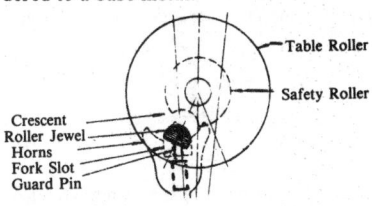

ROLLER JEWEL-The jewel seated in the
roller table, which receives the impulse
from the pallet fork.

ROLLER TABLE-The part of the balance in
which the roller jewel is seated.

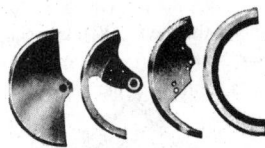

ROTOR-Oscillating weight for self-wind
watches.

SAFETY PINION -A pinion in the center
wheel designed to unscrew if the mainspring
breaks; this protects the train from being
stripped by the great force of the mainspring.

SAFETY ROLLER-The smaller of the two
rollers in a double roller escapement.

SAPPHIRE CRYSTAL - Scratch resistant
glass with a hardness of 9. Mineral glass
has a hardness of 5.

SHAGREEN-The skin of a horse, shark, ray
fish & other animal usually dyed *GREEN* or
a *BLUE GREEN*. Then used as a ornamental
covers for older watch cases.

SIDEREAL TIME-The time of rotation of
the Earth as measured from the stars.

SIDE-WINDER-A mismatched case and
movement.; a term used for a hunting movement that has been placed in an open face
case and winds at 3 o'clock position. Open
face winds at 12 o'clock.

SILVEROID-A type of case composed of alloys to simulate the appearance of silver.

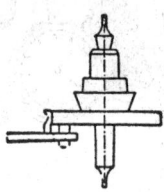

SINGLE ROLLER-The safety roller and the roller jewel are one single table.

SIZE-System used to determine the size of the movement to the case.

SKELETON WATCH-A watch made so the viewer can see the works. Plates are pierced and very decorative.

SKULL WATCH-A antique pendant watch that that is hinged at jaw to reveal a watch.

SLOW TRAIN-A watch with four beats per second or 14,000 per hour.

SNAIL-A cam shaped much like a snail. The snail determines the # of blows to be struck by a repeater.(A count wheel)

SNAILING-Ornamentation of the surface of metals by means of a circle design; also called damaskeening.

SOLAR YEAR-365 days, 5 hours, 48 minutes, 49.7 seconds.

SOUSCRIPTION- The cheapest Breguet watch which he made with high quality made in batches or group lots in advance to lower the cost.(ebauches)

SPOTTING-Decoration used on a watch movement and barrel of movements.

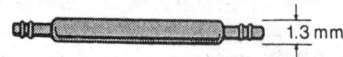

SPRING BAR-The metal keeper that attaches the band to the lugs of a wrist watch & is spring loaded.

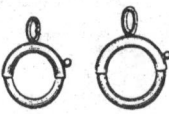

SPRING RING-A circular tube housing a coiled type spring.

STACKFREED-Curved spring and cam to equalize the uneven pull of the mainspring on 16th century German movements.

STAFF-Name for the axle of the balance.

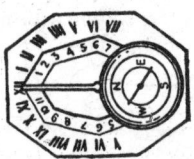

SUN DIAL-A device using a gnomon or style that cast a shadow over a graduated dial as the sun progresses, giving solar time.

SWIVEL-A hinged spring catch with a loop of metal that may be opened to insert a watch bow.

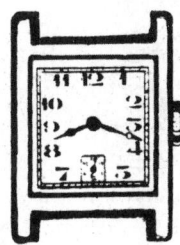

TANK WATCH-A wrist watch case design which the shape looks like the track & body of the military tank.

TOP PLATE-The metal plate that usually contains the name and serial #.

TORSION-A twisting force.

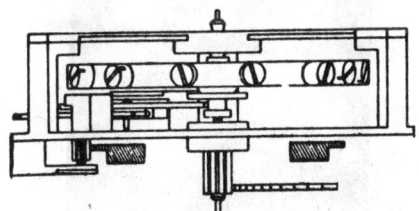

TOURBILLON-A watch with the escapement mounted on a platform pivoted at both ends which revolves most often once a minute. This is designed to eliminate position errors.

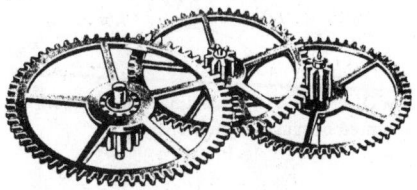

TRAIN-A series of gears that form the works of a watch. The train is used for other functions such as chiming. The time train carries the power to the escapement.

TRIPLE CASE WATCH-18th and 19th century verge escapement, fusee watches made for the Turkish market. A fourth case sometimes added in Turkey.

UP AND DOWN DIAL OR INDICATOR-A dial that shows how much of the mainspring is spent and how far up or down the mainspring is.

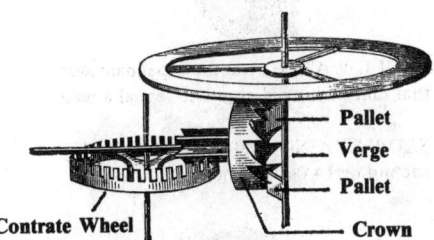

Pallet
Verge
Pallet
Crown
Contrate Wheel

VERGE ESCAPEMENT-Early type of escapement with wheel that is shaped like a crown.

VERMEIL-Gold plated over silver.

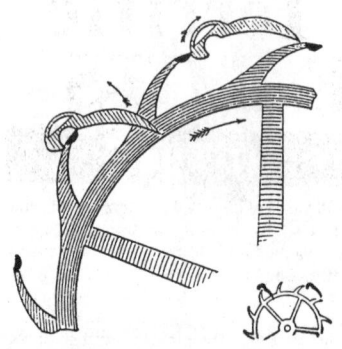

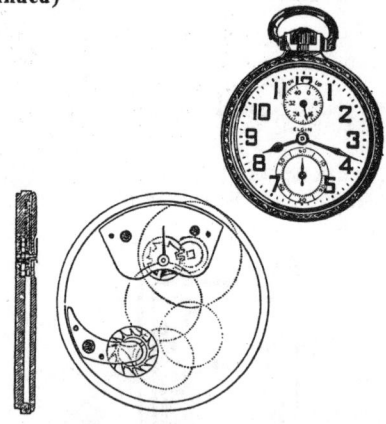

VIRGULE ESCAPEMENT-Early escapement introduced in the mid 1700s .

WIND INDICATOR-A watch that indicates how much of the mainspring is spent. The **illustration** shows a modified Geneva stop works. (see up and down dial)

WATCH GLASS PROTECTOR- A snap on metal grill that covers the crystal .

WOLF TEETH-A winding wheel's teeth so named because of their shape.

WATCH PAPER-A disc of paper with the name of the watchmaker or repairman printed on it; used as a form of advertising and found in pair-cased watches.

ADVERTISE IN THE GUIDE

ATTENTION DEALERS: This book will receive world-wide <u>BOOKSTORE</u> distribution, reaching thousands of people buying & selling watches. It will also be sold directly to THE WATCH COLLECTOR'S MARKET as well. We will be offering limited advertising space in our next edition. Consider advertising in the Guide, as it is an annual publication, your ad will pull all year long or longer. Unlike monthly or quarterly publications, your ad will stay active for years at a *cost savings* to YOU.

PRINTED SIZES
FULL PAGE — 7 1/2 " LONG X 4 3/4" WIDE
HALF PAGE — 3 1/2" LONG X 4 3/4" WIDE
FOURTH PAGE — 1 7/8" LONG X 4 3/4" WIDE

<u>AD RATES</u> ARE SET IN THE LATE SUMMER PRIOR TO EACH EDITION'S RELEASE. CONTACT US FOR AD RATES BETWEEN **(AUGUST & SEPTEMBER)**.

NOTE: Submit your ad on white paper in a version of the actual printed size. We must ask that all ads be neatly & professionally finished, *camera ready.* FULL PAYMENT must be sent with all ads. Your ad will be run as received.

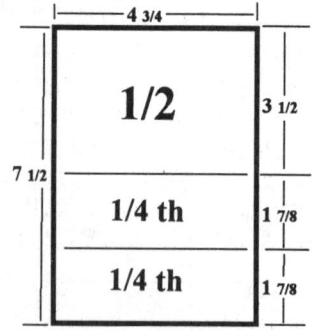

AD DEAD LINE NEXT EDITION IS - OCTOBER 15

This "GUIDE" is the PROFESSIONAL STANDARD and used by collector's and dealer's throughout the world. <u>Do not miss this opportunity to advertise in the guide.</u>

SEND YOUR AD TO:
COOKSEY SHUGART PUBLICATIONS
P. O. BOX 3147
CLEVELAND, TN. 37320-3147
Office: (423) 479-4813 — Fax: (423) 479-4813

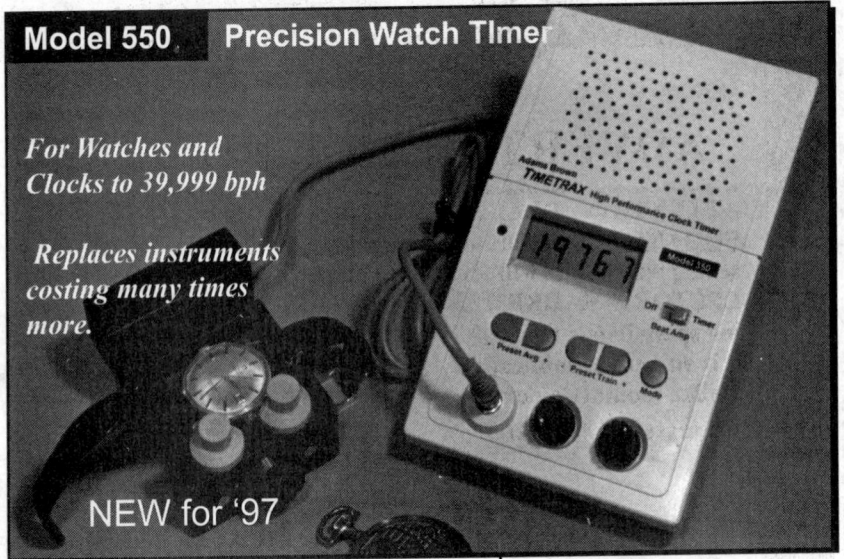

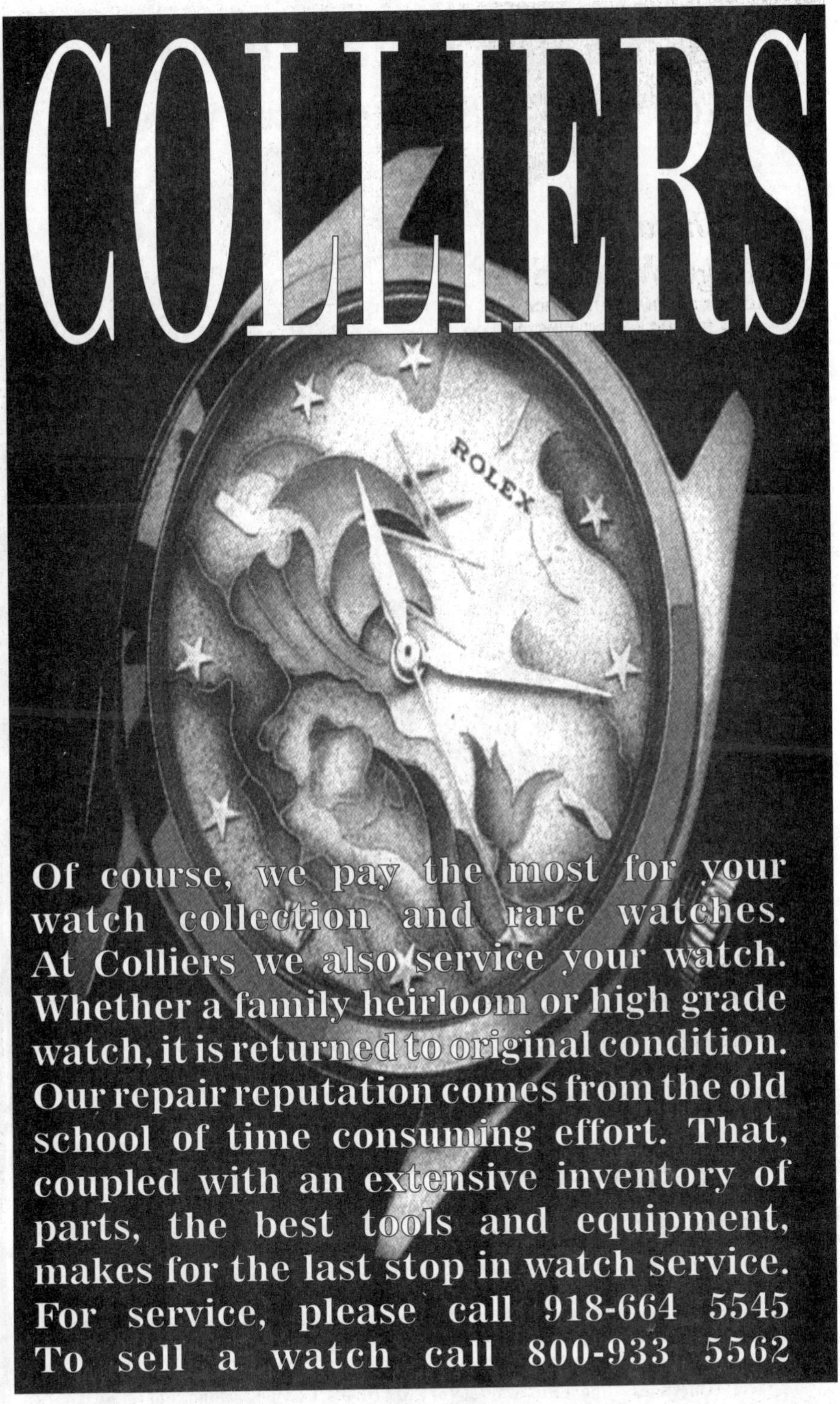
COLLIERS
ROLEX
Of course, we pay the most for your watch collection and rare watches. At Colliers we also service your watch. Whether a family heirloom or high grade watch, it is returned to original condition. Our repair reputation comes from the old school of time consuming effort. That, coupled with an extensive inventory of parts, the best tools and equipment, makes for the last stop in watch service.
For service, please call 918-664 5545
To sell a watch call 800-933 5562

Keep the Fun in Collecting!
Please Elect: Doug Cowan
for NAWCC Second Vice President

If elected, I PLEDGE:
- Sound management of the NAWCC's complex and growing budget.
- More effective communication to the Chapters about "what's going on."
- More effort to support watch collector's interests.
- More young members and less dropout of current members.
- To remind everyone that this Association is supposed to be all about having fun !

A satisfied, growing membership is essential to the future health of the NAWCC.

Qualifications: 35 years in research development, and marketing of consumer products. Retired as CEO of a 500 million dollar company. Member NAWCC 26 years, member AHS, AWI.

Hobby Involvment: Wide range of collecting and research interests. Columnist for Clocks magazine. Done almost every job at the Chapter and large regional levels. Other volunteer work includes many presentations at chapter meetings; Bulletin Answer Box; Promotion for Cincinatti's Taft Museum.

Achievements: Tripled the size of the Southern Ohio Regional while Chairman, Co-authored book, Cofounded the 225 member British Horology Chapter, Several NAWCC slide/tape programs. Now working to modernize the slide/tape library. President Chapter 159, NAWCC Fellow.

Questions ? Phone 513-821-7569 or EMAIL: DCCLOCK@Juno.com

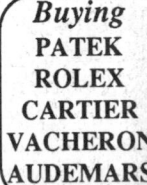

JOIN THE NAWCC

The National Association of Watch & Clock Collectors, Inc. invites you to become an active member of the world's largest horological association.

BENEFITS OF MEMBERSHIP
Subscription to the BULLETIN
Subscription to the MART
Participation in National Conventions
Participation in Regional Conventions
Participation in local Chapter activities
Advance notice of National Seminars
FREE Research services of the NAWCC Library & Museum
FREE Admission to the Watch & Clock Museum
Use of the NAWCC Lending Library

Establish friendships with others who share a fascination for watches and clocks. Time is wasting! **JOIN TODAY !!** Annual NAWCC membership dues are only **$40.00 (US)** or **$50.00 (Non-US)**. Payment must be in US funds drawn on a US bank or International money order.

MEMBERSHIP APPLICATION
To enjoy the benefits of membership, please complete this form and send it, with your check or money order to:
NAWCC, 514 Poplar St, Columbia PA 17512-2130
(717) 684-8261

Name _____

Street _____

City _____ State _____ Zip_____

Phone ( )_____ **Amt Enclosed $40 [ ] $50 [ ]**

Were you previously an NAWCC member? Yes [ ] No [ ]

What was your previous Member Number? _____

If recommended by an NAWCC member, please give name and number:
COOKSEY SHUGART NAWCC # 23843

HENRY FRIED MEMORIAL
THE 24-th ANNUAL HOROLOGICAL TOUR
TO ENGLAND, FRANCE, and BELGIUM

MAY 16 - JUNE 2, 1997   **$3,985.00 P.P.**

HIGHLIGHTS INCLUDE:
- MEETING WITH BRITISH, FRENCH AND BELGIUM A.H.S. AND NAWCC MEMBERS.
- HOROLOGICAL FAIR IN BIRMINGHAM - LARGEST IN THE U.K.
- ANTIQUE FAIRS: PORTOBELLO RD; BERMONDSEY; CAMDEN PASSAGE IN ENGLAND.
- ANTIQUE FAIR IN TONGEREN, BELGIUM.
- VISITS OF MOST IMPORTANT HOROLOGICAL MUSEUMS AND PRIVATE COLLECTIONS, GUIDED BY THEIR RESPECTIVE CURATORS OR CUSTODIANS.
- THE NATIONAL MARITIME MUSEUM AND ROYAL OBSERVATORY, CELEBRATING THE "GREENWICH MERIDIAN 2000" A COMMEMORATION OF THE NEXT MILLENNIUM.
- THE OBSERVATORIE ROYAL de BELGIQUE IN UCCLE, BELGIUM.
- VISIT OF SEVERAL CLOCK MANUFACTURES / FACTORIES.
- VISIT THE ASTRONOMICAL STUDIO AND WONDERCLOCK IN LIER.
- EUROSTAR CHUNNEL CROSSING - THE HIGH SPEED TRAIN UNDER THE ENGLISH CHANNEL.

THERE ARE STILL SEVERAL PLACES AVAILABLE ON THE TOUR. FOR MORE INFORMATION AND A BROCHURE, PLEASE CALL NICK LERESCU AT 1-800-262-4284 OR MAIL THE COUPON BELOW TO **ADVANTAGE TOURS, P.O. BOX 936, HIGHLAND LAKES, NJ. 07422.**

NAME.. TEL. #......../..

ADDRESS...

CITY.. STATE.................... ZIP...................................

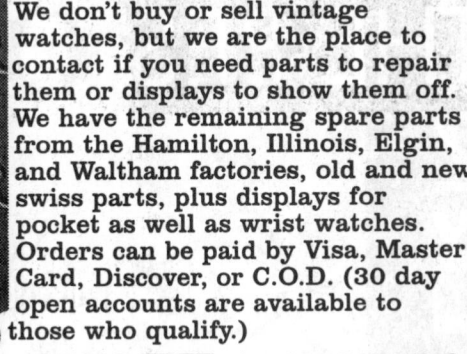

ANTIQUE WATCH CO.
OF ATLANTA
—REPAIR—

Antique Watch Company of Atlanta is an established company specializing in the *RESTORATION* of *"CAN'T BE FIXED"* and complicated Pocket and Wrist Watches including Railroads, Fusees and Repeaters. *ALL WORK GUARANTEED. ESTIMATES FREE OF CHARGE.*

Antique Watch Co. of Atlanta

RUSTY TUGGLE
TEL. 770-457-9686
FAX: 770-457-0163

4335-B N. Shallowford Rd.
Atlanta, GA 30341

– CUSTOM LATHE WORK – APPRAISALS – SALES –

While in Atlanta come visit us in our railroad cabooses.

Member: National Association of Watch & Clock Collectors,
American Watchmakers Institute

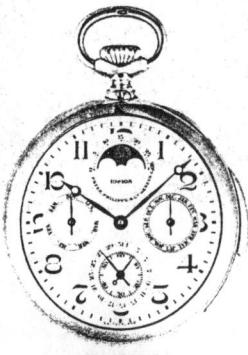

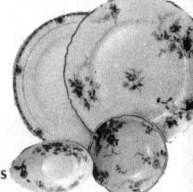

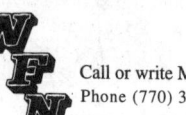
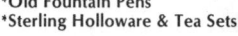

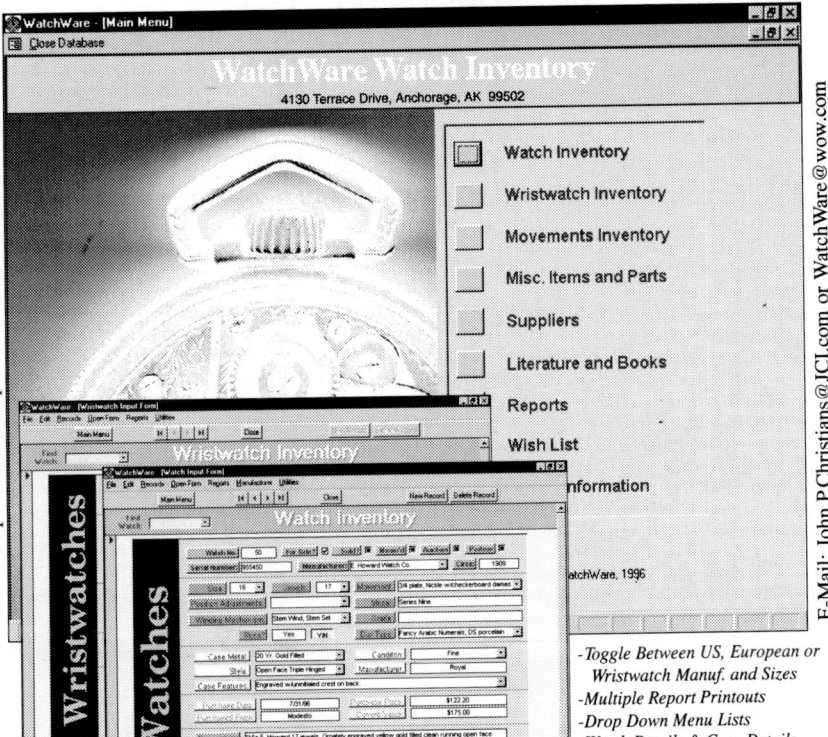

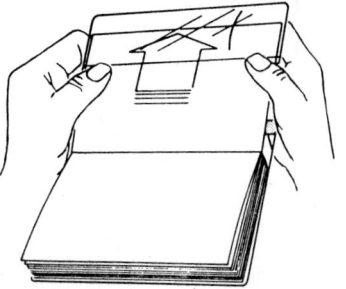